Presented to my

Frank Binns

May he live long to enjoy it

Harold E Schofield

Harold Schofield

Clarissa J Luciano

Selections for Reading.

Deserted Village - Goldsmith.
The Rape of the Lock - Pope.
Robin Hood Ballads
The Battle of Otterburn.
Sir Patrick Spens
The Ancient Mariner, Christabel, Kubla Khan — Coleridge
Childe Harold, The Prisoner of Chillon — Byron.
Marmion, Lady of the Lake — Scott.
Morte D'Arthur - Tennyson.
Cavalier Tunes, The Lost Leader, How they brought the Good News from Ghent to Aix, Home thoughts from Abroad, Home thoughts from the Sea, Incident of the French Camp, My Last Duchess — Browning.
Sohrab and Rustum, The Forsaken Merman — Arnold.
L'Allegro, Il Penseroso, Lycidas — Milton.

ENGLISH POETRY

(1170-1892)

SELECTED BY

JOHN MATTHEWS MANLY, Ph.D.

Professor and Head of the Department of English
in the University of Chicago

GINN & COMPANY

BOSTON · NEW YORK · CHICAGO · LONDON

77.2

The Athenæum Press
GINN & COMPANY · PROPRIETORS · BOSTON · U.S.A.

PREFACE

The idea and plan of the present volume originated ten years ago when Professor Bronson, Professor Dodge, and I were engaged in giving an introductory course in English literature to a class of one hundred and forty freshmen and sophomores in Brown University. We found that we secured the best results by having the students read as widely as their time permitted and then discussing freely with them such points as seemed vital to the interest or the significance of the literature read. We proceeded on the theory that literary productions are vital, organic wholes, and that they must be treated as such to produce the effects intended by their authors. Special beauties of detail were noted and enjoyed, but were subordinated to the main meaning and beauty unless, indeed, as sometimes occurred, the significance of the piece we were reading lay in the beauty of its details, in the nature of its ornamentation, rather than in its meaning or form as a whole. Questions of structure and relation of parts were discussed, but with a view primarily to the main theme. Lectures on authors were given, but the greater part of each lecture was devoted to trying to show what the author meant by his work, what he wished to say, what was significant or interesting in his special way of saying it, and why it was or was not of permanent value. Dates and facts and groups of names were given and required to be learned, but not without an attempt to express their significance in such terms of human experience as had actuality for the students themselves.

That the interest and intelligent coöperation of every member of the class were gained by this method, I will not pretend; but I can testify that I have never seen better results from any class or a larger proportion of interested and intelligent listeners in any audience; and I have good reason to know that this method awakened a love of literature and the habit of reading in many members of the course. Experience with this class and with many classes before and since convinces me that we teachers are inclined to underestimate the capacity of pupils for grasping large ideas and their susceptibility to the beautiful thoughts and forms in which we ourselves have found delight.

For such work as was done in the course of which I speak, it is necessary to have a much larger range of reading matter than is usually given in any single volume of selections. We found no volume that met our needs, and were obliged to ask the class to purchase numerous cheap prints of single pieces. But the expense even of these amounted to more than we could reasonably impose upon the students. I then decided to collect into a single volume all the pieces of nondramatic poetry that any teacher would likely care to have at hand from which to make his own selections. The publishers readily agreed to aid me in bringing the price of the volume within the reach of every student. Circumstances prevented me from beginning the book for several years, but five years ago I began it and have continued to work upon it whenever it was possible to find time and strength for it. Two years of illness sadly interrupted the work, which has, indeed, been much more difficult than I expected. It is now completed, and I hope it will be of service to teachers who believe, with me, that the love of reading and the habit of it are best awakened by treating pieces of literature as living, organic wholes and by subordinating all other considerations to this during the student's first introduction to the study of literature. It may also be useful to that large group of teachers who believe, as I do, that however small may be the number of poems that time permits one to read with his class, they should be chosen by the teacher himself with special reference to the taste and mental development of the pupils he actually has to deal with in each class.

In general the poems in this volume are given without introductory remarks or annotations. Such information can best be supplied by the teacher in the form and amount suggested by his knowledge of his pupils. In regard to most of the authors and poems presented, the most necessary information is to be found in any of the good elementary histories of English literature, and it is presumed that one of them will be used in connection with the course. In certain special cases I have supplied in the Introduction brief remarks intended to supplement the text-book.

Explanations of difficulties of thought or allusion I have avoided altogether. In such reading they are neither welcome nor helpful to a pupil until he feels the need of them, and then they can best be supplied by the teacher.

The earlier poems are provided with notes giving the meanings of unfamiliar words. It is believed that these notes and an ordinary dictionary will enable any student to read intelligently any of these poems. It will be observed that the modern equivalents of prepositions have not usually been given, and that rude English will often result from substituting the words in the notes for those in the text and making no further change. But it is only thus that the student can learn to receive the ancient thought in the ancient forms. Except in vocabulary Middle English is really not very difficult to any intelligent Englishman, and it is hoped that this book may help to remove the prevalent ignorance and fear of it. A little ingenuity and intelligent guessing at the identity of words disguised by their spelling will soon repay the student richly. Authors and poems which have hitherto been mere names to burden the student's memory may easily acquire meaning and interest by reading or even skimming these early poems.

Two principles have determined the choice of authors and poems: none has been omitted that seemed of real importance for the main features of the history of English literature; to these none has been added that had not a clear title to intrinsic beauty and value. It has of course been impossible to include all the poems of this character that exist in English literature, but it is hoped that no teacher will miss any old favorite whose place is not filled by a poem equally deserving of his favor.

Dramatic selections have been excluded because every play that deserves to be read should be read as a whole, and no single volume could contain all the good ones.

The selection from Ford's *The Lover's Melancholy* (p. 163) does not in reality violate this principle of exclusion, for the passage chosen is in no sense dramatic. It is a bit of pure narration, slightly helped in its movement by the interrupting questions, but not dependent upon them. It is highly characteristic of Ford, and under the circumstances there seemed no more impropriety in including it than in including a song from a play.

From some of the longer narrative and reflective poems only extracts are given. An effort has been made to choose extracts characteristic in themselves and, as far as possible, self-explanatory. Usually omissions are indicated by stars, but in a few instances these have been left out where the line numbering makes clear the nature and amount of the omission. Some teachers will be disappointed to find that the familiar *Knight's Tale* is not given among the selections from Chaucer. The authority of Milton, as well as its greater brevity, may be pleaded in justification for making the unfinished *Squire's Tale* the representative of the *Canterbury Tales*.

It is hoped that both teachers and students will approve the inclusion of specimens of the work of some of the living poets who belong to the age of Tennyson. Certainly George Meredith and Swinburne could not have been excluded without serious loss.

All chronological divisions of literature are in some respects unsatisfactory. The division made in this book of the Renaissance in England into the Beginning of the Renaissance, the Renaissance, and the End of the Renaissance is perhaps even more unsatisfactory than usual. The authors are arranged in the order of birth, but unfortunately they neglected to mature and to die at any standard uniform rate or to be equally quick and sensitive in responding to new ideas and new influences in poetical style. Thus it will be found that even before Wyatt and Surrey some writers showed traces, faint indeed but real, of the intellectual awakening that we call the Renaissance. And within the period itself it seems absurd — and from the point of view of style and ideas it is absurd — to find Giles Fletcher the Elder in the division called the Beginning of the Renaissance and William Warner in the Renaissance itself, as if the latter belonged to a more advanced stage of development than the former. Of course the explanation is that the work of Edmund Spenser is generally regarded as the first perfect flower of the epoch, and Fletcher, who happened to be born earlier, naturally finds place in the earlier period, though he outlived Spenser and shows in some of his work the fully developed qualities of the period of Spenser; while, on the other hand, Warner, though born later, seems to have been insensitive to the new ideas and the new style and belongs artistically to the previous generation of crude and antiquated workmanship.

In printing the texts the best accessible editions have been used and great pains have been exercised to avoid errors of every kind, but entire freedom from errors is too much to expect. I shall be grateful for any aid which will enable me to correct such as occur. The spelling of the earlier texts has been scrupulously reproduced with only such modifications as are accepted and used by good editors. In the single case of *The Ormulum* the ancient symbols for *th* and palatal *g* have been used. In it this procedure seemed necessary, as the main value of the work lies in the spelling. It would be inexcusable pedantry to preserve these old forms in other poems in such a book as this.

For aid in making the book I have to thank several friends. My cousin, Louise Manly, began making the selections with me and did a very large amount of work. These selections were revised by me and many were rejected for lack of space, while others were replaced by selections which seemed to me, for one reason or another, better suited to the purposes of the book; but my debt to her is very great, both because her selections were made with taste and judgment and because without her aid I should probably not yet have begun to carry out my plan. To Dr. Hardin Craig, Mr. A. E. Hill, and Miss Elizabeth Calhoun I am indebted for aid in verifying readings while the book was going through the press. To my sister, Annie Manly, I owe the greatest debt for aid in copying and for reading with me every revise of the proofs of the whole book.

J. M. M.

Lake Zurich, Illinois

CONTENTS

THE MIDDLE ENGLISH PERIOD

UNKNOWN AUTHOR (c. 1170)
- The Poema Morale, or Moral Ode...... 1

ORRM (fl. 1200)
- The Ormulum........................ 2

LAYAMON (c. 1205)
- The Brut.......................... 2

UNKNOWN AUTHOR (before 1250)
- King Horn......................... 4

NICHOLAS DE GUILDFORD? (fl. 1250)
- The Owl and the Nightingale........... 7

UNKNOWN AUTHOR (c. 1300)
- Cursor Mundi (The Flight into Egypt).. 9

THOMAS DE HALES (before 1300)
- A Luve Ron........................ 10

A MIDDLE ENGLISH MISCELLANY
- Alysoun (c. 1300).................. 12
- Springtime (c. 1300)................ 13
- The Man in the Moon (c. 1350)........ 13
- Ubi sunt qui ante nos fuerunt? (c. 1350) 14

RICHARD ROLLE DE HAMPOLE (1290?–1349)
- The Pricke of Conscience............ 14

THE AGE OF CHAUCER

UNKNOWN AUTHOR (c. 1350)
- Pearl............................ 15
- Syr Gawayn and the Grene Knyght..... 18

JOHN GOWER (1325?–1408)
- Confessio Amantis (Medea and Eson)... 22

WILLIAM LANGLAND (?) (1332?–1400?)
- Piers the Plowman
  - The Prologue, A-Text.............. 24
  - The Prologue, B-Text: The Fable of Belling the Cat............. 26
  - Passus VI, A-Text................. 27

GEOFFREY CHAUCER (1340?–1400)
- Troilus and Criseyde, Bk. I........... 28
- Troilus and Criseyde, Bk. II.......... 29
- Troilus and Criseyde, Bk. V........... 30
- The Canterbury Tales, The Prologue.... 32
- The Canterbury Tales, The Squieres Tale....................... 38
- A Roundel (from The Parlement of Foules)...................... 45
- Balade de Bon Conseyl................ 45
- The Compleint of Chaucer to his Empty Purse...................... 46
- Moral Balade of Chaucer.............. 46

THE FOLLOWERS OF CHAUCER

THOMAS HOCCLEVE (1370?–1450?)
- De Regimine Principum (On Chaucer).. 47
- To Sir John Oldcastle................. 47

JOHN LYDGATE (1370?–1451?)
- London Lyckpenny................... 48
- The Story of Thebes.................. 49

KING JAMES I OF SCOTLAND (1394–1437)
- The Kingis Quair..................... 50

ROBERT HENRYSON (1430?–1506?)
- The Mouse and the Paddock........... 52

UNKNOWN AUTHOR (c. 1500)
- The Nutbrowne Maide................. 54

WILLIAM DUNBAR (1460?–1513 +)
- The Thrissill and the Rois............. 58

STEPHEN HAWES (d. 1523)
- The Pastime of Pleasure
  - The Mariage betwene Graunde Amour and Labell Pucell....... 59
  - The Epitaph of Graunde Amour.... 59
  - The Excusation of the Aucthoure... 60

THE END OF THE MIDDLE AGES

JOHN SKELTON (1460?–1529)
- A Dirge for Phyllip Sparowe............ 61
- Why Come Ye not to Court?........... 62
- Colyn Cloute......................... 62

EARLY TUDOR LYRICS (c. 1500)
- Religious Lyrics
  - Who shall have my fayr lady?...... 63
  - Quho is at my windo?............. 63
- Christmas Carols
  - Thys ender nyght................. 63
  - Quid petis, O fily?................ 64
  - Make we mery, bothe more and lasse 64
  - What cher? Gud cher!........... 65
- Convivial Songs
  - Pastyme with good companye....... 65
  - Fyll the cuppe, Phylyppe.......... 65
  - Make rome, syrs, and let us be mery 65
- Love Songs
  - Lully, lulley, lulley, lulley.......... 65
  - The lytyll, prety nyghtyngale....... 66

BALLADS
- Robin Hood and Guy of Gisborne...... 66
- The Battle of Otterburn.............. 69
- The Hunting of the Cheviot............ 72
- Sir Patrick Spens..................... 75

BALLADS (*Continued*)
Captain Car; or, Edom o Gordon....... 76
Lord Randal 77
Hind Horn............................. 77
Thomas Rymer.......................... 78
St. Stephen and Herod................. 79

THE BEGINNING OF THE RENAISSANCE

SIR THOMAS WYATT (1503–1542)
A Renouncing of Love.................. 80
Divers doth use, as I have heard and know 80
Unstable dream, according to the place.. 80
My lute, awake........................ 80
A Description of Such a One as He Would Love.......................... 81
Of the Mean and Sure Estate........... 81
HENRY HOWARD, EARL OF SURREY (1517?–1547)
Description of the Restless State of a Lover 82
Description of Spring................. 82
Complaint of a Lover Rebuked.......... 83
Description and Praise of his Love Geraldine........................... 83
The Means to Attain Happy Life........ 83
Of the Death of Sir T. W.............. 83
Virgil's Æneid, Bk. II................ 84
GEORGE GASCOIGNE (1525?–1577)
The Steel Glass (Epilogus)............ 84
THOMAS SACKVILLE, LORD BUCKHURST (1536–1608)
The Mirror for Magistrates (The Induction)........................... 85
GILES FLETCHER, THE ELDER (1549?–1611)
Licia (Sonnet xlvii).................. 87
An Ode................................ 88
SIR EDWARD DYER (1550?–1607)
My mind to me a kingdom is............ 88
SIR WALTER RALEIGH (1552?–1618)
The Silent Lover...................... 88
His Pilgrimage........................ 89
The Conclusion........................ 89

THE RENAISSANCE

EDMUND SPENSER (1552?–1599)
Amoretti (viii, xxiv, lxx, lxxix)..... 90
Prothalamion.......................... 90
An Epithalamion....................... 92
An Hymn in Honour of Beauty........... 95
An Hymn of Heavenly Beauty............ 96
The Shepheards Calender (Februarie)... 96
The Faerie Queene
Bk. I, Canto I...................... 99
Bk. I, Canto III.................... 103
SIR PHILIP SIDNEY (1554–1586)
Astrophel and Stella (i, vii, xv, xxi, xxxi, xxxii, xxxix, xli)............ 104
Eleventh Song......................... 105
Song. The Nightingale................. 106
Love is Dead.......................... 106
Wooing Stuff.......................... 106
Hymn to Apollo........................ 106
JOHN LYLY (1554?–1606)
Apelles' Song......................... 107
Spring's Welcome...................... 107
Hymn to Apollo........................ 107
Fairy Revels.......................... 107
GEORGE PEELE (1558?–1597?)
Song of Paris and Œnone............... 107
Harvestmen a-Singing.................. 108
Farewell to Arms...................... 108
WILLIAM WARNER (1558?–1609)
Albion's England, Bk. IV, Chapter XX. 108
GEORGE CHAPMAN (1559?–1634)
The Sixth Book of Homer's Iliads...... 111
The Twelfth Book of Homer's Odysseys 113
ROBERT GREENE (1560?–1592)
Sweet are the thoughts that savour of content............................ 115
Philomela's Ode....................... 115
Sephestia's Song to her Child......... 116
Menaphon's Song....................... 116
The Shepherd's Wife's Song............ 116
ROBERT SOUTHWELL (1561?–1595)
The Burning Babe...................... 117
SAMUEL DANIEL (1562–1619)
Sonnets to Delia (xix, xxxix, liv, lv).......................... 117
The Complaint of Rosamond............. 118
Epistle to the Countess of Cumberland. 119
Musophilus............................ 119
JOSHUA SYLVESTER (1563–1618)
Were I as base as is the lowly plain.... 120
The Fruits of a Clear Conscience...... 120
MICHAEL DRAYTON (1563–1631)
Idea (To the Reader, and iv, xx, xxiv, xxxvii, xliv, lxi)............ 120
Ode XI (To the Virginian Voyage)..... 121
Ode XII (To the Cambro-Britans: Agincourt)......................... 122
England's Heroical Epistles (Surrey to Geraldine)...................... 123
Nymphidia (The Court of Fairy)....... 124
CHRISTOPHER MARLOWE (1564–1593)
Hero and Leander (The First Sestiad)... 125
ENGLAND'S HELICON (1600)
Phyllida and Corydon (N. Breton, 1545?–1626?)...................... 127
To Colin Clout (Shepherd Tony)....... 127
As it fell upon a day (Ignoto, *i.e.* Richard Barnfield, 1574–1627)........ 127
Happy shepherds, sit and see (W. H., *i.e.* William Hunnis, d. 1597).. 128
Phyllida's Love-Call to her Corydon (Ignoto)......................... 128
The Shepherd's Commendation of his Nymph (Earl of Oxenford, 1550–1604)................. 129
The Shepherd's Description of Love (Ignoto, *i.e.* Sir Walter Raleigh?). 129
Damelus' Song to his Diaphenia (H. C., *i.e.* Henry Constable, 1562–1613) 130
A Nymph's Disdain of Love (Ignoto)... 130
Rosalind's Madrigal (Thom. Lodge, 1558?–1625)................. 130

ENGLAND'S HELICON (*Continued*)
The Herdman's Happy Life (Out of M. Bird's Set Songs) ... 131
The Passionate Shepherd to his Love (Chr. Marlow) ... 131
The Nymph's Reply to the Shepherd (Ignoto) ... 131
The Shepherd's Resolution in Love (Thom. Watson, 1557?–1592) ... 132
WILLIAM SHAKESPEARE (1564–1616)
Venus and Adonis ... 132
The Rape of Lucrece ... 136
A Lover's Complaint ... 137
Sonnets (xii, xv, xvii, xviii, xxv, xxix, xxx, xxxii, xxxiii, lv, lx, lxiv, lxv, lxvi, lxxi, lxxiii, xcvii, xcviii, xcix, cvi, cvii, cix, cx, cxi, cxvi, cxxviii, cxlvi) ... 138
Songs from the Plays ... 143
THOMAS NASH (1567–1601)
Death's Summons ... 145
THOMAS CAMPION (d. 1619)
Chance and Change ... 146
Cherry-Ripe ... 146
SIR HENRY WOTTON (1568–1639)
An Elegy of a Woman's Heart ... 146
The Character of a Happy Life ... 146
On the Sudden Restraint of Robert Carr 147
SIR JOHN DAVIES (1569–1626)
Nosce Teipsum ... 147
THOMAS DEKKER (1570?–1641)
Song from The Shoemaker's Holiday ... 147
Song from Old Fortunatus ... 148
Content (from Patient Grissill) ... 148

THE END OF THE RENAISSANCE

BEN JONSON (1573?–1637)
Song to Celia ... 149
The Triumph of Charis ... 149
To the Memory of my Beloved, Master William Shakespeare ... 149
A Pindaric Ode ... 150
An Epitaph on Salathiel Pavy ... 152
Epitaph on Elizabeth, L. H. ... 152
Ode to Himself upon the Censure of his "New Inn" ... 152
On my First Son ... 152
Inviting a Friend to Supper ... 152
JOHN DONNE (1573–1631)
Go and catch a falling star ... 153
The Indifferent ... 153
The Canonization ... 153
The Dream ... 154
Love's Deity ... 154
The Funeral ... 155
The Computation ... 155
Forget ... 155
Death ... 155
A Hymn to God the Father ... 155
Commendatory Verses on Mr. Thomas Coryat's Crudities ... 156
JOSEPH HALL (1574–1656)
Bk. I, Satire III ... 156
JOHN MARSTON (1575–1634)
The Scourge of Villainy ... 157
GEORGE SANDYS (1578–1644)
A Paraphrase upon the Psalms of David
Psalm XXX, Part II ... 157
Psalm XLVI ... 158
A Paraphrase upon the Song of Solomon
Canto III, Sponsa ... 158
JOHN FLETCHER (1579–1625)
Sweetest Melancholy ... 158
Love's Emblems ... 159
Invocation to Sleep ... 159
Song to Bacchus ... 159
Drink To-day ... 159
Beauty Clear and Fair ... 159
The Charm ... 159
The Sleeping Mistress ... 160
Weep no More ... 160
Dirge ... 160
Marriage Hymn ... 160
FRANCIS BEAUMONT (1584–1616)
On the Life of Man ... 160
Lines on the Tombs in Westminster ... 160
Master Francis Beaumont's letter to Ben Jonson ... 161
EDWARD, LORD HERBERT OF CHERBURY (1583–1648)
An Ode ... 161
WILLIAM DRUMMOND (1585–1649)
A passing glance, a lightning 'long the skies ... 161
The heaven doth not contain so many stars ... 162
Phœbus, arise ... 162
Madrigal I ... 163
Urania ... 163
JOHN FORD (fl. 1639)
The Lover's Melancholy (Act I, Scene I) 163
Song from The Broken Heart ... 164
Dirge from The Broken Heart ... 164

PURITAN AND CAVALIER

GEORGE WITHER (1588–1667)
Fair Virtue (Fair Virtue's Sweet Graces) 165
Shall I, wasting in despair ... 165
Halleluja (For All-Saints' Day) ... 166
THOMAS HEYWOOD (d. 1650?)
Go, Pretty Birds! ... 166
WILLIAM BROWNE (1591–1643)
Britannia's Pastorals, Bk. II, Song IV ... 167
Britannia's Pastorals, Bk. II, Song V ... 167
Epitaph ... 168
On the Countess Dowager of Pembroke. 168
ROBERT HERRICK (1591–1674)
Upon the Loss of his Mistresses ... 168
Cherry-Ripe ... 168
Corinna's Going a-Maying ... 169
To the Virgins to Make Much of Time 169
How Roses Came Red ... 169

Robert Herrick (*Continued*)
To Daffodils........................... 170
Loss from the Least................... 170
Upon Julia's Clothes.................. 170
His Prayer for Absolution............. 170
A Thanksgiving to God for his House.. 170
To Keep a True Lent................... 171
Francis Quarles (1592–1644)
Sweet Phosphor, Bring the Day....... 171
George Herbert (1593–1633)
Virtue.................................. 171
The Collar.............................. 172
Love.................................... 172
Thomas Carew (1598?–1639)
Ask me no more where Jove bestows... 172
Would you know what's soft?.......... 173
Persuasions to Joy: A Song........... 173
Ingrateful Beauty Threatened.......... 173
An Epitaph............................ 173
William Habington (1605–1654)
Nox Nocti Indicat Scientiam........... 173
Sir William Davenant (1606–1668)
The lark now leaves his wat'ry nest.... 174
Praise and Prayer..................... 174
Edmund Waller (1606–1687)
The Story of Phœbus and Daphne, Applied........................ 174
To Phyllis............................ 174
On a Girdle........................... 175
Go, Lovely Rose!...................... 175
John Milton (1608–1674)
On the Morning of Christ's Nativity.... 175
L'Allegro............................. 178
Il Penseroso.......................... 179
Lycidas............................... 181
Sonnets
To the Nightingale.............. 183
At the Age of Twenty-three....... 183
When the Assault was intended to the City.................... 183
On the Detraction which followed Certain Treatises............ 183
On the Same.................... 183
To Mr. H. Lawes on his Airs..... 183
To the Lord General Cromwell.... 184
On the Late Massacre in Piedmont 184
On his Blindness................ 184
To Cyriack Skinner.............. 184
Paradise Lost, Bk. I................. 184
Sir John Suckling (1609–1642)
A Doubt of Martyrdom................ 192
The Constant Lover.................. 192
Why so Pale and Wan?................ 193
Samuel Butler (1612–1680)
Hudibras, Part I, Canto I............ 193
Richard Crashaw (1613?–1649)
In the Holy Nativity of Our Lord God.. 194
Sir John Denham (1615–1669)
Cooper's Hill........................ 196
On Mr. Abraham Cowley's Death...... 196
Richard Lovelace (1618–1658)
To Lucasta, Going to the Wars....... 196
The Grasshopper...................... 197
Richard Lovelace (*Continued*)
To Althea, from Prison............... 197
Abraham Cowley (1618–1667)
The Swallow.......................... 197
On the Death of Mr. William Hervey.. 197
The Wish............................. 198
Andrew Marvell (1621–1678)
The Garden........................... 199
To his Coy Mistress.................. 199
Henry Vaughan (1622–1695)
The Retreat.......................... 200
The World............................ 200
Behind the Veil...................... 200
The Timber........................... 201

THE RESTORATION

John Dryden (1631–1700)
Stanzas on Oliver Cromwell........... 202
Astræa Redux......................... 202
Annus Mirabilis...................... 202
Absalom and Achitophel............... 203
Religio Laici........................ 205
The Hind and the Panther............. 205
A Song for St. Cecilia's Day......... 206
Alexander's Feast; or, The Power of Music......................... 207
Lines under the Portrait of Milton..... 209
Earl of Roscommon (1633?–1685)
An Essay on Translated Verse......... 209
Charles Sackville, Earl of Dorset (1638–1706)
To all you ladies now at land......... 209
Sir Charles Sedley (1639?–1701)
To Celia............................. 210
Love still has something of the sea..... 210
Phillis is my only joy................ 211
John Wilmot, Earl of Rochester (1647–1680)
Love and Life........................ 211
To his Mistress...................... 211
Epitaph on Charles II................ 211
Thomas Otway (1652–1685)
The Enchantment...................... 212
John Oldham (1653–1683)
A Satire Dissuading from Poetry....... 212

THE AGE OF CLASSICISM

Sir Samuel Garth (1661–1719)
The Dispensary....................... 213
Lady Winchilsea (1661–1720)
The Petition for an Absolute Retreat... 213
To the Nightingale................... 214
A Nocturnal Reverie.................. 215
William Walsh (1663–1708)
Death................................ 215
Matthew Prior (1664–1721)
In vain you tell your parting lover........ 215
To a Child of Quality Five Years Old.. 216
A Simile............................. 216
The Remedy Worse than the Disease.. 216
To his Soul.......................... 216

SAMUEL TAYLOR COLERIDGE (1772–1834)
- France: An Ode.................... 353
- Hymn (Before Sunrise in the Vale of Chamouni).................... 353
- Kubla Khan; or, A Vision in a Dream 354
- The Rime of the Ancient Mariner...... 355
- Christabel.................... 361

ROBERT SOUTHEY (1774–1843)
- The Curse of Kehama (The Retreat)... 364
- The Battle of Blenheim.............. 365
- Stanzas Written in his Library........ 366
- The Well of St. Keyne.............. 366

CHARLES LAMB (1775–1834)
- The Old Familiar Faces.............. 367
- Childhood.................... 367
- A Farewell to Tobacco.............. 367

WALTER SAVAGE LANDOR (1775–1864)
- Acon and Rhodope; or, Inconstancy... 368
- Rose Aylmer.................... 369
- A Fiesolan Idyl.................... 369
- To Robert Browning.............. 370
- Why.................... 370
- On his Seventy-Fifth Birthday......... 370
- On Death.................... 370

THOMAS CAMPBELL (1777–1844)
- Hohenlinden.................... 370
- Ye Mariners of England (A Naval Ode) 370
- Exile of Erin.................... 371
- Battle of the Baltic.............. 371
- The Pleasures of Hope.............. 372

THOMAS MOORE (1779–1852)
- The Light of the Harem (Alas! How light a cause).................... 373
- Paradise and the Peri (Syria).......... 373
- Lalla Rookh (The Fire Worshippers)... 373
- The time I've lost in wooing.......... 374
- [illegible] in the stilly night.............. 374
- [illegible]ewell! But whenever.............. 374
- [illegible]ve's Young Dream.............. 375
- [illegible] the last rose of summer.......... 375
- [illegible] harp that once through Tara's [illegible]alls.............. 375
- [illegible]e not his name!.............. 376

[illegible] (1784–1859)
- [illegible] Story of Rimini (A Garden)....... 376
- Rondeau.................... 377
- The Glove and the Lions.............. 377
- Abou Ben Adhem.............. 377
- Fairies' Song.................... 377

GEORGE NOEL GORDON, LORD BYRON (1788–1824)
- English Bards and Scotch Reviewers... 378
- Childe Harold's Pilgrimage.......... 380
- The Prisoner of Chillon.............. 385
- Ode (Oh Venice! Venice! when thy marble walls).............. 389
- Don Juan.................... 391
- The Glory that Was Greece.......... 392
- Know ye the land.............. 392
- She walks in beauty.............. 393
- O! snatch'd away in beauty's bloom... 393
- Stanzas for Music.............. 393
- So we'll go no more a roving.......... 393

CHARLES WOLFE (1791–1823)
- The Burial of Sir John Moore at Corunna 393

PERCY BYSSHE SHELLEY (1792–1822)
- Alastor; or, The Spirit of Solitude...... 394
- Hymn to Intellectual Beauty.......... 396
- Ozymandias.................... 397
- Lines Written among the Euganean Hills 397
- Ode to the West Wind.............. 399
- The Indian Serenade.............. 400
- The Cloud.................... 400
- To a Skylark.................... 401
- Epipsychidion.................... 402
- To — (Music when soft voices die)..... 404
- Adonais.................... 404
- Final Chorus from Hellas.......... 410
- To Night.................... 410
- To — (One word is too often profaned) 410
- Lines (When the lamp is shattered).... 411

JOHN KEBLE (1792–1866)
- St. Thomas the Apostle.............. 411
- The Waterfall.................... 412

FELICIA DOROTHEA (BROWNE) HEMANS (1793–1835)
- A Dirge.................... 412
- The Homes of England.............. 412
- The Landing of the Pilgrim Fathers... 413

JOHN KEATS (1795–1821)
- Ode to a Nightingale.............. 413
- Ode on a Grecian Urn.............. 414
- To Autumn.................... 414
- Ode (Bards of passion and of mirth)... 415
- Lines on the Mermaid Tavern.......... 415
- La Belle Dame sans Merci.......... 416
- Sonnets (The Grasshopper and the Cricket, On First Looking into Chapman's Homer, To Sleep, On the Sea, When I have Fears, Bright Star!).............. 416
- Endymion.................... 417
- Hyperion.................... 418
- Lamia.................... 420
- The Eve of St. Agnes.............. 421

THOMAS HOOD (1799–1845)
- The Bridge of Sighs.............. 425
- The Song of the Shirt.............. 426
- Ruth.................... 427
- The Death-Bed.................... 428

WINTHROP MACKWORTH PRAED (1802–1839)
- The Belle of the Ball-Room.......... 428
- Prologue for an Amateur Performance of "The Honeymoon".......... 429

THOMAS LOVELL BEDDOES (1803–1849)
- Dream Pedlary.................... 430
- Death's Jest-Book (Song).......... 430

THE VICTORIAN AGE

ELIZABETH BARRETT BROWNING (1809–1861)
- The Sleep.................... 431
- Cowper's Grave.................... 431
- The Soul's Expression.............. 432
- Perplexed Music.................... 432

Elizabeth Barrett Browning (*Continued*)
Work 432
To George Sand (A Recognition) 432
A Man's Requirements 432
A Woman's Shortcomings 433
Sonnets from the Portuguese
(i, vii, xiv, xvii, xx, xxi, xxii, xxviii, xliii) 433
The Cry of the Children 435
A Curse for a Nation 436
A Musical Instrument 438
A Child's Thought of God 438
Edward Fitzgerald (1809–1883)
The Rubaiyat of Omar Khayyam 438
Alfred, Lord Tennyson (1809–1892)
Lilian 441
Mariana 441
The Lady of Shalott 442
The Two Voices 444
The Palace of Art 449
A Dream of Fair Women 452
You ask me why 456
Morte d'Arthur 456
Ulysses 459
Locksley Hall 459
St. Agnes' Eve 463
Sir Galahad 464
Break, Break, Break 465
Northern Farmer (New Style) 465
Wages 466
The Higher Pantheism 466
Maud 467
In Memoriam
(Proem, i, xxvii, xxxi, xxxii, liv, lvii, lxxvii, xcvi, cvi, cxxx, Epilogue) 468
Sir John Franklin 471
To Dante 471
The Silent Voices 472
Merlin and the Gleam 472
By an Evolutionist 473
Crossing the Bar 473
Robert Browning (1812–1889)
Cavalier Tunes
Marching Along 474
Give a Rouse 474
Boot and Saddle 474
The Lost Leader 475
"How They Brought the Good News from Ghent to Aix" 475
Meeting at Night 476
Parting at Morning 476
Nay but you, who do not love her 476
Evelyn Hope 476
Home-Thoughts from Abroad 477
Home-Thoughts from the Sea 477
Saul 477
My Star 479
Incident of the French Camp 479
My Last Duchess 479
The Boy and the Angel 480
The Last Ride Together 481
A Grammarian's Funeral 482
Robert Browning (*Continued*)
"Childe Roland to the Dark Tower Came" 483
Fra Lippo Lippi 486
The Bishop Orders his Tomb 490
One Word More 491
Abt Vogler 494
Rabbi Ben Ezra 495
Apparitions 498
Wanting is — What? 498
Never the time and the place 498
The Epilogue to Asolando 498
Philip James Bailey (1816–1902)
Festus, Bk. XV 498
Arthur Hugh Clough (1819–1861)
Qua Cursum Ventus 499
"With Whom is No Variableness" 500
Easter Day, I 500
Easter Day, II 501
"Perchè Pensa?" 502
The Questioning Spirit 502
Bethesda 503
Hope evermore and believe 503
Say not the struggle nought availeth 503
Frederick Locker-Lampson (1821–1895)
To my Grandmother 504
The Unrealized Ideal 504
Matthew Arnold (1822–1888)
To a Friend 505
Shakespeare 505
Stagyrus 505
The Forsaken Merman 506
To Marguerite 507
Morality 507
The Future 508
Sohrab and Rustum [illegible]
Philomela [illegible]
The Scholar Gipsy [illegible]
The Last Word [illegible]
Coventry Patmore (1823–1896)
The Angel in the House
Bk. I, Canto III, Prelude [illegible] Lover) [illegible]
Bk. I, Canto VIII, Prelude[illegible]
(I. Life of Life) [illegible]
(II. The Revelation) [illegible]
(III. The Spirit's Epochs) [illegible]
Bk. I, Canto X (Going to Church) 522
Bk. II, Canto XII, Preludes (I. The Married Lover) 522
The Unknown Eros
The Toys 522
If I were dead 523
Sidney Dobell (1824–1874)
In Wartime (A Prayer of the Understanding) 523
America 524
Dante Gabriel Rossetti (1828–1882)
The Blessed Damozel 524
Jenny 525
Sister Helen 529
The Ballad of Dead Ladies (From François Villon) 532

Dante Gabriel Rossetti (*Continued*)
Francesca da Rimini (From Dante) 533
On Refusal of Aid between Nations 533
The Sonnet 533
Love-Sight 533
Love-Sweetness 533
Mid-Rapture 534
Soul-Light 534
Stillborn Love 534
Inclusiveness 534
Known in Vain 534
The Landmark 535
The Choice (i, ii, iii) 535
Vain Virtues 535
Lost Days 535
A Superscription 536
The One Hope 536
Chimes (i, vi) 536
Three Shadows 536
The Cloud Confines 537
George Meredith (b. 1828)
Love in the Valley 537
Juggling Jerry 540
Bellerophon 541
Lucifer in Starlight 542
Modern Love (xvi, l) 542
Ask, is love divine 542
Song of the Songless 542
Dirge in Woods 542
Christina Rossetti (1830–1894)
The Prince's Progress (The Bride-Song) 543
A Birthday 543
Song (When I am dead) 543
The First Day 544
Remember 544
Rest 544
Christina Rossetti (*Continued*)
The Lowest Place 544
Robert, Lord Lytton ["Owen Meredith"] (1831–1892)
Lucile, Canto III, ii 544
The Portrait 545
Sir Edwin Arnold (1832–1904)
The Light of Asia, Bk. I (The Mystery of Evil) 546
Sir Lewis Morris (b. 1833)
An Ode on a Fair Spring Morning 547
James Thomson (1834–1882)
The City of Dreadful Night 548
Sunday up the River (xv, xviii) 549
Art (i, ii, iii) 550
William Morris (1834–1896)
The Earthly Paradise
The Idle Singer of an Empty Day. 550
Prologue 551
The Lady of the Land 551
Alfred Austin (b. 1835)
Primroses 557
Algernon Charles Swinburne (b. 1837)
Chorus from Atalanta in Calydon 558
The Garden of Proserpine 558
Itylus 559
Hertha 560
The Roundel 561
Étude Réaliste (i, ii, iii) 561
The Salt of the Earth 562
What is Death 562
Sonnets
On Lamb's Specimens of Dramatic Poets 562
Ben Jonson 562
Hope and Fear 562
After Sunset 563

INTRODUCTION

The Poema Morale (p. 1) is the first important English poem after the Norman Conquest. It consists of a large number (about 400 lines) of moral and religious precepts embodying the author's philosophy of life, and was evidently written for the purpose of inculcating right living in all who read or heard it. As the short specimen given here shows, the questions of life, present and future, are treated in a spirit of selfish prudence, and the sentiment most frequently and powerfully appealed to is that of self-preservation. The spirit of the author is a sincere but hard and narrow Christianity, untouched by the tenderness of personal affection for Jesus or of concern for one's friends and fellow-men notable in the best work of Richard Rolle, Thomas de Hales, or even the dull but lovable Orrm. The author has, however, much skill in language and versification, and at times the vigor and vividness of his work is undeniable. The poem must have been very popular in its day, as all peoples in the early stages of development are fond of proverbial sayings and similar forms of practical wisdom. Several copies of it, made in various parts of England, have come down to us.

The Ormulum (p. 2) is interesting almost solely because the author was a theorist about English spelling. He devised a system of his own for representing the pronunciation as exactly as possible and carried it out with much skill and consistency throughout his long poem of 20,000 lines. As scholars are now greatly interested in learning how English was pronounced in early ages, Orrm's work is of the very highest value. As literature, it hardly deserves consideration. It was not intended to be a poem in the modern sense. It was written in verse because verse then seemed the proper form for anything that aspired to be literature. The author merely wished to present to his countrymen an English version of the Gospels read in the services of the church throughout the year, accompanied by explanations which should make clear their whole meaning, figurative as well as literal. Unfortunately, either he was very dull himself or he suspected his audience of almost impenetrable dullness, for he is not content to say a thing once with absolute simplicity and clearness, but must say it over and over again, and, in his anxiety that there shall be no mistake as to what he is talking about, is not satisfied to use pronouns for referring to matters already mentioned, but at each recurrence of them repeats all that he has previously said about them. His poem seems not to have been altogether unprovoked, for it was written at the request of his brother Walter; but there is no evidence that it met with any appreciation, as the single copy that has been preserved seems to be that written by the author himself. In spite of his dullness, however, the gentleness and amiability of Orrm and his real love of God and his fellow-men is manifest in all his work.

Layamon, the author of *The Brut* (p. 2), is a man of much greater ability. His work is a versified chronicle or history of Britain from the destruction of Troy to 689 A.D. It is based mainly upon a similar French poem, the *Roman de Brut* by Wace, but Layamon added much from oral traditions known to him, especially about King Arthur. The merits of the poem at its best are those of a lively and picturesque narrative, rapid, simple, and vigorous, with much of the spirit of the older English epic. The versification also, though not precisely that of the older epic, is thoroughly national.

To us of the present day the most interesting parts of Layamon are those which deal with the story of King Lear, the coming of Hengist and Horsa, and, above all, the wars and death of King Arthur. *The Brut* contains about 30,000 lines and exists in two versions, one of about 1200 A.D., from which our selection is taken, and another of fifty years later, a sort of modernization made necessary by the rapid change of the language in those days.

KING HORN (p. 4) is one of the earliest and best of the metrical romances, — a kind of literature which then filled the place now occupied by the novel. Ancient romances, like early novels, usually begin at the beginning. In our first selection, this part of his subject has been treated with artistic brevity by the author and made essential to the story itself. The second selection gives a part of the love story of the exiled Horn, whose royal descent is kept concealed, and the Princess. Another incident of the same story, slightly modified, is given in the ballad of *Hind Horn* (p. 77). The narrative is full of incident, is well constructed, thoroughly motived, and told with rapidity and directness. The poem contains 1568 lines and, judging from the number of versions, was very popular.

THE OWL AND THE NIGHTINGALE (p. 7) is a work of very different character from any of the preceding. It is poetry in the modern sense of the term and deserves a very high rank when tested by the best standards of modern taste. The strife between the Owl and the Nightingale is in itself such a theme as existed by the hundred in mediæval literature. Strifes and debates, indeed, formed a special literary type, found in every language cultivated in Western Europe. There were strifes between Summer and Winter, between Youth and Age, between Water and Wine; debates as to whether a soldier or a scholar is the better lover, as to whether women are an evil or a good, as to any subject having, or seeming to have, two sides. Only a few of them rise to any considerable dignity or beauty or force. One, *The Debate between the Body and the Soul*, is among the most powerful religious poems of that age and is almost as impressive to-day as when it was first written, though some of its themes have since been worn threadbare. What especially distinguishes *The Owl and the Nightingale* is the astonishing dramatic sympathy of the author. The grief and indignation of the Owl at the failure of the world to recognize the beauty of his song are set forth with the same imaginative simplicity and candor as is the Nightingale's confidence in her own superiority. Such sympathetic imaginative power, such psychological subtlety, and such humor as are shown in this poem, in Chaucer, and in Robert Henryson are rare even in these days when machine-made sympathy and subtlety have been put within the reach of the least endowed. The author's name is unknown; it has been supposed to be Nicholas de Guildford, because towards the end of the poem the birds agree to leave the decision of the strife between them to Master Nicholas of Guildford, who is described as very skillful in music. But obviously Master Nicholas is more probably not the author, but some friend of his. The poem contains 1794 lines.

CURSOR MUNDI (p. 9) is a versified account of biblical history from the Creation to the time of Solomon and from the birth of the Virgin Mary to her Assumption, ending with the Final Judgment. In subject-matter and in the organization of it, *Cursor Mundi* resembles the great dramatic cycles of the Middle Ages; so much so, indeed, that it has been supposed to be the source of some of these plays. The poem is very long, about 25,000 lines, and seems to have been very widely read. The specimen given here exhibits its merits fairly and may serve to show us one of the most agreeable forms in which our ancestors received their knowledge of Bible history. The story here related is, of course, not from any of the canonical books of the Bible, but from the apocryphal pseudo-gospel of Matthew.

Thomas de Hales (p. 10) was a Franciscan friar, known to us by an affectionate message to him in a letter from the famous Adam de Marisco. It is therefore probable that the date ascribed to his poem should have been about 1250. It is certain that he lived before the order of friars had been corrupted by the intrusion of designing and unscrupulous men, and while it still retained the purity and enthusiasm of its great founder. Thomas was a man of great learning, but the sweetness and passionate simplicity of this little poem are not unworthy of the fine spirit of St. Francis himself. The subject of the poem and the circumstances of its composition as given in the first stanza, it may be noted, indicate the nearness of the friars to the people, — that familiar and homely interest in all the affairs of old and young which gave them their tremendous opportunities for good and for evil in the thirteenth and fourteenth centuries. In lines 67–68 Dr. Morris's text is followed. It would have been better to keep the reading of the manuscript:

Amadas and Dideyne (= Idoyne)
Tristram, Yseude and alle theo.

Amadas and Idoyne are almost as famous a pair of lovers as Tristram and Isoude.

The four little Lyrics (p. 12) brought together here are among the best of the multitudinous lyrics of the age. Many of them have been preserved for us in manuscripts, many others are alluded to or quoted in snatches by chroniclers or writers of narrative poems, and many many more must have perished entirely, either through loss of the manuscripts or because they were never written down. Enough remain to prove that the ancient fame of "Merrie England" for song was well deserved and to show that the poetical gifts of mediæval Englishmen are to be studied not in dull didactic poem or prosy rhymed chronicle, but in poems written in the spirit of free and joyous artistry. Better known than any of those given here is the charming *Cuckoo-song*, composed about 1250, of which the music as well as the words has come down to us. Of our selections the first and second are songs of springtime and love, and hardly require any comment, though it may be interesting to compare the second with the Earl of Surrey's treatment of the same theme on page 82. The fourth is an extract from a longer poem, but is a unit in itself and is one of the best lyrical expressions of a theme made famous to the Middle Ages by St. Bernard of Clairvaux and to all ages by François Villon (see Rossetti's translation of Villon's ballade, p. 532). Humorous songs are not rare in Middle English, but it is unusual to find one so thoroughly artistic in conception and execution as our third selection. The poem is uncommonly difficult, partly because of the language, but mainly because the speaker is dramatic and expects you to follow every shifting change of his thought, every fleeting suggestion that comes into his mind to explain the mysterious "man" in the moon. The three first stanzas are a sort of wondering soliloquy about the "man"; the fourth is a direct address; the fifth, an expression of disappointment that the "man" will not accept the author's friendly suggestion. In line 8 the hedge is said to be the only one who knows what clothes the man wears, either because the thorns have retained bits of his rags or because like Autolycus (see *Winter's Tale*, IV, iii, 5, 24) he is conceived as a "snapper-up of unconsidered trifles." Lines 13–14 are, of course, a suggestion as to the reason why the man has a bundle of thorns on his back. Lines 15–16, I take it, explain why he was out late: the man, says the author, felt, as dark came on, that he must cut another truss; without it to complete his pile, all that he had cut would practically count for nothing. The allusion in lines 23–24 is to the fact that it was the duty of the hayward to see that no one trespassed in any of the fields under his charge and to arrest every such offender or take of him a pledge for appearance at the manor court. The friendly proposition in stanza 4 is entirely in keeping with the administration of justice in the Middle Ages, when a little judicious bribery of the officers of the law was recognized as a part of the regular course of business. No one who reads the poem often enough to surmount the initial difficulties of language can fail to recognize in it, not a mere happy accident of composition, but a bit of the work of a genuine artist in comedy floated down to us in the wreckage of time.

RICHARD ROLLE (p. 14) is one of the most interesting figures in English religious history. His mystical experiences of the love of God entitle him to a place beside St. Catharine of Sienna. As a poet, his technical skill is rather unusual for his time; but curiously enough none of his poetry, though he wrote much, rises to the heights of passionate beauty reached by the best of his Latin prose. His longest and best known poem is *The Pricke of Conscience* (9544 lines) dealing, in seven parts, with the wretchedness of human nature, the transitoriness of the world, the death of the body, purgatory, doomsday, the pains of hell, and the joys of heaven. Our selection is from the first part, and is a good specimen of his manner when untouched by strong emotion.

The author of PEARL (p. 15) and SYR GAWAYN AND THE GRENE KNYGHT (p. 18) — if they are really by the same author, as is usually supposed — was not merely a writer of great natural powers but a careful and conscious artist. It is supposed that *Gawayn* was written while the author was still occupied with worldly thoughts and interests and that *Pearl* and two (or three) other religious poems were composed after his conversion to a serious religious life, and this is doubtless true if the poems be all the work of one man. *Gawayn* belongs, of course, to the number of metrical romances dealing with the knights of the Round Table and their adventures, but in one important respect it is very different from most of them. They are as a rule the work of authors who had little qualification for their task beyond a certain ease in narration and versification and a retentive memory. The author of *Gawayn*, however, does not merely repeat a story which he has heard or read; he uses the materials of tradition as freely as Tennyson or Arnold or Swinburne or any other modern artist, and displays a power of construction, a skill in climax, a sense of pictorial effects, fairly comparable with theirs. All this can be seen in the brief episode here given, which we have chosen not because it is better than many others but because it is self-explanatory. The interest of the reader is maintained unflaggingly throughout the 2550 lines of the poem. *Pearl* (1212 lines), though entirely different in subject and tone and manner, is equally admirable. It seems to give the experience of a father who has lost a beloved little daughter, his "Pearl," and who, a few years later, falling asleep in his arbor, sees her in a vision, not as the helpless child he has lost, but as a radiant and beautiful young maiden, the Bride of the Lamb, and talks with her about the joys of her heavenly abode. Recently it has been argued with great learning and ingenuity that the poet is a cleric and can have had no child, and that he is merely a man who, being interested in the theological doctrine of grace, not works, as the basis of rewards in heaven, attempted to illustrate and enforce the doctrine by an imaginary case of a baptised child dying in infancy and receiving in heaven rewards equal to those given the greater saints. There can be no doubt that, whether cleric or not, the poet was deeply versed in theology and believed ardently in the doctrine of grace, but no sufficient reason has been adduced for refusing to recognize the genuine personal tone of the poet's grief and love. That the child was not his own is reasonably clear from his remark that she was nearer to him than aunt or niece (line 233), and from the absence of the terms father and daughter in their conversation. But many a man has loved with great devotion a child not his own. Mr. Swinburne's charming poems (see pp. 561 and 562, and the whole series entitled *A Dark Month*, written when the beloved child was away on a visit) may serve as a notable instance. That the bereaved heart of a lonely man here found consolation in the new and blessed doctrine of grace seems more likely than that a mere theologian devised this most beautiful of poems as the framework for promulgating a favorite dogma.

Gower (p. 22) and Langland (p. 24) are so fully treated in the text-books that only a word on each need be added here. Gower is not a great poet, but through being contrasted with Chaucer he has had less than his due of recognition. Mr. Lowell, one of the most genial of critics, sought to enhance his praise of Chaucer by setting him off against a dark background and playfully celebrating his contemporary and friend Gower as dull with the dullness of super-man. But Chaucer needs no such setting; we now know his age to have been one of extraordinary mental activity and poetical production; and he shines with undiminished brightness above all its light. And Gower, though no artist and undeniably monotonous, is not altogether lacking in power of swift narrative and picturesque description, as the story of Medea and Eson clearly proves.

The poems which go under the name of Langland (p. 24) are the work of several distinct and very different men. One of these men wrote the Prologue and the first eight passus or cantos of the A-text (1800 lines) about 1362. The poem became very popular and was continued by another man who carried it on to about the middle of the twelfth passus and left it unfinished. A certain John But then finished it by a hasty and absurd account of the sudden death of the author. About 1377 another writer, almost equal to the first in picturesqueness of phrasing and vividness of detail, but woefully deficient in power of consecutive thought and constructive ability, revised the whole poem composed by the first two writers, neglecting the passus containing the death of the author. His method of revision was to leave practically unchanged what he found written but to make numerous insertions, expanding suggestions of the original, and numerous additions, developing themes untouched by the earlier writers. The work as he left it is called the B-text. Fifteen or twenty years later a man of greater learning than any of the others and of a more orderly and systematic habit of mind than the author of the B-text, but of much less poetic ability — a pedant, in fact — revised the B-text, rearranging, inserting, and adding. The poem as he left it is called the C-text. The moral earnestness, the satirical power, the picturesque phrasing, of the poem have long been recognized, but, until recently, when it was discovered that it was not all the work of one man, the poem was charged with vagueness, obscurity, formlessness. Now it appears that we ought to read and criticise the different parts separately; and if we do so, we find that the work of the first author (the first half of the A-text) is as clear as it is picturesque, that one need never be at a loss as to its meaning or the relation of its parts, and that its author was a man of remarkable constructive and organizing power. Confusion and uncertainty do not enter until his work has received the well-meant but inartistic insertions and additions of others. His work may be seen in the first and third selections. That of the writer of the B-text is seen at its very best, and free from its usual defects, in the second selection, which constitutes his first insertion in the poem as he found it.

Hoccleve (p. 47) and Lydgate (p. 48) are of historical interest only. Each professed himself a follower and devoted pupil of Chaucer's, and there can be no doubt of their affection and admiration, but both singularly failed to reproduce any of his characteristic qualities. Neither seems to have understood his versification or to have had the ability to adapt it to the language of their time. Chaucer's verse, as everybody now knows, is as smooth and musical as the best verse of any age, if the final vowels which were pronounced in his speech are sounded in his verse. Hoccleve and Lydgate knew that final *e* was sometimes sounded, but in their own speech apparently sounded it much less often than Chaucer, and consequently, when they read his verse with their own pronunciation, it sounded to them as rough and uncertain as their own.

There must have been very great and sudden changes in the pronunciation of English during Chaucer's lifetime, especially in regard to sounding final *e*. He and Gower apparently spoke and wrote the more conservative speech of the upper classes. The younger generation, to which Hoccleve and Lydgate belonged, apparently spoke very differently. This may have been due to the sudden rise in social position of a vast multitude of people in consequence of the general political and social movements of the age. Such people would naturally try to acquire the pronunciation of the new class into which they had risen, but because of the multitude of them their own earlier habits of speech could not fail to exercise some influence upon standard English.

But it is clear also that neither Hoccleve nor Lydgate was possessed of much intellectual fineness or artistic sensibility. Neither of them understood the spirit and aims of Chaucer's work. To them and, sad to relate, to most men for a century to come Chaucer's merits were not those of a great artist, a true poet, but merely those of a voluminous writer of interesting stories and songs. Doubtless they enjoyed his work more than they did Gower's, but he and Gower seemed to them to belong essentially to the same class of writers. It is not strange, therefore, that Hawes and Skelton and other writers of the age of Henry VII and Henry VIII praised Chaucer and Gower and Lydgate in the same breath and with the same note of praise. The matter was all they could understand or appreciate; and Gower and Lydgate had as much material as Chaucer, if not more. In our own day the sudden addition to the reading public of a multitude of readers of uncultivated minds and undeveloped taste has resulted in a somewhat similar state of affairs. The success of a book — that is, of one of "the best sellers" — depends not upon its artistic qualities or its power and beauty of thought, but solely upon its presentation of the sort of material liked by the general public. Now, as in the fifteenth century, it is not even necessary that the material should be novel; the public swallows with avidity to-day absolutely the same story that it swallowed yesterday, provided the names of the hero and the heroine are changed. A century or two hence critics will find it as hard to account for the great vogue of some of our popular novels as we find it to account for the failure of the men of the fifteenth century to distinguish between Chaucer and Gower and Lydgate.

ROBERT HENRYSON, the Scot (p. 52), was also an imitator of Chaucer, and he was one of the few men of the time who at all understood him. Though much inferior to Chaucer in power, he has no little artistic skill, and in humor is a not unworthy follower of the great master. The charming ballad of *Robyn and Maukyn* is perhaps his best known poem, but his beast fables seem more characteristic and better illustrative of his humor and psychological power. *The Mouse and the Paddock* belongs to that peculiar class of beast fables begun in English with Chaucer's *Nonne Prestes Tale* and continued in our own time with Kipling's *Jungle Books*.

THE NUTBROWNE MAIDE (p. 54) is curiously modern in every respect: in versification, in language, in tone, and in sentiment. One would like to know who was the author — to what class of society he belonged, of what education and experience of life he was, whether he ever wrote anything else. The existence of such isolated originality as is shown in this poem, in *The Owl and the Nightingale*, in *The Man in the Moon*, in some of the Early Tudor lyrics, and a few other ancient poems, makes one slow to believe that our remote ancestors were less capable of excellence in literature than we are, and confirms the view that the variation in the number of good writers in different periods is not due so much to differences in intellectual equipment as to variation in the interests that attract the attention of different periods.

WILLIAM DUNBAR, the Scot (p. 58), and STEPHEN HAWES, the Englishman (p. 59), belong also to the list of followers of Chaucer. They, like the rest of these imitators, are insensible to those qualities of the master which make him significant not for the Middle Ages only but for all time. The literary forms and the style which attracted them and which they most frequently try to reproduce are those which Chaucer himself in the course of his marvelous artistic development outgrew and abandoned. They imitate *The Boke of the Duchesse*, *The Prologue to the Legende of Goode Women*, *The Parlement of Foules*, *The Hous of Fame*, and above all the *Roman de la Rose* or the translation of it. Allegory is the chosen form, abstractions are the favorite personages; the ancient conventional machinery of spring mornings and grassy arbors and dreams and troupes of men and fair ladies is used again and again, though all its parts have become loose and worn with use and age and creak audibly at every movement. To all this they add a pretentious diction that smells of schools and musty Latinity. The flowers that deck their fields are withered blossoms that they have picked up and painted and tied to the bare and lifeless stalks. Gaudy they are, but odorless, lifeless, and obviously painted.

DUNBAR's greatest poem is *The Golden Targe*, a long, tedious allegory setting forth the dangers of love and the efficacy of the golden shield of reason. Equally famous and less wearisome is *The Thrissill and the Rois*, a poem celebrating by means of the national flowers of Scotland and England the marriage of James IV of Scotland with Mary Tudor, daughter of Henry VII of England, — a marriage of so much significance later for England and the history of Great Britain. In his satires, such as *The Dance of the Sevin Deidly Sinnis*, and in his shorter poems, such as his *Lament for the Makaris* (i.e. Poets), Dunbar is much more original and vigorous and less pedantic.

STEPHEN HAWES's most important poem is also an elaborate allegory. The full title of it is significant, *The Pastime of Pleasure; or the History of Graunde Amour and La Bell Pucell; conteining the knowledge of the seven Sciences and the course of mans life in this worlde.* All this is set forth in a series of incidents in which the hero Graunde Amour (Love of Knowledge) falls in love with and wins La Bell Pucell (the beautiful maiden, Knowledge). Our first extract gives a fair idea of the method and merits of the poem. After the marriage, Graunde Amour lives happily with his bride for many years; then, summoned by Old Age and Death, he dies and is buried, his epitaph being written by Remembrance. This epitaph is perhaps the most interesting passage of the poem to a modern reader.

That LYRICS (p. 63) were written in great numbers before the influence of Italy seriously affected English poetry in the sixteenth century is well known, but most historians of English literature entirely neglect these lyrics and speak as if England owed all her wealth of song in the age of Elizabeth to Italian influence. That there was much imitation of sonnet and madrigal and other Italian forms of lyric poetry is beyond question, but in many of the most charming of the lyrics of the latter part of the century one hears, I think, the same notes and discovers the same poetic method that had marked English lyrics at the beginning of the century and for ages before. Only a few specimens of these native wood-notes wild are given here, but they will serve to enforce what has just been said. One of them, it will be remarked, is curiously unlike the rest and curiously modern. In both tone and poetic method the love song:

> Lully, lulley, lulley, lulley!
> The fawcon hath born my make away! (p. 65)

smacks, not of the Middle Ages, but of that interesting nineteenth-century imitation of mediævalism associated with the Pre-Raphaelite Movement.

The BALLADS (p. 66) here given are specimens of a kind of literature which has attracted a great deal of attention and aroused a great deal of controversy in modern times. Composed during the Middle Ages for the common people, they attracted scarcely any attention from cultivated readers and played little part in literature until the second half of the eighteenth century. Sir Philip Sidney knew and loved "the old song of Percy and Douglas," Shakespeare and some of the other dramatists quoted brief snatches of them in certain of their plays, and Addison devotes a critique in the *Spectator* to one of the best of them; but they had no general literary standing until some men of the eighteenth century, sick of the conventionalities and prettinesses of the poetry of their day, turned for relief to the rude vigor and simplicity of these old poems. The book most influential in this introduction of them to modern readers was Bishop Percy's *Reliques of Ancient English Poetry*, published in 1765.

But, although obscure until the time of the Romantic Movement, the ballads, as has been said, were composed centuries before that time. Even approximate dates of composition can be set for very few of them, for they were usually not written down but only preserved in memory and transmitted orally through the centuries, and consequently in most cases no certain conclusions as to their dates can be drawn from the forms of the language in which they are expressed. But we know that some of those that have come down to us belong to the fifteenth, the fourteenth, and even the thirteenth centuries. Perhaps the earliest of those printed here is *St. Stephen and Herod* (p. 79), one of the most remarkable for a vivid simplicity which no art could improve. This and *Sir Patrick Spens*, by some curious chance, have precisely the artistic qualities which we look for in the best modern verse; the excellences of some of the others, such as the *Battle of Otterburn* and *Captain Car*, though perhaps as great in their way, belong to an ideal of art entirely different from that of the modern individualistic, conscious artist.

Most of the lyrics of Sir Thomas Wyatt (p. 80) and the Earl of Surrey (p. 82) were first printed in a little volume entitled *Songs and Sonnets, written by the Right Honourable Lord Henry Howard, late Earl of Surrey, and others*, but commonly known, from the publisher's name, as *Tottel's Miscellany*. The significance of this volume is duly emphasized in all histories of English literature.

George Sandys (p. 157) is usually regarded as too unimportant to find a place in a brief history of English literature; but it has seemed worth while to give three brief specimens of his translations, because they show the falsity of the common opinion, shared by some of the best literary critics, that it is impossible to translate the poetry of the Old Testament into English verse and preserve the dignity and simplicity and force which are so finely preserved in the prose of the Authorized Version. The student may also be interested to notice that two of the verse-forms Sandys uses were afterwards made famous by Tennyson.

Lady Winchilsea (p. 213) finds a place here because of recent years the romantic qualities of her work, noted long ago by Wordsworth, have met with general recognition and have received special significance from their existence at a time when the Classical Movement seemed supreme.

William Hamilton of Bangor produced in his paraphrase of Hamlet's soliloquy (p. 260) what has been regarded as the very *reductio ad absurdum* of the "classical" method and style. Hamilton's own lack of ability is of course responsible for the absolute lifelessness of the lines, and bad writers will always write badly; but the tone, the manner of approaching the subject, the choice of imagery and of stylistic devices, are distinctly "classical." A comparison of the soliloquy with its original would be a good elementary exercise in defining the two contrasted ideals of literary art. It would also emphasize anew the great fact that in literature, as in life, the idea is little, while the emotions it awakens, the images it arouses, the associations that accompany it, are everything; for Hamilton has used all the ideas of the great soliloquy and rejected all its means of effectiveness.

David Mallet (p. 260) — his name was originally Malloch — lives in literary history by virtue of three rather curious circumstances: the title of one of his poems (*The Excursion*) had the honor of being used later by Wordsworth; the famous song, *Rule, Britannia!* (p. 258), was first sung in a musical comedy called *Alfred, a Masque*, composed by him and James Thomson; and he was the reputed author of *William and Margaret* (p. 260), the most important ballad in the history of the Romantic Movement. Fate favored him in Wordsworth's choice of a title for his poem. She favored him in the second instance by letting the poet James Thomson die before *Alfred* was printed and before any public claim had been made to the great song which all scholars now ascribe to Thomson. She favored him the third time by allowing him to retain for over one hundred and fifty years credit in literary circles for the authorship of *William and Margaret*, a poem which we now know to have been printed in slightly different form and sold about the streets of London while he was still a child. The importance of the ballad for the history of Romanticism lies partly in its real beauty, partly in the early date at which it attracted public attention and interest, and partly in the large amount of discussion to which it gave rise.

Thomas Warton (p. 283) owes his position in the history of English poetry not to the fact that he was poet laureate but to his having contributed, both by his own verse and by his *History of English Poetry*, to the triumph of Romanticism. His *History of English Poetry*, which is still a standard treatise, brought to the attention of the reading public the rich but forgotten fields of English poetry from the twelfth to the close of the sixteenth century, the influence of which became dominant in the Romantic revival. His best poetry also expresses two of the principal characteristics of Romanticism, — love of antiquity and love of nature. He is further notable as having helped to revive the sonnet as a form of English verse.

Thomas Chatterton (p. 295) wrote under his own name some poems of great promise for a boy (he was only eighteen when he died), but his most important and interesting poems he pretended not to have written but to have discovered. Most of them, he said, were composed by a monk named Rowley in the second half of the fifteenth century, and had been found by himself among old papers in the church of St. Mary Redcliffe at Bristol. In the present state of knowledge of the English language it is easy for any scholar to see that these poems could not possibly have been written in the fifteenth century, and some persons suspected them when they were first produced; but to the majority even of the scholars of that day any imitation of old manuscripts, old writing, and old spelling was good evidence of age, and it seemed absolutely impossible that so young a boy — he was only twelve or thirteen when he began to produce these poems — could have composed the poems and fabricated the manuscripts. When the imposture was discovered the critics, making no allowance for its having been the work of a mere child, were filled with high moral indignation, and the poor boy was allowed to starve, until, being able to endure his neglect no longer, he took poison and died. It has been thought strange that the poems written in this "fake" old English are better than those in the English of his own day; but the explanation seems easy psychologically. The imagination of the boy was specially excited both by the idea of the imposture he was carrying on and by the odd forms of words which he used. He felt himself transported to the times and scenes he was trying to reproduce and wrote with the picturesqueness and vigor which belong to such excited states of mind. Professor Skeat, in his recent edition of Chatterton, has changed the old spelling of the poems to modern spelling, on the ground that the boy really thought in eighteenth-century English and ought to be so represented. This sounds logical, but really is not. He may have thought thus, but we may be sure that he felt and imagined in these pseudo-archaic forms which made the antique world live again for him. Chatterton's method of old spelling is so simple also that it will give hardly any trouble. His first principle is to double letters as often as possible; his second is not to be too regular even in doing this; his third, to use any genuine old spellings that he happened to remember. No difficulty exists in *The Bristowe Tragedie*. *The Accounte of W. Canynges Feast* is harder. In line 1 *han sounde* is intended to mean *has sounded*. The meaning of line 2 is *a fair welcome does befit persons of dignity*, — *Byelecoyle* being a bad spelling of the name of one of the characters in the old Chaucerian translation of the *Roman de la Rose*. *Ealdermenne*, line 3, is of course *aldermen; cheorte*, line 4, really means *dearness* or *scarcity*, but Chatterton thought it could mean *delicious; swotelye*, line 6, means *sweetly* (= *sweet*) and *doe* is for *does*. *Syche coyne*, line 7, means *such food*. Professor Skeat thinks *coyne* means *daintily*, but Chatterton probably got the word from Spenser's *View of the Present State of Ireland*, where Spenser says, "by the woord of Coygnye is understood mans-meat," as opposed to horse-meat. *Coygnye* is also spelled *coyn* and *coyne*. In line 8 *dynne* is *noise*. In line 9 *Heie stylle* means *they* (the minstrels) *cease playing*. In line 11 *echone* is of course *every* (each one), and *deene* is *dine*. Line 12 means *if Rowley*, *Iscamm*, *or Tyb Gorges* (three of his friends) *be not seen*.

The MINOR SCOTTISH POETS represented in pages 304–309 are mainly interesting as a background to Burns. In methods and ideals he was not an isolated phenomenon; freedom and individuality had not perished entirely. In London literary circles and throughout Great Britain wherever people tried to write or to criticise as they thought all "up-to-date" people were writing and criticising, the prevailing fashion of "classicism" was omnipotent. But wherever people wrote for the pleasure of saying a thing as they wished to say it, life, with its old joys and hopes and sorrows and fears and desires, ran fresh and strong, as it always has run and always will.

PRAED (p. 428) and LOCKER-LAMPSON (p. 504) are the advance guard of a host of writers of *vers de société* of exquisite delicacy and refinement. The ideal of such verse is elegant and ingenious trifling with only occasional touches of more serious sentiment, — as a swallow circles bright and swift through the air, dips its wing for a moment in the water, and like a flash is off again in its careless flight. Some of the lighter verse of the sixteenth, seventeenth, and eighteenth centuries bears a close resemblance to the work of these later writers, but there is a difference in tone, in attitude, in personal concern with the sentiments expressed. Locker (or Locker-Lampson, to use the name he assumed upon his marriage to Miss Lampson) was far superior to Praed in tenderness, in reserve, in genuine poetic feeling, and in technique. His range of sentiments, of ideas, and of rhythms was greater; and he has had the greater influence upon later writers.

Fitzgerald's translation of THE RUBAIYAT OF OMAR KHAYYAM (p. 438) has long had a place in the hearts of lovers of high and serious poetry. Although a translation, it is in the truest sense an original poem and expresses as scarcely any other does the strange combination of doubt and defiance and sensuousness and religious yearning characteristic of much of the thought and feeling of the Victorian Age.

Bailey's FESTUS (p. 498) was one of the most successful poems of any age. Published in 1839, it passed through many editions in England, besides thirty in America. In addition to this popular success, it gained the extravagant praises of many critics and poets, even such men as Walter Savage Landor ranking it with the great poems of the world. But it is dead and will never be read again except as a literary curiosity. Three quotations from it still survive as the sum total of its claims upon the future. The poet and dramatist, Westland Marston, said, "I know no poem in any language that can be compared with it in copiousness and variety of imagery." This is true; but the imagery of the poem is the result of intellectual ingenuity, not of poetic imagination, and the movement of it, both in general and in detail, is the movement of machinery, not of life.

Coventry Patmore (p. 521) has been the subject of the most widely divergent judgments. One contemporary critic says, "It may be affirmed that no poet of the present age is more certain of immortality than he." Another regards him as possessor of no spark of the divine fire. The selections here presented seem to justify his claim to a unique and high position among the poets of his time, but his range was narrow — his vocal register had scarcely a tone that does not find utterance in these selections — and his voice obviously lacked resonance and power. Being incapable of self-criticism, he wrote much that is prosaic — some lines that even awaken inextinguishable laughter; but at its best his verse is simple, picturesque, passionate, of exquisite freshness and charm.

Sidney Dobell (p. 523) is a notable example of the rather large class of poets in the nineteenth century who gave evidence of true and even great poetic ability, but who failed in unity, in consistency, in power of final and perfect utterance.

George Meredith (p. 537) is perhaps the most richly and variously endowed writer of the nineteenth century. He is best known as a novelist, but to many of his admirers he seems equally great as a poet. All of his work is notable for its combination of significance and beauty. In depth of insight, in subtle apprehension of life and the problems which it presents to try the hearts of intelligent men and women, even such great writers as Scott, Dickens, Thackeray, and George Eliot are hardly his equals; and his sensitiveness to the beauties of nature and of the soul of man has a wider range and a finer delicacy. The same qualities are manifest in much of his poetry. But the gods gave him also the fatal gift of excessive intellectual ingenuity and a delight in the exercise of it; while the sole gift they denied him was self-restraint. Like his own Bellerophon, he had the winged horse and the golden bridle, and he, too,

Could mount and sit
Flying, and up Olympus midway speed;

but instead of riding straight and hard for the summit he too often, in mere exuberance of power and of delight in his steed, executes difficult feats of horsemanship on the lower slopes of the mountain.

Robert Bulwer Lytton, "Owen Meredith" (p. 544), is notable only as an example of the worthlessness of contemporary popularity, however great, as a test of merit. No one can now read his verses without seeing clearly and at once that he had not a single quality of greatness. He had no power of thought, no sensitiveness to beauty, no real charm of manner. His success was a triumph of the commonplace and of cheap and tawdry sensationalism. That we are all now able to see this does not mean that we are wiser than the preceding generation or endowed with better taste, but only that this particular kind of commonplace and sensationalism does not appeal to us. Most of us are still equally ready to praise work different in badness, but just as bad.

Sir Lewis Morris (p. 547) is not a great poet, but he occupies an honorable place among poets of the second rank. Though lacking in originality and strength he has sincerity and sensitiveness to beauty and truth; and often his verse has the simple, noble charm of genuine poetry.

James Thomson (p. 548) is one of the most curious and interesting figures of the Victorian period. No one has been more successful in catching the true poetic aspect of the pleasures of the lower middle classes of a great city. His "idyls of the London mob," as he calls them, are not echoes of Theocritus or Virgil, of the pastoral of the Italian Renaissance, or of the genuine bucolic poetry of Scotland and England; they are original and independent treatments of the material that he saw actually about him in the holiday excursions of the young people of cockneydom. In striking contrast with these simple and charming pictures is the dark melancholy which finds expression in *The City of Dreadful Night* and other poems of his later years. These poems have often been admired, or condemned, as the ultimate expression of philosophical pessimism, and often the form and the ideas seem to justify such an interpretation; but there can be little doubt that they are in reality devoid of philosophical significance, though full of power and of far-reaching suggestion. The ideas and the imagery have the horrible fascination of a hideous dream. They are indeed the utterance of a poet of splendid original power and infinite aspiration for life and strength and beauty, whose vigor has been sapped by folly and misfortune, who with shattered nerves and strengthless hands strives vainly to clutch some good that has durability and three dimensions. *The City of Dreadful Night* is, as the poet explains, the city of darkness, peopled with sad forms by the insomnia which night after night tortures and weakens him and restores him to the day empty of strength and hope.

Of the extraordinarily high qualities of William Morris (p. 550) and Algernon Charles Swinburne (p. 558) it is hardly necessary to speak, as these poets usually find a place in the histories of English literature, though seldom so high a place as they deserve.

Alfred Austin (p. 557) has had the misfortune as poet laureate to be compared with Tennyson and Wordsworth, and has of course suffered greatly thereby. The selection here given — and there are many other poems as good as this — proves that, though not great, Mr. Austin is nevertheless a true poet and by no means the contemptible versifier he has too often been represented as being.

ENGLISH POETRY

EARLY MIDDLE ENGLISH

From THE POEMA MORALE, OR MORAL ODE (c. 1170)

(Unknown Author)

Ich [1] æm elder then ich [1] wes a wintre and a lore;
Ic [1] wælde [3] more thanne ic dude,[4] mi wit ah [5] to ben more.
Wel lange ic [1] habbe [6] child ibeon [7] a weorde and ech [8] a dede;
Theh [9] ic beo [10] a wintre eald,[11] to ying I eom [10] a rede.[12]
Unnut [13] lyf ic habb ilæd,[14] and yiet, me-thincth, ic lede;
Thanne ic me bethenche,[15] wel sore ic me adrede.[16]
Mest [17] al thæt ic habbe ydon [18] ys idelnesse and chilche;[19]
Wel late ic habbe me bithoht, bute [20] me God do milce.[21]
Fele [22] ydele word ic habbe iqueden [23] syththen [24] ic speke cuthe,[25]
And fale [22] yunge [26] dede ido, thet me of-thinchet [27] nuthe.[28]
Al to lome [29] ic habbe agult [30] a weorche [31] and ec [8] a worde;
Al to muchel ic habbe ispend, to litel yleid [32] an horde.
Mest [17] al thet me licede [33] ær,[34] nu hit me mislicheth;[35]
The [36] mychel [37] folyeth [38] his ywil, him sulfne he biswiketh.[39]
Ich mihte habbe bet [40] idon, hadde ic tho [41] yselthe;[42]

[1] I [2] in years and in knowledge [3] govern [4] did [5] ought [6] have [7] been [8] also [9] though [10] am [11] old [12] counsel [13] useless [14] led [15] bethink [16] I am frightened [17] almost [18] done [19] childishness [20] unless [21] mercy [22] many [23] spoken [24] since [25] could [26] young, silly [27] repents [28] now [29] all too often [30] sinned [31] deed [32] laid [33] pleased [34] formerly [35] displeases [36] who [37] much [38] follows [39] betrays [40] better [41] then [42] good fortune

Nu ic wolde, ac [1] ic ne mei [2] for elde [3] ne for unhelthe;[4]
Ylde [3] me is bistolen on, ær ic hit awyste;[5]
Ne mihte ic iseon [6] before me for smeche [7] ne for miste.
Ærwe [8] we beoth [9] to done god, and to yfele [10] al to thriste;[11]
More æie [12] stent [13] man of manne thanne him do of Criste.
The [14] wel ne deth [15] the hwile he mei,[2] wel oft hit hym scæl ruwen,[16]
Thænne [17] hy [18] mowen sculen [19] and ripen, ther [20] hi ær seowen.[21]
Don ec [22] to Gode wet [23] ye muye,[24] the hwile ye buth [9] a life;
Ne hopie no man [25] to muchel to childe ne to wyfe;
The [14] him selve foryut [26] for wife other for childe,
He sceal cume an uvele stede,[27] bute [28] hym God beo milde.
Sende æch [29] sum god biforen hym, the hwile he mei, to heovene;
Betere is an elmesse [30] bifore thenne beon æfter seovene.
Ne beo the leovre [31] thene the sulf thi mei [32] ne thi maye.[33]
Sot [34] is the [14] is othres mannes freond betre thene his aye.[35]
Ne hopie [36] wif to hire were,[37] ne wer [37] to his wife;
Beo [38] for him sulve ævrich [39] man, the hwyle he beo [40] alive.
Wis [41] is the [42] him sulfne bithencth,[43] the hwile he mote [44] libbe,[45]
For sone [46] wulleth [47] him foryite [48] the fremde [49] and the sibbe.[50]

[1] but [2] may not [3] age [4] weakness [5] before I knew it [6] see [7] smoke [8] timid [9] are [10] evil [11] bold [12] awe, fear [13] arises to [14] who [15] doth [16] shall repent [17] when [18] they [19] shall [20] where [21] sowed [22] also [23] what [24] may [25] let no man hope [26] forgets [27] in evil place [28] unless [29] each [30] one alms [31] dearer [32] kinsman [33] son [34] foolish [35] own [36] hope not [37] man [38] be [39] every [40] is [41] wise [42] who [43] bethinks [44] may [45] live [46] soon [47] will [48] forget [49] stranger [50] kinsman

The [1] wel ne deth [2] the hwile he mei,[3] ne sceal he hwenne he wolde.
Manies mannes sare iswinch habbeth oft unholde.[4]
Ne scolde nan man don a furst,[5] ne sclawen [6] wel to done;
For mani man bihateth [7] wel, the [1] hit foryiteth sone.
The man the [1] siker [8] wule beon to habbe Godes blisse,
Do wel him sulf the hwile he mei, then haveth he mid iwisse.[9]

ORRM (fl. 1200)

From THE ORMULUM

Nu,[10] broþerr Wallterr, broþerr min
Affterr þe flæshess kinde; [11]
& broþerr min i [12] Crisstenndom
Þurrh fulluhht [13] & þurrh trowwþe; [14]
& broþerr min i [12] Godess hus,
Ȝēt o [15] the þride [16] wise,[17]
Þurrh þatt witt [18] hafenn [19] tăkenn ba [20]
An [21] reȝhellboc [22] to follȝhenn,[23]
Unnderr kanunnkess [24] had [25] & lif,
Swa summ [26] Sannt Awwstin sette; [27]
Icc hafe [28] don swa summ [26] þu badd,[29]
& forþedd [30] te [31] þin wille,
Icc hafe [28] wennd [32] inntill [33] Ennglissh
Goddspelless hallȝhe lare,[34]
Affterr þatt little witt [35] tatt [36] me
Min Drihhtin hafeþþ lenedd.[37]
Þu þohhtesst [38] tatt [36] itt mihhte wel
Till [39] mikell frame [40] turrnenn,
Ȝiff [41] Ennglissh follk, forr lufe off Crist,
Itt wollde ȝerne [42] lernenn,
& follȝhenn [23] itt, & fillenn [43] itt
Wiþþ þohht,[44] wiþþ word, wiþþ dede.
& forrþi [45] ȝerrndesst [46] tu þatt icc
Þiss werrc [47] þe shollde wirrkenn;
& icc itt hafe forþedd [30] te,[31]
Acc [48] all þurrh Cristess hellpe;
& unnc birrþ [49] baþe [50] þannkenn Crist
Þatt itt iss brohht till [39] ende.
Icc hafe sammnedd [51] o [52] þiss boc

[1] who [2] doth [3] may [4] many a man's sore labor hath often misfortune [5] no man should postpone [6] delay [7] promises [8] sure [9] then he hath it certainly [10] now [11] nature [12] in [13] through baptism [14] faith [15] on [16] third [17] way, degree [18] we two [19] have [20] both [21] one [22] rule-book [23] follow [24] canon's [25] order [26] just as [27] commanded [28] I have [29] badest [30] accomplished [31] thee [32] turned [33] into [34] holy lore [35] wit, intelligence [36] that [37] my Lord has lent [38] thoughtest [39] to [40] great benefit [41] if [42] eagerly [43] fulfil [44] with thought [45] therefore [46] desiredst [47] work [48] but [49] us two it behooves [50] both [51] collected [52] in

Þa Goddspelless neh [1] alle,
Þatt sinndenn [2] o the messeboc [3]
Inn all the ȝer [4] att messe.
& aȝȝ [5] affterr the Goddspell stannt [6]
Þatt tatt [7] te Goddspell meneþþ,[8]
Þatt mann birrþ spellenn [9] to the follc
Off theȝȝre [10] sawle nede;
& ȝēt tær tekenn mare inoh [11]
Þu shallt tæronne [12] findenn,
Off þatt tatt [7] Cristess hallȝhe þed [13]
Birrþ [14] trowwenn [15] wel & follȝhenn.[16]
Icc hafe sett her o [17] þiss boc
Amang Goddspelless wordess,
All þurrh me sellfenn,[18] maniȝ word
Þe rīme [19] swa [20] to fillenn;
Acc þu shallt finndenn þatt min word,
Eȝȝwhær þær [21] itt iss ekedd,[22]
Maȝȝ hellpenn tha [23] þatt redenn itt
To sen & tunnderrstanndenn [24]
All þess te bettre hu þeȝȝm birrþ [25]
Þe Goddspell unnderrstanndenn;
& forrþi [26] trowwe icc þatt te [27] birrþ
Wel þolenn [28] mine wordess,
Eȝȝwhær þær [21] thu shallt findenn hemm [29]
Amang Godspelless wordess.

LAYAMON (c. 1205)

From THE BRUT

Arthur for [30] to Cornwale
Mid unimete ferde; [31]
Modred that iherde [32]
And him togeines heolde [33]
Mid unimete [34] folke.
Ther weore monie væie! [35]
Uppen there Tambre [36]
Heo [37] tuhten [38] to-gadere;
The stude hatte [39] Camelford, —
Ever-mare ilast that ilke weorde! [40]
And at Camelforde wes isomned [41]
Sixti thusend
And ma thusend there-to; [42]

[1] nigh, near [2] are [3] mass-book [4] year [5] always [6] stands [7] that that, that which [8] means [9] that it behooves one tell [10] of their [11] and besides that enough more [12] therein [13] holy people [14] behooves [15] believe [16] follow [17] here in [18] by myself [19] rhythm, measure [20] so [21] everywhere where [22] added [23] those [24] to understand [25] all the better for this how it behooves them [26] therefore [27] thee [28] endure, permit [29] them [30] went [31] with a numberless army [32] heard [33] and went against him [34] numberless [35] there were many fey (fated to die) [36] upon the Tamar (a river) [37] they [38] came [39] the place was called [40] evermore shall last that same word (name) [41] was gathered [42] and more thousands besides

Modred wes heore ælder.[1]
Tha [2] thiderward gon [3] ride
Arthur the riche [4]
Mid unimete folke,
Væie thah hit weore.[5]
Uppe there Tambre
Heo tuhte [6] to-somne,[7]
Heven here-marken,[8]
Halden [9] to-gadere;
Luken sweord longe,[10]
Leiden o [11] the helmen,
Fur ut sprengen,[12]
Speren brastlien; [13]
Sceldes gonnen scanen,[14]
Scaftes to-breken.[15]
Ther faht [16] al to-somne [17]
Folc unimete.
Tambre wes on flode [18]
Mid unimete [19] blode.
Mon i than fihte
Non [20] ther ne mihte
I-kenne nenne kempe,[21]
No [22] wha dude [23] wurse, no wha bet,[24]
Swa that withe [25] wes imenged; [26]
For ælc [27] sloh [28] adun riht,
Weore he swein,[29] weore he cniht.[30]
Ther wes Modred of-slawe [31]
And idon of lif-dawe [32]

[33] * * * * * * *
* * * in than fihte.
Ther weoren of-slawe [31]
Alle tha snelle,[34]
Arthures hered-men,[35]
Heye and lawe,[36]
And tha Bruttes [37] alle
Of Arthures borde, [38]
And alle his fosterlinges [39]
Of feole kineriches,[40]
And Arthur forwunded
Mid wal-spere brade.[41]
Fiftene he hafde
Feondliche wunden; [42]
Mon mihte i thare lasten [43]

[1] was their leader [2] then [3] did [4] great [5] fey though they were [6] they came [7] together [8] raised battle-standards [9] rushed [10] locked long swords [11] laid on, struck upon [12] made fire leap out [13] rattled spears [14] shields did shiver [15] shafts broke to pieces [16] fought [17] together [18] a-flood [19] measureless [20] no man in the fight [21] recognize no warrior [22] nor [23] did [24] better [25] conflict [26] confused [27] each [28] struck [29] swain [30] knight [31] slain [32] and put from life-days [33] *A line or more is missing here.* [34] the brave [35] retainers [36] high and low [37] the Britons [38] table [39] wards [40] many kingdoms [41] with broad slaughter-spear [42] dreadful wounds [43] in the least

Twa gloven ithraste.[1]
Tha [2] nas ther na mare
I than fehte to lave [3]
Of twa hundred thusend monnen [4]
Tha [5] ther leien [6] to-hauwen [7]
Buten [8] Arthur the king ane [9]
And of his cnihtes tweien.[10]
Arthur wes for-wunded
Wunder ane swithe.[11]
Ther to him com a cnave [12]
The [13] wes of his cunne; [14]
He wes Cadores sune,
The Eorles of Cornwaile.
Constantin hehte [15] the cnave;
He wes than [16] kinge deore.
Arthur him lokede on,
Ther he lai on folden,[17]
And thas word [18] seide
Mid sorhfulle heorte:
"Constantin, thu art wilcume!
Thu weore [19] Cadores sone!
Ich the bitache here [20]
Mine kineriche; [21]
And wite [22] mine Bruttes
A to thines lifes; [23]
And hald heom [24] alle tha lawen [25]
Tha habbeoth istonden a mine dawen,[26]
And alle tha lawen gode
Tha bi Utheres dawen stode.
And ich wulle varen [27] to Avalun
To vairest [28] alre [29] maidene,
To Argante there [30] quene,
Alven swithe sceone; [31]
And heo [32] scal mine wunden
Makien alle isunde,[33]
Al hal [34] me makien
Mid haleweiye drenchen.[35]
And seothe [36] ich cumen wulle
To mine kineriche [37]
And wunien [38] mid Brutten
Mid muchelere wunne." [39]
Æfne than worden [40]
Ther com of se wenden [41]
That wes an sceort bat lithen,[42]

[1] thrust [2] then [3] in the fight remaining [4] men [5] who [6] lay [7] hewed to pieces [8] but [9] alone [10] two [11] wondrously much [12] young man [13] who [14] kin [15] was named [16] to the [17] the ground [18] these words [19] thou wert [20] I commit to thee here [21] kingdom [22] defend [23] ever during thy life [24] keep for them [25] customs, laws [26] that have stood in my days [27] I will go [28] fairest [29] of all [30] the [31] elf very beautiful [32] she [33] well [34] whole [35] with healing draughts [36] afterwards [37] kingdom [38] dwell [39] with great joy [40] even with these words [41] from the sea moving [42] that was a short boat gliding

Sceoven mid uthen;[1]
And twa wimmen ther-inne
Wunderliche idihte.[2]
And heo nomen Arthur anan,[3]
And an eovste hine vereden,[4]
And softe hine adun leiden,
And forth gunnen lithen.[5]
Tha[6] wes hit iwurthen[7]
That Merlin seide whilen,[8]
That weore unimete care[9]
Of Arthures forth-fare.[10]
Bruttes ileveth yete[11]
That he bon on live[12]
And wunnien[13] in Avalun
Mid fairest alre[14] alven;
And lokieth evere Bruttes yete
Whan Arthur cumen lithe.[15]
Nis naver[16] the mon iboren,
Of naver nane burde icoren,[17]
The cunne[18] of than sothe[19]
Of Arthur sugen mare.[20]
Bute while[21] wes an witeye[22]
Mærlin ihate,[23]
He bodede[24] mid worde —
His quithes[25] weoren sothe[26] —
That an Arthur sculde yete
Cum Anglen to fulste.[27]

From KING HORN (before 1250)

(*Unknown Author*)

Alle beon he[28] blithe
That to my song lythe![29]
A sang ihc schal you singe
Of Murry the kinge.
King he was bi weste[30]
So longe so hit laste.
Godhild het[31] his quen;
Fairer ne mihte non ben.[32]
He hadde a sone that het[31] Horn;
Fairer ne mihte non beo born,
Ne no rein upon birine,[33]

[1] impelled by the waves [2] wondrously attired [3] they took Arthur at once [4] and in haste bore him [5] did glide [6] then [7] fulfilled [8] whilom, formerly [9] that there should be measureless sorrow [10] death [11] believe yet [12] is alive [13] dwells [14] of all [15] shall come [16] is never [17] of never no (*i.e.* of no) lady chosen [18] who can [19] the truth [20] say more [21] once [22] wizard [23] named [24] announced [25] sayings [26] true [27] come for a help to the English [28] they [29] listen [30] in the west [31] was named [32] fairer might none be [33] nor any rain rain upon

Ne sunne upon bischine.[1]
Fairer nis non thane he was;
He was brigt so the glas,
He was whit so the flur,
Rose-red was his colur.[2]
In none kinge-riche[3]
Nas non his iliche.[4]
Twelf feren[5] he hadde
That he with him ladde,[6]
Alle riche mannes sones,
And alle hi were faire gomes,[7]
With him for to pleie.
And mest he luvede tweie;[8]
That on him het[9] Hathulf child,
And that other Fikenild.
Athulf was the beste
And Fikenylde the werste.
Hit was upon a someres day,
Also[10] ihc you telle may,
Murri the gode king
Rod on his pleing[11]
Bi the se side,
Ase he was woned[12] ride.[2]
He fond bi the stronde,
Arived on his londe,
Schipes fiftene,
With Sarazins kene,[13]
He axede what hi sohte[14]
Other to londe brohte.
A payn[15] hit of-herde[16]
And hym wel sone answerde,
"Thi lond-folk we schulle slon[17]
And alle that Crist leveth[18] upon,
And the selve[19] rigt anon;
Ne schaltu[20] todai henne[21] gon."
The kyng ligte of his stede,
For tho[22] he havede nede,
And his gode knigtes two;
Al to fewe he hadde tho.[22]
Swerd hi[23] gunne[24] gripe
And to-gadere smite.
Hy[23] smyten[25] under schelde,
That sume hit yfelde.[26]
The king hadde al to fewe
Togenes so vele schrewe.[27]
So fele[28] mihten ythe[29]
Bringe hem thre to dithe.[30]
The pains[31] come to londe
And neme[32] hit in here honde.

[1] shine [2] *After this line other MSS. insert two other lines.* [3] kingdom [4] like [5] companions [6] led [7] fellows [8] two [9] was named [10] as [11] in his sport [12] wont [13] bold [14] they sought [15] pagan [16] heard [17] slay [18] believe [19] thyself [20] thou shalt not [21] hence [22] then [23] they [24] did [25] smote [26] felled [27] against so many wicked [28] many [29] easily [30] death [31] pagans [32] took

That folc hi gunne quelle [1]
And churchen for to felle.
Ther ne moste libbe [2]
The fremde [3] ne the sibbe,[4]
Bute hi here lawe asoke [5]
And to here [6] toke.
Of alle wymmanne
Wurst was Godhild thanne.
For Murri heo weop [7] sore
And for Horn yute [8] more.[9]
He [10] wenten ut of halle,
Fram hire maidenes alle,
Under a roche of stone.
Ther heo livede alone.
Ther heo [10] servede Gode,
Agenes the paynes [11] forbode.[12]
Ther he [10] servede Criste,
That no payn hit ne wiste.[13]
Evere heo bad [14] for Horn Child,
That Jesu Crist him beo myld.
Horn was in paynes honde
With his feren [15] of the londe.
Muchel was his fairhede,[16]
For Jhesu Crist him makede.
Payns him wolde slen [17]
Other al quic flen.[18]
Gef his fairnesse nere,[19]
The children alle aslawe [20] were.
Thanne spak on Admirald,
Of wordes he was bald,[21]
"Horn, thu art wel kene,[22]
And that is wel isene; [23]
Thu art gret and strong,
Fair and evene long.[24]
Thu schalt waxe more,[25]
Bi fulle seve [26] yere,
Gef thu mote [27] to live [28] go,
And thine feren [15] also.
Gef hit so bi-falle,
Ye scholde slen [17] us alle;
Tharvore thu most to stere,[29]
Thu and thine ifere.[15]
To schupe schulle ye funde [30]
And sinke to the grunde.[31]
The se you schal adrenche; [32]
Ne schal hit us noht of-thinche.[33]
For if thu were alive,

[1] did kill [2] there might not live [3] foreigner [4] kinsman [5] unless they forsook their faith [6] theirs [7] she wept [8] yet [9] *See note on* l. 16. [10] she [11] pagans' [12] prohibition [13] knew [14] prayed [15] companions [16] fairness [17] slay [18] flay alive [19] if it were not for his beauty [20] slain [21] bold [22] brave [23] very evident [24] of good height [25] greater [26] seven [27] mayst [28] alive [29] go to ship [30] go [31] bottom [32] drown [33] repent

With swerd other with knive
We scholden alle deie,
And thi fader deth abeie." [1]
The children hi brohte to stronde,
Wringinde here honde,[2]
Into schupes borde
At the furste worde.
Ofte hadde Horn beo wo,[3]
Ac [4] nevere wurs than him was tho.[5]
The se bigan to flowe
And Hornchild to rowe.
The se that schup so faste drof,
The children dradde ther of;
Hi wenden to-wisse [6]
Of here lif to misse,
Al the day and al the niht,
Til hit sprang dai liht,
Til Horn say [7] on the stronde
Men gon in the londe.
"Feren," [8] quath he, "yinge,
Ihc [9] telle you tithinge.
Ihc here fogeles [10] singe
And that gras him springe.
Blithe beo we on lyve,
Ure schup is on ryve." [11]
Of schup hi gunne funde [12]
And setten fout [13] to grunde.[14]
Bi the se side
Hi leten that schup ride.
Thanne spak him Child Horn,
In Suddene he was iborn,
"Schup, bi the se flode
Daies have thu gode;
Bi the se brinke
No water the na drinke.[15]
Gef thu cume to Suddenne,
Gret thu wel of myne kenne; [16]
Gret thu wel my moder,
Godhild, quen the gode.
And seie the paene [17] kyng,
Jesu Cristes withering,[18]
That ihc [9] am hol and fer [19]
On this lond arived her.
And seie that hi [20] schal fonde [21]
The dent of myne honde."

* * * * *

Anon upon Athulf child
Rymenhild gan wexe wild.
He [22] wende [23] that Horn hit were

[1] pay for [2] wringing their hands [3] been sad [4] but [5] then *See note on* l. 16. [6] they expected certainly [7] saw [8] companions [9] I [10] birds [11] shore [12] did go [13] foot [14] ground [15] drown [16] kin [17] pagan [18] enemy [19] far [20] they [21] experience [22] she [23] thought

That heo[1] havede there.
Heo[1] sette him on bedde,
With Athulf child he[1] wedde.[2]
On[3] hire armes tweie
Athulf heo gan[4] leie.
"Horn," quath heo, "wel longe
Ihc habbe the luved stronge.
Thu schalt thi trewthe plihte
On myn hond her-rihte,[5]
Me to spuse holde,[6]
And ihc the lord to wolde."[7]
Athulf sede on hire ire,[8]
So stille so hit were,[9]
"Thi tale nu thu lynne,[10]
For Horn nis noht her inne.
Ne beo we noht iliche,[11]
Horn is fair and riche,
Fairer bi one ribbe[12]
Thane eni man that libbe.[13]
They[14] Horn were under molde,
Other elles[15] wher he wolde,
Other henne[16] a thusend mile,
Ihc nolde[17] him bigile."
Rymenhild hire biwente,[18]
And Athelbrus fule[19] heo schente.[20]
"Hennes[16] thu go, thu fule theof,[21]
Ne wurstu[22] me nevere-more leof.[23]
Went[24] ut of my bur,[25]
With muchel mesaventeur.
Schame mote[26] thu fonge[27]
And on hiye rode[28] anhonge.[29]
Ne spek ihc noht with Horn,
Nis he noht so unorn.[30]
Horn is fairer thane beo he,
With muchel schame mote thu deie."[31]
Athelbrus in a stunde[32]
Fel anon to grunde.
"Lefdi, min owe,[33]
Lithe[34] me a litel throwe.[35]
Lust[36] whi ich wonde[37]
Bringe the Horn to honde.
For Horn is fair and riche,
Nis no whar his iliche.[11]
Aylmar, the gode kyng,
Dude[38] him on mi lokyng.[39]
Gef Horn were her abute,[40]
Sore y[41] me dute[42]

[1] she [2] acted madly [3] in [4] did [5] at once [6] to have me as wife [7] and I to possess thee as lord [8] ear [9] as softly as might be [10] cease [11] alike [12] a rib [13] lives [14] though [15] or else [16] hence [17] I would not [18] turned [19] foully [20] abused [21] foul thief [22] thou shalt not be [23] dear [24] go [25] bower [26] may [27] get [28] cross, gallows [29] hang [30] ugly [31] die [32] moment [33] own [34] listen [35] while [36] list [37] refused [38] put [39] care [40] here-about [41] I [42] fear

With him ye wolden pleie
Bitwex you selve tweie.[1]
Thanne scholde withuten othe[2]
The kyng maken us wrothe.[3]
Forgef me thi tene,[4]
Lefdi, my quene,
And Horn ihc schal the fecche,
Wham-so hit recche."[5]
Rymenhild, yef he cuthe,[6]
Gan lynne[7] with hire muthe.
Heo[8] makede hire wel blithe,
Wel was hire that sithe.[9]
"Go nu," quath heo, "sone,[10]
And send him after none,[11]
On a squieres wise,
Whane the kyng arise,
To wude for to pleie.
Nis non that him biwreie;[12]
He schal with me bileve[13]
Til hit beo nir[14] eve,
To haven of him mi wille.
After ne recche ihc what me telle."[15]
Aylbrus wende[16] hire fro;
Horn in halle fond he tho[17]
Bifore the kyng on benche
Wyn for to schenche.[18]
"Horn," quath he, "so hende,[19]
To bure[20] nu thu wende,[21]
After mete stille,
With Rymenhild to duelle.[22]
Wordes suthe[23] bolde
In herte thu hem holde.
Horn, beo me wel trewe;
Ne schal hit the nevre rewe."[24]
Horn in herte leide
Al that he him seide.
He yeode[25] in wel rigte
To Rymenhild the brigte.
On knes he him sette,[26]
And sweteliche hure grette.[27]
Of his feire sigte
Al the bur gan ligte.
He spac faire speche;
Ne dorte[28] him noman teche.
"Wel thu sitte and softe,
Rymenhild the brigte,
With thine Maidenes sixe
That the sitteth nixte.[29]
Kinges stuard ure[30]

[1] two [2] without oath, certainly [3] afraid [4] sorrow [5] who-ever regrets it [6] if she could [7] cease [8] she [9] time [10] at once [11] noon [12] shall betray [13] remain [14] near [15] afterwards I care not what people may say [16] went [17] then [18] pour [19] courteous [20] bower [21] go [22] remain, be [23] very [24] repent [25] went [26] he kneeled [27] greeted [28] needed [29] that sit nearest thee [30] our

Sende me in to bure.
With the speke ihc scholde;
Seie [1] me what thu woldest.
Seie, and ich schal here,
What thi wille were."
Rymenhild up gan stonde
And tok him bi the honde.
Heo sette him on pelle,[2]
Of wyn to drinke his fulle.[3]
Heo makede him faire chere
And tok him abute the swere.[4]
Ofte heo him custe,[5]
So wel so hire luste.[6]
"Horn," heo sede, "withute strif
Thu schalt have me to thi wif.
Horn, have of me rewthe,[7]
And pligt [8] me thi trewthe."
Horn tho him bithogte
What he speke migte.
"Crist," quath he, "the wisse,[9]
And yive [10] the hevene blisse
Of thine husebonde,
Wher he beo in londe;
Ihc am ibore to lowe
Such wimman to knowe.
Ihc am icome of thralle,
And fundling bifalle.[11]
Ne feolle [12] hit the of cunde [13]
To spuse [14] beo me bunde.[15]
Hit nere no fair wedding
Bitwexe a thral and a king."
Tho gan Rymenhild mis-lyke,
And sore gan to sike.[16]
Armes heo gan buge; [17]
Adun he [18] feol iswoge.[19]
Horn in herte was ful wo,
And tok hire on his armes two.
He gan hire for to kesse,
Wel ofte mid ywisse.[20]
"Lemman," [21] he sede, "dere,
Thin herte nu thu stere.[22]
Help me to knigte,
Bi al thine migte,
To my lord the king,
That he me yive dubbing.
Thanne is mi thralhod
Iwent [23] in to knigthod,
And i schal wexe more,
And do, lemman, thi lore." [24]
Rymenhild, that swete thing,

[1] tell [2] skin, rug [3] fill [4] neck [5] kissed [6] pleased [7] pity [8] plight [9] direct [10] give [11] chanced [12] it would not suit [13] nature [14] spouse [15] bound [16] sigh [17] did bow [18] she [19] a-swoun [20] very often indeed [21] sweetheart [22] direct, control [23] turned [24] teaching

Wakede of hire swowning.[1]
"Horn," quath heo, "wel sone
That schal beon idone.
Thu schal beo dubbed knigt
Are [2] come seve nigt.
Have her this cuppe,
And this ring ther-uppe,[3]
To Aylbrus the stuard,
And se he holde foreward.[4]
Seie [5] ich him biseche,
With loveliche speche,
That he adun falle
Bifore the king in halle,
And bidde [6] the king arigte
Dubbe the to knigte.
With selver and with golde
Hit wurth [7] him wel iyolde.[8]
Crist him lene spede [9]
Thin erende to bede." [10]

* * * * * * *

NICHOLAS DE GUILDFORD (?)
(fl. 1250)

THE OWL AND THE NIGHTINGALE

Ich [11] was in one sumere dale,[12]
In one swithe digele hale,[13]
I-herede [14] ich holde grete tale [15]
An ule and one nigtingale.
That plait [16] was stif and starc and strong,
Sum wile [17] softe, and lud among; [18]
And aither [19] agen other swal,[20]
And let that vule mod ut al.[21]
And either [19] seide of otheres custe [22]
That alre-worste [23] that hi wuste; [24]
And hure and hure [25] of otheres songe
Hi [26] heolde plaiding swithe [27] stronge.
The nigtingale bi-gon the speche,
In one hurne [28] of one beche;
And sat up one vaire bohe,[29]
Thar were abute [30] blosme i-nohe,[31]
In ore waste [32] thicke hegge,
I-meind mid spire [33] and grene segge.
Heo [34] was the gladur vor [35] the rise,[36]
And song a vele cunne wise; [37]

[1] swooning [2] ere [3] besides [4] agreement [5] say [6] pray [7] shall be [8] paid [9] grant success [10] present [11] I [12] a summer dale [13] a very secret corner [14] heard [15] talk [16] strife [17] while [18] at times [19] each [20] swelled [21] the foul spirit all out [22] qualities [23] the very worst [24] knew [25] and indeed and indeed [26] they [27] very [28] corner [29] a fair bough [30] about [31] enough [32] a solitary [33] mixed with sprouts [34] she [35] for [36] spray [37] and sang in many kinds of ways

Bet thuhte the drem [1] that he [2] were
Of harpe and pipe, than he [2] nere,[3]
Bet thuhte [4] that he[2] were i-shote
Of harpe and pipe than of throte.
  Tho [5] stod on old stoc thar bi-side,
Thar tho [6] ule song hire tide,[7]
And was mid ivi al bi-growe,
Hit was thare ule earding-stowe.[8]
  The nihtingale hi [9] i-seh.
And hi [9] bi-heold and over-seh,[10]
And thuhte wel vule [11] of thare ule,
For me hi halt [12] lothlich [13] and fule.
"Unwiht," [14] heo sede, "awei thu fleo!
Me is the wers [15] that ich the seo;
I-wis [16] for thine vule lete [17]
Wel oft ich mine song for-lete; [18]
Min heorte at-flith,[19] and falt [20] mi tunge,
Wonne [21] thu art to me i-thrunge. [22]
Me luste bet speten [23] thane singe,
Of [24] thine fule gogelinge." [25]
  Theos ule abod fort [26] hit was eve,
Heo ne mihte no leng bileve,[27]
Vor hire heorte was so gret,[28]
That wel neh [29] hire fnast at-schet; [30]
And warp [31] a word thar-after longe:
"Hu thincthe [32] nu bi mine songe?
Wenst [33] thu that ich ne cunne [34] singe,
Theh [35] ich ne cunne [36] of writelinge? [37]
I-lome [38] thu dest [39] me grame,[40]
And seist me bothe teone [41] and schame;
Gif [42] ich the heolde on mine vote,[43]
So hit bi-tide [44] that ich mote! [45]
And thu were ut of thine rise,[46]
Thu scholdest singe an other wise."

* * * * * *

"Yet thu me seist of other thinge,
And telst that ich ne can noht singe,
Ac [47] al mi reorde [48] is woning,[49]
And to i-here grislich [50] thing.
That nis noht soth,[51] ich singe efne [52]
Mid fulle dreme [53] and lude stefne.[48]
Thu wenist [54] that ech song beo grislich [55]

[1] the sound seemed rather [2] it [3] was not [4] it seemed rather [5] then [6] where the [7] in her turn [8] the owl's home [9] her [10] despised [11] very foully [12] for everyone holds her [13] hateful [14] monster [15] I am the worse [16] truly [17] appearance [18] give up [19] flies away [20] fails [21] when [22] arrived [23] I feel more like spitting [24] because of [25] screeching [26] waited till [27] no longer wait [28] swollen [29] nigh [30] breath choked [31] threw [32] how does it seem [33] thinkst [34] cannot [35] though [36] know nothing [37] trilling [38] often [39] causest [40] anger [41] injury [42] if [43] foot [44] so may it happen [45] may [46] bough [47] but [48] voice [49] lamentation [50] terrible [51] true [52] precisely [53] sound [54] thinkest [55] harsh

That thine pipinge nis i-lich: [1]
Mi stefne [2] is bold and noht un-orne,[3]
Heo [4] is i-lich [1] one grete horne,
And thin is i-lich [1] one pipe
Of one smale weode un-ripe.[5]
Ich singe bet than thu dest; [6]
Thu chaterest so [7] doth on Irish prest.
Ich singe an eve, a rihte time,
And seoththe [8] won [9] hit is bed-time,
The thridde sithe [10] at middelnihte,
And so ich mine song adihte [11]
Wone [9] ich i-seo arise veorre [12]
Other [13] dai-rim [14] other [15] dai-sterre.
Ich do god mid mine throte,
And warni men to heore note; [16]
Ac [17] thu singest alle longe niht,
From eve fort [18] hit is dai-liht,
And evre lesteth thin o [19] song
So [7] longe so [7] the niht is longe,
And evre croweth thi wrecche crei,[20]
That he ne swiketh [21] niht ne dai;
Mid thine pipinge thu adunest [22]
Thas monnes earen thar [23] thu wunest,[24]
And makest thine song so un-wiht [25]
That me [26] ne telth [27] of the nowiht.[28]
Evrich murhthe [29] mai so longe i-leste,
That heo shal liki [30] wel un-wreste; [31]
Vor harpe and pipe and fugeles [32] songe
Misliketh, gif hit is to longe.
Ne beo the song never so murie,
That he ne shal thinche [33] wel un-murie,[34]
Gef he i-lesteth over un-wille.[35]
So thu miht [36] thine song aspille; [37]
Vor hit is soth,[38] Alvred hit seide,
And me [26] hit mai in boke rede,
'Evrich thing mai leosen [39] his godhede [40]
Mid unmethe [41] and mid over-dede.'" [42]

* * * * * *

  "Ule," heo seide, "wi dostu so?
Thu singest a-winter [43] 'wolawo'; [44]
Thu singest so [7] doth hen a [45] snowe,
Al that heo singeth, hit is for wowe.[46]
A-wintere thu singest wrothe [47] and gomere,[48]
And evre thu art dumb a-sumere.
Hit is for thine fule nithe,[49]

[1] that is not like thy piping [2] voice [3] unpleasing [4] it [5] green [6] dost [7] as [8] afterwards [9] when [10] third time [11] ordain [12] afar [13] either [14] dawn [15] or [16] benefit [17] but [18] till [19] lasteth thy one [20] cry [21] it ceases not [22] dinnest [23] where [24] dwellest [25] horrible [26] one [27] accounts [28] naught [29] every mirth [30] please [31] very badly [32] bird's [33] seem [34] unpleasant [35] if it lasts unto displeasure [36] mayst [37] ruin [38] true [39] lose [40] goodness [41] excess [42] over-doing [43] in winter [44] welaway [45] in the [46] woe [47] wrath [48] grief [49] hatred

That thu ne miht [1] mid us beo blithe,
Vor thu forbernest [2] wel neh [3] for onde,[4]
Wane [5] ure blisse cumeth to londe.
Thu farest so [6] doth the ille; [7]
Evrich blisse him is un-wille; [8]
Grucching and luring [9] him beoth rade,[10]
Gif he i-seoth that men beoth glade;
He wolde that he i-seye [11]
Teres in evrich monnes eye;
Ne rohte he [12] theh [13] flockes were
I-meind [14] bi toppes [15] and bi here.[16]
Al-so thu dost on thire [17] side;
Vor wanne [5] snou lith thicke and wide,
And alle wihtes [18] habbeth sorhe,[19]
Thu singest from eve fort amorhe.[20]
Ac [21] ich alle blisse mid me bringe;
Ech wiht [22] is glad for mine thinge,[23]
And blisseth hit [24] wanne [5] ich cume,
And hihteth agen [25] mine kume.[26]
The blostme ginneth springe and sprede
Bothe ine treo and ek on mede;
The lilie mid hire faire wlite [27]
Wolcumeth me, that thu hit wite,[28]
Bit [29] me mid hire faire bleo [30]
That ich schulle to hire fleo;
The rose also mide hire rude,[31]
That cumeth ut of the thorne wude,
Bit [29] me that ich shulle singe
Vor hire luve one skentinge." [32]

* * * * * *

From CURSOR MUNDI (c. 1300)

(*Unknown Author*)

THE FLIGHT INTO EGYPT

An angel thus til [33] him can [34] sai:
"Rise up, Joseph, and busk [35] and ga,[36]
Maria and thi child al-sua; [37]
For yow be-hoves nu [38] al thre
In land of Egypt for to fle;
Rise up ar [39] it be dai,
And folus [40] forth the wildrin [41] wai.
Herod, that es the child [42] fa,[43]
Fra nu [44] wil sek him for to sla.[45]
Thare sal [46] yee bide stil wit [47] the barn,[48]

[1] mayst not [2] burnest up [3] nigh [4] envy [5] when [6] as [7] wicked man [8] unpleasing [9] louring [10] ready [11] saw [12] he would not care [13] though [14] mixed up [15] heads [16] hair [17] thy [18] creatures [19] sorrow [20] till morning [21] but [22] creature [23] on my account [24] rejoices [25] hopeth for [26] coming [27] face [28] know [29] bids [30] visage [31] redness [32] pastime [33] to [34] did [35] get ready [36] go [37] also [38] now [39] ere [40] follow [41] wilderness [42] child's [43] foe [44] from now [45] slay [46] shall [47] with [48] child

Til that I eft [1] cum yow to warn."
Son [2] was Joseph redi bun; [3]
Wit [4] naghtertale [5] he went o [6] tun,
Wit [4] Maria mild and thair meine,[7]
A maiden and thair suanis [8] thre,
That servid tham in thair servis;
With thaim was nan bot war [9] and wis.
Forth sco rad,[10] that moder mild,
And in hir barm [11] sco ledd [12] hir child,
Til thai come at [13] a cove was [14] depe.
Thar [15] thai tham thoght to rest and slepe;
Thar did [16] thai Mari for to light,[17]
Bot son thai sagh [18] an ugli sight.
Als [19] thai loked tham biside,
Ute o [20] this cove [21] than sagh [18] thai glide
Mani dragons wel [22] sodanli;
The suanis [23] than bi-gan to cri.
Quen [24] Jesus sagh tham glopnid [25] be,
He lighted of [26] his moder kne
And stod a-pon thaa [27] bestes grim,[28]
And thai tham luted [29] under him.
Than com [30] the propheci al cler
To dede [31] that said es in Sauter: [32]
"The dragons, wonand [33] in thair cove,
The Laverd [34] agh [35] yee worthli to lofe." [36]
Jesus he went befor tham than,
Forbed [37] tham harm do ani man.
Maria and Joseph ne-for-thi [38]
For the child war ful dreri; [39]
Bot Jesus ansuard [40] thaim onan: [41]
"For me drednes haf [42] nu yee nan,[43]
Ne haf yee for me na barn-site,[44]
For I am self [45] man al parfite,[46]
And al the bestes that ar wild
For me most [47] be tame and mild."
Leon yode tham als imid; [48]
And pardes,[49] als [19] the dragons did,
Bifor Maria and Joseph yede,[50]
In right wai tham for to lede.
Quen Maria sagh thaa [27] bestes lute,[51]
First sco [52] was gretli in dute,[53]
Til Jesus loked on hir blith
And dridnes [54] bad hir nan to kith.[55]
"Moder," he said, "haf thou na ward [56]

[1] again [2] soon [3] prepared [4] with [5] nighttime [6] from [7] household [8] men-servants [9] none but was wary [10] she rode [11] bosom [12] carried [13] came to [14] cave that was [15] there [16] caused [17] alight [18] saw [19] as [20] out of [21] cave [22] very [23] men [24] when [25] terrified [26] off [27] those [28] fierce [29] bowed [30] came [31] to deed, to realization [32] the Psalter [33] dwelling [34] Lord [35] ought [36] praise [37] forbade [38] nevertheless [39] sad [40] answered [41] at once [42] have [43] none [44] child-sorrow [45] very [46] perfect [47] must [48] a lion went with them also [49] leopards [50] went [51] bow [52] she [53] doubt, fear [54] terror [55] show, feel [56] regard

Nother o [1] leon ne o lepard,
For thai com noght us harm to do,
Bot thair servis at [2] serve us to."
Bath [3] ass and ox that wit [4] tham war [5]
And bestes that thair harnais bar
Ute o Jerusalem, thair kyth,[6]
The leons mekli yod [7] tham wit,[4]
Wit-uten harm of ox or ass,
Or ani best that wit tham was.
Than was fulfild the propheci,
That said was thoru Jeremi,
"Wolf and wether, leon and ox,
Sal [8] comen samen,[9] and lamb and fox."
A wain [10] thai had thair gere wit-in,
That draun [11] was wit oxen tuin.[12]
Forth thair wai thai went fra than [13]
Wit-uten kithing [14] of ani man;
Maria forth tham foluand [15] rade.[16]
Gret hete in wildernes it made;[17]
O [1] gret travail sco was weri;
A palme-tre sco sagh hir bi;
"Joseph," sco said, "fain wald I rest,
Under this tre me-thinc [18] wer best."
"Gladli," said he, "that wil resun;" [19]
Son [20] he stert [21] and tok hir dun.
Quen sco had sitten thar a wei,[22]
Sco bihild a tre was hei,[23]
And sagh a frut thar-on hingand,[24]
Man clepes palmes [25] in that land.
"Joseph," sco said, "fain wald I ete
O this fruit, if I moght gete."
"Maria, me-thinc ferli [26] o the
That se the gret heght o this tre;
The frut hu suld [27] man reche unto
That man his hand mai to nan do? [28]
Bot I site [29] for an other thing,
That we o water has nu wanting;
Ur water purveance [30] es gan,
And in this wildernes es nan,
Nather for us ne for ur fee [31]
Ne for nan of ur meiné." [32]
Jesus satt on his moder kne,
Wit a ful blith cher [33] said he,
"Bogh [34] thou til [2] us suith,[35] thou tre,
And of thi fruit thou give us plenté."
Unnethe [36] had he said the sune,[37]

[1] of [2] to [3] both [4] with [5] were [6] country [7] went [8] shall [9] together [10] wagon [11] drawn [12] two [13] then [14] knowledge [15] following [16] rode [17] it became very hot in the wilderness [18] me-thinks [19] reason wills that [20] immediately [21] came up [22] a short while [23] tall [24] hanging [25] which they call palms [26] strange [27] should [28] to none of which one may put his hand [29] sorrow [30] our provision of water [31] cattle [32] household [33] countenance [34] bow [35] quickly [36] scarcely [37] sound

Quen the tre it boghed dune [1]
Right to Maria, his moder, fote,
The crop was evening to the rote.[2]
Quen all had eten frut i-nogh,
Yeit it boghud [3] dun ilk bogh,[4]
Til he wald comand it to rise,
That gert it lute [5] in his servis.
To that tre than spak Jesu:
"Rise up," he said, "and right the nu,[6]
I wil [7] thou fra nu forward
Be planted in min orcherd
Amang mi tres o paradise,
That thou and thai be of a prise; [8]
Under thi rote thar es a spring,
I wil that ute the water wring; [9]
Mak us a well, for mine sake,
That all mai plente o water take."
Wit this stert [10] up the tre stedfast;
Under the rote a well [11] ute-brast,
Wit strand [12] suete,[13] and clere, and cald.
All dranc i-nogh, ilkan [14] that wald,[15]
Wit all the bestes in that place;
Thai loved ai Drightin of [16] his grace.

THOMAS DE HALES (fl. 1250)

A LUVE RON [17]

A mayde Cristes [18] me bit yorne [19]
  That ich hire [20] wurche [21] a luve ron;
For hwan heo [22] myhte best ileorne [23]
  To taken on [24] other soth [25] lefmon [26]
That treowest were of alle berne,[27]
  And best wyte cuthe [28] a freo wymmon.
Ich hire nule [29] nowiht [30] werne,[31]
  Ich hire wule [32] teche as ic con.

Mayde, her [33] thu myht [34] biholde
  This worldes luve nys [35] bute o res [36]
And is byset so fele-volde,[37]
  Vikel,[38] and frakel,[39] and wok,[40] and les.[41]
Theos theines [42] that her weren bolde
  Beoth aglyden [43] so [44] wyndes bles; [45]
Under molde [46] hi liggeth [47] colde
  And faleweth [48] so [44] doth medewe gres.

* * * * * * *

[1] down [2] the top was even with the root [3] bowed [4] every bough [5] who made it bow [6] straighten thyself now [7] I will that [8] of one value, of equal dignity [9] burst [10] sprang [11] spring [12] stream [13] sweet [14] each one [15] would [16] praised ever the Lord for [17] a love rune (or letter) [18] of Christ's [19] begs me eagerly [20] her [21] make [22] whereby she [23] learn [24] an [25] true [26] lover [27] men [28] could protect [29] will not [30] not at all [31] refuse [32] will [33] here [34] mayst [35] is not [36] a race [37] in so many ways [38] fickle [39] ugly [40] weak [41] false [42] these nobles [43] are passed away [44] as [45] breath [46] the earth [47] they lie [48] wither

Nis non [1] so riche, ne non so freo,[2]
That he ne schal heonne [3] sone away.
Ne may hit never his waraunt beo, —
Gold ne seolver, vouh [4] ne gray;[5]
Ne beo he no the swift,[6] ne may he fleo,
Ne weren [7] his lif enne [8] day.
Thus is thes world, as thu mayht [9] seo,
Al so [10] the schadewe that glyt [11] away.

This world fareth hwilynde.[12]
Hwenne [13] on cumeth, an other goth;
That [14] wes bi-fore nu is bihynde,
That [14] er [15] was leof [16] nu hit is loth;[17]
For-thi [18] he doth as the blynde
That in this world his luve doth.[19]
Ye mowen iseo [20] the world aswynde;[21]
That wouh [22] goth forth, abak that soth.[23]

Theo [24] luve that ne may her abyde,
Thu treowest [25] hire [26] myd muchel wouh,[27]
Al so [28] hwenne hit schal to-glide,[29]
Hit is fals, and mereuh,[30] and frouh,[31]
And fromward [32] in uychon tide.[33]
Hwile hit lesteth, is seorewe [34] inouh;[35]
An ende,[36] ne werie [37] mon [robe] so syde,[38]
He schal to-dreosen [39] so lef on bouh.[40]

* * * * * * *

Hwer is Paris and Heleyne,
That weren so bryht and feyre on bleo;[41]
Amadas, Tristram, and Dideyne,[42]
Yseude and alle theo;[43]
Ector, with his scharpe meyne,[44]
And Cesar, riche of worldes feo?[45]
Heo beoth iglyden [46] ut of the reyne [47]
So [48] the schef [49] is of the cleo.[50]

Hit is of heom [51] al so hit nere;[52]
Of heom [51] me haveth [53] wunder itold,
Nere hit reuthe [54] for to heren
Hw hi [55] were with pyne aquold,[56]
And hwat hi tholeden [57] alyve here.
Al is heore [58] hot iturnd to cold.
Thus is thes world of false fere;[59]
Fol [60] he is the [61] on hire is bold.

[1] there is none [2] free, generous [3] hence [4] ermine [5] vair [6] be he never so swift [7] protect [8] a single [9] mayst [10] just as [11] glides [12] swiftly [13] when [14] what [15] formerly [16] dear [17] hated [18] therefore [19] places [20] may see [21] vanish [22] the wrong [23] the true [24] the [25] trusteth [26] it [27] very wrongly [28] even so [29] pass away [30] delicate [31] capricious [32] hasting away [33] at every time [34] sorrow [35] enough [36] at last [37] wear [38] wide [39] fall [40] bough [41] of face [42] Dido [43] those [44] strength [45] wealth [46] they have slipped away [47] land [48] as [49] sheaf [50] from the hillside [51] them [52] as if they had not existed [53] people have [54] were it not pity [55] how they [56] killed with torture [57] suffered [58] their [59] validity [60] foolish [61] who

Theyh [1] he were so riche mon [2]
As Henry ure [3] kyng,
And al so veyr [4] as Absalon
That nevede [5] on eorthe non evenyng,[6]
Al were sone his prute [7] agon,
Hit nere on ende [8] wurth on heryng.[9]
Mayde, if thu wilnest [10] after leofmon [11]
Ich teche the enne [12] treowe king.

A! swete, if thu iknowe [13]
The gode thewes [14] of thisse childe!
He is feyr and bryht on heowe,[15]
Of glede chere,[16] of mode [17] mylde,
Of lufsum lost,[18] of truste treowe,
Freo of heorte, of wisdom wilde;[19]
Ne thurhte the never rewe,[20]
Myhtestu do the [21] in his hylde.[22]

He is ricchest mon of londe;
So [23] wide so [23] mon speketh with muth,
Alle heo [24] beoth [25] to his honde
Est and west, north and suth.
Henri, king of Engelonde,
Of hym he halt [26] and to hym buhth [27]
Mayde, to the he send [28] his sonde [29]
And wilneth [30] for to beo the cuth.[31]

* * * * * * *

Hwat spekestu of eny bolde [32]
That wrouthe [33] the wise Salomon?
Of jaspe, of saphir, of merede [34] golde,
And of mony on other ston?
Hit is feyrure of feole volde [35]
More than ich eu [36] telle con;
This bold,[32] mayde, the [37] is bihote,[38]
If that thu bist [39] his leovemon.[40]

Hit stont [41] uppon a treowe mote,[42]
Thar hit never truke [43] ne schal;
Ne may no mynur hire underwrote,[44]
Ne never false [45] thene grundwal.[46]
Thar-inne is uich balewes bote,[47]
Blisse and joye, and gleo and gal.[48]
This bold, mayde, is the bihote,
And uych o blisse [49] thar-wyth-al.

[1] though [2] man [3] our [4] beautiful, fair [5] had not [6] equal [7] pride [8] at last [9] a herring [10] longest [11] a lover [12] I will teach thee a [13] didst know [14] qualities [15] hue, appearance [16] countenance [17] mood [18] of lovable desire [19] able [20] thou wouldst never need to repent [21] might'st thou put thyself [22] grace [23] as [24] they [25] are [26] holds [27] bows [28] sends [29] messenger [30] desires [31] known to thee [32] building [33] wrought [34] refined [35] fairer by many fold [36] you [37] to thee [38] promised [39] art [40] beloved [41] stands [42] moat [43] fail [44] undermine [45] make false [46] the foundation [47] each bale's remedy [48] singing [49] every bliss

Ther ne may no freond fleon [1] other,
  Ne non fur-leosen [2] his iryhte; [3]
Ther nys hate ne wreththe nouther,[4]
  Of prude [5] ne of onde [6] of none wihte;
Alle heo schule wyth engles pleye,
  Some and sauhte [7] in heovene lyhte.
Ne beoth heo,[8] mayde, in gode weye
  That wel luveth ure Dryhte? [9]

Ne may no mon hine iseo [10]
  Al so [11] he is in his mihte,
That may with-uten blisse beo
  Hwanne he isihth [12] ure Drihte;
His sihte is al joye and gleo,
  He is day wyth-ute nyhte.
Nere [13] he, mayde, ful seoly [14]
  That myhte wunye [15] myd such a knyhte?

* * * * * * *

Hwen [16] thu me dost [17] in thine rede [18]
  For the to cheose [19] a leofmon,
Ich wile don as thu me bede,[20] —
  The beste that ich fynde con.
Ne doth he, mayde, on uvele [21] dede
  That may cheose [19] of two that on,[22]
And he wile, with-ute neode,
  Take thet wurse, the betere let gon?

This rym, mayde, ich the sende
  Open and with-ute sel;
Bidde ic [23] that thu hit untrende [24]
  And leorny bute [25] bok uych del; [26]
Her-of that thu beo swithe hende,[27]
  And tech hit other maydenes wel.
Hwo-so cuthe [28] hit to than ende,[29]
  Hit wolde him stonde muchel stel.[30]

Hwenne thu sittest in longynge,
  Drauh the [31] forth this ilke [32] wryt,
Mid swete stephne [33] thu hit singe,
  And do al so hit the byt.[34]
To the he haveth send one gretynge,
  God al-myhti the beo myd! [35]
And leve cumen [36] to his brudthinge [37]
  Heye in heovene ther [38] he sit! [39]

[1] flee [2] lose [3] right [4] neither [5] pride [6] envy [7] together and at peace [8] are not they [9] our Lord [10] him see [11] just as [12] sees [13] were not [14] blessed [15] dwell [16] since [17] puttest [18] counsel [19] choose [20] badest [21] an evil [22] the one [23] I pray [24] unroll [25] without [26] each part [27] very courteous [28] knew [29] the end [30] it would help him greatly [31] draw thee [32] same [33] voice [34] bids [35] with [36] permit to come [37] marriage [38] where [39] sits

A MIDDLE ENGLISH MISCELLANY

(*Unknown Authors*)

ALYSOUN (c. 1300)

Bytuene Mersh [1] and Averil,
  When spray biginneth to springe,
The lutel foul [2] hath hire wyl
  On hyre lud [3] to synge.
  Ich libbe [4] in love longinge
  For semlokest [5] of alle thinge.
  He [6] may me blisse bringe;
Icham [7] in hire baundoun.[8]
  An hendy hap ichabbe yhent,[9]
  Ichot,[10] from hevene it is me sent,
  From alle wymmen mi love is lent [11]
And lyht [12] on Alysoun.

On heu [13] hire her is fayr ynoh,
  Hire browe broune, hire eye blake, —
With lossum chere [14] he on me loh! [15] —
  With middel [16] smal, and wel ymake.[17]
  Bote [18] he me wolle [19] to hire take,
  Forte buen [20] hire owen make,[21]
  Longe to lyuen ichulle [22] forsake,
And feye [23] fallen adoun.
  An hendy hap, etc.

Nihtes-when y wende [24] and wake;
  Forthi [25] myn wonges [26] waxeth won.
Levedi,[27] al for thine sake
  Longinge is ylent [28] me on.
  In world nis non so wytermon,[29]
  That al hire bounte [30] telle con.[31]
  Hire swyre [32] is whittore then the swon,
And feyrest may [33] in toune.
  An hendi, etc.

Icham for wowyng al forwake,[34]
  Wery so water in wore,[35]
Lest eny reve [36] me my make.[21]
  Ychabbe y-yir yore,[37]
  Betere is tholien whyle sore [38]

[1] March [2] little bird [3] in her language [4] I live [5] most beautiful [6] she [7] I am [8] power [9] a pleasant fortune I have got [10] I know [11] departed [12] alighted [13] in color [14] with loving look [15] laughed [16] waist [17] made [18] unless [19] will [20] (for) to be [21] mate [22] I will [23] ready to die [24] at night time I turn [25] therefore [26] cheeks [27] lady [28] descended [29] there is no so wise man [30] goodness [31] can [32] neck [33] maid [34] I am for wooing all worn with watching [35] weary as water in weir [36] take away from [37] I have heard long ago [38] it is better to endure hurt for a while

Then [1] mournen evermore.
  Geynest under gore,[2]
Herkne to my roun.[3]
  An hendi, etc.

SPRINGTIME (c. 1300)

Lenten [4] ys come with love to toune,
With blosmen and with briddes roune; [5]
  That al this blisse bryngeth.
Dayes-eyes in this [6] dales;
Notes suete [7] of nyhtegales;
  Uch foul song singeth.[8]
The threstercoc him threteth oo; [9]
Away is huere [10] wynter woo,
  When woderoue [11] springeth.
This [12] foules singeth ferly fele,[13]
And wlyteth [14] on huere wynter wele,[15]
  That al the wode ryngeth.

The rose rayleth [16] hire rode,[17]
The leves on the lyhte wode
  Waxen al with wille.[18]
The mone mandeth [19] hire bleo,[20]
The lilie is lossom [21] to seo,
  The fenyl and the fille; [22]
Wowes this wilde drakes,[23]
Miles murgeth huere makes; [24]
  Ase strem that striketh [25] stille,
Mody meneth, so doht mo; [26]
Ichot ycham on of tho,[27]
  For love that likes ille.[28]

The mone mandeth [29] hire lyht,
So doth the semly sonne bryht,
  When briddes singeth breme; [30]
Deawes donketh [31] the dounes; [32]
Deores with huere derne rounes,[33]
  Domes forte deme; [34]
Wormes woweth under cloude; [35]
Wymmen waxeth wounder proude,
  So wel hit wol hem seme
Yef [36] me shal wonte [37] wille of on,[38]
This wunne weole [39] y wole [40] forgon,
  Ant wyht in wode be fleme.[41]

[1] than [2] most gracious one alive (in clothing) [3] secret [4] spring [5] whisper [6] these [7] sweet [8] each bird sings a song [9] the thrustle cock threatens ever [10] their [11] woodrow [12] these [13] wonderfully many [14] look [15] weal [16] puts on [17] redness [18] vigorously [19] mends [20] complexion [21] beautiful [22] thyme [23] these wild drakes woo [24] beasts gladden their mates [25] runs [26] the moody man laments, — so do others [27] I know I am one of those [28] pleases ill [29] mends, increases [30] loud [31] dews wet [32] hills [33] lovers with their secret whispers [come] [34] cases [of love] to judge [35] worms woo under clod [36] if [37] want [38] one [39] wealth of joy [40] will [41] and be a banished wight in the forest

THE MAN IN THE MOON (c. 1350)

Mon in the mone stond [1] and strit,[2]
  On is bot-forke [3] is burthen he bereth;
Hit is muche wonder that he nadoun slyt,[4]
  For doute [5] leste he valle,[6] he shoddreth and shereth.[7]
When the forst freseth, muche chele [8] he byd; [9]
  The thornes beth kene, is hattren to-tereth; [10]
Nis no wyht [11] in the world that wot [12] when he syt,[13]
  Ne, bote [14] hit bue [15] the hegge,[16] whet wedes [17] he wereth.

Whider trowe [18] this mon ha [19] the wey take?
  He hath set is o fot [20] is other to-foren: [21]
For non hihthe [22] that he hath ne syht me hym ner shake,[23]
  He is the sloweste mon that ever wes yboren.
Wher he were othe feld [24] pycchynde stake,
  For hope of ys [25] thornes to dutten is doren? [26]
He mot [27] myd [28] is twybyl [29] other trous [30] make,
  Other [31] al is dayes werk ther were yloren.[32]

This ilke [33] mon upon heh,[34] wher-er he were,
  Wher [35] he were y the mone boren and yfed,
He leneth on is forke ase a grey frere;
  This crockede caynard,[36] sore he is adred.
Hit is mony day go [37] that he was here;
  Ichot [38] of is ernde [39] he nath [40] nout ysped.
He hath hewe [41] sumwher a burthen of brere,
  Thare-fore sum hayward [42] hath taken ys wed.[43]

Yef [44] thy wed ys ytake, bring hom the trous,[30]
  Sete forth thyn other fot, stryd over sty; [45]
We shule preye [46] the haywart hom to ur [47] hous,
  Ant maken hym at heyse [48] for the maystry,[49]
Drynke to hym deorly of fol god bous,[50]
  Ant oure dame douse [51] shal sitten hym by;
When that he is dronke ase a dreynt [52] mous,
  Thenne we schule borewe [53] the wed ate bayly.[54]

[1] stands [2] strides [3] pitch-fork [4] he doesn't slide down [5] fear [6] fall [7] shakes [8] chill [9] endures [10] they tear his clothes [11] there is nobody [12] knows [13] sits [14] unless [15] be [16] hedge [17] what clothes [18] think you [19] has [20] his one foot [21] before [22] for no haste [23] one never sees him hurry [24] whether he were in the field (*i.e.* was he) [25] his [26] to close his door [27] must [28] with [29] ax [30] truss, bundle [31] or [32] lost [33] same [34] high [35] whether [36] crooked coward [37] it is many a day ago [38] I think [39] errand [40] hath not [41] cut [42] hedge-keeper [43] pawn [44] if [45] stride over the path [46] invite [47] our [48] at ease [49] to the utmost [50] full good drink [51] sweet [52] drowned [53] redeem [54] from the bailiff

This mon hereth me nout, thah [1] ich to hym crye;
Ichot [2] the cherl is def, the del hym to-drawe! [3]
Thah [1] ich yeye upon heh,[4] nulle nout hye,[5] —
The lostlase [6] ladde con [7] nout o lawe!
Hupe forth,[8] Hubert, hoferede [9] pye!
Ichot thart amarstled [10] in-to the mawe.
Thah me teone [11] with hym that myn teth mye,[12]
The cherl nul nout [13] adoun er the day dawe.[14]

UBI SUNT QUI ANTE NOS FUERUNT?
(c. 1350)

Were beth [15] they that biforen us weren,
Houndes ladden [16] and havekes beren,[17]
And hadden feld and wode?
The riche levedies [18] in here [19] bour,
That wereden gold in here [19] tressour,[20]
With here [19] brighte rode; [21]

Eten and drounken, and maden hem glad;
Here lif was al with gamen [22] y-lad,
Men kneleden hem [23] biforen;
They beren hem wel swithe heye; [24]
And in a twincling of an eye
Here soules weren forloren.[25]

Were is that lawhing [26] and that song,
That trayling and that proude gong,[27]
Tho havekes [28] and tho houndes?
Al that joye is went away,
That wele [29] is comen to weylaway [30]
To manye harde stoundes.[31]

Here [19] paradis they nomen [32] here,[33]
And nou they lyen in helle y-fere; [34]
The fyr hit brennes [35] evere:
Long is ay, and long is o,
Long is wy, and long is wo;
Thennes ne cometh they nevere.

RICHARD ROLLE DE HAMPOLE
(1290?–1349)

FROM THE PRICKE OF CONSCIENCE

And [when man] was born til [36] this werldys light,
He ne had nouther [37] strenthe ne myght,

[1] though [2] I believe [3] the devil rend him [4] I cry aloud [5] he will not haste [6] miserable [7] knows [8] hop along [9] humpbacked [10] I believe thou art stuffed [11] though I strive [12] till my teeth ache [13] will not [14] dawns [15] where are [16] led [17] hawks bore [18] ladies [19] their [20] head dress [21] complexion [22] pleasure [23] them [24] bore themselves very high [25] lost [26] laughing [27] gait [28] those hawks [29] weal [30] alas [31] hours [32] took [33] here [34] together [35] burns [36] to [37] neither

Nouther [1] to ga [2] ne yhit [3] to stand,
Ne to crepe with fote ne with hand.
Than [4] has a man les myght than a beste
When he es born, and is sene leste;[5]
For a best, when it es born, may ga
Als-tite [6] aftir, and rýn [7] to and fra;
Bot a man has na myght thar-to,
When he es born, swa [8] to do;
For than may he noght stande ne crepe,
Bot ligge [9] and sprawel, and cry and wepe.
For unnethes [10] es a child born fully
That it ne bygynnes to goule [11] and cry;
And by that cry men may knaw than
Whether it be man or weman,
For when it es born it cryes swa; [8]
If it be man, it says 'a, a,'
That the first letter es of the nam
Of our forme-fader [12] Adam.
And if the child a woman be,
When it es born, it says 'e, e.'
E es the first letter and the hede [13]
Of the name of Eve, that bygan our dede.[14]
Tharfor a clerk made on this manere
This vers of metre that es wreten here:
Dicentes E vel A quotquot nascuntur ab Eva.
"Alle thas," he says, "that comes of Eve,
That es al men that here byhoves leve,[15]
When thai er born, what-swa [16] thai be,
Thai say outher [17] 'a, a,' or 'e, e.'"
Thus es here the bygynnyng,
Of our lyfe sorow and gretyng,[18]
Til whilk [19] our wrechednes stirres us,
And tharfor Innocent says thus:
Omnes nascimur eiulantes, ut nature nostre miseriam exprimamus.
He says, "al er we born gretand,[18]
And makand [20] a sorowful sembland,[21]
For to shew the grete wrechednes
Of our kynd [22] that in us es."
Thus when the tyme come [23] of our birthe,
Al made sorow and na mirthe;
Naked we come [23] hider, and bare,
And pure swa, sal [24] we hethen [25] fare.

* * * * * * *

[1] neither [2] walk [3] yet [4] then [5] smallest [6] immediately [7] run [8] so [9] lie [10] scarcely [11] yell [12] forefather [13] head [14] death [15] are obliged to live here [16] what-so [17] either [18] weeping [19] to which [20] making [21] semblance [22] nature [23] came [24] precisely so, shall [25] hence

THE AGE OF CHAUCER

PEARL (c. 1350)

(*Unknown Author*)

I

Perle plesaunte to prynces paye,[1]
To clanly clos [2] in golde so clere,
Oute of oryent I hardyly saye,
Ne proved I never her precios pere,[3] —
So rounde, so reken in uche a raye,[4]
So smal, so smothe her sydez were, —
Queresoever I jugged gemmez gaye,
I sette hyr sengeley in synglere.[5]
    Allas! I leste [6] hyr in on erbere; [7]
    Thurgh gresse to grounde hit fro me yot; [8]
    I dewyne, for-dokked of luf-daungere [9]
    Of that pryvy perle withouten spot.

II

Sythen [10] in that spote hit fro me sprange,
Ofte haf I wayted wyschande [11] that wele,[12]
That wont wacz whyle [13] devoyde [14] my wrange,
And heven [15] my happe and al my hele; [16]
That docz bot thrych my herte thrange,[17]
My breste in bale [18] bot bolne and bele.[19]
Yet thoght me never so swete a sange
As stylle stounde [20] let to me stele;
    Forsothe ther fleten [21] to me fele,[22] —
    To thenke hir color so clad in clot! [23]
    O moul [24] thou marrez a myry mele,[25] —
    My privy perle withouten spot.

V

Bifore that spot my honde I spennd [26]
For care ful colde that to me caght;[27]
A denely dele in my herte denned,[28]
Thagh resoun sette my selven saght.[29]

[1] delight [2] cleanly enclose? or enclosed? [3] equal [4] fit in every respect [5] alone in uniqueness [6] lost [7] an arbor [8] departed [9] I pine away, deprived of the love-dominion [10] since [11] wishing [12] weal [13] was formerly [14] to remove [15] lift up [16] prosperity [17] does but oppress my heart grievously [18] distress [19] swell and burn [20] the quiet hour [21] float [22] many things [23] clod [24] earth [25] sweet delight [26] stretched out [27] that seized upon me [28] a secret sorrow lay in my heart [29] though reason reconciled all difficulties

I playned [1] my perle that ther wacz spenned [2]
Wyth fyrte skyllez [3] that faste faght; [4]
Thagh kynde of Kryst me comfort kenned,[5]
My wreched wylle in wo ay wraghte.[6]
    I felle upon that floury flaght; [7]
    Suche odour to my hernez [8] schot,
    I slode upon a slepyng-slaghte [9]
    On that precios perle withouten spot.

XIV

More mervayle con my dom adaunt; [10]
I segh [11] by-yonde that myry mere [12]
A crystal clyffe ful relusaunt,[13]
Mony ryal ray con fro hit rere; [14]
At the fote thereof ther sete a faunt,[15]
A mayden of menske,[16] ful debonere,
Blysnande whyte wacz hyr bleaunt,[17] —
I knew hyr wel, I hade sen hyr ere.[18]
    As glysnande golde that man con schere [19]
    So schon that schene anunder schore; [20]
    On lenghe [21] I looked to hyr there, —
    The lenger, I knew hyr more and more.[22]

XV

The more I frayste [23] hyr fayre face,
Her figure fyn quen I had fonte,[24]
Suche gladande glory con to me glace [25]
As lyttel byfore therto wacz wonte;
To calle hyr lyste con me enchace,[26]
Bot baysment [27] gef myn hert a brunt; [28]
I segh hyr in so strange a place,
Such a burre myght make myn herte blunt.[29]
    Thenne verez ho up her fayre frount,[30]
    Hyr vysayge whyt as playn yvore,[31]
    That stonge myn hert ful stray atount,[32]
    And ever the lenger, the more and more.

[1] lamented [2] was taken away [3] timid reasons [4] fought hard [5] though Christ's nature taught me comfort [6] wrought [7] bed of flowers [8] brains [9] I slided into a dream [10] a greater wonder daunted my judgment [11] saw [12] pleasant lake [13] gleaming [14] many a royal gleam arose from it [15] child [16] grace [17] gleaming white was her attire [18] before [19] that one has refined [20] so shone that beautiful one beneath the cliff [21] a long time [22] the longer I looked the more certainly I knew her [23] questioned [24] when I had examined [25] such delight came to me [26] desire to speak to her seized me [27] timidity [28] attack [29] such a surprise might well astound me [30] then she lifts her fair face [31] ivory [32] that struck me into bewilderment

XX

Pyght[1] in perle, that precios pyece
On wyther-half water[2] com doun the schore;[3]
No gladder gome hethen[4] into Grece
Then I quen ho on brymme wore.[5]
Ho wacz me nerre[6] then aunte or nece,
My joy forthy wacz[7] much the more.
Ho profered me speche, that special spece,[8]
Enclynande lowe in wommon lore,[9]
Caghte of her coroun of grete tresore,
And haylsed me wyth a lote lyghte.[10]
Wel wacz me that ever I wacz bore,
To sware[11] that swete in perlez pyghte.

XXI

"O Perle," quoth I, "in perlez pyght,
Art thou my perle that I haf playned,[12]
Regretted by myn one, an nyghte?[13]
Much longeyng haf I for the layned,[14]
Sythen in-to gresse thou me aglyghte;[15]
Pensyf, payred,[16] I am for-payned,[17]
And thou in a lyf of lykyng lyghte[18]
In paradys erde,[19] of stryf unstrayned.
What wyrde hacz hyder my juel wayned,[20]
And don me in thys del[21] and gret daunger?
Fro we in twynne wern towen and twayned[22]
I haf ben a joylez jueler."[23]

XXII

That juel thenne in gemmez gente,[24]
Vered up her vyse[25] with yghen[26] graye,
Set on hyr coroun of perle orient,
And soberly after thenne con ho say:[27]
"Syr, ye haf your tale myse-tente,[28]
To say your perle is al awaye,
That is in cofer, so comly clente,[1]
As in this gardyn gracios gaye,
Here-inne to lenge[29] for-ever and play,
Ther mys nee mornyng[30] com never ner;
Her were a forser[31] for the, in faye,
If thou were a gentyl jueler.

[1] set [2] on the opposite side of the water [3] cliff [4] person from hence [5] than I when she was at the bank [6] she was nearer to me [7] on that account was [8] she spoke to me, that rare one [9] bowing low as women are taught [10] greeted me pleasantly [11] answer [12] lamented [13] alone by night [14] suffered secretly [15] since thou didst slip away from me into the grass [16] weakened [17] worn with grief [18] and thou in a life of delightful pleasure [19] land [20] what fate has brought my jewel hither [21] put me in this grief [22] since we were drawn apart and separated [23] possessor of jewels [24] beautiful [25] lifted her face [26] eyes [27] she said [28] distorted [29] remain [30] where lack nor mourning [31] jewel-box

XXIII

"Bot, jueler gente, if thou schal lose
Thy joy for a gemme that the wacz lef,[1]
Me thynk the put[2] in a mad porpose,
And busyez the aboute a raysoun bref;[3]
For that thou lestez[4] wacz bot a rose,
That flowred and fayled as kynde[5] hit gef;
Now thurgh kynde[5] of the kyste[6] that hyt con[7] close,
To a perle of prys hit is put in pref;[8]
And thou hacz called thy wyrde[9] a thef,
That oght of noght hacz mad the cler;[10]
Thou blamez the bote[11] of thy meschef,
Thou art no kynde jueler."

XXIV

A juel to me then wacz thys geste,
And juelez wern hyr gentyl sawez.[12]
"I-wyse," quoth I, "my blysfol beste,[13]
My grete dystresse thou al to-drawez.[14]
To be excused I make requeste;
I trawed my perle don out of dawez;[15]
Now haf I fonde hyt, I schal ma feste,[16]
And wony[17] with hyt in schyr wod-schawez,[18]
And love my Lorde and all his lawez,
That hacz me broght thys blysse ner.
Now were I at[19] yow byyonde thise wawez,[20]
I were a joyful jueler."

XXV

"Jueler," sayde that gemme clene,
"Wy borde[21] ye men?—so madde ye be.
Thre wordez hacz thou spoken at ene;[22]
Unavysed, for sothe, wern alle thre.
Thou ne woste[23] in worlde quat[24] on[25] docz mene;
Thy worde byfore thy wytte con[26] fle.
Thou says thou trawez[27] me in this dene,[28]
Bycawse thou may with yghen me se;
Another[29] thou says, in thys countre
Thy self schal won[17] with me ryght here;
The thrydde, to passe thys water fre.
That may no joyful jueler."

XXXII

"My blysse, my bale,[30] ye han ben bothe,
Bot much the bygger yet wacz my mon;
Fro thou wacz wroken[31] fro uch a wothe,[32]
I wyste[33] never quere my perle wacz gon.

[1] was dear to thee [2] I regard thee as put [3] small affair [4] didst lose [5] nature [6] chest [7] did [8] put in proof = turned [9] fate [10] that has clearly made for thee something of nothing [11] remedy [12] sayings [13] best [14] takest away [15] done out of days (destroyed) [16] make feast [17] dwell [18] beautiful groves [19] with [20] waves [21] jest [22] once [23] knowest not [24] what [25] one [26] did [27] believest [28] den [29] another thing [30] sorrow [31] banished [32] every field [33] knew

Now I hit se, now lethez [1] my lothe.
And quen we departed, we wern at one;
God forbede we be now wrothe,
We meten so selden by stok other [2] ston.
Thagh [3] cortaysly ye carpe con,[4]
I am bot mol [5] and marez mysse; [6]
Bot Crystes mersy and Mary and Jon,
Thise arne the grounde of all my blysse.

XXXIII

"In blysse I se the blythely blent,[7]
And I a man al mornyf, mate,[8]
Ye take ther-on ful lyttel tente,[9]
Thagh I hente [10] ofte harmez hate.[11]
Bot now I am here in your presente,
I wolde bysech wythouten debate,
Ye wolde me say in sobre asente,
What lyf ye lede, erly and late;
For I am ful fayn that your astate
Is worthen to worschyp and wele [12] iwyss.
Of alle my joy the hyghe gate [13]
Hit is in grounde of alle my blysse."

XXXV

"A blysful lyf thou says I lede,
Thou woldez knaw ther-of the stage;
Thow wost wel when thy perle con schede,[14]
I wacz ful yong and tender of age,
Bot my Lorde, the Lombe, thurgh hys godhede,
He toke myself to hys maryage,
Corounde me quene in blysse to brede,[15]
In lenghe of dayez that ever schal wage,[16]
And sesed in [17] alle hys herytage
Hys lef [18] is, I am holy hysse;
Hys prese,[19] his prys,[20] and hys parage [21]
Is rote and grounde of all my blysse."

LXIII

"O maskelez [22] perle in perlez pure,
That berez," quod I, "the perle of prys,
Quo [23] formed the thy fayre fygure?
That wroght thy wede,[24] he wacz ful wys;
Thy beaute com never of nature;
Pymalyon paynted never thy vys; [25]
Ne Arystotel nawther by hys lettrure
Of carped the kynde these propertez.[26]
Thy colour passez the flour-de-lys,
Thyn angel-havyng so clene cortez; [27]
Breve [28] me, bryght, quat-kyn of triys [29]
Berez the perle so maskellez."

[1] lessens [2] or [3] though [4] did speak [5] earth [6] increase loss [7] mingled [8] mournful, overcome [9] heed [10] receive [11] hot [12] is changed to honor and prosperity [13] way [14] did depart [15] grow [16] last [17] possessed of [18] beloved [19] praise [20] glory [21] rank [22] spotless [23] who [24] garment [25] face [26] described thy beauties of nature [27] courteous [28] inform [29] promise

LXIV

"My maskelez Lambe that al may bete," [1]
Quod scho,[2] "my dere destyne
Me ches [3] to hys make,[4] al-thagh unmete.
Sum tyme semed that assemble,
When I wente fro yor worlde wete: [5]
He calde me to hys bonerte: [6] —
'Cum hyder to me, my lemman [7] swete,
For mote ne spot is non in the.'
He yef [8] me myght and als [9] bewte;
In hys blod he wesch my wede [10] on dese,[11]
And coronde clene in vergynte,
And pyght me in perlez maskellez."

LXXXI

"Motelez [12] may, so meke and mylde,"
Then sayde I to that lufly flor,[13]
"Bryng me to that bygly bylde,[14]
And let me se thy blysful bor." [15]
That schene [16] sayde, that [17] God wyl schylde,
"Thou may not enter with-inne hys tor,[18]
Bot of the Lombe I have the [19] aquylde [20]
For a syght ther-of thurgh gret favor.
Ut-wyth [21] to se that clene cloystor,
Thou may; bot in-wyth [22] not a fote,
To strech in the strete thou hacz no vygour,
Bot thou wer clene with-outen mote."

XCVI

The Lombe delyt non lyste to wene; [23]
Thagh he were hurt and wounde hade,
In his sembelaunt [24] wacz never sene;
So wern his glentez [25] gloryous glade.
I loked among his meyny schene,[26]
How thay wyth lyf wern last and lade,[27]
Thenne sagh I ther my lyttel quene,
That I wende [28] had standen by me in sclade.[29]
Lorde! much of mirthe wacz that ho [30] made,
Among her ferez [31] that wacz so quyt! [32]
That syght me gart [33] to think to wade,
For luf-longyng in gret delyt.

XCVII

Delyt me drof in yghe [34] and ere;
My manez [35] mynde to maddyng malte.[36]
Quen I segh [37] my frely,[38] I wolde be there,
By-yonde the water thagh ho [30] were walte.[39]

[1] amend [2] said she [3] chose [4] mate [5] wet [6] goodness [7] sweetheart [8] gave [9] also [10] garment [11] dais [12] spotless [13] flower [14] great building [15] bower [16] beautiful one [17] whom [18] tower [19] for thee [20] obtained [21] from without [22] within [23] wished to doubt [24] appearance [25] looks [26] beautiful company [27] supplied and laden [28] thought [29] valley [30] she [31] companions [32] white [33] caused [34] eye [35] man's [36] melted [37] saw [38] gracious one [39] kept

I thoght that no-thyng myght me dere,[1]
To fech me bur and take me halt;[2]
And to start in the strem schulde non me stere,[3]
To swymme the remnaunt, thagh I ther swalte;[4]
Bot of that munt[5] I wacz bi-talt;[6]
When I schulde start in the strem astraye,
Out of that caste[7] I wacz by-calt;[8]
Hit wacz not at my pryncez paye.[9]

XCVIII

Hit payed[10] hym not that I so flonc[11]
Over mervelous merez,[12] so mad arayed;
Of raas[13] thagh I were rasch and ronk,[14]
Yet rapely[15] ther-inne I wacz restayed;
For ryght as I sparred un-to the bonc,
That bratthe[16] out of my drem me brayde;[17]
Then wakned I in that erber wlonk,[18]
My hede upon that hylle wacz layde
Ther as my perle to grounde strayd;
I raxled[19] and fel in gret affray,[20]
And sykyng[21] to myself I sayd:—
"Now al be to that pryncez paye."[9]

SYR GAWAYN AND THE GRENE KNYGHT

(*The Same Author?*)

FYTTE THE FIRST

XI

Ther wacz[22] lokyng on lenthe,[23] the lude[24] to beholde,
For uch[25] mon had mervayle quat[26] hit mene myght,
That a hathel[27] and a horse myght such a hwe lach.[28]
As growe grene as the gres[29] and grener hit semed,
Then[30] grene aumayl[31] on golde lowande[32] bryghter.
Al studied that ther stod, and stalked hym nerre,[33]
Wyth al the wonder of the worlde, what he worch[34] schulde;
For fele sellyez[35] had thay sen, bot such never are,[36]
For-thi for fantoum and fayryye[37] the folk there hit demed.
Ther-fore to answare wacz arghe[38] mony athel freke,[39]
And al stouned[40] at his steven,[41] and ston-stil seten,

[1] injure [2] to fetch me an assault and take me lame [3] prevent [4] perished [5] purpose [6] shaken [7] intention [8] recalled [9] pleasure [10] pleased [11] should fling [12] waters [13] onset [14] strong [15] quickly [16] haste [17] moved [18] fair [19] roused [20] fear [21] sighing [22] was [23] long and steadily [24] man [25] each [26] what [27] knight [28] catch such a color [29] grass [30] than [31] enamel [32] gleaming [33] nearer [34] do [35] many strange things [36] before [37] therefore as illusion and magic [38] timid [39] many a noble knight [40] were amazed [41] voice

In a swoghe sylence[1] thurgh the sale[2] riche;
As[3] al were slypped upon slepe, so slaked horgh lotez[4]
In hyye;[5]
I deme hit not al for doute,[6]
Bot sum for cortaysye,
Let hym that al schulde loute,[7]
Cast[8] unto that wyye.[9]

XII

Thenn Arthour bifore the high dece[10] that aventure[11] byholdez,[12]
And rekenly hym reverenced,[13] for rad[14] was he never,
And sayde, "Wyye, welcum iwys[15] to this place;
The hede of this ostel[16] Arthour I hat;[17]
Light luflych[18] adoun, and lenge,[19] I the praye,
And quat-so thy wylle is, we schal wyt[20] after."
"Nay, as help me," quoth the hathel, "He that on hyghe syttes,
To wone[21] any quyle[22] in this won,[23] hit wacz not myn ernde;[24]
Bot for[25] the los[26] of the lede[27] is lyft up so hyghe,
And thy burgh and thy burnes[28] best ar holden,
Stifest under stel-gere[29] on stedes to ryde,
The wyghtest[30] and the worthyest of the worldes kynde,
Preve[31] for to play wyth in other pure laykez;[32]
And here is kydde[33] cortaysye, as I haf herd carp,[34]
And that hacz wayned[35] me hider, iwys, at this tyme.
Ye may be seker[36] bi this braunch that I bere here,
That I passe as in pes, and no plyght seche;[37]
For, had I founded[38] in fere, in feghtyng wyse,
I have a hauberghe[39] at home and a helme[40] bothe,
A schelde, and a scharp spere, schinande bryght,
Ande other weppenes to welde,[41] I wene wel als.[42]
Bot for[25] I wolde no were,[43] my wedez[44] ar softer.
Bot if thou be so bold as alle burnez[28] tellen,
Thou wyl grant me godly[45] the gomen[46] that I ask,
Bi ryght."
Arthour con onsware,[47]
And sayd, "Syr cortays knyght,
If thou crave batayl bare,
Here faylez thou not to fyght."

[1] in a death-like silence [2] hall [3] as if [4] so slackened their actions [5] suddenly [6] fear [7] but let him to whom all should bow (= Arthur) [8] speak [9] man [10] dais [11] happening [12] observes [13] courteously greeted him [14] afraid [15] indeed [16] house [17] I am called [18] alight graciously [19] remain [20] know [21] dwell [22] while [23] place [24] errand [25] because [26] fame [27] people [28] knights [29] steel-gear, armor [30] stoutest [31] proven [32] fine sports [33] shown [34] declare [35] has drawn [36] sure [37] seek no danger [38] come [39] hauberk [40] helmet [41] wield [42] also [43] war [44] garments [45] graciously [46] pleasure [47] answered

XIII

"Nay, frayst[1] I no fyght, in fayth I the telle;
Hit arn[2] aboute on this bench bot berdlez chylder!
If I were hasped[3] in armes on a heghe[4] stede,
Here is no mon me to mach,[5] for myghtez so wayke.[6]
For-thy[7] I crave in this court a Crystemas gomen,[8]
For hit is Yol and Nwe Yer, and here are yep[9] mony;
If any so hardy in this hous holdez hym-selven,
Be so bolde in his blod, brayn[10] in hys hede,
That dar stifly strike a strok for an other,
I schal gif hym of my gyft thys giserne[11] ryche, —
This ax, that is hevé innogh, — to hondele[12] as hym lykes,
And I schal bide[13] the fyrst bur,[14] as bare as I sitte.
If any freke[15] be so felle[16] to fonde[17] that[18] I telle,
Lepe[19] lyghtly me to, and lach[20] this weppen,
I quit-clayme hit for ever, kepe hit as his awen,[21]
And I schal stonde hym a strok, stif on this flet,[22]
Ellez thou wyl dight me the dom[23] to dele hym an other,
Barlay;[24]
And yet gif hym respite,
A twelmonyth and a day;
Now hyghe,[25] and let se tite[26]
Dar any her-inne oght say."

XIV

If he hem stowned[27] upon fyrst,[28] stiller were thanne
Alle the hered-men[29] in halle, the hygh and the lowe;
The renk[15] on his rounce[30] hym ruched[31] in his sadel,
And runischly[32] his rede yyen[33] he reled aboute,
Bende his bresed[34] browez, blycande[35] grene,
Wayved his berde for to wayte[36] quo-so[37] wolde ryse.
When non wolde kepe hym with carp[38] he coghed ful hyghe,[39]
Ande rimed hym ful richely,[40] and ryght hym[41] to speke;
"What, is this Arthures hous," quoth the hathel[42] thenne,
"That al the rous rennes of[43] thurgh ryalmes so mony?

1 ask 2 there are 3 clasped 4 high, tall 5 match 6 weak 7 therefore 8 game, amusement 9 bold, ready 10 mad 11 pole-ax 12 handle 13 abide, endure 14 attack 15 man 16 fierce 17 try 18 what 19 let him leap 20 seize 21 own 22 floor 23 provided thou wilt give me the right 24 by our Lady 25 hasten 26 quickly 27 amazed 28 at first 29 retainers 30 horse 31 settled 32 furiously 33 eyes 34 bristly 35 glittering 36 observe 37 who-so 38 when none would reply 39 coughed aloud 40 and made full preparation 41 got ready 42 knight 43 of which all the fame goes

Where is now your sourquydrye[1] and your conquestes,
Your gryndel-layk,[2] and your greme,[3] and your grete wordes?
Now is the revel and the renoun of the Rounde Table
Over-walt[4] wyth a worde of on wyyes[5] speche;
For al dares[6] for drede, withoute dynt[7] schewed!"
Wyth this he laghes[8] so loude, that the lorde greved, —
The blod schot for scham in-to his schyre[9] face
And lere.[10]
He wex as wroth as wynde;
So did alle that ther were.
The kyng, as kene bi kynde,[11]
Then stod that stif mon nere.[12]

XV

Ande sayde, "Hathel, by heven thyn askyng is nys,[13]
And as thou foly hacz frayst,[14] fynde the be-hoves.[15]
I know no gome[16] that is gast[17] of thy grete wordes.
Gif me now thy geserne,[18] upon Godez halve,[19]
And I schal baythen thy bone,[20] that thou boden[14] habbes."
Lyghtly lepez he hym to, and laght[21] at his honde;
Then feersly that other freke[16] upon fote lyghtis.
Now hacz Arthure his axe, and the halme[22] grypez,
And sturnely sturez[23] hit aboute, that stryke wyth hit thoght.
The stif mon hym bifore stod upon hyght,[24]
Herre[25] then ani in the hous by the hede and more;
Wyth sturne chere[26] ther he stod, he stroked his berde,
And wyth a countenaunce dryye[27] he drow doun his cote,
No more mate[28] ne dismayd for hys mayn dintez,[29]
Then any burne[30] upon bench hade broght hym to drynk
Of wyne.
Gawan, that sate bi the quene,
To the kyng he can[31] enclyne,
"I be-seche now with sawez sene,[32]
This melly mot[33] be myne."

1 haughtiness 2 fierceness 3 grimness 4 overturned 5 one man's 6 all are frightened 7 stroke 8 laughs 9 bright 10 cheek 11 as one bold by nature 12 nearer 13 foolish 14 asked 15 it behooves thee to find 16 man 17 frightened 18 ax 19 in God's name 20 grant thy boon 21 grasped 22 shaft 23 fiercely moves 24 stood tall 25 taller 26 fierce look 27 dry, without emotion 28 dispirited 29 strong blows 30 than if any man 31 did 32 courteous words 33 this encounter may

XVI

"Wolde ye, worthilych[1] lorde," quoth Gawan to the kyng,
"Bid me bowe[2] fro this benche, and stonde by yow there,
That I wyth-oute vylanye myght voyde[3] this table,
And that my legge[4] lady lyked not ille,
I wolde com to your counseyl, bifore your cort ryche;[5]
For me think hit not semly,[6] as hit is soth knawen,[7]
Ther[8] such an askyng is hevened[9] so hyghe in your sale,[10]
Thagh ye your-self be talenttyf[11] to take hit to your-selven,
Whil mony so bolde yow aboute upon bench sytten,
That under heven, I hope,[12] non hagher[13] er[14] of wylle,
Ne better bodyes on bent,[15] ther[8] baret[16] is rered.
I am the wakkest,[17] I wot, and of wyt feblest,
And lest lur[18] of my lyf, quo laytes the sothe;[19]
Bot, for as much as ye ar myn em,[20] I am only to prayse —
No bounté[21] bot your blod I in my bodé knowe, —
And sythen this note[22] is so nys[23] that noght hit yow falles,[24]
And I have frayned[25] hit at yow fyrst, foldez[26] hit to me!
And if I carp[27] not comlyly, let alle this cort rych[28]
Bout[29] blame."
Ryche[30] to-geder con roun,[31]
And sythen thay redden alle same,[32]
To ryd the kyng wyth croun,[33]
And gif Gawan the game.

XVII

Then comaunded the kyng the knyght for to ryse;
And he ful radly[34] up ros, and ruchched hym fayre,[35]
Kneled doun bifore the kyng, and cachez[36] that weppen;
And he luflyly hit hym laft,[37] and lyfte up his honde,
And gef hym Goddez blessyng, and gladly hym biddes
That his hert and his honde schulde hardi be bothe.
"Kepe the, cosyn," quoth the kyng, "that thou on kyrf sette,[1]
And if thou redez[2] hym ryght, redly I trowe
That thou schal byden the bur[3] that he schal bede[4] after."
Gawan gocz[5] to the gome,[6] with giserne[7] in honde,
And he baldly hym bydez,[8] he bayst never the helder.[9]
Then carppez to Syr Gawan the knyght in the grene,
"Refourme we oure forwardes,[10] er we fyrre[11] passe.
Fyrst I ethe[12] the, hathel, how that thou hattes,[13]
That thou me telle truly, as I tryst[14] may."
"In god fayth," quoth the goode knyght, "Gawan I hatte,[15]
That bede[4] the this buffet, quat-so bi-fallez after,
And at this tyme twelmonyth take at the[16] another,
Wyth what weppen so thou wylt, and wyth no wy ellez[17]
On lyve."[18]
That other onswarez[19] agayn,
"Sir Gawan, so mot[20] I thryve,
As I am ferly fayn,[21]
This dint that thou schal dryve.[22]

XVIII

"Bi Gog," quoth the grene knyght, "Syr Gawan, me lykes,[23]
That I schal fange at thy fust[24] that[25] I haf frayst[26] here;
And thou hacz redily rehersed, bi resoun ful trwe,
Clanly[27] al the covenaunt that I the kynge asked,
Saf that thou schal siker[28] me, segge,[6] by thi trawthe,
That thou schal seche[29] me thi-self, where-so thou hopes[30]
I may be funde upon folde,[31] and foch[32] the such wages
As thou deles me to day, bifore this douthe[33] ryche."
"Where schulde I wale[29] the?" quoth Gauan, "Where is thy place?
I wot never where thou wonyes,[34] bi Hym that me wroght,

[1] worthy [2] move [3] leave [4] liege [5] rich (splendid) court [6] fitting [7] is known for truth [8] where [9] raised [10] hall [11] desirous [12] think [13] apter, fitter [14] are [15] in field [16] strife [17] weakest [18] least loss [19] if any one seeks the truth [20] uncle [21] goodness [22] affair [23] foolish [24] becomes [25] requested [26] grant [27] if I speak [28] judge [29] without [30] the great ones [31] did whisper [32] and afterwards they decided unanimously [33] to set aside the crowned king [34] quickly [35] stooped courteously [36] seizes [37] left, gave

[1] take care, cousin, that thou give one stroke [2] greatest [3] attack [4] offer [5] goes [6] man [7] ax [8] awaits [9] he quailed never the more [10] agreements [11] further [12] ask [13] what is thy name [14] believe [15] Gawan is my name [16] from thee [17] no man else [18] alive [19] answers [20] may [21] wonderfully glad [22] that thou shalt deliver this blow [23] it pleases me [24] take from thy fist [25] what [26] asked [27] entirely [28] promise [29] seek [30] believest [31] earth [32] fetch [33] nobility [34] dwellest

Ne I know not the, knyght, thy cort, ne thi name.
Bot teche me truly ther-to, and telle me howe thou hattes,[1]
And I schal ware[2] alle my wyt to wynne me theder,[3]
And that I swere the for sothe, and by my seker[4] traweth."
"That is innogh in Nwe Yer, hit nedes no more,"
Quoth the gome in the grene to Gawan the hende,[5]
"Gif[6] I the telle trwly, quen I the tape[7] have,
And thou me smothely hacz[8] smyten, smartly I the teche
Of my hous, and my home, and myn owen nome,[9]
Then may thou frayst my fare,[10] and forwardez[11] holde.
And if I spende no speche, thenne spedez thou the better,
For thou may leng[12] in thy londe, and layt no fyrre,[13]
Bot slokes.[14]
Ta[15] now thy grymme tole[16] to the,
And let se how thou cnokez."[17]
"Gladly, syr, for sothe,"
Quoth Gawan; his ax he strokes.

XIX

The grene knyght upon grounde graythely hym dresses,[18]
A littel lut[19] with the hede, the lere[20] he diskoverez,
His longe lovelych lokkez he layd over his croun,
Let the naked nec to the note[21] schewe.
Gauan gripped to his ax, and gederes hit on hyght,[22]
The kay[23] fote on the folde[24] he be-fore sette,
Let hit doun lyghtly lyght on the naked,
That the scharp of the schalk[25] schyndered[26] the bones,
And schrank[27] thurgh the schyire grece,[28] and scade[29] hit in twynne,[30]
That the bit of the broun stel bot[31] on the grounde.
The fayre hede fro the halce[32] hit [helde][33] to the erthe,
That fele[34] hit foyned[35] wyth her fete, there[36] hit forth roled;
The blod brayd[37] fro the body, that blykked[38] on the grene;
And nawther[39] faltered ne fel the freke[40] never-the-helder,[41]

[1] what is thy name [2] use [3] to get there [4] sure [5] courteous [6] if [7] tap, stroke [8] hast [9] name [10] ask my state, condition [11] the agreements [12] remain [13] seek no further [14] but cease [15] take [16] instrument [17] knockest [18] readily prepares himself [19] bowed [20] cheek [21] head [22] high [23] left [24] ground [25] edge [26] sundered [27] cut [28] pure gristle [29] divided [30] two [31] bit, cut [32] neck [33] fell [34] many [35] thrust [36] where [37] spouted [38] shone [39] neither [40] man [41] never the more

Bot stythly[1] he start forth upon styf schonkes,[2]
And runyschly[3] he raght[4] out, there-as[5] renkkez[6] stoden,
Laght[4] to his lufly[7] hed, and lyft hit up sone;[8]
And sythen bowez[9] to his blonk,[10] the brydel he cachchez,
Steppez in to stel-bawe[11] and strydez alofte,
And his hede by the here in his honde haldez;
And as sadly[12] the segge[13] hym in his sadel sette,
As[14] non unhap had hym ayled, thagh[15] hedlez he were,
In stedde;[16]
He brayde[17] his blunk[10] aboute,
That ugly bodi that bledde,
Moni on of hym had doute,[18]
Bi that his resounz were redde.[19]

XX

For the hede in his honde he haldez up even,
To-ward the derrest[20] on the dece[21] he dressez[22] the face,
And hit lyfte up the yye-lyddez,[23] and loked ful brode,
And meled[24] thus much with his muthe, as ye may now here.
"Loke, Gawan, thou be graythe[25] to go as thou hettez,[26]
And layte[27] as lelly[28] til thou me, lude,[29] fynde,
As thou hacz hette[30] in this halle, herande[31] thise knyghtes.
To the grene chapel thou chose,[32] I charge the, to fotte;[33]
Such a dunt[34] as thou hacz dalt[35] disserved thou habbez,[36]
To be yederly yolden[37] on Nw Yeres morn.
The Knyght of the Grene Chapel, men knowen me mony;[38]
For-thi[39] me for to fynde, if thou fraystez,[40] faylez thou never;
Ther-fore com, other[41] recreaunt be calde the be-hoves."
With a runisch rout[42] the raynez he tornez,
Halled[43] out at the hal-dor, his hed in his hande,
That the fyr of the flynt flawe[44] from fole hoves.[45]
To quat kyth he be-com,[46] knewe non there,

[1] sturdily [2] shanks [3] hastily [4] reached [5] where [6] men [7] lovely [8] immediately [9] goes [10] horse [11] stirrup [12] steadily [13] fellow [14] as if [15] though [16] in the place [17] turned [18] fear [19] by the time his remarks were made [20] noblest [21] dais [22] directs [23] eye-lids [24] spoke [25] ready [26] didst promise [27] seek [28] faithfully [29] man [30] promised [31] hearing [32] go [33] on foot [34] blow [35] hast dealt [36] hast [37] promptly paid [38] many men know me [39] therefore [40] inquirest [41] or [42] sudden noise [43] rushed [44] flew [45] from the horse's hoofs [46] to what land he went

Never more then thay wyste fram quethen[1] he wacz wonnen.[2]
What thenne?
The kyng and Gawen thare,
At that Grene thay lagh and grenne,
Thet breved[3] wacz hit ful bare[4]
A mervayl among tho[5] menne.

XXI

Thagh[6] Arthur the hende[7] kyng at hert hade wonder,
He let no semblaunt be sene, bot sayde ful hyghe[8]
To the comlych Quene, wyth cortays speche,
"Dere dame, to-day demay[9] yow never;
Wel bycommes[10] such craft upon Cristmasse,
Laykyng[11] of enterludez, to laghe and to syng
Among[12] thise kynde[13] caroles of knyghtez and ladyez;
Never-the-lece[14] to my mete[15] I may me wel dres,[16]
For I haf sen a selly,[17] I may not for-sake."[18]
He glent[19] upon Syr Gawen, and gaynly[20] he sayde,
"Now, syr, heng up thyn ax, that hacz innogh hewen."
And hit wacz don[21] abof the dece, on doser[22] to henge,
Ther alle men for mervayl myght on hit loke,
And bi trwe tytel ther-of[23] to telle the wonder.
Thenne thay bowed[24] to a borde,[25] thise burnes[26] to-geder,
The kyng and the gode kynght; and kene[27] men hem served
Of alle dayntyez double, as derrest[28] myght falle, —
Wyth alle maner of mete and mynstralcie bothe;
Wyth wele walt thay that day, til worthed an ende[29]
In londe.
Now thenk wel, Syr Gawan,
For wothe[30] that thou ne wonde[31]
This aventure forto frayn[32]
That thou hacz tan[33] on honde.

JOHN GOWER (1325?–1408)

From CONFESSIO AMANTIS Bk. V

Jason, which sih[34] his fader old,
Upon Medea made him bold
Of art magique, which sche couthe,[35]
And preith hire that his fader[36] youthe
Sche wolde make ayeinward[1] newe.
And sche, that was toward him trewe,
Behihte[2] him that sche wolde it do
Whan that sche time sawh[3] therto.
Bot[4] what sche dede in that matiere
It is a wonder thing to hiere,
Bot yit for the novellerie[5]
I thenke tellen a partie.[6]
Thus it befell upon a nyht
Whan ther was noght bot sterreliht,[7]
Sche was vanyssht riht as hir liste,[8]
That no wyht bot hirself it wiste,
And that was ate[9] mydnyht tyde.
The world was stille on every side;
With open[10] hed and fot al bare,
Hir her tosprad,[11] sche gan to fare;
Upon hir clothes gert[12] sche was;
Al specheles and[13] on the gras
Sche glod[14] forth as an addre doth —
Non otherwise sche ne goth —
Til sche cam to the freisshe flod,
And there a while sche withstod.[15]
Thries sche torned hire aboute,
And thries ek sche gan doun loute[16]
And in the flod sche wette hir her,
And thries on the water ther
Sche gaspeth with a drecchinge[17] onde,[18]
And tho[19] sche tok hir speche on honde.
Ferst sche began to clepe[20] and calle
Upward unto the sterres alle,
To Wynd, to Air, to See, to Lond
Sche preide, and ek hield up hir hond
To Echates,[21] — and gan to crie, —
Which is goddesse of sorcerie.
Sche seide, "Helpeth at this nede,
And as ye maden me to spede,[22]
Whan Jason cam the Flees[23] to seche,
So help me nou, I you beseche."
With that sche loketh and was war,[24]
Doun fro the sky ther cam a char,[25]
The which dragouns aboute drowe.
And tho[19] sche gan hir hed doun bowe,
And up sche styh,[26] and faire and wel
Sche drof forth bothe char and whel
Above in thair[27] among the skyes.[28]
The lond of Crete and tho parties[29]
Sche soughte, and faste gan hire hye,[30]
And there upon the hulles[31] hyhe

[1] whence [2] come [3] accounted [4] entirely [5] those [6] though [7] courteous [8] loud [9] dismay [10] suits [11] playing [12] now and then [13] suitable [14] nevertheless [15] food [16] address [17] marvel [18] deny [19] glanced [20] kindly [21] put [22] tapestry [23] and on the evidence of it [24] went [25] table [26] knights [27] brave [28] dearest [29] in joy they spent the day, till it came to end [30] injury [31] hesitate [32] seek [33] taken [34] saw [35] knew [36] father's

[1] again [2] promised [3] saw [4] but [5] novelty [6] part [7] starlight [8] as it pleased her [9] at the [10] uncovered [11] her hair unbound [12] girded [13] *Gower often gives* and *a strange position in the sentence; we should place it before* al. [14] glided [15] stood still [16] bow [17] troubling [18] breath [19] then [20] cry [21] Hecate [22] succeed [23] fleece [24] aware [25] chariot [26] rose [27] the air [28] clouds [29] those parts [30] hasten [31] hills

Of Othrin and Olimpe also,
And ek of othre hulles mo,
Sche fond and gadreth herbes suote,[1]
Sche pulleth up som be the rote,
And manye with a knyf sche scherth,[2]
And alle into hir char sche berth.[3]
Thus whan sche hath the hulles sought,
The flodes[4] ther forgat[5] sche nought,
Eridian and Amphrisos,
Peneie and ek Spercheidos.
To hem sche wente and ther sche nom[6]
Bothe of the water and the fom,
The sond and ek the smale stones,
Whiche-as sche ches[7] out for the nones;[8]
And of the Rede See a part
That was behovelich to hire art
Sche tok, and after that aboute
Sche soughte sondri sedes oute
In feldes and in many greves,[9]
And ek a part sche tok of leves;
Bot thing which mihte hire most availe
Sche fond in Crete and in Thessaile.
  In daies and in nyhtes nyne,
With gret travaile and with gret pyne,
Sche was pourveid of every piece,
And torneth homward into Grece.
Before the gates of Eson
Hir char sche let awai to gon,
And tok out ferst that was therinne;
For tho sche thoghte to beginne
Suche thing as semeth impossible,
And made hirselven invisible,
As sche that was with air enclosed
And mihte of noman be desclosed.
Sche tok up turves of the lond
Withoute helpe of mannes hond,
Al heled[10] with the grene gras,
Of which an alter mad ther was
Unto Echates, the goddesse
Of art magique and the maistresse,
And eft[11] an other to Juvente,
As sche which dede hir hole entente.[12]
Tho tok sche fieldwode and verveyne, —
Of herbes ben noght betre tueine;[13]
Of which anon withoute let
These alters ben aboute set.
Tuo sondri puttes[14] faste by
Sche made, and with that hastely
A wether which was blak sche slouh,[15]
And out ther-of the blod sche drouh[16]
And dede[17] into the pettes[14] tuo;
Warm melk sche putte also therto

[1] sweet [2] cuts [3] bears, carries [4] rivers [5] forgot [6] took [7] chose [8] for the purpose [9] groves [10] covered [11] again [12] entire purpose [13] twain, two [14] pits [15] slew [16] drew [17] put

With hony meynd;[1] and in such wise
Sche gan to make hir sacrifice.
And cride and preide forth withal
To Pluto, the god infernal,
And to the queene Proserpine.
And so sche soghte out al the line
Of hem that longen to that craft,
Behinde was no name laft,[2]
And preide hem alle, as sche wel couthe,[3]
To grante Eson his ferste youthe.
  This olde Eson broght forth was tho;[4]
Awei sche bad alle othre go,
Upon peril that mihte falle;
And with that word thei wenten alle,
And leften there hem tuo al-one.
And tho sche gan to gaspe and gone,[5]
And made signes many-on,
And seide hir wordes therupon;
So that with spellinge of hir charmes
Sche took Eson in both hire armes,
And made him forto slepe faste,
And him upon hire herbes caste.
The blake wether tho sche tok,
And hiewh[6] the fleissh, as doth a cok;
On either alter part sche leide,
And with the charmes that sche seide
A fyr doun fro the sky alyhte
And made it forto brenne lyhte.
Bot whan Medea sawh it brenne,
Anon sche gan to sterte and renne[7]
The fyri aulters al aboute.
Ther was no beste which goth oute
More wylde than sche semeth ther:
Aboute hir schuldres hyng[8] hir her,
As thogh sche were oute of hir mynde
And torned in an other kynde.[9]
Tho lay ther certein wode cleft,
Of which the pieces nou and eft[10]
Sche made hem in the pettes wete,
And put hem in the fyri hete,
And tok the brond with al the blase,
And thries sche began to rase
Aboute Eson, ther-as[11] he slepte;
And eft with water, which sche kepte,
Sche made a cercle aboute him thries,
And eft with fyr of sulphre twyes.
Ful many an other thing sche dede,
Which is noght writen in this stede.[12]
Bot tho sche ran so up and doun,
Sche made many a wonder soun,
Somtime lich[13] unto the cock,
Somtime unto the laverock,[14]

[1] mixed [2] left [3] could [4] then [5] walk [6] hewed [7] run [8] hung [9] nature [10] now and again [11] where [12] place [13] like [14] lark

Somtime kacleth as a hen,
Somtime spekth as don the men;
And riht so as hir jargoun strangeth,[1]
In sondri wise hir forme changeth,
Sche semeth faie [2] and no womman;
For with the craftes that sche can
Sche was, as who seith, a goddesse.
And what hir liste, more or lesse,
Sche dede, in bokes as we finde,
That passeth over manneskinde.[3]
Bot who that wole of wondres hiere,
What thing sche wroghte in this matiere,
To make an ende of that sche gan,[4]
Such merveile herde nevere man.
 Apointed in the newe mone,
Whan it was time forto done,
Sche sette a caldron on the fyr,
In which was al the hole atir,[5]
Wheron the medicine stod,
Of jus, of water, and of blod,
And let it buile [6] in such a plit,
Til that sche sawh the spume whyt;
And tho sche caste in rynde [7] and rote,
And sed and flour that was for bote,[8]
With many an herbe and many a ston,
Wherof sche hath ther many on.
And ek Cimpheius the serpent
To hire hath alle his scales lent,
Chelidre hire yaf his addres skin,
And sche to builen caste hem in;
A part ek of the horned oule,
The which men hiere on nyhtes houle;
And of a raven, which was told
Of nyne hundred wynter old,
Sche tok the hed with al the bile;[9]
And as the medicine it wile,
Sche tok therafter the bouele [10]
Of the seewolf, and for the hele [11]
Of Eson, with a thousand mo
Of thinges that sche hadde tho,
In that caldroun togedre as blyve [12]
Sche putte; and tok thanne of olyve
A drie branche hem with to stere,[13]
The which anon gan floure and bere
And waxe al freissh and grene ayein.
Whan sche this vertu hadde sein,
Sche let the leste drope of alle
Upon the bare flor doun falle;
Anon ther sprong up flour and gras,
Where-as the drope falle was,
And wox anon al medwe [14] grene,
So that it mihte wel be sene.

[1] becomes strange [2] fairy [3] that surpasses human nature [4] began [5] equipment [6] boil [7] bark [8] remedy [9] bill [10] intestine [11] healing [12] quickly [13] stir [14] meadow

Medea thanne knew and wiste
Hir medicine is forto triste,[1]
And goth to Eson ther [2] he lay,
And tok a swerd was of assay [3]
With which a wounde upon his side
Sche made, that therout mai slyde
The blod withinne, which was old
And sek and trouble and fieble and cold.
And tho sche tok unto his us [4]
Of herbes al the beste jus,
And poured it into his wounde;
That made his veynes fulle and sounde.
And tho sche made his wounde clos,
And tok his hand, and up he ros.
And tho sche yaf [5] him drinke a drauhte,
Of which his youthe ayein he cauhte,
His hed, his herte and his visage
Lich [6] unto twenty wynter age;
Hise hore heres were away,
And lich unto the freisshe Maii,
Whan passed ben the colde schoures,
Riht so recovereth he his floures.

WILLIAM LANGLAND? (1332?–1400?)

PIERS THE PLOWMAN

FROM THE PROLOGUE (A — TEXT)

In a somer sesun, / whon softe was the sonne,
I schop [7] me into a shroud,[8] / as [9] I a scheep [10] were;
In habite as an hermite / unholy of werkes
Wente I wyde in this world / wondres to here;[11]
Bote [12] in a Mayes morwnynge / on Malverne hulles [13]
Me bifel a ferly,[14] / of fairie,[15] me-thoughte.
 I was wery, forwandred,[16] / and wente me to reste
Undur a brod banke / bi a bourne [17] side;
And as I lay and leonede / and lokede on the watres,
I slumbrede in a slepynge, / hit [18] swyed [19] so murie.[20]
Thenne gon I meeten [21] / a mervelous sweven,[22]
That I was in a wildernesse, / wuste [23] I never where;
And as I beheold into the est / an heigh [24] to the sonne,
I sauh [25] a tour on a toft,[26] / tryelyche [27] i-maket;
A deop dale bineothe, / a dungun ther-inne,
With deop dich and derk / and dredful of sighte.

[1] trust [2] where [3] proof [4] use [5] gave [6] like [7] shaped, arrayed [8] garment [9] as if [10] shepherd [11] hear [12] but [13] hills [14] strange thing [15] enchantment [16] worn out with wandering [17] burn, brook [18] it [19] whispered, made a low sound [20] merry [21] did I dream [22] dream [23] knew [24] on high [25] saw [26] field, building-site [27] choicely, skilfully

A feir feld full of folk / fond[1] I ther bitwene,
Of alle maner of men, / the mene and the riche,
Worchinge[2] and wandringe / as the world asketh.
Summe putten hem[3] to the plough, / pleiden[4] ful seldene,[5] 20
In settynge and in sowynge / swonken[6] ful harde,
And wonnen that[7] theos wasturs[8] / with glotonye distruen.[9]
And summe putten hem to pruide,[10] / apparaylden hem ther-after,[11]
In cuntenaunce[12] of clothinge / comen disgisid.[13]
To preyeres and to penaunce / putten hem monye,[14] 25
For love of ur[15] Lord / liveden ful streite,
In hope for to have / hevene-riche blisse;[16]
As ancres[17] and hermytes / that holdeth hem in heore[18] celles,
Coveyte[19] not in cuntre / to cairen[20] aboute,
For non likerous lyflode[21] / heore licam[22] to plese.
And summe chosen chaffare[23] / to cheeven[24] the bettre, 31
As hit semeth to ure sighte / that suche men thryveth;
And summe, murthhes[25] to maken / as munstrals cunne,[26]
And gete gold with here[18] gle, / giltles, I trowe.
Bote japers[27] and jangelers,[28] / Judas children,
Founden hem fantasyes / and fooles hem maaden,
And habbeth wit at heore[18] wille / to worchen yif hem luste,[29] 37
That[7] Poul precheth of hem, / I dar not preoven[30] heere;
Qui loquitur turpiloquium / he is Luciferes hyne.[31]
Bidders[32] and beggers / faste aboute eoden,[33]
Til heor bagges and heore balies[34] / weren bretful i-crommet;[35] 41
Feyneden hem[36] for heore foode, / foughten atte[37] ale;
In glotonye, God wot, / gon heo[33] to bedde,
And ryseth up with ribaudye[39] / this roberdes knaves;[40]
Sleep and sleughthe[41] / suweth[42] hem evere. 45
Pilgrimes and palmers / plihten[43] hem togederes
For to seche[44] Seint Jame / and seintes at Roome;
Wenten forth in heore wey / with mony wyse tales,
And hedden[1] leve to lyen / al heore lyf aftir. 49
[2] Grete lobres[3] and longe / that loth weore to swynke[4]
Clotheden hem in copes / to beo knowen for bretheren;
And summe schopen hem to[5] hermytes / heore ese to have.
I fond there freres,[6] / all the foure ordres, 55
Prechinge the peple / for profyt of heore wombes,[7]
Glosynge[8] the Gospel / as hem good·liketh,[9]
For covetyse of copes / construeth hit ille;
For monye[10] of this maistres / mowen[11] clothen hem at lyking,
For moneye[12] and heore marchaundie / meeten togedere; 60
Seththe[13] Charite hath be[14] chapmon,[15] / and cheef to schriven[16] lordes,
Mony ferlyes han[17] bifalle / in a fewe yeres.
But[18] Holychirche and heo[19] / holde bet[20] togedere,
The moste mischeef on molde[21] / is mountyng up faste.
Ther prechede a pardoner, / as[22] he a prest were, 65
And brought forth a bulle / with bisschopes seles,
And seide that himself mighte / asoylen[23] hem alle
Of falsnesse and fastinge / and of vouwes i-broken.[24]
The lewede[25] men levide[26] him wel / and likede his speche,
And comen up knelynge / to kissen his bulle; 70
He bonchede[27] hem with his brevet / and blered[28] heore eiyen,[29]
And raughte[30] with his ragemon[31] / ringes and broches.
Thus ye giveth oure[32] gold / glotonis[33] to helpen!
And leveth hit to losels[34] / that lecherie haunten.[35]
Weore the bisschop i-blesset / and worth bothe his eres,[36] 75
His sel shulde not be sent / to deceyve the peple.
Hit is not al bi[37] the bisschop / that the boye precheth,
Bote the parisch prest and the pardoner / parte the selver
That the pore peple of the parisch schulde have / yif that heo ne weore,[38]

[1] found [2] working [3] them [4] played [5] seldom [6] labored [7] what [8] these wasters [9] destroy [10] pride [11] accordingly [12] fashion [13] came disguised [14] many [15] our [16] the joy of the kingdom of heaven [17] nuns [18] their [19] desire [20] roam [21] luxurious food [22] body [23] trade [24] thrive [25] amusements [26] know how [27] jesters [28] buffoons [29] to work if they pleased [30] prove, declare [31] servant [32] beggars [33] went [34] bellies [35] brimful, crammed [36] shammed [37] at the [38] go they [39] ribaldry [40] these robber rascals [41] sloth [42] follow [43] plighted [44] seek

[1] had [2] *I have omitted two lines, which probably were not in the earliest version.* [3] lubbers [4] labor [5] shaped them to, became [6] friars [7] bellies [8] interpreting [9] according to their own desire [10] many [11] may [12] money [13] since [14] been [15] trader [16] shrive, confess [17] many wonders have [18] unless [19] she, *i.e.* Charity [20] better [21] earth [22] as if [23] absolve [24] broken vows [25] ignorant [26] believed [27] banged [28] blinded [29] eyes [30] reached, got [31] licence [32] your [33] gluttons [34] rascals [35] practice [36] ears [37] it is not all the fault of [38] if it were not for them

Persones and parisch prestes / playneth[1] to heore bisschops,
That heore parisch hath ben pore / seththe[2] the pestilence tyme,
To have a lycence and leve / at Londun to dwelle,
To singe ther for simonye, / for selver is swete.
Ther hovide[3] an hundret / in houves[4] of selke,
Serjauns hit semide / to serven atte barre;
Pleden for pens[5] / and poundes the lawe,
Not for love of ur Lord / unloseth heore lippes ones,[6]
Thou mightest beter meten[7] the myst / on Malverne hulles
Then geten a mom[8] of heore mouth / til moneye weore schewed!
I saugh ther bisschops bolde / and bachilers of divyne[9]
Bicoome clerkes of acounte / the king for to serven.
Erchedekenes and denis,[10] / that dignite haven
To preche the peple / and pore men to feede,
Beon lopen[11] to Londun, / bi leve of heore bisschopes,
To ben clerkes of the Kynges Benche / the cuntre to schende.[12]
Barouns and burgeis[13] / and bondages[14] alse[15]
I saugh in that semble,[16] / as ye schul heren aftur,
Bakers, bochers, / and breusters[17] monye,
Wollene-websteris,[18] / and weveris of lynen,
Taillours, tanneris, / and tokkeris[19] bothe,
Masons, minours, / and mony other craftes,
Dykers, and delvers, / that don heore dedes ille,[20]
And driveth forth the longe day / with "*Deu save Dam Emme!*"[21]
Cookes and heore knaves[22] / cryen "Hote pies, hote!
"Goode gees and grys![23] / Go we dyne, go we!"
Taverners to hem tolde / the same tale,
With wyn of Oseye[24] / and win of Gaskoyne,
Of the Ryn[25] and of the Rochel, / the rost to defye,[26]
Al this I saugh slepynge / and seve sithes[27] more.

THE FABLE OF BELLING THE CAT

From THE PROLOGUE (B—TEXT)

With that ran there a route[28] / of ratones[29] at ones,[6]
And smale mys[30] with hem[31] / mo then a thousande,

[1] complain [2] since [3] lingered [4] hoods [5] pence, money [6] once [7] thou mightst more easily measure [8] syllable [9] divinity [10] deans [11] have run [12] injure [13] burgesses [14] bondmen [15] also [16] assembly [17] brewers [18] woollen-weavers [19] tuckers, finishers of cloth [20] that do their work badly [21] A popular song of the time. [22] boys [23] pigs [24] Alsatia [25] Rhine [26] digest [27] seven times [28] crowd [29] rats [30] mice [31] them

And comen[1] to a conseille / for here[2] comune profit;
For a cat of a courte / cam whan hym lyked,
And overlepe hem lyghtlich / and laughte[3] hem at his wille,
And pleyde with hem perilouslych / and possed[4] hem aboute.
"For doute[5] of dyverse dredes[6] / we dar noughte wel loke;
And yif[7] we grucche[8] of his gamen[9] / he wil greve us alle,
Cracche[10] us, or clawe us / and in his cloches[11] holde,
That us lotheth the lyf / or[12] he lete us passe.
Myghte we with any witte / his wille withstonde,
We myghte be lordes aloft / and lyven at owre ese."
A raton[13] of renon,[14] / most renable[15] of tonge,
Seide for a sovereygne / help to hymselve:[16] —
"I have y-sein[17] segges,"[18] quod he, / "in the cité of London
Beren beighes[19] ful brighte / abouten here nekkes,
And some colers of crafty werk; / uncoupled thei wenden[20]
Both in wareine[21] and in waste / where hem leve lyketh;[22]
And otherwhile thei aren elleswhere / as I here telle.
Were there a belle on here beighe,[23] / bi Jesu, as me thynketh,
Men myghte wite[24] where thei went, / and awei renne![25]
And right so," quod this raton, / "reson me sheweth
To bugge[26] a belle of brasse / or of brighte sylver
And knitten on a colere / for owre comune profit,
And hangen it upon the cattes hals;[27] / than here[28] we mowen[29]
Where[30] he ritt[31] or rest / or renneth[32] to playe.
And yif him list for to laike,[33] / thenne loke we mowen,
And peren[34] in his presence / ther-while hym plaie liketh;[35]
And yif him wrattheth,[36] be y-war / and his weye shonye."[37]
Alle this route of ratones / to this reson thei assented.
Ac tho[38] the belle was y-bought / and on the beighe hanged,

[1] came [2] their [3] seized [4] pushed [5] fear [6] dreads [7] if [8] grudge [9] sport [10] scratch [11] clutches [12] before [13] rat [14] renown [15] eloquent [16] themselves [17] seen [18] people (*here* dogs *are meant*) [19] rings [20] went [21] warren [22] wherever they please [23] collar [24] know [25] run [26] buy [27] neck [28] hear [29] may [30] whether [31] rides [32] runs [33] if he wishes to play [34] appear [35] when he pleases to play [36] he is angry [37] shun [38] but when

Ther ne was ratoun in alle the route, / for alle the rewme [1] of Fraunce,
That dorst have y-bounden the belle / aboute the cattis nekke,
Ne hangen it aboute the cattes hals / al Engelond to wynne;
And helden hem unhardy [2] / and here conseille feble,
And leten [3] here laboure lost / and alle here longe studye.
A mous that moche good / couthe,[4] as me thoughte,
Stroke forth sternly / and stode biforn hem alle,
And to the route of ratones / reherced these wordes: —
"Though we culled [5] the catte / yut [6] sholde ther come another
To cracchy us and al owre kynde, / though we croupe [7] under benches.
For-thi [8] I conseille alle the comune / to lat the catte worthe,[9]
And be we never so bolde / the belle hym to shewe;
For I herde my sire seyn,[10] / is sevene yere y-passed,
There [11] the catte is a kitoun / the courte is ful elyng; [12]
That witnisseth Holi-write, / who-so wil it rede,
Ve terre ubi puer rex est,[13] &c.
For may no renke [14] there rest have / for ratones bi nyghte.
The while he caccheth conynges [15] / he coveiteth nought owre caroyne,[16]
But fet [17] hym al with venesoun,[18] / defame we hym nevere.
For better is a litel losse / than a longe sorwe,
The mase [19] amonge us alle / though we mysse [20] a shrewe.[21]
For many mannes malt / we mys wolde destruye,
And also ye route [22] of ratones / rende mennes clothes,
Nere [23] that cat of that courte / that can yow overlepe;
For had ye rattes yowre wille, / ye couthe [24] nought reule [25] yowre-selve.
I sey for me," quod the mous, / "I se so mykel [26] after,
Shal never the cat ne the kitoun / bi my conseille be greved,

[1] realm [2] timid [3] counted [4] knew [5] killed [6] yet [7] should creep [8] therefore [9] be [10] say [11] where [12] ailing [13] woe to the land where the king is a boy. [14] man, person [15] rabbits [16] flesh [17] feeds [18] game [19] confusion [20] get rid of [21] tyrant [22] crowd [23] were it not for [24] could [25] rule [26] much

Ne carpyng [1] of this coler / that costed [2] me nevre.
And though it had coste me catel [3] / biknowen [4] it I nolde,[5]
But suffre as hym-self wolde / to do as hym liketh,
Coupled and uncoupled / to cacche what thei mowe.[6]
For-thi uche [7] a wise wighte I warne / wite [8] wel his owne." —
What this meteles [9] bemeneth,[10] / ye men that be merye,
Devine ye, for I ne dar,[11] / bi dere God in hevene!

From Passus VI (A — Text)

[12] [Now riden this folk / and walken on fote,
To seche [13] that seint [14] / in selcouthe [15] londis;]
Bote [16] ther were fewe men so wys / that couthe [17] the wei thider,
Bote [16] blustrede forth as bestes / over valeyes and hulles;
[12] [For while thei wente here [18] owen wille, / thei wente alle amys,]
Til late and longe / that thei a leod [19] metten
Apparayled as a palmere / in pilgrimes wyse.[20]
He bar a bordun [21] i-bounde / with a brod lyste [22]
In a weth-bondes [23] wyse / i-writhen [24] aboute.
A bagge and a bolle / he bar bi his syde;
An hundred of ampolles [25] / on his hat seten,[26]
Signes of Synay / and schelles of Galys; [27]
Moni [28] cros on his cloke, / and keiyes [29] of Rome,
And the vernicle bi-fore, / for men schulde knowe
And seo be his signes / whom he sought [30] hedde.[31]
This folk fraynede [32] him feire [33] / from whenne that he coome.
"From Synay," he seide, / "and from the Sepulcre;
At Bethleem and at Babiloyne, / I have ben in bothe;
In Armonye, in Alisaundre, / and in mony other places.
Ye mouwe [6] seo be my signes / that sitteth on myn hat
That I have walked ful wyde / in weete and in druye [34]
And sought [35] goode seyntes / for my soule hele." [36]

[1] talking [2] cost [3] property [4] confess [5] would not [6] may [7] each [8] keep [9] dream [10] means [11] dare not [12] *These lines are given by Skeat from one MS.; they do not belong to the original.* [13] seek [14] Saint Truth [15] strange [16] but [17] knew [18] their [19] man [20] fashion [21] staff [22] strip of cloth [23] convolvulus [24] twisted [25] sacred vials [26] sat [27] Galicia [28] many a [29] keys [30] visited [31] had [32] asked [33] courteously [34] dry [35] visited [36] soul's health

"Knowest thou ought [1] a corseynt [2] / that men callen Treuthe?
Const thou wissen [3] us the wey / wher that he dwelleth?" 24
"Nay, so God me helpe," / seide the gome [4] thenne;
"Sauh I nevere palmere / with pyk [5] ne with schrippe [6]
Axen aftir him, / er [7] now in this place."
"Peter!" quod a plough-mon, / and putte forth his hed,
"I knowe him as kuyndeliche [8] / as clerk doth his bokes. 29
Clene concience and wit [9] / kende [10] me to his place,
And dude enseure [11] me seththe [12] / to serve him for evere,
Bothe to sowen and to setten, / while I swynke [13] mighte.
I have ben his folower / this fiftene wynter, 33
Bothe i-sowed his seed / and suwed [14] his beestes,
And eke i-kept his corn, / and cariede hit to house,
I-dyket and i-dolven,[15] / and don what he highte,[16]
With-innen and withouten / i-wayted [17] his profyt.
Ther nis no laborer in this lordschip / that he loveth more; 38
For, thaugh I sigge [18] hit myself, / I serve him to-paye.[19]
I have myn hure [20] of him wel / and otherwhile more.
He is the presteste [21] payere / that pore men knowen; 41
He with-halt [22] non hyne [23] his huire [20] / that he hit nath [24] at even.
He is as louh [25] as a lemb, / lovelich of speche;
And yif ye wolleth [26] i-wite [27] / wher that he dwelleth, 44
I schal wissen ow [28] wel / the righte way to his place."
"Ye, leve Pers," [29] quod the pilgrimes, / and profreden him huire.
"Nai, bi the peril of my soule," quod Pers, / and gon for to swere;
"I nolde fonge [30] a ferthing / for Seynt Thomas schrine;
Treuthe wolde love me the lasse / a gret while after. 49
Bote ye that wendeth [31] to him, / this is the wei thider."

[1] at all [2] saint [3] direct [4] fellow [5] spiked staff [6] scrip, bag [7] before [8] naturally, well [9] intelligence [10] instructed [11] did bind [12] afterwards [13] work [14] followed [15] dyked and delved [16] commanded [17] looked out for [18] say [19] acceptably [20] hire [21] promptest [22] withholds [23] servant [24] has not [25] low, humble [26] will [27] know [28] direct you [29] yea, dear Piers [30] I would not take [31] go

GEOFFREY CHAUCER (1340?–1400)

TROILUS AND CRISEYDE

From BOOK I

And so bifel, whan comen was the tyme
Of Aperil, whan clothed is the mede
With newe grene, of lusty Ver [1] the pryme,
And swote smellen floures whyte and rede,
In sondry wyses shewede, as I rede,
The folk of Troye hir observaunces olde, 160
Palladiones feste for to holde.

And to the temple, in al hir beste wyse,
In general, ther wente many a wight,
To herknen of Palladion the servyse;
And namely,[2] so many a lusty knight, 165
So many a lady fresh and mayden bright,
Ful wel arayed, bothe moste [3] and leste,
Ye, bothe for the seson and the feste.

Among thise othere folk was Criseyda,
In widewes habite blak; but nathelees, 170
Right as our firste lettre is now an A,
In beautee first so stood she, makelees;[4]
Hir goodly looking gladede al the prees.[5]
Nas [6] never seyn thing to ben preysed derre,[7]
Nor under cloude blak so bright a sterre 175

As was Criseyde, as folk seyde everichoon [8]
That hir bihelden in hir blake wede;[9]
And yet she stood ful lowe and stille alloon,
Bihinden othere folk, in litel brede,[10]
And neigh the dore, ay under shames drede,
Simple of atyr, and debonaire of chere, 181
With ful assured loking and manere.

This Troilus, as he was wont to gyde
His yonge knightes, ladde hem up and doun
In thilke [11] large temple on every syde, 185
Biholding ay the ladyes of the toun,
Now here, now there, for no devocioun
Hadde he to noon, to reven [12] him his reste,
But gan to preyse and lakken [13] whom him leste.[14]

And in his walk ful fast he gan to wayten [15]
If knight or squyer of his companye 191
Gan for to syke,[16] or lete his eyen bayten [17]
On any woman that he coude aspye;
He wolde smyle, and holden it folye, 194
And seye him thus, "God wot, she slepeth softe
For love of thee, whan thou tornest ful ofte.

[1] spring [2] especially [3] greatest [4] peerless [5] crowd [6] was not [7] more dearly [8] every one [9] garment [10] space [11] that same [12] take away [13] blame [14] it pleased [15] observe [16] sigh [17] feast

"I have herd told, pardieux, of your livinge,
Ye lovers, and your lewede [1] observaunces,
And which [2] a labour folk han [3] in winninge
Of love, and, in the keping which [2] doutaunces; [4]
And whan your preye is lost, wo and penaunces;
O verrey foles! nyce [5] and blinde be ye;
Ther nis [6] not oon can war [7] by other be."

And with that word he gan cast up the browe,
Ascaunces,[8] "Lo! is this nought wysly spoken?"
At which the god of love gan loken rowe [9]
Right for despyt, and shoop [10] for to ben wroken; [11]
He kidde [12] anoon his bowe nas not broken;
For sodeynly he hit him at the fulle; —
And yet as proud a pekok can he pulle! [13]

O blinde world, O blinde entencioun! [14]
How ofte falleth al theffect [15] contraire
Of surquidrye [16] and foul presumpcioun;
For caught is proud, and caught is debonaire.
This Troilus is clomben on the staire,
And litel weneth that he moot descenden.
But al-day [17] falleth thing that foles ne wenden.[18]

As proude Bayard ginneth for to skippe
Out of the wey, so priketh him his corn,[19]
Til he a lash have of the longe whippe,
Than thenketh he, "Though I praunce al biforn
First in the trays, ful fat and newe shorn,
Yet am I but an hors, and horses lawe
I moot endure, and with my feres [20] drawe."

From BOOK II

With this he took his leve, and hoom he wente;
And lord, how he was glad and wel bigoon! [21]
Criseyde aroos, no lenger she ne stente, [22]
But straught in-to hir closet wente anoon,
And sette here [23] doun as stille as any stoon,
And every word gan up and doun to winde,
That he hadde seyd, as it com hir to minde;

And wex somdel [24] astonied in hir thought,
Right for the newe cas; but whan that she
Was ful avysed,[25] tho [26] fond she right nought
Of peril, why she oughte afered be.
For man may love, of possibilitee,
A womman so his herte may to-breste,[27]
And she nought love ayein, but-if hir leste.[28]

[1] silly [2] what sort of [3] have [4] perplexities [5] foolish [6] is not [7] cautious [8] as if to say [9] cruel [10] planned [11] avenged [12] made known [13] pluck [14] purpose [15] result [16] overweening [17] constantly [18] did not expect [19] food [20] fellows [21] happy [22] delayed [23] her [24] somewhat [25] had considered thoroughly [26] then [27] burst [28] unless it please her

But as she sat allone and thoughte thus,
Thascry [1] aroos at skarmish al with-oute,
And men cryde in the strete, "See, Troilus
Hath right now put to flight the Grekes route!" [2]
With that gan al hir meynee [3] for to shoute,
"A! go we see, caste up the latis [4] wyde;
For thurgh this strete he moot to palays ryde;

"For other wey is fro the yate [5] noon
Of Dardanus, ther [6] open is the cheyne." [7]
With that com he and al his folk anoon
An esy pas rydinge, in routes [8] tweyne,
Right as his happy day was, sooth to seyne,
For which men say, may nought disturbed be
That shal bityden of necessitee.

This Troilus sat on his baye stede,
Al armed, save his heed, ful richely,
And wounded was his hors, and gan to blede,
On whiche he rood a pas, ful softely;
But swych a knightly sighte, trewely,
As was on him, was nought, with-outen faile,
To loke on Mars, that god is of batayle.

So lyk a man of armes and a knight
He was to seen, fulfild of heigh prowesse;
For bothe he hadde a body and a might
To doon that thing, as wel as hardinesse;
And eek to seen him in his gere [9] him dresse,
So fresh, so yong, so weldy [10] semed he,
It was an heven up-on him for to see.

His helm to-hewen [11] was in twenty places,
That by a tissew heng, his bak bihinde,
His sheld to-dasshed was with swerdes and maces,
In which men mighte many an arwe finde
That thirled [12] hadde horn and nerf [13] and rinde; [14]
And ay the peple cryde, "Here cometh our joye,
And, next his brother, holdere up of Troye!"

For which he wex a litel reed for shame,
When he the peple up-on him herde cryen,
That to biholde it was a noble game,
How sobreliche he caste doun his yen.
Cryseyda gan al his chere aspyen,
And leet [15] so softe it in hir herte sinke,
That to hir-self she seyde, "Who yaf [16] me drinke?" [17]

For of hir owene thought she wex al reed,
Remembringe hir right thus, "Lo, this is he
Which that myn uncle swereth he moot be deed,[18]
But I on him have mercy and pitee;"

[1] the shout [2] crowd [3] household [4] lattice [5] gate [6] where [7] chain [8] companies [9] gear, equipment [10] active [11] cut through [12] pierced [13] sinew [14] hide [15] let [16] gave [17] a potion [18] must die

And with that thought, for pure a-shamed,[1] she
Gan in hir heed to pulle, and that as faste,
Whyl he and al the peple for-by paste.

And gan to caste and rollen up and doun
With-inne hir thought his excellent prowesse,
And his estat, and also his renoun,
His wit, his shap, and eek his gentillesse;
But most hir favour was for [2] his distresse
Was al for hir, and thoughte it was a routhe [3]
To sleen [4] swich oon, if that he mente trouthe.

Now mighte some envyous jangle thus,
"This was a sodeyn love, how mighte it be
That she so lightly lovede Troilus
Right for the firste sighte; ye, pardee?"
Now who-so seyeth so, mote [5] he never thee! [6]
For everything, a ginning [7] hath it nede
Er al be wrought, with-outen any drede.

For I sey nought that she so sodeynly
Yaf [8] him her love, but that she gan enclyne
To lyk him first, and I have told yow why;
And after that, his manhood and his pyne
Made love with-inne hir herte for to myne,
For which, by proces and by good servyse,
He gat hir love, and in no sodeyn wyse.

From BOOK V

The morwe [9] com, and goostly [10] for to speke,
This Diomede is come un-to Criseyde,
And shortly, lest that ye my tale breke,
So wel he for him-selve spak and seyde,
That alle hir sykes [11] sore adoun he leyde.
And fynally, the sothe for to seyne,
He refte [12] hir of the grete [13] of al hir payne.

And after this the story telleth us,
That she him yaf [8] the faire baye stede,
The which she ones wan of Troilus;
And eek [14] a broche (and that was litel nede)
That Troilus was, she yaf [8] this Diomede.
And eek, the bet [15] from sorwe him to releve,
She made him were a pencel [16] of hir sleve.

I finde eek in the stories elles-where,
Whan through the body hurt was Diomede
Of [17] Troilus, tho weep [18] she many a tere,
Whan that she saugh his wyde woundes blede;

[1] for very shame [2] because [3] pity [4] slay [5] may [6] thrive [7] beginning [8] gave [9] morrow [10] spiritually [11] sighs [12] deprived [13] great (most) [14] also [15] better [16] pencil, small flag [17] by [18] then wept

And that she took to kepen him good hede;
And for to hele him of his sorwes smerte,
Men seyn, I not,[1] that she yaf him hir herte.

But trewely, the story telleth us,
Ther made never womman more wo
Than she, whan that she falsed Troilus.
She seyde, "Allas! for now is clene a-go [2]
My name of trouthe in love, for ever-mo!
For I have falsed oon the gentileste
That ever was, and oon the worthieste!

"Allas, of me, un-to the worldes ende,
Shal neither been y-writen nor y-songe
No good word, for thise bokes wol me shende.[3]
O, rolled shal I been on many a tonge;
Through-out the world my belle shal be ronge;
And wommen most wol hate me of alle.
Allas, that swich a cas me sholde falle!

"They wol seyn, in as muche as in me is
I have hem don dishonour, weylawey!
Al be I not the firste that dide amis,
What helpeth that to do [4] my blame awey?
But sin [5] I see there is no bettre way,
And that to late is now for me to rewe,[6]
To Diomede algate [7] I wol be trewe.

"But, Troilus, sin [5] I no better may,
And sin [5] that thus departen ye and I,
Yet preye I God, so yeve [8] yow right good day
As for the gentileste, trewely,
That ever I say,[9] to serven feithfully,
And best can ay his lady [10] honour kepe:" —
And with that word she brast [11] anon [12] to wepe.

"And certes, yow ne haten shal I never,
And freendes love, that shal ye han of me,
And my good word, al [13] mighte I liven ever.
And, trewely, I wolde sory be
For to seen yow in adversitee.
And giltelees, I woot [14] wel, I yow leve; [15]
But al shal passe; and thus take I my leve."

But trewely, how longe it was bitwene,
That she for-sook him for this Diomede,
Ther is non auctor telleth it, I wene.[16]
Take every man now to his bokes hede;
He shal no terme finden, out of drede.[17]
For though that he bigan to wowe hir sone,
Er he hir wan, yet was ther more to done.

[1] know not [2] gone [3] shame [4] put [5] since [6] repent [7] at any rate [8] give [9] saw [10] lady's [11] burst [12] at once [13] although [14] know [15] abandon [16] think [17] without doubt

Ne me ne list[1] this sely[2] womman chyde
Ferther than the story wol devyse.
Hir name, allas! is publisshed so wyde
That for hir gilt it oughte y-now[3] suffyse.
And if I mighte excuse hir any wyse,
For she so sory was for hir untrouthe,
Y-wis,[4] I wolde excuse hir yet for routhe.[5]

* * * * * * *

Go, litel book, go litel myn tregedie,
Ther[6] God thy maker yet, er that he dye,
So sende might to make in som comedie!
But litel book, no making[7] thou nenvye,[8]
But subgit be to alle poesye;
And kis the steppes, wher-as thou seest pace[9]
Virgile, Ovyde, Omer, Lucan, and Stace.

And for[10] ther is so greet diversitee
In English and in wryting of our tonge,
So preye I God that noon miswryte thee,
Ne thee mismetre for defaute of tonge.
And red wher-so thou be, or elles songe,
That thou be understonde I God beseche!
But yet to purpos of my rather[11] speche. —

The wraththe, as I began yow for to seye,
Of Troilus, the Grekes boughten dere;
For thousandes his hondes maden deye,
As he that was with-outen any pere,
Save Ector, in his tyme, as I can here.
But weylaway, save only Goddes wille,
Dispitously[12] him slough the fiers Achille.

And whan that he was slayn in this manere,
His lighte goost[13] ful blisfully is went[14]
Up to the holownesse of the eighte spere,[15]
In convers letinge[16] every element;
And ther he saugh,[17] with ful avysement,[18]
The erratik sterres, herkeninge armonye[19]
With sownes fulle of hevenish melodye.

And doun from thennes faste he gan avyse[20]
This litel spot of erthe, that with the see
Enbraced is, and fully gan despyse
This wrecched world, and held al vanitee
To respect of[21] the pleyn[22] felicitee
That is in hevene above; and at the laste,
Ther he was slayn, his loking doun he caste;

And in him-self he lough[23] right at the wo
Of hem that wepten for his deeth so faste;
And dampned al our werk that folweth so
The blinde lust, the which that may not laste,
And sholden al our herte on hevene caste.
And forth he wente, shortly for to telle,
Ther as Mercurie sorted him to dwelle. —

Swich fyn[1] hath, lo, this Troilus for love,
Swich fyn hath al his grete worthinesse;
Swich fyn hath his estat real[2] above,
Swich fyn his lust, swich fyn hath his noblesse;
Swich fyn hath false worldes brotelnesse.[3]
And thus bigan his lovinge of Criseyde,
As I have told, and in this wyse he deyde.

O yonge fresshe folkes, he or she,
In which that love up groweth with your age,
Repeyreth hoom from worldly vanitee,
And of your herte up-casteth the visage
To thilke[4] God that after his image
Yow made, and thinketh al nis but a fayre
This world, that passeth sone as floures fayre.

And loveth Him, the which that right for love
Upon a cros, our soules for to beye,[5]
First starf,[6] and roos, and sit[7] in hevene a-bove;
For He nil[8] falsen no wight, dar I seye,
That wol his herte al hooly[9] on Him leye.
And sin[10] He best to love is, and most meke,
What nedeth feyned loves for to seke?

Lo here, of Payens corsed[11] olde rytes,
Lo here, what alle hir goddes may availle;
Lo here, these wrecched worldes appetytes;
Lo here, the fyn[1] and guerdon for travaille
Of Jove, Apollo, of Mars, of swich rascaille!
Lo here, the forme of olde clerkes speche
In poetrye, if ye hir bokes seche.[12] —

O moral Gower, this book I directe
To thee, and to the philosophical Strode,
To vouchen sauf, ther[13] nede is, to corecte,
Of your benignitees and zeles gode.
And to that sothfast[14] Crist, that starf[15] on rode,[16]
With al myn herte of mercy ever I preye;
And to the Lord right thus I speke and seye:

Thou oon, and two, and three, eterne on-lyve,[17]
That regnest ay in three and two and oon,
Uncircumscript, and al mayst circumscryve,
Us from visible and invisible foon
Defende; and to thy mercy, everichoon,
So make us, Jesus, for thy grace digne,[18]
For love of mayde and moder thyn benigne!
Amen.

[1] nor do I wish [2] poor [3] enough [4] certainly [5] pity [6] where [7] composition [8] envy not [9] pass [10] because [11] former [12] pitilessly [13] spirit [14] gone [15] sphere [16] leaving behind (so that they seemed convex) [17] saw [18] perfect understanding [19] harmony [20] did perceive [21] in comparison with [22] perfect [23] laughed

[1] end [2] royal [3] brittleness, frailty [4] that same [5] buy, redeem [6] died [7] sits [8] will not [9] entirely [10] since [11] cursed [12] examine [13] where [14] true and faithful [15] died [16] cross [17] eternally living [18] worthy

THE CANTERBURY TALES

From THE PROLOGUE

Whan that Aprille with hise shoures soote [1]
The droghte of Marche hath perced to the roote,
And bathed every veyne [2] in swich [3] licour
Of which vertu engendred is the flour;
Whan Zephirus eek with his swete breeth
Inspired hath in every holt [4] and heeth
The tendre croppes,[5] and the yonge sonne
Hath in the Ram his halfe cours [6] y-ronne,
And smale foweles [7] maken melodye
That slepen al the nyght with open eye, —
So priketh hem Nature in hir corages,[8] —
Thanne longen folk to goon on pilgrimages,
And palmeres for to seken straunge strondes,[9]
To ferne halwes,[10] kowthe [11] in sondry londes;
And specially, from every shires ende
Of Engelond, to Caunterbury they wende,
The hooly blisful martir for to seke,
That hem hath holpen whan that they were seeke.
Bifil [12] that in that seson on a day,
In Southwerk at the Tabard as I lay,
Redy to wenden on my pilgrymage
To Caunterbury with ful devout corage,[13]
At nyght was come into that hostelrye
Wel [14] nyne-and-twenty in a compaignye,
Of sondry folk, by aventure [15] y-falle
In felaweshipe, and pilgrimes were they alle,
That toward Caunterbury wolden ryde.
The chambres and the stables weren wyde,
And wel we weren esed atte beste.[16]
And, shortly, whan the sonne was to reste,
So hadde I spoken with hem everychon,
That I was of hir felaweshipe anon,
And made forward [17] erly for to ryse,
To take oure wey, ther-as I yow devyse.[18]
But nathelees, whil I have tyme and space,
Er that I ferther in this tale pace,
Me thynketh it accordaunt to resoun
To telle yow al the condicioun [19]
Of ech of hem, so as it semed me,
And whiche [20] they weren and of what degree,
And eek in what array that they were inne;
And at a knyght than wol I first bigynne.
A Knyght ther was and that a worthy man,
That fro the tyme that he first bigan

[1] showers sweet [2] vein [3] such [4] forest [5] twigs [6] *In April the sun's course lies partly in the zodiacal sign of the Ram and partly in that of the Bull.* [7] birds [8] hearts [9] foreign strands [10] distant shrines [11] known [12] it befell [13] heart [14] full [15] chance [16] made comfortable [17] agreement [18] describe [19] character [20] what sort

To riden out, he lovede chivalrie,
Trouthe and honour, fredom and curteisie.
Ful worthy was he in his lordes werre,
And therto [1] hadde he riden, no man ferre,[2]
As wel in Cristendom as in hethenesse,
And ever honoured for his worthynesse.
At Alisaundre he was whan it was wonne;
Ful ofte tyme he hadde the bord bigonne [3]
Aboven alle nacions in Pruce.[4]
In Lettow [5] hadde he reysed [6] and in Ruce,[7]
No Cristen man so ofte of his degree.[8]
In Gernade [9] at the seege eek hadde he be
Of Algezir, and riden in Belmarye.[10]
At Lyeys [11] was he, and at Satalye,[11]
Whan they were wonne; and in the Grete See [12]
At many a noble armee [13] hadde he be.
At mortal batailles hadde he been fiftene,
And foughten for oure feith at Tramyssene [11]
In lystes thries, and ay slayn his foo.
This ilke [14] worthy knyght hadde been also
Somtyme with the lord of Palatye [11]
Agayn [15] another hethen in Turkye;
And evermoore he hadde a sovereyn prys.[16]
And though that he were worthy, he was wys,
And of his port [17] as meeke as is a mayde.
He never yet no vileynye [18] ne sayde
In al his lyf unto no maner wight.
He was a verray, parfit, gentil knyght.
But for to tellen yow of his array,
His hors were goode, but he was nat gay;
Of fustian [19] he wered a gypon [20]
Al bismotered [21] with his habergeon;[22]
For he was late y-come from his viage,[23]
And wente for to doon his pilgrymage.
With hym ther was his sone, a yong Squier,
A lovyere and a lusty bacheler,
With lokkes crulle,[24] as [25] they were leyd in presse.
Of twenty yeer of age he was, I gesse.
Of his stature he was of evene lengthe,[26]
And wonderly delyvere [27] and greet of strengthe;
And he hadde been somtyme in chyvachye,[28]
In Flaundres, in Artoys and Pycardye,
And born hym weel, as of so litel space,
In hope to stonden in his lady [29] grace.
Embrouded was he, as it were a meede [30]
Al ful of fresshe floures whyte and reede;

[1] besides [2] further [3] begun the board (sat at the head of the table) [4] Prussia [5] Lithuania [6] made expeditions [7] Russia [8] rank [9] Grenada [10] *A Town in Africa.* [11] *Towns in Asia Minor.* [12] Mediterranean. [13] armed expedition [14] same [15] against [16] high esteem [17] bearing [18] discourtesy [19] coarse cloth [20] shirt [21] soiled [22] coat of mail [23] voyage [24] curly [25] as if [26] medium height [27] active [28] cavalry expeditions [29] lady's [30] meadow

Syngynge he was or floytynge[1] al the day;
He was as fressh as is the monthe of May.
Short was his gowne, with sleves longe and wyde;
Wel coude he sitte on hors, and faire ryde;
He coude songes make and wel endite,[2]
Juste and eek daunce and weel purtreye and write.
So hoote he lovede that by nyghtertale[3]
He sleep namoore than dooth a nyghtyngale.
Curteis he was, lowely and servysable,
And carf[4] biforn his fader at the table.
  A Yeman[5] hadde he[6] and servants namo[7]
At that tyme, for hym liste ride soo;
And he was clad in cote and hood of grene;
A sheef[8] of pocok[9] arwes bright and kene
Under his belt he bar ful thriftily —
Wel coude he dresse[10] his takel[11] yemanly;
His arwes drouped noght with fetheres lowe[12] —
And in his hand he bar a myghty bowe.
A not-heed[13] hadde he with a broun visage.
Of woodecraft wel koude he al the usage.
Upon his arm he bar a gay bracer,
And by his syde a swerd and a bokeler,[14]
And on that oother syde a gay daggere
Harneised wel and sharpe as point of spere;
A Cristofre[15] on his brest of silver sheene;
An horn he bar, the bawdryk[16] was of grene.
A forster was he soothly, as I gesse.
  Ther was also a Nonne, a Prioresse,
That of hir smylyng was ful symple and coy;[17]
Hire gretteste ooth was but by Seïnt Loy,[18]
And she was cleped[19] madame Eglentyne.
Ful weel she songe the service dyvyne,
Entuned in hir nose ful semely;
And Frenssh she spak ful faire and fetisly[20]
After the scole of Stratford-atte-Bowe,[21]
For Frenssh of Parys was to hire unknowe.
At mete wel y-taught was she with-alle,
She leet no morsel from hir lippes falle,
Ne wette hir fyngres in hir sauce depe;
Wel coude she carie a morsel and wel kepe,
That no drope ne fille upon hire breste.
In curteisie was set ful muchel hir leste.[22]
Hire over-lippe wyped she so clene,
That in hir coppe ther was no ferthyng sene
Of grece, whan she dronken hadde hir draughte.
Ful semely after hir mete she raughte,[23]
And sikerly[24] she was of greet desport,[25]
And ful plesaunt and amyable of port,[26]
And peyned hire[1] to countrefete[2] cheere[3]
Of court, and been estatlich[4] of manere,
And to ben holden digne[5] of reverence.
But, for to speken of hire conscience,
She was so charitable and so pitous
She wolde wepe if that she saugh[6] a mous
Caught in a trappe, if it were deed or bledde.
Of smale houndes[7] hadde she, that she fedde
With rosted flessh, or milk and wastel-breed;[8]
But sore wepte she, if oon of hem were deed,[9]
Or if men[10] smoot it with a yerde[11] smerte,[12]
And al was conscience and tendre herte.
Ful semyly[13] hir wympul[14] pynched[15] was;
Hire nose tretys,[16] hir eyen greye as glas,
Hir mouth ful smal and ther-to softe and reed
But sikerly she hadde a fair forheed;
It was almoost a spanne brood I trowe,
For, hardily,[17] she was nat undergrowe.
Ful fetys[18] was hir cloke, as I was war;[19]
Of smal coral aboute hire arm she bar
A peire[20] of bedes gauded[21] al with grene,
And ther-on heng a brooch of gold ful sheene,[22]
On which ther was first write a crowned A,
And after *Amor vincit omnia.*
  Another Nonne with hire hadde she,
That was hire chapeleyne; and Preestes thre.
  A Monk ther was, a fair for the maistrie,[23]
An outridere that lovede venerie,[24]
A manly man, to been an abbot able.
Ful many a deyntee[25] hors hadde he in stable,
And whan he rood men myghte his brydel heere
Gynglen in a whistlynge wynd as cleere
And eek as loude as dooth the chapel-belle
Ther-as this lord was kepere of the celle.[26]
The reule of Seint Maure or of Seint Beneit,
By-cause that it was old and som-del streit,[27] —
This ilke monk leet olde thynges pace
And heeld after the newe world the space.
He yaf nat of that text a pulled[28] hen
That seith that hunters beth nat hooly men,
Ne that a monk when he is recchelees[29]
Is likned til a fissh that is waterlees;
This is to seyn, a monk out of his cloystre.
But thilke text heeld he nat worth an oystre;
And I seyde his opinioun was good;
What sholde he studie and make hym-selven wood,[30]
Upon a book in cloystre alwey to poure,
Or swynken[31] with his handes and laboure

[1] whistling [2] compose [3] night-time [4] carved [5] yeoman [6] *the knight* [7] no more [8] bundle of twenty-four [9] peacock [10] take care of [11] equipment [12] worn and clipped short [13] closely cut hair [14] small shield [15] an image of his patron saint [16] cord [17] quiet [18] *St. Loy (St. Eligius) did not swear at all.* [19] named [20] skilfully [21] *A convent near London.* [22] pleasure [23] reached [24] certainly [25] good humor [26] bearing

[1] exerted herself [2] imitate [3] fashions [4] dignified [5] worthy [6] saw [7] little dogs [8] cake bread [9] died [10] any one [11] stick [12] sharply [13] neatly [14] face cloth [15] pinched, plaited [16] well-formed [17] certainly [18] well-made [19] as I perceived [20] set [21] *Every eleventh bead was a large green one.* [22] beautiful [23] an extremely fine one [24] hunting [25] fine [26] *A cell is a branch monastery.* [27] strict [28] plucked [29] vagabond [30] crazy [31] work

As Austyn bit?[1] How shal the world be served?
Lat Austyn have his swynk[2] to him reserved.
Therfore he was a pricasour[3] aright;
Grehoundes he hadde, as swift as fowel in flight:
Of prikyng[4] and of huntyng for the hare
Was al his lust,[5] for no cost wolde he spare.
I seigh[6] his sleves purfiled[7] at the hond
With grys,[8] and that the fyneste of a lond;
And for to festne his hood under his chyn
He hadde of gold y-wroght a curious pyn;
A love-knotte in the gretter ende ther was.
His heed was balled, that shoon as any glas,
And eek his face as it hadde been enoynt.
He was a lord ful fat and in good poynt;[9]
Hise eyen stepe[10] and rollynge in his heed,
That stemed[11] as a forneys of a leed;[12]
His bootes souple, his hors in greet estaat.
Now certeinly he was a fair prelaat.
He was nat pale, as a forpyned[13] goost;
A fat swan loved he best of any roost.
His palfrey was as broun as is a berye.
A Frere ther was, a wantown and a merye,
A lymytour,[14] a ful solempne[15] man.
In alle the ordres foure[16] is noon that can[17]
So muchel of daliaunce and fair langage;
He hadde maad ful many a mariage
Of yonge wommen at his owene cost.
Unto his ordre he was a noble post;
Ful wel biloved and famulier was he
With frankeleyns[18] over-al in his contree;
And eek with worthy wommen of the toun,
For he hadde power of confessioun,
As seyde hym-self, moore than a curat,
For of his ordre he was licenciat.
Ful swetely herde he confessioun,
And plesaunt was his absolucioun.
He was an esy man to yeve penaunce
Ther-as[19] he wiste[20] to have a good pitaunce;[21]
For unto a povre ordre for to yive
Is signe that a man is wel y-shryve.
For, if he[22] yaf, he[23] dorste make avaunt
He wiste that a man was repentaunt;
For many a man so harde is of his herte
He may nat wepe al thogh hym soore smerte.
Therfore in stede of wepynge and preyeres
Men moote yeve silver to the povre freres.
His typet was ay farsed[24] full of knyves
And pynnes, for to yeven faire wyves.

[1] bids [2] work [3] hard rider [4] riding [5] pleasure [6] saw [7] edged [8] gray fur [9] *en bon point*, fleshy [10] large [11] gleamed [12] cauldron [13] tortured to death [14] licensed to beg in a certain district [15] imposing [16] *Dominican, Franciscan, Carmelite and Austin friars* [17] knows [18] rich farmers [19] where [20] knew [21] pittance, gift [22] *the man* [23] *the friar* [24] stuffed

And certeinly he hadde a murye[1] note;
Wel coude he synge and pleyen on a rote;[2]
Of yeddynges[3] he bar outrely the pris.
His nekke whit was as the flour-de-lys;
Ther-to he strong was as a champioun.
He knew the tavernes well in every toun
And everich hostiler and tappestere[4]
Bet[5] than a lazar[6] or a beggestere;[7]
For unto swich a worthy man as he
Acorded nat, as by his facultee,
To have with sike lazars aqueyntaunce;
It is nat honeste,[8] it may nat avaunce
For to deelen with no swiche poraille,[9]
But al with riche and selleres of vitaille.
And over-al,[10] ther-as[11] profit sholde arise,
Curteis he was and lowely of servyse.
Ther nas no man nowher so vertuous;[12]
He was the beste beggere in his hous,
For thogh a wydwe hadde noght a sho,[13]
So plesaunt was his *In principio*,[14]
Yet wolde he have a ferthyng[15] er he wente:
His purchas[16] was wel bettre than his rente.[17]
And rage he koude, as it were right a whelpe.[18]
In love-dayes[19] ther coude he muchel helpe,
For there he was nat lyk a cloysterer
With a thredbare cope, as is a povre scoler,
But he was lyk a maister, or a pope;
Of double worstede was his semi-cope,[20]
That rounded as a belle, out of the presse.[21]
Somwhat he lipsed for his wantownesse,[22]
To make his Englissh swete upon his tonge,
And in his harpyng, whan that he hadde songe,
Hise eyen twynkled in his heed aryght
As doon the sterres in the frosty nyght.
This worthy lymytour was cleped Huberd.

* * * * * * *

A Clerk ther was of Oxenford also
That unto logyk hadde longe y-go.
As leene was his hors as is a rake,
And he nas nat right fat, I undertake,
But looked holwe[23] and ther-to[24] sobrely.
Ful thredbare was his overeste courtepy,[25]
For he hadde geten hym yet no benefice,
Ne was so worldly for to have office;
For hym was levere[26] have at his beddes heed
Twenty bookes clad in blak or reed

[1] merry [2] fiddle [3] proverbial sayings [4] bar-maid [5] better [6] beggar [7] female beggar [8] becoming [9] poor folk [10] everywhere [11] where [12] full of good qualities [13] shoe [14] *St. John* i, 1, *used as a greeting.* [15] bit [16] gettings [17] what he paid for his begging privileges *or* his regular income [18] puppy [19] arbitration days [20] short cape [21] *the press in which the semi-cope was kept.* [22] jollity [23] hollow [24] besides [25] outer short coat [26] he had rather

Of Aristotle and his philosophie,
Than robes riche, or fithele,[1] or gay sautrie.[1]
But al be that he was a philosophre,
Yet hadde he but litel gold in cofre;
But al that he myghte of his freendes hente
On bookes and his lernynge he it spente,
And bisily gan for the soules preye
Of hem that gaf hym wher-with to scoleye.[2]
Of studie took he moost cure[3] and moost heede;
Noght o word spak he moore than was neede,
And that was seyd in forme and reverence,
And short and quyk and ful of hy sentence.[4]
Sownynge in[5] moral vertu was his speche,
And gladly wolde he lerne and gladly teche.

* * * * * * * *

A Frankeleyn[6] was in his compaignye;
Whit was his berd as is the dayesye;
Of his complexioun[7] he was sangwyn.
Wel loved he by the morwe[8] a sope[9] in wyn;
To lyven in delit was evere his wone,[10]
For he was Epicurus owne sone,
That heeld opinioun that pleyn delit
Was verraily felicitee parfit.
An housholdere, and that a greet, was he;
Seint Julian[11] he was in his contree;
His breed, his ale, was alweys after oon;[12]
A bettre envyned[13] man was no-wher noon.
Withoute bake-mete[14] was nevere his hous,
Of fissh and flessh, and that so plentevous
It snewed[15] in his hous of mete and drynke,
Of alle deyntees that men coude thynke
After the sondry sesons of the yeer, —
So chaunged he his mete and his soper.
Ful many a fat partrich hadde he in muwe,[16]
And many a breem[17] and many a luce[17] in stuwe.[18]
Wo was his cook but-if[19] his sauce were
Poynaunt and sharpe, and redy al his geere.
His table dormant[20] in his halle alway
Stood redy covered al the longe day.
At sessiouns ther was he lord and sire;
Ful ofte tyme he was knyght of the shire.
An anlaas,[21] and a gipser[22] al of silk,
Heeng at his girdel whit as morne milk.
A shirreve hadde he been and a countour;[23]
Was no-wher such a worthy vavasour.[24]

* * * * * * * *

[1] musical instrument [2] go to school [3] care [4] meaning [5] tending to [6] rich landowner [7] temperament [8] in the morning [9] sop [10] custom [11] patron saint of hospitality [12] always of the same quality [13] provided with wines [14] pasties [15] snowed [16] coop [17] a kind of fish [18] pond [19] unless [20] a permanent table [21] knife [22] pouch [23] treasurer [24] landholder

A Shipman was ther, wonynge[1] fer by weste;
For aught I woot[2] he was of Dertemouthe.
He rood upon a rouncy[3] as he couthe,[4]
In a gowne of faldyng[5] to the knee.
A daggere hangynge on a laas[6] hadde he
Aboute his nekke under his arm adoun.
The hoote somer hadde maad his hewe al broun.
And certeinly he was a good felawe;[7]
Ful many a draughte of wyn hadde he i-drawe
Fro Burdeuxward, whil that the chapman[8] sleep.
Of nyce conscience took he no keep.[9]
If that he faught, and hadde the hyer hond,
By water he sente hem hoom[10] to every lond.
But of his craft to rekene wel his tydes,
His stremes[11] and his daungers hym bisides,
His herberwe and his moone, his lodemenage,[12]
Ther nas noon swich from Hulle to Cartage.
Hardy he was, and wys to undertake;[13]
With many a tempest hadde his berd been shake;
He knew wel alle the havenes, as they were,
From Gootlond[14] to the Cape of Fynystere,
And every cryke[15] in Britaigne and in Spayne.
His barge y-cleped was the Maudelayne.

* * * * * * *

A Good-wif was ther of biside Bathe,
But she was som-del deef and that was scathe.[16]
Of clooth-makyng she hadde swich an haunt[17]
She passed hem of Ypres and of Gaunt.
In al the parisshe wif ne was ther noon
That to the offrynge bifore hire sholde goon;
And if ther dide, certeyn so wrooth was she
That she was out of alle charitee.
Hir coverchiefs ful fyne weren of ground;
I dorste swere they weyeden ten pound,
That on a Sonday weren upon hir heed.
Hir hosen weren of fyn scarlet reed
Ful streite y-teyd, and shoes ful moyste[18] and newe.
Boold was hir face and fair and reed of hewe.
She was a worthy womman al hir lyve;
Housbondes at chirche dore she hadde fyve,
Withouten oother compaignye in youthe,
But ther-of nedeth nat to speke as nowthe;[19]
And thries hadde she been at Jerusalem;
She hadde passed many a straunge strem;
At Rome she hadde been and at Boloigne,
In Galice at Seint Jame, and at Coloigne;
She coude[20] muche of wandrynge by the weye:
Gat-tothed[21] was she, soothly for to seye.

[1] dwelling [2] know [3] hackney [4] as well as he could [5] cheap cloth [6] lace, cord [7] goodfellow, rascal [8] merchant [9] heed [10] threw them into the sea [11] currents [12] steersmanship [13] cunning in his plans [14] Denmark [15] creek, inlet [16] harm [17] skill [18] soft [19] at present [20] knew [21] teeth set wide apart, *a sign that one will travel.*

Upon an amblere esily she sat,
Y-wympled[1] wel, and on her heed an hat
As brood as is a bokeler or a targe;[2]
A foot-mantel[3] aboute hir hipes large,
And on hire feet a paire of spores sharpe.
In felaweshipe wel coude she laughe and carpe;
Of remedies of love she knew per chaunce,
For she coude[4] of that art the olde daunce.[5]

* * * * * * *

A good man was ther of religioun,
And was a Povre Persoun of a toun;
But riche he was of hooly thoght and werk;
He was also a lerned man, a clerk,
That Cristes gospel trewely wolde preche.
Hise parisshens devoutly wolde he teche;
Benygne he was and wonder diligent,
And in adversitee ful pacient;
And swich he was y-preved[6] ofte sithes.[7]
Ful looth were hym to cursen[8] for hise tithes,
But rather wolde he yeven, out of doute,
Unto his povre parisshens aboute,
Of his offryng and eek of his substaunce.
He coude in litel thyng have suffisaunce.
Wyd was his parisshe, and houses fer asonder,
But he ne lafte[9] nat for reyn ne thonder,
In siknesse nor in meschief to visite
The ferreste[10] in his parisshe, muche and lite,[11]
Upon his feet, and in his hand a staf.
This noble ensample to his sheepe he gaf,
That firste he wroghte and afterward he taughte.
Out of the gospel he tho[12] wordes caughte,
And this figure he added eek[13] therto,
That if gold ruste what shal iren doo?
For if a preest be foul, on whom we truste,
No wonder is a lewed[14] man to ruste;
And shame it is, if a prest take keep,[15]
A [filthy] shepherde and a clene sheep.
Wel oghte a preest ensample for to yeve
By his clennesse, how that his sheepe sholde lyve.
He sette nat his benefice to hyre
And leet his sheep encombred in the myre,
And ran to London unto Seïnt Poules
To seken hym a chaunterie for soules,
Or with a bretherhed to been withholde;[16]
But dwelte at hoom and kepte wel his folde,
So that the wolf ne made it nat myscarie;
He was a shepherde, and noght a mercenarie.
And though he hooly were and vertuous,
He was to synful man nat despitous,[17]
Ne of his speche daungerous[18] ne digne,[19]
But in his techyng descreet and benygne;

[1] with a wimple about her face [2] shield [3] riding-skirt [4] knew [5] *This is a slang phrase.* [6] proved [7] times [8] impose penalties [9] neglected [10] farthest [11] rich and poor [12] those [13] also [14] ignorant [15] heed [16] maintained [17] pitiless [18] overbearing [19] haughty

To drawen folk to hevene by fairnesse,
By good ensample, this was his bisynesse.
But it were any persone obstinat,
What so he were, of heigh or lowe estat,
Hym wolde he snybben[1] sharply for the nonys.[2]
A bettre preest I trowe that no-wher noon ys;
He waited after no pompe and reverence,
Ne maked him a spiced conscience,
But Cristes loore, and his apostles twelve,
He taughte, but first he folwed it hym-selve.

* * * * * * *

The Millere was a stout carl for the nones,[2]
Ful byg he was of brawn and eek of bones;
That proved wel, for over-al[3] ther he cam,
At wrastlynge he wolde have alwey the ram.[4]
He was short-sholdred, brood, a thikke knarre,[5]
Ther nas no dore that he nolde heve of harre,[6]
Or breke it at a rennyng with his heed.
His berd, as any sowe or fox, was reed,
And therto brood, as though it were a spade.
Upon the cop[7] right of his nose he hade
A werte, and theron stood a tuft of herys,
Reed as the bristles of a sowes erys;[8]
His nosethirles[9] blake were and wyde.
A swerd and a bokeler bar he by his syde.
His mouth as wyde was as a greet forneys;
He was a janglere[10] and a goliardeys,[11]
And that was moost of synne and harlotries.
Wel coude he stelen corn and tollen thries,
And yet he hadde a thombe of gold,[12] pardee!
A whit cote and a blew hood wered he;
A baggepipe wel coude he blowe and sowne,
And therwithal he broghte us out of towne.

* * * * * * *

Now have I toold you shortly, in a clause,
Thestaat, tharray, the nombre, and eek the cause
Why that assembled was this compaignye
In Southwerk at this gentil hostelrye,
That highte[13] the Tabard, faste by the Belle.
But now is tyme to you for to telle
How that we baren us that ilke nyght,
Whan we were in that hostelrie alyght;
And after wol I telle of our viage[14]
And al the remenaunt of oure pilgrimage.
But first, I pray yow of youre curteisye,
That ye narette it nat[15] my vileynye,[16]
Thogh that I pleynly speke in this mateere
To telle yow hir wordes and hir cheere,

[1] snub, rebuke [2] for the nones *means* very, extremely. [3] everywhere [4] *the prize* [5] knot [6] heave off its hinges [7] end [8] ears [9] nostrils [10] loud talker [11] jester [12] *As all honest millers have.* [13] was called [14] journey [15] do not ascribe it to [16] lack of breeding

Ne thogh I speke hir wordes proprely;[1]
For this ye knowen al-so wel as I,
Whoso shal telle a tale after a man,
He moote reherce, as ny as evere he can,
Everich a word, if it be in his charge,
Al[2] speke he never so rudeliche and large,[3]
Or ellis he moot telle his tale untrewe,
Or feyne thyng, or fynde wordes newe.
He may nat spare, althogh he were his brother,
He moot as wel seye o word as another.
Crist spak hymself ful brode in hooly writ,
And wel ye woot no vileynye[4] is it.
Eek Plato seith, whoso that can hym rede,
"The wordes moote be cosyn[5] to the dede."
Also I prey yow to foryeve it me
Al[2] have I nat set folk in hir degree
Heere in this tale, as that they sholde stonde;
My wit is short, ye may wel understonde.
Greet chiere made oure hoste us everichon,[6]
And to the soper sette he us anon,
And served us with vitaille at the beste;
Strong was the wyn, and wel to drynke us leste.[7]
A semely man oure Hooste was with-alle
For to han been a marshal in an halle.
A large man he was, with eyen stepe,[8]
A fairer burgeys was ther noon in Chepe;[9]
Boold of his speche, and wys and wel y-taught,
And of manhod hym lakkede right naught.
Eek therto[10] he was right a myrie man,
And after soper pleyen he bigan,
And spak of myrthe amonges othere thynges,
Whan that we hadde maad our rekenynges;
And seyde thus: "Now, lordynges, trewely,
Ye been to me right welcome, hertely;
For by my trouthe, if that I shal nat lye,
I ne saugh this yeer so myrie a compaignye
At ones in this herberwe[11] as is now;
Fayn wolde I doon yow myrthe, wiste I how.[12]
And of a myrthe I am right now bythoght,
To doon yow ese, and it shal coste noght.
"Ye goon to Canterbury; God yow speede,
The blisful martir quite yow youre meede![13]
And, wel I woot,[14] as ye goon by the weye,
Ye shapen yow to talen[15] and to pleye;
For trewely comfort ne myrthe is noon
To ride by the weye doumb as a stoon;
And therfore wol I maken yow disport,
As I seyde erst,[16] and doon yow som comfort.
And if you liketh alle, by oon assent,
Now for to stonden at my juggement,
And for to werken as I shal yow seye,
To-morwe, whan ye riden by the weye,
Now by my fader soule that is deed,
But[1] ye be myrie, I wol yeve yow myn heed!
Hoold up youre hond withouten moore speche."
Oure conseil was nat longe for to seche;
Us thoughte it was noght worth to make it wys,
And graunted hym withouten moore avys,[2]
And bad him seye his verdit, as hym leste.[3]
"Lordynges,"[4] quod he, "now herkneth for the beste,
But taak it nought, I prey yow, in desdeyn;
This is the poynt, to speken short and pleyn,
That ech of yow to shorte with your weye,
In this viage shal telle tales tweye
To Caunterburyward, — I mean it so, —
And homward he shal tellen othere two,
Of aventures that whilom[5] han bifalle.
And which of yow that bereth hym beste of alle,
That is to seyn, that telleth in this caas
Tales of best sentence[6] and moost solaas,
Shal have a soper at oure aller cost,[7]
Heere in this place, sittynge by this post,
Whan that we come agayn fro Caunterbury.
And, for to make yow the moore mury,[8]
I wol myselven gladly with yow ryde
Right at myn owne cost, and be youre gyde.
And whoso wole my juggement withseye[9]
Shal paye al that we spenden by the weye.
And if ye vouche-sauf that it be so
Tel me anon, withouten wordes mo,
And I wol erly shape me[10] therfore."
This thyng was graunted, and oure othes swore
With ful glad herte, and preyden hym also
That he would vouche-sauf for to do so,
And that he wolde been oure governour,
And of our tales juge and reportour,
And sette a soper at a certeyn pris,
And we wol reuled been at his devys
In heigh and lowe; and thus by oon assent
We been acorded to his juggement.
And therupon the wyn was fet[11] anon;
We dronken and to reste wente echon
Withouten any lenger taryynge.
Amorwe, whan that day bigan to sprynge,
Up roos oure Hoost and was oure aller cok,[12]
And gadrede us togidre alle in a flok,
And forth we riden, a litel moore than paas,[13]
Unto the Wateryng of Seint Thomas;
And there oure Hoost bigan his hors areste
And seyde, "Lordynges, herkneth, if yow leste!

[1] accurately [2] although [3] coarsely [4] vulgarity [5] cousin [6] every one [7] it pleased us [8] big [9] Cheapside [10] besides [11] inn [12] if I knew how [13] give you your reward [14] know [15] tell tales [16] before

[1] unless [2] consideration [3] pleased him [4] gentlemen [5] formerly [6] meaning [7] cost of us all [8] merry [9] gainsay [10] prepare myself [11] fetched [12] cock, — *waked us all.* [13] a little faster than a walk

Ye woot youre forward [1] and I it yow recorde.
If even-song and morwe-song accorde,
Lat se now who shal telle the firste tale.
As evere mote I drynke wyn or ale,
Whoso be rebel to my juggement
Shal paye for all that by the wey is spent!
Now draweth cut, er that we ferrer twynne.[2]
He which that hath the shorteste shal bigynne.
Sire Knyght," quod he, "my mayster and my lord,
Now draweth cut, for that is myn accord.
Cometh neer," [3] quod he, "my lady Prioresse,
And ye, sire Clerk, lat be your shamefastnesse,
Ne studieth noght; ley hond to, every man."
  Anon to drawen every wight bigan,
And, shortly for to tellen as it was,
Were it by aventure, or sort,[4] or cas,[5]
The sothe is this, the cut fil to the knyght,
Of which ful blithe and glad was every wyght:
And telle he moste his tale as was resoun
By forward [1] and by composicioun,[6]
As ye han herd; what nedeth wordes mo?
And whan this goode man saugh that it was so,
As he that wys was and obedient
To kepe his forward [1] by his free assent,
He seyde, "Syn [7] I shal bigynne the game,
What, welcome be the cut a [8] Goddes name!
Now lat us ryde, and herkneth what I seye."
And with that word, we ryden forth oure weye;
And he bigan with right a myrie cheere
His tale anon, and seyde in this manere.

* * * * * * *

THE SQUIERES TALE

"Squyer, com neer,[9] if it your wille be,
And sey somwhat of love; for certes ye
Connen [10] ther-on as muche as any man."
"Nay, sir," quod he, "but I wol seye as I can
With hertly wille; for I wol nat rebelle
Agayn your lust;[11] a tale wol I telle.
Have me excused if I speke amis,
My wille is good; and lo, my tale is this."

Heere bigynneth the Squieres Tale

At Sarray, in the londe of Tartarye,
Ther dwelte a king, that werreyed [12] Russye,
Thurgh which ther deyde many a doughty man.
This noble king was cleped Cambyuskan,
Which in his tyme was of so greet renoun
That ther nas no-wher in no regioun
So excellent a lord in alle thing;
Him lakked nought that longeth to a king.

[1] agreement [2] further depart [3] come nearer [4] fate [5] chance [6] compact [7] since [8] in [9] nearer [10] know [11] pleasure [12] ravaged

As of the secte [1] of which that he was born
He kepte his lay,[2] to which that he was sworn;
And ther-to he was hardy, wys, and riche,
Pitous and just, and evermore yliche;[3]
Sooth [4] of his word, benigne and honurable,
Of his corage [5] as any centre stable;[6]
Yong, fresh, and strong, in armes desirous
As any bacheler of al his hous.
A fair persone he was and fortunat,
And kepte alwey so wel roial estat,
That ther was no-wher swich another man.
  This noble king, this Tartre Cambyuskan
Hadde two sones on Elpheta his wyf,
Of whiche the eldeste highte [7] Algarsyf,
That other sone was cleped [8] Cambalo.
A doughter hadde this worthy king also,
That yongest was, and highte Canacee.
But for to telle yow al hir beautee
It lyth nat in my tonge, nin [9] my conning;
I dar nat undertake so hy a thing.
Myn English eek is insufficient;
It moste ben a rethor [10] excellent,
That coude his colours [11] longing for that art,
If he sholde hir discryven every part.
I am non swich, I mot speke as I can.
  And so bifel that, whan this Cambyuskan
Hath twenty winter born his diademe,
As he was wont fro yeer to yeer, I deme,
He leet the feste of his nativitee
Don cryen thurghout Sarray his citee,
The last Idus of March after the yeer.
Phebus the sonne ful joly was and cleer;
For he was neigh his exaltacion,
In Martes face, and in his mansion
In Aries,[12] the colerik hote signe.
Ful lusty was the weder and benigne,
For which the foules, agayn the sonne shene,
What for the seson and the yonge grene,
Ful loude songen hir affeccions;
Hem semed han geten hem proteccions
Agayn the swerd of winter kene and cold.
  This Cambyuskan, of which I have yow told,
In roial vestiment sit [13] on his deys,[14]
With diademe, ful hy in his paleys,
And halt [15] his feste, so solempne and so riche
That in this world ne was ther noon it liche.[16]
Of which if I shal tellen al tharray,
Than wolde it occupye a someres day;
And eek it nedeth nat for to devyse [17]

[1] religion [2] faith [3] alike [4] true [5] heart [6] steadfast [7] was named [8] called [9] nor in [10] rhetorician [11] ornaments [12] *The zodiacal sign Aries is the mansion of Mars, and the first ten degrees are his face. The sign was supposed to be hot and to govern the red bile (cholera).* [13] sits [14] dais [15] holds [16] like [17] describe

At every cours the ordre of her servyse.
I wol nat tellen of her strange sewes,[1]
Ne of her swannes, ne of her heronsewes.[2]
Eek in that lond, as tellen knyghtes olde,
Ther is som mete that is ful deyntee holde,
That in this lond men recche of [3] it but smal;
Ther nis no man that may reporten al.
I wol nat tarien yow, for it is pryme,[4]
And for it is no fruyt [5] but los of tyme;
Un-to my firste I wol have my recours.
  And so bifel that, after the thridde cours,
Whyl that this king sit [6] thus in his nobleye,[7]
Herkning his minstralles her thinges [8] pleye
Biforn him at the bord deliciously,
In at the halle dore al sodeynly
Ther cam a knyght upon a stede of bras,
And in his hond a brood mirour of glas;
Upon his thombe he hadde of gold a ring,
And by his syde a naked swerd hanging;
And up he rydeth to the hye bord.[9]
In al the halle ne was ther spoke a word
For merveille of this knyght; him to biholde
Ful bisily ther wayten yonge and olde.
This strange knyght, that cam thus sodeynly,
Al armed save his heed ful richely,
Salueth king and queen, and lordes alle,
By ordre as they seten [10] in the halle,
With so hy reverence and obeisance
As wel in spechë as in contenance,[11]
That Gawayn with his olde curteisye,
Though he were come ageyn out of Fairye,
Ne coude him nat amende with a word.
And after this, biforn the hye bord,
He with a manly voys seith his message,
After the forme used in his langage,
With-outen vice [12] of sillable or of lettre.
And, for his tale sholde seme the bettre,
Accordant to his wordes was his chere,
As techeth art of speche hem that it lere.[13]
Al-be-it that I can nat soune [14] his style,
Ne can nat clymben over so hy a style,
Yet seye I this, as to commune entente,
Thus much amounteth al that ever he mente,
If it so be that I have it in mynde.
  He seyde, "The king of Arabie and of Ynde,
My lige lord, on this solempne day
Salueth yow as he best can and may,
And sendeth yow, in honour of your feste,
By me, that am al redy at your heste,[15]
This stede of bras, that esily and wel
Can, in the space of o [16] day naturel,

[1] dishes [2] young herons [3] reck of, care for [4] nine o'clock [5] profit [6] sits [7] nobility [8] pieces of music [9] high table [10] sat [11] bearing [12] fault [13] learn [14] sound [15] command [16] one

This is to seyn, in foure and twenty houres,
Wher-so [1] yow list, in droughte or elles shoures,
Beren your body in-to every place
To which your herte wilneth for to pace
With-outen wem [2] of yow, thurgh foul or fair;
Or, if yow list to fleen [3] as hy in the air
As doth an egle, whan him list to sore,
This same stede shal bere yow ever-more
With-outen harm, til ye be ther yow leste,[4]
Though that ye slepen on his bak or reste;
And turne ageyn, with wrything [5] of a pin.
He that it wroughte coude [6] ful many a gin;[7]
He wayted [8] many a constellacion
Er he had don this operacion;
And knew ful many a seel and many a bond.[9]
  "This mirour eek, that I have in myn hond,
Hath swich a myght, that men may in it see
Whan ther shal fallen any adversitee
Un-to your regne or to your-self also;
And openly who is your frend or foo.
And over [10] al this, if any lady bryght
Hath set hir herte on any maner wyght,[11]
If he be fals, she shal his treson see,
His newe love, and al his subtiltee,
So openly that ther shal no thing hyde.
Wherfor, ageyn [12] this lusty someres tyde,
This mirour and this ring, that ye may see,
He hath sent to my lady Canacee,
Your excellente doughter that is here.
  "The vertu of the ring, if ye wol here,
Is this; that, if hir lust [13] it for to were
Up-on hir thombe, or in hir purs it bere,
Ther is no foul that fleeth [14] under the hevene
That she ne shal wel understonde his stevene,[15]
And knowe his mening openly and pleyn,
And answere him in his langage ageyn.
And every gras [16] that groweth up-on rote
She shal eek knowe, and whom it wol do bote,[17]
Al [18] be his woundes never so depe and wyde.
  "This naked swerd, that hangeth by my syde,
Swich vertu hath, that what man so ye smyte,
Thurgh-out his armure it wol kerve and byte,
Were it as thikke as is a branched ook;
And what man that is wounded with the strook
Shal never be hool til that yow list,[19] of grace,
To stroke him with the platte in thilke [20] place
Ther [21] he is hurt: this is as muche to seyn,
Ye mote with the platte swerd ageyn
Stroken him in the wounde, and it wol close;
This is a verray sooth, [22] with-outen glose, [23]

[1] where-ever [2] spot, soilure [3] fly [4] where you please [5] twisting [6] knew [7] device [8] observed [9] magical seals and bonds [10] besides [11] kind of person [12] toward [13] she pleases [14] flies [15] speech [16] plant [17] help [18] although [19] you please [20] the same [21] where [22] truth [23] deceit

It failleth nat whyl it is in your hold."
  And whan this knyght had thus his tale told,
He rydeth out of halle, and doun he lyghte.
His stede, which that shoon as sonne bryghte,
Stant [1] in the courte, stille as any stoon.
This knyght is to his chambre lad [2] anon,
And is unarmed and to mete yset.[3]
  The presentes ben ful roially yfet,[4]
This is to seyn, the swerd and the mirour,
And born anon in-to the hye tour
With certeine officers ordeyned therfore;
And un-to Canacee this ring was bore
Solempnely,[5] ther [6] she sit [7] at the table.
But sikerly,[8] with-outen any fable,
The hors of bras, that may nat be remewed,[9]
It stant [1] as it were to the ground yglewed.
Ther may no man out of the place it dryve
For noon engyn of wyndas [10] or polyve; [11]
And cause why, for they can [12] nat the craft.[13]
And therefor in the place they han it laft [14]
Til that the knyght hath taught hem the manere
To voyden him,[15] as ye shal after here.
  Greet was the pres,[16] that swarmeth to and fro,
To gauren [17] on this hors that standeth so;
For it so hy was, and so brood and long,
So wel proporcioned for to ben strong,
Ryght as it were a stede of Lumbardye;
Ther-with so horsly, and so quik of yë
As it a gentil Poileys [18] courser were;
For certes, fro his tayl un-to his ere,
Nature ne art ne coude him nat amende
In no degree, as al the peple wende.[19]
But evermore her moste [20] wonder was,
How that it coude gon, and was of bras;
It was of Fairye, as the peple semed.[21]
Diverse folk diversely they demed;
As many heedes, as many wittes ther been.
They murmurede as doth a swarm of been,[22]
And maden skiles [23] after her fantasyes,
Rehersinge of thise olde poetryes,
And seyden, it was lyk the Pegasee,
The hors that hadde winges for to flee;
Or elles it was the Grekes hors Synon,[24]
That broughte Troye to destruccion,
As men may in thise olde gestes [25] rede.
"Myn herte," quod oon, "is evermore in drede;
I trowe som men of armes ben ther-inne,
That shapen hem this citee for to winne.
It were ryght good that al swich thing were knowe."

[1] stands [2] led [3] set [4] fetched [5] in state [6] where [7] sits [8] certainly [9] removed [10] windlass [11] pulley [12] know [13] trick [14] left [15] get him away [16] throng [17] gaze [18] Apulian [19] thought [20] their greatest [21] seemed to the people [22] bees [23] explanations [24] the horse of Sinon the Greek [25] tales

Another rowned [1] to his felawe lowe,
And seyde, "He lyeth; it is rather lyk
An apparence ymaad by som magyk,
As jogelours pleyen at thise festes grete."
Of sondry doutes thus they jangle and trete,[2]
As lewed [3] peple demeth comunly
Of thinges that ben maad more subtilly
Than they can in her lewednes [4] comprehende;
They demen gladly to the badder ende.
  And somme of hem wondrede on the mirour,
That born was up in-to the maister tour,
How men myghte in it swiche thinges se.
Another answerde and seyde it myghte wel be
Naturelly, by composicions
Of angles and of slye reflexions,
And seyde that in Rome was swich oon.
They speken of Alocen and Vitulon,
And Aristotle, that writen in her lyves
Of queynte mirours and of prospectyves,[5]
As knowen they that han her bokes herd.
  And othere folk han wondred on the swerd
That wolde percen thurgh-out every-thing;
And fille [6] in speche of Thelophus the king,
And of Achilles with his queynte spere,
For he coude with it bothe hele and dere,[7]
Ryght in swich wyse as men may with the swerd
Of which ryght now ye han your-selven herd.
They speke of sondry harding of metal,
And speke of medicynes ther-with-al,
And how, and whan, it sholde yharded be;
Which is unknowe, algates [8] unto me.
  Tho [9] speke they of Canaceës ring,
And seyden alle, that swich a wonder thing
Of craft of ringes herde they never non,
Save that he Moyses and king Salomon
Hadden a name of cunning in swich art.
Thus seyn the peple, and drawen hem apart.
But natheles somme seyden that it was
Wonder to maken of fern-asshen [10] glas,
And yet nis glas nat lyk asshen of fern;
But for they han yknowen it so fern,[11]
Therfor cesseth her jangling and her wonder.
As sore wondren somme on cause of thonder,
On ebbe, on flood, on gossomer,[12] and on mist,
And on al thing, til that the cause is wist.[13]
Thus jangle they and demen and devyse,
Til that the king gan fro the bord aryse.
  Phebus hath laft the angle meridional,[14]
And yet ascending was the beste roial,
The gentil Leon, with his Aldiran,[15]
Whan that this Tartre king, this Cambyuskan,
Ros fro his bord, ther [16] that he sat ful hye.

[1] whispered [2] discuss [3] ignorant [4] ignorance [5] prospective glasses [6] fell [7] injure [8] at all events [9] then [10] fern ashes [11] long [12] fog [13] known [14] *The thirty degrees just preceding the zenith.* [15] *a star* [16] where

To-forn him goth the loude minstralcye,
Til he cam to his chambre of parementz,[1]
Ther-as they sownen [2] diverse instrumentz,
That it is lyk an heven for to here.
Now dauncen lusty Venus children dere,
For in the Fish her lady sat ful hye,[3]
And loketh on hem with a frendly yë.
This noble king is set up in his trone.
This strange knyght is fet [4] to him ful sone,
And on the daunce he goth with Canacee.
Heer is the revel and the jolitee
That is nat able a dul man to devyse.[5]
He moste han knowen love and his servyse,
And ben a festlich man as fresh as May,
That sholde yow devysen swich array.
Who coude telle yow the forme of daunces,
So uncouthe [6] and so fresshe contenaunces,
Swich subtil loking and dissimulinges
For drede of jalous mennes aperceyvinges?
No man but Launcelot, and he is deed.
Therefor I passe of al this lustiheed;
I seye namore, but in this jolynesse
I lete [7] hem, til men to the soper dresse.[8]
The styward bit [9] the spyces for to hye,[10]
And eek the wyn, in al this melodye.
The usshers and the squyers ben ygon;
The spyces and the wyn is come anon.
They ete and drinke; and whan this hadde an ende,
Un-to the temple, as reson was, they wende.
The service don, they soupen al by day.
What nedeth yow rehercen her array?
Ech man wot wel that at a kinges feste
Hath plentee, to the moste and to the leste,
And deyntees mo than ben in my knowing.
  At after-soper goth this noble king
To sen this hors of bras, with al the route [11]
Of lordes and of ladyes him aboute.
Swich wondring was ther on this hors of bras
That, sin [12] the grete sege of Troye was,
Ther-as [13] men wondreden on an hors also,
Ne was ther swich a wondring as was tho.[14]
But fynally the king axeth this knyght
The vertu [15] of this courser and the myght,
And preyede him to telle his governaunce.
This hors anon bigan to trippe and daunce,
Whan that this knyght leyde hond up-on his reyne,
And seyde, "Sir, ther is namore to seyne,[16]
But, whan yow list [17] to ryden any-where,
Ye moten trille [18] a pin, stant [19] in his ere,

[1] ornaments [2] sound [3] *Their lady, Venus, was in exaltation in Pisces.* [4] fetched [5] describe [6] strange [7] leave [8] prepare [9] bids [10] hasten [11] company [12] since [13] where [14] then [15] excellence [16] say [17] you please [18] turn [19] which stands

Which I shall telle yow bitwixe us two.
Ye mote nempne [1] him to what place also
Or to what contree that yow list [2] to ryde.
And whan ye come ther-as [3] yow list abyde,
Bidde him descende, and trille another pin,—
For ther-in lyth the effect of al the gin,[4] —
And he wol doun descende and don your wille;
And in that place he wol abyde stille;
Though al the world the contrarie hadde yswore,
He shal nat thennes ben ydrawe ne ybore.[5]
Or, if yow liste [2] bidde him thennes gon,
Trille this pin, and he wol vanishe anon
Out of the syghte of every maner wyght,[6]
And come agayn, be it by day or nyght,
When that yow list to clepen [7] him ageyn
In swich a gyse [8] as I shal to yow seyn [9]
Bitwixe yow and me, and that ful sone.
Ryd whan yow list, ther is namore to done."
  Enformed whan the king was of [10] that knyght,
And hath conceyved in his wit aryght
The maner and the forme of al this thing,
Thus glad and blythe this noble doughty king
Repeireth to his revel as biforn.
The brydel is un-to the tour yborn,
And kept among his jewels leve [11] and dere.
The hors vanisshed, I noot [12] in what manere,
Out of her syghte; ye gete namore of me.
But thus I lete [13] in lust [14] and jolitee
This Cambyuskan his lordes festeyinge,
Til wel ny the day bigan to springe.

Explicit prima pars. Sequitur pars secunda

The norice [15] of digestioun, the Slepe,
Gan on hem winke, and bad hem taken kepe [16]
That muchel drink and labour wolde han reste;
And with a galping [17] mouth hem all he keste,
And seyde, it was tyme to lye adoun,
For blood was in his dominacioun;
"Cherissheth blood, natures frend," quod he.
They thanken him galpinge,[17] by two, by thre,
And every wyght gan drawe him to his reste,
As Slepe hem bad; [18] they toke it for the beste.
Her dremes shul nat ben ytold for me;
Ful were her heedes of fumositee,
That causeth dreem of which ther nis no charge.[19]
They slepen til that it was pryme large,[20]
The moste part, but it were Canacee;
She was ful mesurable, as wommen be.
For of hir fader hadde she take leve
To gon to reste, sone after it was eve;

[1] name, mention [2] you please [3] where [4] device [5] drawn nor borne [6] kind of person [7] call [8] wise, way [9] say [10] by [11] precious [12] know not [13] leave [14] pleasure [15] nurse [16] heed [17] gaping [18] bade [19] importance, significance [20] fully nine o'clock

Hir liste nat appalled [1] for to be,
Nor on the morwe [2] unfestlich [3] for to se;
And slepte hir firste slepe, and thanne awook.
For swich a joye she in hir herte took
Bothe of hir queynte ring and hir mirour,
That twenty tyme she changed hir colour;
And in hir slepe, ryght for impression
Of hir mirour, she hadde a vision.
Wherfor, er that the sonne gan up glyde,
She cleped [4] on hir maistresse [5] hir bisyde,
And seyde that hir liste for to ryse.
Thise olde wommen that been gladly wyse,
As is hir maistresse, answerde hir anon,
And seyde, "Madame, whider wole [6] ye gon [7]
Thus erly, for the folk ben alle on reste?"
"I wol," [6] quod she, "aryse, for me leste
No lenger for to slepe; and walke aboute."
Hir maistresse clepeth [8] wommen a gret route,[9]
And up they rysen, wel a ten or twelve;
Up ryseth fresshe Canacee hir-selve,
As rody [10] and bryght as doth the yonge sonne,
That in the Ram [11] is four degrees up-ronne;
Noon hyer was he, whan she redy was;
And forth she walketh esily a pas,
Arrayed after the lusty seson sote [12]
Lyghtly, for to pleye and walke on fote;
Nat but with fyve or six of hir meynee; [13]
And in a trench,[14] forth in the park, goth she.
The vapour, which that fro the erthe glood,[15]
Made the sonne to seme rody [10] and brood;
But natheles, it was so fair a syghte
That it made alle her hertes for to lyghte,
What for the seson and the morweninge,
And for the foules that she herde singe;
For ryght anon she wiste what they mente
Ryght by her song, and knew al her entente.[16]
The knotte why that every tale is told,
If it be taried til that lust [17] be cold
Of hem that han it after herkned yore,[18]
The savour passeth ever lenger the more,
For fulsomnesse of his prolixitee.
And by the same reson, thinketh me,[19]
I sholde to the knotte condescende,
And maken of hir walking sone an ende.
Amidde a tree fordrye,[20] as whyt as chalk,
As Canacee was pleying in hir walk,
Ther sat a faucon over hir heed ful hye,
That with a pitous voys so gan to crye
That all the wode resouned of hir cry.
Ybeten [21] hath she hir-self so pitously
With bothe hir winges til the rede blood

[1] made pale [2] morning [3] unfitting a feast [4] called [5] duenna [6] will [7] go [8] calls [9] company [10] ruddy [11] The zodiacal sign Aries. [12] sweet [13] household [14] closed walk [15] glided [16] meaning [17] desire [18] long [19] me-thinks [20] dried up [21] beaten

Ran endelong [1] the tree ther-as [2] she stood.
And ever-in-oon [3] she cryde alwey and shryghte,[4]
And with hir beek hir-selven so she pryghte,[5]
That ther nis tygre, ne non so cruel beste,
That dwelleth either in wode or in foreste,
That nolde [6] han wept, if that he wepe coude,
For sorwe of hir, she shryghte [4] alwey so loude.
For ther nas never yet no man on lyve [7] —
If that I coude a faucon wel discryve —
That herde of swich another of fairnesse
As wel of plumage as of gentillesse
Of shap, and al that myghte yrekened [8] be.
A faucon peregryn than semed she
Of fremde [9] londe; and evermore, as she stood,
She swowneth now and now for lakke of blood,
Til wel ny is she fallen fro the tree.
This faire kinges doughter, Canacee,
That on hir finger bar the queynte ring,
Thurgh which she understood wel every thing
That any foul may in his ledene [10] seyn,
And coude answere him in his ledene [10] ageyn,
Hath understonde what this faucon seyde,
And wel ny for the rewthe [11] almost she deyde.
And to the tree she goth ful hastily,
And on this faucon loketh pitously,
And held hir lappe abrood, for wel she wiste [12]
The faucon moste fallen fro the twiste,[13]
When that it swowned next, for lakke of blood.
A longe while to wayten [14] hir she stood,
Til atte laste she spak in this manere
Un-to the hauk,[15] as ye shul [16] after here.
"What is the cause, if it be for to telle,
That ye be in this furial pyne [17] of helle?"
Quod Canacee un-to this hauk above.
"Is this for sorwe of deth or los of love?
For, as I trowe, thise ben causes two
That causen most a gentil herte wo.
Of other harm it nedeth nat to speke,
For ye your-self upon your-self yow wreke;
Which proveth wel that either love or drede
Mot ben encheson [18] of your cruel dede,
Sin [19] that I see non other wyght yow chace.
For love of God, as doth your-selven grace!
Or what may ben your help? for West nor Est
Ne sey [20] I never er now no brid ne best
That ferde [21] with him-self so pitously.
Ye sle [22] me with your sorwe, verraily;
I have of yow so gret compassioun.
For Goddes love, com fro the tree adoun;
And, as I am a kinges doughter trewe,
If that I verraily the cause knewe

[1] along [2] where [3] continually [4] shrieked [5] tore [6] would not [7] alive [8] reckoned [9] foreign [10] language [11] pity [12] knew [13] bough [14] watch [15] hawk, falcon [16] shall [17] grievous torture [18] occasion [19] since [20] saw [21] acted [22] slay

Of your disese, if it lay in my myght,
I wolde amende it, er that it were nyght,
As wisly[1] helpe me gret God of kynde![2]
And herbes shal I ryght ynowe[3] yfynde
To hele[4] with your hurtes hastily."
Tho[5] shryghte this faucon yet more pitously
Than ever she dide, and fil[6] to grounde anon,
And lyth aswowne,[7] deed, and lyk a stoon,
Til Canacee hath in hir lappe hir take
Un-to the tyme she gan of swough[8] awake.
And, after that she of hir swough[8] gan breyde,[9]
Ryght in hir haukes ledene[10] thus she seyde:
"That pitee renneth[11] sone in gentil herte,
Feling his similitude in peynes smerte,
Is preved[12] al-day,[13] as men may it see,
As wel by werk as by auctoritee;
For gentil herte kytheth[14] gentillesse.
I se wel, that ye han of my distresse
Compassion, my faire Canacee,
Of verray wommanly benignitee
That Nature in your principles hath set.
But for non hope for to fare the bet,[15]
But for to obeye un-to your herte free,
And for to maken other be war[16] by me,
As by the whelp chasted[17] is the leoun,
Ryght for that cause and that conclusioun,[18]
Whyl that I have a leyser[19] and a space,
Myn harm I wol confessen, er I pace."[20]
And ever, whyl that oon[21] hir sorwe tolde,
That other[22] weep, as[23] she to water wolde,[24]
Til that the faucon bad hir to be stille;
And, with a syk,[25] ryght thus she seyde hir wille.
"Ther[26] I was bred, allas that harde day!
And fostred in a roche[27] of marbul gray
So tendrely, that nothing eyled me,
I niste[28] nat what was adversitee,
Til I coude flee ful hye under the sky.
Tho dwelte a tercelet[29] me faste by,
That semed welle of alle gentillesse;
Al[30] were he ful of treson and falsnesse,
It was so wrapped under humble chere,
And under hewe[31] of trewthe in swich manere,
Under plesance, and under bisy peyne,
That I ne coude han wend[32] he coude feyne,
So depe in greyn he dyed his coloures.
Ryght as a serpent hit[33] him under floures
Til he may sen his tyme for to byte,
Ryght so this god of love, this ypocryte,
Doth so his cerimonies and obeisances,

[1] certainly [2] nature [3] enough [4] heal [5] then [6] fell [7] in a faint [8] swoon [9] started [10] language [11] runs [12] proved [13] constantly [14] makes known, shows [15] better [16] cautious [17] chastised [18] end [19] leisure [20] pass [21] the one [22] the other [23] as if [24] would turn [25] sigh [26] where [27] rock [28] knew not [29] male falcon [30] although [31] color [32] thought [33] hides

And kepeth in semblant alle his observances
That sowneth in-to[1] gentillesse of love.
As in a toumbe is al the faire above,
And under is the corps, swich as ye wot,[2]
Swich was this ypocrite, both cold and hot,
And in this wyse he served his entente,
That (save the feend) non wiste[3] what he mente.
Til he so longe had wopen[4] and compleyned,
And many a yeer his service to me feyned,
Til that myn herte, to pitous and to nyce,[5]
Al innocent of his corouned malice,
For-fered of his deth, as thoughte me,
Upon his othes and his seuretee,
Graunted him love, on this condicioun,
That evermore myn honour and renoun
Were saved, bothe privee and apert;[6]
This is to seyn, that, after his desert,
I yaf[7] him al myn herte and al my thought —
God wot and he, that otherwyse nought —
And took his herte in chaunge for myn for ay.
"But sooth[8] is seyd gon sithen many a day,[9]
'A trew wyght[10] and a theef thenken nat oon.'
And, whan he sey[11] the thing so fer ygon,
That I had graunted him fully my love,
In swich a gyse[12] as I have seyd above,
And yiven[13] him my trewe herte, as fre
As he swoor that he yaf[7] his herte to me;
Anon this tygre, ful of doublenesse,
Fil on his knees with so devout humblesse,
With so hey reverence, and, as by his chere,[14]
So lyk a gentil lovere of manere,
So ravisshed, as it semed, for the joye,
That never Jason, ne Paris of Troye,—
Jason? certes, ne non other man,
Sin[15] Lameth was, that alderfirst[16] bigan
To loven two, as wryten folk biforn,
Ne never, sin[15] the firste man was born,
Ne coude man, by twenty thousand part,
Countrefete the sophimes of his art;
Ne were worthy unbokele his galoche,
Ther doublenesse or feyning sholde approche,
Ne so coude thanke a wyght as he did me!
His maner was an heven for to see
Til[17] any womman, were she never so wys;
So peyntede he and kembde[18] at point-devys
As wel his wordes as his contenance.
And I so lovede him for his obeisance,
And for the trewthe I demede in his herte,
That, if so were that any thing him smerte,
Al were it never so lyte,[19] and I it wiste,[20]
Me thoughte I felte deth myn herte twiste.

[1] belong to [2] know [3] knew [4] wept [5] foolish [6] privately and publicly [7] gave [8] truth [9] long ago [10] honest man [11] saw [12] way [13] given [14] bearing [15] since [16] first of all [17] to [18] combed, made up [19] small [20] if I knew it

And, shortly, so ferforth[1] this thing is went,[2]
That my wil was his willes instrument;
This is to seyn, my wil obeyede his wil
In alle thing, as fer as reson fil,[3]
Keping the boundes of my worshipe ever.
Ne never hadde I thing so leef,[4] ne lever,[5]
As him, God wot! ne never shal namo.[6]
"This lasteth lenger than a yeer or two,
That I supposed of him nought but good.
But fynally, thus atte laste it stood,
That fortune wolde that he moste twinne[7]
Out of that place which that I was inne.
Wher[8] me was wo, that is no questioun;
I can nat make of it discripcioun;
For o thing dar I tellen boldely,
I knowe what is the peyne of deth ther-by;
Swich harm I felte for he ne myghte bileve.[9]
So on a day of me he took his leve,
So sorwefully eek, that I wende[10] verrailly
That he had felt as muche harm as I,
Whan that I herde him speke, and sey[11] his hewe.
But natheles, I thoughte he was so trewe,
And eek that he repaire[12] sholde ageyn
With-inne a litel whyle, soth to seyn;
And reson wolde eek that he moste go
For his honour, as ofte it happeth so,
That I made vertu of necessitee,
And took it wel, sin[13] that it moste be.
As I best myghte, I hidde fro him my sorwe,
And took him by the hond, Seint John to borwe,[14]
And seyde him thus: 'Lo, I am youres al;
Beth[15] swich as I to yow have ben, and shal.'
What he answerde it nedeth nat reherse,
Who can seyn bet[16] than he, who can do werse?
Whan he hath al wel seyd, thanne hath he doon.
'Therfor bihoveth him a ful long spoon
That shal ete with a feend,' thus herde I seye.
So atte laste he moste[17] forth his weye,
And forth he fleeth,[18] til he cam ther him leste.[19]
Whan it cam him to purpos for to reste,
I trowe he hadde thilke[20] text in mynde,
That 'alle thing, repeiring to his kynde,[21]
Gladeth him-self;' thus seyn men, as I gesse.
Men loven of propre kynde[22] newfangelnesse,[23]
As briddes doon that men in cages fede;
For though thou nyght and day take of hem hede,
And strawe hir cage faire and softe as silk,
And yive[24] hem sugre, hony, breed and milk,
Yet ryght anon, as that his dore is uppe,
He with his feet wol spurne adoun his cuppe,
And to the wode he wol[25] and wormes ete;
So newefangel[1] ben they of hir mete,
And loven novelries of propre kynde;[2]
No gentillesse of blood ne may hem bynde.
So ferde[3] this tercelet, allas the day!
Though he were gentil born, and fresh and gay,
And goodly for to seen, and humble and free,
He sey up-on a tyme a kyte[4] flee,
And sodeynly he loved this kyte so,
That al his love is clene fro me ago,
And hath his trewthe falsed in this wyse;
Thus hath the kyte my love in hir servyse,
And I am lorn with-outen remedye!"
And with that word this faucon gan to crye,
And swowned eft[5] in Canaceës barme.[6]
Greet was the sorwe for the haukes harme
That Canacee and alle hir wommen made;
They nisten[7] how they myghte the faucon glade.
But Canacee hom bereth hir in hir lappe,
And softely in plastres gan hir wrappe
Ther-as[8] she with hir beek had hurt hir-selve.
Now can nat Canacee but herbes delve[9]
Out of the grounde, and make salves newe
Of herbes precious, and fyne of hewe,
To helen[10] with this hauk; fro day to nyght
She doth hir bisynesse and al hir myght.
And by hir beddes heed she made a mewe,[11]
And covered it with velouettes[12] blewe,
In signe of trewthe that is in wommen sene.
And al with-oute, the mewe[11] is peynted grene,
In which were peynted alle thise false foules,
As beth thise tidifs,[13] tercelets, and oules;
And pyes,[14] on hem for to crye and chyde,
Ryght for despyt were peynted hem bisyde.
Thus lete[15] I Canacee hir hauk keping;
I wol namore as now[16] speke of hir ring,
Til it come eft[5] to purpos for to seyn
How that this faucon gat hir love ageyn
Repentant, as the storie telleth us,
By mediacion of Cambalus,
The kinges sone, of which that I yow tolde.
But hennes-forth[17] I wol my proces holde
To speke of aventures and of batailles,
That never yet was herd so grete mervailles.
First wol I telle yow of Cambyuskan,
That in his tyme many a citee wan;
And after wol I speke of Algarsyf,
How that he wan Theodora to his wyf,
For whom ful ofte in greet peril he was,
Ne hadde he[18] ben holpen by the stede of bras.
And after wol I speke of Cambalo,
That faught in listes with the bretheren two

[1] far [2] gone [3] fell [4] dear [5] dearer [6] no more [7] depart [8] whether [9] remain [10] thought [11] saw [12] return [13] since [14] St. John as my security [15] be [16] better [17] must go [18] flies [19] where he pleased [20] that [21] nature [22] their own nature [23] novelty [24] give [25] will go

[1] desirous of novelty [2] their own nature [3] acted [4] *a bird* [5] again [6] lap [7] knew not [8] where [9] dig [10] heal [11] cage [12] velvets [13] *small birds* [14] magpies [15] leave [16] for the present [17] henceforth [18] had he not

For Canacee, er that he myghte hir winne.
And ther I lefte[1] I wol ageyn biginne.

Explicit secunda pars. Incipit pars tercia

Appollo whirleth vp his char[2] so hye,
Til that the god Mercurius hous the slye[3] —

[*The poem was not completed by the author.*]

Heere folwen the wordes of the Frankelyn to the Squier, and the wordes of the hoost to the Frankelyn

"In feith, Squyer, thou hast thee wel yquit,[4]
And gentilly I preise wel thy wit,"
Quod the Frankeleyn, "considering thy youthe,
So feelingly thou spekest, sir, I allow[5] the!
As to my doom,[6] ther is noon that is here
Of eloquence that shal be thy pere
If that thou live, — God yive[7] thee good chaunce,
And in vertu sende thee continuaunce!
For of thy speche I have greet deÿntee.[8]
I have a sone, and, by the Trinitee,
I hadde lever than twenty pound worth lond,
Though it ryght now were fallen in myn hond,
He were a man of swich discrecioun
As that ye ben! Fy on possessioun
But-if[9] a man be vertuous with-al.
I have my sone snibbed,[10] and yet shal,
For he to vertu listeth[11] nat entende;
But for to pleye at dees,[12] and to dispende,
And lese[13] al that he hath, is his usage.[14]
And he hath lever talken with a page
Than to comune with any gentil wyght
Ther[15] he myghte lerne gentillesse aryght."
"Straw for your gentillesse," quod our host;
"What, frankeleyn? parde, sir, wel thou wost[16]
That eche of yow mot tellen atte leste[17]
A tale or two, or breken his biheste,"[18]
"That knowe I wel, sir," quod the frankeleyn;
"I preye yow, haveth me nat in disdeyn
Though to this man I speke a word or two."
"Tel on thy tale with-outen wordes mo."
"Gladly, sir host," quod he, "I wol obeye
Un-to your wil; now herkneth what I seye.
I wol yow nat contrarien in no wyse
As fer as that my wittes wol suffyse;
I preye to God that it may plesen yow,
Than wot I[19] wel that it is good ynow."[20]

Explicit

[1] where I left off [2] chariot [3] *The zodiacal sign Gemini was the house of the sly god Mercury.* [4] acquitted [5] praise [6] judgment [7] give [8] pleasure [9] unless [10] reproved [11] cares [12] dice [13] lose [14] habit [15] where [16] knowest [17] at least [18] promise [19] then know I [20] enough

A ROUNDEL

From THE PARLEMENT OF FOULES

"Now welcom, somer, with thy sonne softe,
That hast this wintres weders[1] over-shake,[2]
And driven awey the longe nightes blake!"

Seynt Valentyn, that art ful hy on-lofte,[3]
Thus singen smale foules[4] for thy sake:
"Now welcom, somer, with thy sonne softe,
That hast this wintres weders over-shake."

Wel han[5] they cause for to gladen ofte,
Sith[6] ech of hem recovered hath his make;[7]
Ful blisful may they singen whan they wake:
"Now welcom, somer, with thy sonne softe,
That hast this wintres weders over-shake,
And driven awey the longe nightes blake!"

BALADE DE BON CONSEYL

Fle fro the prees, and dwelle with sothfastnesse,[8]
Suffyce unto thy good, though hit be smal;
For hord hath hate, and clymbing tikelnesse,[9]
Prees[10] hath envye, and wele blent overal;[11]
Savour no more than thee bihove shal;
Werk wel thy-self, that other folk canst rede;[12]
And trouthe shal delivere, hit is no drede.[13]

Tempest[14] thee noght al croked to redresse,
In trust of hir that turneth as a bal;[15]
Gret reste stant[16] in litel besinesse.
And eek be war[17] to sporne[18] ageyn an al;[19]
Strive noght, as doth the crokke[20] with the wal.
Daunte thy-self, that dauntest otheres dede;
And trouthe shal delivere, hit is no drede.

That thee is sent, receyve in buxumnesse,[21]
The wrastling for this worlde axeth a fal.
Her nis non hom, her nis but wildernesse:
Forth, pilgrim, forth! Forth, beste,[22] out of thy stal!
Know thy contree; lok up, thank God of al;
Hold the hye-wey,[23] and lat thy gost[24] thee lede!
And trouthe shal delivere, hit is no drede.

Envoy

Therfore, thou vache,[25] leve thyn old wrecchednesse;
Unto the worlde leve[26] now to be thral;
Crye Him mercy that[27] of His hy goodnesse
Made thee of noght, and in especial

[1] storms [2] overturned [3] above [4] little birds [5] have [6] since [7] mate [8] truth [9] insecurity [10] the crowd [11] prosperity blinds everywhere [12] advise [13] doubt [14] disturb [15] *i.e.* Fortune [16] stands, resides [17] cautious [18] kick [19] awl [20] crock, earthen pot [21] willing obedience [22] beast [23] highway [24] spirit [25] cow [26] cease [27] thank him who

Draw unto Him, and pray in general
For thee, and eek for other, hevenlich mede;[1]
And trouthe shal delivere, hit is no drede.

Explicit Le bon counseill de G. Chaucer

THE COMPLEINT OF CHAUCER TO HIS EMPTY PURSE

To you, my purse, and to non other wight[2]
Compleyne I, for ye be my lady dere!
I am so sory, now that ye be light;
For certes, but[3] ye make me hevy chere,[4]
Me were as leef be leyd up-on my bere;[5]
For whiche un-to your mercy thus I crye:
Beth[6] hevy ageyn, or elles mot I dye!

Now voucheth sauf this day, or[7] hit be night,
That I of you the blisful soun may here,
Or see your colour lyk the sonne bright,
That of yelownesse hadde never pere.
Ye be my lyf, ye be myn hertes stere,[8]
Quene of comfort and of good companye,
Beth hevy ageyn, or elles mot I dye!

Now purs, that be to me my lyves light,
And saveour, as doun in this worlde here,
Out of this toune help me through your might,
Sin that ye wole nat ben my tresorere;
For I am shave as nye[9] as any frere.[10]
But yit I pray un-to your curtesye:
Beth hevy ageyn, or elles mot I dye!

[1] reward [2] creature [3] unless [4] cheer [5] bier [6] be [7] ere [8] guide [9] shaven as close [10] friar

Lenvoy de Chaucer

O conquerour of Brutes Albioun!
Which that by lyne and free eleccioun
Ben[1] verray king, this song to you I sende;
And ye, that mowen[2] al myn harm amende,
Have mynde up-on my supplicacioun!

MORAL BALADE OF CHAUCER

The firste stok,[3] fader of gentilesse—
What man that claymeth gentil for to be,
Must folowe his trace, and all his wittes dresse
Vertu to sewe,[4] and vyces for to flee.
For unto vertu longeth dignitee,
And noght the revers, saufly dar I deme,[5]
Al were he[6] mytre, crowne, or diademe.

This firste stok was ful of rightwisnesse,
Trewe of his word, sobre, pitous, and free,
Clene of his goste,[7] and loved besinesse,
Ageinst the vyce of slouthe, in honestee;
And, but[8] his heir love vertu, as dide he,
He is noght gentil, thogh he riche seme,
Al were he mytre, crowne, or diademe.

Vyce may wel be heir to old richesse;
But ther may no man, as men may wel see,
Bequethe his heir his vertuous noblesse;
That is appropred unto no degree,
But to the Firste Fader in Magestee,
That maketh him his heir, that can him queme,[9]
Al were he mytre, crowne, or diademe.

[1] are [2] may [3] stock, stem [4] follow [5] judge, think [6] though he wear [7] spirit [8] unless [9] please

THE FOLLOWERS OF CHAUCER

THOMAS HOCCLEVE (1370?–1450?)

From DE REGIMINE PRINCIPUM

ON CHAUCER

O maister deere and fadir reverent, 1961
  Mi maister Chaucer, flour of eloquence,
Mirour of fructuous entendement,[1]
  O universel fadir in science,
  Allas, that thou thyn excellent prudence
    In thi bed mortel mightist noght byquethe!
    What eiled deth allas! why wold he sle the?

O deth, thou didest naght harme singuleer[2] 1968
  In slaughtere of him, but al this land it smertith.
But nathelees yit hast thou no power
  His name sle; his hy vertu astertith[3]
  Unslayn fro the, whiche ay us lyfly hertyth[4]
    With bookes of his ornat endytyng,
    That is to al this land enlumynyng. 1974

* * * * * * *

My dere maistir (God his soule quyte!) 2077
  And fadir Chaucer fayn wolde han me taght,
  But I was dul, and lerned lite or naght.

Allas! my worthi maister honorable, 2080
  This landes verray tresor and richesse!
Dethe, by thi deth, hath harme irreparable
  Unto us doon; hir vengeable duresse[5]
  Despoiled hath this land of the swetnesse
    Of rethorik, for unto Tullius
    Was never man so lyk[6] amonges us. 2086

Also who was hier[7] in philosophie 2087
  To Aristotle in our tonge but thow?
The steppes of Virgile in poesie
  Thow folwedist eeke, men wot wel ynow.
  That combre-world[8] that the, my maistir, slow,[9]
    Would I slayne were! Deth was to hastyf,
    To renne[10] on the, and reve[11] the thi lyf.

Deth hath but smal consideracion 2094
  Unto the vertuous, I have espied,
No more, as shewith the probacion,[12]
  Than to a vicious maister losel[13] tried;
  Among an heep[14] every man is maistried[15]
    With[1] hire, as wel the porre[2] as is the riche;
    Lerede[3] and lewde[4] eeke standen al yliche.[5]

She mighte han taryed hir vengeance a while 2101
  Til that some man had egal to the be.[6]
Nay, lat be that! sche knew wel that this yle
  May never man forth brynge lyk to the,
  And hir office[7] nedes do mot[8] she;
    God bad hir do so, I truste as for the beste;
    O maister, maister, God thi soule reste!

* * * * * * *

The firste fyndere of our faire langage 4978
  Hath seyde in caas semblable,[9] and othir moo,[10]
So hyly wel, that it is my dotage
  For to expresse or touche any of thoo.[11]
  Alasse! my fadir fro the worlde is goo,
    My worthi maister Chaucer, hym I mene:
    Be thou advoket[12] for hym, Hevenes Quene!

As thou wel knowest, O Blissid Virgyne, 4985
  With lovyng hert and hye devocion
In thyne honour he wroot ful many a lyne;
  O now thine helpe and thi promocion!
  To God thi Sone make a mocion
    How he thi servaunt was, Mayden Marie,
    And lat his love floure and fructifie! 4991

Al-thogh his lyfe be queynt,[13] the résemblaunce
  Of him hath in me so fressh lyflynesse,
That, to putte othir men in rémembraunce
  Of his persone, I have heere his lyknesse
  Do make,[14] to this ende, in sothfastnesse,
    That thei that have of him lest thought and
        mynde,
    By this peynture may ageyn him fynde. 4998

TO SIR JOHN OLDCASTLE

Lete holy chirche medle of the doctryne
Of Crystes lawes and of his byleeve,[15]
And lete alle othir folke ther-to enclyne,
And of our feith noon argumentes meeve.[16] 140
For if we mighte our feith by reson preeve,[17]
We sholde no meryt of our feith have.
But now-a-dayes a baillif or a reeve
Or man of craft wole in it dote or rave. 144

1 fruitful understanding 2 affecting only one 3 escapes 4 heartens 5 cruel affliction 6 like 7 heir 8 world-cumberer 9 slew 10 run 11 bereave 12 experience 13 rascal 14 in a crowd 15 overcome

1 by 2 poor 3 learned 4 ignorant 5 alike 6 had been equal to thee 7 duty 8 must 9 like cases 10 others also 11 those 12 advocate 13 quenched 14 had made 15 faith 16 move 17 prove

Some wommen eeke, thogh hir wit be thynne,
Wele [1] argumentes make in holy writ!
Lewde calates! [2] sittith down and spynne,
And kakele of sumwhat elles, for your wit
Is al to feeble to despute of it!
To clerkes grete apparteneth [3] that aart;
The knowleche of that God hath fro yow shit; [4]
Stynte [5] and leve of,[6] for right sclendre is your paart.

Oure fadres olde and modres lyved wel,
And taghte hir children as hem self taght were
Of Holy Chirche and axid nat a del [7]
"Why stant [8] this word heere?" and "why this
word there?"
"Why spake God thus and seith thus elles where?"
"Why dide he this wyse and mighte han do thus?"
Our fadres medled no thyng of swich gere: [9]
That oghte been a good mirour to us.

If land to thee be falle of heritage,
Which that thy fadir heeld [10] in reste and pees,
With title just and trewe in al his age,
And his fadir before him brygelees,[11]
And his and his, and so forth douteless,
I am ful seur [12] who-so wolde it thee reve,[13]
Thow woldest thee deffende and putte in prees; [14]
Thy right thow woldest nat, thy thankes,[15] leve.

Right so where-as our goode fadres olde
Possessid were, and hadden the seisyne [16]
Peisible of Crystes feith, and no man wolde
Impugne hir right, it sit [17] us to enclyne
Ther-to. Let us no ferthere ymagyne
But as that they dide; occupie [18] our right;
And in oure hertes fully determyne
Our title good, and keepe it with our might!

JOHN LYDGATE (1370?–1451?)

LONDON LYCKPENY

To London once my steppes I bent,
Where trouth in no wyse should be faynt;
To-Westmynster-ward I forthwith went,
To a man of law to make complaynt;
I sayd, "For Marys love, that holy saynt,
Pyty the poore that wold proceede!"
But for lack of mony I cold not spede.

And as I thrust the prese [19] amonge,
By froward [20] chaunce my hood was gone;
Yet for all that I stayd not longe,
Tyll to the Kynges Bench I was come.
Before the judge I kneled anon,
And prayd hym for Gods sake to take heede;
But for lack of mony I myght not speede.

Beneth hem sat clarkes a great rout,[1]
Which fast dyd wryte by one assent,
There stoode up one and cryed about,
"Rychard, Robert, and John of Kent."
I wyst not well what this man ment,
He cryed so thycke [2] there in dede.
But he that lackt mony myght not spede.

Unto the Common Place [3] I yode thoo,[4]
Where sat one with a sylken hoode;
I dyd hym reverence, for I ought to do so,
And told my case as well as I coode,
How my goodes were defrauded me by falshood.
I gat not a mum of his mouth for my meed,[5]
And for lack of mony I myght not spede.

Unto the Rolles I gat me from thence,
Before the Clarkes of the Chauncerye,
Where many I found earnyng of pence,
But none at all once regarded mee.
I gave them my playnt uppon my knee;
They lyked it well, when they had it reade;
But, lackyng mony, I could not be sped.

In Westmynster-hall I found out one,
Which went in a long gown of raye; [6]
I crowched and kneled before hym anon,
For Maryes love, of help I hym praye.
"I wot not what thou meanest," gan he say.
To get me thence he dyd me bede; [7]
For lack of mony, I cold not speed.

Within this hall, nether rich nor yett poore
Wold do for me ought, although I shold dye.
Which seing, I gat me out of the doore,
Where Flemynges began on me for to cry,
"Master, what will you copen [8] or by?
Fyne felt hattes, or spectacles to reede?
Lay down your sylver, and here you may speede."

Then to Westmynster-gate I presently went,
When the sonne was at hyghe pryme;
Cookes to me they tooke good entente,
And proferred me bread, with ale and wyne,
Rybbes of befe, both fat and ful fyne;
A fayre cloth they gan for to sprede.
But, wantyng mony, I myght not then speede.

Then unto London I dyd me hye; [9]
Of all the land it beareth the pryse.[10]
"Hot pescodes," one began to crye,
"Strabery rype," and "cherryes in the ryse;" [11]
One bad me come nere and by some spyce;

[1] will [2] wenches [3] belongs [4] shut [5] cease [6] leave off [7] not at all [8] stands [9] business [10] held [11] without dispute [12] sure [13] take away [14] make an effort [15] willingly [16] possession [17] behooves [18] make use of [19] crowd [20] perverse

[1] crowd [2] fast [3] Court of Common Pleas [4] went then [5] reward [6] a striped cloth [7] bid [8] buy [9] hasten [10] superiority [11] on the bough

Peper and safforne they gan me bede.
But for lack of mony I myght not spede.

Then to the Chepe [1] I gan me drawne,
  Where mutch people I saw for to stand;
One ofred me velvet, sylke, and lawne,
  An other he taketh me by the hande,
  "Here is Parys thred, the fynest in the land."
I never was used to such thynges in dede,
And, wantyng mony, I myght not speed.

Then went I forth by London stone,
  Thoroughout all Canwyke streete;
Drapers mutch cloth me offred anone.
  Then met I one, cryed "hot shepes feete;"
  One cryde "makerell"; "ryshes [2] grene" an
    other gan greete; [3]
On bad me by a hood to cover my head;
But for want of mony I myght not be sped.

Then I hyed me into Est-Chepe;
  One cryes "rybbes of befe," and many a pye;
Pewter pottes they clattered on a heape;
  There was harpe, pype, and mynstralsye.
  "Yea, by Cock!" "nay, by Cock!" some began
    crye;
Some songe of Jenken and Julyan for there mede.
But for lack of mony I myght not spede.

Then into Cornhyll anon I yode,[4]
  Where was mutch stolen gere [5] amonge; [6]
I saw where honge myne owne hoode,
  That I had lost amonge the thronge;
  To by my own hood I thought it wronge,
I knew it well as I dyd my crede;
But for lack of mony I could not spede.

The taverner tooke me by the sleve,
  "Sir," sayth he, "wyll you our wyne assay?" [7]
I answered, "That can not mutch me greve:
  A peny can do no more then it may;"
  I drank a pynt and for it dyd paye;
Yet sore a-hungerd from thence I yede,[4]
And, wantyng mony, I cold not spede.

Then hyed I me to Belyngsgate,
  And one cryed, "Hoo! go we hence!"
I prayd a barge-man, for Gods sake,
  That he wold spare me my expense.
  "Thou scapst not here," quod he, "under two
    pence;
I lyst not yet bestow my almes dede."
Thus, lackyng mony, I could not speede.

[1] the market [2] rushes [3] cry [4] went [5] goods [6] here and there [7] try

Then I convayd me into Kent,
  For of the law wold I meddle no more;
Because no man to me tooke entent,[1]
  I dyght me [2] to do as I dyd before.
  Now Jesus, that in Bethlem was bore,
Save London, and send trew lawyers there mede!
For who-so wantes mony with them shall not
    spede!

From THE STORY OF THEBES

How falsly Ethyocles leyde a busshement [3] in the way to have slayn Tydeus

At a posterne forth they gan to ryde
By a geyn [4] path, that ley oute a-side,
Secrely, that no man hem espie,
Only of [5] tresoun and of felonye.
They haste hem forth al the longe day,
Of cruel malys, forto stoppe his way,
Thorgh a forest, alle of oon assent,
Ful covartly to leyn a busshement
Under an hille, at a streite passage,
To falle on hym at mor avantage,[6]
The same way that Tydeus gan drawe
At thylke [7] mount wher that Spynx was slawe.[8]
He, nothing war in his opynyoun [9]
Of this conpassed [10] conspiracioun,
But innocent and lich [11] a gentyl knyght,
Rood ay forth to [12] that it drowe [13] to nyght,
Sool by hym-silf with-oute companye,
Havyng no man to wisse [14] hym or to gye.[15]
  But at the last, lifting up his hede,
Toward eve, he gan taken hede;
Mid of his waye, right as eny lyne,
Thoght he saugh, ageyn the mone shyne,
Sheldes fresshe and plates borned [16] bright,
The which environ [17] casten a gret lyght;
Ymagynyng in his fantasye
Ther was treson and conspiracye
Wrought by the kyng, his journe [18] forto lette.[19]

How Tydeus outraged fifty knyghtes that lay in awayt for hym

And of al that he no-thyng ne sette,[20]
But wel assured in his manly herte,
List [21] nat onys a-syde to dyverte,
But kepte his way, his sheld upon his brest,
And cast his spere manly in the rest,

[1] heed [2] prepared myself [3] ambush [4] convenient [5] purely because of [6] greater advantage [7] the same [8] slain [9] not at all aware in his thought [10] arranged, formed [11] like [12] till [13] drew [14] direct [15] guide [16] burnished [17] around [18] journey [19] hinder [20] he cared nothing for it [21] wished

And the first platly [1] that he mette
Thorgh the body proudely he hym smette,
That he fille ded, chief mayster of hem alle;
And than at onys they upon hym falle
On every part, be [2] compas envyroun.
But Tydeus, thorgh his hegh renoun,
His blody swerde lete about hym glyde,
Sleth and kylleth upon every side
In his ire and his mortal tene; [3]
That mervaile was he myght so sustene
Ageyn hem alle, in every half besette; [4]
But his swerde was so sharpe whette,
That his foomen founde ful unsoote.[5]
But he, allas! was mad light a foote,[6]
Be force grounded,[7] in ful gret distresse;
But of knyghthod and of gret prouesse [8]
Up he roos, maugre [9] alle his foon,[10]
And as they cam, he slogh [11] hem oon be oon,
Lik a lyoun rampaunt in his rage,
And on this hille he fond a narow passage,
Which that he took of ful high prudence;
And liche [12] a boor, stondyng at his diffence,
As his foomen proudly hym assaylle,
Upon the pleyn he made her blode to raylle [13]
Al enviroun, that the soyl wex rede,
Now her, now ther, as they fille dede,
That her lay on, and ther lay two or thre,
So mercyles, in his cruelte,
Thilke day he was upon hem founde;
And, attonys [14] his enemyes to confounde,
Wher-as he stood, this myghty champioun,
Be-side he saugh, with water turned doun,
An huge stoon large, rounde, and squar;
And sodeynly, er that thei wer war,
As [15] it hadde leyn ther for the nonys,[16]
Upon his foon he rolled it at onys,
That ten of hem [17] wenten unto wrak,
And the remnaunt amased drogh [18] a-bak;
For on by on they wente to meschaunce.[19]
And fynaly he broght to outraunce [20]
Hem everychoon, Tydeus, as blyve,[21]
That non but on left of ham [17] alyve:
Hym-silf yhurt, and ywounded kene,[22]
Thurgh his harneys bledyng on the grene;
The Theban knyghtes in compas rounde aboute
In the vale lay slayne, alle the hoole route,[23]
Which pitously ageyn the mone [24] gape;
For non of hem, shortly, [25] myght eskape,
But dede [26] echon as thei han deserved,
Save oon excepte, the which was reserved

[1] absolutely [2] by [3] pain [4] beset on every side [5] unsweet, bitter [6] made to alight on foot [7] brought to ground [8] prowess [9] in spite of [10] foes [11] slew [12] like [13] flow [14] at once [15] as if [16] for the purpose [17] them [18] drew [19] defeat [20] destruction [21] quickly [22] sorely [23] crowd [24] moon [25] to tell it briefly [26] died

By Tydeus, of intencioun,
To the kyng to make relacioun
How his knyghtes han on her journe spedde,[1] —
Everich of hem his lyf left for a wedde,[2] —
And at the metyng how they han hem born;
To tellen al he sured [3] was and sworn
To Tydeus, ful lowly on his kne.

KING JAMES I OF SCOTLAND (1394–1437)

From THE KINGIS QUAIR

Quhare-as [4] in ward full oft I wold bewaille
 My dedely lyf, full of peyne and penance,
Saing ryght thus, quhat have I gilt [5] to faille
 My fredome in this warld and my plesance,
 Sen [6] every wight has thereof suffisance,
That I behold, and I a creature
Put from all this? — hard is myn aventure!

The bird, the beste, the fisch eke in the see,
 They lyve in fredome everich in his kynd; [7]
And I a man, and lakkith libertee;
 Quhat schall I seyne,[8] quhat resoun may I fynd,
 That fortune suld [9] do so? thus in my mynd
My folk I wold argewe, bot all for noght;
Was non that myght, that on my peynes rought.[10]

Than wold I say, "Gif [11] God me had devisit [12]
 To lyve my lyf in thraldome thus and pyne,[13]
Quhat was the cause that he me more comprisit
 Than othir folk to lyve in suich ruyne?
 I suffer allone amang the figuris nyne,
Ane wofull wrecche that to no wight may spede,
And yit of every lyvis [14] help hath nede."

The longe dayes and the nyghtis eke
 I wold bewaille my fortune in this wise,
For quhich, agane distresse confort to seke,
 My custum was on mornis for to ryse
 Airly as day; O happy exercise,
By the come I to joye out of turment!
Bot now to purpose of my first entent: —

Bewailing in my chamber thus allone,
 Despeired of all joye and remedye,
For-tirit [15] of my thoght, and wo begone,
 Unto the wyndow gan I walk in hye,[16]
 To se the warld and folk that went forby;
And for the tyme, though I of mirthis fude [17]
Myght have no more, to luke it did me gude.

[1] succeeded, fared [2] pledge [3] assured [4] where [5] sinned [6] since [7] nature [8] say [9] should [10] had pity [11] if [12] planned [13] torture [14] living person's [15] tired out [16] haste [17] food

Now was there maid fast by the touris wall
A gardyn faire, and in the corneris set
Ane herbere grene, with wandis [1] long and small
Railit about; and so with treis set
Was all the place, and hawthorn hegis knet,
That lyf [2] was non walking there forby
That myght within scarse ony wight aspye. 217

So thik the bewis [3] and the leves grene
Beschadit all the aleyes that there were,
And myddis every herbere myght be sene
The scharpe grene suete jenepere,
Growing so faire with branchis here and there,
That, as it semyt to a lyf without,
The bewis [3] spred the herbere all about; 224

And on the smalle grene twistis [4] sat
The lytill suete [5] nyghtingale, and song
So loud and clere, the ympnis [6] consecrat
Off lufis use, now soft, now lowd among,
That all the gardyng and the wallis rong
Ryght of thaire song, and on the copill [7] next
Off thaire suete armony, and lo the text: 231

Cantus

"*Worschippe, ye that loveris bene, this May,*
For of your blisse the kalendis are begonne,
And sing with us, Away, winter, away!
Cum, somer, cum, the suete sesoun and sonne!
Awake for schame! that have your hevynnis wonne,
And amorously lift up your hedis all,
Thank lufe that list you to his merci call." 238

Quhen thai this song had song a lytill thrawe,[8]
Thai stent [9] a quhile, and therewith unaffraid,
As I beheld and kest myn eyne a-lawe,[10]
From beugh to beugh thay hippit [11] and thai plaid,
And freschly in thaire birdis kynd [12] arraid 243
Thaire fetheris new, and fret [13] thame in the sonne,
And thankit lufe, that had thaire makis [14] wonne.

This was the plane ditee of thaire note,
And there-with-all unto my-self I thoght,
"Quhat lyf is this that makis birdis dote?
Quhat may this be, how cummyth it of ought?
Quhat nedith it to be so dere ybought?
It is nothing, trowe I, bot feynit chere,[15]
And that men list to counterfeten chere." [16] 252

[1] wands [2] living creature [3] boughs [4] twigs [5] sweet [6] hymns [7] couplet [8] time [9] ceased [10] below [11] hopped [12] manner [13] adorned [14] mates [15] feigned countenance [16] good manner

Eft [1] wald I think; "O Lord, quhat may this be,
That lufe is of so noble myght and kynde,[2]
Lufing his folk? and suich prosperitee
Is it of him as we in bukis fynd?
May he oure hertes setten and unbynd?
Hath he upon oure hertis suich maistrye?
Or all this is bot feynyt fantasye! 259

"For gif [3] he be of so grete excellence,
That he of every wight hath cure and charge,
Quhat have I gilt [4] to him or doon offense,
That I am thrall, and birdis gone [5] at large,
Sen [6] him to serve he myght set my corage?
And gif he be noght so, than may I seyne,[7]
Quhat makis folk to jangill of him in veyne? 266

"Can I noght elles fynd, bot-gif [8] that he
Be lord, and as a god may lyve and regne,
To bynd and louse, and maken thrallis free,
Than wold I pray his blisfull grace benigne,
To hable [9] me unto his service digne; [10]
And evermore for to be one of tho [11]
Him trewly for to serve in wele and wo." 273

And there-with kest I doun myn eye ageyne,
Quhare-as I sawe, walking under the toure,
Full secretly new cummyn hir to pleyne,[12]
The fairest or the freschest yonge floure
That ever I sawe, me thoght, before that houre,
For quhich sodayn abate,[13] anon astert [14]
The blude of all my body to my hert. 280

And though I stude abaisit [15] tho a lyte,[16]
No wonder was; for-quhy [17] my wittis all
Were so overcom with plesance and delyte,
Onely throu latting of myn eyen fall,
That sudaynly my hert became hir thrall,
For ever, of free wyll; for of manace
There was no takyn [18] in hir suete face. 287

And in my hede I drewe right hastily,
And eft-sones [19] I lent it forth ageyne,
And sawe hir walk, that verray womanly,
With no wight mo, bot onely wommen tueyne.
Than gan I studye in my-self and seyne,[20]
"A! suete, ar ye a warldly [21] creature,
Or hevinly thing in likenesse of nature? 294

"Or ar ye god Cupidis owin princesse,
And cummyn are to louse [22] me out of band?
Or ar ye verray Nature the goddesse,
That have depaynted with your hevinly hand
This gardyn full of flouris, as they stand?

[1] again [2] nature [3] if [4] sinned [5] go [6] since [7] say [8] except [9] enable [10] worthy [11] those [12] play [13] surprise [14] leaped [15] abashed [16] little [17] because [18] token [19] immediately [20] say [21] earthly [22] loose

Quhat sall I think, allace! quhat reverence
Sall I minister to your excellence?

"Gif ye a goddesse be, and that ye like
  To do me payne, I may it noght astert;[1]
Gif[2] ye be warldly wight, that dooth me sike,[3]
  Quhy lest[4] God mak you so, my derrest hert,
  To do a sely prisoner thus smert,
That lufis yow all, and wote[5] of noght bot wo?
And therefor, merci, suete! sen it is so."

Quhen I a lytill thrawe[6] had maid my moon,
  Bewailling myn infortune and my chance,
Unknawin[7] how or quhat was best to doon,
  So ferre i-fallyng into lufis dance,
  That sodeynly my wit, my contenance,
My hert, my will, my nature, and my mynd,
Was changit clene ryght in an-othir kind.

Off hir array the form gif I sall write,
  Toward hir goldin haire and rich atyre
In fret-wyse couchit was with perllis quhite[8]
  And gretë balas[9] lemyng[10] as the fyre,
  With mony ane emeraut and faire saphire;
And on hir hede a chaplet fresch of hewe,
Off plumys partit[11] rede, and quhite, and blewe;

Full of quaking spangis[12] bryght as gold,
  Forgit[13] of schap like to the amorettis,[14]
So new, so fresch, so plesant to behold,
  The plumys eke like to the floure-jonettis,[15]
  And othir of schap like to the round crokettis,[16]
And, above all this, there was, wele I wote,
Beautee eneuch to mak a world to dote.

About hir nek, quhite as the fyne amaille,[17]
  A gudely cheyne of smale orfeverye,[18]
Quhareby there hang[19] a ruby, without faille,
  Lyke to ane herte schapin verily,
  That, as a sperk of lowe,[20] so wantonly
Semyt[21] birnyng upon hir quhytë throte.
Now gif[2] there was gud partye, God it wote!

And forto walk that freschë Mayes morowe,
  An huke[22] sche had upon hir tissew quhite,
That gudeliare had noght bene sene toforowe,[23]
  As I suppose; and girt sche was a lyte;[24]
  Thus halflyng louse[25] for haste, to suich delyte
It was to see hir youth in gudelihede,[26]
That for rudenes to speke thereof I drede.

[1] escape [2] if [3] sigh [4] why did it please [5] knows [6] time [7] ignorant [8] white [9] a kind of ruby [10] gleaming [11] partly [12] spangles [13] forged [14] love-knots [15] yellow flowers [16] locks of hair [17] enamel [18] goldsmith's work [19] hung [20] flame [21] seemed [22] cloak [23] before [24] little [25] half loose [26] goodliness

In hir was youth, beautee, with humble aport,[1]
  Bountee, richesse, and wommanly facture,
God better wote than my pen can report:
  Wisedome, largesse,[2] estate, and connyng[3] sure
  In every poynt so guydit hir mesure,
In word, in dede, in schap, in contenance,
That nature myght no more hir childe avance.

Throw quhich anon I knew and understude
  Wele[4] that sche was a warldly creature;
On quhom[5] to rest myn eye, so mich gude
  It did my wofull hert, I yow assure,
  That it was to me joye without mesure;
And, at the last, my luke unto the hevin
I threwe furthwith, and said thir[6] versis sevin:

"O Venus clere! of goddis stellifyit![7]
  To quhom I yelde homage and sacrifise,
Fro this day forth your grace be magnifyit,
  That me ressavit[8] have in suich a wise,
  To lyve under your law and do service;
Now help me furth, and for your merci lede
My hert to rest, that deis[9] nere for drede."

Quhen I with gude entent this orisoun
  Thus endid had, I stynt[10] a lytill stound;[11]
And eft[12] myn eye full pitously adoun
  I kest, behalding unto hir lytill hound,
  That with his bellis playit on the ground;
Than wold I say, and sigh there-with a lyte,
"A! wele were him that now were in thy plyte!"

An-othir quhile the lytill nyghtingale,
  That sat apon the twiggis, wold I chide,
And say ryght thus; "Quhare are thy notis smale,
  That thou of love has song this morowe-tyde?
  Seis thou noght hire that sittis the besyde?
For Venus sake, the blisfull goddesse clere,
Sing on agane, and mak my lady chere."

ROBERT HENRYSON (1430?–1506?)

THE MOUSE AND THE PADDOCK[13]

Upone a tyme, as Ysop[14] can[15] report,
A littill Mouss come till[16] a rever syd,
Scho[17] mycht nocht waid, hir schankis wer so schort;
Scho cowth nocht sowme;[18] scho had no horss till ryd;
Off verry forss[19] behuvit hir to byd,
And to and fro upone that rever deip
Scho ran, cryand[20] with mony peteuss peip.

[1] bearing [2] liberality [3] intelligence [4] well [5] whom [6] these [7] stellified [8] received [9] dies [10] ceased [11] while [12] again [13] frog [14] Æsop [15] did [16] to [17] she [18] swim [19] of very necessity [32] crying

"Help our![1] help our!" the silly Mowss can[2] cry,
"For Godis lufe, sum-body our[3] this bryme.[4]"
With that ane Paddok, on the wattir by,
Put up hir heid and on the bank cowth[2] clyme,
Quhilk[5] be[6] natur gowth[2] dowk[7] and gaylie swyme.
With voce full rawk,[8] scho said on[9] this maneir,
"Gud morne, Deme[10] Mowss, quhat is your erand heir?"

"Seis[11] thow," quod scho, "of corne yone joly flat,[12]
Of ryp aitis,[13] of beir,[14] of peiss,[15] and quheit;[16]
I am hungry, and fane[17] wald be thairat,
Bot I am stoppit heir be this wattir greit;
And on this syd I get na thing till eit,[18]
Bot hard nutis, quhilk with my teith I boir;
War[19] I beyond, my feist wald be the moir.

"I haif no boit,[20] heir is no mareneir,[21]
And thocht[22] thair ware, I haif no frawcht[23] to pay."
Quod scho, "Sistir, lat be your havy cheir,[24]
Do my counsall,[25] and I sall fynd the way,
Withowttin horss, brig,[26] boit,[20] or yit gallay,[27]
To bring yow our[3] saifly, — be nocht affeird! —
And nocht to weit[28] the campis[29] of your beird."[30]

"I haif mervell,"[31] than quod the silly Mowss,
"How thow can fleit[32] without feddir or fyn;
The rever is so deip and dengerouss,
Me think that thow suld drowin to wed[33] thairin.
Tell me, thairfoir, quhat faculty or gyn[34]
Thow hes[35] to bring me our this wattir wan?"[36]
That to declair the Paddok thus began: —

"With my twa feit,"[37] quod scho, "lukkin and braid,[38]
Insteid of airis,[39] I row the streme full still;
Suppoiss the bruk be perrellus to waid,
Baith to and fro I swyme at my awin will.
I may nocht droun, for-quhy[40] myne oppin gill
Devoydis[41] ay the watter I ressaif;
Thairfoir to droun forsuth[42] no dreid I haif."

The Mowss beheld onto hir fronsyt[43] face,
Hir runclit beik,[44] and hir lippis syd,[45]
Hir hyngand[46] browis, and hir voce so hace,[8]
Hir logrand[47] leggis, and hir harsky[48] hyd.
Scho ran abak, and on the Paddock cryd,

[1] help over [2] did [3] over [4] flood [5] which [6] by [7] dive, duck [8] hoarse [9] in [10] dame [11] seest [12] field [13] oats [14] barley [15] pease [16] wheat [17] fain [18] to eat [19] were [20] boat [21] boat-man [22] though [23] freight [24] heavy countenance [25] advice [26] bridge [27] galley [28] wet [29] whiskers [30] beard [31] I have wonder [32] float [33] wade [34] device [35] hast [36] dark [37] feet [38] webbed and broad [39] oars [40] because [41] empties [42] forsooth [43] wrinkled [44] twisted mouth [45] wide [46] hanging [47] loose-jointed, wobbly [48] rough

"Gife I can any skeill of fysnomy,[1]
Thow hes sum pairte of frawd and als[2] invy.[3]

"For clerkis sayis[4] the inclinatioun
Of manis thocht persavis[5] commounly
Eftir the corporall complexioun[6]
Till gud or yll, as natur will apply;
A frawart[7] will, a thrawin[8] phisnomy.
The auld proverb is witness of this lorum:[9]
'*Distortum vultum sequitur distortio morum.*'"

"Na," quod the Taid,[10] "that proverb is nocht trew,
For fair thingis oft tymes ar fowll fakin;[11]
Thir bla berryis,[12] thocht[13] thay be blak of hew,
Ar gaddrit up quhen[14] prumross is forsakin.
The face may faill to be the hairtis taikin:[15]
Thairfoir I fynd in Scriptour in a place,
'Thow suld nocht juge a man eftir his face.'

"Thocht[13] I unlusty[16] be to luk upone,
I haif na wyt[17] quhy suld I lakkit[18] be;
War[19] I als fare as joly Absalone,
I am nocht caussar of that grit[20] bewte.
This differens in forme and qualite
Almychty God hes cawsit dame Nature
To prent and set in every creature.

"Off[21] sum the face may be rycht flurisand,[22]
With silkin tong and cheir most amorus,
With mynd inconstant, fals and variand,[23]
Full of dissait,[24] and menys cautelus."[25]
"Lat be preching," quod the hungry Mouss;
"And be[26] quhat craft, thow gar[27] me undirstand,
How thow wald gyd[28] me to the yondir land."

"Thow wait,"[29] quod scho, "a body that hes neid,[30]
To help thame selff suld mony wayis cast;[31]
Thairfoir go tak a dowble twynnit[8] threid,
And bind thi leg to myne with knotis fast;
I sall[32] the leir[33] to swyme, be nocht agast."
"Is that thi counsale?" quod the silly Mouss,
"To preif[34] that play it wer our[35] perrellouss!

"Suld I be bund[36] and fast, quhair[37] I am fre,
In howp[38] of help? nay, than eschrew ws baith,[39]
For I mycht loss[40] both lyfe and libertie!
Gife[41] it wer sa, quha mycht amend my skaith?[42]
Bot gife[41] thow sueir[43] to me the murthour aith,[44]

[1] if I have any knowledge of physiognomy [2] also [3] envy [4] learned men say [5] manifests itself [6] bodily temperament [7] perverse [8] twisted [9] lore [10] toad, frog [11] foully deceitful [12] these blueberries [13] though [14] when [15] token [16] unpleasant [17] knowledge [18] blamed [19] were [20] great [21] of [22] flourishing [23] fickle [24] deceit [25] tricky means [26] by [27] make [28] conduct [29] knowest [30] need [31] contrive [32] shall [33] teach [34] prove, test [35] over [36] bound [37] where [38] hope [39] confound us both [40] lose [41] if [42] injury [43] swear [44] oath

But[1] frawd or gyle, to bring me our this flude,
But[1] hurt or harme," quod scho, "in faith I dude.[2]"

Scho golkit[3] up, and to the hevin can[4] cry,
"How[5] Juppiter, of Natur god and king,
I mak ane aith[6] to the trewly, that I
This littill Mouss sall[7] our the wattir bring."
This aith[6] was maid. This Mouss, but persawing[8]
Of fals ingyne[9] of this fals crabit[10] Taid,
Tuk threid and band her leg, as scho hir bad.

Than fute for fute thay lap[11] baith in the brime,[12]
Bot in thair mynd thay wer rycht different;
The Mowss thocht na thing bot to fleit[13] and swyme,
The Padok for to slay set hir intent.
Quhen thai in mydwart of the streme wer went,[14]
With all hir forss the Paddok dowkit[15] doun,
And thocht the Mouss without mercy to droun.

Persevand[16] this, the Mouss on hir gan[4] cry,
"Tratour to God, and mansworne[17] on-to me,
Thow swoir[18] the murthour-aith[19] saifly that I,
But[1] harme or hurt, suld ferreid[20] be and fre."
And quhen scho saw thair wass bot do or dy,
Scho bowtit[21] up and foirsit[22] hir to swyme,
And preisit[23] on the Taidis bak to clyme.

The dreid of deid[24] hir strenthis gart[25] incress,
And fandit[23] hir defend with mony mane;[26]
The Mowss upwart, the Paddok doun can[4] press,
Quhile[27] to, quhile[27] fra, quhile dowk,[28] quhile up agane.
This silly Mouss, this[29] plungit in grit pane,
Can[4] fecht[30] als lang as breth wes in hir breist,
Till at the last scho cryit for a preist.[31]

Sichand thus gait,[32] a Gled[33] sat on a twist,[34]
And to this wrechit battell tuk gud heid,[35]
And with a wisk,[36] or owthir[37] of thame wist,[38]
He claucht[39] his cluke[40] betuene thame in the threid;
Syne[41] to the land he flew with thame gud speid,[42]
Fane[43] of that fang,[44] pypand with mony pew;[45]
Syne[41] lowsit[46] thame, and bayth[47] but[1] pety slew.

[1] without [2] I would do it [3] stared [4] did [5] O [6] oath [7] shall [8] without perceiving [9] device [10] crabbed [11] leaped [12] flood [13] float [14] were gone [15] ducked [16] perceiving [17] perjured [18] sworest [19] murder-oath [20] ferried [21] leaped [22] forced [23] attempted [24] death [25] made [26] moan [27] now . . . now [28] duck [29] thus [30] fight [31] priest [32] sighing thus [33] hawk [34] bough [35] heed [36] whisk, sudden movement [37] ere either [38] knew [39] caught [40] claw [41] afterwards [42] rapidly [43] glad [44] catch [45] cry [46] loosed [47] both

Syne bowellit[1] thame, that bowchir,[2] with his bill
And bellyflawcht full fetly he thame flaid;[3]
Bot baith thair flesche wald skant be half a fill,
And gutis als,[4] unto that gredy Gled.
Off[5] thair debait thus quhen I had owt-red,[6]
He tuk his flicht[7] and our[8] the feildis he flaw.
Gife this be trew, speir[9] ye at thame that saw.

THE NUTBROWNE MAIDE (c. 1500)

(*Unknown Author*)

"Be it right or wrong, these men among[10] on women do complaine,
Affermyng this, how that it is a labour spent in vaine
To love them wele, for never a dele they love a man agayne;
For lete a man do what he can ther favor to attayne,
Yet yf a newe to them pursue, ther furst trew lover than
Laboureth for nought, and from her thought he is a bannisshed man."

"I say not nay but that all day it is both writ and sayde
That woman's fayth is, as who saythe, all utterly decayed;
But nevertheless right good witnes in this case might be layde
That they love trewe and contynew, — recorde the Nutbrowne Maide,
Whiche from her love, whan, her to prove, he cam to make his mone,
Wolde not departe, for in her herte she lovyd but hym allone."

"Than betwene us lete us discusse what was all the maner
Betwene them too, we wyl also telle all the peyne infere[11]
That she was in. Now I begynne, soo that ye me answere.
Wherfore alle ye that present be, I pray you geve an eare.
I am a knyght, I cum be nyght, as secret as I can,
Sayng, 'Alas! thus stondyth the case: I am a bannisshed man.'"

"And I your wylle for to fulfylle, in this wyl not refuse,
Trusting to shewe in wordis fewe that men have an ille use,

[1] disembowelled [2] butcher [3] and skilfully flayed them whole [4] also [5] of [6] disentanglement [7] flight [8] over [9] inquire [10] continually [11] together

To ther owne shame wymen to blame, and causeles them accuse.
Therfore to you I answere now, alle wymen to excuse:
'Myn owne hert dere, with you what chiere? I prey you telle anoon;
For in my mynde of all mankynde I love but you allon.' "

"It stondeth so, a dede is do wherfore moche harme shal growe.
My desteny is for to dey a shamful dethe, I trowe,
Or ellis to flee; the ton[1] must bee, none other wey I knowe
But to withdrawe as an outlaw and take me to my bowe.
Wherfore adew, my owne hert trewe, none other red I can;
For I muste to the grene wode goo, alone, a bannysshed man."

"O Lorde, what is this worldis blisse, that chaungeth as the mone?
My somers day in lusty May is derked before the none.
I here you saye 'farwel;' nay, nay, we departe not soo sone.
Why say ye so? wheder wyl ye goo? alas! what have ye done?
Alle my welfare to sorow and care shulde chaunge if ye were gon;
For in my mynde of all mankynde I love but you alone."

"I can beleve it shal you greve, and somwhat you distrayne;
But aftyrwarde your paynes harde within a day or tweyne
Shal sone aslake, and ye shal take confort to you agayne.
Why shuld ye nought? for to take thought, your labur were in veyne.
And thus I do, and pray you, loo! as hertely as I can;
For I muste too the grene wode goo, alone, a bannysshed man."

"Now syth that ye have shewed to me the secret of your mynde,
I shalbe playne to you agayne, lyke as ye shal me fynde;
Syth it is so that ye wyll goo, I wol not leve[2] behynde;
Shal ne'er be sayd the Nutbrowne Mayd was to her love unkind.
Make you redy, for soo am I, all though it were anoon;
For in my mynde of all mankynde I love but you alone."

"Yet I you rede to take good hede, what men wyl thinke and sey;
Of yonge and olde it shalbe tolde that ye be gone away,
Your wanton wylle for to fulfylle, in grene wood you to play,
And that ye myght from your delyte noo lenger make delay.
Rather than ye shuld thus for me be called an ylle woman,
Yet wolde I to the grenewodde goo, alone, a bannysshed man."

"Though it be songe of olde and yonge that I shuld be to blame,
Theirs be the charge that speke so large in hurting of my name;
For I wyl prove that feythful love it is devoyd of shame,
In your distresse and hevynesse to parte wyth you the same;
And sure all thoo[1] that doo not so, trewe lovers ar they noon;
But in my mynde of all mankynde I love but you alone."

"I councel yow, remembre how it is noo maydens lawe
Nothing to dought, but to renne out to wod with an outlawe;
For ye must there in your hands bere a bowe redy to drawe,
And as a theef thus must ye lyve ever in drede and awe,
By whiche to yow gret harme myght grow; yet had I lever than
That I had too the grenewod goo, alone, a banysshyd man."

"I thinke not nay, but as ye saye, it is noo maydens lore;
But love may make me for your sake, as ye have said before,
To com on fote, to hunte and shote to get us mete and store;
For soo that I your company may have, I aske noo more;
From whiche to parte, it makith myn herte as colde as ony ston;
For in my mynde of all mankynde I love but you alone."

[1] one [2] remain

[1] those

"For an outlawe this is the lawe, that men hym take and binde,
Wythout pytee hanged to bee, and waver wyth the wynde.
Yf I had neede, as God forbede, what rescous[1] coude ye finde?
For sothe I trowe, you and your bowe shul drawe for fere behynde;
And noo merveyle, for lytel avayle were in your councel than;
Wherfore I too the woode wyl goo, alone, a bannysshd man."

"Ful wel knowe ye that wymen bee ful febyl for to fyght;
Noo womanhed is it indeede to bee bolde as a knight;
Yet in suche fere yf that ye were, amonge enemys day and nyght,
I wolde wythstonde, with bowe in hande, to greve them as I myght,
And you to save, as wymen have from deth many one;
For in my mynde of all mankynde I love but you alone."

"Yet take good hede, for ever I drede that ye coude not sustein
The thorney wayes, the depe valeis, the snowe, the frost, the reyn,
The colde, the hete; for, drye or wete, we must lodge on the playn,
And, us above, noon other rove[2] but a brake, bussh, or twayne;
Whiche sone shulde greve you, I beleve, and ye wolde gladly than
That I had too the grenewode goo, alone, a banysshed man."

"Syth I have here ben partynere with you of joy and blysse,
I muste also parte of your woo endure, as reason is;
Yet am I sure of oo[3] plesure, and shortly it is this,
That where ye bee, me semeth, perde, I coude not fare amysse.
Wythout more speche, I you beseche that we were soon agone;
For in my mynde of all mankynde I love but you alone."

"Yef ye goo thedyr, ye must consider, whan ye have lust to dyne,
Ther shal no mete be fore to gete, nor drinke, bere, ale, ne wine,
Ne shetis clene to lye betwene, made of thred and twyne,
Noon other house but levys and bowes, to kever your hed and myn.
Loo! myn herte swete, this ylle dyet shuld make you pale and wan;
Wherfore I to the wood wyl goo, alone, a banysshid man."

"Amonge the wylde dere suche an archier as men say that ye bee
Ne may not fayle of good vitayle, where is so grete plente;
And watir cleere of the ryvere shalbe ful swete to me,
Wyth whiche in hele I shal right wele endure, as ye shal see;
And, er we goo, a bed or twoo I can provide anoon;
For in my mynde of all mankynde I love but you alone."

"Loo! yet before ye must doo more, yf ye wyl goo with me, —
As cutte your here up by your ere, your kirtel by the knee,
Wyth bowe in hande, for to withstonde your enmys, yf nede be,
And this same nyght before daylyght to woodward wyl I flee;
And if ye wyl all this fulfylle, doo it shortely as ye can;
Ellis wil I to the grenewode goo, alone, a banysshyd man."

"I shal, as now, do more for you than longeth to womanhede,
To short my here, a bowe to bere to shote in time of nede.
O my swete moder, before all other, for you have I most drede;
But now adiew! I must ensue, wher fortune doth me leede:
All this make ye; now lete us flee, the day cummeth fast upon;
For in my mynde of all mankynde I love but you alone."

"Nay, nay, not soo, ye shal not goo! and I shal tell you why:
Your appetyte is to be lyght of love, I wele aspie;
For right as ye have sayd to me, in lykewise hardely
Ye wolde answere, whosoever it were, in way of company.
It is sayd of olde, 'sone hote, sone colde,' and so is a woman;
Wherfore I too the woode wyl goo, alone, a banysshid man."

[1] rescue [2] roof [3] one

"Yef ye take hede, yet is noo nede, suche wordis to say bee[1] me,
For oft ye preyd, and longe assayed, or I you lovid, perdee!
And though that I of auncestry a barons doughter bee,
Yet have you proved how I you loved, a squyer of lowe degree,
And ever shal, what so befalle, to dey therfore anoon;
For in my mynde of all mankynde I love but you alone."

"A barons childe to be begyled, it were a curssed dede,
To be felaw with an outlawe, almyghty God forbede!
Yet bettyr were the power[2] squyer alone to forest yede,[3]
Than ye shal say, another day, that be[1] my wyked dede
Ye were betrayed; wherfore, good maide, the best red[4] that I can,
Is that I too the grenewode goo, alone, a banysshed man."

"Whatsoever befalle, I never shal of this thing you upbraid;
But yf ye goo and leve me so, than have ye me betraied.
Remembre you wele how that ye dele, for yf ye, as ye sayde,
Be so unkynde to leve behynde your love, the Notbrowne Maide,
Trust me truly that I shal dey sone after ye be gone;
For in my mynde of all mankynde I love but you alone."

"Yef that ye went, ye shulde repent, for in the forest now
I have purveid me of a maide, whom I love more than you, —
Another fayrer than ever ye were, I dare it wel avowe;
And of you both, eche shuld be wrothe with other, as I trowe.
It were myn ease to lyve in pease; so wyl I yf I can;
Wherfore I to the wode wyl goo, alone, a banysshid man."

"Though in the wood I undirstode ye had a paramour,
All this may nought remeve my thought, but that I wyl be your;

[1] by [2] poor [3] should go [4] advice

And she shal fynde me softe and kynde, and curteis every our,
Glad to fulfylle all that she wyl commaunde me, to my power;
For had ye, loo! an hondred moo, yet wolde I be that one;
For in my mynde of all mankynde I love but you alone."

"Myn owne dere love, I see the prove that ye be kynde and trewe;
Of mayde and wyfe, in all my lyf, the best that ever I knewe!
Be mery and glad, be no more sad, the case is chaunged newe;
For it were ruthe that for your trouth you shuld have cause to rewe.
Be not dismayed, whatsoever I sayd, to you whan I began,
I wyl not too the grenewode goo, I am noo banysshyd man."

"Theis tidingis be more glad to me than to be made a quene,
Yf I were sure they shuld endure; but it is often seen,
When men wyl breke promyse, they speke the wordis on the splene.
Ye shape some wyle, me to begyle, and stele fro me, I wene.
Then were the case wurs than it was, and I more woo-begone;
For in my mynde of al mankynde I love but you alone."

"Ye shal not nede further to drede, I wyl not disparage
You, God defende, sith you descende of so grete a lynage.
Now understonde, to Westmerlande, whiche is my herytage,
I wyle you bringe, and wyth a rynge, be wey of maryage,
I wyl you take, and lady make, as shortly as I can;
Thus have ye wone an erles son, and not a bannysshyd man."

Here may ye see that wymen be in love meke, kinde, and stable,
Late never man repreve them than, or calle them variable,
But rather prey God that we may to them be confortable, —
Whiche somtyme provyth suche as he loveth, yf they be charitable.

For sith men wolde that wymen sholde be meke to them echeon,
Moche more ought they to God obey, and serve but hym alone.

WILLIAM DUNBAR (1460?–1513 +)

From THE THRISSILL AND THE ROIS

Quhen Merch wes with variand [1] windis past,
And Appryll had, with hir silver schouris,
Tane leif at [2] Nature with ane orient blast,
And lusty May, that muddir is of flouris,
Had maid the birdis to begyn thair houris,[3]
Amang the tendir odouris reid and quhyt,[4]
Quhois [5] armony to heir [6] it wes delyt;

In bed at morrow,[7] sleiping as I lay,
Methocht [8] Aurora, with hir cristall ene,[9]
In at the window lukit, by the day,[10]
And halsit [11] me, with visage paill and grene;
On quhois hand a lark sang fro the splene,[12]
"Awalk, luvaris,[13] out of your slomering,
Se how the lusty morrow dois up-spring!"

Me thocht, fresche May befoir my bed up-stude,
In weid depaynt [14] of mony diverss hew,
Sobir, benyng,[15] and full of mansuetude,[16]
In brycht [17] atteir of flouris forgit [18] new,
Hevinly of color, quhyt,[4] reid, broun, and blew,
Balmit [19] in dew, and gilt with Phebus bemys,
Quhill [20] all the houss illumynit of his lemys.[21]

"Slugird," scho said, "awalk annone [22] for schame,
And in my honour sum thing thow go wryt;
The lark hes done the mirry day proclame,
To raiss up luvaris with confort and delyt;
Yit nocht incressis thy curage to indyt,[23]
Quhois hairt sum-tyme hes glaid and blisfull bene,
Sangis [24] to mak undir the levis grene."

"Quhairto," quod I, "sall I upryss at morrow,
For in this May few birdis herd I sing?
Thai haif [25] moir [26] causs to weip and plane thair sorrow,
Thy air it is nocht holsum nor benyng.[15]
Lord Eolus dois [27] in thy sessone [28] ring; [29]
So busteous [30] ar the blastis of his horne
Amang thy bewis,[31] to walk [32] I haif forborne."

[1] varying [2] taken leave of [3] hours, services of praise [4] white [5] whose [6] hear [7] morning [8] methought [9] eyes [10] looked, at dawn [11] greeted [12] from the spleen, fervently [13] awake, lovers [14] in garment colored [15] benign [16] mildness [17] bright [18] forged, made [19] balmed [20] while [21] beams [22] awake at once [23] compose [24] songs [25] have [26] more [27] does [28] season [29] reign [30] noisy [31] boughs [32] wake

With that this lady sobirly did smyll,
And said, "Upryss, and do thy observance;
Thow did promyt,[1] in Mayis lusty quhyle,[2]
For to discryve the Ross of most plesance.
Go se the birdis how thay sing and dance,
Illumynit oure [3] with orient skyis brycht,
Annamyllit [4] richely with new asure [5] lycht."

* * * * * * *

Than callit scho all flouris that grew on feild,
Discirnyng [6] all thair fassionis and effeiris. [7]
Upone the awfull Thrissil scho beheld,
And saw him kepit with [8] a busche of speiris;
Considering him so able for the weiris,[9]
A radius [10] crown of rubeis scho him gaif,
And said, "In feild go furth, and fend the laif.[11]

"And sen thow art a king, thow be discreit;
Herb without vertew thow hald nocht of sic [12] pryce
As herb of vertew and of odor sueit;
And lat no nettill, vyle and full of vyce,
Hir fallow [13] to the gudly flour-de-lyce;
Nor latt no wyld weid,[14] full of churlicheness,
Compair hir till the lilleis nobilness;

"Nor hald non udir flour in sic denty [15]
As the fresche Ross, of cullour reid and quhyt;
For gife [16] thow dois, hurt is thyne honesty,
Considdering that no flour is so perfyt,
So full of vertew, plesans,[17] and delyt,
So full of blisful angellik bewty,
Imperiall birth, honour and dignite."

Than to the Ross scho turnit hir visage,
And said, "O lusty dochtir most benyng,
Aboif the lilly, illustare [18] of lynnage,
Fro the stok ryell [19] rysing fresche and ying,[20]
But [21] ony spot or macull [22] doing spring: [23]
Cum, blowme of joy, with jemis to be cround,
For oure the laif [24] thy bewty is renownd."

A coistly [25] croun, with clarefeid [26] stonis brycht,
This cumly quene did on hir heid incloiss,[27]
Quhill [28] all the land illumynit of the licht;
Quhairfoir, me thocht, all flouris did rejoiss,
Crying attonis, "Haill be thow, richest Ross!
Haill hairbis [29] empryce, haill freschest quene of flouris,
To the be glory and honour at all houris."

[1] promise [2] season [3] over [4] enameled [5] azure [6] distinguishing [7] qualities [8] guarded by [9] wars [10] shining [11] defend the rest [12] such [13] make herself fellow [14] weed [15] such esteem [16] if [17] pleasance [18] illustrious [19] royal [20] young [21] without [22] blemish [23] springing [24] above the rest [25] costly [26] clear [27] inclose [28] while [29] herbs'

Thane all the birdis song with voce on hicht,[1]
Quhois mirthfull soun wes mervelus to heir;
The mavyss sang, "Haill, Ross, most riche and richt,
That dois up-flureiss[2] undir Phebus speir![3]
Haill, plant of yowth! haill, princes dochtir deir!
Haill, blosome breking out of the blud royall,
Quhois pretius vertew is imperiall!"

The merle scho sang, "Haill, Roiss of most delyt!
Haill, of all flouris quene and soverane!"
The lark scho sang, "Haill, Roiss, both reid and quhyt,
Most plesand flour, of michty cullouris twane!"
The nychtingaill sang, "Haill, Naturis suffragane,
In bewty, nurtour,[4] and every nobilness,
In riche array, renown, and gentilness!"

The common voce upraiss[5] of birdis small,
Apon this wyss,[6] "O blissit be the hour
That thow wes chosin to be our principall!
Welcome to be our princes of honour,
Our perle, our plesans, and our paramour,[7]
Our peax,[8] our play, our plane felicite!
Chryst the conserf[9] frome all adversite!"

STEPHEN HAWES (d. 1523)

THE PASTIME OF PLEASURE

OF THE GREAT MARIAGE BETWENE GRAUNDE AMOUR AND LABELL PUCELL

From Capit. XXXIX

Then Perceveraunce in all goodly haste
Unto the stewarde called Liberalitie
Gave warnyng for to make ready fast
Agaynst this tyme of great solemnitie
That on the morowe halowed shoulde be.
She warned the cooke called Temperaunce
And after that the ewres,[10] Observaunce,

With Pleasaunce, the panter,[11] and dame Curtesy,
The gentle butler, with the ladyes all.
Eche in her office was prepared shortly
Agaynst this feast so muche triumphall;
And La Bell Pucell then in speciall
Was up by time in the morowe graye;
Right so was I when I sawe the daye.

And right anone La Bell Pucell me sent
Agaynst my weddyng of the saten fyne,
White as the mylke, a goodly garment
Braudred[1] with pearle that clearely dyd shine.
And so, the mariage for to determine,
Venus me brought to a royal chapell,
Whiche of fine golde was wrought everydell.

And after that the gay and glorious
La Bell Pucell to the chapell was leade
In a white vesture fayre and precious,
With a golden chaplet on her yelowe heade;
And Lex Ecclesie did me to her wedde.
After whiche weddyng then was a great feast;
Nothing we lacked, but had of the best.

What[2] shoulde I tary by longe continuance
Of the fest? for of my joy and pleasure
Wisdome can judge, without variaunce,
That nought I lacked, as ye may be sure,
Paiyng the swete due dette of nature.
Thus with my lady, that was fayre and cleare,
In joy I lived full ryght, many a yere.

O lusty youth and yong tender hart,
The true companion of my lady bryght!
God let us never from other astart,[3]
But all in joye to live bothe daye and nyght.
Thus after sorowe joye arived aryght;
After my payne I had sport and playe;
Full litle thought I that it shoulde decaye,

Tyll that Dame Nature Naturyng[4] had made
All thinges to growe unto their fortitude;[5]
And Nature Naturyng waxt retrograde,
By strength my youthe so far to exclude,
As was ever her olde consuetude
First to augment and then to abate, —
This is the custome of her hye estate.

THE EPITAPH OF GRAUNDE AMOUR

From Capit. XLII

O erth! on erth it is a wonders[6] case
That thou art blynde and wyll not the[7] know;
Though upon erth thou hast thy dwelling place,
Yet erth at last must nedes the[7] overthrow.
Thou thinkest thou do be no erth, I trow;
For if thou diddest, thou woldest than[8] apply
To forsake pleasure and to lerne to dye.

O erth, of erth why art thou so proud?
Now what thou art, call to remembraunce;

[1] aloud [2] flourish [3] sphere [4] nurture [5] uprose [6] wise [7] beloved [8] peace [9] preserve [10] eweress, servant in charge of ewers, napkins, etc. [11] servant in charge of pantry

[1] broidered [2] why [3] start away [4] *Natura naturans*, Nature as a creative being. [5] strength [6] wondrous [7] thee, thyself [8] then

Open thine eares unto my song aloude.
Is not thy beauté, strength, and puyssance,
Though becladde with cloth of pleasaunce,
Very erth and also wormes fode,
When erth to erth shall turne to the blode?

And erth, with erth why art thou so wroth?
Remembre the[1] that it vayleth[2] right nought;
For thou mayst thinke, of a perfyte trothe,
If with the erth thou hast a quarell sought,
Amyddes the erth there is a place ywrought,
Whan erth to erth is torned properly,
The[1] for thy synne to perrysh wonderly.

And erth, for erth why hast thou envy?
And the erth upon erth to be more prosperous
Than thou thyselfe, fretting the[1] inwardly?
It is a sinne right foul and vicious
And unto God also full odious.
Thou thinkest, I trow, there is no punishment
Ordeyned for sinne by egall[3] judgement.

Toward heven to folow on the way
Thou arte full slow, and thinkest nothing[4]
That thy nature doth full sore decaye
And deth right fast is to the comyng.
God graunte the mercy, but no time enlongyng.[5]
Whan thou hast time, take tyme and space;
Whan time is past, lost is the tyme of grace.

And whan erth to erth is nexte to reverte
And nature low in the last age,
Of erthly treasure erth doth sette his herte
Insaciately upon covetyse[6] to rage;
He thynketh not his lyfe shall asswage;[7]
His good is his God, with his great ryches;
He thinketh not for to leve it doutles.[8]

The pomped clerkes, with foles[9] delicious,[10]
Erth often fedeth with corrupt glotony,
And nothing[4] with werkes vertuous;
The soule doth fede ryght well ententifly,[11]
But without mesure full inordinatly
The body lyveth and wyll not remember
Howe erth to erth must his strength surrender.

[1] thee [2] availeth [3] equal, just [4] not at all [5] prolonging [6] covetousness [7] cease [8] doubtless [9] fools [10] fond of pleasure [11] carefully

The vyle carkes[1] set upon a fyre[2]
Doth often haunte the synne of lechery,
Fulfyllyng the foule carnall desyre:
Thus erth with erth is corrupt mervaylously,
And erth on erth wyll nothing purify,
Till erth to erth be nere[3] subverted
For erth with erth is so perverted.

O mortall folke, you may beholde and se
Howe I lye here, sometime a myghty knyght!
The end of joye and all prosperite
Is deth at last, thorough his course and myght!
After the day there cometh the derke night;
For though the day be never so longe,
At last the belles ringeth to even-songe!

THE EXCUSATION OF THE AUCTHOURE

Capit. XLVI

Unto all poetes I do me excuse,
If that I offende for lacke of science.
This little boke yet do ye not refuse,
Though it be devoyde of famous eloquence.
Adde or detray[4] by your hye sapience,
And pardon me of my hye enterprise,
Whiche of late this fable did fayne and devise.

Go, little boke, I pray God the save
From misse-metryng by wrong impression;
And who that ever list the for to have,
That he perceyve well thyne intencion
For to be grounded wythout presumption,
As for to eschue the synne of ydlenes
To make suche bokes I apply my busines,

Besechyng God for to geve me grace
Bokes to compyle of morall vertue,
Of my master Lidgate to folowe the trace,
His noble fame for to laude and renue,
Whiche in his lyfe the slouthe[5] did eschue,
Makyng great bokes to be in memory;
On whose soule I pray God have mercy!

[1] carcass [2] set a-fire [3] near [4] take away [5] sloth

THE END OF THE MIDDLE AGES

JOHN SKELTON (1460?–1529)

From A DIRGE FOR PHYLLIP SPAROWE

Do mi nus,[1]
Helpe nowe, swete Jesus!
Levavi oculos meos in montes:[2]
Wolde God I had Zenophontes,
Or Socrates the wyse,
To shew me their devyse,
Moderatly to take
This sorrow that I make
For Phyllip Sparowes sake!
So fervently I shake,
I fele my body quake;
So urgently I am brought
Into carefull thought.
Like Andromach, Hectors wyfe,
Was wery of her lyfe,
Whan she had lost her joye,
Noble Hector of Troye;
In lyke manner also
Encreaseth my dedly wo,
For my sparowe is go.
It was so prety a fole,[3]
It wold syt on a stole,
And lerned after my scole
For to kepe his cut,[4]
With, "Phyllyp, kepe your cut!"
It had a velvet cap,
And wold syt upon my lap,
And seke after small wormes,
And somtyme white-bred crommes;
And many tymes and ofte
Betwene my brestes softe
It wolde lye and rest;
It was propre and prest.[5]
Somtyme he wolde gaspe
Whan he sawe a waspe;
A fly or a gnat,
He wolde flye at that;

[1] Lord [2] I have lifted up mine eyes to the mountains. [3] fool [4] to act shy? to keep his distance? [5] ready

And prytely he wold pant
Whan he saw an ant;
Lord, how he wolde pry
After the butterfly!
Lorde, how he wolde hop
After the gressop![1]
And whan I sayd, "Phyp! Phyp!"
Than he wold lepe and skyp,
And take me by the lyp.
Alas, it wyll me slo,[2]
That Phillyp is gone me fro!

* * * * *

But my sparowe dyd pas[3]
All the sparows of the wode
That were syns Noes flode;
Was never none so good;
Kynge Phylyp of Macedony
Had no such Phylyp as I,
No, no, syr, hardely.[4]
That vengeaunce I aske and crye,
By way of exclamacyon,
On all the hole nacyon
Of cattes wylde and tame;
God send them sorowe and shame!
The cat specyally
That slew so cruelly
My lytell pretty sparowe
That I brought up at Carowe.
O cat of carlyshe kynde,[5]
The fynde[6] was in thy mynde
Whan thou my byrde untwynde!
I wold thou haddest ben blynde!
The leopardes savage,
The lyons in theyr rage,
Myght[7] catche the in theyr pawes,
And gnawe the in theyr jawes!
The serpentes of Lybany
Myght stynge the venymously!
The dragones with their tonges
Might poyson thy lyver and longes!
The mantycors[8] of the mountaynes
Myght fede them on thy braynes!

[1] grasshopper [2] slay [3] surpass [4] certainly [5] churlish nature [6] fiend [7] I would they might [8] *a fabulous monster, with a human head and the body of a beast of prey.*

From WHY COME YE NOT TO COURT?

Ones yet agayne
Of you I wolde frayne,[1]
Why come ye nat to court? —
To whyche court?
To the kynges courte,
Or to Hampton Court? —
Nay, to the kynges court!
The kynges courte
Shulde have the excellence;
But Hampton Court
Hath the preemynence,
And Yorkes Place,
With my lordes grace,
To whose magnifycence
Is all the conflewence,
Sutys and supplycacyons,
Embassades of all nacyons.
Strawe for lawe canon!
Or for the lawe common!
Or for lawe cyvyll!
It shall be as he wyll:
Stop at law tancrete,[2]
An obstract [3] or a concrete;
Be it soure, be it swete,
His wysdome is so dyscrete,
That in a fume or an hete,
Wardeyn of the Flete,
Set hym fast by the fete!
And of his royall powre
Whan him lyst to lowre,
Than, have him to the Towre,
Saunz aulter [4] *remedy*,
Have hym forthe by and by [5]
To the Marshalsy,
Or to the Kynges Benche!
He dyggeth so in the trenche
Of the court royall,
That he ruleth them all.
So he dothe undermynde,
And suche sleyghtes dothe fynde,
That the kynges mynde
By hym is subverted,
And so streatly coarted [6]
In credensynge his tales,
That all is but nutshales [7]
That any other sayth;
He hath in him suche fayth.
Now, yet all this myght be
Suffred and taken in gre,[8]
If that that he wrought
To any good ende were brought;

[1] inquire [2] transcribed [3] abstract [4] without other [5] immediately [6] coërced [7] nut-shells [8] in good part

But all he bringeth to nought,
By God, that me dere bought!
He bereth the kyng on hand,[1]
That he must pyll [2] his lande,
To make his cofers ryche;
But he laythe all in the dyche,
And useth suche abusyoun,
That in the conclusyoun
All commeth to confusyon.
Perceyve the cause why!
To tell the trouth playnly,
He is so ambicyous,
So shamles, and so vicyous,
And so supersticyous,
And so moche oblivyous
From whens that he came,
That he falleth into a *caeciam*,[3]
Whiche, truly to expresse,
Is a forgetfulnesse,
Or wylfull blyndnesse,
Wherwith the Sodomites
Lost theyr inward syghtes,
The Gommoryans also
Were brought to deedly wo,
As Scrypture recordis.
A caecitate cordis,[4]
In the Latyne synge we,
Libera nos, Domine! [5]
But this madde Amalecke,
Lyke to a Mamelek,
He regardeth lordes
No more than potshordes;[6]
He is in suche elacyon
Of his exaltacyon,
And the supportacyon
Of our soverayne lorde,
That, God to recorde,[7]
He ruleth all at wyll,
Without reason or skyll:
How be it the primordyall
Of his wretched originall,
And his base progeny,
And his gresy genealogy,
He came of the sank royall [8]
That was cast out of a bochers stall.

From COLYN CLOUTE

My name is Colyn Cloute.
I purpose to shake oute
All my connyng bagge,
Lyke a clerkely hagge;

[1] insists to the king. [2] plunder [3] blind vertigo [4] from blindness of heart. [5] free us, O Lord! [6] potsherds [7] I call God to witness. [8] blood royal

For though my ryme be ragged,
Tattered and jagged,
Rudely rayne beaten,
Rusty and moughte [1] eaten,
If ye take well therwith,
It hath in it some pyth.
For, as farre as I can se,
It is wronge with eche degre;
For the temporalte
Accuseth the spiritualte;
The spirituall agayne
Dothe grudge and complayne
Upon the temporall men:
Thus eche of other blother [2]
The tone [3] agayng the tother.
Alas, they make me shoder!
For in hoder moder [4]
The Churche is put in faute. [5]
The prelates ben so haut, [6]
They say, and loke so hy,
As though they wolde fly
Above the sterry skye.
Laye-men say indede,
How they take no hede
Theyr sely shepe to fede,
But plucke away and pull
The fleces of theyr wull;
Unethes [7] they leve a locke
Of wull amonges theyr flocke.
And as for theyr connynge,
A glommynge and a mummynge,
And make therof a jape;
They gaspe and they gape,
All to have promocyon;
There is theyr hole devocyon,
With money, if it wyll hap,
To catche the forked cap.
Forsothe they are to lewd
To say so, all beshrewd!

EARLY TUDOR LYRICS (c. 1500)

I. RELIGIOUS LYRICS

I

Who shall have my fayr lady?
Who but I? Who but I? Who?
Who shall have my fayr lady?
Who hath more ryght therto?

This lady clere
That I sheu [8] here,
Man soul yt ys, trust ye;
To Cryst most dere
It hath no pere;
Therfor thys song syng we.
Who shall, etc.

"For love swetnes
And joy endles
I made my lady fre,
Unto my lyknes
I gave her quicnes [1]
In Paradyse to be.
Who shall, etc.

"O my swet store,
My true love therfore
Thy place yt ys above;
What man may do more
Than only dy therfore,
Lady, for thy love?
Who shall," etc.

II

"Quho [2] is at my windo? Quho? Quho?
Go from my windo, go, go!
Quho callis thair
Sa lyke a strangair?
Go from my windo, go!"

"Lord I am heir, ane wretchit mortall
That for thy mercy dois cry and call
Unto the, my Lord celestiall.
Se quho is at thy windo, quho!"

"How dar thow for mercy cry,
Sa lang in sin as thow dois ly?
Mercy to have thow art not worthy,
Go from my windo, go!"

II. CHRISTMAS CAROLS

I

Thys ender nyght [3]
I saw a syght,
A star as bright as day;
And ever among
A maydyn song:
By-by, baby, lullay!

Thys vyrgyn clere
Wythowtyn pere
Unto hur son gane say:
"My son, my lorde,
My fathere dere,
Why lyest thow in hay?

[1] moth [2] complain [3] the one [4] in secret [5] fault [6] haughty [7] scarcely [8] show, declare

[1] life [2] who [3] the other night

"Methynk by ryght
Thow, kyng and knyght,
Shulde lye in ryche aray,
Yet none the lesse
I wyll not cesse
To syng, By-by, lullay!"

Thys babe full bayne [1]
Aunsweryd agayne,
And thus, me-thought, he sayd:
"I am a kyng
Above all thyng,
Yn hay yff I be layde;

"For ye shall see
That kynges thre
Shall cum on the twelfe day.
For thys behest
Geffe me thy brest
And sing, By-by, lullay!"

"My son, I say
Wythowtyn nay [2]
Thow art my derling dere;
I shall the kepe
Whyle thow dost slepe
And make the goode chere;

"And all thy wylle
I wyll fulfill,
Thou wotyst hyt well yn fay.
Yet more then thys, —
I wyll the kys
And syng, By-by, lullay."

"My moder swete,
When I have slepe,
Then take me up on lofte;
Upon your kne
Thatt ye sett me
And dandell me full soft;

"And in your arme
Lap me ryght warme
And kepe me nyght and day;
And yff I wepe
And cannott slepe,
Syng, By, baby, lullay."

"My son, my lorde,
My fader dere,
Syth all ys at thy wyll,
I pray the, son,
Graunte me a bone,
Yff hyt be ryght and skylle;

[1] readily [2] certainly

"That chylde or man,
Whoever can
Be mery on thys day,
To blys them bryng
And I shall syng:
By-by, baby, lullay!"

"My moder shene,
Of hevyn quene,
Your askyng shall I spede,
So that the myrth
Dysplease me nott
Yn wordes nor in dede.

"Syng what ye wyll,
So ye fullfyll
My ten commaundements ay.
Yow for to please
Let them nott sesse
To syng, Baby, lullay."

II

"*Quid petis, o fily?*"
"*Mater dulcissima, ba-ba!*"
"*Quid petis, o fili?*"
"*Michi plausus oscula da-da!*"

So laughyng in lap layde,
So pretyly, so pertly,
So passyngly well a-payd,
Ful softly and full soberly
Unto her swet son she said:
"Quid petys," etc.

The moder full manerly and mekly as a mayd,
Lokyng on her lytill son so laughyng in lap layd,
So pretyly, so partly, so passingly well apayd,
So passyngly wel apayd,
Full softly and full soberly
Unto her son she saide,
Unto her son saide:
"Quid petis," etc.

I mene this by Mary, our Makers moder of myght,
Full lovely lookyng on our Lord, the lanterne of lyght,
Thus saying to our Savior; this saw I in my syght.

III

Make we mery, bothe more and lasse,
For now ys the tyme of Crystymas!

Let no man cum into this hall,
Grome, page, nor yet marshal,
But that sum sport he bryng withall,
For now ys the tyme of Crystymas.
Make we mery, etc.

Yffe that he say he can not syng,
Sum oder sport then lett hym bryng,
That yt may please at thys festyng,
    For now ys the tyme of Crystymas.
    Make we mery, etc.

Yffe he say he can nowght do,
Then, for my love, aske hym no mo,
But to the stokke then lett hym go,
    For now ys the tyme of Crystymas.
    Make we mery, etc.

IV

What cher? Gud cher! gud cher, gud cher!
Be mery and glad this gud Newyere!

"Lyft up your hartes and be glad,"
In Crystes byrth the angell bad;
Say eche to oder, yf any be sad,
    "What cher," etc.

Now the kyng of hevyn his byrth hath take,
Joy and myrth we owght to make;
Say eche to oder for hys sake,
    "What cher," etc.

I tell you all with hart so fre,
Ryght welcum ye be to me;
Be glad and mery, for charite!
    "What cher," etc.

The gudman of this place in fere [1]
You to be mery he prayth you here,
And with gud hert he doth to you say,
    "What cher," etc.

III. CONVIVIAL SONGS

I

Pastyme with good companye
I love and shall untyll I dye.
Gruche [2] who lust, but none denye.
So God be plesyd, thus leve [3] wyll I,
For my pastance Hunt, syng and dance;
My hart is sett;
All goodly sport For my comfort.
Who schall me lett? [4]

Youthe must have sum daliance,
Off good or yll sum pastance,
Company me-thynkys the best
All thoughtes and fansys to dejest,
For idillness Is cheff mastres
Of vices all!
Then who can say But myrth and play
Is best of all?

[1] together [2] grudge [3] live [4] hinder

Company with honeste
Is vertu vices to fle;
Company is good and ill,
But every man hath hys fre wyll.
The best ensew, The worst eschew!
My mynde shalbe
Vertue to use, Vice to refuce;
Thus schall I use me.

II

Fyll the cuppe, Phylyppe,
    And let us drynke a drame!
Ons or twys abowte the howse
    And leave where we began.
I drynke to your swete harte
    Soo mutche as here is in,
Desyeringe yow to followe me
    And doo as I begyn!
And yf you will not pledge,
    You shall bere the blame.
I drynke to you with all my harte,
    Yf you will pledge me the same.

III

Make rome,[1] syrs, and let us be mery,
    With "Huffa, galand!"
Synge, "Tyrll on the bery,"
And let the wyde worlde wynde!
    Synge, "Fryska joly,"
    With "Hey, troly loly,"
    For I se well it is but foly
For to have a sad mynd!

IV. LOVE SONGS

I

Lully, lulley, lulley, lulley!
The fawcon hath born my make [2] away!

He bare hym up, he bare hym down,
He bare hym into an orchard brown.
    Lully, lulley, etc.

Yn that orchard there was an halle
That was hangid with purpill and pall.
    Lully, lulley, etc.

And in that hall there was a bede,
Hit was hangid with gold so rede.
    Lully, lulley, etc.

And yn that bed there lythe a knyght,
His wowndis bledyng day and nyght.
    Lully, lulley, etc.

[1] room [2] mate, sweetheart

By that bedis side kneleth a may,
And she wepeth both night and day.
Lully, lulley, etc.

And by that beddis side there stondith a ston,
Corpus Christi wretyn theron.
Lully, lulley, etc.

II

The lytyll, prety nyghtyngale,
Among the levys grene,
I wold I were with her all nyght!
But yet ye wote [1] not whome I mene!

The nyghtyngale sat one a brere
Among the thornys sherp and keyn
And comfort me wyth mery cher.
But yet ye wot not whome I mene!

She dyd aper [2] all on [3] hur keynde [4]
A lady ryght well be-seyne,
Wyth wordys of loff tolde me hur mynde.
But yet ye wot not whome I mene.

Hyt dyd me goode upon hur to loke,
Hur corse was closyd all in grene;
Away fro me hur herte she toke,
But yete ye wot not whome I mene.

"Lady!" I cryed, wyth rufull mone,
"Have mynd of me, that true hath bene!
For I loved none but you alone."
But yet ye wot not whome I mene.

BALLADS

(*Authors and Dates Unknown*)

ROBIN HOOD AND GUY OF GISBORNE

1. When shawes [5] beene sheene,[6] and shradds [7] full fayre,
And leeves both large and longe,
It is merry, walking in the fayre fforrest,
To heare the small birds songe.

2. The woodweele [8] sang, and wold not cease,
Amongst the leaves a lyne; [9]
And it is by two wight [10] yeomen,
By deare God, that I meane.

* * * * * * *

[1] know [2] appear [3] in [4] nature [5] groves [6] beautiful [7] coppices [8] woodlark [9] of linden [10] stout

3. "Me thought they did mee beate and binde,
And tooke my bow mee froe;
If I bee Robin a-live in this lande,
I'le be wrocken [1] on both them towe."

4. "Sweavens [2] are swift, master," quoth John,
"As the wind that blowes ore a hill;
For if itt be never soe lowde this night,
To-morrow it may be still."

5. "Buske yee, bowne yee, my merry men all,
For John shall goe with mee;
For I'le goe seeke yond wight yeomen
In greenwood where they bee."

6. They cast on their gowne of greene,
A shooting gone are they,
Until they came to the merry greenwood,
Where they had gladdest bee;
There were they ware of a wight yeoman,
His body leaned to a tree.

7. A sword and a dagger he wore by his side,
Had beene many a mans bane,
And he was cladd in his capull-hyde,[3]
Topp, and tayle, and mayne.

8. "Stand you still, master," quoth Litle John,
"Under this trusty tree,
And I will goe to yond wight yeoman,
To know his meaning trulye."

9. "A, John, by me thou setts noe store,
And that's a ffarley [4] thinge;
How offt send I my men beffore,
And tarry my-selfe behinde?

10. "It is noe cunning a knave to ken;
And a man but heare him speake.
And itt were not for bursting of my bowe,
John, I wold thy head breake."

11. But often words they breeden bale;
That parted Robin and John.
John is gone to Barnesdale,
The gates he knowes eche one.

12. And when hee came to Barnesdale,
Great heavinesse there hee hadd;
He ffound two of his fellowes
Were slaine both in a slade,[5]

13. And Scarlett a-ffoote flyinge was,
Over stockes and stone,
For the sheriffe with seven score men
Fast after him is gone.

[1] avenged [2] dreams [3] horse-hide [4] strange [5] valley

14. "Yett one shoote I'le shoote," sayes Litle John,
"With Crist his might and mayne;
I'le make yond fellow that flyes soe fast
To be both glad and ffaine."

15. John bent up a good veiwe[1] bow,
And ffetteled[2] him to shoote;
The bow was made of a tender boughe,
And fell downe to his foote.

16. "Woe worth thee, wicked wood," sayd Litle John,
"That ere thou grew on a tree!
For this day thou art my bale,
My boote[3] when thou shold bee!"

17. This shoote it was but looselye shott,
The arrowe flew in vaine,
And it mett one of the sheriffes men;
Good William a Trent was slaine.

18. It had beene better for William a Trent
To hange upon a gallowe
Then for to lye in the greenwoode,
There slaine with an arrowe.

19. And it is sayd, when men be mett,
Six can doe more than three:
And they have tane Litle John,
And bound him ffast to a tree.

20. "Thou shalt be drawen by dale and downe," quoth the sheriffe,
"And hanged hye on a hill:"
"But thou may ffayle," quoth Litle John,
"If itt be Christs owne will."

21. Let us leave talking of Litle John,
For hee is bound fast to a tree,
And talke of Guy and Robin Hood
In the green woode where they bee.

22. How these two yeomen together they mett,
Under the leaves of lyne,
To see what marchandise they made
Even at that same time.

23. "Good morrow, good fellow," quoth Sir Guy;
"Good morrow, good ffellow," quoth hee;
"Methinkes by this bow thou beares in thy hand,
A good archer thou seems to bee."

24. "I am wilfull[4] of my way," quoth Sir Guye,
"And of my morning tyde:"
"I'le lead thee through the wood," quoth Robin,
"Good ffellow, I'le be thy guide."

[1] yew [2] made ready [3] help [4] astray

25. "I seeke an outlaw," quoth Sir Guye,
"Men call him Robin Hood;
I had rather meet with him upon a day
Than forty pound of golde."

26. "If you tow mett, itt wold be seene whether were better
Afore yee did part awaye;
Let us some other pastime find,
Good ffellow, I thee pray.

27. "Let us some other masteryes make,
And wee will walke in the woods even;
Wee may chance meet with Robin Hoode
Att some unsett steven."[1]

28. They cutt them downe the summer shroggs[2]
Which grew both under a bryar,
And sett them three score rood in twinn,[3]
To shoote the prickes full neare.

29. "Leade on, good ffellow," sayd Sir Guye,
"Lead on, I doe bidd thee:"
"Nay, by my faith," quoth Robin Hood,
"The leader thou shalt bee."

30. The first good shoot that Robin ledd,
Did not shoote an inch the pricke ffroe;
Guy was an archer good enoughe,
But he cold neere shoote soe.

31. The second shoote Sir Guy shott,
He shott within the garlande;
But Robin Hoode shott it better than hee,
For he clove the good pricke-wande.

32. "Gods blessing on thy heart!" sayes Guye,
"Goode ffellow, thy shooting is goode;
For an thy hart be as good as thy hands,
Thou were better than Robin Hood.

33. "Tell me thy name, good ffellow," quoth Guy,
"Under the leaves of lyne:"
"Nay, by my faith," quoth good Robin,
"Till thou have told me thine."

34. "I dwell by dale and downe," quoth Guye,
"And I have done many a curst turne;
And he that calles me by my right name,
Calles me Guye of good Gysborne."

35. "My dwelling is in the wood," sayes Robin;
"By thee I set right nought;
My name is Robin Hood of Barnesdale,
A ffellow thou has long sought."

[1] hour [2] wands [3] apart

36. He that had neither beene a kithe nor kin
Might have seene a full fayre sight,
To see how together these yeomen went,
With blades both browne and bright;

37. To have seene how these yeomen together fought
Two howers of a summer's day;
Itt was neither Guy nor Robin Hood
That ffettled [1] them to flye away.

38. Robin was reacheles [2] on a roote,
And stumbled at that tyde,
And Guy was quicke and nimble with-all,
And hitt him ore the left side.

39. "Ah, deere Lady!" sayd Robin Hoode,
"Thou art both mother and may! [3]
I thinke it was never mans destinye
To dye before his day."

40. Robin thought on Our Lady deere,
And soone leapt up againe,
And thus he came with an awkwarde [4] stroke;
Good Sir Guy hee has slayne.

41. He tooke Sir Guys head by the hayre,
And sticked itt on his bowes end:
"Thou hast beene traytor all thy liffe,
Which thing must have an ende."

42. Robin pulled forth an Irish kniffe,
And nicked Sir Guy in the fface,
That hee was never on a woman borne
Cold tell who Sir Guye was.

43. Saies, "Lye there, lye there, good Sir Guye,
And with me be not wrothe;
If thou have had the worse stroakes at my hand,
Thou shalt have the better cloathe."

44. Robin did off his gowne of greene,
Sir Guye hee did it throwe;
And hee put on that capull-hyde
That cladd him topp to toe.

45. "The bowe, the arrowes, and litle horne,
And with me now I'le beare;
For now I will goe to Barnesdale,
To see how my men doe ffare."

46. Robin sette Guyes horne to his mouth,
A lowd blast in it he did blow;
That beheard the sheriffe of Nottingham,
As he leaned under a lowe.[5]

[1] made ready [2] careless [3] maiden [4] back-handed [5] hill

47. "Hearken! hearken!" sayd the sheriffe,
"I heard noe tydings but good;
For yonder I heare Sir Guyes horne blowe,
For he hath slaine Robin Hoode.

48. "For yonder I heare Sir Guyes horne blow,
Itt blowes soe well in tyde,
For yonder comes that wighty yeoman,
Cladd in his capull-hyde.

49. "Come hither, thou good Sir Guy,
Aske of mee what thou wilt have:"
"I'le none of thy gold," sayes Robin Hood,
"Nor I'le none of itt have.

50. "But now I have slaine the master," he sayd,
"Let me goe strike the knave;
This is all the reward I aske,
Nor noe other will I have."

51. "Thou art a madman," said the shiriffe,
"Thou sholdest have had a knights ffee;
Seeing thy asking hath beene soe badd,
Well granted it shall be."

52. But Litle John heard his master speake,
Well he knew that was his steven; [1]
"Now shall I be loset," quoth Litle John,
"With Christs might in heaven."

53. But Robin hee hyed him towards Litle John,
Hee thought hee wold loose him belive; [2]
The sheriffe and all his companye
Fast after him did drive.

54. "Stand abacke! stand abacke!" sayd Robin;
"Why draw you mee soe neere?
Itt was never the use in our countrye
Ones shrift another shold heere."

55. But Robin pulled forth an Irysh kniffe,
And losed John hand and ffoote,
And gave him Sir Guyes bow in his hand,
And bade it be his boote.[3]

56. But John tooke Guyes bow in his hand
(His arrowes were rawstye [4] by the roote);
The sherriffe saw Litle John draw a bow
And ffettle him to shoote.

57. Towards his house in Nottingham
He ffled full fast away,
And soe did all his companye,
Not one behind did stay.

[1] voice [2] quickly [3] help [4] clotted

58. But he cold neither soe fast goe,
Nor away soe fast runn,
But Litle John, with an arrow broade,
Did cleave his heart in twinn.

THE BATTLE OF OTTERBURN

1. Yt felle abowght the Lamasse tyde,
When husbondes wynnes[1] ther haye,
The dowghtye Dowglasse bowynd[2] hym to ryde,
In Ynglond to take a praye.

2. The yerlle of Fyffe, wythowghten stryffe,
He bowynd hym over Sulway;
The grete wolde ever to-gether ryde;
That raysse[3] they may rewe for aye.

3. Over Hoppertope hyll they cam in,
And so down by Rodclyffe crage;
Upon Grene Lynton they lyghted dowyn,
Styrande[4] many a stage.

4. And boldely brente[5] Northomberlond,
And haryed many a towyn;
They dyd owr Ynglyssh men grete wrange,
To battell that were not bowyn.

5. Than spake a berne upon the bent,
Of comforte that was not colde,
And sayd, "We have brente Northomberlond,
We have all welth in holde.

6. "Now we have haryed all Bamborowe schyre,
All the welth in the world have wee;
I rede we ryde to Newe Castell,
So styll and stalworthlye."

7. Upon the morowe,[6] when it was day,
The standerds schone fulle bryght;
To the Newe Castell they toke the waye,
And thether they cam fulle ryght.

8. Syr Henry Perssy laye at the New Castell,
I tell yow wythowtten drede;[7]
He had byn a march-man all hys dayes,
And kepte Barwyke upon Twede.

9. To the Newe Castell when they cam,
The Skottes they cryde on hyght,
"Syr Hary Perssy, and thow byste within,
Com to the fylde, and fyght.

10. "For we have brente Northomberlonde,
Thy erytage good and ryght,
And syne[8] my logeyng[9] I have take,
Wyth my brande dubbyd many a knyght."

[1] dry [2] got ready [3] raid [4] arousing [5] burned
[6] morning [7] doubt [8] since [9] lodging

11. Syr Harry Perssy cam to the walles,
The Skottyssch oste for to se,
And sayd, "And thow hast brente Northomberlond,
Full sore it rewyth me.

12. "Yf thou hast haryed all Bamborowe schyre,
Thow hast done me grete envye;[1]
For the trespasse thow hast me done,
The tone[2] of us schall dye."

13. "Where schall I byde the?" sayd the Dowglas,
"Or where wylte thow com to me?"
"At Otterborne, in the hygh way,
Ther mast thow well logeed be.

14. "The roo[3] full rekeles ther sche rinnes,
To make the game and glee;
The fawken and the fesaunt both,
Amonge the holtes on hye.

15. "Ther mast thow have thy welth at wyll,
Well looged ther mast be;
Yt schall not be long or I com the tyll,"
Sayd Syr Harry Perssye.

16. "Ther schall I byde the," sayd the Dowglas,
"By the fayth of my bodye."
"Thether schall I com," sayd Syr Harry Perssy
"My trowth I plyght to the."

17. A pype of wyne he gave them over the walles,
For soth as I yow saye;
Ther he mayd the Dowglasse drynke,
And all hys ost that daye.

18. The Dowglas turnyd hym homewarde agayne,
For soth withowghten naye;
He toke his logeyng at Oterborne,
Upon a Wedynsday.

19. And ther he pyght[4] hys standerd dowyn,
Hys gettyng more and lesse,
And syne he warned hys men to goo
To chose ther geldynges gresse.[5]

20. A Skottysshe knyght hoved[6] upon the bent,[7]
A wache I dare well saye;
So was he ware on the noble Perssy
In the dawnyng of the daye.

21. He prycked to hys pavyleon dore,
As faste as he myght ronne;
"Awaken, Dowglas," cryed the knyght,
"For Hys love that syttes in trone.

[1] hostility [2] the one [3] roe [4] fixed [5] grass
[6] tarried [7] field

22. "Awaken, Dowglas," cryed the knyght,
"For thow maste waken wyth wynne;[1]
Yender have I spyed the prowde Perssye,
And seven stondardes wyth hym."

23. "Nay by my trowth," the Dowglas sayed,
"It ys but a fayned taylle;
He durst not loke on my brede[2] banner
For all Ynglonde so haylle.

24. "Was I not yesterdaye at the Newe Castell,
That stondes so fayre on Tyne?
For all the men the Perssy had,
He coude not garre[3] me ones to dyne."

25. He stepped owt at his pavelyon dore,
To loke and it were lesse:[4]
"Araye yow, lordynges, one and all,
For here bygynnes no peysse.[5]

26. "The yerle of Mentaye, thow arte my eme,[6]
The fowarde[7] I gyve to the:
The yerlle of Huntlay, cawte and kene,[8]
He schall be wyth the.

27. "The lorde of Bowghan, in armure bryght,
On the other hand he schall be;
Lord Jhonstoune and Lorde Maxwell,
They to schall be with me.

28. "Swynton, fayre fylde upon your pryde!
To batell make yow bowen
Syr Davy Skotte, Syr Water Stewarde,
Syr Jhon of Agurstone!"

29. The Perssy cam byfore hys oste,
Wych was ever a gentyll knyght;
Upon the Dowglas lowde can[9] he crye,
"I wyll holde that I have hyght.[10]

30. "For thou haste brente Northomberlonde,
And done me grete envye;
For thys trespasse thou hast me done,
The tone[11] of us schall dye."

31. The Dowglas answerde hym agayne,
Wyth grett wurdes upon hye,
And sayd, "I have twenty agaynst thy one,
Byholde, and thou maste see."

32. Wyth that the Perssy was grevyd sore,
For soth as I yow saye;
He lyghted dowyn upon his foote,
And schoote[12] hys horsse clene awaye.

[1] joy [2] broad [3] make [4] if it might be false [5] peace [6] uncle [7] van [8] wary and bold [9] did [10] promised [11] one [12] sent away

33. Every man sawe that he dyd soo,
That ryall[1] was ever in rowght;[2]
Every man schoote hys horsse hym froo,
And lyght hym rowynde abowght.

34. Thus Syr Hary Perssye toke the fylde,
For soth as I yow saye;
Jhesu Cryste in hevyn on hyght
Dyd helpe hym well that daye.

35. But nyne thowzand, ther was no moo,
The cronykle wyll not layne;[3]
Forty thowsande of Skottes and fowre
That day fowght them agayne.

36. But when the batell byganne to joyne,
In hast ther cam a knyght;
The letters fayre furth hath he tayne,
And thus he sayd full ryght:

37. "My lorde your father he gretes yow well,
Wyth many a noble knyght;
He desyres yow to byde
That he may see thys fyght.

38. "The Baron of Grastoke ys com out of the west,
With hym a noble companye;
All they loge at your fathers thys nyght,
And the batell fayne wolde they see."

39. "For Jhesus love," sayd Syr Harye Perssy,
"That dyed for yow and me,
Wende to my lorde my father agayne,
And saye thow sawe me not with yee.[4]

40. "My trowth ys plyght to yonne Skottysh knyght,
It nedes me not to layne,
That I schulde byde hym upon thys bent,
And I have hys trowth agayne.

41. "And if that I weynde of thys growende,
For soth, onfowghten awaye,
He wolde me call but a kowarde knyght
In hys londe another daye.

42. "Yet had I lever to be rynde and rente,[5]
By Mary, that mykkel maye,[6]
Then ever my manhood schulde be reprovyd
Wyth a Skotte another daye.

43. "Wherefore schote, archars, for my sake,
And let scharpe arowes flee;
Mynstrells, playe up for your waryson,[7]
And well quyt it schall bee.

[1] royal [2] company [3] lie [4] eye [5] flayed and drawn [6] powerful maid [7] reward

44. "Every man thynke on hys trewe-love,
And marke hym to the Trenite;
For to God I make myne avowe
Thys day wyll I not flee."

45. The blodye harte in the Dowglas armes,
Hys standerde stood on hye,
That every man myght full well knowe;
By syde stode starrës thre.

46. The whyte lyon on the Ynglyssh perte,[1]
For soth as I yow sayne,
The lucettes[2] and the cressawntes both;
The Skottes faught them agayne.

47. Upon Sent Androwe lowde can they crye,
And thrysse they schowte on hyght,[3]
And syne merked them one owr Ynglysshe men,
As I have tolde yow ryght.

48. Sent George the bryght, owr Ladyes knyght,
To name they were full fayne;
Owr Ynglyssh men they cryde on hyght,
And thrysse they schowtte agayne.

49. Wyth that scharpe arowes bygan to flee,
I tell yow in sertayne;
Men of armes byganne to joyne,
Many a dowghty man was ther slayne.

50. The Perssy and the Dowglas mette,
That ether of other was fayne;
They swapped[4] together whyll[5] that they swette,
Wyth swordes of fyne collayne:[6]

51. Tyll the bloode from ther bassonnettes ranne,
As the roke[7] doth in the rayne;
"Yelde the to me," sayd the Dowglas,
"Or elles thow schalt be slayne.

52. "For I see by thy bryght bassonet,
Thow arte sum man of myght;
And so I do by thy burnysshed brande;
Thow arte an yerle, or elles a knyght."

53. "By my good faythe," sayd the noble Perssye,
"Now haste thou rede[8] full ryght;
Yet wyll I never yelde me to the,
Whyll I may stonde and fyght."

54. They swapped together whyll that they swette,
Wyth swordës scharpe and long;
Ych on other so faste they beette,
Tyll ther helmes cam in peyses dowyn.

[1] part [2] pike (fish) [3] aloud [4] smote [5] till [6] Cologne steel [7] smoke? distaff? [8] discerned

55. The Perssy was a man of strenghth,
I tell yow in thys stounde;[1]
He smote the Dowglas at the swordes length
That he fell to the growynde.

56. The sworde was scharpe, and sore can byte,
I tell yow in sertayne;
To the harte he cowde[2] hym smyte,
Thus was the Dowglas slayne.

57. The stonderdes stode styll on eke a[3] syde,
Wyth many a grevous grone;
Ther they fowght the day, and all the nyght,
And many a dowghty man was slayne.

58. Ther was no freke[4] that ther wolde flye,
But styffely in stowre[5] can stond,
Ychone hewyng on other whyll they myght drye,[6]
Wyth many a bayllefull bronde.

59. Ther was slayne upon the Skottës syde,
For soth and sertenly,
Syr James a Dowglas ther was slayne,
That day that he cowde[2] dye.

60. The yerlle of Mentaye he was slayne,
Grysely[7] groned upon the growynd;
Syr Davy Skotte, Syr Water Stewarde,
Syr Jhon of Agurstoune.

61. Syr Charllës Morrey in that place,
That never a fote wold flee;
Syr Hewe Maxwell, a lord he was,
Wyth the Dowglas dyd he dye.

62. Ther was slayne upon the Skottës syde,
For soth as I yow saye,
Of fowre and forty thowsande Scottes
Went but eyghtene awaye.

63. Ther was slayne upon the Ynglysshe syde,
For soth and sertenlye,
A gentell knyght, Syr Jhon Fechewe,
Yt was the more pety.

64. Syr James Hardbotell ther was slayne,
For hym ther hartes were sore;
The gentyll Lovell ther was slayne,
That the Perssys standerd bore.

65. Ther was slayne upon the Ynglyssh perte,
For soth as I yow saye,
Of nyne thowsand Ynglyssh men
Fvye hondert cam awaye.

[1] time [2] did [3] every [4] man [5] battle [6] endure [7] fearfully

66. The other were slayne in the fylde;
Cryste kepe ther sowlles from wo!
Seyng [1] ther was so fewe fryndes
Agaynst so many a foo.

67. Then on the morne they mayde them beerys
Of byrch and haysell graye;
Many a wydowe, wyth wepyng teyres,
Ther makes they fette [2] awaye.

68. Thys fraye bygan at Otterborne,
Bytwene the nyght and the day;
Ther the Dowglas lost hys lyffe,
And the Perssy was lede awaye.

69. Then was ther a Scottysh prisoner tayne,
Syr Hewe Mongomery was hys name;
For soth as I yow saye,
He borowed [3] the Perssy home agayne.

70. Now let us all for the Perssy praye
To Jhesu most of myght,
To bryng hys sowlle to the blysse of heven,
For he was a gentyll knyght.

THE HUNTING OF THE CHEVIOT

1. The Persë owt off Northombarlonde,
and avowe to God mayd he
That he wold hunte in the mowntayns
off Chyviat within days thre,
In the magger [4] of doughtë Dogles,
and all that ever with him be.

2. The fattiste hartes in all Cheviat
he sayd he wold kyll, and cary them away:
"Be my feth," sayd the dougheti Doglas agayn,
"I wyll let [5] that hontyng yf that I may."

3. Then the Persë owt off Banborowe cam,
with him a myghtee meany, [6]
With fifteen hondrith archares bold off blood and bone;
the [7] wear chosen owt of shyars thre.

4. This begane on a Monday at morn,
in Cheviat the hillys so he; [8]
The chylde may rue that ys unborn,
it wos the more pittë.

5. The dryvars thorowe the woodës went,
for to reas the dear;
Bomen byckarte [9] uppone the bent [10]
with ther browd aros cleare.

[1] seeing [2] fetched [3] ransomed [4] spite [5] prevent [6] company [7] they [8] high [9] attacked [10] field

6. Then the wyld [1] thorowe the woodës went,
on every sydë shear; [2]
Greahondës thorowe the grevis [3] glent, [4]
for to kyll thear dear.

7. This begane in Chyviat the hyls abone, [5]
yerly on a Monnyn-day;
Be that [6] it drewe to the oware off none, [7]
a hondrith fat hartës ded ther lay.

8. The [8] blewe a mort uppone the bent, [9]
the [8] semblyde on sydis shear; [10]
To the quyrry then the Persë went,
to se the bryttlynge [11] off the deare.

9. He sayd, "It was the Duglas promys,
this day to met me hear;
But I wyste he wolde faylle, verament;"
a great oth the Persë swear.

10. At the laste a squyar off Northomberlonde
lokyde at his hand full ny;
He was war a the doughetie Doglas commynge,
with him a myghttë meany. [12]

11. Both with spear, bylle, and brande,
yt was a myghtti sight to se;
Hardyar men, both off hart nor hande,
wear not in Cristiantë.

12. The wear [13] twenti hondrith spear-men good,
withoute any feale;
The wear borne along be the watter a Twyde,
yth [14] bowndës of Tividale.

13. "Leave of the brytlyng of the dear," he sayd,
"and to your boÿs [15] lock ye tayk good hede;
For never sithe ye wear on your mothars borne
had ye never so mickle nede."

14. The dougheti Dogglas on a stede,
he rode alle his men beforne;
His armor glytteryde as dyd a glede; [16]
a boldar barne was never born.

15. "Tell me whos men ye ar," he says,
"or whos men that ye be:
Who gave youe leave to hunte in this Chyviat chays,
in the spyt of myn and of me."

[1] deer [2] several [3] groves [4] glided [5] above [6] by the time [7] noon [8] they [9] field [10] several, all [11] cutting up [12] company [13] they were [14] in the [15] bows [16] glowing coal

16. The first mane that ever him an answear mayd,
yt was the good lord Persë:
"We wyll not tell the whoys men we ar," he says,
"nor whos men that we be;
But we wyll hounte hear in this chays,
in the spyt of thyne and of the.

17. "The fattiste hartës in all Chyviat
we have kyld, and cast to carry them away.
"Be my troth," sayd the doughetë Dogglas agayn,
"therfor the ton[1] of us shall de this day."

18. Then sayd the doughtë Doglas
unto the lord Persë:
"To kyll alle thes giltles men,
alas, it wear great pittë!

19. "But, Persë, thowe art a lord of lande,
I am a yerle callyd within my contrë;
Let all our men uppone a parti stande,
and do the battell off the and of me."

20. "Nowe Cristes cors on his crowne," sayd the lord Persë,
"who-so-ever ther-to says nay;
Be my troth, doughttë Doglas," he says,
"thow shalt never se that day,

21. "Nethar in Ynglonde, Skottlonde, nar France,
nor for no man of a woman born,
But, and fortune be my chance,
I dar met him, on[1] man for on."[1]

22. Then bespayke a squyar off Northombarlonde,
Richard Wytharyngton was his nam:
"It shall never be told in Sothe-Ynglonde," he says,
"to Kyng Herry the Fourth for sham.

23. "I wat youe byn great lordës twaw,
I am a poor squyar of lande:
I wylle never se my captayne fyght on a fylde,
and stande my selffe and loocke on,
But whylle I may my weppone welde,
I wylle not fayle both hart and hande."

24. That day, that day, that dredfull day!
the first fit here I fynde;
And youe wyll here any mor a the hountyng a the Chyviat,
yet ys ther mor behynde.

25. The Yngglyshe men hade ther bowys yebent,
ther hartes wer good yenoughe;
The first off arros that the shote off,
seven skore spear-men the sloughe.[2]

[1] one [2] they slew

26. Yet byddys the yerle Doglas uppon the bent,
a captayne good yenoughe,
And that was sene verament,
for he wrought hom both woo and wouche.[1]

27. The Dogglas partyd his ost in thre,
lyk a cheffe cheften off pryde;
With suar[2] spears off myghttë tre,
the[3] cum in on every syde:

28. Thrughe our Yngglyshe archery
gave many a wounde fulle wyde;
Many a doughetë the[3] garde[4] to dy,
which ganyde them no pryde.

29. The Ynglyshe men let ther boÿs be,
and pulde owt brandes that wer brighte;
It was a hevy syght to se
bryght swordes on basnites[5] lyght.

30. Thorowe ryche male and myneyeple,[6]
many sterne the[3] strocke done[7] streght;
Many a freyke[8] that was fulle fre,
ther undar foot dyd lyght.

31. At last the Duglas and the Persë met,
lyk to captayns of myght and of mayne;
The[3] swapte[9] togethar tylle the[3] both swat,
with swordes that wear of fyn myllan.[10]

32. Thes worthë freckys for to fyght,
ther-to the[3] wear fulle fayne,
Tylle the bloode owte off thear basnetes sprente
as ever dyd heal or rayn.

33. "Yelde the, Persë," sayde the Doglas,
"and i feth I shalle the brynge
Wher thowe shalte have a yerls wagis
of Jamy our Skottish kynge.

34. "Thou shalte have thy ransom fre,
I hight[11] the hear this thinge;
For the manfullyste man yet art thowe
that ever I conqueryd in filde fighttynge."

35. "Nay," sayd the lord Persë,
"I tolde it the beforne,
That I wolde never yeldyde be
to no man of a woman born."

36. With that ther cam an arrowe hastely,
forthe off a myghttë wane;[12]
Hit hathe strekene the yerle Duglas
in at the brest-bane.

[1] harm [2] trusty [3] they [4] made, caused [5] basinets, a kind of helmet [6] gauntlet [7] struck down [8] man [9] smote [10] Milan steel [11] promise [12] flight

37. Thorowe lyvar[1] and longës bathe[2]
the sharpe arrowe ys gane,
That never after in all his lyffe-days
he spayke mo wordës but ane:
That was, "Fyghte ye, my myrry men, whyllys ye may,
for my lyff-days ben gan."

38. The Persë leanyde on his brande,
and sawe the Duglas de;
He tooke the dede mane by the hande,
and sayd, "Wo ys me for the!

39. "To have savyde thy lyffe, I wolde have partyde with
my landes for years thre,
For a better man, of hart nare of hande,
was nat in all the north contrë."

40. Off all that se a Skottishe knyght,
was callyd Ser Hewe the Monggombyrry;
He sawe the Duglas to the deth was dyght,
he spendyd[3] a spear, a trusti tre.

41. He rod uppone a corsiare
throughe a hondrith archery:
He never stynttyde,[4] nar never blane,[5]
tylle he cam to the good lord Persë.

42. He set uppone the lorde Persë
a dynte that was full soare;
With a suar spear of a myghttë tre
clean thorow the body he the Persë ber,

43. A the tothar syde that a man myght se
a large cloth-yard and mare:[6]
Towe bettar captayns wear nat in Cristiantë
then that day slan wear ther.

44. An archar off Northomberlonde
say[7] slean was the lord Persë;
He bar a bende bowe in his hand,
was made off trusti tre.

45. An arow, that a cloth-yarde was lang,
to the harde stele halyde[8] he;
A dynt that was both sad and soar
he sat[9] on Ser Hewe the Monggombyrry.

46. The dynt yt was both sad and sar,
that he of Monggomberry sete;
The swane-fethars that his arrowe bar
with his hart-blood the[10] wear wete.

[1] liver [2] both [3] grasped [4] stopped [5] ceased
[6] more [7] saw [8] drew [9] set [10] they

47. Ther was never a freake wone foot wolde fle,
but still in stour dyd stand,
Heawyng on yche othar, whylle the[1] myghte dre,[2]
with many a balfull brande.

48. This battell begane in Chyviat
an owar befor the none,
And when even-songe bell was rang,
the battell was nat half done.

49. The tocke . . . on ethar hande
be the lyght off the mone;
Many hade no strenght for to stande,
in Chyviat the hillys abon.

50. Of fifteen hondrith archars of Ynglonde
went away but seventi and thre;
Of twenti hondrith spear-men of Skotlonde,
but even five and fifti.

51. But all wear slayne Cheviat within;
the[1] hade no strengthe to stand on hy;
The chylde may rue that ys unborne,
it was the mor pittë.

52. Thear was slayne, withe the lord Persë,
Sir Johan of Agerstone,
Ser Rogar, the hinde[3] Hartly,
Ser Wyllyam, the bolde Hearone.

53. Ser Jorg, the worthë Loumle,
a knyghte of great renowen,
Ser Raff, the ryche Rugbe,
with dyntes wear beaten dowene.

54. For Wetharryngton my harte was wo,
that ever he slayne shulde be;
For when both his leggis wear hewyne in to,
yet he knyled and fought on hys kny.

55. Ther was slayne, with the dougheti Duglas,
Ser Hewe the Monggombyrry,
Ser Davy Lwdale, that worthë was,
his sistars son was he.

56. Ser Charls a Murrë in that place,
that never a foot wolde fle;
Ser Hewe Maxwelle, a lorde he was,
with the Doglas dyd he dey.

57. So on the morrowe the[1] mayde them byears
off birch and hasell so gray;
Many wedous, with wepyng tears,
cam to fache ther makys[4] away.

[1] they [2] endure [3] courteous [4] mates

58. Tivydale may carpe off care,
 Northombarlond may mayk great mon,
For towe such captayns as slayne wear thear,
 on the March-parti shall never be non.

59. Word ys commen to Eddenburrowe,
 to Jamy the Skottische kynge,
That dougheti Duglas, lyff-tenant of the Marches,
 he lay slean Chyviot within.

60. His handdës dyd he weal[1] and wryng,
 he sayd, "Alas, and woe ys me!
Such an othar captayn Skotland within,"
 he sayd, "ye-feth shuld never be."

61. Worde ys commyn to lovly Londone,
 till the fourth Harry our kynge,
That lord Persë, leyff-tenante of the Marchis,
 he lay slayne Chyviat within.

62. "God have merci on his solle," sayde Kyng Harry,
 "good Lord, yf thy will it be!
I have a hondrith captayns in Ynglonde," he sayd,
 "as good as ever was he:
But, Persë, and I brook my lyffe,
 thy deth well quyte shall be."

63. As our noble kynge mayd his avowe,
 lyke a noble prince of renowen,
For the deth of the lord Persë
 he dyde the battell of Hombyll-down;

64. Wher syx and thrittë Skottishe knyghtes
 on a day wear beaten down:
Glendale glytteryde on ther armor bryght,
 over castille, towar, and town.

65. This was the hontynge off the Cheviat,
 that tear begane this spurn;[2]
Old men that knowen the grownde well yenoughe
 call it the battell of Otterburn.

66. At Otterburn begane this spurne
 uppone a Monnynday;
Ther was the doughtë Doglas slean,
 the Persë never went away.

67. Ther was never a tym on the Marche-partës
 sen the Doglas and the Persë met,
But yt ys mervele and the rede blude ronne not,
 as the reane[3] doys in the stret.

[1] clench [2] that ere began this fight! [3] rain

68. Jhesue Crist our balys bete,[1]
 and to the blys us brynge!
Thus was the hountynge of the Chivyat:
 God sent us alle good endyng!

SIR PATRICK SPENS

1. The king sits in Dumferling toune,
 Drinking the blude-reid wine:
"O whar will I get guid sailor,
 To sail this schip of mine?"

2. Up and spak an eldern knicht,
 Sat at the kings richt kne:
"Sir Patrick Spence is the best sailor,
 That sails upon the se."

3. The king has written a braid letter,
 And signd it wi his hand,
And sent it to Sir Patrick Spence,
 Was walking on the sand.

4. The first line that Sir Patrick red,
 A loud lauch[2] lauched he;
The next line that Sir Patrick red,
 The teir blinded his ee.

5. "O wha is this has don this deid,
 This ill deid don to me,
To send me out this time o' the yeir,
 To sail upon the se!

6. "Mak hast, mak haste, my mirry men all,
 Our guid schip sails the morne:"
"O say na sae, my master deir,
 For I feir a deadlie storme.

7. "Late, late yestreen I saw the new moone,
 Wi the auld moone in hir arme,
And I feir, I feir, my deir master,
 That we will cum to harme."

8. O our Scots nobles wer richt laith[3]
 To weet their cork-heild schoone;
Bot lang owre[4] a' the play wer playd,
 Thair hats they swam aboone.[5]

9. O lang, lang may their ladies sit,
 Wi thair fans into their hand,
Or eir they se Sir Patrick Spence
 Cum sailing to the land.

10. O lang, lang may the ladies stand,
 Wi thair gold kems[6] in their hair,
Waiting for thair ain deir lords,
 For they'll se thame na mair.

[1] amend [2] laugh [3] loth [4] ere [5] above [6] combs

11. Haf owre, haf owre to Aberdour,
It's fiftie fadom deip,
And thair lies guid Sir Patrick Spence,
Wi the Scots lords at his feit.

CAPTAIN CAR, OR, EDOM O GORDON

1. It befell at Martynmas,
When wether waxed colde,
Captaine Care said to his men,
"We must go take a holde."[1]

Syck,[2] sike,[2] and to-towe[3] sike,
And sike and like to die;
The sikest nighte that ever I abode,
God[4] Lord have mercy on me!

2. "Haille, master, and wether you will,
And wether ye like it best."
"To the castle of Crecrynbroghe,
And there we will take our reste."

3. "I knowe wher is a gay castle,
Is builded of lyme and stone;
Within their is a gay ladie,
Her lord is riden and gone."

4. The ladie she lend on her castle-walle,
She loked upp and downe;
There was she ware of an host of men,
Come riding to the towne.

5. "Se yow, my meri men all,
And se yow what I see?
Yonder I see an host of men,
I muse who they shold bee."

6. She thought he had ben her wed lord,
As he comd riding home;
Then was it traitur Captaine Care
The lord of Ester-towne.

7. They wer no soner at supper sett,
Then after said the grace,
Or Captaine Care and all his men
Wer lighte aboute the place.

8. "Gyve over thi howsse, thou lady gay,
And I will make the a bande;
To-nighte thou shall ly within my armes,
To-morrowe thou shall ere[5] my lande."

9. Then bespacke the eldest sonne,
That was both whitt and redde:
"O mother dere, geve over your howsse,
Or elles we shalbe deade."

[1] castle [2] sick [3] too-too [4] good [5] possess

10. "I will not geve over my hous," she saithe,
"Not for feare of my lyffe;
It shalbe talked throughout the land,
The slaughter of a wyffe.

11. "Fetch me my pestilett,[1]
And charge me my gonne,
That I may shott at this bloddy butcher,
The lord of Easter-towne."

12. Styfly upon her wall she stode,
And lett the pellettes flee;
But then she myst the blody bucher,
And she slew other three.

13. "I will not geve over my hous," she saithe,
"Netheir for lord nor lowne;
Nor yet for traitour Captaine Care,
The lord of Easter-towne.

14. "I desire of Captine Care,
And all his bloddye band,
That he would save my eldest sonne,
The eare[2] of all my lande."

15. "Lap him in a shete," he sayth,
"And let him downe to me,
And I shall take him in my armes,
His waran shall I be."

16. The captayne sayd unto him selfe;
Wyth sped, before the rest,
He cut his tonge out of his head,
His hart out of his brest.

17. He lapt them in a handkerchef,
And knet it of knotes three,
And cast them over the castell-wall,
At that gay ladye.

18. "Fye upon the, Captayne Care,
And all thy bloddy band!
For thou hast slayne my eldest sonne,
The ayre of all my land."

19. Then bespake the yongest sonne,
That sat on the nurses knee,
Sayth, "Mother gay, geve over your house;
For the smoake it smoothers me."

20. Out then spake the Lady Margaret,
As she stood on the stair;
The fire was at her goud[3] garters,
The lowe[4] was at her hair.

[1] pistol [2] heir [3] gold [4] flame

21. "I wold geve my gold," she saith,
"And so I wolde my ffee,
For a blaste of the westryn wind,
To dryve the smoke from thee.

22. "Fy upon the, John Hamleton,
That ever I paid the hyre!
For thou hast broken my castle-wall,
And kyndled in the ffyre."

23. The lady gate to her close parler,[1]
The fire fell aboute her head;
She toke up her children two,
Seth, "Babes, we are all dead."

24. Then bespake the hye steward,
That is of hye degree;
Saith, "Ladie gay, you are in close,
Wether ye fighte or flee."

25. Lord Hamleton dremd in his dream,
In Carvall where he laye,
His halle were all of fyre,
His ladie slayne or daye.[2]

26. "Busk and bowne, my mery men all,
Even and go ye with me;
For I dremd that my hall was on fyre,
My lady slayne or day."

27. He buskt him and bownd hym,
And like a worthi knighte;
And when he saw his hall burning,
His harte was no dele lighte.

28. He sett a trumpett till his mouth,
He blew as it plesd his grace;
Twenty score of Hamlentons
Was light aboute the place.

29. "Had I knowne as much yesternighte
As I do to-daye,
Captaine Care and all his men
Should not have gone so quite.

30. "Fye upon the, Captaine Care,
And all thy blody bande!
Thou haste slayne my lady gay,
More wurth then all thy lande.

31. "If thou had ought eny ill will," he saith,
"Thou shoulde have taken my lyffe,
And have saved my children thre,
All and my lovesome wyffe."

[1] parlor [2] ere day

LORD RANDAL

1. "O where hae ye been, Lord Randal, my son?
O where hae ye been, my handsome young man?"
"I hae been to the wild wood; mother, make my bed soon,
For I'm weary wi hunting, and fain wald lie down."

2. "Where gat ye your dinner, Lord Randal, my son?
Where gat ye your dinner, my handsome young man?"
"I din'd wi my true-love; mother, make my bed soon,
For I'm weary wi hunting, and fain wald lie down."

3. "What gat ye to your dinner, Lord Randal, my son?
What gat ye to your dinner, my handsome young man?"
"I gat eels boiled in broo; mother, make my bed soon,
For I'm weary wi hunting, and fain wald lie down."

4. "What became of your bloodhounds, Lord Randal, my son?
What became of your bloodhounds, my handsome young man?"
"O they swelld and they died; mother, make my bed soon,
For I'm weary wi hunting, and fain wald lie down."

5. "O I fear ye are poison'd, Lord Randal, my son!
O I fear ye are poisond, my handsome young man!"
"O yes! I am poisond; mother, make my bed soon,
For I'm sick at the heart and I fain wald lie down."

HIND HORN

1. In Scotland there was a babie born,
Lill lal, etc.
And his name it was called young Hind Horn.
With a fal lal, etc.

2. He sent a letter to our king
That he was in love with his daughter Jean.

3. The king an angry man was he;
He sent young Hind Horn to the sea.

4. He's gien to her a silver wand,
With seven living lavrocks[1] sitting thereon.

5. She's gien to him a diamond ring,
With seven bright diamonds set therein.

6. "When this ring grows pale and wan,
You may know by it my love is gane."

7. One day as he looked his ring upon,
He saw the diamonds pale and wan.

8. He left the sea and came to land,
And the first that he met was an old beggar man.

9. "What news, what news?" said young Hind Horn;
"No news, no news," said the old beggar man.

10. "No news," said the beggar, "no news at a'
But there is a wedding in the king's ha.

11. "But there is a wedding in the king's ha,
That has halden these forty days and twa."

12. "Will ye lend me your begging coat?
And I'll lend you my scarlet cloak.

13. "Will you lend me your beggar's rung?[2]
And I'll gie you my steed to ride upon.

14. "Will you lend me your wig o hair,
To cover mine, because it is fair?"

15. The auld beggar man was bound for the mill,
But young Hind Horn for the king's hall.

16. The auld beggar man was bound for to ride,
But young Hind Horn was bound for the bride.

17. When he came to the king's gate,
He sought a drink for Hind Horn's sake.

18. The bride came down with a glass of wine,
When he drank out the glass, and dropt in the ring.

19. "O got ye this by sea or land?
Or got ye it off a dead man's hand?"

[1] larks [2] staff

20. "I got not it by sea, I got it by land,
And I got it, madam, out of your own hand."

21. "O I'll cast off my gowns of brown,
And beg wi you frae town to town.

22. "O I'll cast off my gowns of red,
And I'll beg wi you to win my bread."

23. "Ye needna cast off your gowns of brown,
For I'll make you lady o many a town.

24. "Ye needna cast off your gowns o red,
It's only a sham, the begging o my bread."

THOMAS RYMER

1. True Thomas lay oer yond grassy bank,
And he beheld a ladie gay,
A ladie that was brisk and bold,
Come riding oer the fernie brae.[1]

2. Her skirt was of the grass-green silk,
Her mantle of the velvet fine,
At ilka tett[2] of her horse's mane
Hung fifty silver bells and nine.

3. True Thomas he took off his hat
And bowed him low down till his knee:
"All hail, thou mighty Queen of Heaven!
For your peer on earth I never did see."

4. "O no, O no, True Thomas," she says,
"That name does not belong to me;
I am but the queen of fair Elfland,
And I'm come here for to visit thee.

5. ["Harp and carp,[3] Thomas," she said,
"Harp and carp along wi me;
But if ye dare to kiss my lips,
Sure of your bodie I will be."

6. "Betide me weal, betide me woe,
That weird[4] shall never daunton me;" —
Syne he has kissed her rosy lips
All underneath the Eildon Tree.]

7. "But ye maun go wi me now, Thomas,
True Thomas, ye maun go wi me,
For ye maun serve me seven years,
Thro weel or wae as may chance to be."

8. She turned about her milk-white steed,
And took True Thomas up behind,
And aye wheneer her bridle rang,
The steed flew swifter than the wind.

[1] ferny hill [2] every lock [3] sing [4] fate

9. For forty days and forty nights
He wade thro red blude to the knee,
And he saw neither sun nor moon,
But heard the roaring of the sea.

10. O they rade on and further on,
Until they came to a garden green:
"Light down, light down, ye ladie free,
Some of that fruit let me pull to thee."

11. "O no, O no, True Thomas," she says,
"That fruit maun not be touched by thee,
For a' the plagues that are in hell
Light on the fruit of this countrie.

12. "But I have a loaf here in my lap,
Likewise a bottle of claret wine,
And here ere we go farther on,
We'll rest a while, and ye may dine."

13. When he had eaten and drunk his fill,
"Lay down your head upon my knee,"
The lady sayd, "ere we climb yon hill,
And I will show you fairlies[1] three.

14. "O see ye not yon narrow road,
So thick beset wi thorns and briers?
That is the path of righteousness,
Tho after it but few enquires.

15. "And see not ye that braid braid road,
That lies across yon lillie leven?[2]
That is the path of wickedness,
Tho some call it the road to heaven.

16. "And see ye not that bonny road,
Which winds about the fernie brae?[3]
That is the road to fair Elfland,
Where you and I this night maun gae.

17. "But Thomas, ye maun hold your tongue,
Whatever ye may hear or see,
For gin ae word you should chance to speak,
You will neer get back to your ain countrie."

18. He has gotten a coat of the even[4] cloth,
And a pair of shoes of velvet green,
And till seven years were past and gone
True Thomas on earth was never seen.

ST. STEPHEN AND HEROD

1. Seynt Stevene was a clerk in Kyng Herowdes halle,
And servyd him of bred and cloth, as every kyng befalle.

[1] marvels [2] lovely lawn [3] hillside [4] smooth

2. Stevyn out of kechone cam, wyth boris[1] hed on honde;
He saw a sterre was fayr and brygt over Bedlem stonde.

3. He kyst[2] adoun the boris hed and went in to the halle:
"I forsak the, Kyng Herowdes, and thi werkes alle.

4. "I forsak the, Kyng Herowdes, and thi werkes alle;
Ther is a chyld in Bedlem born is beter than we alle."

5. "What eylyt[3] the, Stevene? What is the befalle?
Lakkyt the eyther mete or drynk in Kyng Herowdes halle?"

6. "Lakit me neyther mete nor drynk in Kyng Herowdes halle;
Ther is a chyld in Bedlem born is beter than we alle."

7. "What eylyt the, Stevyn? Art thu wod,[4] or thu gynnyst to brede?[5]
Lakkyt the eyther gold or fe,[6] or ony ryche wede?"[7]

8. "Lakyt me neyther gold ne fe, ne non ryche wede;
Ther is a chyld in Bedlem born xal helpyn us at our nede."

9. "That is al so soth,[8] Stevyn, al so soth, iwys,[9]
As this capoun crowe xal that lyth here in myn dysh."

10. That word was not so sone seyd, that word in that halle,
The capoun crew *Cristus natus est!* among the lordes alle.

11. "Rysyt[10] up, myn turmentowres, be to[11] and al be on,
And ledyt Stevyn out of this toun, and stonyt hym wyth ston!"

12. Tokyn he[12] Stevene, and stonyd hym in the way,
And therfore is his evyn on Crystes owyn day.

[1] boar's [2] cast [3] aileth [4] crazy [5] be whimsical [6] property [7] garment [8] true [9] indeed [10] rise [11] by two [12] they

THE BEGINNING OF THE RENAISSANCE

SIR THOMAS WYATT (1503–1542)

A RENOUNCING OF LOVE

Farewell, Love, and all thy laws forever!
Thy baited hooks shall tangle me no more:
Senec and Plato call me from thy lore
To perfect wealth my wit for to endeavour.
In blind error when I did persèver,
Thy sharp repulse, that pricketh aye so sore,
Taught me in trifles that I set no store;
But 'scaped forth thence since, liberty is lever.[1]
Therefore, farewell! go trouble younger hearts,
And in me claim no more authority.
With idle youth go use thy property,
And thereon spend thy many brittle darts;
For hitherto though I have lost my time,
Me list no longer rotten boughs to climb.

THE DESERTED LOVER CONSOLETH HIMSELF WITH REMEMBRANCE THAT ALL WOMEN ARE BY NATURE FICKLE

Divers doth use, as I have heard and know,
When that to change their ladies do begin,
To mourn, and wail, and never for to lynn;[2]
Hoping thereby to 'pease their painful woe.
And some there be that when it chanceth so
That women change, and hate where love hath been,
They call them false, and think with words to win
The hearts of them which otherwhere doth grow.
But as for me, though that by chance indeed
Change hath outworn the favour that I had,
I will not wail, lament, nor yet be sad,
Nor call her false that falsely did me feed;
But let it pass, and think it is of kind[3]
That often change doth please a woman's mind.

THE LOVER HAVING DREAMED OF ENJOYING OF HIS LOVE, COMPLAINETH THAT THE DREAM IS NOT EITHER LONGER OR TRUER

Unstable dream, according to the place,
Be steadfast once, or else at least be true.
By tasted sweetness make me not to rue
The sudden loss of thy false feigned grace.
By good respect in such a dangerous case
Thou broughtst not her into these tossing seas,
But madest my spirit to live, my care t'encrease,
My body in tempest her delight t'embrace.
The body dead, the spirit had his desire;
Painless was th' one, the other in delight.
Why then, alas! did it not keep it right,
But thus return to leap into the fire,
And where it was at wish, could not remain?
Such mocks of dreams do turn to deadly pain!

[1] dearer [2] cease [3] of nature, natural

THE LOVER COMPLAINETH THE UNKINDNESS OF HIS LOVE

My lute, awake, perform the last
Labour that thou and I shall waste,
And end that I have now begun.
And when this song is sung and past,
My lute, be still, for I have done.

As to be heard where ear is none,
As lead to grave in marble stone,
My song may pierce her heart as soon.
Should we then sigh, or sing, or moan?
No, no, my lute, for I have done.

The rocks do not so cruelly
Repulse the waves continually,
As she my suit and affection;
So that I am past remedy,
Whereby my lute and I have done.

Proud of the spoil that thou hast got
Of simple hearts through Lovës shot,
By whom unkind thou hast them won,
Think not he hath his bow forgot,
Although my lute and I have done.

Vengeance shall fall on thy disdain
That makest but game on earnest pain.
Think not alone under the sun
Unquit to cause thy lovers plain,[1]
Although my lute and I have done.

May chance thee lie withered and old
In winter nights that are so cold,
Playning in vain unto the moon;
Thy wishes then dare not be told.
Care then who list, for I have done.

[1] complain

And then may chance thee to repent
The time that thou hast lost and spent
To cause thy lovers sigh and swoon;
Then shalt thou know beauty but lent,
And wish and want, as I have done.

Now cease, my lute, this is the last
Labour that thou and I shall waste,
And ended is that we begun.
Now is this song both sung and past,
My lute, be still, for I have done.

A DESCRIPTION OF SUCH A ONE AS HE WOULD LOVE

A face that should content me wondrous well,
Should not be fair, but lovely to behold,
Of lively look, all grief for to repell,
With right good grace, so would I that it should
Speak without word, such words as none can tell;
The tress also should be of crisped gold.
With wit and these perchance I might be tried,
And knit again with knot that should not slide.

OF THE MEAN AND SURE ESTATE

Written to John Poins

My mother's maids, when they did sew and spin,
They sang sometime a song of the field mouse
That, for because her livelihood was but thin,
Would needs go seek her townish sister's house.
She thought herself endured too much pain;
The stormy blasts her cave so sore did souse
That when the furrows swimmed with the rain,
She must lie cold and wet in sorry plight;
And worse than that, bare meat there did remain
To comfort her when she her house had dight;
Sometime a barly corn; sometime a bean,
For which she laboured hard both day and night
In harvest time whilst she might go and glean;
And where store [1] was stroyed [2] with the flood,
Then welaway! for she undone was clean.
Then was she fain to take instead of food
Sleep, if she might, her hunger to beguile.
"My sister," quoth she, "hath a living good,
And hence from me she dwelleth not a mile.
In cold and storm she lieth warm and dry
In bed of down, the dirt doth not defile
Her tender foot, she laboureth not as I.
Richly she feedeth and at the richman's cost,
And for her meat she needs not crave nor cry.
By sea, by land, of the delicates, the most
Her cater [3] seeks and spareth for no peril,

[1] abundance [2] destroyed [3] caterer

She feedeth on boiled bacon, meat and roast,
And hath thereof neither charge nor travail;
And when she list, the liquor of the grape
Doth glad her heart till that her belly swell."
And at this journey she maketh but a jape; [1]
So forth she goeth, trusting of all this wealth
With her sister her part so for to shape,
That if she might keep herself in health,
To live a lady while her life doth last.
And to the door now is she come by stealth,
And with her foot anon she scrapeth full fast.
Th' other for fear durst not well scarce appear,
Of every noise so was the wretch aghast.
At last she asked softly who was there,
And in her language as well as she could.
"Peep!" quoth the other sister, "I am here."
"Peace," quoth the town mouse, "why speakest thou so loud?"
And by the hand she took her fair and well.
"Welcome," quoth she, "my sister, by the Rood!"
She feasted her, that joy it was to tell
The fare they had; they drank the wine so clear,
And as to purpose now and then it fell,
She cheered her with "Ho, sister, what cheer!"
Amid this joy befell a sorry chance,
That, welaway! the stranger bought full dear
The fare she had, for, as she looks askance,
Under a stool she spied two steaming [2] eyes
In a round head with sharp ears. In France
Was never mouse so fear'd, for, though unwise
Had not i-seen such a beast before,
Yet had nature taught her after her guise
To know her foe and dread him evermore.
The towney mouse fled, she knew whither to go;
Th' other had no shift, but wanders sore
Feard of her life. At home she wished her tho, [3]
And to the door, alas! as she did skip,
The Heaven it would, lo! and eke her chance was so,
At the threshold her silly foot did trip;
And ere she might recover it again,
The traitor cat had caught her by the hip,
And made her there against her will remain,
That had forgotten her poor surety and rest
For seeming wealth wherein she thought to reign.
Alas, my Poines, how men do seek the best
And find the worst by error as they stray!
And no marvel; when sight is so oppressed,
And blind the guide, anon out of the way
Goeth guide and all in seeking quiet life.
O wretched minds, there is no gold that may
Grant that ye seek; no war; no peace; no strife.
No, no, although thy head were hooped with gold,

[1] jest [2] gleaming [3] then

Sergeant with mace, halberd, sword nor knife,
Cannot repulse the care that follow should.
Each kind of life hath with him his disease.
Live in delight even as thy lust would,
And thou shalt find, when lust doth most thee please,
It irketh straight and by itself doth fade.
A small thing it is that may thy mind appease.
None of ye all there is that is so mad
To seek grapes upon brambles or briars;
Nor none, I trow, that hath his wit so bad
To set his hay[1] for conies[2] over rivers,
Nor ye set not a drag-net for an hare;
And yet the thing that most is your desire
Ye do mistake with more travail and care.
Make plain thine heart, that it be not knotted
With hope or dread, and see thy will be bare
From all effects whom vice hath ever spotted.
Thyself content with that is thee assigned,
And use it well that is to thee allotted.
Then seek no more out of thyself to find
The thing that thou hast sought so long before,
For thou shalt feel it sitting in thy mind.
Mad, if ye list to continue your sore,
Let present pass and gape on time to come,
And dip yourself in travail more and more.
  Henceforth, my Poines, this shall be all and some,
These wretched fools shall have nought else of me;
But to the great God and to his high dome,
None other pain pray I for them to be,
But when the rage doth lead them from the right,
That, looking backward, virtue they may see,
Even as she is so goodly fair and bright,
And whilst they clasp their lusts in arms across,
Grant them, good Lord, as Thou mayst of Thy might,
To fret inward for losing such a loss.

[1] snare [2] rabbits

HENRY HOWARD, EARL OF SURREY (1517?–1547)

DESCRIPTION OF THE RESTLESS STATE OF A LOVER

The sun hath twice brought forth his tender green
And clad the earth in lively lustiness,
Once have the winds the trees despoiled clean,
And new again begins their cruelness,
Since I have hid under my breast the harm
That never shall recover healthfulness.
The winter's hurt recovers with the warm,
The parched green restored is with the shade.
What warmth, alas! may serve for to disarm
The frozen heart that mine in flame hath made?
What cold again is able to restore
My fresh green years, that wither thus and fade?
Alas, I see, nothing hath hurt so sore,
But time in time reduceth a return;
In time my harm increaseth more and more,
And seems to have my cure always in scorn.
Strange kinds of death, in life that I do try,
At hand to melt, far off in flame to burn;
And like as time list to my cure apply,
So doth each place my comfort clean refuse.
All thing alive that seeth the heavens with eye
With cloak of night may cover and excuse
Itself from travail of the day's unrest,
Save I, alas! against all others' use,
That then stir up the torments of my breast,
And curse each star as causer of my fate.
And when the sun hath eke the dark oppresst,
And brought the day, it doth nothing abate
The travails of mine endless smart and pain;
For then, as one that hath the light in hate,
I wish for night, more covertly to plain,[1]
And me withdraw from every haunted place,
Lest by my cheer my chance appear too plain.
And in my mind I measure pace by pace,
To seek the place where I myself had lost,
That day that I was tangled in the lace,
In seeming slack, that knitteth ever most.
But never yet the travail of my thought
Of better state could catch a cause to boast;
For if I found, sometime that I have sought,
Those stars by whom I trusted of the port,
My sails do fall, and I advance right nought,
As anchored fast, my spirits do all resort
To stand agazed, and sink in more and more
The deadly harm which she doth take in sport.
Lo, if I seek, how I do find my sore!
And if I flee I carry with me still
The venomed shaft, which doth his force restore
By haste of flight, and I may plain my fill
Unto myself, unless this careful song
Print in your heart some parcel of my teen;[2]
For I, alas! in silence all too long
Of mine old hurt yet feel the wound but green.
Rue on my life; or else your cruel wrong
Shall well appear, and by my death be seen!

DESCRIPTION OF SPRING, WHEREIN EACH THING RENEWS, SAVE ONLY THE LOVER

The soote[3] season that bud and bloom forth brings
With green hath clad the hill and eke the vale;
The nightingale with feathers new she sings;
The turtle to her make[4] hath told her tale:

[1] complain [2] grief [3] sweet [4] mate

Summer is come, for every spray now springs;
The hart hath hung his old head on the pale;
The buck in brake his winter cote he flings;
The fishes flete[1] with new repaired scale;
The adder all her slough away she slings;
The swift swallow pursueth the flies smale;
The busy bee her honey now she mings.[2]
Winter is worn, that was the flowers' bale:
And thus I see among these pleasant things
Each care decays, and yet my sorrow springs!

COMPLAINT OF A LOVER REBUKED

Love, that liveth and reigneth in my thought,
That built his seat within my captive breast,
Clad in the arms wherein with me he fought,
Oft in my face he doth his banner rest.
She that me taught to love and suffer pain,
My doubtful hope and eke my hot desire
With shamefast cloak to shadow and refrain,
Her smiling grace converteth straight to ire.
The coward Love then to the heart apace
Taketh his flight, whereas he lurks and plains,[3]
His purpose lost, and dare not show his face.
For my lord's guilt thus faultless bide I pains.
Yet from my lord shall not my foot remove;
Sweet is his death that takes his end by love.

DESCRIPTION AND PRAISE OF HIS LOVE GERALDINE

From Tuscan came my lady's worthy race;
Fair Florence was sometime her ancient seat;
The Western isle whose pleasant shore doth face
Wild Camber's cliffs did give her lively heat;
Fostered she was with milk of Irish breast;
Her sire, an earl; her dame, of princes' blood;
From tender years in Britain she doth rest,
With a king's child, where she tasteth costly food;
Hunsdon did first present her to mine eyes;
Bright is her hue, and Geraldine she hight;[4]
Hampton me taught to wish her first for mine;
And Windsor, alas, doth chase me from her sight:
Her beauty of kind,[5] her virtues from above.
Happy is he, that can obtain her love!

THE MEANS TO ATTAIN HAPPY LIFE

Martial, the things that do attain
The happy life be these, I find:
The riches left, not got with pain;
The fruitful ground; the quiet mind;

[1] float [2] mixes [3] laments [4] is named [5] from nature

The egall[1] friend; no grudge, no strife;
No charge of rule, no governance;
Without disease, the healthful life;
The household of continuance;
The mean[2] diet, no delicate fare;
True wisdom joined with simpleness;
The night discharged of all care,
Where wine the wit may not oppress;
The faithful wife, without debate;
Such sleeps as may beguile the night:
Contented with thine own estate,
Ne wish for death, ne fear his might.

OF THE DEATH OF SIR T. W.

Resteth here, that quick could never rest;
Whose heavenly gifts, encreased by disdain,
And virtue sank the deeper in his breast;
Such profit he by envy could obtain.
A head where wisdom mysteries did frame;
Whose hammers beat still in that lively brain
As on a stithe[3] where that some work of fame
Was daily wrought to turn to Britain's gain.
A visage stern and mild; where both did grow,
Vice to condemn, in virtue to rejoice;
Amid great storms, whom grace assured so
To live upright and smile at fortune's choice.
A hand that taught what might be said in rhyme;
That reft[4] Chaucer the glory of his wit:
A mark, the which (unperfected, for time)
Some may approach, but never none shall hit.
A tongue that served in foreign realms his king;
Whose courteous talk to virtue did enflame
Each noble heart; a worthy guide to bring
Our English youth by travail unto fame.
An eye whose judgment none affect[5] could blind,
Friends to allure, and foes to reconcile;
Whose piercing look did represent a mind
With virtue fraught, reposed, void of guile.
A heart where dread was never so impressed,
To hide the thought that might the truth advance;
In neither fortune lost, nor yet repressed,
To swell in wealth, or yield unto mischance.
A valiant corse, where force and beauty met;
Happy, alas, too happy, but for foes!
Lived, and ran the race, that Nature set:
Of manhood's shape, where she the mold did lose.
But to the heavens that simple soul is fled,
Which left with such as covet Christ to know
Witness of faith that never shall be dead,
Sent for our health, but not received so.

[1] equal [2] moderate [3] anvil [4] bereft [5] affection

Thus, for our guilt, this jewel have we lost;
The earth his bones, the heavens possess his ghost!

VIRGIL'S ÆNEID

BOOK II

They whisted[1] all, with fixed face attent,
When Prince Æneas from the royal seat
Thus 'gan to speak: "O Queen, it is thy will
I should renew a woe cannot be told;
How that the Greeks did spoil and overthrow
The Phrygian wealth and wailful[2] realm of Troy.
Those ruthful things that I myself beheld,
And whereof no small part fell to my share;
Which to express, who could refrain from tears?
What Myrmidon? or yet what Dolopes?
What stern Ulysses' waged soldier?
And lo! moist night now from the welkin falls,
And stars declining counsel us to rest;
But since so great is thy delight to hear
Of our mishaps and Troyës last decay,
Though to record the same my mind abhors
And plaint eschews, yet thus will I begin: —
The Greekës chieftains, all irked with the war,
Wherein they wasted had so many years,
And oft repulsed by fatal destiny,
A huge horse made, high raised like a hill,
By the divine science of Minerva, —
Of cloven fir compacted were his ribs, —
For their return a feigned sacrifice, —
The fame whereof so wandered it at point.
In the dark bulk they closed bodies of men
Chosen by lot, and did enstuff by stealth
The hollow womb with armed soldiers.
There stands in sight an isle hight Tenedon,
Rich and of fame while Priam's kingdom stood,
Now but a bay and road unsure for ship.
Hither them secretly the Greeks withdrew,
Shrouding themselves under the desert shore;
And, weening we they had been fled and gone,
And with that wind had fet[3] the land of Greece,
Troy discharged her long continued dole.[4]
The gates cast up, we issued out to play,
The Greekish camp desirous to behold,
The places void and the forsaken coasts.
Here Pyrrhus' band, there fierce Achilles pight;[5]
Here rode their ships, there did their battles join.
Astonied some the scathful[6] gift beheld,
Behight[7] by vow unto the chaste Minerve, —
All wondering at the hugeness of the horse.
And first of all Timœtes gan advise
Within the walls to lead and draw the same,
And place it eke amid the palace court, —
Whether of guile, or Troyës fate it would.
Capys, with some of judgment more discreet,
Willed it to drown, or underset with flame,
The suspect present of the Greek's deceit,
Or bore and gauge the hollow caves uncouth;
So diverse ran the giddy people's mind.
Lo! foremost of a rout that followed him,
Kindled Laöcoön hasted from the tower,
Crying far off: 'O wretched citizens,
What so great kind of frenzy freteth you?
Deem ye the Greeks, our enemies, to be gone?
Or any Greekish gifts can you suppose
Devoid of guile? Is so Ulysses known?
Either the Greeks are in this timber hid,
Or this an engine is to annoy our walls,
To view our towers, and overwhelm our town.
Here lurks some craft. Good Troyans give no trust
Unto this horse, for, whatsoever it be,
I dread the Greeks, yea when they offer gifts.'"

* * * * * * *

[1] became silent [2] lamentable [3] fetched, reached [4] sorrow [5] camped, *tendebat* [6] harmful [7] promised

GEORGE GASCOIGNE (1525?–1577)

THE STEEL GLASS

EPILOGUS

Alas, my lord, my haste was all too hot,
I shut my glass before you gazed your fill,
And, at a glimpse, my silly self have spied
A stranger troop than any yet were seen.
Behold, my lord, what monsters muster here,
With angel's face, and harmful hellish hearts,
With smiling looks, and deep deceitful thoughts,
With tender skins, and stony cruel minds,
With stealing steps, yet forward feet to fraud.
Behold, behold, they never stand content,
With God, with kind, with any help of art,
But curl their locks with bodkins and with braids,
But dye their hair with sundry subtle sleights,
But paint and slick till fairest face be foul,
But bumbast, bolster, frizzle, and perfume.
They mar with musk the balm which nature made
And dig for death in delicatest dishes.
The younger sort come piping on apace,
In whistles made of fine enticing wood,
Till they have caught the birds for whom they birded.
The elder sort go stately stalking on,
And on their backs they bear both land and fee,
Castles and towers, revenues and receipts,
Lordships and manors, fines, yea, farms and all.
What should these be? Speak you, my lovely lord.

They be not men: for why? they have no beards.
They be no boys, which wear such side[1] long gowns.
They be no gods, for all their gallant gloss.
They be no devils, I trow, which seem so saintish.
What be they? women? masking in men's weeds?
With Dutchkin doublets, and with jerkins jagged?
With Spanish spangs,[2] and ruffs fetched out of
France,
With high-copped[3] hats, and feathers flaunt-a-flaunt?
They be so sure, even *wo* to *men* indeed.
Nay then, my lord, let shut the glass apace,
High time it were for my poor muse to wink,[4]
Since all the hands, all paper, pen, and ink,
Which ever yet this wretched world possessed,
Cannot describe this sex in colors due!
No, no, my lord, we gazed have enough;
And I too much, God pardon me therefor.
Better look off, than look an ace too far;
And better mum, than meddle overmuch.
But if my glass do like[5] my lovely lord,
We will espy, some sunny summer's day,
To look again, and see some seemly sights.
Meanwhile, my muse right humbly doth beseech,
That my good lord accept this vent'rous verse,
Until my brains may better stuff devise.

THOMAS SACKVILLE, LORD BUCKHURST (1536–1608)

THE MIRROR FOR MAGISTRATES

From THE INDUCTION

Whereby I knew that she a goddess was,
And therewithal resorted to my mind
My thought, that late presented me the glass
Of brittle state, of cares that here we find,
Of thousand woes to silly men assigned;
And how she now bid me come and behold,
To see with eye that erst in thought I rolled.

Flat down I fell, and with all reverence
Adored her, perceiving now that she,
A goddess sent by godly providence,
In earthly shape thus showed herself to me,
To wail and rue this world's uncertainty:
And while I honored thus her god-head's might,
With plaining voice these words to me she shright:[6]

"I shall thee guide first to the griesly[7] lake,
And thence unto the blissful place of rest,
Where thou shalt see and hear the plaint they make,
That whilom here bare swing[8] among the best.
This shalt thou see, but great is the unrest
That thou must bide before thou canst attain
Unto the dreadful place where these remain.

And with these words as I upraised stood,
And 'gan to follow her that straightforth paced,
Ere I was ware, into a desert wood
We now were come; where, hand in hand embraced,
She led the way, and through the thick so
traced,
As, but I had been guided by her might,
It was no way for any mortal wight.

But lo! while thus, amid the desert dark,
We passed on with steps and pace unmeet,
A rumbling roar, confused with howl and bark
Of dogs, shook all the ground under our feet,
And struck the din within our ears so deep,
As half distraught unto the ground I fell,
Besought return, and not to visit hell.

But she forth-with uplifting me apace
Removed my dread, and with a steadfast mind
Bade me come on, for here was now the place,
The place where we our travel's end should find.
Wherewith I arose, and to the place assigned
Astonied I stalk; when straight we approached
near
The dreadful place, that you will dread to hear.

An hideous hole all vast, withouten shape,
Of endless depth, o'erwhelmed with ragged stone,
With ugly mouth, and griesly jaws doth gape,
And to our sight confounds itself in one.
Here entered we, and yeding[1] forth, anon
An horrible lothly lake we might discern
As black as pitch, that cleped[2] is Averne.

A deadly gulf where nought but rubbish grows,
With foul black swelth[3] in thickened lumps that
lies,
Which up in the air such stinking vapours throws,
That over there may fly no fowl but dies,
Choked with the pestilent savours that arise.
Hither we come, whence forth we still did pace,
In dreadful fear amid the dreadful place.

And first within the porch and jaws of Hell
Sat deep Remorse of Conscience, all besprent
With tears: and to herself oft would she tell
Her wretchedness, and cursing never stent[4]
To sob and sigh; but ever thus lament
With thoughful care, as she that all in vain
Would wear and waste continually in pain.

[1] wide [2] spangles [3] high-topped [4] close the eyes [5] please [6] shrieked [7] dreadful [8] bore sway

[1] going [2] called [3] scum [4] cease

Her eyes unsteadfast, rolling here and there,
Whirled on each place, as place that vengeance brought,
So was her mind continually in fear,
Tossed and tormented with the tedious thought
Of those detested crimes which she had wrought;
With dreadful cheer and looks thrown to the sky,
Wishing for death, and yet she could not die. 231

Next saw we Dread, all trembling how he shook,
With foot uncertain proferred here and there;
Benumbed of speech, and with a ghastly look
Searched every place all pale and dead for fear,
His cap borne up with staring [1] of his hair,
Stoynd [2] and amazed at his own shade for dread,
And fearing greater dangers than was need. 238

And next within the entry of this lake
Sat fell Revenge, gnashing her teeth for ire,
Devising means how she may vengeance take,
Never in rest till she have her desire;
But frets within so farforth [3] with the fire
Of wreaking flames, that now determines she
To die by Death, or venged by Death to be. 245

When fell Revenge with bloody foul pretence
Had shown herself as next in order set,
With trembling limbs we softly parted thence,
Till in our eyes another sigh we met:
When from my heart a sight forthwith I fet,[4]
Rueing, alas! upon the woeful plight
Of Misery, that next appeared in sight. 252

His face was lean, and somewhat pined away,
And eke his hands consumed to the bone,
And what his body was I cannot say,
For on his carcass raiment had he none
Save clouts and patches, pieced one by one.
With staff in hand, and scrip on shoulders cast,
His chief defence against the winter's blast. 259

His food, for most,[5] was wild fruits of the trees,
Unless sometime some crumbs fell to his share,
Which in his wallet long, God wot, kept he.
As on the which full daintily would he fare;
His drink the running stream, his cup the bare
Of his palm closed, his bed the hard cold ground.
To this poor life was Misery y-bound. 266

Whose wretched state when we had well beheld
With tender ruth on him and on his feres [6]
In thoughtful cares, forth then our pace we held.
And by and by, another shape appears
Of greedy Care, still brushing up the breres,[7]

[1] standing on end [2] astounded [3] excessively
[4] fetched [5] chiefly [6] companions [7] briars

His knuckles knobbed, his flesh deep dented in,
With tawed hands, and hard y-tanned skin. 273

The morrow gray no sooner hath begun
To spread his light, even peeping in our eyes,
When he is up and to his work y-run;
But let the night's black misty mantels rise,
And with foul dark never so much disguise
The fair bright day, yet ceaseth he no while,
But hath his candles to prolong his toil. 280

By him lay heavy Sleep, the cousin of Death
Flat on the ground, and still as any stone,
A very corpse, save yielding forth a breath.
Small keep [1] took he whom Fortune frowned on
Or whom she lifted up into the throne
Of high renown; but as a living death,
So dead alive, of life he drew the breath. 287

The body's rest, the quiet of the heart,
The travail's ease, the still night's fear was he.
And of our life in earth the better part,
Reaver of sight, and yet in whom we see
Things oft that tide,[2] and oft that never be.
Without respect esteeming equally
King Cresus' pomp, and Irus' poverty. 294

And next in order sad Old Age we found,
His beard all hoar, his eyes hollow and blind,
With drooping cheer still poring on the ground,
As on the place where nature him assigned
To rest, when that the Sisters had untwined
His vital thread, and ended with their knife
The fleeting course of fast declining life. 301

There heard we him with broken and hollow plaint
Rue with himself his end approaching fast,
And all for nought his wretched mind torment
With sweet remembrance of his pleasures past,
And fresh delights of lusty youth forwast.[3]
Recounting which, how would he sob and shriek,
And to be young again of Jove beseek![4] 308

But and [5] the cruel fates so fixed be
That time forepast cannot return again,
This one request of Jove yet prayed he:
That in such withered plight, and wretched pain
As Eld, accompanied with his lothsome train,
Had brought on him, all were it woe and grief,
He might a while yet linger forth his life, 315

And not so soon descend into the pit,
Where Death, when he the mortal corps hath slain,

[1] heed [2] happen [3] wasted away [4] beseech [5] if

With retchless [1] hand in grave doth cover it,
Thereafter never to enjoy again
The gladsome light, but, in the ground y-lain,
In depth of darkness waste and wear to nought,
As he had never into the world been brought.

But who had seen him, sobbing how he stood
Unto himself, and how he would bemoan
His youth forepast, as though it wrought him good
To talk of youth, all were his youth foregone,
He would have mused, and marvelled much whereon
This wretched Age should life desire so fain,
And knows full well life doth but length his pain.

Crookbacked he was, toothshaken, and blear-eyed,
Went on three feet, and sometime crept on four,
With old lame bones, that rattled by his side,
His scalp all piled [2] and he with elde forlore; [3]
His withered fist still knocking at death's door,
Fumbling and drivelling as he draws his breath,
For brief, the shape and messenger of Death.

And fast by him pale Malady was placed,
Sore sick in bed, her colour all foregone,
Bereft of stomach, savour, and of taste,
Ne could she brook no meat but broths alone.
Her breath corrupt, her keepers every one
Abhorring her, her sickness past recure, [4]
Detesting physic and all physic's cure.

But oh! the doleful sight that then we see;
We turned our look, and on the other side
A griesly [5] shape of Famine mought we see,
With greedy looks, and gaping mouth that cried,
And roared for meat as she should there have died;
Her body thin and bare as any bone,
Whereto was left nought but the case alone.

And that, alas! was gnawen on everywhere,
All full of holes, that I ne mought refrain
From tears, to see how she her arms could tear,
And with her teeth gnash on the bones in vain;
When all for nought she fain would so sustain
Her starved corse, that rather seemed a shade
Than any substance of a creature made.

Great was her force, whom stone wall could not stay,
Her tearing nails snatching at all she saw;
With gaping jaws, that by no means y-may
Be satisfied from hunger of her maw,
But eats herself as she that hath no law;
Gnawing, alas! her carcass all in vain,
Where you may count each sinew, bone, and vein.

[1] careless [2] bare [3] worn with age [4] recovery [5] terrible

On her while we thus firmly fixed our eyes,
That bled for ruth of such a dreary sight,
Lo, suddenly she shryght [1] in so huge wise,
As made hell-gates to shiver with the might.
Wherewith a dart we saw, how it did light
Right on her breast, and therewithal pale Death
Enthrilling [2] it, to reave her of her breath.

And by and by a dumb dead corpse we saw,
Heavy and cold, the shape of Death aright,
That daunts all earthly creatures to his law:
Against whose force in vain it is to fight.
Ne peers, ne princes, nor no mortal wight,
Ne towns, ne realms, cities, ne strongest tower,
But all perforce must yield unto his power.

His dart anon out of the corpse he took,
And in his hand (a dreadful sight to see)
With great triumph eftsoons the same he shook,
That most of all my fears affrayed me.
His body dight with nought but bones, perdie,
The naked shape of man there saw I plain,
All save the flesh, the sinew, and the vein.

Lastly stood War, in glittering arms y-clad,
With visage grim, stern looks, and blackly hued;
In his right hand a naked sword he had,
That to the hilts was all with blood embrued:
And in his left (that kings and kingdoms rued)
Famine and fire he held, and therewithal
He razed towns, and threw down towers and all.

Cities he sacked, and realms, that whilom flowered
In honour, glory, and rule above the best,
He overwhelmed, and all their fame devoured,
Consumed, destroyed, wasted, and never ceased,
Till he their wealth, their name, and all oppressed.
His face forhewed [3] with wounds, and by his side
There hung his targe [4] with gashes deep and wide.

GILES FLETCHER THE ELDER
(1549?–1611)

LICIA

SONNET XLVII

Like Memnon's rock, touched with the rising sun,
  Which yields a sound, and echoes forth a voice;
But, when it's drowned in western seas, is dumb,
  And, drowsy-like, leaves off to make a noise:
So I, my love! enlightened with your shine,
  A Poet's skill within my soul I shroud!
Not rude, like that which finer wits decline,
  But such as Muses to the best allowed!

[1] shrieked [2] thrusting in [3] hewed to pieces [4] shield

But when your figure and your shape is gone,
  I speechless am! like as I was before;
Or, if I write, my verse is filled with moan,
  And blurred with tears, by falling in such store.
Then, muse not, Licia! if my Muse be slack;
For when I wrote, I did thy beauty lack!

From an Ode

"False!" She said, "how can it be,
To court another, yet love me?
Crowns and Love no partners brook;
If she be liked, I am forsook.
Farewell, False, and love her still!
Your chance was good, but mine was ill.
No harm to you but this I crave
That your new Love may you deceive,
And jest with you as you have done;
  For light's the love that's quickly won."
"Kind and fair Sweet, once believe me!
Jest I did, but not to grieve thee;
Words and sighs and what I spent
In show to her, to you were meant.
Fond I was, your love to cross, —
Jesting love oft brings this loss!
Forget this fault! and love your friend,
Which vows his truth unto the end!"
"Content," She said, "if this you keep!"
  Thus both did kiss, and both did weep.

SIR EDWARD DYER (1550?–1607)

MY MIND TO ME A KINGDOM IS

My mind to me a kingdom is,
  Such present joys therein I find
That it excels all other bliss
  That earth affords or grows by kind:
Though much I want which most would have,
Yet still my mind forbids to crave.

No princely pomp, no wealthy store,
  No force to win the victory,
No wily wit to salve a sore,
  No shape to feed a loving eye;
To none of these I yield as thrall:
For why? My mind doth serve for all.

I see how plenty [surfeits] oft,
  And hasty climbers soon do fall;
I see that those which are aloft
  Mishap doth threaten most of all;
They get with toil, they keep with fear:
Such cares my mind could never bear.

Content to live, this is my stay;
  I seek no more than may suffice;
I press to bear no haughty sway;
  Look, what I lack my mind supplies:
Lo, thus I triumph like a king,
Content with that my mind doth bring.

Some have too much, yet still do crave;
  I little have, and seek no more.
They are but poor, though much they have,
  And I am rich with little store:
They poor, I rich; they beg, I give;
They lack, I leave; they pine, I live.

I laugh not at another's loss;
  I grudge not at another's pain;
No worldly waves my mind can toss;
  My state at one doth still remain:
I fear no foe, I fawn no friend;
I loathe not life, nor dread my end.

Some weigh their pleasure by their lust,
  Their wisdom by their rage of will;
Their treasure is their only trust;
  A cloaked craft their store of skill:
But all the pleasure that I find
Is to maintain a quiet mind.

My wealth is health and perfect ease;
  My conscience clear my chief defence;
I neither seek by bribes to please,
  Nor by deceit to breed offence:
Thus do I live; thus will I die;
Would all did so as well as I!

SIR WALTER RALEIGH (1552?–1618)

THE SILENT LOVER

I

Passions are liken'd best to floods and streams:
  The shallow murmur, but the deep are dumb.
So, when affection yields discourse, it seems
  The bottom is but shallow whence they come.
They that are rich in words, in words discover
That they are poor in that which makes a lover.

II

Wrong not, sweet empress of my heart,
  The merit of true passion,
With thinking that he feels no smart,
  That sues for no compassion.

Silence in love bewrays more woe
  Than words, though ne'er so witty:
A beggar that is dumb, you know,
  May challenge double pity.

Then wrong not, dearest to my heart,
My true, though secret passion;
He smarteth most that hides his smart,
And sues for no compassion.

HIS PILGRIMAGE

Give me my scallop-shell of quiet,
My staff of faith to walk upon,
My scrip of joy, immortal diet,
My bottle of salvation,
My gown of glory, hope's true gage;
And thus I'll take my pilgrimage.

Blood must be my body's balmer;
No other balm will there be given;
Whilst my soul, like a quiet palmer,
Travelleth towards the land of heaven,
Over the silver mountains,
Where spring the nectar fountains.
There will I kiss
The bowl of bliss;
And drink mine everlasting fill
Upon every milken hill.
My soul will be a-dry before;
But, after, it will thirst no more.

Then by that happy blissful day
More peaceful pilgrims I shall see,
That have cast off their rags of clay,
And walk apparelled fresh like me.
I'll take them first,
To quench their thirst
And taste of nectar suckets,
At those clear wells
Where sweetness dwells,
Drawn up by saints in crystal buckets.

And when our bottles and all we
Are filled with immortality,
Then the blessèd paths we'll travel,
Strowed with rubies thick as gravel;
Ceilings of diamonds, sapphire floors,
High walls of coral, and pearly bowers.

From thence to Heaven's bribeless hall,
Where no corrupted voices brawl;
No conscience molten into gold;
No forged accuser bought or sold;
No cause deferred, no vain-spent journey,
For there Christ is the King's Attorney,
Who pleads for all, without degrees,
And he hath angels but no fees.
And when the grand twelve million jury
Of our sins, with direful fury,
Against our souls black verdicts give,
Christ pleads his death; and then we live.

Be Thou my speaker, taintless Pleader!
Unblotted Lawyer! true Proceeder!
Thou giv'st salvation, even for alms,
Not with a bribèd lawyer's palms.

And this is mine eternal plea
To Him that made heaven and earth and sea:
That, since my flesh must die so soon,
And want a head to dine next noon,
Just at the stroke, when my veins start and spread,
Set on my soul an everlasting head!

Then am I ready, like a palmer fit,
To tread those blest paths; which before I writ.

THE CONCLUSION

Even such is time, that takes in trust
Our youth, our joys, our all we have,
And pays us but with earth and dust;
Who in the dark and silent grave,
When we have wander'd all our ways,
Shuts up the story of our days:
But from this earth, this grave, this dust,
My God shall raise me up, I trust.

(This was written the night before Sir Walter Raleigh was beheaded)

THE RENAISSANCE

EDMUND SPENSER (1552?–1599)

AMORETTI

VIII

More than most fair, full of the living fire
Kindled above unto the Maker near;
No eyes but joys, in which all powers conspire
That to the world naught else be counted dear;
Through your bright beams doth not the blinded guest
Shoot out his darts to base affections wound;
But angels come to lead frail minds to rest
In chaste desires, on heavenly beauty bound.
You frame my thoughts, and fashion me within;
You stop my tongue, and teach my heart to speak;
You calm the storm that passion did begin,
Strong through your cause, but by your virtue weak.
  Dark is the world, where your light shined never;
  Well is he born that may behold you ever.

XXIV

Like as a ship, that through the ocean wide,
By conduct of some star doth make her way,
Whenas a storm hath dimmed her trusty guide,
Out of her course doth wander far astray;
So I, whose star, that wont with her bright ray
Me to direct, with clouds is overcast,
Do wander now, in darkness and dismay,
Through hidden perils round about me placed;
Yet hope I well that, when this storm is past,
My Helicë, the lodestar of my life,
Will shine again, and look on me at last,
With lovely light to clear my cloudy grief:
  Till then I wander careful, comfortless,
  In secret sorrow, and sad pensiveness.

LXX

Fresh Spring, the herald of love's mighty king,
In whose coat-armour richly are displayed
All sorts of flowers the which on earth do spring
In goodly colours gloriously arrayed;
Go to my love, where she is careless laid,
Yet in her winter's bower not well awake;
Tell her the joyous time will not be stayed,
Unless she do him by the forelock take;
Bid her therefore herself soon ready make
To wait on Love amongst his lovely crew;
Where everyone that misseth then her make [1]
Shall be by him amerced with penance due.
  Make haste, therefore, sweet love, whilst it is prime;
  For none can call again the passed time.

LXXIX

Men call you fair, and you do credit it,
For that yourself ye daily such do see:
But the true fair, that is the gentle wit
And virtuous mind, is much more praised of me:
For all the rest, however fair it be,
Shall turn to nought and lose that glorious hue;
But only that is permanent and free
From frail corruption that doth flesh ensue.
That is true beauty; that doth argue you
To be divine, and born of heavenly seed;
Derived from that fair Spirit from whom all true
And perfect beauty did at first proceed:
  He only fair, and what he fair hath made;
  All other fair, like flowers, untimely fade.

PROTHALAMION

Calm was the day, and through the trembling air
Sweet, breathing Zephyrus did softly play
A gentle spirit, that lightly did delay
Hot Titan's beams, which then did glister fair;
When I (whom sullen care,
Through discontent of my long fruitless stay
In princes' court, and expectation vain
Of idle hopes, which still do fly away,
Like empty shadows, did afflict my brain)
Walked forth to ease my pain
Along the shore of silver streaming Thames;
Whose rutty [2] bank, the which his river hems,
Was painted all with variable flowers,
And all the meads adorned with dainty gems
Fit to deck maidens' bowers,
And crown their paramours
Against the bridal day, which is not long:
  Sweet Thames! run softly, till I end my song.

[1] mate [2] rooty

There, in a meadow, by the river's side,
A flock of nymphs I chanced to espy,
All lovely daughters of the flood thereby,
With goodly greenish locks, all loose untied,
As each had been a bride:
And each one had a little wicker basket,
Made of fine twigs, entrailed curiously,
In which they gathered flowers to fill their flasket,
And with fine fingers cropt full feateously [1]
The tender stalks on high.
Of every sort, which in that meadow grew,
They gathered some; the violet, pallid blue,
The little daisy, that at evening closes,
The virgin lily, and the primrose true,
With store of vermeil roses,
To deck their bridegroom's posies
Against the bridal day, which was not long:
Sweet Thames! run softly, till I end my song.

With that I saw two swans of goodly hue
Come softly swimming down along the Lee;
Two fairer birds I yet did never see;
The snow, which doth the top of Pindus strew,
Did never whiter shew,
Nor Jove himself, when he a swan would be
For love of Leda, whiter did appear;
Yet Leda was, they say, as white as he,
Yet not so white as these, nor nothing near;
So purely white they were,
That even the gentle stream, the which them bare,
Seemed foul to them, and bade his billows spare
To wet their silken feathers, lest they might
Soil their fair plumes with water not so fair,
And mar their beauties bright,
That shone as heaven's light,
Against their bridal day, which was not long:
Sweet Thames! run softly, till I end my song.

Eftsoons the nymphs, which now had flowers their fill,
Ran all in haste to see that silver brood,
As they came floating on the crystal flood;
Whom when they saw, they stood amazed still,
Their wondering eyes to fill;
Them seemed they never saw a sight so fair
Of fowls so lovely, that they sure did deem
Them heavenly born, or to be that same pair
Which through the sky draw Venus' silver team;
For sure they did not seem
To be begot of any earthly seed,
But rather angels, or of angels' breed;
Yet were they bred of summer's heat, they say,
In sweetest season, when each flower and weed
The earth did fresh array;
So fresh they seemed as day,
Even as their bridal day, which was not long:
Sweet Thames! run softly, till I end my song.

Then forth they all out of their baskets drew
Great store of flowers, the honour of the field,
That to the sense did fragrant odours yield,
All which upon those goodly birds they threw
And all the waves did strew,
That like old Peneus' waters they did seem,
When down along by pleasant Tempe's shore,
Scattered with flowers, through Thessaly they stream,
That they appear, through lilies' plenteous store,
Like a bride's chamber floor.
Two of those nymphs meanwhile, two garlands bound
Of freshest flowers which in that mead they found,
The which presenting all in trim array,
Their snowy foreheads therewithal they crowned,
Whilst one did sing this lay,
Prepared against that day,
Against their bridal day, which was not long:
Sweet Thames! run softly, till I end my song.

"Ye gentle birds! the world's fair ornament,
And heaven's glory whom this happy hour
Doth lead unto your lover's blissful bower,
Joy may you have, and gentle hearts' content
Of your love's couplement;
And let fair Venus, that is queen of love,
With her heart-quelling son upon you smile,
Whose smile, they say, hath virtue to remove
All love's dislike, and friendship's faulty guile
For ever to assoil;
Let endless peace your steadfast hearts accord,
And blessed plenty wait upon your board;
And let your bed with pleasures chaste abound,
That fruitful issue may to you afford,
Which may your foes confound,
And make your joys redound
Upon your bridal day, which is not long:"
Sweet Thames! run softly, till I end my song.

So ended she: and all the rest around
To her redoubled that her undersong,
Which said their bridal day should not be long:
And gentle Echo from the neighbour ground
Their accents did resound.
So forth those joyous birds did pass along,
Adown the Lee, that to them murmured low,
As he would speak, but that he lacked a tongue,
Yet did by signs his glad affection show,
Making his stream run slow.
And all the fowl which in his flood did dwell
'Gan flock about these twain, that did excel

[1] neatly

The rest, so far as Cynthia doth shend[1]
The lesser stars. So they, enranged well,
Did on those two attend,
And their best service lend
Against their wedding day, which was not long:
Sweet Thames! run softly, till I end my song.

At length they all to merry London came,
To merry London, my most kindly nurse,
That to me gave this life's first native source;
Though from another place I take my name,
An house of ancient fame:
There when they came, whereas[2] those bricky towers
The which on Thames' broad, aged back do ride,
Where now the studious lawyers have their bowers,
There whilom wont the Templar Knights to bide,
Till they decayed through pride:
Next whereunto there stands a stately place,
Where oft I gained gifts and goodly grace
Of that great lord, which therein wont to dwell,
Whose want too well now feels my friendless case;
But ah! here fits not well
Old woes, but joys, to tell
Against the bridal day, which is not long:
Sweet Thames! run softly, till I end my song.

Yet therein now doth lodge a noble peer,
Great England's glory, and the world's wide wonder,
Whose dreadful name late through all Spain did thunder,
And Hercules' two pillars standing near
Did make to quake and fear:
Fair branch of honour, flower of chivalry!
That fillest England with thy triumph's fame,
Joy have thou of thy noble victory,
And endless happiness of thine own name,
That promiseth the same;
That through thy prowess, and victorious arms,
Thy country may be freed from foreign harms;
And great Elisa's glorious name may ring
Through all the world, filled with thy wide alarms,
Which some brave muse may sing
To ages following,
Upon the bridal day, which is not long:
Sweet Thames! run softly, till I end my song.

From those high towers this noble lord issuing,
Like radiant Hesper, when his golden hair
In th' ocean billows he hath bathed fair,
Descended to the river's open viewing,
With a great train ensuing.
Above the rest were goodly to be seen

[1] shame [2] where

Two gentle knights of lovely face and feature
Beseeming well the bower of any queen,
With gifts of wit, and ornaments of nature,
Fit for so goodly stature,
That like the twins of Jove they seemed in sight,
Which deck the baldrick of the heavens bright;
They two, forth pacing to the river's side,
Received those two fair brides, their love's delight;
Which, at th' appointed tide,
Each one did make his bride
Against their bridal day, which is not long:
Sweet Thames! run softly, till I end my song.

From AN EPITHALAMION

Ye learned sisters, which have oftentimes
Been to me aiding, others to adorn,
Whom ye thought worthy of your graceful rimes,
That even the greatest did not greatly scorn
To hear their names sung in your simple lays,
But joyed in their praise;
And when ye list your own mishaps to mourn,
Which Death, or Love, or Fortune's wreck did raise,
Your string could soon to sadder tenor turn,
And teach the woods and waters to lament
Your doleful dreariment:
Now lay those sorrowful complaints aside;
And, having all your heads with garlands crowned,
Help me mine own love's praises to resound;
Ne let the same of any be envied;
So Orpheus did for his own bride!
So I unto myself alone will sing;
The woods shall to me answer, and my echo ring.

Early, before the world's light-giving lamp
His golden beam upon the hills doth spread,
Having dispersed the night's uncheerful damp
Do ye awake, and, with fresh lustihed,[1]
Go to the bower of my beloved love,
My truest turtle dove;
Bid her awake; for Hymen is awake,
And long since ready forth his mask to move,
With his bright tead[2] that flames with many a flake,
And many a bachelor to wait on him,
In their fresh garments trim,
Bid her awake therefore, and soon her dight,
For lo! the wished day is come at last,
That shall, for all the pains and sorrows past,
Pay to her usury of long delight:
And, whilst she doth her dight,
Do ye to her of joy and solace sing,
That all the woods may answer, and your echo ring.

[1] lustiness [2] torch

Bring with you all the nymphs that you can hear,
Both of the rivers and the forests green,
And of the sea that neighbours to her near,
All with gay garlands goodly well beseen.
And let them also with them bring in hand
Another gay garland,
For my fair love, of lilies and of roses,
Bound truelove wise with a blue silk riband;
And let them make great store of bridal posies,
And let them eke bring store of other flowers,
To deck the bridal bowers.
And let the ground whereas[1] her foot shall tread,
For fear the stones her tender foot should wrong,
Be strewed with fragrant flowers all along,
And diapered[2] like the discoloured[3] mead;
Which done, do at her chamber door await,
For she will waken straight;
The whiles do ye this song unto her sing,
The woods shall to you answer, and your echo ring.

* * * * * * *

Wake, now, my love, awake! for it is time;
The rosy morn long since left Tithon's bed,
All ready to her silver coach to climb;
And Phœbus gins to show his glorious head.
Hark, how the cheerful birds do chant their lays
And carol of love's praise.
The merry lark her matins sings aloft;
The thrush replies; the mavis descant plays;
The ouzel shrills; the ruddock warbles soft;
So goodly all agree, with sweet content,
To this day's merriment.
Ah! my dear love, why do ye sleep thus long,
When meeter were that ye should now awake,
T' await the coming of your joyous make,
And hearken to the birds' love-learned song,
The dewy leaves among!
For they of joy and pleasance to you sing,
That all the woods them answer, and their echo ring.

My love is now awake out of her dreams,
And her fair eyes, like stars that dimmed were
With darksome cloud, now show their goodly beams
More bright than Hesperus his head doth rear.
Come now, ye damsels, daughters of delight,
Help quickly her to dight:
But first come, ye fair hours, which were begot,
In Jove's sweet paradise of Day and Night;
Which do the seasons of the year allot,
And all that ever in this world is fair,
Do make and still repair:
And ye three handmaids of the Cyprian queen,
The which do still adorn her beauty's pride,
Help to adorn my beautifulest bride;
And as ye her array, still throw between
Some graces to be seen,
And, as ye use to Venus, to her sing,
The whiles the woods shall answer, and your echo ring.

* * * * * * *

Lo! where she comes along with portly pace,
Like Phœbe, from her chamber of the East,
Arising forth to run her mighty race,
Clad all in white, that seems a virgin best.
So well it her beseems, that ye would ween
Some angel she had been.
Her long loose yellow locks like golden wire,
Sprinkled with pearl, and pearling flowers atween,
Do like a golden mantle her attire;
And, being crowned with a garland green,
Seem like some maiden queen.
Her modest eyes, abashed to behold
So many gazers as on her do stare,
Upon the lowly ground affixed are;
Ne dare lift up her countenance too bold,
But blush to hear her praises sung so loud,
So far from being proud.
Nathless do ye still loud her praises sing,
That all the woods may answer, and your echo ring.

* * * * * * *

But if ye saw that which no eyes can see,
The inward beauty of her lively spright,[1]
Garnished with heavenly gifts of high degree,
Much more then would ye wonder at that sight,
And stand astonished like to those which read
Medusa's mazeful head.
There dwells sweet love, and constant chastity,
Unspotted faith, and comely womanhood,
Regard of honour, and mild modesty;
There virtue reigns as queen in royal throne,
And giveth laws alone,
The which the base affections do obey,
And yield their services unto her will;
Ne thought of thing uncomely ever may
Thereto approach to tempt her mind to ill.
Had ye once seen these her celestial treasures,
And unrevealed pleasures,
Then would ye wonder, and her praises sing,
That all the woods should answer, and your echo ring.

Open the temple gates unto my love,
Open them wide that she may enter in,
And all the posts adorn as doth behove,
And all the pillars deck with garlands trim,
For to receive this Saint with honour due,

[1] where [2] marked [3] vari-colored

[1] spirit

That cometh in to you.
With trembling steps, and humble reverence
She cometh in, before th' Almighty's view;
Of her ye virgins learn obedience,
When so ye come into those holy places,
To humble your proud faces:
Bring her up to th' high altar, that she may
The sacred ceremonies there partake,
The which do endless matrimony make;
And let the roaring organs loudly play
The praises of the Lord in lively notes;
The whiles, with hollow throats,
The choristers the joyous anthem sing,
That all the woods may answer, and their echo ring.

Behold, whiles she before the altar stands,
Hearing the holy priest that to her speaks,
And blesseth her with his two happy hands,
How the red roses flush up in her cheeks,
And the pure snow, with goodly vermeil stain,
Like crimson dyed in grain:
That even th' angels, which continually
About the sacred altar do remain,
Forget their service and about her fly,
Oft peeping in her face, that seems more fair,
The more they on it stare.
But her sad[1] eyes, still fastened on the ground,
Are governed with goodly modesty,
That suffers not one look to glance awry,
Which may let in a little thought unsound.
Why blush ye, love, to give to me your hand,
The pledge of all our band?
Sing, ye sweet angels, Alleluia sing,
That all the woods may answer, and your echo ring.

Now all is done: bring home the bride again;
Bring home the triumph of our victory:
Bring home with you the glory of her gain
With joyance bring her and with jollity.
Never had man more joyful day than this
Whom heaven would heap with bliss;
Make feast therefore now all this live-long day;
This day for ever to me holy is.
Pour out the wine without restraint or stay,
Pour not by cups, but by the bellyful,
Pour out to all that will,
And sprinkle all the posts and walls with wine,
That they may sweat, and drunken be withal.
Crown ye god Bacchus with a coronal,
And Hymen also crown with wreaths of vine;
And let the Graces dance unto the rest,
For they can do it best:
The whiles the maidens do their carol sing,
To which the woods shall answer, and their echo ring.

Ring ye the bells, ye young men of the town,
And leave your wonted labours for this day:
This day is holy; do ye write it down,
That ye forever it remember may;
This day the sun is in his chiefest height,
With Barnaby the bright,
From whence declining daily by degrees,
He somewhat loseth of his heat and light,
When once the Crab behind his back he sees.
But for this time it ill ordained was,
To choose the longest day in all the year,
And shortest night, when longest fitter were:
Yet never day so long, but late would pass.
Ring ye the bells, to make it wear away,
And bonfires make all day;
And dance about them, and about them sing,
That all the woods may answer, and your echo ring.

Ah! when will this long weary day have end,
And lend me leave to come unto my love?
How slowly do the hours their numbers spend!
How slowly does sad Time his feathers move!
Haste thee, O fairest planet, to thy home,
Within the western foam:
Thy tired steeds long since have need of rest.
Long though it be, at last I see it gloom,
And the bright evening-star with golden crest
Appear out of the East.
Fair child of beauty! glorious lamp of love!
That all the hosts of heaven in ranks dost lead,
And guidest lovers through the night's sad dread,
How cheerfully thou lookest from above,
And seem'st to laugh atween thy twinkling light,
As joying in the sight
Of these glad many, which for joy do sing,
That all the woods them answer, and their echo ring!

Now cease, ye damsels, your delights forepast;
Enough it is that all the day was yours:
Now day is done, and night is nighing fast,
Now bring the bride into the bridal bowers.
The night is come, now soon her disarray,
And in her bed her lay;
Lay her in lilies and in violets,
And silken curtains over her display,
And odoured sheets, and Arras coverlets.
Behold how goodly my fair love does lie,
In proud humility!
Like unto Maia, whenas Jove her took
In Tempe, lying on the flowery grass,

[1] serious

Twixt sleep and wake, after she weary was
With bathing in the Acidalian brook.
Now it is night, ye damsels may be gone,
And leave my love alone,
And leave likewise your former lay to sing:
The woods no more shall answer, nor your echo ring.

* * * * * * *

Song! made in lieu of many ornaments,
With which my love should duly have been decked,
Which cutting off through hasty accidents,
Ye would not stay your due time to expect,
But promised both to recompense;
Be unto her a goodly ornament,
And for short time an endless monument!

From AN HYMN IN HONOUR OF BEAUTY

What time this world's great Workmaster did cast
To make all things such as we now behold,
It seems that he before his eyes had placed
A goodly pattern, to whose perfect mould
He fashioned them as comely as he could,
That now so fair and seemly they appear
As nought may be amended anywhere.

That wondrous pattern, wheresoe'er it be,
Whether in earth laid up in secret store,
Or else in heaven, that no man may it see
With sinful eyes, for fear it to deflore,[1]
Is perfect Beauty, which all men adore;
Whose face and feature doth so much excel
All mortal sense, that none the same may tell.

Thereof as every earthly thing partakes
Or more or less, by influence divine,
So it more fair accordingly it makes,
And the gross matter of this earthly mine
Which clotheth it, thereafter doth refine,
Doing away the dross which dims the light
Of that fair beam which therein is empight.[2]

For, through infusion of celestial power,
The duller earth it quickeneth with delight,
And life-full spirits privily doth pour
Through all the parts, that to the looker's sight
They seem to please. That is thy sovereign might,
O Cyprian queen! which, flowing from the beam
Of thy bright star, thou into them dost stream.

That is the thing which giveth pleasant grace
To all things fair, that kindleth lively fire,
Light of thy lamp; which, shining in the face,
Thence to the soul darts amorous desire,
And robs the hearts of those which it admire;

[1] sully [2] placed

Therewith thou pointest thy son's poisoned arrow,
That wounds the life, and wastes the inmost marrow.

How vainly then do idle wits invent,
That beauty is nought else but mixture made
Of colours fair, and goodly temp'rament
Of pure complexions, that shall quickly fade
And pass away, like to a summer's shade;
Or that it is but comely composition
Of parts well measured, with meet disposition!

Hath white and red in it such wondrous power,
That it can pierce through th' eyes unto the heart,
And therein stir such rage and restless stour,[1]
As nought but death can stint his dolour's smart?
Or can proportion of the outward part
Move such affection in the inward mind,
That it can rob both sense, and reason blind?

Why do not then the blossoms of the field,
Which are arrayed with much more orient hue,
And to the sense most dainty odours yield,
Work like impression in the looker's view?
Or why do not fair pictures like power shew,
In which ofttimes we nature see of[2] art
Excelled in perfect limning every part?

But ah! believe me there is more than so,
That works such wonders in the minds of men;
I, that have often prov'd, too well it know,
And whoso list the like assays to ken,
Shall find by trial, and confess it then,
That Beauty is not, as fond men misdeem,
An outward show of things that only seem.

For that same goodly hue of white and red,
With which the cheeks are sprinkled, shall decay,
And those sweet rosy leaves, so fairly spread
Upon the lips, shall fade and fall away
To that they were, even to corrupted clay:
That golden wire, those sparkling stars so bright,
Shall turn to dust, and lose their goodly light.

But that fair lamp, from whose celestial ray
That light proceeds, which kindleth lovers' fire,
Shall never be extinguished nor decay;
But, when the vital spirits do expire,
Unto her native planet shall retire;
For it is heavenly born and cannot die,
Being a parcel of the purest sky.

* * * * * *

So every spirit, as it is most pure,
And hath in it the more of heavenly light,

[1] strife [2] by

So it the fairer body doth procure
To habit in, and it more fairly dight[1]
With cheerful grace and amiable sight;
For of the soul the body form doth take;
For soul is form, and doth the body make.

Therefore wherever that thou dost behold
A comely corps, with beauty fair endued,
Know this for certain, that the same doth hold
A beauteous soul, with fair conditions[2] thewed,
Fit to receive the seed of virtue strewed;
For all that fair is, is by nature good;
That is a sign to know the gentle blood.

Yet oft it falls that many a gentle mind
Dwells in deformed tabernacle drowned,
Either by chance, against the course of kind,
Or through unaptness in the substance found,
Which it assumed of some stubborn ground,
That will not yield unto her form's direction,
But is deformed with some foul imperfection.

And oft it falls, (ay me, the more to rue!)
That goodly beauty, albe heavenly born,
Is foul abused, and that celestial hue,
Which doth the world with her delight adorn,
Made but the bait of sin, and sinners' scorn,
Whilst every one doth seek and sue to have it,
But every one doth seek but to deprave it.

Yet nathemore[3] is that fair beauty's blame,
But theirs that do abuse it unto ill:
Nothing so good, but that through guilty shame
May be corrupt, and wrested unto will:
Natheless the soul is fair and beauteous still,
However flesh's fault it filthy make;
For things immortal no corruption take.

From AN HYMN OF HEAVENLY BEAUTY

The means, therefore, which unto us is lent
Him to behold, is on his works to look,
Which he hath made in beauty excellent,
And in the same, as in a brazen book,
To read enregistered in every nook
His goodness which his beauty doth declare;
For all that's good is beautiful and fair.

Thence gathering plumes of perfect speculation
To imp the wings of thy high-flying mind,
Mount up aloft through heavenly contemplation
From this dark world, whose damps the soul do blind,
And, like the native brood of eagle's kind,
On that bright Sun of Glory fix thine eyes,
Cleared from gross mists of frail infirmities.

Humbled with fear and awful reverence,
Before the footstool of his Majesty
Throw thyself down, with trembling innocence,
Ne dare look up with corruptible eye
On the dread face of that great Deity,
For fear, lest if he chance to look on thee,
Thou turn to nought, and quite confounded be.

But lowly fall before his mercy-seat,
Close covered with the Lamb's integrity
From the just wrath of his avengeful threat
That sits upon the righteous throne on high;
His throne is built upon Eternity,
More firm and durable than steel or brass,
Or the hard diamond, which them both doth pass.

His sceptre is the rod of Righteousness,
With which he bruiseth all his foes to dust
And the great Dragon strongly doth repress,
Under the rigour of his judgment just;
His seat is Truth, to which the faithful trust,
From whence proceed her beams so pure and bright
That all about him sheddeth glorious light.

* * * * * * *

Ah, then, my hungry soul! which long hast fed
On idle fancies of thy foolish thought,
And, with false beauty's flattering bait misled,
Hast after vain deceitful shadows sought,
Which all are fled, and now have left thee nought
But late repentance through thy follies' prief;[1]
Ah! cease to gaze on matter of thy grief:

And look at last up to that Sovereign Light,
From whose pure beams all perfect beauty springs,
That kindleth love in every godly spright,
Even the love of God; which loathing brings
Of this vile world and these gay-seeming things:
With whose sweet pleasures being so possessed,
Thy straying thoughts henceforth forever rest.

From THE SHEPHEARDS CALENDER

FEBRUARIE

Ægloga Secunda

Cuddie. Thenot

Cuddie. Ah for pittie, will rancke Winters rage,
These bitter blasts neuer ginne tasswage?
The kene cold blowes through my beaten hyde,

[1] adorn [2] qualities [3] none the more

[1] proof

All as I were through the body gryde.[1]
My ragged rontes [2] all shiver and shake,
As doen high Towers in an earthquake:
They wont in the wind wagge their wrigle tailes,
Perke [3] as Peacock; but nowe it auales.[4]
THE. Lewdly complainest thou, laesie ladde,
Of Winters wracke for making thee sadde.
Must not the world wend in his commun course,
From good to badd, and from badde to worse,
From worse vnto that is worst of all,
And then returne to his former fall [5]?
Who will not suffer the stormy time,
Where will he liue tyll the lusty prime?
Selfe haue I worne out thrise threttie yeares,
Some in much ioy, many in many teares,
Yet neuer complained of cold nor heate,
Of Sommers flame, nor of Winters threat:
Ne euer was to Fortune foeman,
But gently tooke, that ungently came;
And euer my flocke was my chiefe care,
Winter or Sommer they mought well fare.
CUD. No marueile, Thenot, if thou can beare
Cherefully the Winters wrathfull cheare;
For Age and Winter accord full nie,
This chill, that cold, this crooked, that wrye;
And as the lowring Wether lookes downe,
So semest thou like good fryday to frowne,
But my flowring youth is foe to frost,
My shippe unwont in stormes to be tost.
THE. The soveraigne of seas he blames in vaine,
That, once sea beate, will to sea againe.
So loytring liue you little heardgroomes,
Keeping your beasts in the budded broomes:
And, when the shining sunne laugheth once,
You deemen, the Spring is come attonce;
Tho [6] gynne you, fond flyes, the cold to scorne,
And, crowing in pypes made of greene corne,
You thinken to be Lords of the yeare;
But eft,[7] when ye count you freed from feare,
Comes the breme [8] winter with chamfred [9] browes
Full of wrinckles and frostie furrowes:
Drerily shooting his stormy darte,
Which cruddles [10] the blood, and pricks the harte.
Then is your carelesse corage accoied,[11]
Your carefull heards with cold bene annoied.
Then paye you the price of your surquedrie,[12]
With weeping, and wayling, and misery.
CUD. Ah foolish old man, I scorne thy skill,
That wouldest me, my springing youngth to spil:
I deeme, thy braine emperished bee
Through rusty elde, that hath rotted thee:
Or sicker [13] thy head veray tottie [14] is,

[1] pierced [2] young bullocks [3] pert [4] droops
[5] condition [6] then [7] again, after [8] bitter [9] wrinkled
[10] curdles [11] quieted [12] pride [13] surely [14] unsteady

So on thy corbe [1] shoulder it leanes amisse.
Now thy selfe hast lost both lopp and topp,
Als [2] my budding braunch thou wouldest cropp:
But were thy yeares greene, as now bene myne,
To other delights they would encline.
Tho wouldest thou learne to caroll of Loue,
And hery [3] with hymnes thy lasses gloue.
Tho wouldest thou pype of Phyllis prayse:
But Phyllis is myne for many dayes;
I wonne her with a gyrdle of gelt,[4]
Embost with buegle about the belt.
Such an one shepeheards woulde make full faine:
Such an one would make thee younge againe.
THE. Thou art a fon [5] of thy loue to boste,
All that is lent to loue, wyll be lost.
CUD. Seest, howe brag [6] yond Bullocke beares,
So smirke, so smoothe, his pricked eares?
His hornes bene as broade, as Rainebowe bent,
His dewelap as lythe, as lasse of Kent,
See howe he venteth into the wynd.
Weenest of loue is not his mynd?
Seemeth thy flocke thy counsell can,[7]
So lustlesse bene they, so weake, so wan,
Clothed with cold, and hoary wyth frost,
Thy flockes father his corage hath lost:
Thy Ewes, that wont to haue blowen [8] bags,
Like wailefull widdowes hangen their crags [9]:
The rather [10] lambes bene starved with cold,
All for their Maister is lustlesse and old.
THE. Cuddie, I wote thou kenst [11] little good,
So vainely tadvaunce thy headlesse hood.
For Youngth is a bubble blowne up with breath,
Whose witt is weakenesse, whose wage is death,
Whose way is wildernesse, whose ynne Penaunce,
And stoopegallaunt Age the hoste of Greeuaunce.
But shall I tel thee a tale of truth,
Which I cond [12] of Tityrus in my youth,
Keeping his sheepe on the hils of Kent?
CUD. To nought more, Thenot, my mind is bent,
Then to heare nouells of his deuise:
They bene so well thewed, and so wise,
What euer that good old man bespake.
THE. Many meete tales of youth did he make,
And some of loue, and some of cheualrie:
But none fitter then this to applie.
Now listen a while, and hearken the end.

There grewe an aged Tree on the greene,
A goodly Oake sometime had it bene,
With armes full strong and largely displayd,
But of their leaues they were disarayde:
The bodie bigge, and mightely pight,

[1] crooked [2] also [3] praise [4] gilt [5] fool [6] brisk
[7] know [8] full [9] necks [10] earlier [11] knowest [12] learned

Throughly rooted, and of wonderous hight:
Whilome had bene the King of the field,
And mochell[1] mast to the husband did yielde,
And with his nuts larded many swine.
But now the gray mosse marred his rine,
His bared boughes were beaten with stormes,
His toppe was bald, and wasted with wormes,
His honor decayed, his braunches sere.
  Hard by his side grewe a bragging Brere,
Which prowdly thrust into Thelement,
And seemed to threat the Firmament.
It was embellisht with blossomes fayre,
And thereto aye wonned[2] to repayre
The shepheards daughters to gather flowres,
To peinct their girlonds with his colowres.
And in his small bushes used to shrowde
The sweete Nightingale singing so lowde:
Which made this foolish Brere wexe so bold,
That on a time hee cast him to scold,
And snebbe the good Oake, for he was old.
  'Why standst there (quoth he) thou brutish blocke?
'Nor for fruict nor for shadowe serues thy stocke:
'Seest how fresh my flowers bene spredde,
'Dyed in Lilly white and Cremsin redde,
'With Leaves engrained in lusty greene,
'Colours meete to clothe a mayden Queene.
'Thy wast bignes[3] but combers the grownd,
'And dirks the beautie of my blossomes rownd.
'The mouldie mosse, which thee accloieth,[4]
'My Sinamon smell too much annoieth.
'Wherefore soone I rede[5] thee, hence remoue,
'Least thou the price of my displeasure proue.'
So spake this bold brere with great disdaine:
Little him answered the Oake againe,
But yielded, with shame and greefe adawed,[6]
That of a weede he was ouerawed.
  Yt chaunced after vpon a day,
The Hus-bandman selfe to come that way,
Of custome for to suruewe[7] his grownd,
And his trees of state in compasse rownd.
Him when the spitefull brere had espyed,
Causlesse complayned, and lowdly cryed
Vnto his Lord, stirring up sterne strife:
  'O, my liege Lord! the God of my life,
'Pleaseth you ponder your Suppliants plaint,
'Caused of wrong, and cruell constraint,
'Which I your poore vassall dayly endure:
'And but your goodnes the same recure,[8]
'Am like for desperate doole[9] to dye,
'Through felonous force of mine enemie.'
  Greatly agast with this piteous plea,

[1] much [2] were accustomed [3] vast bigness [4] encumbers [5] advise [6] daunted [7] look over [8] recover [9] grief

Him rested the goodman on the lea,
And badde the Brere in his plaint proceede.
With painted words tho[1] gan this proude weede,
(As most vsen Ambitious folke:)
His colowred crime with craft to cloke.
  'Ah, my soveraigne! Lord of creatures all,
'Thou placer of plants both humble and tall,
'Was not I planted of thine owne hand,
'To be the primrose of all thy land,
'With flowring blossomes, to furnish the prime
'And scarlet berries in Sommer time?
'Howe falls it then that this faded Oake,
'Whose bodie is sere, whose braunches broke,
'Whose naked Armes stretch vnto the fyre,
'Vnto such tyrannie doth aspire.
'Hindering with his shade my louely light,
'And robbing me of the swete sonnes sight?
'So beate his old boughes my tender side,
'That oft the bloud springeth from wounds wyde:
'Untimely my flowres forced to fall,
'That bene the honor of your Coronall.
'And oft he lets his cancker wormes light
'Upon my braunches, to worke me more spight:
'And oft his hoarie locks downe doth cast,
'Where with my fresh flowretts bene defast:
'For this, and many more such outrage,
'Craving your goodlihead[2] to aswage
'The ranckorous rigour of his might,
'Nought aske I, but onely to hold my right:
'Submitting me to your good sufferance,
'And praying to be garded from greeuance.'
  To this the Oake cast him to replie
Well as he couth[3]; but his enemie
Had kindled such coles of displeasure,
That the good man noulde[4] stay his leasure,
But home him hasted with furious heate,
Encreasing his wrath with many a threate.
His harmefull Hatchet he hent[5] in hand,
(Alas, that it so ready should stand)
And to the field alone he speedeth,
(Ay little helpe to harme there needeth)
Anger nould let him speake to the tree,
Enaunter[6] his rage mought cooled be:
But to the roote bent his sturdy stroke,
And made many wounds in the wast[7] Oake.
The Axes edge did oft turne againe,
As halfe unwilling to cutte the graine:
Semed, the sencelesse yron dyd feare,
Or to wrong holy eld did forbeare.
For it had bene an auncient tree,

[1] then [2] goodness [3] could [4] would not [5] seized [6] lest [7] vast

Sacred with many a mysteree,
And often crost with the priestes crewe,
And often halowed with holy water dewe.
But sike [1] fancies weren foolerie,
And broughten this Oake to this miserye.
For nought mought they quitten him from decay:
For fiercely the good man at him did laye.
The blocke oft groned vnder the blow,
And sighed to see his neare ouerthrow.
In fine, the steele had pierced his pitth,
Tho [2] downe to the earth hee fell forthwith.
His wonderous weight made the grounde to quake,
Thearth shronke vnder him, and seemed to shake.
There lyeth the Oake, pitied of none.
Now stands the Brere like a Lord alone,
Puffed vp with pryde and vaine pleasaunce:
But all this glee had no continuaunce:
For eftsones [3] Winter gan to approche,
The blustring Boreas did encroche,
And beate upon the solitarie Brere:
For nowe no succoure was seene him nere.
Now gan he repent his pride to late;
For naked left and disconsolate,
The byting frost nipt his stalke dead,
The watrie wette weighed downe his head,
And heaped snowe burdned him so sore,
That nowe vpright he can stand no more:
And, being downe, is trodde in the durt
Of cattell, and brouzed, and sorely hurt.
Such was thend of this Ambitious brere,
For scorning Eld
CUD. Now I pray thee shepheard, tel it not forth:
Here is a long tale, and little worth.
So longe haue I listened to thy speche,
That graffed to the ground is my breche;
My hartblood is welnigh frorne [4] I feele,
And my galage [5] growne fast to my heele:
But little ease of thy lewd tale I tasted:
Hye thee home shepheard, the day is nigh wasted.

Thenots Embleme.
Iddio perche é vecchio
Fa suoi al suo essempio.[6]

Cuddies Embleme.
Niuno vecchio
Spaventa Iddio.[7]

[1] such [2] then [3] soon again [4] frozen [5] shoe
[6] God, because he is old, Makes his own in his image. [7] No graybeard Fears God

THE FAERIE QUEENE

BOOK I. CANTO I

I

A gentle Knight was pricking [1] on the plaine,
Ycladd in mightie armes and silver shielde,
Wherein old dints of deepe woundes did remaine,
The cruell markes of many a bloody fielde;
Yet armes till that time did he never wield.
His angry steede did chide his foming bitt,
As much disdayning to the curbe to yield:
Full jolly knight he seemd, and faire did sitt,
As one for knightly giusts [2] and fierce encounters fitt.

II

And on his brest a bloodie Crosse he bore,
The deare remembrance of his dying Lord,
For whose sweete sake that glorious badge he wore,
And dead, as living, ever him ador'd:
Upon his shield the like was also scor'd,
For soveraine hope which in his helpe he had.
Right faithfull true he was in deede and word;
But of his cheere did seeme too solemne sad;
Yet nothing did he dread, but ever was ydrad.[3]

III

Upon a great adventure he was bond,[4]
That greatest Gloriana to him gave,
(That greatest Glorious Queene of Faery lond [5])
To winne him worshippe, and her grace to have,
Which of all earthly thinges he most did crave:
And ever as he rode his hart did earne [6]
To prove his puissance in battell brave
Upon his foe, and his new force to learne,
Upon his foe, a Dragon horrible and stearne.

IV

A lovely Ladie rode him faire beside,
Upon a lowly Asse more white then snow,
Yet she much whiter; but the same did hide
Under a vele,[7] that wimpled was full low;
And over all a blacke stole shee did throw:
As one that inly mournd, so was she sad,
And heavie sate upon her palfrey slow;
Seemed in heart some hidden care she had,
And by her, in a line, a milkewhite lambe she lad.[8]

[1] riding [2] jousts [3] dreaded [4] bound [5] land
[6] yearn [7] veil [8] led

V

So pure and innocent as that same lambe
She was in life and every vertuous lore;
And by descent from Royall lynage came
Of ancient Kinges and Queenes, that had of yore
Their scepters stretcht from East to Westerne shore,
And all the world in their subjection held;
Till that infernall feend with foule uprore
Forwasted [1] all their land, and them expeld;
Whom to avenge she had this Knight from far compeld.

VI

Behind her farre away a Dwarfe did lag,
That lasie seemd, in being ever last,
Or wearied with bearing of her bag
Of needments at his backe. Thus as they past,
The day with cloudes was suddeine overcast,
And angry Jove an hideous storme of raine
Did poure into his Lemans [2] lap so fast
That everie wight to shrowd [3] it did constrain;
And this faire couple eke [4] to shroud themselves were fain.[5]

VII

Enforst to seeke some covert nigh at hand,
A shadie grove not farr away they spide,
That promist ayde the tempest to withstand;
Whose loftie trees, yclad with sommers pride,
Did spred so broad that heavens light did hide,
Not perceable with power of any starr:
And all within were pathes and alleies wide,
With footing worne, and leading inward farr.
Faire harbour that them seems; so in they entred ar.

VIII

And foorth they passe, with pleasure forward led,
Joying to heare the birdes sweete harmony,
Which, therein shrouded from the tempest dred,
Seemd in their song to scorne the cruell sky.
Much can they praise the trees so straight and hy,
The sayling Pine; the Cedar proud and tall;
The vine-propp Elme; the Poplar never dry;
The builder Oake, sole king of forrests all;
The Aspine good for staves; the Cypresse funerall;

IX

The Laurell, meed of mightie Conquerours
And Poets sage; the Firre that weepeth still;
The Willow, worne of forlorne Paramours;
The Eugh,[1] obedient to the benders will;
The Birch for shaftes; the Sallow for the mill;
The Mirrhe sweete-bleeding in the bitter wound;
The warlike Beech; the Ash for nothing ill;
The fruitfull Olive; and the Platane round;
The carver Holme; the Maple seeldom inward sound.

X

Led with delight, they thus beguile the way
Untill the blustring storme is overblowne;
When, weening to returne whence they did stray,
They cannot finde that path which first was showne,
But wander too and fro in waies unknowne,
Furthest from end then when they neerest weene,
That makes them doubt their wits be not their owne;
So many pathes, so many turnings seene,
That which of them to take in diverse doubt they been.

XI

At last resolving forward still to fare
Till that some end they finde, or in or out,
That path they take that beaten seemd most bare,
And like to lead the labyrinth about;
Which when by tract they hunted had throughout,
At length it brought them to a hollowe cave
Amid the thickest woods. The Champion stout
Eftsoones [2] dismounted from his courser brave,
And to the Dwarfe a while his needlesse spere he gave.

XII

"Be well aware," quoth then that Ladie milde,
"Least suddaine mischiefe ye too rash provoke:
The danger hid, the place unknowne and wilde,
Breedes dreadfull doubts. Oft fire is without smoke,
And perill without show: therefore your stroke,
Sir Knight, with-hold till further tryall made."
"Ah Ladie," (sayd he) "shame were to revoke
The forward footing for an hidden shade:
Vertue gives her selfe light through darknesse for to wade."

[1] devastated [2] sweetheart's [3] cover [4] also [5] glad

[1] Yew [2] immediately

XIII

"Yea, but" (quoth she) "the perill of this place
I better wot than you: though nowe too late
To wish you backe returne with foule disgrace;
Yet wisdome warnes, whilest foot is in the gate,
To stay the steppe ere forced to retrate.
This is the wandring wood, this Errours den,
A monster vile, whom God and man does hate:
Therefore, I read,[1] beware." "Fly, fly!" (quoth then
The fearefull Dwarfe) "this is no place for living men."

XIV

But, full of fire and greedy hardiment,
The youthfull Knight could not for ought be staide;
But forth unto the darksom hole he went,
And looked in: his glistring armor made
A little glooming light, much like a shade;
By which he saw the ugly monster plaine,
Halfe like a serpent horribly displaide,
But th' other halfe did womans shape retaine,
Most lothsom, filthie, foule, and full of vile disdaine.

* * * * * * *

XXIX

At length they chaunst to meet upon the way
An aged Sire, in long blacke weedes yclad,
His feete all bare, his beard all hoarie gray,
And by his belt his booke he hanging had:
Sober he seemde, and very sagely sad,
And to the ground his eyes were lowly bent,
Simple in shew, and voide of malice bad;
And all the way he prayed as he went,
And often knockt his brest, as one that did repent.

XXX

He faire the knight saluted, louting[2] low,
Who faire him quited, as that courteous was;
And after asked him, if he did know
Of straunge adventures, which abroad did pas?
"Ah! my dear sonne," (quoth he) "how should, alas!
Silly old man, that lives in hidden cell,
Bidding his beades all day for his trespas,
Tydings of warre and worldly trouble tell?
With holy father sits not with such thinges to mell.

[1] advise [2] bowing

XXXI

"But if of daunger, which hereby doth dwell,
And homebredd evil ye desire to heare,
Of a straunge man I can you tidings tell,
That wasteth all this countrie, farre and neare."
"Of such," (saide he,) "I chiefly doe inquere,
And shall thee well rewarde to shew the place,
In which that wicked wight his dayes doth weare;
For to all knighthood it is foule disgrace,
That such a cursed creature lives so long a space."

XXXII

"Far hence" (quoth he) "in wastfull wildernesse
His dwelling is, by which no living wight
May ever passe, but thorough[1] great distresse."
"Now," (saide the Ladie,) "draweth toward night,
And well I wote, that of your later fight
Ye all forwearied be; for what so strong,
But, wanting rest, will also want of might?
The Sunne, that measures heaven all day long,
At night doth baite his steedes the Ocean waves emong.

XXXIII

"Then with the Sunne take, Sir, your timely rest,
And with new day new worke at once begin:
Untroubled night, they say, gives counsell best."
"Right well, Sir knight, ye have advised bin,"
Quoth then that aged man: "the way to win
Is wisely to advise; now day is spent:
Therefore with me ye may take up your In
For this same night." The knight was well content;
So with that godly father to his home they went.

XXXIV

A litle lowly Hermitage it was,
Downe in a dale, hard by a forests side,
Far from resort of people that did pas
In traveill to and froe: a litle wyde
There was an holy chappell edifyde,[2]
Wherein the Hermite dewly wont to say
His holy thinges each morne and eventyde;
Thereby a christall streame did gently play,
Which from a sacred fountaine welled forth alway.

[1] through [2] built

XXXV

Arrived there, the litle house they fill,
Ne looke for entertainement where none was;
Rest is their feast, and all thinges at their will.
The noblest mind the best contentment has.
With faire discourse the evening so they pas;
For that olde man of pleasing wordes had store
And well could file his tongue as smooth as glas:
He told of Saintes and Popes, and evermore
He strowd an Ave-Mary after and before.

XXXVI

The drouping night thus creepeth on them fast,
And the sad humor loading their eyeliddes,
As messenger of Morpheus, on them cast
Sweet slombring deaw, the which to sleep them biddes.
Unto their lodgings then his guestes he riddes:
Where when all drownd in deadly sleepe he findes,
He to his studie goes; and there amiddes
His magick bookes and artes of sundrie kindes,
He seekes out mighty charmes to trouble sleepy minds.

XXXVII

Then choosing out few words most horrible,
(Let none them read) thereof did verses frame;
With which, and other spelles like terrible,
He bad awake blacke Plutoes griesly Dame;
And cursed heven; and spake reprochful shame
Of highest God, the Lord of life and light:
A bold bad man, that dar'd to call by name
Great Gorgon, prince of darknes and dead night;
At which Cocytus quakes, and Styx is put to flight.

XXXVIII

And forth he cald out of deepe darknes dredd
Legions of Sprights, the which, like litle flyes
Fluttring about his ever-damned hedd,
Awaite whereto their service he applyes,
To aide his friendes, or fray his enimies.
Of those he chose out two, the falsest twoo,
And fittest for to forge true-seeming lyes:
The one of them he gave a message too,
The other by him selfe staide, other worke to doo.

XXXIX

He, making speedy way through spersed ayre,
And through the world of waters wide and deepe,
To Morpheus house doth hastily repaire.
Amid the bowels of the earth full steepe,
And low, where dawning day doth never peepe,
His dwelling is; there Tethys his wet bed
Doth ever wash, and Cynthia still doth steepe
In silver deaw his ever-drouping hed,
Whiles sad Night over him her mantle black doth spred.

XL

Whose double gates he findeth locked fast,
The one faire fram'd of burnisht Yvory,
The other all with silver overcast;
And wakeful dogges before them farre doe lye,
Watching to banish Care their enimy,
Who oft is wont to trouble gentle Sleepe.
By them the Sprite doth passe in quietly,
And unto Morpheus comes, whom drowned deepe
In drowsie fit he findes: of nothing he takes keepe.

XLI

And more to lulle him in his slumber soft,
A trickling streame from high rock tumbling downe,
And ever-drizling raine upon the loft,
Mixt with a murmuring winde much like the sowne
Of swarming Bees, did cast him in a swowne.
No other noyse, nor peoples troublous cryes,
As still are wont t'annoy the walled towne,
Might there be heard; but carelesse Quiet lyes
Wrapt in eternall silence farre from enimyes.

XLII

The Messenger approching to him spake;
But his waste wordes retournd to him in vaine:
So sound he slept that nought mought him awake.
Then rudely he him thrust, and pusht with paine,
Whereat he gan to stretch; but he againe
Shook him so hard that forced him to speake.
As one then in a dreame, whose dryer braine
Is tost with troubled sights and fancies weake,
He mumbled soft, but would not all his silence breake.

XLIII

The Sprite then gan more boldly him to wake,
And threatned unto him the dreaded name
Of Hecate: whereat he gan to quake,
And, lifting up his lompish head, with blame
Halfe angrie asked him, for what he came.

"Hether" (quoth he) "me Archimago sent,
He that the stubborne Sprites can wisely tame,
He bids thee to him send for his intent
A fit false dreame, that can delude the sleepers sent."

CANTO III

I

Nought is there under heav'ns wide hollownesse,
That moves more deare compassion of mind,
Then beautie brought t'unworthie wretchednesse
Through envies snares, or fortunes freakes unkind.
I, whether lately through her brightnes blynd,
Or through alleageance, and fast fealty,
Which I do owe unto all womankynd,
Feele my hart perst with so great agony,
When such I see, that all for pitty I could dy.

II

And now it is empassioned so deepe,
For fairest Unaes sake, of whom I sing,
That my frayle eies these lines with teares do steepe,
To thinke how she through guyleful handeling,
Though true as touch, though daughter of a king,
Though faire as ever living wight was fayre,
Though nor in word nor deede ill meriting,
Is from her knight divorced in despayre,
And her dew loves deryv'd to that vile witches shayre.

III

Yet she, most faithfull Ladie, all this while
Forsaken, wofull, solitarie mayd,
Far from all peoples preace,[1] as in exile,
In wildernesse and wastfull deserts strayd,
To seeke her knight; who, subtily betrayd
Through that late vision which th' Enchanter wrought,
Had her abandond. She, of nought affrayd,
Through woods and wastnes wide him daily sought;
Yet wished tydinges none of him unto her brought.

IV

One day, nigh wearie of the yrksome way,
From her unhastie beast she did alight;
And on the grasse her dainty limbs did lay,
In secrete shadow, far from all mens sight:
From her fayre head her fillet she undight,

[1] press, throng

And layd her stole aside. Her angels face,
As the great eye of heaven, shyned bright,
And made a sunshine in the shady place;
Did never mortall eye behold such heavenly grace.

V

It fortuned, out of the thickest wood
A ramping Lyon rushed suddeinly,
Hunting full greedy after salvage blood.
Soone as the royall virgin he did spy,
With gaping mouth at her ran greedily,
To have attonce devoured her tender corse;
But to the pray when as he drew more ny,
His bloody rage aswaged with remorse,[1]
And, with the sight amazd, forgat his furious forse.

VI

In stead thereof he kist her wearie feet,
And lickt her lilly hands with fawning tong,
As he her wronged innocence did weet.[2]
O, how can beautie maister the most strong,
And simple truth subdue avenging wrong!
Whose yielded pryde and proud submission,
Still dreading death, when she had marked long,
Her hart gan melt in great compassion;
And drizling teares did shed for pure affection.

VII

"The Lyon, Lord of everie beast in field,"
Quoth she, "his princely puissance doth abate,
And mightie proud to humble weake does yield,
Forgetfull of the hungry rage, which late
Him prickt, in pittie of my sad estate:
But he, my Lyon, and my noble Lord,
How does he find in cruell hart to hate
Her that him lov'd and ever most adord
As the God of my life? why hath he me abhord?"

VIII

Redounding teares did choke th' end of her plaint,
Which softly ecchoed from the neighbor wood;
And, sad to see her sorrowfull constraint,
The kingly beast upon her gazing stood:
With pittie calmd downe fell his angry mood.
At last, in close hart shutting up her payne,
Arose the virgin, borne of heavenly brood,
And to her snowy Palfrey got agayne,
To seeke her strayed Champion if she might attayne.

[1] pity [2] know

IX

The Lyon would not leave her desolate,
But with her went along, as a strong gard
Of her chast person, and a faythfull mate
Of her sad troubles and misfortunes hard:
Still,[1] when she slept, he kept both watch and ward;
And, when she wakt, he wayted diligent,
With humble service to her will prepard:
From her fayre eyes he tooke commandement,
And ever by her lookes conceived her intent.

* * * * * * *

SIR PHILIP SIDNEY (1554–1586)

ASTROPHEL AND STELLA

I

Loving in truth, and fain in verse my love to show,
That she, dear she, might take some pleasure of my pain, —
Pleasure might cause her read, reading might make her know,
Knowledge might pity win, and pity grace obtain, —
I sought fit words to paint the blackest face of woe;
Studying inventions fine, her wits to entertain,
Oft turning others' leaves, to see if thence would flow
Some fresh and fruitful showers upon my sunburn'd brain.
But words came halting forth, wanting Invention's stay;
Invention, Nature's child, fled step-dame Study's blows;
And others' feet still seem'd but strangers in my way.
Thus, great with child to speak, and helpless in my throes,
Biting my truant pen, beating myself for spite;
"Fool," said my Muse to me, "look in thy heart, and write."

VII

When Nature made her chief work, Stella's eyes,
In color black why wrapt she beams so bright?
Would she, in beamy black, like painter wise,
Frame daintiest lustre, mixed of shades and light?
Or did she else that sober hue devise,
In object best to knit and strength our sight;
Lest, if no veil these brave gleams did disguise,
They, sunlike, should more dazzle than delight?

[1] always

Or would she her miraculous power show,
That, whereas black seems Beauty's contrary,
She even in black doth make all beauties flow?
Both so, and thus, — she, minding Love should be
Placed ever there, gave him this mourning weed
To honor all their deaths who for her bleed.

XV

You that do search for every purling spring
Which from the ribs of old Parnassus flows,
And every flower, not sweet perhaps, which grows
Near thereabouts, into your poesie wring;
Ye that do dictionary's method bring
Into your rimes, running in rattling rows;
You that poor Petrarch's long-deceased woes
With new-born sighs and denizen'd wit do sing;
You take wrong ways; those far-fet[1] helps be such
As do bewray a want of inward touch,
And sure, at length stol'n goods do come to light:
But if, both for your love and skill, your name
You seek to nurse at fullest breasts of Fame,
Stella behold, and then begin to endite.

XXI

Your words, my friend, right healthful caustics, blame
My young mind marred, whom Love doth windlass so;
That mine own writings, like bad servants, show
My wits quick in vain thoughts, in virtue lame;
That Plato I read for nought but-if[2] he tame
Such coltish years; that to my birth I owe
Nobler desires, lest else that friendly foe,
Great expectation, wear a train of shame:
For since mad March great promise made of me,
If now the May of my years much decline,
What can be hoped my harvest-time will be?
Sure, you say well, "Your wisdom's golden mine
Dig deep with Learning's spade." Now tell me this —
Hath this world aught so fair as Stella is?

XXXI

With how sad steps, O Moon, thou climb'st the skies!
How silently, and with how wan a face!
What, may it be that even in heav'nly place
That busy archer his sharp arrows tries!
Sure, if that long-with-love-acquainted eyes

[1] far-fetched [2] unless

Can judge of love, thou feel'st a lover's case,
I read it in thy looks; thy languished grace,
To me, that feel the like, thy state descries.
Then, ev'n of fellowship, O Moon, tell me,
Is constant love deem'd there but want of wit?
Are beauties there as proud as here they be?
Do they above love to be lov'd, and yet
Those lovers scorn whom that love doth possess?
Do they call virtue there ungratefulness?

XXXII

Morpheus, the lively son of deadly Sleep,
Witness of life to them that living die,
A prophet oft, and oft an history,
A poet eke, as humors fly or creep;
Since thou in me so sure a power dost keep,
That never I with clos'd-up sense do lie,
But by thy work my Stella I descry,
Teaching blind eyes both how to smile and weep;
Vouchsafe, of all acquaintance, this to tell,
Whence hast thou ivory, rubies, pearl, and gold,
To show her skin, lips, teeth, and head so well?
"Fool!" answers he; "no Inds such treasures hold;
But from thy heart, while my sire charmeth thee,
Sweet Stella's image I do steal to me."

XXXIX

Come, Sleep! O Sleep, the certain knot of peace,
The baiting-place of wit, the balm of woe,
The poor man's wealth, the prisoner's release,
Th' indifferent judge between the high and low;
With shield of proof shield me from out the prease[1]
Of those fierce darts Despair at me doth throw:
O make in me those civil wars to cease;
I will good tribute pay, if thou do so.
Take thou of me smooth pillows, sweetest bed,
A chamber deaf of noise and blind of light,
A rosy garland and a weary head:
And if these things, as being thine in right,
Move not thy heavy grace, thou shalt in me,
Livelier then else-where, Stella's image see.

XLI

Having this day my horse, my hand, my lance
Guided so well that I obtain'd the prize,
Both by the judgment of the English eyes
And of some sent from that sweet enemy France;
Horsemen my skill in horsemanship advance,
Town folks my strength; a daintier judge applies
His praise too slight which from good use doth rise;
Some lucky wits impute it but to chance;
Others, because of both sides I do take
My blood from them who did excell in this,
Think Nature me a man-at-arms did make.
How far they shot awry! the true cause is,
Stella looked on, and from her heav'nly face
Sent forth the beams which made so fair my race.

[1] throng

ELEVENTH SONG

"Who is it that this dark night
Underneath my window plaineth?"
It is one who from thy sight
Being, ah! exil'd, disdaineth
Every other vulgar light.

"Why, alas! and are you he?
Be not yet those fancies changed?"
Dear, when you find change in me,
Though from me you be estranged,
Let my change to ruin be.

"Well, in absence this will die;
Leave to see, and leave to wonder."
Absence sure will help, if I
Can learn how myself to sunder
From what in my heart doth lie.

"But time will these thoughts remove;
Time doth work what no man knoweth."
Time doth as the subject prove;
With time still the affection groweth
In the faithful turtle-dove.

"What if we new beauties see?
Will not they stir new affection?"
I will think they pictures be,
(Image-like, of saints' perfection)
Poorly counterfeiting thee.

"But your reason's purest light
Bids you leave such minds to nourish."
Dear, do reason no such spite;
Never doth thy beauty flourish
More than in my reason's sight.

"But the wrongs Love bears will make
Love at length leave undertaking."
No, the more fools it do shake,
In a ground of so firm making
Deeper still they drive the stake.

"Peace, I think that some give ear!
Come no more, lest I get anger!"

Bliss, I will my bliss forbear;
Fearing, sweet, you to endanger;
But my soul shall harbor there.

"Well, be gone! be gone, I say,
Lest that Argus' eyes perceive you!"
O unjust is Fortune's sway,
Which can make me thus to leave you;
And from louts to run away.

SONG. THE NIGHTINGALE

The nightingale, as soon as April bringeth
Unto her rested sense a perfect waking,
While late bare earth, proud of new clothing, springeth,
Sings out her woes, a thorn her song-book making,
And mournfully bewailing,
Her throat in tunes expresseth
What grief her breast oppresseth
For Tereus' force on her chaste will prevailing.
O Philomela fair, O take some gladness,
That here is juster cause of painful sadness:
Thine earth now springs, mine fadeth;
Thy thorn without, my thorn my heart invadeth.

LOVE IS DEAD

Ring out your bells, let mourning shows be spread;
For Love is dead:
All Love is dead, infected
With plague of deep disdain:
Worth, as nought worth, rejected,
And Faith fair scorn doth gain.
From so ungrateful fancy,
From such a female franzie,[1]
From them that use men thus,
Good Lord, deliver us!

Weep, neighbors, weep; do you not hear it said
That Love is dead?
His death-bed, peacock's folly;
His winding-sheet is shame;
His will, false-seeming holy;
His sole exec'tor, blame.
From so ungrateful fancy,
From such a female franzie,
From them that use men thus,
Good Lord, deliver us!

Let dirge be sung, and trentals rightly read,
For Love is dead;
Sir Wrong his tomb ordaineth
My mistress' marble heart;
Which epitaph containeth,
"Her eyes were once his dart."

[1] frenzy

From so ungrateful fancy,
From such a female franzie,
From them that use men thus,
Good Lord, deliver us!

Alas, I lie: rage hath this error bred;
Love is not dead;
Love is not dead, but sleepeth
In her unmatched mind,
Where she his counsel keepeth,
Till due deserts she find.
Therefore from so vile fancy,
To call such wit a franzie,
Who Love can temper thus,
Good Lord, deliver us!

WOOING STUFF

Faint Amorist, what! dost thou think
To taste Love's honey, and not drink
One dram of gall? or to devour
A world of sweet, and taste no sour?
Dost thou ever think to enter
Th' Elysian fields, that dar'st not venture
In Charon's barge? a lover's mind
Must use to sail with every wind.
He that loves, and fears to try,
Learns his mistress to deny.
Doth she chide thee? 'tis to show it,
That thy coldness makes her do it;
Is she silent? is she mute?
Silence fully grants thy suit;
Doth she pout, and leave the room?
Then she goes to bid thee come;
Is she sick? why then be sure
She invites thee to the cure;
Doth she cross thy suit with No?
Tush, she loves to hear thee woo;
Doth she call the faith of man
In question? nay, 'uds-foot, she loves thee than;[1]
And if ere she makes a blot,
She's lost if that thou hit'st her not.
He that after ten denials
Dares attempt no farther trials,
Hath no warrant to acquire
The dainties of his chaste desire.

HYMN TO APOLLO

Apollo great, whose beams the greater world do light,
And in our little world do clear our inward sight,

[1] then

Which ever shine, though hid from earth by earthly shade,
Whose lights do ever live, but in our darkness fade;
Thou god whose youth was decked with spoil of Python's skin
(So humble knowledge can throw down the snakish sin);
Latona's son, whose birth in pain and travail long
Doth teach, to learn the good what travails do belong;
In travail of our life (a short but tedious space),
While brickle hour-glass runs, guide thou our panting pace:
Give us foresightful minds; give us minds to obey
What foresight tells; our thoughts upon thy knowledge stay.
Let so our fruits grow up that Nature be maintained,
But so our hearts keep down, with vice they be not stained.
Let this assured hold our judgments overtake,
That nothing wins the heaven but what doth earth forsake.

JOHN LYLY (1554?–1606)

APELLES' SONG

Cupid and my Campaspe played
At cards for kisses; Cupid paid.
He stakes his quiver, bows and arrows,
His mother's doves and team of sparrows:
Loses them too; then down he throws
The coral of his lip, the rose
Growing on's cheek (but none knows how);
With these the crystal of his brow,
And then the dimple of his chin;
All these did my Campaspe win.
At last he set her both his eyes;
She won, and Cupid blind did rise.
O Love, has she done this to thee?
What shall, alas! become of me?

SPRING'S WELCOME

What bird so sings, yet so does wail?
O 'tis the ravished nightingale.
"Jug, jug, jug, jug, tereu," she cries,
And still her woes at midnight rise.
Brave prick-song! who is't now we hear?
None but the lark so shrill and clear;
Now at heaven's gates she claps her wings,
The morn not waking till she sings.
Hark, hark, with what a pretty throat
Poor robin redbreast tunes his note;
Hark how the jolly cuckoos sing,
Cuckoo, to welcome in the spring;
Cuckoo, to welcome in the spring!

HYMN TO APOLLO

Sing to Apollo, god of day,
Whose golden beams with morning play
And make her eyes so brightly shine,
Aurora's face is called divine;
Sing to Phœbus and that throne
Of diamonds which he sits upon.
Io, pæans let us sing
To Physic's and to Poesy's king!

Crown all his altars with bright fire,
Laurels bind about his lyre,
A Daphnean coronet for his head,
The Muses dance about his bed;
When on his ravishing lute he plays,
Strew his temple round with bays.
Io, pæans let us sing
To the glittering Delian king!

FAIRY REVELS

OMNES. Pinch him, pinch him black and blue;
Saucy mortals must not view
What the queen of stars is doing,
Nor pry into our fairy wooing.
1 FAIRY. Pinch him blue —
2 FAIRY. And pinch him black —
3 FAIRY. Let him not lack
Sharp nails to pinch him blue and red,
Till sleep has rocked his addlehead.
4 FAIRY. For the trespass he hath done,
Spots o'er all his flesh shall run.
Kiss Endymion, kiss his eyes,
Then to our midnight heydeguyes.

GEORGE PEELE (1558?–1597?)

SONG OF PARIS AND ŒNONE

ŒNONE. Fair and fair, and twice so fair,
As fair as any may be;
The fairest shepherd on our green,
A love for any lady.
PARIS. Fair and fair, and twice so fair,
As fair as any may be;
Thy love is fair for thee alone,
And for no other lady.

ŒN. My love is fair, my love is gay,
As fresh as bin the flowers in May,
And of my love my roundelay,
My merry, merry roundelay,
Concludes with Cupid's curse,—
"They that do change old love for new,
Pray gods they change for worse!"
AMBO SIMUL. They that do change, etc.
ŒN. Fair and fair, etc.
PAR. Fair and fair, etc.
Thy love is fair, etc.
ŒN. My love can pipe, my love can sing,
My love can many a pretty thing,
And of his lovely praises ring
My merry, merry roundelays,
Amen to Cupid's curse, —
"They that do change," etc.
PAR. They that do change, etc.
AMBO. Fair and fair, etc.

HARVESTMEN A-SINGING

All ye that lovely lovers be,
Pray you for me:
Lo, here we come a-sowing, a-sowing,
And sow sweet fruits of love;
In your sweet hearts well may it prove!

Lo, here we come a-reaping, a-reaping,
To reap our harvest-fruit!
And thus we pass the year so long,
And never be we mute.

FAREWELL TO ARMS

His golden locks time hath to silver turned;
O time too swift, O swiftness never ceasing!
His youth 'gainst time and age hath ever spurned,
But spurned in vain; youth waneth by increasing:
Beauty, strength, youth, are flowers but fading seen;
Duty, faith, love, are roots, and ever green.

His helmet now shall make a hive for bees,
And, lovers' sonnets turned to holy psalms,
A man-at-arms must now serve on his knees,
And feed on prayers, which are age his alms:
But though from court to cottage he depart,
His saint is sure of his unspotted heart.

And when he saddest sits in homely cell,
He'll teach his swains this carol for a song, —
"Blessed be the hearts that wish my sovereign well,
Cursed be the souls that think her any wrong."
Goddess, allow this aged man his right,
To be your beadsman now that was your knight.

WILLIAM WARNER (1558?-1609)

ALBION'S ENGLAND

BOOK IV, CHAPTER XX

The Brutons thus departed hence, seven kingdoms here begun, —
Where diversely in divers broils the Saxons lost and won, —
King Edel and king Adelbright in Diria jointly reign;
In loyal concord during life these kingly friends remain.
When Adelbright should leave his life, to Edel thus he says:
"By those same bonds of happy love, that held us friends always,
By our bi-parted crown, of which the most is mine,
By God, to whom my soul must pass, and so in time may thine,
I pray thee, nay I conjure thee, to nourish as thine own
Thy niece, my daughter Argentile, till she to age be grown;
And then, as thou receivest it, resign to her my throne."
A promise had for this bequest, the testator he dies;
But all that Edel undertook, he afterward denies.
Yet well he fosters for a time the damsel, that was grown
The fairest lady under Heaven; whose beauty being known,
A many princes seek her love, but none might her obtain:
For gripple[1] Edel to himself her kingdom sought to gain,
And for that cause from sight of such he did his ward restrain.
By chance one Curan, son unto a prince in Danske, did see
The maid, with whom he fell in love as much as one might be.
Unhappy youth, what should he do? his saint was kept in mew,
Nor he, nor any noble-man admitted to her view.
One while in melancholy fits he pines himself away,
Anon he thought by force of arms to win her, if he may,
And still against the king's restraint did secretly inveigh.
At length the high controller Love, whom none may disobey,

[1] avaricious

Imbased him from lordliness, unto a kitchen drudge:
That so at least of life or death she might become his judge.
Access so had to see, and speak, he did his love betray,
And tells his birth; her answer was she husbandless would stay.
Meanwhile the king did beat his brains his booty to achieve,
Nor caring what became of her, so he by her might thrive.
At last his resolution was some peasant should her wive.
And (which was working to his wish) he did observe with joy
How Curan, whom he thought a drudge, scaped many an amorous toy.
The king, perceiving such his vein, promotes his vassal still,
Lest that the baseness of the man should let, perhaps, his will.
Assured therefore of his love, but not suspecting who
The lover was, the king himself in his behalf did woo.
The lady, resolute from love, unkindly takes that he
Should bar the noble, and unto so base a match agree;
And therefore shifting out of doors, departed thence by stealth,
Preferring poverty before a dangerous life in wealth.
When Curan heard of her escape, the anguish in his heart
Was more than much, and after her from court he did depart:
Forgetful of himself, his hearth, his country, friends, and all,
And only minding (whom he missed) the foundress of his thrall.
Nor means he after to frequent or court or stately towns,
But solitarily to live amongst the country grounds.
A brace of years he lived thus, well pleased so to live,
And shepherd-like to feed a flock himself did wholly give.
So wasting, love, by work and want, grew almost to the wane;
But then began a second love, the worser of the twain.
A country wench, a neatherd's maid, where Curan kept his sheep,
Did feed her drove: and now on her was all the shepherd's keep.
He borrowed on the working days his holy russets oft;
And of the bacon's fat, to make his startops black and soft;
And lest his tarbox should offend he left it at the fold;
Sweet growte, or whig, his bottle had as much as it might hold;
A sheave of bread as brown as nut, and cheese as white as snow;
And wildings or the season's fruit he did in scrip bestow.
And whilst his pie-bald cur did sleep, and sheephook lay him by,
On hollow quills of oaten straw he piped melody;
But when he spied her, his saint, he wiped his greasy shoes,
And clear'd the drivel from his beard and thus the shepherd woos:
"I have, sweet wench, a piece of cheese, as good as tooth may chaw,
And bread and wildings souling well

* * * * * * * *

"Thou art too elvish, faith thou art too elvish, and too coy;
Am I (I pray thee) beggarly, that such a flock enjoy?
I know I am not ; yet that thou dost hold me in disdain
Is brim abroad, and made a gibe to all that keep this plain.
There be as quaint (at least that think themselves as quaint) that crave
The match, that thou (I know not why) mayst, but dislik'st to have.

* * * * * * * *

"Then choose a shepherd. With the Sun he doth his flock unfold,
And all the day on hill or plain he merry chat can hold;
And with the Sun doth fold again; then jogging home betime,
He turns a crab, or tunes a round, or sings some merry rhyme.
Nor lacks he gleeful tales to tell, whilst round the bowl doth trot;
And sitteth singing care away, till he to bed hath got.
There sleeps he soundly all the night, forgetting morrow cares,
Nor fears he blasting of his corn nor uttering of his wares,
Or storms by seas, or stirs on land, or crack of credit lost,
Not spending franklier than his flock shall still defray the cost.

"Well know I, sooth they say that say, 'More quiet nights and days
The shepherd sleeps and wakes than he whose cattle he doth graze.'
Believe me, lass, a king is but a man, and so am I;
Content is worth a monarchy, and mischiefs hit the high;
As late it did a king and his, not dwelling far from hence,
Who left a daughter, (save thyself) for fair a matchless wench." —
Here did he pause, as if his tongue had done his heart offence. —
The Neatress, longing for the rest, did egg him on to tell
How fair she was, and who she was. "She bore," quoth he, "the bell
For beauty. Though I clownish am, I know what beauty is;
Or did I not, yet seeing thee, I senseless were to miss.
Suppose her beauty Helen's-like, or Helen's somewhat less,
And every star consorting to a pure complexion guess.
Her stature comely tall, her gait well graced, and her wit
To marvel at, not meddle with, as matchless I omit.
A globe-like head, a gold-like hair, a forehead smooth and high,
An even nose, on either side did shine a greyish eye;
Two rosy cheeks, round ruddy lips, white just-set teeth within;
A mouth in mean, and underneath a round and dimpled chin;
Her snowish neck with blueish veins stood bolt upright upon
Her portly shoulders; beating balls, her veined breasts, anon
Add more to beauty; wand-like was her middle;

* * * * * * * * *

"And more, her long and limber arms had white and azure wrists;
And slender fingers answer to her smooth and lily fists.

* * * * * * * * *

"With these (O thing divine) with these, her tongue of speech was spare;
But speaking, Venus seem'd to speak, the ball from Ide to bear.
With Phœbe, Juno, and with both, herself contends in face;
Where equal mixture did not want of mild and stately grace.
Her smiles were sober, and her looks were cheerful unto all;
And such as neither wanton seem, nor wayward, mell, nor gall.
A quiet mind, a patient mood, and not disdaining any;
Not gibing, gadding, gaudy, and her faculties were many.
A nymph, no tongue, no heart, no eye, might praise, might wish, might see
For life, for love, for form, more good, more worth, more fair than she.
Yea such a one, as such was none, save only she was such.
Of Argentile to say the most, were to be silent much."
"I knew the lady very well, but worthless of such praise,"
The Neatress said; "and muse I do, a shepherd thus should blaze
The coat of beauty. Credit me, thy latter speech betrays
Thy clownish shape a coined show. But wherefore dost thou weep?"
The Shepherd wept, and she was woe, and both doth silence keep.
"In truth," quoth he, "I am not such as seeming I profess:
But then for her, and now for thee, I from myself digress.
Her loved I, — wretch that I am and recreant to be! —
I loved her, that hated love. But now I die for thee.
At Kirkland is my father's court, and Curan is my name,
In Edel's court sometimes in pomp, till love controlled the same;
But now — What now? Dear heart, how now? What ailest thou to weep?"
The damsel wept, and he was woe, and both did silence keep.
"I grant," quoth she, "it was too much, that you did love so much;
But whom your former could not move, your second love doth touch.
Thy twice beloved Argentile submitteth her to thee;
And for thy double love presents herself, a single fee;
In passion, not in person chang'd, and I, my lord, am she."
They sweetly surfeiting in joy, and silent for a space,

When as the ecstasy had end did tenderly embrace,
And for their wedding, and their wish got fitting time and place.
Not England (for of Hengest then was named so this land)
Than Curan had an hardier knight, his force could none withstand;
Whose sheep-hook laid apart, he then had higher things in hand,
First, making known his lawful claim in Argentile her right,
He warr'd in Diria, and he won Brentia too in fight;
And so from treacherous Edel took at once his life and crown,
And of Northumberland was king, long reigning in renown.

GEORGE CHAPMAN (1559?–1634)

From THE SIXTH BOOK OF HOMER'S ILIADS

This said, he went to see
The virtuous princess, his true wife, white-arm'd Andromache.
She, with her infant son and maid, was climb'd the tower, about
The sight of him that sought for her, weeping and crying out.
Hector, not finding her at home, was going forth; retired;
Stood in the gate; her woman call'd, and curiously inquired
Where she was gone; bade tell him true, if she were gone to see
His sisters, or his brothers' wives; or whether she should be
At temple with the other dames, t' implore Minerva's ruth.
Her woman answer'd; since he ask'd, and urged so much the truth,
The truth was she was neither gone, to see his brothers' wives,
His sisters, nor t' implore the ruth of Pallas on their lives;
But she (advertised of the bane Troy suffer'd, and how vast
Conquest had made herself for Greece) like one distraught, made haste
To ample Ilion with her son, and nurse, and all the way
Mourn'd, and dissolved in tears for him. Then Hector made no stay,
But trod her path, and through the streets, magnificently built,
All the great city pass'd, and came where, seeing how blood was spilt,
Andromache might see him come; who made as he would pass
The ports without saluting her, not knowing where she was.
She, with his sight, made breathless haste, to meet him; she, whose grace
Brought him withal so great a dower; she that of all the race
Of king Aëtion only lived; Aëtion whose house stood
Beneath the mountain Placius, environ'd with the wood
Of Theban Hypoplace, being court to the Cilician land.
She ran to Hector, and with her, tender of heart and hand,
Her son, borne in his nurse's arms; when, like a heavenly sign,
Compact of many golden stars, the princely child did shine,
Whom Hector call'd Scamandrius; but whom the town did name
Astyanax, because his sire did only prop the same.
Hector, though grief bereft his speech, yet smiled upon his joy.
Andromache cried out, mix'd hands, and to the strength of Troy
Thus wept forth her affection: "O noblest in desire,
Thy mind, inflamed with others' good, will set thyself on fire:
Nor pitiest thou thy son, nor wife, who must thy widow be,
If now thou issue; all the field will only run on thee.
Better my shoulders underwent the earth, than thy decease;
For then would earth bear joys no more; then comes the black increase
Of griefs (like Greeks on Ilion). Alas, what one survives
To be my refuge? one black day bereft seven brothers' lives,
By stern Achilles; by his hand my father breathed his last,
His high-wall'd rich Cilician Thebes sack'd by him, and laid waste;
The royal body yet he left unspoil'd; Religion charm'd
That act of spoil; and all in fire he burn'd him complete arm'd;
Built over him a royal tomb; and to the monument

He left of him, th' Oreades (that are the high descent
Of Ægis-bearing Jupiter) another of their own
Did add to it, and set it round with elms; by which is shown,
In theirs, the barrenness of death; yet might it serve beside
To shelter the sad monument from all the ruffinous pride
Of storms and tempests, used to hurt things of that noble kind.
The short life yet my mother lived he saved, and served his mind
With all the riches of the realm; which not enough esteem'd,
He kept her prisoner; whom small time, but much more wealth, redeem'd;
And she, in sylvan Hypoplace, Cilicia ruled again,
But soon was overruled by death; Diana's chaste disdain
Gave her a lance, and took her life. Yet, all these gone from me,
Thou amply render'st all; thy life makes still my father be,
My mother, brothers; and besides thou art my husband too,
Most loved, most worthy. Pity then, dear love, and do not go,
For thou gone, all these go again; pity our common joy,
Lest, of a father's patronage, the bulwark of all Troy,
Thou leav'st him a poor widow's charge: stay, stay then, in this tower,
And call up to the wild fig-tree all thy retired power;
For there the wall is easiest scal'd, and fittest for surprise,
And there, th' Ajaces, Idomen, th' Atrides, Diomed, thrice
Have both survey'd and made attempt; I know not if induced
By some wise augur, or the fact was naturally infused
Into their wits, or courages." To this great Hector said:
"Be well assur'd, wife, all these things in my kind cares are weigh'd,
But what a shame and fear it is to think how Troy would scorn
(Both in her husbands, and her wives, whom long-train'd gowns adorn)
That I should cowardly fly off! The spirit I first did breathe
Did never teach me that; much less, since the contempt of death
Was settled in me, and my mind knew what a worthy was,
Whose office is to lead in fight, and give no danger pass
Without improvement. In this fire must Hector's trial shine;
Here must his country, father, friends, be, in him, made divine.
And such a stormy day shall come (in mind and soul I know)
When sacred Troy shall shed her towers, for tears of overthrow;
When Priam, all his birth and power, shall in those tears be drown'd.
But neither Troy's posterity so much my soul doth wound,
Priam, nor Hecuba herself, nor all my brothers' woes
(Who, though so many, and so good, must all be food for foes,)
As thy sad state; when some rude Greek shall lead thee weeping hence,
These free days clouded, and a night of captive violence
Loading thy temples, out of which thine eyes must never see,
But spin the Greek wives' webs of task, and their fetch-water be
To Argos, from Messeïdes, or clear Hyperia's spring;
Which howsoever thou abhorr'st, Fate's such a shrewish thing
She will be mistress; whose cursed hands, when they shall crush out cries
From thy oppressions (being beheld by other enemies)
Thus they will nourish thy extremes: 'This dame was Hector's wife,
A man that, at the wars of Troy, did breathe the worthiest life
Of all their army.' This again will rub thy fruitful wounds,
To miss the man that to thy bands could give such narrow bounds.
But that day shall not wound mine eyes; the solid heap of night
Shall interpose, and stop mine ears against thy plaints, and plight."
This said, he reach'd to take his son; who, of his arms afraid,
And then the horse-hair plume, with which he was so overlaid,
Nodded so horribly, he cling'd back to his nurse, and cried.
Laughter affected his great sire, who doff'd, and laid aside

His fearful helm, that on the earth cast round about it light;
Then took and kiss'd his loving son, and (balancing his weight
In dancing him) these loving vows to living Jove he used,
And all the other bench of Gods: "O you that have infused
Soul to this infant, now set down this blessing on his star:
Let his renown be clear as mine; equal his strength in war;
And make his reign so strong in Troy, that years to come may yield
His facts this fame, when, rich in spoils, he leaves the conquer'd field
Sown with his slaughters: 'These high deeds exceed his father's worth.'
And let this echo'd praise supply the comforts to come forth
Of his kind mother with my life." This said, th' heroic sire
Gave him his mother; whose fair eyes fresh streams of love's salt fire
Billow'd on her soft cheeks, to hear the last of Hector's speech,
In which his vows comprised the sum of all he did beseech
In her wish'd comfort. So she took into her odorous breast
Her husband's gift; who, moved to see her heart so much oppress'd,
He dried her tears, and thus desired: "Afflict me not, dear wife,
With these vain griefs. He doth not live, that can disjoin my life
And this firm bosom, but my fate; and Fate whose wings can fly?
Noble, ignoble, Fate controls. Once born, the best must die.
Go home, and set thy housewifery on these extremes of thought;
And drive war from them with thy maids; keep them from doing nought.
These will be nothing; leave the cares of war to men, and me,
In whom, of all the Ilion race, they take their highest degree."

From THE TWELFTH BOOK OF HOMER'S ODYSSEYS

"First to the Sirens ye shall come, that taint
The minds of all men whom they can acquaint
With their attractions. Whosoever shall,
For want of knowledge moved, but hear the call
Of any Siren, he will so despise
Both wife and children, for their sorceries,
That never home turns his affection's stream,
Nor they take joy in him, nor he in them.
The Sirens will so soften with their song
(Shrill, and in sensual appetite so strong)
His loose affections, that he gives them head.
And then observe: They sit amidst a mead,
And round about it runs a hedge or wall
Of dead men's bones, their wither'd skins and all
Hung all along upon it; and these men
Were such as they had fawn'd into their fen,
And then their skins hung on their hedge of bones.
Sail by them therefore, thy companions
Beforehand causing to stop every ear
With sweet soft wax so close, that none may hear
A note of all their charmings. Yet may you,
If you affect it, open ear allow
To try their motion; but presume not so
To trust your judgment, when your senses go
So loose about you, but give strait command
To all your men, to bind you foot and hand
Sure to the mast, that you may safe approve
How strong in instigation to their love
Their rapting tunes are. If so much they move,
That, spite of all your reason, your will stands
To be enfranchised both of feet and hands,
Charge all your men before to slight your charge,
And rest so far from fearing to enlarge
That much more sure they bind you. When your friends
Have outsail'd these, the danger that transcends
Rests not in any counsel to prevent,
Unless your own mind finds the tract and bent
Of that way that avoids it. I can say
That in your course there lies a twofold way,
The right of which your own taught present wit,
And grace divine, must prompt. In general yet
Let this inform you: Near these Sirens' shore
Move two steep rocks, at whose feet lie and roar
The black sea's cruel billows; the bless'd Gods
Call them the Rovers. Their abhorr'd abodes
No bird can pass; no not the doves, whose fear
Sire Jove so loves that they are said to bear
Ambrosia to him, can their ravine scape,
But one of them falls ever to the rape
Of those sly rocks; yet Jove another still
Adds to the rest, that so may ever fill
The sacred number. Never ship could shun
The nimble peril wing'd there, but did run
With all her bulk, and bodies of her men,
To utter ruin. For the seas retain
Not only their outrageous æsture there,
But fierce assistants of particular fear
And supernatural mischief they expire,

And those are whirlwinds of devouring fire
Whisking about still. Th' Argive ship alone,
(Which bore the care of all men) got her gone,
Come from Areta. Yet perhaps even she
Had wrack'd at those rocks, if the Deity,
That lies by Jove's side, had not lent her hand
To their transmission; since the man, that mann'd
In chief that voyage, she in chief did love.
Of these two spiteful rocks, the one doth shove
Against the height of heaven her pointed brow.
A black cloud binds it round, and never show
Lends to the sharp point; not the clear blue sky
Lets ever view it, not the summer's eye,
Not fervent autumn's. None that death could end
Could ever scale it, or, if up, descend,
Though twenty hands and feet he had for hold.
A polish'd ice-like glibness doth enfold
The rock so round, whose midst a gloomy cell
Shrouds so far westward that it sees to hell.
From this keep you as far as from his bow
An able young man can his shaft bestow.
For here the whuling Scylla shrouds her face,
That breathes a voice at all parts no more base
Than are newly-kitten'd kitling's cries,
Herself a monster yet of boundless size,
Whose sight would nothing please a mortal's eyes;
No, nor the eyes of any God, if he
(Whom nought should fright) fell foul on her, and she
Her full shape show'd. Twelve foul feet bear about
Her ugly bulk. Six huge long necks look'd out
Of her rank shoulders; every neck doth let
A ghastly head out; every head three set,
Thick thrust together, of abhorred teeth;
And every tooth stuck with a sable death;
"She lurks in midst of all her den, and streaks
From out a ghastly whirlpool all her necks;
Where (gloating round her rock) to fish she falls;
And up rush dolphins, dogfish; some-whiles whales,
If got within her when her rapine feeds;
For ever-groaning Amphitrite breeds
About her whirlpool an unmeasured store.
No sea-man ever boasted touch of shore
That there touch'd with his ship, but still she fed
Of him and his; a man for every head
Spoiling his ship of. You shall then descry
The other humbler rock, that moves so nigh
Your dart may mete the distance. It receives
A huge wild fig-tree, curl'd with ample leaves,
Beneath whose shades divine Charybdis sits,
Supping the black deeps. Thrice a day her pits
She drinks all dry, and thrice a day again
All up she belches, baneful to sustain.
When she is drinking, dare not near her draught,
For not the force of Neptune (if once caught)
Can force your freedom. Therefore, in your strife
To scape Charybdis, labour all, for life,
To row near Scylla, for she will but have
For her six heads six men; and better save
The rest, than all make offerings to the wave."
This need she told me of my loss, when I
Desired to know, if that Necessity,
When I had scaped Charybdis' outrages,
My powers might not revenge, though not redress.
She answers: "O unhappy! art thou yet
Enflamed with war, and thirst to drink thy sweat?
Not to the Gods give up both arms and will?
She deathless is, and that immortal ill
Grave, harsh, outrageous, not to be subdued,
That men must suffer till they be renew'd.
Nor lives there any virtue that can fly
The vicious outrage of their cruelty.
Shouldst thou put arms on, and approach the rock,
I fear six more must expiate the shock.
Six heads six men ask still. Hoise sail, and fly,
And, in thy flight, aloud on Cratis cry
(Great Scylla's mother, who exposed to light
That bane of men) and she will do such right
To thy observance, that she down will tread
Her daughter's rage, nor let her show a head.
"From henceforth then, for ever past her care,
Thou shalt ascend the isle triangular,
Where many oxen of the Sun are fed,
And fatted flocks. Of oxen fifty head
In every herd feed, and their herds are seven;
And of his fat flocks is their number even.
Increase they yield not, for they never die.
There every shepherdess a Deity.
Fair Phaëthusa, and Lampetie,
The lovely Nymphs are that their guardians be,
Who to the daylight's lofty-going flame
Had gracious birthright from the heavenly dame,
Still young Neæra; who (brought forth and bred)
Far off dismiss'd them, to see duly fed
Their father's herds and flocks in Sicily.
These herds and flocks if to the Deity
Ye leave, as sacred things, untouch'd, and on
Go with all fit care of your home, alone,
(Though through some sufferance) you yet safe shall land
In wished Ithaca. But if impious hand
You lay on those herds to their hurts, I then
Presage sure ruin to thy ship and men.
If thou escapest thyself, extending home
Thy long'd-for landing, thou shalt loaded come
With store of losses, most exceeding late,
And not consorted with a saved mate."
This said, the golden-throned Aurora rose,
She her way went, and I did mine dispose

Up to my ship, weigh'd anchor, and away.
When reverend Circe help'd us to convey
Our vessel safe, by making well inclined
A seaman's true companion, a forewind,
With which she fill'd our sails; when, fitting all
Our arms close by us, I did sadly fall
To grave relation what concern'd in fate
My friends to know, and told them that the state
Of our affairs' success, which Circe had
Presaged to me alone, must yet be made
To one nor only two known, but to all;
That, since their lives and deaths were left to fall
In their elections, they might life elect,
And give what would preserve it fit effect.
  I first inform'd them, that we were to fly
The heavenly-singing Sirens' harmony,
And flower-adorned meadow; and that I
Had charge to hear their song, but fetter'd fast
In bands, unfavour'd, to th' erected mast;
From whence, if I should pray, or use command,
To be enlarged, they should with much more band
Contain my strugglings. This I simply told
To each particular, nor would withhold
What most enjoin'd mine own affection's stay,
That theirs the rather might be taught t' obey.
  In meantime flew our ships, and straight we fetch'd
The Sirens' isle; a spleenless wind so stretch'd
Her wings to waft us, and so urged our keel.
But having reach'd this isle, we could not feel
The least gasp of it, it was stricken dead,
And all the sea in prostrate slumber spread:
The Sirens' devil charm'd all. Up then flew
My friends to work, strook sail, together drew,
And under hatches stow'd them, sat, and plied
Their polish'd oars, and did in curls divide
The white-head waters. My part then came on:
A mighty waxen cake I set upon,
Chopp'd it in fragments with my sword, and wrought
With strong hand every piece, till all were soft.
The great power of the sun, in such a beam
As then flew burning from his diadem,
To liquefaction help'd us. Orderly
I stopp'd their ears: and they as fair did ply
My feet and hands with cords, and to the mast
With other halsers made me soundly fast.
  Then took they seat, and forth our passage strook,
The foamy sea beneath their labour shook.
  Row'd on, in reach of an erected voice,
The Sirens soon took note, without our noise;
Tuned those sweet accents that made charms so strong,
And these learn'd numbers made the Sirens' song:

  "*Come here, thou worthy of a world of praise,*
That dost so high the Grecian glory raise;
Ulysses! stay thy ship, and that song hear
That none pass'd ever but it bent his ear,
But left him ravish'd and instructed more
By us, than any ever heard before.
For we know all things whatsoever were
In wide Troy labour'd; whatsoever there
The Grecians and the Trojans both sustain'd
By those high issues that the Gods ordain'd.
And whatsoever all the earth can show
T' inform a knowledge of desert, we know."
  This they gave accent in the sweetest strain
That ever open'd an enamour'd vein.
When my constrain'd heart needs would have mine ear
Yet more delighted, force way forth, and hear.
To which end I commanded with all sign
Stern looks could make (for not a joint of mine
Had power to stir) my friends to rise, and give
My limbs free way. They freely strived to drive
Their ship still on. When, far from will to loose,
Eurylochus and Perimedes rose
To wrap me surer, and oppress'd me more
With many a halser than had use before.
When, rowing on without the reach of sound,
My friends unstopp'd their ears, and me unbound,
And that isle quite we quitted.

ROBERT GREENE (1560?–1592)

SONG

Sweet are the thoughts that savour of content;
  The quiet mind is richer than a crown;
Sweet are the nights in careless slumber spent;
  The poor estate scorns fortune's angry frown:
Such sweet content, such minds, such sleep, such bliss,
Beggars enjoy, when princes oft do miss.

The homely house that harbours quiet rest;
  The cottage that affords no pride nor care;
The mean that 'grees with country music best;
  The sweet consort of mirth and music's fare;
Obscurèd life sets down a type of bliss:
A mind content both crown and kingdom is.

PHILOMELA'S ODE

Sitting by a river's side,
Where a silent stream did glide,
Muse I did of many things
That the mind in quiet brings.
I 'gan think how some men deem

Gold their god; and some esteem
Honour is the chief content
That to man in life is lent.
And some others do contend,
Quiet none like to a friend.
Others hold there is no wealth
Comparèd to a perfect health.
Some man's mind in quiet stands,
When he is lord of many lands.
But I did sigh, and said all this
Was but a shade of perfect bliss;
And in my thoughts I did approve,
Nought so sweet as is true love.
Love 'twixt lovers passeth these,
When mouth kisseth and heart 'grees,
With folded arms and lips meeting,
Each soul another sweetly greeting;
For by the breath the soul fleeteth,
And soul with soul in kissing meeteth.
If love be so sweet a thing,
That such happy bliss doth bring,
Happy is love's sugared thrall,
But unhappy maidens all,
Who esteem your virgin blisses
Sweeter than a wife's sweet kisses.
No such quiet to the mind
As true Love with kisses kind;
But if a kiss prove unchaste,
Then is true love quite disgraced.
Though love be sweet, learn this of me
No sweet love but honesty.

SEPHESTIA'S SONG TO HER CHILD

Weep not, my wanton, smile upon my knee,
When thou art old there's grief enough for thee.
Mother's wag, pretty boy,
Father's sorrow, father's joy;
When thy father first did see
Such a boy by him and me,
He was glad, I was woe,
Fortune changèd made him so,
When he left his pretty boy
Last his sorrow, first his joy.

Weep not, my wanton, smile upon my knee,
When thou art old there's grief enough for thee.
Streaming tears that never stint,
Like pearl drops from a flint,
Fell by course from his eyes,
That one another's place supplies;
Thus he grieved in every part,
Tears of blood fell from his heart,
When he left his pretty boy,
Father's sorrow, father's joy.

Weep not, my wanton, smile upon my knee,
When thou art old there's grief enough for thee.
The wanton smiled, father wept,
Mother cried, baby leapt;
More he crowed, more he cried,
Nature could not sorrow hide:
He must go, he must kiss
Child and mother, baby bless,
For he left his pretty boy,
Father's sorrow, father's joy.
Weep not, my wanton, smile upon my knee,
When thou art old there's grief enough for thee.

MENAPHON'S SONG

Some say Love,
Foolish Love,
Doth rule and govern all the gods:
I say Love,
Inconstant Love,
Sets men's senses far at odds.
Some swear Love,
Smooth-faced Love,
Is sweetest sweet that men can have:
I say Love,
Sour Love,
Makes virtue yield as beauty's slave.
A bitter sweet, a folly worst of all,
That forceth wisdom to be folly's thrall.

Love is sweet,
Wherein sweet?
In fading pleasures that do pain.
Beauty sweet:
Is that sweet
That yieldeth sorrow for a gain?
If Love's sweet,
Herein sweet,
That minute's joys are monthly woes:
'Tis not sweet,
That is sweet
Nowhere but where repentance grows.
Then love who list, if beauty be so sour;
Labor for me, Love rest in prince's bower.

THE SHEPHERD'S WIFE'S SONG

Ah, what is love? It is a pretty thing,
As sweet unto a shepherd as a king;
And sweeter too:
For kings have cares that wait upon a crown,
And cares can make the sweetest love to frown.
Ah then, ah then,
If country loves such sweet desires do gain,
What lady would not love a shepherd swain?

His flocks are folded, he comes home at night,
As merry as a king in his delight;
And merrier too:
For kings bethink them what the state require,
Where shepherds careless carol by the fire.
Ah then, ah then,
If country loves such sweet desires do gain,
What lady would not love a shepherd swain?

He kisseth first, then sits as blithe to eat
His cream and curds as doth the king his meat;
And blither too:
For kings have often fears when they do sup,
Where shepherds dread no poison in their cup.
Ah then, ah then,
If country loves such sweet desires do gain,
What lady would not love a shepherd swain?

To bed he goes, as wanton then, I ween,
As is a king in dalliance with a queen;
More wanton too:
For kings have many griefs affects to move,
Where shepherds have no greater grief than love.
Ah then, ah then,
If country loves such sweet desires do gain,
What lady would not love a shepherd swain?

Upon his couch of straw he sleeps as sound,
As doth the king upon his bed of down;
More sounder too:
For cares cause kings full oft their sleep to spill,
Where weary shepherds lie and snort their fill.
Ah then, ah then,
If country loves such sweet desires do gain,
What lady would not love a shepherd swain?

Thus with his wife he spends the year, as blithe
As doth the king at every tide or sithe;
And blither too:
For kings have wars and broils to take in hand
When shepherds laugh and love upon the land.
Ah then, ah then,
If country loves such sweet desires do gain,
What lady would not love a shepherd swain?

ROBERT SOUTHWELL (1561?–1595)

THE BURNING BABE

As I in hoary winter's night stood shivering in the snow,
Surprised I was with sudden heat which made my heart to glow;
And lifting up a fearful eye to view what fire was near,
A pretty babe all burning bright did in the air appear,
Who scorchèd with exceeding heat such floods of tears did shed,
As though His floods should quench His flames with what His tears were fed;
"Alas!" quoth He, "but newly born in fiery heats I fry,
Yet none approach to warm their hearts or feel my fire but I!
My faultless breast the furnace is, the fuel wounding thorns;
Love is the fire and sighs the smoke, the ashes shame and scorns;
The fuel Justice layeth on, and Mercy blows the coals;
The metal in this furnace wrought are men's defilèd souls;
For which, as now on fire I am, to work them to their good,
So will I melt into a bath, to wash them in my blood:"
With this He vanish'd out of sight, and swiftly shrunk away,
And straight I callèd unto mind that it was Christmas-day.

SAMUEL DANIEL (1562–1619)

SONNETS TO DELIA

XIX

Restore thy tresses to the golden ore;
Yield Cytherea's son those arcs of love:
Bequeath the heavens the stars that I adore;
And to the orient do thy pearls remove.
Yield thy hands' pride unto the ivory white;
To Arabian odours give thy breathing sweet;
Restore thy blush unto Aurora bright;
To Thetis give the honour of thy feet.
Let Venus have thy graces her resigned;
And thy sweet voice give back unto the spheres:
But yet restore thy fierce and cruel mind
To Hyrcan tigers and to ruthless bears.
Yield to the marble thy hard heart again;
So shalt thou cease to plague and I to pain.

XXXIX

Look, Delia, how we esteem the half-blown rose
The image of thy blush, and summer's honour!
Whilst yet her tender bud doth undisclose
That full of beauty Time bestows upon her.
No sooner spreads her glory in the air
But strait her wide-blown pomp comes to decline;
She then is scorn'd that late adorned the fair;
So fade the roses of those cheeks of thine.

No April can revive thy withered flowers
Whose springing grace adorns thy glory now;
Swift, speedy Time, feathered with flying hours,
Dissolves the beauty of the fairest brow.
Then do not thou such treasure waste in vain,
But love now, whilst thou mayst be loved again.

LIV

Care-charmer Sleep, son of the sable Night,
Brother to Death, in silent darkness born:
Relieve my languish, and restore the light;
With dark forgetting of my care, return!
And let the day be time enough to mourn
The shipwreck of my ill-adventured youth:
Let waking eyes suffice to wail their scorn,
Without the torment of the night's untruth.
Cease, dreams, the images of day-desires,
To model forth the passions of the morrow;
Never let rising sun approve you liars,
To add more grief to aggravate my sorrow.
Still let me sleep, embracing clouds in vain;
And never wake to feel the day's disdain.

LV

Let others sing of Knights and Paladins
In aged accents and untimely words;
Paint shadows in imaginary lines
Which well the reach of their high wits records:
But I must sing of thee, and those fair eyes
Authentic shall my verse in time to come;
When yet th' unborn shall say, "Lo where she lies
Whose beauty made him speak that else was dumb."
These are the arcs, the trophies I erect,
That fortify thy name against old age;
And these thy sacred virtues must protect
Against the dark, and Time's consuming rage.
Though the error of my youth in them appear,
Suffice they shew I lived and loved thee dear.

From THE COMPLAINT OF ROSAMOND

Amazed he stands, nor voice nor body stirs;
Words had no passage, tears no issue found;
For sorrow shut up words, wrath kept in tears;
Confused affects each other do confound;
Oppresst with grief, his passions had no bound.
Striving to tell his woes, words would not come;
For light cares speak when mighty griefs are dumb.

At length extremity breaks out a way
Through which th' imprisoned voice, with tears attended,
Wails out a sound that sorrows do bewray;
With arms across, and eyes to heaven bended,
Vapouring out sighs that to the skies ascended;
Sighs (the poor ease calamity affords)
Which serve for speech when sorrow wanteth words.

"O heavens," quoth he, "why do mine eyes behold
The hateful rays of this unhappy sun?
Why have I light to see my sins controlled
With blood of mine own shame thus vildly done!
How can my sight endure to look thereon?
Why doth not black eternal darkness hide
That from mine eyes my heart cannot abide?

"What saw my life wherein my soul might joy?
What had my days, whom troubles still afflicted,
But only this, to counterpoise annoy?
This joy, this hope, which Death hath interdicted;
This sweet, whose loss hath all distress inflicted;
This, that did season all my sour of life,
Vexed still at home with broils, abroad in strife?

"Vexed still at home with broils, abroad in strife,
Dissension in my blood, jars in my bed;
Distrust at board, suspecting still my life,
Spending the night in horror, days in dread,
Such life hath Tyrants and this life I led;
These miseries go masked in glittering shows,
Which wise men see, the vulgar little knows."

Thus, as these passions do him overwhelm,
He draws him near the body to behold it:
And as the vine married unto the elm
With strict embraces, so doth he enfold it;
And as he in his careful arms doth hold it,
Viewing the face that even Death commends,
On senseless lips millions of kisses spends.

"Pitiful mouth," saith he, "that living gavest
The sweetest comfort that my soul could wish;
O be it lawful now that dead thou havest
This sorrowing farewell of a dying kiss.
And you fair eyes, containers of my bliss,
Motives of love, born to be matched never,
Entombed in your sweet circles sleep forever.

"Ah, how methinks I see Death dallying seeks
To entertain itself in Love's sweet place;
Decayed roses of discoloured cheeks
Do yet retain dear notes of former grace;
And ugly Death sits fair within her face;

Sweet remnants resting of vermilion red,
That Death itself doubts whether she be dead.

"Wonder of beauty, oh, receive these plaints,
These obsequies, the last that I shall make thee;
For lo, my soul that now already faints
(That loved thee living, dead will not forsake thee)
Hastens her speedy course to overtake thee.
I'll meet my death, and free myself thereby;
For, ah, what can he do that cannot die?

"Yet ere I die thus much my soul doth vow,
Revenge shall sweeten death with ease of mind;
And I will cause posterity shall know
How fair thou wert above all women-kind;
And after ages monuments shall find
Shewing thy beauty's title, not thy name,
Rose of the world that sweetened so the same."

EPISTLE TO THE LADY MARGARET, COUNTESS OF CUMBERLAND

He that of such a height hath built his mind,
And rear'd the dwelling of his thoughts so strong,
As neither fear nor hope can shake the frame
Of his resolved pow'rs; nor all the wind
Of vanity or malice pierce to wrong
His settled peace, or to disturb the same:
What a fair seat hath he, from whence he may
The boundless wastes and wilds of man survey!
And with how free an eye doth he look down
Upon these lower regions of turmoil!
Where all the storms of passions mainly beat
On flesh and blood: where honour, pow'r, renown
Are only gay afflictions, golden toil;
Where greatness stands upon as feeble feet
As frailty doth; and only great doth seem
To little minds, who do it so esteem.
He looks upon the mightiest monarchs' wars
But only as on stately robberies;
Where evermore the fortune that prevails
Must be the right: the ill-succeeding mars
The fairest and the best-fac'd enterprise.
Great pirate Pompey lesser pirates quails:
Justice, he sees (as if seducèd), still
Conspires with pow'r, whose cause must not be ill.
He sees the face of Right t' appear as manifold
As are the passions of uncertain man;
Who puts it in all colours, all attires,
To serve his ends, and make his courses hold.
He sees, that let deceit work what it can,
Plot and contrive base ways to high desires,
That the all-guiding Providence doth yet
All disappoint, and mocks this smoke of wit.
Nor is he mov'd with all the thunder-cracks
Of tyrants' threats, or with the surly brow
Of Pow'r, that proudly sits on others' crimes;
Charg'd with more crying sins than those he checks.
The storms of sad confusion, that may grow
Up in the present for the coming times,
Appal not him; that hath no side at all,
But himself, and knows the worst can fall.
Altho' his heart, so near allied to earth,
Cannot but pity the perplexed state
Of troublous and distress'd mortality,
That thus make way unto the ugly birth
Of their own sorrows, and do still beget
Affliction upon imbecility:
Yet seeing thus the course of things must run,
He looks thereon not strange, but as fore-done.
And whilst distraught ambition compasses,
And is encompass'd; whilst as craft deceives,
And is deceiv'd; whilst man doth ransack man,
And builds on blood, and rises by distress;
And th' inheritance of desolation leaves
To great-expecting hopes: he looks thereon,
As from the shore of peace, with unwet eye,
And bears no venture in impiety.

From MUSOPHILUS

Sacred Religion! Mother of Form and Fear!
How gorgeously sometimes dost thou sit decked!
What pompous vestures do we make thee wear,
What stately piles we prodigal erect,
How sweet perfumed thou art, how shining clear,
How solemnly observed, with what respect!
Another time all plain, all quite thread-bare;
Thou must have all within, and nought without;
Sit poorly without light, disrobed, — no care
Of outward grace, to amuse the poor devout;
Powerless, unfollowed; scarcely men can spare
The necessary rites to set thee out!

* * * * * * *

And for the few that only lend their ear,
That few is all the world; which with a few
Do ever live, and move, and work, and stir.
This is the heart doth feel and only know.
The rest of all, that only bodies bear,
Roll up and down, and fill up but the row,
And serve as others members, not their own,
The instruments of those that do direct.
Then what disgrace is this, not to be known
To those know not to give themselves respect?
And though they swell with pomp of folly blown,
They live ungrac'd, and die but in Neglect.
And for my part, if only one allow
The care my labouring spirits take in this,

He is to me a Theater large enow,
And his applause only sufficient is.
All my respect is bent but to his brow,
That is my All; and all I am, is his.
  And if some worthy spirits be pleased too,
It shall more comfort breed, but not more will.
But what if none? It cannot yet undo
The love I bear unto this holy skill.
This is the thing that I was born to do,
This is my Scene, this Part must I fulfil.
  Let those that know not breath, esteem of wind,
And set t' a vulgar air their servile song;
Rating their goodness by the praise they find,
Making their worth on others' fits belong;
As Virtue were the hireling of the mind,
And could not live if Fame had ne'er a tongue.
  Hath that all-knowing power that holds within
The goodly prospective of all this frame,
(Where, whatsoever is, or what hath been,
Reflects a certain image of the same)
No inward pleasures to delight her in,
But she must gad to seek an alms of Fame?

JOSHUA SYLVESTER (1563–1618)

SONNET

Were I as base as is the lowly plain,
  And you, my Love, as high as heaven above,
Yet should the thoughts of me, your humble swain,
  Ascend to heaven in honour of my love.
Were I as high as heaven above the plain,
  And you, my Love, as humble and as low
As are the deepest bottoms of the main,
  Whatsoe'er you were, with you my love should go!
Were you the earth, dear Love! and I, the skies;
  My love should shine on you, like to the sun!
And look upon you, with ten thousand eyes,
  Till heaven waxed blind! and till the world were done!
Wheresoe'er I am, — below, or else above, you, —
  Wheresoe'er you are, my heart shall truly love you!

THE FRUITS OF A CLEAR CONSCIENCE

To shine in silk, and glister all in gold,
  To flow in wealth, and feed on dainty fare,
To have thy houses stately to behold,
  Thy prince's favour, and the people's care:
    The groaning gout, the colic, or the stone,
    Will mar thy mirth, and turn it all to moan!
But, be it that thy body subject be
  To no such sickness or the like annoy,
Yet if thy Conscience be not firm and free,
  Riches are trash, and Honour's but a toy!
  This Peace of Conscience is the perfect joy
    Wherewith God's children in the world be blest:
    Wanting the which, as good want all the rest!

The want thereof made Adam hide his head!
  The want of this made Cain to wail and weep!
This want, alas, makes many go to bed,
  When they, God wot, have little list to sleep.
  Strive, oh, then strive, to entertain and keep
    So rich a jewel, and so rare a guest!
    Which being had, a rush for all the rest!

MICHAEL DRAYTON (1563–1631)

IDEA

TO THE READER OF THESE SONNETS

Into these Loves, who but for Passion looks;
  At this first sight, here let him lay them by,
  And seek elsewhere in turning other books,
  Which better may his labour satisfy.
No far-fetched sigh shall ever wound my breast;
Love from mine eye a tear shall never wring;
Nor in "Ah me's!" my whining sonnets drest!
A libertine! fantasticly I sing!
  My verse is the true image of my mind,
Ever in motion, still desiring change;
And as thus, to variety inclined,
So in all humours sportively I range!
  My Muse is rightly of the English strain,
  That cannot long one fashion entertain.

IV

Bright Star of Beauty! on whose eyelids sit
A thousand nymph-like and enamoured Graces,
The Goddesses of Memory and Wit,
Which there in order take their several places.
  In whose dear bosom, sweet delicious Love
Lays down his quiver, which he once did bear,
Since he that blessèd paradise did prove;
And leaves his mother's lap, to sport him there.
  Let others strive to entertain with words!
My soul is of a braver mettle made:
I hold that vile, which vulgar wit affords,
In me's that faith which Time cannot invade!
  Let what I praise be still made good by you!
  Be you most worthy, whilst I am most true!

XX

An evil Spirit (your Beauty) haunts me still,
Wherewith, alas, I have been long possest;
Which ceaseth not to attempt me to each ill,
Nor give me once, but one poor minute's rest.
In me it speaks, whether I sleep or wake;
And when by means to drive it out I try,
With greater torments then it me doth take,
And tortures me in most extremity.
Before my face, it lays down my despairs,
And hastes me on unto a sudden death;
Now tempting me, to drown myself in tears,
And then in sighing to give up my breath.
Thus am I still provoked to every evil,
By this good-wicked Spirit, sweet Angel-Devil.

XXIV

I hear some say, "This man is not in love!"
"Who! can he love? a likely thing!" they say.
"Read but his verse, and it will easily prove!"
O, judge not rashly, gentle Sir, I pray!
Because I loosely trifle in this sort,
As one that fain his sorrows would beguile,
You now suppose me, all this time, in sport,
And please yourself with this conceit the while.
Ye shallow Censures! sometimes, see ye not,
In greatest perils some men pleasant be?
Where Fame by death is only to be got,
They resolute! So stands the case with me.
Where other men in depth of passion cry,
I laugh at Fortune, as in jest to die!

XXXVII

Dear! why should you command me to my rest,
When now the night doth summon all to sleep?
Methinks this time becometh lovers best!
Night was ordained together friends to keep.
How happy are all other living things,
Which, through the day, disjoined by several flight,
The quiet evening yet together brings,
And each returns unto his Love at night!
O thou that art so courteous else to all,
Why shouldst thou, Night, abuse me only thus?
That every creature to his kind dost call,
And yet 'tis thou dost only sever us!
Well could I wish it would be ever day;
If, when night comes, you bid me go away!

XLIV

Whilst thus my pen strives to eternize thee,
Age rules my lines with wrinkles in my face,
Where, in the map of all my misery,
Is modelled out the world of my disgrace.
Whilst in despite of tyrannizing Times,
Medea-like, I make thee young again,
Proudly thou scorn'st my world-outwearing rhymes,
And murder'st Virtue with thy coy disdain!
And though in youth my youth untimely perish
To keep thee from oblivion and the grave,
Ensuing ages yet my rhymes shall cherish,
Where I entombed, my better part shall save;
And though this earthly body fade and die,
My name shall mount upon Eternity!

LXI

Since there's no help, come, let us kiss and part!
Nay, I have done; you get no more of me!
And I am glad, yea, glad, with all my heart,
That thus so cleanly I myself can free.
Shake hands for ever! Cancel all our vows!
And when we meet at any time again,
Be it not seen in either of our brows,
That we one jot of former love retain!
Now at the last gasp of Love's latest breath,
When, his pulse failing, Passion speechless lies;
When Faith is kneeling by his bed of death,
And Innocence is closing up his eyes,—
Now, if thou wouldst, when all have given him over,
From death to life thou might'st him yet recover!

ODE XI

TO THE VIRGINIAN VOYAGE

You brave heroic minds,
Worthy your country's name,
That honour still pursue;
Go and subdue!
Whilst loitering hinds
Lurk here at home with shame.

Britons, you stay too long;
Quickly aboard bestow you!
And with a merry gale
Swell your stretched sail,
With vows as strong
As the winds that blow you!

Your course securely steer,
West-and-by-south forth keep!
Rocks, lee-shores, nor shoals,
When Eolus scowls,
You need not fear,
So absolute the deep.

And, cheerfully at sea,
Success you still entice,
To get the pearl and gold;
And ours to hold,
Virginia,
Earth's only Paradise.

Where Nature hath in store
Fowl, venison, and fish;
And the fruitful'st soil, —
Without your toil,
Three harvests more,
All greater than your wish.

And the ambitious vine
Crowns with his purple mass
The cedar reaching high
To kiss the sky,
The cypress, pine,
And useful sassafras.

To whom, the Golden Age
Still Nature's laws doth give:
Nor other cares attend,
But them to defend
From winter's rage,
That long there doth not live.

When as the luscious smell
Of that delicious land,
Above the seas that flows,
The clear wind throws,
Your hearts to swell,
Approaching the dear strand.

In kenning of the shore
(Thanks to God first given!)
O you, the happiest men,
Be frolic then!
Let cannons roar,
Frightening the wide heaven!

And in regions far,
Such heroes bring ye forth
As those from whom we came!
And plant our name
Under that star
Not known unto our North!

And where in plenty grows
The laurel everywhere,
Apollo's sacred tree
Your days may see
A poet's brows
To crown, that may sing there.

Thy Voyages attend,
Industrious Hakluyt!
Whose reading shall inflame
Men to seek fame;
And much commend
To after times thy wit.

ODE XII

TO THE CAMBRO-BRITANS AND THEIR HARP, HIS BALLAD OF AGINCOURT

Fair stood the wind for France,
When we our sails advance;
Nor now to prove our chance
Longer will tarry;
But putting to the main,
At Caux, the mouth of Seine,
With all his martial train
Landed King Harry.

And taking many a fort,
Furnished in warlike sort,
Marcheth towards Agincourt
In happy hour;
Skirmishing, day by day,
With those that stopped his way,
Where the French general lay
With all his power.

Which, in his height of pride,
King Henry to deride,
His ransom to provide,
To the King sending;
Which he neglects the while,
As from a nation vile,
Yet, with an angry smile,
Their fall portending.

And turning to his men,
Quoth our brave Henry then:
"Though they to one be ten
Be not amazèd!
Yet have we well begun:
Battles so bravely won
Have ever to the sun
By Fame been raised!"

"And for myself," quoth he,
"This my full rest shall be:
England ne'er mourn for me,
Nor more esteem me!
Victor I will remain,
Or on this earth lie slain;
Never shall She sustain
Loss to redeem me!"

"Poitiers and Cressy tell,
When most their pride did swell,
Under our swords they fell.
No less our skill is,
Than when our Grandsire great,
Claiming the regal seat,
By many a warlike feat
Lopped the French lilies."

The Duke of York so dread
The eager vanward led;
With the main, Henry sped
Amongst his henchmen:
Exeter had the rear,
A braver man not there!
O Lord, how hot they were
On the false Frenchmen!

They now to fight are gone;
Armour on armour shone;
Drum now to drum did groan:
To hear, was wonder;
That, with the cries they make,
The very earth did shake;
Trumpet to trumpet spake;
Thunder to thunder.

Well it thine age became,
O noble Erpingham,
Which didst the signal aim
To our hid forces!
When, from a meadow by,
Like a storm suddenly,
The English archery
Stuck the French horses.

With Spanish yew so strong;
Arrows a cloth-yard long,
That like to serpents stung,
Piercing the weather.
None from his fellow starts;
But, playing manly parts,
And like true English hearts,
Stuck close together.

When down their bows they threw,
And forth their bilboes drew,
And on the French they flew:
Not one was tardy.
Arms were from shoulders sent,
Scalps to the teeth were rent,
Down the French peasants went:
Our men were hardy.

This while our noble King,
His broad sword brandishing,
Down the French host did ding,
As to o'erwhelm it.
And many a deep wound lent;
His arms with blood besprent,
And many a cruel dent
Bruisèd his helmet.

Gloucester, that duke so good,
Next of the royal blood,
For famous England stood
With his brave brother.
Clarence, in steel so bright,
Though but a maiden knight,
Yet in that furious fight
Scarce such another!

Warwick in blood did wade;
Oxford, the foe invade,
And cruel slaughter made,
Still as they ran up.
Suffolk his axe did ply;
Beaumont and Willoughby
Bare them right doughtily;
Ferrers, and Fanhope.

Upon Saint Crispin's Day
Fought was this noble Fray;
Which Fame did not delay
To England to carry.
O when shall English men
With such acts fill a pen?
Or England breed again
Such a King Harry?

ENGLAND'S HISTORICAL EPISTLES

HENRY HOWARD, EARL OF SURREY, TO GERALDINE

From learned Florence (long time rich in fame),
From whence thy race, thy noble grandsires, came
To famous England, the kind nurse of mine,
Thy Surrey sends to heavenly Geraldine.
Yet let not Tuscan think I do her wrong,
That I from thence write in my native tongue,
That in these harsh-tun'd cadences I sing,
Sitting so near the Muses' sacred spring;
But rather think herself adorn'd thereby,
That England reads the praise of Italy.
Though to the Tuscan I the smoothness grant,
Our dialect no majesty doth want,
To set thy praises in as high a key,
As France, or Spain, or Germany, or they.

* * * * * * *

And as that wealthy Germany I passed,
Coming unto the Emperor's court at last,
Great learned Agrippa, so profound in Art,
Who the infernal secrets doth impart,

When of thy health I did desire to know,
Me in a glass my Geraldine did show,
Sick in thy bed, and for thou couldst not sleep,
By a wax taper set thy light to keep.
I do remember thou didst read that Ode,
Sent back whilst I in Thanet made abode;
Where as thou cam'st unto the word of love,
Even in thine eyes I saw how passion strove.
That snowy lawn which covered thy bed,
Me thought looked white, to see thy cheek so red,
Thy rosy cheek oft changing in my sight,
Yet still was red, to see the lawn so white.
The little taper which should give thee light,
Me thought waxed dim, to see thy eye so bright;
Thine eye again supplies the taper's turn,
And with his beams doth make the taper burn.
The shrugging air about thy temple hurls,
And wraps thy breath in little crowded curls,
And as it doth ascend, it straight doth cease it,
And as it sinks, it presently doth raise it.
Canst thou by sickness banish beauty so?
Which if put from thee, knows not where to go
To make her shift, and for her succor seek
To every riveled face, each bankrupt cheek.
If health preserved, thou beauty still dost cherish;
If that neglected, beauty soon doth perish.
Care draws on care, woe comforts woe again,
Sorrow breeds sorrow, one grief brings forth twain.
If live, or die, as thou dost, so do I;
If live, I live, and if thou die, I die;
One heart, one love, one joy, one grief, one troth,
One good, one ill, one life, one death to both.
If Howard's blood thou hold'st as but too vile
Or not esteemst of Norfolk's Princely style,

* * * * * * *

Yet am I one of great Apollo's heirs,
The sacred Muses challenge me for theirs.
By Princes my immortal lines are sung,
My flowing verses graced with every tongue;
The little children, when they learn to go,
By painful mothers guided to and fro,
Are taught my sugar'd numbers to rehearse,
And have their sweet lips seasoned with my verse.
When heaven would strive to do the best it can,
And put an angel's spirit into a man,
The utmost power in that great work doth spend,
When to the world a poet it doth intend.
That little difference 'twixt the Gods and us,
By them confirmed, distinguished only thus;
Whom they in birth ordain to happy days,
The Gods commit their glory to our praise;
To eternal life when they dissolve their breath,
We likewise share a second power by death.
When time shall turn those amber colours to gray,
My verse again shall gild and make them gay,
And trick them up in knotted curls anew,
And in the autumn give a summer's hue.
That sacred power that in my ink remains
Shall put fresh blood into thy withered veins,
And on thy red decayed, thy whiteness dead,
Shall set a white more white, a red more red.
When thy dim sight thy glass cannot descry,
Thy crazed mirror cannot see thine eye,
My verse to tell what eye, what mirror was,
Glass to thine eye, an eye unto thy glass,
Where both thy mirror and thine eye shall see,
What once thou saw'st in that, that saw in thee;
And to them both shall tell the simple truth,
What that in pureness was, what thou in youth.
If Florence once should lose her old renown,
As famous Athens, now a fisher town,
My lines for thee a Florence shall erect,
Which great Apollo ever shall protect;
And with the numbers from my pen that falls,
Bring marble mines to re-erect those walls.

* * * * * * *

I find no cause, nor judge I reason why
My country should give place to Lombardy.
As goodly flowers on Thamisis do grow,
As beautify the banks of wanton Po;
As many Nymphs as haunt rich Arnus' strand,
By silver Sabrine tripping hand in hand;
Our shades as sweet, though not to us so dear,
Because the sun hath greater power here.
This distant place but gives me greater woe;
Far off, my sighs the farther have to go!
Ah absence! why thus shouldst thou seem so long?
Or wherefore shouldst thou offer time such wrong,
Summer so soon should steal on winter's cold
Or winter's blasts so soon make summer old?
Love did us both with one self arrow strike;
Our wounds both one, our cure should be the like;
Except thou hast found out some means by art,
Some powerful medicine to withdraw the dart;
But mine is fixed, and absence, physic proved,
It sticks too fast, it cannot be removed.
Adieu, adieu, from Florence when I go,
By my next letters Geraldine shall know;
Which if good fortune shall my course direct,
From Venice by some messenger expect;
Till when, I leave thee to thy heart's desire.
By him that lives thy virtues to admire.

From NYMPHIDIA

THE COURT OF FAIRY

Old Chaucer doth of Topas tell,
Mad Rabelais of Pantagruel,
A later third of Dowsabel,
With such poor trifles playing;

Others the like have laboured at,
Some of this thing and some of that,
And many of they know not what,
But that they must be saying.

Another sort there be, that will
Be talking of the Fairies still,
Nor never can they have their fill,
As they were wedded to them;
No tales of them their thirst can slake,
So much delight therein they take,
And some strange thing they fain would make,
Knew they the way to do them.

Then since no Muse hath been so bold,
Or of the later or the old,
Those elfish secrets to unfold
Which lie from others' reading;
My active Muse to light shall bring
The court of that proud Fairy King,
And tell there of the reveling.
Jove prosper my proceeding!

* * * * * * *

Which done, the Queen her maids doth call,
And bids them to be ready all:
She would go see her summer hall,
She could no longer tarry.

Her chariot ready straight is made
Each thing therein is fitting laid,
That she by nothing might be stayed,
For nought must her be letting;
Four nimble gnats the horses were,
Their harnesses of gossamer,
Fly Cranion her charioteer
Upon the coach-box getting.

Her chariot of a snail's fine shell,
Which for the colours did excel,
The fair Queen Mab becoming well,
So lively was the limning;
The seat the soft wool of the bee,
The cover, gallantly to see,
The wing of a pied butterflee;
I trow 'twas simple trimming.

The wheels composed of crickets' bones,
And daintily made for the nonce;
For fear of rattling on the stones
With thistle-down they shod it;
For all her maidens much did fear
If Oberon had chanc'd to hear
That Mab his Queen should have been there,
He would not have abode it.

She mounts her chariot with a trice,
Nor would she stay, for no advice,
Until her maids that were so nice
To wait on her were fitted;
But ran herself away alone,
Which when they heard, there was not one
But hasted after to be gone,
As she had been diswitted.

Hop and Mop and Drop so clear
Pip and Trip and Skip that were
To Mab, their sovereign, ever dear,
Her special maids of honour;
Fib and Tib and Pink and Pin,
Tick and Quick and Jill and Jin,
Tit and Nit and Wap and Win,
The train that wait upon her.

Upon a grasshopper they got
And, what with amble and with trot,
For hedge nor ditch they spared not,
But after her they hie them;
A cobweb over them they throw,
To shield the wind if it should blow;
Themselves they wisely could bestow
Lest any should espy them.

CHRISTOPHER MARLOWE[1] (1564–1593)

HERO AND LEANDER

From THE FIRST SESTIAD

On Hellespont, guilty of true love's blood,
In view and opposite two cities stood,
Sea-borderers, disjoin'd by Neptune's might;
The one Abydos, the other Sestos hight.
At Sestos Hero dwelt; Hero the fair,
Whom young Apollo courted for her hair,
And offer'd as a dower his burning throne,
Where she should sit, for men to gaze upon.
The outside of her garments were of lawn,
The lining purple silk, with gilt stars drawn;
Her wide sleeves green, and border'd with a grove,
Where Venus in her naked glory strove
To please the careless and disdainful eyes
Of proud Adonis, that before her lies;
Her kirtle blue, whereon was many a stain,
Made with the blood of wretched lovers slain.
Upon her head she ware a myrtle wreath,
From whence her veil reach'd to the ground beneath;
Her veil was artificial flowers and leaves,

[1] See also p. 131.

Whose workmanship both man and beast deceives.
Many would praise the sweet smell as she past,
When 'twas the odour which her breath forth cast;
And there, for honey, bees have sought in vain,
And, beat from thence, have lighted there again.
About her neck hung chains of pebble-stone,
Which, lighten'd by her neck, like diamonds shone.
She ware no gloves; for neither sun nor wind
Would burn or parch her hands, but, to her mind,
Or warm or cool them, for they took delight
To play upon those hands, they were so white.
Buskins of shells, all silver'd, usèd she,
And branch'd with blushing coral to the knee;
Where sparrows perch'd of hollow pearl and gold,
Such as the world would wonder to behold:
Those with sweet water oft her handmaid fills,
Which as she went, would chirrup through the bills.
Some say, for her the fairest Cupid pin'd,
And, looking in her face, was strooken blind.
But this is true; so like was one the other,
As he imagin'd Hero was his mother;
And oftentimes into her bosom flew,
About her naked neck his bare arms threw,
And laid his childish head upon her breast,
And, with still panting rock, there took his rest.
So lovely-fair was Hero, Venus' nun,
As Nature wept, thinking she was undone,
Because she took more from her than she left,
And of such wondrous beauty her bereft:
Therefore, in sign her treasure suffer'd wrack,
Since Hero's time hath half the world been black.
Amorous Leander, beautiful and young
(Whose tragedy divine Musæus sung),
Dwelt at Abydos; since him dwelt there none
For whom succeeding times make greater moan.
His dangling tresses, that were never shorn,
Had they been cut, and unto Colchos borne,
Would have allur'd the venturous youth of Greece
To hazard more than for the golden fleece.
Fair Cynthia wished his arms might be her Sphere;
Grief makes her pale, because she moves not there.
His body was as straight as Circe's wand;
Jove might have sipt out nectar from his hand.
Even as delicious meat is to the taste,
So was his neck in touching, and surpast
The white of Pelops' shoulder: I could tell ye,
How smooth his breast was, and how white his belly;
And whose immortal fingers did imprint
That heavenly path with many a curious dint
That runs along his back; but my rude pen
Can hardly blazon forth the loves of men,
Much less of powerful gods: Let it suffice
That my slack Muse sings of Leander's eyes;
Those orient cheeks and lips, exceeding his
That leapt into the water for a kiss
Of his own shadow, and, despising many,
Died ere he could enjoy the love of any.
Had wild Hippolytus Leander seen,
Enamour'd of his beauty had he been.
His presence made the rudest peasant melt,
That in the vast uplandish country dwelt;
The barbarous Thracian soldier, mov'd with nought,
Was mov'd with him, and for his favour sought.
Some swore he was a maid in man's attire,
For in his looks were all that men desire, —
A pleasant-smiling cheek, a speaking eye,
A brow for love to banquet royally;
And such as knew he was a man, would say,
"Leander, thou art made for amorous play;
Why art thou not in love, and loved of all?
Though thou be fair, yet be not thine own thrall."
The men of wealthy Sestos every year,
For his sake whom their goddess held so dear,
Rose-cheek'd Adonis, kept a solemn feast.
Thither resorted many a wandering guest
To meet their loves; such as had none at all
Came lovers home from this great festival;
For every street, like to a firmament,
Glister'd with breathing stars, who, where they went,
Frighted the melancholy earth, which deem'd
Eternal heaven to burn, for so it seem'd
As if another Phaëton had got
The guidance of the sun's rich chariot.
But, far above the loveliest, Hero shin'd,
And stole away th' enchanted gazer's mind;
For like sea-nymphs' inveigling harmony,
So was her beauty to the standers by;
Nor that night-wandering, pale, and watery star
(When yawning dragons draw her thirling car
From Latmus' mount up to the gloomy sky,
Where, crown'd with blazing light and majesty,
She proudly sits) more over-rules the flood
Than she the hearts of those that near her stood.
Even as, when gaudy nymphs pursue the chase,
Wretched Ixion's shaggy-footed race,
Incens'd with savage heat, gallop amain
From steep pine-bearing mountains to the plain,
So ran the people forth to gaze upon her,
And all that view'd her were enamour'd on her.
And as, in fury of a dreadful fight,
Their fellows being slain or put to flight,
Poor soldiers stand with fear of death dead-strooken,
So at her presence all surpris'd and tooken,
Await the sentence of her scornful eyes;
He whom she favours lives; the other dies.
There might you see one sigh; another rage;

And some, their violent passions to assuage,
Compile sharp satires; but, alas, too late!
For faithful love will never turn to hate.
And many, seeing great princes were denied,
Pin'd as they went, and thinking on her died.
On this feast-day — O cursèd day and hour! —
Went Hero thorough Sestos, from her tower
To Venus' temple, where unhappily,
As after chanc'd, they did each other spy.
So fair a church as this had Venus none:
The walls were of discolour'd jasper-stone,
Wherein was Proteus carved; and over-head
A lively vine of green sea-agate spread,
Where by one hand light-headed Bacchus hung,
And with the other wine from grapes out-wrung.
Of crystal shining fair the pavement was;
The town of Sestos call'd it Venus' glass:

* * * * * * *

And in the midst a silver altar stood:
There Hero, sacrificing turtles' blood,
Vailed to the ground, veiling her eyelids close;
And modestly they opened as she rose.
Thence flew Love's arrow with the golden head;
And thus Leander was enamourèd.
Stone-still he stood, and evermore he gaz'd,
Till with the fire that from his countenance blaz'd
Relenting Hero's gentle heart was strook:
Such force and virtue hath an amorous look.
It lies not in our power to love or hate,
For will in us is over-rul'd by fate.
When two are stript long ere the course begin,
We wish that one should lose, the other win;
And one especially do we affect
Of two gold ingots, like in each respect:
The reason no man knows, let it suffice,
What we behold is censur'd by our eyes.
Where both deliberate, the love is slight:
Who ever lov'd, that lov'd not at first sight?

ENGLAND'S HELICON (1600)

PHYLLIDA AND CORYDON

In the merry month of May,
In a morn by break of day,
Forth I walk'd by the wood-side,
When as May was in his pride:
There I spiëd all alone,
Phyllida and Corydon.
Much ado there was, God wot!
He would love and she would not.
She said, never man was true;
He said, none was false to you.
He said, he had loved her long;
She said, love should have no wrong.
Corydon would kiss her then;
She said, maids must kiss no men,
Till they did for good and all;
Then she made the shepherd call
All the heavens to witness truth:
Never loved a truer youth.
Thus with many a pretty oath,
Yea and nay, and faith and troth,
Such as silly shepherds use
When they will not love abuse,
Love which had been long deluded,
Was with kisses sweet concluded;
And Phyllida, with garlands gay,
Was made the Lady of the May.

— N. Breton (1545?–1626?)

TO COLIN CLOUT

Beauty sat bathing in a spring,
Where fairest shades did hide her;
The winds blew calm, the birds did sing,
The cool streams ran beside her.
My wanton thoughts enticed mine eye,
To see what was forbidden,
But better memory said, fie:
So, vain desire was chidden.
Hey nonny, nonny, etc.

Into a slumber then I fell,
When fond Imagination
Seem'd to see, but could not tell,
Her feature or her fashion.
But even as babes in dreams do smile,
And sometimes fall a-weeping,
So I awaked, as wise this while
As when I fell a-sleeping.
Hey nonny, nonny, etc.

— Shepherd Tony

AS IT FELL UPON A DAY

As it fell upon a day,
In the merry month of May,
Sitting in a pleasant shade,
Which a group of myrtles made,
Beasts did leap and birds did sing,
Trees did grow and plants did spring,
Everything did banish moan,
Save the nightingale alone;
She, poor bird, as all forlorn,
Lean'd her breast against a thorn,
And there sung the dolefull'st ditty,
That to hear it was great pity.
"Fie, fie, fie!" now would she cry;

"Teru, teru!"[1] by-and-by.
That to hear her so complain
Scarce I could from tears refrain;
For her griefs so lively shown
Made me think upon mine own.
Ah, thought I, thou mourn'st in vain,
None takes pity on thy pain.
Senseless trees, they cannot hear thee;
Ruthless beasts, they will not cheer thee;
King Pandion he is dead,
All thy friends are lapp'd in lead;
All thy fellow birds do sing,
Careless of thy sorrowing;
Even so, poor bird, like thee,
None alive will pity me.

— IGNOTO

HAPPY SHEPHERDS, SIT AND SEE

Happy shepherds, sit and see,
With joy,
The peerless wight
For whose sake Pan keeps from ye
Annoy,
And gives delight,
Blessing this pleasant spring.
Her praises must I sing;
List, you swains, list to me,
The whiles your flocks feeding be.

First, her brow a beauteous globe
I deem,
And golden hair;
And her cheek Aurora's robe
Doth seem,
But far more fair.
Her eyes like stars are bright,
And dazzle with their light;
Rubies her lips to see,
But to taste nectar they be.

Orient pearls her teeth, her smile
Doth link
The Graces three;
Her white neck doth eyes beguile
To think
It ivory.
Alas! her lily hand
How it doth me command!
Softer silk none can be,
And whiter milk none can see.

Circe's wand is not so straight
As is
Her body small;
But two pillars bear the weight
Of this
Majestic hall.
Those be, I you assure,
Of alabaster pure,
Polish'd fine in each part;
Ne'er Nature yet show'd like art.

How shall I her pretty tread
Express,
When she doth walk?
Scarce she does the primrose head
Depress,
Or tender stalk
Of blue-vein'd violets,
Whereon her foot she sets.
Virtuous she is, for we find
In body fair beauteous mind.

Live fair Amargana still
Extoll'd
In all my rhyme;
Hand want art, when I want will
T' unfold
Her worth divine.
But now my muse doth rest,
Despair closed in my breast.
Of the valour I sing;
Weak faith that no hope doth bring.

— W. H.

PHYLLIDA'S LOVE-CALL TO HER CORYDON, AND HIS REPLYING

PHYL. Corydon, arise my Corydon!
Titan shineth clear.
COR. Who is it that calleth Corydon?
Who is it that I hear?
PHYL. Phyllida, thy true love calleth thee,
Arise then, arise then;
Arise and keep thy flock with me!
COR. Phyllida, my true love, is it she?
I come then, I come then,
I come and keep my flock with thee.

PHYL. Here are cherries ripe for my Corydon;
Eat them for my sake.
COR. Here's my oaten pipe, my lovely one,
Sport for thee to make.
PHYL. Here are threads, my true love, fine as silk,
To knit thee, to knit thee,
A pair of stockings white as milk.
COR. Here are reeds, my true love, fine and neat,
To make thee, to make thee,
A bonnet to withstand the heat.

[1] Words supposed to resemble the cry of the nightingale.

PHYL. I will gather flowers, my Corydon,
To set in thy cap.
COR. I will gather pears, my lovely one,
To put in thy lap.
PHYL. I will buy my true love garters gay,
For Sundays, for Sundays,
To wear about his legs so tall.
COR. I will buy my true love yellow say,
For Sundays, for Sundays,
To wear about her middle small.

PHYL. When my Corydon sits on a hill,
Making melody —
COR. When my lovely one goes to her wheel,
Singing cheerily —
PHYL. Sure methinks my true love doth excel
For sweetness, for sweetness,
Our Pan, that old Arcadian knight.
COR. And methinks my true love bears the bell
For clearness, for clearness,
Beyond the nymphs that be so bright.

PHYL. Had my Corydon, my Corydon,
Been, alack! her swain —
COR. Had my lovely one, my lovely one,
Been in Ida plain —
PHYL. Cynthia Endymion had refused,
Preferring, preferring,
My Corydon to play withal.
COR. The queen of love had been excused
Bequeathing, bequeathing,
My Phyllida the golden ball.

PHYL. Yonder comes my mother, Corydon,
Whither shall I fly?
COR. Under yonder beech, my lovely one,
While she passeth by.
PHYL. Say to her thy true love was not here;
Remember, remember,
To-morrow is another day.
COR. Doubt me not, my true love, do not fear;
Farewell then, farewell then,
Heaven keep our loves alway.

— IGNOTO

THE SHEPHERD'S COMMENDATION OF HIS NYMPH

What shepherd can express
The favour of her face,
To whom in this distress
I do appeal for grace?
A thousand Cupids fly
About her gentle eye.
From which each throws a dart
That kindleth soft sweet fire
Within my sighing heart,
Possessèd by desire;
No sweeter life I try
Than in her love to die.

The lily in the field,
That glories in his white,
For pureness now must yield,
And render up his right;
Heaven pictured in her face
Doth promise joy and grace.

Fair Cynthia's silver light,
That beats on running streams,
Compares not with her white,
Whose hairs are all sunbeams.
So bright my nymph doth shine
As day unto my eyne.

With this there is a red,
Exceeds the damask-rose,
Which in her cheeks is spread,
Where every favour grows;
In sky there is no star,
But she surmounts it far.

When Phœbus from the bed
Of Thetis doth arise,
The morning blushing red,
In fair carnation-wise,
He shows in my nymph's face,
As queen of every grace.

This pleasant lily white,
This taint of roseate red,
This Cynthia's silver light,
This sweet fair Dea spread,
These sunbeams in mine eye,
These beauties make me die.

— EARL OF OXENFORD (1550–1604)

THE SHEPHERD'S DESCRIPTION OF LOVE

MELIBŒUS. Shepherd, what's love, I pray thee tell?
FAUSTUS. It is that fountain and that well,
Where pleasure and repentance dwell;
It is perhaps that sauncing bell
That tolls all in to heaven or hell:
And this is Love, as I hear tell.
MELI. Yet what is Love, I prithee say?
FAUST. It is a work on holiday,
It is December match'd with May,

When lusty bloods in fresh array
Hear ten months after of the play:
And this is Love, as I hear say.
MELI. Yet what is Love, good shepherd, sain?
FAUST. It is a sunshine mix'd with rain,
It is a tooth-ache, or like pain,
It is a game, where none doth gain;
The lass saith no, and would full fain:
And this is Love, as I hear sain.
MELI. Yet, shepherd, what is Love, I pray?
FAUST. It is a yea, it is a nay,
A pretty kind of sporting fray,
It is a thing will soon away,
Then, nymphs, take vantage while ye may:
And this is Love, as I hear say.
MELI. Yet what is Love, good shepherd, show?
FAUST. A thing that creeps, it cannot go,
A prize that passeth to and fro,
A thing for one, a thing for moe,
And he that proves shall find it so:
And, shepherd, this is Love, I trow.

— IGNOTO

DAMELUS' SONG TO HIS DIAPHENIA

Diaphenia, like the daffadowndilly,
White as the sun, fair as the lily,
Heigho, how I do love thee!
I do love thee as my lambs
Are belovèd of their dams:
How blest were I if thou wouldst prove me!

Diaphenia, like the spreading roses,
That in thy sweets all sweets encloses,
Fair sweet, how I do love thee!
I do love thee as each flower
Loves the sun's life-giving power;
For dead, thy breath to life might move me.

Diaphenia, like to all things blessèd,
When all thy praises are expressèd,
Dear joy, how I do love thee!
As the birds do love the Spring,
Or the bees their careful king:
Then in requite, sweet virgin, love me!

— H. C.

A NYMPH'S DISDAIN OF LOVE

"Hey, down, a down!" did Dian sing,
Amongst her virgins sitting;
"Than love there is no vainer thing,
For maidens most unfitting."
And so think I, with a down, down, derry.

When women knew no woe,
But lived themselves to please,
Men's feigning guiles they did not know,
The ground of their disease.
Unborn was false suspect,
No thought of jealousy;
From wanton toys and fond affect,
The virgin's life was free.
"Hey, down, a down!" did Dian sing, etc.

At length men usèd charms,
To which what maids gave ear,
Embracing gladly endless harms,
Anon enthrallèd were.
Thus women welcomed woe,
Disguised in name of love,
A jealous hell, a painted show:
So shall they find that prove.
"Hey, down, a down!" did Dian sing,
Amongst her virgins sitting;
"Than love there is no vainer thing,
For maidens most unfitting."
And so think I, with a down, down, derry.

— IGNOTO

ROSALIND'S MADRIGAL

Love in my bosom like a bee,
Doth suck his sweet;
Now with his wings he plays with me,
Now with his feet.
Within mine eyes he makes his nest,
His bed amidst my tender breast;
My kisses are his daily feast,
And yet he robs me of my rest.
Ah, wanton, will ye?

And if I sleep, then percheth he,
With pretty slight,
And makes his pillow of my knee,
The livelong night.
Strike I my lute, he tunes the string;
He music plays if I but sing;
He lends me every lovely thing;
Yet cruel he my heart doth sting.
Whist, wanton, still ye!

Else I with roses every day
Will ship ye hence,
And bind ye, when ye long to play,
For your offence.
I'll shut my eyes to keep ye in,
I'll make you fast it for your sin,
I'll count your power not worth a pin.
Alas! what hereby shall I win
If he gainsay me?

What if I beat the wanton boy
With many a rod?
He will repay me with annoy,
Because a god.
Then sit thou safely on my knee,
And let thy bower my bosom be;
Lurk in mine eyes, I like of thee.
O Cupid! so thou pity me,
Spare not, but play thee.

— Thom. Lodge (1558?–1625)

THE HERDMAN'S HAPPY LIFE

What pleasure have great princes
More dainty to their choice
Than herdmen wild, who careless
In quiet life rejoice?
And fortune's fate not fearing,
Sing sweet in summer morning.

Their dealings plain and rightful,
Are void of all deceit;
They never know how spiteful
It is to kneel and wait
On favourite presumptuous,
Whose pride is vain and sumptuous.

All day their flocks each tendeth,
At night they take their rest,
More quiet than who sendeth
His ship into the east,
Where gold and pearl are plenty,
But getting very dainty.

For lawyers and their pleading,
They 'steem it not a straw;
They think that honest meaning,
Is of itself a law;
Where conscience judgeth plainly,
They spend no money vainly.

Oh, happy who thus liveth!
Not caring much for gold;
With clothing which sufficeth,
To keep him from the cold.
Though poor and plain his diet,
Yet merry it is and quiet.

— Out of M. Bird's Set Songs

THE PASSIONATE SHEPHERD TO HIS LOVE

Come live with me and be my love,
And we will all the pleasures prove,
That valleys, groves, hills, and fields,
Woods, or steepy mountains yields.

And we will sit upon the rocks,
Seeing the shepherds feed their flocks,
By shallow rivers, to whose falls
Melodious birds sings madrigals.

And I will make thee beds of roses,
And a thousand fragrant posies,
A cap of flowers and a kirtle
Embroider'd all with leaves of myrtle:

A gown made of the finest wool,
Which from our pretty lambs we pull;
Fair lined slippers for the cold,
With buckles of the purest gold;

A belt of straw and ivy buds,
With coral clasps and amber studs;
And if these pleasures may thee move,
Come live with me and be my love.

The shepherd swains shall dance and sing
For thy delights each May morning;
If these delights thy mind may move,
Then live with me and be my love.

— Chr. Marlow (1564–1593)

THE NYMPH'S REPLY TO THE SHEPHERD

If all the world and love were young,
And truth in every shepherd's tongue,
These pretty pleasures might me move,
To live with thee and be thy love.

Time drives the flocks from field to fold,
When rivers rage, and rocks grow cold;
And Philomel becometh dumb;
The rest complains of cares to come.

The flowers do fade, and wanton fields
To wayward Winter reckoning yields;
A honey tongue, a heart of gall,
Is fancy's spring, but sorrow's fall.

Thy gowns, thy shoes, thy beds of roses,
Thy cap, thy kirtle, and thy posies,
Soon break, soon wither, soon forgotten,
In folly ripe, in reason rotten.

Thy belt of straw and ivy buds,
Thy coral clasps and amber studs,
All these in me no means can move,
To come to thee and be thy love.

But could youth last, and love still breed,
Had joys no date, nor age no need,
Then these delights my mind might move,
To live with thee and be thy love.

— Ignoto

THE SHEPHERD'S RESOLUTION IN LOVE

If Jove himself be subject unto Love,
And range the woods to find a mortal prey;
If Neptune from the seas himself remove,
And seek on sands with earthly wights to play:
  Then may I love my shepherdess by right,
  Who far excels each other mortal wight? 6

If Pluto could by Love be drawn from hell
To yield himself a silly virgin's thrall;
If Phœbus could vouchsafe on earth to dwell,
To win a rustic maid unto his call:
  Then how much more should I adore the sight
  Of her in whom the heavens themselves delight? 12

If country Pan might follow nymphs in chase,
And yet through Love remain devoid of blame;
If satyrs were excused for seeking grace
To joy the fruits of any mortal dame:
  My shepherdess why should not I love still, 17
  On whom nor gods nor men can gaze their fill?

— THOM. WATSON (1557?–1592)

WILLIAM SHAKESPEARE (1564–1616)

FROM VENUS AND ADONIS

This said, she hasteth to a myrtle grove,
Musing the morning is so much o'erworn,
And yet she hears no tidings of her love:
She hearkens for his hounds and for his horn:
  Anon she hears them chant it lustily,
  And all in haste she coasteth to the cry. 870

And as she runs, the bushes in the way
Some catch her by the neck, some kiss her face,
Some twine about her thigh to make her stay:
She wildly breaketh from their strict embrace,
  Like a milch doe, whose swelling dugs do ache,
  Hasting to feed her fawn hid in some brake.

By this, she hears the hounds are at a bay;
Whereat she starts, like one that spies an adder
Wreathed up in fatal folds just in his way,
The fear whereof doth make him shake and shudder; 880
  Even so the timorous yelping of the hounds
  Appals her senses and her spirit confounds.

For now she knows it is no gentle chase,
But the blunt boar, rough bear, or lion proud,
Because the cry remaineth in one place,
Where fearfully the dogs exclaim aloud:
  Finding their enemy to be so curst,
  They all strain courtesy who shall cope him first.

This dismal cry rings sadly in her ear,
Through which it enters to surprise her heart;
Who, overcome by doubt and bloodless fear, 891
With cold-pale weakness numbs each feeling part:
  Like soldiers, when their captain once doth yield,
  They basely fly and dare not stay the field.

Thus stands she in a trembling ecstasy;
Till, cheering up her senses all dismay'd,
She tells them 'tis a causeless fantasy,
And childish error, that they are afraid;
  Bids them leave quaking, bids them fear no more: — 899
  And with that word she spied the hunted boar,

Whose frothy mouth, bepainted all with red,
Like milk and blood being mingled both together,
A second fear through all her sinews spread,
Which madly hurries her she knows not whither:
  This way she runs, and now she will no further,
  But back retires to rate the boar for murther.

A thousand spleens bear her a thousand ways;
She treads the path that she untreads again;
Her more than haste is mated with delays,
Like the proceedings of a drunken brain, 910
  Full of respects, yet nought at all respecting;
  In hand with all things, nought at all effecting.

Here kennell'd in a brake she finds a hound,
And asks the weary caitiff for his master,
And there another licking of his wound,
'Gainst venom'd sores the only sovereign plaster;
  And here she meets another sadly scowling,
  To whom she speaks, and he replies with howling.

When he hath ceased his ill-resounding noise,
Another flap-mouth'd mourner, black and grim,
Against the welkin volleys out his voice; 921
Another and another answer him,
  Clapping their proud tails to the ground below,
  Shaking their scratch'd ears, bleeding as they go.

Look, how the world's poor people are amazed
At apparitions, signs, and prodigies,
Whereon with fearful eyes they long have gazed,
Infusing them with dreadful prophecies;
  So she at these sad signs draws up her breath
  And sighing it again, exclaims on Death. 930

"Hard-favour'd tyrant, ugly, meagre, lean,
Hateful divorce of love," — thus chides she Death, —
"Grim-grinning ghost, earth's worm, what dost thou mean
To stifle beauty and to steal his breath,
Who when he lived, his breath and beauty set
Gloss on the rose, smell to the violet?

"If he be dead, — O no, it cannot be,
Seeing his beauty, thou shouldst strike at it: —
O yes, it may; thou hast no eyes to see,
But hatefully at random dost thou hit.
Thy mark is feeble age, but thy false dart
Mistakes that aim and cleaves an infant's heart.

"Hadst thou but bid beware, then he had spoke,
And, hearing him, thy power had lost his power.
The Destinies will curse thee for this stroke;
They bid thee crop a weed, thou pluck'st a flower:
Love's golden arrow at him should have fled,
And not Death's ebon dart, to strike him dead.

"Dost thou drink tears, that thou provokest such weeping?
What may a heavy groan advantage thee?
Why hast thou cast into eternal sleeping
Those eyes that taught all other eyes to see?
Now Nature cares not for thy mortal vigour,
Since her best work is ruin'd with thy rigour."

Here overcome, as one full of despair,
She vail'd her eyelids, who, like sluices, stopt
The crystal tide that from her two cheeks fair
In the sweet channel of her bosom dropt;
But through the flood-gates breaks the silver rain,
And with his strong course opens them again.

O, how her eyes and tears did lend and borrow!
Her eyes seen in the tears, tears in her eye;
Both crystals, where they view'd each other's sorrow,
Sorrow that friendly sighs sought still to dry;
But like a stormy day, now wind, now rain,
Sighs dry her cheeks, tears make them wet again.

Variable passions throng her constant woe,
As striving who should best become her grief;
All entertain'd, each passion labours so,
That every present sorrow seemeth chief,
But none is best: then join they all together,
Like many clouds consulting for foul weather.

By this, far off she hears some huntsman hollo;
A nurse's song ne'er pleased her babe so well:
The dire imagination she did follow
This sound of hope doth labour to expel;
For now reviving joy bids her rejoice,
And flatters her it is Adonis' voice.

Whereat her tears began to turn their tide,
Being prison'd in her eye like pearls in glass;
Yet sometimes falls an orient drop beside,
Which her cheek melts, as scorning it should pass,
To wash the foul face of the sluttish ground,
Who is but drunken when she seemeth drown'd.

O hard-believing love, how strange it seems
Not to believe, and yet too credulous!
Thy weal and woe are both of them extremes;
Despair and hope makes thee ridiculous:
The one doth flatter thee in thoughts unlikely,
In likely thoughts the other kills thee quickly.

Now she unweaves the web that she hath wrought;
Adonis lives, and Death is not to blame;
It was not she that call'd him all-to naught:
Now she adds honours to his hateful name;
She clepes him king of graves and grave for kings,
Imperious supreme of all mortal things.

"No, no," quoth she, "sweet Death, I did but jest;
Yet pardon me I felt a kind of fear
When-as I met the boar, that bloody beast,
Which knows no pity, but is still severe;
Then, gentle shadow, — truth I must confess, —
I rail'd on thee, fearing my love's decease.

"'Tis not my fault: the boar provoked my tongue;
Be wreak'd on him, invisible commander;
'Tis he, foul creature, that hath done thee wrong;
I did but act, he's author of thy slander;
Grief hath two tongues, and never woman yet
Could rule them both without ten women's wit."

Thus hoping that Adonis is alive,
Her rash suspect she doth extenuate;
And that his beauty may the better thrive,
With Death she humbly doth insinuate;
Tells him of trophies, statues, tombs, and stories;
His victories, his triumphs, and his glories.

"O Jove," quoth she, "how much a fool was I
To be of such a weak and silly mind
To wail his death who lives and must not die
Till mutual overthrow of mortal kind!
For he being dead, with him is beauty slain,
And, beauty dead, black chaos comes again.

"Fie, fie, fond love, thou art so full of fear
As one with treasure laden, hemm'd with thieves;
Trifles, unwitnessed with eye or ear,
Thy coward heart with false bethinking grieves."
  Even at this word she hears a merry horn,
  Whereat she leaps that was but late forlorn.

As falcon to the lure, away she flies;
The grass stoops not, she treads on it so light;
And in her haste unfortunately spies
The foul boar's conquest on her fair delight;
  Which seen, her eyes, as murder'd with the view,
  Like stars ashamed of day, themselves withdrew;

Or, as the snail, whose tender horns being hit,
Shrinks backward in his shelly cave with pain,
And there, all smother'd up, in shade doth sit,
Long after fearing to creep forth again;
  So, at his bloody view, her eyes are fled
  Into the deep dark cabins of her head:

Where they resign their office and their light
To the disposing of her troubled brain;
Who bids them still consort with ugly night,
And never wound the heart with looks again;
  Who, like a king perplexed in his throne,
  By their suggestion gives a deadly groan,

Whereat each tributary subject quakes;
As when the wind, imprison'd in the ground,
Struggling for passage, earth's foundation shakes,
Which with cold terror doth men's minds confound.
  This mutiny each part doth so surprise
  That from their dark beds once more leap her eyes;

And, being open'd, threw unwilling light
Upon the wide wound that the boar had trench'd
In his soft flank; whose wonted lily white
With purple tears, that his wound wept, was drench'd.
  No flower was nigh, no grass, herb, leaf, or weed,
  But stole his blood and seem'd with him to bleed.

This solemn sympathy poor Venus noteth;
Over one shoulder doth she hang her head;
Dumbly she passions, franticly she doteth;
She thinks he could not die, he is not dead:
  Her voice is stopt, her joints forget to bow;
  Her eyes are mad that they have wept till now.

Upon his hurt she looks so steadfastly,
That her sight dazzling makes the wound seem three;
And then she reprehends her mangling eye,
That makes more gashes where no breach should be:
  His face seems twain, each several limb is doubled;
  For oft the eye mistakes, the brain being troubled.

"My tongue cannot express my grief for one,
And yet," quoth she, "behold two Adons dead!
My sighs are blown away, my salt tears gone,
Mine eyes are turn'd to fire, my heart to lead:
  Heavy heart's lead, melt at mine eyes' red fire!
  So shall I die by drops of hot desire.

"Alas, poor world, what treasure hast thou lost!
What face remains alive that's worth the viewing?
Whose tongue is music now? what canst thou boast
Of things long since, or any thing ensuing?
  The flowers are sweet, their colours fresh and trim;
  But true-sweet beauty lived and died with him.

"Bonnet nor veil henceforth no creature wear!
Nor sun nor wind will ever strive to kiss you:
Having no fair to lose, you need not fear;
The sun doth scorn you and the wind doth hiss you:
  But when Adonis lived, sun and sharp air
  Lurk'd like two thieves, to rob him of his fair:

"And therefore would he put his bonnet on,
Under whose brim the gaudy sun would peep;
The wind would blow it off and, being gone,
Play with his locks: then would Adonis weep;
  And straight, in pity of his tender years,
  They both would strive who first should dry his tears.

"To see his face the lion walk'd along
Behind some hedge, because he would not fear him;
To recreate himself when he hath sung,
The tiger would be tame and gently hear him;
  If he had spoke, the wolf would leave his prey
  And never fright the silly lamb that day.

"When he beheld his shadow in the brook,
The fishes spread on it their golden gills;
When he was by, the birds such pleasure took,
That some would sing, some other in their bills

Would bring him mulberries and ripe-red cherries;
He fed them with his sight, they him with berries.

"But this foul, grim, and urchin-snouted boar,
Whose downward eye still looketh for a grave,
Ne'er saw the beauteous livery that he wore;
Witness the entertainment that he gave:
If he did see his face, why then I know
He thought to kiss him, and hath kill'd him so.

"'Tis true, 'tis true; thus was Adonis slain:
He ran upon the boar with his sharp spear,
Who did not whet his teeth at him again,
But by a kiss thought to persuade him there;
And nuzzling in his flank, the loving swine
Sheathed unaware the tusk in his soft groin.

"Had I been tooth'd like him, I must confess,
With kissing him I should have kill'd him first;
But he is dead, and never did he bless
My youth with his; the more am I accurst."
With this, she falleth in the place she stood,
And stains her face with his congealed blood.

She looks upon his lips, and they are pale;
She takes him by the hand, and that is cold;
She whispers in his ears a heavy tale,
As if they heard the woeful words she told;
She lifts the coffer-lids that close his eyes,
Where, lo, two lamps, burnt out, in darkness lies;

Two glasses, where herself herself beheld
A thousand times, and now no more reflect;
Their virtue lost, wherein they late excell'd,
And every beauty robb'd of his effect:
"Wonder of time," quoth she, "this is my spite,
That, thou being dead, the day should yet be light.

"Since thou art dead, lo, here I prophesy:
Sorrow on love hereafter shall attend:
It shall be waited on with jealousy,
Find sweet beginning, but unsavoury end,
Ne'er settled equally, but high or low,
That all love's pleasure shall not match his woe.

"It shall be fickle, false, and full of fraud,
Bud and be blasted in a breathing-while;
The bottom poison, and the top o'erstraw'd
With sweets that shall the truest sight beguile:
The strongest body shall it make most weak,
Strike the wise dumb and teach the fool to speak.

"It shall be sparing and too full of riot
Teaching decrepit age to tread the measures;
The staring ruffian shall it keep in quiet,
Pluck down the rich, enrich the poor with treasures;
It shall be raging-mad and silly-mild,
Make the young old, the old become a child.

"It shall suspect where is no cause of fear;
It shall not fear where it should most mistrust;
It shall be merciful and too severe,
And most deceiving when it seems most just;
Perverse it shall be where it shows most toward;
Put fear to valour, courage to the coward.

"It shall be cause of war and dire events,
And set dissension 'twixt the son and sire;
Subject and servile to all discontents,
As dry combustious matter is to fire:
Sith in his prime Death doth my love destroy,
They that love best their loves shall not enjoy."

By this, the boy that by her side lay kill'd
Was melted like a vapour from her sight,
And in his blood that on the ground lay spill'd,
A purple flower sprung up, chequer'd with white,
Resembling well his pale cheeks and the blood
Which in round drops upon their whiteness stood.

She bows her head, the new-sprung flower to smell,
Comparing it to her Adonis' breath,
And says, within her bosom it shall dwell,
Since he himself is reft from her by death:
She crops the stalk, and in the breach appears
Green dropping sap, which she compares to tears.

"Poor flower," quoth she, "this was thy father's guise —
Sweet issue of a more sweet-smelling sire —
For every little grief to wet his eyes:
To grow unto himself was his desire,
And so 'tis thine; but know, it is as good
To wither in my breast as in his blood.

"Here was thy father's bed, here in my breast;
Thou art the next of blood, and 'tis thy right:
Lo, in this hollow cradle take thy rest,
My throbbing heart shall rock thee day and night;
There shall not be one minute in an hour
Wherein I will not kiss my sweet love's flower."

Thus weary of the world, away she hies,
And yokes her silver doves; by whose swift aid
Their mistress mounted through the empty skies
In her light chariot quickly is convey'd;
  Holding their course to Paphos, where their queen
  Means to immure herself and not be seen.

From THE RAPE OF LUCRECE

But now the mindful messenger, come back,
Brings home his lord and other company;
Who finds his Lucrece clad in mourning black:
And round about her tear-distained eye
Blue circles stream'd, like rainbows in the sky:
  These water-galls in her dim element
  Foretell new storms to those already spent.

Which when her sad-beholding husband saw,
Amazedly in her sad face he stares:
Her eyes, though sod in tears, look'd red and raw,
Her lively colour kill'd with deadly cares.
He hath no power to ask her how she fares:
  Both stood, like old acquaintance in a trance,
  Met far from home, wondering each other's chance.

At last he takes her by the bloodless hand,
And thus begins: "What uncouth ill event
Hath thee befall'n, that thou dost trembling stand?
Sweet love, what spite hath thy fair colour spent?
Why art thou thus attired in discontent?
  Unmask, dear dear, this moody heaviness,
  And tell thy grief, that we may give redress."

Three times with sighs she gives her sorrow fire,
Ere once she can discharge one word of woe:
At length address'd to answer his desire,
She modestly prepares to let them know
Her honour is ta'en prisoner by the foe;
  While Collatine and his consorted lords
  With sad attention long to hear her words.

And now this pale swan in her watery nest
Begins the sad dirge of her certain ending;
"Few words," quoth she, "shall fit the trespass best,
Where no excuse can give the fault amending:
In me moe woes than words are now depending;
  And my laments would be drawn out too long,
  To tell them all with one poor tired tongue.

"Then be this all the task it hath to say:
Dear husband, in the interest of thy bed
A stranger came, and on that pillow lay
Where thou wast wont to rest thy weary head;
And what wrong else may be imagined
  By foul enforcement might be done to me,
  From that, alas, thy Lucrece is not free.

"For in the dreadful dead of dark midnight,
With shining falchion in my chamber came
A creeping creature, with a flaming light,
And softly cried 'Awake, thou Roman dame,
And entertain my love; else lasting shame
  On thee and thine this night I will inflict,
  If thou my love's desire do contradict.

"'For some hard-favour'd groom of thine,' quoth he,
'Unless thou yoke thy liking to my will,
I'll murder straight, and then I'll slaughter thee
And swear I found you where you did fulfil
The loathsome act of lust, and so did kill
  The lechers in their deed: this act will be
  My fame and thy perpetual infamy.'

"With this, I did begin to start and cry;
And then against my heart he sets his sword,
Swearing, unless I took all patiently,
I should not live to speak another word;
So should my shame still rest upon record,
  And never be forgot in mighty Rome
  Th' adulterate death of Lucrece and her groom.

"Mine enemy was strong, my poor self weak,
And far the weaker with so strong a fear:
My bloody judge forbade my tongue to speak;
No rightful plea might plead for justice there:
His scarlet lust came evidence to swear
  That my poor beauty had purloin'd his eyes;
  And when the judge is robb'd the prisoner dies.

"O, teach me how to make mine own excuse!
Or at the least this refuge let me find;
Though my gross blood be stain'd with this abuse,
Immaculate and spotless is my mind;
That was not forced; that never was inclined
  To accessary yieldings, but still pure
  Doth in her poison'd closet yet endure."

Lo, here, the hopeless merchant of this loss,
With head declined, and voice damm'd up with woe,
With sad set eyes, and wretched arms across,
From lips new-waxen pale begins to blow
The grief away that stops his answer so:
  But, wretched as he is, he strives in vain;
  What he breathes out his breath drinks up again.

As through an arch the violent roaring tide
Outruns the eye that doth behold his haste,
Yet in the eddy boundeth in his pride
Back to the strait that forced him on so fast;
In rage sent out, recall'd in rage, being past:

Even so his sighs, his sorrows, make a saw,
To push grief on, and back the same grief draw.

Which speechless woe of his poor she attendeth,
And his untimely frenzy thus awaketh:
"Dear lord, thy sorrow to my sorrow lendeth
Another power; no flood by raining slaketh.
My woe too sensible thy passion maketh
More feeling-painful: let it then suffice
To drown one woe, one pair of weeping eyes.

"And for my sake, when I might charm thee so
For she that was thy Lucrece, now attend me:
Be suddenly revenged on my foe,
Thine, mine, his own: suppose thou dost defend me
From what is past: the help that thou shalt lend me
Comes all too late, yet let the traitor die;
For sparing justice feeds iniquity.

"But ere I name him, you fair lords," quoth she,
Speaking to those that came with Collatine,
"Shall plight your honourable faiths to me,
With swift pursuit to venge this wrong of mine;
For 'tis a meritorious fair design
To chase injustice with revengeful arms:
Knights, by their oaths, should right poor ladies' harms."

At this request, with noble disposition
Each present lord began to promise aid,
As bound in knighthood to her imposition,
Longing to hear the hateful foe bewray'd.
But she, that yet her sad task hath not said,
The protestation stops. "O, speak," quoth she,
"How may this forced stain be wiped from me?

"What is the quality of mine offence,
Being constrain'd with dreadful circumstance?
May my pure mind with the foul act dispense,
My low-declined honour to advance?
May any terms acquit me from this chance?
The poison'd fountain clears itself again;
And why not I from this compelled stain?"

With this, they all at once began to say,
Her body's stain her mind untainted clears;
While with a joyless smile she turns away
The face, that map which deep impression bears
Of hard misfortune, carved in it with tears.
"No, no," quoth she, "no dame, hereafter living,
By my excuse shall claim excuse's giving."

Here with a sigh, as if her heart would break,
She throws forth Tarquin's name: "He, he," she says,
But more than "he" her poor tongue could not speak;
Till after many accents and delays,
Untimely breathings, sick and short assays,
She utters this, "He, he, fair lords, 'tis he,
That guides this hand to give this wound to me."

Even here she sheathed in her harmless breast
A harmful knife, that thence her soul unsheathed:
That blow did bail it from the deep unrest
Of that polluted prison where it breathed:
Her contrite sighs unto the clouds bequeathed
Her winged sprite, and through her wounds doth fly
Life's lasting date from cancell'd destiny.

From A LOVER'S COMPLAINT

"Yet did I not, as some my equals did,
Demand of him, nor being desired yielded;
Finding myself in honour so forbid,
With safest distance I mine honour shielded:
Experience for me many bulwarks builded
Of proofs new-bleeding, which remain'd the foil
Of this false jewel, and his amorous spoil.

"But, ah, who ever shunn'd by precedent
The destined ill she must herself assay?
Or forced examples, 'gainst her own content,
To put the by-past perils in her way?
Counsel may stop awhile what will not stay;
For when we rage, advice is often seen
By blunting us to make our wits more keen.

"Nor gives it satisfaction to our blood,
That we must curb it upon others' proof:
To be forbod the sweets that seem so good,
For fear of harms that preach in our behoof.
O appetite, from judgement stand aloof!
The one a palate hath that needs will taste,
Though Reason weep, and cry 'It is thy last.'

"For further I could say 'This man's untrue,'
And knew the patterns of his foul beguiling;
Heard where his plants in others' orchards grew,
Saw how deceits were gilded in his smiling;
Knew vows were ever brokers to defiling;
Thought characters and words merely but art,
And bastards of his foul adulterate heart.

"And long upon these terms I held my city,
Till thus he gan besiege me: 'Gentle maid,
Have of my suffering youth some feeling pity,
And be not of my holy vows afraid:
That's to ye sworn to none was ever said;
For feasts of love I have been call'd unto,
Till now did ne'er invite, nor never woo.

"'All my offences that abroad you see
Are errors of the blood, none of the mind;
Love made them not: with acture they may be,
Where neither party is nor true nor kind:
They sought their shame that so their shame did find;
And so much less of shame in me remains,
By how much of me their reproach contains.

"'Among the many that mine eyes have seen,
Not one whose flame my heart so much as warm'd,
Or my affection put to the smallest teen,
Or any of my leisures ever charm'd:
Harm have I done to them, but ne'er was harm'd;
Kept hearts in liveries, but mine own was free,
And reign'd, commanding in his monarchy.

"'Look here, what tributes wounded fancies sent me,
Of paled pearls and rubies red as blood;
Figuring that they their passions likewise lent me
Of grief and blushes, aptly understood
In bloodless white and the encrimson'd mood;
Effects of terror and dear modesty,
Encamp'd in hearts, but fighting outwardly.

"'And, lo, behold these talents of their hair,
With twisted metal amorously impleach'd,
I have received from many a several fair,
Their kind acceptance weepingly beseech'd,
With the annexions of fair gems enrich'd,
And deep-brain'd sonnets that did amplify
Each stone's dear nature, worth, and quality.

"'The diamond, — why, 'twas beautiful and hard,
Whereto his invised properties did tend;
The deep-green emerald, in whose fresh regard
Weak sights their sickly radiance do amend;
The heaven-hued sapphire and the opal blend
With objects manifold: each several stone,
With wit well blazon'd, smiled or made some moan.

"'Lo, all these trophies of affections hot,
Of pensived and subdued desires the tender,
Nature hath charged me that I hoard them not,
But yield them up where I myself must render,
That is, to you, my origin and ender;
For these, of force, must your oblations be,
Since I their altar, you enpatron me.'

* * * * * * *

"This said, his watery eyes he did dismount,
Whose sights till then were levell'd on my face;
Each cheek a river running from a fount
With brinish current downward flow'd apace:
O, how the channel to the stream gave grace!
Who glazed with crystal gate the glowing roses
That flame through water which their hue encloses.

"O father, what a hell of witchcraft lies
In the small orb of one particular tear!
But with the inundation of the eyes
What rocky heart to water will not wear?
What breast so cold that is not warmed here?
O cleft effect! cold modesty, hot wrath,
Both fire from hence and chill extincture hath.

"For, lo, his passion, but an art of craft,
Even there resolved my reason into tears;
There my white stole of chastity I daff'd,
Shook off my sober guards and civil fears;
Appear to him, as he to me appears,
All melting; though our drops this difference bore,
His poison'd me, and mine did him restore.

"In him a plenitude of subtle matter,
Applied to cautels, all strange forms receives,
Of burning blushes, or of weeping water,
Or swooning paleness; and he takes and leaves,
In either's aptness, as it best deceives,
To blush at speeches rank, to weep at woes,
Or to turn white and swoon at tragic shows:

"That not a heart which in his level came
Could 'scape the hail of his all-hurting aim,
Showing fair nature is both kind and tame;
And, veil'd in them, did win whom he would maim:
Against the thing he sought he would exclaim;
When he most burn'd in heart-wish'd luxury,
He preach'd pure maid, and praised cold chastity.

"Thus merely with the garment of a Grace
The naked and concealed fiend he cover'd;
That th' unexperient gave the tempter place,
Which like a cherubin above them hover'd.
Who, young and simple, would not be so lover'd?
Ay me! I fell; and yet do question make
What I should do again for such a sake.

"O, that infected moisture of his eye,
O, that false fire which in his cheek so glow'd,
O, that forced thunder from his heart did fly,
O, that sad breath his spongy lungs bestow'd,
O, all that borrow'd motion seeming owed,
Would yet again betray the fore-betray'd,
And new pervert a reconciled maid!"

SONNETS

XII

When I do count the clock that tells the time,
And see the brave day sunk in hideous night;
When I behold the violet past prime,
And sable curls all silver'd o'er with white;

When lofty trees I see barren of leaves,
Which erst from heat did canopy the herd,
And summer's green all girded up in sheaves
Borne on the bier with white and bristly beard,
Then of thy beauty do I question make,
That thou among the wastes of time must go,
Since sweets and beauties do themselves forsake
And die as fast as they see others grow;
And nothing 'gainst Time's scythe can make defence
Save breed, to brave him when he takes thee hence.

XV

When I consider every thing that grows
Holds in perfection but a little moment,
That this huge stage presenteth nought but shows
Whereon the stars in secret influence comment;
When I perceive that men as plants increase,
Cheered and check'd even by the self-same sky,
Vaunt in their youthful sap, at height decrease,
And wear their brave state out of memory;
Then the conceit of this inconstant stay
Sets you most rich in youth before my sight,
Where wasteful Time debateth with Decay,
To change your day of youth to sullied night;
And all in war with Time for love of you,
As he takes from you, I engraft you new.

XVII

Who will believe my verse in time to come,
If it were fill'd with your most high deserts?
Though yet, heaven knows, it is but as a tomb
Which hides your life and shows not half your parts.
If I could write the beauty of your eyes
And in fresh numbers number all your graces,
The age to come would say "This poet lies;
Such heavenly touches ne'er touch'd earthly faces."
So should my papers yellow'd with their age
Be scorn'd like old men of less truth than tongue,
And your true rights be term'd a poet's rage
And stretchèd metre of an antique song:
But were some child of yours alive that time,
You should live twice; in it and in my rhyme.

XVIII

Shall I compare thee to a summer's day?
Thou art more lovely and more temperate:
Rough winds do shake the darling buds of May,
And summer's lease hath all too short a date:
Sometime too hot the eye of heaven shines,
And often is his gold complexion dimm'd;
And every fair from fair sometime declines,
By chance or nature's changing course untrimm'd;
But thy eternal summer shall not fade
Nor lose possession of that fair thou owest;
Nor shall Death brag thou wander'st in his shade,
When in eternal lines to time thou growest:
So long as men can breathe or eyes can see,
So long lives this and this gives life to thee.

XXV

Let those who are in favour with their stars
Of public honour and proud titles boast,
Whilst I, whom fortune of such triumph bars,
Unlook'd for joy in that I honour most.
Great princes' favourites their fair leaves spread
But as the marigold at the sun's eye,
And in themselves their pride lies burièd,
For at a frown they in their glory die.
The painful warrior famousèd for fight,
After a thousand victories once foil'd,
Is from the book of honour razèd quite,
And all the rest forgot for which he toil'd:
Then happy I, that love and am beloved
Where I may not remove nor be removed.

XXIX

When, in disgrace with fortune and men's eyes,
I all alone beweep my outcast state
And trouble deaf heaven with my bootless cries
And look upon myself and curse my fate,
Wishing me like to one more rich in hope,
Featured like him, like him with friends possess'd,
Desiring this man's art and that man's scope,
With what I most enjoy contented least;
Yet in these thoughts myself almost despising,
Haply I think on thee, and then my state,
Like to the lark at break of day arising
From sullen earth, sings hymns at heaven's gate;
For thy sweet love remember'd such wealth brings
That then I scorn to change my state with kings.

XXX

When to the sessions of sweet silent thought
I summon up remembrance of things past,
I sigh the lack of many a thing I sought,
And with old woes new wail my dear time's waste:
Then can I drown an eye, unused to flow,
For precious friends hid in death's dateless night,
And weep afresh love's long since cancell'd woe,
And moan the expense of many a vanish'd sight:
Then can I grieve at grievances foregone,
And heavily from woe to woe tell o'er

The sad account of fore-bemoanèd moan,
Which I new pay as if not paid before.
But if the while I think on thee, dear friend,
All losses are restored and sorrows end.

XXXII

If thou survive my well-contented day,
When that churl Death my bones with dust shall cover,
And shalt by fortune once more re-survey
These poor rude lines of thy deceasèd lover,
Compare them with the bettering of the time,
And though they be outstripp'd by every pen,
Reserve them for my love, not for their rhyme,
Exceeded by the height of happier men.
O, then vouchsafe me but this loving thought:
"Had my friend's Muse grown with this growing age,
A dearer birth than this his love had brought,
To march in ranks of better equipage:
But since he died and poets better prove,
Theirs for their style I'll read, his for his love."

XXXIII

Full many a glorious morning have I seen
Flatter the mountain-tops with sovereign eye,
Kissing with golden face the meadows green,
Gilding pale streams with heavenly alchemy;
Anon permit the basest clouds to ride
With ugly rack on his celestial face,
And from the forlorn world his visage hide,
Stealing unseen to west with this disgrace:
Even so my sun one early morn did shine
With all-triumphant splendour on my brow;
But out, alack! he was but one hour mine;
The region cloud hath mask'd him from me now.
Yet him for this my love no whit disdaineth;
Suns of the world may stain when heaven's sun staineth.

LV

Not marble, nor the gilded monuments
Of princes, shall outlive this powerful rhyme;
But you shall shine more bright in these contents
Than unswept stone besmear'd with sluttish time.
When wasteful war shall statues overturn,
And broils root out the work of masonry,
Nor Mars his sword nor war's quick fire shall burn
The living record of your memory.
'Gainst death and all-oblivious enmity
Shall you pace forth; your praise shall still find room
Even in the eyes of all posterity
That wear this world out to the ending doom.
So, till the judgement that yourself arise,
You live in this, and dwell in lovers' eyes.

LX

Like as the waves make towards the pebbled shore,
So do our minutes hasten to their end;
Each changing place with that which goes before,
In sequent toil all forwards do contend.
Nativity, once in the main of light,
Crawls to maturity, wherewith being crown'd,
Crooked eclipses 'gainst his glory fight,
And Time that gave doth now his gift confound.
Time doth transfix the flourish set on youth
And delves the parallels in beauty's brow,
Feeds on the rarities of nature's truth,
And nothing stands but for his scythe to mow:
And yet to times in hope my verse shall stand,
Praising thy worth, despite his cruel hand.

LXIV

When I have seen by Time's fell hand defaced
The rich proud cost of outworn buried age;
When sometime lofty towers I see down-razed
And brass eternal slave to mortal rage;
When I have seen the hungry ocean gain
Advantage on the kingdom of the shore,
And the firm soil win of the watery main,
Increasing store with loss and loss with store;
When I have seen such interchange of state,
Or state itself confounded to decay;
Ruin hath taught me thus to ruminate,
That Time will come and take my love away.
This thought is as a death, which cannot choose
But weep to have that which it fears to lose.

LXV

Since brass, nor stone, nor earth, nor boundless sea,
But sad mortality o'er-sways their power,
How with this rage shall beauty hold a plea,
Whose action is no stronger than a flower?
O, how shall summer's honey breath hold out
Against the wreckful siege of battering days,
When rocks impregnable are not so stout,
Nor gates of steel so strong, but Time decays?
O fearful meditation! where, alack,
Shall Time's best jewel from Time's chest lie hid?
Or what strong hand can hold his swift foot back?
Or who his spoil of beauty can forbid?
O, none, unless this miracle have might,
That in black ink my love may still shine bright.

LXVI

Tired with all these, for restful death I cry, —
As, to behold desert a beggar born,
And needy nothing trimm'd in jollity,
And purest faith unhappily forsworn,
And gilded honour shamefully misplaced,
And maiden virtue rudely strumpeted,
And right perfection wrongfully disgraced,
And strength by limping sway disablèd,
And art made tongue-tied by authority,
And folly doctor-like controlling skill,
And simple truth miscall'd simplicity,
And captive good attending captain ill:
Tired with all these, from these would I be gone,
Save that, to die, I leave my love alone.

LXXI

No longer mourn for me when I am dead
Than you shall hear the surly sullen bell
Give warning to the world that I am fled
From this vile world, with vilest worms to dwell:
Nay, if you read this line, remember not
The hand that writ it; for I love you so
That I in your sweet thoughts would be forgot
If thinking on me then should make you woe.
O, if, I say, you look upon this verse
When I perhaps compounded am with clay,
Do not so much as my poor name rehearse,
But let your love even with my life decay,
Lest the wise world should look into your moan
And mock you with me after I am gone.

LXXIII

That time of year thou mayst in me behold
When yellow leaves, or none, or few, do hang
Upon those boughs which shake against the cold,
Bare ruin'd choirs, where late the sweet birds sang.
In me thou see'st the twilight of such day
As after sunset fadeth in the west,
Which by and by black night doth take away,
Death's second self, that seals up all in rest.
In me thou see'st the glowing of such fire
That on the ashes of his youth doth lie,
As the death-bed whereon it must expire,
Consumed with that which it was nourish'd by.
This thou perceivest, which makes thy love more strong,
To love that well which thou must leave ere long.

XCVII

How like a winter hath my absence been
From thee, the pleasure of the fleeting year!
What freezings have I felt, what dark days seen!
What old December's bareness every where!
And yet this time removed was summer's time,
The teeming autumn, big with rich increase,
Bearing the wanton burthen of the prime,
Like widow'd wombs after their lords' decease:
Yet this abundant issue seem'd to me
But hope of orphans and unfather'd fruit;
For summer and his pleasures wait on thee,
And, thou away, the very birds are mute;
Or, if they sing, 'tis with so dull a cheer
That leaves look pale, dreading the winter's near.

XCVIII

From you have I been absent in the spring,
When proud-pied April dress'd in all his trim
Hath put a spirit of youth in every thing,
That heavy Saturn laugh'd and leap'd with him.
Yet nor the lays of birds nor the sweet smell
Of different flowers in odour and in hue
Could make me any summer's story tell,
Or from their proud lap pluck them where they grew;
Nor did I wonder at the lily's white,
Nor praise the deep vermilion in the rose;
They were but sweet, but figures of delight,
Drawn after you, you pattern of all those.
Yet seem'd it winter still, and, you away,
As with your shadow, I with these did play.

XCIX

The forward violet thus did I chide:
Sweet thief, whence didst thou steal thy sweet that smells,
If not from my love's breath? The purple pride
Which on thy soft cheek for complexion dwells
In my love's veins thou hast too grossly dyed.
The lily I condemnèd for thy hand,
And buds of marjoram had stol'n thy hair.
The roses fearfully on thorns did stand,
One blushing shame, another white despair;
A third, nor red nor white, had stol'n of both
And to his robbery had annex'd thy breath;
But, for his theft, in pride of all his growth
A vengeful canker eat him up to death.
More flowers I noted, yet I none could see
But sweet or colour it had stol'n from thee.

CVI

When in the chronicle of wasted time
I see descriptions of the fairest wights,
And beauty making beautiful old rhyme
In praise of ladies dead and lovely knights,
Then, in the blazon of sweet beauty's best,
Of hand, of foot, of lip, of eye, of brow,
I see their antique pen would have express'd

Even such a beauty as you master now.
So all their praises are but prophecies
Of this our time, all you prefiguring;
And, for they look'd but with divining eyes,
They had not skill enough your worth to sing:
For we, which now behold these present days,
Have eyes to wonder, but lack tongues to praise.

CVII

Not mine own fears, nor the prophetic soul
Of the wide world dreaming on things to come,
Can yet the lease of my true love control,
Supposed as forfeit to a confined doom.
The mortal moon hath her eclipse endured
And the sad augurs mock their own presage;
Incertainties now crown themselves assured
And peace proclaims olives of endless age.
Now with the drops of this most balmy time
My love looks fresh, and Death to me subscribes,
Since, spite of him, I'll live in this poor rhyme,
While he insults o'er dull and speechless tribes:
And thou in this shalt find thy monument,
When tyrants' crests and tombs of brass are spent.

CIX

O, never say that I was false of heart,
Though absence seem'd my flame to qualify.
As easy might I from myself depart
As from my soul, which in thy breast doth lie:
That is my home of love: if I have ranged,
Like him that travels I return again,
Just to the time, not with the time exchanged,
So that myself bring water for my stain.
Never believe, though in my nature reign'd
All frailties that besiege all kinds of blood,
That it could so preposterously be stain'd,
To leave for nothing all thy sum of good;
For nothing this wide universe I call,
Save thou, my rose; in it thou art my all.

CX

Alas, 'tis true I have gone here and there
And made myself a motley to the view,
Gored mine own thoughts, sold cheap what is most dear,
Made old offences of affections new;
Most true it is that I have look'd on truth
Askance and strangely; but, by all above,
These blenches gave my heart another youth,
And worse essays proved thee my best of love.
Now all is done, have what shall have no end:
Mine appetite I never more will grind
On newer proof, to try an older friend,
A god in love, to whom I am confin'd.
Then give me welcome, next my heaven the best,
Even to thy pure and most most loving breast.

CXI

O, for my sake do you with Fortune chide,
The guilty goddess of my harmful deeds,
That did not better for my life provide
Than public means which public manners breeds.
Thence comes it that my name receives a brand,
And almost thence my nature is subdued
To what it works in, like the dyer's hand.
Pity me then and wish I were renew'd;
Whilst, like a willing patient, I will drink
Potions of eisel 'gainst my strong infection;
No bitterness that I will bitter think,
Nor double penance, to correct correction.
Pity me then, dear friend, and I assure ye
Even that your pity is enough to cure me.

CXVI

Let me not to the marriage of true minds
Admit impediments. Love is not love
Which alters when it alteration finds,
Or bends with the remover to remove:
O, no! it is an ever-fixèd mark
That looks on tempests and is never shaken;
It is the star to every wandering bark,
Whose worth's unknown, although his height be taken.
Love's not Time's fool, though rosy lips and cheeks
Within his bending sickle's compass come;
Love alters not with his brief hours and weeks,
But bears it out even to the edge of doom.
If this be error and upon me proved,
I never writ, nor no man ever loved.

CXXVIII

How oft, when thou, my music, music play'st,
Upon that blessed wood whose motion sounds
With thy sweet fingers, when thou gently sway'st
The wiry concord that mine ear confounds,
Do I envy those jacks that nimble leap
To kiss the tender inward of thy hand,
Whilst my poor lips, which should that harvest reap,
At the wood's boldness by thee blushing stand!
To be so tickled, they would change their state
And situation with those dancing chips,
O'er whom thy fingers walk with gentle gait,
Making dead wood more blest than living lips.
Since saucy jacks so happy are in this,
Give them thy fingers, me thy lips to kiss.

CXLVI

Poor soul, the centre of my sinful earth,
[Amidst] these rebel powers that thee array,
Why dost thou pine within and suffer dearth,
Painting thy outward walls so costly gay?
Why so large cost, having so short a lease,
Dost thou upon thy fading mansion spend?
Shall worms, inheritors of this excess,
Eat up thy charge? is this thy body's end?
Then, soul, live thou upon thy servant's loss,
And let that pine to aggravate thy store;
Buy terms divine in selling hours of dross;
Within be fed, without be rich no more:
So shalt thou feed on Death, that feeds on men,
And Death once dead, there's no more dying then.

SONGS FROM THE PLAYS

FROM LOVE'S LABOUR'S LOST

When icicles hang by the wall,
And Dick the shepherd blows his nail,
And Tom bears logs into the hall,
And milk comes frozen home in pail,
When blood is nipped and ways be foul,
Then nightly sings the staring owl,
Tu-whit, tu-who! a merry note,
While greasy Joan doth keel the pot.

When all aloud the wind doth blow,
And coughing drowns the parson's saw,
And birds sit brooding in the snow,
And Marian's nose looks red and raw,
When roasted crabs hiss in the bowl,
Then nightly sings the staring owl,
Tu-whit, tu-who! a merry note,
While greasy Joan doth keel the pot.

FROM A MIDSUMMER NIGHT'S DREAM

Over hill, over dale,
Thorough bush, thorough brier,
Over park, over pale,
Thorough flood, thorough fire,
I do wander everywhere,
Swifter than the moonës sphere;
And I serve the Fairy Queen,
To dew her orbs upon the green.
The cowslips tall her pensioners be;
In their gold coats spots you see:
Those be rubies, fairy favours,
In those freckles live their savours.
I must go seek some dewdrops here,
And hang a pearl in every cowslip's ear.

FROM TWO GENTLEMEN OF VERONA

Who is Silvia? what is she,
That all our swains commend her?
Holy, fair, and wise is she;
The heaven such grace did lend her,
That she might admired be.

Is she kind as she is fair?
For beauty lives with kindness.
Love doth to her eyes repair
To help him of his blindness,
And, being help'd, inhabits there.

Then to Silvia let us sing,
That Silvia is excelling;
She excels each mortal thing
Upon the dull earth dwelling:
To her let us garlands bring.

FROM THE MERCHANT OF VENICE

Tell me, where is fancy bred,
Or in the heart, or in the head?
How begot, how nourishèd?
Reply, reply.

It is engendered in the eyes,
With gazing fed; and fancy dies
In the cradle where it lies:
Let us all ring fancy's knell;
I'll begin it, — Ding-dong, bell.
Ding, dong, bell.

FROM AS YOU LIKE IT

Under the greenwood tree
Who loves to lie with me,
And turn his merry note
Unto the sweet bird's throat,
Come hither! come hither! come hither!
Here shall he see
No enemy
But winter and rough weather.

Who doth ambition shun
And loves to live i' the sun,
Seeking the food he eats
And pleased with what he gets,
Come hither! come hither! come hither!
Here shall he see
No enemy
But winter and rough weather.

From AS YOU LIKE IT

Blow, blow, thou winter wind!
Thou art not so unkind
As man's ingratitude;
Thy tooth is not so keen,
Because thou art not seen,
Although thy breath be rude.

Heigh ho! sing, heigh ho! unto the green holly:
Most friendship is feigning, most loving mere folly:
Then, heigh ho, the holly!
This life is most jolly.

Freeze, freeze, thou bitter sky!
That dost not bite so nigh
As benefits forgot;
Though thou the waters warp,
Thy sting is not so sharp
As friend remembered not.

Heigh ho! sing, heigh ho! etc.

From MUCH ADO ABOUT NOTHING

Sigh no more, ladies, sigh no more!
Men were deceivers ever,
One foot in sea and one on shore,
To one thing constant never:
Then sigh not so, but let them go,
And be you blithe and bonny,
Converting all your sounds of woe
Into Hey nonny, nonny!

Sing no more ditties, sing no moe
Of dumps so dull and heavy!
The fraud of men was ever so,
Since summer first was leavy:
Then sigh not so, but let them go,
And be you blithe and bonny,
Converting all your sounds of woe
Into Hey nonny, nonny!

From TWELFTH NIGHT

O Mistress mine, where are you roaming?
O, stay and hear; your true love's coming,
That can sing both high and low:
Trip no further, pretty sweeting,
Journeys end in lovers meeting,
Every wise man's son doth know.

What is love? 'tis not hereafter;
Present mirth hath present laughter;
What's to come is still unsure:
In delay there lies no plenty;
Then come kiss me, sweet and twenty,
Youth's a stuff will not endure.

From MEASURE FOR MEASURE

Take, O, take those lips away,
That so sweetly were forsworn;
And those eyes, the break of day,
Lights that do mislead the morn:
But my kisses bring again,
Bring again;
Seals of love, but sealed in vain,
Sealed in vain!

From TWELFTH NIGHT

Come away, come away, Death!
And in sad cypress let me be laid;
Fly away, fly away, breath;
I am slain by a fair cruel maid.
My shroud of white, stuck all with yew,
O, prepare it!
My part of death, no one so true
Did share it.

Not a flower, not a flower sweet,
On my black coffin let there be strown;
Not a friend, not a friend greet
My poor corpse, where my bones shall be thrown:
A thousand thousand sighs to save,
Lay me, O, where
Sad true lover never find my grave,
To weep there!

From HAMLET

How should I your true love know
From another one?
By his cockle hat and staff,
And his sandal shoon.

He is dead and gone, lady,
He is dead and gone;
At his head a grass-green turf,
At his heels a stone.

White his shroud as the mountain snow,
Larded with sweet flowers,
Which bewept to the grave did go
With true-love showers.

From CYMBELINE

Hark, hark! the lark at heaven's gate sings,
  And Phœbus 'gins arise,
His steeds to water at those springs
  On chaliced flowers that lies;
And winking Mary-buds begin
  To ope their golden eyes:
With every thing that pretty is,
  My lady sweet, arise!
    Arise, arise!

From CYMBELINE

Fear no more the heat o' th' sun,
  Nor the furious winter's rages;
Thou thy worldly task hast done,
  Home art gone, and ta'en thy wages:
Golden lads and girls all must,
As chimney-sweepers, come to dust.

Fear no more the frown o' th' great;
  Thou art past the tyrant's stroke;
Care no more to clothe and eat;
  To thee the reed is as the oak:
The Sceptre, Learning, Physic, must
All follow this, and come to dust.

Fear no more the lightning-flash,
  Nor th' all-dreaded thunder-stone;
Fear not slander, censure rash;
  Thou hast finished joy and moan:
All lovers young, all lovers must
Consign to thee, and come to dust.

No exorciser harm thee!
  Nor no witchcraft charm thee!
Ghost unlaid forbear thee!
  Nothing ill come near thee!
Quiet consummation have;
And renowned be thy grave!

From THE TEMPEST

A Sea Dirge

Full fathom five thy father lies:
    Of his bones are coral made;
Those are pearls that were his eyes;
    Nothing of him that doth fade
But doth suffer a sea change
Into something rich and strange.
Sea-nymphs hourly ring his knell:
                Ding-dong!
Hark! now I hear them, — Ding-dong, bell!

From THE TEMPEST

  Where the bee sucks, there suck I;
  In a cowslip's bell I lie;
  There I couch when owls do cry.
  On the bat's back I do fly
  After summer merrily.
Merrily, merrily, shall I live now
Under the blossom that hangs on the bough.

THOMAS NASH (1567–1601)

DEATH'S SUMMONS

Adieu, farewell, earth's bliss,
This world uncertain is:
Fond are life's lustful joys,
Death proves them all but toys.
None from his darts can fly:
I am sick, I must die.
    Lord, have mercy on us!

Rich men, trust not in wealth,
Gold cannot buy you health;
Physic himself must fade;
All things to end are made;
The plague full swift goes by:
I am sick, I must die.
    Lord, have mercy on us!

Beauty is but a flower,
Which wrinkles will devour:
Brightness falls from the air;
Queens have died young and fair;
Dust hath closed Helen's eye:
I am sick, I must die.
    Lord, have mercy on us!

Strength stoops unto the grave;
Worms feed on Hector brave;
Swords may not fight with fate;
Earth still holds ope her gate;
Come, come, the bells do cry.
I am sick, I must die.
    Lord, have mercy on us!

Wit with his wantonness,
Tasteth death's bitterness;
Hell's executioner
Hath no ears for to hear
What vain art can reply;
I am sick, I must die:
    Lord, have mercy on us!

Haste therefore each degree
To welcome destiny!

Heaven is our heritage,
Earth but a player's stage;
Mount we unto the sky:
I am sick, I must die.
Lord, have mercy on us!

THOMAS CAMPION (d. 1619)

CHANCE AND CHANGE

What if a day, or a month, or a year,
Crown thy delights, with a thousand sweet contentings!
Cannot a chance of a night, or an hour,
Cross thy desires, with as many sad tormentings?
Fortune, honour, beauty, youth,
Are but blossoms dying!
Wanton pleasure, doting love,
Are but shadows flying!
All our joys are but toys;
Idle thoughts deceiving!
None have power, of an hour,
In their life's bereaving.

Earth's but a point to the world; and a man
Is but a point to the world's comparèd centre!
Shall then, a point of a point be so vain
As to triumph in a silly point's adventure!
All is hazard that we have!
There is nothing biding!
Days of pleasure are like streams,
Through fair meadows gliding!
Weal and woe, Time doth go!
Time is never turning!
Secret fates guide our states;
Both in mirth and mourning!

CHERRY-RIPE

There is a garden in her face
Where roses and white lilies blow;
A heavenly paradise is that place,
Wherein all pleasant fruits do flow:
There cherries grow which none may buy
Till "Cherry-ripe" themselves do cry.

Those cherries fairly do enclose
Of orient pearl a double row,
Which when her lovely laughter shows,
They look like rosebuds fill'd with snow;
Yet them nor peer nor prince can buy
Till "Cherry-ripe" themselves do cry.

Her eyes like angels watch them still;
Her brows like bended bows do stand,
Threat'ning with piercing frowns to kill
All that attempt with eye or hand
Those sacred cherries to come nigh
Till "Cherry-ripe" themselves do cry.

SIR HENRY WOTTON (1568–1639)

AN ELEGY OF A WOMAN'S HEART

O, faithless World! and thy more faithless part,
A woman's heart!
The true shop of variety! where sits
Nothing but fits
And fevers of desire, and pangs of love;
Which toys remove!
Why was she born to please! or I, to trust
Words writ in dust!
Suff'ring her eyes to govern my despair;
My pain, for air!
And fruit of time rewarded with untruth,
The food of youth!
Untrue She was: yet I believed her eyes,
(Instructed spies!)
Till I was taught, that love was but a school
To breed a fool!
Or sought She more, by triumphs of denial,
To make a trial,
How far her smiles commanded my weakness!
Yield, and confess!
Excuse no more thy folly! But, for cure,
Blush, and endure
As well thy shame, as passions that were vain!
And think, 'tis gain
To know, that love, lodged in a woman's breast,
Is but a guest!

THE CHARACTER OF A HAPPY LIFE

How happy is he born and taught
That serveth not another's will;
Whose armour is his honest thought,
And simple truth his utmost skill!

Whose passions not his masters are;
Whose soul is still prepared for death,
Untied unto the world by care
Of public fame or private breath;

Who envies none that chance doth raise;
Nor vice hath ever understood
(How deepest wounds are given by praise!)
Nor rules of State, but rules of good;

Who hath his life from rumours freed;
Whose conscience is his strong retreat;
Whose state can neither flatterers feed,
Nor ruin make oppressors great;

Who God doth late and early pray,
  More of his grace, than gifts, to lend,
And entertains the harmless day
  With a religious book or friend!

This man is freed from servile bands
  Of hope to rise or fear to fall!
Lord of himself, though not of lands;
  And having nothing, yet hath all!

ON THE SUDDEN RESTRAINT OF ROBERT CARR, EARL OF SOMERSET; THEN FALLING FROM FAVOUR

Dazzled thus with height of Place,
  Whilst our hopes our wits beguile,
No man marks the narrow space
  'Twixt a Prison and a Smile!

Then, since Fortune's favours fade,
  You that in her arms do sleep,
Learn to swim, and not to wade;
  For the hearts of kings are deep.

But if Greatness be so blind
  As to trust in Towers of Air,
Let it be with Goodness lined,
  That, at least, the Fall be fair.

Then, though darkened, you shall say,
  When friends fail and princes frown:
"Virtue is the roughest way,
  But proves, at night, a bed of down!"

SIR JOHN DAVIES (1569–1626)

From NOSCE TEIPSUM!

OF THE SOUL OF MAN AND THE IMMORTALITY THEREOF

O Light! (which mak'st the light, which mak'st the day;
  Which sett'st the eye without, and mind within)
  Lighten my spirit with one clear heavenly ray!
  Which now to view itself doth first begin.

For her true form how can my spark discern?
  Which, dim by nature, art did never clear;
  When the great wits, of whom all skill we learn,
  Are ignorant both what she is and where!

* * * * * * *

Thus these great clerks their little wisdom show,
  While with their doctrines they at hazard play;
  Tossing their light opinions to and fro,
  To mock the lewd; as learned in this as they!

For no crazed brain could ever yet propound,
  Touching the soul, so vain and fond a thought,
  But some among these masters have been found
  Which in their schools the selfsame thing have taught.

God, only-wise! to punish pride of wit,
  Among men's wits hath this confusion wrought!
  As the proud tower whose points the clouds did hit
  By tongues' confusion was to ruin brought.

But, Thou! which didst man's soul of nothing make!
  And when to nothing it was fallen again,
  To make it new the form of man didst take,
  And, God with God, becam'st a man with men!

Thou! that hast fashioned twice this soul of ours,
  So that she is by double title Thine!
  Thou only knowest her nature and her powers;
  Her subtle form Thou only canst define!

To judge herself, she must herself transcend;
  As greater circles comprehend the less:
  But she wants power her own powers to extend;
  As fettered men cannot their strength express.

But Thou, bright morning Star! Thou, rising Sun!
  Which, in these later times, has brought to light
  Those mysteries that, since the world begun,
  Lay hid in darkness and eternal night!

Thou, like the sun, dost with indifferent ray
  Into the palace and the cottage shine,
  And showest the soul, both to the clerk and lay,
  By the clear lamp of thy oracle divine!

This lamp, through all the regions of my brain,
  Where my soul sits, doth spread such beams of grace,
  As now, methinks, I do distinguish plain
  Each subtle line of her immortal face!

THOMAS DEKKER (1570?–1641)

From THE SHOEMAKER'S HOLIDAY

THE SECOND THREE MEN'S SONG

Cold's the wind, and wet's the rain,
  Saint Hugh be our good speed!
Ill is the weather that bringeth no gain,
  Nor helps good hearts in need.

Trowl the bowl, the jolly nut-brown bowl,
 And here, kind mate, to thee:
Let's sing a dirge for Saint Hugh's soul,
 And down it merrily.

Down a down! hey down a down!
 Hey derry derry, down a down!
Ho, well done; to me let come!
 Ring, compass, gentle joy.

Trowl the bowl, the nut-brown bowl,
 And here, kind mate, to thee: etc.

(*Repeat as often as there be men to drink; and at last when all have drunk, this verse:*)

Cold's the wind, and wet's the rain,
 Saint Hugh be our good speed!
Ill is the weather that bringeth no gain,
 Nor helps good hearts in need.

From OLD FORTUNATUS

SONG

Virtue smiles: cry holiday,
Dimples on her cheeks do dwell,
Virtue frowns, cry welladay,
Her love is heaven, her hate is hell,
Since heaven and hell obey her power,
Tremble when her eyes do lower.
Since heaven and hell her power obey,
Where she smiles, cry holiday.
Holiday with joy we cry,
And bend, and bend, and merrily
Sing hymns to Virtue's deity:
Sing hymns to Virtue's deity.

From PATIENT GRISSILL

CONTENT

Art thou poor, yet hast thou golden slumbers?
  O sweet content!
Art thou rich, yet is thy mind perplexed?
  O punishment!
Dost laugh to see how fools are vexed
To add to golden numbers golden numbers?
 O sweet content, O sweet, O sweet content!

 Work apace! apace! apace! apace!
 Honest labour bears a lovely face.
 Then hey noney, noney; hey noney, noney!

Canst drink the waters of the crispèd spring?
  O sweet content!
Swim'st thou in wealth, yet sink'st in thine own tears?
  O punishment!
Then he that patiently want's burden bears
No burden bears, but is a king, a king.
 O sweet content, O sweet, O sweet content!

 Work apace, apace, etc.

THE END OF THE RENAISSANCE

BEN JONSON (1573?–1637)

SONG TO CELIA

Drink to me only with thine eyes,
  And I will pledge with mine;
Or leave a kiss but in the cup,
  And I'll not look for wine.
The thirst that from the soul doth rise
  Doth ask a drink divine;
But might I of Jove's nectar sup,
  I would not change for thine.

I sent thee late a rosy wreath,
  Not so much honouring thee
As giving it a hope, that there
  It could not wither'd be.
But thou thereon didst only breathe,
  And sent'st it back to me;
Since when it grows, and smells, I swear,
  Not of itself, but thee.

THE TRIUMPH OF CHARIS

See the chariot at hand here of Love,
  Wherein my Lady rideth!
Each that draws is a swan or a dove,
  And well the car Love guideth.
As she goes, all hearts do duty
          Unto her beauty;
And enamour'd, do wish, so they might
          But enjoy such a sight,
That they still were to run by her side,
Through swords, through seas, whither she would ride.

Do but look on her eyes, they do light
  All that Love's world compriseth!
Do but look on her hair, it is bright
  As Love's star when it riseth!
Do but mark, her forehead's smoother
          Than words that soothe her;
And from her arched brows, such a grace
          Sheds itself through the face
As alone there triumphs to the life
All the gain, all the good, of the elements' strife.

Have you seen but a bright lily grow,
  Before rude hands have touched it?
Have you marked but the fall of the snow
  Before the soil hath smutched it?
Have you felt the wool of the beaver?
          Or swan's down ever?
Or have smelt o' the bud of the briar?
          Or the nard in the fire?
Or have tasted the bag of the bee?
Oh so white! Oh so soft! Oh so sweet is she!

TO THE MEMORY OF MY BELOVED, MASTER WILLIAM SHAKESPEARE

To draw no envy, Shakespeare, on thy name,
Am I thus ample to thy book and fame;
While I confess thy writings to be such
As neither man, nor muse, can praise too much.
'Tis true, and all men's suffrage. But these ways
Were not the paths I meant unto thy praise;
For silliest ignorance on these may light,
Which, when it sounds at best, but echoes right;
Or blind affection, which doth ne'er advance
The truth, but gropes, and urgeth all by chance;
Or crafty malice might pretend this praise,
And think to ruin, where it seemed to raise.
These are, as some infamous bawd or whore
Should praise a matron. What could hurt her more?
But thou art proof against them, and, indeed,
Above the ill fortune of them, or the need.
I therefore will begin. Soul of the age!
The applause, delight, the wonder of our stage!
My Shakespeare, rise! I will not lodge thee by
Chaucer, or Spenser, or bid Beaumont lie
A little further, to make thee a room:
Thou art a monument without a tomb,
And art alive still while thy book doth live
And we have wits to read and praise to give.
That I not mix thee so, my brain excuses,
I mean with great, but disproportioned Muses;
For if I thought my judgment were of years,
I should commit thee surely with thy peers,
And tell how far thou didst our Lily outshine,
Or sporting Kyd, or Marlowe's mighty line.

And though thou hadst small Latin and less Greek,
From thence to honour thee, I would not seek
For names; but call forth thundering Æschylus,
Euripides, and Sophocles to us;
Pacuvius, Accius, him of Cordova dead,
To life again, to hear thy buskin tread,
And shake a stage; or, when thy socks were on,
Leave thee alone for the comparison
Of all that insolent Greece or haughty Rome
Sent forth, or since did from their ashes come.
Triumph, my Britain, thou hast one to show
To whom all scenes of Europe homage owe.
He was not of an age, but for all time!
And all the Muses still were in their prime,
When, like Apollo, he came forth to warm
Our ears, or like a Mercury to charm!
Nature herself was proud of his designs
And joyed to wear the dressing of his lines!
Which were so richly spun, and woven so fit,
As, since, she will vouchsafe no other wit.
The merry Greek, tart Aristophanes,
Neat Terence, witty Plautus, now not please;
But antiquated and deserted lie,
As they were not of Nature's family.
Yet must I not give Nature all; thy art,
My gentle Shakespeare, must enjoy a part.
For though the poet's matter nature be,
His art doth give the fashion; and, that he
Who casts to write a living line, must sweat,
(Such as thine are) and strike the second heat
Upon the Muses' anvil; turn the same
(And himself with it) that he thinks to frame,
Or, for the laurel, he may gain a scorn;
For a good poet's made, as well as born.
And such wert thou! Look how the father's face
Lives in his issue, even so the race
Of Shakespeare's mind and manners brightly shines
In his well turnèd, and true filèd lines;
In each of which he seems to shake a lance,
As brandished at the eyes of ignorance.
Sweet Swan of Avon! what a sight it were
To see thee in our waters yet appear,
And make those flights upon the banks of Thames,
That so did take Eliza, and our James!
But stay, I see thee in the hemisphere
Advanced, and made a constellation there!
Shine forth, thou Star of poets, and with rage
Or influence, chide or cheer the drooping stage,
Which, since thy flight from hence, hath mourned like night,
And despairs day, but for thy volume's light.

A PINDARIC ODE

To the immortal memory and friendship of that noble pair, Sir Lucius Cary and Sir H. Morison.

I

The Strophe, or Turn

Brave infant of Saguntum, clear
Thy coming forth in that great year,
When the prodigious Hannibal did crown
His rage with razing your immortal town.
Thou looking then about,
Ere thou wert half got out,
Wise child, didst hastily return,
And mad'st thy mother's womb thine urn.
How summ'd a circle didst thou leave mankind
Of deepest lore, could we the centre find!

The Antistrophe, or Counter-Turn

Did wiser nature draw thee back,
From out the horror of that sack;
Where shame, faith, honour, and regard of right,
Lay trampled on? the deeds of death and night
Urged, hurried forth, and hurl'd
Upon the affrighted world;
Fire, famine, and fell fury met,
And all on utmost ruin set:
As, could they but life's miseries foresee,
No doubt all infants would return like thee.

The Epode, or Stand

For what is life, if measured by the space,
Not by the act?
Or maskèd man, if valued by his face,
Above his fact?
Here's one outlived his peers
And told forth fourscore years:
He vexèd time, and busied the whole state;
Troubled both foes and friends;
But ever to no ends:
What did this stirrer but die late?
How well at twenty had he fallen or stood!
For three of his four score he did no good.

II

The Strophe, or Turn

He entered well by virtuous parts,
Got up, and thrived with honest arts,
He purchased friends, and fame, and honours then,
And had his noble name advanced with men;
But weary of that flight,
He stooped in all men's sight

To sordid flatteries, acts of strife,
And sunk in that dead sea of life,
So deep, as he did then death's waters sup,
But that the cork of title buoyed him up.

The Antistrophe, or Counter-Turn

Alas! but Morison fell young!
He never fell, — thou fall'st, my tongue.
He stood a soldier to the last right end,
A perfect patriot and a noble friend;
But most, a virtuous son.
All offices were done
By him, so ample, full, and round,
In weight, in measure, number, sound,
As, though his age imperfect might appear,
His life was of humanity the sphere.

The Epode, or Stand

Go now, and tell our days summed up with fears,
And make them years;
Produce thy mass of miseries on the stage,
To swell thine age;
Repeat of things a throng,
To show thou hast been long,
Not lived; for life doth her great actions spell,
By what was done and wrought
In season, and so brought
To light: her measures are, how well
Each syllabe answered, and was formed, how fair;
These make the lines of life, and that's her air!

III

The Strophe, or Turn

It is not growing like a tree
In bulk, doth make men better be;
Or standing long an oak, three hundred year,
To fall a log at last, dry, bald, and sear:
A lily of a day,
Is fairer far, in May,
Although it fall and die that night;
It was the plant and flower of light.
In small proportions we just beauties see;
And in short measures life may perfect be.

The Antistrophe, or Counter-Turn

Call, noble Lucius, then, for wine,
And let thy locks with gladness shine;
Accept this garland, plant it on thy head,
And think, nay know, thy Morison's not dead.
He leaped the present age,
Possest with holy rage,
To see that bright eternal day;
Of which we priests and poets say
Such truths as we expect for happy men;
And there he lives with memory and Ben——

The Epode, or Stand

Jonson, who sung this of him, ere he went,
Himself, to rest,
Or taste a part of that full joy he meant
To have exprest,
In this bright asterism; —
Where it were friendship's schism,
Were not his Lucius long with us to tarry,
To separate these twi-
Lights, the Dioscuri;
And keep the one half from his Harry.
But fate doth so alternate the design,
Whilst that in heaven, this light on earth must shine, —

IV

The Strophe, or Turn

And shine as you exalted are;
Two names of friendship, but one star:
Of hearts the union, and those not by chance
Made, or indenture, or leased out t' advance
The profits for a time.
No pleasures vain did chime,
Of rhymes, or riots, at your feasts,
Orgies of drink, or feigned protests;
But simple love of greatness and of good,
That knits brave minds and manners more than blood.

The Antistrophe, or Counter-Turn

This made you first to know the why
You liked, then after, to apply
That liking; and approach so one the t' other,
Till either grew a portion of the other;
Each styled by his end,
The copy of his friend.
You lived to be the great sir-names
And titles by which all made claims
Unto the Virtue: nothing perfect done,
But as a Cary or a Morison.

The Epode, or Stand

And such a force the fair example had,
As they that saw
The good and durst not practise it, were glad
That such a law
Was left yet to mankind;
Where they might read and find
Friendship, indeed, was written not in words;
And with the heart, not pen,
Of two so early men,

Whose lines her rolls were, and records;
Who, ere the first down bloomèd on the chin,
Had sowed these fruits, and got the harvest in.

AN EPITAPH ON SALATHIEL PAVY

Weep with me, all you that read
This little story:
And know, for whom a tear you shed
Death's self is sorry.
'Twas a child that so did thrive
In grace and feature,
As heaven and nature seem'd to strive
Which owned the creature.
Years he numbered scarce thirteen
When fates turned cruel,
Yet three filled zodiacs had he been
The stage's jewel;
And did act, what now we moan,
Old men so duly,
As, sooth, the Parcæ thought him one,
He played so truly.
So, by error, to his fate
They all consented;
But viewing him since, alas, too late!
They have repented;
And have sought, to give new birth,
In baths to steep him;
But being so much too good for earth,
Heaven vows to keep him.

EPITAPH ON ELIZABETH, L. H.

Would'st thou hear what man can say
In a little? Reader, stay.

Underneath this stone doth lie
As much beauty as could die:
Which in life did harbour give
To more virtue than doth live.

If at all she had a fault,
Leave it buried in this vault.
One name was Elizabeth,
The other, let it sleep with death!
Fitter, where it died, to tell,
Than that it lived at all. Farewell!

FROM ODE TO HIMSELF UPON THE CENSURE OF HIS "NEW INN"

JANUARY, 1630

Come, leave the loathèd stage,
And the more loathsome age;
Where pride and impudence, in faction knit,
Usurp the chair of wit!
Indicting and arraigning every day
Something they call a play.
Let their fastidious, vain
Commission of the brain
Run on and rage, sweat, censure and condemn;
They were not made for thee, less thou for them.

Say that thou pour'st them wheat,
And they will acorns eat;
'Twere simple fury still thyself to waste
On such as have no taste!
To offer them a surfeit of pure bread
Whose appetites are dead!
No, give them grains their fill,
Husks, draff to drink and swill;
If they love lees, and leave the lusty wine,
Envy them not, their palate's with the swine.

No doubt some mouldy tale,
Like Pericles and stale
As the shrieve's crusts, and nasty as his fish —
Scraps, out of every dish
Thrown forth, and raked into the common tub,
May keep up the Play-club.
There, sweepings do as well
As the best-ordered meal;
For who the relish of these guests will fit,
Needs set them but the alms-basket of wit.

ON MY FIRST SON

Farewell, thou child of my right hand, and joy;
My sin was too much hope of thee, lov'd boy:
Seven years thou wert lent to me, and I thee pay,
Exacted by thy fate, on the just day.
Oh, could I lose all father now! for why
Will man lament the state he should envy?
To have so soon 'scaped world's and flesh's rage,
And, if no other misery, yet age!
Rest in soft peace, and ask'd, say here doth lie
Ben Jonson his best piece of poetry:
For whose sake henceforth all his vows be such,
As what he loves may never like too much.

INVITING A FRIEND TO SUPPER

To-night, grave sir, both my poor house and I
Do equally desire your company, —
Not that we think us worthy such a guest,
But that your worth will dignify our feast,
With those that come; whose grace may make that seem
Something, which else would hope for no esteem.
It is the fair acceptance, sir, creates
The entertainment perfect, not the cates.

Yet shall you have, to rectify your palate,
An olive, capers, or some better sallet
Ushering the mutton; with a short-legged hen,
If we can get her full of eggs, and then
Lemons and wine for sauce; to these, a coney
Is not to be despaired of for our money;
And though fowl now be scarce, yet there are clerks,
The sky not falling, think we may have larks.
I'll tell you of more, and lie, so you will come:
Of partridge, pheasant, woodcock, of which some
May yet be there; and god-wit if we can;
Knat, rail, and ruff too. Howsoe'er, my man
Shall read a piece of Virgil, Tacitus,
Livy, or of some better book to us,
Of which we'll speak our minds, amidst our meat;
And I'll profess no verses to repeat.
To this if aught appear, which I not know of,
That will the pastry, not my paper, show of.
Digestive cheese, and fruit there sure will be;
But that which most doth take my muse and me
Is a pure cup of rich Canary wine,
Which is the Mermaid's now, but shall be mine:
Of which had Horace or Anacreon tasted,
Their lives, as do their lines, till now had lasted.
Tobacco, nectar, or the Thespian spring,
Are all but Luther's beer to this I sing.
Of this we will sup free, but moderately,
And we will have no Pooly, or Parrot by;
Nor shall our cups make any guilty men,
But at our parting we will be as when
We innocently met. No simple word,
That shall be uttered at our mirthful board,
Shall make us sad next morning, or affright
The liberty that we'll enjoy to-night.

JOHN DONNE (1573-1631)

SONG

Go and catch a falling star,
  Get with child a mandrake root,
Tell me where all past years are,
  Or who cleft the Devil's foot;
Teach me to hear mermaids singing,
Or to keep off envy's stinging,
    And find
    What wind
Serves to advance an honest mind.

If thou be'st born to strange sights,
  Things invisible go see,
Ride ten thousand days and nights
  Till Age snow white hairs on thee;
Thou, when thou return'st, wilt tell me
All strange wonders that befell thee,
    And swear
    No where
Lives a woman true and fair.

If thou find'st one, let me know;
  Such a pilgrimage were sweet.
Yet do not; I would not go,
  Though at next door we might meet.
Though she were true when you met her,
And last till you write your letter,
    Yet she
    Will be
False, ere I come, to two or three.

THE INDIFFERENT

I can love both fair and brown;
Her whom abundance melts, and her whom want betrays;
Her who loves loneness best, and her who masks and plays;
Her whom the country form'd, and whom the town;
Her who believes, and her who tries;
Her who still weeps with spongy eyes,
And her who is dry cork and never cries.
I can love her, and her, and you, and you;
I can love any, so she be not true.

Will no other vice content you?
Will it not serve your turn to do as did your mothers?
Or have you all old vices spent and now would find out others?
Or doth a fear that men are true torment you?
O we are not, be not you so;
Let me — and do you — twenty know;
Rob me, but bind me not, and let me go.
Must I, who came to travel thorough you,
Grow your fix'd subject, because you are true?

Venus heard me sigh this song;
And by love's sweetest part, variety, she swore,
She heard not this till now; it should be so no more.
She went, examined, and return'd ere long,
And said, "Alas! some two or three
Poor heretics in love there be,
Which think to stablish dangerous constancy.
But I have told them, 'Since you will be true,
You shall be true to them who're false to you.'"

THE CANONIZATION

For God's sake hold your tongue, and let me love;
  Or chide my palsy, or my gout;
  My five grey hairs, or ruin'd fortune flout;

With wealth your state, your mind with arts improve;
Take you a course, get you a place,
Observe his Honour, or his Grace;
Or the king's real, or his stamp'd face
Contemplate; what you will, approve,
So you will let me love. 9

Alas! alas! who's injured by my love?
What merchant's ships have my sighs drown'd?
Who says my tears have overflow'd his ground?
When did my colds a forward spring remove?
When did the heats which my veins fill
Add one more to the plaguy bill?
Soldiers find wars, and lawyers find out still
Litigious men, which quarrels move,
Though she and I do love. 18

Call's what you will, we are made such by love;
Call her one, me another fly,
We're tapers too, and at our own cost die,
And we in us find th' eagle and the dove.
The phoenix riddle hath more wit
By us; we two being one, are it;
So, to one neutral thing both sexes fit.
We die and rise the same, and prove
Mysterious by this love. 27

We can die by it, if not live by love,
And if unfit for tomb or hearse
Our legend be, it will be fit for verse;
And if no piece of chronicle we prove,
We'll build in sonnets pretty rooms;
As well a well-wrought urn becomes
The greatest ashes, as half-acre tombs,
And by these hymns all shall approve
Us canonized for love; 36

And thus invoke us, "You, whom reverend love
Made one another's hermitage;
You, to whom love was peace, that now is rage;
Who did the whole world's soul contract, and drove
Into the glasses of your eyes;
So made such mirrors, and such spies,
That they did all to you epitomize —
Countries, towns, courts beg from above
A pattern of your love." 45

THE DREAM

Dear love, for nothing less than thee
Would I have broke this happy dream;
It was a theme
For reason, much too strong for fantasy.
Therefore thou waked'st me wisely; yet
My dream thou brok'st not, but continued'st it.
Thou art so true that thoughts of thee suffice
To make dreams truths and fables histories;
Enter these arms, for since thou thought'st it best
Not to dream all my dream, let's act the rest. 10

As lightning, or a taper's light,
Thine eyes, and not thy noise, waked me;
Yet I thought thee —
For thou lov'st truth — an angel, at first sight;
But when I saw thou saw'st my heart,
And knew'st my thoughts beyond an angel's art,
When thou knew'st what I dreamt, when thou knew'st when
Excess of joy would wake me, and cam'st then,
I must confess it could not choose but be
Profane to think thee anything but thee. 20

Coming and staying show'd thee thee,
But rising makes me doubt that now
Thou art not thou.
That Love is weak where Fear's as strong as he;
'Tis not all spirit pure and brave
If mixture it of Fear, Shame, Honour have.
Perchance as torches, which must ready be,
Men light and put out, so thou deal'st with me.
Thou cam'st to kindle, go'st to come: then I 29
Will dream that hope again, but else would die.

LOVE'S DEITY

I long to talk with some old lover's ghost
Who died before the god of love was born.
I cannot think that he who then loved most
Sunk so low as to love one which did scorn.
But since this god produced a destiny,
And that vice-nature, custom, lets it be,
I must love her that loves not me. 7

Sure, they which made him god, meant not so much,
Nor he in his young godhead practiced it.
But when an even flame two hearts did touch,
His office was indulgently to fit
Actives to passives. Correspondency
Only his subject was; it cannot be
Love till I love her who loves me. 14

But every modern god will not extend
His vast prerogative as far as Jove.
To rage, to lust, to write to, to commend,
All is the purlieu of the god of love.
O! were we waken'd by this tyranny
To ungod this child again, it could not be
I should love her who loves not me. 21

Rebel and atheist too, why murmur I,
As though I felt the worst that love could do?
Love may make me leave loving, or might try
A deeper plague, to make her love me too;
Which, since she loves before, I'm loth to see.
Falsehood is worse than hate; and that must be,
If she whom I love, should love me. 28

THE FUNERAL

Whoever comes to shroud me, do not harm
Nor question much
That subtle wreath of hair about mine arm;
The mystery, the sign you must not touch,
For 'tis my outward soul,
Viceroy to that which, unto heav'n being gone,
Will leave this to control
And keep these limbs, her provinces, from dissolution. 8

For if the sinewy thread my brain lets fall
Through every part
Can tie those parts, and make me one of all;
Those hairs, which upward grew, and strength and art
Have from a better brain,
Can better do't: except she meant that I
By this should know my pain,
As prisoners then are manacled, when they're condemn'd to die. 16

Whate'er she meant by't, bury it with me,
For since I am
Love's martyr, it might breed idolatry
If into other hands these reliques came.
As 'twas humility
T'afford to it all that a soul can do,
So 'tis some bravery
That, since you would have none of me, I bury some of you. 24

THE COMPUTATION

For my first twenty years, since yesterday,
I scarce believed thou couldst be gone away;
For forty more I fed on favours past,
And forty on hopes that thou wouldst they might last;
Tears drown'd one hundred, and sighs blew out two;
A thousand I did neither think nor do,
Or not divide, all being one thought of you;
Or in a thousand more, forgot that too.
Yet call not this long life; but think that I 9
Am, by being dead, immortal; can ghosts die?

FORGET

If poisonous minerals, and if that tree
Whose fruit threw death on else immortal us,
If lecherous goats, if serpents envious
Cannot be damn'd, alas! why should I be?
Why should intent or reason, born in me,
Make sins, else equal, in me more heinous?
And, mercy being easy and glorious
To God, in His stern wrath why threatens He? 8
But who am I, that dare dispute with Thee?
O God, O! of Thine only worthy blood
And my tears make a heavenly Lethean flood,
And drown in it my sin's black memory.
That Thou remember them, some claim as debt;
I think it mercy if Thou wilt forget.

DEATH

Death, be not proud, though some have callèd thee
Mighty and dreadful, for thou art not so;
For those whom thou think'st thou dost overthrow
Die not, poor Death; nor yet canst thou kill me.
From Rest and Sleep, which but thy picture be,
Much pleasure; then from thee much more must flow;
And soonest our best men with thee do go —
Rest of their bones and souls' delivery! 8
Thou'rt slave to Fate, chance, kings, and desperate men,
And dost with poison, war, and sickness dwell;
And poppy or charms can make us sleep as well
And better than thy stroke. Why swell'st thou then?
One short sleep past, we wake eternally,
And Death shall be no more: Death, thou shalt die!

A HYMN TO GOD THE FATHER

Wilt Thou forgive that sin where I begun,
Which was my sin, though it were done before?
Wilt Thou forgive that sin through which I run,
And do run still, though still I do deplore?
When Thou hast done, Thou hast not done;
For I have more. 6

Wilt Thou forgive that sin which I have won
Others to sin, and made my sins their door?
Wilt Thou forgive that sin which I did shun
A year or two, but wallow'd in a score?
When Thou hast done, Thou hast not done;
For I have more. 12

I have a sin of fear, that when I've spun
  My last thread, I shall perish on the shore;
But swear by Thyself that at my death Thy Son
  Shall shine as He shines now and heretofore;
And having done that, Thou hast done;
  I fear no more.

From COMMENDATORY VERSES UPON MR. THOMAS CORYAT'S CRUDITIES

Oh, to what height will love of greatness drive
Thy learned spirit, sesqui-superlative?
Venice' vast lake thou'st seen, and wouldst seek then
Some vaster thing, and found'st a courtesan.
That inland sea having discover'd well,
A cellar-gulf, where one might sail to hell
From Heidelberg, thou longed'st to see; and thou
This book, greater than all, producest now.
Infinite work! which doth so far extend,
That none can study it to any end.
'Tis no one thing; it is not fruit nor root,
Nor poorly limited with head or foot.
If man be therefore man, because he can
Reason and laugh, thy book doth half make man.
One-half being made, thy modesty was such,
That thou on th' other half wouldst never touch.
When wilt thou be at full, great lunatic?
Not till thou exceed the world? Canst thou be like
A prosperous nose-born wen, which sometimes grows
To be far greater than the mother-nose?
Go then, and as to thee, when thou didst go,
Münster did towns and Gesner authors show,
Mount now to Gallo-Belgicus; appear
As deep a statesman as a gazeteer.
Homely and familiarly, when thou comest back,
Talk of Will Conqueror, and Prester Jack.
Go, bashful man, lest here thou blush to look
Upon the progress of thy glorious book.

JOSEPH HALL (1574–1656)

BOOK I, SATIRE III

With some pot-fury, ravish'd from their wit,
They sit and muse on some no-vulgar writ:
As frozen dunghills in a winter's morn,
That void of vapours seemèd all beforn,
Soon as the sun sends out his piercing beams,
Exhale out filthy smoke and stinking steams;
So doth the base, and the fore-barren brain,
Soon as the raging wine begins to reign.
One higher pitch'd doth set his soaring thought
On crownèd kings, that fortune hath low brought;
Or some upreared, high-aspiring swain,
As it might be the Turkish Tamberlain:
Then weeneth he his base drink-drowned spright,
Rapt to the threefold loft of heaven hight,
When he conceives upon his feigned stage
The stalking steps of his great personage,
Gracèd with huff-cap terms and thund'ring threats,
That his poor hearers' hair quite upright sets.
Such soon as some brave-minded hungry youth
Sees fitly frame to his wide-strained mouth,
He vaunts his voice upon an hired stage,
With high-set steps and princely carriage;
Now swooping in side robes of royalty,
That erst did scrub in lousy brokery.
There if he can with terms Italianate,
Big-sounding sentences and words of state,
Fair patch me up his pure iambic verse,
He ravishes the gazing scaffolders.
Then certes was the famous Corduban
Never but half so high tragedian.
Now, lest such frightful shows of Fortune's fall,
And bloody tyrant's rage, should chance appall
The dead-struck audience, midst the silent rout,
Comes leaping in a self-misformed lout,
And laughs, and grins, and frames his mimic face,
And justles straight into the prince's place;
Then doth the theatre echo all aloud,
With gladsome noise of that applauding crowd.
A goodly hotch-potch! when vile russetings
Are match'd with monarchs, and with mighty kings.
A goodly grace to sober tragic muse,
When each base clown his clumsy fist doth bruise,
And show his teeth in double rotten row,
For laughter at his self-resembled show.
Meanwhile our poets in high parliament
Sit watching every word and gesturement,
Like curious censors of some doughty gear,
Whispering their verdict in their fellow's ear.
Woe to the word whose margent in their scroll
Is noted with a black condemning coal.
But if each period might the synod please,
Ho! — bring the ivy boughs, and bands of bays.
Now when they part and leave the naked stage,
'Gins the bare hearer, in a guilty rage,
To curse and ban, and blame his likerous eye,
That thus hath lavish'd his late halfpenny.
Shame that the Muses should be bought and sold,
For every peasant's brass, on each scaffold.

JOHN MARSTON (1575–1634)

FROM THE SCOURGE OF VILLAINY

In Lectores prorsus indignos

Fie, Satire, fie! shall each mechanic slave,
Each dunghill peasant, free perusal have
Of thy well-labour'd lines? — each satin suit,
Each quaint fashion-monger, whose sole repute
Rests in his trim gay clothes, lie slavering,
Tainting thy lines with his lewd censuring?
Shall each odd puisne of the lawyer's inn,
Each barmy-froth, that last day did begin
To read his little, or his ne'er a whit,
Or shall some greater ancient, of less wit
That never turn'd but brown tobacco leaves,
Whose senses some damn'd occupant bereaves,
Lie gnawing on thy vacant time's expense,
Tearing thy rhymes, quite altering the sense?
Or shall perfum'd Castilio censure thee,
Shall he o'erview thy sharp-fang'd poesy
Who ne'er read further than his mistress lips,
Ne'er practised ought but some spruce cap'ring skips,
Ne'er in his life did other language use,
But "Sweet lady, fair mistress, kind heart, dear cuz" —
Shall this phantasma, this Coloss peruse,
And blast, with stinking breath, my budding muse?
Fie! wilt thou make thy wit a courtezan
For every broken handcraft's artisan?
Shall brainless cittern-heads, each jobbernoul,
Pocket the very genius of thy soul?
Ay, Phylo, ay, I'll keep an open hall,
A common and a sumptuous festival.
Welcome all eyes, all ears, all tongues to me!
Gnaw peasants on my scraps of poesy!
Castilios, Cyprians, court-boys, Spanish blocks,
Ribanded ears, Granado netherstocks,
Fiddlers, scriveners, pedlars, tinkering knaves,
Base blue-coats, tapsters, broad-cloth-minded slaves —
Welcome, i' faith; but may you ne'er depart
Till I have made your gallèd hides to smart.
Your gallèd hides? avaunt, base muddy scum,
Think you a satire's dreadful sounding drum
Will brace itself, and deign to terrify
Such abject peasants' basest roguery?
No, no, pass on, ye vain fantastic troop
Of puffy youths; know I do scorn to stoop
To rip your lives. Then hence, lewd nags, away,
Go read each post, view what is play'd to-day,
Then to Priapus' gardens. You, Castilio,
I pray thee let my lines in freedom go;
Let me alone, the madams call for thee,
Longing to laugh at thy wit's poverty.
Sirra livery cloak, you lazy slipper-slave,
Thou fawning drudge, what, wouldst thou satires have?
Base mind, away, thy master calls, be gone.
Sweet Gnato, let my poesy alone;
Go buy some ballad of the Fairy King,
And of the beggar wench some roguy thing,
Which thou mayst chant unto the chamber-maid
To some vile tune, when that thy master's laid.
But will you needs stay? am I forced to bear
The blasting breath of each lewd censurer?
Must naught but clothes, and images of men,
But spriteless trunks, be judges of thy pen?
Nay then, come all! I prostitute my muse,
For all the swarms of idiots to abuse.
Read all, view all; even with my full consent,
So you will know that which I never meant;
So you will ne'er conceive, and yet dispraise
That which you ne'er conceived, and laughter raise,
Where I but strive in honest seriousness
To scourge some soul-polluting beastliness.
So you will rail, and find huge errors lurk
In every corner of my cynic work.
Proface! read on, for your extrem'st dislikes
Will add a pinion to my praise's flights.
O how I bristle up my plumes of pride,
O how I think my satire's dignifi'd,
When I once hear some quaint Castilio,
Some supple-mouth'd slave, some lewd Tubrio,
Some spruce pedant, or some span-new-come fry
Of inns-o'court, striving to vilify
My dark reproofs! Then do but rail at me,
No greater honour craves my poesy.

GEORGE SANDYS (1578–1644)

A PARAPHRASE UPON THE PSALMS OF DAVID

PSALM XXX, PART II

In my prosperity I said,
My feet shall ever fix'd abide;
I, by Thy favour fortifi'd,
Am like a steadfast mountain made.

But when Thou hid'st Thy cheerful face,
How infinite my troubles grew;
My cries then with my grief renew,
Which thus implor'd Thy saving grace.

What profit can my blood afford,
When I shall to the grave descend?
Can senseless dust Thy praise extend?
Can death Thy living truth record?

To my complaints attentive be,
Thy mercy in my aid advance;
O perfect my deliverance,
That have no other hope but Thee!

Thou, Lord, hast made th' afflicted glad;
My sorrow into dancing turn'd:
The sack-cloth torn wherein I mourn'd,
And me in Tyrian purple clad:

That so my glory might proclaim
Thy favours in a joyful verse;
Incessantly Thy praise rehearse,
And magnify Thy sacred Name.

PSALM XLVI

God is our refuge, our strong tow'r,
Securing by His mighty pow'r,
When dangers threaten to devour.

Thus arm'd no fears shall chill our blood,
Though earth no longer steadfast stood,
And shook her hills into the flood;

Although the troubled ocean rise
In foaming billows to the skies,
And mountains shake with horrid noise.

Clear streams purl from a crystal spring,
Which gladness to God's city bring,
The mansion of th' Eternal King;

He in her centre takes His place,
What foe can her fair tow'rs deface,
Protected by His early grace?

Tumultuary nations rose,
And armèd troops our walls enclose,
But His fear'd Voice unnerv'd our foes.

The Lord of Hosts is on our side,
The God by Jacob magnified,
Our Strength, on Whom we have relied.

Come, see the wonders He hath wrought;
Who hath to desolation brought
Those kingdoms which our ruin sought.

He makes destructive war surcease,
The earth, deflower'd of her increase,
Restores with universal peace.

He breaks their bows, unarms their quivers,
The bloody spear in pieces shivers,
Their chariots to the flame delivers.

Forbear, and know that I, the Lord,
Will by all nations be ador'd,
Prais'd with unanimous accord.

The Lord of Hosts is on our side,
The God by Jacob magnified,
Our Strength on Whom we have relied.

A PARAPHRASE UPON THE SONG OF SOLOMON

CANTO III

SPONSA

Stretched on my restless bed all night,
I vainly sought my soul's delight.
Then rose, the city search'd: no street,
No angle my unwearied feet
Untracèd left: yet could not find
The only solace of my mind.
When lo! the watch, who walk the round,
Me in my soul's distemper found;
Of whom, with passion, I inquir'd,
Saw you the man so much desir'd?
Nor many steps had farther past,
But found my love, and held him fast;
Fast held, till I the so-long-sought
Had to my mother's mansion brought.
In that adornèd chamber laid
Of her who gave me life, I said:
You daughters of Jerusalem,
You branches of that holy stem,
I, by the mountain roes, and by
The hinds which through the forest fly,
Adjure you that you silence keep,
Nor, till he call, disturb his sleep.

JOHN FLETCHER (1579–1625)

SWEETEST MELANCHOLY

Hence, all you vain delights,
As short as are the nights
Wherein you spend your folly!
There's nought in this life sweet,
If man were wise to see't,
But only melancholy;
O sweetest melancholy!

Welcome, folded arms and fixèd eyes,
A sigh that piercing mortifies,

A look that's fastened to the ground,
A tongue chained up without a sound!
Fountain heads and pathless groves,
Places which pale passion loves!
Moonlight walks, when all the fowls
Are warmly housed save bats and owls!

A midnight bell, a parting groan,
These are the sounds we feed upon.
Then stretch our bones in a still gloomy valley;
Nothing's so dainty sweet as lovely melancholy.

LOVE'S EMBLEMS

Now the lusty spring is seen;
Golden yellow, gaudy blue,
Daintily invite the view,
Everywhere on every green,
Roses blushing as they blow,
And enticing men to pull
Lilies whiter than the snow,
Woodbines of sweet honey full:
All love's emblems, and all cry,
"Ladies, if not plucked, we die."

Yet the lusty spring hath stayed;
Blushing red and purest white
Daintily to love invite
Every woman, every maid.
Cherries kissing as they grow,
And inviting men to taste,
Apples even ripe below,
Winding gently to the waist:
All love's emblems, and all cry,
"Ladies, if not plucked, we die."

INVOCATION TO SLEEP

Care-charming Sleep, thou easer of all woes,
Brother to Death, sweetly thyself dispose
On this afflicted prince; fall like a cloud
In gentle showers; give nothing that is loud
Or painful to his slumbers; — easy, sweet,
And as a purling stream, thou son of Night,
Pass by his troubled senses; sing his pain
Like hollow murmuring wind or silver rain;
Into this prince gently, oh, gently slide,
And kiss him into slumbers like a bride!

SONG TO BACCHUS

God Lyæus, ever young,
Ever honoured, ever sung;
Stained with blood of lusty grapes,
In a thousand lusty shapes,
Dance upon the mazer's brim,
In the crimson liquor swim;
From thy plenteous hand divine
Let a river run with wine;
God of youth, let this day here
Enter neither care nor fear!

DRINK TO-DAY

Drink to-day, and drown all sorrow;
You shall perhaps not do it to-morrow:
Best, while you have it, use your breath;
There is no drinking after death.

Wine works the heart up, wakes the wit,
There is no cure 'gainst age but it:
It helps the headache, cough, and phthisic,
And is for all diseases physic.

Then let us swill, boys, for our health;
Who drinks well, loves the commonwealth.
And he that will to bed go sober
Falls with the leaf still in October.

BEAUTY CLEAR AND FAIR

Beauty clear and fair,
Where the air
Rather like a perfume dwells;
Where the violet and the rose
Their blue veins and blush disclose,
And come to honour nothing else.

Where to live near,
And planted there,
Is to live, and still live new;
Where to gain a favour is
More than light, perpetual bliss, —
Make me live by serving you.

Dear, again back recall
To this light
A stranger to himself and all;
Both the wonder and the story
Shall be yours, and eke the glory:
I am your servant, and your thrall.

THE CHARM

This way, this way come, and hear,
You that hold these pleasures dear;
Fill your ears with our sweet sound
Whilst we melt the frozen ground.
This way come; make haste, O fair!
Let your clear eyes gild the air;
Come, and bless us with your sight;
This way, this way, seek delight!

THE SLEEPING MISTRESS

O, fair sweet face! O, eyes celestial bright,
Twin stars in heaven, that now adorn the night!
Oh, fruitful lips, where cherries ever grow,
And damask cheeks, where all sweet beauties blow!
O, thou, from head to foot divinely fair!
Cupid's most cunning net's made of that hair;
And, as he weaves himself for curious eyes,
"O me, O me, I'm caught myself!" he cries:
Sweet rest about thee, sweet and golden sleep,
Soft peaceful thoughts, your hourly watches keep,
Whilst I in wonder sing this sacrifice,
To beauty sacred, and those angel eyes!

WEEP NO MORE

Weep no more, nor sigh, nor groan,
Sorrow calls no time that's gone;
Violets plucked the sweetest rain
Makes not fresh nor grow again;
Trim thy locks, look cheerfully;
Fate's hid ends eyes cannot see;
Joys as wingèd dreams fly fast,
Why should sadness longer last?

Grief is but a wound to woe;
Gentlest fair, mourn, mourn no mo.

DIRGE

Lay a garland on my hearse
  Of the dismal yew;
Maidens, willow branches bear;
  Say, I died true.

My love was false, but I was firm
  From my hour of birth.
Upon my buried body lie
  Lightly, gentle earth!

MARRIAGE HYMN

Roses, their sharp spines being gone,
Not royal in their smells alone,
    But in their hue;
Maiden-pinks, of odour faint,
Daisies smell-less yet most quaint,
    And sweet thyme true;

Primrose, first-born child of Ver
Merry spring-time's harbinger,
    With her bells dim;
Oxlips in their cradles growing,
Marigolds on death-beds blowing,
    Larks'-heels trim.

All, dear Nature's children sweet,
Lie, 'fore bride and bridegroom's feet,
    Blessing their sense!
Not an angel of the air,
Bird melodious or bird fair,
    Be absent hence!

The crow, the slanderous cuckoo, nor
The boding raven, nor chough hoar,
    Nor chattering pie,
May on our bride-house perch or sing,
Or with them any discord bring,
    But from it fly!

FRANCIS BEAUMONT (1584-1616)

ON THE LIFE OF MAN

Like to the falling of a star,
Or as the flights of eagles are,
Or like the fresh spring's gaudy hue,
Or silver drops of morning dew,
Or like a wind that chafes the flood,
Or bubbles which on water stood:
Even such is man, whose borrowed light
Is straight called in and paid to night:
The wind blows out, the bubble dies,
The spring intombed in autumn lies;
The dew's dried up, the star is shot,
The flight is past, and man forgot.

LINES ON THE TOMBS IN WEST-MINSTER

Mortality, behold and fear!
What a change of flesh is here!
Think how many royal bones
Sleep within this heap of stones;
Here they lie had realms and lands,
Who now want strength to stir their hands;
Where from their pulpits sealed with dust
They preach, "In greatness is no trust."
Here's an acre sown indeed
With the richest royal'st seed
That the earth did e'er suck in,
Since the first man died for sin;
Here the bones of birth have cried,
"Though gods they were, as men they died."
Here are sands, ignoble things,
Dropt from the ruined sides of kings.
Here's a world of pomp and state,
Buried in dust, once dead by fate.

MASTER FRANCIS BEAUMONT'S LETTER TO BEN JONSON

The sun (which doth the greatest comfort bring
To absent friends, because the selfsame thing
They know they see, however absent) is
Here our best haymaker! Forgive me this;
It is our country's style! In this warm shine
I lie and dream of your full Mermaid Wine!

* * * * * * *

Methinks the little wit I had is lost
Since I saw you! For wit is like a rest
Held up at tennis, which men do the best
With the best gamesters. What things have we seen
Done at the Mermaid! heard words that have been
So nimble and so full of subtle flame,
As if that every one from whence they came
Had meant to put his whole wit in a jest
And had resolved to live a fool the rest
Of his dull life! Then, when there hath been thrown
Wit able enough to justify the town
For three days past! Wit, that might warrant be
For the whole city to talk foolishly
Till that were cancelled! And, when we were gone,
We left an air behind us, which alone
Was able to make the two next companies
Right witty! though but downright fools, more wise!
When I remember this, and see that now
The country gentlemen begin to allow
My wit for dry bobs; then I needs must cry,
"I see my days of ballading grow nigh!"
I can already riddle; and can sing
Catches, sell bargains; and I fear shall bring
Myself to speak the hardest words I find
Over as oft as any, with one wind,
That takes no medicines! But one thought of thee
Makes me remember all these things to be
The wit of our young men, fellows that show
No part of good, yet utter all they know!
Who, like trees of the guard, have growing souls.
Only strong Destiny, which all controls,
I hope hath left a better fate in store
For me, thy friend, than to live ever poor,
Banished unto this home! Fate, once again,
Bring me to thee, who canst make smooth and plain
The way of knowledge for me; and then I,
Who have no good but in thy company,
Protest it will my greatest comfort be
To acknowledge all I have to flow from thee!
Ben, when these scenes are perfect, we'll taste wine!
I'll drink thy Muse's health! thou shalt quaff mine!

EDWARD LORD HERBERT OF CHERBURY (1583–1648)

From AN ODE UPON A QUESTION MOVED WHETHER LOVE SHOULD CONTINUE FOR EVER

* * * * * * *

O no, Belov'd, I am most sure
Those virtuous habits we acquire
As being with the soul entire
Must with it evermore endure.

* * * * * * *

Else should our souls in vain elect,
And vainer yet were Heaven's laws,
When to an everlasting cause
They gave a perishing effect.

Nor here on earth then, or above,
Our good affection can impair;
For where God doth admit the fair,
Think you that He excludeth love?

These eyes again then eyes shall see,
These hands again these hands enfold,
And all chaste pleasures can be told
Shall with us everlasting be.

For if no use of sense remain
When bodies once this life forsake,
Or they could no delight partake,
Why should they ever rise again?

And if every imperfect mind
Make love the end of knowledge here,
How perfect will our love be, where
All imperfection is refin'd.

Let then no doubt, Celinda, touch,
Much less your fairest mind invade;
Were not our souls immortal made,
Our equal loves can make them such.

* * * * * * *

So when from hence we shall be gone,
And be no more, nor you, nor I;
As one another's mystery,
Each shall be both, yet both but one.

* * * * * * *

WILLIAM DRUMMOND (1585–1649)

SONNET

A passing glance, a lightning 'long the skies,
That, ush'ring thunder, dies straight to our sight;
A spark, of contraries which doth arise,
Then drowns in the huge depths of day and night:

Is this small Small call'd life, held in such price
Of blinded wights, who nothing judge aright.
Of Parthian shaft so swift is not the flight
As life, that wastes itself, and living dies.
O! what is human greatness, valour, wit?
What fading beauty, riches, honour, praise?
To what doth serve in golden thrones to sit,
Thrall earth's vast round, triumphal arches raise?
All is a dream, learn in this prince's fall,
In whom, save death, nought mortal was at all.

SEXTAIN I

The heaven doth not contain so many stars,
So many leaves not prostrate lie in woods,
When autumn's old and Boreas sounds his wars,
So many waves have not the ocean floods,
As my rent mind hath torments all the night,
And heart spends sighs, when Phœbus brings the light.

Why should I been a partner of the light,
Who, crost in birth by bad aspects of stars,
Have never since had happy day nor night?
Why was not I a liver in the woods,
Or citizen of Thetis' crystal floods,
Than made a man for love and fortune's wars?

I look each day when death should end the wars,
Uncivil wars, 'twixt sense and reason's light;
My pains I count to mountains, meads, and floods,
And of my sorrow partners make the stars;
All desolate I haunt the fearful woods,
When I should give myself to rest at night.

With watchful eyes I ne'er behold the night,
Mother of peace, but ah! to me of wars,
And Cynthia queen-like shining through the woods,
When straight those lamps come in my thought, whose light
My judgment dazzled, passing brightest stars,
And then mine eyes en-isle themselves with floods.

Turn to their springs again first shall the floods,
Clear shall the sun the sad and gloomy night,
To dance about the pole cease shall the stars,
The elements renew their ancient wars
Shall first, and be depriv'd of place and light,
Ere I find rest in city, fields, or woods.

End these my days, indwellers of the woods,
Take this my life, ye deep and raging floods;
Sun, never rise to clear me with thy light,
Horror and darkness, keep a lasting night;
Consume me, care, with thy intestine wars,
And stay your influence o'er me, bright stars!

In vain the stars, indwellers of the woods,
Care, horror, wars, I call, and raging floods,
For all have sworn no night shall dim my light.

SONG II

Phœbus, arise,
And paint the sable skies
With azure, white, and red;
Rouse Memnon's mother from her Tithon's bed,
That she thy career may with roses spread;
The nightingales thy coming each where sing;
Make an eternal spring,
Give life to this dark world which lieth dead;
Spread forth thy golden hair
In larger locks than thou wast wont before,
And, emperor-like, decore
With diadem of pearl thy temples fair;
Chase hence the ugly night,
Which serves but to make dear thy glorious light.
This is that happy morn,
That day, long-wished day,
Of all my life so dark
(If cruel stars have not my ruin sworn,
And fates not hope betray),
Which, only white, deserves
A diamond forever should it mark;
This is the morn should bring unto this grove
My love, to hear and recompense my love.
Fair king, who all preserves,
But show thy blushing beams,
And thou two sweeter eyes
Shalt see, than those which by Peneus' streams
Did once thy heart surprise;
Nay, suns, which shine as clear
As thou when two thou did to Rome appear.
Now, Flora, deck thyself in fairest guise;
If that ye, winds, would hear
A voice surpassing far Amphion's lyre,
Your stormy chiding stay;
Let zephyr only breathe,
And with her tresses play,
Kissing sometimes those purple ports of death.
The winds all silent are,
And Phœbus in his chair,
Ensaffroning sea and air,
Makes vanish every star;
Night like a drunkard reels
Beyond the hills to shun his flaming wheels;
The fields with flow'rs are deck'd in every hue,
The clouds bespangle with bright gold their blue;
Here is the pleasant place,
And ev'ry thing, save her, who all should grace.

MADRIGAL I

This life, which seems so fair,
Is like a bubble blown up in the air
By sporting children's breath,
Who chase it everywhere,
And strive who can most motion it bequeath;
And though it sometime seem of its own might,
Like to an eye of gold, to be fix'd there,
And firm to hover in that empty height,
That only is because it is so light.
But in that pomp it doth not long appear;
For even when most admir'd, it in a thought,
As swell'd from nothing, doth dissolve in nought.

From URANIA

IX

Thrice happy he, who by some shady grove,
Far from the clamorous world doth live his own,
Though solitare, yet who is not alone,
But doth converse with that eternal love.
O how more sweet is birds' harmonious moan,
Or the soft sobbings of the widow'd dove,
Than those smooth whisp'rings near a prince's throne,
Which good make doubtful, do the evil approve!
O how more sweet is zephyr's wholesome breath,
And sighs perfum'd, which do the flowers unfold,
Than that applause vain honour doth bequeath!
How sweet are streams to poison drunk in gold!
The world is full of horrors, falsehoods, slights;
Woods' silent shades have only true delights.

JOHN FORD (fl. 1639)

From THE LOVER'S MELANCHOLY

ACT I, SCENE I

MEN. Passing from Italy to Greece, the tales
Which poets of an elder time have feigned
To glorify their Tempe, bred in me
Desire of visiting that paradise.
To Thessaly I came; and living private,
Without acquaintance of more sweet companions
Than the old inmates to my love, my thoughts,
I day by day frequented silent groves
And solitary walks. One morning early
This accident encountered me: I heard
The sweetest and most ravishing contention
That art and nature ever were at strife in.
AMET. I cannot yet conceive what you infer
By art and nature.
MEN. I shall soon resolve ye.
A sound of music touched mine ears, or rather
Indeed entranced my soul. As I stole nearer,
Invited by the melody, I saw
This youth, this fair-faced youth, upon his lute,
With strains of strange variety and harmony,
Proclaiming, as it seemed, so bold a challenge
To the clear quiristers of the woods, the birds,
That, as they flocked about him, all stood silent,
Wondering at what they heard. I wondered too.
AMET. And so do I; good, on!
MEN. A nightingale,
Nature's best skilled musician, undertakes
The challenge, and for every several strain
The well-shaped youth could touch, she sung her own;
He could not run division with more art
Upon his quaking instrument than she,
The nightingale, did with her various notes
Reply to; for a voice and for a sound,
Amethus, 'tis much easier to believe
That such they were than hope to hear again.
AMET. How did the rivals part?
MEN. You term them rightly;
For they were rivals, and their mistress, harmony.
Some time thus spent, the young man grew at last
Into a pretty anger, that a bird,
Whom art had never taught cliffs, moods, or notes,
Should vie with him for mastery, whose study
Had busied many hours to perfect practice:
To end the controversy, in a rapture
Upon his instrument he plays so swiftly,
So many voluntaries and so quick,
That there was curiosity and cunning,
Concord in discord, lines of differing method
Meeting in one full centre of delight.
AMET. Now for the bird!
MEN. The bird, ordained to be
Music's first martyr, strove to imitate
These several sounds; which when her warbling throat
Failed in, for grief down dropped she on his lute,
And brake her heart. It was the quaintest sadness,
To see the conqueror upon her hearse
To weep a funeral elegy of tears;
That, trust me, my Amethus, I could chide
Mine own unmanly weakness, that made me
A fellow-mourner with him.
AMET. I believe thee.
MEN. He looked upon the trophies of his art,
Then sighed, then wiped his eyes, then sighed and cried,
"Alas, poor creature! I will soon revenge
This cruelty upon the author of it;
Henceforth this lute, guilty of innocent blood,
Shall never more betray a harmless peace
To an untimely end;" and in that sorrow,

As he was dashing it against a tree,
I suddenly stept in.

SONG

From THE BROKEN HEART

Can you paint a thought? or number
Every fancy in a slumber?
Can you count soft minutes roving
From a dial's point by moving?
Can you grasp a sigh? or, lastly,
Rob a virgin's honour chastely?
  No, O, no! yet you may
Sooner do both that and this,
This and that, and never miss,
  Than by any praise display
Beauty's beauty; such a glory,
As beyond all fate, all story,
  All arms, all arts,
  All loves, all hearts,
Greater than those or they,
Do, shall, and must obey.

DIRGE

From THE BROKEN HEART

Chor. Glories, pleasures, pomps, delights, and ease,
  Can but please
The outward senses, when the mind
Is or untroubled or by peace refined.
1st Voice. Crowns may flourish and decay,
Beauties shine, but fade away.
2nd Voice. Youth may revel, yet it must
Lie down in a bed of dust.
3rd Voice. Earthly honours flow and waste,
Time alone doth change and last.
Chor. Sorrows mingled with contents prepare
  Rest for care;
Love only reigns in death; though art
Can find no comfort for a broken heart.

PURITAN AND CAVALIER

GEORGE WITHER (1588–1667)

From FAIR VIRTUE, THE MISTRESS OF PHILARETÉ

FAIR VIRTUE'S SWEET GRACES

Think not, though, my Muse now sings
Mere absurd or feignèd things!
If to gold I like her hair,
Or to stars her eyes so fair,
Though I praise her skin by snow,
Or by pearls her double-row,
'Tis that you might gather thence
Her unmatchèd excellence.
Eyes as fair (for eyes) hath she
As stars fair (for stars) may be.
And each part as fair doth show
In its kind as white in snow.
'Tis no grace to her at all,
If her hair I sunbeams call;
For, were there power in art
So to portrait every part,
All men might those beauties see
As they do appear to me,
I would scorn to make compare
With the glorious'st things that are.
Nought I e'er saw fair enow
But the hair the hair to show;
Yet some think him over bold
That compares it but to gold.
He from reason seems to err
Who, commending of his dear,
Gives her lips the rubies' hue,
Or by pearls her teeth doth shew;
But what pearls, what rubies can
Seem so lovely fair to man
As her lips whom he doth love,
When in sweet discourse they move?
Or her lovelier teeth, the while
She doth bless him with a smile?
Stars, indeed, fair creatures be!
Yet, amongst us, where is he
Joys not more, the while he lies
Sunning in his mistress' eyes
Than in all the glimmering light
Of a starry winter's night?
Him to flatter most suppose,
That prefers before the rose,
Or the lilies while they grow,
Or the flakes of new-fall'n snow,
Her complexion whom he loveth;
And yet this, my Muse approveth.
For in such a beauty meets
Unexpressèd moving sweets,
That the like unto them no man
Ever saw but in a woman.
Look on moon! on stars! or sun!
All God's creatures overrun!
See if all of them presents
To your mind, such sweet contents;
Or if you from them can take
Ought that may a beauty make,
Shall one half so pleasing prove
As is hers whom you do love!

SONNET IV

Shall I, wasting in despair,
Die, because a woman's fair?
Or make pale my cheeks with care,
'Cause another's rosy are?
Be she fairer than the day,
Or the flowery meads in May!
If she be not so to me,
What care I how fair she be?

Should my heart be grieved or pined,
'Cause I see a woman kind?
Or a well disposèd nature
Joinèd with a lovely feature?
Be she meeker, kinder than
Turtle dove, or pelican!
If she be not so to me,
What care I how kind she be?

Shall a woman's virtues move
Me to perish for her love?
Or her well deserving known,
Make me quite forget mine own?
Be she with that goodness blest
Which may gain her, name of best!
If she be not such to me,
What care I how good she be?

'Cause her fortune seems too high,
Shall I play the fool, and die?
Those that bear a noble mind,
Where they want of riches find,
Think "What, with them, they would do
That, without them, dare to woo!"
And unless that mind I see,
What care I though great she be?

Great, or good, or kind, or fair,
I will ne'er the more despair!
If she love me (this believe!)
I will die, ere she shall grieve!
If she slight me, when I woo,
I can scorn, and let her go!
For if she be not for me,
What care I for whom she be?

From HALLELUJA

FOR ALL-SAINTS' DAY

No bliss can so contenting prove
As universal love to gain,
If we, with full requiting love,
Could such affection entertain;
But such a love the heart of man
Nor comprehend nor merit can:

For though to all we might be dear,
Which cannot in this life befall,
We discontented should appear,
Because we had not heart for all;
That we might all men love, as we
Belovèd would of all men be.

For love in loving joys as much
As love for loving to obtain;
The perfect love is alway such,
And cannot part itself in twain,
Or love receive, but where it may
With truest love true love repay.

Love cannot in itself be two,
The object of true love, therefore,
An unity is, which cannot grow
To be in essence two or more.
In rivals' loves no love is known,
And love divided loveth none.

By love in fraction vex'd are we
Whilst here on earth we do remain,
And if in heaven such love could be,
Sure heaven would be a place of pain,
And saints, perhaps, would jealous prove
Of God's or of each other's love.

But he whose wisdom hath contrived
His glory with our full content,
Hath from himself a means derived
Our love's distractions to prevent;
One body of all saints he makes,
And for his bride that one he takes.

So every member doth obtain
Full love from all, returning too
Full love to all of them again,
As members of one body do!
None jealous, but all striving how
Most love to others to allow.

For as the soul is all in all,
And all through ev'ry member too,
Love, in that body mystical,
Is as the soul, and fits it so:
Uniting them to God as near
As to each other they are dear.

The love they want to entertain
Such overflowing love as His,
He adds, which they return again,
To make up love which perfect is;
That He may His own love employ,
And both find perfect love and joy.

The seed of this content was sown
When God the spacious world did frame,
And ever since that seed hath grown,
To be an honour to His name.
And when the saints are sealed all,
This hidden truth unseal He shall.

THOMAS HEYWOOD (d. 1650?)

GO, PRETTY BIRDS!

Ye little birds, that sit and sing
Amidst the shady valleys,
And see how Phillis sweetly walks
Within her garden alleys,
Go, pretty birds, about her bower!
Sing, pretty birds, she may not lower!
Ah me! methinks, I see her frown!
Ye pretty wantons, warble!

Go, tell her, through your chirping bills,
As you by me are bidden,
To her is only known my love;
Which from the world is hidden.
Go, pretty birds, and tell her so!
See that your notes strain not too low!
For still, methinks, I see her frown!
Ye pretty wantons, warble!

Go, tune your voices' harmony,
  And sing, I am her lover!
Strain loud and sweet, that every note
  With sweet content may move her!
And she that hath the sweetest voice,
Tell her, I will not change my choice!
Yet still, methinks, I see her frown!
  Ye pretty wantons, warble!

O, fly! Make haste! See, see, she falls
  Into a pretty slumber!
Sing round about her rosy bed,
  That, waking, she may wonder!
Say to her, 'Tis her lover true,
That sendeth love to you! to you!
And when you hear her kind reply,
  Return with pleasant warblings!

WILLIAM BROWNE (1591–1643)

BRITANNIA'S PASTORALS

From BOOK II, SONG IV

  Yet as when I with other swains have been
Invited by the maidens of our green
To wend to yonder wood, in time of year
When cherry-trees enticing burdens bear,
He that with wreathed legs doth upwards go,
Plucks not alone for those which stand below;
But now and then is seen to pick a few
To please himself as well as all his crew:
Or if from where he is he do espy
Some apricock upon a bough thereby,
Which overhangs the tree on which he stands,
Climbs up and strives to take it with his hands:
So if to please myself I somewhat sing,
Let it not be to you less pleasuring.
No thirst of glory tempts me, for my strains
Befit poor shepherds on the lowly plains;
The hope of riches cannot draw from me
One line that tends to servile flattery,
Nor shall the most in titles on the earth
Blemish my Muse with an adulterate birth,
Nor make me lay pure colours on a ground
Where nought substantial can be ever found.
No; such as sooth a base and dunghill spirit
With attributes fit for the most of merit,
Cloud their free Muse; as, when the sun doth
    shine
On straw and dirt mix'd by the sweating hyne,
It nothing gets from heaps so much impure
But noisome steams that do his light obscure.
  My freeborn Muse will not like Danae be,
Won with base dross to clip with slavery;
Nor lend her choicer balm to worthless men,
Whose names would die but for some hired pen.
No; if I praise, virtue shall draw me to it,
And not a base procurement make me do it.
What now I sing is but to pass away
A tedious hour, as some musicians play;
Or make another my own griefs bemoan;
Or to be least alone when most alone.
In this can I as oft as I will choose
Hug sweet content by my retired Muse,
And in a study find as much to please
As others in the greatest palaces.
Each man that lives, according to his power,
On what he loves bestows an idle hour.
Instead of hounds that make the wooded hills
Talk in a hundred voices to the rills,
I like the pleasing cadence of a line
Struck by the consort of the sacred Nine.
In lieu of hawks, the raptures of my soul
Transcend their pitch and baser earth's control.
For running horses, Contemplation flies
With quickest speed to win the greatest prize.
For courtly dancing, I can take more pleasure
To hear a verse keep time and equal measure.
For winning riches, seek the best directions
How I may well subdue mine own affections.
For raising stately piles for heirs to come,
Here in this poem I erect my tomb.
And Time may be so kind in these weak lines
To keep my name enroll'd past his that shines
In gilded marble or in brazen leaves:
Since verse preserves, when stone and brass de-
    ceives.
Or if (as worthless) Time not lets it live
To those full days which others' Muses give,
Yet I am sure I shall be heard and sung
Of most severest eld and kinder young
Beyond my days; and, maugre Envy's strife,
Add to my name some hours beyond my life.

From BOOK II, SONG V

  Now was the Lord and Lady of the May
Meeting the May-pole at the break of day,
And Cælia, as the fairest on the green,
Not without some maids' envy chosen queen.
Now was the time com'n, when our gentle swain
Must in his harvest or lose all again.
Now must he pluck the rose lest other hands,
Or tempests, blemish what so fairly stands:
And therefore, as they had before decreed,
Our shepherd gets a boat, and with all speed,
In night, that doth on lovers' actions smile,
Arrivèd safe on Mona's fruitful isle.
  Between two rocks (immortal, without mother,)
That stand as if out-facing one another,

There ran a creek up, intricate and blind,
As if the waters hid them from the wind;
Which never wash'd but at a higher tide
The frizzled coats which do the mountains hide;
Where never gale was longer known to stay
Than from the smooth wave it had swept away
The new divorced leaves, that from each side
Left the thick boughs to dance out with the tide.
At further end the creek a stately wood
Gave a kind shadow to the brackish flood
Made up of trees, not less kenn'd by each skiff
Than that sky-scaling Peak of Teneriffe,
Upon whose tops the hernshaw bred her young,
And hoary moss upon their branches hung;
Whose rugged rinds sufficient were to show,
Without their height, what time they 'gan to grow;
And if dry eld by wrinkled skin appears,
None could allot them less than Nestor's years.
As under their command the thronged creek
Ran lessen'd up. Here did the shepherd seek
Where he his little boat might safely hide,
Till it was fraught with what the world beside
Could not outvalue; nor give equal weight
Though in the time when Greece was at her height.
The ruddy horses of the rosy Morn
Out of the Eastern gates had newly borne
Their blushing mistress in her golden chair,
Spreading new light throughout our hemisphere,
When fairest Cælia with a lovelier crew
Of damsels than brave Latmus ever knew
Came forth to meet the youngsters, who had here
Cut down an oak that long withouten peer
Bore his round head imperiously above
His other mates there, consecrate to Jove.
The wished time drew on: and Cælia now,
That had the fame for her white arched brow,
While all her lovely fellows busied were
In picking off the gems from Tellus' hair,
Made tow'rds the creek, where Philocel, unspied
Of maid or shepherd that their May-games plied,
Receiv'd his wish'd-for Cælia, and begun
To steer his boat contrary to the sun,
Who could have wish'd another in his place
To guide the car of light, or that his race
Were to have end (so he might bless his hap)
In Cælia's bosom, not in Thetis' lap.
The boat oft danc'd for joy of what it held:
The hoist-up sail not quick but gently swell'd,
And often shook, as fearing what might fall,
Ere she deliver'd what she went withal.
Winged Argestes, fair Aurora's son,
Licens'd that day to leave his dungeon,
Meekly attended and did never err,
Till Cælia grac'd our land, and our land her.
As through the waves their love-fraught wherry ran,
A many Cupids, each set on his swan,
Guided with reins of gold and silver twist
The spotless birds about them as they list:
Which would have sung a song (ere they were gone)
Had unkind Nature given them more than one;
Or in bestowing that had not done wrong,
And made their sweet lives forfeit one sad song.

EPITAPH

May, be thou never graced with birds that sing,
Nor Flora's pride!
In thee all flowers and roses spring,
Mine only died.

ON THE COUNTESS DOWAGER OF PEMBROKE

Underneath this sable herse
Lies the subject of all verse:
Sidney's sister, Pembroke's mother:
Death, ere thou hast slain another
Fair and learn'd and good as she,
Time shall throw a dart at thee.

ROBERT HERRICK (1591–1674)

UPON THE LOSS OF HIS MISTRESSES

I have lost, and lately, these
Many dainty mistresses:
Stately Julia, prime of all;
Sapho next, a principal;
Smooth Anthea, for a skin
White and heaven-like crystalline;
Sweet Electra, and the choice
Myrha, for the lute and voice.
Next, Corinna, for her wit,
And the graceful use of it;
With Perilla: all are gone,
Only Herrick's left alone,
For to number sorrow by
Their departures hence, and die.

CHERRY-RIPE

Cherry-ripe, ripe, ripe, I cry,
Full and fair ones; come and buy;
If so be you ask me where
They do grow? I answer, there,
Where my Julia's lips do smile;
There's the land, or cherry-isle,
Whose plantations fully show
All the year where cherries grow.

CORINNA'S GOING A-MAYING

Get up, get up for shame, the blooming morn
Upon her wings presents the god unshorn.
See how Aurora throws her fair
Fresh-quilted colours through the air:
Get up, sweet slug-a-bed, and see
The dew bespangling herb and tree.
Each flower has wept and bow'd toward the east
Above an hour since: yet you not dress'd;
Nay! not so much as out of bed?
When all the birds have matins said
And sung their thankful hymns, 'tis sin,
Nay, profanation, to keep in,
Whereas a thousand virgins on this day
Spring, sooner than the lark, to fetch in May.

Rise and put on your foliage, and be seen
To come forth, like the spring-time, fresh and green,
And sweet as Flora. Take no care
For jewels for your gown or hair:
Fear not; the leaves will strew
Gems in abundance upon you:
Besides, the childhood of the day has kept,
Against you come, some orient pearls unwept;
Come and receive them while the light
Hangs on the dew-locks of the night:
And Titan on the eastern hill
Retires himself, or else stands still
Till you come forth. Wash, dress, be brief in praying:
Few beads are best when once we go a-Maying.

Come, my Corinna, come; and, coming, mark
How each field turns a street, each street a park
Made green and trimm'd with trees; see how
Devotion gives each house a bough
Or branch: each porch, each door ere this
An ark, a tabernacle is,
Made up of white-thorn, neatly interwove;
As if here were those cooler shades of love.
Can such delights be in the street
And open fields and we not see't?
Come, we'll abroad; and let's obey
The proclamation made for May:
And sin no more, as we have done, by staying;
But, my Corinna, come, let's go a-Maying.

There's not a budding boy or girl this day
But is got up, and gone to bring in May.
A deal of youth, ere this, is come
Back, and with white-thorn laden home.
Some have despatched their cakes and cream
Before that we have left to dream;
And some have wept, and woo'd, and plighted troth,
And chose their priest, ere we can cast off sloth:
Many a green-gown has been given;
Many a kiss, both odd and even:
Many a glance too has been sent
From out the eye, love's firmament;
Many a jest told of the keys betraying
This night, and locks pick'd, yet we're not a-Maying.

Come, let us go while we are in our prime;
And take the harmless folly of the time.
We shall grow old apace, and die
Before we know our liberty.
Our life is short, and our days run
As fast away as does the sun;
And, as a vapour or a drop of rain,
Once lost, can ne'er be found again,
So when or you or I are made
A fable, song, or fleeting shade,
All love, all liking, all delight
Lies drowned with us in endless night.
Then while time serves, and we are but decaying,
Come, my Corinna, come, let's go a-Maying.

TO THE VIRGINS, TO MAKE MUCH OF TIME

Gather ye rosebuds while ye may,
Old Time is still a-flying;
And this same flower that smiles to-day,
To-morrow will be dying.

The glorious lamp of heaven, the sun,
The higher he's a-getting,
The sooner will his race be run,
And nearer he's to setting.

That age is best which is the first,
When youth and blood are warmer;
But being spent, the worse and worst
Times still succeed the former.

Then be not coy, but use your time,
And while ye may, go marry;
For, having lost but once your prime,
You may forever tarry.

HOW ROSES CAME RED

Roses at first were white,
Till they could not agree,
Whether my Sapho's breast
Or they more white should be.

But being vanquish'd quite,
A blush their cheeks bespread;
Since which, believe the rest,
The roses first came red.

TO DAFFODILS

Fair Daffodils, we weep to see
You haste away so soon;
As yet the early rising sun
Has not attain'd his noon.
Stay, stay,
Until the hasting day
Has run
But to the even-song;
And, having prayed together, we
Will go with you along.

We have short time to stay, as you,
We have as short a spring;
As quick a growth to meet decay,
As you, or anything.
We die
As your hours do, and dry
Away,
Like to the summer's rain;
Or as the pearls of morning's dew,
Ne'er to be found again.

LOSS FROM THE LEAST

Great men by small means oft are overthrown;
He's lord of thy life who contemns his own.

UPON JULIA'S CLOTHES

When-as in silks my Julia goes,
Then, then, methinks, how sweetly flows
The liquefaction of her clothes.

Next, when I cast mine eyes, and see
That brave vibration, each way free,
O, how that glittering taketh me!

HIS PRAYER FOR ABSOLUTION

For those my unbaptizèd rhymes,
Writ in my wild unhallowed times,
For every sentence, clause, and word,
That's not inlaid with Thee, my Lord,
Forgive me, God, and blot each line
Out of my book that is not Thine.
But if, 'mongst all, Thou find'st here one
Worthy thy benediction,
That one of all the rest shall be
The glory of my work and me.

A THANKSGIVING TO GOD FOR HIS HOUSE

Lord, Thou hast given me a cell
Wherein to dwell,
A little house, whose humble roof
Is weather-proof,
Under the spars of which I lie
Both soft and dry;
Where Thou, my chamber for to ward,
Hast set a guard
Of harmless thoughts, to watch and keep
Me while I sleep.
Low is my porch, as is my fate,
Both void of state;
And yet the threshold of my door
Is worn by th' poor,
Who thither come and freely get
Good words or meat.
Like as my parlor so my hall
And kitchen's small;
A little buttery, and therein
A little bin,
Which keeps my little loaf of bread
Unchipped, unflead;
Some little sticks of thorn or briar
Make me a fire,
Close by whose living coal I sit,
And glow like it.
Lord, I confess too, when I dine,
The pulse is Thine,
And all those other bits that be
There plac'd by Thee;
The worts, the purslain, and the mess
Of water-cress,
Which of Thy kindness Thou hast sent;
And my content
Makes those, and my beloved beet,
To be more sweet.
'Tis Thou that crown'st my glittering hearth
With guiltless mirth,
And giv'st me wassail bowls to drink,
Spiced to the brink.
Lord, 'tis Thy plenty-dropping hand
That soils my land,
And giv'st me, for my bushel sown,
Twice ten for one;
Thou mak'st my teeming hen to lay
Her egg each day;
Besides my healthful ewes to bear
Me twins each year;
The while the conduits of my kine
Run cream, for wine.
All these, and better Thou dost send
Me, to this end,

That I should render, for my part,
A thankful heart,
Which, fir'd with incense, I resign,
As wholly Thine;
But the acceptance, that must be,
My Christ, by Thee.

TO KEEP A TRUE LENT

Is this a fast, to keep
The larder lean,
And clean
From fat of veals and sheep?

Is it to quit the dish
Of flesh, yet still
To fill
The platter high with fish?

Is it to fast an hour,
Or ragg'd to go,
Or show
A downcast look, and sour?

No; 'tis a fast, to dole
Thy sheaf of wheat
And meat
Unto the hungry soul.

It is to fast from strife,
From old debate,
And hate;
To circumcise thy life.

To show a heart grief-rent;
To starve thy sin,
Not bin;
And that's to keep thy Lent.

FRANCIS QUARLES (1592–1644)

SWEET PHOSPHOR, BRING THE DAY

"*Lighten mine eyes, O Lord, lest I sleep the sleep of death.*" — Ps. 13. 3.

Will 't ne'er be morning? Will that promis'd light
Ne'er break, and clear these clouds of night?
Sweet Phosphor, bring the day,
Whose conqu'ring ray
May chase these fogs; sweet Phosphor, bring the day.

How long! how long shall these benighted eyes
Languish in shades, like feeble flies
Expecting Spring! How long shall darkness soil
The face of earth, and thus beguile
The souls of sprightful action; when will day
Begin to dawn, whose new-born ray
May gild the weathercocks of our devotion,
And give our unsoul'd souls new motion!
Sweet Phosphor, bring the day,
Thy light will fray
These horrid mists; sweet Phosphor, bring the day.

Let those have night that silly love t'immure
Their cloister'd crimes, and sin secure;
Let those have night that blush to let men know
The baseness they ne'er blush to do;
Let those have night that love to take a nap
And loll in Ignorance's lap;
Let those whose eyes, like owls, abhor the light,
Let those have night that love the night!
Sweet Phosphor, bring the day;
How sad delay
Afflicts dull hopes! sweet Phosphor, bring the day.

Alas! my light-in-vain-expecting eyes
Can find no objects but what rise
From this poor mortal blaze, a dying spark
Of Vulcan's forge, whose flames are dark
And dangerous, a dull blue-burning light,
As melancholy as the night:
Here's all the suns that glisten in the sphere
Of earth: Ah me! what comfort's here?
Sweet Phosphor, bring the day;
Haste, haste away
Heav'n's loitering lamp; sweet Phosphor, bring the day.

Blow, Ignorance: O thou, whose idle knee
Rocks earth into a lethargy,
And with thy sooty fingers hast bedight
The world's fair cheeks, blow, blow thy spite;
Since thou hast puffed our greater taper, do
Puff on, and out the lesser too;
If e'er that breath-exilèd flame return,
Thou hast not blown, as it will burn.
Sweet Phosphor, bring the day;
Light will repay
The wrongs of night; sweet Phosphor, bring the day.

GEORGE HERBERT (1593–1633)

VIRTUE

Sweet day, so cool, so calm, so bright,
The bridal of the earth and sky!
The dew shall weep thy fall to-night;
For thou must die.

Sweet rose, whose hue, angry and brave,
Bids the rash gazer wipe his eye,
Thy root is ever in its grave,
And thou must die.

Sweet spring, full of sweet days and roses,
A box where sweets compacted lie,
My music shows ye have your closes,
And all must die.

Only a sweet and virtuous soul,
Like seasoned timber, never gives;
But though the whole world turn to coal,
Then chiefly lives.

THE COLLAR

I struck the board, and cried, "No more;
I will abroad!
What! shall I ever sigh and pine?
My lines and life are free; free as the road,
Loose as the wind, as large as store.
Shall I be still in suit?
Have I no harvest but a thorn
To let me blood, and not restore
What I have lost with cordial fruit?
Sure there was wine
Before my sighs did dry it; there was corn
Before my tears did drown it;
Is the year only lost to me?
Have I no bays to crown it,
No flowers, no garlands gay? all blasted,
All wasted?
Not so, my heart; but there is fruit,
And thou hast hands.
Recover all thy sigh-blown age
On double pleasures; leave thy cold dispute
Of what is fit and not; forsake thy cage,
Thy rope of sands
Which petty thoughts have made; and made to thee
Good cable, to enforce and draw,
And be thy law,
While thou didst wink and wouldst not see.
Away! take heed;
I will abroad.
Call in thy death's-head there, tie up thy fears:
He that forbears
To suit and serve his need
Deserves his load."
But as I raved, and grew more fierce and wild
At every word,
Methought I heard one calling, "Child";
And I replied, "My Lord."

LOVE

Love bade me welcome; yet my soul drew back,
Guilty of dust and sin.
But quick-eyed Love, observing me grow slack
From my first entrance in,
Drew nearer to me, sweetly questioning,
If I lacked anything.

"A guest," I answered, "worthy to be here:"
Love said, "You shall be he."
"I, the unkind, ungrateful? Ah, my dear,
I cannot look on Thee!"
Love took my hand and smiling did reply,
"Who made the eyes but I?"

"Truth, Lord; but I have marred them: let my shame
Go where it doth deserve."
"And know you not," says Love, "who bore the blame?"
"My dear, then I will serve."
"You must sit down," says Love, "and taste my meat."
So I did sit and eat.

THOMAS CAREW (1598?–1639?)

SONG

Ask me no more where Jove bestows,
When June is past, the fading rose,
For in your beauty's orient deep
These flowers, as in their causes, sleep.

Ask me no more whither do stray
The golden atoms of the day,
For, in pure love, heaven did prepare
Those powders to enrich your hair.

Ask me no more whither doth haste
The nightingale when May is past,
For in your sweet dividing throat
She winters and keeps warm her note.

Ask me no more where those stars light
That downwards fall in dead of night,
For in your eyes they sit, and there
Fixèd become as in their sphere.

Ask me no more if east or west
The Phœnix builds her spicy nest,
For unto you at last she flies,
And in your fragrant bosom dies.

SONG

Would you know what's soft? I dare
Not bring you to the down, or air,
Nor to stars to show what's bright,
Nor to snow to teach you white;

Nor, if you would music hear,
Call the orbs to take your ear;
Nor, to please your sense, bring forth
Bruisèd nard, or what's more worth;

Or on food were your thoughts placed,
Bring you nectar for a taste;
Would you have all these in one,
Name my mistress, and 'tis done!

PERSUASIONS TO JOY: A SONG

If the quick spirits in your eye
Now languish and anon must die;
If every sweet and every grace
Must fly from that forsaken face;
Then, Celia, let us reap our joys
Ere Time such goodly fruit destroys.

Or if that golden fleece must grow
For ever free from agèd snow;
If those bright suns must know no shade,
Nor your fresh beauties ever fade;
Then fear not, Celia, to bestow
What, still being gather'd, still must grow.

Thus either Time his sickle brings
In vain, or else in vain his wings.

INGRATEFUL BEAUTY THREATENED

Know, Celia, since thou art so proud,
'Twas I that gave thee thy renown.
Thou hadst in the forgotten crowd
Of common beauties lived unknown,
Had not my verse extoll'd thy name,
And with it imp'd the wings of Fame.

That killing power is none of thine;
I gave it to thy voice and eyes;
Thy sweets, thy graces, all are mine;
Thou art my star, shin'st in my skies;
Then dart not from thy borrow'd sphere
Lightning on him that fix'd thee there.

Tempt me with such affrights no more,
Lest what I made I uncreate;
Let fools thy mystic form adore,
I know thee in thy mortal state.
Wise poets, that wrapt Truth in tales,
Knew her themselves through all her veils.

AN EPITAPH

This little vault, this narrow room,
Of love and beauty is the tomb;
The dawning beam, that 'gan to clear
Our clouded sky, lies darken'd here,
For ever set to us: by death
Sent to enflame the world beneath.
'Twas but a bud, yet did contain
More sweetness than shall spring again;
A budding star, that might have grown
Into a sun when it had blown.
This hopeful beauty did create
New life in love's declining state;
But now his empire ends, and we
From fire and wounding darts are free;
His brand, his bow, let no man fear:
The flames, the arrows, all lie here.

WILLIAM HABINGTON (1605–1654)

NOX NOCTI INDICAT SCIENTIAM

When I survey the bright
Celestial sphere;
So rich with jewels hung, that night
Doth like an Ethiop bride appear:

My soul her wings doth spread
And heavenward flies,
Th' Almighty's mysteries to read
In the large volumes of the skies.

For the bright firmament
Shoots forth no flame
So silent, but is eloquent
In speaking the Creator's name.

No unregarded star
Contracts its light
Into so small a character,
Removed far from our human sight,

But if we steadfast look
We shall discern
In it, as in some holy book,
How man may heavenly knowledge learn.

It tells the conqueror
That far-stretch'd power,
Which his proud dangers traffic for,
Is but the triumph of an hour;

That from the farthest North,
Some nation may,
Yet undiscover'd, issue forth,
And o'er his new-got conquest sway:

Some nation yet shut in
With hills of ice
May be let out to scourge his sin,
Till they shall equal him in vice.

And then they likewise shall
Their ruin have;
For as yourselves your empires fall,
And every kingdom hath a grave.

Thus those celestial fires,
Though seeming mute,
The fallacy of our desires
And all the pride of life confute: —

For they have watch'd since first
The world had birth;
And found sin in itself accurst,
And nothing permanent on earth.

SIR WILLIAM DAVENANT (1606–1668)

SONG

The lark now leaves his wat'ry nest,
And climbing shakes his dewy wings.
He takes this window for the East,
And to implore your light he sings —
Awake, awake! the morn will never rise
Till she can dress her beauty at your eyes.

The merchant bows unto the seaman's star,
The ploughman from the sun his season takes;
But still the lover wonders what they are
Who look for day before his mistress wakes.
Awake, awake! break thro' your veils of lawn!
Then draw your curtains, and begin the dawn!

PRAISE AND PRAYER

Praise is devotion fit for mighty minds,
The diff'ring world's agreeing sacrifice;
Where Heaven divided faiths united finds:
But Prayer in various discord upward flies.

For Prayer the ocean is where diversely
Men steer their course, each to a sev'ral coast;
Where all our interests so discordant be
That half beg winds by which the rest are lost.

By Penitence when we ourselves forsake,
'Tis but in wise design on piteous Heaven;
In Praise we nobly give what God may take,
And are, without a beggar's blush, forgiven.

EDMUND WALLER (1606–1687)

THE STORY OF PHŒBUS AND DAPHNE, APPLIED

Thyrsis, a youth of the inspired train,
Fair Sacharissa loved, but loved in vain.
Like Phœbus sung the no less amorous boy;
Like Daphne she, as lovely, and as coy!
With numbers he the flying nymph pursues,
With numbers such as Phœbus' self might use!
Such is the chase when Love and Fancy leads,
O'er craggy mountains, and through flowery meads;
Invoked to testify the lover's care,
Or form some image of his cruel fair.
Urged with his fury, like a wounded deer,
O'er these he fled; and now approaching near,
Had reached the nymph with his harmonious lay,
Whom all his charms could not incline to stay.
Yet what he sung in his immortal strain,
Though unsuccessful, was not sung in vain;
All, but the nymph that should redress his wrong,
Attend his passion, and approve his song.
Like Phœbus thus, acquiring unsought praise,
He catched at love, and filled his arm with bays.

TO PHYLLIS

Phyllis! why should we delay
Pleasures shorter than the day?
Could we (which we never can)
Stretch our lives beyond their span,
Beauty like a shadow flies,
And our youth before us dies.
Or would youth and beauty stay,
Love hath wings, and will away.
Love hath swifter wings than Time;
Change in love to heaven does climb.
Gods, that never change their state,
Vary oft their love and hate.
Phyllis! to this truth we owe
All the love betwixt us two.
Let not you and I inquire
What has been our past desire;
On what shepherds you have smiled,
Or what nymphs I have beguiled;
Leave it to the planets too,
What we shall hereafter do;
For the joys we now may prove,
Take advice of present love.

ON A GIRDLE

That which her slender waist confined,
Shall now my joyful temples bind;
No monarch but would give his crown,
His arms might do what this has done.

It was my heaven's extremest sphere,
The pale which held that lovely deer.
My joy, my grief, my hope, my love,
Did all within this circle move!

A narrow compass! and yet there
Dwelt all that's good, and all that's fair;
Give me but what this ribband bound,
Take all the rest the sun goes round.

GO, LOVELY ROSE!

Go, lovely Rose!
Tell her that wastes her time and me,
That now she knows,
When I resemble her to thee,
How sweet and fair she seems to be.

Tell her that's young,
And shuns to have her graces spied,
That hadst thou sprung
In deserts, where no men abide,
Thou must have uncommended died.

Small is the worth
Of beauty from the light retired;
Bid her come forth,
Suffer herself to be desired,
And not blush so to be admired.

Then die! that she
The common fate of all things rare
May read in thee;
How small a part of time they share
That are so wondrous sweet and fair!

JOHN MILTON (1608–1674)

ON THE MORNING OF CHRIST'S NATIVITY

(Composed 1629)

This is the month, and this the happy morn,
Wherein the Son of Heaven's eternal King,
Of wedded maid and virgin mother born,
Our great redemption from above did bring;
For so the holy sages once did sing,
That he our deadly forfeit should release,
And with his Father work us a perpetual peace.

That glorious form, that light unsufferable,
And that far-beaming blaze of majesty,
Wherewith he wont at Heaven's high council-table
To sit the midst of Trinal Unity,
He laid aside; and here with us to be,
Forsook the courts of everlasting day,
And chose with us a darksome house of mortal clay.

Say, Heavenly Muse, shall not thy sacred vein
Afford a present to the Infant God?
Hast thou no verse, no hymn, or solemn strain,
To welcome him to this his new abode,
Now while the heaven, by the sun's team untrod,
Hath took no print of the approaching light,
And all the spangled host keep watch in squadrons bright?

See how from far upon the eastern road
The star-led wizards haste with odours sweet!
O run, prevent them with thy humble ode,
And lay it lowly at his blessed feet;
Have thou the honour first thy Lord to greet,
And join thy voice unto the angel quire,
From out his secret altar touched with hallowed fire.

THE HYMN

It was the winter wild,
While the heaven-born child
All meanly wrapt in the rude manger lies;
Nature, in awe to him,
Had doffed her gaudy trim,
With her great Master so to sympathize:
It was no season then for her
To wanton with the sun, her lusty paramour.

Only with speeches fair
She woos the gentle air
To hide her guilty front with innocent snow,
And on her naked shame,
Pollute with sinful blame,
The saintly veil of maiden white to throw;
Confounded, that her Maker's eyes
Should look so near upon her foul deformities.

But he, her fears to cease,
Sent down the meek-eyed Peace:
She, crowned with olive green, came softly sliding
Down through the turning sphere,
His ready harbinger,
With turtle wing the amorous clouds dividing;
And waving wide her myrtle wand,
She strikes a universal peace through sea and land.

No war, or battle's sound,
Was heard the world around;
The idle spear and shield were high uphung;
The hookèd chariot stood
Unstained with hostile blood;
The trumpet spake not to the armèd throng;
And kings sat still with awful eye,
As if they surely knew their sovran Lord was by.

But peaceful was the night
Wherein the Prince of Light
His reign of peace upon the earth began:
The winds, with wonder whist,
Smoothly the waters kissed,
Whispering new joys to the mild ocean,
Who now hath quite forgot to rave,
While birds of calm sit brooding on the charmèd wave.

The stars, with deep amaze,
Stand fixed in steadfast gaze,
Bending one way their precious influence,
And will not take their flight,
For all the morning light,
Or Lucifer that often warned them thence;
But in their glimmering orbs did glow,
Until their Lord himself bespake and bid them go.

And though the shady gloom
Had given day her room,
The sun himself withheld his wonted speed,
And hid his head for shame,
As his inferior flame
The new-enlightened world no more should need:
He saw a greater Sun appear
Than his bright throne or burning axletree could bear.

The shepherds on the lawn,
Or ere the point of dawn,
Sat simply chatting in a rustic row;
Full little thought they than,
That the mighty Pan
Was kindly come to live with them below:
Perhaps their loves, or else their sheep,
Was all that did their silly thoughts so busy keep.

When such music sweet
Their hearts and ears did greet
As never was by mortal finger strook,
Divinely-warbled voice
Answering the stringèd noise,
As all their souls in blissful rapture took:
The air, such pleasure loath to lose,
With thousand echoes still prolongs each heavenly close.

Nature, that heard such sound
Beneath the hollow round
Of Cynthia's seat the airy region thrilling,
Now was almost won
To think her part was done,
And that her reign had here its last fulfilling:
She knew such harmony alone
Could hold all heaven and earth in happier union.

At last surrounds their sight
A globe of circular light,
That with long beams the shamefaced night arrayed;
The helmèd cherubim
And sworded seraphim
Are seen in glittering ranks with wings displayed,
Harping in loud and solemn quire,
With unexpressive notes, to Heaven's new-born heir.

Such music (as 'tis said)
Before was never made,
But when of old the sons of morning sung,
While the Creator great
His constellations set,
And the well-balanced world on hinges hung,
And cast the dark foundations deep,
And bid the weltering waves their oozy channel keep.

Ring out, ye crystal spheres!
Once bless our human ears
(If ye have power to touch our senses so),
And let your silver chime
Move in melodious time;
And let the bass of heaven's deep organ blow;
And with your ninefold harmony
Make up full consort to the angelic symphony.

For if such holy song
Enwrap our fancy long,
Time will run back and fetch the age of gold;
And speckled Vanity
Will sicken soon and die,
And leprous Sin will melt from earthly mould;
And Hell itself will pass away,
And leave her dolorous mansions to the peering day.

Yea, Truth and Justice then
Will down return to men,
Orbed in a rainbow; and, like glories wearing,
Mercy will sit between,
Throned in celestial sheen,
With radiant feet the tissued clouds down steering;

And Heaven, as at some festival
Will open wide the gates of her high Palace Hall.

But wisest Fate says no,
This must not yet be so;
The Babe yet lies in smiling infancy
That on the bitter cross
Must redeem our loss,
So both himself and us to glorify:
Yet first, to those ychained in sleep,
The wakeful trump of doom must thunder through the deep,

With such a horrid clang
As on Mount Sinai rang,
While the red fire and smouldering clouds outbrake:
The aged earth, aghast
With terror of that blast,
Shall from the surface to the centre shake,
When at the world's last session,
The dreadful Judge in middle air shall spread his throne.

And then at last our bliss
Full and perfect is,
But now begins; for from this happy day
The old Dragon under ground,
In straiter limits bound,
Not half so far casts his usurpèd sway;
And wroth to see his kingdom fail,
Swinges the scaly horror of his folded tail.

The oracles are dumb;
No voice or hideous hum
Runs through the archèd roof in words deceiving.
Apollo from his shrine
Can no more divine,
With hollow shriek the steep of Delphos leaving.
No nightly trance, or breathèd spell,
Inspires the pale-eyed priest from the prophetic cell.

The lonely mountains o'er,
And the resounding shore,
A voice of weeping heard and loud lament;
From haunted spring, and dale
Edged with poplar pale,
The parting Genius is with sighing sent;
With flower-inwoven tresses torn
The Nymphs in twilight shade of tangled thickets mourn.

In consecrated earth,
And on the holy hearth,
The Lars and Lemures moan with midnight plaint;
In urns and altars round,
A drear and dying sound
Affrights the flamens at their service quaint;
And the chill marble seems to sweat,
While each peculiar power forgoes his wonted seat.

Peor and Baälim
Forsake their temples dim,
With that twice-battered god of Palestine;
And moonèd Ashtaroth,
Heaven's queen and mother both,
Now sits not girt with tapers' holy shine;
The Libyc Hammon shrinks his horn;
In vain the Tyrian maids their wounded Thammuz mourn.

And sullen Moloch, fled,
Hath left in shadows dread
His burning idol all of blackest hue;
In vain with cymbals' ring
They call the grisly king,
In dismal dance about the furnace blue;
The brutish gods of Nile as fast,
Isis and Orus and the dog Anubis, haste.

Nor is Osiris seen
In Memphian grove or green,
Trampling the unshowered grass with lowings loud;
Nor can he be at rest
Within his sacred chest;
Naught but profoundest Hell can be his shroud;
In vain, with timbrelled anthems dark,
The sable-stolèd sorcerers bear his worshipped ark.

He feels from Juda's land
The dreaded Infant's hand;
The rays of Bethlehem blind his dusky eyn;
Nor all the gods beside
Longer dare abide,
Not Typhon huge ending in snaky twine:
Our Babe, to show his Godhead true,
Can in his swaddling bands control the damnèd crew.

So when the sun in bed,
Curtained with cloudy red,
Pillows his chin upon an orient wave,
The flocking shadows pale
Troop to the infernal jail,
Each fettered ghost slips to his several grave,
And the yellow-skirted fays
Fly after the night-steeds, leaving their moon-loved maze.

But see! the Virgin blest
Hath laid her Babe to rest.
Time is our tedious song should here have ending:
Heaven's youngest-teemèd star
Hath fixed her polished car,
Her sleeping Lord with handmaid lamp attending;
And all about the courtly stable
Bright-harnessed angels sit in order serviceable.

L'ALLEGRO

Hence, loathèd Melancholy,
Of Cerberus and blackest Midnight born
In Stygian cave forlorn,
'Mongst horrid shapes and shrieks and sights unholy!
Find out some uncouth cell,
Where brooding darkness spreads his jealous wings,
And the night-raven sings;
There under ebon shades and low-browed rocks,
As ragged as thy locks,
In dark Cimmerian desert ever dwell.
But come, thou Goddess fair and free,
In heaven yclept Euphrosyne,
And by men heart-easing Mirth;
Whom lovely Venus, at a birth,
With two sister Graces more,
To ivy-crownèd Bacchus bore;
Or whether (as some sager sing)
The frolic wind that breathes the spring,
Zephyr, with Aurora playing,
As he met her once a-Maying,
There on beds of violets blue
And fresh-blown roses washed in dew,
Filled her with thee, a daughter fair,
So buxom, blithe, and debonair.
Haste thee, nymph, and bring with thee
Jest, and youthful Jollity,
Quips and cranks and wanton wiles,
Nods and becks and wreathèd smiles,
Such as hang on Hebe's cheek,
And love to live in dimple sleek;
Sport that wrinkled Care derides,
And Laughter holding both his sides.
Come, and trip it as you go,
On the light fantastic toe;
And in thy right hand lead with thee
The mountain nymph, sweet Liberty;
And if I give thee honour due,
Mirth, admit me of thy crew,
To live with her, and live with thee,
In unreprovèd pleasures free:
To hear the lark begin his flight,
And singing, startle the dull night,
From his watch-tower in the skies,
Till the dappled dawn doth rise;
Then to come in spite of sorrow,
And at my window bid good-morrow,
Through the sweet-briar or the vine,
Or the twisted eglantine;
While the cock, with lively din,
Scatters the rear of darkness thin,
And to the stack, or the barn-door,
Stoutly struts his dames before:
Oft listening how the hounds and horn
Cheerly rouse the slumbering morn,
From the side of some hoar hill,
Through the high wood echoing shrill:
Sometime walking, not unseen,
By hedge-row elms, on hillocks green,
Right against the eastern gate
Where the great sun begins his state,
Robed in flames and amber light,
The clouds in thousand liveries dight;
While the ploughman, near at hand,
Whistles o'er the furrowed land,
And the milkmaid singeth blithe,
And the mower whets his scythe,
And every shepherd tells his tale
Under the hawthorn in the dale.
Straight mine eye hath caught new pleasures
Whilst the landskip round it measures:
Russet lawns and fallows grey,
Where the nibbling flocks do stray;
Mountains on whose barren breast
The labouring clouds do often rest;
Meadows trim with daisies pied,
Shallow brooks and rivers wide;
Towers and battlements it sees
Bosomed high in tufted trees,
Where perhaps some beauty lies,
The cynosure of neighbouring eyes.
Hard by, a cottage chimney smokes
From betwixt two aged oaks,
Where Corydon and Thyrsis met
Are at their savoury dinner set
Of herbs and other country messes,
Which the neat-handed Phillis dresses;
And then in haste her bower she leaves,
With Thestylis to bind the sheaves;
Or, if the earlier season lead,
To the tanned haycock in the mead.
Sometimes, with secure delight,
The upland hamlets will invite,
When the merry bells ring round,
And the jocund rebecks sound
To many a youth and many a maid
Dancing in the chequered shade;

And young and old come forth to play
On a sunshine holiday,
Till the livelong daylight fail:
Then to the spicy nut-brown ale,
With stories told of many a feat,
How faery Mab the junkets eat.
She was pinched and pulled, she said;
And he, by friar's lantern led,
Tells how the drudging goblin sweat
To earn his cream-bowl duly set,
When in one night, ere glimpse of morn,
His shadowy flail hath threshed the corn
That ten day-labourers could not end;
Then lies him down, the lubber fiend,
And, stretched out all the chimney's length,
Basks at the fire his hairy strength,
And crop-full out of doors he flings,
Ere the first cock his matin rings.
Thus done the tales, to bed they creep,
By whispering winds soon lulled asleep.
Towered cities please us then,
And the busy hum of men,
Where throngs of knights and barons bold,
In weeds of peace high triumphs hold,
With store of ladies, whose bright eyes
Rain influence, and judge the prize
Of wit or arms, while both contend
To win her grace whom all commend.
There let Hymen oft appear
In saffron robe, with taper clear,
And pomp and feast and revelry,
With mask and antique pageantry;
Such sights as youthful poets dream
On summer eves by haunted stream.
Then to the well-trod stage anon,
If Jonson's learnèd sock be on,
Or sweetest Shakespear, Fancy's child,
Warble his native wood-notes wild.
And ever, against eating cares,
Lap me in soft Lydian airs,
Married to immortal verse,
Such as the meeting soul may pierce,
In notes with many a winding bout
Of linkèd sweetness long drawn out,
With wanton heed and giddy cunning,
The melting voice through mazes running,
Untwisting all the chains that tie
The hidden soul of harmony;
That Orpheus' self may heave his head
From golden slumber on a bed
Of heaped Elysian flowers, and hear
Such strains as would have won the ear
Of Pluto to have quite set free
His half-regained Eurydice.
These delights if thou canst give,
Mirth, with thee I mean to live.

IL PENSEROSO

Hence, vain deluding Joys,
The brood of Folly without father bred!
How little you bested,
Or fill the fixèd mind with all your toys!
Dwell in some idle brain,
And fancies fond with gaudy shapes possess,
As thick and numberless
As the gay motes that people the sun-beams,
Or likest hovering dreams,
The fickle pensioners of Morpheus' train.
But hail, thou Goddess sage and holy,
Hail, divinest Melancholy!
Whose saintly visage is too bright
To hit the sense of human sight,
And therefore to our weaker view
O'erlaid with black, staid Wisdom's hue;
Black, but such as in esteem
Prince Memnon's sister might beseem,
Or that starred Ethiop queen that strove
To set her beauty's praise above
The sea nymphs, and their powers offended.
Yet thou art higher far descended:
Thee bright-haired Vesta long of yore
To solitary Saturn bore;
His daughter she (in Saturn's reign
Such mixture was not held a stain).
Oft in glimmering bowers and glades
He met her, and in secret shades
Of woody Ida's inmost grove,
Whilst yet there was no fear of Jove.
Come, pensive Nun, devout and pure,
Sober, steadfast, and demure,
All in a robe of darkest grain,
Flowing with majestic train,
And sable stole of cypress lawn
Over thy decent shoulders drawn.
Come, but keep thy wonted state,
With even step, and musing gait,
And looks commercing with the skies,
Thy rapt soul sitting in thine eyes:
There, held in holy passion still,
Forget thyself to marble, till
With a sad leaden downward cast
Thou fix them on the earth as fast.
And join with thee calm Peace, and Quiet,
Spare Fast, that oft with gods doth diet,
And hears the Muses in a ring
Aye round about Jove's altar sing;
And add to these retired Leisure,
That in trim gardens takes his pleasure;
But first, and chiefest, with thee bring
Him that yon soars on golden wing,
Guiding the fiery-wheelèd throne,
The cherub Contemplation;

And the mute Silence hist along,
'Less Philomel will deign a song,
In her sweetest, saddest plight,
Smoothing the rugged brow of Night,
While Cynthia checks her dragon yoke
Gently o'er the accustomed oak:
Sweet bird, that shunn'st the noise of folly,
Most musical, most melancholy!
Thee, chauntress, oft the woods among,
I woo to hear thy even-song;
And missing thee, I walk unseen
On the dry smooth-shaven green,
To behold the wandering moon,
Riding near her highest noon,
Like one that had been led astray
Through the heaven's wide pathless way,
And oft, as if her head she bowed,
Stooping through a fleecy cloud.
Oft on a plat of rising ground,
I hear the far-off curfew sound,
Over some wide-watered shore,
Swinging slow with sullen roar;
Or if the air will not permit,
Some still removèd place will fit,
Where glowing embers through the room
Teach light to counterfeit a gloom,
Far from all resort of mirth,
Save the cricket on the hearth,
Or the bellman's drowsy charm
To bless the doors from nightly harm.
Or let my lamp at midnight hour
Be seen in some high lonely tower,
Where I may oft out-watch the Bear,
With thrice-great Hermes; or unsphere
The spirit of Plato, to unfold
What worlds or what vast regions hold
The immortal mind that hath forsook
Her mansion in this fleshly nook;
And of those demons that are found
In fire, air, flood, or underground,
Whose power hath a true consent
With planet or with element.
Sometime let gorgeous Tragedy
In sceptred pall come sweeping by,
Presenting Thebes, or Pelops' line,
Or the tale of Troy divine,
Or what (though rare) of later age
Ennobled hath the buskined stage.
But, O sad Virgin! that thy power
Might raise Musæus from his bower;
Or bid the soul of Orpheus sing
Such notes as, warbled to the string,
Drew iron tears down Pluto's cheek,
And made Hell grant what love did seek;
Or call up him that left half-told
The story of Cambuscan bold,
Of Camball, and of Algarsife,
And who had Canace to wife,
That owned the virtuous ring and glass,
And of the wondrous horse of brass
On which the Tartar king did ride;
And if aught else great bards beside
In sage and solemn tunes have sung,
Of turneys, and of trophies hung,
Of forests, and enchantments drear,
Where more is meant than meets the ear.
Thus, Night, oft see me in thy pale career,
Till civil-suited Morn appear,
Not tricked and frounced as she was wont
With the Attic boy to hunt,
But kerchieft in a comely cloud,
While rocking winds are piping loud,
Or ushered with a shower still,
When the gust hath blown his fill,
Ending on the rustling leaves,
With minute-drops from off the eaves.
And when the sun begins to fling
His flaring beams, me, Goddess, bring
To archèd walks of twilight groves,
And shadows brown, that Sylvan loves,
Of pine, or monumental oak,
Where the rude axe with heavèd stroke
Was never heard the nymphs to daunt,
Or fright them from their hallowed haunt.
There in close covert by some brook,
Where no profaner eye may look,
Hide me from day's garish eye,
While the bee with honeyed thigh,
That at her flowery work doth sing,
And the waters murmuring,
With such consort as they keep,
Entice the dewy-feathered Sleep;
And let some strange mysterious dream
Wave at his wings in airy stream
Of lively portraiture displayed,
Softly on my eyelids laid;
And as I wake, sweet music breathe
Above, about, or underneath,
Sent by some spirit to mortals good,
Or the unseen Genius of the wood.
But let my due feet never fail
To walk the studious cloister's pale,
And love the high embowèd roof,
With antique pillars massy proof,
And storied windows richly dight,
Casting a dim religious light.
There let the pealing organ blow,
To the full-voiced quire below,
In service high and anthems clear,
As may with sweetness, through mine ear,
Dissolve me into ecstasies,
And bring all Heaven before mine eyes.

And may at last my weary age
Find out the peaceful hermitage,
The hairy gown, and mossy cell,
Where I may sit and rightly spell
Of every star that heaven doth shew,
And every herb that sips the dew,
Till old experience do attain
To something like prophetic strain.
These pleasures, Melancholy, give,
And I with thee will choose to live.

LYCIDAS

In this Monody the Author bewails a learned Friend, unfortunately drowned in his passage from Chester on the Irish Seas, 1637; and by occasion foretells the ruin of our corrupted Clergy, then in their height.

Yet once more, O ye laurels, and once more,
Ye myrtles brown, with ivy never sere,
I come to pluck your berries harsh and crude,
And with forced fingers rude
Shatter your leaves before the mellowing year.
Bitter constraint and sad occasion dear
Compels me to disturb your season due;
For Lycidas is dead, dead ere his prime,
Young Lycidas, and hath not left his peer.
Who would not sing for Lycidas? he knew
Himself to sing, and build the lofty rhyme.
He must not float upon his watery bier
Unwept, and welter to the parching wind,
Without the meed of some melodious tear.
Begin then, Sisters of the sacred well
That from beneath the seat of Jove doth spring;
Begin, and somewhat loudly sweep the string.
Hence with denial vain and coy excuse;
So may some gentle Muse
With lucky words favour my destined urn,
And as he passes turn,
And bid fair peace be to my sable shroud.
For we were nursed upon the self-same hill,
Fed the same flock, by fountain, shade, and rill;
Together both, ere the high lawns appeared
Under the opening eyelids of the morn,
We drove a-field, and both together heard
What time the gray-fly winds her sultry horn,
Battening our flocks with the fresh dews of night,
Oft till the star that rose at evening, bright,
Toward heaven's descent had sloped his westering wheel.
Meanwhile the rural ditties were not mute,
Tempered to the oaten flute;
Rough Satyrs danced, and Fauns with cloven heel
From the glad sound would not be absent long;
And old Damœtas loved to hear our song.
But O the heavy change, now thou art gone,
Now thou art gone, and never must return!
Thee, Shepherd, thee the woods and desert caves,
With wild thyme and the gadding vine o'ergrown,
And all their echoes, mourn.
The willows and the hazel copses green
Shall now no more be seen,
Fanning their joyous leaves to thy soft lays.
As killing as the canker to the rose,
Or taint-worm to the weanling herds that graze,
Or frost to flowers, that their gay wardrobe wear,
When first the white-thorn blows;
Such, Lycidas, thy loss to shepherd's ear.
Where were ye, Nymphs, when the remorseless deep
Closed o'er the head of your loved Lycidas?
For neither were ye playing on the steep
Where your old bards, the famous Druids, lie,
Nor on the shaggy top of Mona high,
Nor yet where Deva spreads her wizard stream.
Ay me, I fondly dream!
Had ye been there — for what could that have done?
What could the Muse herself that Orpheus bore,
The Muse herself, for her enchanting son,
Whom universal nature did lament,
When by the rout that made the hideous roar
His gory visage down the stream was sent,
Down the swift Hebrus to the Lesbian shore?
Alas! what boots it with uncessant care
To tend the homely, slighted, shepherd's trade,
And strictly meditate the thankless Muse?
Were it not better done, as others use,
To sport with Amaryllis in the shade,
Or with the tangles of Neæra's hair?
Fame is the spur that the clear spirit doth raise
(That last infirmity of noble mind)
To scorn delights and live laborious days;
But the fair guerdon when we hope to find,
And think to burst out into sudden blaze,
Comes the blind Fury with the abhorrèd shears,
And slits the thin-spun life. "But not the praise,"
Phœbus replied, and touched my trembling ears:
"Fame is no plant that grows on mortal soil,
Nor in the glistering foil
Set off to the world, nor in broad rumour lies;
But lives and spreads aloft by those pure eyes
And perfect witness of all-judging Jove;
As he pronounces lastly on each deed,
Of so much fame in heaven expect thy meed."
O fountain Arethuse, and thou honoured flood,
Smooth-sliding Mincius, crowned with vocal reeds,
That strain I heard was of a higher mood:
But now my oat proceeds,
And listens to the herald of the sea,
That came in Neptune's plea.
He asked the waves, and asked the felon winds,
What hard mishap hath doomed this gentle swain?

And questioned every gust of rugged wings
That blows from off each beakèd promontory:
They knew not of his story;
And sage Hippotades their answer brings,
That not a blast was from his dungeon strayed;
The air was calm, and on the level brine
Sleek Panope with all her sisters played.
It was that fatal and perfidious bark,
Built in the eclipse, and rigged with curses dark,
That sunk so low that sacred head of thine.
  Next Camus, reverend sire, went footing slow,
His mantle hairy, and his bonnet sedge,
Inwrought with figures dim, and on the edge
Like to that sanguine flower inscribed with woe.
"Ah! who hath reft," quoth he, "my dearest pledge?"
Last came, and last did go,
The pilot of the Galilean lake;
Two massy keys he bore of metals twain
(The golden opes, the iron shuts amain).
He shook his mitred locks, and stern bespake:
"How well could I have spared for thee, young swain,
Enough of such as for their bellies' sake,
Creep and intrude and climb into the fold!
Of other care they little reckoning make
Than how to scramble at the shearers' feast,
And shove away the worthy bidden guest.
Blind mouths! that scarce themselves know how to hold
A sheep-hook, or have learnt aught else the least
That to the faithful herdman's art belongs!
What recks it them? What need they? They are sped;
And when they list, their lean and flashy songs
Grate on their scrannel pipes of wretched straw;
The hungry sheep look up, and are not fed,
But swoln with wind and the rank mist they draw,
Rot inwardly, and foul contagion spread;
Besides what the grim wolf with privy paw
Daily devours apace, and nothing said.
But that two-handed engine at the door
Stands ready to smite once, and smite no more."
  Return, Alpheus; the dread voice is past
That shrunk thy streams; return, Sicilian Muse,
And call the vales, and bid them hither cast
Their bells and flowrets of a thousand hues.
Ye valleys low, where the mild whispers use
Of shades and wanton winds and gushing brooks,
On whose fresh lap the swart star sparely looks,
Throw hither all your quaint enamelled eyes,
That on the green turf suck the honeyed showers,
And purple all the ground with vernal flowers.
Bring the rathe primrose that forsaken dies,
The tufted crow-toe, and pale jessamine,
The white pink, and the pansy freaked with jet,
The glowing violet,
The musk-rose, and the well-attired woodbine,
With cowslips wan that hang the pensive head,
And every flower that sad embroidery wears;
Bid amaranthus all his beauty shed,
And daffodillies fill their cups with tears,
To strew the laureate hearse where Lycid lies.
For so to interpose a little ease,
Let our frail thoughts dally with false surmise,
Ay me! whilst thee the shores and sounding seas
Wash far away, where'er thy bones are hurled;
Whether beyond the stormy Hebrides,
Where thou perhaps under the whelming tide
Visit'st the bottom of the monstrous world;
Or whether thou, to our moist vows denied,
Sleep'st by the fable of Bellerus old,
Where the great vision of the guarded mount
Looks toward Namancos and Bayona's hold.
Look homeward, Angel, now, and melt with ruth;
And O ye dolphins, waft the hapless youth.
  Weep no more, woeful shepherds, weep no more,
For Lycidas, your sorrow, is not dead,
Sunk though he be beneath the watery floor;
So sinks the day-star in the ocean bed,
And yet anon repairs his drooping head,
And tricks his beams, and with new-spangled ore
Flames in the forehead of the morning sky:
So Lycidas sunk low, but mounted high,
Through the dear might of him that walked the waves,
Where, other groves and other streams along,
With nectar pure his oozy locks he laves,
And hears the unexpressive nuptial song,
In the blest kingdoms meek of joy and love.
There entertain him all the saints above,
In solemn troops and sweet societies,
That sing, and singing in their glory move,
And wipe the tears for ever from his eyes.
Now, Lycidas, the shepherds weep no more;
Henceforth thou art the Genius of the shore,
In thy large recompense, and shalt be good
To all that wander in that perilous flood.
  Thus sang the uncouth swain to the oaks and rills,
While the still morn went out with sandals gray;
He touched the tender stops of various quills,
With eager thought warbling his Doric lay:
And now the sun had stretched out all the hills,
And now was dropt into the western bay.
At last he rose, and twitched his mantle blue:
To-morrow to fresh woods and pastures new.

SONNETS

TO THE NIGHTINGALE

O Nightingale, that on yon bloomy spray
Warblest at eve, when all the woods are still,
Thou with fresh hope the lover's heart dost fill,
While the jolly hours lead on propitious May.
Thy liquid notes that close the eye of day,
First heard before the shallow cuckoo's bill,
Portend success in love. O, if Jove's will
Have linked that amorous power to thy soft lay,
Now timely sing, ere the rude bird of hate
Foretell my hopeless doom, in some grove nigh;
As thou from year to year hast sung too late
For my relief, yet hadst no reason why.
Whether the Muse or Love call thee his mate,
Both them I serve, and of their train am I.

ON HIS HAVING ARRIVED AT THE AGE OF TWENTY-THREE

How soon hath Time, the subtle thief of youth,
Stolen on his wing my three and twentieth year!
My hasting days fly on with full career,
But my late spring no bud or blossom shew'th.
Perhaps my semblance might deceive the truth
That I to manhood am arrived so near;
And inward ripeness doth much less appear,
That some more timely-happy spirits endu'th.
Yet be it less or more, or soon or slow,
It shall be still in strictest measure even
To that same lot, however mean or high,
Toward which Time leads me, and the will of Heaven;
All is, if I have grace to use it so,
As ever in my great Task-Master's eye.

WHEN THE ASSAULT WAS INTENDED TO THE CITY

Captain, or Colonel, or Knight in arms,
Whose chance on these defenceless doors may seize,
If ever deed of honour did thee please,
Guard them, and him within protect from harms.
He can requite thee; for he knows the charms
That call fame on such gentle acts as these,
And he can spread thy name o'er lands and seas,
Whatever clime the sun's bright circle warms.
Lift not thy spear against the Muses' bower:
The great Emathian conqueror bid spare
The house of Pindarus, when temple and tower
Went to the ground; and the repeated air
Of sad Electra's poet had the power
To save the Athenian walls from ruin bare.

ON THE DETRACTION WHICH FOLLOWED UPON MY WRITING CERTAIN TREATISES

A book was writ of late called Tetrachordon,
And woven close, both matter, form, and style;
The subject new: it walked the town a while,
Numbering good intellects; now seldom pored on.
Cries the stall-reader, "Bless us! what a word on
A title-page is this!"; and some in file
Stand spelling false, while one might walk to Mile-
End Green. Why, is it harder, sirs, than Gordon,
Colkitto, or Macdonnel, or Galasp?
Those rugged names to our like mouths grow sleek
That would have made Quintilian stare and gasp.
Thy age, like ours, O soul of Sir John Cheek,
Hated not learning worse than toad or asp,
When thou taught'st Cambridge and King Edward Greek.

ON THE SAME

I did but prompt the age to quit their clogs
By the known rules of ancient liberty,
When straight a barbarous noise environs me
Of owls and cuckoos, asses, apes, and dogs;
As when those hinds that were transformed to frogs
Railed at Latona's twin-born progeny,
Which after held the sun and moon in fee.
But this is got by casting pearl to hogs,
That bawl for freedom in their senseless mood,
And still revolt when truth would set them free.
License they mean when they cry Liberty;
For who loves that must first be wise and good:
But from that mark how far they rove we see,
For all this waste of wealth and loss of blood.

TO MR. H. LAWES ON HIS AIRS

Harry, whose tuneful and well-measured song
First taught our English music how to span
Words with just note and accent, not to scan
With Midas' ears, committing short and long:
Thy worth and skill exempts thee from the throng,
With praise enough for Envy to look wan:

To after age thou shalt be writ the man
That with smooth air couldst humour best our tongue.
Thou honour'st verse, and verse must lend her wing
To honour thee, the priest of Phœbus' quire,
That tun'st their happiest lines in hymn or story.
Dante shall give Fame leave to set thee higher
Than his Casella, whom he wooed to sing,
Met in the milder shades of Purgatory.

TO THE LORD GENERAL CROMWELL

MAY, 1652

On the Proposals of Certain Ministers at the Committee for Propagation of the Gospel

Cromwell, our chief of men, who through a cloud
Not of war only, but detractions rude,
Guided by faith and matchless fortitude,
To peace and truth thy glorious way hast ploughed,
And on the neck of crownèd Fortune proud
Hast reared God's trophies, and his work pursued,
While Darwen stream, with blood of Scots imbrued,
And Dunbar field, resounds thy praises loud,
And Worcester's laureate wreath: yet much remains
To conquer still; peace hath her victories
No less renowned than war: new foes arise,
Threatening to bind our souls with secular chains.
Help us to save free conscience from the paw
Of hireling wolves, whose gospel is their maw.

ON THE LATE MASSACRE IN PIEDMONT

Avenge, O Lord, thy slaughtered saints, whose bones
Lie scattered on the Alpine mountains cold;
Even them who kept thy truth so pure of old,
When all our fathers worshipped stocks and stones,
Forget not: in thy book record their groans
Who were thy sheep, and in their ancient fold
Slain by the bloody Piemontese, that rolled
Mother with infant down the rocks. Their moans
The vales redoubled to the hills, and they
To heaven. Their martyred blood and ashes sow
O'er all the Italian fields, where still doth sway
The triple tyrant; that from these may grow
A hundredfold, who, having learnt thy way,
Early may fly the Babylonian woe.

ON HIS BLINDNESS

When I consider how my light is spent
Ere half my days, in this dark world and wide,
And that one talent which is death to hide
Lodged with me useless, though my soul more bent
To serve therewith my Maker, and present
My true account, lest he returning chide;
"Doth God exact day-labour, light denied?"
I fondly ask. But Patience, to prevent
That murmur, soon replies, "God doth not need
Either man's work or his own gifts. Who best
Bear his mild yoke, they serve him best. His state
Is kingly: thousands at his bidding speed,
And post o'er land and ocean without rest;
They also serve who only stand and wait."

TO CYRIACK SKINNER

Cyriack, this three years' day these eyes, though clear
To outward view, of blemish or of spot,
Bereft of light, their seeing have forgot;
Nor to their idle orbs doth sight appear
Of sun or moon or star throughout the year,
Or man or woman. Yet I argue not
Against Heaven's hand or will, nor bate a jot
Of heart or hope, but still bear up and steer
Right onward. What supports me, dost thou ask?
The conscience, friend, to have lost them overplied
In liberty's defence, my noble task,
Of which all Europe talks from side to side.
This thought might lead me through the world's vain mask
Content, though blind, had I no better guide.

PARADISE LOST

BOOK I

Of Man's first disobedience, and the fruit
Of that forbidden tree, whose mortal taste
Brought death into the world, and all our woe,
With loss of Eden, till one greater Man
Restore us, and regain the blissful seat,
Sing, Heavenly Muse, that on the secret top
Of Oreb, or of Sinai, didst inspire

That shepherd who first taught the chosen seed
In the beginning how the Heavens and Earth
Rose out of Chaos: or, if Sion hill
Delight thee more, and Siloa's brook that flowed
Fast by the oracle of God, I thence
Invoke thy aid to my adventurous song,
That with no middle flight intends to soar
Above the Aonian mount, while it pursues
Things unattempted yet in prose or rhyme.
And chiefly Thou, O Spirit, that dost prefer
Before all temples the upright heart and pure,
Instruct me, for Thou know'st; Thou from the first
Wast present, and, with mighty wings outspread,
Dove-like sat'st brooding on the vast Abyss,
And mad'st it pregnant: what in me is dark
Illumine, what is low raise and support;
That to the highth of this great argument
I may assert Eternal Providence,
And justify the ways of God to men.
  Say first — for Heaven hides nothing from Thy view,
Nor the deep tract of Hell — say first what cause
Moved our grand parents, in that happy state,
Favoured of Heaven so highly, to fall off
From their Creator, and transgress his will
For one restraint, lords of the world besides.
Who first seduced them to that foul revolt?
  The infernal Serpent; he it was, whose guile,
Stirred up with envy and revenge, deceived
The mother of mankind, what time his pride
Had cast him out from Heaven, with all his host
Of rebel Angels, by whose aid, aspiring
To set himself in glory above his peers,
He trusted to have equalled the Most High,
If he opposed; and with ambitious aim
Against the throne and monarchy of God
Raised impious war in Heaven, and battle proud,
With vain attempt. Him the Almighty Power
Hurled headlong flaming from the ethereal sky,
With hideous ruin and combustion, down
To bottomless perdition; there to dwell
In adamantine chains and penal fire,
Who durst defy the Omnipotent to arms.
  Nine times the space that measures day and night
To mortal men, he with his horrid crew
Lay vanquished, rolling in the fiery gulf,
Confounded, though immortal. But his doom
Reserved him to more wrath; for now the thought
Both of lost happiness and lasting pain
Torments him; round he throws his baleful eyes,
That witnessed huge affliction and dismay,
Mixed with obdurate pride and steadfast hate.
At once, as far as Angels ken, he views
The dismal situation waste and wild:
A dungeon horrible on all sides round
As one great furnace flamed; yet from those flames
No light; but rather darkness visible
Served only to discover sights of woe,
Regions of sorrow, doleful shades, where peace
And rest can never dwell, hope never comes
That comes to all; but torture without end
Still urges, and a fiery deluge, fed
With ever-burning sulphur unconsumed.
Such place Eternal Justice had prepared
For those rebellious; here their prison ordained
In utter darkness, and their portion set,
As far removed from God and light of Heaven
As from the centre thrice to the utmost pole.
Oh how unlike the place from whence they fell!
There the companions of his fall, o'erwhelmed
With floods and whirlwinds of tempestuous fire,
He soon discerns; and, weltering by his side,
One next himself in power, and next in crime,
Long after known in Palestine, and named
Beëlzebub. To whom the Arch-Enemy,
And thence in Heaven called Satan, with bold words
Breaking the horrid silence, thus began: —
  "If thou beest he — but Oh how fallen! how changed
From him, who in the happy realms of light,
Clothed with transcendent brightness, didst outshine
Myriads, though bright! — if he whom mutual league,
United thoughts and counsels, equal hope
And hazard in the glorious enterprise,
Joined with me once, now misery hath joined
In equal ruin — into what pit thou seest
From what highth fallen: so much the stronger proved
He with his thunder: and till then who knew
The force of those dire arms? Yet not for those,
Nor what the potent Victor in his rage
Can else inflict, do I repent, or change,
Though changed in outward lustre, that fixed mind,
And high disdain from sense of injured merit,
That with the Mightiest raised me to contend,
And to the fierce contention brought along
Innumerable force of Spirits armed,
That durst dislike his reign, and, me preferring,
His utmost power with adverse power opposed
In dubious battle on the plains of Heaven,
And shook his throne. What though the field be lost?
All is not lost: the unconquerable will,
And study of revenge, immortal hate,
And courage never to submit or yield,
And what is else not to be overcome;

That glory never shall his wrath or might
Extort from me. To bow and sue for grace
With suppliant knee, and deify his power
Who, from the terror of this arm, so late
Doubted his empire — that were low indeed;
That were an ignominy and shame beneath
This downfall; since by fate the strength of gods
And this empyreal substance cannot fail;
Since, through experience of this great event,
In arms not worse, in foresight much advanced,
We may with more successful hope resolve
To wage by force or guile eternal war,
Irreconcilable to our grand Foe,
Who now triumphs, and in the excess of joy
Sole reigning holds the tyranny of Heaven."

So spake the apostate Angel, though in pain,
Vaunting aloud, but racked with deep despair;
And him thus answered soon his bold compeer: —
"O Prince! O Chief of many thronèd powers,
That led the embattled Seraphim to war
Under thy conduct, and, in dreadful deeds
Fearless, endangered Heaven's perpetual King,
And put to proof his high supremacy,
Whether upheld by strength, or chance, or fate!
Too well I see and rue the dire event
That with sad overthrow and foul defeat
Hath lost us Heaven, and all this mighty host
In horrible destruction laid thus low,
As far as gods and Heavenly essences
Can perish: for the mind and spirit remains
Invincible, and vigor soon returns,
Though all our glory extinct, and happy state
Here swallowed up in endless misery.
But what if he our Conqueror (whom I now
Of force believe almighty, since no less
Than such could have o'erpowered such force as ours)
Have left us this our spirit and strength entire,
Strongly to suffer and support our pains,
That we may so suffice his vengeful ire;
Or do him mightier service, as his thralls
By right of war, whate'er his business be,
Here in the heart of Hell to work in fire,
Or do his errands in the gloomy Deep?
What can it then avail, though yet we feel
Strength undiminished, or eternal being
To undergo eternal punishment?"

Whereto with speedy words the Arch-Fiend replied: —
"Fallen Cherub, to be weak is miserable,
Doing or suffering: but of this be sure —
To do aught good never will be our task,
But ever to do ill our sole delight,
As being the contrary to his high will
Whom we resist. If then his providence
Out of our evil seek to bring forth good,
Our labour must be to pervert that end,
And out of good still to find means of evil;
Which ofttimes may succeed so as perhaps
Shall grieve him, if I fail not, and disturb
His inmost counsels from their destined aim.
But see! the angry Victor hath recalled
His ministers of vengeance and pursuit
Back to the gates of Heaven; the sulphurous hail,
Shot after us in storm, o'erblown hath laid
The fiery surge that from the precipice
Of Heaven received us falling; and the thunder,
Winged with red lightning and impetuous rage,
Perhaps hath spent his shafts, and ceases now
To bellow through the vast and boundless Deep.
Let us not slip the occasion, whether scorn
Or satiate fury yield it from our Foe.
Seest thou yon dreary plain, forlorn and wild,
The seat of desolation, void of light,
Save what the glimmering of these livid flames
Casts pale and dreadful? Thither let us tend
From off the tossing of these fiery waves;
There rest, if any rest can harbour there;
And, reassembling our afflicted powers,
Consult how we may henceforth most offend
Our Enemy, our own loss how repair,
How overcome this dire calamity,
What reinforcement we may gain from hope,
If not, what resolution from despair."

Thus Satan, talking to his nearest mate,
With head uplift above the wave, and eyes
That sparkling blazed; his other parts besides,
Prone on the flood, extended long and large,
Lay floating many a rood, in bulk as huge
As whom the fables name of monstrous size,
Titanian, or Earth-born, that warred on Jove,
Briareos or Typhon, whom the den
By ancient Tarsus held, or that sea-beast
Leviathan, which God of all his works
Created hugest that swim the ocean-stream.
Him, haply slumbering on the Norway foam,
The pilot of some small night-foundered skiff
Deeming some island, oft, as seamen tell,
With fixèd anchor in his scaly rind,
Moors by his side under the lee, while night
Invests the sea, and wishèd morn delays.
So stretched out huge in length the Arch-Fiend lay,
Chained on the burning lake; nor ever thence
Had risen or heaved his head, but that the will
And high permission of all-ruling Heaven
Left him at large to his own dark designs,
That with reiterated crimes he might
Heap on himself damnation, while he sought
Evil to others, and enraged might see
How all his malice served but to bring forth
Infinite goodness, grace, and mercy, shewn

On Man by him seduced; but on himself
Treble confusion, wrath, and vengeance poured.
  Forthwith upright he rears from off the pool
His mighty stature; on each hand the flames
Driven backward slope their pointing spires, and, rolled
In billows, leave in the midst a horrid vale.
Then with expanded wings he steers his flight
Aloft, incumbent on the dusky air,
That felt unusual weight; till on dry land
He lights — if it were land that ever burned
With solid, as the lake with liquid fire,
And such appeared in hue, as when the force
Of subterranean wind transports a hill
Torn from Pelorus, or the shattered side
Of thundering Ætna, whose combustible
And fuelled entrails thence conceiving fire,
Sublimed with mineral fury, aid the winds,
And leave a singèd bottom all involved
With stench and smoke: such resting found the sole
Of unblest feet. Him followed his next mate,
Both glorying to have 'scaped the Stygian flood
As gods, and by their own recovered strength,
Not by the sufferance of supernal power.
  "Is this the region, this the soil, the clime,"
Said then the lost Archangel, "this the seat
That we must change for Heaven? this mournful gloom
For that celestial light? Be it so, since he
Who now is sovran can dispose and bid
What shall be right: farthest from him is best,
Whom reason hath equalled, force hath made supreme
Above his equals. Farewell, happy fields,
Where joy forever dwells! Hail, horrors! hail,
Infernal world! and thou, profoundest Hell,
Receive thy new possessor, one who brings
A mind not to be changed by place or time.
The mind is its own place, and in itself
Can make a Heaven of Hell, a Hell of Heaven.
What matter where, if I be still the same,
And what I should be, all but less than he
Whom thunder hath made greater? Here at least
We shall be free; the Almighty hath not built
Here for his envy, will not drive us hence:
Here we may reign secure, and in my choice
To reign is worth ambition, though in Hell:
Better to reign in Hell, than serve in Heaven.
But wherefore let we then our faithful friends,
The associates and co-partners of our loss,
Lie thus astonished on the oblivious pool,
And call them not to share with us their part
In this unhappy mansion, or once more
With rallied arms to try what may be yet
Regained in Heaven, or what more lost in Hell?"
  So Satan spake; and him Beëlzebub
Thus answered: — "Leader of those armies bright
Which but the Omnipotent none could have foiled,
If once they hear that voice, their liveliest pledge
Of hope in fears and dangers — heard so oft
In worst extremes, and on the perilous edge
Of battle when it raged, in all assaults
Their surest signal — they will soon resume
New courage and revive, though now they lie
Grovelling and prostrate on yon lake of fire,
As we erewhile, astounded and amazed:
No wonder, fallen such a pernicious highth!"
  He scarce had ceased when the superior Fiend
Was moving toward the shore; his ponderous shield,
Ethereal temper, massy, large, and round,
Behind him cast. The broad circumference
Hung on his shoulders like the moon, whose orb
Through optic glass the Tuscan artist views
At evening from the top of Fesole,
Or in Valdarno, to descry new lands,
Rivers, or mountains, in her spotty globe.
His spear — to equal which the tallest pine
Hewn on Norwegian hills, to be the mast
Of some great ammiral, were but a wand —
He walked with, to support uneasy steps
Over the burning marle, not like those steps
On Heaven's azure; and the torrid clime
Smote on him sore besides, vaulted with fire.
Nathless he so endured, till on the beach
Of that inflamèd sea he stood, and called
His legions, angel forms, who lay entranced,
Thick as autumnal leaves that strow the brooks
In Vallombrosa, where the Etrurian shades
High over-arched embower; or scattered sedge
Afloat, when with fierce winds Orion armed
Hath vexed the Red-Sea coast, whose waves o'erthrew
Busiris and his Memphian chivalry,
While with perfidious hatred they pursued
The sojourners of Goshen, who beheld
From the safe shore their floating carcases
And broken chariot-wheels: so thick bestrown,
Abject and lost, lay these, covering the flood,
Under amazement of their hideous change.
He called so loud that all the hollow deep
Of Hell resounded: — "Princes, Potentates,
Warriors, the Flower of Heaven — once yours, now lost,
If such astonishment as this can seize
Eternal Spirits! Or have ye chosen this place
After the toil of battle to repose
Your wearied virtue, for the ease you find
To slumber here, as in the vales of Heaven?
Or in this abject posture have ye sworn
To adore the Conqueror, who now beholds

Cherub and Seraph rolling in the flood
With scattered arms and ensigns, till anon
His swift pursuers from Heaven-gates discern
The advantage, and descending tread us down
Thus drooping, or with linkèd thunderbolts
Transfix us to the bottom of this gulf?
Awake, arise, or be forever fallen!"
They heard, and were abashed, and up they sprung
Upon the wing, as when men wont to watch,
On duty sleeping found by whom they dread,
Rouse and bestir themselves ere well awake.
Nor did they not perceive the evil plight
In which they were, or the fierce pains not feel;
Yet to their General's voice they soon obeyed
Innumerable. As when the potent rod
Of Amram's son, in Egypt's evil day,
Waved round the coast, up called a pitchy cloud
Of locusts, warping on the eastern wind,
That o'er the realm of impious Pharaoh hung
Like night, and darkened all the land of Nile:
So numberless were those bad angels seen
Hovering on wing under the cope of Hell,
'Twixt upper, nether, and surrounding fires;
Till, as a signal given, the uplifted spear
Of their great Sultan waving to direct
Their course, in even balance down they light
On the firm brimstone, and fill all the plain:
A multitude like which the populous North
Poured never from her frozen loins, to pass
Rhene or the Danaw, when her barbarous sons
Came like a deluge on the South, and spread
Beneath Gibraltar to the Libyan sands.
Forthwith, from every squadron and each band,
The heads and leaders thither haste where stood
Their great Commander; godlike shapes, and forms
Excelling human, princely Dignities,
And Powers that erst in Heaven sat on thrones;
Though of their names in Heavenly records now
Be no memorial, blotted out and rased
By their rebellion from the Books of Life.
Nor had they yet among the sons of Eve
Got them new names, till, wandering o'er the earth,
Through God's high sufferance for the trial of man,
By falsities and lies the greatest part
Of mankind they corrupted to forsake
God their Creator, and the invisible
Glory of him that made them, to transform
Oft to the image of a brute, adorned
With gay religions full of pomp and gold,
And devils to adore for deities:
Then were they known to men by various names,
And various idols through the heathen world.
Say, Muse, their names then known, who first, who last,
Roused from the slumber on that fiery couch,
At their great Emperor's call, as next in worth,
Came singly where he stood on the bare strand,
While the promiscuous crowd stood yet aloof.
The chief were those who, from the pit of Hell
Roaming to seek their prey on Earth, durst fix
Their seats, long after, next the seat of God,
Their altars by his altar, gods adored
Among the nations round, and durst abide
Jehovah thundering out of Sion, throned
Between the Cherubim; yea, often placed
Within his sanctuary itself their shrines,
Abominations; and with cursèd things
His holy rites and solemn feasts profaned,
And with their darkness durst affront his light.
First Moloch, horrid king, besmeared with blood
Of human sacrifice, and parents' tears,
Though, for the noise of drums and timbrels loud,
Their children's cries unheard that passed through fire
To his grim idol. Him the Ammonite
Worshipped in Rabba and her watery plain,
In Argob and in Basan, to the stream
Of utmost Arnon. Nor content with such
Audacious neighbourhood, the wisest heart
Of Solomon he led by fraud to build
His temple right against the temple of God
On that opprobrious hill, and made his grove
The pleasant valley of Hinnom, Tophet thence
And black Gehenna called, the type of Hell.
Next Chemos, the obscene dread of Moab's sons,
From Aroar to Nebo and the wild
Of southmost Abarim; in Hesebon
And Horonaim, Seon's realm, beyond
The flowery dale of Sibma clad with vines,
And Elealè to the Asphaltic pool.
Peor his other name, when he enticed
Israel in Sittim, on their march from Nile,
To do him wanton rites, which cost them woe.
Yet thence his lustful orgies he enlarged
Even to that hill of scandal, by the grove
Of Moloch homicide, lust hard by hate,
Till good Josiah drove them thence to Hell.
With these came they who, from the bordering flood
Of old Euphrates to the brook that parts
Egypt from Syrian ground, had general names
Of Baälim and Ashtaroth — those male,
These feminine. For Spirits, when they please,
Can either sex assume, or both; so soft
And uncompounded is their essence pure,
Not tied or manacled with joint or limb,
Nor founded on the brittle strength of bones,

Like cumbrous flesh; but, in what shape they choose,
Dilated or condensed, bright or obscure,
Can execute their aery purposes,
And works of love or enmity fulfil.
For those the race of Israel oft forsook
Their living Strength, and unfrequented left
His righteous altar, bowing lowly down
To bestial gods; for which their heads as low
Bowed down in battle, sunk before the spear
Of despicable foes. With these in troop
Came Astoreth, whom the Phœnicians called
Astarte, Queen of Heaven, with crescent horns;
To whose bright image nightly by the moon
Sidonian virgins paid their vows and songs;
In Sion also not unsung, where stood
Her temple on the offensive mountain, built
By that uxorious king whose heart, though large,
Beguiled by fair idolatresses, fell
To idols foul. Thammuz came next behind,
Whose annual wound in Lebanon allured
The Syrian damsels to lament his fate
In amorous ditties all a summer's day,
While smooth Adonis from his native rock
Ran purple to the sea, supposed with blood
Of Thammuz yearly wounded: the love-tale
Infected Sion's daughters with like heat,
Whose wanton passions in the sacred porch
Ezekiel saw, when, by the vision led,
His eye surveyed the dark idolatries
Of alienated Judah. Next came one
Who mourned in earnest, when the captive ark
Maimed his brute image, head and hands lopt off
In his own temple, on the grunsel-edge,
Where he fell flat, and shamed his worshippers:
Dagon his name, sea-monster, upward man
And downward fish; yet had his temple high
Reared in Azotus, dreaded through the coast
Of Palestine, in Gath and Ascalon,
And Accaron and Gaza's frontier bounds.
Him followed Rimmon, whose delightful seat
Was fair Damascus, on the fertile banks
Of Abbana and Pharphar, lucid streams.
He also against the house of God was bold:
A leper once he lost, and gained a king,
Ahaz, his sottish conqueror, whom he drew
God's altar to disparage and displace
For one of Syrian mode, whereon to burn
His odious offerings, and adore the gods
Whom he had vanquished. After these appeared
A crew who, under names of old renown,
Osiris, Isis, Orus, and their train,
With monstrous shapes and sorceries abused
Fanatic Egypt and her priests, to seek
Their wandering gods disguised in brutish forms
Rather than human. Nor did Israel 'scape
The infection, when their borrowed gold composed
The calf in Oreb; and the rebel king
Doubled that sin in Bethel and in Dan,
Likening his Maker to the grazèd ox —
Jehovah, who, in one night, when he passed
From Egypt marching, equalled with one stroke
Both her first-born and all her bleating gods.
Belial came last, than whom a Spirit more lewd
Fell not from Heaven, or more gross to love
Vice for itself. To him no temple stood
Or altar smoked; yet who more oft than he
In temples and at altars, when the priest
Turns atheist, as did Eli's sons, who filled
With lust and violence the house of God?
In courts and palaces he also reigns,
And in luxurious cities, where the noise
Of riot ascends above their loftiest towers,
And injury and outrage; and when night
Darkens the streets, then wander forth the sons
Of Belial, flown with insolence and wine.
Witness the streets of Sodom, and that night
In Gibeah, when the hospitable door
Exposed a matron, to avoid worse rape.

These were the prime in order and in might;
The rest were long to tell, though far renowned
The Ionian gods — of Javan's issue held
Gods, yet confessed later than Heaven and Earth,
Their boasted parents; — Titan, Heaven's first-born,
With his enormous brood, and birthright seized
By younger Saturn; he from mightier Jove,
His own and Rhea's son, like measure found;
So Jove usurping reigned. These, first in Crete
And Ida known, thence on the snowy top
Of cold Olympus ruled the middle air,
Their highest Heaven; or on the Delphian cliff,
Or in Dodona, and through all the bounds
Of Doric land; or who with Saturn old
Fled over Adria to the Hesperian fields,
And o'er the Celtic roamed the utmost isles.

All these and more came flocking; but with looks
Downcast and damp, yet such wherein appeared
Obscure some glimpse of joy, to have found their Chief
Not in despair, to have found themselves not lost
In loss itself; which on his countenance cast
Like doubtful hue. But he, his wonted pride
Soon recollecting, with high words that bore
Semblance of worth, not substance, gently raised
Their fainting courage, and dispelled their fears:
Then straight commands that at the warlike sound
Of trumpets loud and clarions, be upreared
His mighty standard. That proud honour claimed
Azazel as his right, a Cherub tall:
Who forthwith from the glittering staff unfurled

The imperial ensign, which, full high advanced,
Shone like a meteor streaming to the wind,
With gems and golden lustre rich emblazed,
Seraphic arms and trophies; all the while
Sonorous metal blowing martial sounds:
At which the universal host up-sent
A shout that tore Hell's concave, and beyond
Frighted the reign of Chaos and old Night.
All in a moment through the gloom were seen
Ten thousand banners rise into the air,
With orient colours waving; with them rose
A forest huge of spears; and thronging helms
Appeared, and serried shields in thick array
Of depth immeasurable. Anon they move
In perfect phalanx to the Dorian mood
Of flutes and soft recorders — such as raised
To highth of noblest temper heroes old
Arming to battle, and instead of rage
Deliberate valour breathed, firm and unmoved
With dread of death to flight or foul retreat;
Nor wanting power to mitigate and swage,
With solemn touches, troubled thoughts, and chase
Anguish and doubt and fear and sorrow and pain
From mortal or immortal minds. Thus they,
Breathing united force with fixèd thought,
Moved on in silence to soft pipes that charmed
Their painful steps o'er the burnt soil; and now
Advanced in view they stand, a horrid front
Of dreadful length and dazzling arms, in guise
Of warriors old, with ordered spear and shield,
Awaiting what command their mighty Chief
Had to impose. He through the armèd files
Darts his experienced eye, and soon traverse
The whole battalion views — their order due,
Their visages and stature as of gods;
Their number last he sums. And now his heart
Distends with pride, and hardening in his strength
Glories; for never, since created man,
Met such embodied force as, named with these,
Could merit more than that small infantry
Warred on by cranes: though all the giant brood
Of Phlegra with the heroic race were joined
That fought at Thebes and Ilium, on each side
Mixed with auxiliar gods; and what resounds
In fable or romance of Uther's son,
Begirt with British and Armoric knights;
And all who since, baptized or infidel,
Jousted in Aspramont, or Montalban,
Damasco, or Marocco, or Trebisond;
Or whom Biserta sent from Afric shore
When Charlemain with all his peerage fell
By Fontarabbia. Thus far these beyond
Compare of mortal prowess, yet observed
Their dread commander. He, above the rest
In shape and gesture proudly eminent,
Stood like a tower; his form had yet not lost
All her original brightness, nor appeared
Less than Archangel ruined, and the excess
Of glory obscured: as when the sun new-risen
Looks through the horizontal misty air
Shorn of his beams, or from behind the moon,
In dim eclipse, disastrous twilight sheds
On half the nations, and with fear of change
Perplexes monarchs. Darkened so, yet shone
Above them all the Archangel; but his face
Deep scars of thunder had intrenched, and care
Sat on his faded cheek, but under brows
Of dauntless courage, and considerate pride
Waiting revenge. Cruel his eye, but cast
Signs of remorse and passion, to behold
The fellows of his crime, the followers rather
(Far other once beheld in bliss), condemned
Forever now to have their lot in pain;
Millions of Spirits for his fault amerced
Of Heaven, and from eternal splendors flung
For his revolt; yet faithful how they stood,
Their glory withered: as, when Heaven's fire
Hath scathed the forest oaks or mountain pines,
With singèd top their stately growth, though bare,
Stands on the blasted heath. He now prepared
To speak; whereat their doubled ranks they bend
From wing to wing, and half enclose him round
With all his peers: attention held them mute.
Thrice he assayed, and thrice, in spite of scorn,
Tears, such as Angels weep, burst forth: at last
Words interwove with sighs found out their way:—
"O myriads of immortal Spirits! O powers
Matchless, but with the Almighty! — and that strife
Was not inglorious, though the event was dire,
As this place testifies, and this dire change,
Hateful to utter. But what power of mind,
Foreseeing or presaging, from the depth
Of knowledge past or present, could have feared
How such united force of gods, how such
As stood like these, could ever know repulse?
For who can yet believe, though after loss,
That all these puissant legions, whose exile
Hath emptied Heaven, shall fail to reascend,
Self-raised, and repossess their native seat?
For me, be witness all the host of Heaven,
If counsels different, or dangers shunned
By me, have lost our hopes. But he who reigns
Monarch in Heaven, till then as one secure
Sat on his throne, upheld by old repute,
Consent or custom, and his regal state
Put forth at full, but still his strength concealed;
Which tempted our attempt, and wrought our fall.
Henceforth his might we know, and know our own,
So as not either to provoke, or dread
New war provoked. Our better part remains

To work in close design, by fraud or guile,
What force effected not; that he no less
At length from us may find, who overcomes
By force hath overcome but half his foe.
Space may produce new worlds; whereof so rife
There went a fame in Heaven that he erelong
Intended to create, and therein plant
A generation whom his choice regard
Should favour equal to the Sons of Heaven.
Thither, if but to pry, shall be perhaps
Our first eruption: thither or elsewhere;
For this infernal pit shall never hold
Celestial Spirits in bondage, nor the Abyss
Long under darkness cover. But these thoughts,
Full counsel must mature. Peace is despaired,
For who can think submission? War, then, war
Open or understood, must be resolved."
He spake; and, to confirm his words, out-flew
Millions of flaming swords, drawn from the thighs
Of mighty Cherubim; the sudden blaze
Far round illumined Hell. Highly they raged
Against the Highest, and fierce with graspèd arms
Clashed on their sounding shields the din of war,
Hurling defiance toward the vault of Heaven.
There stood a hill not far, whose grisly top
Belched fire and rolling smoke; the rest entire
Shone with a glossy scurf, undoubted sign
That in his womb was hid metallic ore,
The work of sulphur. Thither, winged with speed,
A numerous brigade hastened: as when bands
Of pioneers, with spade and pickaxe armed,
Forerun the royal camp, to trench a field,
Or cast a rampart. Mammon led them on,
Mammon, the least erected Spirit that fell
From Heaven, for even in Heaven his looks and thoughts
Were always downward bent, admiring more
The riches of Heaven's pavement, trodden gold,
Than aught divine or holy else enjoyed
In vision beatific. By him first
Men also, and by his suggestion taught,
Ransacked the Centre, and with impious hands
Rifled the bowels of their mother Earth
For treasures better hid. Soon had his crew
Opened into the hill a spacious wound,
And digged out ribs of gold. Let none admire
That riches grow in Hell; that soil may best
Deserve the precious bane. And here let those
Who boast in mortal things, and wondering tell
Of Babel, and the works of Memphian kings,
Learn how their greatest monuments of fame,
And strength, and art, are easily outdone
By Spirits reprobate, and in an hour
What in an age they, with incessant toil
And hands innumerable, scarce perform.
Nigh on the plain, in many cells prepared,
That underneath had veins of liquid fire
Sluiced from the lake, a second multitude
With wondrous art founded the massy ore,
Severing each kind, and scummed the bullion dross.
A third as soon had formed within the ground
A various mould, and from the boiling cells
By strange conveyance filled each hollow nook:
As in an organ, from one blast of wind,
To many a row of pipes the sound-board breathes.
Anon out of the earth a fabric huge
Rose like an exhalation, with the sound
Of dulcet symphonies and voices sweet —
Built like a temple, where pilasters round
Were set, and Doric pillars overlaid
With golden architrave; nor did there want
Cornice or frieze, with bossy sculptures graven:
The roof was fretted gold. Not Babylon,
Nor great Alcairo, such magnificence
Equalled in all their glories, to enshrine
Belus or Serapis their gods, or seat
Their kings, when Egypt with Assyria strove
In wealth and luxury. The ascending pile
Stood fixed her stately highth, and straight the doors,
Opening their brazen folds, discover, wide
Within, her ample spaces o'er the smooth
And level pavement: from the archèd roof,
Pendent by subtle magic, many a row
Of starry lamps and blazing cressets, fed
With naphtha and asphaltus, yielded light
As from a sky. The hasty multitude
Admiring entered, and the work some praise,
And some the architect. His hand was known
In Heaven by many a towered structure high,
Where sceptred Angels held their residence,
And sat as Princes, whom the supreme King
Exalted to such power, and gave to rule,
Each in his Hierarchy, the Orders bright.
Nor was his name unheard or unadored
In ancient Greece; and in Ausonian land
Men called him Mulciber; and how he fell
From Heaven they fabled, thrown by angry Jove
Sheer o'er the crystal battlements: from morn
To noon he fell, from noon to dewy eve,
A summer's day; and with the setting sun
Dropt from the zenith, like a falling star,
On Lemnos, the Ægæan isle. Thus they relate,
Erring; for he with this rebellious rout
Fell long before; nor aught availed him now
To have built in Heaven high towers; nor did he 'scape
By all his engines, but was headlong sent

With his industrious crew to build in Hell.
  Meanwhile the wingèd heralds, by command
Of sovran power, with awful ceremony
And trumpet's sound, throughout the host proclaim
A solemn council forthwith to be held
At Pandemonium, the high capital
Of Satan and his peers. Their summons called
From every band and squarèd regiment
By place or choice the worthiest; they anon
With hundreds and with thousands trooping came
Attended. All access was thronged, the gates
And porches wide, but chief the spacious hall
(Though like a covered field, where champions bold
Wont ride in armed, and at the Soldan's chair
Defied the best of Panim chivalry
To mortal combat, or career with lance)
Thick swarmed, both on the ground and in the air,
Brushed with the hiss of rustling wings. As bees
In spring-time, when the Sun with Taurus rides,
Pour forth their populous youth about the hive
In clusters; they among fresh dews and flowers
Fly to and fro, or on the smoothèd plank,
The suburb of their straw-built citadel,
New rubbed with balm, expatiate and confer
Their state-affairs. So thick the aery crowd
Swarmed and were straightened; till, the signal given,
Behold a wonder! they but now who seemed
In bigness to surpass Earth's giant sons,
Now less than smallest dwarfs, in narrow room
Throng numberless, like that pygmean race
Beyond the Indian mount; or faery elves,
Whose midnight revels, by a forest-side
Or fountain, some belated peasant sees,
Or dreams he sees, while overhead the Moon
Sits arbitress, and nearer to the Earth
Wheels her pale course; they, on their mirth and dance
Intent, with jocund music charm his ear;
At once with joy and fear his heart rebounds.
Thus incorporeal Spirits to smallest forms
Reduced their shapes immense, and were at large,
Though without number still, amidst the hall
Of that infernal court. But far within,
And in their own dimensions like themselves,
The great Seraphic Lords and Cherubim
In close recess and secret conclave sat,
A thousand demi-gods on golden seats,
Frequent and full. After short silence then,
And summons read, the great consult began.

SIR JOHN SUCKLING (1609–1642)

A DOUBT OF MARTYRDOM

O for some honest lover's ghost,
  Some kind unbodied post
    Sent from the shades below!
    I strangely long to know
Whether the noble chaplets wear
Those that their mistress' scorn did bear
    Or those that were used kindly.

For whatsoe'er they tell us here
  To make those sufferings dear,
    'Twill there, I fear, be found
    That to the being crown'd
T' have loved alone will not suffice,
Unless we also have been wise
    And have our loves enjoy'd.

What posture can we think him in
  That, here unloved, again
    Departs, and 's thither gone
    Where each sits by his own?
Or how can that Elysium be
Where I my mistress still must see
    Circled in other's arms?

For there the judges all are just,
  And Sophronisba must
    Be his whom she held dear,
    Not his who loved her here.
The sweet Philoclea, since she died,
Lies by her Pirocles his side,
    Not by Amphialus.

Some bays, perchance, or myrtle bough
  For difference crowns the brow
    Of those kind souls that were
    The noble martyrs here:
And if that be the only odds
(As who can tell?), ye kinder gods,
    Give me the woman here!

THE CONSTANT LOVER

Out upon it, I have loved
  Three whole days together!
And am like to love three more,
  If it prove fair weather.

Time shall moult away his wings
  Ere he shall discover
In the whole wide world again
  Such a constant lover.

But the spite on't is, no praise
  Is due at all to me:
Love with me had made no stays,
  Had it any been but she.

Had it any been but she,
  And that very face,
There had been at least ere this
  A dozen dozen in her place.

WHY SO PALE AND WAN?

Why so pale and wan, fond lover?
  Prithee, why so pale?
Will, when looking well can't move her,
  Looking ill prevail?
  Prithee, why so pale?

Why so dull and mute, young sinner?
  Prithee, why so mute?
Will, when speaking well can't win her,
  Saying nothing do 't?
  Prithee, why so mute?

Quit, quit for shame! This will not move;
  This cannot take her.
If of herself she will not love,
  Nothing can make her:
  The devil take her!

SAMUEL BUTLER (1612–1680)

HUDIBRAS

PART I. From CANTO I

We grant, altho' he had much wit,
H' was very shy of using it,
As being loath to wear it out;
And therefore bore it not about,
Unless on holidays or so,
As men their best apparel do.
Beside, 'tis known he could speak Greek
As naturally as pigs squeak;
That Latin was no more difficile,
Than to a blackbird 'tis to whistle:
Being rich in both, he never scanted
His bounty unto such as wanted;
But much of either would afford
To many that had not one word.
For Hebrew roots, altho' they're found
To flourish most in barren ground,
He had such plenty as sufficed
To make some think him circumcised:
And truly so perhaps he was,
'Tis many a pious Christian's case.
  He was in logic a great critic,
Profoundly skill'd in analytic:
He could distinguish, and divide
A hair 'twixt south and south-west side;
On either which he would dispute,
Confute, change hands, and still confute.
He'd undertake to prove, by force
Of argument, a man's no horse;
He'd prove a buzzard is no fowl,
And that a lord may be an owl,
A calf an alderman, a goose a justice,
And rooks committee-men and trustees.
He'd run in debt by disputation,
And pay with ratiocination.
All this by syllogism, true
In mood and figure, he would do.
  For rhetoric, he could not ope
His mouth, but out there flew a trope;
And when he happen'd to break off
I' th' middle of his speech, or cough,
H' had hard words ready to show why,
And tell what rules he did it by;
Else, when with greatest art he spoke,
You'd think he talk'd like other folk:
For all a rhetorician's rules
Teach nothing but to name his tools.
But, when he pleased to show't, his speech
In loftiness of sound was rich;
A Babylonish dialect,
Which learnèd pedants much affect;
It was a party-colour'd dress
Of patch'd and piebald languages:
'Twas English cut on Greek and Latin,
Like fustian heretofore on satin;
It had an odd promiscuous tone,
As if h' had talk'd three parts in one;
Which made some think, when he did gabble,
Th' had heard three labourers of Babel,
Or Cerberus himself pronounce
A leash of languages at once.
This he as volubly would vent
As if his stock would ne'er be spent;
And truly, to support that charge,
He had supplies as vast and large;
For he could coin or counterfeit
New words, with little or no wit;
Words so debased and hard, no stone
Was hard enough to touch them on;
And, when with hasty noise he spoke 'em,
The ignorant for current took 'em;
That had the orator, who once
Did fill his mouth with pebble stones
When he harangued, but known his phrase,
He would have used no other ways.
  In mathematics he was greater

Than Tycho Brahe, or Erra Pater;
For he, by geometric scale,
Could take the size of pots of ale;
Resolve by sines and tangents, straight,
If bread or butter wanted weight;
And wisely tell what hour o' th' day
The clock does strike, by algebra.
Beside, he was a shrewd philosopher,
And had read every text and gloss over;
Whate'er the crabbed'st author hath,
He understood b' implicit faith;
Whatever sceptic could inquire for,
For every why he had a wherefore;
Knew more than forty of them do,
As far as words and terms could go;
All which he understood by rote,
And, as occasion served, would quote;
No matter whether right or wrong,
They might be either said or sung,
His notions fitted things so well,
That which was which he could not tell,
But oftentimes mistook the one
For th' other, as great clerks have done.
He could reduce all things to acts,
And knew their natures by abstracts;
Where Entity and Quiddity,
The ghosts of defunct bodies, fly;
Where truth in person does appear,
Like words congeal'd in northern air.
He knew what's what, and that's as high
As metaphysic wit can fly:
In school divinity as able
As he that hight Irrefragable;
A second Thomas, or at once
To name them all, another Dunce:
Profound in all the Nominal
And Real ways beyond them all;
For he a rope of sand could twist
As tough as learnèd Sorbonist;
And weave fine cobwebs, fit for skull
That's empty when the moon is full;
Such as take lodgings in a head
That's to be let unfurnishèd.
He could raise scruples dark and nice,
And after solve 'em in a trice;
As if Divinity had catch'd
The itch, on purpose to be scratch'd;
Or, like a mountebank, did wound
And stab herself with doubts profound,
Only to show with how small pain
The sores of Faith are cured again;
Altho' by woful proof we find
They always leave a scar behind.
He knew the seat of Paradise,
Could tell in what degree it lies;
And, as he was disposed, could prove it
Below the moon, or else above it;
What Adam dreamt of, when his bride
Came from her closet in his side;
Whether the devil tempted her
By a High Dutch interpreter;
If either of them had a navel;
Who first made music malleable;
Whether the Serpent, at the Fall,
Had cloven feet, or none at all:
All this, without a gloss or comment,
He could unriddle in a moment,
In proper terms, such as men smatter
When they throw out, and miss the matter.
For his religion, it was fit
To match his learning and his wit:
'Twas Presbyterian true blue;
For he was of that stubborn crew
Of errant Saints, whom all men grant
To be the true Church Militant;
Such as do build their faith upon
The holy text of pike and gun;
Decide all controversies by
Infallible artillery;
And prove their doctrine orthodox
By apostolic blows and knocks;
Call fire, and sword, and desolation,
A godly, thorough Reformation,
Which always must be carried on,
And still be doing, never done;
As if Religion were intended
For nothing else but to be mended.

RICHARD CRASHAW (1613?–1649)

IN THE HOLY NATIVITY OF OUR LORD GOD

A HYMN SUNG AS BY THE SHEPHERDS

CHORUS

Come, we shepherds, whose blest sight
Hath met Love's noon in Nature's night;
Come, lift we up our loftier song
And wake the sun that lies too long.

To all our world of well-stol'n joy
He slept, and dreamt of no such thing;
While we found out heaven's fairer eye
And kissed the cradle of our King.
Tell him he rises now, too late
To show us aught worth looking at.

Tell him we now can show him more
Than he e'er showed to mortal sight;

Than he himself e'er saw before;
Which to be seen needs not his light.
Tell him, Tityrus, where th' hast been
Tell him, Thyrsis, what th' hast seen.

TITYRUS. Gloomy night embraced the place
Where the noble Infant lay.
The Babe looked up and showed His face;
In spite of darkness, it was day.
It was Thy day, Sweet! and did rise
Not from the east, but from Thine eyes.

CHORUS. It was Thy day, Sweet . . .

THYRSIS. Winter chid aloud; and sent
The angry North to wage his wars.
The North forgot his fierce intent;
And left perfumes instead of scars.
By those sweet eyes' persuasive powers,
Where he meant frost he scattered flowers.

CHO. By those sweet eyes . . .

BOTH. We saw Thee in Thy balmy nest,
Young Dawn of our Eternal Day!
We saw Thine eyes break from their east
And chase the trembling shades away.
We saw Thee, and we blest the sight,
We saw Thee by Thine own sweet light.

TIT. Poor World, said I, what wilt thou do
To entertain this starry Stranger?
Is this the best thou canst bestow?
A cold, and not too cleanly, manger?
Contend, the powers of heaven and earth,
To fit a bed for this huge birth!

CHO. Contend the powers . . .

THYR. Proud World, said I; cease your contest
And let the mighty Babe alone;
The phœnix builds the phœnix' nest,
Love's architecture is his own;
The Babe whose birth embraves this morn,
Made His own bed e'er He was born.

CHO. The Babe whose . . .

TIT. I saw the curl'd drops, soft and slow,
Come hovering o'er the place's head;
Off'ring their whitest sheets of snow
To furnish the fair Infant's bed.
Forbear, said I; be not too bold;
Your fleece is white, but 'tis too cold.

CHO. Forbear, said I . . .

THYR. I saw the obsequious seraphim
Their rosy fleece of fire bestow,
For well they now can spare their wings
Since Heaven itself lies here below.
Well done, said I; but are you sure
Your down so warm, will pass for pure?

CHO. Well done, said I . . .

TIT. No, no, your King's not yet to seek
Where to repose His royal head;
See, see how soon His new-bloomed cheek
'Twixt mother's breasts is gone to bed!
Sweet choice, said we! no way but so
Not to lie cold, yet sleep in snow.

CHO. Sweet choice, said we . . .

BOTH. We saw Thee in Thy balmy nest,
Bright Dawn of our Eternal Day!
We saw Thine eyes break from their east
And chase the trembling shades away.
We saw Thee, and we blest the sight,
We saw Thee by Thine own sweet Light.

CHO. We saw Thee . . .

FULL CHORUS

Welcome, all wonders in one night!
Eternity shut in a span,
Summer in winter, day in night,
Heaven in earth, and God in man.
Great Little One! Whose all-embracing birth
Lifts earth to heaven, stoops heaven to earth.

Welcome — though nor to gold nor silk,
To more than Cæsar's birthright is;
Two sister-seas of virgin-milk
With many a rarely-tempered kiss
That breathes at once both maid and mother,
Warms in the one, cools in the other.

Welcome — though not to those gay flies
Gilded i' th' beams of earthly kings,
Slippery souls in smiling eyes —
But to poor shepherds, homespun things,
Whose wealth's their flock, whose wit's to be
Well read in their simplicity.

Yet, when young April's husband show'rs
Shall bless the fruitful Maia's bed,
We'll bring the first-born of her flow'rs
To kiss Thy feet and crown Thy head.

To Thee, dread Lamb! Whose love must keep
The shepherds, more than they the sheep.

To Thee, meek Majesty! soft King
Of simple graces and sweet loves!
Each of us his lamb will bring,
Each his pair of silver doves!
Till burnt at last in fire of Thy fair eyes,
Ourselves become our own best sacrifice!

SIR JOHN DENHAM (1615–1669)

FROM COOPER'S HILL

My eye, descending from the hill, surveys
Where Thames amongst the wanton valleys strays;
Thames, the most loved of all the Ocean's sons,
By his old sire to his embraces runs,
Hasting to pay his tribute to the sea,
Like mortal life to meet eternity;
Though with those streams he no resemblance hold,
Whose foam is amber, and their gravel gold,
His genuine and less guilty wealth to explore,
Search not his bottom, but survey his shore,
O'er which he kindly spreads his spacious wing,
And hatches plenty for th' ensuing spring;
Nor then destroys it with too fond a stay,
Like mothers which their infants overlay,
Nor, with a sudden and impetuous wave,
Like profuse kings, resumes the wealth he gave;
No unexpected inundations spoil
The mower's hopes, nor mock the ploughman's toil,
But godlike his unwearied bounty flows,
First loves to do, then loves the good he does;
Nor are his blessings to his banks confined,
But free and common as the sea or wind;
When he to boast or to disperse his stores,
Full of the tributes of his grateful shores,
Visits the world, and in his flying towers,
Brings home to us, and makes both Indies ours,
Finds wealth where 'tis, bestows it where it wants,
Cities in deserts, woods in cities plants;
So that to us no thing, no place is strange,
While his fair bosom is the world's exchange.
O could I flow like thee, and make thy stream
My great example, as it is my theme!
Though deep, yet clear, though gentle, yet not dull,
Strong without rage, without o'erflowing full.

ON MR. ABRAHAM COWLEY'S DEATH AND BURIAL AMONGST THE ANCIENT POETS

Old Chaucer, like the morning star,
To us discovers day from far.
His light those mists and clouds dissolved,
Which our dark nation long involved;
But he descending to the shades,
Darkness again the age invades.
Next (like Aurora) Spenser rose,
Whose purple blush the day foreshews;
The other three, with his own fires
Phœbus, the poets' God, inspires;
By Shakespear, Jonson, Fletcher's lines,
Our stage's lustre Rome's outshines:
These poets near our princes sleep,
And in one grave their mansion keep;
They liv'd to see so many days,
Till time had blasted all their bays;
But cursèd be the fatal hour
That pluck'd the fairest, sweetest flower
That in the muses' garden grew,
And amongst wither'd laurels threw.
Time, which made them their fame outlive,
To Cowley scarce did ripeness give.
Old mother wit, and nature, gave
Shakespear and Fletcher all they have;
In Spenser, and in Jonson, art
Of slower nature got the start;
But both in him so equal are,
None knows which bears the happiest share;
To him no author was unknown,
Yet what he wrote was all his own;
He melted not the ancient gold,
Nor, with Ben Jonson, did make bold
To plunder all the Roman stores
Of poets, and of orators:
Horace's wit, and Virgil's state,
He did not steal, but emulate:
And when he would like them appear,
Their garb, but not their clothes, did wear:

* * * * * * * *

RICHARD LOVELACE (1618–1658)

TO LUCASTA, GOING TO THE WARS

Tell me not, Sweet, I am unkind,
That from the nunnery
Of thy chaste breast and quiet mind
To war and arms I fly.

True, a new mistress now I chase,
The first foe in the field;
And with a stronger faith embrace
A sword, a horse, a shield.

Yet this inconstancy is such
As thou too shalt adore;
I could not love thee, Dear, so much,
Loved I not Honour more.

From THE GRASSHOPPER

O Thou that swing'st upon the waving hair
Of some well-fillèd oaten beard,
Drunk every night with a delicious tear
Dropt thee from heaven, where thou wert rear'd.

The joys of earth and air are thine entire,
That with thy feet and wings dost hop and fly;
And when thy poppy works, thou dost retire
To thy carved acorn-bed to lie.

Up with the day, the sun thou welcom'st then,
Sport'st in the gilt plaits of his beams,
And all these merry days mak'st merry, men,
Thyself, and melancholy streams.

TO ALTHEA, FROM PRISON

When Love with unconfinèd wings
Hovers within my gates,
And my divine Althea brings
To whisper at the grates;
When I lie tangled in her hair
And fetter'd to her eye,
The birds that wanton in the air
Know no such liberty.

When flowing cups run swiftly round
With no allaying Thames,
Our careless heads with roses bound,
Our hearts with loyal flames;
When thirsty grief in wine we steep,
When healths and draughts go free —
Fishes that tipple in the deep
Know no such liberty.

When, like committed linnets, I
With shriller throat shall sing
The sweetness, mercy, majesty,
And glories of my King;
When I shall voice aloud how good
He is, how great should be,
Enlargèd winds, that curl the flood,
Know no such liberty.

Stone walls do not a prison make,
Nor iron bars a cage;
Minds innocent and quiet take
That for an hermitage;
If I have freedom in my love
And in my soul am free,
Angels alone, that soar above,
Enjoy such liberty.

ABRAHAM COWLEY (1618–1667)

THE SWALLOW

Foolish prater, what dost thou
So early at my window do?
Cruel bird, thou'st ta'en away
A dream out of my arms to-day;
A dream that ne'er must equall'd be
By all that waking eyes may see.
Thou this damage to repair
Nothing half so sweet and fair,
Nothing half so good, canst bring,
Tho' men say thou bring'st the Spring.

ON THE DEATH OF MR. WILLIAM HERVEY

It was a dismal and a fearful night:
Scarce could the Morn drive on th' unwilling Light,
When Sleep, Death's image, left my troubled breast
By something liker Death possest.
My eyes with tears did uncommanded flow,
And on my soul hung the dull weight
Of some intolerable fate.
What bell was that? Ah me! too much I know!

My sweet companion and my gentle peer,
Why hast thou left me thus unkindly here,
Thy end forever and my life to moan?
O, thou hast left me all alone!
Thy soul and body, when death's agony
Besieged around thy noble heart,
Did not with more reluctance part
Than I, my dearest friend, do part from thee.

My dearest friend, would I had died for thee!
Life and this world henceforth will tedious be!
Nor shall I know hereafter what to do
If once my griefs prove tedious too.
Silent and sad I walk about all day,
As sullen ghosts stalk speechless by
Where their hid treasures lie;
Alas! my treasure's gone; why do I stay?

Say, for you saw us, ye immortal lights,
How oft unwearied have we spent the nights,

Till the Ledæan stars, so famed for love,
Wonder'd at us from above!
We spent them not in toys, in lusts, or wine;
But search of deep philosophy,
With eloquence, and poetry —
Arts which I loved, for they, my friend, were thine.

Ye fields of Cambridge, our dear Cambridge, say
Have ye not seen us walking every day?
Was there a tree about which did not know
The love betwixt us two?
Henceforth, ye gentle trees, forever fade;
Or your sad branches thicker join
And into darksome shades combine,
Dark as the grave wherein my friend is laid!

Large was his soul: as large a soul as e'er
Submitted to inform a body here;
High as the place 'twas shortly in heaven to have,
But low and humble as his grave.
So high that all the virtues there did come,
As to their chiefest seat
Conspicuous and great;
So low, that for me too it made a room.

Knowledge he only sought, and so soon caught
As if for him knowledge had rather sought;
Nor did more learning ever crowded lie
In such a short mortality.
Whene'er the skilful youth discoursed or writ,
Still did the notions throng
About his eloquent tongue;
Nor could his ink flow faster than his wit.

His mirth was the pure spirits of various wit,
Yet never did his God or friends forget;
And when deep talk and wisdom came in view,
Retired, and gave to them their due,
For the rich help of books he always took,
Though his own searching mind before
Was so with notions written o'er,
As if wise Nature had made that her book.

With as much zeal, devotion, piety,
He always lived, as other saints do die.
Still with his soul severe account he kept,
Weeping all debts out ere he slept.
Then down in peace and innocence he lay,
Like the sun's laborious light,
Which still in water sets at night,
Unsullied with his journey of the day.

But happy thou, ta'en from this frantic age,
Where ignorance and hypocrisy does rage!
A fitter time for heaven no soul e'er chose —
The place now only free from those.
There 'mong the blest thou dost forever shine;
And wheresoe'er thou casts thy view
Upon that white and radiant crew,
See'st not a soul clothed with more light than thine.

THE WISH

Well then! I now do plainly see
This busy world and I shall ne'er agree.
The very honey of all earthly joy
Does of all meats the soonest cloy;
And they, methinks, deserve my pity
Who for it can endure the stings,
The crowd and buzz and murmurings,
Of this great hive, the city.

Ah, yet, ere I descend to the grave
May I a small house and large garden have;
And a few friends, and many books, both true,
Both wise, and both delightful too!
And since love ne'er will from me flee,
A Mistress moderately fair,
And good as guardian angels are,
Only beloved and loving me.

O fountains! when in you shall I
Myself eased of unpeaceful thoughts espy?
O fields! O woods! when, when shall I be made
The happy tenant of your shade?
Here's the spring-head of Pleasure's flood:
Here's wealthy Nature's treasury,
Where all the riches lie that she
Has coin'd and stamp'd for good.

Pride and ambition here
Only in far-fetch'd metaphors appear;
Here nought but winds can hurtful murmurs scatter,
And nought but Echo flatter.
The gods, when they descended, hither
From heaven did always choose their way:
And therefore we may boldly say
That 'tis the way too thither.

How happy here should I
And one dear She live, and embracing die!
She who is all the world, and can exclude
In deserts solitude.
I should have then this only fear:
Lest men, when they my pleasures see,
Should hither throng to live like me,
And so make a city here.

ANDREW MARVELL (1621–1678)

THE GARDEN

How vainly men themselves amaze,
To win the palm, the oak, or bays,
And their incessant labours see
Crowned from some single herb or tree
Whose short and narrow-vergèd shade
Does prudently their toils upbraid,
While all the flowers and trees do close
To weave the garlands of repose!

Fair Quiet, have I found thee here,
And Innocence, thy sister dear?
Mistaken long, I sought you then
In busy companies of men.
Your sacred plants, if here below,
Only among the plants will grow;
Society is all but rude
To this delicious solitude.

No white nor red was ever seen
So amorous as this lovely green.
Fond lovers, cruel as their flame,
Cut in these trees their mistress' name.
Little, alas! they know or heed,
How far these beauties hers exceed!
Fair trees! wheres'e'er your barks I wound
No name shall but your own be found.

When we have run our passion's heat,
Love hither makes his best retreat.
The gods, that mortal beauty chase,
Still in a tree did end their race;
Apollo hunted Daphne so,
Only that she might laurel grow;
And Pan did after Syrinx speed,
Not as a nymph, but for a reed.

What wondrous life is this I lead!
Ripe apples drop about my head;
The luscious clusters of the vine
Upon my mouth do crush their wine;
The nectarine, and curious peach,
Into my hands themselves do reach;
Stumbling on melons, as I pass,
Insnared with flowers, I fall on grass.

Meanwhile the mind, from pleasure less,
Withdraws into its happiness; —
The mind, that ocean where each kind
Does straight its own resemblance find;
Yet it creates, transcending these,
Far other worlds, and other seas,
Annihilating all that's made
To a green thought in a green shade.

Here at the fountain's sliding foot,
Or at some fruit-tree's mossy root,
Casting the body's vest aside,
My soul into the boughs does glide:
There, like a bird, it sits and sings,
Then whets and combs its silver wings,
And, till prepared for longer flight,
Waves in its plumes the various light.

Such was that happy garden-state,
While man there walked without a mate
After a place so pure and sweet,
What other help could yet be meet!
But 'twas beyond a mortal's share
To wander solitary there:
Two paradises 'twere in one,
To live in paradise alone.

How well the skilful gardener drew
Of flowers, and herbs, this dial new;
Where, from above, the milder sun
Does through a fragrant zodiac run,
And, as it works, the industrious bee
Computes its time as well as we!
How could such sweet and wholesome hours
Be reckoned but with herbs and flowers?

TO HIS COY MISTRESS

Had we but world enough, and time,
This coyness, Lady, were no crime,
We would sit down and think which way
To walk and pass our long love's day.
Thou by the Indian Ganges' side
Shouldst rubies find; I by the tide
Of Humber would complain. I would
Love you ten years before the Flood,
And you should, if you please, refuse
Till the conversion of the Jews.
My vegetable love should grow
Vaster than empires, and more slow;
An hundred years should go to praise
Thine eyes and on thy forehead gaze;
Two hundred to adore each breast,
But thirty thousand to the rest;
An age at least to every part,
And the last age should show your heart.
For, Lady, you deserve this state,
Nor would I love at lower rate.
  But at my back I always hear
Time's wingèd chariot hurrying near;
And yonder all before us lie
Deserts of vast eternity.
Thy beauty shall no more be found,
Nor, in thy marble vault, shall sound
My echoing song; then worms shall try

That long preserved virginity,
And your quaint honour turn to dust,
And into ashes all my lust:
The grave's a fine and private place,
But none, I think, do there embrace.
  Now therefore, while the youthful hue
Sits on thy skin like morning dew,
And while thy willing soul transpires
At every pore with instant fires,
Now let us sport us while we may,
And now, like amorous birds of prey,
Rather at once our time devour
Than languish in his slow-chapt power.
Let us roll all our strength and all
Our sweetness up into one ball,
And tear our pleasures with rough strife
Thorough the iron gates of life:
Thus, though we cannot make our sun
Stand still, yet we will make him run.

HENRY VAUGHAN (1622–1695)

THE RETREAT

Happy those early days, when I
Shined in my angel-infancy!
Before I understood this place
Appointed for my second race,
Or taught my soul to fancy ought
But a white, celestial thought;
When yet I had not walked above
A mile or two from my first love,
And looking back — at that short space —
Could see a glimpse of His bright face;
When on some gilded cloud or flower
My gazing soul would dwell an hour,
And in those weaker glories spy
Some shadows of eternity;
Before I taught my tongue to wound
My conscience with a sinful sound,
Or had the black art to dispense,
A several sin to every sense,
But felt through all this fleshly dress
Bright shoots of everlastingness.
  O how I long to travel back,
And tread again that ancient track!
That I might once more reach that plain,
Where first I left my glorious train;
From whence the enlightened spirit sees
That shady city of palm trees.
But ah! my soul with too much stay
Is drunk, and staggers in the way!
Some men a forward motion love,
But I by backward steps would move;
And when this dust falls to the urn,
In that state I came, return.

From THE WORLD

I saw Eternity the other night,
Like a great ring of pure and endless light,
All calm, as it was bright;
And round beneath it Time in hours, days, years,
    Driven by the spheres
Like a vast shadow moved; in which the world
    And all her train were hurled.

BEHIND THE VEIL

They are all gone into the world of light!
  And I alone sit lingering here;
Their very memory is fair and bright,
  And my sad thoughts doth clear.

It glows and glitters in my cloudy breast,
  Like stars upon some gloomy grove,
Or those faint beams in which this hill is drest,
  After the sun's remove.

I see them walking in an air of glory,
  Whose light doth trample on my days:
My days, which are at best but dull and hoary,
  Mere glimmering and decays.

O holy Hope! and high Humility,
  High as the heavens above!
These are your walks, and you have showed them me,
  To kindle my cold love.

Dear, beauteous Death! the jewel of the just,
  Shining nowhere, but in the dark,
What mysteries do lie beyond thy dust,
  Could man outlook that mark!

He that hath found some fledged bird's nest, may know
  At first sight if the bird be flown;
But what fair well or grove he sings in now,
  That is to him unknown.

And yet as angels in some brighter dreams
  Call to the soul, when man doth sleep,
So some strange thoughts transcend our wonted themes,
  And into glory peep.

If a star were confined into a tomb,
  The captive flames must needs burn there;
But when the hand that locked her up, gives room,
  She'll shine through all the sphere.

O Father of eternal life, and all
  Created glories under Thee,
Resume Thy spirit from this world of thrall
  Into true liberty. 36

Either disperse these mists, which blot and fill
  My perspective still as they pass;
Or else remove me hence unto that hill,
  Where I shall need no glass. 40

THE TIMBER

Sure thou didst flourish once; and many springs,
  Many bright mornings, much dew, many showers,
Pass'd o'er thy head; many light hearts and wings,
  Which now are dead, lodged in thy living bowers.

And still a new succession sings and flies;
  Fresh groves grow up, and their green branches shoot
Towards the old and still enduring skies,
  While the low violet thrives at their root.

But thou beneath the sad and heavy line 9
  Of death dost waste, all senseless, cold, and dark;
Where not so much as dreams of light may shine,
  Nor any thought of greenness, leaf, or bark.

And yet — as if some deep hate and dissent,
  Bred in thy growth betwixt high winds and thee,
Were still alive — thou dost great storms resent
  Before they come, and know'st how near they be.

Else all at rest thou liest, and the fierce breath
  Of tempests can no more disturb thy ease;
But this thy strange resentment after death 19
  Means only those who broke in life thy peace.

THE RESTORATION

JOHN DRYDEN (1631–1700)

From STANZAS ON OLIVER CROMWELL

And now 'tis time; for their officious haste
  Who would before have borne him to the sky,
Like eager Romans, ere all rites were past,
  Did let too soon the sacred eagle fly.

Though our best notes are treason to his fame
  Joined with the loud applause of public voice,
Since Heaven what praise we offer to his name
  Hath rendered too authentic by its choice;

Though in his praise no arts can liberal be,
  Since they, whose Muses have the highest flown,
Add not to his immortal memory,
  But do an act of friendship to their own;

Yet 'tis our duty and our interest too
  Such monuments as we can build to raise,
Lest all the world prevent what we should do,
  And claim a title in him by their praise.

How shall I then begin or where conclude
  To draw a fame so truly circular?
For in a round what order can be shewed,
  Where all the parts so equal-perfect are?

His grandeur he derived from Heaven alone,
  For he was great, ere Fortune made him so;
And wars, like mists that rise against the sun,
  Made him but greater seem, not greater grow.

No borrowed bays his temples did adorn,
  But to our crown he did fresh jewels bring;
Nor was his virtue poisoned, soon as born,
  With the too early thoughts of being king.

From ASTRÆA REDUX

  And welcome now, great Monarch, to your own!
Behold the approaching cliffs of Albion.
It is no longer motion cheats your view;
As you meet it, the land approacheth you.
The land returns, and in the white it wears
The marks of penitence and sorrow bears.
But you, whose goodness your descent doth show,
Your heavenly parentage and earthly too,
By that same mildness which your father's crown
Before did ravish shall secure your own.
Not tied to rules of policy, you find
Revenge less sweet than a forgiving mind.
Thus, when the Almighty would to Moses give
A sight of all he could behold and live,
A voice before His entry did proclaim
Long-suffering, goodness, mercy, in His name.
Your power to justice doth submit your cause,
Your goodness only is above the laws,
Whose rigid letter, while pronounced by you,
Is softer made. So winds that tempests brew,
When through Arabian groves they take their flight,
Made wanton with rich odours, lose their spite.
And as those lees that trouble it refine
The agitated soul of generous wine,
So tears of joy, for your returning spilt,
Work out and expiate our former guilt.
Methinks I see those crowds on Dover's strand,
Who in their haste to welcome you to land
Choked up the beach with their still growing store
And made a wilder torrent on the shore:
While, spurred with eager thoughts of past delight,
Those who had seen you, court a second sight,
Preventing still your steps and making haste
To meet you often wheresoe'er you past.
How shall I speak of that triumphant day,
When you renewed the expiring pomp of May!
A month that owns an interest in your name;
You and the flowers are its peculiar claim.
That star, that at your birth shone out so bright
It stained the duller sun's meridian light,
Did once again its potent fires renew,
Guiding our eyes to find and worship you.

From ANNUS MIRABILIS

The morn they look on with unwilling eyes,
  Till from their maintop joyful news they hear
Of ships which by their mould bring new supplies
  And in their colours Belgian lions bear.

Our watchful General had discerned from far
  This mighty succour, which made glad the foe;
He sighed, but, like a father of the war,
  His face spake hope, while deep his sorrows flow.

His wounded men he first sends off to shore,
  Never till now unwilling to obey:
They not their wounds but want of strength deplore
  And think them happy who with him can stay.

Then to the rest, "Rejoice," said he, "to-day!
  In you the fortune of Great Britain lies;
Among so brave a people you are they
  Whom Heaven has chose to fight for such a prize.

"If number English courages could quell,
  We should at first have shunned, not met our foes,
Whose numerous sails the fearful only tell;
  Courage from hearts and not from numbers grows."

He said, nor needed more to say: with haste
  To their known stations cheerfully they go;
And all at once, disdaining to be last,
  Solicit every gale to meet the foe.

Nor did the encouraged Belgians long delay,
  But bold in others, not themselves, they stood,
So thick our navy scarce could sheer their way,
  But seemed to wander in a moving wood.

Our little fleet was now engaged so far
  That like the sword-fish in the whale they fought;
The combat only seemed a civil war,
  Till through their bowels we our passage wrought.

Never had valour, no, not ours before,
  Done aught like this upon the land or main;
Where not to be o'ercome was to do more
  Than all the conquests former kings did gain.

* * * * * * *
* * * * * * *

No help avails; for, hydra-like, the fire
  Lifts up his hundred heads to aim his way;
And scarce the wealthy can one half retire
  Before he rushes in to share the prey.

The rich grow suppliant and the poor grow proud:
  Those offer mighty gain and these ask more;
So void of pity is the ignoble crowd,
  When others' ruin may increase their store.

As those who live by shores with joy behold
  Some wealthy vessel split or stranded nigh,
And from the rocks leap down for shipwrecked gold
  And seek the tempest which the others fly:

So these but wait the owners' last despair
  And what's permitted to the flames invade;
Even from their jaws they hungry morsels tear
  And on their backs the spoils of Vulcan lade.

The days were all in this lost labour spent;
  And when the weary King gave place to night,
His beams he to his royal brother lent,
  And so shone still in his reflective light.

Night came, but without darkness or repose,
  A dismal picture of the general doom;
Where souls distracted, when the trumpet blows,
  And half unready, with their bodies come.

Those who have homes, when home they do repair,
  To a last lodging call their wandering friends;
Their short uneasy sleeps are broke with care,
  To look how near their own destruction tends:

Those who have none sit round where once it was
  And with full eyes each wonted room require,
Haunting the yet warm ashes of the place,
  As murdered men walk where they did expire.

Some stir up coals and watch the vestal fire,
  Others in vain from sight of ruin run
And, while through burning labyrinths they retire,
  With loathing eyes repeat what they would shun.

The most in fields like herded beasts lie down,
  To dews obnoxious on the grassy floor;
And while their babes in sleep their sorrows drown,
  Sad parents watch the remnants of their store.

While by the motion of the flames they guess
  What streets are burning now, and what are near,
An infant, waking, to the paps would press
  And meets instead of milk a falling tear.

No thought can ease them but their Sovereign's care
  Whose praise the afflicted as their comfort sing;
Even those whom want might drive to just despair
  Think life a blessing under such a King.

From ABSALOM AND ACHITOPHEL

Of these the false Achitophel was first,
A name to all succeeding ages curst:
For close designs and crooked counsels fit,
Sagacious, bold, and turbulent of wit,
Restless, unfixed in principles and place,
In power unpleased, impatient of disgrace:
A fiery soul, which, working out its way,
Fretted the pigmy body to decay
And o'er-informed the tenement of clay.
A daring pilot in extremity,

Pleased with the danger, when the waves went high,
He sought the storms; but, for a calm unfit,
Would steer too nigh the sands to boast his wit.
Great wits are sure to madness near allied
And thin partitions do their bounds divide;
Else, why should he, with wealth and honour blest,
Refuse his age the needful hours of rest?
Punish a body which he could not please,
Bankrupt of life, yet prodigal of ease?
And all to leave what with his toil he won
To that unfeathered two-legg'd thing, a son,
Got, while his soul did huddled notions try,
And born a shapeless lump, like anarchy.
In friendship false, implacable in hate,
Resolved to ruin or to rule the state;
To compass this the triple bond he broke,
The pillars of the public safety shook,
And fitted Israel for a foreign yoke;
Then, seized with fear, yet still affecting fame,
Usurped a patriot's all-atoning name.
So easy still it proves in factious times
With public zeal to cancel private crimes.
How safe is treason and how sacred ill,
Where none can sin against the people's will,
Where crowds can wink and no offence be known,
Since in another's guilt they find their own!
Yet fame deserved no enemy can grudge;
The statesman we abhor, but praise the judge.
In Israel's courts ne'er sat an Abbethdin
With more discerning eyes or hands more clean,
Unbribed, unsought, the wretched to redress,
Swift of despatch and easy of access.
Oh! had he been content to serve the crown
With virtues only proper to the gown,
Or had the rankness of the soil been freed
From cockle that oppressed the noble seed,
David for him his tuneful harp had strung
And Heaven had wanted one immortal song.
But wild ambition loves to slide, not stand,
And fortune's ice prefers to virtue's land.
Achitophel, grown weary to possess
A lawful fame and lazy happiness,
Disdained the golden fruit to gather free
And lent the crowd his arm to shake the tree.
Now, manifest of crimes contrived long since,
He stood at bold defiance with his prince,
Held up the buckler of the people's cause
Against the crown, and skulked behind the laws.
The wished occasion of the plot he takes;
Some circumstances finds, but more he makes;
By buzzing emissaries fills the ears
Of listening crowds with jealousies and fears
Of arbitrary counsels brought to light,
And proves the king himself a Jebusite.
Weak arguments! which yet he knew full well
Were strong with people easy to rebel.
For governed by the moon, the giddy Jews
Tread the same track when she the prime renews;
And once in twenty years their scribes record,
By natural instinct they change their lord.
Achitophel still wants a chief, and none
Was found so fit as warlike Absalon.
Not that he wished his greatness to create,
For politicians neither love nor hate;
But, for he knew his title not allowed
Would keep him still depending on the crowd,
That kingly power, thus ebbing out, might be
Drawn to the dregs of a democracy.

* * * * * * *

A numerous host of dreaming saints succeed
Of the true old enthusiastic breed:
'Gainst form and order they their power employ,
Nothing to build and all things to destroy.
But far more numerous was the herd of such
Who think too little and who talk too much.
These out of mere instinct, they knew not why,
Adored their fathers' God and property,
And by the same blind benefit of Fate
The Devil and the Jebusite did hate:
Born to be saved even in their own despite,
Because they could not help believing right.
Such were the tools; but a whole Hydra more
Remains of sprouting heads too long to score.
Some of their chiefs were princes of the land;
In the first rank of these did Zimri stand,
A man so various that he seemed to be
Not one, but all mankind's epitome:
Stiff in opinions, always in the wrong,
Was everything by starts and nothing long;
But in the course of one revolving moon
Was chymist, fiddler, statesman, and buffoon;
Then all for women, painting, rhyming, drinking,
Besides ten thousand freaks that died in thinking.
Blest madman, who could every hour employ
With something new to wish or to enjoy!
Railing and praising were his usual themes,
And both, to show his judgment, in extremes:
So over violent or over civil
That every man with him was God or Devil.
In squandering wealth was his peculiar art;
Nothing went unrewarded but desert.
Beggared by fools whom still he found too late,
He had his jest, and they had his estate.
He laughed himself from Court; then sought relief
By forming parties, but could ne'er be chief:
For spite of him, the weight of business fell
On Absalom and wise Achitophel;
Thus wicked but in will, of means bereft,
He left not faction, but of that was left.

* * * * * * * *

From RELIGIO LAICI

Oh, but, says one, Tradition set aside,
Where can we hope for an unerring guide?
For since the original Scripture has been lost
All copies disagreeing, maimed the most,
Or Christian faith can have no certain ground
Or truth in Church tradition must be found.
Such an omniscient Church we wish indeed;
'Twere worth both Testaments, and cast in the Creed;
But if this mother be a guide so sure
As can all doubts resolve, all truth secure,
Then her infallibility as well
Where copies are corrupt or lame can tell;
Restore lost canon with as little pains,
As truly explicate what still remains;
Which yet no Council dare pretend to do,
Unless, like Esdras, they could write it new;
Strange confidence, still to interpret true,
Yet not be sure that all they have explained
Is in the blest original contained.
More safe and much more modest 'tis to say,
God would not leave mankind without a way;
And that the Scriptures, though not everywhere
Free from corruption, or entire, or clear,
Are uncorrupt, sufficient, clear, entire,
In all things which our needful faith require.
If others in the same glass better see,
'Tis for themselves they look, but not for me;
For my salvation must its doom receive,
Not from what others, but what I, believe.
Must all tradition then be set aside?
This to affirm were ignorance or pride.
Are there not many points, some needful sure
To saving faith, that Scripture leaves obscure,
Which every sect will wrest a several way?
For what one sect interprets, all sects may.
We hold, and say we prove from Scripture plain,
That Christ is God; the bold Socinian
From the same Scripture urges he's but man.
Now what appeal can end the important suit?
Both parts talk loudly, but the rule is mute.
Shall I speak plain, and in a nation free
Assume an honest layman's liberty?
I think, according to my little skill,
To my own mother Church submitting still,
That many have been saved, and many may,
Who never heard this question brought in play.
The unlettered Christian, who believes in gross,
Plods on to Heaven and ne'er is at a loss;
For the strait gate would be made straiter yet,
Were none admitted there but men of wit.
The few by Nature formed, with learning fraught,
Born to instruct, as others to be taught,
Must study well the sacred page; and see
Which doctrine, this or that, does best agree
With the whole tenour of the work divine,
And plainliest points to Heaven's revealed design;
Which exposition flows from genuine sense,
And which is forced by wit and eloquence.

From THE HIND AND THE PANTHER

A milk-white Hind, immortal and unchanged,
Fed on the lawns and in the forest ranged;
Without unspotted, innocent within,
She feared no danger, for she knew no sin.
Yet had she oft been chased with horns and hounds
And Scythian shafts, and many wingèd wounds
Aimed at her heart; was often forced to fly,
And doomed to death, though fated not to die.
Not so her young; for their unequal line
Was hero's make, half human, half divine.
Their earthly mould obnoxious was to fate,
The immortal part assumed immortal state.
Of these a slaughtered army lay in blood,
Extended o'er the Caledonian wood,
Their native walk; whose vocal blood arose
And cried for pardon on their perjured foes.
Their fate was fruitful, and the sanguine seed,
Endued with souls, increased the sacred breed.
So captive Israel multiplied in chains,
A numerous exile, and enjoyed her pains.
With grief and gladness mixed, their mother viewed
Her martyred offspring and their race renewed;
Their corps to perish, but their kind to last,
So much the deathless plant the dying fruit surpassed.
Panting and pensive now she ranged alone,
And wandered in the kingdoms once her own.
The common hunt, though from their rage restrained
By sovereign power, her company disdained,
Grinned as they passed, and with a glaring eye
Gave gloomy signs of secret enmity.
'Tis true she bounded by and tripped so light,
They had not time to take a steady sight;
For truth has such a face and such a mien
As to be loved needs only to be seen.
The bloody Bear, an Independent beast,
Unlicked to form, in groans her hate expressed.
Among the timorous kind the quaking Hare
Professed neutrality, but would not swear.
Next her the buffoon Ape, as atheists use,
Mimicked all sects and had his own to choose;
Still when the Lion looked, his knees he bent,
And paid at church a courtier's compliment.
The bristled Baptist Boar, impure as he,
But whitened with the foam of sanctity,
With fat pollutions filled the sacred place,

And mountains levelled in his furious race:
So first rebellion founded was in grace.
But, since the mighty ravage which he made
In German forests had his guilt betrayed,
With broken tusks and with a borrowed name,
He shunned the vengeance and concealed the shame,
So lurked in sects unseen. With greater guile
False Reynard fed on consecrated spoil;
The graceless beast by Athanasius first
Was chased from Nice, then by Socinus nursed,
His impious race their blasphemy renewed,
And nature's king through nature's optics viewed;
Reversed they viewed him lessened to their eye,
Nor in an infant could a God descry.
New swarming sects to this obliquely tend,
Hence they began, and here they all will end.

* * * * * * *

But if they think at all, 'tis sure no higher
Than matter put in motion may aspire;
Souls that can scarce ferment their mass of clay,
So drossy, so divisible are they
As would but serve pure bodies for allay,
Such souls as shards produce, such beetle things
As only buzz to heaven with evening wings,
Strike in the dark, offending but by chance,
Such are the blindfold blows of ignorance.
They know not beings, and but hate a name;
To them the Hind and Panther are the same.
 The Panther, sure the noblest next the Hind,
And fairest creature of the spotted kind;
Oh, could her inborn stains be washed away,
She were too good to be a beast of prey!
How can I praise or blame, and not offend,
Or how divide the frailty from the friend?
Her faults and virtues lie so mixed, that she
Nor wholly stands condemned nor wholly free.
Then, like her injured Lion, let me speak;
He cannot bend her and he would not break.
Unkind already, and estranged in part,
The Wolf begins to share her wandering heart.
Though unpolluted yet with actual ill,
She half commits who sins but in her will.
If, as our dreaming Platonists report,
There could be spirits of a middle sort,
Too black for heaven and yet too white for hell,
Who just dropped half-way down, nor lower fell;
So poised, so gently she descends from high,
It seems a soft dismission from the sky.
Her house not ancient, whatsoe'er pretence
Her clergy heralds make in her defence;
A second century not half-way run,
Since the new honours of her blood begun.

A SONG FOR ST. CECILIA'S DAY, NOVEMBER 22, 1687

From harmony, from heavenly harmony
 This universal frame began;
When Nature underneath a heap
 Of jarring atoms lay,
And could not heave her head,
The tuneful voice was heard from high,
 Arise, ye more than dead.

Then cold and hot and moist and dry
 In order to their stations leap,
 And Music's power obey.
From harmony, from heavenly harmony,
 This universal frame began:
 From harmony to harmony
Through all the compass of the notes it ran,
The diapason closing full in Man.

What passion cannot Music raise and quell?
 When Jubal struck the chorded shell,
His listening brethren stood around,
 And, wondering, on their faces fell
To worship that celestial sound:
Less than a god they thought there could not dwell
 Within the hollow of that shell,
 That spoke so sweetly, and so well.
What passion cannot Music raise and quell?

The trumpet's loud clangour
 Excites us to arms
With shrill notes of anger
 And mortal alarms.
The double, double, double beat
 Of the thundering drum
 Cries, hark! the foes come;
Charge, charge, 'tis too late to retreat!
 The soft complaining flute
 In dying notes discovers
 The woes of hopeless lovers,
Whose dirge is whispered by the warbling lute.

Sharp violins proclaim
Their jealous pangs and desperation,
Fury, frantic indignation,
Depth of pains and height of passion,
 For the fair, disdainful dame.

But oh! what art can teach,
What human voice can reach
 The sacred organ's praise?
Notes inspiring holy love,
Notes that wing their heavenly ways
 To mend the choirs above.

Orpheus could lead the savage race,
And trees unrooted left their place,
Sequacious of the lyre;
But bright Cecilia raised the wonder higher;
When to her organ vocal breath was given,
An angel heard, and straight appeared,
Mistaking earth for heaven.

GRAND CHORUS

As from the power of sacred lays
The spheres began to move,
And sung the great Creator's praise
To all the bless'd above;
So when the last and dreadful hour
This crumbling pageant shall devour,
The trumpet shall be heard on high,
The dead shall live, the living die,
And Music shall untune the sky.

ALEXANDER'S FEAST; OR, THE POWER OF MUSIC

A SONG IN HONOUR OF ST. CECILIA'S DAY, 1697

'Twas at the royal feast for Persia won
By Philip's warlike son:
Aloft in awful state
The godlike hero sate
On his imperial throne;
His valiant peers were placed around;
Their brows with roses and with myrtles bound:
(So should desert in arms be crowned.)
The lovely Thais, by his side,
Sate like a blooming Eastern bride,
In flower of youth and beauty's pride.
Happy, happy, happy pair!
None but the brave,
None but the brave,
None but the brave deserves the fair.

CHORUS

Happy, happy, happy pair!
None but the brave,
None but the brave,
None but the brave deserves the fair.

Timotheus, placed on high
Amid the tuneful quire,
With flying fingers touched the lyre:
The trembling notes ascend the sky,
And heavenly joys inspire.
The song began from Jove,
Who left his blissful seats above,
(Such is the power of mighty love)
A dragon's fiery form belied the god:
Sublime on radiant spires he rode,
When he to fair Olympia pressed;
And while he sought her snowy breast,
Then round her slender waist he curled,
And stamped an image of himself, a sovereign of the world.
The listening crowd admire the lofty sound,
A present deity, they shout around;
A present deity, the vaulted roofs rebound:
With ravished ears
The monarch hears,
Assumes the god,
Affects to nod,
And seems to shake the spheres.

CHORUS

With ravished ears
The monarch hears,
Assumes the god,
Affects to nod,
And seems to shake the spheres.

The praise of Bacchus then the sweet musician sung,
Of Bacchus ever fair, and ever young.
The jolly god in triumph comes;
Sound the trumpets, beat the drums;
Flushed with a purple grace
He shows his honest face:
Now give the hautboys breath; he comes, he comes.
Bacchus, ever fair and young,
Drinking joys did first ordain;
Bacchus' blessings are a treasure,
Drinking is the soldier's pleasure;
Rich the treasure,
Sweet the pleasure,
Sweet is pleasure after pain.

CHORUS

Bacchus' blessings are a treasure,
Drinking is the soldier's pleasure;
Rich the treasure,
Sweet the pleasure,
Sweet is pleasure after pain.

Soothed with the sound the king grew vain;
Fought all his battles o'er again;

And thrice he routed all his foes, and thrice he slew the slain.
The master saw the madness rise,
His glowing cheeks, his ardent eyes;
And while he heaven and earth defied,
Changed his hand, and checked his pride.
He chose a mournful Muse,
Soft pity to infuse;
He sung Darius great and good,
By too severe a fate,
Fallen, fallen, fallen, fallen,
Fallen from his high estate,
And weltering in his blood;
Deserted at his utmost need
By those his former bounty fed;
On the bare earth exposed he lies,
With not a friend to close his eyes.
With downcast looks the joyless victor sate,
Revolving in his altered soul
The various turns of chance below:
And, now and then, a sigh he stole,
And tears began to flow.

CHORUS

Revolving in his altered soul
The various turns of chance below;
And, now and then, a sigh he stole,
And tears began to flow.

The mighty master smiled to see
That love was in the next degree;
'Twas but a kindred-sound to move,
For pity melts the mind to love.
Softly sweet, in Lydian measures,
Soon he soothed his soul to pleasures.
War, he sung, is toil and trouble;
Honour but an empty bubble;
Never ending, still beginning,
Fighting still, and still destroying:
If the world be worth thy winning,
Think, O think it worth enjoying:
Lovely Thais sits beside thee,
Take the good the gods provide thee.
The many rend the skies with loud applause:
So Love was crowned, but Music won the cause.
The prince, unable to conceal his pain,
Gazed on the fair
Who caused his care,
And sighed and looked, sighed and looked,
Sighed and looked, and sighed again;
At length, with love and wine at once oppressed,
The vanquished victor sunk upon her breast.

CHORUS

The prince, unable to conceal his pain,
Gazed on the fair
Who caused his care,
And sighed and looked, sighed and looked,
Sighed and looked, and sighed again;
At length, with love and wine at once oppressed,
The vanquished victor sunk upon her breast.

Now strike the golden lyre again;
A louder yet, and yet a louder strain.
Break his bands of sleep asunder,
And rouse him, like a rattling peal of thunder.
Hark, hark, the horrid sound
Has raised up his head;
As awaked from the dead,
And, amazed, he stares around.
"Revenge, revenge!" Timotheus cries;
"See the Furies arise;
See the snakes that they rear,
How they hiss in their hair,
And the sparkles that flash from their eyes?
Behold a ghastly band,
Each a torch in his hand!
Those are Grecian ghosts, that in battle were slain,
And unburied remain
Inglorious on the plain:
Give the vengeance due
To the valiant crew.
Behold how they toss their torches on high,
How they point to the Persian abodes,
And glittering temples of their hostile gods."
The princes applaud with a furious joy;
And the king seized a flambeau with zeal to destroy;
Thais led the way,
To light him to his prey,
And, like another Helen, fired another Troy.

CHORUS

And the king seized a flambeau with zeal to destroy;
Thais led the way,
To light him to his prey,
And, like another Helen, fired another Troy.

Thus long ago,
Ere heaving bellows learned to blow,
While organs yet were mute,
Timotheus, to his breathing flute
And sounding lyre,
Could swell the soul to rage, or kindle soft desire.
At last divine Cecilia came,
Inventress of the vocal frame;
The sweet enthusiast, from her sacred store,
Enlarged the former narrow bounds,

And added length to solemn sounds,
With Nature's mother-wit, and arts unknown before.
Let old Timotheus yield the prize,
Or both divide the crown:
He raised a mortal to the skies;
She drew an angel down.

Grand Chorus

At last divine Cecilia came,
Inventress of the vocal frame;
The sweet enthusiast, from her sacred store,
Enlarged the former narrow bounds,
And added length to solemn sounds,
With Nature's mother-wit, and arts unknown before.
Let old Timotheus yield the prize,
Or both divide the crown:
He raised a mortal to the skies;
She drew an angel down.

LINES PRINTED UNDER THE ENGRAVED PORTRAIT OF MILTON

(In Tonson's folio edition of the Paradise Lost, 1688)

Three poets, in three distant ages born,
Greece, Italy, and England did adorn.
The first in loftiness of thought surpassed,
The next in majesty, in both the last.
The force of Nature could no farther go;
To make a third she joined the former two.

EARL OF ROSCOMMON (1633?–1685)

From AN ESSAY ON TRANSLATED VERSE

What I have instanced only in the best,
Is, in proportion, true of all the rest.
Take pains the genuine meaning to explore;
There sweat, there strain; tug the laborious oar;
Search every comment that your care can find;
Some here, some there, may hit the poet's mind.
Yet be not blindly guided by the throng;
The multitude is always in the wrong.
When things appear unnatural or hard,
Consult your author, with himself compared.
Who knows what blessing Phœbus may bestow,
And future ages to your labours owe?
Such secrets are not easily found out;
But, once discover'd, leave no room for doubt.
Truth stamps conviction in your ravish'd breast;
And peace and joy attend the glorious guest.
Truth still is one; Truth is divinely bright;
No cloudy doubts obscure her native light;
While in your thoughts you find the least debate,
You may confound, but never can translate.
Your style will this through all disguises show;
For none explain more clearly than they know.
He only proves he understands a text,
Whose exposition leaves it unperplex'd.
They who too faithfully on names insist,
Rather create than dissipate the mist;
And grow unjust by being over nice,
(For superstitious virtue turns to vice.)
Let Crassus' ghost and Labienus tell
How twice in Parthian plains their legions fell.
Since Rome hath been so jealous of her fame,
That few know Pacorus' or Monæses' name.
Words in one language elegantly used,
Will hardly in another be excused;
And some that Rome admired in Cæsar's time
May neither suit our genius nor our clime.
The genuine sense, intelligibly told,
Shows a translator both discreet and bold.
Excursions are inexpiably bad;
And 'tis much safer to leave out than add.
Abstruse and mystic thought you must express
With painful care, but seeming easiness;
For Truth shines brightest through the plainest dress.

CHARLES SACKVILLE, EARL OF DORSET (1638–1706)

SONG

To all you ladies now at land
We men at sea indite;
But first would have you understand
How hard it is to write:
The Muses now, and Neptune too,
We must implore to write to you —
With a fa, la, la, la, la!

For though the Muses should prove kind,
And fill our empty brain,
Yet if rough Neptune rouse the wind
To wave the azure main,
Our paper, pen, and ink, and we,
Roll up and down our ships at sea —
With a fa, la, la, la, la!

Then if we write not by each post,
Think not we are unkind;
Nor yet conclude our ships are lost
By Dutchmen or by wind:

Our tears we'll send a speedier way,
The tide shall bring them twice a day —
With a fa, la, la, la, la!

The King with wonder and surprise
Will swear the seas grow bold,
Because the tides will higher rise
Than e'er they did of old;
But let him know it is our tears
Bring floods of grief to Whitehall stairs —
With a fa, la, la, la, la!

Should foggy Opdam chance to know
Our sad and dismal story,
The Dutch would scorn so weak a foe,
And quit their fort at Goree;
For what resistance can they find
From men who've left their hearts behind? —
With a fa, la, la, la, la!

Let wind and weather do its worst,
Be you to us but kind;
Let Dutchmen vapour, Spaniards curse,
No sorrow we shall find;
'Tis then no matter how things go,
Or who's our friend, or who's our foe —
With a fa, la, la, la, la!

To pass our tedious hours away
We throw a merry main,
Or else at serious ombre play;
But why should we in vain
Each other's ruin thus pursue?
We were undone when we left you —
With a fa, la, la, la, la!

But now our fears tempestuous grow
And cast our hopes away,
Whilst you, regardless of our woe,
Sit careless at a play,
Perhaps permit some happier man
To kiss your hand, or flirt your fan —
With a fa, la, la, la, la!

When any mournful tune you hear
That dies in every note,
As if it sigh'd with each man's care
For being so remote,
Think then how often love we've made
To you, when all those tunes were play'd —
With a fa, la, la, la, la!

In justice you cannot refuse
To think of our distress,
When we for hopes of honour lose
Our certain happiness:
All those designs are but to prove
Ourselves more worthy of your love —
With a fa, la, la, la, la!

And now we've told you all our loves,
And likewise all our fears,
In hopes this declaration moves
Some pity for our tears:
Let's hear of no inconstancy —
We have too much of that at sea —
With a fa, la, la, la, la!

SIR CHARLES SEDLEY (1639?–1701)

TO CELIA

Not, Celia, that I juster am,
Or better than the rest;
For I would change each hour like them
Were not my heart at rest.

But I am tied to very thee,
By every thought I have;
Thy face I only care to see,
Thy heart I only crave.

All that in woman is adored
In thy dear self I find;
For the whole sex can but afford
The handsome and the kind.

Why then should I seek further store
And still make love anew?
When change itself can give no more,
'Tis easy to be true.

SONG

Love still has something of the sea,
From whence his Mother rose;
No time his slaves from love can free,
Nor give their thoughts repose.

They are becalm'd in clearest days,
And in rough weather tost;
They wither under cold delays,
Or are in tempests lost.

One while they seem to touch the port,
Then straight into the main
Some angry wind in cruel sport
Their vessel drives again.

At first disdain and pride they fear,
Which, if they chance to 'scape,
Rivals and falsehood soon appear
In a more dreadful shape.

By such degrees to joy they come,
And are so long withstood,
So slowly they receive the sum,
It hardly does them good.

'Tis cruel to prolong a pain;
  And to defer a bliss,
Believe me, gentle Hermione,
  No less inhuman is.

An hundred thousand oaths your fears
  Perhaps would not remove,
And if I gazed a thousand years,
  I could no deeper love.

SONG

Phillis is my only joy,
  Faithless as the winds or seas,
Sometimes cunning, sometimes coy,
  Yet she never fails to please;
    If with a frown
    I am cast down,
    Phillis smiling
    And beguiling
Makes me happier than before.

Though alas! too late I find
  Nothing can her fancy fix,
Yet the moment she is kind
  I forgive her with her tricks;
    Which though I see,
    I can't get free, —
    She deceiving,
    I believing, —
What need lovers wish for more?

JOHN WILMOT, EARL OF ROCHESTER (1647-1680)

LOVE AND LIFE

All my past life is mine no more;
  The flying hours are gone,
Like transitory dreams given o'er,
Whose images are kept in store
  By memory alone.

The time that is to come is not;
  How can it then be mine?
The present moment's all my lot;
And that, as fast as it is got,
  Phillis, is only thine.

Then talk not of inconstancy,
  False hearts, and broken vows;
If I by miracle can be
This live-long minute true to thee,
  'Tis all that Heaven allows.

TO HIS MISTRESS

Why dost thou shade thy lovely face? O why
Does that eclipsing hand of thine deny
The sunshine of the Sun's enlivening eye?

Without thy light what light remains in me?
Thou art my life; my way, my light's in thee;
I live, I move, and by thy beams I see.

Thou art my life — if thou but turn away
My life's a thousand deaths. Thou art my way —
Without thee, Love, I travel not but stray.

My light thou art — without thy glorious sight
My eyes are darken'd with eternal night.
My Love, thou art my way, my life, my light.

Thou art my way; I wander if thou fly.
Thou art my light; if hid, how blind am I!
Thou art my life; if thou withdraw'st, I die.

My eyes are dark and blind, I cannot see:
To whom or whither should my darkness flee,
But to that light? — and who's that light but thee?

If I have lost my path, dear lover, say,
Shall I still wander in a doubtful way?
Love, shall a lamb of Israel's sheepfold stray?

My path is lost, my wandering steps do stray;
I cannot go, nor can I safely stay;
Whom should I seek but thee, my path, my way?

And yet thou turn'st thy face away and fly'st me!
And yet I sue for grace and thou deny'st me!
Speak, art thou angry, Love, or only try'st me?

Thou art the pilgrim's path, the blind man's eye,
The dead man's life. On thee my hopes rely:
If I but them remove, I surely die.

Dissolve thy sunbeams, close thy wings and stay!
See, see how I am blind, and dead, and stray!
— O thou art my life, my light, my way!

Then work thy will! If passion bid me flee,
My reason shall obey, my wings shall be
Stretch'd out no farther than from me to thee!

EPITAPH ON CHARLES II

Here lies our Sovereign Lord the King,
  Whose word no man relies on,
Who never said a foolish thing,
  Nor ever did a wise one.

THOMAS OTWAY (1652–1685)

THE ENCHANTMENT

I did but look and love awhile,
  'Twas but for one half-hour;
Then to resist I had no will,
  And now I have no power.

To sigh and wish is all my ease;
  Sighs which do heat impart
Enough to melt the coldest ice,
  Yet cannot warm your heart.

O would your pity give my heart
  One corner of your breast,
'Twould learn of yours the winning art
  And quickly steal the rest.

JOHN OLDHAM (1653–1683)

From A SATIRE DISSUADING FROM POETRY

'Tis so, 'twas ever so, since heretofore
The blind old bard, with dog and bell before,
Was fain to sing for bread from door to door:
The needy muses all turn'd Gipsies then,
And, of the begging-trade, e'er since have been:

*   *   *   *   *   *   *

My own hard usage here I need not press
Where you have ev'ry day before your face
Plenty of fresh resembling instances:
Great Cowley's muse the same ill treatment had,
Whose verse shall live forever to upbraid
Th' ungrateful world, that left such worth unpaid.
Waller himself may thank inheritance,
For what he else had never got by sense.
On Butler who can think without just rage,
The glory, and the scandal of the age?
Fair stood his hopes, when first he came to town,
Met, ev'ry where, with welcomes of renown,
Courted, caress'd by all, with wonder read,
And promises of princely favour fed;
But what reward for all had he at last,
After a life in dull expectance pass'd?
The wretch, at summing up his misspent days,
Found nothing left, but poverty, and praise?
Of all his gains by verse he could not save
Enough to purchase flannel, and a grave:
Reduc'd to want, he, in due time, fell sick,
Was fain to die, and be interr'd on tick;
And well might bless the fever that was sent,
To rid him hence, and his worse fate prevent.
  You've seen what fortune other poets share;
View next the factors of the theatre:
That constant mart, which all the year does hold,
Where staple wit is barter'd, bought, and sold.
Here trading scriblers for their maintenance,
And livelihood, trust to a lott'ry-chance.
But who his parts would in the service spend,
Where all his hopes on vulgar breath depend?
Where ev'ry sot, for paying half a crown,
Has the prerogative to cry him down.
Sedley indeed may be content with fame,
Nor care, should an ill-judging audience damn;
But Settle, and the rest, that write for pence,
Whose whole estate's an ounce or two of brains,
Should a thin house on the third day appear,
Must starve, or live in tatters all the year.
And what can we expect that's brave and great,
From a poor needy wretch, that writes to eat?
Who the success of the next play must wait
For lodging, food, and clothes, and whose chief care
Is how to spunge for the next meal, and where?

THE AGE OF CLASSICISM

SIR SAMUEL GARTH (1661–1719)

From THE DISPENSARY

Speak, Goddess! since 'tis thou that best canst tell
How ancient leagues to modern discord fell;
And why physicians were so cautious grown
Of others' lives, and lavish of their own;
How by a journey to the Elysian plain,
Peace triumphed, and old time returned again.
  Not far from that most celebrated place
Where angry Justice shews her awful face;
Where little villains must submit to fate,
That great ones may enjoy the world in state;
There stands a dome, majestic to the sight,
And sumptuous arches bear its oval height;
A golden globe, placed high with artful skill,
Seems to the distant sight a gilded pill;
This pile was, by the pious patron's aim,
Raised for a use as noble as its frame;
Nor did the learn'd Society decline
The propagation of that great design;
In all her mazes, Nature's face they viewed,
And, as she disappeared, their search pursued.
Wrapt in the shade of night the goddess lies,
Yet to the learn'd unveils her dark disguise,
But shuns the gross access of vulgar eyes.
  Now she unfolds the faint and dawning strife
Of infant atoms kindling into life;
How ductile matter new meanders takes,
And slender trains of twisting fibres makes;
And how the viscous seeks a closer tone,
By just degrees to harden into bone;
While the more loose flow from the vital urn,
And in full tides of purple streams return;
How lambent flames from life's bright lamps arise,
And dart in emanations through the eyes;
How from each sluice a gentle torrent pours,
To slake a feverish heat with ambient showers;
Whence their mechanic powers the spirits claim;
How great their force, how delicate their frame;
How the same nerves are fashioned to sustain
The greatest pleasure and the greatest pain;
Why bilious juice a golden light puts on,
And floods of chyle in silver currents run;
How the dim speck of entity began
To extend its recent form, and stretch to man;

* * * * * * *

  Hence 'tis we wait the wondrous cause to find
How body acts upon impassive mind;
How fumes of wine the thinking part can fire,
Past hopes revive, and present joys inspire;
Why our complexions oft our soul declare,
And how the passions in the features are;
How touch and harmony arise between
Corporeal figure and a form unseen;
How quick their faculties the limbs fulfil,
And act at every summons of the will;
With mighty truths, mysterious to descry,
Which in the womb of distant causes lie.

LADY WINCHILSEA (1661–1720)

THE PETITION FOR AN ABSOLUTE RETREAT

Give me, O indulgent Fate!
Give me yet, before I die,
A sweet, but absolute retreat,
'Mongst paths so lost, and trees so high,
That the world may ne'er invade,
Through such windings and such shade,
My unshaken liberty.

  No intruders thither come,
Who visit, but to be from home;
None who their vain moments pass,
Only studious of their glass.
News, that charm to listning ears,
That false alarm to hopes and fears,
That common theme for every fop,
From the statesman to the shop,
In those coverts ne'er be spread.
Of who's deceas'd, or who's to wed,
Be no tidings thither brought,
But silent, as a midnight thought,
Where the world may ne'er invade,
Be those windings, and that shade!

Courteous Fate! afford me there
A table spread without my care
With what the neighb'ring fields impart,
Whose cleanliness be all its art.
When of old the calf was drest —
Tho' to make an angel's feast —
In the plain, unstudied sauce
Nor truffle, nor morillia was;
Nor could the mighty patriarch's board
One far-fetch'd ortolane afford.
Courteous Fate, then give me there
Only plain and wholesome fare.
Fruits indeed, would Heaven bestow,
All, that did in Eden grow, —
All, but the forbidden tree,
Would be coveted by me:
Grapes, with juice so crowded up
As breaking thro' the native cup;
Figs, yet growing, candied o'er
By the sun's attracting power;
Cherries, with the downy peach,
All within my easy reach;
Whilst, creeping near the humble ground,
Should the strawberry be found,
Springing wheresoe'er I strayed,
Thro' those windings and that shade.

For my garments, let them be
What may with the time agree;
Warm, when Phœbus does retire,
And is ill-supplied by fire;
But when he renews the year
And verdant all the fields appear,
Beauty every thing resumes,
Birds have dropt their winter-plumes;
When the lily full displayed
Stands in purer white arrayed
Than that vest which heretofore
The luxurious monarch wore
When from Salem's gates he drove
To the soft retreat of love,
Lebanon's all burnish'd house,
And the dear Egyptian spouse, —
Clothe me, Fate, tho' not so gay,
Clothe me light, and fresh as May.
In the fountains let me view
All my habit cheap and new,
Such as, when sweet zephyrs fly,
With their motions may comply,
Gently waving, to express
Unaffected carelessness.
No perfumes have there a part,
Borrow'd from the chymist's art;
But such as rise from flow'ry beds,
Or the falling jasmin sheds!
'Twas the odour of the field
Esau's rural coat did yield
That inspir'd his Father's prayer
For blessings of the earth and air.
Of gums or powders had it smelt,
The supplanter, then unfelt,
Easily had been descry'd
For one that did in tents abide,
For some beauteous handmaid's joy
And his mother's darling boy.
Let me then no fragrance wear
But what the winds from gardens bear
In such kind, surprising gales
As gather'd from Fidentia's vales
All the flowers that in them grew;
Which intermixing, as they flew,
In wreathen garlands dropt again
On Lucullus, and his men,
Who, cheer'd by the victorious sight
Trebled numbers put to flight.
Let me, when I must be fine,
In such natural colours shine;
Wove, and painted by the sun,
Whose resplendent rays to shun,
When they do too fiercely beat,
Let me find some close retreat
Where they have no passage made
Thro' those windings, and that shade.

TO THE NIGHTINGALE

Exert thy voice, sweet harbinger of Spring!
This moment is thy time to sing,
This moment I attend to praise,
And set my numbers to thy lays.
Free as thine shall be my song;
As thy music, short, or long.
Poets, wild as thee, were born,
Pleasing best when unconfin'd,
When to please is least design'd,
Soothing but their cares to rest;
Cares do still their thoughts molest,
And still th' unhappy poet's breast,
Like thine, when best he sings, is plac'd against a thorn.
She begins, let all be still!
Muse, thy promise now fulfil!
Sweet, oh! sweet, still sweeter yet!
Can thy words such accents fit?
Canst thou syllables refine,
Melt a sense that shall retain
Still some spirit of the brain,
Till with sounds like these it join?
'Twill not be! then change thy note;
Let division shake thy throat.
Hark! division now she tries;

Yet as far the muse outflies.
Cease then, prithee, cease thy tune;
Trifler, wilt thou sing till June?
Till thy bus'ness all lies waste,
And the time of building's past!
Thus we poets that have speech,
Unlike what thy forests teach,
If a fluent vein be shown
That's transcendent to our own,
Criticise, reform, or preach,
Or censure what we cannot reach.

A NOCTURNAL REVERIE

In such a night, when every louder wind
Is to its distant cavern safe confin'd,
And only gentle zephyr fans his wings,
And lonely Philomel, still waking, sings;
Or from some tree, fam'd for the owl's delight,
She, hollowing clear, directs the wand'rer right;
In such a night, when passing clouds give place,
Or thinly vail the Heav'ns mysterious face;
When in some river, overhung with green,
The waving moon and trembling leaves are seen;
When freshen'd grass now bears itself upright,
And makes cool banks to pleasing rest invite,
Whence springs the woodbind and the bramble-rose,
And where the sleepy cowslip shelter'd grows;
Whilst now a paler hue the foxglove takes,
Yet chequers still with red the dusky brakes;
When scatter'd glow-worms, but in twilight fine,
Show trivial beauties watch their hour to shine,
Whilst Salisb'ry stands the test of every light
In perfect charms and perfect virtue bright;
When odours which declin'd repelling day
Thro' temp'rate air uninterrupted stray;
When darken'd groves their softest shadows wear,
And falling waters we distinctly hear;
When thro' the gloom more venerable shows
Some ancient fabric, awful in repose,
While sunburnt hills their swarthy looks conceal
And swelling haycocks thicken up the vale;
When the loos'd horse now, as his pasture leads,
Comes slowly grazing thro' th' adjoining meads,
Whose stealing pace, and lengthen'd shade we fear,
Till torn up forage in his teeth we hear;
When nibbling sheep at large pursue their food,
And unmolested kine re-chew the cud;
When curlews cry beneath the village-walls,
And to her straggling brood the partridge calls;
Their shortliv'd jubilee the creatures keep,
Which but endures whilst tyrant-man does sleep;
When a sedate content the spirit feels,
And no fierce light disturb, whilst it reveals;
But silent musings urge the mind to seek
Something too high for syllables to speak;
Till the free soul to a compos'dness charm'd,
Finding the elements of rage disarm'd,
O'er all below a solemn quiet grown,
Joys in th' inferior world and thinks it like her own:
In such a night let me abroad remain
Till morning breaks and all's confus'd again;
Our cares, our toils, our clamours are renew'd,
Or pleasures, seldom reach'd, again pursu'd.

WILLIAM WALSH (1663–1708)

DEATH

What has this bugbear Death that's worth our care?
After a life in pain and sorrow past,
After deluding hope and dire despair,
Death only gives us quiet at the last.

How strangely are our love and hate misplaced!
Freedom we seek, and yet from freedom flee;
Courting those tyrant sins that chain us fast,
And shunning Death, that only sets us free.

'Tis not a foolish fear of future pains,
(Why should they fear who keep their souls from stains?)
That makes me dread thy terrors, Death, to see:
'Tis not the loss of riches, or of fame,
Or the vain toys the vulgar pleasures name;
'Tis nothing, Cælia, but the losing thee.

MATTHEW PRIOR (1664–1721)

A SONG

In vain you tell your parting lover,
You wish fair winds may waft him over.
Alas! what winds can happy prove,
That bear me far from what I love?
Alas! what dangers on the main
Can equal those that I sustain,
From slighted vows, and cold disdain?

Be gentle, and in pity choose
To wish the wildest tempests loose:
That thrown again upon the coast,
Where first my shipwrecked heart was lost,
I may once more repeat my pain;
Once more in dying notes complain
Of slighted vows, and cold disdain.

TO A CHILD OF QUALITY FIVE YEARS OLD

Lords, knights, and 'squires, the numerous band,
  That wear the fair Miss Mary's fetters,
Were summoned by her high command,
  To show their passions by their letters.

My pen among the rest I took,
  Lest those bright eyes that cannot read
Should dart their kindling fires, and look
  The power they have to be obeyed.

Nor quality, nor reputation,
  Forbid me yet my flame to tell,
Dear Five-years-old befriends my passion,
  And I may write till she can spell.

For, while she makes her silk-worms beds
  With all the tender things I swear;
Whilst all the house my passion reads,
  In papers round her baby's hair;

She may receive and own my flame,
  For, though the strictest prudes should know it,
She'll pass for a most virtuous dame,
  And I for an unhappy poet.

Then too, alas! when she shall tear
  The lines some younger rival sends;
She'll give me leave to write, I fear,
  And we shall still continue friends.

For, as our different ages move,
  'Tis so ordained, (would Fate but mend it!)
That I shall be past making love,
  When she begins to comprehend it.

A SIMILE

Dear Thomas, did'st thou never pop
Thy head into a tin-man's shop?
There, Thomas, did'st thou never see
('Tis but by way of simile!)
A squirrel spend his little rage
In jumping round a rolling cage?
The cage, as either side turned up,
Striking a ring of bells a-top? —
  Moved in the orb, pleased with the chimes,
The foolish creature thinks he climbs:
But here or there, turn wood or wire,
He never gets two inches higher.

  So fares it with those merry blades,
That frisk it under Pindus's shades.
In noble songs, and lofty odes,
They tread on stars, and talk with gods;
Still dancing in an airy round,
Still pleased with their own verses' sound;
Brought back, how fast soe'er they go,
Always aspiring, always low.

THE REMEDY WORSE THAN THE DISEASE

I sent for Ratcliffe; was so ill,
  That other doctors gave me over:
He felt my pulse, prescribed his pill,
  And I was likely to recover.

But when the wit began to wheeze,
  And wine had warm'd the politician,
Cured yesterday of my disease,
  I died last night of my physician.

TO HIS SOUL

TRANSLATED FROM THE LATIN OF HADRIAN

Poor little, pretty, fluttering thing,
  Must we no longer live together?
And dost thou prune thy trembling wing,
  To take thy flight thou know'st not whither?

Thy humorous vein, thy pleasing folly
  Lie all neglected, all forgot:
And pensive, wavering, melancholy,
  Thou dread'st and hop'st thou know'st not what.

JONATHAN SWIFT (1667–1745)

From VERSES ON THE DEATH OF DR. SWIFT

Vain human kind! fantastic race!
Thy various follies who can trace?
Self-love, ambition, envy, pride,
Their empire in our hearts divide.
Give others riches, power, and station,
'Tis all on me a usurpation.
I have no title to aspire;
Yet, when you sink, I seem the higher.
In Pope I cannot read a line
But with a sigh I wish it mine;
When he can in one couplet fix
More sense than I can do in six,
It gives me such a jealous fit
I cry, "Pox take him and his wit!"
I grieve to be outdone by Gay
In my own humorous biting way.

Arbuthnot is no more my friend,
Who dares to irony pretend,
Which I was born to introduce,
Refined it first, and show'd its use.
St. John, as well as Pultney, knows
That I had some repute for prose;
And, till they drove me out of date,
Could maul a minister of state.
If they have mortified my pride,
And made me throw my pen aside:
If with such talents Heaven has bless'd 'em,
Have I not reason to detest 'em?

* * * * * * *

From Dublin soon to London spread,
'Tis told at court, "the Dean is dead."
And Lady Suffolk, in the spleen,
Runs laughing up to tell the queen.
The queen, so gracious, mild, and good,
Cries, "Is he gone: 'tis time he should.
He's dead, you say; then let him rot:
I'm glad the medals were forgot.
I promised him, I own; but when?
I only was the princess then;
But now, as consort of the king,
You know, 'tis quite another thing."
Now Chartres, at Sir Robert's levee,
Tells with a sneer the tidings heavy:
"Why, if he died without his shoes,"
Cries Bob, "I'm sorry for the news:
O, were the wretch but living still,
And in his place my good friend Will!
Or had a mitre on his head,
Provided Bolingbroke were dead!"
Now Curll his shop from rubbish drains:
Three genuine tomes of Swift's remains!
And then, to make them pass the glibber,
Revised by Tibbalds, Moore, and Cibber.
He'll treat me as he does my betters,
Publish my will, my life, my letters:
Revive the libels born to die;
Which Pope must bear, as well as I.
Here shift the scene, to represent
How those I love my death lament.
Poor Pope would grieve a month, and Gay
A week, and Arbuthnot a day.
St. John himself will scarce forbear
To bite his pen, and drop a tear.
The rest will give a shrug, and cry,
"I'm sorry — but we all must die!"

* * * * * * *

Suppose me dead; and then suppose
A club assembled at the Rose;
Where, from discourse of this and that,
I grow the subject of their chat.
And while they toss my name about,
With favour some, and some without,
One, quite indifferent in the cause,
My character impartial draws:
"The Dean, if we believe report,
Was never ill-received at court.
As for his works in verse and prose,
I own myself no judge of those;
Nor can I tell what critics thought 'em,
But this I know, all people bought 'em.
As with a moral view design'd
To cure the vices of mankind,
His vein, ironically grave,
Exposed the fool, and lash'd the knave.
To steal a hint was never known,
But what he writ was all his own.
"He never thought an honour done him,
Because a duke was proud to own him;
Would rather slip aside and choose
To talk with wits in dirty shoes;
Despised the fools with stars and garters,
So often seen caressing Chartres.
He never courted men in station,
Nor persons held in admiration;
Of no man's greatness was afraid,
Because he sought for no man's aid.
Though trusted long in great affairs
He gave himself no haughty airs.
Without regarding private ends,
Spent all his credit for his friends;
And only chose the wise and good;
No flatterers; no allies in blood:
But succour'd virtue in distress,
And seldom fail'd of good success;
As numbers in their hearts must own,
Who, but for him, had been unknown.

* * * * * * *

"Perhaps I may allow the Dean
Had too much satire in his vein;
And seem'd determined not to starve it,
Because no age could more deserve it.
Yet malice never was his aim;
He lash'd the vice, but spared the name;
No individual could resent,
Where thousands equally were meant;
His satire points at no defect,
But what all mortals may correct;
For he abhorr'd that senseless tribe
Who call it humour when they gibe:
He spared a hump, or crooked nose,
Whose owners set not up for beaux.
True genuine dullness moved his pity,
Unless it offer'd to be witty.
Those who their ignorance confest,
He ne'er offended with a jest;
But laugh'd to hear an idiot quote

A verse from Horace learn'd by rote.
"He knew a hundred pleasing stories,
With all the turns of Whigs and Tories:
Was cheerful to his dying day;
And friends would let him have his way.
"He gave the little wealth he had
To build a house for fools and mad;
And show'd by one satiric touch,
No nation wanted it so much."

STELLA'S BIRTHDAY, MARCH 13, 1726

This day, whate'er the Fates decree,
Shall still be kept with joy by me.
This day then let us not be told
That you are sick, and I grown old;
Nor think on our approaching ills,
And talk of spectacles and pills.
To-morrow will be time enough
To hear such mortifying stuff.
Yet, since from reason may be brought
A better and more pleasing thought,
Which can in spite of all decays
Support a few remaining days,
From not the gravest of divines
Accept for once some serious lines.
Altho' we now can form no more
Long schemes of life, as heretofore;
Yet you, while time is running fast,
Can look with joy on what is past.
Were future happiness and pain
A mere contrivance of the brain,
As atheists argue, to entice
And fit their proselytes for vice,
(The only comfort they propose,
To have companions in their woes)
Grant this the case; yet sure 'tis hard
That virtue, styled its own reward
And by all sages understood
To be the chief of human good,
Should acting die, nor leave behind
Some lasting pleasure in the mind,
Which, by remembrance, will assuage
Grief, sickness, poverty, and age;
And strongly shoot a radiant dart
To shine thro' life's declining part.
Say, Stella, feel you no content,
Reflecting on a life well spent?
Your skilful hand employ'd to save
Despairing wretches from the grave;
And then supporting with your store
Those whom you dragg'd from death before.
So Providence on mortals waits,
Preserving what it first creates.
Your generous boldness to defend
An innocent and absent friend;
That courage which can make you just
To merit humbled in the dust;
The detestation you express
For vice in all its glittering dress;
That patience under torturing pain,
Where stubborn stoics would complain:
Must these like empty shadows pass,
Or forms reflected from a glass?
Or mere chimæras in the mind,
That fly and leave no marks behind?
Does not the body thrive and grow
By food of twenty years ago?
And, had it not been still supplied,
It must a thousand times have died.
Then who with reason can maintain
That no effects of food remain?
And is not virtue in mankind
The nutriment that feeds the mind;
Upheld by each good action past,
And still continued by the last?
Then, who with reason can pretend
That all effects of virtue end?
Believe me, Stella, when you show
That true contempt for things below,
Nor prize your life for other ends
Than merely to oblige your friends;
Your former actions claim their part,
And join to fortify your heart.
For virtue in her daily race,
Like Janus, bears a double face;
Looks back with joy where she has gone,
And therefore goes with courage on.
She at your sickly couch will wait,
And guide you to a better state.
O then, whatever Heaven intends,
Take pity on your pitying friends!
Nor let your ills affect your mind,
To fancy they can be unkind.
Me, surely me, you ought to spare,
Who gladly would your suffering share,
Or give my scrap of life to you,
And think it far beneath your due;
You, to whose care so oft I owe
That I'm alive to tell you so.

JOSEPH ADDISON (1672–1719)

FROM AN ACCOUNT OF THE GREATEST ENGLISH POETS

Long had our dull forefathers slept supine,
Nor felt the raptures of the tuneful Nine;
Till Chaucer first, the merry bard, arose,
And many a story told in rhyme and prose.

But age has rusted what the poet writ,
Worn out his language, and obscured his wit;
In vain he jests in his unpolished strain,
And tries to make his readers laugh, in vain.
Old Spenser next, warmed with poetic rage,
In ancient tales amused a barbarous age;
An age that yet uncultivate and rude,
Where'er the poet's fancy led, pursued
Through pathless fields, and unfrequented floods,
To dens of dragons and enchanted woods.
But now the mystic tale, that pleased of yore,
Can charm an understanding age no more;
The long-spun allegories fulsome grow,
While the dull moral lies too plain below.
We view well-pleased at distance all the sights
Of arms and palfreys, battles, fields, and fights,
And damsels in distress, and courteous knights;
But when we look too near, the shades decay,
And all the pleasing landscape fades away.
Great Cowley then, a mighty genius, wrote,
O'er-run with wit, and lavish of his thought:
His turns too closely on the reader press;
He more had pleased us, had he pleased us less.
One glittering thought no sooner strikes our eyes
With silent wonder, but new wonders rise;
As in the milky-way a shining white
O'er-flows the heavens with one continued light,
That not a single star can show his rays,
Whilst jointly all promote the common blaze.
Pardon, great poet, that I dare to name
The unnumbered beauties of thy verse with blame;
Thy fault is only wit in its excess,
But wit like thine in any shape will please.
What muse but thine can equal hints inspire,
And fit the deep-mouthed Pindar to thy lyre;
Pindar, whom others, in a laboured strain
And forced expression, imitate in vain?
Well-pleased in thee he soars with new delight,
And plays in more unbounded verse, and takes a nobler flight.
Blest man! whose spotless life and charming lays
Employed the tuneful prelate in thy praise:
Blest man! who now shalt be forever known
In Sprat's successful labours and thy own.

From A LETTER TO THE RIGHT HONOURABLE CHARLES LORD HALIFAX

O Liberty, thou goddess heavenly bright,
Profuse of bliss, and pregnant with delight!
Eternal pleasures in thy presence reign,
And smiling Plenty leads thy wanton train;
Eased of her load, Subjection grows more light,
And Poverty looks cheerful in thy sight;
Thou mak'st the gloomy face of nature gay,
Giv'st beauty to the sun, and pleasure to the day.
Thee, goddess, thee, Britannia's isle adores;
How has she oft exhausted all her stores,
How oft in fields of death thy presence sought,
Nor thinks the mighty prize too dearly bought!
On foreign mountains may the sun refine
The grape's soft juice, and mellow it to wine;
With citron groves adorn a distant soil,
And the fat olive swell with floods of oil:
We envy not the warmer clime, that lies
In ten degrees of more indulgent skies,
Nor at the coarseness of our heaven repine,
Though o'er our heads the frozen Pleiads shine:
'Tis liberty that crowns Britannia's isle,
And makes her barren rocks and her bleak mountains smile.
Others with towering piles may please the sight,
And in their proud, aspiring domes delight;
A nicer touch to the stretched canvas give,
Or teach their animated rocks to live:
'Tis Britain's care to watch o'er Europe's fate,
And hold in balance each contending state,
To threaten bold, presumptuous kings with war,
And answer her afflicted neighbours' prayer.
The Dane and Swede, roused up by fierce alarms,
Bless the wise conduct of her pious arms:
Soon as her fleets appear, their terrors cease,
And all the northern world lies hushed in peace.

The ambitious Gaul beholds with secret dread
Her thunder aimed at his aspiring head,
And fain her godlike sons would disunite
By foreign gold, or by domestic spite;
But strives in vain to conquer or divide,
Whom Nassau's arms defend and counsels guide.

Fired with the name, which I so oft have found
The distant climes and different tongues resound,
I bridle in my struggling muse with pain,
That longs to launch into a bolder strain.
But I've already troubled you too long,
Nor dare attempt a more adventurous song.
My humble verse demands a softer theme,
A painted meadow, or a purling stream;
Unfit for heroes, whom immortal lays,
And lines like Virgil's, or like yours, should praise.

From THE CAMPAIGN, A POEM TO HIS GRACE THE DUKE OF MARLBOROUGH

But, O my muse, what numbers wilt thou find
To sing the furious troops in battle joined!

Methinks I hear the drum's tumultuous sound
The victor's shouts and dying groans confound,
The dreadful burst of cannon rend the skies,
And all the thunder of the battle rise!
'Twas then great Marlborough's mighty soul was
proved.
That, in the shock of charging hosts unmoved,
Amidst confusion, horror, and despair,
Examined all the dreadful scenes of war;
In peaceful thought the field of death surveyed,
To fainting squadrons sent the timely aid,
Inspired repulsed battalions to engage,
And taught the doubtful battle where to rage.
So when an angel by divine command
With rising tempests shakes a guilty land,
Such as of late o'er pale Britannia past,
Calm and serene he drives the furious blast;
And, pleased the Almighty's orders to perform,
Rides in the whirlwind, and directs the storm.
But see the haughty household-troops advance!
The dread of Europe, and the pride of France.
The war's whole art each private soldier knows,
And with a general's love of conquest glows;
Proudly he marches on, and, void of fear,
Laughs at the shaking of the British spear:
Vain insolence! with native freedom brave,
The meanest Briton scorns the highest slave.

HYMN

The spacious firmament on high,
With all the blue ethereal sky,
And spangled heavens, a shining frame,
Their great Original proclaim.
Th' unwearied Sun from day to day
Does his Creator's power display;
And publishes to every land
The work of an Almighty hand.

Soon as the evening shades prevail,
The Moon takes up the wondrous tale;
And nightly to the listening Earth
Repeats the story of her birth:
Whilst all the stars that round her burn,
And all the planets in their turn,
Confirm the tidings as they roll,
And spread the truth from pole to pole.

What though in solemn silence all
Move round the dark terrestrial ball;
What though no real voice nor sound
Amidst their radiant orbs be found?
In Reason's ear they all rejoice,
And utter forth a glorious voice;
Forever singing as they shine,
"The Hand that made us is divine."

ISAAC WATTS (1674–1748)

THE DAY OF JUDGMENT

When the fierce North-wind with his airy forces
Rears up the Baltic to a foaming fury;
And the red lightning with a storm of hail comes
Rushing amain down;

How the poor sailors stand amazed and tremble,
While the hoarse thunder, like a bloody trumpet,
Roars a loud onset to the gaping waters,
Quick to devour them.

Such shall the noise be, and the wild disorder
(If things eternal may be like these earthly),
Such the dire terror when the great Archangel
Shakes the creation;

Tears the strong pillars of the vault of Heaven,
Breaks up old marble, the repose of princes,
Sees the graves open, and the bones arising,
Flames all around them.

Hark, the shrill outcries of the guilty wretches!
Lively bright horror and amazing anguish
Stare thro' their eyelids, while the living worm lies
Gnawing within them.

Thoughts, like old vultures, prey upon their heart-
strings,
And the smart twinges, when the eye beholds the
Lofty Judge frowning, and a flood of vengeance
Rolling afore Him.

Hopeless immortals! how they scream and shiver,
While devils push them to the pit wide-yawning
Hideous and gloomy, to receive them headlong
Down to the centre!

Stop here, my fancy: (all away, ye horrid
Doleful ideas!) come, arise to Jesus,
How He sits God-like! and the saints around Him
Throned, yet adoring!

O may I sit there when He comes triumphant,
Dooming the nations! then ascend to glory,
While our Hosannas all along the passage
Shout the Redeemer.

A CRADLE HYMN

Hush! my dear, lie still and slumber,
Holy angels guard thy bed!
Heavenly blessings without number
Gently falling on thy head.

Sleep, my babe; thy food and raiment,
House and home, thy friends provide;
All without thy care or payment:
All thy wants are well supplied.

How much better thou'rt attended
Than the Son of God could be,
When from heaven He descended
And became a child like thee!

Soft and easy is thy cradle:
Coarse and hard thy Saviour lay,
When His birthplace was a stable
And His softest bed was hay.

Blessèd babe! what glorious features —
Spotless fair, divinely bright!
Must He dwell with brutal creatures?
How could angels bear the sight?

Was there nothing but a manger
Cursèd sinners could afford
To receive the heavenly stranger?
Did they thus affront their Lord?

Soft, my child: I did not chide thee,
Though my song might sound too hard;
'Tis thy mother sits beside thee,
And her arms shall be thy guard.

Yet to read the shameful story
How the Jews abused their King,
How they served the Lord of Glory,
Makes me angry while I sing.

See the kinder shepherds round Him,
Telling wonders from the sky!
Where they sought Him, there they found Him,
With His Virgin mother by.

See the lovely babe a-dressing;
Lovely infant, how He smiled!
When He wept, the mother's blessing
Soothed and hush'd the holy child.

Lo, He slumbers in His manger,
Where the hornèd oxen fed;
Peace, my darling; here's no danger,
Here's no ox anear thy bed.

'Twas to save thee, child, from dying,
Save my dear from burning flame,
Bitter groans and endless crying,
That thy blest Redeemer came.

May'st thou live to know and fear Him,
Trust and love Him all thy days;
Then go dwell forever near Him,
See His face, and sing His praise!

AMBROSE PHILIPS (1675–1749)

TO MISS CHARLOTTE PULTENEY, IN HER MOTHER'S ARMS

Timely blossom, infant fair,
Fondling of a happy pair,
Every morn and every night
Their solicitous delight;
Sleeping, waking, still at ease,
Pleasing, without skill to please;
Little gossip, blithe and hale,
Tattling many a broken tale,
Singing many a tuneless song,
Lavish of a heedless tongue.
Simple maiden, void of art,
Babbling out the very heart,
Yet abandoned to thy will,
Yet imagining no ill,
Yet too innocent to blush;
Like the linnet in the bush,
To the mother-linnet's note
Moduling her slender throat,
Chirping forth thy pretty joys;
Wanton in the change of toys,
Like the linnet green, in May,
Flitting to each bloomy spray;
Wearied then, and glad of rest,
Like the linnet in the nest.
This thy present happy lot,
This, in time, will be forgot;
Other pleasures, other cares,
Ever-busy Time prepares;
And thou shalt in thy daughter see
This picture once resembled thee.

JOHN PHILIPS (1676–1709)

From THE SPLENDID SHILLING

Happy the man who, void of cares and strife,
In silken or in leathern purse retains
A Splendid Shilling. He nor hears with pain
New oysters cried, nor sighs for cheerful ale;
But with his friends, when nightly mists arise,
To Juniper's Magpie or Town-hall repairs:
Where, mindful of the nymph whose wanton eye
Transfixed his soul and kindled amorous flames,
Chloe or Phillis, he each circling glass
Wishes her health, and joy, and equal love.
Meanwhile he smokes, and laughs at merry tale
Or pun ambiguous, or conundrum quaint.
But I, whom griping penury surrounds,
And hunger, sure attendant upon want,
With scanty offals, and small acid tiff,

Wretched repast! my meagre corps sustain:
Then solitary walk, or doze at home
In garret vile, and with a warming puff
Regale chilled fingers; or from tube as black
As winter-chimney, or well-polished jet,
Exhale mundungus, ill-perfuming scent:
Not blacker tube nor of a shorter size
Smokes Cambro-Briton, versed in pedigree,
Sprung from Cadwalador and Arthur, kings
Full famous in romantic tale, when he
O'er many a craggy hill and barren cliff,
Upon a cargo of famed Cestrian cheese,
High overshadowing rides, with a design
To vend his wares, or at th' Arvonian mart,
Or Maridunum, or the ancient town
Ycleped Brechinia, or where Vaga's stream
Encircles Ariconium, fruitful soil!
Whence flows nectareous wines that well may vie
With Massic, Setin, or renowned Falern.
Thus, while my joyless minutes tedious flow
With looks demure and silent pace, a dun,
Horrible monster! hated by gods and men,
To my aërial citadel ascends.
With vocal heel thrice thundering at my gate,
With hideous accent thrice he calls; I know
The voice ill-boding, and the solemn sound.
What should I do? or whither turn? Amazed,
Confounded, to the dark recess I fly
Of wood-hole; straight my bristling hairs erect
Thro' sudden fear: a chilly sweat bedews
My shuddering limbs, and, wonderful to tell!
My tongue forgets her faculty of speech;
So horrible he seems! His faded brow
Entrench'd with many a frown, and conic beard,
And spreading band, admired by modern saints,
Disastrous acts forebode; in his right hand
Long scrolls of paper solemnly he waves,
With characters and figures dire inscribed,
Grievous to mortal eyes; ye gods, avert
Such plagues from righteous men! Behind him stalks
Another monster, not unlike himself,
Sullen of aspect, by the vulgar called
A catchpole, whose polluted hands the gods
With force incredible and magic charms
First have endued: if he his ample palm
Should haply on ill-fated shoulder lay
Of debtor, straight his body, to the touch
Obsequious, as whilom knights were wont,
To some enchanted castle is conveyed,
Where gates impregnable and coercive chains
In durance strict detain him till, in form
Of money, Pallas sets the captive free.

THOMAS PARNELL (1679–1718)

From A NIGHT-PIECE ON DEATH

By the blue taper's trembling light,
No more I waste the wakeful night,
Intent with endless view to pore
The schoolmen and the sages o'er;
Their books from wisdom widely stray,
Or point at best the longest way.
I'll seek a readier path, and go
Where wisdom's surely taught below.

How deep yon azure dyes the sky,
Where orbs of gold unnumber'd lie,
While through their ranks in silver pride
The nether crescent seems to glide!
The slumbering breeze forgets to breathe,
The lake is smooth and clear beneath,
Where once again the spangled show
Descends to meet our eyes below.
The grounds which on the right aspire,
In dimness from the view retire:
The left presents a place of graves,
Whose wall the silent water laves.
That steeple guides thy doubtful sight
Among the livid gleams of night.
There pass, with melancholy state,
By all the solemn heaps of fate,
And think, as softly-sad you tread
Above the venerable dead,
"Time was, like thee they life possest,
And time shall be, that thou shalt rest."

Those graves, with bending osier bound,
That nameless heave the crumbled ground,
Quick to the glancing thought disclose,
Where toil and poverty repose.
The flat smooth stones that bear a name,
The chisel's slender help to fame,
(Which ere our set of friends decay
Their frequent steps may wear away;)
A middle race of mortals own,
Men, half ambitious, all unknown.
The marble tombs that rise on high,
Whose dead in vaulted arches lie,
Whose pillars swell with sculptur'd stones,
Arms, angels, epitaphs, and bones,
These, all the poor remains of state,
Adorn the rich, or praise the great;
Who while on earth in fame they live,
Are senseless of the fame they give.

Ha! while I gaze, pale Cynthia fades,
The bursting earth unveils the shades!

All slow, and wan, and wrapp'd with shrouds,
They rise in visionary crowds,
And all with sober accent cry,
"Think, mortal, what it is to die."

From A HYMN OF CONTENTMENT

Lovely, lasting peace of mind!
Sweet delight of human-kind!
Heavenly-born, and bred on high,
To crown the favourites of the sky
With more of happiness below,
Than victors in a triumph know!
Whither, O whither art thou fled,
To lay thy meek, contented head?
What happy region dost thou please
To make the seat of calms and ease?

Ambition searches all its sphere
Of pomp and state, to meet thee there.
Encreasing Avarice would find
Thy presence in its gold enshrined.
The bold adventurer ploughs his way,
Through rocks amidst the foaming sea,
To gain thy love; and then perceives
Thou wert not in the rocks and waves.
The silent heart, which grief assails,
Treads soft and lonesome o'er the vales,
Sees daisies open, rivers run,
And seeks, as I have vainly done.
Amusing thought; but learns to know
That solitude's the nurse of woe.
No real happiness is found
In trailing purple o'er the ground;
Or in a soul exalted high,
To range the circuit of the sky,
Converse with stars above, and know
All nature in its forms below;
The rest it seeks, in seeking dies,
And doubts at last, for knowledge, rise.

Lovely, lasting peace, appear!
This world itself, if thou art here,
Is once again with Eden blest,
And man contains it in his breast.

'Twas thus, as under shade I stood,
I sung my wishes to the wood,
And lost in thought, no more perceiv'd
The branches whisper as they wav'd:
It seem'd, as all the quiet place
Confess'd the presence of the Grace.
When thus she spoke — "Go rule thy will,
Bid thy wild passions all be still,
Know God, and bring thy heart to know
The joys which from religion flow;
Then every Grace shall prove its guest,
And I'll be there to crown the rest."

Oh! by yonder mossy seat,
In my hours of sweet retreat,
Might I thus my soul employ,
With sense of gratitude and joy!
Rais'd as ancient prophets were,
In heavenly vision, praise, and prayer;
Pleasing all men, hurting none,
Pleas'd and bless'd with God alone:
Then while the gardens take my sight,
With all the colours of delight;
While silver waters glide along,
To please my ear, and court my song;
I'll lift my voice, and tune my string,
And thee, great Source of nature, sing.

The sun that walks his airy way,
To light the world, and give the day;
The moon that shines with borrow'd light;
The stars that gild the gloomy night;
The seas that roll unnumber'd waves;
The wood that spreads its shady leaves;
The field whose ears conceal the grain,
The yellow treasure of the plain;
All of these, and all I see,
Should be sung, and sung by me:
They speak their maker as they can,
But want and ask the tongue of man.

Go search among your idle dreams,
Your busy or your vain extremes;
And find a life of equal bliss,
Or own the next begun in this.

SONG

When thy beauty appears
In its graces and airs
All bright as an angel new dropp'd from the sky,
At distance I gaze and am awed by my fears:
So strangely you dazzle my eye!

But when without art
Your kind thoughts you impart,
When your love runs in blushes through every vein;
When it darts from your eyes, when it pants in your heart,
Then I know you're a woman again.

"There's a passion and pride
In our sex," she replied,
"And thus, might I gratify both, I would do:
Still an angel appear to each lover beside,
But still be a woman to you."

EDWARD YOUNG (1683–1765)

THE OLD COQUETTE

From SATIRE V

"But adoration! give me something more,"
Cries Lycè, on the borders of threescore.
Nought treads so silent as the foot of Time:
Hence we mistake our autumn for our prime.
'Tis greatly wise to know, before we're told,
The melancholy news that we grow old.
Autumnal Lycè carries in her face
Memento mori to each public place.
Oh! how your beating breast a mistress warms
Who looks through spectacles to see your charms,
While rival undertakers hover round
And with his spade the sexton marks the ground!
Intent not on her own, but others' doom,
She plans new conquests and defrauds the tomb.
In vain the cock has summoned sprites away,
She walks at noon and blasts the bloom of day.
Gay rainbow silks her mellow charms infold,
And nought of Lycè but herself is old.
Her grizzled locks assume a smirking grace,
And art has levelled her deep furrowed face.
Her strange demand no mortal can approve,
We'll ask her blessing, but can't ask her love.
She grants, indeed, a lady may decline
(All ladies but herself) at ninety-nine.

TIME

From NIGHT THOUGHTS

Night I

The bell strikes one: we take no note of time,
But from its loss. To give it, then, a tongue,
Is wise in man. As if an angel spoke,
I feel the solemn sound. If heard aright,
It is the knell of my departed hours:
Where are they? With the years beyond the flood.
It is the signal that demands despatch;
How much is to be done! my hopes and fears
Start up alarmed, and o'er life's narrow verge
Look down — on what? a fathomless abyss;
A dread eternity; how surely mine!
And can eternity belong to me,
Poor pensioner on the bounties of an hour?

Night II

Time the supreme! — Time is eternity;
Pregnant with all eternity can give;
Pregnant with all that makes archangels smile.
Who murders time, he crushes in the birth
A power ethereal, only not adored.
Ah! how unjust to Nature and himself,
Is thoughtless, thankless, inconsistent man!
Like children babbling nonsense in their sports,
We censure Nature for a span too short:
That span too short, we tax as tedious too;
Torture invention, all expedients tire,
To lash the lingering moments into speed,
And whirl us (happy riddance!) from ourselves.
Art, brainless Art! our furious charioteer
(For Nature's voice, unstifled, would recall),
Drives headlong towards the precipice of death!
Death, most our dread; death, thus more dreadful made:
O, what a riddle of absurdity!
Leisure is pain; takes off our chariot wheels:
How heavily we drag the load of life!
Blest leisure is our curse: like that of Cain,
It makes us wander; wander earth around
To fly that tyrant, Thought. As Atlas groaned
The world beneath, we groan beneath an hour.
We cry for mercy to the next amusement:
The next amusement mortgages our fields;
Slight inconvenience! prisons hardly frown,
From hateful Time if prisons set us free.
Yet when Death kindly tenders us relief,
We call him cruel; years to moments shrink,
Ages to years. The telescope is turned.
To man's false optics (from his folly false)
Time, in advance, behind him hides his wings,
And seems to creep, decrepit with his age;
Behold him when past by; what then is seen
But his broad pinions, swifter than the winds?
And all mankind, in contradiction strong,
Rueful, aghast, cry out on his career.

PROCRASTINATION

From THE COMPLAINT

Night I

By nature's law, what may be, may be now;
There's no prerogative in human hours.
In human hearts what bolder thought can rise
Than man's presumption on to-morrow's dawn?
Where is to-morrow? In another world.
For numbers this is certain; the reverse
Is sure to none; and yet on this 'perhaps,'
This 'peradventure,' infamous for lies,
As on a rock of adamant, we build
Our mountian hopes, spin out eternal schemes
As we the fatal sisters could out-spin,
And big with life's futurities, expire.
Not e'en Philander had bespoke his shroud,

Nor had he cause; a warning was denied:
How many fall as sudden, not as safe;
As sudden, though for years admonish'd home!
Of human ills the last extreme beware;
Beware, Lorenzo, a slow sudden death.
How dreadful that deliberate surprise!
Be wise to-day; 'tis madness to defer;
Next day the fatal precedent will plead;
Thus on, till wisdom is push'd out of life.
Procrastination is the thief of time;
Year after year it steals, till all are fled,
And to the mercies of a moment leaves
The vast concerns of an eternal scene.
If not so frequent, would not this be strange?
That 'tis so frequent, this is stranger still.
Of man's miraculous mistakes this bears
The palm, "That all men are about to live,
Forever on the brink of being born."
All pay themselves the compliment to think
They one day shall not drivel: and their pride
On this reversion takes up ready praise;
At least, their own; their future selves applaud
How excellent that life they ne'er will lead.
Time lodg'd in their own hands is folly's vails;
That lodg'd in fate's to wisdom they consign.
The thing they can't but purpose, they postpone.
'Tis not in folly not to scorn a fool,
And scarce in human wisdom to do more.
All promise is poor dilatory man,
And that through every stage: when young indeed
In full content we sometimes nobly rest,
Unanxious for ourselves; and only wish,
As duteous sons our fathers were more wise.
At thirty man suspects himself a fool,
Knows it at forty and reforms his plan;
At fifty chides his infamous delay,
Pushes his prudent purpose to resolve;
In all the magnanimity of thought
Resolves, and re-resolves; then dies the same.

MAN

From NIGHT THOUGHTS

Night I

How poor, how rich, how abject, how august,
How complicate, how wonderful, is man!
How passing wonder He who made him such!
Who centred in our make such strange extremes,
From different natures marvellously mixed,
Connection exquisite of distant worlds!
Distinguished link in being's endless chain!
Midway from nothing to the Deity!
A beam ethereal, sullied, and absorpt!
Though sullied and dishonoured, still divine!
Dim miniature of greatness absolute!
An heir of glory! a frail child of dust!
Helpless immortal! insect infinite!
A worm! a god! — I tremble at myself,
And in myself am lost! At home a stranger,
Thought wanders up and down, surprised, aghast,
And wondering at her own. How reason reels!
O, what a miracle to man is man!
Triumphantly distressed! What joy! what dread!
Alternately transported and alarmed!
What can preserve my life? or what destroy?
An angel's arm can't snatch me from the grave;
Legions of angels can't confine me there.

JOHN GAY (1685–1732)

THE HARE WITH MANY FRIENDS

Friendship, like love, is but a name,
Unless to one you stint the flame.
The child whom many fathers share,
Hath seldom known a father's care.
'Tis thus in friendship; who depend
On many rarely find a friend.
  A Hare, who, in a civil way,
Complied with everything, like Gay,
Was known by all the bestial train,
Who haunt the wood, or graze the plain.
Her care was, never to offend,
And every creature was her friend.
  As forth she went at early dawn,
To taste the dew-besprinkled lawn,
Behind she hears the hunter's cries,
And from the deep-mouthed thunder flies.
She starts, she stops, she pants for breath;
She hears the near advance of death;
She doubles, to mislead the hound,
And measures back her mazy round:
Till, fainting in the public way,
Half dead with fear she gasping lay.
What transport in her bosom grew,
When first the Horse appeared in view!
"Let me," says she, "your back ascend,
And owe my safety to a friend.
You know my feet betray my flight;
To friendship every burden's light."
The Horse replied: "Poor honest Puss,
It grieves my heart to see thee thus;
Be comforted; relief is near,
For all your friends are in the rear."
  She next the stately Bull implored;
And thus replied the mighty lord,
"Since every beast alive can tell
That I sincerely wish you well,
I may, without offence, pretend,
To take the freedom of a friend;

Love calls me hence; a favourite cow
Expects me near yon barley-mow:
And when a lady's in the case,
You know, all other things give place.
To leave you thus might seem unkind;
But see, the Goat is just behind."
  The Goat remarked her pulse was high,
Her languid head, her heavy eye;
"My back," says he, "may do you harm;
The Sheep's at hand, and wool is warm."
  The Sheep was feeble, and complained
His sides a load of wool sustained:
Said he was slow, confessed his fears,
For hounds eat sheep as well as hares.
  She now the trotting Calf addressed,
To save from death a friend distressed.
"Shall I," says he, "of tender age,
In this important care engage?
Older and abler passed you by;
How strong are those, how weak am I!
Should I presume to bear you hence,
Those friends of mine may take offence.
Excuse me, then. You know my heart.
But dearest friends, alas, must part!
How shall we all lament! Adieu!
For see, the hounds are just in view."

BLACK-EYED SUSAN

All in the Downs the fleet was moored,
  The streamers waving in the wind,
When Black-eyed Susan came aboard,
  "Oh! where shall I my true love find?
Tell me, ye jovial sailors, tell me true,
If my sweet William sails among the crew?"

William, who high upon the yard
  Rocked with the billow to and fro,
Soon as her well-known voice he heard
  He sighed, and cast his eyes below:
The cord slides swiftly through his glowing hands
And, quick as lightning, on the deck he stands.

So the sweet lark, high poised in air,
  Shuts close his pinions to his breast —
If chance his mate's shrill call he hear —
  And drops at once into her nest.
The noblest captain in the British fleet
Might envy William's lips those kisses sweet.

"O Susan, Susan, lovely dear,
  My vows shall ever true remain;
Let me kiss off that falling tear;
  We only part to meet again.
Change as ye list, ye winds! my heart shall be
The faithful compass that still points to thee.

"Believe not what the landsmen say,
  Who tempt with doubts thy constant mind;
They'll tell thee, sailors, when away,
  In every port a mistress find;
Yes, yes, believe them when they tell thee so,
For thou art present wheresoe'er I go.

"If to fair India's coast we sail,
  Thy eyes are seen in diamonds bright;
Thy breath is Afric's spicy gale,
  Thy skin is ivory so white.
Thus every beauteous object that I view,
Wakes in my soul some charm of lovely Sue.

"Though battle call me from thy arms,
  Let not my pretty Susan mourn;
Though cannons roar, yet safe from harms,
  William shall to his dear return.
Love turns aside the balls that round me fly,
Lest precious tears should drop from Susan's eye."

The boatswain gave the dreadful word;
  The sails their swelling bosom spread;
No longer must she stay aboard;
  They kissed — she sighed — he hung his head.
Her lessening boat unwilling rows to land,
"Adieu!" she cries, and waved her lily hand.

THE FAN

From Book I

Now Venus mounts her car, she shakes the reins,
And steers her turtles to Cythera's plains;
Straight to the grot with graceful step she goes,
Her loose ambrosial hair behind her flows.
The swelling bellows heave for breath no more;
All drop their silent hammers on the floor;
In deep suspense the mighty labour stands,
While thus the goddess spoke her mild commands:
  "Industrious Loves, your present toils forbear,
A more important task demands your care;
Long has the scheme employ'd my thoughtful mind,
By judgment ripen'd, and by time refined.
That glorious bird have ye not often seen
Who draws the car of the celestial Queen?
Have ye not oft survey'd his varying dyes,
His tail all gilded o'er with Argus' eyes?
Have ye not seen him in the sunny day
Unfurl his plumes, and all his pride display,
Then suddenly contract his dazzling train,
And with long-trailing feathers sweep the plain?
Learn from this hint, let this instruct your art:
Thin taper sticks must from one centre part;
Let these into the quadrant's form divide,

The spreading ribs with snowy paper hide;
Here shall the pencil bid its colours flow,
And make a miniature creation grow.
Let the machine in equal foldings close,
And now its plaited surface wide dispose.
So shall the fair her idle hand employ,
And grace each motion with the restless toy,
With various play bid grateful Zephyrs rise,
While love in ev'ry grateful Zephyr flies."
  The master Cupid traces out the lines,
And with judicious hand the draught designs;
Th' expecting Loves with joy the model view,
And the joint labour eagerly pursue.
Some slit their arrows with the nicest art,
And into sticks convert the shiver'd dart;
The breathing bellows wake the sleeping fire,
Blow off the cinders, and the sparks aspire;
Their arrow's point they soften in the flame,
And sounding hammers break its barbèd frame:
Of this, the little pin they neatly mould,
From whence their arms the spreading sticks unfold;
In equal plaits they now the paper bend,
And at just distance the wide ribs extend;
Then on the frame they mount the limber screen
And finish instantly the new machine.

THOMAS TICKELL (1686–1740)

From THE ELEGY ON ADDISON

Can I forget the dismal night that gave
My soul's best part forever to the grave?
How silent did his old companions tread,
By midnight lamps, the mansions of the dead,
Through breathing statues, then unheeded things,
Through rows of warriors, and through walks of kings!
What awe did the slow solemn knell inspire;
The pealing organ, and the pausing choir;
The duties by the lawn-robed prelate paid;
And the last words, that dust to dust conveyed!
While speechless o'er thy closing grave we bend,
Accept these tears, thou dear departed friend.
Oh, gone forever! take this long adieu;
And sleep in peace next thy loved Montague.
  To strew fresh laurels, let the task be mine,
A frequent pilgrim at thy sacred shrine;
Mine with true sighs thy absence to bemoan,
And grave with faithful epitaphs thy stone.
If e'er from me thy loved memorial part,
May shame afflict this alienated heart;
Of thee forgetful if I form a song,
My lyre be broken, and untuned my tongue,
My griefs be doubled from thy image free,
And mirth a torment, unchastised by thee!
  Oft let me range the gloomy aisles alone,
Sad luxury to vulgar minds unknown,
Along the walls where speaking marbles show
What worthies form the hallowed mould below;
Proud names, who once the reins of empire held;
In arms who triumphed, or in arts excelled;
Chiefs graced with scars and prodigal of blood;
Stern patriots who for sacred freedom stood;
Just men by whom impartial laws were given;
And saints who taught and led the way to heaven.
Ne'er to these chambers, where the mighty rest,
Since their foundation came a nobler guest;
Nor e'er was to the bowers of bliss conveyed
A fairer spirit or more welcome shade.
  In what new region to the just assigned,
What new employments please th' unbodied mind?
A wingèd Virtue, through th' ethereal sky
From world to world unwearied does he fly?
Or curious trace the long laborious maze
Of heaven's decrees, where wondering angels gaze?
Does he delight to hear bold seraphs tell
How Michael battled, and the dragon fell?
Or, mixed with milder cherubim, to glow
In hymns of love, not ill essayed below?
Or dost thou warn poor mortals left behind,
A task well suited to thy gentle mind?
Oh, if sometimes thy spotless form descend,
To me thy aid, thou guardian genius, lend!
When rage misguides me, or when fear alarms,
When pain distresses or when pleasure charms,
In silent whisperings purer thoughts impart,
And turn from ill a frail and feeble heart:
Led through the paths thy virtue trod before,
Till bliss shall join, nor death can part us more.
  That awful form which, so the heavens decree,
Must still be loved and still deplored by me,
In nightly visions seldom fails to rise,
Or, roused by fancy, meets my waking eyes.
If business calls or crowded courts invite,
Th' unblemished statesman seems to strike my sight;
If in the stage I seek to soothe my care,
I meet his soul which breathes in Cato there;
If pensive to the rural shades I rove,
His shape o'ertakes me in the lonely grove;
'Twas there of just and good he reasoned strong,
Cleared some great truth, or raised some serious song:
There patient showed us the wise course to steer,
A candid censor, and a friend severe;
There taught us how to live, and (oh! too high
The price for knowledge) taught us how to die.

ALLAN RAMSAY (1686–1758)

PEGGY

My Peggy is a young thing,
  Just enter'd in her teens,
Fair as the day, and sweet as May,
Fair as the day, and always gay;
  My Peggy is a young thing,
  And I'm not very auld,
Yet well I like to meet her at
  The wawking[1] of the fauld.

My Peggy speaks sae sweetly
  Whene'er we meet alane,
I wish nae mair to lay my care,
I wish nae mair of a' that's rare;
  My Peggy speaks sae sweetly,
  To a' the lave[2] I'm cauld,
But she gars[3] a' my spirits glow
  At wawking of the fauld.

My Peggy smiles sae kindly
  Whene'er I whisper love,
That I look down on a' the town,
That I look down upon a crown;
  My Peggy smiles sae kindly,
  It makes me blyth and bauld,
And naething gives me sic[4] delight
  As wawking of the fauld.

My Peggy sings sae saftly
  When on my pipe I play,
By a' the rest it is confest,
By a' the rest, that she sings best;
  My Peggy sings sae saftly,
  And in her sangs are tauld
With innocence the wale[5] of sense,
  At wawking of the fauld.

ALEXANDER POPE (1688–1744)

AN ESSAY ON CRITICISM

From PART I

'Tis hard to say, if greater want of skill
Appear in writing or in judging ill;
But, of the two, less dangerous is th' offence
To tire our patience, than mislead our sense.
Some few in that, but numbers err in this,
Ten censure wrong for one who writes amiss;
A fool might once himself alone expose,
Now one in verse makes many more in prose.
'Tis with our judgments as our watches, none
Go just alike, yet each believes his own.
In poets as true genius is but rare,
True taste as seldom is the critic's share;
Both must alike from Heaven derive their light,
These born to judge, as well as those to write.
Let such teach others who themselves excel,
And censure freely who have written well.
Authors are partial to their wit, 'tis true,
But are not critics to their judgment too?

* * * * * * *

  First follow Nature, and your judgment frame
By her just standard, which is still the same:
Unerring Nature, still divinely bright,
One clear, unchanged, and universal light,
Life, force, and beauty, must to all impart,
At once the source, and end, and test of Art.
Art from that fund each just supply provides,
Works without show, and without pomp presides:
In some fair body thus th' informing soul
With spirits feeds, with vigour fills the whole,
Each motion guides, and every nerve sustains;
Itself unseen, but in th' effects, remains.
Some, to whom Heaven in wit has been profuse,
Want as much more, to turn it to its use;
For wit and judgment often are at strife,
Though meant each other's aid, like man and wife.
'Tis more to guide than spur the Muse's steed;
Restrain his fury, than provoke his speed;
The winged courser, like a generous horse,
Shows most true mettle when you check his course.
  Those rules of old discovered, not devised,
Are Nature still, but Nature methodized;
Nature, like liberty, is but restrained
By the same laws which first herself ordained.

* * * * * * *

  You, then, whose judgment the right course would steer,
Know well each ancient's proper character;
His fable, subject, scope in every page;
Religion, country, genius of his age:
Without all these at once before your eyes,
Cavil you may, but never criticise.
Be Homer's works your study and delight,
Read them by day, and meditate by night;
Thence form your judgment, thence your maxims bring,
And trace the Muses upward to their spring.
Still with itself compared, his text peruse;
And let your comment be the Mantuan Muse.
  When first young Maro in his boundless mind
A work t' outlast immortal Rome designed,
Perhaps he seemed above the critic's law,
And but from nature's fountains scorned to draw:
But when t' examine every part he came,

[1] watching [2] rest [3] makes [4] such [5] choice

Nature and Homer were, he found, the same.
Convinced, amazed, he checks the bold design;
And rules as strict his laboured work confine,
As if the Stagirite o'erlooked each line.
Learn hence for ancient rules a just esteem;
To copy nature is to copy them.
Some beauties yet no precepts can declare,
For there's a happiness as well as care.
Music resembles poetry, in each
Are nameless graces which no methods teach,
And which a master-hand alone can reach.
If, where the rules not far enough extend,
(Since rules were made but to promote their end)
Some lucky license answer to the full
Th' intent proposed, that license is a rule.
Thus Pegasus, a nearer way to take,
May boldly deviate from the common track;
From vulgar bounds with brave disorder part,
And snatch a grace beyond the reach of art,
Which without passing through the judgment, gains
The heart, and all its end at once attains.
In prospects thus, some objects please our eyes,
Which out of nature's common order rise,
The shapeless rock, or hanging precipice.
Great wits sometimes may gloriously offend,
And rise to faults true critics dare not mend.
But tho' the ancients thus their rules invade,
(As kings dispense with laws themselves have made)
Moderns, beware! or if you must offend
Against the precept, ne'er transgress its end;
Let it be seldom and compelled by need;
And have, at least, their precedent to plead.
The critic else proceeds without remorse,
Seizes your fame, and puts his laws in force.
I know there are, to whose presumptuous thoughts
Those freer beauties, e'en in them, seem faults.
Some figures monstrous and misshaped appear,
Considered singly, or beheld too near,
Which, but proportioned to their light or place,
Due distance reconciles to form and grace.
A prudent chief not always must display
His powers in equal ranks, and fair array,
But with th' occasion and the place comply,
Conceal his force, nay, seem sometimes to fly.
Those oft are stratagems which errors seem,
Nor is it Homer nods, but we that dream.

From PART II

A little learning is a dangerous thing;
Drink deep, or taste not the Pierian spring:
There shallow draughts intoxicate the brain,
And drinking largely sobers us again.
Fired at first sight with what the Muse imparts,
In fearless youth we tempt the heights of arts,
While from the bounded level of our mind,
Short views we take, nor see the lengths behind;
But more advanced, behold with strange surprise
New distant scenes of endless science rise!
So pleased at first the towering Alps we try,
Mount o'er the vales, and seem to tread the sky,
Th' eternal snows appear already past,
And the first clouds and mountains seem the last;
But, those attained, we tremble to survey
The growing labours of the lengthened way,
Th' increasing prospects tire our wandering eyes,
Hills peep o'er hills, and Alps on Alps arise!
A perfect judge will read each work of wit
With the same spirit that its author writ:
Survey the whole, nor seek slight faults to find
Where nature moves, and rapture warms the mind;
Nor lose, for that malignant dull delight,
The generous pleasure to be charmed with wit.
But in such lays as neither ebb, nor flow,
Correctly cold, and regularly low,
That shunning faults, one quiet tenor keep;
We cannot blame indeed —— but we may sleep.
In wit, as nature, what affects our hearts
Is not th' exactness of peculiar parts;
'Tis not a lip, or eye, we beauty call,
But the joint force and full result of all.
Thus when we view some well-proportioned dome,
(The world's just wonder, and e'en thine, O Rome!)
No single parts unequally surprise,
All comes united to th' admiring eyes;
No monstrous height, or breadth, or length appear;
The whole at once is bold, and regular.
Whoever thinks a faultless piece to see,
Thinks what ne'er was, nor is, nor e'er shall be.
In every work regard the writer's end,
Since none can compass more than they intend;
And if the means be just, the conduct true,
Applause, in spite of trivial faults, is due;
As men of breeding, sometimes men of wit,
T' avoid great errors, must the less commit:
Neglect the rules each verbal critic lays,
For not to know some trifles, is a praise.
Most critics, fond of some subservient art,
Still make the whole depend upon a part:
They talk of principles, but notions prize,
And all to one loved folly sacrifice.

* * * * * * *

Some to conceit alone their taste confine,
And glittering thoughts struck out at every line;
Pleased with a work where nothing's just or fit;
One glaring chaos and wild heap of wit.

Poets like painters, thus unskilled to trace
The naked nature and the living grace,
With gold and jewels cover every part,
And hide with ornaments their want of art.
True wit is nature to advantage dressed,
What oft was thought, but ne'er so well expressed;
Something, whose truth convinced at sight we find,
That gives us back the image of our mind.
As shades more sweetly recommend the light,
So modest plainness sets off sprightly wit.
For works may have more wit than does 'em good,
As bodies perish thro' excess of blood.
Others for language all their care express,
And value books, as women, men, for dress:
Their praise is still, — the style is excellent;
The sense, they humbly take upon content.
Words are like leaves; and where they most abound,
Much fruit of sense beneath is rarely found.
False eloquence, like the prismatic glass,
Its gaudy colours spreads on every place;
The face of nature we no more survey,
All glares alike, without distinction gay:
But true expression, like th' unchanging sun,
Clears and improves whate'er it shines upon,
It gilds all objects, but it alters none.
Expression is the dress of thought, and still
Appears more decent, as more suitable;
A vile conceit in pompous words expressed,
Is like a clown in regal purple dressed:
For different styles with different subjects sort,
As several garbs with country, town, and court.
Some by old words to fame have made pretence,
Ancients in phrase, mere moderns in their sense;
Such laboured nothings, in so strange a style,
Amaze th' unlearn'd, and make the learnèd smile.
Unlucky, as Fungoso in the play,
These sparks with awkward vanity display
What the fine gentleman wore yesterday;
And but so mimic ancient wits at best,
As apes our grandsires, in their doublets dressed.
In words, as fashions, the same rule will hold;
Alike fantastic, if too new, or old:
Be not the first by whom the new are tried,
Nor yet the last to lay the old aside.
But most by numbers judge a poet's song;
And smooth or rough, with them, is right or wrong:
In the bright Muse though thousand charms conspire,
Her voice is all these tuneful fools admire;
Who haunt Parnassus but to please their ear,
Not mend their minds; as some to church repair,
Not for the doctrine, but the music there.
These equal syllables alone require,
Tho' oft the ear the open vowels tire;
While expletives their feeble aid do join,
And ten low words oft creep in one dull line:
While they ring round the same unvaried chimes,
With sure returns of still expected rhymes;
Where'er you find "the cooling western breeze,"
In the next line, it "whispers through the trees;"
If crystal streams "with pleasing murmurs creep,"
The reader's threatened (not in vain) with "sleep:"
Then, at the last and only couplet fraught
With some unmeaning thing they call a thought,
A needless Alexandrine ends the song,
That, like a wounded snake, drags its slow length along.
Leave such to tune their own dull rhymes, and know
What's roundly smooth or languishingly slow;
And praise the easy vigour of a line,
Where Denham's strength, and Waller's sweetness join.
True ease in writing comes from art, not chance,
As those move easiest who have learned to dance.
'Tis not enough no harshness gives offence,
The sound must seem an echo to the sense.
Soft is the strain when Zephyr gently blows,
And the smooth stream in smoother numbers flows;
But when loud surges lash the sounding shore,
The hoarse, rough verse should like the torrent roar.
When Ajax strives some rock's vast weight to throw,
The line too labours, and the words move slow;
Not so, when swift Camilla scours the plain,
Flies o'er th' unbending corn, and skims along the main.
Hear how Timotheus' varied lays surprise,
And bid alternate passions fall and rise!
While, at each change, the son of Libyan Jove
Now burns with glory, and then melts with love;
Now his fierce eyes with sparkling fury glow,
Now sighs steal out, and tears begin to flow:
Persians and Greeks like turns of nature found,
And the world's victor stood subdued by sound!
The power of music all our hearts allow,
And what Timotheus was, is Dryden now.
Avoid extremes; and shun the fault of such,
Who still are pleased too little or too much.
At every trifle scorn to take offence,
That always shows great pride, or little sense;
Those heads, as stomachs, are not sure the best,
Which nauseate all, and nothing can digest.
Yet let not each gay turn thy rapture move;
For fools admire, but men of sense approve:

As things seem large which we through mists descry,
Dullness is ever apt to magnify.

From PART III

The bookful blockhead, ignorantly read,
With loads of learnèd lumber in his head,
With his own tongue still edifies his ears,
And always listening to himself appears.
All books he reads, and all he reads assails,
From Dryden's Fables down to Durfey's Tales.
With him, most authors steal their works, or buy;
Garth did not write his own Dispensary.
Name a new play, and he's the poet's friend,
Nay, showed his faults — but when would poets mend?
No place so sacred from such fops is barred,
Nor is Paul's church more safe than Paul's church yard:
Nay, fly to altars; there they'll talk you dead:
For fools rush in where angels fear to tread.
Distrustful sense with modest caution speaks,
It still looks home, and short excursions makes;
But rattling nonsense in full volleys breaks,
And never shocked, and never turned aside,
Bursts out, resistless, with a thundering tide.
But where's the man, who counsel can bestow,
Still pleased to teach, and yet not proud to know?
Unbiassed, or by favour, or by spite;
Not dully prepossessed, nor blindly right;
Though learn'd, well-bred; and though well-bred, sincere,
Modestly bold, and humanly severe:
Who to a friend his faults can freely show,
And gladly praise the merit of a foe?
Blest with a taste exact, yet unconfined;
A knowledge both of books and human kind:
Generous converse; a soul exempt from pride;
And love to praise, with reason on his side?

* * * * * * *

THE RAPE OF THE LOCK

An Heroi-Comical Poem

Canto I

What dire offence from amorous causes springs,
What mighty contests rise from trivial things,
I sing. — This verse to Caryl, Muse! is due;
This, e'en Belinda may vouchsafe to view.
Slight is the subject, but not so the praise,
If she inspire, and he approve my lays.
Say what strange motive, Goddess! could compel
A well-bred lord t' assault a gentle belle?
Oh, say what stranger cause, yet unexplored,
Could make a gentle belle reject a lord?
In tasks so bold, can little men engage,
And in soft bosoms dwells such mighty rage?
Sol through white curtains shot a timorous ray,
And oped those eyes that must eclipse the day.
Now lap-dogs give themselves the rousing shake,
And sleepless lovers, just at twelve, awake.
Thrice rung the bell, the slipper knocked the ground,
And the pressed watch returned a silver sound.
Belinda still her downy pillow pressed,
Her guardian sylph prolonged the balmy rest;
'Twas he had summoned to her silent bed
The morning dream that hovered o'er her head;
A youth more glittering than a birth-night beau,
(That e'en in slumber caused her cheek to glow)
Seemed to her ear his winning lips to lay,
And thus in whispers said, or seemed to say:
"Fairest of mortals, thou distinguished care
Of thousand bright inhabitants of air!
If e'er one vision touched thy infant thought,
Of all the nurse and all the priest have taught,
Of airy elves by moonlight shadows seen,
The silver token, and the circled green,
Or virgins visited by angel powers,
With golden crowns and wreaths of heavenly flowers;
Hear and believe! thy own importance know,
Nor bound thy narrow views to things below.
Some secret truths, from learnèd pride concealed,
To maids alone and children are revealed.
What though no credit doubting wits may give?
The fair and innocent shall still believe.
Know, then, unnumbered spirits round thee fly,
The light militia of the lower sky.
These, though unseen, are ever on the wing,
Hang o'er the box, and hover round the Ring.
Think what an equipage thou hast in air,
And view with scorn two pages and a chair.
As now your own, our beings were of old,
And once enclosed in woman's beauteous mould;
Thence, by a soft transition, we repair
From earthly vehicles to these of air.
Think not, when woman's transient breath is fled,
That all her vanities at once are dead;
Succeeding vanities she still regards,
And though she plays no more, o'erlooks the cards.
Her joy in gilded chariots, when alive,
And love of ombre, after death survive.
For when the fair in all their pride expire,
To their first elements their souls retire:
The sprites of fiery termagants in flame
Mount up, and take a salamander's name.
Soft yielding minds to water glide away,

And sip, with nymphs, their elemental tea.
The graver prude sinks downward to a gnome,
In search of mischief still on earth to roam.
The light coquettes in sylphs aloft repair,
And sport and flutter in the fields of air.
"Know further yet: whoever fair and chaste
Rejects mankind, is by some sylph embraced;
For spirits, freed from mortal laws, with ease
Assume what sexes and what shapes they please.
What guards the purity of melting maids,
In courtly balls, and midnight masquerades,
Safe from the treacherous friend, the daring spark,
The glance by day, the whisper in the dark,
When kind occasion prompts their warm desires,
When music softens, and when dancing fires?
'Tis but their sylph, the wise celestials know,
Though honour is the word with men below.
Some nymphs there are, too conscious of their face,
For life predestined to the gnomes' embrace.
These swell their prospects and exalt their pride,
When offers are disdained, and love denied:
Then gay ideas crowd the vacant brain,
While peers, and dukes, and all their sweeping train,
And garters, stars, and coronets appear,
And in soft sounds 'Your Grace' salutes their ear.
'Tis these that early taint the female soul,
Instruct the eyes of young coquettes to roll,
Teach infant cheeks a bidden blush to know,
And little hearts to flutter at a beau.
"Oft when the world imagine women stray,
The sylphs through mystic mazes guide their way,
Through all the giddy circle they pursue,
And old impertinence expel by new.
What tender maid but must a victim fall
To one man's treat, but for another's ball?
When Florio speaks, what virgin could withstand,
If gentle Damon did not squeeze her hand?
With varying vanities, from every part,
They shift the moving toyshop of their heart;
Where wigs with wigs, with sword-knots sword-knots strive,
Beaux banish beaux, and coaches coaches drive.
This erring mortals levity may call;
Oh, blind to truth! the sylphs contrive it all.
"Of these am I, who thy protection claim,
A watchful sprite, and Ariel is my name.
Late, as I ranged the crystal wilds of air,
In the clear mirror of thy ruling star
I saw, alas! some dread event impend,
Ere to the main this morning sun descend,
But Heaven reveals not what, or how, or where.
Warned by the sylph, O pious maid, beware!
This to disclose is all thy guardian can:
Beware of all, but most beware of man!"
He said; when Shock, who thought she slept too long,
Leaped up, and waked his mistress with his tongue.
'Twas then, Belinda, if report say true,
Thy eyes first opened on a billet-doux;
Wounds, charms, and ardours were no sooner read,
But all the vision vanished from thy head.
And now, unveiled, the toilet stands displayed,
Each silver vase in mystic order laid.
First, robed in white, the nymph intent adores,
With head uncovered, the cosmetic powers.
A heavenly image in the glass appears,
To that she bends, to that her eyes she rears;
Th' inferior priestess, at her altar's side,
Trembling begins the sacred rites of pride.
Unnumbered treasures ope at once, and here
The various offerings of the world appear;
From each she nicely culls with curious toil,
And decks the goddess with the glittering spoil.
This casket India's glowing gems unlocks,
And all Arabia breathes from yonder box.
The tortoise here and elephant unite,
Transformed to combs, the speckled, and the white.
Here files of pins extend their shining rows,
Puffs, powders, patches, bibles, billets-doux.
Now awful beauty puts on all its arms;
The fair each moment rises in her charms,
Repairs her smiles, awakens every grace,
And calls forth all the wonders of her face;
Sees by degrees a purer blush arise,
And keener lightnings quicken in her eyes.
The busy sylphs surround their darling care,
These set the head, and those divide the hair,
Some fold the sleeve, whilst others plait the gown;
And Betty's praised for labours not her own.

Canto II

Not with more glories, in th' ethereal plain,
The sun first rises o'er the purpled main,
Than, issuing forth, the rival of his beams
Launched on the bosom of the silver Thames.
Fair nymphs, and well-dressed youths around her shone,
But every eye was fixed on her alone.
On her white breast a sparkling cross she wore,
Which Jews might kiss, and infidels adore.
Her lively looks a sprightly mind disclose,
Quick as her eyes, and as unfixed as those;
Favours to none, to all she smiles extends;
Oft she rejects, but never once offends.
Bright as the sun, her eyes the gazers strike,

And, like the sun, they shine on all alike.
Yet graceful ease, and sweetness void of pride,
Might hide her faults, if belles had faults to hide;
If to her share some female errors fall,
Look on her face, and you 'll forget 'em all.
This nymph, to the destruction of mankind,
Nourished two locks, which graceful hung behind
In equal curls, and well conspired to deck
With shining ringlets the smooth ivory neck.
Love in these labyrinths his slaves detains,
And mighty hearts are held in slender chains.
With hairy springes, we the birds betray,
Slight lines of hair surprise the finny prey,
Fair tresses man's imperial race ensnare,
And beauty draws us with a single hair.
Th' adventurous baron the bright locks admired;
He saw, he wished, and to the prize aspired.
Resolved to win, he meditates the way,
By force to ravish, or by fraud betray;
For when success a lover's toil attends,
Few ask, if fraud or force attained his ends.
For this, ere Phœbus rose, he had implored
Propitious Heaven, and every power adored,
But chiefly Love; to Love an altar built,
Of twelve vast French romances, neatly gilt.
There lay three garters, half a pair of gloves,
And all the trophies of his former loves;
With tender billets-doux he lights the pyre,
And breathes three amorous sighs to raise the fire.
Then prostrate falls, and begs with ardent eyes
Soon to obtain, and long possess the prize.
The powers gave ear, and granted half his prayer;
The rest the winds dispersed in empty air.
But now secure the painted vessel glides,
The sunbeams trembling on the floating tides;
While melting music steals upon the sky,
And softened sounds along the waters die;
Smooth flow the waves, the zephyrs gently play,
Belinda smiled, and all the world was gay.
All but the sylph — with careful thoughts oppressed,
Th' impending woe sat heavy on his breast.
He summons straight his denizens of air;
The lucid squadrons round the sails repair;
Soft o'er the shrouds aërial whispers breathe,
That seemed but zephyrs to the train beneath.
Some to the sun their insect wings unfold,
Waft on the breeze, or sink in clouds of gold;
Transparent forms, too fine for mortal sight,
Their fluid bodies half dissolved in light.
Loose to the wind their airy garments flew,
Thin glittering textures of the filmy dew,
Dipt in the richest tincture of the skies,
Where light disports in ever-mingling dyes,
While every beam new transient colours flings,
Colours that change whene'er they wave their wings.
Amid the circle, on the gilded mast,
Superior by the head, was Ariel placed;
His purple pinions opening to the sun,
He raised his azure wand, and thus begun:
"Ye sylphs and sylphids, to your chief give ear!
Fays, fairies, genii, elves, and demons, hear!
Ye know the spheres, and various tasks assigned
By laws eternal to th' aërial kind.
Some in the fields of purest æther play,
And bask and whiten in the blaze of day.
Some guide the course of wandering orbs on high,
Or roll the planets through the boundless sky.
Some less refined, beneath the moon's pale light
Pursue the stars that shoot athwart the night,
Or suck the mists in grosser air below,
Or dip their pinions in the painted bow,
Or brew fierce tempests on the wintry main,
Or o'er the glebe distil the kindly rain;
Others on earth o'er human race preside,
Watch all their ways, and all their actions guide:
Of these the chief the care of nations own,
And guard with arms divine the British throne.
"Our humbler province is to tend the fair,
Not a less pleasing, though less glorious care;
To save the powder from too rude a gale,
Nor let th' imprisoned essences exhale;
To draw fresh colours from the vernal flowers;
To steal from rainbows, ere they drop in showers,
A brighter wash; to curl their waving hairs,
Assist their blushes, and inspire their airs;
Nay, oft in dreams, invention we bestow,
To change a flounce, or add a furbelow.
"This day, black omens threat the brightest fair
That e'er deserved a watchful spirit's care;
Some dire disaster, or by force, or sleight;
But what, or where, the fates have wrapped in night.
Whether the nymph shall break Diana's law,
Or some frail china jar receive a flaw;
Or stain her honour, or her new brocade;
Forget her prayers, or miss a masquerade;
Or lose her heart, or necklace, at a ball;
Or whether Heaven has doomed that Shock must fall.
Haste, then, ye spirits! to your charge repair;
The fluttering fan be Zephyretta's care;
The drops to thee, Brillante, we consign;
And, Momentilla, let the watch be thine;
Do thou, Crispissa, tend her favourite lock;
Ariel himself shall be the guard of Shock.
To fifty chosen sylphs, of special note,
We trust th' important charge, the petticoat:

Oft have we known that seven-fold fence to fail,
Though stiff with hoops, and armed with ribs of whale;
Form a strong line about the silver bound,
And guard the wide circumference around.
"Whatever spirit, careless of his charge,
His post neglects, or leaves the fair at large,
Shall feel sharp vengeance soon o'ertake his sins,
Be stopped in vials, or transfixed with pins;
Or plunged in lakes of bitter washes lie,
Or wedged whole ages in a bodkin's eye;
Gums and pomatums shall his flight restrain,
While clogged he beats his silken wings in vain;
Or alum styptics with contracting power
Shrink his thin essence like a rivelled flower;
Or, as Ixion fixed, the wretch shall feel
The giddy motion of the whirling mill,
In fumes of burning chocolate shall glow,
And tremble at the sea that froths below!"
He spoke; the spirits from the sails descend;
Some, orb in orb, around the nymph extend;
Some thrid the mazy ringlets of her hair;
Some hang upon the pendants of her ear;
With beating hearts the dire event they wait,
Anxious, and trembling for the birth of fate.

Canto III

Close by those meads, forever crowned with flowers,
Where Thames with pride surveys his rising towers,
There stands a structure of majestic frame,
Which from the neighbouring Hampton takes its name.
Here Britain's statesmen oft the fall foredoom
Of foreign tyrants and of nymphs at home;
Here thou, great Anna! whom three realms obey,
Dost sometimes counsel take — and sometimes tea.
Hither the heroes and the nymphs resort,
To taste awhile the pleasures of a court;
In various talk th' instructive hours they passed,
Who gave the ball, or paid the visit last;
One speaks the glory of the British Queen,
And one describes a charming Indian screen;
A third interprets motions, looks, and eyes;
At every word a reputation dies.
Snuff, or the fan, supply each pause of chat,
With singing, laughing, ogling, and all that.
Meanwhile, declining from the noon of day,
The sun obliquely shoots his burning ray;
The hungry judges soon the sentence sign,
And wretches hang that jurymen may dine;
The merchant from th' Exchange returns in peace,
And the long labours of the toilet cease.
Belinda now, whom thirst of fame invites,
Burns to encounter two adventurous knights,
At ombre singly to decide their doom;
And swells her breast with conquests yet to come.
Straight the three bands prepare in arms to join,
Each band the number of the sacred nine.
Soon as she spreads her hand, th' aërial guard
Descend, and sit on each important card:
First, Ariel perched upon a Matadore,
Then each, according to the rank they bore;
For sylphs, yet mindful of their ancient race,
Are, as when women, wondrous fond of place.
Behold, four kings in majesty revered,
With hoary whiskers and a forky beard;
And four fair queens whose hands sustain a flower,
The expressive emblem of their softer power;
Four knaves in garbs succinct, a trusty band,
Caps on their heads, and halberts in their hand;
And parti-coloured troops, a shining train,
Draw forth to combat on the velvet plain.
The skilful nymph reviews her force with care:
Let spades be trumps! she said, and trumps they were.
Now moved to war her sable Matadores,
In show like leaders of the swarthy Moors.
Spadillio first, unconquerable lord!
Led off two captive trumps, and swept the board.
As many more Manillio forced to yield
And marched a victor from the verdant field.
Him Basto followed, but his fate more hard
Gained but one trump and one plebeian card.
With his broad sabre next, a chief in years,
The hoary majesty of spades appears,
Puts forth one manly leg, to sight revealed,
The rest, his many-coloured robe concealed.
The rebel knave, who dares his prince engage,
Proves the just victim of his royal rage.
E'en mighty Pam, that kings and queens o'erthrew,
And mowed down armies in the fights of Loo,
Sad chance of war! now destitute of aid,
Falls undistinguished by the victor spade!
Thus far both armies to Belinda yield;
Now to the baron fate inclines the field.
His warlike Amazon her host invades,
The imperial consort of the crown of spades;
The club's black tyrant first her victim died,
Spite of his haughty mien, and barbarous pride.
What boots the regal circle on his head,
His giant limbs, in state unwieldy spread;
That long behind he trails his pompous robe,
And, of all monarchs, only grasps the globe?
The baron now his diamonds pours apace;
Th' embroidered king who shows but half his face,
And his refulgent queen, with powers combined,
Of broken troops an easy conquest find.

Clubs, diamonds, hearts, in wild disorder seen,
With throngs promiscuous strew the level green.
Thus when dispersed a routed army runs,
Of Asia's troops, and Afric's sable sons,
With like confusion different nations fly,
Of various habit, and of various dye,
The pierced battalions disunited fall,
In heaps on heaps; one fate o'erwhelms them all.
The knave of diamonds tries his wily arts,
And wins (oh shameful chance!) the queen of hearts.
At this the blood the virgin's cheek forsook,
A livid paleness spreads o'er all her look;
She sees, and trembles at th' approaching ill,
Just in the jaws of ruin, and codille.
And now (as oft in some distempered state)
On one nice trick depends the general fate.
An ace of hearts steps forth; the king unseen
Lurked in her hand, and mourned his captive queen:
He springs to vengeance with an eager pace,
And falls like thunder on the prostrate ace.
The nymph exulting fills with shouts the sky;
The walls, the woods, and long canals reply.
Oh thoughtless mortals! ever blind to fate,
Too soon dejected, and too soon elate.
Sudden, these honours shall be snatched away,
And cursed forever this victorious day.
For lo! the board with cups and spoons is crowned,
The berries crackle, and the mill turns round;
On shining altars of Japan they raise
The silver lamp; the fiery spirits blaze;
From silver spouts the grateful liquors glide,
While China's earth receives the smoking tide:
At once they gratify their scent and taste,
And frequent cups prolong the rich repast.
Straight hover round the fair her airy band;
Some, as she sipped, the fuming liquor fanned,
Some o'er her lap their careful plumes displayed,
Trembling, and conscious of the rich brocade.
Coffee (which makes the politician wise,
And see through all things with his half-shut eyes)
Sent up in vapours to the baron's brain
New stratagems the radiant lock to gain.
Ah, cease, rash youth! desist ere 'tis too late,
Fear the just gods, and think of Scylla's fate!
Changed to a bird, and sent to flit in air,
She dearly pays for Nisus' injured hair!
But when to mischief mortals bend their will,
How soon they find fit instruments of ill!
Just then Clarissa drew with tempting grace
A two-edged weapon from her shining case:
So ladies in romance assist their knight,
Present the spear, and arm him for the fight.
He takes the gift with reverence, and extends
The little engine on his fingers' ends;
This just behind Belinda's neck he spread,
As o'er the fragrant steams she bends her head.
Swift to the lock a thousand sprites repair,
A thousand wings, by turns, blow back the hair;
And thrice they twitched the diamond in her ear;
Thrice she looked back, and thrice the foe drew near.
Just in that instant, anxious Ariel sought
The close recesses of the virgin's thought;
As on the nosegay in her breast reclined,
He watched th' ideas rising in her mind,
Sudden he viewed, in spite of all her art,
An earthly lover lurking at her heart.
Amazed, confused, he found his power expired,
Resigned to fate, and with a sigh retired.
The peer now spreads the glittering forfex wide,
T' inclose the lock; now joins it, to divide.
E'en then, before the fatal engine closed,
A wretched sylph too fondly interposed;
Fate urged the shears, and cut the sylph in twain,
(But airy substance soon unites again).
The meeting points the sacred hair dissever
From the fair head, forever, and forever!
Then flashed the living lightning from her eyes,
And screams of horror rend th' affrighted skies.
Not louder shrieks to pitying Heaven are cast,
When husbands, or when lap-dogs breathe their last;
Or when rich China vessels, fallen from high,
In glittering dust and painted fragments lie!
"Let wreaths of triumph now my temples twine,"
The victor cried; "the glorious prize is mine!
While fish in streams, or birds delight in air,
Or in a coach and six the British fair,
As long as Atalantis shall be read,
Or the small pillow grace a lady's bed,
While visits shall be paid on solemn days,
When numerous wax-lights in bright order blaze,
While nymphs take treats, or assignations give,
So long my honour, name, and praise shall live!
What Time would spare, from steel receives its date,
And monuments, like men, submit to fate!
Steel could the labour of the gods destroy,
And strike to dust th' imperial towers of Troy;
Steel could the works of mortal pride confound,
And hew triumphal arches to the ground.
What wonder then, fair nymph! thy hairs should feel,
The conquering force of unresisted steel?"

Canto IV

But anxious cares the pensive nymph oppressed,
And secret passions laboured in her breast.
Not youthful kings in battle seized alive,
Not scornful virgins who their charms survive,
Not ardent lovers robbed of all their bliss,
Not ancient ladies when refused a kiss,
Not tyrants fierce that unrepenting die,
Not Cynthia when her manteau's pinned awry,
E'er felt such rage, resentment, and despair,
As thou, sad virgin, for thy ravished hair.
For, that sad moment, when the sylphs withdrew
And Ariel weeping from Belinda flew,
Umbriel, a dusky, melancholy sprite,
As ever sullied the fair face of light,
Down to the central earth, his proper scene,
Repaired to search the gloomy cave of Spleen.
Swift on his sooty pinions flits the gnome,
And in a vapour reached the dismal dome.
No cheerful breeze this sullen region knows,
The dreaded east is all the wind that blows.
Here in a grotto, sheltered close from air,
And screened in shades from day's detested glare,
She sighs forever on her pensive bed,
Pain at her side, and Megrim at her head.
Two handmaids wait the throne, alike in place,
But differing far in figure and in face.
Here stood Ill-nature like an ancient maid,
Her wrinkled form in black and white arrayed;
With store of prayers, for mornings, nights, and noons
Her hand is filled; her bosom with lampoons.
There Affectation, with a sickly mien,
Shows in her cheek the roses of eighteen,
Practised to lisp, and hang the head aside,
Faints into airs, and languishes with pride,
On the rich quilt sinks with becoming woe,
Wrapped in a gown, for sickness, and for show.
The fair ones feel such maladies as these,
When each new night-dress gives a new disease.
A constant vapour o'er the palace flies;
Strange phantoms rising as the mists arise;
Dreadful, as hermit's dreams in haunted shades,
Or bright, as visions of expiring maids.
Now glaring fiends, and snakes on rolling spires,
Pale spectres, gaping tombs, and purple fires;
Now lakes of liquid gold, Elysian scenes,
And crystal domes, and angels in machines.
Unnumbered throngs on every side are seen,
Of bodies changed to various forms by Spleen.
Here living tea-pots stand, one arm held out,
One bent; the handle this, and that the spout.
A pipkin there, like Homer's tripod, walks;
Here sighs a jar, and there a goose-pie talks;
Men prove with child, as powerful fancy works,
And maids, turned bottles, call aloud for corks.
Safe past the gnome through this fantastic band,
A branch of healing spleenwort in his hand.
Then thus addressed the power: "Hail, wayward queen!
Who rule the sex, to fifty from fifteen:
Parent of vapours and of female wit;
Who give th' hysteric, or poetic fit;
On various tempers act by various ways,
Make some take physic, others scribble plays;
Who cause the proud their visits to delay,
And send the godly in a pet to pray.
A nymph there is, that all thy power disdains,
And thousands more in equal mirth maintains.
But oh! if e'er thy gnome could spoil a grace,
Or raise a pimple on a beauteous face,
Like citron-waters matrons' cheeks inflame,
Or change complexions at a losing game;
If e'er with airy horns I planted heads,
Or rumpled petticoats, or tumbled beds,
Or caused suspicion when no soul was rude,
Or discomposed the head-dress of a prude,
Or e'er to costive lap-dog gave disease,
Which not the tears of brightest eyes could ease:
Hear me, and touch Belinda with chagrin,
That single act gives half the world the spleen."
The goddess with a discontented air
Seems to reject him, though she grants his prayer.
A wondrous bag with both her hands she binds,
Like that where once Ulysses held the winds;
There she collects the force of female lungs,
Sighs, sobs, and passions, and the war of tongues.
A vial next she fills with fainting fears,
Soft sorrows, melting griefs, and flowing tears.
The gnome rejoicing bears her gifts away,
Spreads his black wings, and slowly mounts to day.
Sunk in Thalestris' arms the nymph he found,
Her eyes dejected and her hair unbound.
Full o'er their heads the swelling bag he rent,
And all the furies issued at the vent.
Belinda burns with more than mortal ire,
And fierce Thalestris fans the rising fire.
"O wretched maid!" she spread her hands, and cried,
(While Hampton's echoes, "Wretched maid!" replied)
"Was it for this you took such constant care
The bodkin, comb, and essence to prepare?
For this your locks in paper durance bound,
For this with torturing irons wreathed around?
For this with fillets strained your tender head,
And bravely bore the double loads of lead?
Gods! shall the ravisher display your hair,
While the fops envy, and the ladies stare!
Honour forbid! at whose unrivalled shrine

Ease, pleasure, virtue, all our sex resign.
Methinks already I your tears survey,
Already hear the horrid things they say,
Already see you a degraded toast,
And all your honour in a whisper lost!
How shall I, then, your helpless fame defend?
'Twill then be infamy to seem your friend!
And shall this prize, th' inestimable prize,
Exposed through crystal to the gazing eyes,
And heightened by the diamond's circling rays,
On that rapacious hand forever blaze?
Sooner shall grass in Hyde Park Circus grow,
And wits take lodgings in the sound of Bow;
Sooner let earth, air, sea, to chaos fall,
Men, monkeys, lap-dogs, parrots, perish all!"
She said; then raging to Sir Plume repairs,
And bids her beau demand the precious hairs
(Sir Plume, of amber snuff-box justly vain,
And the nice conduct of a clouded cane).
With earnest eyes, and round unthinking face,
He first the snuff-box opened, then the case,
And thus broke out — "My lord, why, what the devil?
Zounds! damn the lock! 'fore Gad, you must be civil!
Plague on't! 'tis past a jest — nay prithee, pox!
Give her the hair," he spoke, and rapped his box.
"It grieves me much," replied the peer again,
"Who speaks so well should ever speak in vain.
But by this lock, this sacred lock, I swear,
(Which never more shall join its parted hair;
Which never more its honours shall renew,
Clipped from the lovely head where late it grew)
That while my nostrils draw the vital air,
This hand, which won it, shall forever wear."
He spoke, and speaking, in proud triumph spread
The long-contended honours of her head.
But Umbriel, hateful gnome! forbears not so;
He breaks the vial whence the sorrows flow.
Then see! the nymph in beauteous grief appears,
Her eyes half languishing, half drowned in tears;
On her heaved bosom hung her drooping head,
Which, with a sigh, she raised; and thus she said:
"Forever curs'd be this detested day,
Which snatched my best, my favourite curl away!
Happy! ah, ten times happy had I been,
If Hampton Court these eyes had never seen!
Yet am not I the first mistaken maid,
By love of courts to numerous ills betrayed.
Oh, had I rather unadmired remained
In some lone isle or distant northern land;
Where the gilt chariot never marks the way,
Where none learn ombre, none e'er taste bohea!
There kept my charms concealed from mortal eye,
Like roses, that in deserts bloom and die.
What moved my mind with youthful lords to roam?
Oh, had I stayed, and said my prayers at home!
'Twas this, the morning omens seemed to tell:
Thrice from my trembling hand the patch-box fell;
The tottering china shook without a wind;
Nay, Poll sat mute, and Shock was most unkind!
A sylph, too, warned me of the threats of fate,
In mystic visions, now believed too late!
See the poor remnants of these slighted hairs!
My hands shall rend what e'en thy rapine spares;
These in two sable ringlets taught to break,
Once gave new beauties to the snowy neck;
The sister lock now sits uncouth, alone,
And in its fellow's fate foresees its own;
Uncurled it hangs, the fatal shears demands,
And tempts once more, thy sacrilegious hands.
Oh, hadst thou, cruel! been content to seize
Hairs less in sight, or any hairs but these!"

Canto V

She said: the pitying audience melt in tears.
But Fate and Jove had stopped the baron's ears.
In vain Thalestris with reproach assails,
For who can move when fair Belinda fails?
Not half so fixed the Trojan could remain,
While Anna begged and Dido raged in vain.
Then grave Clarissa graceful waved her fan;
Silence ensued, and thus the nymph began:
"Say, why are beauties praised and honoured most,
The wise man's passion, and the vain man's toast?
Why decked with all that land and sea afford,
Why angels called, and angel-like adored?
Why round our coaches crowd the white-gloved beaux,
Why bows the side-box from its inmost rows?
How vain are all these glories, all our pains,
Unless good sense preserve what beauty gains;
That men may say, when we the front-box grace,
'Behold the first in virtue as in face!'
Oh! if to dance all night, and dress all day,
Charmed the small-pox, or chased old age away,
Who would not scorn what housewife's cares produce,
Or who would learn one earthly thing of use?
To patch, nay ogle, might become a saint,
Nor could it sure be such a sin to paint.
But since, alas! frail beauty must decay;
Curled or uncurled, since locks will turn to grey;
Since painted, or not painted, all shall fade,
And she who scorns a man must die a maid;

What then remains but well our power to use,
And keep good humour still whate'er we lose?
And trust me, dear! good humour can prevail,
When airs, and flights, and screams, and scolding fail.
Beauties in vain their pretty eyes may roll;
Charms strike the sight, but merit wins the soul."
 So spoke the dame, but no applause ensued;
Belinda frowned, Thalestris called her prude.
"To arms, to arms!" the fierce virago cries,
And swift as lightning to the combat flies.
All side in parties, and begin th' attack;
Fans clap, silks rustle, and tough whalebones crack;
Heroes' and heroines' shouts confus'dly rise,
And bass and treble voices strike the skies.
No common weapons in their hands are found,
Like gods they fight, nor dread a mortal wound.
 So when bold Homer makes the gods engage,
And heavenly breasts with human passions rage;
'Gainst Pallas, Mars; Latona, Hermes arms;
And all Olympus rings with loud alarms:
Jove's thunder roars, Heaven trembles all around,
Blue Neptune storms, the bellowing deeps resound:
Earth shakes her nodding towers, the ground gives way,
And the pale ghosts start at the flash of day!
 Triumphant Umbriel on a sconce's height
Clapped his glad wings, and sat to view the fight;
Propped on their bodkin spears, the sprites survey
The growing combat, or assist the fray.
 While through the press enraged Thalestris flies,
And scatters death around from both her eyes,
A beau and witling perished in the throng,
One died in metaphor, and one in song.
"O cruel nymph! a living death I bear,"
Cried Dapperwit, and sunk beside his chair.
A mournful glance Sir Fopling upwards cast,
"Those eyes are made so killing" — was his last.
Thus on Mæander's flowery margin lies
Th' expiring swan, and as he sings he dies.
 When bold Sir Plume had drawn Clarissa down,
Chloe stepped in and killed him with a frown;
She smiled to see the doughty hero slain,
But, at her smile, the beau revived again.
 Now Jove suspends his golden scales in air,
Weighs the men's wits against the lady's hair;
The doubtful beam long nods from side to side;
At length the wits mount up, the hairs subside.
 See, fierce Belinda on the Baron flies,
With more than usual lightning in her eyes;
Nor feared the chief th' unequal fight to try,
Who sought no more than on his foe to die.
But this bold lord with manly strength endued,
She with one finger and a thumb subdued:
Just where the breath of life his nostrils drew,
A charge of snuff the wily virgin threw;
The gnomes direct, to every atom just,
The pungent grains of titillating dust.
Sudden, with starting tears each eye o'erflows,
And the high dome re-echoes to his nose.
 "Now meet thy fate," incensed Belinda cried,
And drew a deadly bodkin from her side.
(The same, his ancient personage to deck,
Her great great grandsire wore about his neck,
In three seal-rings; which after, melted down,
Formed a vast buckle for his widow's gown;
Her infant grandame's whistle next it grew,
The bells she jingled, and the whistle blew;
Then in a bodkin graced her mother's hairs,
Which long she wore, and now Belinda wears.)
 "Boast not my fall," he cried, "insulting foe!
Thou by some other shalt be laid as low;
Nor think to die dejects my lofty mind:
All that I dread is leaving you behind!
Rather than so, ah, let me still survive,
And burn in Cupid's flames — but burn alive."
 "Restore the lock!" she cries; and all around
"Restore the lock!" the vaulted roofs rebound.
Not fierce Othello in so loud a strain
Roared for the handkerchief that caused his pain.
But see how oft ambitious aims are crossed,
And chiefs contend till all the prize is lost!
The lock, obtained with guilt, and kept with pain,
In every place is sought, but sought in vain:
With such a prize no mortal must be blessed,
So Heaven decrees! with Heaven who can contest?
 Some thought it mounted to the lunar sphere,
Since all things lost on earth are treasured there.
There heroes' wits are kept in ponderous vases,
And beaux' in snuff-boxes and tweezer cases;
There broken vows and death-bed alms are found,
And lovers' hearts with ends of riband bound,
The courtier's promises, and sick man's prayers,
The smiles of harlots, and the tears of heirs,
Cages for gnats, and chains to yoke a flea,
Dried butterflies, and tomes of casuistry.
 But trust the Muse — she saw it upward rise,
Though marked by none but quick, poetic eyes:
(So Rome's great founder to the heavens withdrew,
To Proculus alone confessed in view)
A sudden star, it shot through liquid air,
And drew behind a radiant trail of hair.
Not Berenice's locks first rose so bright,
The heavens bespangling with dishevelled light.
The sylphs behold it kindling as it flies,
And pleased pursue its progress through the skies
 This the beau monde shall from the Mall survey,

And hail with music its propitious ray.
This the blest lover shall for Venus take,
And send up vows from Rosamonda's lake.
This Partridge soon shall view in cloudless skies,
When next he looks through Galileo's eyes;
And hence th' egregious wizard shall foredoom
The fate of Louis and the fall of Rome.
Then cease, bright nymph! to mourn thy ravished hair,
Which adds new glory to the shining sphere!
Not all the tresses that fair head can boast,
Shall draw such envy as the lock you lost.
For, after all the murders of your eye,
When, after millions slain, yourself shall die;
When those fair suns shall set, as set they must,
And all those tresses shall be laid in dust:
This lock, the Muse shall consecrate to fame,
And 'midst the stars inscribe Belinda's name.

From ELOÏSA TO ABELARD

In these deep solitudes and awful cells,
Where heavenly-pensive contemplation dwells,
And ever-musing melancholy reigns,
What means this tumult in a vestal's veins?
Why rove my thoughts beyond this last retreat?
Why feels my heart its long-forgotten heat?
Yet, yet I love! — from Abelard it came,
And Eloïsa yet must kiss the name.
Dear fatal name! rest ever unrevealed,
Nor pass these lips in holy silence sealed!
Hide it, my heart, within that close disguise,
Where mixed with God's, his loved idea lies!
Oh, write it not, my hand — the name appears
Already written — wash it out, my tears!
In vain lost Eloïsa weeps and prays;
Her heart still dictates, and her hand obeys.
Relentless walls! whose darksome round contains
Repentant sighs, and voluntary pains:
Ye rugged rocks! which holy knees have worn;
Ye grots and caverns shagg'd with horrid thorn!
Shrines! where their vigils pale-eyed virgins keep,
And pitying saints, whose statues learn to weep!
Though cold like you, unmoved and silent grown,
I have not yet forgot myself to stone.
All is not Heaven's while Abelard has part,
Still rebel nature holds out half my heart;
Nor prayers nor fasts its stubborn pulse restrain,
Nor tears, for ages taught to flow in vain.
Soon as thy letters trembling I unclose,
That well-known name awakens all my woes.
Oh, name forever sad! forever dear!
Still breathed in sighs, still ushered with a tear.
I tremble too, where'er my own I find;
Some dire misfortune follows close behind.
Line after line my gushing eyes o'erflow,
Led through a sad variety of woe:
Now warm in love, now withering in my bloom,
Lost in a convent's solitary gloom!
There stern religion quenched th' unwilling flame,
There died the best of passions, love and fame.
Yet write, oh! write me all, that I may join
Griefs to thy griefs, and echo sighs to thine.
Nor foes nor fortune take this power away;
And is my Abelard less kind than they?
Tears still are mine, and those I need not spare,
Love but demands what else were shed in prayer;
No happier task these faded eyes pursue;
To read and weep is all they now can do.
Then share thy pain, allow that sad relief;
Ah, more than share it, give me all thy grief.
Heaven first taught letters for some wretch's aid,
Some banished lover, or some captive maid;
They live, they speak, they breathe what love inspires,
Warm from the soul, and faithful to its fires,
The virgin's wish without her fears impart,
Excuse the blush, and pour out all the heart,
Speed the soft intercourse from soul to soul,
And waft a sigh from Indus to the Pole.
Thou know'st how guiltless first I met thy flame,
When love approached me under friendship's name;
My fancy formed thee of angelic kind,
Some emanation of th' all-beauteous Mind.
Those smiling eyes, attempering every ray,
Shone sweetly lambent with celestial day.
Guiltless I gazed; Heaven listened while you sung;
And truths divine came mended from that tongue.
From lips like those what precept failed to move?
Too soon they taught me 'twas no sin to love;
Back through the paths of pleasing sense I ran,
Nor wished an angel whom I loved a man.
Dim and remote the joys of saints I see;
Nor envy them that Heaven I lose for thee.

* * * * * * *

How happy is the blameless vestal's lot!
The world forgetting, by the world forgot:
Eternal sunshine of the spotless mind!
Each prayer accepted, and each wish resigned;
Labour and rest, that equal periods keep;
"Obedient slumbers that can wake and weep;"
Desires composed, affections ever even;
Tears that delight, and sighs that waft to Heaven.
Grace shines around her with serenest beams,
And whispering angels prompt her golden dreams.
For her th' unfading rose of Eden blooms,
And wings of seraphs shed divine perfumes;
For her the Spouse prepares the bridal ring;

For her white virgins hymenæals sing;
To sounds of heavenly harps she dies away,
And melts in visions of eternal day.
  Far other dreams my erring soul employ,
Far other raptures, of unholy joy.
When at the close of each sad, sorrowing day,
Fancy restores what vengeance snatched away,
Then conscience sleeps, and leaving nature free
All my loose soul unbounded springs to thee.
O curs'd, dear horrors of all-conscious night!
How glowing guilt exalts the keen delight!
Provoking demons all restraint remove,
And stir within me every source of love.
I hear thee, view thee, gaze o'er all thy charms,
And round thy phantom glue my clasping arms.
I wake: — no more I hear, no more I view;
The phantom flies me, as unkind as you.
I call aloud; it hears not what I say:
I stretch my empty arms; it glides away.
To dream once more I close my willing eyes;
Ye soft illusions, dear deceits, arise!
Alas, no more! methinks we wandering go
Through dreary wastes, and weep each other's woe,
Where round some mouldering tower pale ivy creeps,
And low-browed rocks hang nodding o'er the deeps.
Sudden you mount, you beckon from the skies;
Clouds interpose, waves roar, and winds arise.
I shriek, start up, the same sad prospect find,
And wake to all the griefs I left behind.
  For thee the fates, severely kind, ordain
A cool suspense from pleasure and from pain;
Thy life, a long, dead calm of fixed repose;
No pulse that riots, and no blood that glows;
Still as the sea, ere winds were taught to blow,
Or moving spirit bade the waters flow;
Soft as the slumbers of a saint forgiven,
And mild as opening gleams of promised Heaven.

* * * * * * *

  I come, I come! prepare your roseate bowers,
Celestial palms, and ever-blooming flowers.
Thither, where sinners may have rest, I go,
Where flames refined in breasts seraphic glow.
Thou, Abelard! the last sad office pay,
And smooth my passage to the realms of day.
See my lips tremble, and my eye-balls roll,
Suck my last breath, and catch my flying soul!
Ah, no; in sacred vestments may'st thou stand,
The hallowed taper trembling in thy hand,
Present the cross before my lifted eye,
Teach me at once, and learn of me to die.
Ah, then thy once-loved Eloïsa see!
It will be then no crime to gaze on me.
See from my cheek the transient roses fly!
See the last sparkle languish in my eye!
Till every motion, pulse, and breath be o'er;
And e'en my Abelard be loved no more.
O Death all-eloquent! you only prove
What dust we dote on, when 'tis man we love.
  Then too, when fate shall thy fair frame destroy,
(That cause of all my guilt, and all my joy)
In trance ecstatic may thy pangs be drowned,
Bright clouds descend, and angels watch thee round,
From opening skies may streaming glories shine,
And saints embrace thee with a love like mine.
  May one kind grave unite each hapless name,
And graft my love immortal on thy fame!
Then, ages hence, when all my woes are o'er,
When this rebellious heart shall beat no more;
If ever chance two wandering lovers brings
To Paraclete's white walls and silver springs,
O'er the pale marble shall they join their heads,
And drink the falling tears each other sheds;
Then sadly say, with mutual pity moved,
"Oh, may we never love as these have loved!"
From the full choir when loud hosannas rise,
And swell the pomp of dreadful sacrifice,
Amid that scene if some relenting eye
Glance on the stone where our cold relics lie,
Devotion's self shall steal a thought from Heaven,
One human tear shall drop and be forgiven.
  And sure if fate some future bard shall join
In sad similitude of griefs to mine,
Condemned whole years in absence to deplore,
And image charms he must behold no more;
Such if there be, who loves so long, so well;
Let him our sad, our tender story tell;
The well-sung woes will soothe my pensive ghost;
He best can paint them who shall feel them most.

From AN ESSAY ON MAN

BOOK I

Awake, my St. John! leave all meaner things
To low ambition, and the pride of kings.
Let us (since life can little more supply
Than just to look about us and to die)
Expatiate free o'er all this scene of man;
A mighty maze! but not without a plan;
A wild, where weeds and flowers promiscuous shoot;
Or garden, tempting with forbidden fruit.
Together let us beat this ample field,
Try what the open, what the covert yield;
The latent tracts, the giddy heights, explore
Of all who blindly creep, or sightless soar;

Eye nature's walks, shoot folly as it flies,
And catch the manners living as they rise;
Laugh where we must, be candid where we can;
But vindicate the ways of God to man.
I. Say first, of God above, or man below,
What can we reason, but from what we know?
Of man, what see we but his station here
From which to reason or to which refer?
Through worlds unnumbered though the God be known,
'Tis ours to trace him only in our own.
He, who through vast immensity can pierce,
See worlds on worlds compose one universe,
Observe how system into system runs,
What other planets circle other suns,
What varied being peoples every star,
May tell why Heaven has made us as we are.
But of this frame the bearings, and the ties,
The strong connections, nice dependencies,
Gradations just, has thy pervading soul
Looked through? or can a part contain the whole?
Is the great chain, that draws all to agree,
And drawn supports, upheld by God, or thee?
II. Presumptuous man! the reason wouldst thou find,
Why formed so weak, so little, and so blind?
First, if thou canst, the harder reason guess,
Why formed no weaker, blinder, and no less?
Ask of thy mother earth, why oaks are made
Taller or stronger than the weeds they shade?
Or ask of yonder argent fields above,
Why Jove's satellites are less than Jove.
Of systems possible, if 'tis confessed
That wisdom infinite must form the best,
Where all must full or not coherent be,
And all that rises, rise in due degree;
Then, in the scale of reasoning life, 'tis plain,
There must be, somewhere, such a rank as man:
And all the question (wrangle e'er so long)
Is only this, if God has placed him wrong?
Respecting man, whatever wrong we call,
May, must be right, as relative to all.
In human works, though laboured on with pain,
A thousand movements scarce one purpose gain;
In God's, one single can its end produce;
Yet serves to second too some other use.
So man, who here seems principal alone,
Perhaps acts second to some sphere unknown,
Touches some wheel, or verges to some goal;
'Tis but a part we see, and not a whole.
When the proud steed shall know why man restrains
His fiery course, or drives him o'er the plains;
When the dull ox, why now he breaks the clod,
Is now a victim, and now Egypt's god:
Then shall man's pride and dullness comprehend
His actions', passions', being's, use and end;
Why doing, suffering, checked, impelled; and why
This hour a slave, the next a deity.
Then say not man's imperfect, Heaven in fault;
Say rather, man's as perfect as he ought:
His knowledge measured to his state and place,
His time a moment, and a point his space.
If to be perfect in a certain sphere,
What matter, soon or late, or here or there?
The blest to-day is as completely so,
As who began a thousand years ago.
III. Heaven from all creatures hides the book of fate,
All but the page prescribed, their present state:
From brutes what men, from men what spirits know:
Or who could suffer being here below?
The lamb thy riot dooms to bleed to-day,
Had he thy reason, would he skip and play?
Pleased to the last, he crops the flowery food,
And licks the hand just raised to shed his blood.
Oh, blindness to the future! kindly given,
That each may fill the circle marked by Heaven:
Who sees with equal eye, as God of all,
A hero perish, or a sparrow fall,
Atoms or systems into ruin hurled,
And now a bubble burst, and now a world.
Hope humbly then; with trembling pinions soar;
Wait the great teacher Death; and God adore.
What future bliss, he gives not thee to know,
But gives that hope to be thy blessing now.
Hope springs eternal in the human breast:
Man never is, but always to be blest.
The soul, uneasy and confined from home,
Rests and expatiates in a life to come.
Lo, the poor Indian! whose untutored mind
Sees God in clouds, or hears him in the wind;
His soul, proud science never taught to stray
Far as the solar walk, or milky way;
Yet simple nature to his hope has given,
Behind the cloud-topped hill, an humbler Heaven;
Some safer world in depths of woods embraced,
Some happier island in the watery waste,
Where slaves once more their native land behold
No fiends torment, no Christians thirst for gold.
To be, contents his natural desire,
He asks no angel's wing, no seraph's fire;
But thinks, admitted to that equal sky,
His faithful dog shall bear him company.
IV. Go, wiser thou! and, in thy scale of sense
Weigh thy opinion against Providence;
Call imperfection what thou fanciest such,
Say, "Here he gives too little, there too much;"
Destroy all creatures for thy sport or gust,
Yet cry, "If man's unhappy, God's unjust;"

If man alone engross not Heaven's high care,
Alone made perfect here, immortal there,
Snatch from his hand the balance and the rod,
Re-judge his justice, be the god of God.
In pride, in reasoning pride, our error lies;
All quit their sphere, and rush into the skies.
Pride still is aiming at the blest abodes,
Men would be angels, angels would be gods.
Aspiring to be gods, if angels fell,
Aspiring to be angels, men rebel:
And who but wishes to invert the laws
Of order, sins against the Eternal Cause.
V. Ask for what end the heavenly bodies shine,
Earth for whose use? Pride answers, "'Tis for mine:
For me kind nature wakes her genial power,
Suckles each herb, and spreads out every flower;
Annual for me, the grape, the rose renew
The juice nectareous, and the balmy dew;
For me, the mine a thousand treasures brings;
For me, health gushes from a thousand springs;
Seas roll to waft me, suns to light me rise;
My footstool earth, my canopy the skies."
But errs not Nature from this gracious end,
From burning suns when livid deaths descend,
When earthquakes swallow, or when tempests sweep
Towns to one grave, whole nations to the deep?
No ('tis replied), the first Almighty Cause
Acts not by partial, but by general laws;
Th' exceptions few; some change, since all began:
And what created perfect? — Why then man?
If the great end be human happiness,
Then nature deviates; and can man do less?
As much that end a constant course requires
Of showers and sunshine, as of man's desires;
As much eternal springs and cloudless skies,
As men forever temperate, calm, and wise.
If plagues or earthquakes break not Heaven's design,
Why then a Borgia, or a Catiline?
Who knows but He, whose hand the lightning forms,
Who heaves old ocean, and who wings the storms;
Pours fierce ambition in a Cæsar's mind,
Or turns young Ammon loose to scourge mankind?
From pride, from pride, our very reasoning springs.
Account for moral, as for natural things:
Why charge we Heaven in those, in these acquit?
In both, to reason right is to submit,
Better for us, perhaps, it might appear,
Were there all harmony, all virtue here;
That never air or ocean felt the wind;
That never passion discomposed the mind.
But all subsists by elemental strife;
And passions are the elements of life.
The general order, since the whole began,
Is kept in nature, and is kept in man.
VI. What would this man? Now upward will he soar,
And little less than angel, would be more;
Now looking downwards, just as grieved appears
To want the strength of bulls, the fur of bears.
Made for his use all creatures if he call,
Say what their use, had he the powers of all?
Nature to these, without profusion, kind,
The proper organs, proper powers assigned;
Each seeming want compensated of course,
Here with degrees of swiftness, there of force;
All in exact proportion to the state;
Nothing to add, and nothing to abate.
Each beast, each insect, happy in its own:
Is Heaven unkind to man, and man alone?
Shall he alone, whom rational we call,
Be pleased with nothing, if not blessed with all?
The bliss of man (could pride that blessing find)
Is not to act or think beyond mankind;
No powers of body or of soul to share,
But what his nature and his state can bear.
Why has not man a microscopic eye?
For this plain reason, man is not a fly.
Say what the use, were finer optics given,
T' inspect a mite, not comprehend the heaven?
Or touch, if tremblingly alive all o'er,
To smart and agonize at every pore?
Or, quick effluvia darting through the brain,
Die of a rose in aromatic pain?
If nature thundered in his opening ears,
And stunned him with the music of the spheres,
How would he wish that Heaven had left him still
The whispering zephyr, and the purling rill?
Who finds not Providence all good and wise,
Alike in what it gives, and what denies?
VII. Far as creation's ample range extends,
The scale of sensual, mental power ascends.
Mark how it mounts, to man's imperial race,
From the green myriads in the peopled grass:
What modes of sight betwixt each wide extreme,
The mole's dim curtain, and the lynx's beam:
Of smell, the headlong lioness between
And hound sagacious on the tainted green:
Of hearing, from the life that fills the flood,
To that which warbles through the vernal wood:
The spider's touch, how exquisitely fine!
Feels at each thread, and lives along the line:
In the nice bee, what sense so subtly true
From poisonous herbs extracts the healing dew?
How instinct varies in the grovelling swine,
Compared, half-reasoning elephant, with thine!

'Twixt that and reason, what a nice barrier,
Forever separate, yet forever near!
Remembrance and reflection how allied;
What thin partitions sense from thought divide:
And middle natures, how they long to join,
Yet never pass th' insuperable line!
Without this just gradation, could they be
Subjected, these to those, or all to thee?
The powers of all subdued by thee alone,
Is not thy reason all these powers in one?
VIII. See, through this air, this ocean, and this earth
All matter quick, and bursting into birth.
Above, how high, progressive life may go!
Around, how wide! how deep extend below!
Vast chain of being! which from God began,
Natures ethereal, human, angel, man,
Beast, bird, fish, insect, what no eye can see,
No glass can reach; from infinite to thee,
From thee to nothing. — On superior powers
Were we to press, inferior might on ours;
Or in the full creation leave a void,
Where, one step broken, the great scale's destroyed:
From nature's chain whatever link you strike,
Tenth, or ten thousandth, breaks the chain alike.
And, if each system in gradation roll
Alike essential to th' amazing whole,
The least confusion but in one, not all
That system only but the whole must fall.
Let earth unbalanced from her orbit fly,
Planets and suns run lawless through the sky;
Let ruling angels from their spheres be hurled,
Being on being wrecked, and world on world;
Heaven's whole foundations to their centre nod,
And nature tremble to the throne of God.
All this dread order break — for whom? for thee?
Vile worm! — Oh, madness! pride! impiety!
IX. What if the foot, ordained the dust to tread,
Or hand, to toil, aspired to be the head?
What if the head, the eye, or ear repined
To serve mere engines to the ruling mind?
Just as absurd for any part to claim
To be another, in this general frame;
Just as absurd, to mourn the tasks or pains,
The great directing Mind of all ordains.
All are but parts of one stupendous whole,
Whose body nature is, and God the soul;
That, changed through all, and yet in all the same;
Great in the earth, as in th' ethereal frame;
Warms in the sun, refreshes in the breeze,
Glows in the stars, and blossoms in the trees,
Lives through all life, extends through all extent,
Spreads undivided, operates unspent;
Breathes in our soul, informs our mortal part,
As full, as perfect, in a hair as heart;
As full, as perfect, in vile man that mourns,
As the rapt seraph that adores and burns:
To him no high, no low, no great, no small;
He fills, he bounds, connects, and equals all.
X. Cease then, nor order imperfection name:
Our proper bliss depends on what we blame.
Know thy own point: this kind, this due degree
Of blindness, weakness, Heaven bestows on thee.
Submit. — In this, or any other sphere,
Secure to be as blest as thou canst bear:
Safe in the hand of one disposing Power,
Or in the natal, or the mortal hour.
All nature is but art, unknown to thee;
All chance, direction, which thou canst not see;
All discord, harmony not understood;
All partial evil, universal good:
And, spite of pride, in erring reason's spite,
One truth is clear, Whatever is, is right.

EPISTLE TO DR. ARBUTHNOT

P. Shut, shut the door, good John! fatigued, I said?
Tie up the knocker, say I'm sick, I'm dead.
The Dog-star rages! nay, 'tis past a doubt,
All Bedlam, or Parnassus, is let out:
Fire in each eye, and papers in each hand,
They rave, recite, and madden round the land.
What walls can guard me, or what shades can hide?
They pierce my thickets, through my grot they glide;
By land, by water, they renew the charge,
They stop the chariot, and they board the barge.
No place is sacred, not the church is free;
E'en Sunday shines no Sabbath day to me:
Then from the Mint walks forth the man of rhyme,
Happy to catch me just at dinner-time.
Is there a parson, much bemused in beer,
A maudlin poetess, a rhyming peer,
A clerk, foredoomed his father's soul to cross,
Who pens a stanza, when he should engross?
Is there, who, locked from ink and paper, scrawls
With desperate charcoal round his darkened walls?
All fly to Twit'nam, and in humble strain
Apply to me, to keep them mad or vain.
Arthur, whose giddy son neglects the laws,
Imputes to me and my damn'd works the cause:
Poor Cornus sees his frantic wife elope,
And curses wit, and poetry, and Pope.
Friend to my life! (which did not you prolong,
The world had wanted many an idle song)
What drop or nostrum can this plague remove?
Or which must end me, a fool's wrath or love?

A dire dilemma! either way I'm sped:
If foes, they write, if friends, they read me dead.
Seized and tied down to judge, how wretched I!
Who can't be silent, and who will not lie.
To laugh, were want of goodness and of grace,
And to be grave, exceeds all power of face.
I sit with sad civility, I read
With honest anguish, and an aching head;
And drop at last, but in unwilling ears,
This saving counsel, "Keep your piece nine years."
  "Nine years!" cries he, who high in Drury Lane,
Lulled by soft zephyrs through the broken pane,
Rhymes ere he wakes, and prints before term ends,
Obliged by hunger, and request of friends:
"The piece, you think, is incorrect? why, take it,
I'm all submission, what you'd have it, make it."
  Three things another's modest wishes bound,
My friendship, and a prologue, and ten pound.
  Pitholeon sends to me: "You know his Grace,
I want a patron; ask him for a place."
"Pitholeon libelled me" — "But here's a letter
Informs you, sir, 'twas when he knew no better.
Dare you refuse him? Curll invites to dine,
He'll write a journal, or he'll turn divine."
  Bless me! a packet. — "'Tis a stranger sues,
A virgin tragedy, an orphan Muse."
If I dislike it, "Furies, death and rage!"
If I approve, "Commend it to the stage."
There (thank my stars) my whole commission ends,
The players and I are, luckily, no friends.
Fired that the house reject him, "'Sdeath I'll print it,
And shame the fools —— Your interest, sir, with Lintot!"
"Lintot, dull rogue! will think your price too much:"
"Not, sir, if you revise it, and retouch."
All my demurs but double his attacks;
At last he whispers, "Do; and we go snacks."
Glad of a quarrel, straight I clap the door;
"Sir, let me see your works and you no more."
  'Tis sung, when Midas' ears began to spring,
(Midas, a sacred person and a king)
His very minister who spied them first,
(Some say his queen) was forced to speak, or burst.
And is not mine, my friend, a sorer case,
When every coxcomb perks them in my face?
A. Good friend, forbear! you deal in dangerous things.
I'd never name queens, ministers, or kings;
Keep close to ears, and those let asses prick;
'Tis nothing — *P*. Nothing? if they bite and kick?
Out with it, Dunciad! let the secret pass,
That secret to each fool, that he's an ass:
The truth once told (and wherefore should we lie?),
The Queen of Midas slept, and so may I.
  You think this cruel? take it for a rule,
No creature smarts so little as a fool.
Let peals of laughter, Codrus! round thee break,
Thou unconcerned canst hear the mighty crack:
Pit, box, and gallery in convulsions hurled,
Thou stand'st unshook amidst a bursting world.
Who shames a scribbler? break one cobweb through,
He spins the slight, self-pleasing thread anew:
Destroy his fib or sophistry, in vain,
The creature's at his dirty work again,
Throned in the centre of his thin designs,
Proud of a vast extent of flimsy lines!
Whom have I hurt? has poet yet, or peer,
Lost the arched eyebrow, or Parnassian sneer?

* * * * * * * *
* * * * * * * *

Does not one table Bavius still admit?
Still to one bishop Philips seem a wit?
Still Sappho —— *A*. Hold! for God's sake — you'll offend,
No names! — be calm! — learn prudence of a friend:
I too could write, and I am twice as tall;
But foes like these —— *P*. One flatterer's worse than all.
Of all mad creatures, if the learned are right,
It is the slaver kills, and not the bite.
A fool quite angry is quite innocent:
Alas! 'tis ten times worse when they repent.
  One dedicates in high heroic prose,
And ridicules beyond a hundred foes;
One from all Grub Street will my fame defend,
And, more abusive, calls himself my friend.
This prints my letters, that expects a bribe,
And others roar aloud, "Subscribe, subscribe!"
  There are, who to my person pay their court:
I cough like Horace, and, though lean, am short,
Ammon's great son one shoulder had too high,
Such Ovid's nose, and "Sir! you have an eye" —
Go on, obliging creatures, make me see
All that disgraced my betters, met in me.
Say for my comfort, languishing in bed,
"Just so immortal Maro held his head:"
And when I die, be sure you let me know
Great Homer died three thousand years ago.
  Why did I write? what sin to me unknown
Dipped me in ink, my parents', or my own?
As yet a child, nor yet a fool to fame,
I lisped in numbers, for the numbers came.
I left no calling for this idle trade,
No duty broke, no father disobeyed.
The Muse but served to ease some friend, not wife,
To help me through this long disease, my life,

To second, Arbuthnot! thy art and care,
And teach the being you preserved, to bear.
But why then publish? Granville the polite,
And knowing Walsh, would tell me I could write;
Well-natured Garth inflamed with early praise,
And Congreve loved, and Swift endured my lays;
The courtly Talbot, Somers, Sheffield, read;
E'en mitred Rochester would nod the head,
And St. John's self (great Dryden's friends before)
With open arms received one poet more.
Happy my studies, when by these approved!
Happier their author, when by these beloved!
From these the world will judge of men and books,
Not from the Burnets, Oldmixons, and Cookes.
Soft were my numbers; who could take offence
While pure description held the place of sense?
Like gentle Fanny's was my flowery theme,
A painted mistress, or a purling stream.
Yet then did Gildon draw his venal quill; —
I wished the man a dinner, and sat still.
Yet then did Dennis rave in furious fret;
I never answered — I was not in debt.
If want provoked, or madness made them print,
I waged no war with Bedlam or the Mint.
Did some more sober critic come aboard;
If wrong, I smiled; if right, I kissed the rod.
Pains, reading, study, are their just pretence,
And all they want is spirit, taste, and sense.
Commas and points they set exactly right,
And 'twere a sin to rob them of their mite;
Yet ne'er one sprig of laurel graced these ribalds,
From slashing Bentley down to piddling Tibbalds.
Each wight, who reads not, and but scans and spells,
Each word-catcher, that lives on syllables,
E'en such small critics some regard may claim,
Preserved in Milton's or in Shakespeare's name.
Pretty! in amber to observe the forms
Of hairs, or straws, or dirt, or grubs, or worms!
The things, we know, are neither rich nor rare,
But wonder how the devil they got there.
Were others angry: I excused them too;
Well might they rage, I gave them but their due.
A man's true merit 'tis not hard to find;
But each man's secret standard in his mind,—
That casting-weight pride adds to emptiness,—
This, who can gratify? for who can guess?
The bard whom pilfered Pastorals renown,
Who turns a Persian tale for half a crown,
Just writes to make his barrenness appear,
And strains from hard-bound brains, eight lines a year;
He, who still wanting, though he lives on theft,
Steals much, spends little, yet has nothing left;
And he, who now to sense, now nonsense leaning,
Means not, but blunders round about a meaning;
And he, whose fustian's so sublimely bad,
It is not poetry, but prose run mad:
All these, my modest satire bade translate,
And owned that nine such poets made a Tate.
How did they fume, and stamp, and roar, and chafe!
And swear, not Addison himself was safe.
Peace to all such! but were there one whose fires
True genius kindles, and fair fame inspires;
Blessed with each talent and each art to please,
And born to write, converse, and live with ease:
Should such a man, too fond to rule alone,
Bear, like the Turk, no brother near the throne,
View him with scornful, yet with jealous eyes,
And hate for arts that caused himself to rise;
Damn with faint praise, assent with civil leer,
And without sneering, teach the rest to sneer;
Willing to wound, and yet afraid to strike,
Just hint a fault, and hesitate dislike;
Alike reserved to blame, or to commend,
A timorous foe, and a suspicious friend;
Dreading e'en fools, by flatterers besieged,
And so obliging, that he ne'er obliged;
Like Cato, give his little senate laws,
And sit attentive to his own applause;
While wits and Templars every sentence raise,
And wonder with a foolish face of praise —
Who but must laugh, if such a man there be?
Who would not weep, if Atticus were he!
What though my name stood rubric on the walls,
Or plastered posts, . . . in capitals?
Or smoking forth, a hundred hawkers' load,
On wings of winds came flying all abroad?
I sought no homage from the race that write;
I kept, like Asian monarchs, from their sight:
Poems I heeded (now be-rhymed so long)
No more than thou, great George! a birthday song.
I ne'er with wits or witlings passed my days,
To spread about the itch of verse and praise;
Nor like a puppy, daggled through the town,
To fetch and carry sing-song up and down;
Nor at rehearsals sweat, and mouthed, and cried,
With handkerchief and orange at my side;
But sick of fops, and poetry, and prate,
To Bufo left the whole Castalian state.
Proud as Apollo on his forked hill,
Sat full-blown Bufo, puffed by every quill;
Fed with soft dedication all day long,
Horace and he went hand in hand in song.
His library (where busts of poets dead
And a true Pindar stood without a head)
Received of wits an undistinguished race,
Who first his judgment asked, and then a place.
Much they extolled his pictures, much his seat,
And flattered every day, and some days eat;
Till grown more frugal in his riper days,

He paid some bards with port, and some with praise;
To some a dry rehearsal was assigned;
And others (harder still) he paid in kind.
Dryden alone (what wonder?) came not nigh,
Dryden alone escaped this judging eye:
But still the great have kindness in reserve,
He helped to bury whom he helped to starve.
  May some choice patron bless each grey goose quill!
May every Bavius have his Bufo still!
So, when a statesman wants a day's defence,
Or envy holds a whole week's war with sense,
Or simple pride for flattery makes demands,
May dunce by dunce be whistled off my hands!
Bless'd be the great! for those they take away,
And those they left me; for they left me Gay;
Left me to see neglected genius bloom,
Neglected die, and tell it on his tomb:
Of all thy blameless life the sole return
My verse, and Queensbury weeping o'er thy urn!
  Oh, let me live my own, and die so too!
(To live and die is all I have to do!)
Maintain a poet's dignity and ease,
And see what friends, and read what books I please;
Above a patron, though I condescend
Sometimes to call a minister my friend.
I was not born for courts or great affairs;
I pay my debts, believe, and say my prayers;
Can sleep without a poem in my head,
Nor know, if Dennis be alive or dead.
  Why am I asked what next shall see the light?
Heavens! was I born for nothing but to write?
Has life no joys for me? or (to be grave)
Have I no friend to serve, no soul to save?
"I found him close with Swift." — "Indeed? no doubt,"
Cries prating Balbus, "something will come out."
'Tis all in vain, deny it as I will.
"No, such a genius never can lie still;"
And then for mine obligingly mistakes
The first lampoon Sir Will or Bubo makes.
Poor guiltless I! and can I choose but smile,
When every coxcomb knows me by my style?
  Curs'd be the verse, how well soe'er it flow,
That tends to make one worthy man my foe,
Give virtue scandal, innocence a fear,
Or from the soft-eyed virgin steal a tear!
But he who hurts a harmless neighbour's peace,
Insults fallen worth, or beauty in distress;
Who loves a lie, lame slander helps about;
Who writes a libel, or who copies out;
That fop, whose pride affects a patron's name,
Yet absent, wounds an author's honest fame;
Who can your merit selfishly approve,
And show the sense of it without the love;
Who has the vanity to call you friend,
Yet wants the honour, injured, to defend;
Who tells whate'er you think, whate'er you say,
And, if he lie not, must at least betray;
Who to the Dean and silver bell can swear,
And sees at Canons what was never there;
Who reads, but with a lust to misapply,
Make satire a lampoon, and fiction, lie:
A lash like mine no honest man shall dread,
But all such babbling blockheads in his stead.
  Let Sporus tremble —— *A*. What? that thing of silk,
Sporus, that mere white curd of ass's milk?
Satire or sense, alas! can Sporus feel?
Who breaks a butterfly upon a wheel?
  P. Yet let me flap this bug with gilded wings,
This painted child of dirt, that stinks and stings;
Whose buzz the witty and the fair annoys,
Yet wit ne'er tastes, and beauty ne'er enjoys:
So well-bred spaniels civilly delight
In mumbling of the game they dare not bite.
Eternal smiles his emptiness betray,
As shallow streams run dimpling all the way.
Whether in florid impotence he speaks,
And, as the prompter breathes, the puppet squeaks;
Or at the ear of Eve, familiar toad,
Half froth, half venom, spits himself abroad,
In puns, or politics, or tales, or lies,
Or spite, or smut, or rhymes, or blasphemies.
His wit all see-saw, between that and this,
Now high, now low, now master up, now miss,
And he himself one vile antithesis.
Amphibious thing! that acting either part,
The trifling head, or the corrupted heart,
Fop at the toilet, flatterer at the board,
Now trips a lady, and now struts a lord.
Eve's tempter thus the rabbins have expressed,
A cherub's face, a reptile all the rest:
Beauty that shocks you, parts that none will trust,
Wit that can creep, and pride that licks the dust.
  Not fortune's worshipper, nor fashion's fool,
Not lucre's madman, nor ambition's tool,
Not proud, nor servile; — be one poet's praise,
That, if he pleased, he pleased by manly ways:
That flattery, e'en to kings, he held a shame,
And thought a lie in verse or prose the same;
That not in fancy's maze he wandered long,
But stooped to truth, and moralized his song;
That not for fame, but virtue's better end,
He stood the furious foe, the timid friend,
The damning critic, half approving wit,
The coxcomb hit, or fearing to be hit;
Laughed at the loss of friends he never had,
The dull, the proud, the wicked, and the mad;
The distant threats of vengeance on his head,

The blow unfelt, the tear he never shed;
The tale revived, the lie so oft o'erthrown,
Th' imputed trash, and dullness not his own;
The morals blackened when the writings scape,
The libelled person, and the pictured shape;
Abuse, on all he loved, or loved him, spread,
A friend in exile, or a father dead;
The whisper, that to greatness still too near,
Perhaps, yet vibrates on his Sovereign's ear —
Welcome for thee, fair virtue! all the past;
For thee, fair virtue! welcome e'en the last!
A. But why insult the poor, affront the great?
P. A knave's a knave, to me, in every state:
Alike my scorn, if he succeed or fail,
Sporus at Court, or Japhet in a jail,
A hireling scribbler, or a hireling peer,
Knight of the post corrupt, or of the shire;
If on a pillory, or near a throne,
He gain his prince's ear, or lose his own.
Yet soft by nature, more a dupe than wit,
Sappho can tell you how this man was bit:
This dreaded satirist Dennis will confess
Foe to his pride, but friend to his distress:
So humble, he has knocked at Tibbald's door,
Has drunk with Cibber, nay has rhymed for Moore.
Full ten years slandered, did he once reply?
Three thousand suns went down on Welsted's lie.
To please a mistress one aspersed his life;
He lashed him not, but let her be his wife.
Let Budgell charge low Grub Street on his quill,
And write whate'er he pleased, except his will;
Let the two Curlls of town and court, abuse
His father, mother, body, soul, and Muse.
Yet why? that father held it for a rule,
It was a sin to call our neighbour fool.

* * * * * * *

Hear this, and spare his family, James Moore!
Unspotted names, and memorable long!
If there be force in virtue, or in song.
Of gentle blood (part shed in honour's cause,
While yet in Britain honour had applause)
Each parent sprung —— *A*. What fortune, pray? — *P*. Their own,
And better got, than Bestia's from the throne.
Born to no pride, inheriting no strife,
Nor marrying discord in a noble wife,
Stranger to civil and religious rage,
The good man walked innoxious through his age.
No courts he saw, no suits would ever try,
Nor dared an oath, nor hazarded a lie.
Unlearn'd, he knew no schoolman's subtle art,
No language, but the language of the heart.
By nature honest, by experience wise,
Healthy by temperance, and by exercise;
His life, though long, to sickness passed unknown,
His death was instant, and without a groan.
O grant me thus to live, and thus to die!
Who sprung from kings shall know less joy than I.
O friend! may each domestic bliss be thine!
Be no unpleasing melancholy mine:
Me, let the tender office long engage,
To rock the cradle of reposing age,
With lenient arts extend a mother's breath,
Make languor smile, and smooth the bed of death,
Explore the thought, explain the asking eye,
And keep awhile one parent from the sky!
On cares like these if length of days attend,
May Heaven, to bless those days, preserve my friend,
Preserve him social, cheerful, and serene,
And just as rich as when he served a queen.
A. Whether that blessing be denied or given,
Thus far was right, the rest belongs to Heaven.

MORAL ESSAYS

From EPISTLE II

To a Lady

Of the Characters of Women

Nothing so true as what you once let fall,
"Most women have no characters at all."
Matter too soft a lasting mark to bear,
And best distinguished by black, brown, or fair.
How many pictures of one nymph we view,
All how unlike each other, all how true!
Arcadia's countess here in ermined pride
Is there Pastora by a fountain side;
Here Fannia, leering on her own good man,
And there, a naked Leda with a swan.
Let then the fair one beautifully cry,
In Magdalen's loose hair and lifted eye,
Or dressed in smiles of sweet Cecilia shine,
With simpering angels, palms, and harps divine;
Whether the charmer sinner it, or saint it,
If folly grow romantic, I must paint it.
Come then, the colours and the ground prepare!
Dip in the rainbow, trick her off in air;
Choose a firm cloud, before it fall, and in it
Catch, ere she change, the Cynthia of this minute.

* * * * * * *

Flavia's a wit, has too much sense to pray;
To toast our wants and wishes, is her way;
Nor asks of God, but of her stars, to give
The mighty blessing, "while we live, to live."
Then all for death, that opiate of the soul!
Lucretia's dagger, Rosamonda's bowl.
Say, what can cause such impotence of mind?
A spark too fickle, or a spouse too kind.

Wise wretch! with pleasures too refined to please;
With too much spirit to be e'er at ease;
With too much quickness ever to be taught;
With too much thinking to have common thought:
You purchase pain with all that joy can give,
And die of nothing but a rage to live.
  Turn then from wits; and look on Simo's mate,
No ass so meek, no ass so obstinate;
Or her, that owns her faults, but never mends,
Because she's honest, and the best of friends;
Or her, whose life the Church and scandal share,
Forever in a passion, or a prayer;
Or her, who laughs at hell, but (like her Grace)
Cries, "Ah! how charming, if there's no such place!"
Or who in sweet vicissitude appears
Of mirth and opium, ratafie and tears,
The daily anodyne, and nightly draught,
To kill those foes to fair ones, time and thought.
Woman and fool are two hard things to hit;
For true no-meaning puzzles more than wit.
  But what are these to great Atossa's mind?
Scarce once herself, by turns all womankind!
Who, with herself, or others, from her birth
Finds all her life one warfare upon earth;
Shines, in exposing knaves, and painting fools,
Yet is, whate'er she hates and ridicules.
No thought advances, but her eddy brain
Whisks it about, and down it goes again.
Full sixty years the world has been her trade,
The wisest fool much time has ever made.
From loveless youth to unrespected age,
No passion gratified except her rage.
So much the fury still outran the wit,
The pleasure missed her, and the scandal hit.
Who breaks with her, provokes revenge from hell,
But he's a bolder man who dares be well.
Her every turn with violence pursued,
Nor more a storm her hate than gratitude:
To that each passion turns, or soon or late;
Love, if it makes her yield, must make her hate:
Superiors? death! and equals? what a curse!
But an inferior not dependent? worse.
Offend her, and she knows not to forgive;
Oblige her, and she'll hate you while you live;
But die, and she'll adore you — then the bust
And temple rise — then fall again to dust.
Last night, her lord was all that's good and great;
A knave this morning, and his will a cheat.
Strange! by the means defeated of the ends,
By spirit robbed of power, by warmth of friends,
By wealth of followers! without one distress,
Sick of herself through very selfishness!
Atossa, cursed with every granted prayer,
Childless with all her children, wants an heir.
To heirs unknown descends the unguarded store,
Or wanders, Heaven-directed, to the poor.
  Pictures like these, dear Madam, to design,
Asks no firm hand, and no unerring line;
Some wandering touches, some reflected light,
Some flying stroke alone can hit them right:
For how should equal colours do the knack?
Chameleons who can paint in white and black?
  "Yet Chloe sure was formed without a spot" —
Nature in her then erred not, but forgot.
"With every pleasing, every prudent part,
Say, what can Chloe want?" — She wants a heart.
She speaks, behaves, and acts just as she ought;
But never, never, reached one generous thought.
Virtue she finds too painful an endeavour,
Content to dwell in decencies forever.
So very reasonable, so unmoved,
As never yet to love, or to be loved.
She, while her lover pants upon her breast,
Can mark the figures on an Indian chest;
And when she sees her friend in deep despair,
Observes how much a chintz exceeds mohair.
Forbid it Heaven, a favour or a debt
She e'er should cancel — but she may forget.
Safe is your secret still in Chloe's ear;
But none of Chloe's shall you ever hear.
Of all her dears she never slandered one,
But cares not if a thousand are undone.
Would Chloe know if you're alive or dead?
She bids her footman put it in her head.
Chloe is prudent — would you too be wise?
Then never break your heart when Chloe dies.

* * * * * * *

  In men, we various ruling passions find;
In women, two almost divide the kind;
Those, only fixed, they first or last obey,
The love of pleasure, and the love of sway.
  That, Nature gives; and where the lesson taught
Is but to please, can pleasure seem a fault?
Experience, this; by man's oppression cursed,
They seek the second not to lose the first.
  Men, some to business, some to pleasure take;
But every woman is at heart a rake:
Men, some to quiet, some to public strife;
But every lady would be queen for life.

* * * * * * *

  Pleasures the sex, as children birds, pursue,
Still out of reach, yet never out of view;
Sure, if they catch, to spoil the toy at most,
To covet flying, and regret when lost:
At last, to follies youth could scarce defend,
It grows their age's prudence to pretend;
Ashamed to own they gave delight before,
Reduced to feign it, when they give no more:
As hags hold Sabbaths, less for joy than spite,
So these their merry, miserable night;

Still round and round the ghosts of beauty glide,
And haunt the places where their honour died.
See how the world its veterans rewards!
A youth of frolics, an old age of cards;
Fair to no purpose, artful to no end,
Young without lovers, old without a friend;
A fop their passion, but their prize a sot;
Alive, ridiculous, and dead, forgot!
Ah! Friend! to dazzle let the vain design;
To raise the thought and touch the heart be thine!
That charm shall grow, while what fatigues the Ring
Flaunts and goes down, an unregarded thing:
So when the sun's broad beam has tired the sight,
All mild ascends the moon's more sober light,
Serene in virgin modesty she shines,
And unobserved the glaring orb declines.
Oh! blest with temper whose unclouded ray
Can make to-morrow cheerful as to-day;
She, who can love a sister's charms, or hear
Sighs for a daughter with unwounded ear;
She, who ne'er answers till a husband cools,
Or, if she rules him, never shows she rules;
Charms by accepting, by submitting, sways,
Yet has her humour most, when she obeys;
Let fops or fortune fly which way they will;
Disdains all loss of tickets, or Codille;
Spleen, vapours, or small-pox, above them all,
And mistress of herself, though China fall.
And yet, believe me, good as well as ill,
Woman's at best a contradiction still.
Heaven, when it strives to polish all it can
Its last best work, but forms a softer man;
Picks from each sex, to make the favorite blest,
Your love of pleasure, our desire of rest:
Blends, in exception to all general rules,
Your taste of follies, with our scorn of fools:
Reserve with frankness, art with truth allied,
Courage with softness, modesty with pride;
Fixed principles, with fancy ever new;
Shakes all together, and produces — You.

THE UNIVERSAL PRAYER

Father of all! in every age,
In every clime adored,
By saint, by savage, and by sage,
Jehovah, Jove, or Lord!

Thou Great First Cause, least understood:
Who all my sense confined
To know but this, that Thou art good,
And that myself am blind;

Yet gave me, in this dark estate,
To see the good from ill;
And binding nature fast in fate,
Left free the human will.

What conscience dictates to be done,
Or warns me not to do,
This, teach me more than hell to shun,
That, more than Heaven pursue.

What blessings Thy free bounty gives,
Let me not cast away;
For God is paid when man receives,
T' enjoy is to obey.

Yet not to earth's contracted span
Thy goodness let me bound,
Or think Thee Lord alone of man,
When thousand worlds are round:

Let not this weak, unknowing hand
Presume Thy bolts to throw,
And deal damnation round the land,
On each I judge Thy foe.

If I am right, Thy grace impart,
Still in the right to stay;
If I am wrong, oh! teach my heart
To find that better way.

Save me alike from foolish pride,
Or impious discontent,
At aught Thy wisdom has denied,
Or aught Thy goodness lent.

Teach me to feel another's woe,
To hide the fault I see;
That mercy I to others show,
That mercy show to me.

Mean though I am, not wholly so,
Since quickened by Thy breath;
Oh, lead me wheresoe'er I go,
Through this day's life or death.

This day, be bread and peace my lot:
All else beneath the sun,
Thou know'st if best bestowed or not,
And let Thy will be done.

To Thee, whose temple is all space,
Whose altar earth, sea, skies,
One chorus let all being raise,
All nature's incense rise!

THE DUNCIAD

From BOOK IV

Then thus. "Since man from beast by words is known,
Words are man's province, words we teach alone.
When reason doubtful, like the Samian letter,
Points him two ways, the narrower is the better.
Placed at the door of learning, youth to guide,
We never suffer it to stand too wide.
To ask, to guess, to know, as they commence,
As fancy opens the quick springs of sense,
We ply the memory, we load the brain,
Bind rebel wit, and double chain on chain,
Confine the thought, to exercise the breath;
And keep them in the pale of words till death.
Whate'er the talents, or howe'er designed,
We hang one jingling padlock on the mind:
A poet the first day he dips his quill;
And what the last? A very poet still.
Pity! the charm works only in our wall,
Lost, lost too soon in yonder House or Hall.
There truant Wyndham every muse gave o'er,
There Talbot sunk, and was a wit no more!
How sweet an Ovid, Murray, was our boast!
How many Martials were in Pulteney lost!
Else sure some bard, to our eternal praise,
In twice ten thousand rhyming nights and days,
Had reached the work, the all that mortal can,
And South beheld that masterpiece of man."
"Oh," cried the goddess, "for some pedant reign!
Some gentle James, to bless the land again;
To stick the doctor's chair into the throne,
Give law to words, or war with words alone,
Senates and courts with Greek and Latin rule,
And turn the council to a grammar school!
For sure, if Dullness sees a grateful day,
'Tis in the shade of arbitrary sway.
O! if my sons may learn one earthly thing,
Teach but that one, sufficient for a king;
That which my priests, and mine alone, maintain,
Which as it dies, or lives, we fall, or reign:
May you, may Cam and Isis, preach it long!
'The right divine of kings to govern wrong.'"
Prompt at the call, around the goddess roll
Broad hats, and hoods, and caps, a sable shoal:
Thick and more thick the black blockade extends,
A hundred head of Aristotle's friends.
Nor wert thou, Isis! wanting to the day,
Though Christ Church long kept prudishly away.
Each staunch polemic, stubborn as a rock,
Each fierce logician, still expelling Locke,
Came whip and spur, and dashed through thin and thick
On German Crousaz, and Dutch Burgersdyck.
As many quit the streams that murmuring fall
To lull the sons of Margaret and Clare Hall,
Where Bentley late tempestuous wont to sport
In troubled waters, but now sleeps in port.
Before them marched that awful Aristarch;
Ploughed was his front with many a deep remark;
His hat, which never vailed to human pride,
Walker with reverence took, and laid aside.
Low bowed the rest: he, kingly, did but nod;
So upright Quakers please both man and God.
"Mistress! dismiss that rabble from your throne:
Avaunt —— is Aristarchus yet unknown?
Thy mighty scholiast, whose unwearied pains
Made Horace dull, and humbled Milton's strains.
Turn what they will to verse, their toil is vain,
Critics like me shall make it prose again.
Roman and Greek grammarians, know your better!
Author of something yet more great than letter;
While towering o'er your alphabet, like Saul,
Stands our Digamma, and o'ertops them all.
'Tis true, on words is still our whole debate,
Disputes of *me* or *te*, of *aut* or *at*,
To sound or sink in *cano*, O or A,
Or give up Cicero to C or K.
Let Freind affect to speak as Terence spoke,
And Alsop never but like Horace joke;
For me, what Virgil, Pliny may deny,
Manilius or Solinus shall supply.
For Attic phrase in Plato let them seek,
I poach in Suidas for unlicensed Greek.
In ancient sense if any needs will deal,
Be sure I give them fragments, not a meal;
What Gellius or Stobæus hashed before,
Or chewed by blind old scholiasts o'er and o'er.
The critic eye, that microscope of wit,
Sees hairs and pores, examines bit by bit.
How parts relate to parts, or they to whole,
The body's harmony, the beaming soul, —
All things which Kuster, Burman, Wasse shall see,
When man's whole frame is obvious to a flea.
"Ah, think not, mistress! more true dullness lies
In folly's cap, than wisdom's grave disguise.
Like buoys, that never sink into the flood,
On learning's surface we but lie and nod.
Thine is the genuine head of many a house,
And much divinity without a Νοῦς.
Nor could a Barrow work on every block,
Nor has one Atterbury spoiled the flock.
See, still thy own, the heavy cannon roll,
And metaphysic smokes involve the pole.
For thee we dim the eyes, and stuff the head
With all such reading as was never read;

For thee explain a thing till all men doubt it,
And write about it, goddess, and about it:
So spins the silk-worm small its slender store,
And labours till it clouds itself all o'er.
"What though we let some better sort of fool
Thrid every science, run through every school?
Never by tumbler through the hoops was shown
Such skill in passing all, and touching none.
He may indeed (if sober all this time)
Plague with dispute, or persecute with rhyme.
We only furnish what he cannot use,
Or wed to what he must divorce, a Muse;
Full in the midst of Euclid dip at once,
And petrify a genius to a dunce;
Or set on metaphysic ground to prance,
Show all his paces, not a step advance.
With the same cement, ever sure to bind
We bring to one dead level every mind.
Then take him to develop, if you can,
And hew the block off, and get out the man.

* * * * * * * *

"Be that my task (replies a gloomy clerk,
Sworn foe to mystery, yet divinely dark;
Whose pious hope aspires to see the day
When moral evidence shall quite decay,
And damns implicit faith, and holy lies,
Prompt to impose, and fond to dogmatize)
Let others creep by timid steps, and slow,
On plain experience lay foundations low,
By common sense to common knowledge bred,
And last, to nature's cause through nature led.
All-seeing in thy mists, we want no guide,
Mother of arrogance, and source of pride!
We nobly take the high priori road,
And reason downward, till we doubt of God;
Make nature still encroach upon his plan,
And shove him off as far as e'er we can;
Thrust some mechanic cause into his place;
Or bind in matter, or diffuse in space:
Or, at one bound o'erleaping all his laws,
Make God man's image, man the final cause,
Find virtue local, all relation scorn,
See all in self, and but for self be born,—
Of nought so certain as our reason still,
Of nought so doubtful as of soul and will.
Oh, hide the God still more! and make us se
Such as Lucretius drew, a God like thee,—
Wrapped up in self, a God without a thought,
Regardless of our merit or default:
Or that bright image to our fancy draw,
Which Theocles in raptured vision saw,
While through poetic scenes the Genius roves,
Or wanders wild in academic groves;
That Nature, our society adores,
Where Tindal dictates, and Silenus snores."

Next bidding all draw near on bended knees,
The queen confers her titles and degrees.
Her children first of more distinguished sort,
Who study Shakespeare at the Inns of Court,
Impale a glow-worm, or vertù profess,
Shine in the dignity of F.R.S.
Some, deep free masons, join the silent race
Worthy to fill Pythagoras's place;
Some botanists, or florists at the least,
Or issue members of an annual feast.
Nor passed the meanest unregarded, one
Rose a Gregorian, one a Gormogon.
The last, not least in honour or applause,
Isis and Cam made doctors of her laws.
Then, blessing all, "Go, children of my care!
To practice now from theory repair.
All my commands are easy, short, and full:
My sons! be proud, be selfish, and be dull.
Guard my prerogative, assert my throne:
This nod confirms each privilege your own.
The cap and switch be sacred to his Grace;
With staff and pumps the marquis lead the race;
From stage to stage the licensed earl may run,
Paired with his fellow-charioteer the sun;
The learned baron butterflies design,
Or draw to silk Arachne's subtle line;
The judge to dance his brother sergeant call;
The senator at cricket urge the ball;
The bishop stow (pontific luxury!)
An hundred souls of turkeys in a pie;
The sturdy squire to Gallic masters stoop,
And drown his lands and manors in a soup.
Others import yet nobler arts from France,
Teach kings to fiddle, and make senates dance.
Perhaps more high some daring son may soar,
Proud to my list to add one monarch more;
And nobly conscious, princes are but things
Born for first ministers, as slaves for kings,
Tyrant supreme! shall three estates command,
And make one mighty Dunciad of the land!"
More she had spoke, but yawned — All nature nods:
What mortal can resist the yawn of gods?
Churches and chapels instantly it reached,
(St. James's first, for leaden G—— preached)
Then catched the schools; the Hall scarce kept awake:
The Convocation gaped, but could not speak.
Lost was the nation's sense, nor could be found,
While the long solemn unison went round;
Wide, and more wide, it spread o'er all the realm;
E'en Palinurus nodded at the helm.
The vapour mild o'er each committee crept;
Unfinished treaties in each office slept;
And chiefless armies dozed out the campaign,
And navies yawned for orders on the main.

O Muse! relate (for you can tell alone;
Wits have short memories, and dunces none)
Relate, who first, who last resigned to rest,
Whose heads she partly, whose completely, blest;
What charms could faction, what ambition lull,
The venal quiet, and entrance the dull;
Till drowned was sense, and shame, and right, and wrong —
O sing, and hush the nations with thy song!

In vain, in vain — the all-composing hour
Resistless falls: the Muse obeys the power.
She comes! she comes! the sable throne behold
Of Night primeval and of Chaos old!
Before her, Fancy's gilded clouds decay,
And all its varying rainbows die away.
Wit shoots in vain its momentary fires,
The meteor drops, and in a flash expires.
As one by one, at dread Medea's strain,
The sickening stars fade off th' ethereal plain;
As Argus' eyes, by Hermes' wand oppressed,
Closed one by one to everlasting rest:
Thus at her felt approach, and secret might,
Art after art goes out, and all is night.
See skulking Truth to her old cavern fled,
Mountains of casuistry heaped o'er her head!
Philosophy, that leaned on Heaven before,
Shrinks to her second cause, and is no more.
Physic of Metaphysic begs defence,
And Metaphysic calls for aid on Sense!
See Mystery to Mathematics fly!
In vain! they gaze, turn giddy, rave, and die.
Religion blushing veils her sacred fires,
And unawares Morality expires.
Nor public flame, nor private, dares to shine;
Nor human spark is left, nor glimpse divine!
Lo! thy dread empire, Chaos! is restored;
Light dies before thy uncreating word:
Thy hand, great Anarch! lets the curtain fall;
And universal darkness buries all.

THE ILIAD

From BOOK VI

He said, and pass'd with sad presaging heart
To seek his spouse, his soul's far dearer part;
At home he sought her, but he sought in vain:
She, with one maid of all her menial train,
Had thence retir'd; and, with her second joy,
The young Astyanax, the hope of Troy,
Pensive she stood on Ilion's tow'ry height,
Beheld the war, and sicken'd at the sight;
There her sad eyes in vain her lord explore,
Or weep the wounds her bleeding country bore.
But he, who found not whom his soul desir'd,
Whose virtue charm'd him as her beauty fir'd,
Stood in the gates, and ask'd what way she bent
Her parting steps; if to the fane she went,
Where late the mourning matrons made resort,
Or sought her sisters in the Trojan court.
"Not to the court" replied th' attendant train,
"Nor, mix'd with matrons, to Minerva's fane;
To Ilion's steepy tow'r she bent her way,
To mark the fortunes of the doubtful day.
Troy fled, she heard, before the Grecian sword;
She heard, and trembled for her distant lord.
Distracted with surprise, she seem'd to fly,
Fear on her cheek and sorrow in her eye.
The nurse attended with her infant boy,
The young Astyanax, the hope of Troy."
Hector, this heard, return'd without delay;
Swift through the town he trod his former way,
Through streets of palaces and walks of state,
And met the mourner at the Scæan gate.
With haste to meet him sprung the joyful fair,
His blameless wife, Eëtion's wealthy heir
(Cilician Thebè great Eëtion sway'd,
And Hippoplacus' wide-extended shade);
The nurse stood near, in whose embraces press'd
His only hope hung smiling at her breast,
Whom each soft charm and early grace adorn,
Fair as the new-born star that gilds the morn.
To this lov'd infant Hector gave the name
Scamandrius, from Scamander's honour'd stream;
Astyanax the Trojans call'd the boy,
From his great father, the defence of Troy.
Silent the warrior smil'd, and pleas'd, resign'd,
To tender passions all his mighty mind:
His beauteous princess cast a mournful look,
Hung on his hand, and then dejected spoke;
Her bosom labour'd with a boding sigh,
And the big tear stood trembling in her eye.
"Too daring prince! ah whither dost thou run?
Ah, too forgetful of thy wife and son!
And think'st thou not how wretched we shall be,
A widow I, a helpless orphan he!
For sure such courage length of life denies,
And thou must fall, thy virtue's sacrifice.
Greece in her single heroes strove in vain;
Now hosts oppose thee, and thou must be slain!
Oh, grant me, gods! e'er Hector meets his doom,
All I can ask of heav'n, an early tomb!
So shall my days in one sad tenor run,
And end with sorrows as they first begun.
No parent now remains, my griefs to share,
No father's aid, no mother's tender care.
The fierce Achilles wrapt our walls in fire,
Laid Thebè waste, and slew my warlike sire!
His fate compassion in the victor bred;
Stern as he was, he yet rever'd the dead,
His radiant arms preserv'd from hostile spoil,

And laid him decent on the fun'ral pile;
Then rais'd a mountain where his bones were burn'd:
The mountain nymphs the rural tomb adorn'd;
Jove's sylvan daughters bade their elms bestow
A barren shade, and in his honour grow.
"By the same arm my seven brave brothers fell;
In one sad day beheld the gates of hell:
While the fat herds and snowy flocks they fed,
Amid their fields the hapless heroes bled!
My mother liv'd to bear the victor's bands,
The queen of Hippoplacia's sylvan lands;
Redeem'd too late, she scarce beheld again
Her pleasing empire and her native plain,
When, ah! oppress'd by life-consuming woe,
She fell a victim to Diana's bow.
"Yet while my Hector still survives, I see
My father, mother, brethren, all, in thee:
Alas! my parents, brothers, kindred, all
Once more will perish if my Hector fall.
Thy wife, thy infant, in thy danger share:
Oh, prove a husband's and a father's care!
That quarter most the skilful Greeks annoy,
Where yon wild fig-trees join the wall of Troy:
Thou from this tow'r defend th' important post.
There Agamemnon points his dreadful host,
That pass Tydides, Ajax, strive to gain,
And there the vengeful Spartan fires his train.
Thrice our bold foes the fierce attack have giv'n,
Or led by hopes, or dictated from heav'n.
Let others in the field their arms employ,
But stay my Hector here, and guard his Troy."
The chief replied: "That post shall be my care,
Not that alone, but all the works of war.
How would the sons of Troy, in arms renown'd,
And Troy's proud dames, whose garments sweep the ground,
Attaint the lustre of my former name,
Should Hector basely quit the field of fame?
My early youth was bred to martial pains,
My soul impels me to th' embattled plains:
Let me be foremost to defend the throne,
And guard my father's glories and my own.
Yet come it will, the day decreed by fates,
(How my heart trembles while my tongue relates!)
The day when thou, imperial Troy! must bend,
And see thy warriors fall, thy glories end.
And yet no dire presage so wounds my mind,
My mother's death, the ruin of my kind,
Not Priam's hoary hairs defil'd with gore,
Not all my brothers gasping on the shore,
As thine, Andromache! Thy griefs I dread:
I see thee trembling, weeping, captive led,
In Argive looms our battles to design,
And woes of which so large a part was thine!
To bear the victor's hard commands, or bring
The weight of waters from Hyperia's spring!
There, while you groan beneath the load of life,
They cry, 'Behold the mighty Hector's wife!'
Some haughty Greek, who lives thy tears to see,
Embitters all thy woes by naming me.
The thoughts of glory past and present shame,
A thousand griefs, shall waken at the name!
May I lie cold before that dreadful day,
Press'd with a load of monumental clay!
Thy Hector, wrapp'd in everlasting sleep,
Shall neither hear thee sigh, nor see thee weep."
Thus having spoke, th' illustrious chief of Troy
Stretch'd his fond arms to clasp the lovely boy.
The babe clung crying to his nurse's breast,
Scar'd at the dazzling helm and nodding crest.
With secret pleasure each fond parent smil'd,
And Hector hasted to relieve his child;
The glitt'ring terrors from his brows unbound,
And plac'd the beaming helmet on the ground.
Then kiss'd the child, and, lifting high in air,
Thus to the gods preferr'd a father's pray'r:
"O thou! whose glory fills th' ethereal throne,
And all ye deathless pow'rs! protect my son!
Grant him, like me, to purchase just renown,
To guard the Trojans, to defend the crown,
Against his country's foes the war to wage,
And rise the Hector of the future age!
So when, triumphant from successful toils,
Of heroes slain he bears the reeking spoils,
Whole hosts may hail him with deserv'd acclaim,
And say, 'This chief transcends his father's fame':
While pleas'd, amidst the gen'ral shouts of Troy,
His mother's conscious heart o'erflows with joy."
He spoke, and fondly gazing on her charms,
Restor'd the pleasing burthen to her arms;
Soft on her fragrant breast the babe she laid,
Hush'd to repose, and with a smile survey'd.
The troubled pleasure soon chastis'd by fear,
She mingled with the smile a tender tear.
The soften'd chief with kind compassion view'd,
And dried the falling drops, and thus pursued:
"Andromache! my soul's far better part,
Why with untimely sorrows heaves thy heart?
No hostile hand can antedate my doom,
Till fate condemns me to the silent tomb.
Fix'd is the term to all the race of earth,
And such the hard condition of our birth.
No force can then resist, no flight can save;
All sink alike, the fearful and the brave.
No more — but hasten to thy tasks at home,
There guide the spindle, and direct the loom;
Me glory summons to the martial scene,
The field of combat is the sphere for men.
Where heroes war, the foremost place I claim,
The first in danger as the first in fame."

CLASSICISTS AND ROMANTICISTS

ROBERT BLAIR (1699–1746)

From THE GRAVE

While some affect the sun, and some the shade,
Some flee the city, some the hermitage,
Their aims as various as the roads they take
In journeying through life; the task be mine
To paint the gloomy horrors of the tomb;
Th' appointed place of rendezvous, where all
These travellers meet. Thy succours I implore,
Eternal King! whose potent arm sustains
The keys of hell and death. — The Grave, dread thing!
Men shiver when thou'rt nam'd: nature, appall'd,
Shakes off her wonted firmness. — Ah! how dark
Thy long-extended realms, and rueful wastes!
Where nought but silence reigns, and night, dark night,
Dark as was chaos, ere the infant sun
Was roll'd together, or had tried his beams
Athwart the gloom profound. — The sickly taper
By glimmering through thy low-brow'd misty vaults,
(Furr'd round with mouldy damps and ropy slime)
Lets fall a supernumerary horror,
And only serves to make thy night more irksome.
Well do I know thee by thy trusty yew,
Cheerless, unsocial plant! that loves to dwell
Midst skulls and coffins, epitaphs and worms:
Where light-heel'd ghosts, and visionary shades,
Beneath the wan cold moon (as fame reports)
Embodied, thick, perform their mystic rounds.
No other merriment, dull tree! is thine.
  See yonder hallow'd fane; — the pious work
Of names once fam'd, now dubious or forgot,
And buried midst the wreck of things which were;
There lie interr'd the more illustrious dead.
The wind is up: hark! how it howls! Methinks
Till now I never heard a sound so dreary:
Doors creak, and windows clap, and night's foul bird,
Rook'd in the spire, screams loud: the gloomy aisles,
Black-plaster'd, and hung round with shreds of 'scutcheons
And tatter'd coats of arms, send back the sound
Laden with heavier airs, from the low vaults,
The mansions of the dead. — Rous'd from their slumbers,
In grim array the grisly spectres rise,
Grin horrible, and, obstinately sullen,
Pass and repass, hush'd as the foot of night.
Again the screech-owl shrieks: ungracious sound!
I'll hear no more; it makes one's blood run chill.
  Quite round the pile, a row of reverend elms,
(Coeval near with that) all ragged show,
Long lash'd by the rude winds. Some rift half down
Their branchless trunks; others so thin a-top,
That scarce two crows could lodge in the same tree.
Strange things, the neighbours say, have happen'd here:
Wild shrieks have issued from the hollow tombs:
Dead men have come again, and walk'd about;
And the great bell has toll'd, unrung, untouch'd.
(Such tales their cheer, at wake or gossiping,
When it draws near the witching time of night.)
  Oft in the lone church-yard at night I've seen,
By glimpse of moonshine chequering through the trees,
The school-boy, with his satchel in his hand,
Whistling aloud to bear his courage up,
And lightly tripping o'er the long flat stones,
(With nettles skirted, and with moss o'ergrown,)
That tell in homely phrase who lie below.
Sudden he starts, and hears, or thinks he hears,
The sound of something purring at his heels;
Full fast he flies, and dares not look behind him,
Till out of breath he overtakes his fellows;
Who gather round, and wonder at the tale
Of horrid apparition, tall and ghastly,
That walks at dead of night, or takes his stand
O'er some new-open'd grave; and (strange to tell!)
Evanishes at crowing of the cock.
  The new-made widow, too, I've sometimes 'spied,
Sad sight! slow moving o'er the prostrate dead:
Listless, she crawls along in doleful black,
Whilst bursts of sorrow gush from either eye,
Fast falling down her now untasted cheek:
Prone on the lowly grave of the dear man
She drops; whilst busy, meddling memory,
In barbarous succession musters up
The past endearments of their softer hours,

Tenacious of its theme. Still, still she thinks
She sees him, and indulging the fond thought,
Clings yet more closely to the senseless turf,
Nor heeds the passenger who looks that way.

* * * * * * *

JAMES THOMSON (1700–1748)

A SNOW SCENE

From WINTER

The keener tempests come: and fuming dun
From all the livid east, or piercing north,
Thick clouds ascend — in whose capacious womb
A vapoury deluge lies, to snow congealed.
Heavy they roll their fleecy world along;
And the sky saddens with the gathered storm.
Through the hushed air the whitening shower descends,
At first thin wavering; till at last the flakes
Fall broad, and wide, and fast, dimming the day
With a continual flow. The cherished fields
Put on their winter-robe of purest white.
'Tis brightness all; save where the new snow melts
Along the mazy current. Low, the woods
Bow their hoar head; and, ere the languid sun
Faint from the west emits his evening ray,
Earth's universal face, deep-hid and chill,
Is one wild dazzling waste, that buries wide
The works of man. Drooping, the labourer-ox
Stands covered o'er with snow, and then demands
The fruit of all his toil. The fowls of heaven,
Tamed by the cruel season, crowd around
The winnowing store, and claim the little boon
Which Providence assigns them. One alone,
The redbreast, sacred to the household gods,
Wisely regardful of the embroiling sky,
In joyless fields and thorny thickets leaves
His shivering mates, and pays to trusted man
His annual visit. Half-afraid, he first
Against the window beats; then, brisk, alights
On the warm hearth; then, hopping o'er the floor,
Eyes all the smiling family askance,
And pecks, and starts, and wonders where he is —
Till, more familiar grown, the table-crumbs
Attract his slender feet. The foodless wilds
Pour forth their brown inhabitants. The hare,
Though timorous of heart, and hard beset
By death in various forms, dark snares, and dogs,
And more unpitying men, the garden seeks,
Urged on by fearless want. The bleating kind
Eye the black heaven, and next the glistening earth
With looks of dumb despair; then, sad dispersed,
Dig for the withered herb through heaps of snow.

* * * * * * *

THE SHEEP-WASHING

From SUMMER

Or rushing thence, in one diffusive band,
They drive the troubled flocks, by many a dog
Compelled, to where the mazy-running brook
Forms a deep pool; this bank abrupt and high,
And that, fair-spreading in a pebbled shore.
Urged to the giddy brink, much is the toil,
The clamour much, of men, and boys, and dogs,
Ere the soft, fearful people to the flood
Commit their woolly sides. And oft the swain,
On some impatient seizing, hurls them in:
Emboldened then, nor hesitating more,
Fast, fast, they plunge amid the flashing wave,
And panting labour to the farther shore.
Repeated this, till deep the well-washed fleece
Has drunk the flood, and from his lively haunt
The trout is banished by the sordid stream,
Heavy and dripping, to the breezy brow
Slow move the harmless race; where, as they spread
Their swelling treasures to the sunny ray,
Inly disturbed, and wondering what this wild
Outrageous tumult means, their loud complaints
The country fill — and, tossed from rock to rock,
Incessant bleatings run around the hills.
At last, of snowy white, the gathered flocks
Are in the wattled pen innumerous pressed,
Head above head; and ranged in lusty rows
The shepherds sit, and whet the sounding shears.
The housewife waits to roll her fleecy stores,
With all her gay-drest maids attending round.
One, chief, in gracious dignity enthroned,
Shines o'er the rest, the pastoral queen, and rays
Her smiles, sweet-beaming, on her shepherd-king;
While the glad circle round them yield their souls
To festive mirth, and wit that knows no gall.
Meantime, their joyous task goes on apace:
Some mingling stir the melted tar, and some,
Deep on the new-shorn vagrant's heaving side,
To stamp his master's cypher ready stand;
Others the unwilling wether drag along;
And, glorying in his might, the sturdy boy
Holds by the twisted horns the indignant ram.
Behold where bound, and of its robe bereft,
By needy man, that all-depending lord,
How meek, how patient, the mild creature lies!
What softness in its melancholy face,
What dumb complaining innocence appears!
Fear not, ye gentle tribes, 'tis not the knife
Of horrid slaughter that is o'er you waved;
No, 'tis the tender swain's well-guided shears,
Who having now, to pay his annual care,
Borrowed your fleece, to you a cumbrous load,
Will send you bounding to your hills again.

THE COMING OF THE RAIN

From SPRING

At first a dusky wreath they seem to rise,
Scarce staining ether; but by fast degrees,
In heaps on heaps, the doubling vapour sails
Along the loaded sky, and mingling deep,
Sits on the horizon round, a settled gloom:
Not such as wintry storms on mortals shed,
Oppressing life; but lovely, gentle, kind,
And full of every hope and every joy,
The wish of Nature. Gradual sinks the breeze
Into a perfect calm; that not a breath
Is heard to quiver through the closing woods,
Or rustling turn the many twinkling leaves
Of aspen tall. The uncurling floods, diffused
In glassy breadth, seem through delusive lapse
Forgetful of their course. 'Tis silence all,
And pleasing expectation. Herds and flocks
Drop the dry sprig, and, mute-imploring, eye
The fallen verdure. Hushed in short suspense
The plumy people streak their wings with oil,
To throw the lucid moisture trickling off;
And wait the approaching sign to strike, at once,
Into the general choir. Even mountains, vales,
And forests seem, impatient, to demand
The promised sweetness. Man superior walks
Amid the glad creation, musing praise,
And looking lively gratitude. At last,
The clouds consign their treasures to the fields;
And, softly shaking on the dimpled pool
Prelusive drops, let all their moisture flow,
In large effusion, o'er the freshened world.

STORM IN HARVEST

From AUTUMN

Defeating oft the labours of the year,
The sultry south collects a potent blast.
At first, the groves are scarcely seen to stir
Their trembling tops, and a still murmur runs
Along the soft-inclining fields of corn;
But as the aërial tempest fuller swells,
And in one mighty stream, invisible,
Immense, the whole excited atmosphere
Impetuous rushes o'er the sounding world,
Strained to the root, the stooping forest pours
A rustling shower of yet untimely leaves.
High-beat, the circling mountains eddy in,
From the bare wild, the dissipated storm,
And send it in a torrent down the vale.
Exposed, and naked, to its utmost rage,
Through all the sea of harvest rolling round,
The billowy plain floats wide; nor can evade,
Though pliant to the blast, its seizing force —
Or whirled in air, or into vacant chaff
Shook waste. And sometimes too a burst of rain,
Swept from the black horizon, broad, descends
In one continuous flood. Still over head
The mingling tempest weaves its gloom, and still
The deluge deepens; till the fields around
Lie sunk, and flatted, in the sordid wave.
Sudden, the ditches swell; the meadows swim.
Red, from the hills, innumerable streams
Tumultuous roar; and high above its banks
The river lift; before whose rushing tide,
Herds, flocks, and harvests, cottages, and swains,
Roll mingled down: all that the winds had spared,
In one wild moment ruined; the big hopes,
And well-earned treasures of the painful year.
Fled to some eminence, the husbandman,
Helpless, beholds the miserable wreck
Driving along; his drowning ox at once
Descending, with his labours scattered round,
He sees; and instant o'er his shivering thought
Comes Winter unprovided, and a train
Of clamant children dear. Ye masters, then,
Be mindful of the rough laborious hand
That sinks you soft in elegance and ease;
Be mindful of those limbs, in russet clad,
Whose toil to yours is warmth and graceful pride;
And, oh, be mindful of that sparing board
Which covers yours with luxury profuse,
Makes your glass sparkle, and your sense rejoice!
Nor cruelly demand what the deep rains
And all-involving winds have swept away.

From THE CASTLE OF INDOLENCE

In lowly dale, fast by a river's side
With woody hill o'er hill encompassed round,
A most enchanting wizard did abide,
Than whom a fiend more fell is nowhere found.
It was, I ween, a lovely spot of ground;
And there a season atween June and May,
Half prankt with spring, with summer half imbrowned,
A listless climate made, where, sooth to say,
No living wight could work, ne cared for play.

Was nought around but images of rest:
Sleep-soothing groves, and quiet lawns between;
And flowery beds, that slumbrous influence kest,
From poppies breathed; and beds of pleasant green,
Where never yet was creeping creature seen.
Meantime unnumbered glittering streamlets played,
And hurled everywhere their waters sheen;

That, as they bickered through the sunny glade,
Though restless still themselves, a lulling murmur made.

Joined to the prattle of the purling rills,
Were heard the lowing herds along the vale,
And flocks loud-bleating from the distant hills,
And vacant shepherds piping in the dale:
And now and then sweet Philomel would wail,
Or stock-doves plain amid the forest deep,
That drowsy rustled to the sighing gale;
And still a coil the grasshopper did keep:
Yet all the sounds yblent inclined all to sleep.

Full in the passage of the vale, above,
A sable, silent, solemn forest stood;
Where nought but shadowy forms were seen to move,
As Idless fancied in her dreaming mood:
And up the hills, on either side, a wood
Of blackening pines, aye waving to and fro,
Sent forth a sleepy horror through the blood;
And where this valley winded out below,
The murmuring main was heard, and scarcely heard, to flow.

A pleasing land of drowsy-head it was:
Of dreams that wave before the half-shut eye;
And of gay castles in the clouds that pass,
Forever flushing round a summer-sky.
There eke the soft delights, that witchingly
Instil a wanton sweetness through the breast,
And the calm pleasures, always hovered nigh;
But whate'er smackt of noyance, or unrest,
Was far, far off expelled from this delicious nest.

The landscape such, inspiring perfect ease,
Where Indolence (for so the wizard hight)
Close-hid his castle mid embowering trees,
That half shut out the beams of Phœbus bright,
And made a kind of checkered day and night.
Meanwhile, unceasing at the massy gate,
Beneath a spacious palm, the wicked wight
Was placed; and to his lute, of cruel fate
And labour harsh, complained, lamenting man's estate.

Thither continual pilgrims crowded still,
From all the roads of earth that pass there by:
For, as they chanced to breathe on neighbouring hill,
The freshness of this valley smote their eye,
And drew them ever and anon more nigh;
Till clustering round the enchanter false they hung,
Ymolten with his syren melody;
While o'er the enfeebling lute his hand he flung,
And to the trembling chords these tempting verses sung:

"Behold! ye pilgrims of this earth, behold!
See all but man with unearned pleasure gay:
See her bright robes the butterfly unfold,
Broke from her wintry tomb in prime of May!
What youthful bride can equal her array?
Who can with her for easy pleasure vie?
From mead to mead with gentle wing to stray,
From flower to flower on balmy gales to fly,
Is all she has to do beneath the radiant sky.

"Behold the merry minstrels of the morn,
The swarming songsters of the careless grove;
Ten thousand throats that, from the flowering thorn,
Hymn their good God, and carol sweet of love,
Such grateful kindly raptures them emove!
They neither plough, nor sow; ne, fit for flail,
E'er to the barn the nodding sheaves they drove;
Yet theirs each harvest dancing in the gale,
Whatever crowns the hill, or smiles along the vale.

"Outcast of Nature, man! the wretched thrall
Of bitter-dropping sweat, of sweltry pain,
Of cares that eat away the heart with gall,
And of the vices, an inhuman train,
That all proceed from savage thirst of gain:
For when hard-hearted Interest first began
To poison earth, Astræa left the plain;
Guile, Violence, and Murder, seized on man,
And, for soft milky streams, with blood the rivers ran.

"Come, ye who still the cumbrous load of life
Push hard up-hill; but as the farthest steep
You trust to gain, and put an end to strife,
Down thunders back the stone with mighty sweep,
And hurls your labours to the valley deep,
Forever vain: come, and, withouten fee,
I in oblivion will your sorrows steep,
Your cares, your toils; will steep you in a sea
Of full delight: O come, ye weary wights, to me!

"With me, you need not rise at early dawn,
To pass the joyless day in various stounds;
Or louting low, on upstart Fortune fawn,
And sell fair Honour for some paltry pounds;
Or through the city take your dirty rounds,
To cheat, and dun, and lie, and visit pay,
Now flattering base, now giving secret wounds;
Or prowl in courts of law for human prey,
In venal senate thieve, or rob on broad highway.

"No cocks, with me, to rustic labour call,
From village on to village sounding clear; 119
To tardy swain no shrill-voiced matrons squall;
No dogs, no babes, no wives, to stun your ear;
No hammers thump; no horrid blacksmith sear;
Ne noisy tradesman your sweet slumbers start
With sounds that are a misery to hear;
But all is calm, — as would delight the heart
Of Sybarite of old, — all Nature, and all Art.

* * * * * * *

"The best of men have ever loved repose:
They hate to mingle in the filthy fray;
Where the soul sours, and gradual rancour grows,
Embittered more from peevish day to day,
Even those whom Fame has lent her fairest ray,
The most renowned of worthy wights of yore,
From a base world at last have stolen away:
So Scipio, to the soft Cumæan shore 152
Retiring, tasted joy he never knew before.

"But if a little exercise you choose,
Some zest for ease, 'tis not forbidden here.
Amid the groves you may indulge the Muse,
Or tend the blooms, and deck the vernal year;
Or, softly stealing, with your watery gear,
Along the brooks, the crimson-spotted fry
You may delude; the whilst, amused, you hear
Now the hoarse stream, and now the Zephyr's sigh, 161
Attunèd to the birds, and woodland melody.

"O grievous folly! to heap up estate,
Losing the days you see beneath the sun;
When, sudden, comes blind unrelenting Fate,
And gives the untasted portion you have won,
With ruthless toil and many a wretch undone,
To those who mock you gone to Pluto's reign,
There with sad ghosts to pine, and shadows dun;
But sure it is of vanities most vain, 170
To toil for what you here untoiling may obtain."

He ceased. But still their trembling ears retained
The deep vibrations of his witching song,
That, by a kind of magic power, constrained
To enter in, pell-mell, the listening throng.
Heaps poured on heaps, and yet they slipped along,
In silent ease: as when beneath the beam
Of summer-moons, the distant woods among,
Or by some flood all silvered with the gleam,
The soft-embodied Fays through airy portal stream. 180

* * * * * * *

A certain music, never known before,
Here lulled the pensive, melancholy mind;
Full easily obtained. Behoves no more,
But sidelong to the gently-waving wind
To lay the well-tuned instrument reclined;
From which, with airy flying fingers light,
Beyond each mortal touch the most refined,
The god of winds drew sounds of deep delight:
Whence, with just cause, the harp of Æolus it hight. 360

* * * * * * *

Near the pavilions where we slept, still ran
Soft-tinkling streams, and dashing waters fell,
And sobbing breezes sighed, and oft began 381
(So worked the wizard) wintry storms to swell,
As heaven and earth they would together mell:
At doors and windows, threatening, seemed to call
The demons of the tempest, growling fell,
Yet the least entrance found they none at all;
Whence sweeter grew our sleep, secure in massy hall.

And hither Morpheus sent his kindest dreams,
Raising a world of gayer tinct and grace; 389
O'er which were shadowy cast Elysian gleams,
That played, in waving lights, from place to place,
And shed a roseate smile on Nature's face.
Not Titian's pencil e'er could so array,
So fleece with clouds, the pure ethereal space;
Ne could it e'er such melting forms display,
As loose on flowery beds all languishingly lay.

AN ODE

From ALFRED, A MASQUE

When Britain first, at Heaven's command,
Arose from out the azure main,
This was the charter of the land,
And guardian angels sang this strain:
Rule, Britannia, rule the waves!
Britons never will be slaves!

The nations not so blest as thee,
Must in their turns to tyrants fall,
Whilst thou shalt flourish great and free,
The dread and envy of them all.
Rule, Britannia, etc.

Still more majestic shalt thou rise,
More dreadful from each foreign stroke;
As the loud blast that tears the skies,
Serves but to root thy native oak.
Rule, Britannia, etc.

Thee haughty tyrants ne'er shall tame;
All their attempts to bend thee down
Will but arouse thy generous flame,
But work their woe and thy renown.
Rule, Britannia, etc.

To thee belongs the rural reign;
Thy cities shall with commerce shine;
All thine shall be the subject main,
And every shore it circles thine.
Rule, Britannia, etc.

The Muses, still with freedom found,
Shall to thy happy coast repair;
Blest isle, with matchless beauty crowned,
And manly hearts to guard the fair!
Rule, Britannia, etc.

JOHN DYER (1700?–1758)

From GRONGAR HILL

Silent Nymph, with curious eye,
Who, the purple evening, lie
On the mountain's lonely van,
Beyond the noise of busy man,
Painting fair the form of things,
While the yellow linnet sings;
Or the tuneful nightingale
Charms the forest with her tale;
Come with all thy various hues,
Come, and aid thy sister Muse;
Now while Phœbus riding high
Gives lustre to the land and sky!
Grongar Hill invites my song,
Draw the landskip bright and strong;
Grongar, in whose mossy cells
Sweetly musing Quiet dwells;
Grongar, in whose silent shade,
For the modest Muses made,
So oft I have, the evening still,
At the fountain of a rill,
Sate upon a flowery bed,
With my hand beneath my head;
While strayed my eyes o'er Towy's flood,
Over mead, and over wood,
From house to house, from hill to hill,
'Till Contemplation had her fill.
About his chequered sides I wind,
And leave his brooks and meads behind,
And groves, and grottoes where I lay,
And vistas shooting beams of day:
Wide and wider spreads the vale;
As circles on a smooth canal:
The mountains round, unhappy fate!
Sooner or later, of all height,
Withdraw their summits from the skies,
And lessen as the others rise:
Still the prospect wider spreads,
Adds a thousand woods and meads,
Still it widens, widens still,
And sinks the newly-risen hill.
Now, I gain the mountain's brow,
What a landskip lies below!
No clouds, no vapours intervene,
But the gay, the open scene
Does the face of nature show,
In all the hues of heaven's bow!
And, swelling to embrace the light,
Spreads around beneath the sight.
Old castles on the cliffs arise,
Proudly towering in the skies;
Rushing from the woods, the spires
Seem from hence ascending fires;
Half his beams Apollo sheds
On the yellow mountain-heads,
Gilds the fleeces of the flocks,
And glitters on the broken rocks.
Below me trees unnumbered rise,
Beautiful in various dyes:
The gloomy pine, the poplar blue,
The yellow beach, the sable yew,
The slender fir, that taper grows,
The sturdy oak with broad-spread boughs;
And beyond the purple grove,
Haunt of Phillis, queen of love,
Gaudy as the opening dawn,
Lies a long and level lawn
On which a dark hill, steep and high,
Holds and charms the wandering eye.
Deep are his feet in Towy's flood,
His sides are cloth'd with waving wood,
And ancient towers crown his brow,
That cast an aweful look below;
Whose ragged walls the ivy creeps,
And with her arms from falling keeps;
So both a safety from the wind
On mutual dependence find.

THE FLEECE

From BOOK I

Ah, gentle shepherd, thine the lot to tend,
Of all, that feel distress, the most assail'd,
Feeble, defenceless: lenient be thy care:
But spread around thy tenderest diligence
In flow'ry spring-time, when the new-dropt lamb,
Tottering with weakness by his mother's side,
Feels the fresh world about him; and each thorn,
Hillock, or furrow, trips his feeble feet:

Oh, guard his meek sweet innocence from all
Th' innumerous ills, that rush around his life;
Mark the quick kite, with beak and talons prone,
Circling the skies to snatch him from the plain;
Observe the lurking crows; beware the brake,
There the sly fox the careless minute waits;
Nor trust thy neighbor's dog, nor earth, nor sky:
Thy bosom to a thousand cares divide.
Eurus oft sings his hail; the tardy fields
Pay not their promised food; and oft the dam
O'er her weak twins with empty udder mourns,
Or fails to guard, when the bold bird of prey
Alights, and hops in many turns around,
And tires her also turning: to her aid
Be nimble, and the weakest in thine arms
Gently convey to the warm cote, and oft,
Between the lark's note and the nightingale's,
His hungry bleating still with tepid milk:
In this soft office may thy children join,
And charitable habits learn in sport:
Nor yield him to himself, ere vernal airs
Sprinkle thy little croft with daisy flowers:
Nor yet forget him: life has rising ills:
Various as ether is the pastoral care:
Through slow experience, by a patient breast,
The whole long lesson gradual is attained,
By precept after precept, oft received
With deep attention: such as Nuceus sings
To the full vale near Soare's enamour'd brook,
While all is silence: sweet Hincklean swain!
Whom rude obscurity severely clasps:
The muse, howe'er, will deck thy simple cell
With purple violets and primrose flowers,
Well-pleased thy faithful lessons to repay.

WILLIAM HAMILTON OF BANGOR (1704–1754)

A SOLILOQUY

IN IMITATION OF HAMLET

My anxious soul is tore with doubtful strife,
And hangs suspended betwixt death and life;
Life! death! dread objects of mankind's debate;
Whether superior to the shocks of fate,
To bear its fiercest ills with stedfast mind,
To Nature's order piously resign'd,
Or, with magnanimous and brave disdain,
Return her back th' injurious gift again.
O! if to die, this mortal bustle o'er,
Were but to close one's eyes, and be no more;
From pain, from sickness, sorrows, safe withdrawn,
In night eternal that shall know no dawn;
This dread, imperial, wondrous frame of man,
Lost in still nothing, whence it first began:
Yes, if the grave such quiet could supply,
Devotion's self might even dare to die,
Lest hapless victors in the mortal strife,
Through death we struggle but to second life.
But, fearful here, though curious to explore,
Thought pauses, trembling on the hither shore:
What scenes may rise, awake the human fear;
Being again resum'd, and God more near;
If awful thunders the new guest appal,
Or the soft voice of gentle mercy call.
This teaches life with all its ills to please,
Afflicting poverty, severe disease;
To lowest infamy gives power to charm,
And strikes the dagger from the boldest arm.
Then, Hamlet, cease; thy rash resolves forego;
God, Nature, Reason, all will have it so:
Learn by this sacred horror, well suppress,
Each fatal purpose in the traitor's breast.
This damps revenge with salutary fear,
And stops ambition in its wild career,
Till virtue for itself begin to move,
And servile fear exalt to filial love.
Then in thy breast let calmer passions rise,
Pleas'd with thy lot on earth, absolve the skies.
The ills of life see Friendship can divide;
See angels warring on the good man's side.
Alone to Virtue happiness is given,
On earth self-satisfied, and crown'd in Heaven.

DAVID MALLET (1705–1765)

WILLIAM AND MARGARET

'Twas at the silent solemn hour,
  When night and morning meet;
In glided Margaret's grimly ghost,
  And stood at William's feet.

Her face was like an April morn
  Clad in a wintry cloud;
And clay-cold was her lily hand
  That held her sable shroud.

So shall the fairest face appear,
  When youth and years are flown:
Such is the robe that kings must wear,
  When death has reft their crown.

Her bloom was like the springing flower,
  That sips the silver dew;
The rose was budded in her cheek,
  Just opening to the view.

But love had, like the canker-worm,
  Consumed her early prime;
The rose grew pale, and left her cheek,
  She died before her time.

"Awake!" she cried, "thy true love calls,
Come from her midnight grave:
Now let thy pity hear the maid
Thy love refused to save.

"This is the dark and dreary hour
When injured ghosts complain;
When yawning graves give up their dead,
To haunt the faithless swain.

"Bethink thee, William, of thy fault,
Thy pledge and broken oath!
And give me back my maiden vow,
And give me back my troth.

"Why did you promise love to me,
And not that promise keep?
Why did you swear my eyes were bright,
Yet leave those eyes to weep?

"How could you say my face was fair,
And yet that face forsake?
How could you win my virgin heart,
Yet leave that heart to break?

"Why did you say my lip was sweet,
And make the scarlet pale?
And why did I, young, witless maid!
Believe the flattering tale?

"That face, alas! no more is fair,
Those lips no longer red:
Dark are my eyes, now closed in death,
And every charm is fled.

"The hungry worm my sister is;
This winding-sheet I wear:
And cold and weary lasts our night,
Till that last morn appear.

"But hark! the cock has warned me hence;
A long and last adieu!
Come see, false man, how low she lies,
Who died for love of you."

The lark sung loud; the morning smiled
With beams of rosy red:
Pale William quaked in every limb,
And raving left his bed.

He hied him to the fatal place
Where Margaret's body lay;
And stretched him on the green-grass turf
That wrapt her breathless clay.

And thrice he called on Margaret's name,
And thrice he wept full sore;
Then laid his cheek to her cold grave,
And word spake never more!

CHARLES WESLEY (1707–1788)

FOR THE YOUNGEST

Gentle Jesus, meek and mild,
Look upon a little child;
Pity my simplicity,
Suffer me to come to Thee.

Fain I would to Thee be brought;
Dearest God, forbid it not:
Give me, dearest God, a place
In the kingdom of Thy grace.

Put Thy hands upon my head,
Let me in Thine arms be stayed;
Let me lean upon Thy breast,
Lull me, lull me, Lord, to rest.

Hold me fast in Thy embrace,
Let me see Thy smiling face.
Give me, Lord, Thy blessing give;
Pray for me, and I shall live.

I shall live the simple life,
Free from sin's uneasy strife,
Sweetly ignorant of ill,
Innocent and happy still.

O that I may never know
What the wicked people do!
Sin is contrary to Thee,
Sin is the forbidden tree.

Keep me from the great offence,
Guard my helpless innocence;
Hide me, from all evil hide,
Self, and stubbornness, and pride.

Lamb of God, I look to Thee;
Thou shalt my Example be;
Thou art gentle, meek and mild,
Thou wast once a little Child.

Fain I would be as Thou art;
Give me Thy obedient heart.
Thou art pitiful and kind;
Let me have Thy loving mind.

Meek and lowly may I be;
Thou art all humility.
Let me to my betters bow;
Subject to Thy parents Thou.

Let me above all fulfil
God my heavenly Father's will;
Never His good Spirit grieve,
Only to His glory live.

Thou didst live to God alone,
Thou didst never seek Thine own;
Thou Thyself didst never please.
God was all Thy happiness.

Loving Jesu, gentle Lamb,
In Thy gracious hands I am.
Make me, Saviour, what Thou art,
Live Thyself within my heart.

I shall then show forth Thy praise,
Serve Thee all my happy days:
Then the world shall always see
Christ, the holy Child, in me.

FOR A WOMAN NEAR HER TRAVAIL

Full of trembling expectation,
  Feeling much, and fearing more,
Author, God of my salvation,
  I Thy timely aid implore.
Suffering Son of Man, be near me,
  All my sufferings to sustain;
By Thy sorer griefs to cheer me,
  By Thy more than mortal pain.

Call to mind that unknown anguish,
  In Thy days of flesh below,
When Thy troubled soul did languish
  Under a whole world of woe:
When Thou didst our curse inherit,
  Groan beneath our guilty load,
Burthened with a wounded spirit,
  Bruised by all the wrath of God.

By Thy most severe temptation
  In that dark satanic hour;
By Thy last mysterious Passion,
  Screen me from the adverse power.
By Thy fainting in the garden,
  By Thy bloody sweat, I pray,
Write upon my heart the pardon;
  Take my sins and fears away.

By the travail of Thy spirit,
  By Thine outcry on the tree,
By Thine agonizing merit,
  In my pangs remember me!
By Thy Death I Thee conjure,
  A weak, dying soul befriend;
Make me patient to endure,
  Make me faithful to the end.

SAMUEL JOHNSON (1709–1784)

FROM LONDON

By numbers here from shame or censure free
All crimes are safe, but hated poverty.
This, only this, the rigid law pursues;
This, only this, provokes the snarling muse.
The sober trader at a tatter'd cloak
Wakes from his dream, and labours for a joke;
With brisker air the silken courtiers gaze,
And turn the varied taunt a thousand ways.
Of all the griefs that harass the distress'd,
Sure the most bitter is a scornful jest;
Fate never wounds more deep the gen'rous heart,
Than when a blockhead's insult points the dart.
  Has heaven reserv'd, in pity to the poor,
No pathless waste, or undiscover'd shore?
No secret island in the boundless main?
No peaceful desert yet unclaim'd by Spain?
Quick let us rise, the happy seats explore,
And bear oppression's insolence no more.
This mournful truth is ev'ry where confess'd,
Slow rises worth, by poverty depress'd;
But here more slow, where all are slaves to gold,
Where looks are merchandise, and smiles are sold;
Where won by bribes, by flatteries implor'd,
The groom retails the favours of his lord.
  But hark! th' affrighted crowd's tumultuous cries
Roll through the streets, and thunder to the skies.
Rais'd from some pleasing dream of wealth and pow'r,
Some pompous palace, or some blissful bow'r,
Aghast you start, and scarce with aching sight
Sustain the approaching fire's tremendous light;
Swift from pursuing horrors take your way,
And leave your little All to flames a prey;
Then thro' the world a wretched vagrant roam,
For where can starving merit find a home?
In vain your mournful narrative disclose,
While all neglect, and most insult your woes.

FROM THE VANITY OF HUMAN WISHES

Let observation, with extensive view,
Survey mankind, from China to Peru;
Remark each anxious toil, each eager strife,
And watch the busy scenes of crowded life:
Then say how hope and fear, desire and hate,
O'erspread with snares the clouded maze of fate,
Where wav'ring man, betray'd by vent'rous pride
To tread the dreary paths without a guide,
As treach'rous phantoms in the mist delude,
Shuns fancied ills, or chases airy good;
How rarely reason guides the stubborn choice,
Rules the bold hand, or prompts the suppliant voice;
How nations sink, by darling schemes oppress'd,
When Vengeance listens to the fool's request.
Fate wings with ev'ry wish th' afflictive dart,

Each gift of nature and each grace of art;
With fatal heat impetuous courage glows,
With fatal sweetness elocution flows,
Impeachment stops the speaker's pow'rful breath,
And restless fire precipitates on death.
But scarce observ'd, the knowing and the bold
Fall in the gen'ral massacre of gold;
Wide-wasting pest! that rages unconfin'd,
And crowds with crimes the records of mankind;
For gold his sword the hireling ruffian draws,
For gold the hireling judge distorts the laws:
Wealth heap'd on wealth nor truth nor safety buys;
The dangers gather as the treasures rise.

* * * * * * *

On what foundation stands the warrior's pride,
How just his hopes, let Swedish Charles decide:
A frame of adamant, a soul of fire,
No dangers fright him, and no labours tire;
O'er love, o'er fear, extends his wide domain,
Unconquer'd lord of pleasure and of pain;
No joys to him pacific sceptres yield, —
War sounds the trump, he rushes to the field;
Behold surrounding kings their pow'rs combine,
And one capitulate, and one resign:
Peace courts his hand, but spreads her charms in vain;
"Think nothing gain'd," he cries, "till naught remain,
On Moscow's walls till Gothic standards fly,
And all be mine beneath the polar sky."
The march begins in military state,
And nations on his eye suspended wait;
Stern Famine guards the solitary coast,
And Winter barricades the realms of Frost:
He comes; nor want nor cold his course delay; —
Hide, blushing Glory, hide Pultowa's day:
The vanquish'd hero leaves his broken bands,
And shows his miseries in distant lands;
Condemn'd a needy supplicant to wait,
While ladies interpose and slaves debate.
But did not Chance at length her error mend?
Did no subverted empire mark his end?
Did rival monarchs give the fatal wound?
Or hostile millions press him to the ground?
His fall was destin'd to a barren strand,
A petty fortress, and a dubious hand.
He left the name, at which the world grew pale,
To point a moral, or adorn a tale.

* * * * * * *

But grant, the virtues of a temp'rate prime
Bless with an age exempt from scorn or crime;
An age that melts with unperceiv'd decay,
And glides in modest innocence away;
Whose peaceful day Benevolence endears,
Whose night congratulating Conscience cheers;
The gen'ral fav'rite as the gen'ral friend:
Such age there is, and who shall wish its end?
Yet ev'n on this her load Misfortune flings,
To press the weary minutes' flagging wings;
New sorrow rises as the day returns,
A sister sickens, or a daughter mourns.
Now kindred Merit fills the sable bier,
Now lacerated Friendship claims a tear.
Year chases year, decay pursues decay,
Still drops some joy from with'ring life away;
New forms arise, and diff'rent views engage,
Superfluous lags the vet'ran on the stage,
Till pitying Nature signs the last release,
And bids afflicted worth retire to peace.
But few there are whom hours like these await,
Who set unclouded in the gulphs of Fate.
From Lydia's monarch should the search descend,
By Solon caution'd to regard his end,
In life's last scene what prodigies surprise —
Fears of the brave, and follies of the wise!
From Marlb'rough's eyes the streams of dotage flow,
And Swift expires a driv'ler and a show.

* * * * * * *

Where then shall Hope and Fear their objects find?
Must dull Suspense corrupt the stagnant mind?
Must helpless man, in ignorance sedate,
Roll darkling down the torrent of his fate?
Must no dislike alarm, no wishes rise,
No cries invoke the mercies of the skies? —
Enquirer, cease; petitions yet remain,
Which heav'n may hear; nor deem religion vain.
Still raise for good the supplicating voice,
But leave to heav'n the measure and the choice;
Safe in his pow'r, whose eyes discern afar
The secret ambush of a specious pray'r.
Implore his aid, in his decisions rest,
Secure, whate'er he gives, he gives the best.
Yet when the sense of sacred presence fires,
And strong devotion to the skies aspires,
Pour forth thy fervours for a healthful mind,
Obedient passions, and a will resign'd;
For love, which scarce collective man can fill;
For patience, sov'reign o'er transmuted ill;
For faith, that, panting for a happier seat,
Counts death kind Nature's signal of retreat:
These goods for man the laws of heav'n ordain;
These goods He grants, who grants the pow'r to gain;
With these celestial Wisdom calms the mind,
And makes the happiness she does not find.

WILLIAM SHENSTONE (1714–1763)

WRITTEN AT AN INN AT HENLEY

To thee, fair freedom! I retire
  From flattery, cards, and dice, and din;
Nor art thou found in mansions higher
  Than the low cot, or humble inn.

'Tis here with boundless pow'r I reign;
  And every health which I begin,
Converts dull port to bright champagne;
  Such freedom crowns it, at an inn.

I fly from pomp, I fly from plate!
  I fly from falsehood's specious grin!
Freedom I love, and form I hate,
  And choose my lodgings at an inn.

Here, waiter! take my sordid ore,
  Which lacqueys else might hope to win;
It buys, what courts have not in store;
  It buys me freedom at an inn.

Whoe'er has travell'd life's dull round,
  Where'er his stages may have been,
May sigh to think he still has found
  The warmest welcome, at an inn.

From THE SCHOOL-MISTRESS

IN IMITATION OF SPENSER

Ah me! full sorely is my heart forlorn,
To think how modest worth neglected lies;
While partial fame doth with her blasts adorn
Such deeds alone, as pride and pomp disguise;
Deeds of ill sort, and mischievous emprize:
Lend me thy clarion, goddess! let me try
To sound the praise of merit, ere it dies;
Such as I oft have chaunced to espy,
Lost in the dreary shades of dull obscurity.

In ev'ry village mark'd with little spire,
Embow'r'd in trees, and hardly known to fame,
There dwells, in lowly shed, and mean attire,
A matron old, whom we school-mistress name;
Who boasts unruly brats with birch to tame;
They grieven sore, in piteous durance pent,
Aw'd by the pow'r of this relentless dame;
And oft-times, on vagaries idly bent,
For unkempt hair, or talk unconn'd, are sorely shent.

And all in sight doth rise a birchen tree,
Which learning near her little dome did stowe;
Whilom a twig of small regard to see,
Tho' now so wide its waving branches flow;
And work the simple vassals mickle woe;
For not a wind might curl the leaves that blew,
But their limbs shudder'd, and their pulse beat low;
And as they look'd they found their horror grew,
And shap'd it into rods, and tingled at the view.

* * * * * * *

A russet stole was o'er her shoulders thrown;
A russet kirtle fenc'd the nipping air;
'Twas simple russet, but it was her own;
'Twas her own country bred the flock so fair;
'Twas her own labour did the fleece prepare;
And, sooth to say, her pupils, rang'd around,
Thro' pious awe, did term it passing rare;
For they in gaping wonderment abound,
And think, no doubt, she been the greatest wight on ground.

Albeit ne flatt'ry did corrupt her truth,
Ne pompous title did debauch her ear;
Goody, good-woman, gossip, n'aunt, forsooth,
Or dame, the sole additions she did hear;
Yet these she challeng'd, these she held right dear:
Ne would esteem him act as mought behove,
Who should not honour'd eld with these revere:
For never title yet so mean could prove,
But there was eke a mind which did that title love.

One ancient hen she took delight to feed,
The plodding pattern of the busy dame;
Which, ever and anon, impell'd by need,
Into her school, begirt with chickens, came;
Such favour did her past deportment claim:
And, if neglect had lavish'd on the ground
Fragment of bread, she would collect the same;
For well she knew, and quaintly could expound,
What sin it were to waste the smallest crumb she found.

* * * * * * *

In elbow chair, like that of Scottish stem
By the sharp tooth of cank'ring eld defac'd,
In which, when he receives his diadem,
Our sov'reign prince and liefest liege is plac'd,
The matron sate; and some with rank she grac'd,
(The source of children's and of courtier's pride!)
Redress'd affronts, for vile affronts there pass'd;
And warn'd them not the fretful to deride,
But love each other dear, whatever them betide.

Right well she knew each temper to descry;
To thwart the proud, and the submiss to raise;
Some with vile copper prize exalt on high,
And some entice with pittance small of praise;
And other some with baleful sprig she 'frays:

Ev'n absent, she the reins of pow'r doth hold,
While with quaint arts the giddy crowd she sways;
Forewarn'd, if little bird their pranks behold,
'Twill whisper in her ear, and all the scene unfold.

Lo, now with state she utters the command!
Eftsoons the urchins to their tasks repair;
Their books of stature small they take in hand,
Which with pellucid horn secured are;
To save from finger wet the letters fair:
The work so gay, that on their back is seen,
St. George's high atchievements does declare;
On which thilk wight that has y-gazing been
Kens the forth-coming rod, unpleasing sight, I ween!

Ah, luckless he, and born beneath the beam
Of evil star! it irks me whilst I write!
As erst the bard by Mulla's silver stream,
Oft, as he told of deadly dolorous plight,
Sigh'd as he sung, and did in tears indite.
For brandishing the rod, she doth begin
To loose the brogues, the stripling's late delight!
And down they drop; appears his dainty skin,
Fair as the furry coat of whitest ermilin.

O ruthful scene! when from a nook obscure,
His little sister doth his peril see:
All playful as she sate, she grows demure;
She finds full soon her wonted spirits flee;
She meditates a pray'r to set him free:
Nor gentle pardon could this dame deny,
(If gentle pardon could with dames agree)
To her sad grief that swells in either eye,
And wrings her so that all for pity she could die.

No longer can she now her shrieks command;
And hardly she forbears thro' aweful fear,
To rushen forth, and, with presumptuous hand,
To stay harsh justice in its mid career.
On thee she calls, on thee, her parent dear!
(Ah! too remote to ward the shameful blow!)
She sees no kind domestic visage near,
And soon a flood of tears begins to flow;
And gives a loose at last to unavailing woe.

* * * * * * *

The other tribe, aghast, with sore dismay,
Attend, and conn their tasks with mickle care:
By turns, astony'd, ev'ry twig survey,
And, from their fellow's hateful wounds, beware;
Knowing, I wist, how each the same may share;
'Till fear has taught them a performance meet,
And to the well-known chest the dame repair;
Whence oft with sugar'd cates she doth 'em greet,
And ginger-bread y-rare; now, certes, doubly sweet!

* * * * * * *

Ah me! how much I fear lest pride it be!
But if that pride it be, which thus inspires,
Beware, ye dames, with nice discernment see,
Ye quench not too the sparks of nobler fires:
Ah! better far than all the muses' lyres,
All coward arts, is valour's gen'rous heat;
The firm fixt breast which fit and right requires,
Like Vernon's patriot soul; more justly great
Than craft that pimps for ill, or flow'ry false deceit.

Yet nurs'd with skill, what dazzling fruits appear!
Ev'n now sagacious foresight points to show
A little bench of heedless bishops here,
And there a chancellour in embryo,
Or bard sublime, if bard may e'er be so,
As Milton, Shakespeare, names that ne'er shall die!
Tho' now he crawl along the ground so low,
Nor weeting how the muse should soar on high,
Wisheth, poor starv'ling elf! his paper kite may fly.

THOMAS GRAY (1716–1771)

AN ODE

ON THE SPRING

Lo! where the rosy-bosom'd Hours,
Fair Venus' train appear,
Disclose the long-expecting flowers,
And wake the purple year!
The Attic warbler pours her throat,
Responsive to the cuckow's note,
The untaught harmony of spring:
While whisp'ring pleasure as they fly,
Cool Zephyrs thro' the clear blue sky
Their gather'd fragrance fling.

Where'er the oak's thick branches stretch
A broader browner shade;
Where'er the rude and moss-grown beech
O'er-canopies the glade
Beside some water's rushy brink
With me the Muse shall sit, and think
(At ease reclin'd in rustic state)
How vain the ardour of the Crowd,
How low, how little are the Proud,
How indigent the Great!

Still is the toiling hand of Care:
The panting herds repose:
Yet hark, how thro' the peopled air
The busy murmur glows!

The insect youth are on the wing,
Eager to taste the honied spring,
And float amid the liquid noon:
Some lightly o'er the current skim,
Some shew their gaily-gilded trim
Quick-glancing to the sun.

To Contemplation's sober eye
Such is the race of Man:
And they that creep, and they that fly,
Shall end where they began.
Alike the Busy and the Gay
But flutter thro' life's little day,
In fortune's varying colours drest:
Brush'd by the hand of rough Mischance,
Or chill'd by age, their airy dance
They leave, in dust to rest.

Methinks I hear in accents low
The sportive kind reply:
Poor moralist! and what art thou?
A solitary fly!
Thy Joys no glittering female meets,
No hive hast thou of hoarded sweets,
No painted plumage to display:
On hasty wings thy youth is flown;
Thy sun is set, thy spring is gone —
We frolick, while 'tis May.

AN ODE

ON A DISTANT PROSPECT OF ETON COLLEGE

Ye distant spires, ye antique towers,
That crown the watry glade,
Where grateful Science still adores
Her Henry's holy Shade;
And ye, that from the stately brow
Of Windsor's heights th' expanse below
Of grove, of lawn, of mead survey,
Whose turf, whose shade, whose flowers among
Wanders the hoary Thames along
His silver-winding way.

Ah, happy hills, ah, pleasing shade,
Ah, fields belov'd in vain,
Where once my careless childhood stray'd,
A stranger yet to pain!
I feel the gales, that from ye blow,
A momentary bliss bestow,
As waving fresh their gladsome wing,
My weary soul they seem to sooth,
And, redolent of joy and youth,
To breathe a second spring.

Say, Father Thames, for thou hast seen
Full many a sprightly race
Disporting on thy margent green
The paths of pleasure trace,
Who foremost now delight to cleave
With pliant arm thy glassy wave?
The captive linnet which enthrall?
What idle progeny succeed
To chase the rolling circle's speed,
Or urge the flying ball?

While some on earnest business bent
Their murm'ring labours ply
'Gainst graver hours, that bring constraint
To sweeten liberty:
Some bold adventurers disdain
The limits of their little reign,
And unknown regions dare descry:
Still as they run they look behind,
They hear a voice in every wind,
And snatch a fearful joy.

Gay hope is theirs by fancy fed,
Less pleasing when possest;
The tear forgot as soon as shed,
The sunshine of the breast:
Theirs buxom health of rosy hue,
Wild wit, invention ever-new,
And lively cheer of vigour born;
The thoughtless day, the easy night,
The spirits pure, the slumbers light,
That fly th' approach of morn.

Alas, regardless of their doom,
The little victims play!
No sense have they of ills to come,
Nor care beyond to-day:
Yet see how all around 'em wait
The Ministers of human fate,
And black Misfortune's baleful train!
Ah, shew them where in ambush stand
To seize their prey the murth'rous band!
Ah, tell them, they are men!

These shall the fury Passions tear,
The vultures of the mind,
Disdainful Anger, pallid Fear,
And Shame that skulks behind;
Or pining Love shall waste their youth,
Or Jealousy with rankling tooth,
That inly gnaws the secret heart,
And Envy wan, and faded Care,
Grim-visag'd comfortless Despair,
And Sorrow's piercing dart.

Ambition this shall tempt to rise,
Then whirl the wretch from high,

To bitter Scorn a sacrifice,
  And grinning Infamy.
The stings of Falsehood those shall try,
And hard Unkindness' alter'd eye,
  That mocks the tear it forc'd to flow;
And keen Remorse with blood defil'd,
And moody Madness laughing wild
  Amid severest woe.

Lo, in the vale of years beneath
  A griesly troop are seen,
The painful family of Death,
  More hideous than their Queen:
This racks the joints, this fires the veins,
That every labouring sinew strains,
  Those in the deeper vitals rage:
Lo, Poverty, to fill the band,
That numbs the soul with icy hand,
  And slow-consuming Age.

To each his suff'rings: all are men,
  Condemn'd alike to groan,
The tender for another's pain;
  Th' unfeeling for his own.
Yet ah! why should they know their fate?
Since sorrow never comes too late,
  And happiness too swiftly flies.
Thought would destroy their paradise.
No more; where ignorance is bliss,
  'Tis folly to be wise.

ELEGY

WRITTEN IN A COUNTRY CHURCHYARD

The Curfew tolls the knell of parting day,
  The lowing herd wind slowly o'er the lea,
The plowman homeward plods his weary way,
  And leaves the world to darkness and to me.

Now fades the glimmering landscape on the sight,
  And all the air a solemn stillness holds,
Save where the beetle wheels his droning flight,
  And drowsy tinklings lull the distant folds;

Save that from yonder ivy-mantled tow'r
  The moping owl does to the moon complain
Of such, as wand'ring near her secret bow'r,
  Molest her ancient solitary reign.

Beneath those rugged elms, that yew-tree's shade,
  Where heaves the turf in many a mould'ring heap,
Each in his narrow cell for ever laid,
  The rude Forefathers of the hamlet sleep.

The breezy call of incense-breathing Morn,
  The swallow twitt'ring from the straw-built shed,
The cock's shrill clarion, or the echoing horn,
  No more shall rouse them from their lowly bed.

For them no more the blazing hearth shall burn,
  Or busy housewife ply her evening care:
No children run to lisp their sire's return,
  Or climb his knees the envied kiss to share.

Oft did the harvest to their sickle yield,
  Their furrow oft the stubborn glebe has broke;
How jocund did they drive their team afield!
  How bow'd the woods beneath their sturdy stroke!

Let not Ambition mock their useful toil,
  Their homely joys, and destiny obscure;
Nor Grandeur hear with a disdainful smile,
  The short and simple annals of the poor.

The boast of heraldry, the pomp of pow'r,
  And all that beauty, all that wealth e'er gave,
Awaits alike th' inevitable hour.
  The paths of glory lead but to the grave.

Nor you, ye Proud, impute to These the fault,
  If Mem'ry o'er their Tomb no Trophies raise,
Where thro' the long-drawn isle and fretted vault
  The pealing anthem swells the note of praise.

Can storied urn or animated bust
  Back to its mansion call the fleeting breath?
Can Honour's voice provoke the silent dust,
  Or Flatt'ry sooth the dull cold ear of Death?

Perhaps in this neglected spot is laid
  Some heart once pregnant with celestial fire;
Hands, that the rod of empire might have sway'd,
  Or wak'd to extasy the living lyre.

But Knowledge to their eyes her ample page
  Rich with the spoils of time did ne'er unroll;
Chill Penury repress'd their noble rage,
  And froze the genial current of the soul.

Full many a gem of purest ray serene,
  The dark unfathom'd caves of ocean bear:
Full many a flower is born to blush unseen,
  And waste its sweetness on the desert air.

Some village-Hampden, that with dauntless breast
  The little Tyrant of his fields withstood;
Some mute inglorious Milton here may rest,
  Some Cromwell guiltless of his country's blood.

Th' applause of list'ning senates to command,
  The threats of pain and ruin to despise,
To scatter plenty o'er a smiling land,
  And read their hist'ry in a nation's eyes,

Their lot forbade: nor circumscrib'd alone
Their growing virtues, but their crimes confin'd;
Forbade to wade through slaughter to a throne,
And shut the gates of mercy on mankind,

The struggling pangs of conscious truth to hide,
To quench the blushes of ingenuous shame,
Or heap the shrine of Luxury and Pride
With incense kindled at the Muse's flame.

Far from the madding crowd's ignoble strife,
Their sober wishes never learn'd to stray;
Along the cool sequester'd vale of life
They kept the noiseless tenor of their way.

Yet ev'n these bones from insult to protect,
Some frail memorial still erected nigh,
With uncouth rhymes and shapeless sculpture deck'd,
Implores the passing tribute of a sigh.

Their name, their years, spelt by th' unletter'd muse,
The place of fame and elegy supply:
And many a holy text around she strews,
That teach the rustic moralist to die.

For who to dumb Forgetfulness a prey,
This pleasing anxious being e'er resign'd,
Left the warm precincts of the cheerful day,
Nor cast one longing ling'ring look behind?

On some fond breast the parting soul relies,
Some pious drops the closing eye requires;
Ev'n from the tomb the voice of Nature cries,
Ev'n in our Ashes live their wonted Fires.

For thee, who mindful of th' unhonour'd Dead
Dost in these lines their artless tale relate;
If chance, by lonely contemplation led,
Some kindred Spirit shall inquire thy fate,

Haply some hoary-headed Swain may say,
"Oft have we seen him at the peep of dawn
Brushing with hasty steps the dews away
To meet the sun upon the upland lawn.

"There at the foot of yonder nodding beech
That wreathes its old fantastic roots so high,
His listless length at noontide would he stretch,
And pore upon the brook that babbles by.

"Hard by yon wood, now smiling as in scorn,
Mutt'ring his wayward fancies he would rove,
Now drooping, woeful wan, like one forlorn,
Or craz'd with care, or cross'd in hopeless love.

"One morn I miss'd him on the custom'd hill,
Along the heath and near his fav'rite tree;
Another came; nor yet beside the rill,
Nor up the lawn, nor at the wood was he;

"The next with dirges due in sad array
Slow thro' the church-way path we saw him borne.
Approach and read (for thou can'st read) the lay,
Grav'd on the stone beneath yon aged thorn."

THE EPITAPH

Here rests his head upon the lap of Earth
A Youth to Fortune and to Fame unknown.
Fair Science frown'd not on his humble birth,
And Melancholy mark'd him for her own.

Large was his bounty, and his soul sincere,
Heav'n did a recompense as largely send:
He gave to Mis'ry all he had, a tear,
He gain'd from Heav'n ('twas all he wish'd) a friend.

No farther seek his merits to disclose,
Or draw his frailties from their dread abode,
(There they alike in trembling hope repose)
The bosom of his Father and his God.

THE PROGRESS OF POESY

A PINDARIC ODE

I

The Strophe

Awake, Æolian lyre, awake,
And give to rapture all thy trembling strings.
From Helicon's harmonious springs
A thousand rills their mazy progress take:
The laughing flowers, that round them blow,
Drink life and fragrance as they flow.
Now the rich stream of music winds along
Deep, majestic, smooth, and strong,
Thro' verdant vales, and Ceres' golden reign:
Now rolling down the steep amain,
Headlong, impetuous, see it pour:
The rocks, and nodding groves rebellow to the roar.

The Antistrophe

Oh! Sovereign of the willing soul,
Parent of sweet and solemn-breathing airs,
Enchanting shell! the sullen Cares,
And frantic Passions hear thy soft control.
On Thracia's hills the Lord of War,

Has curb'd the fury of his car,
And dropp d his thirsty lance at thy command.
Perching on the scept'red hand
Of Jove, thy magic lulls the feather'd king
With ruffled plumes, and flagging wing:
Quench'd in dark clouds of slumber lie
The terror of his beak, and light'nings of his eye.

The Epode

Thee the voice, the dance, obey,
Temper'd to thy warbled lay.
O'er Idalia's velvet-green
The rosy-crownèd Loves are seen
On Cytherea's day
With antic Sports, and blue-eyed Pleasures,
Frisking light in frolic measures;
Now pursuing, now retreating,
Now in circling troops they meet:
To brisk notes in cadence beating
Glance their many-twinkling feet.
Slow melting strains their Queen's approach declare:
Where'er she turns the Graces homage pay.
With arms sublime, that float upon the air,
In gliding state she wins her easy way:
O'er her warm cheek, and rising bosom, move
The bloom of young Desire, and purple light of Love.

II

The Strophe

Man's feeble race what Ills await,
Labour, and Penury, the racks of Pain,
Disease, and Sorrow's weeping train,
And Death, sad refuge from the storms of Fate!
The fond complaint, my Song, disprove,
And justify the laws of Jove.
Say, has he giv'n in vain the heav'nly Muse?
Night, and all her sickly dews,
Her Spectres wan, and Birds of boding cry,
He gives to range the dreary sky:
Till down the eastern cliffs afar
Hyperion's march they spy, and glitt'ring shafts of war.

The Antistrophe

In climes beyond the solar road,
Where shaggy forms o'er ice-built mountains roam,
The Muse has broke the twilight-gloom
To cheer the shiv'ring Native's dull abode.
And oft, beneath the od'rous shade
Of Chili's boundless forests laid,
She deigns to hear the savage Youth repeat
In loose numbers wildly sweet
Their feather-cinctured Chiefs, and dusky Loves.
Her track, where'er the Goddess roves,
Glory pursue, and generous Shame,
Th' unconquerable Mind, and Freedom's holy flame.

The Epode

Woods, that wave o'er Delphi's steep,
Isles, that crown th' Ægean deep,
Fields, that cool Ilissus laves,
Or where Mæander's amber waves
In lingering Lab'rinths creep,
How do your tuneful Echo's languish,
Mute, but to the voice of Anguish?
Where each old poetic Mountain
Inspiration breath'd around:
Ev'ry shade and hallow'd Fountain
Murmur'd deep a solemn sound:
Till the sad Nine in Greece's evil hour
Left their Parnassus for the Latian plains.
Alike they scorn the pomp of tyrant-Power,
And coward Vice, that revels in her chains.
When Latium had her lofty spirit lost,
They sought, O Albion! next thy sea-encircled coast.

III

The Strophe

Far from the sun and summer-gale,
In thy green lap was Nature's Darling laid,
What time, where lucid Avon stray'd,
To Him the mighty Mother did unveil
Her awful face: The dauntless Child
Stretch'd forth his little arms, and smiled.
This pencil take (she said) whose colours clear
Richly paint the vernal year:
Thine too these golden keys, immortal Boy!
This can unlock the gates of Joy;
Of Horror that, and thrilling Fears,
Or ope the sacred source of sympathetic Tears.

The Antistrophe

Nor second He, that rode sublime
Upon the seraph-wings of Ecstasy,
The secrets of th' Abyss to spy.
He pass'd the flaming bounds of Place and Time:
The living Throne, the sapphire-blaze,
Where Angels tremble, while they gaze,
He saw; but blasted with excess of light,
Closed his eyes in endless night.
Behold, where Dryden's less presumptuous car,
Wide o'er the fields of Glory bear
Two Coursers of ethereal race,
With necks in thunder cloth'd, and long-resounding pace.

The Epode

Hark, his hands the lyre explore!
Bright-eyed Fancy hovering o'er
Scatters from her pictur'd urn
Thoughts that breathe, and words that burn.
But ah! 'tis heard no more ———
O Lyre divine, what daring Spirit
Wakes thee now? tho' he inherit
Nor the pride, nor ample pinion,
That the Theban Eagle bear
Sailing with supreme dominion
Thro' the azure deep of air:
Yet oft before his infant eyes would run
Such forms, as glitter in the Muse's ray
With orient hues, unborrow'd of the Sun:
Yet shall he mount, and keep his distant way
Beyond the limits of a vulgar fate,
Beneath the Good how far — but far above the Great.

THE BARD

A PINDARIC ODE

I

The Strophe

"Ruin seize thee, ruthless King!
Confusion on thy banners wait,
Tho' fann'd by Conquest's crimson wing
They mock the air with idle state.
Helm, nor Hauberk's twisted mail,
Nor even thy virtues, Tyrant, shall avail
To save thy secret soul from nightly fears,
From Cambria's curse, from Cambria's tears!"
Such were the sounds, that o'er the crested pride
Of the first Edward scatter'd wild dismay,
As down the steep of Snowdon's shaggy side
He wound with toilsome march his long array.
Stout Glo'ster stood aghast in speechless trance;
To arms! cried Mortimer, and couch'd his quiv'ring lance.

The Antistrophe

On a rock, whose haughty brow
Frowns o'er old Conway's foaming flood,
Robed in the sable garb of woe,
With haggard eyes the Poet stood;
(Loose his beard, and hoary hair
Stream'd, like a meteor, to the troubled air)
And with a Master's hand, and Prophet's fire,
Struck the deep sorrows of his lyre:
"Hark, how each giant-oak, and desert cave,
Sighs to the torrent's awful voice beneath!
O'er thee, O King! their hundred arms they wave,
Revenge on thee in hoarser murmurs breathe;
Vocal no more, since Cambria's fatal day,
To high-born Hoel's harp, or soft Llewellyn's lay.

The Epode

"Cold is Cadwallo's tongue,
That hush'd the stormy main;
Brave Urien sleeps upon his craggy bed:
Mountains, ye mourn in vain
Modred, whose magic song
Made huge Plinlimmon bow his cloud-topp'd head.
On dreary Arvon's shore they lie,
Smear'd with gore, and ghastly pale:
Far, far aloof th' affrighted ravens sail;
The famish'd Eagle screams, and passes by.
Dear lost companions of my tuneful art,
Dear, as the light that visits these sad eyes,
Dear, as the ruddy drops that warm my heart,
Ye died amidst your dying country's cries —
No more I weep. They do not sleep.
On yonder cliffs, a griesly band,
I see them sit, they linger yet,
Avengers of their native land:
With me in dreadful harmony they join,
And weave with bloody hands the tissue of thy line:—

II

The Strophe

"'Weave the warp, and weave the woof,
The winding sheet of Edward's race.
Give ample room, and verge enough
The characters of hell to trace.
Mark the year, and mark the night,
When Severn shall re-echo with affright
The shrieks of death, thro' Berkley's roofs that ring,
Shrieks of an agonising King!
She-Wolf of France, with unrelenting fangs,
That tear'st the bowels of thy mangled Mate,
From thee be born, who o'er thy country hangs
The scourge of Heav'n. What Terrors round him wait!
Amazement in his van, with Flight combined,
And Sorrow's faded form, and Solitude behind.

The Antistrophe

"'Mighty Victor, mighty Lord,
Low on his funeral couch he lies!
No pitying heart, no eye, afford
A tear to grace his obsequies.
Is the sable Warriour fled?
Thy son is gone. He rests among the Dead.

The Swarm, that in thy noon-tide beam were born?
Gone to salute the rising Morn.
Fair laughs the Morn, and soft the Zephyr blows,
While proudly riding o'er the azure realm
In gallant trim the gilded Vessel goes;
Youth on the prow, and Pleasure at the helm;
Regardless of the sweeping Whirlwind's sway,
That, hush'd in grim repose, expects his evening-prey.

The Epode

"'Fill high the sparkling bowl,
The rich repast prepare;
Reft of a crown, he yet may share the feast.
Close by the regal chair
Fell Thirst and Famine scowl
A baleful smile upon their baffled Guest.
Heard ye the din of battle bray,
Lance to lance, and horse to horse?
Long Years of havock urge their destined course,
And thro' the kindred squadrons mow their way.
Ye Towers of Julius, London's lasting shame,
With many a foul and midnight murther fed,
Revere his Consort's faith, his Father's fame,
And spare the meek Usurper's holy head.
Above, below, the rose of snow,
Twined with her blushing foe, we spread:
The bristled Boar in infant-gore
Wallows beneath the thorny shade.
Now, brothers, bending o'er th' accursed loom
Stamp we our vengeance deep, and ratify his doom.

III

The Strophe

"'Edward, lo! to sudden fate
(Weave we the woof. The thread is spun)
Half of thy heart we consecrate.
(The web is wove. The work is done.)'—
Stay, oh stay! nor thus forlorn
Leave me unbless'd, unpitied, here to mourn!
In yon bright track, that fires the western skies,
They melt, they vanish from my eyes.
But oh! what solemn scenes on Snowdon's height
Descending slow their glitt'ring skirts unroll?
Visions of glory, spare my aching sight,
Ye unborn Ages, crowd not on my soul!
No more our long-lost Arthur we bewail.
All-hail, ye genuine Kings, Britannia's Issue, hail!

The Antistrophe

"Girt with many a baron bold
Sublime their starry fronts they rear;
And gorgeous Dames, and Statesmen old
In bearded majesty, appear.
In the midst a Form divine!
Her eye proclaims her of the Briton-Line;
Her lion-port, her awe-commanding face,
Attemper'd sweet to virgin-grace.
What strings symphonious tremble in the air,
What strains of vocal transport round her play!
Hear from the grave, great Taliessin, hear;
They breathe a soul to animate thy clay.
Bright Rapture calls, and soaring, as she sings,
Waves in the eye of Heav'n her many-colour'd wings.

The Epode

"The verse adorn again
Fierce War, and faithful Love,
And Truth severe, by fairy Fiction drest.
In buskin'd measures move
Pale Grief, and pleasing Pain,
With Horror, Tyrant of the throbbing breast.
A Voice, as of the Cherub-Choir,
Gales from blooming Eden bear;
And distant warblings lessen on my ear,
That lost in long futurity expire.
Fond impious Man, think'st thou, yon sanguine cloud,
Rais'd by thy breath, has quench'd the Orb of day?
To-morrow he repairs the golden flood,
And warms the nations with redoubled ray.
Enough for me: With joy I see
The different doom our Fates assign.
Be thine Despair, and scept'red Care,
To triumph, and to die, are mine."——
He spoke, and headlong from the mountain's height
Deep in the roaring tide he plung'd to endless night.

AN ODE

FROM THE NORSE TONGUE

Now the storm begins to lower,
(Haste, the loom of hell prepare,)
Iron-sleet of arrowy shower
Hurtles in the darken'd air.

Glitt'ring lances are the loom,
Where the dusky warp we strain,
Weaving many a soldier's doom,
Orkney's woe, and Randver's bane.

See the griesly texture grow,
('Tis of human entrails made,)
And the weights, that play below,
Each a gasping warrior's head.

Shafts for shuttles, dipt in gore,
Shoot the trembling cords along.
Sword, that once a monarch bore,
Keep the tissue close and strong.

Mista black, terrific maid,
Sangrida, and Hilda see,
Join the wayward work to aid:
'Tis the woof of victory.

Ere the ruddy sun be set,
Pikes must shiver, javelins sing,
Blade with clattering buckler meet,
Hauberk crash, and helmet ring.

(Weave the crimson web of war)
Let us go, and let us fly,
Where our friends the conflict share,
Where they triumph, where they die.

As the paths of fate we tread,
Wading thro' th' ensanguin'd field:
Gondula, and Geira, spread
O'er the youthful king your shield.

We the reins to slaughter give,
Ours to kill, and ours to spare:
Spite of danger he shall live.
(Weave the crimson web of war.)

They, whom once the desert-beach
Pent within its bleak domain,
Soon their ample sway shall stretch
O'er the plenty of the plain.

Low the dauntless earl is laid,
Gor'd with many a gaping wound:
Fate demands a nobler head;
Soon a king shall bite the ground.

Long his loss shall Eirin weep,
Ne'er again his likeness see;
Long her strains in sorrow steep,
Strains of immortality!

Horror covers all the heath,
Clouds of carnage blot the sun.
Sisters, weave the web of death;
Sisters, cease, the work is done.

Hail the task, and hail the hands!
Songs of joy and triumph sing!
Joy to the victorious bands;
Triumph to the younger king.

Mortal, thou that hear'st the tale,
Learn the tenor of our song.
Scotland, thro' each winding vale
Far and wide the notes prolong.

Sisters, hence with spurs of speed:
Each her thundering falchion wield;
Each bestride her sable steed.
Hurry, hurry to the field.

WILLIAM COLLINS (1721–1759)

A SONG FROM SHAKESPEARE'S CYMBELYNE

Sung by Guiderus and Arviragus over Fidele, supposed to be dead

To fair Fidele's grassy tomb
  Soft maids and village hinds shall bring
Each op'ning sweet, of earliest bloom,
  And rifle all the breathing spring.

No wailing ghost shall dare appear,
  To vex with shrieks this quiet grove;
But shepherd lads assemble here,
  And melting virgins own their love.

No wither'd witch shall here be seen,
  No goblins lead their nightly crew;
The female fays shall haunt the green,
  And dress thy grave with pearly dew.

The redbreast oft at ev'ning hours
  Shall kindly lend his little aid,
With hoary moss, and gather'd flow'rs,
  To deck the ground where thou art laid.

When howling winds, and beating rain,
  In tempests shake the sylvan cell,
Or midst the chase on ev'ry plain,
  The tender thought on thee shall dwell,

Each lonely scene shall thee restore,
  For thee the tear be duly shed:
Belov'd, till life could charm no more;
  And mourn'd, till Pity's self be dead.

ODE

WRITTEN IN THE BEGINNING OF THE YEAR 1746

How sleep the brave who sink to rest
By all their country's wishes blest!
When Spring, with dewy fingers cold,
Returns to deck their hallow'd mold,
She there shall dress a sweeter sod
Than Fancy's feet have ever trod.

By fairy hands their knell is rung,
By forms unseen their dirge is sung;

There Honour comes, a pilgrim grey,
To bless the turf that wraps their clay;
And Freedom shall awhile repair,
To dwell a weeping hermit there!

ODE TO EVENING

If ought of oaten stop, or pastoral song,
May hope, chaste Eve, to sooth thy modest ear,
Like thy own solemn springs,
Thy springs and dying gales,

O nymph reserv'd, while now the bright-hair'd sun
Sits in yon western tent, whose cloudy skirts,
With brede ethereal wove,
O'erhang his wavy bed:

Now air is hush'd, save where the weak-ey'd bat,
With short shrill shriek, flits by on leathern wing,
Or where the beetle winds
His small but sullen horn,

As oft he rises 'midst the twilight path,
Against the pilgrim borne in heedless hum:
Now teach me, maid compos'd,
To breathe some soften'd strain,

Whose numbers, stealing thro' thy dark'ning vale
May not unseemly with its stillness suit,
As, musing slow, I hail
Thy genial lov'd return!

For when thy folding-star arising shews
His paly circlet, at his warning lamp
The fragrant Hours, and elves
Who slept in flow'rs the day,

And many a nymph who wreaths her brows with sedge,
And sheds the fresh'ning dew, and, lovelier still
The pensive Pleasures sweet,
Prepare thy shadowy car.

Then lead, calm vot'ress, where some sheety lake
Cheers the lone heath, or some time-hallow'd pile
Or upland fallows grey
Reflect its last cool gleam.

But when chill blust'ring winds, or driving rain,
Forbid my willing feet, be mine the hut
That from the mountain's side
Views wilds, and swelling floods,

And hamlets brown, and dim-discover'd spires,
And hears their simple bell, and marks o'er all
Thy dewy fingers draw
The gradual dusky veil.

While Spring shall pour his show'rs, as oft he wont,
And bathe thy breathing tresses, meekest Eve;
While Summer loves to sport
Beneath thy ling'ring light;

While sallow Autumn fills thy lap with leaves;
Or Winter, yelling thro' the troublous air,
Affrights thy shrinking train,
And rudely rends thy robes;

So long, sure-found beneath the sylvan shed,
Shall Fancy, Friendship, Science, rose-lipp'd Health,
Thy gentlest influence own,
And hymn thy fav'rite name!

THE PASSIONS

AN ODE TO MUSIC

When Music, heav'nly maid, was young,
While yet in early Greece she sung,
The Passions oft, to hear her shell,
Throng'd around her magic cell,
Exulting, trembling, raging, fainting,
Possest beyond the Muse's painting;
By turns they felt the glowing mind
Disturb'd, delighted, rais'd, refin'd:
Till once, 'tis said, when all were fir'd,
Fill'd with fury, rapt, inspir'd,
From the supporting myrtles round
They snatch'd her instruments of sound;
And as they oft had heard apart
Sweet lessons of her forceful art,
Each, for madness rul'd the hour,
Would prove his own expressive pow'r.

First Fear his hand, its skill to try,
Amid the chords bewilder'd laid,
And back recoil'd, he knew not why,
Ev'n at the sound himself had made.

Next Anger rush'd; his eyes, on fire,
In lightnings own'd his secret stings;
In one rude clash he struck the lyre,
And swept with hurried hand the strings.

With woful measures wan Despair
Low sullen sounds his grief beguil'd;
A solemn, strange, and mingled air;
'Twas sad by fits, by starts 'twas wild.

But thou, O Hope, with eyes so fair,
What was thy delightful measure?
Still it whisper'd promis'd pleasure,
And bade the lovely scenes at distance hail!

Still would her touch the strain prolong,
And from the rocks, the woods, the vale,
She call'd on Echo still thro' all the song;
And where her sweetest theme she chose,
A soft responsive voice was heard at ev'ry close,
And Hope enchanted smil'd, and wav'd her golden hair.

And longer had she sung, — but with a frown
Revenge impatient rose;
He threw his blood-stain'd sword in thunder down
And with a with'ring look
The war-denouncing trumpet took,
And blew a blast so loud and dread,
Were ne'er prophetic sounds so full of woe.
And ever and anon he beat
The doubling drum with furious heat;
And tho' sometimes, each dreary pause between,
Dejected Pity, at his side,
Her soul-subduing voice applied,
Yet still he kept his wild unalter'd mien,
While each strain'd ball of sight seem'd bursting from his head.

Thy numbers, Jealousy, to nought were fix'd,
Sad proof of thy distressful state;
Of diff'ring themes the veering song was mix'd,
And now it courted Love, now raving call'd on Hate.

With eyes uprais'd, as one inspir'd,
Pale Melancholy sate retir'd,
And from her wild sequester'd seat,
In notes by distance made more sweet,
Pour'd thro' the mellow horn her pensive soul:
And, dashing soft from rocks around,
Bubbling runnels join'd the sound;
Thro' glades and glooms the mingled measure stole;
Or o'er some haunted stream with fond delay
Round an holy calm diffusing,
Love of peace and lonely musing,
In hollow murmurs died away.

But oh, how alter'd was its sprightlier tone,
When Cheerfulness, a nymph of healthiest hue,
Her bow across her shoulder flung,
Her buskins gemm'd with morning dew,
Blew an inspiring air, that dale and thicket rung,
The hunter's call to faun and dryad known!
The oak-crown'd sisters, and their chaste-ey'd queen,
Satyrs, and sylvan boys, were seen,
Peeping from forth their alleys green;
Brown Exercise rejoic'd to hear,
And Sport leapt up, and seiz'd his beechen spear.

Last came Joy's ecstatic trial.
He, with viny crown advancing,
First to the lively pipe his hand addrest;
But soon he saw the brisk awak'ning viol,
Whose sweet entrancing voice he lov'd the best.
They would have thought, who heard the strain,
They saw in Tempe's vale her native maids
Amidst the vestal sounding shades,
To some unwearied minstrel dancing,
While, as his flying fingers kiss'd the strings,
Love fram'd with Mirth a gay fantastic round;
Loose were her tresses seen, her zone unbound,
And he, amidst his frolic play,
As if he would the charming air repay,
Shook thousand odours from his dewy wings.

O Music, sphere-descended maid,
Friend of Pleasure, Wisdom's aid,
Why, goddess, why, to us denied,
Lay'st thou thy ancient lyre aside?
As in that lov'd Athenian bow'r
You learn'd an all-commanding pow'r,
Thy mimic soul, O nymph endear'd,
Can well recall what then it heard.
Where is thy native simple heart,
Devote to Virtue, Fancy, Art?
Arise as in that elder time,
Warm, energic, chaste, sublime!
Thy wonders, in that godlike age,
Fill thy recording sister's page. —
'Tis said, and I believe the tale,
Thy humblest reed could more prevail,
Had more of strength, diviner rage,
Than all which charms this laggard age,
Ev'n all at once together found,
Cæcilia's mingled world of sound.
O bid our vain endeavours cease,
Revive the just designs of Greece,
Return in all thy simple state,
Confirm the tales her sons relate!

AN ODE

ON THE POPULAR SUPERSTITIONS OF THE HIGHLANDS OF SCOTLAND, CONSIDERED AS THE SUBJECT OF POETRY

I

H——, thou return'st from Thames, whose naiads long
Have seen thee ling'ring, with a fond delay,
'Mid those soft friends, whose hearts, some future day,

Shall melt, perhaps, to hear thy tragic song.
Go, not unmindful of that cordial youth
Whom, long-endear'd, thou leav'st by Lavant's side;
Together let us wish him lasting truth,
And joy untainted, with his destined bride.
Go! nor regardless, while these numbers boast
My short-liv'd bliss, forget my social name;
But think, far off, how on the Southern coast
I met thy friendship with an equal flame!
Fresh to that soil thou turn'st, whose ev'ry vale
Shall prompt the poet, and his song demand:
To thee thy copious subjects ne'er shall fail;
Thou need'st but take the pencil to thy hand,
And paint what all believe who own thy genial land.

II

There must thou wake perforce thy Doric quill;
'Tis Fancy's land to which thou sett'st thy feet,
Where still, 'tis said, the fairy people meet
Beneath each birken shade on mead or hill.
There each trim lass that skims the milky store
To the swart tribes their creamy bowl allots;
By night they sip it round the cottage door,
While airy minstrels warble jocund notes.
There ev'ry herd, by sad experience, knows
How, wing'd with fate, their elf-shot arrows fly;
When the sick ewe her summer food foregoes,
Or, stretch'd on earth, the heart-smit heifers lie.
Such airy beings awe th' untutor'd swain:
Nor thou, thou learn'd, his homelier thoughts neglect;
Let thy sweet Muse the rural faith sustain:
These are the themes of simple, sure effect,
That add new conquests to her boundless reign,
And fill, with double force, her heart-commanding strain.

III

Ev'n yet preserv'd, how often may'st thou hear,
Where to the pole the boreal mountains run,
Taught by the father to his list'ning son,
Strange lays, whose pow'r had charm'd a Spenser's ear.
At ev'ry pause, before thy mind possest,
Old Runic bards shall seem to rise around,
With uncouth lyres, in many-colour'd vest,
Their matted hair with boughs fantastic crown'd:
Whether thou bid'st the well-taught hind repeat
The choral dirge that mourns some chieftain brave,
When ev'ry shrieking maid her bosom beat,
And strew'd with choicest herbs his scented grave;
Or whether, sitting in the shepherd's shiel,
Thou hear'st some sounding tale of war's alarms,
When, at the bugle's call, with fire and steel,
The sturdy clans pour'd forth their bony swarms,
And hostile brothers met to prove each other's arms.

IV

'Tis thine to sing, how, framing hideous spells,
In Sky's lone isle the gifted wizard seer,
Lodg'd in the wintry cave with Fate's fell spear;
Or in the depth of Uist's dark forests dwells:
How they whose sight such dreary dreams engross,
With their own visions oft astonish'd droop,
When o'er the wat'ry strath or quaggy moss
They see the gliding ghosts unbodied troop;
Or if in sports, or on the festive green,
Their [destined] glance some fated youth descry,
Who, now perhaps in lusty vigour seen
And rosy health, shall soon lamented die.
For them the viewless forms of air obey,
Their bidding heed, and at their beck repair.
They know what spirit brews the stormful day,
And, heartless, oft like moody madness stare
To see the phantom train their secret work prepare.

V

[To monarchs dear, some hundred miles astray,[1]
Oft have they seen Fate give the fatal blow!
The seer, in Sky, shriek'd as the blood did flow,
When headless Charles warm on the scaffold lay!
As Boreas threw his young Aurora forth,
In the first year of the first George's reign,
And battles rag'd in welkin of the North,
They mourn'd in air, fell, fell Rebellion slain!
And as, of late, they joy'd in Preston's fight,
Saw at sad Falkirk all their hopes near crown'd,
They rav'd, divining, thro' their second sight,
Pale, red Culloden, where these hopes were drown'd!
Illustrious William! Britain's guardian name!
One William sav'd us from a tyrant's stroke;
He, for a sceptre, gain'd heroic fame;
But thou, more glorious, Slavery's chain hast broke,
To reign a private man, and bow to Freedom's yoke!

[1] This Ode was first published after the death of Collins. The bracketed passages are missing in the original and are here supplied from an unauthorized edition, London, 1788.

VI

These, too, thou'lt sing! for well thy magic Muse
Can to the topmost heav'n of grandeur soar!
Or stoop to wail the swain that is no more!
Ah, homely swains! your homeward steps ne'er lose;
Let not dank Will mislead you to the heath:
Dancing in mirky night, o'er fen and lake,
He glows, to draw you downward to your death,
In his bewitch'd, low, marshy willow brake!]
What tho' far off, from some dark dell espied,
His glimm'ring mazes cheer th' excursive sight,
Yet turn, ye wand'rers, turn your steps aside,
Nor trust the guidance of that faithless light;
For, watchful, lurking 'mid th' unrustling reed,
At those mirk hours the wily monster lies,
And listens oft to hear the passing steed,
And frequent round him rolls his sullen eyes,
If chance his savage wrath may some weak wretch surprise.

VII

Ah, luckless swain, o'er all unblest indeed!
Whom, late bewilder'd in the dank, dark fen,
Far from his flocks and smoking hamlet then,
To that sad spot [where hums the sedgy weed]
On him, enrag'd, the fiend, in angry mood,
Shall never look with Pity's kind concern,
But instant, furious, raise the whelming flood
O'er its drown'd bank, forbidding all return.
Or, if he meditate his wish'd escape
To some dim hill that seems uprising near,
To his faint eye the grim and grisly shape,
In all its terrors clad, shall wild appear.
Meantime, the wat'ry surge shall round him rise,
Pour'd sudden forth from ev'ry swelling source.
What now remains but tears and hopeless sighs?
His fear-shook limbs have lost their youthly force,
And down the waves he floats, a pale and breathless corse.

VIII

For him, in vain, his anxious wife shall wait,
Or wander forth to meet him on his way;
For him, in vain, at to-fall of the day,
His babes shall linger at th' unclosing gate.
Ah, ne'er shall he return! Alone, if night
Her travell'd limbs in broken slumbers steep,
With dropping willows drest, his mournful sprite
Shall visit sad, perchance, her silent sleep:
Then he, perhaps, with moist and wat'ry hand,
Shall fondly seem to press her shudd'ring cheek
And with his blue-swoln face before her stand,
And, shiv'ring cold, these piteous accents speak:
"Pursue, dear wife, thy daily toils pursue
At dawn or dusk, industrious as before;
Nor e'er of me one hapless thought renew,
While I lie welt'ring on the ozier'd shore,
Drown'd by the kelpie's wrath, nor e'er shall aid thee more!"

IX

Unbounded is thy range; with varied style
Thy Muse may, like those feath'ry tribes which spring
From their rude rocks, extend her skirting wing
Round the moist marge of each cold Hebrid isle
To that hoar pile which still its ruin shows:
In whose small vaults a pigmy-folk is found,
Whose bones the delver with his spade upthrows,
And culls them, wond'ring, from the hallow'd ground!
Or thither, where, beneath the show'ry West,
The mighty kings of three fair realms are laid:
Once foes, perhaps, together now they rest;
No slaves revere them, and no wars invade:
Yet frequent now, at midnight's solemn hour,
The rifted mounds their yawning cells unfold,
And forth the monarchs stalk with sov'reign pow'r,
In pageant robes, and wreath'd with sheeny gold,
And on their twilight tombs aërial council hold.

X

But oh, o'er all, forget not Kilda's race,
On whose bleak rocks, which brave the wasting tides,
Fair Nature's daughter, Virtue, yet abides.
Go, just as they, their blameless manners trace!
Then to my ear transmit some gentle song
Of those whose lives are yet sincere and plain,
Their bounded walks the rugged cliffs along,
And all their prospect but the wintry main.
With sparing temp'rance, at the needful time,
They drain the sainted spring, or, hunger-prest,
Along th' Altantic rock undreading climb,
And of its eggs despoil the solan's nest.
Thus blest in primal innocence they live,
Suffic'd and happy with that frugal fare
Which tasteful toil and hourly danger give.
Hard is their shallow soil, and bleak and bare;
Nor ever vernal bee was heard to murmur there!

XI

Nor need'st thou blush, that such false themes engage
Thy gentle mind, of fairer stores possest:

For not alone they touch the village breast,
But fill'd in elder time th' historic page.
There Shakespeare's self, with ev'ry garland crown'd, —
[Flew to those fairy climes his fancy sheen!]—
In musing hour, his wayward Sisters found,
And with their terrors drest the magic scene.
From them he sung, when, 'mid his bold design,
Before the Scot afflicted and aghast,
The shadowy kings of Banquo's fated line
Thro' the dark cave in gleamy pageant past.
Proceed, nor quit the tales which, simply told,
Could once so well my answ'ring bosom pierce;
Proceed! in forceful sounds and colours bold,
The native legends of thy land rehearse;
To such adapt thy lyre and suit thy pow'rful verse.

XII

In scenes like these, which, daring to depart
From sober truth, are still to nature true,
And call forth fresh delight to Fancy's view,
Th' heroic muse employ'd her Tasso's art!
How have I trembled, when, at Tancred's stroke,
Its gushing blood the gaping cypress pour'd;
When each live plant with mortal accents spoke,
And the wild blast upheav'd the vanish'd sword!
How have I sat, when pip'd the pensive wind,
To hear his harp, by British Fairfax strung, —
Prevailing poet, whose undoubting mind
Believ'd the magic wonders which he sung!
Hence at each sound imagination glows;
[*The MS. lacks a line here.*]
Hence his warm lay with softest sweetness flows;
Melting it flows, pure, num'rous, strong, and clear,
And fills th' impassion'd heart, and wins th' harmonious ear.

XIII

All hail, ye scenes that o'er my soul prevail,
Ye [splendid] friths and lakes which, far away,
Are by smooth Annan fill'd, or past'ral Tay,
Or Don's romantic springs; at distance, hail!
The time shall come when I, perhaps, may tread
Your lowly glens, o'erhung with spreading broom,
Or o'er your stretching heaths by fancy led:
[*The MS. lacks a line here.*]
Then will I dress once more the faded bow'r,
Where Jonson sat in Drummond's [classic] shade,
Or crop from Tiviot's dale each [lyric flower]
And mourn on Yarrow's banks [where Willy's laid!]
Meantime, ye Pow'rs that on the plains which bore
The cordial youth, on Lothian's plains, attend,
Where'er he dwell, on hill or lowly muir,
To him I lose your kind protection lend,
And, touch'd with love like mine, preserve my absent friend!

MARK AKENSIDE (1721–1770)

THE NIGHTINGALE

To-night retired, the queen of heaven
With young Endymion stays;
And now to Hesper it is given
Awhile to rule the vacant sky,
Till she shall to her lamp supply
A stream of brighter rays.

Propitious send thy golden ray,
Thou purest light above!
Let no false flame seduce to stray
Where gulf or steep lie hid for harm;
But lead where music's healing charm
May soothe afflicted love.

To them, by many a grateful song
In happier seasons vow'd,
These lawns, Olympia's haunts, belong:
Oft by yon silver stream we walk'd,
Or fix'd, while Philomela talk'd,
Beneath yon copses stood.

Nor seldom, where the beechen boughs
That roofless tower invade,
We came, while her enchanting Muse
The radiant moon above us held:
Till, by a clamorous owl compell'd
She fled the solemn shade.

But hark! I hear her liquid tone!
Now Hesper guide my feet!
Down the red marl with moss o'ergrown,
Through yon wild thicket next the plain,
Whose hawthorns choke the winding lane
Which leads to her retreat.

See the green space: on either hand
Enlarged it spreads around:
See, in the midst she takes her stand,
Where one old oak his awful shade
Extends o'er half the level mead,
Enclosed in woods profound.

Hark! how through many a melting note
She now prolongs her lays:
How sweetly down the void they float!

The breeze their magic path attends;
The stars shine out; the forest bends;
The wakeful heifers graze.

Whoe'er thou art whom chance may bring
To this sequester'd spot,
If then the plaintive Siren sing,
Oh softly tread beneath her bower
And think of Heaven's disposing power,
Of man's uncertain lot.

Oh think, o'er all this mortal stage
What mournful scenes arise:
What ruin waits on kingly rage;
How often virtue dwells with woe;
How many griefs from knowledge flow;
How swiftly pleasure flies!

Oh sacred bird! let me at eve,
Thus wandering all alone,
Thy tender counsel oft receive,
Bear witness to thy pensive airs,
And pity Nature's common cares,
Till I forget my own.

OLIVER GOLDSMITH (1728–1774)

THE DESERTED VILLAGE

Sweet Auburn! loveliest village of the plain;
Where health and plenty cheered the labouring swain,
Where smiling spring its earliest visit paid,
And parting summer's lingering blooms delayed:
Dear lovely bowers of innocence and ease,
Seats of my youth, when every sport could please,
How often have I loitered o'er thy green,
Where humble happiness endeared each scene!
How often have I paused on every charm,
The sheltered cot, the cultivated farm,
The never-failing brook, the busy mill,
The decent church that topt the neighbouring hill,
The hawthorn bush, with seats beneath the shade
For talking age and whispering lovers made!
How often have I blest the coming day,
When toil remitting lent its turn to play,
And all the village train, from labour free,
Led up their sports beneath the spreading tree
While many a pastime circled in the shade,
The young contending as the old surveyed;
And many a gambol frolicked o'er the ground,
And sleights of art and feats of strength went round.
And still, as each repeated pleasure tired,
Succeeding sports the mirthful band inspired;
The dancing pair that simply sought renown
By holding out to tire each other down;
The swain mistrustless of his smutted face,
While secret laughter tittered round the place;
The bashful virgin's side-long looks of love,
The matron's glance that would those looks reprove:
These were thy charms, sweet village! sports like these,
With sweet succession, taught even toil to please:
These round thy bowers their cheerful influence shed:
These were thy charms — but all these charms are fled.

Sweet smiling village, loveliest of the lawn,
Thy sports are fled, and all thy charms withdrawn;
Amidst thy bowers the tyrant's hand is seen,
And desolation saddens all thy green:
One only master grasps the whole domain,
And half a tillage stints thy smiling plain.
No more thy glassy brook reflects the day,
But, choked with sedges, works its weedy way;
Along the glades, a solitary guest,
The hollow sounding bittern guards its nest;
Amidst thy desert walks the lapwing flies,
And tires their echoes with unvaried cries;
Sunk are thy bowers in shapeless ruin all,
And the long grass o'ertops the mouldering wall;
And trembling, shrinking from the spoiler's hand,
Far, far away thy children leave the land.

Ill fares the land, to hastening ills a prey,
Where wealth accumulates, and men decay:
Princes and lords may flourish, or may fade;
A breath can make them, as a breath has made:
But a bold peasantry, their country's pride,
When once destroyed, can never be supplied.

A time there was, ere England's griefs began,
When every rood of ground maintained its man;
For him light labour spread her wholesome store,
Just gave what life required, but gave no more:
His best companions, innocence and health;
And his best riches, ignorance of wealth.

But times are altered; trade's unfeeling train
Usurp the land and dispossess the swain;
Along the lawn, where scattered hamlets rose,
Unwieldy wealth and cumbrous pomp repose,
And every want to opulence allied,
And every pang that folly pays to pride.
These gentle hours that plenty bade to bloom,
Those calm desires that asked but little room,
Those healthful sports that graced the peaceful scene,
Lived in each look, and brightened all the green;
These, far departing, seek a kinder shore,
And rural mirth and manners are no more.

Sweet Auburn! parent of the blissful hour,

Thy glades forlorn confess the tyrant's power.
Here, as I take my solitary rounds
Amidst thy tangling walks and ruined grounds,
And, many a year elapsed, return to view
Where once the cottage stood, the hawthorn grew,
Remembrance wakes with all her busy train,
Swells at my breast, and turns the past to pain.
In all my wanderings round this world of care,
In all my griefs — and God has given my share —
I still had hopes, my latest hours to crown,
Amidst these humble bowers to lay me down;
To husband out life's taper at the close,
And keep the flame from wasting by repose:
I still had hopes, for pride attends us still,
Amidst the swains to show my book-learned skill,
Around my fire an evening group to draw,
And tell of all I felt, and all I saw;
And, as an hare whom hounds and horns pursue
Pants to the place from whence at first she flew,
I still had hopes, my long vexations past,
Here to return — and die at home at last.
O blest retirement, friend to life's decline,
Retreats from care, that never must be mine,
How happy he who crowns in shades like these
A youth of labour with an age of ease;
Who quits a world where strong temptations try,
And, since 'tis hard to combat, learns to fly!
For him no wretches, born to work and weep,
Explore the mine, or tempt the dangerous deep;
No surly porter stands in guilty state,
To spurn imploring famine from the gate;
But on he moves to meet his latter end,
Angels around befriending Virtue's friend;
Bends to the grave with unperceived decay,
While resignation gently slopes the way;
And, all his prospects brightening to the last,
His heaven commences ere the world be past!
Sweet was the sound, when oft at evening's close
Up yonder hill the village murmur rose.
There, as I passed with careless steps and slow,
The mingling notes came softened from below;
The swain responsive as the milk-maid sung,
The sober herd that lowed to meet their young,
The noisy geese that gabbled o'er the pool,
The playful children just let loose from school,
The watch-dog's voice that bayed the whispering wind,
And the loud laugh that spoke the vacant mind; —
These all in sweet confusion sought the shade,
And filled each pause the nightingale had made.
But now the sounds of population fail,
No cheerful murmurs fluctuate in the gale,
No busy steps the grass-grown foot-way tread,
For all the bloomy flush of life is fled.
All but yon widowed, solitary thing,
That feebly bends beside the plashy spring:
She, wretched matron, forced in age, for bread,
To strip the brook with mantling cresses spread,
To pick her wintry faggot from the thorn,
To seek her nightly shed, and weep till morn;
She only left of all the harmless train,
The sad historian of the pensive plain.
Near yonder copse, where once the garden smiled,
And still where many a garden flower grows wild;
There, where a few torn shrubs the place disclose,
The village preacher's modest mansion rose.
A man he was to all the country dear,
And passing rich with forty pounds a year;
Remote from towns he ran his godly race,
Nor e'er had changed, nor wished to change his place;
Unpractised he to fawn, or seek for power,
By doctrines fashioned to the varying hour;
Far other aims his heart had learned to prize,
More skilled to raise the wretched than to rise.
His house was known to all the vagrant train;
He chid their wanderings but relieved their pain:
The long-remembered beggar was his guest,
Whose beard descending swept his aged breast;
The ruined spendthrift, now no longer proud,
Claimed kindred there, and had his claims allowed;
The broken soldier, kindly bade to stay,
Sat by the fire, and talked the night away,
Wept o'er his wounds or, tales of sorrow done,
Shouldered his crutch and showed how fields were won.
Pleased with his guests, the good man learned to glow,
And quite forgot their vices in their woe;
Careless their merits or their faults to scan,
His pity gave ere charity began.
Thus to relieve the wretched was his pride,
And e'en his failings leaned to Virtue's side;
But in his duty prompt at every call,
He watched and wept, he prayed and felt for all;
And, as a bird each fond endearment tries
To tempt its new-fledged offspring to the skies,
He tried each art, reproved each dull delay,
Allured to brighter worlds, and led the way.
Beside the bed where parting life was laid,
And sorrow, guilt, and pain by turns dismayed,
The reverend champion stood. At his control
Despair and anguish fled the struggling soul;
Comfort came down the trembling wretch to raise,
And his last faltering accents whispered praise.
At church, with meek and unaffected grace,
His looks adorned the venerable place;
Truth from his lips prevailed with double sway,
And fools, who came to scoff, remained to pray.

The service past, around the pious man,
With steady zeal, each honest rustic ran;
Even children followed with endearing wile,
And plucked his gown to share the good man's smile.
His ready smile a parent's warmth exprest;
Their welfare pleased him, and their cares distrest:
To them his heart, his love, his griefs were given,
But all his serious thoughts had rest in heaven.
As some tall cliff that lifts its awful form,
Swells from the vale, and midway leaves the storm,
Tho' round its breast the rolling clouds are spread,
Eternal sunshine settles on its head.

Beside yon straggling fence that skirts the way,
With blossom'd furze unprofitably gay,
There, in his noisy mansion, skill'd to rule,
The village master taught his little school.
A man severe he was, and stern to view;
I knew him well, and every truant knew;
Well had the boding tremblers learned to trace
The day's disasters in his morning face;
Full well they laughed with counterfeited glee
At all his jokes, for many a joke had he;
Full well the busy whisper circling round
Conveyed the dismal tidings when he frowned.
Yet he was kind, or, if severe in aught,
The love he bore to learning was in fault;
The village all declared how much he knew:
'Twas certain he could write, and cipher too;
Lands he could measure, terms and tides presage,
And even the story ran that he could gauge;
In arguing, too, the parson owned his skill,
For, even tho' vanquished, he could argue still;
While words of learned length and thundering sound
Amazed the gazing rustics ranged around;
And still they gazed, and still the wonder grew,
That one small head could carry all he knew.

But past is all his fame. The very spot
Where many a time he triumphed is forgot.
Near yonder thorn, that lifts its head on high,
Where once the sign-post caught the passing eye,
Low lies that house where nut-brown draughts inspired,
Where graybeard mirth and smiling toil retired,
Where village statesmen talked with looks profound,
And news much older than their ale went round.
Imagination fondly stoops to trace
The parlour splendours of that festive place:
The white-washed wall, the nicely sanded floor,
The varnished clock that clicked behind the door;
The chest contrived a double debt to pay,
A bed by night, a chest of drawers by day;
The pictures placed for ornament and use,
The twelve good rules, the royal game of goose;
The hearth, except when winter chill'd the day,
With aspen boughs and flowers and fennel gay;
While broken tea-cups, wisely kept for show,
Ranged o'er the chimney, glistened in a row.

Vain transitory splendours! could not all
Reprieve the tottering mansion from its fall?
Obscure it sinks, nor shall it more impart
An hour's importance to the poor man's heart.
Thither no more the peasant shall repair
To sweet oblivion of his daily care;
No more the farmer's news, the barber's tale,
No more the woodman's ballad shall prevail;
No more the smith his dusky brow shall clear,
Relax his ponderous strength, and lean to hear;
The host himself no longer shall be found
Careful to see the mantling bliss go round;
Nor the coy maid, half willing to be prest,
Shall kiss the cup to pass it to the rest.

Yes! let the rich deride, the proud disdain,
These simple blessings of the lowly train;
To me more dear, congenial to my heart,
One native charm, than all the gloss of art.
Spontaneous joys, where Nature has its play,
The soul adopts, and owns their first born sway;
Lightly they frolic o'er the vacant mind,
Unenvied, unmolested, unconfined.
But the long pomp, the midnight masquerade,
With all the freaks of wanton wealth arrayed —
In these, ere triflers half their wish obtain,
The toiling pleasure sickens into pain;
And, e'en while fashion's brightest arts decoy,
The heart distrusting asks if this be joy.

Ye friends to truth, ye statesmen who survey
The rich man's joy increase, the poor's decay,
'Tis yours to judge, how wide the limits stand
Between a splendid and an happy land.
Proud swells the tide with loads of freighted ore,
And shouting Folly hails them from her shore;
Hoards e'en beyond the miser's wish abound,
And rich men flock from all the world around.
Yet count our gains! This wealth is but a name
That leaves our useful products still the same.
Not so the loss. The man of wealth and pride
Takes up a space that many poor supplied;
Space for his lake, his park's extended bounds,
Space for his horses, equipage, and hounds:
The robe that wraps his limbs in silken sloth
Has robbed the neighbouring fields of half their growth;
His seat, where solitary sports are seen,
Indignant spurns the cottage from the green:
Around the world each needful product flies,
For all the luxuries the world supplies;
While thus the land adorned for pleasure all

In barren splendour feebly waits the fall.

As some fair female unadorned and plain,
Secure to please while youth confirms her reign,
Slights every borrowed charm that dress supplies,
Nor shares with art the triumph of her eyes;
But when those charms are past, for charms are frail,
When time advances, and when lovers fail,
She then shines forth, solicitous to bless,
In all the glaring impotence of dress.
Thus fares the land by luxury betrayed:
In nature's simplest charms at first arrayed,
But verging to decline, its splendours rise,
Its vistas strike, its palaces surprise;
While, scourged by famine from the smiling land
The mournful peasant leads his humble band,
And while he sinks, without one arm to save,
The country blooms — a garden and a grave.

Where then, ah! where, shall poverty reside,
To 'scape the pressure of contiguous pride?
If to some common's fenceless limits strayed
He drives his flock to pick the scanty blade,
Those fenceless fields the sons of wealth divide,
And even the bare-worn common is denied.

If to the city sped — what waits him there?
To see profusion that he must not share;
To see ten thousand baneful arts combined
To pamper luxury, and thin mankind;
To see those joys the sons of pleasure know
Extorted from his fellow-creature's woe.
Here while the courtier glitters in brocade,
There the pale artist plies the sickly trade;
Here while the proud their long-drawn pomps display,
There the black gibbet glooms beside the way.
The dome where pleasure holds her midnight reign
Here, richly deckt, admits the gorgeous train:
Tumultuous grandeur crowds the blazing square,
The rattling chariots clash, the torches glare.
Sure scenes like these no troubles e'er annoy!
Sure these denote one universal joy!
Are these thy serious thoughts? — Ah, turn thine eyes
Where the poor houseless shivering female lies.
She once, perhaps, in village plenty blest,
Has wept at tales of innocence distrest;
Her modest looks the cottage might adorn,
Sweet as the primrose peeps beneath the thorn:
Now lost to all; her friends, her virtue fled,
Near her betrayer's door she lays her head,
And, pinch'd with cold, and shrinking from the shower,
With heavy heart deplores that luckless hour,
When idly first, ambitious of the town,
She left her wheel and robes of country brown.

Do thine, sweet Auburn, — thine, the loveliest train, —
Do thy fair tribes participate her pain?
Even now, perhaps, by cold and hunger led,
At proud men's doors they ask a little bread!

Ah, no! To distant climes, a dreary scene,
Where half the convex world intrudes between,
Through torrid tracts with fainting steps they go,
Where wild Altama murmurs to their woe.
Far different there from all that charm'd before
The various terrors of that horrid shore;
Those blazing suns that dart a downward ray,
And fiercely shed intolerable day;
Those matted woods, where birds forget to sing,
But silent bats in drowsy clusters cling;
Those poisonous fields with rank luxuriance crowned,
Where the dark scorpion gathers death around;
Where at each step the stranger fears to wake
The rattling terrors of the vengeful snake;
Where crouching tigers wait their hapless prey,
And savage men more murderous still than they;
While oft in whirls the mad tornado flies,
Mingling the ravaged landscape with the skies.
Far different these from every former scene,
The cooling brook, the grassy vested green,
The breezy covert of the warbling grove,
That only sheltered thefts of harmless love.

Good Heaven! what sorrows gloom'd that parting day,
That called them from their native walks away;
When the poor exiles, every pleasure past,
Hung round the bowers, and fondly looked their last,
And took a long farewell, and wished in vain
For seats like these beyond the western main,
And shuddering still to face the distant deep,
Returned and wept, and still returned to weep.
The good old sire the first prepared to go
To new found worlds, and wept for others' woe;
But for himself, in conscious virtue brave,
He only wished for worlds beyond the grave.
His lovely daughter, lovelier in her tears,
The fond companion of his helpless years,
Silent went next, neglectful of her charms,
And left a lover's for a father's arms.
With louder plaints the mother spoke her woes,
And blest the cot where every pleasure rose,
And kist her thoughtless babes with many a tear
And claspt them close, in sorrow doubly dear,
Whilst her fond husband strove to lend relief
In all the silent manliness of grief.

O luxury! thou curst by Heaven's decree,
How ill exchanged are things like these for thee!
How do thy potions, with insidious joy,
Diffuse their pleasure only to destroy!

Kingdoms by thee, to sickly greatness grown,
Boast of a florid vigour not their own.
At every draught more large and large they grow,
A bloated mass of rank unwieldy woe;
Till sapped their strength, and every part unsound,
Down, down, they sink, and spread a ruin round.
  Even now the devastation is begun,
And half the business of destruction done;
Even now, methinks, as pondering here I stand,
I see the rural virtues leave the land.
Down where yon anchoring vessel spreads the sail,
That idly waiting flaps with every gale,
Downward they move, a melancholy band,
Pass from the shore, and darken all the strand.
Contented toil, and hospitable care,
And kind connubial tenderness, are there;
And piety with wishes placed above,
And steady loyalty, and faithful love.
And thou, sweet Poetry, thou loveliest maid,
Still first to fly where sensual joys invade;
Unfit in these degenerate times of shame
To catch the heart, or strike for honest fame;
Dear charming nymph, neglected and decried,
My shame in crowds, my solitary pride;
Thou source of all my bliss, and all my woe,
That found'st me poor at first, and keep'st me so;
Thou guide by which the nobler arts excel,
Thou nurse of every virtue, fare thee well!
Farewell, and oh! where'er thy voice be tried,
On Torno's cliffs, or Pambamarca's side,
Whether where equinoctial fervours glow,
Or winter wraps the polar world in snow,
Still let thy voice, prevailing over time,
Redress the rigours of the inclement clime;
Aid slighted truth with thy persuasive strain;
Teach erring man to spurn the rage of gain;
Teach him, that states of native strength possest,
Tho' very poor, may still be very blest;
That trade's proud empire hastes to swift decay,
As ocean sweeps the laboured mole away;
While self-dependent power can time defy,
As rocks resist the billows and the sky.

ELEGY ON MADAM BLAISE

Good people all, with one accord,
  Lament for Madam Blaize;
Who never wanted a good word —
  From those who spoke her praise.

The needy seldom passed her door,
  And always found her kind;
She freely lent to all the poor —
  Who left a pledge behind.

She strove the neighbourhood to please,
  With manners wondrous winning;
She never followed wicked ways —
  Unless when she was sinning.

At church, in silk and satins new,
  With hoop of monstrous size,
She never slumbered in her pew —
  But when she shut her eyes.

Her love was sought, I do aver,
  By twenty beaux, or more;
The king himself has followed her —
  When she has walked before.

But now, her wealth and finery fled,
  Her hangers-on cut short all,
Her doctors found, when she was dead —
  Her last disorder mortal.

Let us lament, in sorrow sore;
  For Kent Street well may say,
That, had she lived a twelvemonth more —
  She had not died to-day.

SONG

When lovely woman stoops to folly,
  And finds too late that men betray,
What charm can soothe her melancholy?
  What art can wash her guilt away?

The only art her guilt to cover,
  To hide her shame from every eye,
To give repentance to her lover,
  And wring his bosom, is — to die.

From THE RETALIATION

  At a dinner so various, at such a repast,
Who'd not be a glutton, and stick to the last?
Here, waiter, more wine, let me sit while I'm able,
Till all my companions sink under the table;
Then, with chaos and blunders encircling my head,
Let me ponder, and tell what I think of the dead.
  Here lies the good Dean, reunited to earth,
Who mix'd reason with pleasure, and wisdom with mirth.
If he had any faults, he has left us in doubt,
At least in six weeks I could not find them out;
Yet some have declared, and it can't be denied them,
That Slyboots was cursedly cunning to hide them.

Here lies our good Edmund, whose genius was such,
We scarcely can praise it, or blame it too much;
Who, born for the universe, narrow'd his mind,
And to party gave up what was meant for mankind:
Though fraught with all learning, yet straining his throat
To persuade Tommy Townshend to lend him a vote;
Who, too deep for his hearers, still went on refining,
And thought of convincing, while they thought of dining;
Tho' equal to all things, for all things unfit;
Too nice for a statesman, too proud for a wit;
For a patriot too cool; for a drudge disobedient;
And too fond of the right to pursue the expedient.
In short, 'twas his fate, unemploy'd or in place, Sir,
To eat mutton cold, and cut blocks with a razor.

* * * * * * * *

Here Cumberland lies, having acted his parts,
The Terence of England, the mender of hearts;
A flattering painter, who made it his care
To draw men as they ought to be, not as they are.
His gallants are all faultless, his women divine,
And Comedy wonders at being so fine;
Like a tragedy-queen he has dizen'd her out,
Or rather like tragedy giving a rout.
His fools have their follies so lost in a crowd
Of virtues and feelings, that folly grows proud;
And coxcombs, alike in their failings alone,
Adopting his portraits, are pleased with their own.
Say, where has our poet this malady caught?
Or wherefore his characters thus without fault?
Say, was it, that vainly directing his view
To find out men's virtues, and finding them few,
Quite sick of pursuing each troublesome elf,
He grew lazy at last, and drew from himself?

* * * * * * * *

Here lies David Garrick, describe him who can?
An abridgment of all that was pleasant in man;
As an actor, confest without rival to shine;
As a wit, if not first, in the very first line;
Yet with talents like these, and an excellent heart,
The man had his failings, a dupe to his art;
Like an ill-judging beauty his colours he spread,
And beplaster'd with rouge his own natural red.
On the stage he was natural, simple, affecting,
'Twas only that when he was off he was acting;
With no reason on earth to go out of his way,
He turn'd and he varied full ten times a day:
Tho' secure of our hearts, yet confoundedly sick
If they were not his own by finessing and trick;
He cast off his friends as a huntsman his pack,
For he knew when he pleased he could whistle them back.
Of praise a mere glutton, he swallow'd what came,
And the puff of a dunce he mistook it for fame;
Till his relish grown callous, almost to disease,
Who pepper'd the highest was surest to please.
But let us be candid, and speak out our mind:
If dunces applauded, he paid them in kind.
Ye Kenricks, ye Kellys, and Woodfalls so grave,
What a commerce was yours, while you got and you gave!
How did Grub Street re-echo the shouts that you raised,
When he was be-Roscius'd, and you were be-praised!
But peace to his spirit, wherever it flies,
To act as an angel, and mix with the skies!
Those poets who owe their best fame to his skill,
Shall still be his flatterers, go where he will;
Old Shakespeare receive him with praise and with love,
And Beaumonts and Bens be his Kellys above.

* * * * * * * *

Here Reynolds is laid, and to tell you my mind,
He has not left a wiser or better behind.
His pencil was striking, resistless, and grand;
His manners were gentle, complying, and bland;
Still born to improve us in every part,
His pencil our faces, his manners our heart.
To coxcombs averse, yet most civilly steering,
When they judged without skill he was still hard of hearing;
When they talk'd of their Raphaels, Correggios and stuff,
He shifted his trumpet, and only took snuff.

THOMAS WARTON (1728–1790)

From THE CRUSADE

Bound for holy Palestine,
Nimbly we brush'd the level brine,
All in azure steel array'd;
O'er the wave our weapons play'd,
And made the dancing billows glow;
High upon the trophied prow,
Many a warrior-minstrel swung
His sounding harp, and boldly sung:
"Syrian virgins, wail and weep,
English Richard ploughs the deep!
Tremble, watchmen, as ye spy,
From distant towers, with anxious eye,
The radiant range of shield and lance
Down Damascus' hills advance:

From Sion's turrets as afar
Ye ken the march of Europe's war!
Saladin, thou paynim king,
From Albion's isle revenge we bring!
On Acon's spiry citadel,
Though to the gale thy banners swell,
Pictur'd with the silver moon;
England shall end thy glory soon!
In vain, to break our firm array,
Thy brazen drums hoarse discord bray:
Those sounds our rising fury fan:
English Richard in the van,
On to victory we go,
A vaunting infidel the foe."
Blondel led the tuneful band,
And swept the wire with glowing hand.
Cyprus, from her rocky mound,
And Crete, with piny verdure crown'd,
Far along the smiling main
Echoed the prophetic strain.
Soon we kiss'd the sacred earth
That gave a murder'd Saviour birth;
Then, with ardour fresh endu'd,
Thus the solemn song renew'd:—
"Lo, the toilsome voyage past,
Heaven's favour'd hills appear at last!
Object of our holy vow,
We tread the Tyrian valleys now.
From Carmel's almond-shaded steep
We feel the cheering fragrance creep:
O'er Engaddi's shrubs of balm
Waves the date-empurpled palm;
See Lebanon's aspiring head
Wide his immortal umbrage spread!
Hail Calvary, thou mountain hoar,
Wet with our Redeemer's gore!
Ye trampled tombs, ye fanes forlorn,
Ye stones, by tears of pilgrims worn;
Your ravish'd honours to restore,
Fearless we climb this hostile shore!
And thou, the sepulchre of God!
By mocking pagans rudely trod,
Bereft of every awful rite,
And quench'd thy lamps that beam'd so bright;
For thee, from Britain's distant coast,
Lo, Richard leads his faithful host!
Aloft in his heroic hand,
Blazing, like the beacon's brand,
O'er the far-affrighted fields,
Resistless Kaliburn he wields.
Proud Saracen, pollute no more
The shrines by martyrs built of yore.
From each wild mountain's trackless crown
In vain thy gloomy castles frown:
Thy battering engines, huge and high,
In vain our steel-clad steeds defy;
And, rolling in terrific state,
On giant-wheels harsh thunders grate.
When eve has hush'd the buzzing camp,
Amid the moonlight vapours damp,
Thy necromantic forms, in vain,
Haunt us on the tented plain:
We bid those spectre-shapes avaunt,
Ashtaroth, and Termagaunt!
With many a demon, pale of hue,
Doom'd to drink the bitter dew
That drops from Macon's sooty tree,
'Mid the dread grove of ebony.
Nor magic charms, nor fiends of hell,
The Christian's holy courage quell.
Salem, in ancient majesty
Arise, and lift thee to the sky!
Soon on thy battlements divine
Shall wave the badge of Constantine.
Ye Barons, to the sun unfold
Our Cross with crimson wove and gold!"

SONNET IV

WRITTEN AT STONEHENGE

Thou noblest monument of Albion's isle!
Whether by Merlin's aid from Scythia's shore,
To Amber's fatal plain Pendragon bore,
Huge frame of giant-hands, the mighty pile,
T' entomb his Britons slain by Hengist's guile:
Or Druid priests, sprinkled with human gore,
Taught 'mid thy massy maze their mystic lore:
Or Danish chiefs, enrich'd with savage spoil,
To Victory's idol vast, an unhewn shrine,
Rear'd the rude heap: or, in thy hallow'd round,
Repose the kings of Brutus' genuine line;
Or here those kings in solemn state were crown'd:
Studious to trace thy wondrous origine,
We muse on many an ancient tale renown'd.

SONNET VII

While summer suns o'er the gay prospect play'd,
Through Surry's verdant scenes, where Epsom spreads
'Mid intermingling elms her flowery meads,
And Hascombe's hill, in towering groves array'd,
Rear'd its romantic steep, with mind serene,
I journey'd blithe. Full pensive I return'd;
For now my breast with hopeless passion burn'd,
Wet with hoar mists appear'd the gaudy scene,
Which late in careless indolence I pass'd;
And Autumn all around those hues had cast
Where past delight my recent grief might trace.
Sad change, that Nature a congenial gloom

Should wear, when most, my cheerless mood to chase,
I wish'd her green attire, and wonted bloom!

SONNET IX

TO THE RIVER LODON

Ah! what a weary race my feet have run,
Since first I trod thy banks with alders crown'd,
And thought my way was all through fairy ground,
Beneath thy azure sky, and golden sun:
Where first my Muse to lisp her notes begun!
While pensive Memory traces back the round,
Which fills the varied interval between;
Much pleasure, more of sorrow, marks the scene.
Sweet native stream! those skies and suns so pure
No more return, to cheer my evening road!
Yet still one joy remains: that not obscure,
Nor useless, all my vacant days have flow'd,
From youth's gay dawn to manhood's prime mature;
Nor with the Muse's laurel unbestow'd.

CHARLES CHURCHILL (1731–1764)

From THE APOLOGY

The stage I choose — a subject fair and free —
'Tis yours — 'tis mine — 'tis public property,
All common exhibitions open lie
For praise or censure to the common eye.
Hence are a thousand hackney writers fed;
Hence Monthly Critics earn their daily bread.
This is a general tax which all must pay,
From those who scribble, down to those who play.
Actors, a venal crew, receive support
From public bounty for the public sport.
To clap or hiss, all have an equal claim,
The cobbler's and his lordship's right the same.
All join for their subsistence; all expect
Free leave to praise their worth, their faults correct.
When active Pickle Smithfield stage ascends,
The three days' wonder of his laughing friends,
Each, or as judgment or as fancy guides,
The lively witling praises or derides.
And where's the mighty difference, tell me where,
Betwixt a Merry Andrew and a play'r?
The strolling tribe, a despicable race!
Like wandering Arabs, shift from place to place.
Vagrants by law, to justice open laid,
They tremble, of the beadle's lash afraid,
And, fawning, cringe for wretched means of life
To Madam Mayoress, or his Worship's wife.
The mighty monarch, in theatric sack,
Carries his whole regalia at his back;
His royal consort heads the female band,
And leads the heir apparent in her hand;
The pannier'd ass creeps on with conscious pride,
Bearing a future prince on either side.
No choice musicians in this troop are found,
To varnish nonsense with the charms of sound;
No swords, no daggers, not one poison'd bowl;
No lightning flashes here, no thunders roll;
No guards to swell the monarch's train are shown;
The monarch here must be a host alone:
No solemn pomp, no slow processions here;
No Ammon's entry, and no Juliet's bier.
By need compell'd to prostitute his art,
The varied actor flies from part to part;
And, strange disgrace to all theatric pride!
His character is shifted with his side.
Question and answer he by turns must be,
Like that small wit in Modern Tragedy
Who, to patch up his fame — or fill his purse —
Still pilfers wretched plans, and makes them worse;
Like gipsies, lest the stolen brat be known,
Defacing first, then claiming for his own.
In shabby state they strut, and tatter'd robe,
The scene a blanket, and a barn the globe:
No high conceits their moderate wishes raise,
Content with humble profit, humble praise.
Let dowdies simper, and let bumpkins stare,
The strolling pageant hero treads in air:
Pleas'd for his hour, he to mankind gives law,
And snores the next out on a truss of straw.

* * * * * * * *

WILLIAM COWPER (1731–1800)

From CONVERSATION

Ye powers who rule the tongue, if such there are,
And make colloquial happiness your care,
Preserve me from the thing I dread and hate,
A duel in the form of a debate.
The clash of arguments and jar of words,
Worse than the mortal brunt of rival swords,
Decide no question with their tedious length,
(For opposition gives opinion strength)
Divert the champions prodigal of breath,
And put the peaceably disposed to death.
Oh, thwart me not, Sir Soph, at every turn,
Nor carp at every flaw you may discern;
Though syllogisms hang not on my tongue,
I am not surely always in the wrong;
'Tis hard if all is false that I advance,
A fool must now and then be right by chance.

Not that all freedom of dissent I blame;
No, — there I grant the privilege I claim.

* * * * * * * *

Perhaps at last close scrutiny may show
The practice dastardly, and mean, and low,
That men engage in it compelled by force,
And fear, not courage, is its proper source:
The fear of tyrant custom, and the fear
Lest fops should censure us, and fools should sneer.
At least to trample on our Maker's laws,
And hazard life for any or no cause,
To rush into a fixed eternal state
Out of the very flames of rage and hate,
Or send another shivering to the bar
With all the guilt of such unnatural war, —
Whatever use may urge, or honour plead, —
On reason's verdict is a madman's deed.
Am I to set my life upon a throw,
Because a bear is rude and surly? No.
A moral, sensible, and well-bred man
Will not affront me, — and no other can.
Were I empowered to regulate the lists,
They should encounter with well-loaded fists;
A Trojan combat would be something new,
Let Dares beat Entellus black and blue;
Then each might show to his admiring friends
In honourable bumps his rich amends,
And carry in contusions of his skull
A satisfactory receipt in full.

* * * * * * * *

THE TASK

From BOOK I

There often wanders one, whom better days
Saw better clad, in cloak of satin trimmed
With lace, and hat with splendid riband bound.
A serving-maid was she, and fell in love
With one who left her, went to sea, and died.
Her fancy followed him through foaming waves
To distant shores, and she would sit and weep
At what a sailor suffers; fancy too,
Delusive most where warmest wishes are,
Would oft anticipate his glad return,
And dream of transports she was not to know.
She heard the doleful tidings of his death,
And never smiled again. And now she roams
The dreary waste; there spends the livelong day,
And there, unless when charity forbids,
The livelong night. A tattered apron hides,
Worn as a cloak, and hardly hides, a gown
More tattered still; and both but ill conceal
A bosom heaved with never-ceasing sighs.
She begs an idle pin of all she meets,
And hoards them in her sleeve; but needful food,
Though pressed with hunger oft, or comelier clothes,
Though pinched with cold, asks never. — Kate is crazed.

I see a column of slow-rising smoke
O'ertop the lofty wood that skirts the wild.
A vagabond and useless tribe there eat
Their miserable meal. A kettle, slung
Between two poles upon a stick transverse,
Receives the morsel; flesh obscene of dog,
Or vermin, or, at best, of cock purloined
From his accustomed perch. Hard-faring race!
They pick their fuel out of every hedge,
Which, kindled with dry leaves, just saves unquenched
The spark of life. The sportive wind blows wide
Their fluttering rags, and shows a tawny skin,
The vellum of the pedigree they claim.
Great skill have they in palmistry, and more
To conjure clean away the gold they touch,
Conveying worthless dross into its place;
Loud when they beg, dumb only when they steal.
Strange! that a creature rational, and cast
In human mould, should brutalize by choice
His nature, and, though capable of arts
By which the world might profit and himself,
Self banished from society, prefer
Such squalid sloth to honourable toil!
Yet even these, though, feigning sickness oft,
They swathe the forehead, drag the limping limb,
And vex their flesh with artificial sores,
Can change their whine into a mirthful note
When safe occasion offers; and with dance,
And music of the bladder and the bag,
Beguile their woes, and make the woods resound.
Such health and gaiety of heart enjoy
The houseless rovers of the sylvan world;
And breathing wholesome air, and wandering much,
Need other physic none to heal the effects
Of loathsome diet, penury, and cold.

* * * * * * * *

From BOOK II

Oh for a lodge in some vast wilderness,
Some boundless contiguity of shade,
Where rumour of oppression and deceit,
Of unsuccessful or successful war,
Might never reach me more! My ear is pained,
My soul is sick with every day's report
Of wrong and outrage with which earth is filled.
There is no flesh in man's obdurate heart,
It does not feel for man; the natural bond
Of brotherhood is severed as the flax

That falls asunder at the touch of fire.
He finds his fellow guilty of a skin
Not coloured like his own, and, having power
To enforce the wrong, for such a worthy cause
Dooms and devotes him as his lawful prey.
Lands intersected by a narrow frith
Abhor each other. Mountains interposed
Make enemies of nations who had else
Like kindred drops been mingled into one.
Thus man devotes his brother, and destroys;
And worse than all, and most to be deplored,
As human nature's broadest, foulest blot,
Chains him, and tasks him, and exacts his sweat
With stripes that Mercy, with a bleeding heart,
Weeps when she sees inflicted on a beast.
Then what is man? And what man seeing this,
And having human feelings, does not blush
And hang his head, to think himself a man?
I would not have a slave to till my ground,
To carry me, to fan me while I sleep,
And tremble when I wake, for all the wealth
That sinews bought and sold have ever earned.
No: dear as freedom is, and in my heart's
Just estimation prized above all price,
I had much rather be myself the slave
And wear the bonds, than fasten them on him.
We have no slaves at home. — Then why abroad?
And they themselves once ferried o'er the wave
That parts us, are emancipate and loosed.
Slaves cannot breathe in England; if their lungs
Receive our air, that moment they are free,
They touch our country, and their shackles fall.
That's noble, and bespeaks a nation proud
And jealous of the blessing. Spread it then,
And let it circulate through every vein
Of all your empire; that where Britain's power
Is felt, mankind may feel her mercy too.

* * * * * * * *

Would I describe a preacher, such as Paul,
Were he on earth, would hear, approve, and own,
Paul should himself direct me. I would trace
His master-strokes, and draw from his design.
I would express him simple, grave, sincere;
In doctrine uncorrupt; in language plain,
And plain in manner; decent, solemn, chaste,
And natural in gesture; much impressed
Himself, as conscious of his awful charge,
And anxious mainly that the flock he feeds
May feel it too; affectionate in look,
And tender in address, as well becomes
A messenger of grace to guilty men.
Behold the picture! Is it like? — Like whom?
The things that mount the rostrum with a skip,
And then skip down again; pronounce a text,
Cry — hem! and reading what they never wrote,
Just fifteen minutes, huddle up their work,
And with a well-bred whisper close the scene!
In man or woman, but far most in man,
And most of all in man that ministers
And serves the altar, in my soul I loathe
All affectation. 'Tis my perfect scorn;
Object of my implacable disgust.
What! — will a man play tricks, will he indulge
A silly fond conceit of his fair form
And just proportion, fashionable mien,
And pretty face, in presence of his God?
Or will he seek to dazzle me with tropes,
As with the diamond on his lily hand,
And play his brilliant parts before my eyes,
When I am hungry for the bread of life?
He mocks his Maker, prostitutes and shames
His noble office, and, instead of truth,
Displaying his own beauty, starves his flock.
Therefore, avaunt all attitude and stare,
And start theatric, practised at the glass!
I seek divine simplicity in him
Who handles things divine; and all besides,
Though learned with labour, and though much admired
By curious eyes and judgments ill informed,
To me is odious as the nasal twang
Heard at conventicle, where worthy men,
Misled by custom, strain celestial themes
Through the pressed nostril, spectacle-bestrid.
Some, decent in demeanour while they preach,
That task performed, relapse into themselves,
And, having spoken wisely, at the close
Grow wanton, and give proof to every eye —
Whoe'er was edified, themselves were not.
Forth comes the pocket mirror. First we stroke
An eyebrow; next, compose a straggling lock;
Then with an air, most gracefully performed,
Fall back into our seat, extend an arm,
And lay it at its ease with gentle care,
With handkerchief in hand, depending low.
The better hand, more busy, gives the nose
Its bergamot, or aids the indebted eye
With opera-glass to watch the moving scene,
And recognise the slow-retiring fair.
Now this is fulsome, and offends me more
Than in a churchman slovenly neglect
And rustic coarseness would. A heavenly mind
May be indifferent to her house of clay,
And slight the hovel as beneath her care;
But how a body so fantastic, trim,
And quaint in its deportment and attire,
Can lodge a heavenly mind — demands a doubt.
He that negotiates between God and man,
As God's ambassador, the grand concerns
Of judgment and of mercy, should beware
Of lightness in his speech. 'Tis pitiful

To court a grin, when you should woo a soul;
To break a jest, when pity would inspire
Pathetic exhortation; and to address
The skittish fancy with facetious tales,
When sent with God's commission to the heart.
So did not Paul. Direct me to a quip
Or merry turn in all he ever wrote,
And I consent you take it for your text,
Your only one, till sides and benches fail.
No: he was serious in a serious cause,
And understood too well the weighty terms
That he had ta'en in charge. He would not stoop
To conquer those by jocular exploits,
Whom truth and soberness assailed in vain.

* * * * * * * *

The Rout is Folly's circle, which she draws
With magic wand. So potent is the spell,
That none decoyed into that fatal ring,
Unless by Heaven's peculiar grace, escape.
There we grow early grey, but never wise;
There form connections, but acquire no friend;
Solicit pleasure, hopeless of success;
Waste youth in occupations only fit
For second childhood; and devote old age
To sports which only childhood could excuse.
There they are happiest who dissemble best
Their weariness; and they the most polite
Who squander time and treasure with a smile,
Though at their own destruction. She that asks
Her dear five hundred friends, contemns them all,
And hates their coming. They (what can they less?)
Make just reprisals, and with cringe and shrug,
And bow obsequious, hide their hate of her.
All catch the frenzy, downward from her Grace,
Whose flambeaux flash against the morning skies
And gild our chamber ceilings as they pass,
To her who, frugal only that her thrift
May feed excesses she can ill afford,
Is hackneyed home unlackeyed; who in haste
Alighting, turns the key in her own door,
And at the watchman's lantern borrowing light,
Finds a cold bed her only comfort left.
Wives beggar husbands, husbands starve their wives,
On Fortune's velvet altar offering up
Their last poor pittance — Fortune, most severe
Of goddesses yet known, and costlier far
Than all that held their routs in Juno's heaven!
So fare we in this prison-house the world.
And 'tis a fearful spectacle to see
So many maniacs dancing in their chains.
They gaze upon the links that hold them fast,
With eyes of anguish, execrate their lot,
Then shake them in despair, and dance again.

* * * * * * * *

From BOOK V

'Tis morning; and the sun with ruddy orb
Ascending, fires the horizon: while the clouds
That crowd away before the driving wind,
More ardent as the disk emerges more,
Resemble most some city in a blaze,
Seen through the leafless wood. His slanting ray
Slides ineffectual down the snowy vale,
And tinging all with his own rosy hue,
From every herb and every spiry blade
Stretches a length of shadow o'er the field.
Mine, spindling into longitude immense,
In spite of gravity, and sage remark
That I myself am but a fleeting shade,
Provokes me to a smile. With eye askance
I view the muscular proportioned limb
Transformed to a lean shank. The shapeless pair,
As they designed to mock me, at my side
Take step for step; and as I near approach
The cottage, walk along the plastered wall,
Preposterous sight! the legs without the man.
The verdure of the plain lies buried deep
Beneath the dazzling deluge; and the bents
And coarser grass, upspearing o'er the rest,
Of late unsightly and unseen, now shine
Conspicuous, and in bright apparel clad,
And fledged with icy feathers, nod superb.
The cattle mourn in corners where the fence
Screens them, and seem half-petrified to sleep
In unrecumbent sadness. There they wait
Their wonted fodder, not like hungering man,
Fretful if unsupplied, but silent, meek,
And patient of the slow-paced swain's delay.
He from the stack carves out the accustomed load,
Deep-plunging, and again deep-plunging oft,
His broad keen knife into the solid mass;
Smooth as a wall the upright remnant stands,
With such undeviating and even force
He severs it away: no needless care
Lest storms should overset the leaning pile
Deciduous, or its own unbalanced weight.
Forth goes the woodman, leaving unconcerned
The cheerful haunts of man, to wield the axe
And drive the wedge in yonder forest drear,
From morn to eve his solitary task.
Shaggy, and lean, and shrewd, with pointed ears
And tail cropped short, half lurcher and half cur,
His dog attends him. Close behind his heel
Now creeps he slow; and now with many a frisk
Wide scampering, snatches up the drifted snow
With ivory teeth, or ploughs it with his snout;
Then shakes his powdered coat, and barks for joy.

Heedless of all his pranks, the sturdy churl
Moves right toward the mark; nor stops for aught,
But now and then with pressure of his thumb
To adjust the fragrant charge of a short tube
That fumes beneath his nose: the trailing cloud
Streams far behind him, scenting all the air.
Now from the roost, or from the neighbouring pale,
Where, diligent to catch the first faint gleam
Of smiling day, they gossiped side by side,
Come trooping at the housewife's well-known call
The feathered tribes domestic. Half on wing,
And half on foot, they brush the fleecy flood,
Conscious, and fearful of too deep a plunge.
The sparrows peep; and quit the sheltering eaves
To seize the fair occasion. Well they eye
The scattered grain, and thievishly resolved
To escape the impending famine, often scared
As oft return, a pert voracious kind.
Clean riddance quickly made, one only care
Remains to each, the search of sunny nook,
Or shed impervious to the blast. Resigned
To sad necessity, the cock foregoes
His wonted strut, and wading at their head
With well-considered steps, seems to resent
His altered gait and stateliness retrenched.
How find the myriads that in summer cheer
The hills and valleys with their ceaseless songs
Due sustenance, or where subsist they now?
Earth yields them nought: the imprisoned worm is safe
Beneath the frozen clod; all seeds of herbs
Lie covered close; and berry-bearing thorns
That feed the thrush (whatever some suppose)
Afford the smaller minstrels no supply.
The long-protracted rigour of the year
Thins all their numerous flocks. In chinks and holes
Ten thousand seek an unmolested end,
As instinct prompts, self-buried ere they die.
The very rooks and daws forsake the fields,
Where neither grub nor root nor earth-nut now
Repays their labour more; and perched aloft
By the wayside, or stalking in the path,
Lean pensioners upon the traveller's track,
Pick up their nauseous dole, though sweet to them,
Of voided pulse or half-digested grain.
The streams are lost amid the splendid blank,
O'erwhelming all distinction. On the flood,
Indurated and fixed, the snowy weight
Lies undissolved; while silently beneath,
And unperceived, the current steals away.
Not so, where scornful of a check it leaps
The mill-dam, dashes on the restless wheel,
And wantons in the pebbly gulf below:
No frost can bind it there; its utmost force
Can but arrest the light and smoky mist
That in its fall the liquid sheet throws wide.
And see where it has hung the embroidered banks
With forms so various that no powers of art,
The pencil or the pen, may trace the scene!
Here glittering turrets rise, upbearing high
(Fantastic misarrangement!) on the roof
Large growth of what may seem the sparkling trees
And shrubs of fairy land. The crystal drops
That trickle down the branches, fast congealed,
Shoot into pillars of pellucid length,
And prop the pile they but adorned before.
Here grotto within grotto safe defies
The sunbeam; there embossed and fretted wild,
The growing wonder takes a thousand shapes
Capricious, in which fancy seeks in vain
The likeness of some object seen before.
Thus Nature works as if to mock at Art,
And in defiance of her rival powers;
By these fortuitous and random strokes
Performing such inimitable feats,
As she with all her rules can never reach.

* * * * * *

ON THE LOSS OF THE ROYAL GEORGE

Toll for the brave!
The brave that are no more!
All sunk beneath the wave,
Fast by their native shore!

Eight hundred of the brave,
Whose courage well was tried,
Had made the vessel heel,
And laid her on her side.

A land-breeze shook the shrouds,
And she was overset;
Down went the Royal George,
With all her crew complete.

Toll for the brave!
Brave Kempenfelt is gone;
His last sea-fight is fought;
His work of glory done.

It was not in the battle;
No tempest gave the shock;
She sprang no fatal leak;
She ran upon no rock.

His sword was in its sheath;
His fingers held the pen,
When Kempenfelt went down
With twice four hundred men.

Weigh the vessel up,
  Once dreaded by our foes!
And mingle with our cup
  The tears that England owes.

Her timbers yet are sound,
  And she may float again
Full charged with England's thunder,
  And plough the distant main.

But Kempenfelt is gone,
  His victories are o'er;
And he and his eight hundred
  Shall plough the wave no more.

THE ROSE

The rose had been washed, just washed in a shower,
  Which Mary to Anna conveyed,
The plentiful moisture encumbered the flower,
  And weighed down its beautiful head.

The cup was all filled, and the leaves were all wet,
  And it seemed, to a fanciful view,
To weep for the buds it had left with regret
  On the flourishing bush where it grew.

I hastily seized it, unfit as it was
  For a nosegay, so dripping and drowned;
And swinging it rudely, too rudely, alas!
  I snapped it — it fell to the ground.

"And such," I exclaimed, "is the pitiless part
  Some act by the delicate mind,
Regardless of wringing and breaking a heart
  Already to sorrow resigned!

"This elegant rose, had I shaken it less,
  Might have bloomed with its owner awhile;
And the tear that is wiped with a little address
  May be followed perhaps by a smile."

ON THE RECEIPT OF MY MOTHER'S PICTURE

Oh that those lips had language! Life has passed
With me but roughly since I heard thee last.
Those lips are thine — thy own sweet smile I see,
The same that oft in childhood solaced me;
Voice only fails, else how distinct they say,
"Grieve not, my child, chase all thy fears away!"
The meek intelligence of those dear eyes
(Bless'd be the art that can immortalise,
The art that baffles Time's tyrannic claim
To quench it) here shines on me still the same.
  Faithful remembrancer of one so dear,
O welcome guest, though unexpected here!
Who bidst me honour with an artless song,
Affectionate, a mother lost so long,
I will obey, not willingly alone,
But gladly, as the precept were her own:
And, while that face renews my filial grief,
Fancy shall weave a charm for my relief,
Shall steep me in Elysian reverie,
A momentary dream that thou art she.
  My mother! when I learnt that thou wast dead
Say, wast thou conscious of the tears I shed?
Hovered thy spirit o'er thy sorrowing son,
Wretch even then, life's journey just begun?
Perhaps thou gavest me, though unfelt, a kiss:
Perhaps a tear, if souls can weep in bliss —
Ah, that maternal smile! It answers — Yes.
I heard the bell tolled on thy burial day,
I saw the hearse that bore thee slow away,
And turning from my nursery window, drew
A long, long sigh, and wept a last adieu!
But was it such? — It was. — Where thou art gone
Adieus and farewells are a sound unknown.
May I but meet thee on that peaceful shore,
The parting word shall pass my lips no more!
Thy maidens, grieved themselves at my concern,
Oft gave me promise of thy quick return.
What ardently I wished I long believed,
And, disappointed still, was still deceived.
By expectation every day beguiled,
Dupe of *to-morrow* even from a child.
Thus many a sad to-morrow came and went,
Till, all my stock of infant sorrow spent,
I learned at last submission to my lot;
But, though I less deplored thee, ne'er forgot.
  Where once we dwelt our name is heard no more,
Children not thine have trod my nursery floor;
And where the gardener Robin, day by day,
Drew me to school along the public way,
Delighted with my bauble coach, and wrapped
In scarlet mantle warm, and velvet capped,
'Tis now become a history little known,
That once we called the pastoral house our own.
Short-lived possession! but the record fair
That memory keeps, of all thy kindness there,
Still outlives many a storm that has effaced
A thousand other themes less deeply traced.
Thy nightly visits to my chamber made,
That thou mightst know me safe and warmly laid;
Thy morning bounties ere I left my home,
The biscuit, or confectionary plum;
The fragrant waters on my cheek bestowed
By thy own hand, till fresh they shone and glowed;
All this, and more endearing still than all,
Thy constant flow of love, that knew no fall,

Ne'er roughened by those cataracts and brakes
That humour interposed too often makes;
All this still legible in memory's page,
And still to be so to my latest age,
Adds joy to duty, makes me glad to pay
Such honours to thee as my numbers may;
Perhaps a frail memorial, but sincere,
Not scorned in heaven, though little noticed here.
  Could Time, his flight reversed, restore the hours,
When, playing with thy vesture's tissued flowers,
The violet, the pink, and jassamine,
I pricked them into paper with a pin
(And thou wast happier than myself the while,
Wouldst softly speak, and stroke my head and smile),
Could those few pleasant days again appear,
Might one wish bring them, would I wish them here?
I would not trust my heart — the dear delight
Seems so to be desired, perhaps I might. —
But no — what here we call our life is such,
So little to be loved, and thou so much,
That I should ill requite thee to constrain
Thy unbound spirit into bonds again.
  Thou, as a gallant bark from Albion's coast
(The storms all weathered and the ocean crossed)
Shoots into port at some well-havened isle,
Where spices breathe, and brighter seasons smile,
There sits quiescent on the floods that show
Her beauteous form reflected clear below,
While airs impregnated with incense play
Around her, fanning light her streamers gay;
So thou, with sails how swift! hast reached the shore,
"Where tempests never beat nor billows roar."
And thy loved consort on the dangerous tide
Of life long since has anchored by thy side.
But me, scarce hoping to attain that rest,
Always from port withheld, always distressed —
Me howling blasts drive devious, tempest tost,
Sails ripped, seams opening wide, and compass lost,
And day by day some current's thwarting force
Sets me more distant from a prosperous course.
Yet, oh, the thought that thou art safe, and he!
That thought is joy, arrive what may to me.
My boast is not, that I deduce my birth
From loins enthroned and rulers of the earth;
But higher far my proud pretensions rise —
The son of parents passed into the skies!
And now, farewell — Time unrevoked has run
His wonted course, yet what I wished is done.
By contemplation's help, not sought in vain,
I seem to have lived my childhood o'er again;
To have renewed the joys that once were mine,
Without the sin of violating thine:
And, while the wings of Fancy still are free,
And I can view this mimic show of thee,
Time has but half succeeded in his theft —
Thyself removed, thy power to soothe me left.

YARDLEY OAK

Survivor sole, and hardly such, of all
That once lived here, thy brethren! — at my birth
(Since which I number threescore winters past)
A shattered veteran, hollow-trunked perhaps,
As now, and with excoriate forks deform,
Relics of ages! — could a mind, imbued
With truth from Heaven, created thing adore,
I might with reverence kneel and worship thee.
  It seems idolatry with some excuse,
When our forefather Druids in their oaks
Imagined sanctity. The conscience, yet
Unpurified by an authentic act
Of amnesty, the meed of blood divine,
Loved not the light, but, gloomy, into gloom
Of thickest shades, like Adam after taste
Of fruit proscribed, as to a refuge, fled.
  Thou wast a bauble once; a cup and ball,
Which babes might play with; and the thievish jay,
Seeking her food, with ease might have purloined
The auburn nut that held thee, swallowing down
Thy yet close-folded latitude of boughs,
And all thine embryo vastness, at a gulp.
But fate thy growth decreed; autumnal rains
Beneath thy parent tree mellowed the soil
Designed thy cradle; and a skipping deer,
With pointed hoof dibbling the glebe, prepared
The soft receptacle, in which, secure,
Thy rudiments should sleep the winter through.
  So fancy dreams. Disprove it, if ye can,
Ye reasoners broad awake, whose busy search
Of argument, employed too oft amiss,
Sifts half the pleasures of short life away!
  Thou fell'st mature; and in the loamy clod
Swelling with vegetative force instinct
Didst burst thine egg, as theirs the fabled Twins,
Now stars; two lobes, protruding, paired exact;
A leaf succeeded, and another leaf,
And, all the elements thy puny growth
Fostering propitious, thou becamst a twig.
  Who lived when thou wast such? Oh, couldst thou speak,
As in Dodona once thy kindred trees
Oracular, I would not curious ask
The future, best unknown, but at thy mouth
Inquisitive, the less ambiguous past.
  By thee I might correct, erroneous oft,

The clock of history, facts and events
Timing more punctual, unrecorded facts
Recovering, and misstated setting right—
Desperate attempt, till trees shall speak again!
  Time made thee what thou wast, king of the woods,
And Time hath made thee what thou art — a cave
For owls to roost in. Once thy spreading boughs
O'erhung the champaign; and the numerous flocks
That grazed it stood beneath that ample cope
Uncrowded, yet safe-sheltered from the storm.
No flock frequents thee now. Thou hast outlived
Thy popularity, and art become
(Unless verse rescue thee awhile) a thing
Forgotten, as the foliage of thy youth.
  While thus through all the stages thou hast pushed
Of treeship — first a seedling, hid in grass;
Then twig; then sapling; and, as century rolled
Slow after century, a giant-bulk
Of girth enormous, with moss-cushioned root
Upheaved above the soil, and sides embossed
With prominent wens globose, — till at the last
The rottenness, which Time is charged to inflict
On other mighty ones, found also thee.
  What exhibitions various hath the world
Witnessed, of mutability in all
That we account most durable below!
Change is the diet on which all subsist,
Created changeable, and change at last
Destroys them. Skies uncertain, now the heat
Transmitting cloudless, and the solar beam
Now quenching in a boundless sea of clouds, —
Calm and alternate storm, moisture and drought,
Invigorate by turns the springs of life
In all that live, plant, animal, and man,
And in conclusion mar them. Nature's threads,
Fine passing thought, even in her coarsest works,
Delight in agitation, yet sustain
The force that agitates, not unimpaired;
But, worn by frequent impulse, to the cause
Of their best tone their dissolution owe.
  Thought cannot spend itself, comparing still
The great and little of thy lot, thy growth
From almost nullity into a state
Of matchless grandeur, and declension thence,
Slow, into such magnificent decay.
Time was when, settling on thy leaf, a fly
Could shake thee to the root — and time has been
When tempests could not. At thy firmest age
Thou hadst within thy bole solid contents,
That might have ribbed the sides and planked the deck
Of some flagged admiral; and tortuous arms,
The shipwright's darling treasure, didst present
To the four-quartered winds, robust and bold,
Warped into tough knee-timber, many a load!
But the axe spared thee. In those thriftier days
Oaks fell not, hewn by thousands, to supply
The bottomless demands of contest waged
For senatorial honours. Thus to Time
The task was left to whittle thee away
With his sly scythe, whose ever-nibbling edge,
Noiseless, an atom, and an atom more,
Disjoining from the rest, has, unobserved,
Achieved a labour, which had, far and wide,
By man performed, made all the forest ring.
  Embowelled now, and of thy ancient self
Possessing nought but the scooped rind, — that seems
A huge throat calling to the clouds for drink,
Which it would give in rivulets to thy root, —
Thou temptest none, but rather much forbiddest
The feller's toil, which thou couldst ill requite.
Yet is thy root sincere, sound as the rock,
A quarry of stout spurs and knotted fangs,
Which, crook'd into a thousand whimsies, clasp
The stubborn soil, and hold thee still erect.
  So stands a kingdom, whose foundation yet
Fails not, in virtue and in wisdom laid,
Though all the superstructure, by the tooth
Pulverised of venality, a shell
Stands now, and semblance only of itself!
  Thine arms have left thee. Winds have rent them off
Long since, and rovers of the forest wild
With bow and shaft have burnt them. Some have left
A splintered stump, bleached to a snowy white:
And some memorial none, where once they grew.
Yet life still lingers in thee, and puts forth
Proof not contemptible of what she can,
Even where death predominates. The Spring
Finds thee not less alive to her sweet force
Than yonder upstarts of the neighbouring wood,
So much thy juniors, who their birth received
Half a millennium since the date of thine.
  But since, although well qualified by age
To teach, no spirit dwells in thee, nor voice
May be expected from thee, seated here
On thy distorted root, with hearers none,
Or prompter, save the scene, I will perform
Myself the oracle, and will discourse
In my own ear such matter as I may.
  One man alone, the father of us all,
Drew not his life from woman; never gazed,
With mute unconsciousness of what he saw,
On all around him; learned not by degrees,
Nor owed articulation to his ear;
But moulded by his Maker into man
At once, upstood intelligent, surveyed
All creatures, with precision understood

Their purport, uses, properties; assigned
To each his name significant, and, filled
With love and wisdom, rendered back to Heaven
In praise harmonious the first air he drew.
He was excused the penalties of dull
Minority. No tutor charged his hand
With the thought-tracing quill, or tasked his mind
With problems. History, not wanted yet,
Leaned on her elbow, watching Time, whose course,
Eventful, should supply her with a theme.

[The poem was left incomplete.]

TO MARY

The twentieth year is well-nigh past,
Since first our sky was overcast;
Ah, would that this might be the last!
My Mary!

Thy spirits have a fainter flow,
I see thee daily weaker grow;
'Twas my distress that brought thee low,
My Mary!

Thy needles, once a shining store,
For my sake restless heretofore,
Now rust disused, and shine no more,
My Mary!

For though thou gladly wouldst fulfil
The same kind office for me still,
Thy sight now seconds not thy will,
My Mary!

But well thou playedst the housewife's part,
And all thy threads with magic art
Have wound themselves about this heart,
My Mary!

Thy indistinct expressions seem
Like language uttered in a dream;
Yet me they charm, whate'er the theme,
My Mary!

Thy silver locks, once auburn bright,
Are still more lovely in my sight
Than golden beams of orient light,
My Mary!

For, could I view nor them nor thee,
What sight worth seeing could I see?
The sun would rise in vain for me,
My Mary!

Partakers of thy sad decline,
Thy hands their little force resign,
Yet, gently prest, press gently mine,
My Mary!

Such feebleness of limbs thou provest,
That now at every step thou movest
Upheld by two, yet still thou lovest,
My Mary!

And still to love, though prest with ill,
In wintry age to feel no chill,
With me is to be lovely still,
My Mary!

But ah! by constant heed I know,
How oft the sadness that I show
Transforms thy smiles to looks of woe,
My Mary!

And should my future lot be cast
With much resemblance of the past,
Thy worn-out heart will break at last,
My Mary!

THE CASTAWAY

Obscurest night involved the sky,
The Atlantic billows roared,
When such a destined wretch as I,
Washed headlong from on board,
Of friends, of hope, of all bereft,
His floating home forever left.

No braver chief could Albion boast
Than he with whom he went,
Nor ever ship left Albion's coast
With warmer wishes sent.
He loved them both, but both in vain,
Nor him beheld, nor her again.

Not long beneath the whelming brine,
Expert to swim, he lay;
Nor soon he felt his strength decline,
Or courage die away;
But waged with death a lasting strife,
Supported by despair of life.

He shouted: nor his friends had failed
To check the vessel's course,
But so the furious blast prevailed,
That, pitiless perforce,
They left their outcast mate behind,
And scudded still before the wind.

Some succour yet they could afford;
And such as storms allow,
The cask, the coop, the floated cord,
Delayed not to bestow.
But he (they knew) nor ship nor shore,
Whate'er they gave, should visit more.

Nor, cruel as it seemed, could he
Their haste himself condemn,
Aware that flight, in such a sea,
Alone could rescue them;
Yet bitter felt it still to die
Deserted, and his friends so nigh.

He long survives, who lives an hour
In ocean, self-upheld;
And so long he, with unspent power,
His destiny repelled;
And ever, as the minutes flew,
Entreated help, or cried "Adieu!"

At length, his transient respite past,
His comrades, who before
Had heard his voice in every blast,
Could catch the sound no more:
For then, by toil subdued, he drank
The stifling wave, and then he sank.

No poet wept him; but the page
Of narrative sincere,
That tells his name, his worth, his age,
Is wet with Anson's tear:
And tears by bards or heroes shed
Alike immortalize the dead.

I therefore purpose not, or dream,
Descanting on his fate,
To give the melancholy theme
A more enduring date:
But misery still delights to trace
Its semblance in another's case.

No voice divine the storm allayed,
No light propitious shone,
When, snatched from all effectual aid,
We perished, each alone:
But I beneath a rougher sea,
And whelmed in deeper gulfs than he.

JAMES BEATTIE (1735–1803)

THE MINSTREL

From BOOK I

There lived in Gothic days, as legends tell,
A shepherd swain, a man of low degree,
Whose sires, perchance, in Fairyland might dwell,
Sicilian groves, or vales of Arcady;
But he, I ween, was of the north countrie;
A nation famed for song, and beauty's charms;
Zealous, yet modest; innocent, though free;
Patient of toil: serene amidst alarms;
Inflexible in faith: invincible in arms.

The shepherd swain of whom I mention made,
On Scotia's mountains fed his little flock;
The sickle, scythe, or plough he never swayed;
An honest heart was almost all his stock;
His drink the living water from the rock;
The milky dams supplied his board, and lent
Their kindly fleece to baffle winter's shock;
And he, though oft with dust and sweat besprent,
Did guide and guard their wanderings, wheresoe'er they went.

* * * * * * *

And yet poor Edwin was no vulgar boy.
Deep thought oft seemed to fix his infant eye.
Dainties he heeded not, nor gaud, nor toy,
Save one short pipe of rudest minstrelsy;
Silent when glad; affectionate, though shy;
And now his look was most demurely sad;
And now he laughed aloud, yet none knew why.
The neighbors stared and sighed, yet blessed the lad;
Some deemed him wondrous wise, and some believed him mad.

But why should I his childish feats display?
Concourse, and noise, and toil he ever fled;
Nor cared to mingle in the clamorous fray
Of squabbling imps; but to the forest sped,
Or roamed at large the lonely mountain's head,
Or where the maze of some bewildered stream
To deep untrodden groves his footsteps led,
There would he wander wild, till Phœbus' beam,
Shot from the western cliff, released the weary team.

The exploit of strength, dexterity, or speed,
To him nor vanity nor joy could bring:
His heart, from cruel sport estranged, would bleed
To work the woe of any living thing,
By trap or net, by arrow or by sling;
These he detested; those he scorned to wield:
He wished to be the guardian, not the king,
Tyrant far less, or traitor of the field,
And sure the sylvan reign unbloody joy might yield.

Lo! where the stripling, rapt in wonder, roves
Beneath the precipice o'erhung with pine;
And sees on high, amidst the encircling groves,
From cliff to cliff the foaming torrents shine;
While waters, woods, and winds in concert join,
And echo swells the chorus to the skies.
Would Edwin this majestic scene resign
For aught the huntsman's puny craft supplies?
Ah, no! he better knows great Nature's charms to prize.

And oft he traced the uplands to survey,
When o'er the sky advanced the kindling dawn,
The crimson cloud, blue main, and mountain gray,
And lake, dim-gleaming on the smoky lawn:
Far to the west the long, long vale withdrawn,
Where twilight loves to linger for a while;
And now he faintly kens the bounding fawn,
And villager abroad at early toil:
But, lo! the sun appears, and heaven, earth, ocean smile.

And oft the craggy cliff he loved to climb,
When all in mist the world below was lost.
What dreadful pleasure! there to stand sublime,
Like shipwrecked mariner on desert coast,
And view the enormous waste of vapour, tost
In billows, lengthening to the horizon round,
Now scooped in gulfs, with mountains now embossed!
And hear the voice of mirth and song rebound,
Flocks, herds, and waterfalls, along the hoar profound!

In truth he was a strange and wayward wight,
Fond of each gentle and each dreadful scene.
In darkness and in storm he found delight;
Nor less than when on ocean-wave serene
The southern sun diffused his dazzling sheen.
Even sad vicissitude amused his soul;
And if a sigh would sometimes intervene,
And down his cheek a tear of pity roll,
A sigh, a tear, so sweet, he wished not to control.

ANNA LÆTITIA BARBAULD

(1743–1825)

LIFE

Life! I know not what thou art,
But know that thou and I must part;
And when, or how, or where we met,
I own to me's a secret yet.
But this I know, when thou art fled,
Where'er they lay these limbs, this head,
No clod so valueless shall be
As all that then remains of me.

O whither, whither, dost thou fly?
Where bend unseen thy trackless course?
And in this strange divorce,
Ah, tell where I must seek this compound I?
To the vast ocean of empyreal flame
From whence thy essence came
Dost thou thy flight pursue, when freed
From matter's base encumbering weed?
Or dost thou, hid from sight,
Wait, like some spell-bound knight,
Through blank oblivious years th' appointed hour
To break thy trance and reassume thy power?
Yet canst thou without thought or feeling be?
O say, what art thou, when no more thou'rt thee?

Life! we have been long together,
Through pleasant and through cloudy weather;
'Tis hard to part when friends are dear;
Perhaps 'twill cost a sigh, a tear; —
Then steal away, give little warning,
Choose thine own time;
Say not Good-night, but in some brighter clime
Bid me Good-morning!

THOMAS CHATTERTON (1752–1770)

BRISTOWE TRAGEDIE; OR, THE DETHE OF SYR CHARLES BAWDIN

The feathered songster chaunticleer
Han wounde hys bugle horne,
And tolde the earlie villager
The commynge of the morne:

Kynge Edwarde sawe the ruddie streakes
Of lyghte eclypse the greie;
And herde the raven's crokynge throte
Proclayme the fated daie.

"Thou'rt ryghte," quod he, "for, by the Godde
That syttes enthron'd on hyghe!
Charles Bawdin, and hys fellowes twaine,
To-daie shall surelie die."

Thenne wythe a jugge of nappy ale
Hys knyghtes dydd onne hymm waite;
"Goe tell the traytour, thatt to-daie
Hee leaves thys mortall state."

Sir Canterlone thenne bendedd lowe,
With harte brymm-fulle of woe;
Hee journey'd to the castle-gate,
And to Syr Charles dydd goe.

Butt whenne hee came, hys children twaine,
And eke hys lovynge wyfe,
Wythe brinie tears dydd wett the floore,
For goode Syr Charleses lyfe.

"O goode Syr Charles!" sayd Canterlone,
"Badde tydyngs I doe brynge."
"Speke boldlie, manne," sayd brave Syr Charles,
"Whatte says the traytor kynge?"

"I greeve to telle; before yonne Sonne
  Does fromme the welkinn flye,
Hee hathe uppon hys honour sworne,
  Thatt thou shalt surelie die."

"Wee all must die," quod brave Syr Charles;
  "Of thatte I'm not affearde;
Whatte bootes to lyve a little space?
  Thanke Jesu, I'm prepar'd:

"Butt telle thye kynge, for myne hee's not,
  I'de sooner die to-daie
Thanne lyve hys slave, as manie are,
  Though I shoulde lyve for aie."

Thenne Canterlone hee dydd goe out,
  To telle the maior straite
To gett all thynges ynne redyness
  For goode Syr Charleses fate.

Thenne Maisterr Canynge saughte the kynge,
  And felle down onne hys knee;
"I'm come," quod hee, "unto your grace
  To move your clemencye."

Thenne quod the kynge, "Youre tale speke out,
  You have been much oure friende;
Whatever youre request may bee,
  Wee wylle to ytte attende."

"My nobile leige! alle my request,
  Ys for a nobile knyghte,
Who, though may hap hee has donne wronge,
  Hee thoughte ytte stylle was ryghte:

"He has a spouse and children twaine,
  Alle rewyn'd are for aie;
Yff that you are resolved to lett
  Charles Bawdin die to-dai."

"Speke not of such a traytour vile,"
  The kynge ynn furie sayde;
"Before the evening starre doth sheene,
  Bawdin shall loose hys hedde:

"Justice does loudlie for hym calle,
  And hee shalle have hys meede:
Speke, maister Canynge! Whatte thynge else
  Att present doe you neede?"

"My nobile leige!" goode Canynge sayde,
  "Leave justice to our Godde,
And laye the yronne rule asyde;
  Be thyne the olyve rodde.

"Was Godde to serche our hertes and reines,
  The best were synners grete;
Christ's vicarr only knowes ne synne,
  Ynne alle thys mortall state.

"Lett mercie rule thyne infante reigne,
  'Twylle faste thye crowne fulle sure;
From race to race thye familie
  Alle sov'reigns shall endure:

"But yff wythe bloode and slaughter thou
  Beginne thy infante reigne,
Thy crowne upponne thy childrennes brows
  Wylle never long remayne."

"Canynge, awaie! thys traytour vile
  Has scorn'd my power and mee;
Howe canst thou then for such a manne
  Entreate my clemencye?"

"My nobile leige! the trulie brave
  Wylle val'rous actions prize;
Respect a brave and nobile mynde,
  Although ynne enemies."

"Canynge, awaie! By Godde ynne Heav'n
  That dydd mee beinge gyve,
I wylle nott taste a bitt of breade
  Whilst thys Syr Charles dothe lyve.

"By Marie, and alle Seinctes ynne Heav'n,
  Thys sunne shall be hys laste,"
Thenne Canynge dropt a brinie teare,
  And from the presence paste.

With herte brymm-fulle of gnawynge grief,
  Hee to Syr Charles dydd goe,
And sat hymm downe uponne a stoole,
  And teares beganne to flowe.

"Wee all must die," quod brave Syr Charles;
  "Whatte bootes ytte howe or whenne;
Dethe ys the sure, the certaine fate
  Of all wee mortall menne.

"Saye why, my friende, thie honest soul
  Runns overr att thyne eye;
Is ytte for my most welcome doome
  Thatt thou dost child-lyke crye?"

Quod godlie Canynge, "I doe weepe,
  Thatt thou soe soone must dye,
And leave thy sonnes and helpless wyfe;
  'Tys thys thatt wettes myne eye."

"Thenne drie the tears thatt out thyne eye
  From godlie fountaines sprynge;
Dethe I despise, and alle the power
  Of Edwarde, traytour kynge.

"Whan through the tyrant's welcom means
  I shall resigne my lyfe,
The Godde I serve wylle soone provyde
  For bothe mye sonnes and wyfe.

"Before I sawe the lyghtsome sunne,
Thys was appointed mee;
Shall mortall manne repyne or grudge
What Godde ordeynes to bee?

"Howe oft ynne battaile have I stoode,
Whan thousands dy'd arounde;
Whan smokynge streemes of crimson bloode
Imbrew'd the fatten'd grounde:

"Howe dydd I knowe thatt ev'ry darte,
That cutte the airie waie,
Myghte nott fynde passage toe my harte,
And close myne eyes for aie?

"And shall I nowe, forr feere of dethe,
Looke wanne and bee dysmayde?
Ne! fromm my herte flie childyshe feere,
Bee alle the manne display'd.

"Ah! goddelyke Henrie! Godde forefende,
And guarde thee and thye sonne,
Yff 'tis hys wylle; but yff 'tis nott,
Why thenne hys wylle bee donne.

"My honest friende, my faulte has beene
To serve Godde and mye prynce;
And thatt I no tyme-server am,
My dethe wylle soone convynce.

"Ynne Londonne citye was I borne,
Of parents of grete note;
My fadre dydd a nobile armes
Emblazon onne hys cote:

"I make ne doubte butt hee ys gone
Where soone I hope to goe;
Where wee for ever shall bee blest,
From oute the reech of woe.

"Hee taughte mee justice and the laws
Wyth pitie to unite;
And eke hee taughte mee howe to knowe
The wronge cause fromm the ryghte:

"Hee taughte mee wyth a prudent hande
To feede the hungrie poore,
Ne lett mye sarvants dryve awaie
The hungrie fromme my doore:

"And none can saye butt alle mye lyfe
I have hys wordyes kept;
And summ'd the actyonns of the daie
Eche nyghte before I slept.

"I have a spouse, goe aske of her
Yff I defyl'd her bedde?
I have a kynge, and none can laie
Black treason onne my hedde.

"Ynne Lent, and onne the holie eve,
Fromm fleshe I dydd refrayne;
Whie should I thenne appeare dismay'd
To leave thys worlde of payne?

"Ne, hapless Henrie! I rejoyce,
I shall ne see thye dethe;
Moste willynglie ynne thye just cause
Doe I resign my brethe.

"Oh, fickle people! rewyn'd londe!
Thou wylt kenne peace ne moe;
Whyle Richard's sonnes exalt themselves,
Thye brookes wythe bloude wylle flowe.

"Saie, were ye tyr'd of godlie peace,
And godlie Henrie's reigne,
Thatt you dyd choppe your easie daies
For those of bloude and peyne?

"Whatte though I onne a sledde be drawne,
And mangled by a hynde,
I doe defye the traytor's pow'r,
Hee can ne harm my mynd;

"Whatte though, uphoisted onne a pole,
Mye lymbes shall rotte ynne ayre,
And ne ryche monument of brasse
Charles Bawdin's name shall bear;

"Yett ynne the holie booke above,
Whyche tyme can't eate awaie,
There wythe the sarvants of the Lord
Mye name shall lyve for aie.

"Thenne welcome dethe! for lyfe eterne
I leave thys mortall lyfe:
Farewell vayne world, and alle that's deare,
Mye sonnes and lovynge wyfe!

"Nowe dethe as welcome to mee comes,
As e'er the moneth of Maie;
Nor woulde I even wyshe to lyve,
Wyth my dere wyfe to staie."

Quod Canynge, "'Tys a goodlie thynge
To bee prepar'd to die;
And from thys world of peyne and grefe
To Godde ynne heav'n to flie."

And nowe the belle began to tolle,
And claryonnes to sound;
Syr Charles hee herde the horses feete
A prauncyng onne the grounde:

And just before the officers
His lovynge wyfe came ynne,
Weepynge unfeigned teeres of woe,
Wythe loude and dysmalle dynne.

"Sweet Florence! nowe I praie forbere,
Ynn quiet lett mee die;
Praie Godde thatt ev'ry Christian soule
Maye looke onne dethe as I.

"Sweet Florence! why these brinie teers?
Theye washe my soule awaie,
And almost make mee wyshe for lyfe,
Wyth thee, sweete dame, to staie.

"'Tys butt a journie I shalle goe
Untoe the lande of blysse;
Nowe, as a proofe of husbande's love,
Receive thys holie kysse."

Thenne Florence, fault'ring ynne her saie,
Tremblynge these wordyes spoke,
"Ah, cruele Edwarde! bloudie kynge!
Mye herte ys welle nyghe broke:

"Ah, sweete Syr Charles! why wylt thou goe,
Wythoute thye lovynge wyfe?
The cruelle axe thatt cuttes thy necke,
Ytte eke shall ende mye lyfe."

And nowe the officers came ynne
To brynge Syr Charles awaie,
Whoe turnedd toe hys lovynge wyfe,
And thus to her dydd saie:

"I goe to lyfe, and nott to dethe;
Truste thou ynne Godde above,
And teache thy sonnes to feare the Lorde,
And ynne theyre hertes hym love:

"Teache them to runne the nobile race
Thatt I theyre fader runne;
Florence! shou'd dethe thee take — adieu!
Yee officers leade onne."

Thenne Florence rav'd as anie madde,
And dydd her tresses tere;
"Oh staie, mye husbande, lorde, and lyfe!"
Syr Charles thenne dropt a teare.

'Tyll tyredd oute wythe ravynge loude,
Shee fellen onne the flore;
Syr Charles exerted alle hys myghte,
And march'd fromm oute the dore.

Uponne a sledde hee mounted thenne,
Wythe lookes full brave and swete;
Lookes thatt enshone ne more concern
Thanne anie ynne the strete.

Before hym went the council-menne,
Ynne scarlett robes and golde,
And tassils spanglynge ynne the sunne,
Muche glorious to beholde:

The Freers of Seincte Augustyne next
Appeared to the syghte,
Alle cladd ynne homelie russett weedes,
Of godlie monkysh plyghte:

Ynne diffraunt partes a godlie psaume
Moste sweetlie theye dydd chaunt;
Behynde theyre backes syx mynstrelles came,
Who tun'd the strunge bataunt.

Thenne fyve-and-twentye archers came;
Echone the bowe dydd bende,
From rescue of Kynge Henries friends
Syr Charles forr to defend.

Bolde as a lyon came Syr Charles,
Drawne onne a cloth-layde sledde,
Bye two blacke stedes ynne trappynges white,
Wyth plumes uponne theyre hedde:

Behynde hym five-and-twenty moe
Of archers stronge and stoute,
Wyth bended bowe echone ynne hande,
Marched ynne goodlie route;

Seincte Jameses Freers marched next,
Echone hys parte dydd chaunt;
Behynde theyre backes syx mynstrelles came,
Who tun'd the strunge bataunt:

Thenne came the maior and eldermenne,
Ynne clothe of scarlett deck't;
And theyre attendynge menne echone,
Lyke easterne princes trickt:

And after them, a multitude
Of citizens dydd thronge;
The wyndowes were alle fulle of heddes,
As hee dydd passe alonge.

And whenne hee came to the hyghe crosse,
Syr Charles dydd turne and saie,
"O thou, thatt savest manne fromme synne,
Washe mye soule clean thys daie!"

Att the grete mynster wyndowe sat
The kynge ynne myckle state,
To see Charles Bawdin goe alonge
To hys most welcom fate.

Soone as the sledde drewe nyghe enowe,
Thatt Edwarde hee myghte heare,
The brave Syr Charles hee dydd stande uppe,
And thus hys wordes declare:

"Thou seest me, Edwarde! traytour vile!
Expos'd to infamie;
Butt bee assur'd, disloyall manne!
I'm greaterr nowe thanne thee.

"Bye foule proceedyngs, murdre, bloude,
Thou wearest nowe a crowne;
And hast appoynted mee to die,
By power nott thyne owne.

"Thou thynkest I shall die to-daie;
I have beene dede 'till nowe,
And soone shall lyve to weare a crowne
For aie uponne my browe:

"Whylst thou, perhapps, for som few yeares,
Shalt rule thys fickle lande,
To lett them knowe howe wyde the rule
'Twixt kynge and tyrant hande:

"Thye pow'r unjust, thou traytour slave!
Shall falle onne thye owne hedde" —
Fromm out of hearyng of the kynge
Departed thenne the sledde.

Kynge Edwarde's soule rush'd to hys face,
Hee turn'd hys hedde awaie,
And to hys broder Gloucester
Hee thus dydd speke and saie:

"To hym that soe much dreaded dethe
Ne ghastlie terrors brynge,
Beholde the manne! hee spake the truthe,
Hee's greater thanne a kynge!"

"Soe let hym die!" Duke Richarde sayde;
"And maye echone oure foes
Bende downe theyre neckes to bloudie axe
And feede the carryon crowes."

And nowe the horses gentlie drewe
Syr Charles uppe the hyghe hylle;
The axe dydd glysterr ynne the sunne,
His pretious bloude to spylle.

Syrr Charles dydd uppe the scaffold goe,
As uppe a gilded carre
Of victorye, bye val'rous chiefs
Gayn'd ynne the bloudie warre:

And to the people hee dyd saie,
"Beholde you see mee dye,
For servynge loyally mye kynge,
Mye kynge most ryghtfullie.

"As longe as Edwarde rules thys land,
Ne quiet you wylle knowe:
Your sonnes and husbandes shalle bee slayne
And brookes wythe bloude shall flowe.

"You leave youre goode and lawfulle kynge,
Whenne ynne adversitye;
Lyke mee, untoe the true cause stycke,
And for the true cause dye."

Thenne hee, wyth preestes, uponne hys knees,
A prayer to Godde dyd make,
Beseechynge hym unto hymselfe
Hys partynge soule to take.

Thenne, kneelynge downe, hee layd hys hedde
Most seemlie onne the blocke;
Whyche fromme hys bodie fayre at once
The able heddes-manne stroke:

And oute the bloude beganne to flowe,
And rounde the scaffolde twyne;
And teares, enow to washe 't awaie,
Dydd flowe fromme each mann's eyne.

The bloudie axe hys bodie fayre
Ynnto foure partes cutte;
And ev'rye parte, and eke hys hedde,
Uponne a pole was putte.

One parte dydd rotte onne Kynwulph-hylle,
One onne the mynster-tower,
And one from off the castle-gate
The crowen dydd devoure;

The other onne Seyncte Powle's goode gate,
A dreery spectacle;
Hys hedde was plac'd onne the hyghe crosse,
Ynne hyghe-streete most nobile.

Thus was the ende of Bawdin's fate:
Godde prosper longe oure kynge,
And grante hee maye, wyth Bawdin's soule,
Ynne heav'n Godd's mercie synge!

THE ACCOUNTE OF W. CANYNGES FEAST

Thorowe the halle the belle han sounde;
Byelecoyle doe the grave beseeme;
The ealdermenne doe sytte arounde,
Ande snoffelle oppe the cheorte steeme.
Lyche asses wylde ynne desarte waste
Swotelye the morneynge ayre doe taste.

Syche coyne thie ate; the minstrels plaie,
The dynne of angelles doe theie keepe;
Heie stylle; the guestes ha ne to saie,
Butte nodde yer thankes ande falle aslape.
Thos echone daie bee I to deene,
Gyf Rowley, Iscamm, or Tyb Gorges be ne seene.

GEORGE CRABBE (1754–1832)

From THE VILLAGE

BOOK I

Fled are those times, when, in harmonious strains
The rustic poet praised his native plains:

No shepherds now, in smooth alternate verse,
Their country's beauty, or their nymph's rehearse;
Yet still for these we frame the tender strain, 11
Still in our lays fond Corydons complain,
And shepherds' boys their amorous pains reveal,
The only pains, alas! they never feel.
  On Mincio's banks, in Cæsar's bounteous reign,
If Tityrus found the golden age again,
Must sleepy bards the flattering dream prolong,
Mechanic echoes of the Mantuan song? 18
From Truth and Nature shall we widely stray,
Where Virgil, not where fancy, leads the way?

* * * * * * * * *

No; cast by fortune on a frowning coast, 49
Which neither groves nor happy valleys boast;
Where other cares than those the Muse relates,
And other shepherds dwell with other mates;
By such examples taught, I paint the cot,
As Truth will paint it and as bards will not:
Nor you, ye poor, of lettered scorn complain,
To you the smoothest song is smooth in vain;
O'ercome by labour, and bowed down by time,
Feel you the barren flattery of a rhyme?
Can poets soothe you, when you pine for bread,
By winding myrtles round your ruin'd shed?—
Can their light tales your weighty griefs o'erpower. 61
Or glad with airy mirth the toilsome hour?
Lo! where the heath, with withering brake grown o'er,
Lends the light turf that warms the neighbouring poor;
From thence a length of burning sand appears,
Where the thin harvest waves its withered ears;
Rank weeds, that every art and care defy,
Reign o'er the land and rob the blighted rye:
There thistles stretch their prickly arms afar,
And to the ragged infant threaten war; 70
There poppies nodding, mock the hope of toil;
There the blue bugloss paints the sterile soil;
Hardy and high, above the slender sheaf,
The slimy mallow waves her silky leaf;
O'er the young shoot the charlock throws a shade,
And clasping tares cling round the sickly blade;
With mingled tints the rocky coasts abound,
And a sad splendour vainly shines around.

* * * * * * * * *

From TALES

TALE X—THE LOVER'S JOURNEY

On either side
Is level fen, a prospect wild and wide,
With dikes on either hand by ocean's self supplied:
Far on the right the distant sea is seen,
And salt the springs that feed the marsh between.
Beneath an ancient bridge the straitened flood
Rolls through its sloping banks of slimy mud;
Near it a sunken boat resists the tide, 111
That frets and hurries to th' opposing side;
The rushes sharp, that on the borders grow,
Bend their brown flow'rets to the stream below,
Impure in all its course, in all its progress slow:
Here a grave Flora scarcely deigns to bloom,
Nor wears a rosy blush, nor sheds perfume:
The few dull flowers that o'er the place are spread
Partake the nature of their fenny bed;
Here on its wiry stem, in rigid bloom, 120
Grows the salt lavender that lacks perfume:
Here the dwarf sallows creep, the septfoil harsh,
And the soft slimy mallow of the marsh;
Low on the ear the distant billows sound,
And just in view appears their stony bound;
No hedge nor tree conceals the glowing run;
Birds, save a wat'ry tribe, the district shun,
Nor chirp among the reeds where bitter waters run.

* * * * * * *

  Again, the country was enclosed, a wide
And sandy road has banks on either side;
Where, lo! a hollow on the left appeared,
And there a gipsy tribe their tent had reared;
'Twas open spread, to catch the morning sun,
And they had now their early meal begun,
When two brown boys just left their grassy seat,
The early traveller with their prayers to greet:
While yet Orlando held his pence in hand,
He saw their sister on her duty stand; 150
Some twelve years old, demure, affected, sly,
Prepared the force of early powers to try;
Sudden a look of languor he descries,
And well-feigned apprehension in her eyes;
Trained but yet savage, in her speaking face
He marked the features of her vagrant race;
When a light laugh and roguish leer expressed
The vice implanted in her youthful breast:
Forth from the tent her elder brother came,
Who seemed offended, yet forbore to blame 160
The young designer, but could only trace
The looks of pity in the traveller's face:
Within, the father, who from fences nigh
Had brought the fuel for the fire's supply,
Watched now the feeble blaze, and stood dejected by.
On ragged rug, just borrowed from the bed,
And by the hand of coarse indulgence fed,
In dirty patchwork negligently dressed,
Reclined the wife, an infant at her breast;
In her wild face some touch of grace remained,
Of vigour palsied and of beauty stained; 171
Her bloodshot eyes on her unheeding mate

Were wrathful turned, and seemed her wants to state,
Cursing his tardy aid — her mother there
With gipsy-state engrossed the only chair;
Solemn and dull her look; with such she stands,
And reads the milk-maid's fortune in her hands,
Tracing the lines of life; assumed through years,
Each feature now the steady falsehood wears;
With hard and savage eye she views the food,
And grudging pinches their intruding brood;
Last in the group, the worn-out grandsire sits
Neglected, lost, and living but by fits:
Useless, despised, his worthless labours done,
And half protected by the vicious son,
Who half supports him; he with heavy glance
Views the young ruffians who around him dance;
And, by the sadness in his face, appears
To trace the progress of their future years:
Through what strange course of misery, vice, deceit,
Must wildly wander each unpractised cheat!
What shame and grief, what punishment and pain,
Sport of fierce passions, must each child sustain —
Ere they like him approach their latter end,
Without a hope, a comfort, or a friend!

WILLIAM BLAKE (1757–1827)

SONGS OF INNOCENCE

INTRODUCTION

Piping down the valleys wild,
Piping songs of pleasant glee,
On a cloud I saw a child,
And he laughing said to me:

"Pipe a song about a Lamb!"
So I piped with merry cheer.
"Piper, pipe that song again;"
So I piped: he wept to hear.

"Drop thy pipe, thy happy pipe;
Sing thy songs of happy cheer!"
So I sung the same again,
While he wept with joy to hear.

"Piper, sit thee down and write
In a book, that all may read."
So he vanished from my sight;
And I plucked a hollow reed,

And I made a rural pen,
And I stained the water clear,
And I wrote my happy songs
Every child may joy to hear.

ON ANOTHER'S SORROW

Can I see another's woe,
And not be in sorrow too?
Can I see another's grief,
And not seek for kind relief?

Can I see a falling tear,
And not feel my sorrow's share?
Can a father see his child
Weep, nor be with sorrow filled?

Can a mother sit and hear
An infant groan, an infant fear?
No, no! never can it be!
Never, never can it be!

And can He who smiles on all
Hear the wren with sorrows small,
Hear the small bird's grief and care,
Hear the woes that infants bear —

And not sit beside the nest,
Pouring pity in their breast,
And not sit the cradle near,
Weeping tear on infant's tear?

And not sit both night and day,
Wiping all our tears away?
O no! never can it be!
Never, never can it be!

He doth give His joy to all:
He becomes an infant small,
He becomes a man of woe,
He doth feel the sorrow too.

Think not thou canst sigh a sigh,
And thy Maker is not by:
Think not thou canst weep a tear,
And thy Maker is not near.

Oh, He gives to us His joy,
That our grief He may destroy:
Till our grief is fled and gone
He doth sit by us and moan.

SONGS OF EXPERIENCE

THE CLOD AND THE PEBBLE

"Love seeketh not itself to please,
Nor for itself hath any care,
But for another gives its ease,
And builds a heaven in hell's despair."

So sung a little clod of clay,
  Trodden with the cattle's feet,
But a pebble of the brook
  Warbled out these metres meet:

"Love seeketh only Self to please,
  To bind another to its delight,
Joys in another's loss of ease,
  And builds a hell in heaven's despite."

THE SICK ROSE

O Rose, thou art sick!
  The invisible worm,
That flies in the night,
  In the howling storm,

Has found out thy bed
  Of crimson joy,
And his dark secret love
  Does thy life destroy.

THE TIGER

Tiger, tiger, burning bright
In the forests of the night,
What immortal hand or eye
Could frame thy fearful symmetry?

In what distant deeps or skies
Burnt the fire of thine eyes?
On what wings dare he aspire?
What the hand dare seize the fire?

And what shoulder and what art
Could twist the sinews of thy heart?
And, when thy heart began to beat,
What dread hand and what dread feet?

What the hammer? what the chain?
In what furnace was thy brain?
What the anvil? what dread grasp
Dare its deadly terrors clasp?

When the stars threw down their spears,
And watered heaven with their tears,
Did He smile His work to see?
Did He who made the lamb make thee?

Tiger, tiger, burning bright
In the forests of the night,
What immortal hand or eye
Dare frame thy fearful symmetry?

A POISON TREE

I was angry with my friend:
I told my wrath, my wrath did end.
I was angry with my foe:
I told it not, my wrath did grow.

And I watered it in fears
Night and morning with my tears,
And I sunnèd it with smiles
And with soft deceitful wiles.

And it grew both day and night,
Till it bore an apple bright,
And my foe beheld it shine,
And he knew that it was mine, —

And into my garden stole
When the night had veiled the pole;
In the morning, glad, I see
My foe outstretched beneath the tree.

IDEAS OF GOOD AND EVIL

AUGURIES OF INNOCENCE

To see the world in a grain of sand,
  And a heaven in a wild flower;
Hold infinity in the palm of your hand,
  And eternity in an hour.

PROVERBS

A Robin Redbreast in a cage
Puts all heaven in a rage;
A dove-house filled with doves and pigeons
Shudders hell through all its regions.
A dog starved at his master's gate
Predicts the ruin of the state;
A game-cock clipped and armed for fight
Doth the rising sun affright;
A horse misused upon the road
Calls to heaven for human blood.
Every wolf's and lion's howl
Raises from hell a human soul;
Each outcry of the hunted hare
A fibre from the brain does tear;
A skylark wounded on the wing
Doth make a cherub cease to sing.

He who shall hurt the little wren
Shall never be beloved by men;
He who the ox to wrath has moved
Shall never be by woman loved;
He who shall train the horse to war

Shall never pass the polar bar.
The wanton boy that kills the fly
Shall feel the spider's enmity;
He who torments the chafer's sprite
Weaves a bower in endless night.
The caterpillar on the leaf
Repeats to thee thy mother's grief;
The wild deer wandering here and there
Keep the human soul from care;
The lamb misused breeds public strife,
And yet forgives the butcher's knife.
Kill not the moth nor butterfly,
For the last judgment draweth nigh.
The beggar's dog and widow's cat,
Feed them and thou shalt grow fat.
Every tear from every eye
Becomes a babe in eternity;
The bleat, the bark, bellow, and roar,
Are waves that beat on heaven's shore.

The bat that flits at close of eve
Has left the brain that won't believe;
The owl that calls upon the night
Speaks the unbeliever's fright;
The gnat that sings his summer's song
Poison gets from Slander's tongue;
The poison of the snake and newt
Is the sweat of Envy's foot;
The poison of the honey-bee
Is the artist's jealousy;
The strongest poison ever known
Came from Cæsar's laurel crown.

Nought can deform the human race
Like to the armourer's iron brace;
The soldier armed with sword and gun
Palsied strikes the summer's sun.
When gold and gems adorn the plough,
To peaceful arts shall Envy bow.
The beggar's rags fluttering in air
Do to rags the heavens tear;
The prince's robes and beggar's rags
Are toadstools on the miser's bags.

One mite wrung from the labourer's hands
Shall buy and sell the miser's lands,
Or, if protected from on high,
Shall that whole nation sell and buy;
The poor man's farthing is worth more
Than all the gold on Afric's shore.
The whore and gambler, by the state
Licensed, build that nation's fate;
The harlot's cry from street to street
Shall weave Old England's winding-sheet;
The winner's shout, the loser's curse,
Shall dance before dead England's hearse.

He who mocks the infant's faith
Shall be mocked in age and death;
He who shall teach the child to doubt
The rotting grave shall ne'er get out;
He who respects the infant's faith
Triumphs over hell and death.
The babe is more than swaddling-bands
Throughout all these human lands;
Tools were made, and born were hands,
Every farmer understands.

The questioner who sits so sly
Shall never know how to reply;
He who replies to words of doubt
Doth put the light of knowledge out;
A riddle, or the cricket's cry,
Is to doubt a fit reply.
The child's toys and the old man's reasons
Are the fruits of the two seasons.
The emmet's inch and eagle's mile
Make lame philosophy to smile.
A truth that's told with bad intent
Beats all the lies you can invent.
He who doubts from what he sees
Will ne'er believe, do what you please;
If the sun and moon should doubt,
They'd immediately go out.

Every night and every morn
Some to misery are born;
Every morn and every night
Some are born to sweet delight;
Some are born to sweet delight,
Some are born to endless night;
Joy and woe are woven fine,
A clothing for the soul divine;
Under every grief and pine
Runs a joy with silken twine.
It is right it should be so;
Man was made for joy and woe;
And, when this we rightly know,
Safely through the world we go.

We are led to believe a lie
When we see with, not through, the eye,
Which was born in a night to perish in a night
When the soul slept in beams of light.
God appears, and God is light
To those poor souls who dwell in night,
But doth a human form display
To those who dwell in realms of day.

TWO KINDS OF RICHES

Since all the riches of all this world
May be gifts from the devil and earthly kings,

I should suspect that I worshipped the devil
If I thanked God for worldly things.

The countless gold of a merry heart,
The rubies and pearls of a loving eye,
The idle man never can bring to the mart,
Nor the cunning hoard up in his treasury.

THE TWO SONGS

I heard an angel singing,
When the day was springing:
"Mercy, pity, and peace,
Are the world's release."

Thus he sang all day
Over the new-mown hay,
Till the sun went down,
And haycocks looked brown.

I heard a devil curse
Over the heath and the furze:
"Mercy could be no more
If there were nobody poor,
And pity no more could be
If all were happy as ye:
And mutual fear brings peace.
Misery's increase
Are mercy, pity, peace."

At his curse the sun went down,
And the heavens gave a frown.

LOVE'S SECRET

Never seek to tell thy love,
Love that never told shall be;
For the gentle wind does move
Silently, invisibly.

I told my love, I told my love,
I told her all my heart,
Trembling, cold, in ghastly fears.
Ah! she did depart!

Soon after she was gone from me,
A traveller came by,
Silently, invisibly:
He took her with a sigh.

PROPHETIC BOOKS

UNIVERSAL HUMANITY

And as the seed waits eagerly watching for its flower and fruit,
Anxious its little soul looks out into the clear expanse
To see if hungry winds are abroad with their invisible array;
So Man looks out in tree, and herb, and fish, and bird, and beast,
Collecting up the scattered portions of his immortal body
Into the elemental forms of everything that grows.
He tries the sullen North wind, riding on its angry furrows,
The sultry South when the sun rises, and the angry East
When the sun sets, and the clods harden, and the cattle stand
Drooping, and the birds hide in their silent nests.
He stores his thoughts
As in store-houses in his memory. He regulates the forms
Of all beneath and all above, and in the gentle West
Reposes where the sun's heat dwells. He rises to the sun,
And to the planets of the night, and to the stars that gild
The zodiacs, and the stars that sullen stand to North and South,
He touches the remotest pole, and in the centre weeps
That Man should labour and sorrow, and learn and forget, and return
To the dark valley whence he came, and begin his labours anew.
In pain he sighs, in pain he labours in his universe;
Sorrowing in birds over the deep, or howling in the wolf
Over the slain, and moaning in the cattle, and in the winds,
And weeping over Orc and Urizen in clouds and dismal fires,
And in cries of birth and in the groans of death his voice
Is heard throughout the universe. Wherever a grass grows
Or a leaf buds the Eternal Man is seen, is heard, is felt,
And all his sorrows, till he reassumes his ancient bliss.

JOHN SKINNER (1721–1807)

TULLOCHGORUM

Come gie's a sang, Montgomery cried,
And lay your disputes all aside,
What signifies't for folk to chide
For what's been done before them?

Let Whig and Tory all agree!
Whig and Tory! Whig and Tory!
Let Whig and Tory all agree,
To drop their Whig-mig-morum;
Let Whig and Tory all agree,
To spend the night in mirth and glee,
And cheerfu' sing, alang wi' me,
The reel o' Tullochgorum.

O, Tullochgorum's my delight,
It gars [1] us a' in ane unite,
And ony sumph' [2] that keeps up spite,
In conscience I abhor him.
For blythe and cheery we's be a'!
Blythe and cheery! blythe and cheery!
Blythe and cheery we's be a',
And make a happy quorum.
For blythe and cheery we's be a',
As lang as we hae breath to draw,
And dance, till we be like to fa',
The reel of Tullochgorum.

There needs na' be sae great a phrase,
Wi' dringing dull Italian lays,
I wadna gi'e our ain strathspeys [3]
For half a hundred score o' 'em.
They're douff [4] and dowie [5] at the best!
Douff and dowie! douff and dowie!
They're douff and dowie at the best,
Wi' a' their variorum.
They're douff and dowie at the best,
Their allegros and a' the rest,
They cannot please a Scottish taste,
Compar'd wi' Tullochgorum.

Let warldly minds themselves oppress
Wi' fears of want and double cess, [6]
And sullen sots themselves distress
Wi' keeping up decorum.
Shall we sae sour and sulky sit?
Sour and sulky! sour and sulky!
Shall we sae sour and sulky sit,
Like old Philosophorum?
Shall we so sour and sulky sit,
Wi' neither sense, nor mirth, nor wit,
Nor ever rise to shake a fit
To the reel of Tullochgorum?

May choicest blessings still attend
Each honest open-hearted friend,
And calm and quiet be his end,
And a' that's good watch o'er him!
May peace and plenty be his lot!
Peace and plenty! peace and plenty!

[1] makes [2] any surly person [3] lively Scotch dances [4] dreary [5] dull [6] taxes

May peace and plenty be his lot,
And dainties a great store o' 'em;
May peace and plenty be his lot,
Unstain'd by any vicious spot!
And may he never want a groat
That's fond of Tullochgorum.

But for the dirty, yawning fool,
Who wants to be oppression's tool,
May envy gnaw his rotten soul,
And discontent devour him!
May dool [1] and sorrow be his chance!
Dool and sorrow! dool and sorrow!
May dool and sorrow be his chance,
And nane say wae's me for 'im!
May dool and sorrow be his chance,
Wi' a' the ills that come frae France,
Whae'er he be, that winna dance
The reel of Tullochgorum.

WILLIAM JULIUS MICKLE (1735–1788)

THERE'S NAE LUCK ABOUT THE HOUSE [2]

And are ye sure the news is true?
And are ye sure he's weel?
Is this a time to think of wark?
Ye jauds, [3] fling by your wheel.
Is this the time to think of wark.
When Colin's at the door?
Gi'e me my cloak! I'll to the quay
And see him come ashore.

For there's nae luck about the house,
There's nae luck ava; [4]
There's little pleasure in the house,
When our gudeman's awa.'

Rise up and mak' a clean fireside;
Put on the muckle pot;
Gi'e little Kate her cotton gown,
And Jock his Sunday coat:
And mak' their shoon as black as slaes, [5]
Their hose as white as snaw;
It's a' to please my ain gudeman,
For he's been long awa'.

There's twa fat hens upon the bauk, [6]
Been fed this month and mair;
Mak' haste and thraw [7] their necks about,
That Colin weel may fare;

[1] grief [2] *This poem is often wrongly ascribed to Jean Adams.* [3] jades [4] at all [5] sloes [6] cross-beam [7] twist

And mak' the table neat and clean,
Gar [1] ilka thing look braw;
It's a' for love of my gudeman,
For he's been long awa'.

O gi'e me down my bigonet,[2]
My bishop satin gown,
For I maun tell the bailie's wife
That Colin's come to town.
My Sunday's shoon they maun [3] gae on,
My hose o' pearl blue;
'Tis a' to please my ain gudeman,
For he's baith leal and true.

Sae true his words, sae smooth his speech,
His breath's like caller [4] air!
His very foot has music in't,
As he comes up the stair.
And will I see his face again?
And will I hear him speak?
I'm downright dizzy with the thought, —
In troth, I'm like to greet.[5]

The cauld blasts o' the winter wind,
That thrilled through my heart,
They're a' blawn by; I ha'e him safe,
Till death we'll never part:
But what puts parting in my head?
It may be far awa';
The present moment is our ain,
The neist [6] we never saw.

Since Colin's weel, I'm weel content,
I ha'e nae more to crave;
Could I but live to mak' him blest,
I'm blest above the lave:[7]
And will I see his face again?
And will I hear him speak?
I'm downright dizzy wi' the thought, —
In troth, I'm like to greet.

ISOBEL PAGAN (d. 1821)

CA' THE YOWES

Ca' the yowes [8] to the knowes,[9]
Ca' them whare the heather grows,
Ca' them whare the burnie [10] rows,[11]
My bonnie dearie.

As I gaed down the water side,
There I met my shepherd lad,
He rowed [12] me sweetly in his plaid,
And he ca'd me his dearie.

[1] make [2] bonnet [3] must [4] fresh [5] weep [6] next [7] rest [8] yews [9] knolls [10] brook [11] rolls [12] rolled

"Will ye gang down the water side,
And see the waves sae sweetly glide
Beneath the hazels spreading wide,
The moon it shines fu' clearly."

"I was bred up at nae sic school,
My shepherd lad, to play the fool;
And a' the day to sit in dool,
And naebody to see me."

"Ye shall get gowns and ribbons meet,
Cauf-leather shoon [1] upon your feet,
And in my arms ye'se [2] lie and sleep,
And ye shall be my dearie."

"If ye'll but stand to what ye've said,
I'se gang wi' you, my shepherd lad;
And ye may row me in your plaid,
And I shall be your dearie."

"While waters wimple [3] to the sea,
While day blinks in the lift [4] sae hie;
Till clay-cauld death shall blin' my e'e,
Ye aye shall be my dearie."

JANE ELLIOT (1727–1805)

THE FLOWERS OF THE FOREST

I've heard them lilting,[5] at our ewe-milking,
Lasses a-lilting, before the dawn of day;
But now they are moaning, on ilka green loaning;[6]
The Flowers of the Forest are a' wede [7] away.

At bughts [8] in the morning nae blythe lads are scorning;[9]
The lasses are lanely, and dowie,[10] and wae;
Nae daffing,[11] nae gabbing, but sighing and sabbing,
Ilk ane lifts her leglin,[12] and hies her away.

In hairst,[13] at the shearing, nae youths now are jeering,
The bandsters [14] are lyart,[15] and runkled and grey;
At fair or at preaching, nae wooing, nae fleeching [16] —
The Flowers of the Forest are a' wede away.

At e'en, in the gloaming, nae swankies [17] are roaming
'Bout stacks wi' the lasses at bogle [18] to play;
But ilk ane sits eerie, lamenting her dearie —
The Flowers of the Forest are a' wede away.

[1] shoes [2] ye shall [3] ripple [4] air [5] singing [6] meadow path [7] vanished [8] sheep-pens [9] bantering [10] dull [11] jesting [12] pail [13] harvest [14] binders [15] old [16] coaxing [17] young men [18] bugbear

Dool and wae for the order sent our lads to the Border!
The English, for ance, by guile wan the day;
The Flowers of the Forest, that fought aye the foremost,
The prime of our land, lie cauld in the clay.

We'll hear nae more lilting at our ewe-milking,
Women and bairns are heartless and wae;
Sighing and moaning on ilka green loaning,
The Flowers of the Forest are a' wede away.

JOHN MAYNE (1759–1836)

LOGAN BRAES

By Logan's streams that rin sae deep
Fu' aft, wi' glee, I've herded sheep,
I've herded sheep, or gather'd slaes,[1]
Wi' my dear lad, on Logan braes.
But wae's my heart! thae[2] days are gane,
And fu' o' grief I herd[3] alane,
While my dear lad maun face his faes,
Far, far frae me and Logan braes.

Nae mair, at Logan kirk, will he,
Atween the preachings, meet wi' me —
Meet wi' me, or when it's mirk,
Convoy me hame frae Logan kirk.
I weel may sing thae days are gane —
Frae kirk and fair I come alane,
While my dear lad maun face his faes,
Far, far frae me and Logan braes!

At e'en when hope amaist is gane,
I dander[4] dowie[5] and forlane,[6]
Or sit beneath the trysting-tree,
Where first he spak of love to me.
O! cou'd I see thae days again,
My lover skaithless,[7] and my ain;
Rever'd by friends, and far frae faes,
We'd live in bliss on Logan braes.

ADAM SKIRVING (1719–1803)

JOHNNIE COPE

Cope sent a challenge frae Dunbar: —
Charlie, meet me an ye daur,[8]
And I'll learn you the art o' war,
If you'll meet wi' me i' the mornin.

Hey, Johnnie Cope, are ye wauking yet?
Or are your drums a-beating yet?
If ye were wauking, I wad wait
To gang to the coals i' the morning.

[1] sloes [2] those [3] keep company [4] saunter [5] dreary [6] very lonely [7] uninjured [8] dare

When Charlie looked the letter upon,
He drew his sword the scabbard from:
Come follow me, my merry, merry men,
And we'll meet Johnnie Cope in the morning.

Now, Johnnie, be as good's your word,
Come let us try both fire and sword;
And dinna flee away like a frighted bird,
That's chased from its nest in the morning.

When Johnnie Cope he heard of this,
He thought it wadna be amiss,
To ha'e a horse in readiness,
To flee awa' in the morning.

Fy now, Johnnie, get up and rin,
The Highland bagpipes mak' a din;
It is best to sleep in a hale skin,
For 'twill be bluidy in the morning.

When Johnnie Cope to Dunbar came,
They speer'd[1] at him, Where's a' your men?
"The deil confound me gin I ken,
For I left them a' i' the morning."

Now, Johnnie, troth ye are na blate,[2]
To come wi' the news o' your ain defeat,
And leave your men in sic a strait,
Sae early in the morning.

"O! faith," quo' Johnnie, "I got sic flegs[3]
Wi' their claymores[4] and philabegs;[5]
If I face them again, deil break my legs —
So I wish you a' gude morning."

ROBERT FERGUSSON (1750–1774)

THE DAFT DAYS

Now mirk December's dowie[6] face
Glowrs owr the rigs[7] wi' sour grimace,
While, thro' his miminum of space,
The bleer-ey'd sun,
Wi' blinkin light and stealing pace,
His race doth run.

From naked groves nae birdie sings;
To shepherd's pipe nae hillock rings;
The breeze nae od'rous flavour brings
From Borean cave;
And dwyning[8] Nature droops her wings,
Wi' visage grave.

Mankind but scanty pleasure glean
Frae snawy hill or barren plain,
Whan Winter, 'midst his nipping train,
Wi' frozen spear,

[1] inquired [2] bashful [3] such scares [4] swords [5] kilts [6] dreary [7] ridges [8] dwindling

Sends drift owr a' his bleak domain,
And guides[1] the weir.[2]

Auld Reikie! thou'rt the canty[3] hole,
A bield[4] for mony caldrife[5] soul,
Wha snugly at thine ingle[6] loll,
Baith warm and couth;[7]
While round they gar[8] the bicker[9] roll
To weet their mouth.

When merry Yule-day comes, I trow,
You'll scantlins find a hungry mou;
Sma' are our cares, our stamacks fou
O' gusty gear,[10]
And kickshaws, strangers to our view,
Sin' fairn-year.[11]

Ye browster[12] wives! now busk[13] ye bra,[14]
And fling your sorrows far awa';
Then, come and gie's the tither blaw[15]
Of reaming[16] ale,
Mair precious than the Well of Spa,
Our hearts to heal.

Then, tho' at odds wi' a' the warl',
Amang oursells we'll never quarrel;
Tho' Discord gie a canker'd snarl
To spoil our glee,
As lang's there's pith into the barrel
We'll drink and 'gree.

Fiddlers! your pins in temper fix,
And roset[17] weel your fiddlesticks,
But banish vile Italian tricks
From out your quorum,
Nor *fortes* wi' *pianos* mix —
Gie's *Tullochgorum*.

For nought can cheer the heart sae weel
As can a canty Highland reel;
It even vivifies the heel
To skip and dance:
Lifeless is he wha canna feel
Its influence.

Let mirth abound; let social cheer
Invest the dawning of the year;
Let blithesome innocence appear
To crown our joy:
Nor envy, wi' sarcastic sneer,
Our bliss destroy.

And thou, great god of *aqua vitæ!*
Wha sways the empire of this city —
When fou[1] we're sometimes capernoity[2] —
Be thou prepar'd
To hedge us frae that black banditti,
The City Guard.

[1] controls [2] milldam [3] cosy [4] protection [5] freezing [6] fireside [7] comfortable [8] make [9] wooden bowl [10] tasty food [11] long ago [12] brewer [13] attire [14] fine [15] the other draught [16] foaming [17] rosin

From CALLER WATER

Whan father Adie first pat[3] spade in
The bonny yeard of antient Eden
His amry[4] had nae liquor laid in,
To fire his mou',
Nor did he thole[5] his wife's upbraidin'
For being fou.

A caller[6] burn o' siller sheen,
Ran cannily out o'er the green,
And whan our gutcher's[7] drouth had been
To bide right sair,
He loutit[8] down and drank bedeen[9]
A dainty skair.[10]

His bairns a' before the flood
Had langer tack[11] o' flesh and blood,
And on mair pithy shanks they stood
Than Noah's line,
Wha still hae been a feckless brood
Wi' drinking wine.

The fuddlin' Bardies now-a-days
Rin maukin-mad[12] in Bacchus' praise,
And limp and stoiter thro' their lays
Anacreontic,
While each his sea of wine displays
As big's the Pontic.

My muse will no gang far frae hame,
Or scour a' airths[13] to hound for fame;
In troth, the jillet[14] ye might blame
For thinking on't,
Whan eithly[15] she can find the theme
Of *aqua font*.

This is the name that doctors use
Their patients' noddles to confuse;
Wi' simples clad in terms abstruse,
They labour still,
In kittle[16] words to gar[17] you roose[18]
Their want o' skill.

But we'll hae nae sick[19] clitter-clatter,
And briefly to expound the matter,
It shall be ca'd good Caller Water,
Than whilk,[20] I trow,
Few drogs in doctors' shops are better
For me or you.

[1] drunk [2] ill-tempered [3] put [4] cupboard [5] endure [6] fresh [7] grandfather's [8] bent [9] quickly [10] share [11] lease [12] mad as a hare [13] regions [14] huzzy [15] easily [16] ticklish [17] make [18] praise [19] such [20] which

LADY ANNE LINDSAY (1750–1825)

AULD ROBIN GRAY

When the sheep are in the fauld, and the kye at hame,
And a' the warld to rest are gane,
The waes o' my heart fa' in showers frae my e'e,
While my gudeman[1] lies sound by me.

Young Jamie lo'ed me weel, and sought me for his bride;
But saving a croun he had naething else beside;
To make the croun a pund, young Jamie gaid to sea;
And the croun and the pund were baith for me.

He hadna been awa' a week but only twa,
When my father brak his arm, and the cow was stown awa';
My mother she fell sick, — and my Jamie at the sea —
And auld Robin Gray came a-courtin' me.

My father couldna work, and my mother couldna spin;
I toil'd day and night, but their bread I couldna win;
Auld Rob maintain'd them baith, and wi' tears in his e'e
Said, "Jennie, for their sakes, O, marry me!"

My heart it said nay; I look'd for Jamie back;
But the wind it blew high, and the ship it was a wrack;
His ship it was a wrack — Why didna Jamie dee?
Or why do I live to cry, Wae's me!

My father urged me sair: my mother didna speak;
But she look'd in my face till my heart was like to break:
They gi'ed him my hand, tho' my heart was in the sea;
Sae auld Robin Gray he was gudeman to me.

I hadna been a wife a week but only four,
When mournfu' as I sat on the stane at the door,
I saw my Jamie's wraith, — for I couldna think it he,
Till he said, "I'm come hame to marry thee."

O sair, sair did we greet, and muckle did we say;
We took but ae kiss, and we tore ourselves away:
I wish that I were dead, but I'm no like to dee;
And why was I born to say, Wae's me!

[1] husband

I gang like a ghaist, and I carena to spin;
I daurna think on Jamie, for that wad be a sin;
But I'll do my best a gude wife aye to be,
For auld Robin Gray he is kind unto me.

ROBERT BURNS (1759–1796)

SONG, — MARY MORISON

O Mary, at thy window be,
It is the wish'd, the trysted hour!
Those smiles and glances let me see,
That make the miser's treasure poor:
How blythely wad I bide the stoure,[1]
A weary slave frae sun to sun,
Could I the rich reward secure,
The lovely Mary Morison.

Yestreen when to the trembling string
The dance gaed thro' the lighted ha',
To thee my fancy took its wing,
I sat, but neither heard nor saw:
Tho' this was fair, and that was braw,[2]
And yon the toast of a' the town,
I sigh'd, and said amang them a',
"Ye are na Mary Morison."

O Mary, canst thou wreck his peace,
Wha for thy sake wad gladly die?
Or canst thou break that heart of his,
Whase only faut is loving thee?
If love for love thou wilt na gie
At least be pity to me shown:
A thought ungentle canna be
The thought o' Mary Morison.

THE DEATH AND DYING WORDS OF POOR MAILIE,

THE AUTHOR'S ONLY PET YOWE:[3]

AN UNCO[4] MOURNFU' TALE

As Mailie an' her lambs thegither
Was ae day nibblin on the tether,
Upon her cloot[5] she coost a hitch,[6]
An' owre[7] she warsl'd[8] in the ditch:
There, groanin, dyin, she did lie,
When Hughoc he cam doytin[9] by.

Wi' glowrin een[10] and lifted han's,
Poor Hughoc like a statue stan's;

[1] endure the struggle [2] handsome [3] ewe [4] very [5] hoof [6] cast a loop [7] over [8] tumbled [9] strolling [10] eyes

He saw her days were near-hand ended,
But, wae's my heart! he could na mend it.
He gapèd wide but naething spak —
At length poor Mailie silence brak.

"O thou, whase lamentable face
Appears to mourn my woefu' case!
My dying words attentive hear,
An' bear them to my Master dear.

"Tell him, if e'er again he keep
As muckle gear [1] as buy a sheep —
Oh, bid him never tie them mair [2]
Wi' wicked strings o' hemp or hair!

"But ca' [3] them out to park or hill,
An' let them wander at their will:
So may his flock increase and grow
To scores o' lambs and packs o' woo'!

"Tell him, he was a Master kin',[4]
An' aye was guid to me an' mine;
An' now my dying charge I gie him —
My helpless lambs, I trust them wi' him.

"O bid him save their harmless lives
Frae dogs, an' tods,[5] an' butchers' knives!
But gie them guid cow-milk their fill,
Till they be fit to fend [6] themsel;
An' tent [7] them duly, e'en an' morn,
Wi' taets [8] o' hay, an' ripps [9] o' corn.

"An' may they never learn the gaets [10]
Of ither vile, wanrestfu' [11] pets,
To slink through slaps,[12] an' reave [13] an' steal
At stacks o' peas, or stocks o' kail.
So may they, like their great forbears,[14]
For monie a year come thro' the shears:
So wives will gie them bits o' bread,
An' bairns greet [15] for them when they're dead.

"My poor toop-lamb,[16] my son an' heir,
Oh, bid him breed him up wi' care;
An' if he live to be a beast,
To pit some havins [17] in his breast!

"An' warn him, what I winna name,
To stay content wi' yowes at hame;
An' no to rin [18] an' wear his cloots,
Like ither menseless,[19] graceless brutes.

"And niest,[20] my yowie,[21] silly thing,
Gude [22] keep thee frae a tether string!

[1] much wealth [2] more [3] drive [4] kind [5] foxes [6] provide for [7] tend [8] trusses [9] handfuls [10] ways [11] restless [12] gaps [13] rob [14] ancestors [15] weep [16] male lamb [17] manners [18] run [19] silly [20] next [21] little ewe [22] God

Oh, may thou ne'er forgather up [1]
Wi' ony blastit, moorland toop,[2]
But ay keep mind to moop [3] and mell [4]
Wi' sheep o' credit like thysel!

"And now, my bairns, wi' my last breath
I lea'e my blessin wi' you baith;[5]
And when you think upo' your mither,
Mind to be kin' to ane anither.

"Now honest Hughoc, dinna fail
To tell my master a' my tale;
An' bid him burn this cursed tether,
An' for thy pains thou'se get my blether."[6]

This said, poor Mailie turn'd her head,
An' clos'd her een amang the dead!

SONG, — MY NANIE, O

Behind yon hills where Lugar flows,
'Mang moors an' mosses many, O,
The wintry sun the day has clos'd,
An' I'll awa to Nanie, O.

The westlin wind blaws loud an' shill:
The night's baith [5] mirk an' rainy, O;
But I'll get my plaid an' out I'll steal,
An' owre [7] the hill to Nanie, O.

My Nanie's charming, sweet, an' young;
Nae artfu' wiles to win ye, O:
May ill befa' the flattering tongue
That wad beguile my Nanie, O.

Her face is fair, her heart is true,
As spotless as she's bonie, O:
The op'ning gowan,[8] wat wi' dew,
Nae purer is than Nanie, O.

A country lad is my degree,
An' few there be that ken [9] me, O;
But what care I how few they be?
I'm welcome aye to Nanie, O.

My riches a's [10] my penny-fee,
An' I maun guide it cannie, O;
But warl's gear [11] ne'er troubles me,
My thoughts are a' my Nanie, O.

Our auld guidman delights to view
His sheep an' kye [12] thrive bonie, O;
But I'm as blythe that hauds [13] his pleugh,
And has nae care but Nanie, O.

[1] associate [2] ram [3] nibble [4] mix [5] both [6] bladder [7] over [8] daisy [9] know [10] all is [11] world's goods [12] cows [13] holds

Come weel, come woe, I care na by,[1]
I'll tak what Heav'n will sen' me, O;
Nae ither care in life hae I,
But live, an' love my Nanie, O.

SONG, — GREEN GROW THE RASHES

CHORUS. — Green grow the rashes, O!
Green grow the rashes, O!
The sweetest hours that e'er I spend
Are spent amang the lasses, O.

There's nought but care on ev'ry han',
In every hour that passes, O:
What signifies the life o' man,
An 'twere na for the lasses, O?

The war'ly[2] race may riches chase,
An' riches still may fly them, O;
An' tho' at last they catch them fast,
Their hearts can ne'er enjoy them, O

But gie me a cannie[3] hour at e'en,
My arms about my dearie, O;
An' war'ly cares, an' war'ly men,
May a' gae tapsalteerie,[4] O.

For you sae douce,[5] ye sneer at this;
Ye're nought but senseless asses, O:
The wisest man the warl' e'er saw,
He dearly lov'd the lasses, O.

Auld Nature swears, the lovely dears
Her noblest work she classes, O:
Her prentice han' she try'd on man,
An' then she made the lasses, O.

ADDRESS TO THE DEIL

O Prince! O Chief of many thronèd pow'rs!
That led th' embattled seraphim to war. — MILTON.

O thou! whatever title suit thee, —
Auld Hornie, Satan, Nick, or Clootie!
Wha in yon cavern, grim an' sootie,
Clos'd under hatches,
Spairges[6] about the brunstane cootie[7]
To scaud[8] poor wretches!

Hear me, auld Hangie, for a wee,
An' let poor damnèd bodies be;
I'm sure sma' pleasure it can gie,
E'en to a deil,
To skelp[9] an' scaud poor dogs like me,
An' hear us squeel!

[1] not for that [2] worldly [3] quiet [4] topsy-turvy [5] solemn [6] splashes [7] brimstone tub [8] scald [9] slap

Great is thy pow'r, an' great thy fame;
Far ken'd[1] an' noted is thy name;
An' tho' yon lowin heugh's[2] thy hame,[3]
Thou travels far;
An' faith! thou's neither lag[4] nor lame,
Nor blate[5] nor scaur.[6]

Whyles,[7] rangin like a roarin lion,
For prey a' holes an' corners tryin;
Whyles, on the strong-wing'd tempest flyin,
Tirlin'[8] the kirks;[9]
Whyles, in the human bosom pryin,
Unseen thou lurks.

I've heard my rev'rend grannie say,
In lanely[10] glens ye like to stray;
Or whare auld ruin'd castles gray
Nod to the moon,
Ye fright the nightly wand'rer's way
Wi' eldritch[11] croon.

When twilight did my grannie summon
To say her pray'rs, douce[12] honest woman!
Aft yont[13] the dike she's heard you bummin,
Wi' eerie drone;
Or, rustlin, thro' the boortrees[14] comin,
Wi' heavy groan.

Ae[15] dreary, windy, winter night,
The stars shot down wi' sklentin[16] light,
Wi' you mysel I gat a fright
Ayont[17] the lough;[18]
Ye like a rash-buss[19] stood in sight
Wi' waving sough.

The cudgel in my nieve[20] did shake,
Each bristl'd hair stood like a stake,
When wi' an eldritch,[11] stoor[21] "Quaick, quaick,"
Amang the springs,
Awa ye squatter'd like a drake,
On whistlin wings.

Let warlocks[22] grim an' wither'd hags
Tell how wi' you on ragweed nags
They skim the muirs an' dizzy crags
Wi' wicked speed;
And in kirk-yards[23] renew their leagues,
Owre howket[24] dead.

Thence, countra wives wi' toil an' pain
May plunge an' plunge the kirn[25] in vain;

[1] known [2] flaming ravine [3] home [4] sluggish [5] shy [6] timid [7] sometimes [8] unroofing [9] churches [10] lonely [11] unearthly [12] grave [13] often beyond [14] elders [15] one [16] slanting [17] beyond [18] lake [19] rush-bush [20] fist [21] harsh [22] wizards [23] church-yards [24] dug up [25] churn

For oh! the yellow treasure's taen
By witchin skill;
An' dawtet,[1] twal-pint hawkie's[2] gaen
As yell's[3] the bill.[4]

Thence, mystic knots mak great abuse,
On young guidmen, fond, keen, an' crouse;[5]
When the best wark-lume[6] i' the house,
By cantrip[7] wit,
Is instant made no worth a louse,
Just at the bit.

When thowes[8] dissolve the snawy hoord,[9]
An' float the jinglin icy-boord,
Then water-kelpies[10] haunt the foord
By your direction,
An' nighted trav'lers are allur'd
To their destruction.

And aft[11] your moss-traversing spunkies[12]
Decoy the wight that late and drunk is:
The bleezin,[13] curst, mischievous monkeys
Delude his eyes,
Till in some miry slough he sunk is,
Ne'er mair to rise.

When masons' mystic word and grip
In storms an' tempests raise you up,
Some cock or cat your rage maun stop,
Or, strange to tell,
The youngest brither[14] ye wad whip
Aff[15] straught to hell!

Lang syne, in Eden's bonie yard,
When youthfu' lovers first were pair'd,
And all the soul of love they shar'd,
The raptur'd hour,
Sweet on the fragrant flow'ry swaird,[16]
In shady bow'r;

Then you, ye auld sneck-drawin[17] dog!
Ye cam to Paradise incog,
And play'd on man a cursed brogue,[18]
(Black be your fa'!)
And gied the infant warld a shog,[19]
Maist[20] ruin'd a'.

D'ye mind that day, when in a bizz,[21]
Wi' reeket[22] duds and reestet gizz,[23]
Ye did present your smoutie phiz
Mang better folk,
An' sklented[24] on the man of Uz
Your spitefu' joke?

[1] petted [2] twelve-pint cow [3] dry as [4] bull [5] bold [6] work-loom [7] mischievous [8] thaws [9] snowy hoard [10] water-spirits [11] often [12] will-o'-the-wisps [13] blazing [14] brother [15] off [16] sward [17] latch-lifting [18] trick [19] shock [20] almost [21] flurry [22] smoked [23] singed face [24] directed

An' how ye gat him i' your thrall,
An' brak him out o' house and hal',
While scabs and blotches did him gall,
Wi' bitter claw,
An' lows'd[1] his ill-tongued, wicked scaul,[2]
Was warst ava?[3]

But a' your doings to rehearse,
Your wily snares an' fechtin fierce,
Sin' that day Michael did you pierce,
Down to this time,
Wad ding[4] a Lallan tongue, or Erse,
In prose or rhyme.

An' now, auld Cloots, I ken ye're thinkin,
A certain Bardie's rantin, drinkin,
Some luckless hour will send him linkin,[5]
To your black pit;
But faith! he'll turn a corner jinkin,[6]
An' cheat you yet.

But fare you weel, auld Nickie-ben!
O wad ye tak a thought an' men'!
Ye aiblins[7] might — I dinna ken —
Still hae a stake:
I'm wae[8] to think upo' yon den,
Ev'n for your sake!

From LINES TO JOHN LAPRAIK

I am nae Poet, in a sense,
But just a Rhymer like by chance,
An' hae to learning nae pretence;
Yet what the matter?
Whene'er my Muse does on me glance,
I jingle at her.

Your critic-folk may cock their nose,
And say, "How can you e'er propose,
You wha ken hardly verse frae prose,
To mak a sang?"
But, by your leave, my learned foes,
Ye're maybe wrang.

What's a' your jargon o' your schools,
Your Latin names for horns an' stools?
If honest nature made you fools,
What sairs[9] your grammars?
Ye'd better taen up spades and shools,
Or knappin-hammers.[10]

A set o' dull, conceited hashes[11]
Confuse their brains in college classes!

[1] loosed [2] scold [3] worst of all [4] baffle [5] tripping [6] darting [7] possibly [8] sad [9] serves [10] stone breakers [11] fools

They gang in stirks[1] and come out asses,
Plain truth to speak;
An' syne[2] they think to climb Parnassus
By dint o' Greek!

Gie me ae[3] spark o' Nature's fire,
That's a' the learnin I desire;
Then, tho' I drudge thro' dub[4] an' mire
At pleugh or cart,
My Muse, though hamely in attire,
May touch the heart.

THE HOLY FAIR

Upon a simmer[5] Sunday morn,
When Nature's face is fair,
I walkèd forth to view the corn
An' snuff the caller[6] air.
The risin' sun owre Galston muirs
Wi' glorious light was glintin,
The hares were hirplin[7] down the furrs,[8]
The lav'rocks[9] they were chantin
Fu' sweet that day.

As lightsomely I glowr'd[10] abroad
To see a scene sae gay,
Three hizzies,[11] early at the road,
Cam skelpin[12] up the way.
Twa had manteeles o' dolefu' black,
But ane wi' lyart[13] linin;
The third, that gaed a wee a-back,
Was in the fashion shinin
Fu' gay that day.

The twa appear'd like sisters twin
In feature, form, an' claes;[14]
Their visage wither'd, lang an' thin,
An' sour as ony slaes.[15]
The third cam up, hap-step-an'-lowp,[16]
As light as ony lambie,
An' wi' a churchie[17] low did stoop,
As soon as e'er she saw me,
Fu' kind that day.

Wi' bonnet aff, quoth I, "Sweet lass,
I think ye seem to ken me;
I'm sure I've seen that bonie face,
But yet I canna name ye."
Quo' she, an' laughin as she spak,
An' taks me by the han's,
"Ye, for my sake, hae gien the feck[18]
Of a' the ten comman's
A screed[19] some day.

[1] steers [2] then [3] one [4] puddle [5] summer [6] fresh [7] limping [8] furrows [9] larks [10] stared [11] women [12] clattering [13] grey [14] clothes [15] sloes [16] hop step and leap [17] curtsy [18] substance [19] rent

"My name is Fun — your cronie dear,
The nearest friend ye hae;
An' this is Superstition here,
An' that's Hypocrisy.
I'm gaun to Mauchline Holy Fair,
To spend an hour in daffin:[1]
Gin[2] ye'll go there, yon runkl'd[3] pair,
We will get famous laughin
At them this day."

Quoth I, "With a' my heart, I'll do't:
I'll get my Sunday's sark[4] on,
An' meet you on the holy spot;
Faith, we'se hae fine remarkin!"
Then I gaed hame at crowdie-time,[5]
An' soon I made me ready;
For roads were clad frae side to side
Wi' mony a wearie body
In droves that day.

Here farmers gash[6] in ridin graith[7]
Gaed hoddin[8] by their cotters,[9]
There swankies[10] young in braw[11] braid-claith
Are springin owre the gutters.
The lasses, skelpin[12] barefit, thrang,
In silks an' scarlets glitter,
Wi' sweet-milk cheese in mony a whang,[13]
An' farls[14] bak'd wi' butter,
Fu' crump[15] that day.

When by the plate we set our nose,
Weel heapèd up wi' ha'pence,
A greedy glowr Black Bonnet throws,
An' we maun draw our tippence.
Then in we go to see the show:
On ev'ry side they're gath'rin,
Some carryin dails,[16] some chairs an' stools,
An' some are busy bleth'rin[17]
Right loud that day.

* * * * * * * *

Here some are thinkin on their sins,
An' some upo' their claes;
Ane curses feet that fyl'd[18] his shins,
Anither sighs and prays:
On this hand sits a chosen swatch,[19]
Wi' screw'd-up grace-proud faces;
On that a set o' chaps at watch,
Thrang winkin on the lasses
To chairs that day.

O happy is that man and blest!
(Nae wonder that it pride him!)

[1] romping [2] if [3] wrinkled [4] shirt [5] porridge time [6] shrewd [7] attire [8] jogging [9] cottagers [10] strapping fellows [11] fine [12] scampering [13] thick slice [14] coarse cakes [15] crisp [16] boards [17] chattering [18] soiled [19] sample

Whase ain dear lass that he likes best,
  Comes clinkin doun beside him!
Wi' arm repos'd on the chair back,
  He sweetly does compose him;
Which by degrees slips round her neck,
  An's loof [1] upon her bosom,
      Unken'd that day.

Now a' the congregation o'er
  Is silent expectation;
For Moodie speels [2] the holy door,
  Wi' tidings o' damnation.
Should Hornie, as in ancient days,
  'Mang sons o' God present him,
The vera sight o' Moodie's face
  To's ain het [3] hame had sent him
      Wi' fright that day.

Hear how he clears the points o' faith
  Wi' rattlin an' wi' thumpin!
Now meekly calm, now wild in wrath
  He's stampin an' he's jumpin!
His lengthen'd chin, his turn'd-up snout,
  His eldritch [4] squeal and gestures,
Oh, how they fire the heart devout,
  Like cantharidian plaisters,
      On sic [5] a day!

But hark! the tent has chang'd its voice:
  There's peace and rest nae langer;
For a' the real judges rise,
  They canna sit for anger.
Smith opens out his cauld harangues,
  On practice and on morals;
An' aff the godly pour in thrangs,
  To gie the jars an' barrels
      A lift that day.

What signifies his barren shine
  Of moral pow'rs and reason?
His English style an' gesture fine
  Are a' clean out o' season.
Like Socrates or Antonine
  Or some auld pagan heathen,
The *moral man* he does define,
  But ne'er a word o' *faith* in
      That 's richt [6] that day.

In guid time comes an antidote
  Against sic poison'd nostrum;
For Peebles, frae the water-fit, [7]
  Ascends the holy rostrum:
See, up he's got the word o' God
  An' meek an' mim [8] has view'd it,

[1] hand [2] climbs [3] hot [4] unearthly [5] such [6] right [7] river's mouth [8] prim

While Common Sense has ta'en the road,
  An's aff, an' up the Cowgate
      Fast, fast that day.

Wee Miller niest [1] the Guard relieves,
  An' Orthodoxy raibles, [2]
Tho' in his heart he weel believes
  An' thinks it auld wives' fables:
But faith! the birkie [3] wants a Manse,
  So cannilie [4] he hums them;
Altho' his carnal wit an' sense
  Like hafflins-wise [5] o'ercomes him
      At times that day.

Now butt [6] an' ben [7] the change-house [8] fills
  Wi' yill-caup [9] commentators:
Here's cryin out for bakes [10] an gills,
  An' there the pint-stowp [11] clatters;
While thick an' thrang, an' loud an' lang,
  Wi' logic an' wi' Scripture,
They raise a din, that in the end
  Is like to breed a rupture
      O' wrath that day.

Leeze me [12] on Drink! it gies us mair
  Than either school or college:
It ken'les wit, it waukens lair, [13]
  It pangs [14] us fou [15] o' knowledge.
Be't whisky-gill or penny-wheep, [16]
  Or ony stronger potion,
It never fails, on drinkin deep,
  To kittle [17] up our notion
      By night or day.

The lads an' lasses, blythely bent
  To mind baith saul an' body,
Sit round the table weel content,
  An' steer about the toddy.
On this ane's dress an' that ane's leuk
  They're makin observations;
While some are cozie i' the neuk,
  An' formin assignations
      To meet some day.

But now the Lord's ain trumpet touts,
  Till a' the hills are rairin, [18]
An' echoes back return the shouts —
  Black Russell is na sparin.
His piercing words, like highlan' swords,
  Divide the joints an' marrow;
His talk o' hell, whare devils dwell,
  Our vera "sauls does harrow"
      Wi' fright that day.

[1] next [2] rattles off [3] smart young fellow [4] cunningly [5] partly [6] without [7] within [8] tavern [9] ale-mug [10] biscuits [11] pint-cup [12] my blessing [13] learning [14] crams [15] full [16] small ale [17] tickle [18] roaring

A vast, unbottom'd, boundless pit,
Fill'd fou o' lowin brunstane,[1]
Whase ragin flame, an' scorchin heat
Wad melt the hardest whun-stane![2]
The half-asleep start up wi' fear
An' think they hear it roarin,
When presently it does appear
'Twas but some neibor snorin,
Asleep that day.

'Twad be owre lang a tale, to tell
How mony stories past,
An' how they crouded to the yill,[3]
When they were a' dismist:
How drink gaed round in cogs[4] and caups[5]
Amang the furms[6] an' benches:
An' cheese and bread frae women's laps
Was dealt about in lunches
An' dauds[7] that day.

In comes a gaucie,[8] gash[9] guidwife
An' sits down by the fire.
Syne[10] draws her kebbuck[11] an' her knife;
The lasses they are shyer:
The auld guidmen about the grace
Frae side to side they bother,
Till some ane by his bonnet lays,
And gi'es them't like a tether
Fu' lang that day.

Waesucks![12] for him that gets nae lass,
Or lasses that hae naething!
Sma' need has he to say a grace,
Or melvie[13] his braw claithing!
O wives, be mindfu' ance[14] yoursel
How bonie lads ye wanted,
An' dinna for a kebbuck-heel[15]
Let lasses be affronted
On sic a day!

Now Clinkumbell, wi' rattlin tow,[16]
Begins to jow[17] an' croon;
Some swagger hame the best they dow,[18]
Some wait the afternoon.
At slaps[19] the billies[20] halt a blink,
Till lasses strip their shoon:
Wi' faith an' hope, an' love an' drink,
They're a' in famous tune
For crack[21] that day.

How monie hearts this day converts
O' sinners and o' lasses!
Their hearts o' stane,[1] gin night, are gane
As saft as ony flesh is.
There's some are fou o' love divine,
There's some are fou o' brandy;
An' monie jobs that day begin,
May end in houghmagandie[2]
Some ither day.

[1] flaming brimstone [2] mill-stone [3] ale [4] wooden bowls [5] small bowls [6] forms [7] hunks [8] jolly [9] shrewd [10] then [11] cheese [12] alas [13] soil [14] once [15] last piece of a cheese [16] rope [17] swing [18] can [19] gaps [20] young fellows [21] talk

TO A MOUSE

ON TURNING UP HER NEST WITH THE PLOUGH, NOVEMBER, 1785

Wee, sleekit,[3] cowrin, tim'rous beastie,
Oh, what a panic's in thy breastie!
Thou need na start awa sae hasty
Wi' bickerin[4] brattle![5]
I wad be laith[6] to rin an' chase thee
Wi' murd'rin pattle![7]

I'm truly sorry man's dominion
Has broken nature's social union,
An' justifies that ill opinion
Which makes thee startle
At me, thy poor earth-born companion,
An' fellow-mortal!

I doubt na, whyles,[8] but thou may thieve:
What then? poor beastie, thou maun live!
A daimen[9] icker[10] in a thrave[11]
'S a sma' request;
I'll get a blessin wi' the lave,[12]
An' never miss 't!

Thy wee bit housie, too, in ruin!
Its silly wa's the win's are strewin
An' naething, now, to big[13] a new ane,
O' foggage[14] green!
An' bleak December's winds ensuin
Baith snell[15] an' keen!

Thou saw the fields laid bare and waste,
An' weary winter comin fast,
An' cozie here beneath the blast
Thou thought to dwell,
Till crash! the cruel coulter past
Out thro' thy cell.

That wee bit heap o' leaves an' stibble
Has cost thee mony a weary nibble!
Now thou's turn'd out for a' thy trouble,
But[16] house or hald,
To thole[17] the winter's sleety dribble
An' cranreuch[18] cauld!

[1] stone [2] disgrace [3] sleek [4] hurrying [5] scamper [6] loth [7] paddle [8] sometimes [9] occasional [10] ear of grain [11] twenty-four sheaves [12] rest [13] build [14] rank grass [15] piercing [16] without [17] endure [18] hoar-frost

But, Mousie, thou art no thy lane[1]
In proving foresight may be vain:
The best laid schemes o' mice an' men
Gang aft a-gley,[2]
An' lea'e us nought but grief an' pain
For promis'd joy.

Still thou art blest, compar'd wi' me!
The present only toucheth thee:
But, och! I backward cast my ee
On prospects drear!
An' forward, tho' I canna see,
I guess an' fear!

THE COTTER'S SATURDAY NIGHT

INSCRIBED TO ROBERT AIKEN, ESQ.

Let not Ambition mock their useful toil,
Their homely joys and destiny obscure;
Nor Grandeur hear with a disdainful smile,
The short and simple annals of the poor. — GRAY.

My lov'd, my honour'd, much respected friend!
No mercenary bard his homage pays;
With honest pride, I scorn each selfish end:
My dearest meed a friend's esteem and praise.
To you I sing, in simple Scottish lays,
The lowly train in life's sequester'd scene;
The native feelings strong, the guileless ways;
What Aiken in a cottage would have been;
Ah! tho' his worth unknown, far happier there, I ween!

November chill blaws loud wi' angry sugh,[3]
The short'ning winter day is near a close;
The miry beasts retreating frae the pleugh,
The black'ning trains o' craws to their repose;
The toil-worn Cotter frae his labour goes, —
This night his weekly moil is at an end, —
Collects his spades, his mattocks and his hoes,
Hoping the morn in ease and rest to spend,
And weary, o'er the moor, his course does hameward bend.

At length his lonely cot appears in view,
Beneath the shelter of an agèd tree;
Th' expectant wee-things, toddlin, stacher[4] through
To meet their dad, wi' flichterin[5] noise an' glee.
His wee bit ingle,[6] blinkin bonilie,
His clean hearth-stane, his thrifty wifie's smile,
The lisping infant prattling on his knee,
Does a' his weary kiaugh[7] and care beguile,
An' makes him quite forget his labour an' his toil.

[1] lone [2] amiss [3] sound [4] stagger [5] fluttering [6] fire-place [7] anxiety

Belyve,[1] the elder bairns come drappin in,
At service out amang the farmers roun';
Some ca[2] the pleugh, some herd, some tentie[3] rin
A cannie errand to a neibor toun:
Their eldest hope, their Jenny, woman-grown,
In youthfu' bloom, love sparkling in her ee,
Comes hame, perhaps to shew a braw[4] new gown,
Or deposite her sair-won[5] penny-fee,
To help her parents dear, if they in hardship be.

With joy unfeign'd brothers and sisters meet,
An' each for other's weelfare kindly spiers:[6]
The social hours, swift-wing'd, unnotic'd fleet;
Each tells the uncos[7] that he sees or hears.
The parents, partial, eye their hopeful years;
Anticipation forward points the view;
The mother, wi' her needle an' her sheers,
Gars[8] auld claes look amaist as weel's the new;
The father mixes a' wi' admonition due.

Their master's an' their mistress's command
The younkers a' are warnèd to obey;
An' mind their labours wi' an eydent[9] hand,
An' ne'er tho' out o' sight, to jauk or play:
"An' O! be sure to fear the Lord alway,
An' mind your duty, duly, morn an' night!
Lest in temptation's path ye gang astray,
Implore His counsel and assisting might:
They never sought in vain that sought the Lord aright!"

But hark! a rap comes gently to the door.
Jenny, wha kens the meaning o' the same,
Tells how a neibor lad cam o'er the moor,
To do some errands, and convoy her hame.
The wily mother sees the conscious flame
Sparkle in Jenny's ee, and flush her cheek;
Wi' heart-struck, anxious care, inquires his name,
While Jenny hafflins[10] is afraid to speak;
Weel pleas'd the mother hears it's nae wild worthless rake.

Wi' kindly welcome Jenny brings him ben,[11]
A strappin youth; he takes the mother's eye;
Blythe Jenny sees the visit's no ill taen;
The father cracks of horses, pleughs, and kye.[12]

[1] presently [2] drive [3] careful [4] fine [5] hard-won [6] asks [7] odds and ends [8] makes [9] diligent [10] partly [11] within [12] cows

The youngster's artless heart o'erflows wi' joy,
But, blate [1] and laithfu',[2] scarce can weel behave;
The mother wi' a woman's wiles can spy
What maks the youth sae bashfu' an' sae grave,
Weel-pleas'd to think her bairn's respected like the lave.[3]

O happy love! where love like this is found!
O heart-felt raptures! bliss beyond compare!
I've pacèd much this weary, mortal round,
And sage experience bids me this declare —
"If Heaven a draught of heavenly pleasure spare,
One cordial in this melancholy vale,
'Tis when a youthful, loving, modest pair,
In other's arms breathe out the tender tale,
Beneath the milk-white thorn that scents the ev'ning gale."

Is there, in human form, that bears a heart,
A wretch! a villain! lost to love and truth!
That can with studied, sly, ensnaring art
Betray sweet Jenny's unsuspecting youth?
Curse on his perjur'd arts! dissembling smooth!
Are honour, virtue, conscience, all exil'd?
Is there no pity, no relenting ruth,
Points to the parents fondling o'er their child,
Then paints the ruin'd maid, and their distraction wild?

But now the supper crowns their simple board,
The halesome parritch,[4] chief of Scotia's food;
The sowpe [5] their only hawkie [6] does afford,
That yont [7] the hallan [8] snugly chows her cud.
The dame brings forth, in complimental mood,
To grace the lad, her weel-hain'd [9] kebbuck fell,[10]
An' aft [11] he's prest, an' aft he ca's it guid;
The frugal wifie, garrulous, will tell,
How 'twas a towmond [12] auld, sin' lint [13] was i' the bell.

The cheerfu' supper done, wi' serious face,
They round the ingle form a circle wide;
The sire turns o'er with patriarchal grace
The big ha'-bible,[14] ance his father's pride;
His bonnet rev'rently is laid aside,
His lyart [15] haffets [16] wearing thin and bare;
Those strains that once did sweet in Zion glide,

[1] shy [2] bashful [3] rest [4] porridge [5] milk [6] cow [7] beyond [8] partition [9] well-saved [10] strong cheese [11] often [12] twelve-month [13] since flax [14] hall Bible [15] gray [16] locks

He wales [1] a portion with judicious care;
And, "Let us worship God," he says with solemn air.

They chant their artless notes in simple guise;
They tune their hearts, by far the noblest aim:
Perhaps *Dundee's* wild-warbling measures rise,
Or plaintive *Martyrs*, worthy of the name,
Or noble *Elgin* beets [2] the heaven-ward flame,
The sweetest far of Scotia's holy lays.
Compar'd with these, Italian trills are tame;
The tickl'd ear no heart-felt raptures raise;
Nae unison hae they with our Creator's praise.

The priest-like father reads the sacred page, —
How Abram was the friend of God on high;
Or Moses bade eternal warfare wage
With Amalek's ungracious progeny;
Or how the royal bard did groaning lie
Beneath the stroke of heaven's avenging ire;
Or Job's pathetic plaint, and wailing cry;
Or rapt Isaiah's wild, seraphic fire;
Or other holy seers that tune the sacred lyre.

Perhaps the Christian volume is the theme, —
How guiltless blood for guilty man was shed;
How He, who bore in heav'n the second name,
Had not on earth whereon to lay His head:
How His first followers and servants sped;
The precepts sage they wrote to many a land
How he, who lone in Patmos banishèd,
Saw in the sun a mighty angel stand,
And heard great Bab'lon's doom pronounced by Heav'n's command.

Then kneeling down to Heaven's Eternal King,
The saint, the father, and the husband prays:
Hope "springs exulting on triumphant wing,"
That thus they all shall meet in future days:
There ever bask in uncreated rays,
No more to sigh or shed the bitter tear,
Together hymning their Creator's praise,
In such society, yet still more dear,
While circling Time moves round in an eternal sphere.

Compar'd with this, how poor Religion's pride
In all the pomp of method and of art,
When men display to congregations wide
Devotion's ev'ry grace except the heart!
The Pow'r, incens'd, the pageant will desert,
The pompous strain, the sacerdotal stole;
But haply in some cottage far apart

[1] chooses [2] incites, kindles

May hear, well pleased, the language of the soul,
And in His book of life the inmates poor enrol.

Then homeward all take off their sev'ral way;
The youngling cottagers retire to rest;
The parent-pair their secret homage pay,
And proffer up to Heav'n the warm request,
That He, who stills the raven's clam'rous nest
And decks the lily fair in flow'ry pride,
Would, in the way His wisdom sees the best,
For them and for their little ones provide;
But chiefly, in their hearts with grace divine preside.

From scenes like these old Scotia's grandeur springs,
That makes her lov'd at home, rever'd abroad:
Princes and lords are but the breath of kings,
"An honest man's the noblest work of God":
And certes, in fair Virtue's heavenly road,
The cottage leaves the palace far behind:
What is a lordling's pomp? a cumbrous load,
Disguising oft the wretch of human kind,
Studied in arts of hell, in wickedness refin'd!

O Scotia! my dear, my native soil!
For whom my warmest wish to Heaven is sent!
Long may thy hardy sons of rustic toil
Be blest with health, and peace, and sweet content!
And, oh! may Heaven their simple lives prevent
From luxury's contagion, weak and vile!
Then, howe'er crowns and coronets be rent,
A virtuous populace may rise the while,
And stand a wall of fire around their much-lov'd isle.

O Thou! who pour'd the patriotic tide
That stream'd thro' Wallace's undaunted heart,
Who dar'd to nobly stem tyrannic pride,
Or nobly die, the second glorious part, —
(The patriot's God peculiarly thou art,
His friend, inspirer, guardian, and reward!)
O never, never Scotia's realm desert,
But still the patriot, and the patriot-bard,
In bright succession raise, her ornament and guard!

ADDRESS TO THE UNCO GUID, OR THE RIGIDLY RIGHTEOUS

O ye wha are sae guid yoursel,
Sae pious and sae holy,
Ye've nought to do but mark and tell
Your neibour's fauts and folly!
Whase life is like a weel-gaun mill,
Supply'd wi' store o' water,
The heapet happer's ebbing still,
And still the clap plays clatter, —

Hear me, ye venerable core,[1]
As counsel for poor mortals,
That frequent pass douce [2] Wisdom's door
For glaiket [3] Folly's portals;
I for their thoughtless, careless sakes
Would here propone defences —
Their donsie [4] tricks, their black mistakes,
Their failings and mischances.

Ye see your state wi' theirs compar'd,
And shudder at the niffer; [5]
But cast a moment's fair regard,
What maks the mighty differ? [6]
Discount what scant occasion gave,
That purity ye pride in,
And (what's aft [7] mair than a' the lave [8])
Your better art o' hidin.

Think, when your castigated pulse
Gies now and then a wallop,
What ragings must his veins convulse
That still eternal gallop:
Wi' wind and tide fair i' your tail,
Right on ye scud your sea-way;
But in the teeth o' baith [9] to sail,
It maks an unco [10] leeway.

See Social Life and Glee sit down,
All joyous and unthinking,
Till, quite transmugrify'd,[11] they're grown
Debauchery and Drinking:
O would they stay to calculate
Th' eternal consequences;
Or — your more dreaded hell to state —
Damnation of expenses!

Ye high, exalted, virtuous Dames,
Tied up in godly laces,
Before you gie poor Frailty names,
Suppose a change o' cases:

[1] company [2] grave [3] giddy [4] reckless [5] exchange [6] difference [7] often [8] rest [9] both [10] wonderful [11] metamorphosed

A dear lov'd lad, convenience snug,
A treacherous inclination —
But, let me whisper i' your lug,[1]
Ye're aiblins [2] nae temptation.

Then gently scan your brother man,
Still gentler sister woman;
Tho' they may gang a kennin [3] wrang,
To step aside is human:
One point must still be greatly dark,
The moving Why they do it;
And just as lamely can ye mark,
How far perhaps they rue it.

Who made the heart, 'tis He alone
Decidedly can try us,
He knows each chord, its various tone,
Each spring, its various bias:
Then at the balance, let's be mute,
We never can adjust it;
What's done we partly can compute,
But know not what's resisted.

TO A MOUNTAIN DAISY,

ON TURNING ONE DOWN WITH THE PLOUGH, IN APRIL, 1786

Wee, modest, crimson-tippèd flow'r,
Thou's met me in an evil hour;
For I maun crush amang the stoure [4]
Thy slender stem:
To spare thee now is past my pow'r,
Thou bonie gem.

Alas! it's no thy neibor sweet,
The bonie lark, companion meet,
Bending thee 'mang the dewy weet
Wi' spreckl'd breast,
When upward-springing, blythe, to greet
The purpling east.

Cauld blew the bitter-biting north
Upon thy early, humble birth;
Yet cheerfully thou glinted forth
Amid the storm,
Scarce rear'd above the parent-earth
Thy tender form.

The flaunting flowers our gardens yield
High shelt'ring woods an' wa's [5] maun shield:
But thou, beneath the random bield [6]
O' clod or stane,
Adorns the histie [7] stibble-field
Unseen, alane.

[1] ear [2] perhaps [3] trifle [4] dust [5] walls [6] shelter [7] dry

There, in thy scanty mantle clad,
Thy snawie bosom sun-ward spread,
Thou lifts thy unassuming head
In humble guise;
But now the share uptears thy bed,
And low thou lies!

Such is the fate of artless maid,
Sweet flow'ret of the rural shade!
By love's simplicity betray'd
And guileless trust;
Till she, like thee, all soil'd, is laid
Low i' the dust.

Such is the fate of simple bard,
On life's rough ocean luckless starr'd!
Unskilful he to note the card
Of prudent lore,
Till billows rage and gales blow hard,
And whelm him o'er!

Such fate to suffering Worth is giv'n,
Who long with wants and woes has striv'n,
By human pride or cunning driv'n
To mis'ry's brink;
Till, wrench'd of ev'ry stay but Heav'n,
He ruin'd sink!

Ev'n thou who mourn'st the Daisy's fate,
That fate is thine — no distant date;
Stern Ruin's ploughshare drives elate,
Full on thy bloom,
Till crush'd beneath the furrow's weight
Shall be thy doom.

A BARD'S EPITAPH

Is there a whim-inspirèd fool,
Owre fast for thought, owre hot for rule,
Owre blate [1] to seek, owre proud to snool? [2] —
Let him draw near;
And owre this grassy heap sing dool,[3]
And drap a tear.

Is there a bard of rustic song,
Who, noteless, steals the crowds among,
That weekly this area throng? —
Oh, pass not by!
But with a frater-feeling strong
Here heave a sigh.

Is there a man whose judgment clear
Can others teach the course to steer,
Yet runs himself life's mad career
Wild as the wave? —

[1] bashful [2] cringe [3] sorrow

Here pause — and thro' the starting tear
Survey this grave.

The poor inhabitant below
Was quick to learn and wise to know,
And keenly felt the friendly glow
And softer flame;
But thoughtless follies laid him low,
And stain'd his name!

Reader, attend! whether thy soul
Soars fancy's flights beyond the pole,
Or darkling grubs this earthly hole
In low pursuit;
Know, prudent, cautious self-control
Is wisdom's root.

AULD LANG SYNE

Should auld acquaintance be forgot,
And never brought to min'?
Should auld acquaintance be forgot,
And auld lang syne?

CHO. — For auld lang syne, my dear,
For auld lang syne,
We'll tak a cup o' kindness yet
For auld lang syne.

And surely ye'll be your pint-stowp,[1]
And surely I'll be mine!
And we'll tak a cup o' kindness yet
For auld lang syne.

We twa hae run about the braes,[2]
And pu'd the gowans [3] fine;
But we've wander'd mony a weary fit [4]
Sin' auld lang syne.

We twa hae paidl't [5] i' the burn,[6]
From mornin' sun till dine;
But seas between us braid [7] hae roar'd
Sin' auld lang syne.

And there's a hand, my trusty fier,[8]
And gie's a hand o' thine;
And we'll tak a right guid willie-waught [9]
For auld lang syne.

OF A' THE AIRTS THE WIND CAN BLAW

Of a' the airts [10] the wind can blaw
I dearly like the west,
For there the bonie lassie lives,
The lassie I lo'e best:

[1] cup [2] slopes [3] daisies [4] foot [5] paddled [6] brook [7] broad [8] comrade [9] hearty draught [10] directions

There's wild woods grow an' rivers row,[1]
An' mony a hill between;
But day and night my fancy's flight
Is ever wi' my Jean.

I see her in the dewy flow'rs,
I see her sweet an' fair:
I hear her in the tunefu' birds,
I hear her charm the air:
There's not a bonie flow'r that springs
By fountain, shaw,[2] or green;
There's not a bonie bird that sings,
But minds me o' my Jean.

GO FETCH TO ME A PINT O' WINE

Go fetch to me a pint o' wine,
And fill it in a silver tassie; [3]
That I may drink, before I go,
A service to my bonie lassie:
The boat rocks at the pier o' Leith,
Fu' loud the wind blaws frae the Ferry;
The ship rides by the Berwick-law,
And I maun leave my bonie Mary.

The trumpets sound, the banners fly,
The glittering spears are rankèd ready,
The shouts o' war are heard afar,
The battle closes deep and bloody;
It's not the roar o' sea or shore
Would mak me langer wish to tarry;
Nor shouts o' war that's heard afar —
It's leaving thee, my bonie Mary!

JOHN ANDERSON MY JO

John Anderson my jo,[4] John,
When we were first acquent,
Your locks were like the raven,
Your bonie brow was brent; [5]
But now your brow is beld,[6] John,
Your locks are like the snaw;
But blessings on your frosty pow,[7]
John Anderson my jo.

John Anderson my jo, John,
We clamb the hill thegither;
And monie a canty [8] day, John,
We've had wi' ane anither:
Now we maun totter down, John,
And hand in hand we'll go,
And sleep thegither at the foot,
John Anderson my jo.

[1] roll [2] wood [3] goblet [4] sweetheart [5] smooth [6] bald [7] head [8] happy

TAM GLEN

My heart is a-breaking, dear tittie,[1]
Some counsel unto me come len';
To anger them a' is a pity,
But what will I do wi' Tam Glen?

I'm thinking, wi' sic[2] a braw[3] fellow,
In poortith[4] I might mak a fen':[5]
What care I in riches to wallow,
If I maunna marry Tam Glen?

There's Lowrie, the laird o' Dumeller,
"Guid-day to you," — brute! he comes ben:[6]
He brags and he blaws o' his siller,
But when will he dance like Tam Glen?

My minnie[7] does constantly deave[8] me,
And bids me beware o' young men;
They flatter, she says, to deceive me;
But wha can think sae o' Tam Glen?

My daddie says, gin I'll forsake him,
He'll gie me guid hunder marks ten:
But, if it's ordain'd I maun take him,
O wha will I get but Tam Glen?

Yestreen at the valentines' dealing,
My heart to my mou[9] gied a sten:[10]
For thrice I drew ane without failing,
And thrice it was written, "Tam Glen"!

The last Halloween I was waukin[11]
My droukit[12] sark-sleeve,[13] as ye ken:
His likeness cam up the house staukin,[14]
And the very gray breeks[15] o' Tam Glen!

Come counsel, dear tittie, don't tarry;
I'll gie ye my bonie black hen,
Gif ye will advise me to marry
The lad I lo'e dearly, Tam Glen.

[1] sister [2] such [3] fine [4] poverty [5] shift [6] in [7] mother [8] deafen [9] mouth [10] leap [11] watching [12] drenched [13] shirt-sleeve [14] stalking [15] breeches

TO MARY IN HEAVEN

Thou ling'ring star, with less'ning ray,
That lov'st to greet the early morn,
Again thou usher'st in the day
My Mary from my soul was torn.
O Mary! dear departed shade!
Where is thy place of blissful rest?
See'st thou thy lover lowly laid?
Hear'st thou the groans that rend his breast?

That sacred hour can I forget,
Can I forget the hallowed grove,
Where by the winding Ayr we met
To live one day of parting love?
Eternity will not efface
Those records dear of transports past,
Thy image at our last embrace —
Ah! little thought we 'twas our last!

Ayr, gurgling, kiss'd his pebbl'd shore,
O'erhung with wild woods, thick'ning green;
The fragrant birch and hawthorn hoar
Twin'd amorous round the raptur'd scene:
The flow'rs sprang wanton to be prest,
The birds sang love on every spray,
Till too, too soon the glowing west
Proclaim'd the speed of winged day.

Still o'er these scenes my mem'ry wakes,
And fondly broods with miser care!
Time but th' impression stronger makes,
As streams their channels deeper wear.
My Mary, dear departed shade!
Where is thy place of blissful rest?
See'st thou thy lover lowly laid?
Hear'st thou the groans that rend his breast?

TAM O' SHANTER

A TALE

Of Brownyis and of Bogillis full is this buke.
— Gawin Douglas.

When chapman billies[1] leave the street,
And drouthy[2] neibors neibors meet,
As market-days are wearing late,
And folk begin to tak the gate;
While we sit bousin at the nappy,[3]
And gettin fou and unco[4] happy,
We think na on the lang Scots miles,
The mosses, waters, slaps,[5] and stiles,
That lie between us and our hame,
Whare sits our sulky, sullen dame,
Gathering her brows like gathering storm,
Nursing her wrath to keep it warm

This truth fand honest Tam o' Shanter,
As he frae Ayr ae night did canter:
(Auld Ayr, wham ne'er a town surpasses,
For honest men and bonie lasses.)

O Tam! had'st thou but been sae wise
As taen thy ain wife Kate's advice!

[1] shopkeepers [2] thirsty [3] ale [4] marvellously [5] gaps

She tauld thee weel thou was a skellum,[1]
A bletherin, blusterin, drunken blellum;[2]
That frae November till October,
Ae[3] market-day thou was na sober;
That ilka[4] melder[5] wi' the miller,
Thou sat as lang as thou had siller;
That ev'ry naig[6] was ca'd[7] a shoe on,
The smith and thee gat roarin fou on;
That at the Lord's house, ev'n on Sunday,
Thou drank wi' Kirkton Jean till Monday.
She prophesied, that, late or soon,
Thou would be found deep drown'd in Doon;
Or catch't wi' warlocks[8] in the mirk,[9]
By Alloway's auld haunted kirk.

Ah, gentle dames! it gars[10] me greet,[11]
To think how mony counsels sweet,
How mony lengthened sage advices,
The husband frae the wife despises!

But to our tale: — Ae market night,
Tam had got planted unco right,
Fast by an ingle,[12] bleezin finely,
Wi' reamin swats[13] that drank divinely;
And at his elbow, Souter Johnie,
His ancient, trusty, drouthy crony:
Tam lo'ed him like a vera brither;[14]
They had been fou[15] for weeks thegither.
The night drave on wi' sangs and clatter;
And ay the ale was growing better:
The landlady and Tam grew gracious
Wi' secret favours, sweet, and precious:
The souter[16] tauld his queerest stories;
The landlord's laugh was ready chorus:
The storm without might rair and rustle
Tam did na mind the storm a whistle.

Care, mad to see a man sae happy,
E'en drown'd himsel amang the nappy:[17]
As bees flee hame wi' lades o' treasure,
The minutes wing'd their way wi' pleasure;
Kings may be blest, but Tam was glorious,
O'er a' the ills o' life victorious!

But pleasures are like poppies spread,
You seize the flow'r, its bloom is shed;
Or like the snow falls in the river,
A moment white — then melts forever;
Or like the borealis race,
That flit ere you can point their place;
Or like the rainbow's lovely form
Evanishing amid the storm.

[1] wretch [2] idle-talker [3] one [4] every [5] grinding [6] nag [7] driven [8] wizards [9] dark [10] makes [11] weep [12] fireside [13] foaming ale [14] brother [15] full [16] cobbler [17] ale

Nae man can tether time or tide:
The hour approaches Tam maun ride, —
That hour, o' night's black arch the key-stane,
That dreary hour he mounts his beast in;
And sic a night he taks the road in,
As ne'er poor sinner was abroad in.

The wind blew as 't wad blawn its last;
The rattling show'rs rose on the blast;
The speedy gleams the darkness swallow'd;
Loud, deep, and lang the thunder bellow'd:
That night, a child might understand,
The Deil had business on his hand.

Weel mounted on his grey mear, Meg, —
A better never lifted leg, —
Tam skelpit[1] on thro' dub[2] and mire,
Despising wind and rain and fire;
Whiles holding fast his guid blue bonnet,
Whiles crooning o'er some auld Scots sonnet,
Whiles glowrin round wi' prudent cares,
Lest bogles[3] catch him unawares.
Kirk-Alloway was drawing nigh,
Whare ghaists and houlets[4] nightly cry.

By this time he was cross the ford,
Whare in the snaw the chapman smoor'd;[5]
And past the birks[6] and meikle[7] stane,
Whare drucken[8] Charlie brak's neck-bane;[9]
And thro' the whins,[10] and by the cairn,[11]
Whare hunters fand the murder'd bairn;[12]
And near the thorn, aboon[13] the well,
Whare Mungo's mither hang'd hersel.
Before him Doon pours all his floods;
The doubling storm roars thro' the woods;
The lightnings flash from pole to pole,
Near and more near the thunders roll;
When, glimmering thro' the groaning trees,
Kirk-Alloway seemed in a bleeze:[14]
Thro' ilka bore[15] the beams were glancing,
And loud resounded mirth and dancing.

Inspiring bold John Barleycorn!
What dangers thou can'st make us scorn!
Wi' tippenny[16] we fear nae evil;
Wi' usquebae[17] we'll face the devil!
The swats[18] sae ream'd[19] in Tammie's noddle,
Fair play, he car'd na deils a boddle.[20]
But Maggie stood right sair astonish'd,
Till, by the heel and hand admonish'd,
She ventur'd forward on the light;
And, wow! Tam saw an unco[21] sight!

[1] clattered [2] puddle [3] goblins [4] owls [5] smothered [6] birches [7] big [8] drunken [9] bone [10] gorse [11] pile of stones [12] child [13] above [14] blaze [15] every crevice [16] twopenny ale [17] whiskey [18] ale [19] foamed [20] copper [21] marvellous

Warlocks and witches in a dance;
Nae cotillon brent-new [1] frae France,
But hornpipes, jigs, strathspeys, and reels
Put life and mettle in their heels:
A winnock [2] bunker [3] in the east,
There sat Auld Nick in shape o' beast;
A towzie tyke,[4] black, grim, and large,
To gie them music was his charge;
He screw'd the pipes and gart [5] them skirl,[6]
Till roof and rafters a' did dirl.[7] —
Coffins stood round like open presses,
That shaw'd the dead in their last dresses;
And by some devilish cantraip [8] sleight
Each in its cauld hand held a light,
By which heroic Tam was able
To note upon the haly table
A murderer's banes in gibbet airns; [9]
Twa span-lang, wee, unchristen'd bairns;
A thief, new-cutted frae the rape [10] —
Wi' his last gasp his gab [11] did gape;
Five tomahawks, wi' blude red-rusted;
Five scymitars, wi' murder crusted;
A garter, which a babe had strangled;
A knife, a father's throat had mangled,
Whom his ain son o' life bereft —
The grey hairs yet stack to the heft;
Wi' mair o' horrible and awfu',
Which ev'n to name wad be unlawfu'.

As Tammie glowr'd, amaz'd and curious,
The mirth and fun grew fast and furious:
The piper loud and louder blew,
The dancers quick and quicker flew;
They reel'd, they set, they cross'd, they cleekit,[12]
Till ilka carlin [13] swat [14] and reekit [15]
And coost [16] her duddies [17] to the wark [18]
And linket at it in her sark! [19]

Now Tam, O Tam! had thae been queans,[20]
A' plump and strapping in their teens!
Their sarks, instead o' creeshie [21] flannen,
Been snaw-white seventeen hunder linen! —
Thir [22] breeks o' mine, my only pair,
That ance were plush, o' gude blue hair,
I wad hae gien them aff my hurdies,[23]
For ae blink o' the bonie burdies! [20]

* * * * * * * *

But Tam ken'd what was what fu' brawlie; [24]
There was ae winsom wench and walie,[25]
That night enlisted in the core [26]
(Lang after ken'd on Carrick shore:

[1] brand-new [2] window [3] seat [4] shaggy cur [5] made [6] scream [7] throb [8] tricksy [9] irons [10] rope [11] mouth [12] clutched [13] old woman [14] sweated [15] steamed [16] cast [17] clothes [18] work [19] chemise [20] girls [21] greasy [22] these [23] hips [24] well [25] goodly [26] company

For mony a beast to dead she shot,
And perish'd mony a bonie boat,
And shook baith meikle [1] corn and bear,[2]
And kept the country-side in fear);
Her cutty sark [3] o' Paisley harn,[4]
That while a lassie she had worn,
In longitude tho' sorely scanty,
It was her best, and she was vauntie.[5]
Ah! little kent thy reverend grannie,
That sark she coft [6] for her wee Nannie,
Wi' twa pund Scots ('twas a' her riches),
Wad ever graced a dance o' witches!

But here my Muse her wing maun cow'r,
Sic flights are far beyond her pow'r;
To sing how Nannie lap and flang,
(A souple jad she was and strang,)
And how Tam stood like ane bewitch'd,
And thought his very een [7] enrich'd;
Even Satan glowr'd and fidg'd [8] fu' fain,[9]
And hotch'd [10] and blew wi' might and main:
Till first ae caper, syne [11] anither,
Tam tint [12] his reason a' thegither,
And roars out, "Weel done, Cutty-sark!"
And in an instant all was dark:
And scarcely had he Maggie rallied,
When out the hellish legion sallied.

As bees bizz out wi' angry fyke,[13]
When plundering herds assail their byke; [14]
As open pussie's [15] mortal foes,
When, pop! she starts before their nose;
As eager runs the market-crowd,
When "Catch the thief!" resounds aloud;
So Maggie runs, the witches follow,
Wi' mony an eldritch [16] skriech and hollo.

Ah, Tam! ah, Tam! thou'll get thy fairin! [17]
In hell they'll roast thee like a herrin!
In vain thy Kate awaits thy comin!
Kate soon will be a woefu' woman!
Now, do thy speedy utmost, Meg,
And win the key-stane of the brig: [18]
There at them thou thy tail may toss,
A running stream they dare na cross.
But ere the key-stane she could make,
The fient [19] a tail she had to shake!
For Nannie, far before the rest,
Hard upon noble Maggie prest,
And flew at Tam wi' furious ettle; [20]
But little wist she Maggie's mettle —
Ae spring brought aff her master hale,
But left behind her ain grey tail:

[1] much [2] barley [3] short shirt [4] linen [5] proud [6] bought [7] eyes [8] fidgeted [9] eagerly [10] squirmed [11] then [12] lost [13] fuss [14] hive [15] the hare's [16] unearthly [17] reward [18] bridge [19] devil [20] aim

The carlin claught her by the rump,
And left poor Maggie scarce a stump.

Now, wha this tale o' truth shall read,
Ilk [1] man and mother's son, take heed,
Whene'er to drink you are inclin'd,
Or cutty-sarks run in your mind
Think, ye may buy the joys owre [2] dear,
Remember Tam o' Shanter's mear.

BONIE DOON

Ye flowery banks o' bonie Doon,
How can ye blume sae fair?
How can ye chant, ye little birds,
And I sae fu' o' care?

Thou'll break my heart, thou bonie bird,
That sings upon the bough;
Thou minds me o' the happy days,
When my fause luve was true.

Thou'll break my heart, thou bonie bird,
That sings beside thy mate;
For sae I sat, and sae I sang,
And wist na o' my fate.

Aft hae I rov'd by bonie Doon
To see the wood-bine twine,
And ilka [3] bird sang o' its luve,
And sae did I o' mine.

Wi' lightsome heart I pu'd a rose
Frae aff its thorny tree;
And my fause luver staw [4] my rose
But left the thorn wi' me.

FLOW GENTLY, SWEET AFTON

Flow gently, sweet Afton, among thy green braes,[5]
Flow gently, I'll sing thee a song in thy praise;
My Mary's asleep by thy murmuring stream,
Flow gently, sweet Afton, disturb not her dream.

Thou stock-dove, whose echo resounds thro' the glen,
Ye wild whistling blackbirds in yon thorny den,
Thou green-crested lapwing, thy screaming forbear,
I charge you disturb not my slumbering fair.

How lofty, sweet Afton, thy neighbouring hills,
Far mark'd with the courses of clear winding rills;
There daily I wander as noon rises high,
My flocks and my Mary's sweet cot in my eye.

[1] every [2] over [3] every [4] stole [5] slopes

How pleasant thy banks and green valleys below,
Where wild in the woodlands the primroses blow;
There oft, as mild Evening weeps over the lea,
The sweet-scented birk [1] shades my Mary and me.

Thy crystal stream, Afton, how lovely it glides,
And winds by the cot where my Mary resides;
How wanton thy waters her snowy feet lave,
As gathering sweet flow'rets she stems thy clear wave.

Flow gently, sweet Afton, among thy green braes,
Flow gently, sweet river, the theme of my lays;
My Mary's asleep by thy murmuring stream,
Flow gently, sweet Afton, disturb not her dream.

AE FOND KISS

Ae fond kiss, and then we sever;
Ae fareweel, and then forever!
Deep in heart-wrung tears I'll pledge thee,
Warring sighs and groans I'll wage thee.
Who shall say that Fortune grieves him,
While the star of hope she leaves him?
Me, nae cheerfu' twinkle lights me;
Dark despair around benights me.

I'll ne'er blame my partial fancy,
Naething could resist my Nancy;
But to see her was to love her;
Love but her, and love forever.
Had we never lov'd sae kindly,
Had we never lov'd sae blindly,
Never met — or never parted —
We had ne'er been broken-hearted.

Fare thee weel, thou first and fairest!
Fare thee weel, thou best and dearest!
Thine be ilka [2] joy and treasure,
Peace, enjoyment, love, and pleasure!
Ae one fond kiss, and then we sever;
Ae fareweel, alas, forever!
Deep in heart-wrung tears I'll pledge thee.
Warring sighs and groans I'll wage thee!

BONIE LESLEY

O saw ye bonie Lesley
As she gaed o'er the border?
She's gane, like Alexander,
To spread her conquests farther.

To see her is to love her,
And love but her forever;
For Nature made her what she is,
And never made anither!

[1] birch [2] every

Thou art a queen, fair Lesley,
  Thy subjects, we before thee:
Thou art divine, fair Lesley,
  The hearts o' men adore thee.

The Deil he could na scaith thee,
  Or aught that wad belang thee;
He'd look into thy bonie face,
  And say, "I canna wrang thee."

The Powers aboon will tent[1] thee;
  Misfortune sha' na steer[2] thee;
Thou'rt like themselves sae lovely,
  That ill they'll ne'er let near thee.

Return again, fair Lesley,
  Return to Caledonie!
That we may brag, we hae a lass
  There's nane again sae bonie.

HIGHLAND MARY

Ye banks, and braes,[3] and streams around
  The castle o' Montgomery,
Green be your woods and fair your flowers,
  Your waters never drumlie![4]
There simmer first unfauld her robes,
  And there the langest tarry;
For there I took the last fareweel,
  O' my sweet Highland Mary.

How sweetly bloom'd the gay green birk,[5]
  How rich the hawthorn's blossom,
As underneath their fragrant shade
  I clasp'd her to my bosom!
The golden hours, on angel wings,
  Flew o'er me and my dearie;
For dear to me as light and life,
  Was my sweet Highland Mary.

Wi' monie a vow and lock'd embrace
  Our parting was fu' tender;
And, pledging aft to meet again,
  We tore oursels asunder;
But O! fell death's untimely frost,
  That nipt my flower sae early!
Now green's the sod, and cauld's the clay,
  That wraps my Highland Mary!

O pale, pale now, those rosy lips,
  I aft hae kiss'd sae fondly!
And closed for aye the sparkling glance,
  That dwelt on me sae kindly!
And mould'ring now in silent dust,
  That heart that lo'ed me dearly!
But still within my bosom's core
  Shall live my Highland Mary.

[1] tend [2] hurt [3] slopes [4] muddy [5] birch

DUNCAN GRAY

Duncan Gray came here to woo,
    Ha, ha, the wooin o't!
On blythe Yule night when we were fou,[1]
    Ha, ha, the wooin o't!
Maggie coost her head fu hiegh,
Look'd asklent[2] and unco skiegh,[3]
Gart[4] poor Duncan stand abiegh;[5]
    Ha, ha, the wooin o't!

Duncan fleech'd,[6] and Duncan pray'd;
    Ha, ha, the wooin o't!
Meg was deaf as Ailsa Craig,
    Ha, ha, the wooin o't!
Duncan sigh'd baith out and in,
Grat[7] his een[8] baith bleer't[9] and blin',
Spak o' lowpin[10] owre a linn;[11]
    Ha, ha, the wooin o't!

Time and chance are but a tide,
    Ha, ha, the wooin o't!
Slighted love is sair to bide,[12]
    Ha, ha, the wooin o't!
"Shall I, like a fool," quoth he,
"For a haughty hizzie[13] die?
She may gae to — France for me!"
    Ha, ha, the wooin o't!

How it comes let doctors tell,
    Ha, ha, the wooin o't!
Meg grew sick as he grew hale,
    Ha, ha, the wooin o't!
Something in her bosom wrings,
For relief a sigh she brings;
And O! her een, they spak sic things!
    Ha, ha, the wooin o't!

Duncan was a lad o' grace,
    Ha, ha, the wooin o't!
Maggie's was a piteous case,
    Ha, ha, the wooin o't!
Duncan could na be her death,
Swelling pity smoor'd[14] his wrath;
Now they're crouse[15] and cantie[16] baith;
    Ha, ha, the wooin o't!

SCOTS WHA HAE

Scots, wha hae wi' Wallace bled,
Scots, wham Bruce has aften led;
Welcome to your gory bed,
  Or to victory!

[1] full [2] sidewise [3] wondrous shy [4] made [5] off [6] flattered [7] wept [8] eyes [9] bleared [10] leaping [11] waterfall [12] hard to endure [13] lass [14] smothered [15] bright [16] happy

Now's the day, and now's the hour;
See the front o' battle lour;
See approach proud Edward's power —
Chains and slavery!

Wha will be a traitor knave?
Wha can fill a coward's grave?
Wha sae base as be a slave?
Let him turn and flee!
Wha for Scotland's king and law
Freedom's sword will strongly draw,
Freeman stand, or Freeman fa',
Let him follow me!

By oppression's woes and pains
By your sons in servile chains!
We will drain our dearest veins,
But they shall be free!
Lay the proud usurpers low!
Tyrants fall in every foe!
Liberty's in every blow! —
Let us do or die!

A MAN'S A MAN FOR A' THAT

Is there, for honest poverty,
That hings his head, an' a' that?
The coward slave, we pass him by,
We dare be poor for a' that!
For a' that, an' a' that,
Our toils obscure, an' a' that;
The rank is but the guinea's stamp;
The man's the gowd [1] for a' that.

What tho' on hamely fare we dine,
Wear hodden-gray,[2] an' a' that;
Gie fools their silks, and knaves their wine,
A man's a man for a' that.
For a' that, an' a' that,
Their tinsel show, an' a' that;
The honest man, tho' e'er sae poor,
Is king o' men for a' that.

Ye see yon birkie,[3] ca'd a lord,
Wha struts, an' stares, an' a' that;
Tho' hundreds worship at his word,
He's but a coof [4] for a' that:
For a' that, an' a' that,
His riband, star, an' a' that,
The man o' independent mind,
He looks and laughs at a' that.

A prince can mak a belted knight,
A marquis, duke, an' a' that;
But an honest man's aboon [5] his might,
Guid faith he mauna fa' [6] that!
For a' that, an' a' that,
Their dignities, an' a' that,
The pith o' sense, an' pride o' worth,
Are higher rank than a' that.

Then let us pray that come it may,
As come it will for a' that,
That sense and worth, o'er a' the earth,
May bear the gree,[1] an' a' that.
For a' that, an' a' that,
It's coming yet, for a' that,
That man to man, the warld o'er,
Shall brothers be for a' that.

[1] gold [2] coarse grey cloth [3] young fellow [4] fool [5] above [6] cannot accomplish

JOANNA BAILLIE (1762–1851)

WOO'D AND MARRIED AND A'

The bride she is winsome and bonny,
Her hair it is snooded [2] sae sleek,
And faithfu' and kind is her Johnny,
Yet fast fa' the tears on her cheek.
New pearlins [3] are cause of her sorrow,
New pearlins and plenishing [4] too;
The bride that has a' to borrow
Has e'en right mickle ado.
Woo'd and married and a'!
Woo'd and married and a'!
Is na' she very weel aff
To be woo'd and married at a'?

Her mither then hastily spak,
"The lassie is glaikit [5] wi' pride;
In my pouch I had never a plack [6]
On the day when I was a bride.
E'en tak to your wheel and be clever,
And draw out your thread in the sun;
The gear that is gifted [7] it never
Will last like the gear that is won.
Woo'd and married and a'!
Wi' havins and tocher [8] sae sma'!
I think ye are very weel aff
To be woo'd and married at a'."

"Toot, toot," quo' her grey-headed faither,
"She's less o' a bride than a bairn,
She's ta'en like a cout [9] frae the heather,
Wi' sense and discretion to learn.
Half husband, I trow, and half daddy,
As humour inconstantly leans,
The chiel [10] maun be patient and steady
That yokes wi' a mate in her teens.
A kerchief sae douce and sae neat
O'er her locks that the wind used to blaw!

[1] prize [2] bound up in a riband [3] finery, laces, linen [4] furnishings [5] befooled [6] small coin [7] given [8] goods and dowry [9] colt [10] fellow

I'm baith like to laugh and to greet
When I think of her married at a'!"

Then out spak the wily bridegroom,
Weel waled [1] were his wordies, I ween,
"I'm rich, though my coffer be toom,[2]
Wi' the blinks o' your bonny blue e'en.
I'm prouder o' thee by my side
Though thy ruffles or ribbons be few,
Than if Kate o' the Croft were my bride
Wi' purfles and pearlins enow.
Dear and dearest of ony!
Ye're woo'd and buikit [3] and a'!
And do ye think scorn o' your Johnny,
And grieve to be married at a'?"

She turn'd, and she blush'd, and she smiled,
And she looked sae bashfully down;
The pride o' her heart was beguiled,
And she played wi' the sleeves o' her gown.
She twirled the tag o' her lace,
And she nipped her boddice sae blue,
Syne [4] blinkit sae sweet in his face,
And aff like a maukin [5] she flew.
Woo'd and married and a'!
Wi' Johnny to roose [6] her and a'!
She thinks hersel very weel aff
To be woo'd and married at a'!

SAMUEL ROGERS (1763–1855)

From ITALY AND BERGAMO

. . . But who comes,
Brushing the floor with what was once, methinks,
A hat of ceremony? On he glides,
Slip-shod, ungartered; his long suit of black
Dingy, thread-bare, tho', patch by patch, renewed
Till it has almost ceased to be the same.
At length arrived, and with a shrug that pleads
"'Tis my necessity!" he stops and speaks,
Screwing a smile into his dinnerless face.
"Blame not a Poet, Signor, for his zeal —
When all are on the wing, who would be last?
The splendour of thy name has gone before thee;
And Italy from sea to sea exults,
As well indeed she may! But I transgress.
He, who has known the weight of praise himself,
Should spare another." Saying so, he laid
His sonnet, an impromptu, at my feet,
(If his, then Petrarch must have stolen it from him)
And bowed and left me; in his hollow hand
Receiving my small tribute, a zecchine,
Unconsciously, as doctors do their fees.
My omelet, and a flagon of hill-wine,
Pure as the virgin-spring, had happily
Fled from all eyes; or, in a waking dream,
I might have sat as many a great man has,
And many a small, like him of Santillane,
Bartering my bread and salt for empty praise.

[1] well chosen [2] empty [3] registered as intending to marry [4] afterwards [5] hare [6] praise

From ITALY

Am I in Italy? Is this the Mincius?
Are those the distant turrets of Verona?
And shall I sup where Juliet at the Masque
Saw her loved Montague, and now sleeps by him?
Such questions hourly do I ask myself;
And not a stone, in a cross-way, inscribed
"To Manua" — "To Ferrara" — but excites
Surprise, and doubt, and self-congratulation.

O Italy, how beautiful thou art!
Yet I could weep — for thou art lying, alas,
Low in the dust; and we admire thee now
As we admire the beautiful in death.
Thine was a dangerous gift, when thou wert born,
The gift of Beauty. Would thou hadst it not;
Or wert as once, awing the caitiffs vile
That now beset thee, making thee their slave!
Would they had loved thee less, or feared thee more!
But why despair? Twice hast thou lived already;
Twice shone among the nations of the world,
As the sun shines among the lesser lights
Of heaven; and shalt again. The hour shall come,
When they who think to bind the ethereal spirit,
Who, like the eagle cowering o'er his prey,
Watch with quick eye, and strike and strike again
If but a sinew vibrate, shall confess
Their wisdom folly. Even now the flame
Bursts forth where once it burnt so gloriously,
And, dying, left a splendour like the day,
That like the day diffused itself, and still
Blesses the earth — the light of genius, virtue,
Greatness in thought and act, contempt of death,
God-like example. Echoes that have slept
Since Athens, Lacedæmon were themselves, —
Since men invoked "By those in Marathon!" —

Awake along the Ægean; and the dead;
They of that sacred shore, have heard the call,
And thro' the ranks, from wing to wing, are seen
Moving as once they were — instead of rage
Breathing deliberate valour.

A TEAR

O that the chemist's magic art
  Could crystallize this sacred treasure!
Long should it glitter near my heart,
  A secret source of pensive pleasure.

The little brilliant, ere it fell,
  Its lustre caught from Chloe's eye;
Then, trembling, left its coral cell, —
  The spring of Sensibility!

Sweet drop of pure and pearly light!
  In thee the rays of Virtue shine,
More calmly clear, more mildly bright,
  Than any gem that gilds the mine.

Benign restorer of the soul!
  Who ever fliest to bring relief,
When first we feel the rude control
  Of Love or Pity, Joy or Grief.

The sage's and the poet's theme,
  In every clime, in every age,
Thou charm'st in Fancy's idle dream,
  In Reason's philosophic page.

That very law which moulds a tear,
  And bids it trickle from its source, —
That law preserves the earth a sphere,
  And guides the planets in their course.

CAROLINA, LADY NAIRNE
(1766–1845)

THE LAND O' THE LEAL

I'm wearin' awa', John,
Like snaw-wreaths in thaw, John,
I'm wearin' awa'
  To the land o' the leal.
There's nae sorrow there, John,
There's neither cauld nor care, John,
The day is aye fair
  In the land o' the leal.

Our bonnie bairn's there, John,
She was baith gude and fair, John;
And oh! we grudged her sair
  To the land o' the leal.
But sorrow's sel' wears past, John,
And joy's a-coming fast, John,
The joy that's aye to last
  In the land o' the leal.

Sae dear's the joy was bought, John,
Sae free the battle fought, John,
That sinfu' man e'er brought
  To the land o' the leal.
Oh, dry your glistening e'e, John!
My saul langs to be free, John,
And angels beckon me
  To the land o' the leal.

Oh, haud ye leal and true, John!
Your day it's wearin' through, John,
And I'll welcome you
  To the land o' the leal.
Now fare-ye-weel, my ain John,
This warld's cares are vain, John,
We'll meet, and we'll be fain,
  In the land o' the leal.

THE AGE OF ROMANTICISM

WILLIAM WORDSWORTH
(1770–1850)

WE ARE SEVEN

——— A simple child,
That lightly draws its breath,
And feels its life in every limb,
What should it know of death?

I met a little cottage girl:
She was eight years old, she said;
Her hair was thick with many a curl
That clustered round her head.

She had a rustic, woodland air,
And she was wildly clad:
Her eyes were fair, and very fair;
— Her beauty made me glad.

"Sisters and brothers, little maid,
How many may you be?"
"How many? Seven in all," she said,
And wondering looked at me.

"And where are they? I pray you tell."
She answered, "Seven are we;
And two of us at Conway dwell,
And two are gone to sea.

"Two of us in the church-yard lie,
My sister and my brother;
And, in the church-yard cottage, I
Dwell near them with my mother."

"You say that two at Conway dwell,
And two are gone to sea,
Yet ye are seven! — I pray you tell,
Sweet maid, how this may be."

Then did the little maid reply,
"Seven boys and girls are we;
Two of us in the church-yard lie,
Beneath the church-yard tree."

"You run about, my little maid,
Your limbs they are alive;
If two are in the church-yard laid,
Then ye are only five."

"Their graves are green, they may be seen,"
The little maid replied,
"Twelve steps or more from my mother's door,
And they are side by side.

"My stockings there I often knit,
My kerchief there I hem;
And there upon the ground I sit,
And sing a song to them.

"And often after sunset, sir,
When it is light and fair,
I take my little porringer,
And eat my supper there.

"The first that died was sister Jane;
In bed she moaning lay,
Till God released her of her pain;
And then she went away.

"So in the church-yard she was laid;
And, when the grass was dry,
Together round her grave we played,
My brother John and I.

"And when the ground was white with snow,
And I could run and slide,
My brother John was forced to go,
And he lies by her side."

"How many are you, then," said I,
"If they two are in heaven?"
Quick was the little maid's reply,
"O master! we are seven."

"But they are dead; those two are dead!
Their spirits are in heaven!"
'Twas throwing words away; for still
The little maid would have her will,
And said, "Nay, we are seven!"

EXPOSTULATION AND REPLY

"Why, William, on that old grey stone,
Thus for the length of half a day,
Why, William, sit you thus alone,
And dream your time away?

"Where are your books? — that light bequeathed
To beings else forlorn and blind!
Up! up! and drink the spirit breathed
From dead men to their kind.

"You look round on your Mother Earth,
As if she for no purpose bore you;
As if you were her first-born birth,
And none had lived before you!"

One morning thus, by Esthwaite lake,
When life was sweet, I knew not why,
To me my good friend Matthew spake,
And thus I made reply:

"The eye — it cannot choose but see;
We cannot bid the ear be still;
Our bodies feel, where'er they be,
Against or with our will.

"Nor less I dream that there are Powers
Which of themselves our minds impress;
That we can feed this mind of ours
In a wise passiveness.

"Think you, 'mid all this mighty sum
Of things forever speaking,
That nothing of itself will come,
But we must still be seeking?

"— Then ask not wherefore, here, alone,
Conversing as I may,
I sit upon this old grey stone,
And dream my time away."

THE TABLES TURNED

An Evening Scene on the same Subject

Up! up! my friend, and quit your books;
Or surely you'll grow double:
Up! up! my friend, and clear your looks;
Why all this toil and trouble?

The sun, above the mountain's head,
A freshening lustre mellow
Through all the long green fields has spread,
His first sweet evening yellow.

Books! 'tis a dull and endless strife:
Come, hear the woodland linnet,
How sweet his music! on my life
There's more of wisdom in it.

And hark! how blithe the throstle sings!
He, too, is no mean preacher:
Come forth into the light of things,
Let Nature be your teacher.

She has a world of ready wealth,
Our minds and hearts to bless —
Spontaneous wisdom breathed by health,
Truth breathed by cheerfulness.

One impulse from a vernal wood
May teach you more of man,
Of moral evil and of good,
Than all the sages can.

Sweet is the lore which Nature brings;
Our meddling intellect
Misshapes the beauteous forms of things: —
We murder to dissect.

Enough of Science and of Art;
Close up those barren leaves;
Come forth, and bring with you a heart
That watches and receives.

LINES COMPOSED A FEW MILES ABOVE TINTERN ABBEY, ON REVISITING THE BANKS OF THE WYE DURING A TOUR

JULY 13, 1798

Five years have past; five summers, with the length
Of five long winters! and again I hear
These waters, rolling from their mountain-springs
With a soft inland murmur. — Once again
Do I behold these steep and lofty cliffs,
That on a wild secluded scene impress
Thoughts of more deep seclusion; and connect
The landscape with the quiet of the sky.
The day is come when I again repose
Here, under this dark sycamore, and view
These plots of cottage-ground, these orchard-tufts,
Which at this season, with their unripe fruits,
Are clad in one green hue, and lose themselves
'Mid groves and copses. Once again I see
These hedgerows, hardly hedgerows, little lines
Of sportive wood run wild: these pastoral farms,
Green to the very door; and wreaths of smoke
Sent up, in silence, from among the trees!
With some uncertain notice, as might seem
Of vagrant dwellers in the houseless woods,
Or of some hermit's cave, where by his fire
The hermit sits alone.
These beauteous forms,
Through a long absence, have not been to me
As is a landscape to a blind man's eye:
But oft, in lonely rooms, and 'mid the din
Of towns and cities, I have owed to them
In hours of weariness, sensations sweet,

Felt in the blood, and felt along the heart;
And passing even into my purer mind,
With tranquil restoration: — feelings too
Of unremembered pleasure: such, perhaps,
As have no slight or trivial influence
On that best portion of a good man's life,
His little, nameless, unremembered acts
Of kindness and of love. Nor less, I trust,
To them I may have owed another gift,
Of aspect more sublime; that blessed mood,
In which the burthen of the mystery,
In which the heavy and the weary weight
Of all this unintelligible world,
Is lightened: — that serene and blessed mood
In which the affections gently lead us on, —
Until, the breath of this corporeal frame
And even the motion of our human blood
Almost suspended, we are laid asleep
In body, and become a living soul:
While with an eye made quiet by the power
Of harmony, and the deep power of joy,
We see into the life of things.
If this
Be but a vain belief, yet, oh! how oft —
In darkness and amid the many shapes
Of joyless daylight; when the fretful stir
Unprofitable, and the fever of the world,
Have hung upon the beatings of my heart —
How oft, in spirit, have I turned to thee,
O sylvan Wye! thou wanderer thro' the woods,
How often has my spirit turned to thee!
And now, with gleams of half-extinguished thought,
With many recognitions dim and faint,
And somewhat of a sad perplexity,
The picture of the mind revives again:
While here I stand, not only with the sense
Of present pleasure, but with pleasing thoughts
That in this moment there is life and food
For future years. And so I dare to hope,
Though changed, no doubt, from what I was when first
I came among these hills; when like a roe
I bounded o'er the mountains, by the sides
Of the deep rivers, and the lonely streams,
Wherever nature led: more like a man
Flying from something that he dreads, than one
Who sought the thing he loved. For nature then
(The coarser pleasures of my boyish days,
And their glad animal movements all gone by)
To me was all in all. — I cannot paint
What then I was. The sounding cataract
Haunted me like a passion; the tall rock,
The mountain, and the deep and gloomy wood,
Their colours and their forms, were then to me
An appetite; a feeling and a love,
That had no need of a remoter charm,
By thought supplied, nor any interest
Unborrowed from the eye. — That time is past,
And all its aching joys are now no more,
And all its dizzy raptures. Not for this
Faint I, nor mourn, nor murmur; other gifts
Have followed; for such loss, I would believe,
Abundant recompense. For I have learned
To look on nature, not as in the hour
Of thoughtless youth; but hearing oftentimes
The still, sad music of humanity,
Nor harsh nor grating, though of ample power
To chasten and subdue. And I have felt
A presence that disturbs me with the joy
Of elevated thoughts; a sense sublime,
Of something far more deeply interfused,
Whose dwelling is the light of setting suns,
And the round ocean and the living air,
And the blue sky, and in the mind of man;
A motion and a spirit, that impels
All thinking things, all objects of all thought,
And rolls through all things. Therefore am I still
A lover of the meadows and the woods,
And mountains; and of all that we behold
From this green earth; of all the mighty world
Of eye, and ear, — both what they half create,
And what perceive; well pleased to recognise
In nature and the language of the sense,
The anchor of my purest thoughts, the nurse,
The guide, the guardian of my heart, and soul
Of all my moral being.
Nor perchance,
If I were not thus taught, should I the more
Suffer my genial spirits to decay:
For thou art with me here upon the banks
Of this fair river; thou my dearest friend,
My dear, dear friend; and in thy voice I catch
The language of my former heart, and read
My former pleasures in the shooting lights
Of thy wild eyes. Oh! yet a little while
May I behold in thee what I was once,
My dear, dear sister! and this prayer I make,
Knowing that Nature never did betray
The heart that loved her; 'tis her privilege,
Through all the years of this our life, to lead
From joy to joy: for she can so inform
The mind that is within us, so impress
With quietness and beauty, and so feed
With lofty thoughts, that neither evil tongues,
Rash judgments, nor the sneers of selfish men,
Nor greetings where no kindness is, nor all

The dreary intercourse of daily life,
Shall e'er prevail against us, or disturb
Our cheerful faith, that all which we behold
Is full of blessings. Therefore let the moon
Shine on thee in thy solitary walk;
And let the misty mountain-winds be free
To blow against thee: and, in after years,
When these wild ecstasies shall be matured
Into a sober pleasure; when thy mind
Shall be a mansion for all lovely forms,
Thy memory be as a dwelling-place
For all sweet sounds and harmonies; oh! then,
If solitude, or fear, or pain, or grief,
Should be thy portion, with what healing thoughts
Of tender joy wilt thou remember me,
And these my exhortations! Nor, perchance —
If I should be where I no more can hear
Thy voice, nor catch from thy wild eyes these gleams
Of past existence — wilt thou then forget
That on the banks of this delightful stream
We stood together; and that I, so long
A worshipper of Nature, hither came
Unwearied in that service: rather say
With warmer love — oh! with far deeper zeal
Of holier love. Nor wilt thou then forget,
That after many wanderings, many years
Of absence, these steep woods and lofty cliffs,
And this green pastoral landscape, were to me
More dear, both for themselves and for thy sake!

SHE DWELT AMONG

She dwelt among the untrodden ways
  Beside the springs of Dove,
A maid whom there were none to praise
  And very few to love:

A violet by a mossy stone
  Half hidden from the eye!
— Fair as a star, when only one
  Is shining in the sky.

She lived unknown, and few could know
  When Lucy ceased to be;
But she is in her grave, and, oh,
  The difference to me!

THREE YEARS SHE GREW

Three years she grew in sun and shower,
Then Nature said, "A lovelier flower
  On earth was never sown;
This child I to myself will take;
She shall be mine, and I will make
  A lady of my own.

"Myself will to my darling be
Both law and impulse: and with me
  The girl, in rock and plain,
In earth and heaven, in glade and bower,
Shall feel an overseeing power
  To kindle or restrain.

"She shall be sportive as the fawn
That wild with glee across the lawn,
  Or up the mountain springs;
And hers shall be the breathing balm,
And hers the silence and the calm
  Of mute insensate things.

"The floating clouds their state shall lend
To her; for her the willow bend;
  Nor shall she fail to see
Even in the motions of the storm
Grace that shall mould the maiden's form
  By silent sympathy.

"The stars of midnight shall be dear
To her; and she shall lean her ear
  In many a secret place
Where rivulets dance their wayward round,
And beauty born of murmuring sound
  Shall pass into her face.

"And vital feelings of delight
Shall rear her form to stately height,
  Her virgin bosom swell;
Such thoughts to Lucy I will give
While she and I together live
  Here in this happy dell."

Thus Nature spake — the work was done —
How soon my Lucy's race was run!
  She died, and left to me
This heath, this calm, and quiet scene;
The memory of what has been,
  And never more will be.

A SLUMBER DID MY SPIRIT SEAL

A slumber did my spirit seal;
  I had no human fears;
She seemed a thing that could not feel
  The touch of earthly years.

No motion has she now, no force;
  She neither hears nor sees;
Rolled round in earth's diurnal course,
  With rocks, and stones, and trees.

LUCY GRAY; OR, SOLITUDE

Oft I had heard of Lucy Gray:
And, when I crossed the wild,
I chanced to see at break of day
The solitary child.

No mate, no comrade Lucy knew
She dwelt on a wide moor,
— The sweetest thing that ever grew
Beside a human door!

You yet may spy the fawn at play
The hare upon the green;
But the sweet face of Lucy Gray
Will never more be seen.

"To-night will be a stormy night —
You to the town must go;
And take a lantern, child, to light
Your mother through the snow."

"That, Father! will I gladly do:
'Tis scarcely afternoon —
The minster-clock has just struck two,
And yonder is the moon!"

At this the father raised his hook,
And snapped a faggot-band;
He plied his work; — and Lucy took
The lantern in her hand.

Not blither is the mountain roe:
With many a wanton stroke
Her feet disperse the powdery snow,
That rises up like smoke.

The storm came on before its time:
She wandered up and down;
And many a hill did Lucy climb:
But never reached the town.

The wretched parents all that night
Went shouting far and wide;
But there was neither sound nor sight
To serve them for a guide.

At daybreak on a hill they stood
That overlooked the moor;
And thence they saw the bridge of wood,
A furlong from their door.

They wept — and, turning homeward, cried,
"In heaven we all shall meet;"
— When in the snow the mother spied
The print of Lucy's feet.

Then downwards from the steep hill's edge
They tracked the footmarks small;
And through the broken hawthorn hedge,
And by the long stone-wall;

And then an open field they crossed:
The marks were still the same;
They tracked them on, nor ever lost;
And to the bridge they came.

They followed from the snowy bank
Those footmarks, one by one,
Into the middle of the plank;
And further there were none!

— Yet some maintain that to this day
She is a living child;
That you may see sweet Lucy Gray
Upon the lonesome wild.

O'er rough and smooth she trips along,
And never looks behind;
And sings a solitary song
That whistles in the wind.

THE RECLUSE

From BOOK I

On Man, on Nature, and on Human Life,
Musing in solitude, I oft perceive
Fair trains of imagery before me rise,
Accompanied by feelings of delight
Pure, or with no unpleasing sadness mixed;
And I am conscious of affecting thoughts
And dear remembrances, whose presence soothes
Or elevates the mind, intent to weigh
The good and evil of our mortal state.
— To these emotions, whencesoe'er they come,
Whether from breath of outward circumstance,
Or from the soul — an impulse to herself —
I would give utterance in numerous verse.
Of Truth, of Grandeur, Beauty, Love, and Hope,
And melancholy Fear subdued by Faith;
Of blessèd consolations in distress;
Of moral strength, and intellectual power;
Of joy in widest commonalty spread;
Of the individual mind that keeps her own
Inviolate retirement, subject there
To conscience only, and the law supreme
Of that Intelligence which governs all —
I sing: — "fit audience let me find though few!"
So prayed, more gaining than he asked, the bard —
In holiest mood. Urania, I shall need
Thy guidance, or a greater muse, if such
Descend to earth or dwell in highest heaven!

For I must tread on shadowy ground, must sink
Deep — and, aloft ascending, breathe in worlds
To which the heaven of heavens is but a veil.
All strength — all terror, single or in bands,
That ever was put forth in personal form —
Jehovah — with his thunder, and the choir
Of shouting angels, and the empyreal thrones —
I pass them unalarmed. Not Chaos, not
The darkest pit of lowest Erebus,
Nor aught of blinder vacancy, scooped out
By help of dreams — can breed such fear and awe
As falls upon us often when we look
Into our minds, into the mind of Man —
My haunt, and the main region of my song.
— Beauty — a living Presence of the earth,
Surpassing the most fair ideal forms
Which craft of delicate Spirits hath composed
From earth's materials — waits upon my steps;
Pitches her tents before me as I move,
An hourly neighbour. Paradise, and groves
Elysian, Fortunate Fields — like those of old
Sought in the Atlantic Main — why should they be
A history only of departed things,
Or a mere fiction of what never was?
For the discerning intellect of Man,
When wedded to this goodly universe
In love and holy passion, shall find these
A simple produce of the common day.
— I, long before the blissful hour arrives,
Would chant, in lonely peace, the spousal verse
Of this great consummation: — and, by words
Which speak of nothing more than what we are,
Would I arouse the sensual from their sleep
Of death, and win the vacant and the vain
To noble raptures; while my voice proclaims
How exquisitely the individual mind
(And the progressive powers perhaps no less
Of the whole species) to the external world
Is fitted: — and how exquisitely, too —
Theme this but little heard of among men —
The external world is fitted to the mind;
And the creation (by no lower name
Can it be called) which they with blended might
Accomplish: — this is our high argument.
— Such grateful haunts foregoing, if I oft
Must turn elsewhere — to travel near the tribes
And fellowships of men, and see ill sights
Of madding passions mutually inflamed;
Must hear Humanity in fields and groves
Pipe solitary anguish; or must hang
Brooding above the fierce confederate storm
Of sorrow, barricadoed evermore
Within the walls of cities — may these sounds
Have their authentic comment; that even these
Hearing, I be not downcast or forlorn! —
Descend, prophetic Spirit! that inspir'st
The human Soul of universal earth,
Dreaming on things to come; and dost possess
A metropolitan temple in the hearts
Of mighty poets; upon me bestow
A gift of genuine insight; that my song
With star-like virtue in its place may shine,
Shedding benignant influence, and secure
Itself from all malevolent effect
Of those mutations that extend their sway
Throughout the nether sphere! — And if with this
I mix more lowly matter; with the thing
Contemplated, describe the Mind and Man
Contemplating; and who, and what he was —
The transitory being that beheld
This vision; — when and where, and how he lived;
Be not this labour useless. If such theme
May sort with highest objects, then — dread Power!
Whose gracious favour is the primal source
Of all illumination — may my life
Express the image of a better time,
More wise desires, and simpler manners; — nurse
My heart in genuine freedom: — all pure thoughts
Be with me; — so shall thy unfailing love
Guide, and support, and cheer me to the end!

TO THE CUCKOO

O blithe New-comer! I have heard,
I hear thee and rejoice.
O Cuckoo! shall I call thee Bird,
Or but a wandering Voice?

While I am lying on the grass
Thy twofold shout I hear,
From hill to hill it seems to pass,
At once far off, and near.

Though babbling only to the Vale,
Of sunshine and of flowers,
Thou bringest unto me a tale
Of visionary hours.

Thrice welcome, darling of the Spring!
Even yet thou art to me
No bird, but an invisible thing,
A voice, a mystery;

The same whom in my school-boy days
I listened to; that Cry
Which made me look a thousand ways
In bush, and tree, and sky.

To seek thee did I often rove
Through woods and on the green;
And thou wert still a hope, a love;
Still longed for, never seen.

And I can listen to thee yet;
Can lie upon the plain
And listen, till I do beget
That golden time again.

O blessèd Bird! the earth we pace
Again appears to be
An unsubstantial faery place,
That is fit home for thee!

MY HEART LEAPS UP WHEN I BEHOLD

My heart leaps up when I behold
A rainbow in the sky:
So was it when my life began;
So is it now I am a man;
So be it when I shall grow old,
Or let me die!
The Child is father of the Man;
And I could wish my days to be
Bound each to each by natural piety.

AT THE GRAVE OF BURNS

SEVEN YEARS AFTER HIS DEATH

I shiver, Spirit fierce and bold,
At thought of what I now behold:
As vapours breathed from dungeons cold
Strike pleasure dead,
So sadness comes from out the mould
Where Burns is laid.

And have I then thy bones so near,
And thou forbidden to appear?
As if it were thyself that's here
I shrink with pain;
And both my wishes and my fear
Alike are vain.

Off weight — nor press on weight! — away
Dark thoughts! — they came, but not to stay;
With chastened feelings would I pay
The tribute due
To him, and aught that hides his clay
From mortal view.

Fresh as the flower, whose modest worth
He sang, his genius "glinted" forth,
Rose like a star that touching earth,
For so it seems,
Doth glorify its humble birth
With matchless beams.

The piercing eye, the thoughtful brow,
The struggling heart, where be they now? —
Full soon the Aspirant of the plough,
The prompt, the brave,
Slept, with the obscurest, in the low
And silent grave.

I mourned with thousands, but as one
More deeply grieved, for He was gone
Whose light I hailed when first it shone,
And showed my youth
How Verse may build a princely throne
On humble truth.

Alas! where'er the current tends,
Regret pursues and with it blends, —
Huge Criffel's hoary top ascends
By Skiddaw seen, —
Neighbours we were, and loving friends
We might have been;

True friends though diversely inclined;
But heart with heart and mind with mind,
Where the main fibres are entwined,
Through Nature's skill,
May even by contraries be joined
More closely still.

The tear will start, and let it flow;
Thou "poor Inhabitant below,"
At this dread moment — even so —
Might we together
Have sate and talked where gowans blow,
Or on wild heather.

What treasures would have then been placed
Within my reach; of knowledge graced
By fancy what a rich repast!
But why go on? —
Oh! spare to sweep, thou mournful blast,
His grave grass-grown.

There, too, a son, his joy and pride,
(Not three weeks past the stripling died,)
Lies gathered to his father's side,
Soul-moving sight!
Yet one to which is not denied
Some sad delight:

For he is safe, a quiet bed
Hath early found among the dead,

Harboured where none can be misled,
Wronged, or distrest;
And surely here it may be said
That such are blest.

And oh! for Thee, by pitying grace
Checked oft-times in a devious race
May He who halloweth the place
Where man is laid
Receive thy spirit in the embrace
For which it prayed!

Sighing I turned away; but ere
Night fell I heard, or seemed to hear,
Music that sorrow comes not near,
A ritual hymn,
Chaunted in love that casts out fear
By Seraphim.

THE SOLITARY REAPER

Behold her, single in the field,
Yon solitary Highland Lass!
Reaping and singing by herself;
Stop here, or gently pass!
Alone she cuts and binds the grain
And sings a melancholy strain;
O listen! for the vale profound
Is overflowing with the sound.

No nightingale did ever chaunt
More welcome notes to weary bands
Of travellers in some shady haunt,
Among Arabian sands:
A voice so thrilling ne'er was heard
In spring-time from the cuckoo-bird
Breaking the silence of the seas
Among the farthest Hebrides.

Will no one tell me what she sings?—
Perhaps the plaintive numbers flow
For old, unhappy, far-off things,
And battles long ago:
Or is it some more humble lay,
Familiar matter of to-day?
Some natural sorrow, loss, or pain,
That has been, and may be again?

Whate'er the theme, the maiden sang
As if her song could have no ending;
I saw her singing at her work,
And o'er the sickle bending;—
I listened, motionless and still;
And, as I mounted up the hill
The music in my heart I bore,
Long after it was heard no more.

YARROW UNVISITED[1]

From Stirling castle we had seen
The mazy Forth unravelled;
Had trod the banks of Clyde, and Tay,
And with the Tweed had travelled;
And when we came to Clovenford,
Then said my "winsome marrow,"
"Whate'er betide, we'll turn aside,
And see the Braes of Yarrow."

"Let Yarrow folk, frae Selkirk town,
Who have been buying, selling,
Go back to Yarrow, 'tis their own;
Each maiden to her dwelling!
On Yarrow's banks let herons feed,
Hares couch, and rabbits burrow!
But we will downward with the Tweed,
Nor turn aside to Yarrow.

"There's Galla Water, Leader Haughs,
Both lying right before us;
And Dryborough, where with chiming Tweed
The lintwhites sing in chorus;
There's pleasant Tiviot-dale, a land
Made blithe with plough and harrow:
Why throw away a needful day
To go in search of Yarrow?

"What's Yarrow but a river bare,
That glides the dark hills under?
There are a thousand such elsewhere
As worthy of your wonder."
—Strange words they seemed of slight and scorn
My True-love sighed for sorrow;
And looked me in the face, to think
I thus could speak of Yarrow!

"Oh! green," said I, "are Yarrow's holms,
And sweet is Yarrow flowing!
Fair hangs the apple frae the rock,
But we will leave it growing.
O'er hilly path, and open Strath,
We'll wander Scotland thorough;
But, though so near, we will not turn
Into the dale of Yarrow.

"Let beeves and home-bred kine partake
The sweets of Burn-mill meadow;
The swan on still St. Mary's Lake
Float double, swan and shadow!

[1] See the various poems the scene of which is laid upon the banks of the Yarrow; in particular, the exquisite ballad of Hamilton beginning,—

"Busk ye, busk ye, my bonny bonny Bride.
Busk ye, busk ye, my winsome Marrow!"

We will not see them; will not go,
To-day, nor yet to-morrow,
Enough if in our hearts we know
There's such a place as Yarrow.

"Be Yarrow stream unseen, unknown!
It must, or we shall rue it:
We have a vision of our own;
Ah! why should we undo it?
The treasured dreams of times long past,
We'll keep them, winsome marrow!
For when we're there, although 'tis fair,
'Twill be another Yarrow!

"If care with freezing years should come,
And wandering seem but folly, —
Should we be loth to stir from home,
And yet be melancholy;
Should life be dull, and spirits low,
'Twill soothe us in our sorrow,
That earth has something yet to show,
The bonny holms of Yarrow!"

SHE WAS A PHANTOM OF DELIGHT

She was a phantom of delight
When first she gleamed upon my sight:
A lovely apparition, sent
To be a moment's ornament;
Her eyes as stars of twilight fair;
Like twilight's, too, her dusky hair;
But all things else about her drawn
From May-time and the cheerful dawn;
A dancing shape, an image gay,
To haunt, to startle, and way-lay.

I saw her upon nearer view,
A spirit, yet a woman too!
Her household motions light and free,
And steps of virgin-liberty;
A countenance in which did meet
Sweet records, promises as sweet;
A creature not too bright or good
For human nature's daily food;
For transient sorrows, simple wiles,
Praise, blame, love, kisses, tears, and smiles.

And now I see with eye serene
The very pulse of the machine;
A being breathing thoughtful breath,
A traveller between life and death;
The reason firm, the temperate will,
Endurance, foresight, strength, and skill;
A perfect woman, nobly planned,
To warn, to comfort, and command;
And yet a spirit still, and bright
With something of angelic light.

I WANDERED LONELY AS A CLOUD

I wandered lonely as a cloud
That floats on high o'er vales and hills,
When all at once I saw a crowd,
A host, of golden daffodils;
Beside the lake, beneath the trees,
Fluttering and dancing in the breeze.

Continuous as the stars that shine
And twinkle on the milky way,
They stretched in never-ending line
Along the margin of a bay:
Ten thousand saw I at a glance,
Tossing their heads in sprightly dance.

The waves beside them danced; but they
Out-did the sparkling waves in glee:
A poet could not but be gay
In such a jocund company:
I gazed — and gazed — but little thought
What wealth the show to me had brought:

For oft, when on my couch I lie
In vacant or in pensive mood,
They flash upon that inward eye
Which is the bliss of solitude;
And then my heart with pleasure fills,
And dances with the daffodils.

ODE TO DUTY

"Jam non consilio bonus, sed more eo perductus, ut non tantum recte facere possim, sed nisi recte facere non possim."

Stern Daughter of the Voice of God!
O Duty! if that name thou love
Who art a light to guide, a rod
To check the erring, and reprove;
Thou, who art victory and law
When empty terrors overawe;
From vain temptations dost set free;
And calm'st the weary strife of frail humanity!

There are who ask not if thine eye
Be on them; who, in love and truth,
Where no misgiving is, rely
Upon the genial sense of youth:
Glad Hearts! without reproach or blot
Who do thy work, and know it not:
Oh! if through confidence misplaced
They fail, thy saving arms, dread Power! around them cast.

Serene will be our days and bright,
And happy will our nature be,

When love is an unerring light,
And joy its own security.
And they a blissful course may hold
Even now, who, not unwisely bold,
Live in the spirit of this creed;
Yet seek thy firm support, according to their need.

I, loving freedom, and untried;
No sport of every random gust,
Yet being to myself a guide,
Too blindly have reposed my trust:
And oft, when in my heart was heard
Thy timely mandate, I deferred
The task, in smoother walks to stray;
But thee I now would serve more strictly, if I may.

Through no disturbance of my soul,
Or strong compunction in me wrought,
I supplicate for thy control;
But in the quietness of thought:
Me this unchartered freedom tires;
I feel the weight of chance-desires:
My hopes no more must change their name,
I long for a repose that ever is the same.

Stern Lawgiver! yet thou dost wear
The Godhead's most benignant grace;
Nor know we anything so fair
As is the smile upon thy face:
Flowers laugh before thee on their beds
And fragrance in thy footing treads;
Thou dost preserve the stars from wrong;
And the most ancient heavens, through thee, are fresh and strong.

To humbler functions, awful Power!
I call thee: I myself commend
Unto thy guidance from this hour;
Oh, let my weakness have an end!
Give unto me, made lowly wise,
The spirit of self-sacrifice;
The confidence of reason give;
And in the light of truth thy bondman let me live!

PERSONAL TALK

I

I am not one who much or oft delight
To season my fireside with personal talk, —
Of friends, who live within an easy walk,
Or neighbours, daily, weekly, in my sight:
And, for my chance-acquaintance, ladies bright,
Sons, mothers, maidens withering on the stalk,
These all wear out of me, like forms, with chalk
Painted on rich men's floors, for one feast-night.
Better than such discourse doth silence long,
Long, barren silence, square with my desire;
To sit without emotion, hope, or aim,
In the loved presence of my cottage fire,
And listen to the flapping of the flame,
Or kettle whispering its faint undersong.

II

"Yet life," you say, "is life; we have seen and see,
And with a living pleasure we describe;
And fits of sprightly malice do but bribe
The languid mind into activity.
Sound sense, and love itself, and mirth and glee
Are fostered by the comment and the gibe."
Even be it so; yet still among your tribe,
Our daily world's true worldings, rank not me!
Children are blest, and powerful; their world lies
More justly balanced; partly at their feet,
And part far from them: sweetest melodies
Are those that are by distance made more sweet;
Whose mind is but the mind of his own eyes,
He is a slave; the meanest we can meet!

III

Wings have we, — and as far as we can go,
We may find pleasure: wilderness and wood,
Blank ocean and mere sky, support that mood
Which with the lofty sanctifies the low.
Dreams, books, are each a world; and books, we know,
Are a substantial world, both pure and good:
Round these, with tendrils strong as flesh and blood,
Our pastime and our happiness will grow.
There find I personal themes, a plenteous store,
Matter wherein right voluble I am,
To which I listen with a ready ear;
Two shall be named, pre-eminently dear, —
The gentle Lady married to the Moor;
And heavenly Una with her milk-white Lamb.

IV

Nor can I not believe but that hereby
Great gains are mine; for thus I live remote
From evil-speaking; rancour, never sought,
Comes to me not; malignant truth, or lie.
Hence have I genial seasons, hence have I
Smooth passions, smooth discourse, and joyous thought:
And thus from day to day my little boat
Rocks in its harbour, lodging peaceably.

Blessings be with them — and eternal praise,
Who gave us nobler loves, and nobler cares —
The Poets, who on earth have made us heirs
Of truth and pure delight by heavenly lays!
Oh! might my name be numbered among theirs,
Then gladly would I end my mortal days.

ODE

INTIMATIONS OF IMMORTALITY FROM RECOLLECTIONS OF EARLY CHILDHOOD

"The Child is father of the Man;
And I could wish my days to be
Bound each to each by natural piety."

I

There was a time when meadow, grove and stream,
The earth, and every common sight,
To me did seem
Apparelled in celestial light,
The glory and the freshness of a dream.
It is not now as it hath been of yore; —
Turn wheresoe'er I may,
By night or day,
The things which I have seen I now can see no more.

II

The Rainbow comes and goes,
And lovely is the Rose;
The Moon doth with delight
Look round her when the heavens are bare;
Waters on a starry night
Are beautiful and fair;
The sunshine is a glorious birth;
But yet I know, where'er I go,
That there hath past away a glory from the earth.

III

Now, while the birds thus sing a joyous song,
And while the young lambs bound
As to the tabor's sound,
To me alone there came a thought of grief;
A timely utterance gave that thought relief,
And I again am strong:
The cataracts blow their trumpets from the steep;
No more shall grief of mine the season wrong;
I hear the echoes through the mountains throng,
The winds come to me from the fields of sleep,
And all the earth is gay;
Land and sea
Give themselves up to jollity,
And with the heart of May
Doth every beast keep holiday; —
Thou child of joy,
Shout round me, let me hear thy shouts, thou happy shepherd-boy!

IV

Ye blessèd creatures, I have heard the call
Ye to each other make; I see
The heavens laugh with you in your jubilee:
My heart is at your festival,
My head hath its coronal,
The fullness of your bliss, I feel — I feel it all.
Oh evil day! if I were sullen
While Earth herself is adorning,
This sweet May-morning,
And the children are culling
On every side,
In a thousand valleys far and wide,
Fresh flowers; while the sun shines warm,
And the babe leaps up on his mother's arm: —
I hear, I hear, with joy I hear!
— But there's a tree, of many, one,
A single field which I have looked upon,
Both of them speak of something that is gone:
The pansy at my feet
Doth the same tale repeat:
Whither is fled the visionary gleam?
Where is it now, the glory and the dream?

V

Our birth is but a sleep and a forgetting:
The Soul that rises with us, our life's Star,
Hath had elsewhere its setting,
And cometh from afar:
Not in entire forgetfulness,
And not in utter nakedness,
But trailing clouds of glory do we come
From God, who is our home:
Heaven lies about us in our infancy!
Shades of the prison-house begin to close
Upon the growing boy,
But he beholds the light, and whence it flows,
He sees it in his joy;
The Youth, who daily farther from the east
Must travel, still is Nature's priest,
And by the vision splendid
Is on his way attended;
At length the Man perceives it die away,
And fade into the light of common day.

VI

Earth fills her lap with pleasures of her own;
Yearnings she hath in her own natural kind,
And, even with something of a mother's mind,
And no unworthy aim,
The homely nurse doth all she can
To make her foster-child, her inmate Man,
Forget the glories he hath known,
And that imperial palace whence he came.

VII

Behold the Child among his new-born blisses,
A six years' darling of a pigmy size!
See, where 'mid work of his own hand he lies,
Fretted by sallies of his mother's kisses,
With light upon him from his father's eyes!
See, at his feet, some little plan or chart,
Some fragment from his dream of human life,
Shaped by himself with newly-learnèd art;
A wedding or a festival,
A mourning or a funeral;
And this hath now his heart,
And unto this he frames his song:
Then will he fit his tongue
To dialogues of business, love, or strife;
But it will not be long
Ere this be thrown aside,
And with new joy and pride
The little Actor cons another part;
Filling from time to time his "humorous stage"
With all the Persons, down to palsied Age,
That Life brings with her in her equipage;
As if his whole vocation
Were endless imitation.

VIII

Thou, whose exterior semblance doth belie
Thy soul's immensity;
Thou best philosopher, who yet dost keep
Thy heritage, thou eye among the blind,
That, deaf and silent, read'st the eternal deep,
Haunted forever by the eternal mind, —
Mighty prophet! Seer blest!
On whom those truths do rest,
Which we are toiling all our lives to find,
In darkness lost, the darkness of the grave;
Thou, over whom thy immortality
Broods like the day, a master o'er a slave,
A presence which is not to be put by;
Thou little Child, yet glorious in the might
Of heaven-born freedom on thy being's height,
Why with such earnest pains dost thou provoke
The years to bring the inevitable yoke,
Thus blindly with thy blessedness at strife?
Full soon thy Soul shall have her earthly freight,
And custom lie upon thee with a weight,
Heavy as frost, and deep almost as life!

IX

O joy! that in our embers
Is something that doth live,
That nature yet remembers
What was so fugitive!
The thought of our past years in me doth breed
Perpetual benediction: not indeed
For that which is most worthy to be blest —
Delight and liberty, the simple creed
Of childhood, whether busy or at rest,
With new-fledged hope still fluttering in his breast: —
Not for these I raise
The song of thanks and praise;
But for those obstinate questionings
Of sense and outward things,
Fallings from us, vanishings;
Blank misgivings of a Creature
Moving about in worlds not realised,
High instincts before which our mortal nature
Did tremble like a guilty thing surprised:
But for those first affections,
Those shadowy recollections,
Which, be they what they may,
Are yet the fountain light of all our day,
Are yet a master light of all our seeing;
Uphold us, cherish, and have power to make
Our noisy years seem moments in the being
Of the eternal Silence: truths that wake,
To perish never;
Which neither listlessness, nor mad endeavour,
Nor Man nor Boy,
Nor all that is at enmity with joy,
Can utterly abolish or destroy!
Hence in a season of calm weather
Though inland far we be,
Our Souls have sight of that immortal sea
Which brought us hither,
Can in a moment travel thither,
And see the Children sport upon the shore,
And hear the mighty waters rolling evermore.

X

Then sing, ye Birds, sing, sing a joyous song!
And let the young lambs bound
As to the tabor's sound!
We in thought will join your throng,
Ye that pipe and ye that play,

Ye that through your hearts to-day
Feel the gladness of the May!
What though the radiance which was once so bright
Be now forever taken from my sight,
Though nothing can bring back the hour
Of splendour in the grass, of glory in the flower;
We will grieve not, rather find
Strength in what remains behind;
In the primal sympathy
Which having been must ever be;
In the soothing thoughts that spring
Out of human suffering;
In the faith that looks through death,
In years that bring the philosophic mind.

XI

And O ye Fountains, Meadows, Hills, and Groves,
Forebode not any severing of our loves!
Yet in my heart of hearts I feel your might;
I only have relinquished one delight
To live beneath your more habitual sway.
I love the Brooks which down their channels fret,
Even more than when I tripped lightly as they;
The innocent brightness of a new-born Day
Is lovely yet;
The Clouds that gather round the setting sun
Do take a sober colouring from an eye
That hath kept watch o'er man's mortality;
Another race hath been, and other palms are won.
Thanks to the human heart by which we live,
Thanks to its tenderness, its joys, and fears,
To me the meanest flower that blows can give
Thoughts that do often lie too deep for tears.

LAODAMIA

"With sacrifice before the rising morn
Vows have I made by fruitless hope inspired;
And from the infernal gods, 'mid shades forlorn
Of night, my slaughtered lord have I required:
Celestial pity I again implore; —
Restore him to my sight — great Jove, restore!"

So speaking, and by fervent love endowed
With faith, the suppliant heavenward lifts her hands;
While, like the sun emerging from a cloud,
Her countenance brightens — and her eye expands;
Her bosom heaves and spreads, her stature grows;
And she expects the issue in repose.

O terror! what hath she perceived? — O joy!
What doth she look on? — whom doth she behold?
Her hero slain upon the beach of Troy?
His vital presence? his corporeal mould?
It is — if sense deceive her not — 'tis He?
And a god leads him, wingèd Mercury!

Mild Hermes spake — and touched her with his wand
That calms all fear; "Such grace hath crowned thy prayer,
Laodamia! that at Jove's command
Thy husband walks the paths of upper air:
He comes to tarry with thee three hours' space;
Accept the gift, behold him face to face!"

Forth sprang the impassioned queen her lord to clasp;
Again that consummation she essayed;
But unsubstantial form eludes her grasp
As often as that eager grasp was made.
The phantom parts — but parts to re-unite,
And re-assume his place before her sight.

"Protesilaüs, lo! thy guide is gone!
Confirm, I pray, the vision with thy voice:
This is our palace, — yonder is thy throne;
Speak, and the floor thou tread'st on will rejoice.
Not to appal me have the gods bestowed
This precious boon; and blest a sad abode."

"Great Jove, Laodamia! doth not leave
His gifts imperfect: — Spectre though I be,
I am not sent to scare thee or deceive;
But in reward of thy fidelity.
And something also did my worth obtain;
For fearless virtue bringeth boundless gain.

"Thou knowest, the Delphic oracle foretold
That the first Greek who touched the Trojan strand
Should die; but me the threat could not withhold:
A generous cause a victim did demand;
And forth I leapt upon the sandy plain;
A self-devoted chief — by Hector slain."

"Supreme of heroes — bravest, noblest, best!
Thy matchless courage I bewail no more,
Which then, when tens of thousands were deprest
By doubt, propelled thee to the fatal shore;
Thou found'st — and I forgive thee — here thou art —
A nobler counsellor than my poor heart.

"But thou, though capable of sternest deed,
Wert kind as resolute, and good as brave;
And he, whose power restores thee, hath decreed
Thou should'st elude the malice of the grave:
Redundant are thy locks, thy lips as fair
As when their breath enriched Thessalian air.

"No spectre greets me, — no vain shadow this;
Come, blooming hero, place thee by my side!

Give, on this well-known couch, one nuptial kiss
To me, this day, a second time thy bride!"
Jove frowned in heaven: the conscious Parcæ threw
Upon those roseate lips a Stygian hue.

"This visage tells thee that my doom is past:
Nor should the change be mourned, even if the joys
Of sense were able to return as fast
And surely as they vanish. Earth destroys
Those raptures duly — Erebus disdains:
Calm pleasures there abide — majestic pains.

"Be taught, O faithful consort, to control
Rebellious passion: for the gods approve
The depth, and not the tumult, of the soul;
A fervent, not ungovernable, love.
Thy transports moderate; and meekly mourn
When I depart, for brief is my sojourn —"

"Ah, wherefore? — Did not Hercules by force
Wrest from the guardian Monster of the tomb
Alcestis, a reanimated corse,
Given back to dwell on earth in vernal bloom?
Medea's spells dispersed the weight of years,
And Æson stood a youth 'mid youthful peers.

"The gods to us are merciful — and they
Yet further may relent: for mightier far
Than strength of nerve and sinew, or the sway
Of magic potent over sun and star,
Is love, though oft to agony distrest,
And though his favourite seat be feeble woman's breast.

"But if thou goest, I follow —" "Peace!" he said, —
She looked upon him and was calmed and cheered;
The ghastly colour from his lips had fled;
In his deportment, shape, and mien, appeared
Elysian beauty, melancholy grace,
Brought from a pensive though a happy place.

He spake of love, such love as spirits feel
In worlds whose course is equable and pure;
No fears to beat away — no strife to heal —
The past unsighed for, and the future sure;
Spake of heroic arts in graver mood
Revived, with finer harmony pursued;

Of all that is most beauteous — imaged there
In happier beauty; more pellucid streams,
An ampler ether, a diviner air,
And fields invested with purpureal gleams;
Climes which the sun, who sheds the brightest day
Earth knows, is all unworthy to survey.

Yet there the soul shall enter which hath earned
That privilege by virtue. — "Ill," said he,
"The end of man's existence I discerned,
Who from ignoble games and revelry
Could draw, when we had parted, vain delight,
While tears were thy best pastime, day and night;

"And while my youthful peers before my eyes
(Each hero following his peculiar bent)
Prepared themselves for glorious enterprise
By martial sports, — or, seated in the tent,
Chieftains and kings in council were detained;
What time the fleet at Aulis lay enchained.

"The wished-for wind was given: — I then revolved
The oracle, upon the silent sea;
And, if no worthier led the way, resolved
That, of a thousand vessels, mine should be
The foremost prow in pressing to the strand, —
Mine the first blood that tinged the Trojan sand.

"Yet bitter, oft-times bitter, was the pang
When of thy loss I thought, belovèd wife!
On thee too fondly did my memory hang,
And on the joys we shared in mortal life, —
The paths which we had trod — these fountains, flowers,
My new-planned cities, and unfinished towers.

"But should suspense permit the foe to cry,
'Behold they tremble! — haughty their array,
Yet of their number no one dares to die'?
In soul I swept the indignity away:
Old frailties then recurred: — but lofty thought,
In act embodied, my deliverance wrought.

"And thou, though strong in love, art all too weak
In reason, in self-government too slow;
I counsel thee by fortitude to seek
Our blest re-union in the shades below.
The invisible world with thee hath sympathised;
Be thy affections raised and solemnised.

"Learn, by a mortal yearning, to ascend —
Seeking a higher object. Love was given,
Encouraged, sanctioned, chiefly for that end;
For this the passion to excess was driven —
That self might be annulled: her bondage prove
The fetters of a dream, opposed to love." ——

Aloud she shrieked! for Hermes reappears!
Round the dear Shade she would have clung — 'tis vain:
The hours are past — too brief had they been years;
And him no mortal effort can detain:

Swift, toward the realms that know not earthly day,
He through the portal takes his silent way,
And on the palace-floor a lifeless corse she lay.

Thus all in vain exhorted and reproved,
She perished; and, as for a wilful crime,
By the just gods, whom no weak pity moved,
Was doomed to wear out her appointed time,
Apart from happy ghosts, that gather flowers
Of blissful quiet 'mid unfading bowers.

— Yet tears to human suffering are due;
And mortal hopes defeated and o'erthrown
Are mourned by man, and not by man alone,
As fondly he believes. — Upon the side
Of Hellespont (such faith was entertained)
A knot of spiry trees for ages grew
From out the tomb of him for whom she died;
And ever, when such stature they had gained
That Ilium's walls were subject to their view,
The trees' tall summits withered at the sight;
A constant interchange of growth and blight!

TO A SKY-LARK

Ethereal minstrel! pilgrim of the sky!
Dost thou despise the earth where cares abound?
Or, while the wings aspire, are heart and eye
Both with thy nest upon the dewy ground?
Thy nest which thou canst drop into at will,
Those quivering wings composed, that music still!

Leave to the nightingale her shady wood;
A privacy of glorious light is thine;
Whence thou dost pour upon the world a flood
Of harmony, with instinct more divine;
Type of the wise who soar, but never roam;
True to the kindred points of Heaven and Home!

SONNETS

ON THE EXTINCTION OF THE VENETIAN REPUBLIC

Once did She hold the gorgeous east in fee;
And was the safeguard of the west: the worth
Of Venice did not fall below her birth,
Venice, the eldest child of Liberty.
She was a maiden city, bright and free;
No guile seduced, no force could violate;
And, when she took unto herself a Mate,
She must espouse the everlasting Sea.
And what if she had seen those glories fade,
Those titles vanish, and that strength decay;
Yet shall some tribute of regret be paid
When her long life hath reached its final day:
Men are we, and must grieve when even the Shade
Of that which once was great is passed away.

TO TOUSSAINT L'OUVERTURE

Toussaint, the most unhappy man of men!
Whether the whistling rustic tend his plough
Within thy hearing, or thy head be now
Pillowed in some deep dungeon's earless den; —
O miserable chieftain! where and when
Wilt thou find patience? Yet die not; do thou
Wear rather in thy bonds a cheerful brow:
Though fallen thyself, never to rise again,
Live, and take comfort. Thou hast left behind
Powers that will work for thee; air, earth, and skies;
There's not a breathing of the common wind
That will forget thee; thou hast great allies;
Thy friends are exultations, agonies,
And love, and man's unconquerable mind.

SEPTEMBER, 1802, NEAR DOVER

Inland, within a hollow vale, I stood;
And saw, while sea was calm and air was clear,
The coast of France — the coast of France how near!
Drawn almost into frightful neighbourhood.
I shrunk; for verily the barrier flood
Was like a lake, or river bright and fair,
A span of waters; yet what power is there!
What mightiness for evil and for good!
Even so doth God protect us if we be
Virtuous and wise. Winds blow, and waters roll,
Strength to the brave, and Power, and Deity;
Yet in themselves are nothing! One decree
Spake laws to them, and said that by the soul
Only, the nations shall be great and free.

THOUGHT OF A BRITON ON THE SUBJUGATION OF SWITZERLAND

Two voices are there; one is of the sea,
One of the mountains; each a mighty voice:
In both from age to age thou didst rejoice,
They were thy chosen music, Liberty!
There came a tyrant, and with holy glee
Thou fought'st against him; but hast vainly striven:
Thou from thy Alpine holds at length art driven,
Where not a torrent murmurs heard by thee.
Of one deep bliss thine ear hath been bereft:
Then cleave, O cleave to that which still is left;
For, high-souled Maid, what sorrow would it be
That mountain floods should thunder as before,
And ocean bellow from his rocky shore,
And neither awful voice be heard by thee.

LONDON, 1802

Milton! thou should'st be living at this hour:
England hath need of thee: she is a fen
Of stagnant waters: altar, sword, and pen,
Fireside, the heroic wealth of hall and bower,
Have forfeited their ancient English dower
Of inward happiness. We are selfish men;
Oh! raise us up, return to us again;
And give us manners, virtue, freedom, power.
Thy soul was like a Star, and dwelt apart:
Thou hadst a voice whose sound was like the sea:
Pure as the naked heavens, majestic, free,
So didst thou travel on life's common way,
In cheerful godliness; and yet thy heart
The lowliest duties on herself did lay.

COMPOSED UPON WESTMINSTER BRIDGE, SEPT. 3, 1802

Earth has not anything to show more fair:
Dull would he be of soul who could pass by
A sight so touching in its majesty:
This City now doth, like a garment, wear
The beauty of the morning; silent, bare,
Ships, towers, domes, theatres, and temples lie
Open unto the fields, and to the sky;
All bright and glittering in the smokeless air.
Never did sun more beautifully steep
In his first splendour, valley, rock, or hill;
Ne'er saw I, never felt, a calm so deep!
The river glideth at his own sweet will:
Dear God! the very houses seem asleep;
And all that mighty heart is lying still!

ON THE SEA-SHORE NEAR CALAIS

It is a beauteous evening, calm and free,
The holy time is quiet as a Nun
Breathless with adoration; the broad sun
Is sinking down in its tranquillity;
The gentleness of heaven broods o'er the Sea:
Listen! the mighty Being is awake,
And doth with his eternal motion make
A sound like thunder — everlastingly.
Dear Child! dear Girl! that walkest with me here,
If thou appear untouched by solemn thought,
Thy nature is not therefore less divine:
Thou liest in Abraham's bosom all the year;
And worship'st at the temple's inner shrine,
God being with thee when we know it not.

ON THE SONNET

Nuns fret not at their convent's narrow room;
And hermits are contented with their cells;
And students with their pensive citadels;
Maids at the wheel, the weaver at his loom,
Sit blithe and happy; bees that soar for bloom,
High as the highest Peak of Furness-fells,
Will murmur by the hour in foxglove bells:
In truth the prison, unto which we doom
Ourselves, no prison is: and hence for me,
In sundry moods, 'twas pastime to be bound
Within the Sonnet's scanty plot of ground;
Pleased if some Souls (for such there needs must be)
Who have felt the weight of too much liberty,
Should find brief solace there, as I have found.

ADMONITION

Intended more particularly for the perusal of those who may have happened to be enamoured of some beautiful Place of Retreat, in the Country of the Lakes.

Well may'st thou halt — and gaze with brightening eye!
The lovely Cottage in the guardian nook
Hath stirred thee deeply; with its own dear brook,
Its own small pasture, almost its own sky!
But covet not the Abode: — forbear to sigh,
As many do, repining while they look;
Intruders — who would tear from Nature's book
This precious leaf, with harsh impiety.
Think what the Home must be if it were thine,
Even thine, though few thy wants! — Roof, window, door,
The very flowers are sacred to the Poor,
The roses to the porch which they entwine:
Yea, all that now enchants thee, from the day
On which it should be touched, would melt away.

THE WORLD IS TOO MUCH WITH US

The world is too much with us: late and soon,
Getting and spending, we lay waste our powers:
Little we see in Nature that is ours;
We have given our hearts away, a sordid boon!
This Sea that bares her bosom to the moon;
The winds that will be howling at all hours,
And are up-gathered now like sleeping flowers;
For this, for everything, we are out of tune;
It moves us not. — Great God! I'd rather be
A Pagan suckled in a creed outworn;
So might I, standing on this pleasant lea,
Have glimpses that would make me less forlorn;
Have sight of Proteus rising from the sea;
Or hear old Triton blow his wreathèd horn.

TO SLEEP

A flock of sheep that leisurely pass by,
One after one; the sound of rain, and bees
Murmuring; the fall of rivers, winds and seas,
Smooth fields, white sheets of water, and pure sky:
I have thought of all by turns, and yet do lie
Sleepless! and soon the small birds' melodies
Must hear, first uttered from my orchard trees;
And the first cuckoo's melancholy cry.
Even thus last night, and two nights more, I lay,
And could not win thee, Sleep! by any stealth:
So do not let me wear to-night away:
Without Thee what is all the morning's wealth?
Come, blessed barrier between day and day,
Dear mother of fresh thoughts and joyous health!

TO B. R. HAYDON

High is our calling, Friend! — Creative Art
(Whether the instrument of words she use,
Or pencil pregnant with ethereal hues,)
Demands the service of a mind and heart,
Though sensitive, yet, in their weakest part,
Heroically fashioned — to infuse
Faith in the whispers of the lonely Muse,
While the whole world seems adverse to desert.
And, oh! when Nature sinks, as oft she may,
Through long-lived pressure of obscure distress,
Still to be strenuous for the bright reward,
And in the soul admit of no decay,
Brook no continuance of weak-mindedness —
Great is the glory, for the strife is hard!

THE RIVER DUDDON

I

Sole listener, Duddon! to the breeze that played
With thy clear voice, I caught the fitful sound
Wafted o'er sullen moss and craggy mound —
Unfruitful solitudes, that seemed to upbraid
The sun in heaven! — but now, to form a shade
For Thee, green alders have together wound
Their foliage; ashes flung their arms around;
And birch-trees risen in silver colonnade.
And thou hast also tempted here to rise,
'Mid sheltering pines, this cottage rude and grey;
Whose ruddy children, by the mother's eyes
Carelessly watched, sport through the summer day,
Thy pleased associates: — light as endless May
On infant bosoms lonely Nature lies.

II

The old inventive Poets, had they seen,
Or rather felt, the entrancement that detains
Thy waters, Duddon! 'mid these flowery plains —
The still repose, the liquid lapse serene,
Transferred to bowers imperishably green,
Had beautified Elysium! But these chains
Will soon be broken; — a rough course remains,
Rough as the past; where thou, of placid mien,
Innocuous as a firstling of the flock,
And countenanced like a soft cerulean sky,
Shalt change thy temper; and with many a shock
Given and received in mutual jeopardy,
Dance, like a Bacchanal, from rock to rock,
Tossing her frantic thyrsus wide and high!

III

Return, Content! for fondly I pursued,
Even when a child, the Streams — unheard, unseen;
Through tangled woods, impending rocks between;
Or, free as air, with flying inquest viewed
The sullen reservoirs whence their bold brood —
Pure as the morning, fretful, boisterous, keen,
Green as the salt-sea billows, white and green —
Poured down the hills, a choral multitude!
Nor have I tracked their course for scanty gains;
They taught me random cares and truant joys,
That shield from mischief and preserve from stains
Vague minds, while men are growing out of boys;
Maturer fancy owes to their rough noise
Impetuous thoughts that brook not servile reins.

IV

I thought of thee, my partner and my guide,
As being past away. — Vain sympathies!
For, backward, Duddon! as I cast my eyes,
I see what was, and is, and will abide;
Still glides the Stream, and shall forever glide;
The Form remains, the Function never dies;
While we, the brave, the mighty, and the wise,
We Men, who in our morn of youth defied
The elements, must vanish; — be it so!
Enough, if something from our hands have power
To live, and act, and serve the future hour;
And if, as toward the silent tomb we go,
Through love, through hope, and faith's transcendent dower,
We feel that we are greater than we know.

SCORN NOT THE SONNET

Scorn not the Sonnet; Critic, you have frowned,
Mindless of its just honours; with this key
Shakespeare unlocked his heart: the melody
Of this small lute gave ease to Petrarch's wound;
A thousand times this pipe did Tasso sound;
With it Camoëns soothed an exile's grief;
The Sonnet glittered a gay myrtle leaf
Amid the cypress with which Dante crowned
His visionary brow: a glow-worm lamp,
It cheered mild Spenser, called from Faeryland
To struggle through dark ways; and, when a damp
Fell round the path of Milton, in his hand
The Thing became a trumpet; whence he blew
Soul-animating strains — alas, too few!

MOST SWEET IT IS

Most sweet it is with unuplifted eyes
To pace the ground, if path be there or none,
While a fair region round the traveller lies
Which he forbears again to look upon;
Pleased rather with some soft ideal scene,
The work of Fancy, or some happy tone
Of meditation, slipping in between
The beauty coming and the beauty gone.
If Thought and Love desert us, from that day
Let us break off all commerce with the Muse:
With Thought and Love companions of our way,
Whate'er the senses take or may refuse,
The Mind's internal heaven shall shed her dews
Of inspiration on the humblest lay.

COMPOSED ON A MAY MORNING

Life with yon Lambs, like day, is just begun
Yet Nature seems to them a heavenly guide.
Does joy approach? they meet the coming tide,
And sullenness avoid, as now they shun
Pale twilight's lingering glooms, — and in the sun
Couch near their dams, with quiet satisfied;
Or gambol — each with his shadow at his side,
Varying its shape wherever he may run.
As they from turf yet hoar with sleepy dew
All turn, and court the shining and the green,
Where herbs look up, and opening flowers are seen;
Why to God's goodness cannot We be true,
And so, His gifts and promises between,
Feed to the last on pleasures ever new?

THE POET

A Poet! — He hath put his heart to school,
Nor dares to move unpropped upon the staff
Which Art hath lodged within his hand — must laugh
By precept only, and shed tears by rule.
Thy Art be Nature; the live current quaff,
And let the groveller sip his stagnant pool,
In fear that else, when Critics grave and cool
Have killed him, Scorn should write his epitaph.
How does the Meadow-flower its bloom unfold?
Because the lovely little flower is free
Down to its root, and, in that freedom, bold;
And so the grandeur of the Forest-tree
Comes not by casting in a formal mould,
But from its own divine vitality.

SIR WALTER SCOTT (1771–1832)

THE LAY OF THE LAST MINSTREL

From CANTO I

The feast was over in Branksome tower,
And the Ladye had gone to her secret bower;
Her bower that was guarded by word and by spell,
Deadly to hear, and deadly to tell —
Jesu Maria, shield us well!
No living wight, save the Ladye alone,
Had dared to cross the threshold stone.

The tables were drawn, it was idlesse all;
  Knight, and page, and household squire,
Loiter'd through the lofty hall,
  Or crowded round the ample fire:
The staghounds, weary with the chase,
  Lay stretch'd upon the rushy floor,
And urged, in dreams, the forest race,
  From Teviot-stone to Eskdale-moor.

Nine-and-twenty knights of fame
  Hung their shields in Branksome-Hall;
Nine-and-twenty squires of name
  Brought them their steeds to bower from stall;
    Nine-and-twenty yeomen tall
    Waited, duteous, on them all;
    They were all knights of mettle true,
    Kinsmen to the bold Buccleuch.

Ten of them were sheathed in steel,
With belted sword, and spur on heel:
They quitted not their harness bright,
Neither by day, nor yet by night:
      They lay down to rest,
      With corslet laced,
Pillow'd on buckler cold and hard;

They carved at the meal
With gloves of steel,
And they drank the red wine through the helmet barr'd.

Ten squires, ten yeomen, mail-clad men,
Waited the beck of the warders ten;
Thirty steeds, both fleet and wight,
Stood saddled in stable day and night,
Barbed with frontlet of steel, I trow,
And with Jedwood-axe at saddlebow;
A hundred more fed free in stall: —
Such was the custom of Branksome-Hall.

From CANTO VI

The Lay of Rosabelle

O listen, listen, ladies gay!
No haughty feat of arms I tell;
Soft is the note, and sad the lay,
That mourns the lovely Rosabelle;

"Moor, moor the barge, ye gallant crew!
And, gentle ladye, deign to stay,
Rest thee in Castle Ravensheuch,
Nor tempt the stormy firth to-day.

"The blackening wave is edged with white:
To inch and rock the sea-mews fly;
The fishers have heard the Water-Sprite,
Whose screams forbode that wreck is nigh.

"Last night the gifted Seer did view
A wet shroud swathed round ladye gay;
Then stay thee, Fair, in Ravensheuch:
Why cross the gloomy firth to-day?" —

"'Tis not because Lord Lindesay's heir
To-night at Roslin leads the ball,
But that my ladye-mother there
Sits lonely in her castle-hall.

"'Tis not because the ring they ride,
And Lindesay at the ring rides well,
But that my sire the wine will chide,
If 'tis not fill'd by Rosabelle." —

O'er Roslin all that dreary night
A wondrous blaze was seen to gleam;
'Twas broader than the watch-fire's light,
And redder than the bright moonbeam.

It glared on Roslin's castled rock,
It ruddied all the copse-wood glen;
'Twas seen from Dryden's groves of oak,
And seen from cavern'd Hawthornden.

Seem'd all on fire that chapel proud,
Where Roslin's chiefs uncoffin'd lie,
Each Baron, for a sable shroud,
Sheathed in his iron panoply.

Seem'd all on fire, within, around,
Deep sacristy and altar's pale,
Shone every pillar foliage-bound,
And glimmer'd all the dead men's mail.

Blazed battlement and pinnet high,
Blazed every rose-carved buttress fair —
So still they blaze, when fate is nigh
The lordly line of high St. Clair.

There are twenty of Roslin's barons bold
Lie buried within that proud chapelle;
Each one the holy vault doth hold —
But the sea holds lovely Rosabelle!

And each St. Clair was buried there,
With candle, with book, and with knell;
But the sea-caves rung, and the wild winds sung,
The dirge of lovely Rosabelle.

LOCHINVAR

From MARMION, CANTO V

O, young Lochinvar is come out of the west,
Through all the wide Border his steed was the best;
And, save his good broadsword, he weapon had none,
He rode all unarmed, and he rode all alone.
So faithful in love, and so dauntless in war,
There never was knight like the young Lochinvar.

He stayed not for brake, and he stopped not for stone,
He swam the Eske River where ford there was none;
But, ere he alighted at Netherby gate,
The bride had consented, the gallant came late;
For a laggard in love, and a dastard in war,
Was to wed the fair Ellen of brave Lochinvar.

So boldly he entered the Netherby Hall,
Among bridesmen, and kinsmen, and brothers, and all.
Then spoke the bride's father, his hand on his sword
(For the poor craven bridegroom said never a word),
"O, come ye in peace here, or come ye in war,
Or to dance at our bridal, young Lord Lochinvar?"

"I long wooed your daughter, my suit you denied; —
Love swells like the Solway, but ebbs like its tide, —
And now I am come, with this lost love of mine,
To lead but one measure, drink one cup of wine.
There are maidens in Scotland more lovely by far,
That would gladly be bride to the young Lochinvar."

The bride kissed the goblet; the knight took it up,
He quaffed off the wine, and threw down the cup.
She looked down to blush, and she looked up to sigh,
With a smile on her lips, and a tear in her eye.
He took her soft hand, ere her mother could bar, —
"Now tread we a measure," said young Lochinvar.

So stately his form, and so lovely her face,
That never a hall such a galliard did grace;
While her mother did fret, and her father did fume,
And the bridegroom stood dangling his bonnet and plume;
And the bridemaidens whispered, "'Twere better by far
To have matched our fair cousin with young Lochinvar."

One touch to her hand, and one word in her ear,
When they reached the hall-door, and the charger stood near;
So light to the croupe the fair lady he swung,
So light to the saddle before her he sprung;
"She is won! we are gone! over bank, bush, and scaur;
They'll have fleet steeds that follow," quoth young Lochinvar.

There was mounting 'mong Græmes of the Netherby clan;
Forsters, Fenwicks, and Musgraves, they rode and they ran:
There was racing and chasing on Cannobie Lee,
But the lost bride of Netherby ne'er did they see.
So daring in love, and so dauntless in war,
Have ye e'er heard of gallant like young Lochinvar?

CHRISTMAS IN THE OLDEN TIME

From MARMION, INTRODUCTION TO CANTO VI

Heap on more wood! — the wind is chill;
But let it whistle as it will,
We'll keep our Christmas merry still.
Each age has deemed the new-born year
The fittest time for festal cheer:
Even, heathen yet, the savage Dane
At Iol more deep the mead did drain;
High on the beach his galleys drew,
And feasted all his pirate crew;
Then in his low and pine-built hall,
Where shields and axes decked the wall,
They gorged upon the half-dressed steer;
Caroused in seas of sable beer;
While round, in brutal jest, were thrown
The half-gnawed rib and marrow-bone;
Or listened all, in grim delight,
While Scalds yelled out the joys of fight.
Then forth in frenzy would they hie,
While wildly-loose their red locks fly;
And, dancing round the blazing pile,
They make such barbarous mirth the while,
As best might to the mind recall
The boisterous joys of Odin's hall.
And well our Christian sires of old
Loved when the year its course had rolled
And brought blithe Christmas back again
With all its hospitable train.
Domestic and religious rite
Gave honour to the holy night:
On Christmas eve the bells were rung;
On Christmas eve the mass was sung;
That only night, in all the year,
Saw the stoled priest the chalice rear.
The damsel donned her kirtle sheen;
The hall was dressed with holly green;
Forth to the wood did merry-men go,
To gather in the mistletoe.
Then opened wide the baron's hall
To vassal, tenant, serf, and all;
Power laid his rod of rule aside;
And Ceremony doffed her pride.
The heir, with roses in his shoes,
That night might village partner choose;
The lord, underogating, share
The vulgar game of "post and pair."
All hailed with uncontrolled delight,
And general voice, the happy night
That to the cottage, as the crown,
Brought tidings of salvation down.
The fire, with well-dried logs supplied,
Went roaring up the chimney wide;
The huge hall-table's oaken face,
Scrubbed till it shone, the day of grace,
Bore then upon its massive board
No mark to part the squire and lord.
Then was brought in the lusty brawn,
By old blue-coated serving-man;
Then the grim boar's-head frowned on high
Crested with bays and rosemary.

Well can the green-garbed ranger tell
How, when, and where the monster fell;
What dogs before his death he tore,
And all the baiting of the boar.
The wassail round, in good brown bowls,
Garnished with ribbons, blithely trowls.
There the huge sirloin reeked; hard by
Plum-porridge stood, and Christmas pie;
Nor failed old Scotland to produce,
At such high-tide, her savoury goose.
Then came the merry maskers in,
And carols roared with blithesome din;
If unmelodious was the song,
It was a hearty note, and strong.
Who lists may in their mumming see
Traces of ancient mystery;
White skirts supplied the masquerade,
And smutted cheeks the visors made:
But, O! what maskers richly dight
Can boast of bosoms half so light!
England was merry England, when
Old Christmas brought his sports again.
'Twas Christmas broached the mightiest ale;
'Twas Christmas told the merriest tale;
A Christmas gambol oft could cheer
The poor man's heart through half the year.

MARMION AND DOUGLAS

From MARMION, CANTO VI

XIII

Not far advanced was morning day,
When Marmion did his troop array
To Surrey's camp to ride;
He had safe conduct for his band,
Beneath the royal seal and hand,
And Douglas gave a guide:
The ancient Earl, with stately grace,
Would Clara on her palfrey place,
And whispered in an undertone,
"Let the hawk stoop, his prey is flown."
The train from out the castle drew,
But Marmion stopped to bid adieu: —
"Though something I might plain," he said,
"Of cold respect to stranger guest,
Sent hither by your king's behest,
While in Tantallon's towers I stayed,
Part we in friendship from your land,
And, noble Earl, receive my hand." —
But Douglas round him drew his cloak,
Folded his arms, and thus he spoke: —
"My manors, halls, and bowers shall still
Be open, at my sovereign's will,
To each one whom he lists, howe'er
Unmeet to be the owner's peer.
My castles are my king's alone,
From turret to foundation-stone, —
The hand of Douglas is his own;
And never shall in friendly grasp
The hand of such as Marmion clasp."

XIV

Burned Marmion's swarthy cheek like fire,
And shook his very frame for ire,
And — "This to me!" he said, —
"An't were not for thy hoary beard,
Such hand as Marmion's had not spared
To cleave the Douglas' head!
And, first, I tell thee, haughty Peer,
He who does England's message here.
Although the meanest in her state,
May well, proud Angus, be thy mate:
And, Douglas, more I tell thee here,
Even in thy pitch of pride,
Here in thy hold, thy vassals near,
(Nay, never look upon your lord,
And lay your hands upon your sword,)
I tell thee, thou'rt defied!
And if thou said'st I am not peer
To any lord in Scotland here,
Lowland or Highland, far or near,
Lord Angus, thou hast lied!" —
On the Earl's cheek the flush of rage
O'ercame the ashen hue of age:
Fierce he broke forth, — "And dar'st thou then
To beard the lion in his den,
The Douglas in his hall?
And hop'st thou hence unscathed to go?
No, by St. Bride of Bothwell, no!
Up drawbridge, grooms, — what, warder, ho!
Let the portcullis fall." —
Lord Marmion turned, — well was his need! —
And dashed the rowels in his steed;
Like arrow through the archway sprung;
The ponderous grate behind him rung:
To pass there was such scanty room,
The bars, descending, razed his plume.

XV

The steed along the drawbridge flies,
Just as it trembled on the rise;
Not lighter does the swallow skim
Along the smooth lake's level brim;
And when Lord Marmion reached his band,
He halts, and turns with clenchèd hand,
And shout of loud defiance pours,
And shook his gauntlet at the towers.

SOLDIER, REST! THY WARFARE O'ER

From THE LADY OF THE LAKE

Canto I

Soldier, rest! thy warfare o'er,
Sleep the sleep that knows not breaking;
Dream of battled fields no more,
Days of danger, nights of waking.
In our isle's enchanted hall,
Hands unseen thy couch are strewing,
Fairy strains of music fall,
Every sense in slumber dewing.
Soldier, rest! thy warfare o'er,
Dream of fighting fields no more;
Sleep the sleep that knows not breaking,
Morn of toil, nor night of waking.

No rude sound shall reach thine ear,
Armour's clang, or war-steed champing,
Trump nor pibroch summon here
Mustering clan, or squadron tramping.
Yet the lark's shrill fife may come
At the daybreak from the fallow,
And the bittern sound his drum,
Booming from the sedgy shallow.
Ruder sounds shall none be near
Guards nor warders challenge here;
Here's no war-steed's neigh and champing,
Shouting clans or squadrons stamping.

Huntsman, rest! thy chase is done,
While our slumbrous spells assail ye,
Dream not, with the rising sun,
Bugles here shall sound reveille.[1]
Sleep! the deer is in his den;
Sleep! thy hounds are by thee lying;
Sleep! nor dream in yonder glen
How thy gallant steed lay dying.
Huntsman, rest! thy chase is done;
Think not of the rising sun,
For, at dawning to assail ye,
Here no bugles sound reveille.

FITZ-JAMES AND RODERICK DHU

From THE LADY OF THE LAKE

Canto V

VIII

"Enough, I am by promise tied
To match me with this man of pride:
Twice have I sought Clan-Alpine's glen
In peace; but when I come again,
I come with banner, brand, and bow,
As leader seeks his mortal foe.
For lovelorn swain, in lady's bower,
Ne'er panted for the appointed hour,
As I, until before me stand
This rebel Chieftain and his band."

IX

"Have, then, thy wish!" — He whistled shrill,
And he was answered from the hill;
Wild as the scream of the curlew,
From crag to crag the signal flew.
Instant, through copse and heath, arose
Bonnets and spears and bended bows;
On right, on left, above, below,
Sprung up at once the lurking foe;
From shingles grey their lances start,
The bracken bush sends forth the dart,
The rushes and the willow wand
Are bristling into axe and brand,
And every tuft of broom gives life
To plaided warrior armed for strife.
That whistle garrisoned the glen
At once with full five hundred men,
As if the yawning hill to heaven
A subterranean host had given.
Watching their leader's beck and will,
All silent there they stood, and still.
Like the loose crags whose threatening mass
Lay tottering o'er the hollow pass,
As if an infant's touch could urge
Their headlong passage down the verge,
With step and weapon forward flung,
Upon the mountain-side they hung.
The Mountaineer cast glance of pride
Along Benledi's living side,
Then fixed his eye and sable brow
Full on Fitz-James: "How say'st thou now?
These are Clan-Alpine's warriors true;
And, Saxon, — I am Roderick Dhu!"

X

Fitz-James was brave; — though to his heart
The life-blood thrilled with sudden start,
He manned himself with dauntless air,
Returned the Chief his haughty stare,
His back against a rock he bore,
And firmly placed his foot before: —
"Come one, come all! this rock shall fly
From its firm base as soon as I."
Sir Roderick marked, — and in his eyes
Respect was mingled with surprise,
And the stern joy which warriors feel
In foeman worthy of their steel.

[1] Note the rhyme

Short space he stood, — then waved his hand:
Down sunk the disappearing band;
Each warrior vanished where he stood,
In broom or bracken, heath or wood:
Sunk brand and spear, and bended bow,
In osiers pale and copses low:
It seemed as if their mother Earth
Had swallowed up her warlike birth.
The wind's last breath had tossed in air
Pennon and plaid and plumage fair, —
The next but swept a lone hillside,
Where heath and fern were waving wide;
The sun's last glance was glinted back,
From spear and glaive, from targe and jack, —
The next, all unreflected, shone
On bracken green, and cold grey stone.

XI

Fitz-James looked round, — yet scarce believed
The witness that his sight received;
Such apparition well might seem
Delusion of a dreadful dream.
Sir Roderick in suspense he eyed,
And to his look the Chief replied:
"Fear naught — nay, that I need not say —
But — doubt not aught from mine array.
Thou art my guest; — I pledged my word
As far as Coilantogle ford:
Nor would I call a clansman's brand
For aid against one valiant hand,
Though on our strife lay every vale
Rent by the Saxon from the Gael.
So move we on; — I only meant
To show the reed on which you leant,
Deeming this path you might pursue
Without a pass from Roderick Dhu."
They moved; — I said Fitz-James was brave,
As ever knight that belted glaive;
Yet dare not say that now his blood
Kept on its wont and tempered flood,
As, following Roderick's stride, he drew
That seeming lonesome pathway through,
Which yet, by fearful proof, was rife
With lances, that, to take his life,
Waited but signal from a guide,
So late dishonoured and defied.
Ever, by stealth, his eye sought round
The vanished guardians of the ground,
And still, from copse and heather deep,
Fancy saw spear and broadsword peep,
And in the plover's shrilly strain
The signal whistle heard again.
Nor breathed he free till far behind
The pass was left; for then they wind
Along a wide and level green,
Where neither tree nor tuft was seen,
Nor rush nor bush of broom was near,
To hide a bonnet or a spear.

XII

The Chief in silence strode before,
And reached that torrent's sounding shore,
Which, daughter of three mighty lakes,
From Vennachar in silver breaks,
Sweeps through the plain, and ceaseless mines
On Bochastle the mouldering lines,
Where Rome, the Empress of the world,
Of yore her eagle wings unfurled.
And here his course the Chieftain stayed,
Threw down his target and his plaid,
And to the Lowland warrior said:
"Bold Saxon! to his promise just,
Vich-Alpine has discharged his trust.
This murderous Chief, this ruthless man,
This head of a rebellious clan,
Hath led thee safe through watch and ward,
Far past Clan-Alpine's outmost guard.
Now, man to man, and steel to steel,
A Chieftain's vengeance thou shalt feel.
See, here, all vantageless I stand,
Armed, like thyself, with single brand;
For this is Coilantogle ford,
And thou must keep thee with thy sword."

XIII

The Saxon paused: "I ne'er delayed,
When foeman bade me draw my blade;
Nay more, brave Chief, I vowed thy death:
Yet sure thy fair and generous faith,
And my deep debt for life preserved,
A better meed have well deserved:
Can naught but blood our feud atone?
Are there no means?" "No, Stranger, none.
And hear, — to fire thy flagging zeal, —
The Saxon cause rests on thy steel;
For thus spoke Fate, by prophet bred
Between the living and the dead:
'Who spills the foremost foeman's life
His party conquers in the strife.'"
"Then, by my word," the Saxon said,
"The riddle is already read.
Seek yonder brake beneath the cliff, —
There lies Red Murdock, stark and stiff.
Thus Fate hath solved her prophecy,
Then yield to Fate, and not to me.
To James, at Stirling, let us go,
When, if thou wilt be still his foe,
Or if the King shall not agree
To grant thee grace and favour free,

I plight my honour, oath, and word,
That, to thy native strengths restored,
With each advantage shalt thou stand,
That aids thee now to guard thy land."

XIV

Dark lightning flashed from Roderick's eye:
"Soars thy presumption, then, so high,
Because a wretched kern ye slew,
Homage to name to Roderick Dhu?
He yields not, he, to man nor fate!
Thou add'st but fuel to my hate: —
My clansman's blood demands revenge.
Not yet prepared? — By Heaven, I change
My thought, and hold thy valour light
As that of some vain carpet knight,
Who ill deserved my courteous care,
And whose best boast is but to wear
A braid of his fair lady's hair."
"I thank thee, Roderick, for the word!
It nerves my heart, it steels my sword;
For I have sworn this braid to stain
In the best blood that warms thy vein.
Now, truce, farewell! and, ruth, begone! —
Yet think not that by thee alone,
Proud Chief! can courtesy be shown;
Though not from copse, nor heath, nor cairn,
Start at my whistle clansmen stern,
Of this small horn one feeble blast
Would fearful odds against thee cast.
But fear not — doubt not — which thou wilt —
We try this quarrel hilt to hilt."
Then each at once his falchion drew,
Each on the ground his scabbard threw,
Each looked to sun and stream and plain,
And what they ne'er might see again;
Then, foot and point and eye opposed,
In dubious strife they darkly closed.

XV

Ill fared it then with Roderick Dhu,
That on the field his targe he threw,
Whose brazen studs and tough bull-hide
Had death so often dashed aside;
For, trained abroad his arms to wield,
Fitz-James's blade was sword and shield.
He practised every pass and ward,
To thrust, to strike, to feint, to guard;
While less expert, though stronger far,
The Gael maintained unequal war.
Three times in closing strife they stood,
And thrice the Saxon blade drank blood:
No stinted draught, no scanty tide,
The gushing floods the tartans dyed.
Fierce Roderick felt the fatal drain,
And showered his blows like wintry rain;
And, as firm rock or castle-roof
Against the winter shower is proof,
The foe, invulnerable still,
Foiled his wild rage by steady skill;
Till, at advantage ta'en, his brand
Forced Roderick's weapon from his hand,
And, backwards borne upon the lea,
Brought the proud Chieftain to his knee.

XVI

"Now yield thee, or, by Him who made
The world, thy heart's blood dyes my blade!"
"Thy threats, thy mercy, I defy!
Let recreant yield, who fears to die."
Like adder darting from his coil,
Like wolf that dashes through the toil,
Like mountain-cat who guards her young,
Full at Fitz-James's throat he sprung;
Received, but recked not of a wound,
And locked his arms his foeman round.
Now, gallant Saxon, hold thine own!
No maiden's hand is round thee thrown!
That desperate grasp thy frame might feel
Through bars of brass and triple steel!
They tug! They strain! Down, down they go,
The Gael above, Fitz-James below.
The Chieftain's gripe his throat compressed,
His knee was planted in his breast;
His clotted locks he backward threw,
Across his brow his hand he drew,
From blood and mist to clear his sight,
Then gleamed aloft his dagger bright!
But hate and fury ill supplied
The stream of life's exhausted tide,
And all too late the advantage came,
To turn the odds of deadly game;
For, while the dagger gleamed on high,
Reeled soul and sense, reeled brain and eye.
Down came the blow! but in the heath
The erring blade found bloodless sheath.
The struggling foe may now unclasp
The fainting Chief's relaxing grasp;
Unwounded from the dreadful close,
But breathless all, Fitz-James arose.

COUNTY GUY

Ah! County Guy, the hour is nigh,
The sun has left the lea,
The orange-flower perfumes the bower,
The breeze is on the sea.
The lark, his lay who trill'd all day,
Sits hush'd his partner nigh;

Breeze, bird, and flower, confess the hour,
But where is County Guy?

The village maid steals through the shade,
Her shepherd's suit to hear;
To beauty shy, by lattice high,
Sings high-born Cavalier.
The star of Love, all stars above,
Now reigns o'er earth and sky;
And high and low the influence know —
But where is County Guy?

SAMUEL TAYLOR COLERIDGE
(1772–1834)

From FRANCE: AN ODE

II

When France in wrath her giant-limbs up-rear'd,
And with that oath, which smote air, earth, and sea,
Stamp'd her strong foot and said she would be free,
Bear witness for me, how I hoped and fear'd!
With what a joy my lofty gratulation
Unawed I sang, amid a slavish band:
And when to whelm the disenchanted nation,
Like fiends embattled by a wizard's wand,
The Monarchs march'd in evil day,
And Britain join'd the dire array;
Though dear her shores and circling ocean,
Though many friendships, many youthful loves,
Had swoln the patriot emotion,
And flung a magic light o'er all her hills and groves;
Yet still my voice, unalter'd, sang defeat
To all that braved the tyrant-quelling lance,
And shame too long delay'd and vain retreat!
For ne'er, O Liberty! with partial aim
I dimm'd thy light or damp'd thy holy flame;
But bless'd the pæans of deliver'd France,
And hung my head and wept at Britain's name.

IV

Forgive me, Freedom! O forgive those dreams!
I hear thy voice, I hear thy loud lament,
From bleak Helvetia's icy caverns sent —
I hear thy groans upon her blood-stain'd streams!
Heroes, that for your peaceful country perish'd,
And ye that, fleeing, spot your mountain-snows
With bleeding wounds; forgive me, that I cherish'd
One thought that ever bless'd your cruel foes!
To scatter rage and traitorous guilt,
Where Peace her jealous home had built;
A patriot-race to disinherit
Of all that made their stormy wilds so dear;
And with inexpiable spirit
To taint the bloodless freedom of the mountaineer —
O France, that mockest Heaven, adulterous, blind,
And patriot only in pernicious toils,
Are these thy boasts, champion of human kind?
To mix with kings in the low lust of sway,
Yell in the hunt, and share the murderous prey;
To insult the shrine of Liberty with spoils
From freemen torn; to tempt and to betray?

HYMN

BEFORE SUNRISE IN THE VALE OF CHAMOUNI

Hast thou a charm to stay the morning-star
In his steep course? So long he seems to pause
On thy bald awful head, O sovran Blanc!
The Arve and Arveiron at thy base
Rave ceaselessly; but thou, most awful Form!
Risest from forth thy silent sea of pines,
How silently! Around thee and above
Deep is the air and dark, substantial, black,
An ebon mass: methinks thou piercest it,
As with a wedge! But when I look again,
It is thine own calm home, thy crystal shrine,
Thy habitation from eternity!
O dread and silent Mount! I gazed upon thee,
Till thou, still present to the bodily sense,
Didst vanish from my thought: entranced in prayer
I worshipp'd the Invisible alone.

Yet, like some sweet beguiling melody,
So sweet, we know not we are listening to it,
Thou, the meanwhile, wast blending with my thought,
Yea, with my life and life's own secret joy:
Till the dilating Soul, enrapt, transfused,
Into the mighty vision passing — there,
As in her natural form, swell'd vast to Heaven!
Awake, my soul! not only passive praise
Thou owest! not alone these swelling tears,
Mute thanks and secret ecstasy! Awake,
Voice of sweet song! Awake, my heart, awake!
Green vales and icy cliffs, all join my Hymn.

Thou first and chief, sole sovran of the Vale!
O struggling with the darkness all the night,
And visited all night by troops of stars,
Or when they climb the sky or when they sink:

Companion of the morning-star at dawn,
Thyself earth's rosy star, and of the dawn
Co-herald! wake, O wake, and utter praise!
Who sank thy sunless pillars deep in Earth?
Who fill'd thy countenance with rosy light?
Who made thee parent of perpetual streams?

And you, ye five wild torrents fiercely glad!
Who call'd you forth from night and utter death,
From dark and icy caverns call'd you forth,
Down those precipitous, black, jagged rocks,
Forever shatter'd and the same forever?
Who gave you your invulnerable life,
Your strength, your speed, your fury, and your joy,
Unceasing thunder and eternal foam?
And who commanded (and the silence came),
Here let the billows stiffen, and have rest?

Ye ice-falls! ye that from the mountain's brow
Adown enormous ravines slope amain —
Torrents, methinks, that heard a mighty voice,
And stopp'd at once amid their maddest plunge!
Motionless torrents! silent cataracts!
Who made you glorious as the gates of Heaven
Beneath the keen full moon? Who bade the sun
Clothe you with rainbows? Who, with living flowers
Of loveliest blue, spread garlands at your feet? —
God! let the torrents, like a shout of nations,
Answer! and let the ice-plains echo, God!
God! sing, ye meadow-streams, with gladsome voice!
Ye pine-groves, with your soft and soul-like sounds!
And they too have a voice, yon piles of snow,
And in their perilous fall shall thunder, God!

Ye living flowers that skirt the eternal frost!
Ye wild goats sporting round the eagle's nest!
Ye eagles, play-mates of the mountain-storm!
Ye lightnings, the dread arrows of the clouds!
Ye signs and wonders of the element!
Utter forth God, and fill the hills with praise!
Thou too, hoar Mount! with thy sky-pointing peaks,
Oft from whose feet the avalanche, unheard,
Shoots downward, glittering through the pure serene,
Into the depth of clouds that veil thy breast —
Thou too again, stupendous Mountain! thou
That as I raise my head, awhile bow'd low
In adoration, upward from thy base
Slow-travelling with dim eyes suffused with tears,
Solemnly seemest, like a vapoury cloud,
To rise before me — Rise, O ever rise,
Rise like a cloud of incense, from the earth!
Thou kingly spirit throned among the hills,
Thou dread ambassador from earth to heaven,
Great hierarch! tell thou the silent sky,
And tell the stars, and tell yon rising sun,
Earth, with her thousand voices, praises God.

KUBLA KHAN: OR, A VISION IN A DREAM

A FRAGMENT

In Xanadu did Kubla Khan
A stately pleasure-dome decree:
Where Alph, the sacred river, ran
Through caverns measureless to man
Down to a sunless sea.

So twice five miles of fertile ground
With walls and towers were girdled round:
And there were gardens bright with sinuous rills,
Where blossom'd many an incense-bearing tree;
And here were forests ancient as the hills,
Enfolding sunny spots of greenery.

But oh! that deep romantic chasm which slanted
Down the green hill athwart a cedarn cover!
A savage place! as holy and enchanted
As e'er beneath a waning moon was haunted
By woman wailing for her demon-lover!
And from this chasm, with ceaseless turmoil seething,
As if this earth in fast thick pants were breathing,
A mighty fountain momently was forced:
Amid whose swift half-intermitted burst
Huge fragments vaulted like rebounding hail,
Or chaffy grain beneath the thresher's flail:
And 'mid these dancing rocks at once and ever
It flung up momently the sacred river.
Five miles meandering with a mazy motion
Through wood and dale the sacred river ran,
Then reach'd the caverns measureless to man,
And sank in tumult to a lifeless ocean:
And 'mid this tumult Kubla heard from far
Ancestral voices prophesying war!

The shadow of the dome of pleasure
Floated midway on the waves;
Where was heard the mingled measure
From the fountain and the caves.
It was a miracle of rare device,
A sunny pleasure-dome with caves of ice!

A damsel with a dulcimer
In a vision once I saw:
It was an Abyssinian maid,
And on her dulcimer she play'd,
Singing of Mount Abora.

Could I revive within me
Her symphony and song,
To such a deep delight 'twould win me,
That with music loud and long,
I would build that dome in air,
That sunny dome! those caves of ice!
And all who heard should see them there,—
And all should cry, Beware! Beware!—
His flashing eyes, his floating hair!
Weave a circle round him thrice,
And close your eyes with holy dread,
For he on honey-dew hath fed,
And drunk the milk of Paradise.

THE RIME OF THE ANCIENT MARINER

IN SEVEN PARTS

PART I

It is an ancient Mariner,
And he stoppeth one of three.
"By thy long gray beard and glittering eye,
Now wherefore stopp'st thou me?

"The Bridegroom's doors are open'd wide,
And I am next of kin;
The guests are met, the feast is set:
May'st hear the merry din."

He holds him with his skinny hand,
"There was a ship," quoth he.
"Hold off! unhand me, graybeard loon!"
Eftsoons his hand dropt he.

He holds him with his glittering eye —
The wedding-guest stood still,
And listens like a three years' child:
The Mariner hath his will.

The wedding-guest sat on a stone:
He cannot choose but hear;
And thus spake on that ancient man,
The bright-eyed Mariner.

"The ship was cheer'd, the harbour clear'd,
Merrily did we drop
Below the kirk, below the hill,
Below the lighthouse top.

"The sun came up upon the left,
Out of the sea came he!
And he shone bright, and on the right
Went down into the sea.

"Higher and higher every day,
Till over the mast at noon —"
The wedding-guest here beat his breast,
For he heard the loud bassoon.

The bride hath paced into the hall,
Red as a rose is she;
Nodding their heads before her goes
The merry minstrelsy.

The wedding-guest he beat his breast,
Yet he cannot choose but hear;
And thus spake on that ancient man,
The bright-eyed Mariner:

"And now the storm-blast came, and he
Was tyrannous and strong:
He struck with his o'ertaking wings,
And chased us south along.

"With sloping masts and dipping prow,
As who pursued with yell and blow
Still treads the shadow of his foe,
And forward bends his head,
The ship drove fast, loud roar'd the blast,
And southward aye we fled.

"And now there came both mist and snow,
And it grew wondrous cold;
And ice, mast-high, came floating by,
As green as emerald;

"And through the drifts the snowy clifts
Did send a dismal sheen:
Nor shapes of men nor beasts we ken —
The ice was all between.

"The ice was here, the ice was there,
The ice was all around:
It crack'd and growl'd, and roar'd and howl'd,
Like noises in a swound!

"At length did cross an Albatross:
Thorough the fog it came:
As if it had been a Christian soul,
We hail'd it in God's name.

"It ate the food it ne'er had eat,
And round and round it flew.
The ice did split with a thunder-fit;
The helmsman steer'd us through!

"And a good south wind sprung up behind;
The Albatross did follow,
And every day, for food or play,
Came to the mariners' hollo!

"In mist or cloud, on mast or shroud,
It perch'd for vespers nine;
Whiles all the night, through fog-smoke white,
Glimmer'd the white moon-shine."

"God save thee, ancient Mariner!
From the fiends, that plague thee thus! —
Why look'st thou so?" — "With my cross-bow
I shot the Albatross!"

Part II

"The sun now rose upon the right:
Out of the sea came he,
Still hid in mist, and on the left
Went down into the sea.

"And the good south wind still blew behind,
But no sweet bird did follow,
Nor any day, for food or play,
Came to the mariners' hollo!

"And I had done a hellish thing,
And it would work 'em woe;
For all averr'd, I had kill'd the bird
That made the breeze to blow.
Ah wretch! said they, the bird to slay
That made the breeze to blow!

"Nor dim nor red, like God's own head,
The glorious sun uprist:
Then all averr'd, I had kill'd the bird
That brought the fog and mist.
'Twas right, said they, such birds to slay,
That bring the fog and mist.

"The fair breeze blew, the white foam flew,
The furrow follow'd free:
We were the first that ever burst
Into that silent sea.

"Down dropt the breeze, the sails dropt down,
'Twas sad as sad could be;
And we did speak only to break
The silence of the sea!

"All in a hot and copper sky,
The bloody sun, at noon,
Right up above the mast did stand,
No bigger than the moon.

"Day after day, day after day,
We stuck, nor breath nor motion;
As idle as a painted ship
Upon a painted ocean.

"Water, water, everywhere,
And all the boards did shrink;
Water, water, everywhere,
Nor any drop to drink.

"The very deep did rot: O Christ!
That ever this should be!
Yea, slimy things did crawl with legs
Upon the slimy sea.

"About, about, in reel and rout,
The death-fires danced at night;
The water, like a witch's oils,
Burnt green, and blue and white.

"And some in dreams assured were
Of the spirit that plagued us so:
Nine fathom deep he had follow'd us,
From the land of mist and snow.

"And every tongue, through utter drought,
Was wither'd at the root;
We could not speak, no more than if
We had been choked with soot.

"Ah! well-a-day! what evil looks
Had I from old and young!
Instead of the cross, the Albatross
About my neck was hung.

Part III

"There pass'd a weary time. Each throat
Was parch'd, and glazed each eye.
A weary time! A weary time!
How glazed each weary eye!
When looking westward I beheld
A something in the sky.

"At first it seem'd a little speck,
And then it seem'd a mist:
It moved and moved, and took at last
A certain shape, I wist.

"A speck, a mist, a shape, I wist!
And still it near'd and near'd:
As if it dodged a water-sprite,
It plunged and tack'd and veer'd.

"With throats unslaked, with black lips baked,
We could nor laugh nor wail;
Through utter drought all dumb we stood!
I bit my arm, I suck'd the blood,
And cried, 'A sail! a sail!'

"With throats unslaked, with black lips baked,
Agape they heard me call:
Gramercy! they for joy did grin,
And all at once their breath drew in,
As they were drinking all.

"'See! see! (I cried) she tacks no more!
Hither to work us weal;
Without a breeze, without a tide,
She steadies with upright keel!'

"The western wave was all a-flame:
The day was well nigh done:
Almost upon the western wave
Rested the broad bright sun;
When that strange shape drove suddenly
Betwixt us and the sun.

"And straight the sun was fleck'd with bars,
(Heaven's Mother send us grace!)
As if through a dungeon grate he peer'd,
With broad and burning face.

"Alas! (thought I, and my heart beat loud)
How fast she nears and nears!
Are those her sails that glance in the sun,
Like restless gossameres?

"Are those her ribs through which the sun
Did peer, as through a grate?
And is that Woman all her crew?
Is that a Death? and are there two?
Is Death that woman's mate?

"Her lips were red, her looks were free,
Her locks were yellow as gold:
Her skin was as white as leprosy,
The nightmare Life-in-Death was she,
Who thicks man's blood with cold.

"The naked hulk alongside came,
And the twain were casting dice;
'The game is done! I've won, I've won!'
Quoth she, and whistles thrice.

"The sun's rim dips; the stars rush out:
At one stride comes the dark;
With far-heard whisper, o'er the sea,
Off shot the spectre-bark.

"We listen'd and look'd sideways up!
Fear at my heart, as at a cup,
My life-blood seem'd to sip!
The stars were dim, and thick the night,
The steersman's face by his lamp gleam'd white;
From the sails the dew did drip —
Till clomb above the eastern bar
The horned moon, with one bright star
Within the nether tip.

"One after one, by the star-dogg'd moon,
Too quick for groan or sigh,
Each turn'd his face with a ghastly pang,
And cursed me with his eye.

"Four times fifty living men,
(And I heard nor sigh nor groan)
With heavy thump, a lifeless lump,
They dropp'd down one by one.

"The souls did from their bodies fly, —
They fled to bliss or woe!
And every soul, it pass'd me by,
Like the whiz of my cross-bow!"

PART IV

"I fear thee, ancient Mariner!
I fear thy skinny hand!
And thou art long, and lank, and brown,
As is the ribb'd sea-sand.

"I fear thee and thy glittering eye,
And thy skinny hand, so brown." —
"Fear not, fear not, thou wedding-guest!
This body dropt not down.

"Alone, alone, all, all alone,
Alone on a wide wide sea!
And never a saint took pity on
My soul in agony.

"The many men, so beautiful!
And they all dead did lie:
And a thousand thousand slimy things
Lived on; and so did I.

"I look'd upon the rotting sea,
And drew my eyes away;
I look'd upon the rotting deck,
And there the dead men lay.

"I look'd to Heaven, and tried to pray;
But or ever a prayer had gusht,
A wicked whisper came, and made
My heart as dry as dust.

"I closed my lids, and kept them close,
And the balls like pulses beat;
For the sky and the sea, and the sea and the sky,
Lay like a load on my weary eye,
And the dead were at my feet.

"The cold sweat melted from their limbs,
Nor rot nor reek did they:
The look with which they look'd on me
Had never pass'd away.

"An orphan's curse would drag to hell
A spirit from on high;
But oh! more horrible than that
Is the curse in a dead man's eye!
Seven days, seven nights, I saw that curse,
And yet I could not die.

"The moving moon went up the sky,
And nowhere did abide:
Softly she was going up,
And a star or two beside —

"Her beams bemock'd the sultry main,
Like April hoar-frost spread;
But where the ship's huge shadow lay,
The charmèd water burnt alway
A still and awful red.

"Beyond the shadow of the ship,
I watch'd the water-snakes:
They moved in tracks of shining white,
And when they rear'd, the elfish light
Fell off in hoary flakes.

"Within the shadow of the ship
I watch'd their rich attire:
Blue, glossy green, and velvet black,
They coil'd and swam; and every track
Was a flash of golden fire.

"O happy living things! no tongue
Their beauty might declare:
A spring of love gush'd from my heart,
And I bless'd them unaware!
Sure my kind saint took pity on me,
And I bless'd them unaware.

"The selfsame moment I could pray;
And from my neck so free
The Albatross fell off, and sank
Like lead into the sea.

Part V

"Oh sleep! it is a gentle thing,
Beloved from pole to pole!
To Mary Queen the praise be given!
She sent the gentle sleep from Heaven,
That slid into my soul.

"The silly buckets on the deck,
That had so long remain'd,
I dreamt that they were fill'd with dew;
And when I awoke, it rain'd.

"My lips were wet, my throat was cold,
My garments all were dank;
Sure I had drunken in my dreams,
And still my body drank.

"I moved, and could not feel my limbs:
I was so light — almost
I thought that I had died in sleep,
And was a blessèd ghost.

"And soon I heard a roaring wind:
It did not come anear;
But with its sound it shook the sails,
That were so thin and sear.

"The upper air burst into life!
And a hundred fire-flags sheen,
To and fro they were hurried about;
And to and fro, and in and out,
The wan stars danced between.

"And the coming wind did roar more loud,
And the sails did sigh like sedge;
And the rain pour'd down from one black cloud;
The moon was at its edge.

"The thick black cloud was cleft, and still
The moon was at its side:
Like waters shot from some high crag,
The lightning fell with never a jag,
A river steep and wide.

"The loud wind never reach'd the ship,
Yet now the ship moved on!
Beneath the lightning and the moon
The dead men gave a groan.

"They groan'd, they stirr'd, they all uprose,
Nor spake, nor moved their eyes;
It had been strange, even in a dream,
To have seen those dead men rise.

"The helmsman steer'd, the ship moved on;
Yet never a breeze up-blew;
The mariners all 'gan work the ropes,
Where they were wont to do:
They raised their limbs like lifeless tools —
We were a ghastly crew.

"The body of my brother's son
Stood by me, knee to knee:
The body and I pull'd at one rope,
But he said nought to me."

"I fear thee, ancient Mariner!"
"Be calm, thou Wedding-Guest!
'Twas not those souls that fled in pain,
Which to their corses came again,
But a troop of spirits blest:

"For when it dawn'd — they dropp'd their arms,
And cluster'd round the mast;
Sweet sounds rose slowly through their mouths,
And from their bodies pass'd.

"Around, around, flew each sweet sound,
Then darted to the sun;
Slowly the sounds come back again,
Now mix'd, now one by one.

"Sometimes a-dropping from the sky
I heard the skylark sing;
Sometimes all little birds that are,
How they seem'd to fill the sea and air
With their sweet jargoning!

"And now 'twas like all instruments,
Now like a lonely flute;
And now it is an angel's song,
That makes the heavens be mute.

"It ceased; yet still the sails made on
A pleasant noise till noon,
A noise like of a hidden brook
In the leafy month of June,
That to the sleeping woods all night
Singeth a quiet tune.

"Till noon we quietly sail'd on,
Yet never a breeze did breathe:
Slowly and smoothly went the ship,
Moved onward from beneath.

"Under the keel nine fathom deep,
From the land of mist and snow,
The spirit slid; and it was he
That made the ship to go.
The sails at noon left off their tune,
And the ship stood still also.

"The sun, right up above the mast,
Had fix'd her to the ocean;
But in a minute she 'gan stir,
With a short uneasy motion —
Backwards and forwards half her length,
With a short uneasy motion.

"Then like a pawing horse let go,
She made a sudden bound:
It flung the blood into my head,
And I fell down in a swound.

"How long in that same fit I lay,
I have not to declare;
But ere my living life return'd,
I heard, and in my soul discern'd
Two voices in the air.

"'Is it he?' quoth one, 'is this the man?
By Him who died on cross,
With his cruel bow he laid full low
The harmless Albatross.

"'The spirit who bideth by himself
In the land of mist and snow,
He loved the bird that loved the man
Who shot him with his bow.'

"The other was a softer voice,
As soft as honey-dew:
Quoth he, 'The man hath penance done,
And penance more will do.'

Part VI

First Voice

"'But tell me, tell me! speak again,
Thy soft response renewing —
What makes that ship drive on so fast?
What is the ocean doing?'

Second Voice

"'Still as a slave before his lord,
The ocean hath no blast;
His great bright eye most silently
Up to the moon is cast —

"'If he may know which way to go;
For she guides him, smooth or grim.
See, brother, see! how graciously
She looketh down on him.'

First Voice

"'But why drives on that ship so fast,
Without or wave or wind?'

Second Voice

"'The air is cut away before,
And closes from behind.

"'Fly, brother, fly! more high, more high!
Or we shall be belated:
For slow and slow that ship will go,
When the Mariner's trance is abated.'

"I woke, and we were sailing on,
As in a gentle weather:
'Twas night, calm night, the moon was high;
The dead men stood together.

"All stood together on the deck,
For a charnel-dungeon fitter:
All fix'd on me their stony eyes,
That in the moon did glitter.

"The pang, the curse, with which they died,
Had never pass'd away:
I could not draw my eyes from theirs,
Nor turn them up to pray.

"And now this spell was snapt: once more
I view'd the ocean green,
And look'd far forth, yet little saw
Of what had else been seen —

"Like one, that on a lonesome road
Doth walk in fear and dread,
And having once turn'd round, walks on,
And turns no more his head;
Because he knows a frightful fiend
Doth close behind him tread.

"But soon there breathed a wind on me,
Nor sound nor motion made:
Its path was not upon the sea,
In ripple or in shade.

"It raised my hair, it fann'd my cheek
Like a meadow-gale of spring —
It mingled strangely with my fears,
Yet it felt like a welcoming.

"Swiftly, swiftly flew the ship,
Yet she sail'd softly too:
Sweetly, sweetly blew the breeze —
On me alone it blew.

"Oh! dream of joy! is this indeed
The lighthouse top I see?
Is this the hill? is this the kirk?
Is this mine own countree?

"We drifted o'er the harbour-bar,
And I with sobs did pray —
'O let me be awake, my God!
Or let me sleep alway.'

"The harbour-bay was clear as glass,
So smoothly it was strewn!
And on the bay the moonlight lay,
And the shadow of the moon.

"The rock shone bright, the kirk no less,
That stands above the rock:
The moonlight steep'd in silentness
The steady weathercock.

"And the bay was white with silent light,
Till rising from the same,
Full many shapes, that shadows were,
In crimson colours came.

"A little distance from the prow
Those crimson shadows were:
I turn'd my eyes upon the deck —
Oh, Christ! what saw I there!

"Each corse lay flat, lifeless and flat,
And, by the holy rood!
A man all light, a seraph-man,
On every corse there stood.

"This seraph-band, each waved his hand:
It was a heavenly sight!
They stood as signals to the land,
Each one a lovely light:

"This seraph-band, each waved his hand,
No voice did they impart —
No voice; but oh! the silence sank
Like music on my heart.

"But soon I heard the dash of oars,
I heard the pilot's cheer;
My head was turn'd perforce away,
And I saw a boat appear.

"The pilot, and the pilot's boy,
I heard them coming fast:
Dear Lord in Heaven! it was a joy
The dead men could not blast.

"I saw a third — I heard his voice:
It is the Hermit good!
He singeth loud his godly hymns
That he makes in the wood.
He'll shrieve my soul, he'll wash away
The Albatross's blood.

Part VII

"This Hermit good lives in that wood
Which slopes down to the sea.
How loudly his sweet voice he rears!
He loves to talk with marineres
That come from a far countree.

"He kneels at morn, and noon, and eve —
He hath a cushion plump:
It is the moss that wholly hides
The rotted old oak-stump.

"The skiff-boat near'd: I heard them talk,
'Why, this is strange, I trow!
Where are those lights so many and fair,
That signal made but now?'

"'Strange, by my faith!' the Hermit said —
'And they answer'd not our cheer!
The planks look warp'd! and see those sails,
How thin they are and sere!
I never saw aught like to them,
Unless perchance it were

"'Brown skeletons of leaves that lag
My forest-brook along:
When the ivy-tod is heavy with snow,
And the owlet whoops to the wolf below,
That eats the she-wolf's young.'

"'Dear Lord! it hath a fiendish look' —
(The pilot made reply)
'I am a-fear'd' — 'Push on, push on!'
Said the Hermit cheerily.

"The boat came closer to the ship,
But I nor spake nor stirr'd;
The boat came close beneath the ship,
And straight a sound was heard.

"Under the water it rumbled on,
Still louder and more dread:
It reach'd the ship, it split the bay;
The ship went down like lead.

"Stunn'd by that loud and dreadful sound,
Which sky and ocean smote,
Like one that hath been seven days drown'd,
My body lay afloat;
But swift as dreams, myself I found
Within the pilot's boat.

"Upon the whirl, where sank the ship,
The boat spun round and round;
And all was still, save that the hill
Was telling of the sound.

"I moved my lips — the pilot shriek'd,
And fell down in a fit;
The holy Hermit raised his eyes,
And pray'd where he did sit.

"I took the oars: the pilot's boy,
Who now doth crazy go,
Laugh'd loud and long, and all the while
His eyes went to and fro.
'Ha! ha!' quoth he, 'full plain I see,
The Devil knows how to row.'

"And now, all in my own countree,
I stood on the firm land!
The Hermit stepp'd forth from the boat,
And scarcely he could stand.

"'O shrieve me, shrieve me, holy man!'
The Hermit cross'd his brow.
'Say quick,' quoth he, 'I bid thee say —
What manner of man art thou?'

"Forthwith this frame of mine was wrench'd
With a woeful agony,
Which forced me to begin my tale;
And then it left me free.

"Since then at an uncertain hour,
That agony returns;
And till my ghastly tale is told,
This heart within me burns.

"I pass, like night, from land to land;
I have strange power of speech;
That moment that his face I see,
I know the man that must hear me:
To him my tale I teach.

"What loud uproar bursts from that door:
The wedding-guests are there;
But in the garden-bower the bride
And bride-maids singing are;
And hark the little vesper bell,
Which biddeth me to prayer!

"O Wedding-Guest! this soul hath been
Alone on a wide wide sea:
So lonely 'twas, that God himself
Scarce seemed there to be.

"O sweeter than the marriage-feast,
'Tis sweeter far to me,
To walk together to the kirk
With a goodly company! —

"To walk together to the kirk,
And all together pray,
While each to his great Father bends,
Old men, and babes, and loving friends,
And youths and maidens gay!

"Farewell, farewell! but this I tell
To thee, thou Wedding-Guest!
He prayeth well, who loveth well
Both man and bird and beast.

"He prayeth best, who loveth best
All things both great and small;
For the dear God who loveth us,
He made and loveth all."

The Mariner, whose eye is bright,
Whose beard with age is hoar,
Is gone; and now the Wedding-Guest
Turn'd from the bridegroom's door.

He went like one that hath been stunn'd,
And is of sense forlorn:
A sadder and a wiser man
He rose the morrow morn.

CHRISTABEL

From Part I

'Tis the middle of night by the castle clock,
And the owls have awaken'd the crowing cock;
Tu-whit! — Tu-whoo!
And hark, again! the crowing cock,
How drowsily it crew.

Sir Leoline, the Baron rich,
Hath a toothless mastiff bitch;
From her kennel beneath the rock
She maketh answer to the clock,
Four for the quarters, and twelve for the hour;
Ever and aye, by shine and shower,
Sixteen short howls, not over loud;
Some say, she sees my lady's shroud.

Is the night chilly and dark?
The night is chilly, but not dark.
The thin grey cloud is spread on high,
It covers but not hides the sky.
The moon is behind, and at the full;
And yet she looks both small and dull.
The night is chill, the cloud is grey:
'Tis a month before the month of May,
And the Spring comes slowly up this way.

The lovely lady, Christabel,
Whom her father loves so well,
What makes her in the wood so late,
A furlong from the castle gate?
She had dreams all yesternight
Of her own betrothed knight;
And she in the midnight wood will pray
For the weal of her lover that's far away.

She stole along, she nothing spoke,
The sighs she heaved were soft and low,
And naught was green upon the oak,
But moss and rarest misletoe:
She kneels beneath the huge oak tree,
And in silence prayeth she.

The lady sprang up suddenly,
The lovely lady, Christabel!
It moan'd as near, as near can be,
But what it is she cannot tell. —
On the other side it seems to be,
Of the huge, broad-breasted, old oak tree.

The night is chill; the forest bare;
Is it the wind that moaneth bleak?
There is not wind enough in the air
To move away the ringlet curl
From the lovely lady's cheek —
There is not wind enough to twirl
The one red leaf, the last of its clan,
That dances as often as dance it can,
Hanging so light, and hanging so high,
On the topmost twig that looks up at the sky.

Hush, beating heart of Christabel!
Jesu, Maria, shield her well!
She folded her arms beneath her cloak,
And stole to the other side of the oak.
What sees she there?

There she sees a damsel bright,
Drest in a silken robe of white,
That shadowy in the moonlight shone:
The neck that made that white robe wan,
Her stately neck, and arms were bare;
Her blue-vein'd feet unsandal'd were;
And wildly glitter'd here and there
The gems entangled in her hair.
I guess, 'twas frightful there to see
A lady so richly clad as she —
Beautiful exceedingly!

"Mary mother, save me now!"
Said Christabel, "and who art thou?"

The lady strange made answer meet,
And her voice was faint and sweet: —
"Have pity on my sore distress,
I scarce can speak for weariness:
Stretch forth thy hand, and have no fear!"
Said Christabel, "How camest thou here?"
And the lady, whose voice was faint and sweet,
Did thus pursue her answer meet: —
"My sire is of a noble line,
And my name is Geraldine:
Five warriors seized me yestermorn,
Me, even me, a maid forlorn:
They choked my cries with force and fright,
And tied me on a palfrey white.
The palfrey was as fleet as wind,
And they rode furiously behind.
They spurr'd amain, their steeds were white:
And once we cross'd the shade of night.
As sure as Heaven shall rescue me,
I have no thought what men they be;
Nor do I know how long it is
(For I have lain entranced, I wis)
Since one, the tallest of the five,
Took me from the palfrey's back,
A weary woman, scarce alive.
Some mutter'd words his comrades spoke:
He placed me underneath this oak;
He swore they would return with haste;
Whither they went I cannot tell —
I thought I heard, some minutes past,
Sounds as of a castle bell.
Stretch forth thy hand," thus ended she,
"And help a wretched maid to flee."

Then Christabel stretch'd forth her hand,
And comforted fair Geraldine:
"O well, bright dame, may you command
The service of Sir Leoline;
And gladly our stout chivalry
Will he send forth, and friends withal,
To guide and guard you safe and free
Home to your noble father's hall."

She rose: and forth with steps they pass'd
That strove to be, and were not, fast.
Her gracious stars the lady blest,
And thus spake on sweet Christabel:
"All our household are at rest,
The hall as silent as the cell;
Sir Leoline is weak in health,
And may not well awaken'd be,
But we will move as if in stealth;
And I beseech your courtesy,
This night, to share your couch with me."

They cross'd the moat, and Christabel
Took the key that fitted well;
A little door she open'd straight,
All in the middle of the gate;
The gate that was iron'd within and without,
Where an army in battle array had march'd out.
The lady sank, belike through pain,
And Christabel with might and main
Lifted her up, a weary weight,
Over the threshold of the gate:
Then the lady rose again,
And moved, as she were not in pain.

So, free from danger, free from fear,
They cross'd the court: right glad they were.
And Christabel devoutly cried
To the Lady by her side;
"Praise we the Virgin all divine,
Who hath rescued thee from thy distress!"
"Alas, alas!" said Geraldine,
"I cannot speak for weariness."
So, free from danger, free from fear,
They cross'd the court: right glad they were.

Outside her kennel the mastiff old
Lay fast asleep, in moonshine cold.
The mastiff old did not awake,
Yet she an angry moan did make.
And what can ail the mastiff bitch?
Never till now she utter'd yell
Beneath the eye of Christabel.
Perhaps it is the owlet's scritch:
For what can ail the mastiff bitch?

They pass'd the hall, that echoes still,
Pass as lightly as you will.
The brands were flat, the brands were dying,
Amid their own white ashes lying;
But when the lady pass'd, there came
A tongue of light, a fit of flame;
And Christabel saw the lady's eye,
And nothing else saw she thereby,
Save the boss of the shield of Sir Leoline tall,
Which hung in a murky old niche in the wall.
"O softly tread," said Christabel,
"My father seldom sleepeth well."
Sweet Christabel her feet doth bare,
And, jealous of the listening air,
They steal their way from stair to stair,
Now in glimmer, and now in gloom,
And now they pass the Baron's room,
As still as death, with stifled breath!
And now have reach'd her chamber door;
And now doth Geraldine press down
The rushes of the chamber floor.

The moon shines dim in the open air,
And not a moonbeam enters here.
But they without its light can see
The chamber carved so curiously,
Carved with figures strange and sweet,
All made out of the carver's brain,
For a lady's chamber meet:
The lamp with twofold silver chain
Is fasten'd to an angel's feet.
The silver lamp burns dead and dim;
But Christabel the lamp will trim.
She trimm'd the lamp, and made it bright,
And left it swinging to and fro,
While Geraldine, in wretched plight,
Sank down upon the floor below.

"O weary lady, Geraldine,
I pray you, drink this cordial wine!
It is a wine of virtuous powers;
My mother made it of wild flowers."

"And will your mother pity me,
Who am a maiden most forlorn?"
Christabel answer'd — "Woe is me!
She died the hour that I was born.
I have heard the grey-hair'd friar tell,
How on her death-bed she did say,
That she should hear the castle-bell
Strike twelve upon my wedding-day.
O mother dear! that thou wert here!"
"I would," said Geraldine, "she were!"

But soon, with alter'd voice, said she —
"Off, wandering mother! Peak and pine!
I have power to bid thee flee."
Alas! what ails poor Geraldine?
Why stares she with unsettled eye?
Can she the bodiless dead espy?
And why with hollow voice cries she,
"Off, woman, off! this hour is mine —
Though thou her guardian spirit be,
Off, woman, off! 'tis given to me."

Then Christabel knelt by the lady's side,
And raised to heaven her eyes so blue —

"Alas!" said she, "this ghastly ride —
Dear lady! it hath wilder'd you!"
The lady wiped her moist cold brow,
And faintly said, "'Tis over now!"

Again the wild-flower wine she drank:
Her fair large eyes 'gan glitter bright,
And from the floor, whereon she sank,
The lofty lady stood upright:
She was most beautiful to see,
Like a lady of a far countree.

And thus the lofty lady spake —
"All they, who live in the upper sky,
Do love you, holy Christabel!
And you love them, and for their sake,
And for the good which me befell,
Even I in my degree will try,
Fair maiden, to requite you well.
But now unrobe yourself; for I
Must pray, ere yet in bed I lie."

Quoth Christabel, "So let it be!"
And as the lady bade, did she.
Her gentle limbs did she undress,
And lay down in her loveliness.
But through her brain, of weal and woe,
So many thoughts moved to and fro,
That vain it were her lids to close;
So half-way from the bed she rose,
And on her elbow did recline,
To look at the lady Geraldine.

Beneath the lamp the lady bow'd,
And slowly roll'd her eyes around;
Then drawing in her breath aloud,
Like one that shudder'd, she unbound
The cincture from beneath her breast:
Her silken robe, and inner vest,
Dropt to her feet, and full in view,
Behold! her bosom and half her side —
A sight to dream of, not to tell!
O shield her! shield sweet Christabel!

Yet Geraldine nor speaks nor stirs:
Ah! what a stricken look was hers!
Deep from within she seems half-way
To lift some weight with sick assay,
And eyes the maid and seeks delay;
Then suddenly, as one defied,
Collects herself in scorn and pride,
And lay down by the maiden's side! —
And in her arms the maid she took,
Ah wel-a-day!
And with low voice and doleful look
These words did say:

"In the touch of this bosom there worketh a spell,
Which is lord of thy utterance, Christabel!
Thou knowest to-night, and wilt know to-morrow,
This mark of my shame, this seal of my sorrow;
But vainly thou warrest,
For this is alone in
Thy power to declare,
That in the dim forest
Thou heard'st a low moaning,
And found'st a bright lady, surpassingly fair:
And didst bring her home with thee, in love and in charity,
To shield her and shelter her from the damp air."

* * * * * * *

ROBERT SOUTHEY (1774–1843)

From THE CURSE OF KEHAMA

XIII. THE RETREAT

O force of faith! O strength of virtuous will!
Behold him in his endless martyrdom,
Triumphant still!
The curse still burning in his heart and brain,
And yet doth he remain
Patient the while, and tranquil, and content!
The pious soul hath framed unto itself
A second nature, to exist in pain
As in its own allotted element.

Such strength the will reveal'd had given
This holy pair, such influxes of grace,
That to their solitary resting place
They brought the peace of Heaven.
Yea, all around was hallow'd! Danger, Fear,
Nor thought of evil ever enter'd here.
A charm was on the Leopard when he came
Within the circle of that mystic glade;
Submiss he crouch'd before the heavenly maid,
And offer'd to her touch his speckled side;
Or with arch'd back erect, and bending head,
And eyes half-closed for pleasure, would he stand
Courting the pressure of her gentle hand.

Trampling his path through wood and brake,
And canes which crackling fall before his way,
And tassel-grass, whose silvery feathers play
O'ertopping the young trees,
On comes the Elephant to slake
His thirst at noon in yon pellucid springs.
Lo! from his trunk upturn'd, aloft he flings
The grateful shower; and now
Plucking the broad-leaved bough

Of yonder plane, with wavy motion slow,
Fanning the languid air,
He moves it to and fro.
But when that form of beauty meets his sight,
The trunk its undulating motion stops, 169
From his forgetful hold the plane-branch drops,
Reverent he kneels, and lifts his rational eyes
To her as if in prayer;
And when she pours her angel voice in song
Entranced he listens to the thrilling notes,
Till his strong temples, bathed with sudden dews,
Their fragrance of delight and love diffuse.

Lo! as the voice melodious floats around,
The Antelope draws near,
The Tigress leaves her toothless cubs to hear;
The Snake comes gliding from the secret brake,
Himself in fascination forced along 181
By that enchanting song;
The antic Monkeys, whose wild gambols late,
When not a breeze waved the tall jungle grass,
Shook the whole wood, are hush'd, and silently
Hang on the cluster'd tree.
All things in wonder and delight are still;
Only at times the nightingale is heard,
Not that in emulous skill that sweetest bird
Her rival strain would try, 190
A mighty songster, with the Maid to vie;
She only bore her part in powerful sympathy.

Well might they thus adore that heavenly Maid!
For never Nymph of Mountain,
Or Grove, or Lake, or Fountain,
With a diviner presence fill'd the shade.
No idle ornaments deface
Her natural grace,
Musk-spot, nor sandal-streak, nor scarlet stain,
Ear-drop nor chain, nor arm nor ankle-ring, 200
Nor trinketry on front, or neck, or breast,
Marring the perfect form: she seem'd a thing
Of Heaven's prime uncorrupted work, a child
Of early nature undefiled,
A daughter of the years of innocence.
And therefore all things loved her. When she stood
Beside the glassy pool, the fish, that flies
Quick as an arrow from all other eyes,
Hover'd to gaze on her. The mother bird,
When Kailyal's step she heard, 210
Sought not to tempt her from her secret nest,
But hastening to the dear retreat, would fly
To meet and welcome her benignant eye.

THE BATTLE OF BLENHEIM

It was a summer evening,
Old Kaspar's work was done,
And he before his cottage door
Was sitting in the sun,
And by him sported on the green
His little grandchild Wilhelmine. 6

She saw her brother Peterkin
Roll something large and round,
Which he beside the rivulet
In playing there had found;
He came to ask what he had found, 11
That was so large, and smooth, and round.

Old Kaspar took it from the boy,
Who stood expectant by;
And then the old man shook his head,
And with a natural sigh,
"'Tis some poor fellow's skull," said he,
"Who fell in the great victory. 18

"I find them in the garden,
For there's many here about;
And often when I go to plough,
The ploughshare turns them out!
For many thousand men," said he,
"Were slain in that great victory." 24

"Now tell me what 'twas all about,"
Young Peterkin, he cries;
And little Wilhelmine looks up
With wonder-waiting eyes;
"Now tell us all about the war,
And what they fought each other for." 30

"It was the English," Kaspar cried,
"Who put the French to rout;
But what they fought each other for,
I could not well make out;
But everybody said," quoth he,
"That 'twas a famous victory. 36

"My father lived at Blenheim then,
Yon little stream hard by;
They burnt his dwelling to the ground,
And he was forced to fly;
So with his wife and child he fled,
Nor had he where to rest his head. 42

"With fire and sword the country round
Was wasted far and wide,
And many a childing mother then,
And new-born baby died;
But things like that, you know, must be
At every famous victory. 48

"They say it was a shocking sight
After the field was won;
For many thousand bodies here
Lay rotting in the sun;
But things like that, you know, must be
After a famous victory.

"Great praise the Duke of Marlbro' won,
And our good Prince Eugene."
"Why 'twas a very wicked thing!"
Said little Wilhelmine.
"Nay, nay, my little girl," quoth he.
"It was a famous victory.

"And everybody praised the Duke
Who this great fight did win."
"But what good came of it at last?"
Quoth little Peterkin.
"Why that I cannot tell," said he,
"But 'twas a famous victory."

STANZAS WRITTEN IN HIS LIBRARY

My days among the Dead are past;
Around me I behold,
Where'er these casual eyes are cast,
The mighty minds of old;
My never failing friends are they,
With whom I converse day by day.

With them I take delight in weal,
And seek relief in woe;
And while I understand and feel
How much to them I owe,
My cheeks have often been bedew'd
With tears of thoughtful gratitude.

My thoughts are with the Dead, with them
I live in long-past years,
Their virtues love, their faults condemn,
Partake their hopes and fears,
And from their lessons seek and find
Instruction with an humble mind.

My hopes are with the Dead, anon
My place with them will be,
And I with them shall travel on
Through all Futurity;
Yet leaving here a name, I trust,
That will not perish in the dust.

THE WELL OF ST. KEYNE

A well there is in the West country,
And a clearer one never was seen;
There is not a wife in the West country
But has heard of the Well of St. Keyne.

An oak and an elm tree stand beside,
And behind does an ash-tree grow,
And a willow from the bank above
Droops to the water below.

A traveller came to the Well of St. Keyne;
Joyfully he drew nigh,
For from cock-crow he had been travelling,
And there was not a cloud in the sky.

He drank of the water so cool and clear,
For thirsty and hot was he,
And he sat down upon the bank,
Under the willow-tree.

There came a man from the house hard by
At the well to fill his pail,
On the well-side he rested it,
And he bade the stranger hail.

"Now art thou a bachelor, stranger?" quoth he,
"For an if thou hast a wife,
The happiest draught thou hast drank this day
That ever thou didst in thy life.

"Or has thy good woman, if one thou hast,
Ever here in Cornwall been?
For an if she have, I'll venture my life
She has drunk of the Well of St. Keyne."

"I have left a good woman who never was here,"
The stranger he made reply;
"But that my draught should be the better for that,
I pray you answer me why."

"St. Keyne," quoth the Cornish-man, "many a time
Drank of this crystal well,
And before the Angel summoned her
She laid on the water a spell.

"If the Husband of this gifted well
Shall drink before his Wife,
A happy man thenceforth is he,
For he shall be Master for life.

"But if the Wife should drink of it first,
God help the Husband then!"
The stranger stooped to the Well of St. Keyne,
And drank of the waters again.

"You drank of the well, I warrant, betimes?"
He to the Cornish-man said.
But the Cornish-man smiled as the stranger spake,
And sheepishly shook his head.

"I hastened, as soon as the wedding was done,
And left my wife in the porch.
But i' faith, she had been wiser than me,
For she took a bottle to Church."

CHARLES LAMB (1775–1834)

THE OLD FAMILIAR FACES

I have had playmates, I have had companions,
In my days of childhood, in my joyful school-days;
All, all are gone, the old familiar faces.

I have been laughing, I have been carousing,
Drinking late, sitting late, with my bosom cronies;
All, all are gone, the old familiar faces.

I loved a love once, fairest among women;
Closed are her doors on me, I must not see her —
All, all are gone, the old familiar faces.

I have a friend, a kinder friend has no man;
Like an ingrate, I left my friend abruptly;
Left him, to muse on the old familiar faces.

Ghost-like I paced round the haunts of my childhood,
Earth seemed a desert I was bound to traverse,
Seeking to find the old familiar faces.

Friend of my bosom, thou more than a brother,
Why wert not thou born in my father's dwelling?
So might we talk of the old familiar faces —

How some they have died, and some they have left me,
And some are taken from me; all are departed;
All, all are gone, the old familiar faces.

CHILDHOOD

In my poor mind it is most sweet to muse
Upon the days gone by; to act in thought
Past seasons o'er, and be again a child;
To sit in fancy on the turf-clad slope,
Down which the child would roll; to pluck gay flowers,
Make posies in the sun, which the child's hand
(Childhood offended soon, soon reconciled),
Would throw away and straight take up again,
Then fling them to the winds, and o'er the lawn
Bound with so playful and so light a foot,
That the pressed daisy scarce declined her head.

From A FAREWELL TO TOBACCO

May the Babylonish curse
Straight confound my stammering verse,
If I can a passage see
In this word-perplexity,
Or a language to my mind
(Still the phrase is wide or scant),
To take leave of thee, Great Plant!
Or in any terms relate
Half my love, or half my hate;
For I hate, yet love, thee so,
That, whichever thing I show,
The plain truth will seem to be
A constrain'd hyperbole,
And the passion to proceed
More from a mistress than a weed.

Sooty retainer to the vine!
Bacchus' black servant, negro fine!
Sorcerer! that mak'st us dote upon
Thy begrimed complexion,
And, for thy pernicious sake,
More and greater oaths to break
Than reclaimèd lovers take
'Gainst women! Thou thy siege dost lay
Much, too, in the female way,
While thou suck'st the labouring breath
Faster than kisses, or than death.

Thou in such a cloud dost bind us
That our worst foes cannot find us,
And ill fortune, that would thwart us,
Shoots at rovers, shooting at us;
While each man, through thy heightening steam,
Does like a smoking Etna seem;
And all about us does express
(Fancy and wit in richest dress)
A Sicilian fruitfulness.

Thou through such a mist dost show us
That our best friends do not know us,
And, for those allowèd features
Due to reasonable creatures,
Liken'st us to fell Chimeras,
Monsters, — that who see us, fear us;
Worse than Cerberus or Geryon,
Or, who first loved a cloud, Ixion.

Bacchus we know, and we allow
His tipsy rites. But what art thou,
That but by reflex canst show
What his deity can do, —
As the false Egyptian spell
Aped the true Hebrew miracle?
Some few vapours thou mayst raise
The weak brain may serve to amaze;

But to the reins and nobler heart
Canst nor life nor heat impart.

Brother of Bacchus, later born!
The old world was sure forlorn,
Wanting thee, that aidest more
The god's victories than before
All his panthers, and the brawls
Of his piping Bacchanals.
These, as stale, we disallow,
Or judge of thee meant: only thou
His true Indian conquest art;
And, for ivy round his dart,
The reformèd god now weaves
A finer thyrsus of thy leaves.

WALTER SAVAGE LANDOR
(1775–1864)

From ACON AND RHODOPE; OR, INCONSTANCY

The Year's twelve daughters had in turn gone by,
Of measured pace though varying mien all twelve,
Some froward, some sedater, some adorn'd
For festival, some reckless of attire.
The snow had left the mountain-top; fresh flowers
Had withered in the meadow; fig and prune
Hung wrinkling; the last apple glow'd amid
Its freckled leaves; and weary oxen blink'd
Between the trodden corn and twisted vine,
Under whose bunches stood the empty crate,
To creak ere long beneath them carried home.
This was the season when twelve months before,
O gentle Hamadryad, true to love!
Thy mansion, thy dim mansion in the wood
Was blasted and laid desolate: but none
Dared violate its precincts, none dared pluck
The moss beneath it, which alone remain'd
Of what was thine.
Old Thallinos sat mute
In solitary sadness. The strange tale
(Not until Rhaicos died, but then the whole)
Echion had related, whom no force
Could ever make look back upon the oaks.
The father said, "Echion! thou must weigh,
Carefully, and with steady hand, enough
(Although no longer comes the store as once!)
Of wax to burn all day and night upon
That hollow stone where milk and honey lie:
So may the gods, so may the dead, be pleas'd!"
Thallinos bore it thither in the morn,
And lighted it and left it.
First of those
Who visited upon this solemn day
The Hamadryad's oak, were Rhodopè
And Acon; of one age, one hope, one trust.
Graceful was she as was the nymph whose fate
She sorrowed for: he slender, pale, and first
Lapp'd by the flame of love: his father's lands
Were fertile, herds lowed over them afar.
Now stood the two aside the hollow stone
And look'd with steadfast eyes toward the oak
Shivered and black and bare.
"May never we
Love as they loved!" said Acon. She at this
Smiled, for he said not what he meant to say,
And thought not of its bliss, but of its end.
He caught the flying smile, and blush'd, and vow'd
Nor time nor other power, whereto the might
Of love hath yielded and may yield again,
Should alter his.
The father of the youth
Wanted not beauty for him, wanted not
Song, that could lift earth's weight from off his heart,
Discretion, that could guide him thro' the world,
Innocence, that could clear his way to heaven;
Silver and gold and land, not green before
The ancestral gate, but purple under skies
Bending far off, he wanted for his heir.
Fathers have given life, but virgin heart
They never gave; and dare they then control
Or check it harshly? dare they break a bond
Girt round it by the holiest Power on high?

Acon was grieved, he said, grieved bitterly,
But Acon had complied — 'twas dutiful!
Crush thy own heart, Man! Man! but fear to wound
The gentler, that relies on thee alone,
By thee created, weak or strong by thee;
Touch it not but for worship; watch before
Its sanctuary; nor leave it till are closed
The temple doors and the last lamp is spent.
Rhodopè, in her soul's waste solitude,
Sate mournful by the dull-resounding sea,
Often not hearing it, and many tears
Had the cold breezes hardened on her cheek.
Meanwhile he sauntered in the wood of oaks,
Nor shunn'd to look upon the hollow stone
That held the milk and honey, nor to lay
His plighted hand where recently 'twas laid
Opposite hers, when finger playfully
Advanced and push'd back finger, on each side.
He did not think of this, as she would do
If she were there alone. The day was hot;
The moss invited him; it cool'd his cheek,
It cool'd his hands; he thrust them into it
And sank to slumber. Never was there dream
Divine as his. He saw the Hamadryad.
She took him by the arm and led him on

Along a valley, where profusely grew
The smaller lilies with their pendant bells,
And, hiding under mint, chill drosera,
The violet, shy of butting cyclamen,
The feathery fern, and, browser of moist banks,
Her offspring round her, the soft strawberry;
The quivering spray of ruddy tamarisk,
The oleander's light-hair'd progeny
Breathing bright freshness in each other's face,
And graceful rose, bending her brow, with cup
Of fragrance and of beauty, boon for gods.
The fragrance fill'd his breast with such delight
His senses were bewildered, and he thought
He saw again the face he most had loved.
He stopp'd: the Hamadryad at his side
Now stood between; then drew him farther off:
He went, compliant as before: but soon
Verdure had ceased: although the ground was smooth,
Nothing was there delightful. At this change
He would have spoken, but his guide repress'd
All questioning, and said,
"Weak youth! what brought
Thy footstep to this wood, my native haunt,
My life-long residence? this bank, where first
I sate with him — the faithful (now I know
Too late!) the faithful Rhaicos. Haste thee home;
Be happy, if thou canst; but come no more
Where those whom death alone could sever, died."
He started up: the moss whereon he slept
Was dried and withered: deadlier paleness spread
Over his cheek; he sickened: and the sire
Had land enough; it held his only son.

ROSE AYLMER

Ah, what avails the sceptred race,
Ah, what the form divine!
What every virtue, every grace!
Rose Aylmer, all were thine.
Rose Aylmer, whom these wakeful eyes
May weep, but never see,
A night of memories and of sighs
I consecrate to thee.

A FIESOLAN IDYL

Here, where precipitate Spring with one light bound
Into hot Summer's lusty arms expires,
And where go forth at morn, at eve, at night,
Soft airs that want the lute to play with 'em,
And softer sighs that know not what they want,
Aside a wall, beneath an orange-tree,
Whose tallest flowers could tell the lowlier ones
Of sights in Fiesole right up above,
While I was gazing a few paces off
At what they seem'd to show me with their nods,
Their frequent whispers and their pointing shoots,
A gentle maid came down the garden-steps
And gathered the pure treasure in her lap.
I heard the branches rustle, and stepp'd forth
To drive the ox away, or mule, or goat,
Such I believed it must be. How could I
Let beast o'erpower them? when hath wind or rain
Borne hard upon weak plant that wanted me,
And I (however they might bluster round)
Walk'd off? 'Twere most ungrateful: for sweet scents
Are the swift vehicles of still sweeter thoughts,
And nurse and pillow the dull memory
That would let drop without them her best stores.
They bring me tales of youth and tones of love,
And 'tis and ever was my wish and way
To let all flowers live freely, and all die
(Whene'er their Genius bids their souls depart)
Among their kindred in their native place.
I never pluck the rose; the violet's head
Hath shaken with my breath upon its bank
And not reproach'd me; the ever-sacred cup
Of the pure lily hath between my hands
Felt safe, unsoil'd, nor lost one grain of gold.
I saw the light that made the glossy leaves
More glossy; the fair arm, the fairer cheek
Warmed by the eye intent on its pursuit;
I saw the foot that, although half-erect
From its grey slipper, could not lift her up
To what she wanted: I held down a branch
And gather'd her some blossoms; since their hour
Was come, and bees had wounded them, and flies
Of harder wing were working their way thro'
And scattering them in fragments under foot.
So crisp were some, they rattled unevolved,
Others, ere broken off, fell into shells,
For such appear the petals when detach'd,
Unbending, brittle, lucid, white like snow,
And like snow not seen through, by eye or sun:
Yet every one her gown received from me
Was fairer than the first. I thought not so,
But so she praised them to reward my care.
I said, "You find the largest." "This indeed,"
Cried she, "is large and sweet." She held one forth,
Whether for me to look at or to take
She knew not, nor did I; but taking it
Would best have solved (and this she felt) her doubt.
I dared not touch it; for it seemed a part
Of her own self; fresh, full, the most mature
Of blossoms, yet a blossom; with a touch

To fall, and yet unfallen. She drew back
The boon she tender'd, and then finding not
The ribbon at her waist to fix it in,
Dropp'd it, as loth to drop it, on the rest.

TO ROBERT BROWNING

There is delight in singing, though none hear
Beside the singer; and there is delight
In praising, though the praiser sit alone
And see the prais'd far off him, far above.
Shakespeare is not our poet, but the world's,
Therefore on him no speech! and brief for thee,
Browning! Since Chaucer was alive and hale,
No man hath walk'd along our roads with step
So active, so inquiring eye, or tongue
So varied in discourse. But warmer climes
Give brighter plumage, stronger wing: the breeze
Of Alpine highths thou playest with, borne on
Beyond Sorrento and Amalfi, where
The Siren waits thee, singing song for song.

WHY

Why do our joys depart
For cares to seize the heart?
I know not. Nature says,
Obey; and Man obeys.
I see, and know not why,
Thorns live and roses die.

ON HIS SEVENTY-FIFTH BIRTHDAY

I strove with none, for none was worth my strife,
  Nature I loved, and next to Nature, Art;
I warmed both hands before the fire of life,
  It sinks, and I am ready to depart.

ON DEATH

Death stands above me, whispering low
  I know not what into my ear:
Of his strange language all I know
  Is, there is not a word of fear.

THOMAS CAMPBELL (1777–1844)

HOHENLINDEN

On Linden, when the sun was low,
All bloodless lay the untrodden snow,
And dark as winter was the flow
Of Iser, rolling rapidly.

But Linden saw another sight,
When the drum beat at dead of night,
Commanding fires of death to light
The darkness of her scenery.

By torch and trumpet fast arrayed,
Each horseman drew his battle blade,
And furious every charger neighed,
To join the dreadful revelry.

Then shook the hills with thunder riven,
Then rushed the steed to battle driven,
And louder than the bolts of heaven,
Far flashed the red artillery.

But redder yet that light shall glow,
On Linden's hills of stained snow,
And bloodier yet the torrent flow
Of Iser, rolling rapidly.

'Tis morn, but scarce yon level sun
Can pierce the war-clouds, rolling dun,
Where furious Frank, and fiery Hun,
Shout in their sulphurous canopy.

The combat deepens. On, ye brave,
Who rush to glory, or the grave!
Wave, Munich! all thy banners wave!
And charge with all thy chivalry!

Few, few, shall part where many meet!
The snow shall be their winding sheet,
And every turf beneath their feet
Shall be a soldier's sepulchre.

YE MARINERS OF ENGLAND

A NAVAL ODE

Ye mariners of England
That guard our native seas,
Whose flag has braved a thousand years
The battle and the breeze!
Your glorious standard launch again
To match another foe,
And sweep through the deep,
While the stormy winds do blow;
While the battle rages loud and long,
And the stormy winds do blow.

The spirits of your fathers
Shall start from every wave! —
For the deck it was their field of fame,
And Ocean was their grave:
Where Blake and mighty Nelson fell
Your manly hearts shall glow,
As ye sweep through the deep,
While the stormy winds do blow;
While the battle rages loud and long,
And the stormy winds do blow.

Britannia needs no bulwark,
No towers along the steep;
Her march is o'er the mountain waves,
Her home is on the deep.
With thunders from her native oak
She quells the floods below —
As they roar on the shore,
When the stormy winds do blow;
When the battle rages loud and long,
And the stormy winds do blow.

The meteor flag of England
Shall yet terrific burn,
Till danger's troubled night depart
And the star of peace return.
Then, then, ye ocean-warriors!
Our song and feast shall flow
To the fame of your name,
When the storm has ceased to blow;
When the fiery fight is heard no more,
And the storm has ceased to blow.

EXILE OF ERIN

There came to the beach a poor exile of Erin,
The dew on his thin robe was heavy and chill;
For his country he sighed, when at twilight repairing
To wander alone by the wind-beaten hill.
But the day-star attracted his eye's sad devotion,
For it rose o'er his own native isle of the ocean,
Where once, in the fire of his youthful emotion,
He sang the bold anthem of Erin go bragh.

Sad is my fate! said the heart-broken stranger;
The wild deer and wolf to a covert can flee,
But I have no refuge from famine and danger,
A home and a country remain not to me.
Never again in the green sunny bowers
Where my forefathers lived shall I spend the sweet hours,
Or cover my harp with the wild-woven flowers,
And strike to the numbers of Erin go bragh!

Erin, my country! though sad and forsaken,
In dreams I revisit thy sea-beaten shore;
But, alas! in a far foreign land I awaken,
And sigh for the friends who can meet me no more!
O cruel fate! wilt thou never replace me
In a mansion of peace, where no perils can chase me?
Never again shall my brothers embrace me?
They died to defend me, or live to deplore!

Where is my cabin door, fast by the wildwood?
Sisters and sire, did ye weep for its fall?
Where is the mother that looked on my childhood?
And where is the bosom-friend, dearer than all?
O my sad heart! long abandoned by pleasure,
Why did it dote on a fast-fading treasure?
Tears, like the rain-drop, may fall without measure,
But rapture and beauty they cannot recall.

Yet, all its sad recollections suppressing,
One dying wish my lone bosom can draw, —
Erin, an exile bequeaths thee his blessing!
Land of my forefathers, Erin go bragh!
Buried and cold, when my heart stills her motion,
Green be thy fields, sweetest isle of the ocean!
And thy harp-striking bards sing aloud with devotion, —
Erin mavournin, Erin go bragh!

BATTLE OF THE BALTIC

Of Nelson and the North
Sing the glorious day's renown,
When to battle fierce came forth
All the might of Denmark's crown,
And her arms along the deep proudly shone;
By each gun the lighted brand
In a bold determin'd hand,
And the Prince of all the land
Led them on.

Like leviathans afloat
Lay their bulwarks on the brine,
While the sign of battle flew
On the lofty British line:
It was ten of April morn by the chime:
As they drifted on their path,
There was silence deep as death,
And the boldest held his breath
For a time.

But the might of England flushed
To anticipate the scene,
And her van the fleeter rushed
O'er the deadly space between —
"Hearts of oak," our captains cried, when each gun
From its adamantine lips
Spread a death-shade round the ships,
Like the hurricane eclipse
Of the sun.

Again! again! again!
And the havoc did not slack,
Till a feeble cheer the Dane
To our cheering sent us back; —
Their shots along the deep slowly boom: —

Then ceased — and all is wail,
As they strike the shattered sail,
Or in conflagration pale
Light the gloom.

Out spoke the victor then,
As he hailed them o'er the wave;
"Ye are brothers! ye are men!
And we conquer but to save;
So peace instead of death let us bring:
But yield, proud foe, thy fleet
With the crews at England's feet,
And make submission meet
To our King."

Then Denmark blest our chief,
That he gave her wounds repose;
And the sounds of joy and grief,
From her people wildly rose,
As death withdrew his shades from the day;
While the sun looked smiling bright
O'er a wide and woeful sight,
Where the fires of funeral light
Died away.

Now joy, old England, raise!
For the tidings of thy might,
By the festal cities' blaze,
While the wine cup shines in light;
And yet amidst that joy and uproar,
Let us think of them that sleep,
Full many a fathom deep,
By thy wild and stormy steep,
Elsinore!

Brave hearts! to Britain's pride
Once so faithful and so true,
On the deck of fame that died, —
With the gallant good Riou,
Soft sigh the winds of heaven o'er their grave!
While the billow mournful rolls,
And the mermaid's song condoles,
Singing glory to the souls
Of the brave!

From THE PLEASURES OF HOPE

Where Barbarous hordes on Scythian mountains roam,
Truth, Mercy, Freedom, yet shall find a home;
Where'er degraded Nature bleeds and pines,
From Guinea's coast to Sibir's dreary mines,
Truth shall pervade th' unfathom'd darkness there,
And light the dreadful features of despair. —
Hark! the stern captive spurns his heavy load,
And asks the image back that Heaven bestow'd!
Fierce in his eye the fire of valour burns,
And as the slave departs, the man returns.
Oh! sacred Truth! thy triumph ceased awhile,
And Hope, thy sister, ceased with thee to smile,
When leagued Oppression pour'd to Northern wars
Her whisker'd pandoors and her fierce hussars,
Waved her dread standard to the breeze of morn,
Peal'd her loud drum, and twang'd her trumpet horn,
Tumultuous horror brooded o'er her van,
Presaging wrath to Poland — and to man!
Warsaw's last champion from her height survey'd,
Wide o'er the fields, a waste of ruin laid, —
"O Heaven!" he cried, "my bleeding country save! —
Is there no hand on high to shield the brave?
Yet, though destruction sweep those lovely plains,
Rise, fellow-men! our country yet remains!
By that dread name, we wave the sword on high!
And swear for her to live! — with her to die!"
He said, and on the rampart-heights array'd
His trusty warriors, few, but undismay'd;
Firm-paced and slow, a horrid front they form,
Still as the breeze, but dreadful as the storm;
Low murmuring sounds along their banners fly,
Revenge, or death, — the watchword and reply;
Then peal'd the notes, omnipotent to charm,
And the loud tocsin toll'd their last alarm! —
In vain, alas! in vain, ye gallant few!
From rank to rank your volley'd thunder flew: —
Oh, bloodiest picture in the book of Time,
Sarmatia fell, unwept, without a crime;
Found not a generous friend, a pitying foe,
Strength in her arms, nor mercy in her woe!
Dropp'd from her nerveless grasp the shatter'd spear,
Closed her bright eye, and curb'd her high career; —
Hope, for a season, bade the world farewell,
And Freedom shriek'd — as Kosciusko fell!
The sun went down, nor ceased the carnage there,
Tumultuous Murder shook the midnight air —
On Prague's proud arch the fires of ruin glow,
His blood-dyed waters murmuring far below;
The storm prevails, the rampart yields a way,
Bursts the wild cry of horror and dismay!
Hark, as the smouldering piles with thunder fall,
A thousand shrieks for hopeless mercy call!
Earth shook — red meteors flash'd along the sky,
And conscious Nature shudder'd at the cry!
Oh! righteous Heaven; ere Freedom found a grave,
Why slept the sword omnipotent to save?
Where was thine arm, O Vengeance! where thy rod,

That smote the foes of Zion and of God;
That crush'd proud Ammon, when his iron car
Was yoked in wrath, and thunder'd from afar?
Where was the storm that slumber'd till the host
Of blood-stain'd Pharaoh left their trembling coast:
Then bade the deep in wild commotion flow,
And heaved an ocean on their march below?

THOMAS MOORE (1779–1852)

ALAS! HOW LIGHT A CAUSE MAY MOVE

From THE LIGHT OF THE HAREM

Alas! — how light a cause may move
Dissension between hearts that love!
Hearts that the world in vain had tried,
And sorrow but more closely tied;
That stood the storm when waves were rough,
Yet in a sunny hour fall off,
Like ships that have gone down at sea,
When heaven was all tranquillity!
A something light as air — a look,
A word unkind or wrongly taken —
O, love, that tempests never shook,
A breath, a touch like this has shaken!
And ruder words will soon rush in
To spread the breach that words begin;
And eyes forget the gentle ray
They wore in courtship's smiling day;
And voices lose the tone that shed
A tenderness round all they said;
Till fast declining, one by one,
The sweetnesses of love are gone,
And hearts, so lately mingled, seem
Like broken clouds, — or like the stream,
That smiling left the mountain's brow
As though its waters ne'er could sever,
Yet, ere it reach the plain below,
Breaks into floods, that part forever.

O you, that have the charge of Love,
Keep him in rosy bondage bound,
As in the Fields of Bliss above
He sits, with flowerets fettered round; —
Loose not a tie that round him clings,
Nor ever let him use his wings;
For even an hour, a minute's flight
Will rob the plumes of half their light.
Like that celestial bird, — whose nest
Is found beneath far Eastern skies, —
Whose wings, though radiant when at rest,
Lose all their glory when he flies!

SYRIA

From PARADISE AND THE PERI

Now, upon Syria's land of roses,
Softly the light of eve reposes,
And, like a glory, the broad sun
Hangs over sainted Lebanon;
Whose head in wintry grandeur towers,
And whitens with eternal sleet,
While summer, in a vale of flowers,
Is sleeping rosy at his feet.

To one who looked from upper air
O'er all the enchanted regions there,
How beauteous must have been the glow,
The life, how sparkling from below!
Fair gardens, shining streams, with ranks
Of golden melons on their banks,
More golden where the sunlight falls; —
Gay lizards, glittering on the walls
Of ruined shrines, busy and bright
As they were all alive with light;
And, yet more splendid, numerous flocks
Of pigeons, settling on the rocks,
With their rich restless wings that gleam
Variously in the crimson beam
Of the warm west, — as if inlaid
With brilliants from the mine, or made
Of tearless rainbows, such as span
The unclouded skies of Peristan.
And then the mingling sounds that come,
Of shepherd's ancient reed, with hum
Of the wild bees of Palestine,
Banqueting through the flowery vales;
And, Jordan, those sweet banks of thine,
And woods, so full of nightingales!

THE FIRE-WORSHIPPERS

From LALLA ROOKH

"How sweetly," said the trembling maid,
Of her own gentle voice afraid,
So long had they in silence stood,
Looking upon that tranquil flood —
"How sweetly does the moonbeam smile
To-night upon yon leafy isle!
Oft, in my fancy's wanderings,
I've wish'd that little isle had wings,
And we, within its fairy bowers,
Were wafted off to seas unknown,
Where not a pulse would beat but ours,
And we might live, love, die alone!
Far from the cruel and the cold, —
Where the bright eyes of angels only

Should come around us, to behold
A paradise so pure and lonely.
Would this be world enough for thee?"
Playful she turned, that he might see
The passing smile her cheek put on;
But when she marked how mournfully
His eyes met hers, that smile was gone;
And, bursting into heartfelt tears,
"Yes, yes," she cried, "my hourly fears,
My dreams, have boded all too right —
We part — forever part — to-night!
I knew, I knew it could not last —
'Twas bright, 'twas heavenly, but 'tis past!
Oh! ever thus, from childhood's hour,
I've seen my fondest hopes decay;
I never loved a tree or flower,
But 'twas the first to fade away.
I never nursed a dear gazelle,
To glad me with its soft black eye,
But when it came to know me well,
And love me, it was sure to die!
Now too — the joy most like divine
Of all I ever dreamt or knew,
To see thee, hear thee, call thee mine, —
Oh, misery! must I lose that too?
Yet go — on peril's brink we meet; —
Those frightful rocks — that treacherous sea —
No, never come again — though sweet,
Though heaven, it may be death to thee.
Farewell — and blessings on thy way,
Where'er thou go'st, beloved stranger!
Better to sit and watch that ray,
And think thee safe, though far away,
Than have thee near me, and in danger!"

THE TIME I'VE LOST IN WOOING

The time I've lost in wooing,
In watching and pursuing
The light, that lies
In woman's eyes,
Has been my heart's undoing.
Tho' Wisdom oft has sought me,
I scorn'd the lore she brought me,
My only books
Were woman's looks,
And folly's all they've taught me.

Her smile when Beauty granted,
I hung with gaze enchanted,
Like him the Sprite,
Whom maids by night
Oft meet in glen that's haunted.
Like him, too, Beauty won me,
But while her eyes were on me;
If once their ray
Was turned away,
Oh, winds could not outrun me.

And are those follies going?
And is my proud heart growing
Too cold or wise
For brilliant eyes
Again to set it glowing?
No, vain, alas! th' endeavour
From bonds so sweet to sever
Poor Wisdom's chance
Against a glance
Is now as weak as ever.

OFT IN THE STILLY NIGHT

Oft, in the stilly night,
Ere Slumber's chain has bound me,
Fond Memory brings the light
Of other days around me;
The smiles, the tears,
Of boyhood's years,
The words of love then spoken;
The eyes that shone,
Now dimm'd and gone,
The cheerful hearts now broken!
Thus, in the stilly night,
Ere Slumber's chain has bound me,
Sad Memory brings the light
Of other days around me.

When I remember all
The friends, so link'd together,
I've seen around me fall,
Like leaves in wintry weather;
I feel like one
Who treads alone
Some banquet-hall deserted,
Whose lights are fled,
Whose garlands dead,
And all but he departed!
Thus, in the stilly night,
Ere Slumber's chain has bound me,
Sad Memory brings the light
Of other days around me.

FAREWELL! BUT WHENEVER

Farewell! — but whenever you welcome the hour
That awakens the night-song of mirth in your bower,
Then think of the friend who once welcomed it too,
And forgot his own griefs to be happy with you.

His griefs may return, not a hope may remain
Of the few that have brightened his pathway of pain,
But he ne'er will forget the short vision that threw
Its enchantment around him, while lingering with you.

And still on that evening, when pleasure fills up
To the highest top sparkle each heart and each cup,
Where'er my path lies, be it gloomy or bright,
My soul, happy friends, shall be with you that night;
Shall join in your revels, your sports, and your wiles,
And return to me, beaming all o'er with your smiles —
Too blest, if it tells me that, 'mid the gay cheer
Some kind voice has murmured, "I wish he were here!"

Let Fate do her worst, there are relics of joy,
Bright dreams of the past, which she cannot destroy;
Which come, in the night-time of sorrow and care,
And bring back the features that joy used to wear.
Long, long be my heart with such memories filled!
Like the vase in which roses have once been distilled —
You may break, you may shatter the vase, if you will,
But the scent of the roses will hang round it still.

LOVE'S YOUNG DREAM

Oh! the days are gone when beauty bright
My heart's chain wove.
When my dream of life, from morn till night,
Was love, still love!
New hope may bloom,
And days may come,
Of milder, calmer beam,
But there's nothing half so sweet in life
As love's young dream!
No, there's nothing half so sweet in life
As love's young dream.

Though the bard to purer fame may soar,
When wild youth's past;
Though he win the wise, who frowned before,
To smile at last;
He'll never meet
A joy so sweet
In all his noon of fame
As when first he sung to woman's ear
His soul-felt flame,
And, at every close, she blushed to hear
The one loved name!

No, — that hallowed form is ne'er forgot
Which first love traced;
Still it lingering haunts the greenest spot
On memory's waste.
'Twas odour fled
As soon as shed;
'Twas morning's wing'd dream;
'Twas a light that ne'er can shine again
On life's dull stream!
Oh! 'twas a light that ne'er can shine again
On life's dull stream.

'TIS THE LAST ROSE OF SUMMER

'Tis the last rose of summer,
Left blooming alone;
All her lovely companions
Are faded and gone;
No flower of her kindred,
No rosebud, is nigh
To reflect back her blushes,
Or give sigh for sigh!

I'll not leave thee, thou lone one,
To pine on the stem;
Since the lovely are sleeping,
Go, sleep thou with them;
Thus kindly I scatter
Thy leaves o'er the bed
Where thy mates of the garden
Lie scentless and dead.

So soon may I follow,
When friendships decay,
And from love's shining circle
The gems drop away!
When true hearts lie withered,
And fond ones are flown,
O, who would inhabit
This bleak world alone!

THE HARP THAT ONCE THROUGH TARA'S HALLS

The harp that once through Tara's halls
The soul of music shed,
Now hangs as mute on Tara's walls
As if that soul were fled.
So sleeps the pride of former days,
So glory's thrill is o'er,
And hearts that once beat high for praise
Now feel that pulse no more!

No more to chiefs and ladies bright
The harp of Tara swells;

The chord alone that breaks at night
  Its tale of ruin tells.
Thus Freedom now so seldom wakes,
  The only throb she gives
Is when some heart indignant breaks,
  To show that still she lives.

OH, BREATHE NOT HIS NAME!

ROBERT EMMET

Oh, breathe not his name! let it sleep in the shade,
Where cold and unhonoured his relics are laid;
Sad, silent, and dark be the tears that we shed,
As the night-dew that falls on the grass o'er his head.

But the night-dew that falls, though in silence it weeps,
Shall brighten with verdure the grave where he sleeps;
And the tear that we shed, though in secret it rolls,
Shall long keep his memory green in our souls.

LEIGH HUNT (1784–1859)

A GARDEN

From THE STORY OF RIMINI

Canto III

A noble range it was, of many a rood,
Walled and tree-girt, and ending in a wood.
A small sweet house o'erlooked it from a nest
Of pines: — all wood and garden was the rest,
Lawn, and green lane, and covert: — and it had
A winding stream about it, clear and glad,
With here and there a swan, the creature born
To be the only graceful shape of scorn.
The flower-beds all were liberal of delight:
Roses in heaps were there, both red and white,
Lilies angelical, and gorgeous glooms
Of wall-flowers, and blue hyacinths, and blooms
Hanging thick clusters from light boughs; in short,
All the sweet cups to which the bees resort,
With plots of grass, and leafier walks between
Of red geraniums, and of jessamine,
And orange, whose warm leaves so finely suit,
And look as if they shade a golden fruit;
And midst the flowers, turfed round beneath a shade
Of darksome pines, a babbling fountain played,
And 'twixt their shafts you saw the water bright,
Which through the tops glimmered with showering light
So now you stood to think what odours best
Made the air happy in that lovely nest;
And now you went beside the flowers, with eyes
Earnest as bees, restless as butterflies;
And then turned off into a shadier walk,
Close and continuous, fit for lovers' talk;
And then pursued the stream, and as you trod
Onward and onward o'er the velvet sod,
Felt on your face an air, watery and sweet,
And a new sense in your soft-lighting feet.
At last you entered shades indeed, the wood,
Broken with glens and pits, and glades far-viewed,
Through which the distant palace now and then
Look'd lordly forth with many-windowed ken;
A land of trees, — which reaching round about
In shady blessing stretched their old arms out;
With spots of sunny openings, and with nooks
To lie and read in, sloping into brooks,
Where at her drink you startled the slim deer,
Retreating lightly with a lovely fear.
And all about, the birds kept leafy house,
And sung and darted in and out the boughs;
And all about, a lovely sky of blue
Clearly was felt, or down the leaves laughed through.
And here and there, in every part, were seats,
Some in the open walks, some in retreats, —
With bowering leaves o'erhead, to which the eye
Looked up half sweetly and half awfully, —
Places of nestling green, for poets made,
Where, when the sunshine struck a yellow shade,
The rugged trunks, to inward peeping sight,
Thronged in dark pillars up the gold green light.

But 'twixt the wood and flowery walks, half-way,
And formed of both, the loveliest portion lay, —
A spot, that struck you like enchanted ground: —
It was a shallow dell, set in a mound
Of sloping orchards, — fig, and almond trees,
Cherry and pine, with some few cypresses;
Down by whose roots, descending darkly still,
(You saw it not, but heard) there gushed a rill,
Whose low sweet talking seemed as if it said,
Something eternal to that happy shade.
The ground within was lawn, with fruits and flowers
Heaped towards the centre, half of citron bowers;
And in the middle of those golden trees,
Half seen amidst the globy oranges,
Lurked a rare summer-house, a lovely sight, —
Small, marble, well-proportioned, creamy white,

Its top with vine-leaves sprinkled, — but no more, —
And a young bay-tree either side the door.
The door was to the wood, forward and square,
The rest was domed at top, and circular;
And through the dome the only light came in,
Tinged as it entered by the vine-leaves thin.

RONDEAU

Jenny kissed me when we met,
    Jumping from the chair she sat in;
Time, you thief, who love to get
    Sweets into your list, put that in:
Say I'm weary, say I'm sad,
    Say that health and wealth have missed me,
Say I'm growing old, but add,
    Jenny kissed me.

THE GLOVE AND THE LIONS

King Francis was a hearty king, and loved a royal sport,
And one day, as his lions fought, sat looking on the court.
The nobles filled the benches, with the ladies in their pride,
And 'mongst them sat the Count de Lorge, with one for whom he sighed:
And truly 'twas a gallant thing to see that crowning show,
Valour and love, and a king above, and the royal beasts below.

Ramped and roared the lions, with horrid laughing jaws;
They bit, they glared, gave blows like beams, a wind went with their paws;
With wallowing might and stifled roar they rolled on one another,
Till all the pit with sand and mane was in a thunderous smother;
The bloody foam above the bars came whisking through the air;
Said Francis then, "Faith, gentlemen, we're better here than there."

De Lorge's love o'erheard the King, a beauteous lively dame,
With smiling lips and sharp bright eyes, which always seemed the same;
She thought, the Count, my lover, is brave as brave can be;
He surely would do wondrous things to show his love of me;
King, ladies, lovers, all look on; the occasion is divine;
I'll drop my glove, to prove his love; great glory will be mine.

She dropped her glove, to prove his love, then looked at him and smiled;
He bowed, and in a moment leaped among the lions wild;
The leap was quick, return was quick, he has regained his place,
Then threw the glove, but not with love, right in the lady's face.
"By Heaven," said Francis, "rightly done!" and he rose from where he sat;
"No love," quoth he, "but vanity, sets love a task like that."

ABOU BEN ADHEM

Abou Ben Adhem (may his tribe increase!)
Awoke one night from a deep dream of peace,
And saw within the moonlight in his room,
Making it rich and like a lily in bloom,
An angel writing in a book of gold: —
Exceeding peace had made Ben Adhem bold,
And to the presence in the room he said,
"What writest thou?" The vision raised its head,
And, with a look made of all sweet accord,
Answered, "The names of those who love the Lord."
"And is mine one?" said Abou. "Nay, not so,"
Replied the angel. Abou spoke more low,
But cheerly still; and said, "I pray thee, then,
Write me as one that loves his fellow-men."

The angel wrote, and vanished. The next night
It came again, with a great wakening light,
And showed the names whom love of God had blessed, —
And, lo! Ben Adhem's name led all the rest!

FAIRIES' SONG

We the fairies blithe and antic,
Of dimensions not gigantic,
Though the moonshine mostly keep us
Oft in orchards frisk and peep us.

Stolen sweets are always sweeter;
Stolen kisses much completer;
Stolen looks are nice in chapels;
Stolen, stolen be your apples.

When to bed the world are bobbing,
Then's the time for orchard-robbing;
Yet the fruit were scarce worth peeling
Were it not for stealing, stealing.

GEORGE NOEL GORDON, LORD BYRON (1788–1824)

From ENGLISH BARDS AND SCOTCH REVIEWERS

Still must I hear? — shall hoarse Fitzgerald bawl
His creaking couplets in a tavern hall,
And I not sing, lest, haply, Scotch Reviews
Should dub me scribbler, and denounce my Muse?
Prepare for rhyme — I'll publish, right or wrong:
Fools are my theme, let Satire be my song.

* * * * * * * *

A man must serve his time to every trade,
Save censure — critics all are ready made.
Take hackney'd jokes from Miller, got by rote,
With just enough of learning to misquote;
A mind well skill'd to find or forge a fault;
A turn for punning, call it Attic salt;
To Jeffrey go, be silent and discreet,
His pay is just ten sterling pounds per sheet:
Fear not to lie, 'twill seem a lucky hit;
Shrink not from blasphemy, 'twill pass for wit:
Care not for feeling — pass your proper jest,
And stand a critic, hated yet caress'd.
And shall we own such judgment? no — as soon
Seek roses in December, ice in June;
Hope constancy in wind, or corn in chaff,
Believe a woman, or an epitaph,
Or any other thing that's false, before
You trust in critics who themselves are sore;
Or yield one single thought to be misled
By Jeffrey's heart, or Lambe's Bœotian head.

* * * * * * * *

Behold! in various throngs the scribbling crew,
For notice eager, pass in long review;
Each spurs his jaded Pegasus apace,
And rhyme and blank maintain an equal race,
Sonnets on sonnets crowd, and ode on ode;
And tales of terror jostle on the road;
Immeasurable measures move along;
For simpering Folly loves a varied song,
To strange mysterious Dullness still the friend,
Admires the strain she cannot comprehend.
Thus Lays of Minstrels — may they be the last!
On half-strung harps whine mournful to the blast.
While mountain spirits prate to river sprites,
That dames may listen to their sound at nights;
And goblin brats of Gilpin Horner's brood,
Decoy young border-nobles through the wood.
And skip at every step, Lord knows how high,
And frighten foolish babes, the Lord knows why;
While high-born ladies in their magic cell,
Forbidding knights to read who cannot spell,
Despatch a courier to a wizard's grave,
And fight with honest men to shield a knave.
Next view in state, proud prancing on his roan,
The golden-crested haughty Marmion,
Now forging scrolls, now foremost in the fight,
Not quite a felon, yet but half a knight,
The gibbet or the field prepared to grace —
A mighty mixture of the great and base.
And think'st thou, Scott! by vain conceit perchance,
On public taste to foist thy stale romance,
Though Murray with his Miller may combine
To yield thy muse just half-a-crown per line?
No! when the sons of song descend to trade,
Their bays are sear, their former laurels fade.
Let such forego the poet's sacred name,
Who rack their brains for lucre, not for fame:
Low may they sink to merited contempt,
And scorn remunerate the mean attempt!
Such be their meed, such still the just reward
Of prostituted muse and hireling bard!
For this we spurn Apollo's venal son,
And bid a long "good night to Marmion."
These are the themes that claim our plaudits now;
These are the bards to whom the muse must bow:
While Milton, Dryden, Pope, alike forgot,
Resign their hallow'd bays to Walter Scott.

* * * * * * * *

With eagle pinions soaring to the skies,
Behold the ballad monger, Southey, rise!
To him let Camoëns, Milton, Tasso, yield,
Whose annual strains, like armies, take the field.
First in the ranks see Joan of Arc advance,
The scourge of England, and the boast of France!
Though burnt by wicked Bedford for a witch,
Behold her statue placed in glory's niche,
Her fetters burst, and just released from prison,
A virgin Phœnix from her ashes risen.
Next see tremendous Thalaba come on,
Arabia's monstrous, wild, and wondrous son;
Domdaniel's dread destroyer, who o'erthrew
More mad magicians than the world e'er knew.
Immortal hero! all thy foes o'ercome,
Forever reign — the rival of Tom Thumb!
Since startled metre fled before thy face,
Well wert thou doom'd the last of all thy race!
Well might triumphant Genii bear thee hence,
Illustrious conqueror of common sense!
Now, last and greatest, Madoc spreads his sails,
Cacique in Mexico, and Prince in Wales;
Tells us strange tales, as other travellers do,
More old than Mandeville's, and not so true.
Oh! Southey, Southey! cease thy varied song!
A Bard may chaunt too often and too long:

As thou art strong in verse, in mercy spare!
A fourth, alas! were more than we could bear.
But if, in spite of all the world can say,
Thou still wilt verseward plod thy weary way;
If still in Berkley ballads, most uncivil,
Thou wilt devote old women to the devil,
The babe unborn thy dread intent may rue;
"God help thee," Southey, and thy readers too.

Next comes the dull disciple of thy school,
That mild apostate from poetic rule,
The simple Wordsworth, framer of a lay
As soft as evening in his favourite May;
Who warns his friend "to shake off toil and trouble;
And quit his books, for fear of growing double;"
Who, both by precept and example, shows
That prose is verse, and verse is merely prose,
Convincing all, by demonstration plain,
Poetic souls delight in prose insane;
And Christmas stories, tortured into rhyme,
Contain the essence of the true sublime:
Thus when he tells the tale of Betty Foy,
The idiot mother of "an idiot Boy;"
A moon-struck silly lad who lost his way,
And, like his bard, confounded night with day;
So close on each pathetic part he dwells,
And each adventure so sublimely tells,
That all who view the "idiot in his glory,"
Conceive the Bard the hero of the story.

Shall gentle Coleridge pass unnoticed here,
To turgid ode and tumid stanza dear?
Though themes of innocence amuse him best,
Yet still obscurity's a welcome guest.
If Inspiration should her aid refuse
To him who takes a Pixy for a Muse,
Yet none in lofty numbers can surpass
The bard who soars to elegize an ass.
How well the subject suits his noble mind!
"A fellow-feeling makes us wondrous kind!"

* * * * * * * *

Another Epic! who inflicts again
More books of blank upon the sons of men?
Bœotian Cottle, rich Bristowa's boast,
Imports old stories from the Cambrian coast,
And sends his goods to market — all alive!
Lines forty thousand, Cantos twenty-five!
Fresh fish from Helicon! who'll buy? who'll buy?
The precious bargain's cheap — in faith, not I.
Too much in turtle Bristol's sons delight,
Too much o'er bowls of 'rack prolong the night:
If commerce fills the purse, she clogs the brain,
And Amos Cottle strikes the lyre in vain.
In him an author's luckless lot behold!
Condemn'd to make the books which once he sold.
Oh! Amos Cottle! — Phœbus! what a name
To fill the speaking-trump of future fame! —
Oh! Amos Cottle! for a moment think
What meagre profits spread from pen and ink!
When thus devoted to poetic dreams,
Who will peruse thy prostituted reams?
Oh! pen perverted! paper misapplied!
Had Cottle still adorn'd the counter's side,
Bent o'er the desk, or, born to useful toils,
Been taught to make the paper which he soils,
Plough'd, delved, or plied the oar with lusty limb,
He had not sung of Wales, nor I of him.

* * * * * * * *

Health to immortal Jeffrey! once, in name,
England could boast a judge almost the same:
In soul so like, so merciful, yet just,
Some think that Satan has resigned his trust,
And given the Spirit to the world again,
To sentence letters as he sentenced men;
With hand less mighty, but with heart as black,
With voice as willing to decree the rack;
Bred in the courts betimes, though all that law
As yet hath taught him is to find a flaw.
Since well instructed in the patriot school
To rail at party, though a party tool,
Who knows, if chance his patrons should restore
Back to the sway they forfeited before,
His scribbling toils some recompense may meet,
And raise this Daniel to the Judgment Seat.
Let Jeffries' shade indulge the pious hope,
And greeting thus, present him with a rope:
"Heir to my virtues! man of equal mind!
Skill'd to condemn as to traduce mankind,
This cord receive — for thee reserved with care,
To yield in judgment, and at length to wear."

* * * * * * * *

To the famed throng now paid the tribute due,
Neglected Genius! let me turn to you.
Come forth, O Campbell! give thy talents scope;
Who dares aspire if thou must cease to hope?
And thou, melodious Rogers! rise at last,
Recall the pleasing memory of the past;
Arise! let blest remembrance still inspire,
And strike to wonted tones thy hallow'd lyre!
Restore Apollo to his vacant throne,
Assert thy country's honour and thine own.
What! must deserted Poesy still weep
Where her last hopes with pious Cowper sleep?
Unless, perchance, from his cold bier she turns,
To deck the turf that wraps her minstrel, Burns!
No! though contempt hath mark'd the spurious brood,
The race who rhyme from folly, or for food;
Yet still some genuine sons, 'tis hers to boast,
Who, least affecting, still effect the most;

Feel as they write, and write but as they feel —
Bear witness, Gifford, Sotheby, Macneil.

* * * * * * * * *

There be who say in these enlighten'd days
That splendid lies are all the poet's praise;
That strain'd invention, ever on the wing,
Alone impels the modern bard to sing:
'Tis true that all who rhyme, nay, all who write,
Shrink from that fatal word to genius — trite;
Yet truth sometimes will lend her noblest fires,
And decorate the verse herself inspires:
This fact in virtue's name let Crabbe attest —
Though Nature's sternest painter, yet the best.

CHILDE HAROLD'S PILGRIMAGE

From CANTO I

Oh, thou! in Hellas deem'd of heavenly birth,
Muse! form'd or fabled at the minstrel's will!
Since shamed full oft by later lyres on earth,
Mine dares not call thee from thy sacred hill;
Yet there I've wander'd by thy vaunted rill;
Yes! sigh'd o'er Delphi's long-deserted shrine,
Where, save that feeble fountain, all is still;
Nor mote my shell awake the weary Nine
To grace so plain a tale — this lowly lay of mine.

Whilome in Albion's isle there dwelt a youth,
Who ne in virtue's ways did take delight;
But spent his days in riot most uncouth,
And vex'd with mirth the drowsy ear of Night.
Ah, me! in sooth he was a shameless wight,
Sore given to revel and ungodly glee;
Few earthly things found favour in his sight
Save concubines and carnal companie
And flaunting wassailers of high and low degree.

Childe Harold was he hight: — but whence his name
And lineage long, it suits me not to say;
Suffice it, that perchance they were of fame,
And had been glorious in another day:
But one sad losel soils a name for aye,
However mighty in the olden time;
Nor all that heralds rake from coffin'd clay,
Nor florid prose, nor honey'd lies of rhyme,
Can blazon evil deeds, or consecrate a crime.

Childe Harold bask'd him in the noontide sun,
Disporting there like any other fly,
Nor deem'd before his little day was done
One blast might chill him into misery.
But long ere scarce a third of his pass'd by,
Worse than adversity the Childe befell;
He felt the fullness of satiety:
Then loathed he in his native land to dwell,
Which seem'd to him more lone than Eremite's sad cell.

For he through Sin's long labyrinth had run,
Nor made atonement when he did amiss,
Had sigh'd to many, though he loved but one,
And that lov'd one, alas, could ne'er be his.
Ah, happy she! to 'scape from him whose kiss
Had been pollution unto aught so chaste;
Who soon had left her charms for vulgar bliss,
And spoil'd her goodly lands to gild his waste,
Nor calm domestic peace had ever deign'd to taste.

And now Childe Harold was sore sick at heart,
And from his fellow bacchanals would flee;
'Tis said, at times the sullen tear would start,
But Pride congeal'd the drop within his e'e;
Apart he stalk'd in joyless reverie,
And from his native land resolv'd to go,
And visit scorching climes beyond the sea:
With pleasure drugg'd, he almost long'd for woe,
And e'en for change of scene would seek the shades below.

The Childe departed from his father's hall;
It was a vast and venerable pile;
So old, it seemèd only not to fall,
Yet strength was pillar'd in each massy aisle.
Monastic dome! condemn'd to uses vile!
Where Superstition once had made her den,
Now Paphian girls were known to sing and smile;
And monks might deem their time was come agen,
If ancient tales say true, nor wrong these holy men.

Yet ofttimes, in his maddest mirthful mood,
Strange pangs would flash along Childe Harold's brow,
As if the memory of some deadly feud
Or disappointed passion lurk'd below:
But this none knew, nor haply cared to know;
For his was not that open, artless soul
That feels relief by bidding sorrow flow;
Nor sought he friend to counsel or condole,
Whate'er this grief mote be, which he could not control.

And none did love him — though to hall and bower
He gather'd revellers from far and near,
He knew them flatterers of the festal hour;
The heartless parasites of present cheer.
Yea! none did love him — not his lemans dear —

But pomp and power alone are woman's care,
And where these are light Eros finds a feere;
Maidens, like moths, are ever caught by glare,
And Mammon wins his way where Seraphs might despair. 81

Childe Harold had a mother — not forgot,
Though parting from that mother he did shun:
A sister whom he loved, but saw her not
Before his weary pilgrimage begun:
If friends he had, he bade adieu to none,
Yet deem not thence his breast a breast of steel;
Ye, who have known what 'tis to dote upon
A few dear objects, will in sadness feel
Such partings break the heart they fondly hope to heal. 90

His house, his home, his heritage, his lands,
The laughing dames in whom he did delight,
Whose large blue eyes, fair locks, and snowy hands,
Might shake the saintship of an anchorite,
And long had fed his youthful appetite;
His goblets brimm'd with every costly wine,
And all that mote to luxury invite,
Without a sigh he left to cross the brine,
And traverse Paynim shores, and pass Earth's central line. 99

The sails were fill'd, and fair the light winds blew,
As glad to waft him from his native home;
And fast the white rocks faded from his view,
And soon were lost in circumambient foam;
And then, it may be, of his wish to roam
Repented he, but in his bosom slept 105
The silent thought, nor from his lips did come
One word of wail, whilst others sate and wept,
And to the reckless gales unmanly moaning kept.

But when the sun was sinking in the sea,
He seized his harp, which he at times could string,
And strike, albeit with untaught melody,
When deem'd he no strange ear was listening;
And now his fingers o'er it he did fling,
And tuned his farewell in the dim twilight,
While flew the vessel on her snowy wing,
And fleeting shores receded from his sight,
Thus to the elements he pour'd his last "Good Night." 117

Adieu, adieu! my native shore
Fades o'er the waters blue;
The night-winds sigh, the breakers roar,
And shrieks the wild sea-mew.
Yon sun that sets upon the sea
We follow in his flight;
Farewell awhile to him and thee,
My native land — Good night! 125

A few short hours, and he will rise,
To give the morrow birth;
And I shall hail the main and skies,
But not my mother earth.
Deserted is my own good hall,
Its hearth is desolate;
Wild weeds are gathering on the wall,
My dog howls at the gate. 133

* * * * * * *

And now I'm in the world alone,
Upon the wide, wide sea;
But why should I for others groan,
When none will sigh for me?
Perchance my dog will whine in vain,
Till fed by stranger hands;
But long ere I come back again
He'd tear me where he stands. 189

With thee, my bark, I'll swiftly go
Athwart the foaming brine;
Nor care what land thou bear'st me to,
So not again to mine.
Welcome, welcome, ye dark blue waves!
And when you fail my sight,
Welcome, ye deserts, and ye caves!
My native land — Good night! 197

* * * * * * *

From CANTO III

There was a sound of revelry by night,
And Belgium's capital had gather'd then
Her Beauty and her Chivalry, and bright
The lamps shone o'er fair women and brave men;
A thousand hearts beat happily; and when
Music arose with its voluptuous swell,
Soft eyes look'd love to eyes which spake again,
And all went merry as a marriage bell;
But hush! hark! a deep sound strikes like a rising knell! 189

Did ye not hear it? — No; 'twas but the wind,
Or the car rattling o'er the stony street;
On with the dance! let joy be unconfined;
No sleep till morn, when Youth and Pleasure meet
To chase the glowing Hours with flying feet. —

But hark! that heavy sound breaks in once more,
As if the clouds its echo would repeat;
And nearer, clearer, deadlier than before!
Arm! arm! it is — it is — the cannon's opening roar!

Within a window'd niche of that high hall
Sate Brunswick's fated chieftain; he did hear
That sound the first amidst the festival,
And caught its tone with Death's prophetic ear,
And when they smiled because he deem'd it near,
His heart more truly knew that peal too well
Which stretch'd his father on a bloody bier,
And roused the vengeance blood alone could quell.
He rush'd into the field, and, foremost fighting, fell.

Ah! then and there was hurrying to and fro,
And gathering tears, and tremblings of distress,
And cheeks all pale, which but an hour ago
Blush'd at the praise of their own loveliness;
And there were sudden partings, such as press
The life from out young hearts, and choking sighs
Which ne'er might be repeated: who could guess
If ever more should meet those mutual eyes,
Since upon night so sweet such awful morn could rise!

And there was mounting in hot haste: the steed,
The mustering squadron, and the clattering car,
Went pouring forward with impetuous speed,
And swiftly forming in the ranks of war;
And the deep thunder peal on peal afar;
And near, the beat of the alarming drum
Roused up the soldier ere the morning star;
While throng'd the citizens with terror dumb,
Or whispering with white lips — "The foe! They come! they come!"

And wild and high the "Cameron's Gathering" rose,
The war-note of Lochiel, which Albyn's hills
Have heard, and heard, too, have her Saxon foes;
How in the noon of night that pibroch thrills
Savage and shrill! But with the breath which fills
Their mountain pipe, so fill the mountaineers
With the fierce native daring which instils
The stirring memory of a thousand years,
And Evan's, Donald's fame rings in each clansman's ears!

And Ardennes waves above them her green leaves,
Dewy with Nature's tear-drops, as they pass,
Grieving, if aught inanimate e'er grieves,
Over the unreturning brave, — alas!
Ere evening to be trodden like the grass
Which now beneath them, but above shall grow
In its next verdure, when this fiery mass
Of living valour, rolling on the foe,
And burning with high hope, shall moulder cold and low.

Last noon beheld them full of lusty life,
Last eve in Beauty's circle proudly gay,
The midnight brought the signal-sound of strife,
The morn the marshalling in arms — the day
Battle's magnificently stern array!
The thunder-clouds close o'er it, which when rent
The earth is cover'd thick with other clay,
Which her own clay shall cover, heap'd and pent,
Rider and horse — friend, foe, — in one red burial blent!

* * * * * * * *

Lake Leman woos me with its crystal face,
The mirror where the stars and mountains view
The stillness of their aspect in each trace
Its clear depth yields of their far height and hue;
There is too much of man here, to look through
With a fit mind the might which I behold;
But soon in me shall Loneliness renew
Thoughts hid, but not less cherish'd than of old,
Ere mingling with the herd had penn'd me in their fold.

To fly from, need not be to hate, mankind;
All are not fit with them to stir and toil,
Nor is it discontent to keep the mind
Deep in its fountain, lest it overboil
In the hot throng, where we become the spoil
Of our infection, till too late and long
We may deplore and struggle with the coil,
In wretched interchange of wrong for wrong
'Midst a contentious world, striving where none are strong.

There, in a moment, we may plunge our years
In fatal penitence, and in the blight
Of our own soul turn all our blood to tears,
And colour things to come with hues of Night:
The race of life becomes a hopeless flight
To those that walk in darkness; on the sea
The boldest steer but where their ports invite,
But there are wanderers o'er Eternity
Whose bark drives on and on, and anchor'd ne'er shall be.

Is it not better, then, to be alone,
And love Earth only for its earthly sake?
By the blue rushing of the arrowy Rhone,
Or the pure bosom of its nursing lake,
Which feeds it as a mother who doth make
A fair but froward infant her own care,
Kissing its cries away as these awake; —
Is it not better thus our lives to wear,
Than join the crushing crowd, doom'd to inflict or bear?

I live not in myself, but I become
Portion of that around me: and to me,
High mountains are a feeling, but the hum
Of human cities torture; I can see
Nothing to loathe in Nature, save to be
A link reluctant in a fleshly chain,
Class'd among creatures, when the soul can flee,
And with the sky, the peak, the heaving plain
Of ocean, or the stars, mingle, and not in vain.

And thus I am absorb'd, and this is life:
I look upon the peopled desert past,
As on a place of agony and strife,
Where, for some sin, to Sorrow I was cast,
To act and suffer, but remount at last
With a fresh pinion; which I feel to spring,
Though young, yet waxing vigorous as the blast
Which it would cope with, on delighted wing,
Spurning the clay-cold bonds which round our being cling.

And when, at length, the mind shall be all free
From what it hates in this degraded form,
Reft of its carnal life, save what shall be
Existent happier in the fly and worm, —
When elements to elements conform,
And dust is as it should be, shall I not
Feel all I see, less dazzling, but more warm?
The bodiless thought? the Spirit of each spot?
Of which, even now, I share at times the immortal lot?

Are not the mountains, waves, and skies, a part
Of me and of my soul, as I of them?
Is not the love of these deep in my heart
With a pure passion? should I not contemn
All objects, if compared with these? and stem
A tide of suffering rather than forego
Such feelings for the hard and worldly phlegm
Of those whose eyes are only turn'd below,
Gazing upon the ground, with thoughts which dare not glow?

* * * * * * * *

It is the hush of night, and all between
Thy margin and the mountains, dusk, yet clear,
Mellow'd and mingling, yet distinctly seen,
Save darken'd Jura, whose capt heights appear
Precipitously steep; and drawing near,
There breathes a living fragrance from the shore,
Of flowers yet fresh with childhood; on the ear
Drops the light drip of the suspended oar,
Or chirps the grasshopper one good-night carol more;

He is an evening reveller, who makes
His life an infancy, and sings his fill;
At intervals, some bird from out the brakes
Starts into voice a moment, then is still.
There seems a floating whisper on the hill,
But that is fancy, for the starlight dews
All silently their tears of love instil,
Weeping themselves away, till they infuse
Deep into Nature's breast the spirit of her hues.

Ye stars! which are the poetry of heaven!
If in your bright leaves we would read the fate
Of men and empires, — 'tis to be forgiven,
That in our aspirations to be great,
Our destinies o'erleap their mortal state,
And claim a kindred with you; for ye are
A beauty and a mystery, and create
In us such love and reverence from afar,
That fortune, fame, power, life, have named themselves a star.

All heaven and earth are still — though not in sleep,
But breathless, as we grow when feeling most;
And silent, as we stand in thoughts too deep: —
All heaven and earth are still: From the high host
Of stars, to the lull'd lake and mountain-coast,
All is concenter'd in a life intense,
Where not a beam, nor air, nor leaf is lost,
But hath a part of being, and a sense
Of that which is of all Creator and Defence.

Then stirs the feeling infinite, so felt
In solitude, where we are *least* alone;
A truth which through our being then doth melt,
And purifies from self: it is a tone,
The soul and source of music, which makes known
Eternal harmony, and sheds a charm,
Like to the fabled Cytherea's zone,
Binding all things with beauty; — 'twould disarm
The spectre Death, had he substantial power to harm.

Not vainly did the early Persian make
His altar the high places and the peak
Of earth-o'ergazing mountains, and thus take
A fit and unwall'd temple, there to seek
The Spirit, in whose honour shrines are weak,
Uprear'd of human hands. Come, and compare
Columns and idol dwellings, Goth or Greek,
With Nature's realms of worship, earth and air,
Nor fix on fond abodes to circumscribe thy prayer!

The sky is changed! — and such a change! O night,
And storm, and darkness, ye are wondrous strong,
Yet lovely in your strength, as is the light
Of a dark eye in woman! Far along,
From peak to peak, the rattling crags among
Leaps the live thunder! Not from one lone cloud,
But every mountain now hath found a tongue,
And Jura answers, through her misty shroud,
Back to the joyous Alps, who call to her aloud!

From CANTO IV

O Rome! my country! city of the soul!
The orphans of the heart must turn to thee,
Lone mother of dead empires! and control
In their shut breasts their petty misery.
What are our woes and sufferance? Come and see
The cypress, hear the owl, and plod your way
O'er steps of broken thrones and temples, — Ye!
Whose agonies are evils of a day —
A world is at our feet as fragile as our clay.

The Niobe of nations! there she stands,
Childless and crownless in her voiceless woe;
An empty urn within her wither'd hands,
Whose holy dust was scatter'd long ago;
The Scipio's tomb contains no ashes now;
The very sepulchres lie tenantless
Of their heroic dwellers: dost thou flow,
Old Tiber! through a marble wilderness?
Rise, with thy yellow waves, and mantle her distress.

The Goth, the Christian, Time, War, Flood, and Fire,
Have dealt upon the seven-hill'd city's pride:
She saw her glories star by star expire,
And up the steep barbarian monarchs ride,
Where the car climb'd the Capitol; far and wide
Temple and tower went down, nor left a site: —
Chaos of ruins! who shall trace the void,
O'er the dim fragments cast a lunar light,
And say, "Here was, or is," where all is doubly night?

* * * * * * * *

O Love! no habitant of earth thou art —
An unseen seraph, we believe in thee, —
A faith whose martyrs are the broken heart,
But never yet hath seen, nor e'er shall see,
The naked eye, thy form, as it should be:
The mind hath made thee, as it peopled heaven,
Even with its own desiring phantasy,
And to a thought such shape and image given,
As haunts the unquench'd soul — parch'd — wearied — wrung — and riven.

Of its own beauty is the mind diseased,
And fevers into false creation; — where,
Where are the forms the sculptor's soul hath seized?
In him alone. Can Nature show so fair?
Where are the charms and virtues which we dare
Conceive in boyhood and pursue as men,
The unreach'd Paradise of our despair,
Which o'er-informs the pencil and the pen,
And overpowers the page where it would bloom again?

Who loves, raves — 'tis youth's frenzy — but the cure
Is bitterer still; as charm by charm unwinds
Which robed our idols, and we see too sure
Nor worth nor beauty dwells from out the mind's
Ideal shape of such; yet still it binds
The fatal spell, and still it draws us on,
Reaping the whirlwind from the oft-sown winds;
The stubborn heart, its alchemy begun,
Seems ever near the prize — wealthiest when most undone.

We wither from our youth, we gasp away —
Sick — sick; unfound the boon — unslaked the thirst,
Though to the last, in verge of our decay,
Some phantom lures, such as we sought at first —
But all too late, — so are we doubly curst,
Love, fame, ambition, avarice — 'tis the same —
Each idle, and all ill, and none the worst —
For all are meteors with a different name,
And Death the sable smoke where vanishes the flame.

Few — none — find what they love or could have loved:
Though accident, blind contact, and the strong
Necessity of loving, have removed
Antipathies — but to recur, ere long,
Envenom'd with irrevocable wrong;
And Circumstance, that unspiritual god
And miscreator, makes and helps along

Our coming evils with a crutch-like rod,
Whose touch turns Hope to dust — the dust we all have trod.

* * * * * * * *

Oh! that the Desert were my dwelling-place
With one fair Spirit for my minister,
That I might all forget the human race,
And, hating no one, love but only her!
Ye Elements! — in whose ennobling stir
I feel myself exalted — can ye not
Accord me such a being? Do I err
In deeming such inhabit many a spot?
Though with them to converse can rarely be our lot.

There is a pleasure in the pathless woods,
There is a rapture on the lonely shore,
There is society where none intrudes,
By the deep Sea, and music in its roar:
I love not man the less, but Nature more,
From these our interviews, in which I steal
From all I may be, or have been before,
To mingle with the Universe, and feel
What I can ne'er express, yet cannot all conceal.

Roll on, thou deep and dark blue Ocean — roll!
Ten thousand fleets sweep over thee in vain;
Man marks the earth with ruin — his control
Stops with the shore; — upon the watery plain
The wrecks are all thy deed, nor doth remain
A shadow of man's ravage, save his own,
When for a moment, like a drop of rain,
He sinks into thy depths with bubbling groan,
Without a grave, unknell'd, uncoffin'd and unknown.

His steps are not upon thy paths — thy fields
Are not a spoil for him — thou dost arise
And shake him from thee; the vile strength he wields
For earth's destruction thou dost all despise,
Spurning him from thy bosom to the skies,
And send'st him, shivering in thy playful spray,
And howling, to his Gods, where haply lies
His petty hope in some near port or bay,
And dashest him again to earth — there let him lay.

The armaments which thunderstrike the walls
Of rock-built cities, bidding nations quake,
And monarchs tremble in their capitals,
The oak leviathans, whose huge ribs make
Their clay creator the vain title take
Of lord of thee, and arbiter of war;
These are thy toys, and, as the snowy flake,
They melt into thy yeast of waves, which mar
Alike the Armada's pride, or spoils of Trafalgar.

Thy shores are empires, changed in all save thee —
Assyria, Greece, Rome, Carthage, what are they?
Thy waters washed them power while they were free.
And many a tyrant since: their shores obey
The stranger, slave or savage; their decay
Has dried up realms to deserts: — not so thou,
Unchangeable save to thy wild waves' play —
Time writes no wrinkle on thine azure brow —
Such as creation's dawn beheld, thou rollest now.

Thou glorious mirror, where the Almighty's form
Glasses itself in tempests: in all time,
Calm or convulsed — in breeze, or gale, or storm,
Icing the pole, or in the torrid clime
Dark-heaving; — boundless, endless, and sublime —
The image of Eternity — the throne
Of the Invisible; even from out thy slime
The monsters of the deep are made; each zone
Obeys thee; thou goest forth, dread, fathomless, alone.

And I have loved thee, Ocean! and my joy
Of youthful sports was on thy breast to be
Borne, like thy bubbles, onward: from a boy
I wanton'd with thy breakers — they to me
Were a delight; and if the freshening sea
Made them a terror — 'twas a pleasing fear,
For I was as it were a child of thee,
And trusted to thy billows far and near,
And laid my hand upon thy mane — as I do here.

THE PRISONER OF CHILLON

SONNET ON CHILLON

Eternal Spirit of the chainless Mind!
Brightest in dungeons, Liberty! thou art,
For there thy habitation is the heart —
The heart which love of thee alone can bind;
And when thy sons to fetters are consign'd —
To fetters, and the damp vault's dayless gloom,
Their country conquers with their martyrdom,
And Freedom's fame finds wings on every wind.
Chillon! thy prison is a holy place,
And thy sad floor an altar — for 'twas trod,
Until his very steps have left a trace
Worn, as if thy cold pavement were a sod,
By Bonnivard! May none those marks efface!
For they appeal from tyranny to God.

THE PRISONER OF CHILLON

My hair is gray, but not from years;
Nor grew it white
In a single night,
As men's have grown from sudden fears:
My limbs are bow'd, though not with toil,
But rusted with a vile repose,
For they have been a dungeon's spoil,
And mine has been the fate of those
To whom the goodly earth and air
Are bann'd, and barr'd — forbidden fare;
But this was for my father's faith
I suffer'd chains and courted death:
That father perish'd at the stake
For tenets he would not forsake;
And for the same his lineal race
In darkness found a dwelling-place.
We were seven — who now are one;
Six in youth, and one in age,
Finish'd as they had begun,
Proud of Persecution's rage;
One in fire, and two in field,
Their belief with blood have seal'd
Dying as their father died,
For the God their foes denied; —
Three were in a dungeon cast,
Of whom this wreck is left the last.

There are seven pillars of Gothic mould,
In Chillon's dungeon deep and old;
There are seven columns, massy and gray,
Dim with a dull imprison'd ray,
A sunbeam which hath lost its way,
And through the crevice and the cleft
Of the thick wall is fallen and left:
Creeping o'er the floor so damp,
Like a marsh's meteor lamp:
And in each pillar there is a ring,
And in each ring there is a chain;
That iron is a cankering thing,
For in these limbs its teeth remain,
With marks that will not wear away,
Till I have done with this new day,
Which now is painful to these eyes,
Which have not seen the sun so rise
For years — I cannot count them o'er;
I lost their long and heavy score
When my last brother droop'd and died,
And I lay living by his side.

They chain'd us each to a column stone,
And we were three — yet each alone;
We could not move a single pace,
We could not see each other's face,
But with that pale and livid light
That made us strangers in our sight:
And thus together — yet apart,
Fetter'd in hand, but join'd in heart,
'Twas still some solace in the dearth
Of the pure elements of earth,
To hearken to each other's speech,
And each turn comforter to each,
With some new hope, or legend old,
Or song heroically bold;
But even these at length grew cold.
Our voices took a dreary tone,
An echo of the dungeon-stone,
A grating sound — not full and free
As they of yore were wont to be:
It might be fancy — but to me
They never sounded like our own.

I was the eldest of the three;
And to uphold and cheer the rest
I ought to do — and did — my best,
And each did well in his degree.
The youngest, whom my father loved,
Because our mother's brow was given
To him — with eyes as blue as heaven, —
For him my soul was sorely moved.
And truly might it be distress'd
To see such bird in such a nest;
For he was beautiful as day —
(When day was beautiful to me
As to young eagles, being free) —
A polar day, which will not see
A sunset till its summer's gone,
Its sleepless summer of long light,
The snow-clad offspring of the sun:
And thus he was as pure and bright,
And in his natural spirit gay,
With tears for naught but others' ills,
And then they flow'd like mountain rills,
Unless he could assuage the woe
Which he abhorr'd to view below.

The other was as pure of mind,
But form'd to combat with his kind;
Strong in his frame, and of a mood
Which 'gainst the world in war had stood,
And perish'd in the foremost rank
With joy — but not in chains to pine:
His spirit wither'd with their clank,
I saw it silently decline —
And so perchance in sooth did mine;
But yet I forced it on to cheer
Those relics of a home so dear.
He was a hunter of the hills,
Had follow'd there the deer and wolf;
To him this dungeon was a gulf,
And fetter'd feet the worst of ills.

Lake Leman lies by Chillon's walls:
A thousand feet in depth below
Its massy waters meet and flow;
Thus much the fathom line was sent
From Chillon's snow-white battlement,
Which round about the wave enthralls:
A double dungeon wall and wave
Have made — and like a living grave.
Below the surface of the lake
The dark vault lies wherein we lay,
We heard it ripple night and day;
Sounding o'er our heads it knock'd;
And I have felt the winter's spray
Wash through the bars when winds were high
And wanton in the happy sky;
And then the very rock hath rock'd,
And I have felt it shake, unshock'd,
Because I could have smiled to see
The death that would have set me free.

I said my nearer brother pined,
I said his mighty heart declined,
He loathed and put away his food:
It was not that 'twas coarse and rude
For we were used to hunters' fare,
And for the like had little care:
The milk drawn from the mountain goat
Was changed for water from the moat;
Our bread was such as captives' tears
Have moisten'd many a thousand years,
Since man first pent his fellow-men
Like brutes within an iron den;
But what were these to us or him?
These wasted not his heart or limb;
My brother's soul was of that mould
Which in a palace had grown cold,
Had his free-breathing been denied
The range of the steep mountain's side.
But why delay the truth? — he died.
I saw, and could not hold his head,
Nor reach his dying hand — nor dead —
Though hard I strove, but strove in vain,
To rend and gnash my bonds in twain.
He died — and they unlock'd his chain
And scoop'd for him a shallow grave
Even from the cold earth of our cave.
I begg'd them, as a boon, to lay
His corse in dust whereon the day
Might shine — it was a foolish thought,
But then within my brain it wrought,
That even in death his free-born breast
In such a dungeon could not rest.
I might have spared my idle prayer —
They coldly laugh'd — and laid him there:
The flat and turfless earth above
The being we so much did love;
His empty chain above it leant,
Such murder's fitting monument!

But he, the favourite and the flower,
Most cherish'd since his natal hour,
His mother's image in fair face,
The infant love of all his race,
His martyr'd father's dearest thought,
My latest care, for whom I sought
To hoard my life, that his might be
Less wretched now, and one day free;
He, too, who yet had held untired
A spirit natural or inspired —
He, too, was struck, and day by day
Was wither'd on the stalk away.
O God! it is a fearful thing
To see the human soul take wing
In any shape, in any mood: —
I've seen it rushing forth in blood,
I've seen it on the breaking ocean
Strive with a swoll'n convulsive motion,
I've seen the sick and ghastly bed
Of Sin delirious with its dread:
But these were horrors — this was woe
Unmix'd with such, — but sure and slow:
He faded, and so calm and meek,
So softly worn, so sweetly weak,
So tearless, yet so tender, — kind,
And grieved for those he left behind;
With all the while a cheek whose bloom
Was as a mockery of the tomb,
Whose tints as gently sunk away
As a departing rainbow's ray —
An eye of most transparent light,
That almost made the dungeon bright,
And not a word of murmur — not
A groan o'er his untimely lot!
A little talk of better days,
A little hope my own to raise,
For I was sunk in silence — lost
In this last loss, of all the most:
And then the sighs he would suppress
Of fainting nature's feebleness,
More slowly drawn, grew less and less
I listen'd, but I could not hear —
I call'd, for I was wild with fear;
I knew 'twas hopeless, but my dread
Would not be thus admonishèd;
I call'd, and thought I heard a sound —
I burst my chain with one strong bound,
And rush'd to him; — I found him not;
I only stirr'd in this black spot,
I only lived — *I* only drew
The accursed breath of dungeon-dew;
The last, — the sole, — the dearest link
Between me and the eternal brink

Which bound me to my failing race,
Was broken in this fatal place.
One on the earth, and one beneath —
My brothers — both had ceased to breathe:
I took that hand which lay so still;
Alas, my own was full as chill;
I had not strength to stir or strive,
But felt that I was still alive —
A frantic feeling, when we know
That what we love shall ne'er be so.
I know not why
I could not die;
I had no earthly hope — but faith,
And that forbade a selfish death.

What next befell me then and there
I know not well — I never knew: —
First came the loss of light, and air,
And then of darkness too:
I had no thought, no feeling — none —
Among the stones I stood a stone,
And was, scarce conscious what I wist,
As shrubless crags within the mist;
For all was blank, and bleak, and gray,
It was not night — it was not day;
It was not even the dungeon-light,
So hateful to my heavy sight,
But vacancy absorbing space,
And fixedness, without a place:
There were no stars, — no earth, — no time, —
No check, — no change, — no good, — no crime, —
But silence, and a stirless breath
Which neither was of life nor death;
A sea of stagnant idleness,
Blind, boundless, mute, and motionless!

A light broke in upon my brain —
It was the carol of a bird;
It ceased, and then it came again,
The sweetest song ear ever heard;
And mine was thankful, till my eyes
Ran over with the glad surprise,
And they that moment could not see
I was the mate of misery;
But then by dull degrees came back
My senses to their wonted track,
I saw the dungeon walls and floor
Close slowly round me as before,
I saw the glimmer of the sun
Creeping as it before had done,
But through the crevice where it came
That bird was perch'd, as fond and tame,
And tamer than upon the tree;
A lovely bird, with azure wings,
And song that said a thousand things,
And seem'd to say them all for me!
I never saw its like before,
I ne'er shall see its likeness more:
It seem'd, like me, to want a mate,
But was not half so desolate,
And it was come to love me when
None lived to love me so again,
And cheering from my dungeon's brink,
Had brought me back to feel and think.
I know not if it late were free,
Or broke its cage to perch on mine,
But knowing well captivity,
Sweet bird, I could not wish for thine!
Or if it were, in wingèd guise,
A visitant from Paradise;
For — Heaven forgive that thought! the while
Which made me both to weep and smile;
I sometimes deem'd that it might be
My brother's soul come down to me;
But then at last away it flew,
And then 'twas mortal — well I knew,
For he would never thus have flown,
And left me twice so doubly lone —
Lone, — as the corse within its shroud;
Lone, — as a solitary cloud,
A single cloud on a sunny day,
While all the rest of heaven is clear,
A frown upon the atmosphere,
That hath no business to appear
When skies are blue and earth is gay.

A kind of change came in my fate,
My keepers grew compassionate:
I know not what had made them so,
They were inured to sights of woe;
But so it was — my broken chain
With links unfasten'd did remain,
And it was liberty to stride
Along my cell from side to side,
And up and down, and then athwart,
And tread it over every part;
And round the pillars one by one,
Returning where my walk begun,
Avoiding only, as I trod,
My brothers' graves without a sod;
For if I thought with heedless tread
My step profaned their lowly bed,
My breath came gaspingly and thick,
And my crush'd heart fell blind and sick.

I made a footing in the wall,
It was not therefrom to escape,
For I had buried one and all
Who loved me in a human shape;
And the whole earth would henceforth be
A wider prison unto me:
No child — no sire — no kin had I,

No partner in my misery;
I thought of this, and I was glad,
For thought of them had made me mad;
But I was curious to ascend
To my barr'd windows, and to bend
Once more, upon the mountains high,
The quiet of a loving eye.

I saw them — and they were the same,
They were not changed like me in frame;
I saw their thousand years of snow
On high — their wide long lake below,
And the blue Rhone in fullest flow;
I heard the torrents leap and gush
O'er channell'd rock and broken bush;
I saw the white-wall'd distant town,
And whiter sails go skimming down;
And then there was a little isle,
Which in my very face did smile,
The only one in view:
A small green isle, it seem'd no more,
Scarce broader than my dungeon floor;
But in it there were three tall trees,
And o'er it blew the mountain breeze,
And by it there were waters flowing,
And on it there were young flowers growing,
Of gentle breath and hue.
The fish swam by the castle wall,
And they seem'd joyous, each and all;
The eagle rode the rising blast,
Methought he never flew so fast
As then to me he seem'd to fly,
And then new tears came in my eye,
And I felt troubled — and would fain
I had not left my recent chain;
And when I did descend again,
The darkness of my dim abode
Fell on me as a heavy load;
It was as is a new-dug grave,
Closing o'er one we sought to save.
And yet my glance, too much opprest,
Had almost need of such a rest.

It might be months, or years, or days,
I kept no count — I took no note,
I had no hope my eyes to raise,
And clear them of their dreary mote;
At last men came to set me free,
I ask'd not why, and reck'd not where;
It was at length the same to me,
Fetter'd or fetterless to be,
I learn'd to love despair.
And thus, when they appear'd at last,
And all my bonds aside were cast,
These heavy walls to me had grown
A hermitage — and all my own!
And half I felt as they were come
To tear me from a second home:
With spiders I had friendship made,
And watch'd them in their sullen trade,
Had seen the mice by moonlight play,
And why should I feel less than they?
We were all inmates of one place,
And I, the monarch of each race,
Had power to kill — yet, strange to tell!
In quiet we had learn'd to dwell —
My very chains and I grew friends,
So much a long communion tends
To make us what we are: — even I
Regain'd my freedom with a sigh.

ODE

Oh Venice! Venice! when thy marble walls
Are level with the waters, there shall be
A cry of nations o'er thy sunken halls,
A loud lament along the sweeping sea!
If I, a northern wanderer, weep for thee,
What should thy sons do? — any thing but weep:
And yet they only murmur in their sleep.
In contrast with their fathers — as the slime,
The dull green ooze of the receding deep,
Is with the dashing of the spring-tide foam,
That drives the sailor shipless to his home,
Are they to those that were; and thus they creep,
Crouching and crab-like, through their sapping streets.
Oh! agony — that centuries should reap
No mellower harvest! Thirteen hundred years
Of wealth and glory turn'd to dust and tears;
And every monument the stranger meets,
Church, palace, pillar, as a mourner greets;
And even the Lion all subdued appears,
And the harsh sound of the barbarian drum,
With dull and daily dissonance, repeats
The echo of thy tyrant's voice along
The soft waves, once all musical to song,
That heaved beneath the moonlight with the throng
Of gondolas — and to the busy hum
Of cheerful creatures, whose most sinful deeds
Were but the overbeating of the heart,
And flow of too much happiness, which needs
The aid of age to turn its course apart
From the luxuriant and voluptuous flood
Of sweet sensations battling with the blood.
But these are better than the gloomy errors.
The weeds of nations in their last decay,
When vice walks forth with her unsoften'd terrors.
And mirth is madness, and but smiles to slay;
And hope is nothing but a false delay,
The sick man's lightning half an hour ere death,

When faintness, the last mortal birth of pain,
And apathy of limb, the dull beginning
Of the cold staggering race which death is winning
Steals vein by vein and pulse by pulse away;
Yet so relieving the o'ertortured clay,
To him appears renewal of his breath,
And freedom the mere numbness of his chain; —
And then he talks of life, and how again
He feels his spirit soaring; albeit weak,
And of the fresher air, which he would seek;
And as he whispers knows not that he gasps,
That his thin finger feels not what it clasps,
And so the film comes o'er him — and the dizzy
Chamber swims round and round — and shadows busy,
At which he vainly catches, flit and gleam,
Till the last rattle chokes the strangled scream.
And all is ice and blackness, — and the earth
That which it was the moment ere our birth.
There is no hope for nations! Search the page
Of many thousand years — the daily scene,
The flow and ebb of each recurring age,
The everlasting to be which hath been,
Hath taught us nought or little: still we lean
On things that rot beneath our weight, and wear
Our strength away in wrestling with the air;
For 'tis our nature strikes us down: the beasts
Slaughter'd in hourly hecatombs for feasts
Are of as high an order — they must go
Even where their driver goads them, though to slaughter.
Ye men, who pour your blood for kings as water,
What have they given your children in return?
A heritage of servitude and woes,
A blindfold bondage where your hire is blows.
What? do not yet the red-hot ploughshares burn,
O'er which you stumble in a false ordeal,
And deem this proof of loyalty the real;
Kissing the hand that guides you to your scars,
And glorying as you tread the glowing bars?
All that your sires have left you, all that time
Bequeaths of free, and history of sublime,
Spring from a different theme! — Ye see and read,
Admire and sigh, and then succumb and bleed!
Save the few spirits, who, despite of all,
And worse than all, the sudden crimes engender'd
By the down-thundering of the prison-wall,
And thirst to swallow the sweet waters tender'd,
Gushing from freedom's fountains — when the crowd,
Madden'd with centuries of drought, are loud,
And trample on each other to obtain
The cup which brings oblivion of a chain
Heavy and sore, — in which long yoked the plough'd
The sand, — or if there sprung the yellow grain,
'Twas not for them, their necks were too much bow'd,
And their dead palates chew'd the cud of pain: —
Yes! the few spirits — who, despite of deeds
Which they abhor, confound not with the cause
Those momentary starts from Nature's laws,
Which, like the pestilence and earthquake, smite
But for a term, then pass, and leave the earth
With all her seasons to repair the blight
With a few summers, and again put forth
Cities and generations — fair, when free —
For, tyranny, there blooms no bud for thee!

III

Glory and empire! once upon these towers
With freedom — godlike triad! how ye sate!
The league of mightiest nations, in those hours
When Venice was an envy, might abate,
But did not quench, her spirit — in her fate
All were enwrapp'd: the feasted monarchs knew
And loved their hostess, nor could learn to hate,
Although they humbled — with the kingly few
The many felt, for from all days and climes
She was the voyager's worship; — even her crimes
Were of the softer order — born of love,
She drank no blood, nor fatten'd on the dead,
But gladden'd where her harmless conquests spread;
For these restored the cross, that from above
Hallow'd her sheltering banners, which incessant
Flew between earth and the unholy crescent,
Which, if it waned and dwindled, earth may thank
The city it has clothed in chains, which clank
Now, creaking in the ears of those who owe
The name of freedom to her glorious struggles;
Yet she but shares with them a common woe,
And call'd the "kingdom" of a conquering foe, —
But knows what all — and, most of all, we know —
With what set gilded terms a tyrant juggles!

IV

The name of commonwealth is past and gone
O'er the three fractions of the groaning globe;
Venice is crush'd, and Holland deigns to own
A sceptre, and endures the purple robe;
If the free Switzer yet bestrides alone
His chainless mountains, 'tis but for a time,
For tyranny of late is cunning grown,
And in its own good season tramples down
The sparkles of our ashes. One great clime,
Whose vigorous offspring by dividing ocean,
Are kept apart and nursed in the devotion
Of freedom, which their fathers fought for, and

Bequeath'd — a heritage of heart and hand,
And proud distinction from each other land,
Whose sons must bow them at a monarch's motion,
As if his senseless sceptre were a wand
Full of the magic of exploded science —
Still one great clime, in full and free defiance,
Yet rears her crest, unconquer'd and sublime,
Above the far Atlantic! — She has taught
Her Esau-brethren that the haughty flag,
The floating fence of Albion's feebler crag,
May strike to those whose red right hands have bought
Rights cheaply earn'd with blood. Still, still, forever
Better, though each man's life-blood were a river,
That it should flow, and overflow, than creep
Through thousand lazy channels in our veins,
Damn'd like the dull canal with locks and chains,
And moving, as a sick man in his sleep,
Three paces, and then faltering: — better be
Where the extinguish'd Spartans still are free,
In their proud charnel of Thermopylæ,
Than stagnate in our marsh, — or o'er the deep
Fly, and one current to the ocean add,
One spirit to the souls our fathers had,
One freeman more, America, to thee!

DON JUAN

From CANTO III

And when his bones are dust, his grave a blank,
  His station, generation, even his nation,
Become a thing, or nothing, save to rank
  In chronological commemoration,
Some dull MS. oblivion long has sank,
  Or graven stone found in a barrack's station
In digging the foundation of a closet,
May turn his name up as a rare deposit.

And glory long has made the sages smile;
  'Tis something, nothing, words, illusion, wind —
Depending more upon the historian's style,
  Than on the name a person leaves behind.
Troy owes to Homer what whist owes to Hoyle:
  The present century was growing blind
To the great Marlborough's skill in giving knocks,
Until his late Life by Archdeacon Coxe.

Milton's the prince of poets — so we say;
  A little heavy, but no less divine:
An independent being in his day —
  Learn'd, pious, temperate in love and wine:
But his life falling into Johnson's way,
  We're told this great high priest of all the Nine
Was whipt at college, — a harsh sire, — odd spouse,
For the first Mrs. Milton left his house.

All these are, *certes*, entertaining facts,
  Like Shakespeare's stealing deer, Lord Bacon's bribes;
Like Titus' youth, and Cæsar's earliest acts;
  Like Burns (whom Doctor Currie well describes);
Like Cromwell's pranks; — but although truth exacts
  These amiable descriptions from the scribes,
As most essential to their hero's story,
They do not much contribute to his glory.

All are not moralists, like Southey, when
  He prated to the world of "Pantisocracy";
Or Wordsworth, unexcised, unhired, who then
  Season'd his peddler poems with democracy:
Or Coleridge, long before his flighty pen
  Let to the *Morning Post* its aristocracy;
When he and Southey, following the same path,
Espoused two partners (milliners of Bath).

Such names at present cut a convict figure,
  The very Botany Bay in moral geography;
Their loyal treason, renegado rigour,
  Are good manure for their more bare biography.
Wordsworth's last quarto, by the way, is bigger
  Than any since the birthday of typography;
A drowsy, frowzy poem call'd *The Excursion*,
Writ in a manner which is my aversion.

He there builds up a formidable dike
  Between his own and others' intellect;
But Wordsworth's poem, and his followers, like
  Johanna Southcote's Shiloh, and her sect,
Are things which in this century don't strike
  The public mind — so few are the elect;
And the new births of both their stale virginities
Have proved but dropsies, taken for divinities.

But let me to my story: I must own,
  If I have any fault, it is digression —
Leaving my people to proceed alone,
  While I soliloquize beyond expression;
But these are my addresses from the throne,
  Which put off business to the ensuing session,
Forgetting each omission is a loss to
The world, not quite so great as Ariosto.

I know that what our neighbours called *longueurs*
  (We've not so good a *word*, but have the *thing*,
In that complete perfection which ensures
  An epic from Bob Southey every spring —)
Form not the true temptation which allures
  The reader; but 'twould not be hard to bring

Some fine examples of the *épopée*
To prove its grand ingredient is *ennui.*

We learn from Horace, "Homer sometimes sleeps";
We feel without him, Wordsworth sometimes wakes, —
To show with what complacency he creeps,
With his dear "*Waggoners,*" around his lakes.
He wishes for "a boat" to sail the deeps —
Of ocean? — No, of air; and then he makes
Another outcry for "a little boat,"
And drivels seas to set it well afloat.

If he must fain sweep o'er the ethereal plain,
And Pegasus runs restive in his "Waggon,"
Could he not beg the loan of Charles's Wain,
Or pray Medea for a single dragon?
Or if too classic for his vulgar brain,
He fear'd his neck to venture such a nag on,
And he must needs mount nearer to the moon,
Could not the blockhead ask for a balloon?

* * * * * * * *

O Hesperus! thou bringest all good things —
Home to the weary, to the hungry cheer,
To the young bird the parent's brooding wings,
The welcome stall to the o'erlabour'd steer;
Whate'er of peace about our hearthstone clings,
Whate'er our household gods protect of dear,
Are gather'd round us by thy look of rest;
Thou bring'st the child, too, to the mother's breast.

Soft hour! which wakes the wish and melts the heart
Of those who sail the seas, on the first day
When they from their sweet friends are torn apart;
Or fills with love the pilgrim on his way
As the far bell of vesper makes him start,
Seeming to weep the dying day's decay;
Is this a fancy which our reason scorns?
Ah! surely nothing dies but something mourns.

When Nero perish'd by the justest doom
Which ever the destroyer yet destroy'd,
Amidst the roar of liberated Rome,
Of nations freed, and the world overjoy'd,
Some hands unseen strew'd flowers upon his tomb;
Perhaps the weakness of a heart not void
Of feeling for some kindness done, when power
Had left the wretch an uncorrupted hour.

But I'm digressing; what on earth has Nero,
Or any such like sovereign buffoons,
To do with the transactions of my hero,
More than such madmen's fellow-man — the moon's?
Sure my invention must be down at zero,
And I grown one of many "wooden spoons"
Of verse (the name with which we Cantabs please
To dub the last of honours in degrees).

THE GLORY THAT WAS GREECE

Clime of the unforgotten brave!
Whose land from plain to mountain-cave
Was Freedom's home, or Glory's grave!
Shrine of the mighty! can it be
That this is all remains of thee?
Approach, thou craven crouching slave:
Say, is not this Thermopylæ?
These waters blue that round you lave,
O servile offspring of the free —
Pronounce what sea, what shore is this?
The gulf, the rock of Salamis!
These scenes, their story not unknown,
Arise, and make again your own;
Snatch from the ashes of your sires
The embers of their former fires;
And he who in the strife expires
Will add to theirs a name of fear,
That Tyranny shall quake to hear,
And leave his sons a hope, a fame,
They too will rather die than shame
For Freedom's battle once begun,
Bequeathed by bleeding sire to son,
Though baffled oft is ever won.
Bear witness, Greece, thy living page!
Attest it many a deathless age!
While kings, in dusty darkness hid,
Have left a nameless pyramid,
Thy heroes, though the general doom
Hath swept the column from their tomb,
A mightier monument command,
The mountains of their native land!
There points thy Muse to stranger's eye
The graves of those that cannot die!
'Twere long to tell, and sad to trace,
Each step from splendour to disgrace;
Enough — no foreign foe could quell
Thy soul, till from itself it fell;
Yes! Self-abasement paved the way
To villain-bonds and despot sway.

KNOW YE THE LAND?

Know ye the land where the cypress and myrtle
Are emblems of deeds that are done in their clime?
Where the rage of the vulture, the love of the turtle,
Now melt into sorrow, now madden to crime?

Know ye the land of the cedar and vine,
Where the flowers ever blossom, the beams ever shine;
Where the light wings of Zephyr, oppress'd with perfume,
Wax faint o'er the gardens of Gúl in her bloom;
Where the citron and olive are fairest of fruit,
And the voice of the nightingale never is mute:
Where the tints of the earth, and the hues of the sky,
In colour though varied, in beauty may vie,
And the purple of ocean is deepest in dye;
Where the virgins are soft as the roses they twine,
And all, save the spirit of man, is divine?
'Tis the clime of the East; 'tis the land of the Sun —
Can he smile on such deeds as his children have done?
Oh! wild as the accents of lovers' farewell
Are the hearts which they bear, and the tales which they tell.

SHE WALKS IN BEAUTY

She walks in beauty, like the night
Of cloudless climes and starry skies;
And all that's best of dark and bright
Meet in her aspect and her eyes:
Thus mellow'd to that tender light
Which heaven to gaudy day denies.

One shade the more, one ray the less,
Had half impair'd the nameless grace
Which waves in every raven tress,
Or softly lightens o'er her face;
Where thoughts serenely sweet express
How pure, how dear, their dwelling-place.

And on that cheek, and o'er that brow,
So soft, so calm, yet eloquent,
The smiles that win, the tints that glow,
But tell of days in goodness spent,
A mind at peace with all below,
A heart whose love is innocent!

O! SNATCH'D AWAY IN BEAUTY'S BLOOM

O! snatch'd away in beauty's bloom,
On thee shall press no ponderous tomb,
But on thy turf shall roses rear
Their leaves, the earliest of the year;
And the wild cypress wave in tender gloom;

And oft by yon blue gushing stream
Shall Sorrow lean her drooping head,
And feed deep thought with many a dream,
And lingering pause and lightly tread;
Fond wretch! as if her step disturb'd the dead!

Away! we know that tears are vain,
That Death nor heeds nor hears distress;
Will this unteach us to complain!
Or make one mourner weep the less!
And thou — who tell'st me to forget,
Thy looks are wan, thine eyes are wet.

STANZAS FOR MUSIC

There be none of Beauty's daughters
With a magic like thee;
And like music on the waters
Is thy sweet voice to me:
When, as if its sound were causing
The charmèd ocean's pausing,
The waves lie still and gleaming,
And the lull'd winds seem dreaming.

And the midnight moon is weaving
Her bright chain o'er the deep;
Whose breast is gently heaving,
As an infant's asleep:
So the spirit bows before thee,
To listen and adore thee;
With a full but soft emotion,
Like the swell of Summer's ocean.

SO, WE'LL GO NO MORE A ROVING

So, we'll go no more a roving
So late into the night,
Though the heart be still as loving.
And the moon be still as bright.

For the sword outwears its sheath,
And the soul wears out the breast,
And the heart must pause to breathe,
And love itself have rest.

Though the night was made for loving,
And the day returns too soon,
Yet we'll go no more a roving
By the light of the moon.

CHARLES WOLFE (1791–1823)

THE BURIAL OF SIR JOHN MOORE AT CORUNNA

Not a drum was heard, not a funeral note,
As his corse to the rampart we hurried;
Not a soldier discharged his farewell shot
O'er the grave where our hero we buried.

We buried him darkly at dead of night,
The sods with our bayonets turning;
By the struggling moonbeam's misty light,
And the lantern dimly burning.

No useless coffin enclosed his breast,
Not in sheet nor in shroud we wound him,
But he lay like a warrior taking his rest
With his martial cloak around him.

Few and short were the prayers we said,
And we spoke not a word of sorrow;
But we steadfastly gazed on the face that was dead,
And we bitterly thought of the morrow.

We thought as we hollowed his narrow bed,
And smoothed down his lonely pillow,
That the foe and the stranger would tread o'er his head,
And we far away on the billow!

Lightly they'll talk of the spirit that's gone,
And o'er his cold ashes upbraid him, —
But little he'll reck, if they let him sleep on
In the grave where a Briton has laid him.

But half of our weary task was done
When the clock struck the hour for retiring;
And we heard the distant and random gun
That the foe was sullenly firing.

Slowly and sadly we laid him down,
From the field of his fame fresh and gory;
We carved not a line, and we raised not a stone —
But we left him alone with his glory.

PERCY BYSSHE SHELLEY
(1792–1822)

From ALASTOR; OR, THE SPIRIT OF SOLITUDE

Nondum amabam, et amare amabam, quærebam quid amarem, amans amare. — *Confess. St. August.*

Earth, ocean, air, belovèd brotherhood!
If our great Mother has imbued my soul
With aught of natural piety to feel
Your love, and recompense the boon with mine;
If dewy morn, and odorous noon, and even,
With sunset and its gorgeous ministers,
And solemn midnight's tingling silentness;
If autumn's hollow sighs in the sere wood,
And winter robing with pure snow and crowns
Of starry ice the gray grass and bare boughs;
If spring's voluptuous pantings when she breathes
Her first sweet kisses, have been dear to me;
If no bright bird, insect, or gentle beast
I consciously have injured, but still loved
And cherished these my kindred; then forgive
This boast, belovèd brethren, and withdraw
No portion of your wonted favour now!

Mother of this unfathomable world!
Favour my solemn song, for I have loved
Thee ever, and thee only; I have watched
Thy shadow, and the darkness of thy steps,
And my heart ever gazes on the depth
Of thy deep mysteries. I have made my bed
In charnels and on coffins, where black death
Keeps record of the trophies won from thee,
Hoping to still these obstinate questionings
Of thee and thine, by forcing some lone ghost,
Thy messenger, to render up the tale
Of what we are. In lone and silent hours,
When night makes a weird sound of its own stillness,
Like an inspired and desperate alchemist
Staking his very life on some dark hope,
Have I mixed awful talk and asking looks
With my most innocent love, until strange tears
Uniting with those breathless kisses, made
Such magic as compels the charmèd night
To render up thy charge: . . . and, though ne'er yet
Thou hast unveiled thy inmost sanctuary,
Enough from incommunicable dream,
And twilight phantasms, and deep noonday thought,
Has shone within me, that serenely now
And moveless, as a long-forgotten lyre
Suspended in the solitary dome
Of some mysterious and deserted fane,
I wait thy breath, Great Parent, that my strain
May modulate with murmurs of the air,
And motions of the forests and the sea,
And voice of living beings, and woven hymns
Of night and day, and the deep heart of man.

There was a Poet whose untimely tomb
No human hands with pious reverence reared,
But the charmed eddies of autumnal winds
Built o'er his mouldering bones a pyramid
Of mouldering leaves in the waste wilderness: —
A lovely youth, — no mourning maiden decked
With weeping flowers, or votive cypress wreath,
The lone couch of his everlasting sleep: —
Gentle, and brave, and generous, — no lorn bard
Breathed o'er his dark fate one melodious sigh:
He lived, he died, he sung, in solitude.
Strangers have wept to hear his passionate notes,
And virgins, as unknown he passed, have pined

And wasted for fond love of his wild eyes.
The fire of those soft orbs has ceased to burn,
And Silence, too enamoured of that voice,
Locks its mute music in her rugged cell.

By solemn vision, and bright silver dream,
His infancy was nurtured. Every sight
And sound from the vast earth and ambient air,
Sent to his heart its choicest impulses.
The fountains of divine philosophy
Fled not his thirsting lips, and all of great,
Or good, or lovely, which the sacred past
In truth or fable consecrates, he felt
And knew. When early youth had passed, he left
His cold fireside and alienated home
To seek strange truths in undiscovered lands.
Many a wide waste and tangled wilderness
Has lured his fearless steps; and he has bought
With his sweet voice and eyes, from savage men,
His rest and food. Nature's most secret steps
He like her shadow has pursued, where'er
The red volcano overcanopies
Its fields of snow and pinnacles of ice
With burning smoke, or where bitumen lakes
On black bare pointed islets ever beat
With sluggish surge, or where the secret caves
Rugged and dark, winding among the springs
Of fire and poison, inaccessible
To avarice or pride, their starry domes
Of diamond and of gold expand above
Numberless and immeasurable halls,
Frequent with crystal column, and clear shrines
Of pearl, and thrones radiant with chrysolite.
Nor had that scene of ampler majesty
Than gems or gold, the varying roof of heaven
And the green earth, lost in his heart its claims
To love and wonder; he would linger long
In lonesome vales, making the wild his home,
Until the doves and squirrels would partake
From his innocuous hand his bloodless food,
Lured by the gentle meaning of his looks,
And the wild antelope, that starts whene'er
The dry leaf rustles in the brake, suspend
Her timid steps to gaze upon a form
More graceful than her own.
His wandering step,
Obedient to high thoughts, has visited
The awful ruins of the days of old:
Athens, and Tyre, and Balbec, and the waste
Where stood Jerusalem, the fallen towers
Of Babylon, the eternal pyramids,
Memphis and Thebes, and whatsoe'er of strange
Sculptured on alabaster obelisk,
Or jasper tomb, or mutilated sphinx,
Dark Æthiopia in her desert hills
Conceals. Among the ruined temples there,
Stupendous columns, and wild images
Of more than man, where marble dæmons watch
The Zodiac's brazen mystery, and dead men
Hang their mute thoughts on the mute walls around,
He lingered, poring on memorials
Of the world's youth, through the long burning day
Gazed on those speechless shapes, nor, when the moon
Filled the mysterious halls with floating shades,
Suspended he that task, but ever gazed
And gazed, till meaning on his vacant mind
Flashed like strong inspiration, and he saw
The thrilling secrets of the birth of time.

* * * * * * * *

The Poet wandering on, through Arabie
And Persia, and the wild Carmanian waste,
And o'er the aërial mountains which pour down
Indus and Oxus from their icy caves,
In joy and exultation held his way;
Till in the vale of Cashmire, far within
Its loneliest dell, where odorous plants entwine
Beneath the hollow rocks a natural bower,
Beside a sparkling rivulet he stretched
His languid limbs. A vision on his sleep
There came, a dream of hopes that never yet
Had flushed his cheek. He dreamed a veilèd maid
Sate near him, talking in low solemn tones.
Her voice was like the voice of his own soul
Heard in the calm of thought; its music long,
Like woven sounds of streams and breezes, held
His inmost sense suspended in its web
Of many-coloured woof and shifting hues.
Knowledge and truth and virtue were her theme,
And lofty hopes of divine liberty,
Thoughts the most dear to him, and poesy,
Herself a poet. Soon the solemn mood
Of her pure mind kindled through all her frame
A permeating fire: wild numbers then
She raised, with voice stifled in tremulous sobs
Subdued by its own pathos: her fair hands
Were bare alone, sweeping from some strange harp
Strange symphony, and in their branching veins
The eloquent blood told an ineffable tale.
The beating of her heart was heard to fill
The pauses of her music, and her breath
Tumultuously accorded with those fits
Of intermitted song. Sudden she rose,
As if her heart impatiently endured
Its bursting burthen: at the sound he turned,
And saw by the warm light of their own life
Her glowing limbs beneath the sinuous veil
Of woven wind, her outspread arms now bare,

Her dark locks floating in the breath of night,
Her beamy bending eyes, her parted lips
Outstretched, and pale, and quivering eagerly.
His strong heart sunk and sickened with excess
Of love. He reared his shuddering limbs and quelled
His gasping breath, and spread his arms to meet
Her panting bosom: . . . she drew back awhile,
Then, yielding to the irresistible joy,
With frantic gesture and short breathless cry
Folded his frame in her dissolving arms.
Now blackness veiled his dizzy eyes, and night
Involved and swallowed up the vision; sleep,
Like a dark flood suspended in its course,
Rolled back its impulse on his vacant brain.

* * * * * * * *

HYMN TO INTELLECTUAL BEAUTY

The awful shadow of some unseen Power
  Floats though unseen amongst us, — visiting
  This various world with as inconstant wing
As summer winds that creep from flower to flower; —
Like moonbeams that behind some piny mountain shower,
    It visits with inconstant glance
    Each human heart and countenance;
Like hues and harmonies of evening, —
    Like clouds in starlight widely spread, —
    Like memory of music fled, —
    Like aught that for its grace may be
Dear, and yet dearer for its mystery.

Spirit of Beauty, that dost consecrate
  With thine own hues all thou dost shine upon
  Of human thought or form, — where art thou gone?
Why dost thou pass away and leave our state,
This dim vast vale of tears, vacant and desolate?
    Ask why the sunlight not forever
    Weaves rainbows o'er yon mountain river,
Why aught should fail and fade that once is shown,
    Why fear and dream and death and birth
    Cast on the daylight of this earth
    Such gloom, — why man has such a scope
For love and hate, despondency and hope?

No voice from some sublimer world hath ever
  To sage or poet these responses given —
  Therefore the names of Dæmon, Ghost, and Heaven,
Remain the records of their vain endeavour,
Frail spells — whose uttered charm might not avail to sever,
    From all we hear and all we see,
    Doubt, chance, and mutability.
Thy light alone — like mist o'er mountains driven,
    Or music by the night wind sent,
    Through strings of some still instrument,
    Or moonlight on a midnight stream,
Gives grace and truth to life's unquiet dream.

Love, Hope, and Self-esteem, like clouds depart
  And come, for some uncertain moments lent,
  Man were immortal, and omnipotent,
Didst thou, unknown and awful as thou art,
Keep with thy glorious train firm state within his heart.
    Thou messenger of sympathies,
    That wax and wane in lovers' eyes —
Thou — that to human thought art nourishment,
    Like darkness to a dying flame!
    Depart not as thy shadow came,
    Depart not — lest the grave should be,
Like life and fear, a dark reality.

While yet a boy I sought for ghosts, and sped
  Through many a listening chamber, cave and ruin,
  And starlight wood, with fearful steps pursuing
Hopes of high talk with the departed dead.
I called on poisonous names with which our youth is fed,
    I was not heard — I saw them not —
    When musing deeply on the lot
Of life, at the sweet time when winds are wooing
    All vital things that wake to bring
    News of birds and blossoming, —
    Sudden, thy shadow fell on me;
I shrieked, and clasped my hands in ecstasy!

I vowed that I would dedicate my powers
  To thee and thine — have I not kept the vow?
  With beating heart and streaming eyes, even now
I call the phantoms of a thousand hours
Each from his voiceless grave: they have in visioned bower
    Of studious zeal or love's delight
    Outstretched with me the envious night —
They know that never joy illumed my brow
    Unlinked with hope that thou wouldst free
    This world from its dark slavery,
    That thou — O awful Loveliness,
Wouldst give whate'er these words cannot express.

The day becomes more solemn and serene
  When noon is past — there is a harmony
  In autumn, and a lustre in its sky,
Which through the summer is not heard or seen,
As if it could not be, as if it had not been!
    Thus let thy power, which like the truth

Of nature on my passive youth
Descended, to my onward life supply
Its calm — to one who worships thee,
And every form containing thee,
Whom, Spirit fair, thy spells did bind
To fear himself, and love all human kind.

SONNET

OZYMANDIAS

I met a traveller from an antique land
Who said: Two vast and trunkless legs of stone
Stand in the desert. Near them, on the sand,
Half sunk, a shattered visage lies, whose frown,
And wrinkled lip, and sneer of cold command,
Tell that its sculptor well those passions read
Which yet survive, (stamped on these lifeless things,)
The hand that mocked them and the heart that fed:
And on the pedestal these words appear:
"My name is Ozymandias, king of kings:
Look on my works, ye Mighty, and despair!"
Nothing beside remains. Round the decay
Of that colossal wreck, boundless and bare
The lone and level sands stretch far away.

From LINES WRITTEN AMONG THE EUGANEAN HILLS

Many a green isle needs must be
In the deep wide sea of misery,
Or the mariner, worn and wan,
Never thus could voyage on
Day and night, and night and day,
Drifting on his dreary way,
With the solid darkness black
Closing round his vessel's track;
Whilst, above, the sunless sky,
Big with clouds, hangs heavily,
And behind, the tempest fleet
Hurries on with lightning feet,
Riving sail, and cord, and plank,
Till the ship has almost drank
Death from the o'er-brimming deep;
And sinks down, down, like that sleep
When the dreamer seems to be
Weltering through eternity;
And the dim low line before
Of a dark and distant shore
Still recedes, as ever still
Longing with divided will,
But no power to seek or shun,
He is ever drifted on
O'er the unreposing wave
To the haven of the grave.
What if there no friends will greet;
What if there no heart will meet
His with love's impatient beat;
Wander wheresoe'er he may,
Can he dream before that day
To find refuge from distress
In friendship's smile, in love's caress?

* * * * * * *

Lo, the sun floats up the sky
Like thought-wingèd Liberty,
Till the universal light
Seems to level plain and height;
From the sea a mist has spread,
And the beams of morn lie dead
On the towers of Venice now,
Like its glory long ago.
By the skirts of that gray cloud
Many-domèd Padua proud
Stands, a peopled solitude,
'Mid the harvest-shining plain,
Where the peasant heaps his grain
In the garner of his foe,
And the milk-white oxen slow
With the purple vintage strain,
Heaped upon the creaking wain,
That the brutal Celt may swill
Drunken sleep with savage will;
And the sickle to the sword
Lies unchanged, though many a lord,
Like a weed whose shade is poison,
Overgrows this region's foison,
Sheaves of whom are ripe to come
To destruction's harvest home:
Men must reap the things they sow,
Force from force must ever flow,
Or worse; but 'tis a bitter woe
That love or reason cannot change
The despot's rage, the slave's revenge.

Padua, thou within whose walls
Those mute guests at festivals,
Son and Mother, Death and Sin,
Played at dice for Ezzelin,
Till Death cried, "I win, I win!"
And Sin cursed to lose the wager,
But Death promised, to assuage her,
That he would petition for
Her to be made Vice-Emperor,
When the destined years were o'er,
Over all between the Po
And the eastern Alpine snow,
Under the mighty Austrian.
Sin smiled so as Sin only can,
And since that time, aye, long before,
Both have ruled from shore to shore.

That incestuous pair, who follow
Tyrants as the sun the swallow,
As Repentance follows Crime,
And as changes follow Time.

In thine halls the lamp of learning,
Padua, now no more is burning;
Like a meteor, whose wild way
Is lost over the grave of day,
It gleams betrayed and to betray:
Once remotest nations came
To adore that sacred flame,
When it lit not many a hearth
On this cold and gloomy earth:
Now new fires from antique light
Spring beneath the wide world's might;
But their spark lies dead in thee,
Trampled out by tyranny.
As the Norway woodman quells,
In the depth of piny dells,
One light flame among the brakes,
While the boundless forest shakes,
And its mighty trunks are torn
By the fire thus lowly born:
The spark beneath his feet is dead,
He starts to see the flames it fed
Howling through the darkened sky
With a myriad tongues victoriously,
And sinks down in fear: so thou,
O Tyranny, beholdest now
Light around thee, and thou hearest
The loud flames ascend, and fearest:
Grovel on the earth: aye, hide
In the dust thy purple pride!

Noon descends around me now:
'Tis the noon of autumn's glow,
When a soft and purple mist
Like a vaporous amethyst,
Or an air-dissolvèd star
Mingling light and fragrance, far
From the curved horizon's bound
To the point of heaven's profound,
Fills the overflowing sky;
And the plains that silent lie
Underneath, the leaves unsodden
Where the infant frost has trodden
With his morning-wingèd feet,
Whose bright print is gleaming yet;
And the red and golden vines,
Piercing with their trellised lines
The rough, dark-skirted wilderness;
The dun and bladed grass no less,
Pointing from this hoary tower
In the windless air; the flower
Glimmering at my feet; the line
Of the olive-sandalled Apennine
In the south dimly islanded;
And the Alps, whose snows are spread
High between the clouds and sun;
And of living things each one;
And my spirit which so long
Darkened this swift stream of song,
Interpenetrated lie
By the glory of the sky:
Be it love, light, harmony,
Odour, or the soul of all
Which from heaven like dew doth fall,
Or the mind which feeds this verse
Peopling the lone universe.
Noon descends, and after noon
Autumn's evening meets me soon,
Leading the infantine moon,
And that one star, which to her
Almost seems to minister
Half the crimson light she brings
From the sunset's radiant springs:
And the soft dreams of the morn,
(Which like wingèd winds had borne
To that silent isle, which lies
'Mid remembered agonies,
The frail bark of this lone being,)
Pass, to other sufferers fleeing,
And its ancient pilot, Pain,
Sits beside the helm again.

Other flowering isles must be
In the sea of life and agony:
Other spirits float and flee
O'er that gulph: even now, perhaps,
On some rock the wild wave wraps,
With folded wings they waiting sit
For my bark, to pilot it
To some calm and blooming cove,
Where for me, and those I love,
May a windless bower be built,
Far from passion, pain, and guilt,
In a dell 'mid lawny hills,
Which the wild sea-murmur fills,
And soft sunshine, and the sound
Of old forests echoing round,
And the light and smell divine
Of all flowers that breathe and shine:
We may live so happy there,
That the spirits of the air,
Envying us, may even entice
To our healing paradise
The polluting multitude;
But their rage would be subdued
By that clime divine and calm,
And the winds whose wings rain balm
On the uplifted soul, and leaves

Under which the bright sea heaves;
While each breathless interval
In their whisperings musical
The inspired soul supplies
With its own deep melodies,
And the love which heals all strife
Circling, like the breath of life,
All things in that sweet abode
With its own mild brotherhood:
They, not it, would change; and soon
Every sprite beneath the moon
Would repent its envy vain,
And the earth grow young again.

ODE TO THE WEST WIND

I

O, wild West Wind, thou breath of Autumn's being,
Thou, from whose unseen presence the leaves dead
Are driven, like ghosts from an enchanter fleeing,

Yellow, and black, and pale, and hectic red,
Pestilence-stricken multitudes: O, thou,
Who chariotest to their dark wintry bed

The wingèd seeds, where they lie cold and low,
Each like a corpse within its grave, until
Thine azure sister of the spring shall blow

Her clarion o'er the dreaming earth, and fill
(Driving sweet buds like flocks to feed in air)
With living hues and odours plain and hill:

Wild Spirit, which art moving everywhere;
Destroyer and preserver; hear, O, hear!

II

Thou on whose stream, 'mid the steep sky's commotion,
Loose clouds like earth's decaying leaves are shed,
Shook from the tangled boughs of Heaven and Ocean,

Angels of rain and lightning: there are spread
On the blue surface of thine airy surge,
Like the bright hair uplifted from the head

Of some fierce Mænad, even from the dim verge
Of the horizon to the zenith's height
The locks of the approaching storm. Thou dirge

Of the dying year, to which this closing night
Will be the dome of a vast sepulchre,
Vaulted with all thy congregated might

Of vapours, from whose solid atmosphere
Black rain, and fire, and hail will burst: O, hear!

III

Thou who didst waken from his summer dreams
The blue Mediterranean, where he lay,
Lulled by the coil of his crystalline streams,

Beside a pumice isle in Baiæ's bay,
And saw in sleep old palaces and towers
Quivering within the wave's intenser day.

All overgrown with azure moss and flowers
So sweet, the sense faints picturing them! Thou
For whose path the Atlantic's level powers

Cleave themselves into chasms, while far below
The sea-blooms and the oozy woods which wear
The sapless foliage of the ocean, know

Thy voice, and suddenly grow gray with fear,
And tremble and despoil themselves: O, hear!

IV

If I were a dead leaf thou mightest bear;
If I were a swift cloud to fly with thee;
A wave to pant beneath thy power, and share

The impulse of thy strength, only less free
Than thou, O, uncontrollable! If even
I were as in my boyhood, and could be

The comrade of thy wanderings over heaven,
As then, when to outstrip thy skiey speed
Scarce seemed a vision; I would ne'er have striven

As thus with thee in prayer in my sore need.
Oh! lift me as a wave, a leaf, a cloud!
I fall upon the thorns of life! I bleed!

A heavy weight of hours has chained and bowed
One too like thee: tameless, and swift, and proud.

V

Make me thy lyre, even as the forest is:
What if my leaves are falling like its own!
The tumult of thy mighty harmonies

Will take from both a deep, autumnal tone,
Sweet though in sadness. Be thou, spirit fierce,
My spirit! Be thou me, impetuous one!

Drive my dead thoughts over the universe
Like withered leaves to quicken a new birth!
And, by the incantation of this verse,

Scatter, as from an unextinguished hearth
Ashes and sparks, my words among mankind!
Be through my lips to unawakened earth

The trumpet of a prophecy! O, wind,
If Winter comes, can Spring be far behind?

THE INDIAN SERENADE

I arise from dreams of thee
In the first sweet sleep of night,
When the winds are breathing low,
And the stars are shining bright:
I arise from dreams of thee,
And a spirit in my feet
Hath led me — who knows how?
To thy chamber window, Sweet!

The wandering airs they faint
On the dark, the silent stream —
The Champak odours fail
Like sweet thoughts in a dream;
The nightingale's complaint,
It dies upon her heart; —
As I must on thine,
O! belovèd as thou art!

O lift me from the grass!
I die! I faint! I fail!
Let thy love in kisses rain
On my lips and eyelids pale.
My cheek is cold and white, alas!
My heart beats loud and fast; —
Oh! press it to thine own again,
Where it will break at last.

THE CLOUD

I bring fresh showers for the thirsting flowers,
From the seas and the streams;
I bear light shade for the leaves when laid
In their noon-day dreams.
From my wings are shaken the dews that waken
The sweet buds every one,
When rocked to rest on their mother's breast,
As she dances about the sun.
I wield the flail of the lashing hail,
And whiten the green plains under,
And then again I dissolve it in rain,
And laugh as I pass in thunder.

I sift the snow on the mountains below,
And their great pines groan aghast;
And all the night 'tis my pillow white,
While I sleep in the arms of the blast.
Sublime on the towers of my skiey bowers,
Lightning my pilot sits;
In a cavern under is fettered the thunder, —
It struggles and howls at fits;
Over earth and ocean, with gentle motion,
This pilot is guiding me,
Lured by the love of the genii that move
In the depths of the purple sea;
Over the rills, and the crags, and the hills,
Over the lakes and the plains,
Wherever he dream, under mountain or stream,
The Spirit he loves remains;
And I all the while bask in heaven's blue smile,
Whilst he is dissolving in rains.

The sanguine sunrise, with his meteor eyes,
And his burning plumes outspread,
Leaps on the back of my sailing rack,
When the morning star shines dead,
As on the jag of a mountain crag,
Which an earthquake rocks and swings,
An eagle alit one moment may sit
In the light of its golden wings.
And when sunset may breathe, from the lit sea beneath,
Its ardours of rest and of love,
And the crimson pall of eve may fall
From the depth of heaven above,
With wings folded I rest, on mine airy nest,
As still as a brooding dove.

That orbèd maiden with white fire laden,
Whom mortals call the moon,
Glides glimmering o'er my fleece-like floor,
By the midnight breezes strewn;
And wherever the beat of her unseen feet,
Which only the angels hear,
May have broken the woof of my tent's thin roof,
The stars peep behind her and peer;
And I laugh to see them whirl and flee,
Like a swarm of golden bees,
When I widen the rent in my wind-built tent,
Till the calm rivers, lakes, and seas,
Like strips of the sky fallen through me on high,
Are each paved with the moon and these.

I bind the sun's throne with a burning zone,
And the moon's with a girdle of pearl;
The volcanoes are dim, and the stars reel and swim,
When the whirlwinds my banner unfurl.
From cape to cape, with a bridge-like shape,
Over a torrent sea,
Sunbeam-proof, I hang like a roof,
The mountains its columns be.

The triumphal arch through which I march
With hurricane, fire, and snow,
When the powers of the air are chained to my chair,
Is the million-coloured bow;
The sphere-fire above its soft colours wove,
While the moist earth was laughing below.

I am the daughter of earth and water,
And the nursling of the sky;
I pass through the pores of the ocean and shores;
I change, but I cannot die.
For after the rain when, with never a stain,
The pavilion of heaven is bare,
And the winds and sunbeams with their convex gleams
Build up the blue dome of air,
I silently laugh at my own cenotaph,
And out of the caverns of rain,
Like a child from the womb, like a ghost from the tomb,
I arise and unbuild it again.

TO A SKYLARK

Hail to thee, blithe spirit!
Bird thou never wert,
That from heaven, or near it,
Pourest thy full heart
In profuse strains of unpremeditated art.

Higher still and higher
From the earth thou springest
Like a cloud of fire;
The blue deep thou wingest,
And singing still dost soar, and soaring ever singest.

In the golden lightning
Of the sunken sun,
O'er which clouds are brightning,
Thou dost float and run;
Like an unbodied joy whose race is just begun.

The pale purple even
Melts around thy flight;
Like a star of heaven
In the broad day-light
Thou art unseen, but yet I hear thy shrill delight,

Keen as are the arrows
Of that silver sphere,
Whose intense lamp narrows
In the white dawn clear,
Until we hardly see, we feel that it is there.

All the earth and air
With thy voice is loud,
As, when night is bare,
From one lonely cloud
The moon rains out her beams, and heaven is overflowed.

What thou art we know not;
What is most like thee?
From rainbow clouds there flow not
Drops so bright to see
As from thy presence showers a rain of melody.

Like a poet hidden
In the light of thought,
Singing hymns unbidden,
Till the world is wrought
To sympathy with hopes and fears it heeded not:

Like a high-born maiden
In a palace tower,
Soothing her love-laden
Soul in secret hour
With music sweet as love, which overflows her bower:

Like a glow-worm golden
In a dell of dew,
Scattering unbeholden
Its aërial hue
Among the flowers and grass which screen it from the view:

Like a rose embowered
In its own green leaves,
By warm winds deflowered,
Till the scent it gives
Makes faint with too much sweet these heavy-wingèd thieves.

Sound of vernal showers
On the twinkling grass,
Rain-awakened flowers,
All that ever was
Joyous, and clear, and fresh, thy music doth surpass.

Teach us, sprite or bird,
What sweet thoughts are thine;
I have never heard
Praise of love or wine
That panted forth a flood of rapture so divine:

Chorus Hymenæal,
Or triumphal chaunt,
Matched with thine, would be all
But an empty vaunt,
A thing wherein we feel there is some hidden want.

What objects are the fountains
Of thy happy strain?
What fields, or waves, or mountains?
What shapes of sky or plain?
What love of thine own kind? what ignorance of pain?

With thy clear keen joyance
Languor cannot be —
Shadow of annoyance
Never came near thee:
Thou lovest — but ne'er knew love's sad satiety.

Waking or asleep,
Thou of death must deem
Things more true and deep
Than we mortals dream,
Or how could thy notes flow in such a crystal stream?

We look before and after
And pine for what is not:
Our sincerest laughter
With some pain is fraught;
Our sweetest songs are those that tell of saddest thought.

Yet if we could scorn
Hate, and pride, and fear;
If we were things born
Not to shed a tear,
I know not how thy joy we ever should come near.

Better than all measures
Of delightful sound —
Better than all treasures
That in books are found —
Thy skill to poet were, thou scorner of the ground!

Teach me half the gladness
That thy brain must know,
Such harmonious madness
From my lips would flow,
The world should listen then — as I am listening now.

From EPIPSYCHIDION

True Love in this differs from gold and clay,
That to divide is not to take away.
Love is like understanding, that grows bright,
Gazing on many truths; 'tis like thy light,
Imagination! which from earth and sky,
And from the depths of human phantasy,
As from a thousand prisms and mirrors, fills
The Universe with glorious beams, and kills
Error, the worm, with many a sun-like arrow
Of its reverberated lightning. Narrow
The heart that loves, the brain that contemplates,
The life that wears, the spirit that creates
One object, and one form, and builds thereby
A sepulchre for its eternity.

Mind from its object differs most in this:
Evil from good; misery from happiness;
The baser from the nobler; the impure
And frail, from what is clear and must endure.
If you divide suffering and dross, you may
Diminish till it is consumed away;
If you divide pleasure and love and thought,
Each part exceeds the whole; and we know not
How much, while any yet remains unshared,
Of pleasure may be gained, of sorrow spared:
This truth is that deep well, whence sages draw
The unenvied light of hope; the eternal law
By which those live, to whom this world of life
Is as a garden ravaged, and whose strife
Tills for the promise of a later birth
The wilderness of this Elysian earth.

There was a Being whom my spirit oft
Met on its visioned wanderings, far aloft,
In the clear golden prime of my youth's dawn,
Upon the fairy isles of sunny lawn,
Amid the enchanted mountains, and the caves
Of divine sleep, and on the air-like waves
Of wonder-level dream, whose tremulous floor
Paved her light steps; — on an imagined shore,
Under the gray beak of some promontory
She met me, robed in such exceeding glory,
That I beheld her not. In solitudes
Her voice came to me through the whispering woods,
And from the fountains, and the odours deep
Of flowers, which, like lips murmuring in their sleep
Of the sweet kisses which had lulled them there,
Breathed but of *her* to the enamoured air;
And from the breezes whether low or loud,
And from the rain of every passing cloud,
And from the singing of the summer-birds,
And from all sounds, all silence. In the words
Of antique verse and high romance, — in form,
Sound, colour — in whatever checks that Storm
Which with the shattered present chokes the past;
And in that best philosophy, whose taste
Makes this cold common hell, our life, a doom
As glorious as a fiery martyrdom;
Her Spirit was the harmony of truth. —

Then, from the caverns of my dreamy youth
I sprang, as one sandalled with plumes of fire,
And towards the lodestar of my one desire,
I flitted, like a dizzy moth, whose flight

Is as a dead leaf's in the owlet light,
When it would seek in Hesper's setting sphere
A radiant death, a fiery sepulchre,
As if it were a lamp of earthly flame. —
But She, whom prayers or tears then could not tame,
Passed, like a God throned on a wingèd planet,
Whose burning plumes to tenfold swiftness fan it,
Into the dreary cone of our life's shade;
And as a man with mighty loss dismayed,
I would have followed, though the grave between
Yawned like a gulph whose spectres are unseen:
When a voice said: — "O Thou of hearts the weakest,
The phantom is beside thee whom thou seekest."
Then I — "Where?" the world's echo answered "Where!"
And in that silence, and in my despair,
I questioned every tongueless wind that flew
Over my tower of mourning, if it knew
Whither 'twas fled, this soul out of my soul;
And murmured names and spells which have control
Over the sightless tyrants of our fate;
But neither prayer nor verse could dissipate
The night which closed on her; nor uncreate
That world within this Chaos, mine and me,
Of which she was the veiled Divinity,
The world I say of thoughts that worshipped her:
And therefore I went forth, with hope and fear
And every gentle passion sick to death,
Feeding my course with expectation's breath,
Into the wintry forest of our life;
And struggling through its error with vain strife,
And stumbling in my weakness and my haste,
And half bewildered by new forms, I passed
Seeking among those untaught foresters
If I could find one form resembling hers,
In which she might have masked herself from me.
There, — One, whose voice was venomed melody,
Sate by a well, under blue night-shade bowers;
The breath of her false mouth was like faint flowers,
Her touch was as electric poison, — flame
Out of her looks into my vitals came,
And from her living cheeks and bosom flew
A killing air, which pierced like honey-dew
Into the core of my green heart, and lay
Upon its leaves; until, as hair grown grey
O'er a young brow, they hid its unblown prime
With ruins of unseasonable time.

In many mortal forms I rashly sought
The shadow of that idol of my thought.
And some were fair — but beauty dies away:
Others were wise — but honeyed words betray:
And One was true — oh! why not true to me?
Then, as a hunted deer that could not flee,
I turned upon my thoughts, and stood at bay,
Wounded and weak and panting; the cold day
Trembled, for pity of my strife and pain.
When, like a noon-day dawn, there shone again
Deliverance. One stood on my path who seemed
As like the glorious shape which I had dreamed,
As is the Moon, whose changes ever run
Into themselves, to the eternal Sun;
The cold chaste Moon, the Queen of Heaven's bright isles,
Who makes all beautiful on which she smiles,
That wandering shrine of soft yet icy flame
Which ever is transformed, yet still the same,
And warms not but illumines. Young and fair
As the descended Spirit of that sphere,
She hid me, as the Moon may hide the night
From its own darkness, until all was bright
Between the Heaven and Earth of my calm mind,
And, as a cloud charioted by the wind,
She led me to a cave in that wild place,
And sate beside me, with her downward face
Illumining my slumbers, like the Moon
Waxing and waning o'er Endymion.
And I was laid asleep, spirit and limb,
And all my being became bright or dim
As the Moon's image in a summer sea,
According as she smiled or frowned on me;
And there I lay, within a chaste cold bed:
Alas, I then was nor alive nor dead: —
For at her silver voice came Death and Life,
Unmindful each of their accustomed strife,
Masked like twin babes, a sister and a brother,
The wandering hopes of one abandoned mother,
And through the cavern without wings they flew,
And cried "Away, he is not of our crew."
I wept, and though it be a dream, I weep.

* * * * * * * *

At length, into the obscure Forest came
The Vision I had sought through grief and shame.
Athwart that wintry wilderness of thorns
Flashed from her motion splendour like the Morn's,
And from her presence life was radiated
Through the grey earth and branches bare and dead;
So that her way was paved, and roofed above
With flowers as soft as thoughts of budding love;
And music from her respiration spread
Like light, — all other sounds were penetrated
By the small, still, sweet spirit of that sound,
So that the savage winds hung mute around;
And odours warm and fresh fell from her hair
Dissolving the dull cold in the frore air:

Soft as an Incarnation of the Sun,
When light is changed to love, this glorious One
Floated into the cavern where I lay,
And called my Spirit, and the dreaming clay
Was lifted by the thing that dreamed below
As smoke by fire, and in her beauty's glow
I stood, and felt the dawn of my long night
Was penetrating me with living light:
I knew it was the Vision veiled from me
So many years — that it was Emily.

* * * * * * *

TO ———

Music, when soft voices die,
Vibrates in the memory —
Odours, when sweet violets sicken,
Live within the sense they quicken.
Rose-leaves, when the rose is dead,
Are heaped for the belovèd's bed;
And so thy thoughts, when thou art gone,
Love itself shall slumber on.

ADONAIS

I weep for Adonais — he is dead!
O, weep for Adonais! though our tears
Thaw not the frost which binds so dear a head!
And thou, sad Hour, selected from all years
To mourn our loss, rouse thy obscure compeers,
And teach them thine own sorrow, say: "With me
Died Adonais; till the Future dares
Forget the Past, his fate and fame shall be
An echo and a light unto eternity."

Where wert thou, mighty Mother, when he lay,
When thy Son lay, pierced by the shaft which flies
In darkness? where was lorn Urania
When Adonais died? With veilèd eyes,
'Mid listening Echoes, in her Paradise
She sate, while one, with soft enamoured breath,
Rekindled all the fading melodies,
With which, like flowers that mock the corse beneath,
He had adorned and hid the coming bulk of death.

O, weep for Adonais — he is dead!
Wake, melancholy Mother, wake and weep!
Yet wherefore? Quench within their burning bed
Thy fiery tears, and let thy loud heart keep
Like his, a mute and uncomplaining sleep;
For he is gone, where all things wise and fair
Descend; — oh, dream not that the amorous Deep
Will yet restore him to the vital air;
Death feeds on his mute voice, and laughs at our despair.

Most musical of mourners, weep again!
Lament anew, Urania! — He died, —
Who was the Sire of an immortal strain,
Blind, old, and lonely, when his country's pride,
The priest, the slave, and the liberticide,
Trampled and mocked with many a loathèd rite
Of lust and blood; he went, unterrified,
Into the gulph of death; but his clear Sprite
Yet reigns o'er earth; the third among the sons of light.

Most musical of mourners, weep anew!
Not all to that bright station dared to climb;
And happier they their happiness who knew,
Whose tapers yet burn through that night of time
In which suns perished; others more sublime,
Struck by the envious wrath of man or God,
Have sunk, extinct in their refulgent prime;
And some yet live, treading the thorny road,
Which leads, through toil and hate, to Fame's serene abode.

But now, thy youngest, dearest one has perished,
The nursling of thy widowhood, who grew,
Like a pale flower by some sad maiden cherished,
And fed with true love tears, instead of dew;
Most musical of mourners, weep anew!
Thy extreme hope, the loveliest and the last,
The bloom, whose petals, nipped before they blew,
Died on the promise of the fruit, is waste;
The broken lily lies — the storm is overpast.

To that high Capital, where kingly Death
Keeps his pale court in beauty and decay,
He came; and bought, with price of purest breath,
A grave among the eternal. — Come away!
Haste, while the vault of blue Italian day
Is yet his fitting charnel-roof! while still
He lies, as if in dewy sleep he lay;
Awake him not! surely he takes his fill
Of deep and liquid rest, forgetful of all ill.

He will awake no more, oh, never more! —
Within the twilight chamber spreads apace,
The shadow of white Death, and at the door
Invisible Corruption waits to trace
His extreme way to her dim dwelling-place;
The eternal Hunger sits, but pity and awe
Soothe her pale rage, nor dares she to deface

So fair a prey, till darkness, and the law
Of change, shall o'er his sleep the mortal curtain draw.

O, weep for Adonais! — The quick Dreams,
The passion-wingèd Ministers of thought,
Who were his flocks, whom near the living streams
Of his young spirit he fed, and whom he taught
The love which was its music, wander not, —
Wander no more, from kindling brain to brain,
But droop there, whence they sprung; and mourn their lot
Round the cold heart, where, after their sweet pain,
They ne'er will gather strength, or find a home again.

And one with trembling hands clasps his cold head,
And fans him with her moonlight wings, and cries:
"Our love, our hope, our sorrow, is not dead;
See, on the silken fringe of his faint eyes,
Like dew upon a sleeping flower, there lies
A tear some Dream has loosened from his brain."
Lost Angel of a ruined Paradise!
She knew not 'twas her own; as with no stain
She faded, like a cloud which had outwept its rain.

One from a lucid urn of starry dew
Washed his light limbs as if embalming them;
Another clipped her profuse locks, and threw
The wreath upon him, like an anadem,
Which frozen tears instead of pearls begem;
Another in her wilful grief would break
Her bow and wingèd reeds, as if to stem
A greater loss with one which was more weak;
And dull the barbèd fire against his frozen cheek.

Another Splendour on his mouth alit,
That mouth, whence it was wont to draw the breath
Which gave it strength to pierce the guarded wit,
And pass into the panting heart beneath
With lightning and with music: the damp death
Quenched its caress upon his icy lips;
And, as a dying meteor stains a wreath
Of moonlight vapour, which the cold night clips,
It flushed through his pale limbs, and passed to its eclipse.

And others came . . . Desires and Adorations,
Wingèd Persuasions and veiled Destinies,
Splendours, and Glooms, and glimmering Incarnations
Of hopes and fears, and twilight Phantasies;
And Sorrow, with her family of Sighs,
And Pleasure, blind with tears, led by the gleam
Of her own dying smile instead of eyes,
Came in slow pomp; — the moving pomp might seem
Like pageantry of mist on an autumnal stream.

All he had loved, and moulded into thought,
From shape, and hue, and odour, and sweet sound,
Lamented Adonais. Morning sought
Her eastern watch-tower, and her hair unbound,
Wet with the tears which should adorn the ground,
Dimmed the aërial eyes that kindle day;
Afar the melancholy thunder moaned,
Pale Ocean in unquiet slumber lay,
And the wild winds flew round, sobbing in their dismay.

Lost Echo sits amid the voiceless mountains,
And feeds her grief with his remembered lay,
And will no more reply to winds or fountains,
Or amorous birds perched on the young green spray,
Or herdsman's horn, or bell at closing day;
Since she can mimic not his lips, more dear
Than those for whose disdain she pined away
Into a shadow of all sounds: — a drear
Murmur, between their songs, is all the woodmen hear.

Grief made the young Spring wild, and she threw down
Her kindling buds, as if she Autumn were,
Or they dead leaves; since her delight is flown,
For whom should she have waked the sullen year?
To Phœbus was not Hyacinth so dear
Nor to himself Narcissus, as to both
Thou, Adonais: wan they stand and sere
Amid the faint companions of their youth,
With dew all turned to tears; odour, to sighing ruth.

Thy spirit's sister, the lorn nightingale,
Mourns not her mate with such melodious pain;
Not so the eagle, who like thee could scale
Heaven, and could nourish in the sun's domain
Her mighty youth with morning, doth complain,
Soaring and screaming round her empty nest,
As Albion wails for thee: the curse of Cain

Light on his head who pierced thy innocent breast,
And scared the angel soul that was its earthly guest!

Ah, woe is me! Winter is come and gone,
But grief returns with the revolving year;
The airs and streams renew their joyous tone;
The ants, the bees, the swallows reappear;
Fresh leaves and flowers deck the dead Seasons' bier;
The amorous birds now pair in every brake,
And build their mossy homes in field and brere;
And the green lizard, and the golden snake,
Like unimprisoned flames, out of their trance awake.

Through wood and stream and field and hill and Ocean
A quickening life from the Earth's heart has burst,
As it has ever done, with change and motion
From the great morning of the world when first
God dawned on Chaos; in its stream immersed
The lamps of Heaven flash with a softer light;
All baser things pant with life's sacred thirst;
Diffuse themselves; and spend in love's delight
The beauty and the joy of their renewèd might.

The leprous corpse touched by this spirit tender
Exhales itself in flowers of gentle breath;
Like incarnations of the stars, when splendour
Is changed to fragrance, they illumine death
And mock the merry worm that wakes beneath;
Naught we know, dies. Shall that alone which knows
Be as a sword consumed before the sheath
By sightless lightning? — th' intense atom glows
A moment, then is quenched in a most cold repose.

Alas! that all we loved of him should be,
But for our grief, as if it had not been,
And grief itself be mortal! Woe is me!
Whence are we, and why are we? of what scene
The actors or spectators? Great and mean
Meet massed in death, who lends what life must borrow.
As long as skies are blue, and fields are green,
Evening must usher night, night urge the morrow,
Month follow month with woe, and year wake year to sorrow.

He will awake no more, oh, never more!
"Wake thou," cried Misery, "childless Mother, rise
Out of thy sleep, and slake, in thy heart's core,
A wound more fierce than his with tears and sighs."
And all the Dreams that watched Urania's eyes,
And all the Echoes whom their sister's song
Had held in holy silence, cried: "Arise!"
Swift as a Thought by the snake Memory stung,
From her ambrosial rest the fading Splendour sprung.

She rose like an autumnal Night, that springs
Out of the East, and follows wild and drear
The golden Day, which, on eternal wings,
Even as a ghost abandoning a bier,
Had left the Earth a corpse. Sorrow and fear
So struck, so roused, so rapt Urania;
So saddened round her like an atmosphere
Of stormy mist; so swept her on her way
Even to the mournful place where Adonais lay.

Out of her secret Paradise she sped,
Through camps and cities rough with stone, and steel,
And human hearts, which to her aëry tread
Yielding not, wounded the invisible
Palms of her tender feet where'er they fell:
And barbèd tongues, and thoughts more sharp than they,
Rent the soft Form they never could repel,
Whose sacred blood, like the young tears of May,
Paved with eternal flowers that undeserving way.

In the death chamber for a moment Death,
Shamed by the presence of that living Might,
Blushed to annihilation, and the breath
Revisited those lips, and life's pale light
Flashed through those limbs, so late her dear delight.
"Leave me not wild and drear and comfortless,
As silent lightning leaves the starless night!
Leave me not!" cried Urania: her distress
Roused Death: Death rose and smiled, and met her vain caress.

"Stay yet awhile! speak to me once again;
Kiss me, so long but as a kiss may live;
And in my heartless breast and burning brain
That word, that kiss shall all thoughts else survive,
With food of saddest memory kept alive,
Now thou art dead, as if it were a part
Of thee, my Adonais! I would give
All that I am to be as thou now art!
But I am chained to Time, and cannot thence depart!

"Oh gentle child, beautiful as thou wert,
Why didst thou leave the trodden paths of men
Too soon, and with weak hands though mighty heart
Dare the unpastured dragon in his den?
Defenceless as thou wert, oh where was then
Wisdom the mirrored shield, or scorn the spear?
Or hadst thou waited the full cycle, when
Thy spirit should have filled its crescent sphere,
The monsters of life's waste had fled from thee like deer.

"The herded wolves, bold only to pursue;
The obscene ravens, clamorous o'er the dead;
The vultures to the conqueror's banner true,
Who feed where Desolation first has fed,
And whose wings rain contagion; — how they fled,
When like Apollo, from his golden bow,
The Pythian of the age one arrow sped
And smiled! — The spoilers tempt no second blow;
They fawn on the proud feet that spurn them lying low.

"The sun comes forth, and many reptiles spawn;
He sets, and each ephemeral insect then
Is gathered into death without a dawn,
And the immortal stars awake again;
So is it in the world of living men:
A godlike mind soars forth, in its delight
Making earth bare and veiling heaven, and when
It sinks, the swarms that dimmed or shared its light
Leave to its kindred lamps the spirit's awful night."

Thus ceased she: and the mountain shepherds came,
Their garlands sere, their magic mantles rent;
The Pilgrim of Eternity, whose fame
Over his living head like Heaven is bent,
An early but enduring monument,
Came, veiling all the lightnings of his song
In sorrow; from her wilds Ierne sent
The sweetest lyrist of her saddest wrong,
And love taught grief to fall like music from his tongue.

Midst others of less note, came one frail Form,
A phantom among men, companionless
As the last cloud of an expiring storm
Whose thunder is its knell; he, as I guess,
Had gazed on Nature's naked loveliness,
Actæon-like, and now he fled astray
With feeble steps o'er the world's wilderness,
And his own thoughts, along that rugged way,
Pursued, like raging hounds, their father and their prey.

A pardlike Spirit beautiful and swift —
A Love in desolation masked; — a Power
Girt round with weakness; — it can scarce uplift
The weight of the superincumbent hour;
It is a dying lamp, a falling shower,
A breaking billow; — even whilst we speak
Is it not broken? On the withering flower
The killing sun smiles brightly; on a cheek
The life can burn in blood, even while the heart may break.

His head was bound with pansies overblown,
And faded violets, white, and pied, and blue;
And a light spear topped with a cypress cone,
Round whose rude shaft dark ivy tresses grew
Yet dripping with the forest's noonday dew,
Vibrated, as the ever-beating heart
Shook the weak hand that grasped it; of that crew
He came the last, neglected and apart;
A herd-abandoned deer, struck by the hunter's dart.

All stood aloof, and at his partial moan
Smiled through their tears; well knew that gentle band
Who in another's fate now wept his own;
As, in the accents of an unknown land,
He sung new sorrow; sad Urania scanned
The Stranger's mien, and murmured: "Who art thou?"
He answered not, but with a sudden hand
Made bare his branded and ensanguined brow,
Which was like Cain's or Christ's — Oh! that it should be so!

What softer voice is hushed over the dead?
Athwart what brow is that dark mantle thrown?
What form leans sadly o'er the white death-bed,
In mockery of monumental stone,
The heavy heart heaving without a moan?
If it be He, who, gentlest of the wise,
Taught, soothed, loved, honoured the departed one,
Let me not vex with inharmonious sighs
The silence of that heart's accepted sacrifice.

Our Adonais has drunk poison — oh!
What deaf and viperous murderer could crown

Life's early cup with such a draught of woe?
The nameless worm would now itself disown:
It felt, yet could escape the magic tone
Whose prelude held all envy, hate, and wrong,
But what was howling in one breast alone,
Silent with expectation of the song,
Whose master's hand is cold, whose silver lyre unstrung.

Live thou, whose infamy is not thy fame!
Live! fear no heavier chastisement from me,
Thou noteless blot on a remembered name!
But be thyself, and know thyself to be!
And ever at thy season be thou free
To spill the venom when thy fangs o'erflow:
Remorse and Self-contempt shall cling to thee;
Hot Shame shall burn upon thy secret brow,
And like a beaten hound tremble thou shalt — as now.

Nor let us weep that our delight is fled
Far from these carrion kites that scream below;
He wakes or sleeps with the enduring dead;
Thou canst not soar where he is sitting now. —
Dust to the dust! but the pure spirit shall flow
Back to the burning fountain whence it came,
A portion of the Eternal, which must glow
Through time and change, unquenchably the same,
Whilst thy cold embers choke the sordid hearth of shame.

Peace, peace! he is not dead, he doth not sleep —
He hath awakened from the dream of life —
'Tis we who, lost in stormy visions, keep
With phantoms an unprofitable strife,
And in mad trance strike with our spirit's knife
Invulnerable nothings. — *We* decay
Like corpses in a charnel; fear and grief
Convulse us and consume us day by day,
And cold hopes swarm like worms within our living clay.

He has outsoared the shadow of our night;
Envy and calumny and hate and pain,
And that unrest which men miscall delight,
Can touch him not and torture not again;
From the contagion of the world's slow stain
He is secure, and now can never mourn
A heart grown cold, a head grown grey in vain;
Nor, when the spirit's self has ceased to burn,
With sparkless ashes load an unlamented urn.

He lives, he wakes — 'tis Death is dead, not he;
Mourn not for Adonais. — Thou young Dawn,
Turn all thy dew to splendour, for from thee
The spirit thou lamentest is not gone;
Ye caverns and ye forests, cease to moan!
Cease ye faint flowers and fountains, and thou Air,
Which like a mourning veil thy scarf hadst thrown
O'er the abandoned Earth, now leave it bare
Even to the joyous stars which smile on its despair!

He is made one with Nature: there is heard
His voice in all her music, from the moan
Of thunder, to the song of night's sweet bird;
He is a presence to be felt and known
In darkness and in light, from herb and stone,
Spreading itself where'er that Power may move
Which has withdrawn his being to its own;
Which wields the world with never wearied love,
Sustains it from beneath, and kindles it above.

He is a portion of the loveliness
Which once he made more lovely: he doth bear
His part, while the one Spirit's plastic stress
Sweeps through the dull dense world, compelling there
All new successions to the forms they wear;
Torturing th' unwilling dross that checks its flight
To its own likeness, as each mass may bear;
And bursting in its beauty and its might
From trees and beasts and men into the Heaven's light.

The splendours of the firmament of time
May be eclipsed, but are extinguished not;
Like stars to their appointed height they climb
And death is a low mist which cannot blot
The brightness it may veil. When lofty thought
Lifts a young heart above its mortal lair,
And love and life contend in it, for what
Shall be its earthly doom, the dead live there
And move like winds of light on dark and stormy air.

The inheritors of unfulfilled renown
Rose from their thrones, built beyond mortal thought,
Far in the Unapparent. Chatterton
Rose pale, his solemn agony had not
Yet faded from him; Sidney, as he fought
And as he fell and as he lived and loved,
Sublimely mild, a Spirit without spot,

Arose; and Lucan, by his death approved:
Oblivion, as they rose, shrank like a thing reproved.

And many more, whose names on Earth are dark
But whose transmitted effluence cannot die
So long as fire outlives the parent spark,
Rose, robed in dazzling immortality.
"Thou art become as one of us," they cry,
"It was for thee yon kingless sphere has long
Swung blind in unascended majesty,
Silent alone amid an Heaven of Song.
Assume thy wingèd throne, thou Vesper of our throng!"

Who mourns for Adonais? oh come forth,
Fond wretch! and know thyself and him aright.
Clasp with thy panting soul the pendulous Earth;
As from a centre, dart thy spirit's light
Beyond all worlds, until its spacious might
Satiate the void circumference: then shrink
Even to a point within our day and night;
And keep thy heart light, lest it make thee sink,
When hope has kindled hope, and lured thee to the brink.

Or go to Rome, which is the sepulchre,
O, not of him, but of our joy: 'tis naught
That ages, empires, and religions there
Lie buried in the ravage they have wrought;
For such as he can lend, — they borrow not
Glory from those who made the world their prey;
And he is gathered to the kings of thought
Who waged contention with their time's decay,
And of the past are all that cannot pass away.

Go thou to Rome, — at once the Paradise,
The grave, the city, and the wilderness;
And where its wrecks like shattered mountains rise
And flowering weeds and fragrant copses dress
The bones of Desolation's nakedness
Pass, till the Spirit of the spot shall lead
Thy footsteps to a slope of green access
Where, like an infant's smile, over the dead,
A light of laughing flowers along the grass is spread.

And grey walls moulder round, on which dull Time
Feeds, like slow fire upon a hoary brand;
And one keen pyramid with wedge sublime,
Pavilioning the dust of him who planned
This refuge for his memory, doth stand
Like flame transformed to marble; and beneath,
A field is spread, on which a newer band
Have pitched in Heaven's smile their camp of death,
Welcoming him we lose with scarce extinguished breath.

Here pause: these graves are all too young as yet
To have outgrown the sorrow which consigned
Its charge to each; and if the seal is set,
Here, on one fountain of a mourning mind,
Break it not thou! too surely shalt thou find
Thine own well full, if thou returnest home,
Of tears and gall. From the world's bitter wind
Seek shelter in the shadow of the tomb.
What Adonais is, why fear we to become?

The One remains, the many change and pass;
Heaven's light forever shines, Earth's shadows fly;
Life, like a dome of many-coloured glass,
Stains the white radiance of Eternity,
Until Death tramples it to fragments. — Die,
If thou wouldst be with that which thou dost seek!
Follow where all is fled! — Rome's azure sky,
Flowers, ruins, statues, music, words, are weak
The glory they transfuse with fitting truth to speak.

Why linger, why turn back, why shrink, my Heart?
Thy hopes are gone before: from all things here
They have departed; thou shouldst now depart!
A light is past from the revolving year,
And man, and woman; and what still is dear
Attracts to crush, repels to make thee wither.
The soft sky smiles, — the low wind whispers near;
'Tis Adonais calls! oh, hasten thither,
No more let Life divide what Death can join together.

That Light whose smile kindles the Universe,
That Beauty in which all things work and move,
That Benediction which the eclipsing Curse
Of birth can quench not, that sustaining Love
Which, through the web of being blindly wove
By man and beast and earth and air and sea,
Burns bright or dim, as each are mirrors of
The fire for which all thirst, now beams on me,
Consuming the last clouds of cold mortality.

The breath whose might I have invòked in song
Descends on me; my spirit's bark is driven,
Far from the shore, far from the trembling throng
Whose sails were never to the tempest given;
The massy earth and spherèd skies are riven!
I am borne darkly, fearfully, afar:
Whilst burning through the inmost veil of Heaven,
The soul of Adonais, like a star,
Beacons from the abode where the Eternal are.

FINAL CHORUS FROM HELLAS

The world's great age begins anew,
The golden years return,
The earth doth like a snake renew
Her winter weeds outworn:
Heaven smiles, and faiths and empires gleam,
Like wrecks of a dissolving dream.

A brighter Hellas rears its mountains
From waves serener far;
A new Peneus rolls his fountains
Against the morning-star.
Where fairer Tempes bloom, there sleep
Young Cyclads on a sunnier deep.

A loftier Argo cleaves the main,
Fraught with a later prize;
Another Orpheus sings again,
And loves, and weeps, and dies.
A new Ulysses leaves once more
Calypso for his native shore.

O, write no more the tale of Troy,
If earth Death's scroll must be!
Nor mix with Laian rage the joy
Which dawns upon the free:
Although a subtler Sphinx renew
Riddles of death Thebes never knew.

Another Athens shall arise,
And to remoter time
Bequeath, like sunset to the skies,
The splendour of its prime;
And leave, if naught so bright may live,
All earth can take or Heaven can give.

Saturn and Love their long repose
Shall burst, more bright and good
Than all who fell, than One who rose,
Than many unsubdued:
Not gold, not blood, their altar dowers,
But votive tears and symbol flowers.

O cease! must hate and death return?
Cease! must men kill and die?
Cease! drain not to its dregs the urn
Of bitter prophecy.
The world is weary of the past,
O might it die or rest at last!

TO NIGHT

Swiftly walk o'er the western wave,
Spirit of Night!
Out of the misty eastern cave,
Where all the long and lone daylight
Thou wovest dreams of joy and fear,
Which make thee terrible and dear, —
Swift be thy flight!

Wrap thy form in a mantle grey,
Star in-wrought!
Blind with thine hair the eyes of Day;
Kiss her until she be wearied out;
Then wander o'er city, and sea, and land,
Touching all with thine opiate wand —
Come, long sought!

When I arose and saw the dawn,
I sighed for thee;
When light rode high, and the dew was gone,
And noon lay heavy on flower and tree,
And the weary Day turned to his rest,
Lingering like an unloved guest,
I sighed for thee.

Thy brother Death came, and cried,
Wouldst thou me?
Thy sweet child Sleep, the filmy-eyed,
Murmured like a noon-tide bee,
Shall I nestle near thy side?
Wouldst thou me? — And I replied,
No, not thee!

Death will come when thou art dead,
Soon, too soon —
Sleep will come when thou art fled;
Of neither would I ask the boon
I ask of thee, belovèd Night —
Swift be thine approaching flight,
Come soon, soon!

TO ———

One word is too often profaned
For me to profane it,
One feeling too falsely disdained
For thee to disdain it.
One hope is too like despair
For prudence to smother,
And pity from thee more dear
Than that from another.

I can give not what men call love,
But wilt thou accept not
The worship the heart lifts above
And the Heavens reject not, —
The desire of the moth for the star,
Of the night for the morrow,
The devotion to something afar
From the sphere of our sorrow?

LINES

When the lamp is shattered,
The light in the dust lies dead —
When the cloud is scattered,
The rainbow's glory is shed.
When the lute is broken,
Sweet tones are remembered not;
When the lips have spoken,
Loved accents are soon forgot.

As music and splendour
Survive not the lamp and the lute,
The heart's echoes render
No song when the spirit is mute, —
No song but sad dirges,
Like the wind through a ruined cell,
Or the mournful surges
That ring the dead seaman's knell.

When hearts have once mingled,
Love first leaves the well-built nest, —
The weak one is singled
To endure what it once possessed.
O, Love! who bewailest
The frailty of all things here,
Why choose you the frailest
For your cradle, your home, and your bier?

Its passions will rock thee
As the storms rock the ravens on high:
Bright reason will mock thee,
Like the sun from a wintry sky.
From thy nest every rafter
Will rot, and thine eagle home
Leave thee naked to laughter,
When leaves fall and cold winds come.

JOHN KEBLE (1792–1866)

ST. THOMAS THE APOSTLE

We were not by when Jesus came,
But round us, far and near,
We see His trophies, and His name
In choral echoes hear.
In a fair ground our lot is cast,
As in the solemn week that past,
While some might doubt, but all adored,
Ere the whole widowed Church had seen her risen Lord.

Slowly, as then, His bounteous hand
The golden chain unwinds,
Drawing to Heaven with gentlest band
Wise hearts and loving minds.
Love sought Him first; at dawn of morn
From her sad couch she sprang forlorn,
She sought to weep with Thee alone,
And saw Thine open grave, and knew that Thou wert gone.

Reason and Faith at once set out
To search the Saviour's tomb;
Faith faster runs, but waits without,
As fearing to presume
Till Reason enter in, and trace
Christ's relics round the holy place —
"Here lay His limbs, and here His sacred head:
And who was by, to make his new-forsaken bed?"

Both wonder, one believes — but while
They muse on all at home,
No thought can tender Love beguile
From Jesus' grave to roam.
Weeping she stays till He appear —
Her witness first the Church must hear —
All joy to souls that can rejoice
With her at earliest call of His dear gracious voice.

Joy too to those who love to talk
In secret how He died,
Though with sealed eyes, awhile they walk,
Nor see Him at their side;
Most like the faithful pair are they,
Who once to Emmaus took their way,
Half darkling, till their Master shed
His glory on their souls, made known in breaking bread.

Thus, ever brighter and more bright,
On those He came to save
The Lord of new-created light
Dawned gradual from the grave:
Till passed the inquiring daylight hour,
And with closed door in silent bower
The Church in anxious musing sate,
As one who for redemption still had long to wait.

Then, gliding through the unopening door,
Smooth without step or sound,
"Peace to your souls!" He said — no more;
They own Him, kneeling round.
Eye, ear, and hand, and loving heart,
Body and soul in every part,
Successive made His witnesses that hour,
Cease not in all the world to show His saving power.

Is there, on earth, a spirit frail,
Who fears to take their word,
Scarce daring, through the twilight pale,
To think he sees the Lord?
With eyes too tremblingly awake
To bear with dimness for His sake?
Read and confess the Hand Divine
That drew thy likeness here so true in every line.

For all thy rankling doubts so sore,
Love thou thy Saviour still,
Him for thy Lord and God adore,
And ever do His will.
Though vexing thoughts may seem to last,
Let not thy soul be quite o'ercast; —
Soon will He show thee all His wounds, and say,
"Long have I known thy name — know thou My face alway."

From THE WATERFALL

Go where the waters fall,
Sheer from the mountain's height —

Mark how a thousand streams in one, —
One in a thousand on they fare,
Now flashing to the sun,
Now still as beast in lair.

Now round the rock, now mounting o'er
In lawless dance they win their way,
Still seeming more and more
To swell as we survey.

They rush and roar, they whirl and leap,
Not wilder drives the wintry storm;
Yet a strong law they keep,
Strange powers their course inform.

Even so the mighty skyborn stream,
Its living waters from above
All marred and broken seem,
No union and no love.

Yet in dim caves they softly blend
In dreams of mortals unespied:
One is their awful end,
One their unfailing Guide.

FELICIA DOROTHEA (BROWNE) HEMANS (1793–1835)

A DIRGE

Calm on the bosom of thy God,
Fair spirit, rest thee now!
E'en while with ours thy footsteps trod
His seal was on thy brow.

Dust, to its narrow house beneath!
Soul, to its place on high!
They that have seen thy look in death
No more may fear to die.

THE HOMES OF ENGLAND

The stately Homes of England,
How beautiful they stand!
Amidst their tall ancestral trees,
O'er all the pleasant land;
The deer across their greensward bound
Through shade and sunny gleam,
And the swan glides past them with the sound
Of some rejoicing stream.

The merry Homes of England!
Around their hearths by night,
What gladsome looks of household love
Meet in the ruddy light.
There woman's voice flows forth in song,
Or childish tale is told;
Or lips move tunefully along
Some glorious page of old.

The blessèd Homes of England!
How softly on their bowers
Is laid the holy quietness
That breathes from Sabbath hours!
Solemn, yet sweet, the church-bell's chime
Floats through their woods at morn;
All other sounds, in that still time,
Of breeze and leaf are born.

The cottage Homes of England!
By thousands on her plains,
They are smiling o'er the silvery brooks,
And round the hamlet-fanes.
Through glowing orchards forth they peep,
Each from its nook of leaves;
And fearless there the lowly sleep,
As the bird beneath their eaves.

The free, fair Homes of England!
Long, long in hut and hall,
May hearts of native proof be reared
To guard each hallowed wall!

And green forever be the groves,
And bright the flowery sod,
Where first the child's glad spirit loves
Its country and its God!

THE LANDING OF THE PILGRIM FATHERS IN NEW ENGLAND

The breaking waves dashed high
  On a stern and rock-bound coast,
And the woods against a stormy sky
  Their giant branches tossed;

And the heavy night hung dark
  The hills and waters o'er,
When a band of exiles moored their bark
  On the wild New England shore.

Not as the conqueror comes,
  They, the true-hearted, came;
Not with the roll of the stirring drums,
  And the trumpet that sings of fame:

Not as the flying come,
  In silence and in fear; —
They shook the depths of the desert gloom
  With their hymns of lofty cheer.

Amidst the storm they sang,
  And the stars heard, and the sea;
And the sounding aisles of the dim woods rang
  To the anthem of the free.

The ocean eagle soared
  From his nest by the white wave's foam,
And the rocking pines of the forest roared, —
  This was their welcome home.

There were men with hoary hair
  Amidst that pilgrim-band:
Why had *they* come to wither there,
  Away from their childhood's land?

There was woman's fearless eye,
  Lit by her deep love's truth;
There was manhood's brow serenely high,
  And the fiery heart of youth.

What sought they thus afar?
  Bright jewels of the mine?
The wealth of seas, the spoils of war? —
  They sought a faith's pure shrine!

Ay, call it holy ground,
  The soil where first they trod;
They have left unstained what there they found, —
  Freedom to worship God.

JOHN KEATS (1795–1821)

ODE TO A NIGHTINGALE

My heart aches, and a drowsy numbness pains
  My sense, as though of hemlock I had drunk,
Or emptied some dull opiate to the drains
  One minute past, and Lethe-wards had sunk:
'Tis not through envy of thy happy lot,
  But being too happy in thine happiness, —
    That thou, light-wingèd Dryad of the trees,
        In some melodious plot
  Of beechen green, and shadows numberless,
    Singest of summer in full-throated ease.

O for a draught of vintage! that hath been
  Cool'd a long age in the deep-delvèd earth,
Tasting of Flora and the country green,
  Dance, and Provençal song, and sunburnt mirth!
O for a beaker full of the warm South,
  Full of the true, the blushful Hippocrene,
    With beaded bubbles winking at the brim,
        And purple-stainèd mouth;
  That I might drink, and leave the world unseen,
    And with thee fade away into the forest dim:

Fade far away, dissolve, and quite forget,
  What thou among the leaves hast never known,
The weariness, the fever, and the fret
  Here, where men sit and hear each other groan;
Where palsy shakes a few, sad, last grey hairs,
  Where youth grows pale, and spectre-thin, and dies;
    Where but to think is to be full of sorrow
        And leaden-eyed despairs,
  Where Beauty cannot keep her lustrous eyes,
    Or new Love pine at them beyond to-morrow.

Away! away! for I will fly to thee,
  Not charioted by Bacchus and his pards,
But on the viewless wings of Poesy,
  Though the dull brain perplexes and retards:
Already with thee! tender is the night,
  And haply the Queen-Moon is on her throne,
    Cluster'd around by all her starry Fays;
        But here there is no light,
  Save what from heaven is with the breezes blown
    Through verdurous glooms and winding mossy ways.

I cannot see what flowers are at my feet,
  Nor what soft incense hangs upon the boughs,
But, in embalmèd darkness, guess each sweet
  Wherewith the seasonable month endows

The grass, the thicket, and the fruit-tree wild;
White hawthorn, and the pastoral eglantine;
Fast fading violets cover'd up in leaves;
And mid-May's eldest child,
The coming musk-rose, full of dewy wine,
The murmurous haunt of flies on summer eves.

Darkling I listen; and, for many a time
I have been half in love with easeful Death,
Call'd him soft names in many a musèd rhyme,
To take into the air my quiet breath;
Now more than ever seems it rich to die,
To cease upon the midnight with no pain,
While thou art pouring forth thy soul abroad
In such an ecstasy!
Still wouldst thou sing, and I have ears in vain —
To thy high requiem become a sod.

Thou wast not born for death, immortal Bird!
No hungry generations tread thee down;
The voice I hear this passing night was heard
In ancient days by emperor and clown:
Perhaps the self-same song that found a path
Through the sad heart of Ruth, when, sick for home,
She stood in tears amid the alien corn;
The same that oft-times hath
Charm'd magic casements, opening on the foam
Of perilous seas, in faery lands forlorn.

Forlorn! the very word is like a bell
To toll me back from thee to my sole self!
Adieu! the fancy cannot cheat so well
As she is fam'd to do, deceiving elf.
Adieu! adieu! thy plaintive anthem fades
Past the near meadows, over the still stream,
Up the hill-side; and now 'tis buried deep
In the next valley-glades:
Was it a vision, or a waking dream?
Fled is that music: — Do I wake or sleep?

ODE ON A GRECIAN URN

Thou still unravish'd bride of quietness,
Thou foster-child of silence and slow time,
Sylvan historian, who canst thus express
A flowery tale more sweetly than our rhyme:
What leaf-fring'd legend haunts about thy shape
Of deities or mortals, or of both,
In Tempe or the dales of Arcady?
What men or gods are these? What maidens loth?
What mad pursuit? What struggle to escape?
What pipes and timbrels? What wild ecstasy?

Heard melodies are sweet, but those unheard
Are sweeter; therefore, ye soft pipes, play on;
Not to the sensual ear, but, more endear'd,
Pipe to the spirit ditties of no tone:
Fair youth, beneath the trees, thou canst not leave
Thy song, nor ever can those trees be bare;
Bold Lover, never, never canst thou kiss,
Though winning near the goal — yet, do not grieve;
She cannot fade, though thou hast not thy bliss,
Forever wilt thou love, and she be fair!

Ah, happy, happy boughs! that cannot shed
Your leaves, nor ever bid the Spring adieu:
And, happy melodist, unwearied,
Forever piping songs forever new;
More happy love! more happy, happy love!
Forever warm and still to be enjoy'd,
Forever panting, and forever young;
All breathing human passion far above,
That leaves a heart high-sorrowful and cloy'd,
A burning forehead, and a parching tongue.

Who are these coming to the sacrifice?
To what green altar, O mysterious priest,
Lead'st thou that heifer lowing at the skies,
And all her silken flanks with garlands drest?
What little town by river or sea shore,
Or mountain-built with peaceful citadel,
Is emptied of this folk, this pious morn?
And, little town, thy streets for evermore
Will silent be; and not a soul to tell
Why thou art desolate, can e'er return.

O Attic shape! Fair attitude! with brede
Of marble men and maidens overwrought,
With forest branches and the trodden weed;
Thou, silent form, dost tease us out of thought
As doth eternity: Cold Pastoral!
When old age shall this generation waste,
Thou shalt remain, in midst of other woe
Than ours, a friend to man, to whom thou say'st,
"Beauty is truth, truth beauty," — that is all,
Ye know on earth, and all ye need to know.

TO AUTUMN

Season of mists and mellow fruitfulness,
Close bosom-friend of the maturing sun;
Conspiring with him how to load and bless
With fruit the vines that round the thatch-eaves run;
To bend with apples the moss'd cottage-trees,
And fill all fruit with ripeness to the core;

To swell the gourd, and plump the hazel shells
With a sweet kernel; to set budding more,
And still more, later flowers for the bees,
Until they think warm days will never cease,
For Summer has o'er-brimm'd their clammy cells.

Who hath not seen thee oft amid thy store?
Sometimes whoever seeks abroad may find
Thee sitting careless on a granary floor,
Thy hair soft-lifted by the winnowing wind;
Or on a half-reap'd furrow sound asleep,
Drows'd with the fume of poppies, while thy hook
Spares the next swath and all its twinèd flowers:
And sometimes like a gleaner thou dost keep
Steady thy laden head across a brook;
Or by a cider-press, with patient look,
Thou watchest the last oozings hours by hours.

Where are the songs of Spring? Ay, where are they?
Think not of them, thou hast thy music too, —
While barrèd clouds bloom the soft-dying day,
And touch the stubble-plains with rosy hue;
Then in a wailful choir the small gnats mourn
Among the river sallows, borne aloft
Or sinking as the light wind lives or dies;
And full-grown lambs loud bleat from hilly bourn;
Hedge-crickets sing; and now with treble soft
The red-breast whistles from a garden-croft;
And gathering swallows twitter in the skies.

ODE

Bards of Passion and of Mirth,
Ye have left your souls on earth!
Have ye souls in heaven too,
Double-lived in regions new?
Yes, and those of heaven commune
With the spheres of sun and moon;
With the noise of fountains wond'rous,
And the parle of voices thund'rous;
With the whisper of heaven's trees
And one another, in soft ease
Seated on Elysian lawns
Brows'd by none but Dian's fawns;
Underneath large bluebells tented,
Where the daisies are rose-scented,
And the rose herself has got
Perfume which on earth is not;
Where the nightingale doth sing
Not a senseless, tranced thing,
But divine melodious truth;
Philosophic numbers smooth;
Tales and golden histories
Of heaven and its mysteries.

Thus ye live on high, and then
On the earth ye live again;
And the souls ye left behind you
Teach us, here, the way to find you
Where your other souls are joying,
Never slumber'd, never cloying.
Here, your earth-born souls still speak
To mortals, of their little week;
Of their sorrows and delights;
Of their passions and their spites;
Of their glory and their shame;
What doth strengthen and what maim.
Thus ye teach us, every day,
Wisdom, though fled far away.

Bards of Passion and of Mirth,
Ye have left your souls on earth
Ye have souls in heaven too,
Double-lived in regions new!

LINES ON THE MERMAID TAVERN

Souls of Poets dead and gone,
What Elysium have ye known,
Happy field or mossy cavern,
Choicer than the Mermaid Tavern
Have ye tippled drink more fine
Than mine host's Canary wine?
Or are fruits of Paradise
Sweeter than those dainty pies
Of venison? O generous food!
Drest as though bold Robin Hood
Would, with his maid Marian,
Sup and bowse from horn and can.

I have heard that on a day
Mine host's sign-board flew away,
Nobody knew whither, till
An astrologer's old quill
To a sheepskin gave the story,
Said he saw you in your glory,
Underneath a new old-sign
Sipping beverage divine,
And pledging with contented smack
The Mermaid in the Zodiac.

Souls of Poets dead and gone,
What Elysium have ye known,
Happy field or mossy cavern,
Choicer than the Mermaid Tavern?

LA BELLE DAME SANS MERCI

O what can ail thee, knight-at-arms,
  Alone and palely loitering?
The sedge has wither'd from the lake,
  And no birds sing.

O what can ail thee, knight-at-arms,
  So haggard and so woe-begone?
The squirrel's granary is full,
  And the harvest's done.

I see a lily on thy brow
  With anguish moist and fever dew,
And on thy cheeks a fading rose
  Fast withereth too.

"I met a lady in the meads,
  Full beautiful — a faery's child;
Her hair was long, her foot was light,
  And her eyes were wild.

"I made a garland for her head,
  And bracelets too, and fragrant zone;
She look'd at me as she did love,
  And made sweet moan.

"I set her on my pacing steed,
  And nothing else saw all day long,
For sideways would she lean, and sing
  A faery's song.

"She found me roots of relish sweet,
  And honey wild, and manna-dew,
And sure in language strange she said —
  'I love thee true.'

"She took me to her elfin grot,
  And there she wept and sigh'd full sore,
And there I shut her wild, wild eyes,
  With kisses four.

"And there she lullèd me asleep,
  And there I dream'd — ah! woe betide! —
The latest dream I ever dream'd
  On the cold hill's side.

"I saw pale kings and princes too,
  Pale warriors, death-pale were they all;
They cried — 'La Belle Dame sans Merci
  Hath thee in thrall!'

"I saw their starved lips in the gloom,
  With horrid warning gapèd wide;
And I awoke, and found me here
  On the cold hill's side.

"And this is why I sojourn here,
  Alone and palely loitering,
Though the sedge is wither'd from the lake,
  And no birds sing."

SONNETS

THE GRASSHOPPER AND THE CRICKET

The poetry of earth is never dead:
  When all the birds are faint with the hot sun,
  And hide in cooling trees, a voice will run
From hedge to hedge about the new-mown mead;
That is the Grasshopper's — he takes the lead
  In summer luxury, — he has never done
  With his delights; for when tired out with fun
He rests at ease beneath some pleasant weed.
The poetry of earth is ceasing never:
  On a lone winter evening, when the frost
    Has wrought a silence, from the stove there shrills
The Cricket's song, in warmth increasing ever,
  And seems to one in drowsiness half lost,
    The Grasshopper's among some grassy hills.

ON FIRST LOOKING INTO CHAPMAN'S HOMER

Much have I travell'd in the realms of gold,
  And many goodly states and kingdoms seen;
  Round many western islands have I been
Which bards in fealty to Apollo hold.
Oft of one wide expanse had I been told
  That deep-brow'd Homer ruled as his demesne;
  Yet did I never breathe its pure serene
Till I heard Chapman speak out loud and bold:
Then felt I like some watcher of the skies
  When a new planet swims into his ken;
Or like stout Cortez when with eagle eyes
  He star'd at the Pacific — and all his men
Look'd at each other with a wild surmise —
  Silent, upon a peak in Darien.

TO SLEEP

O soft embalmer of the still midnight!
  Shutting with careful fingers and benign
Our gloom-pleased eyes, embower'd from the light,
  Enshaded in forgetfulness divine;
O soothest Sleep! if so it please thee, close,
  In midst of this thine hymn, my willing eyes,
Or wait the amen, ere thy poppy throws
  Around my bed its lulling charities;
  Then save me, or the passèd day will shine
Upon my pillow, breeding many woes;
Save me from curious conscience, that still lords
  Its strength for darkness, burrowing like a mole;
Turn the key deftly in the oilèd wards,
  And seal the hushèd casket of my soul.

ON THE SEA

It keeps eternal whisperings around
Desolate shores, and with its mighty swell
Gluts twice ten thousand caverns, till the spell
Of Hecate leaves them their old shadowy sound.
Often 'tis in such gentle temper found
That scarcely will the very smallest shell
Be mov'd for days from whence it sometime fell,
When last the winds of heaven were unbound.
Oh, ye, who have your eye-balls vex'd and tir'd,
Feast them upon the wideness of the sea;
O, ye, whose ears are dinn'd with uproar rude,
Or fed too much with cloying melody, —
Sit ye near some old cavern's mouth, and brood
Until ye start, as if the sea-nymphs quir'd!

WHEN I HAVE FEARS

When I have fears that I may cease to be
Before my pen has glean'd my teeming brain,
Before high pilèd books, in charact'ry,
Hold like rich garners the full-ripen'd grain;
When I behold, upon the night's starr'd face,
Huge cloudy symbols of a high romance,
And think that I may never live to trace
Their shadows, with the magic hand of chance;
And when I feel, fair creature of an hour!
That I shall never look upon thee more,
Never have relish in the faery power
Of unreflecting love! — then on the shore
Of the wide world I stand alone, and think
Till love and fame to nothingness do sink.

BRIGHT STAR!

Bright star! would I were steadfast as thou art —
Not in lone splendour hung aloft the night,
And watching, with eternal lids apart,
Like Nature's patient sleepless Eremite,
The moving waters at their priestlike task
Of pure ablution round earth's human shores,
Or gazing on the new soft fallen mask
Of snow upon the mountains and the moors —
No — yet still steadfast, still unchangeable,
Pillow'd upon my fair love's ripening breast,
To feel forever its soft fall and swell,
Awake forever in a sweet unrest,
Still, still to hear her tender-taken breath,
And so live ever — or else swoon to death.

ENDYMION

From BOOK I

A thing of beauty is a joy forever:
Its loveliness increases; it will never
Pass into nothingness; but still will keep
A bower quiet for us, and a sleep
Full of sweet dreams, and health, and quiet breathing.
Therefore, on every morrow, are we wreathing
A flowery band to bind us to the earth,
Spite of despondence, of the inhuman dearth
Of noble natures, of the gloomy days,
Of all the unhealthy and o'er-darkened ways
Made for our searching: yes, in spite of all,
Some shape of beauty moves away the pall
From our dark spirits. Such the sun, the moon,
Trees old and young, sprouting a shady boon
For simple sheep; and such are daffodils
With the green world they live in; and clear rills
That for themselves a cooling covert make
'Gainst the hot season; the mid forest brake,
Rich with a sprinkling of fair musk-rose blooms:
And such too is the grandeur of the dooms
We have imagined for the mighty dead;
All lovely tales that we have heard or read:
An endless fountain of immortal drink,
Pouring unto us from the heaven's brink.

Nor do we merely feel these essences
For one short hour; no, even as the trees
That whisper round a temple become soon
Dear as the temple's self, so does the moon,
The passion poesy, glories infinite,
Haunt us till they become a cheering light
Unto our souls, and bound to us so fast,
That, whether there be shine, or gloom o'ercast,
They alway must be with us, or we die.

* * * * * * * *

"This river does not see the naked sky,
Till it begins to progress silverly
Around the western border of the wood,
Whence, from a certain spot, its winding flood
Seems at the distance like a crescent moon:
And in that nook, the very pride of June,
Had I been us'd to pass my weary eyes;
The rather for the sun unwilling leaves
So dear a picture of his sovereign power,
And I could witness his most kingly hour,
When he doth tighten up the golden reins,
And paces leisurely down amber plains
His snorting four. Now when his chariot last
Its beams against the zodiac-lion cast,
There blossom'd suddenly a magic bed
Of sacred ditamy, and poppies red:

At which I wondered greatly, knowing well
That but one night had wrought this flowery spell;
And, sitting down close by, began to muse
What it might mean.

* * * * * * * * *

And lo! from opening clouds, I saw emerge
The loveliest moon that ever silver'd o'er
A shell for Neptune's goblet: she did soar
So passionately bright, my dazzled soul
Commingling with her argent spheres did roll
Through clear and cloudy, even when she went
At last into a dark and vapoury tent —
Whereat, methought, the lidless-eyèd train
Of planets all were in the blue again.
To commune with those orbs, once more I rais'd
My sight right upward: but it was quite dazed
By a bright something, sailing down apace,
Making me quickly veil my eyes and face:
Again I look'd, and, O ye deities,
Who from Olympus watch our destinies!
Whence that completed form of all completeness?
Whence came that high perfection of all sweetness?
Speak, stubborn earth, and tell me where, O where
Hast thou a symbol of her golden hair?
Not oat-sheaves drooping in the western sun;
Not — thy soft hand, fair sister! let me shun
Such follying before thee — yet she had,
Indeed, locks bright enough to make me mad;
And they were simply gordian'd up and braided,
Leaving, in naked comeliness, unshaded,
Her pearl round ears, white neck, and orbèd brow;
The which were blended in, I know not how,
With such a paradise of lips and eyes,
Blush-tinted cheeks, half smiles, and faintest sighs,
That, when I think thereon, my spirit clings
And plays about its fancy, till the stings
Of human neighbourhood envenom all.
Unto what awful power shall I call?
To what high fane? — Ah! see her hovering feet,
More bluely vein'd, more soft, more whitely sweet
Than those of sea-born Venus, when she rose
From out her cradle shell. The wind out-blows
Her scarf into a fluttering pavilion;
'Tis blue, and over-spangled with a million
Of little eyes, as though thou wert to shed
Over the darkest, lushest bluebell bed,
Handfuls of daisies." — "Endymion, how strange!
Dream within dream!" — "She took an airy range,
And then, towards me, like a very maid,
Came blushing, waning, willing, and afraid,
And press'd me by the hand: Ah! 'twas too much;
Methought I fainted at the charmèd touch,
Yet held my recollection, even as one
Who dives three fathoms where the waters run
Gurgling in beds of coral: for anon,
I felt upmounted in that region
Where falling stars dart their artillery forth,
And eagles struggle with the buffeting north
That balances the heavy meteor-stone; —
Felt too, I was not fearful, nor alone,
But lapp'd and lull'd along the dangerous sky.
Soon, as it seem'd, we left our journeying high,
And straightway into frightful eddies swoop'd;
Such as ay muster where grey time has scoop'd
Huge dens and caverns in a mountain's side:
There hollow sounds arous'd me, and I sigh'd
To faint once more by looking on my bliss —
I was distracted; madly did I kiss
The wooing arms which held me, and did give
My eyes at once to death: but 'twas to live,
To take in draughts of life from the gold fount
Of kind and passionate looks; to count, and count
The moments, by some greedy help that seem'd
A second self, that each might be redeem'd
And plunder'd of its load of blessedness.
Ah, desperate mortal! I e'en dar'd to press
Her very cheek against my crownèd lip,
And, at that moment, felt my body dip
Into a warmer air: a moment more,
Our feet were soft in flowers. There was store
Of newest joys upon that alp. Sometimes
A scent of violets, and blossoming limes,
Loiter'd around us; then of honey cells,
Made delicate from all white-flower bells;
And once, above the edges of our nest,
An arch face peep'd, — an Oread as I guess'd.

HYPERION

A FRAGMENT

From Book I

Deep in the shady sadness of a vale
Far sunken from the healthy breath of morn,
Far from the fiery noon, and eve's one star,
Sat gray-hair'd Saturn, quiet as a stone,
Still as the silence round about his lair;
Forest on forest hung about his head
Like cloud on cloud. No stir of air was there,
Not so much life as on a summer's day
Robs not one light seed from the feather'd grass,
But where the dead leaf fell, there did it rest.
A stream went voiceless by, still deadened more
By reason of his fallen divinity

Spreading a shade: the Naiad 'mid her reeds
Press'd her cold finger closer to her lips.

Along the margin-sand large foot-marks went,
No further than to where his feet had stray'd,
And slept there since. Upon the sodden ground
His old right hand lay nerveless, listless, dead,
Unsceptred; and his realmless eyes were closed;
While his bow'd head seem'd list'ning to the Earth,
His ancient mother, for some comfort yet.

It seem'd no force could wake him from his place;
But there came one, who with a kindred hand
Touch'd his wide shoulders, after bending low
With reverence, though to one who knew it not.
She was a Goddess of the infant world;
By her in stature the tall Amazon
Had stood a pigmy's height: she would have ta'en
Achilles by the hair and bent his neck;
Or with a finger stay'd Ixion's wheel.
Her face was large as that of Memphian sphinx,
Pedestal'd haply in a palace court,
When sages look'd to Egypt for their lore.
But oh! how unlike marble was that face:
How beautiful, if sorrow had not made
Sorrow more beautiful than Beauty's self.
There was a listening fear in her regard,
As if calamity had but begun;
As if the vanward clouds of evil days
Had spent their malice, and the sullen rear
Was with its stored thunder labouring up.
One hand she press'd upon that aching spot
Where beats the human heart, as if just there,
Though an immortal, she felt cruel pain:
The other upon Saturn's bended neck
She laid, and to the level of his ear
Leaning with parted lips, some words she spake
In solemn tenor and deep organ tone:
Some mourning words, which in our feeble tongue
Would come in these like accents; O how frail
To that large utterance of the early Gods!
"Saturn, look up! — though wherefore, poor old King?
I have no comfort for thee, no, not one:
I cannot say, 'O wherefore sleepest thou?'
For heaven is parted from thee, and the earth
Knows thee not, thus afflicted, for a God;
And ocean too, with all its solemn noise,
Has from thy sceptre pass'd; and all the air
Is emptied of thine hoary majesty.
Thy thunder, conscious of the new command,
Rumbles reluctant o'er our fallen house;
And thy sharp lightning in unpractised hands
Scorches and burns our once serene domain.
O aching time! O moments big as years!
All as ye pass swell out the monstrous truth,
And press it so upon our weary griefs
That unbelief has not a space to breathe.
Saturn, sleep on: — O thoughtless, why did I
Thus violate thy slumbrous solitude?
Why should I ope thy melancholy eyes?
Saturn, sleep on! while at thy feet I weep."

As when, upon a trancèd summer night,
Those green-rob'd senators of mighty woods,
Tall oaks, branch-charmèd by the earnest stars,
Dream, and so dream all night without a stir,
Save from one gradual solitary gust
Which comes upon the silence, and dies off,
As if the ebbing air had but one wave;
So came these words and went; the while in tears
She touch'd her fair large forehead to the ground,
Just where her falling hair might be outspread
A soft and silken mat for Saturn's feet.
One moon, with alteration slow, had shed
Her silver seasons four upon the night,
And still these two were postured motionless,
Like natural sculpture in cathedral cavern;
The frozen God still couchant on the earth,
And the sad Goddess weeping at his feet:
Until at length old Saturn lifted up
His faded eyes, and saw his kingdom gone,
And all the gloom and sorrow of the place,
And that fair kneeling Goddess; and then spake,
As with a palsied tongue, and while his beard
Shook horrid with such aspen-malady:
"O tender spouse of gold Hyperion,
Thea, I feel thee ere I see thy face;
Look up, and let me see our doom in it;
Look up, and tell me if this feeble shape
Is Saturn's; tell me, if thou hear'st the voice
Of Saturn; tell me, if this wrinkling brow,
Naked and bare of its great diadem,
Peers like the front of Saturn. Who had power
To make me desolate? whence came the strength?
How was it nurtur'd to such bursting forth,
While Fate seem'd strangled in my nervous grasp?
But it is so; and I am smother'd up,
And buried from all godlike exercise
Of influence benign on planets pale,
Of admonitions to the winds and seas,
Of peaceful sway above man's harvesting,
And all those acts which Deity supreme
Doth ease its heart of love in. — I am gone
Away from my own bosom: I have left
My strong identity, my real self,
Somewhere between the throne, and where I sit,
Here on this spot of earth. Search, Thea, search!
Open thine eyes eterne, and sphere them round
Upon all space: space starr'd, and lorn of light;

Space region'd with life-air; and barren void;
Spaces of fire, and all the yawn of hell. —
Search, Thea, search! and tell me, if thou seest
A certain shape or shadow, making way
With wings or chariot fierce to repossess
A heaven he lost erewhile: it must — it must
Be of ripe progress — Saturn must be King.
Yes, there must be a golden victory;
There must be Gods thrown down, and trumpets blown
Of triumph calm, and hymns of festival
Upon the gold clouds metropolitan,
Voices of soft proclaim, and silver stir
Of strings in hollow shells; and there shall be
Beautiful things made new, for the surprise
Of the sky-children; I will give command:
Thea! Thea! Thea! where is Saturn?"

This passion lifted him upon his feet,
And made his hands to struggle in the air,
His Druid locks to shake and ooze with sweat,
His eyes to fever out, his voice to cease.
He stood, and heard not Thea's sobbing deep;
A little time, and then again he snatch'd
Utterance thus. — "But cannot I create?
Cannot I form? Cannot I fashion forth
Another world, another universe,
To overbear and crumble this to naught?
Where is another chaos? Where?" — That word
Found way unto Olympus, and made quake
The rebel three. — Thea was startled up,
And in her bearing was a sort of hope.

* * * * * * * *

"O brightest of my children dear, earth-born
And sky-engendered, Son of Mysteries
All unrevealed even to the powers
Which met at thy creating; at whose joys
And palpitations sweet, and pleasures soft,
I, Cœlus, wonder, how they came and whence;
And at the fruits thereof what shapes they be,
Distinct, and visible; symbols divine,
Manifestations of that beauteous life
Diffus'd unseen throughout eternal space:
Of these new-form'd art thou, O brightest child!
Of these, thy brethren and the Goddesses!
There is sad feud among ye, and rebellion
Of son against his sire. I saw him fall,
I saw my first-born tumbled from his throne!
To me his arms were spread, to me his voice
Found way from forth the thunders round his head!
Pale wox I, and in vapours hid my face.
Art thou, too, near such doom? vague fear there is:
For I have seen my sons most unlike Gods.
Divine ye were created, and divine
In sad demeanour, solemn, undisturb'd,
Unruffled, like high Gods, ye liv'd and ruled:
Now I behold in you fear, hope, and wrath;
Actions of rage and passion; even as
I see them, on the mortal world beneath,
In men who die. — This is the grief, O Son!
Sad sign of ruin, sudden dismay, and fall!
Yet do thou strive; as thou art capable,
As thou canst move about, an evident God;
And canst oppose to each malignant hour
Ethereal presence: — I am but a voice;
My life is but the life of winds and tides,
No more than winds and tides can I avail: —
But thou canst. — Be thou therefore in the van
Of circumstance; yea, seize the arrow's barb
Before the tense string murmur. — To the earth!
For there thou wilt find Saturn, and his woes.
Meantime I will keep watch on thy bright sun,
And of thy seasons be a careful nurse." —
Ere half this region-whisper had come down,
Hyperion arose, and on the stars
Lifted his curvèd lids, and kept them wide
Until it ceas'd; and still he kept them wide:
And still they were the same bright, patient stars.
Then with a slow incline of his broad breast,
Like to a diver in the pearly seas,
Forward he stoop'd over the airy shore,
And plung'd all noiseless into the deep night.

LAMIA

From PART I

Over the solitary hills he fared,
Thoughtless at first, but ere eve's star appear'd
His phantasy was lost, where reason fades,
In the calmed twilight of Platonic shades.
Lamia beheld him coming near, more near —
Close to her passing, in indifference drear,
His silent sandals swept the mossy green;
So neighboured to him, and yet so unseen
She stood: he pass'd, shut up in mysteries,
His mind wrapp'd like his mantle, while her eyes
Follow'd his steps, and her neck regal white
Turn'd — syllabling thus, "Ah, Lycius bright,
And will you leave me on the hills alone?
Lycius, look back! and be some pity shown."
He did; not with cold wonder fearingly,
But Orpheus-like at an Eurydice;
For so delicious were the words she sung,
It seem'd he had lov'd them a whole summer long:
And soon his eyes had drunk her beauty up,
Leaving no drop in the bewildering cup,
And still the cup was full, — while he, afraid
Lest she should vanish ere his lip had paid
Due adoration, thus began to adore;

Her soft look growing coy, she saw his chain so sure:
"Leave thee alone! Look back! Ah, Goddess, see
Whether my eyes can ever turn from thee!
For pity do not this sad heart belie —
Even as thou vanishest so I shall die.
Stay! though a Naiad of the rivers, stay!
To thy far wishes will thy streams obey:
Stay! though the greenest woods be thy domain,
Alone they can drink up the morning rain:
Though a descended Pleiad, will not one
Of thine harmonious sisters keep in tune
Thy spheres, and as thy silver proxy shine?
So sweetly to these ravished ears of mine
Came thy sweet greeting, that if thou shouldst fade,
Thy memory will waste me to a shade: —
For pity do not melt!"

* * * * * * * *

From PART II

By her glad Lycius sitting, in chief place,
Scarce saw in all the room another face,
Till, checking his love trance, a cup he took
Full brimmed, and opposite sent forth a look
'Cross the broad table, to beseech a glance
From his old teacher's wrinkled countenance,
And pledge him. The bald-head philosopher
Had fix'd his eye, without a twinkle or stir
Full on the alarmèd beauty of the bride,
Brow-beating her fair form, and troubling her sweet pride.
Lycius then press'd her hand, with devout touch,
As pale it lay upon the rosy couch:
'Twas icy, and the cold ran through his veins;
Then sudden it grew hot, and all the pains
Of an unnatural heat shot to his heart.
"Lamia, what means this? Wherefore dost thou start?
Know'st thou that man?" Poor Lamia answer'd not.
He gaz'd into her eyes, and not a jot
Own'd they the lovelorn piteous appeal:
More, more he gaz'd: his human senses reel:
Some hungry spell that loveliness absorbs;
There was no recognition in those orbs.
"Lamia!" he cried — and no soft-toned reply.
The many heard, and the loud revelry
Grew hush; the stately music no more breathes;
The myrtle sicken'd in a thousand wreaths.
By faint degrees, voice, lute, and pleasure ceas'd;
A deadly silence step by step increas'd,
Until it seem'd a horrid presence there,
And not a man but felt the terror in his hair.
"Lamia!" he shriek'd; and nothing but the shriek
With its sad echo did the silence break.

THE EVE OF ST. AGNES

St. Agnes' Eve — Ah, bitter chill it was!
The owl, for all his feathers, was a-cold;
The hare limp'd trembling through the frozen grass,
And silent was the flock in woolly fold:
Numb were the Beadsman's fingers, while he told
His rosary, and while his frosted breath,
Like pious incense from a censer old,
Seem'd taking flight for heaven, without a death,
Past the sweet Virgin's picture, while his prayer he saith.

His prayer he saith, this patient, holy man;
Then takes his lamp, and riseth from his knees,
And back returneth, meagre, barefoot, wan,
Along the chapel aisle by slow degrees:
The sculptured dead, on each side, seem to freeze,
Emprison'd in black, purgatorial rails:
Knights, ladies, praying in dumb orat'ries,
He passeth by; and his weak spirit fails
To think how they may ache in icy hoods and mails.

Northward he turneth through a little door,
And scarce three steps, ere Music's golden tongue
Flatter'd to tears this agèd man and poor;
But no — already had his deathbell rung;
The joys of all his life were said and sung:
His was harsh penance on St. Agnes' Eve:
Another way he went, and soon among
Rough ashes sat he for his soul's reprieve,
And all night kept awake, for sinners' sake to grieve.

That ancient Beadsman heard the prelude soft;
And so it chanc'd, for many a door was wide,
From hurry to and fro. Soon, up aloft,
The silver, snarling trumpets 'gan to chide:
The level chambers, ready with their pride,
Were glowing to receive a thousand guests:
The carvèd angels, ever eager-eyed,
Star'd, where upon their heads the cornice rests,
With hair blown back, and wings put cross-wise on their breasts.

At length burst in the argent revelry,
With plume, tiara, and all rich array,
Numerous as shadows haunting fairily
The brain, new stuff'd, in youth, with triumphs gay

Of old romance. These let us wish away,
And turn, sole-thoughted, to one Lady there,
Whose heart had brooded, all that wintry day,
On love, and winged St. Agnes' saintly care,
As she had heard old dames full many times declare.

They told her how, upon St. Agnes' Eve,
Young virgins might have visions of delight,
And soft adorings from their loves receive
Upon the honeyed middle of the night,
If ceremonies due they did aright;
As, supperless to bed they must retire,
And couch supine their beauties, lily white;
Nor look behind, nor sideways, but require
Of Heaven with upward eyes for all that they desire.

Full of this whim was thoughtful Madeline:
The music, yearning like a God in pain,
She scarcely heard: her maiden eyes divine,
Fix'd on the floor, saw many a sweeping train
Pass by — she heeded not at all: in vain
Came many a tiptoe, amorous cavalier,
And back retir'd; not cool'd by high disdain,
But she saw not: her heart was otherwhere:
She sigh'd for Agnes' dreams, the sweetest of the year.

She danc'd along with vague, regardless eyes,
Anxious her lips, her breathing quick and short:
The hallowed hour was near at hand: she sighs
Amid the timbrels, and the thronged resort
Of whisperers in anger, or in sport;
'Mid looks of love, defiance, hate, and scorn,
Hoodwink'd with fairy fancy; all amort,
Save to St. Agnes and her lambs unshorn,
And all the bliss to be before to-morrow morn.

So, purposing each moment to retire,
She linger'd still. Meantime, across the moors,
Had come young Porphyro, with heart on fire
For Madeline. Beside the portal doors,
Buttress'd from moonlight, stands he, and implores
All saints to give him sight of Madeline,
But for one moment in the tedious hours,
That he might gaze and worship all unseen;
Perchance speak, kneel, touch, kiss — in sooth such things have been.

He ventures in: let no buzzed whisper tell:
All eyes be muffled, or a hundred swords
Will storm his heart, Love's fev'rous citadel:
For him, those chambers held barbarian hordes,
Hyena foemen, and hot-blooded lords,
Whose very dogs would execrations howl
Against his lineage: not one breast affords
Him any mercy, in that mansion foul,
Save one old beldame, weak in body and in soul.

Ah, happy chance! the aged creature came,
Shuffling along with ivory-headed wand,
To where he stood, hid from the torch's flame,
Behind a broad hall-pillar, far beyond
The sound of merriment and chorus bland:
He startled her; but soon she knew his face,
And grasp'd his fingers in her palsied hand,
Saying, "Mercy, Porphyro! hie thee from this place;
They are all here to-night, the whole blood-thirsty race!

"Get hence! get hence! there's dwarfish Hildebrand;
He had a fever late, and in the fit
He cursèd thee and thine, both house and land:
Then there's that old Lord Maurice, not a whit
More tame for his grey hairs — Alas me! flit!
Flit like a ghost away." — "Ah, Gossip dear,
We're safe enough; here in this armchair sit,
And tell me how" — "Good Saints! not here, not here;
Follow me, child, or else these stones will be thy bier."

He follow'd through a lowly archèd way,
Brushing the cobwebs with his lofty plume;
And as she mutter'd "Well-a — well-a-day!"
He found him in a little moonlight room,
Pale, lattic'd, chill, and silent as a tomb.
"Now tell me where is Madeline," said he,
"O tell me, Angela, by the holy loom
Which none but secret sisterhood may see,
When they St. Agnes' wool are weaving piously."

"St. Agnes! Ah! it is St. Agnes' Eve —
Yet men will murder upon holy days:
Thou must hold water in a witch's sieve,
And be liege-lord of all the Elves and Fays,
To venture so: it fills me with amaze
To see thee, Porphyro! — St. Agnes' Eve!
God's help! my lady fair the conjurer plays
This very night: good angels her deceive!
But let me laugh awhile, I've mickle time to grieve."

Feebly she laugheth in the languid moon,
While Porphyro upon her face doth look,
Like puzzled urchin on an aged crone
Who keepeth clos'd a wond'rous riddle-book,
As spectacled she sits in chimney nook.

But soon his eyes grew brilliant, when she told
His lady's purpose; and he scarce could brook
Tears, at the thought of those enchantments cold,
And Madeline asleep in lap of legends old.

Sudden a thought came like a full-blown rose,
Flushing his brow, and in his painèd heart
Made purple riot: then doth he propose
A stratagem, that makes the beldame start:
"A cruel man and impious thou art:
Sweet lady, let her pray, and sleep, and dream
Alone with her good angels, far apart
From wicked men like thee. Go, go! — I deem
Thou canst not surely be the same that thou didst seem."

"I will not harm her, by all saints I swear,"
Quoth Porphyro: "O may I ne'er find grace
When my weak voice shall whisper its last prayer,
If one of her soft ringlets I displace,
Or look with ruffian passion in her face:
Good Angela, believe me by these tears;
Or I will, even in a moment's space,
Awake, with horrid shout, my foemen's ears,
And beard them, though they be more fang'd than wolves and bears."

"Ah! why wilt thou affright a feeble soul?
A poor, weak, palsy-stricken, churchyard thing, —
Whose passing-bell may ere the midnight toll;
Whose prayers for thee, each morn and evening,
Were never miss'd." — Thus plaining, doth she bring
A gentler speech from burning Porphyro;
So woeful, and of such deep sorrowing,
That Angela gives promise she will do
Whatever he shall wish, betide her weal or woe.

Which was, to lead him, in close secrecy,
Even to Madeline's chamber, and there hide
Him in a closet, of such privacy
That he might see her beauty unespied,
And win perhaps that night a peerless bride,
While legioned fairies pac'd the coverlet,
And pale enchantment held her sleepy-eyed.
Never on such a night have lovers met,
Since Merlin paid his Demon all the monstrous debt.

"It shall be as thou wishest," said the dame:
"All cates and dainties shall be storèd there
Quickly on this feast-night: by the tambour frame
Her own lute thou wilt see: no time to spare,
For I am slow and feeble, and scarce dare
On such a catering trust my dizzy head.
Wait here, my child, with patience; kneel in prayer
The while. Ah! thou must needs the lady wed,
Or may I never leave my grave among the dead."

So saying, she hobbled off with busy fear.
The lover's endless minutes slowly pass'd;
The dame return'd, and whisper'd in his ear
To follow her; with agèd eyes aghast
From fright of dim espial. Safe at last,
Through many a dusky gallery, they gain
The maiden's chamber, silken, hushed, and chaste;
Where Porphyro took covert, pleas'd amain.
His poor guide hurried back with agues in her brain.

Her falt'ring hand upon the balustrade,
Old Angela was feeling for the stair,
When Madeline, St. Agnes' charmèd maid,
Rose, like a missioned spirit, unaware:
With silver taper's light, and pious care,
She turn'd, and down the agèd gossip led
To a safe level matting. Now prepare,
Young Porphyro, for gazing on that bed;
She comes, she comes again, like ring-dove fray'd and fled.

Out went the taper as she hurried in;
Its little smoke, in pallid moonshine, died:
She closed the door, she panted, all akin
To spirits of the air, and visions wide:
No uttered syllable, or, woe betide!
But to her heart, her heart was voluble,
Paining with eloquence her balmy side;
As though a tongueless nightingale should swell
Her throat in vain, and die, heart-stifled, in her dell.

A casement high and triple-arched there was,
All garlanded with carven imag'ries
Of fruits, and flowers, and bunches of knot-grass,
And diamonded with panes of quaint device,
Innumerable of stains and splendid dyes,
As are the tiger-moth's deep-damasked wings;
And in the midst, 'mong thousand heraldries,
And twilight saints, and dim emblazonings,
A shielded scutcheon blush'd with blood of queens and kings.

Full on this casement shone the wintry moon,
And threw warm gules on Madeline's fair breast,
As down she knelt for heaven's grace and boon;
Rose-bloom fell on her hands, together prest,
And on her silver cross soft amethyst,
And on her hair a glory, like a saint:
She seem'd a splendid angel, newly drest,
Save wings, for heaven: — Porphyro grew faint:
She knelt, so pure a thing, so free from mortal taint.

Anon his heart revives: her vespers done,
Of all its wreathèd pearls her hair she frees;
Unclasps her warmèd jewels one by one;
Loosens her fragrant bodice; by degrees
Her rich attire creeps rustling to her knees:
Half-hidden, like a mermaid in sea-weed,
Pensive awhile she dreams awake, and sees,
In fancy, fair St. Agnes in her bed,
But dares not look behind, or all the charm is fled.

Soon, trembling in her soft and chilly nest,
In sort of wakeful swoon, perplex'd she lay,
Until the poppied warmth of sleep oppress'd
Her soothèd limbs, and soul fatigued away;
Flown, like a thought, until the morrow-day;
Blissfully haven'd both from joy and pain;
Clasp'd like a missal where swart Paynims pray;
Blinded alike from sunshine and from rain,
As though a rose should shut, and be a bud again.

Stol'n to this paradise, and so entranced,
Porphyro gazed upon her empty dress,
And listen'd to her breathing, if it chanc'd
To wake into a slumberous tenderness;
Which when he heard, that minute did he bless,
And breath'd himself: then from the closet crept,
Noiseless as fear in a wide wilderness,
And over the hush'd carpet, silent, stept,
And 'tween the curtains peep'd, where, lo! — how fast she slept.

Then by the bedside, where the faded moon
Made a dim, silver twilight, soft he set
A table, and, half anguish'd, threw thereon
A cloth of woven crimson, gold, and jet: —
O for some drowsy Morphean amulet!
The boisterous, midnight, festive clarion,
The kettle-drum, and far-heard clarionet,
Affray his ears, though but in dying tone: —
The hall door shuts again, and all the noise is gone.

And still she slept an azure-lidded sleep,
In blanchèd linen, smooth, and lavender'd,
While he from forth the closet brought a heap
Of candied apple, quince, and plum, and gourd;
With jellies soother than the creamy curd,
And lucent syrups, tinct with cinnamon;
Manna and dates, in argosy transferr'd
From Fez; and spicèd dainties, every one,
From silken Samarcand to cedared Lebanon.

These delicates he heap'd with glowing hand
On golden dishes and in baskets bright
Of wreathèd silver: sumptuous they stand
In the retirèd quiet of the night,
Filling the chilly room with perfume light. —
"And now, my love, my seraph fair, awake!
Thou art my heaven, and I thine eremite:
Open thine eyes, for meek St. Agnes' sake,
Or I shall drowse beside thee, so my soul doth ache."

Thus whispering, his warm, unnervèd arm
Sank in her pillow. Shaded was her dream
By the dusk curtains: — 'twas a midnight charm
Impossible to melt as icèd stream:
The lustrous salvers in the moonlight gleam;
Broad golden fringe upon the carpet lies:
It seem'd he never, never could redeem
From such a steadfast spell his lady's eyes;
So mus'd awhile, entoil'd in woofèd phantasies.

Awakening up, he took her hollow lute, —
Tumultuous, — and, in chords that tenderest be,
He play'd an ancient ditty, long since mute,
In Provence call'd, "La belle dame sans merci,"
Close to her ear touching the melody; —
Wherewith disturb'd, she utter'd a soft moan:
He ceased — she panted quick — and suddenly
Her blue affrayèd eyes wide open shone:
Upon his knees he sank, pale as smooth-sculptured stone.

Her eyes were open, but she still beheld,
Now wide awake, the vision of her sleep:
There was a painful change, that night expell'd
The blisses of her dream so pure and deep,
At which fair Madeline began to weep,
And moan forth witless words with many a sigh;
While still her gaze on Porphyro would keep;
Who knelt, with joinèd hands and piteous eye,
Fearing to move or speak, she look'd so dreamingly.

"Ah, Porphyro!" said she, "but even now
Thy voice was at sweet tremble in mine ear,
Made tunable with every sweetest vow;
And those sad eyes were spiritual and clear:
How chang'd thou art! how pallid, chill, and drear!
Give me that voice again, my Porphyro,
Those looks immortal, those complainings dear!
Oh leave me not in this eternal woe,
For if thou diest, my Love, I know not where to go."

Beyond a mortal man impassion'd far
At these voluptuous accents, he arose,
Ethereal, flushed, and like a throbbing star
Seen 'mid the sapphire heaven's deep repose;
Into her dream he melted, as the rose
Blendeth its odour with the violet, —
Solution sweet: meantime the frost-wind blows
Like Love's alarum, pattering the sharp sleet
Against the window-panes; St. Agnes' moon hath set.

'Tis dark: quick pattereth the flaw-blown sleet:
"This is no dream, my bride, my Madeline!"
'Tis dark: the icèd gusts still rave and beat:
"No dream, alas! alas! and woe is mine!
Porphyro will leave me here to fade and pine. —
Cruel! what traitor could thee hither bring?
I curse not, for my heart is lost in thine,
Though thou forsakest a deceivèd thing; —
A dove forlorn and lost with sick unprunèd wing."

"My Madeline! sweet dreamer! lovely bride!
Say, may I be for aye thy vassal blest?
Thy beauty's shield, heart-shaped and vermeil dyed?
Ah, silver shrine, here will I take my rest
After so many hours of toil and quest,
A famished pilgrim, — sav'd by miracle.
Though I have found, I will not rob thy nest
Saving of thy sweet self; if thou think'st well
To trust, fair Madeline, to no rude infidel.

"Hark! 'tis an elfin-storm from fairy land,
Of haggard seeming, but a boon indeed:
Arise — arise! the morning is at hand; —
The bloated wassailers will never heed: —
Let us away, my love, with happy speed;
There are no ears to hear, or eyes to see, —
Drown'd all in Rhenish and the sleepy mead:
Awake! arise! my love, and fearless be,
For o'er the southern moors I have a home for thee."

She hurried at his words, beset with fears,
For there were sleeping dragons all around,
At glaring watch, perhaps, with ready spears —
Down the wide stairs a darkling way they found. —
In all the house was heard no human sound.
A chain-drooped lamp was flickering by each door;
The arras, rich with horseman, hawk, and hound,
Flutter'd in the besieging wind's uproar;
And the long carpets rose along the gusty floor.

They glide, like phantoms, into the wide hall;
Like phantoms, to the iron porch they glide;
Where lay the Porter, in uneasy sprawl,
With a huge empty flagon by his side:
The wakeful bloodhound rose, and shook his hide,
But his sagacious eye an inmate owns:
By one, and one, the bolts full easy slide: —
The chains lie silent on the footworn stones; —
The key turns, and the door upon its hinges groans.

And they are gone: ay, ages long ago
These lovers fled away into the storm.
That night the Baron dreamt of many a woe,
And all his warrior-guests, with shade and form
Of witch, and demon, and large coffin-worm,
Were long be-nightmar'd. Angela the old
Died palsy-twitch'd, with meagre face deform;
The Beadsman, after thousand avès told,
For aye unsought for slept among his ashes cold.

THOMAS HOOD (1798–1845)

THE BRIDGE OF SIGHS

One more Unfortunate,
Weary of breath,
Rashly importunate,
Gone to her death!

Take her up tenderly,
Lift her with care;
Fashion'd so slenderly,
Young, and so fair!

Look at her garments
Clinging like cerements;
Whilst the wave constantly
Drips from her clothing;
Take her up instantly,
Loving, not loathing.

Touch her not scornfully;
Think of her mournfully,
Gently and humanly;
Not of the stains of her,
All that remains of her
Now is pure womanly.

Make no deep scrutiny
Into her mutiny
Rash and undutiful:
Past all dishonour,
Death has left on her
Only the beautiful.

Still, for all slips of hers,
One of Eve's family —
Wipe those poor lips of hers
Oozing so clammily.

Loop up her tresses
Escaped from the comb,
Her fair auburn tresses;
Whilst wonderment guesses
Where was her home?

Who was her father?
Who was her mother?
Had she a sister?
Had she a brother?
Or was there a dearer one
Still, and a nearer one
Yet, than all other?

Alas! for the rarity
Of Christian charity
Under the sun!
O, it was pitiful!
Near a whole city full,
Home she had none.

Sisterly, brotherly,
Fatherly, motherly
Feelings had changed:
Love, by harsh evidence,
Thrown from its eminence;
Even God's providence
Seeming estranged.

Where the lamps quiver
So far in the river,
With many a light
From window to casement,
From garret to basement,
She stood with amazement,
Houseless by night.

The bleak wind of March
Made her tremble and shiver;
But not the dark arch,
Or the black flowing river:
Mad from life's history,
Glad to death's mystery,
Swift to be hurl'd —
Anywhere, anywhere
Out of the world!

In she plunged boldly —
No matter how coldly
The rough river ran —
Over the brink of it,
Picture it — think of it,
Dissolute Man!
Lave in it, drink of it,
Then, if you can!

Take her up tenderly,
Lift her with care;
Fashion'd so slenderly,
Young, and so fair!

Ere her limbs frigidly
Stiffen too rigidly,
Decently, kindly,
Smooth and compose them;
And her eyes, close them,
Staring so blindly!

Dreadfully staring
Thro' muddy impurity,
As when with the daring
Last look of despairing
Fix'd on futurity.

Perishing gloomily,
Spurr'd by contumely,
Cold inhumanity,
Burning insanity,
Into her rest. —
Cross her hands humbly,
As if praying dumbly,
Over her breast!

Owning her weakness,
Her evil behaviour,
And leaving with meekness,
Her sins to her Saviour!

THE SONG OF THE SHIRT

With fingers weary and worn,
With eyelids heavy and red,

A woman sat, in unwomanly rags,
Plying her needle and thread —
Stitch! stitch! stitch!
In poverty, hunger, and dirt,
And still with a voice of dolorous pitch
She sang the "Song of the Shirt."

"Work! work! work!
While the cock is crowing aloof!
And work — work — work,
Till the stars shine through the roof!
It's Oh! to be a slave
Along with the barbarous Turk,
Where woman has never a soul to save,
If this is Christian work!

"Work — work — work,
Till the brain begins to swim;
Work — work — work,
Till the eyes are heavy and dim!
Seam, and gusset, and band,
Band, and gusset, and seam,
Till over the buttons I fall asleep,
And sew them on in a dream!

"Oh, Men, with Sisters dear!
Oh, Men, with Mothers and Wives!
It is not linen you're wearing out
But human creatures' lives!
Stitch — stitch — stitch,
In poverty, hunger, and dirt,
Sewing at once, with a double thread,
A Shroud as well as a Shirt.

"But why do I talk of Death?
That Phantom of grisly bone,
I hardly fear its terrible shape,
It seems so like my own —
It seems so like my own,
Because of the fasts I keep;
Oh, God! that bread should be so dear,
And flesh and blood so cheap!

"Work — work — work!
My labour never flags;
And what are its wages? A bed of straw,
A crust of bread — and rags.
That shatter'd roof — this naked floor —
A table — a broken chair —
And a wall so blank, my shadow I thank
For sometimes falling there!

"Work — work — work!
From weary chime to chime,
Work — work — work,
As prisoners work for crime!
Band, and gusset, and seam,
Seam, and gusset, and band,
Till the heart is sick, and the brain benumb'd,
As well as the weary hand.

"Work — work — work,
In the dull December light,
And work — work — work,
When the weather is warm and bright —
While underneath the eaves
The brooding swallows cling
As if to show me their sunny backs
And twit me with the spring.

"Oh! but to breathe the breath
Of the cowslip and primrose sweet —
With the sky above my head,
And the grass beneath my feet;
For only one short hour
To feel as I used to feel,
Before I knew the woes of want
And the walk that costs a meal.

"Oh! but for one short hour!
A respite however brief!
No blessèd leisure for Love or Hope,
But only time for Grief!
A little weeping would ease my heart,
But in their briny bed
My tears must stop, for every drop
Hinders needle and thread!"

With fingers weary and worn,
With eyelids heavy and red,
A woman sat, in unwomanly rags,
Plying her needle and thread —
Stitch! stitch! stitch!
In poverty, hunger, and dirt,
And still with a voice of dolorous pitch, —
Would that its tone could reach the Rich! —
She sang this "Song of the Shirt!"

RUTH

She stood breast-high amid the corn,
Clasped by the golden light of morn,
Like the sweetheart of the sun,
Who many a glowing kiss had won.

On her cheek an autumn flush,
Deeply ripen'd; — such a blush
In the midst of brown was born,
Like red poppies grown with corn.

Round her eyes her tresses fell,
Which were blackest none could tell,

But long lashes veiled a light,
That had else been all too bright.

And her hat, with shady brim,
Made her tressy forehead dim; —
Thus she stood amid the stooks,
Praising God with sweetest looks.

Sure, I said, Heav'n did not mean,
Where I reap thou should'st but glean;
Lay thy sheaf adown and come,
Share my harvest and my home.

THE DEATH-BED

We watched her breathing through the night,
Her breathing soft and low,
As in her breast the wave of life
Kept heaving to and fro.

So silently we seem'd to speak,
So slowly moved about,
As we had lent her half our powers
To eke her living out.

Our very hopes belied our fears,
Our fears our hopes belied —
We thought her dying when she slept,
And sleeping when she died.

For when the morn came dim and sad,
And chill with early showers,
Her quiet eyelids closed — she had
Another morn than ours.

WINTHROP MACKWORTH PRAED
(1802–1839)

THE BELLE OF THE BALL-ROOM

Years — years ago, — ere yet my dreams
Had been of being wise or witty, —
Ere I had done with writing themes,
Or yawned o'er this infernal Chitty; —
Years — years ago, — while all my joy
Was in my fowling-piece and filly, —
In short, while I was yet a boy,
I fell in love with Laura Lily.

I saw her at the County Ball:
There, when the sounds of flute and fiddle
Gave signal sweet in that old hall
Of hands across and down the middle,
Hers was the subtlest spell by far
Of all that set young hearts romancing;
She was our queen, our rose, our star;
And then she danced — O Heaven, her dancing!

Dark was her hair, her hand was white;
Her voice was exquisitely tender;
Her eyes were full of liquid light;
I never saw a waist so slender!
Her every look, her every smile,
Shot right and left a score of arrows;
I thought 'twas Venus from her isle,
And wondered where she'd left her sparrows.

She talked, — of politics or prayers, —
Of Southey's prose or Wordsworth's sonnets, —
Of danglers — or of dancing bears,
Of battles — or the last new bonnets,
By candlelight, at twelve o'clock,
To me it mattered not a tittle;
If those bright lips had quoted Locke,
I might have thought they murmured Little.

Through sunny May, through sultry June,
I loved her with a love eternal;
I spoke her praises to the moon,
I wrote them to the Sunday Journal:
My mother laughed; I soon found out
That ancient ladies have no feeling:
My father frowned; but how should gout
See any happiness in kneeling?

She was the daughter of a Dean,
Rich, fat, and rather apoplectic;
She had one brother, just thirteen,
Whose colour was extremely hectic;
Her grandmother for many a year
Had fed the parish with her bounty;
Her second cousin was a peer,
And Lord Lieutenant of the County.

But titles, and the three per cents,
And mortgages, and great relations,
And India bonds, and tithes, and rents,
Oh, what are they to love's sensations?
Black eyes, fair forehead, clustering locks —
Such wealth, such honours, Cupid chooses;
He cares as little for the Stocks,
As Baron Rothschild for the Muses.

She sketched; the vale, the wood, the beach,
Grew lovelier from her pencil's shading:
She botanised; I envied each
Young blossom in her boudoir fading:
She warbled Handel; it was grand;
She made the Catalani jealous:
She touched the organ; I could stand
For hours and hours to blow the bellows.

She kept an album, too, at home,
Well filled with all an album's glories;
Paintings of butterflies, and Rome,
Patterns for trimmings, Persian stories;
Soft songs to Julia's cockatoo,
Fierce odes to Famine and to Slaughter;
And autographs of Prince Leboo,
And recipes for elder-water.

And she was flattered, worshipped, bored;
Her steps were watched, her dress was noted,
Her poodle dog was quite adored,
Her sayings were extremely quoted;
She laughed, and every heart was glad,
As if the taxes were abolished;
She frowned, and every look was sad,
As if the Opera were demolished.

She smiled on many, just for fun, —
I knew that there was nothing in it;
I was the first — the only one
Her heart had thought of for a minute. —
I knew it, for she told me so,
In phrase which was divinely moulded;
She wrote a charming hand, — and oh!
How sweetly all her notes were folded!

Our love was like most other loves; —
A little glow, a little shiver,
A rose-bud, and a pair of gloves,
And "Fly not yet" — upon the river;
Some jealousy of some one's heir,
Some hopes of dying broken-hearted;
A miniature, a lock of hair,
The usual vows, — and then we parted.

We parted; months and years rolled by;
We met again four summers after:
Our parting was all sob and sigh;
Our meeting was all mirth and laughter:
For in my heart's most secret cell
There had been many other lodgers;
And she was not the ball-room's belle,
But only — Mrs. Something Rogers!

PROLOGUE

FOR AN AMATEUR PERFORMANCE OF "THE HONEYMOON"

"We want" — the Duchess said to me to-day,
"We want, fair sir, a prologue for our play. —
A charming play to show a charming robe in.
'The Honeymoon'" — "By Phœbus!" — "No: by Tobin."
"A prologue!" I made answer; "if you need one,
In every street and square your Grace may read one."

"Cruel Papa! don't talk about Sir Harry!" —
So Araminta lisped; — "I'll never marry;
I loathe all men; such unromantic creatures!
The coarsest tastes, and ah! the coarsest features!
Betty! — the salts! — I'm sick with mere vexation,
To hear them called the Lords of the Creation:
They swear fierce oaths, they seldom say their prayers;
And then, they shed no tears, — unfeeling bears! —
I, and the friend I share my sorrows with,
Medora Gertrude Wilhelmina Smith,
Will weep together through the world's disasters,
In some green vale, unplagued by Lords and Masters,
And hand in hand repose at last in death,
As chaste and cold as Queen Elizabeth."
She spoke in May, and people found in June,
This was her Prologue to the Honeymoon!

"Frederic is poor, I own it." Fanny sighs,
"But then he loves me, and has deep blue eyes.
Since I was nine years old, and he eleven,
We've loved each other, — 'Love is light from Heaven.'
And penury with love, I will not doubt it,
Is better far than palaces without it.
We'll have a quiet curacy in Kent;
We'll keep a cow; and we'll be *so* content.
Forgetting that my father drove fine horses,
And that my mother dined upon three courses,
There I shall sit, perusing Frederic's verses,
Dancing in spring, in winter knitting purses;
Mending the children's pinafores and frills,
Wreathing sweet flowers, and paying butcher's bills."
Alas, poor Fanny! — she will find too soon
Her Prologue's better than her Honeymoon.

But lo! where Laura, with a frenzied air,
Seeks her kind cousin in her pony chair,
And, in a mournful voice, by thick sobs broke
Cries, "Yes, dear Anne! the favours are bespoke,
I am to have him; — so my friends decided;
The stars knew quite as much of it as I did!
You know him, love; — he is so like a mummy: —
I wonder whether diamonds will become me!
He talks of nothing but the price of stocks;
However, I'm to have my opera box

That pert thing, Ellen, thought she could secure him, —
I wish she had, I'm sure I can't endure him!
The cakes are ordered; — how my lips will falter
When I stand fainting at the marriage altar!
But I'm to have him! — Oh, the vile baboon!"
Strange Prologue this for Laura's Honeymoon!

Enough of prologues; surely I should say
One word, before I go, about the play.
Instead of hurrying madly after marriage
To some lord's villa in a travelling carriage,
Instead of seeking earth's remotest ends
To hide their blushes and avoid their friends,
Instead of haunting lonely lanes and brooks
With no companions but the doves and rooks, —
Our Duke and Duchess open wide their Hall,
And bid you warmly welcome, one and all,
Who come with hearts of kindness, eyes of light,
To see, and share, *their* Honeymoon to-night.

THOMAS LOVELL BEDDOES
(1803–1849)

DREAM-PEDLARY

If there were dreams to sell,
  What would you buy?
Some cost a passing bell;
  Some a light sigh,
That shakes from Life's fresh crown
Only a rose-leaf down.
If there were dreams to sell,
Merry and sad to tell,
And the crier rang the bell,
  What would you buy?

A cottage lone and still,
  With bowers nigh,
Shadowy, my woes to still,
  Until I die.
Such pearl from Life's fresh crown
Fain would I shake me down.
Were dreams to have at will,
This would best heal my ill,
  This would I buy.

But there were dreams to sell
  Ill didst thou buy;
Life is a dream, they tell,
  Waking, to die.
Dreaming a dream to prize,
Is wishing ghosts to rise;
And, if I had the spell
To call the buried well,
  Which one would I?

If there are ghosts to raise,
  What shall I call,
Out of hell's murky haze,
  Heaven's blue pall?
Raise my loved long-lost boy
To lead me to his joy. —
There are no ghosts to raise;
Out of death lead no ways;
  Vain is the call.

Know'st thou not ghosts to sue,
  No love thou hast.
Else lie, as I will do,
  And breathe thy last.
So out of Life's fresh crown
Fall like a rose-leaf down.
Thus are the ghosts to woo;
Thus are all dreams made true,
  Ever to last!

From DEATH'S JEST-BOOK

SONG

Old Adam, the carrion crow,
  The old crow of Cairo;
He sat in the shower, and let it flow
  Under his tail and over his crest;
    And through every feather
    Leaked the wet weather;
  And the bough swung under his nest;
  For his beak it was heavy with marrow.
    Is that the wind dying? O no;
    It's only two devils, that blow
    Through a murderer's bones, to and fro,
      In the ghosts' moonshine.

Ho! Eve, my grey carrion wife,
  When we have supped on kings' marrow,
Where shall we drink and make merry our life?
  Our nest it is Queen Cleopatra's skull,
    'Tis cloven and cracked,
    And battered and hacked,
  But with tears of blue eyes it is full:
  Let us drink then, my raven of Cairo.
    Is that the wind dying? O no;
    It's only two devils, that blow
    Through a murderer's bones, to and fro,
      In the ghosts' moonshine

THE VICTORIAN AGE

ELIZABETH BARRETT BROWNING (1809–1861)

THE SLEEP

He giveth His beloved sleep. — Ps. 127. 2.

Of all the thoughts of God that are
Borne inward unto souls afar,
Along the Psalmist's music deep,
Now tell me if that any is,
For gift or grace, surpassing this —
"He giveth His belovèd sleep"?

What would we give to our beloved?
The hero's heart, to be unmoved,
The poet's star-tuned harp, to sweep,
The patriot's voice, to teach and rouse,
The monarch's crown, to light the brows? —
"He giveth *His* belovèd sleep."

What do we give to our beloved?
A little faith all undisproved,
A little dust to overweep,
And bitter memories to make
The whole earth blasted for our sake.
"He giveth *His* belovèd sleep."

"Sleep soft, beloved!" we sometimes say,
But have no tune to charm away
Sad dreams that through the eyelids creep;
But never doleful dream again
Shall break the happy slumber when
"He giveth *His* belovèd sleep."

O earth, so full of dreary noises!
O men, with wailing in your voices!
O delvèd gold, the wailers heap!
O strife, O curse, that o'er it fall!
God strikes a silence through you all,
And "giveth *His* belovèd sleep."

His dews drop mutely on the hill,
His cloud above it saileth still,
Though on its slope men sow and reap.
More softly than the dew is shed,
Or cloud is floated overhead,
"He giveth *His* belovèd sleep."

For me, my heart that erst did go
Most like a tired child at a show,
That sees through tears the mummers leap,
Would now its wearied vision close,
Would childlike on *His* love repose,
Who "giveth *His* belovèd sleep!"

And, friends, dear friends, — when it shall be
That this low breath is gone from me,
And round my bier ye come to weep,
Let one, most loving of you all,
Say, "Not a tear must o'er her fall —
'He giveth *His* belovèd sleep.'"

From COWPER'S GRAVE

It is a place where poets crowned may feel the heart's decaying.
It is a place where happy saints may weep amid their praying:
Yet let the grief and humbleness, as low as silence languish!
Earth surely now may give her calm to whom she gave her anguish.

O poets! from a maniac's tongue was poured the deathless singing!
O Christians! at your cross of hope, a hopeless hand was clinging!
O men! this man in brotherhood your weary paths beguiling,
Groaned inly while he taught you peace and died while ye were smiling!
And now, what time ye all may read through dimming tears his story,
How discord on the music fell, and darkness on the glory,
And how, when, one by one, sweet sounds and wandering lights departed,
He wore no less a loving face because so broken-hearted;

He shall be strong to sanctify the poet's high vocation,
And bow the meekest Christian down in meeker adoration;

Nor ever shall he be, in praise, by wise or good forsaken;
Named softly as the household name of one whom God hath taken.

THE SOUL'S EXPRESSION

With stammering lips and insufficient sound
I strive and struggle to deliver right
That music of my nature, day and night
With dream and thought and feeling interwound,
And inly answering all the senses round
With octaves of a mystic depth and height
Which step out grandly to the infinite
From the dark edges of the sensual ground!
This song of soul I struggle to outbear
Through portals of the sense, sublime and whole,
And utter all myself into the air:
But if I did it, — as the thunder-roll
Breaks its own cloud, — my flesh would perish there,
Before that dread apocalypse of soul.

PERPLEXED MUSIC

Experience, like a pale musician holds
A dulcimer of patience in his hand
Whence harmonies we cannot understand,
Of God's will in His worlds, the strain unfolds
In sad perplexèd minors. Deathly colds
Fall on us while we hear and countermand
Our sanguine heart back from the fancy-land
With nightingales in visionary wolds.
We murmur, "Where is any certain tune
Of measured music, in such notes as these?" —
But angels, leaning from the golden seat,
Are not so minded: their fine ear hath won
The issue of completed cadences;
And, smiling down the stars, they whisper — SWEET.

WORK

What are we set on earth for? Say, to toil —
Nor seek to leave thy tending of the vines,
For all the heat o' the day, till it declines,
And Death's mild curfew shall from work assoil.
God did anoint thee with His odorous oil,
To wrestle, not to reign; and He assigns
All thy tears over, like pure crystallines,
For younger fellow-workers of the soil
To wear for amulets. So others shall
Take patience, labour, to their heart and hand
From thy hand, and thy heart, and thy brave cheer,
And God's grace fructify through thee to all.
The least flower, with a brimming cup, may stand
And share its dew-drop with another near.

TO GEORGE SAND

A RECOGNITION

True genius, but true woman! dost deny
Thy woman's nature with a manly scorn,
And break away the gauds and armlets worn
By weaker women in captivity?
Ah, vain denial! that revolted cry
Is sobbed in by a woman's voice forlorn:
Thy woman's hair, my sister, all unshorn,
Floats back dishevelled strength in agony,
Disproving thy man's name: and while before
The world thou burnest in a poet fire,
We see thy woman's heart beat evermore
Through the large flame. Beat purer, heart, and higher,
Till God unsex thee on the heavenly shore,
Where unincarnate spirits purely aspire!

A MAN'S REQUIREMENTS

Love me, sweet, with all thou art,
Feeling, thinking, seeing, —
Love me in the lightest part,
Love me in full being.

Love me with thine open youth
In its frank surrender;
With the vowing of thy mouth,
With its silence tender.

Love me with thine azure eyes,
Made for earnest granting!
Taking colour from the skies,
Can Heaven's truth be wanting?

Love me with their lids, that fall
Snow-like at first meeting:
Love me with thine heart, that all
The neighbours then see beating.

Love me with thine hand stretched out
Freely — open-minded:
Love me with thy loitering foot, —
Hearing one behind it.

Love me with thy voice, that turns
Sudden faint above me;
Love me with thy blush that burns
When I murmur "Love me!"

Love me with thy thinking soul —
Break it to love-sighing;
Love me with thy thoughts that roll
On through living — dying.

Love me in thy gorgeous airs,
When the world has crowned thee!
Love me, kneeling at thy prayers,
With the angels round thee.

Love me pure, as musers do,
Up the woodlands shady:
Love me gaily, fast, and true,
As a winsome lady.

Through all hopes that keep us brave,
Further off or nigher,
Love me for the house and grave,
And for something higher.

Thus, if thou wilt prove me, dear,
Woman's love no fable,
I will love *thee* — half-a-year —
As a man is able.

A WOMAN'S SHORTCOMINGS

She has laughed as softly as if she sighed!
She has counted six and over,
Of a purse well filled, and a heart well tried —
Oh, each a worthy lover!
They "give her time;" for her soul must slip
Where the world has set the grooving:
She will lie to none with her fair red lip —
But love seeks truer loving.

She trembles her fan in a sweetness dumb,
As her thoughts were beyond recalling;
With a glance for *one*, and a glance for *some*,
From her eyelids rising and falling.
Speaks common words with a blushful air;
Hears bold words, unreproving:
But her silence says — what she never will swear —
And love seeks better loving.

Go, lady! lean to the night-guitar,
And drop a smile on the bringer;
Then smile as sweetly, when he is far,
At the voice of an in-door singer!
Bask tenderly beneath tender eyes;
Glance lightly, on their removing:
And join new vows to old perjuries —
But dare not call it loving!

Unless you can think, when the song is done,
No other is soft in the rhythm;
Unless you can feel, when left by One,
That all men else go with him;
Unless you can know, when unpraised by his breath,
That your beauty itself wants proving;
Unless you can swear — "For life, for death!" —
Oh, fear to call it loving!

Unless you can muse in a crowd all day,
On the absent face that fixed you;
Unless you can love, as the angels may,
With the breadth of heaven betwixt you;
Unless you can dream that his faith is fast,
Through behooving and unbehooving;
Unless you can *die* when the dream is past —
Oh, never call it loving!

SONNETS FROM THE PORTUGUESE

I

I thought once how Theocritus had sung
Of the sweet years, the dear and wished-for years,
Who each one in a gracious hand appears
To bear a gift for mortals, old or young:
And, as I mused it in his antique tongue,
I saw in gradual vision through my tears,
The sweet, sad years, the melancholy years,
Those of my own life, who by turns had flung
A shadow across me. Straightway I was 'ware,
So weeping, how a mystic Shape did move
Behind me, and drew me backward by the hair;
And a voice said in mastery while I strove,
"Guess now who holds thee?" — "Death!" I said. But there,
The silver answer rang: "Not Death, but Love."

VII

The face of all the world is changed, I think,
Since first I heard the footsteps of thy soul
Move still, oh, still, beside me; as they stole
Betwixt me and the dreadful outer brink
Of obvious death, where I who thought to sink
Was caught up into love and taught the whole
Of life in a new rhythm. The cup of dole
God gave for baptism, I am fain to drink,
And praise its sweetness, sweet, with thee anear.
The name of country, heaven, are changed away
For where thou art or shalt be, there or here;
And this — this lute and song — loved yesterday,
(The singing angels know) are only dear
Because thy name moves right in what they say.

XIV

If thou must love me, let it be for nought
Except for love's sake only. Do not say,
"I love her for her smile — her look — her way
Of speaking gently, — for a trick of thought
That falls in well with mine, and certes brought
A sense of pleasant ease on such a day;" —
For these things in themselves, Belovèd, may

Be changed, or change for thee, — and love so wrought,
May be unwrought so. Neither love me for
Thine own dear pity's wiping my cheeks dry:
A creature might forget to weep, who bore
Thy comfort long, and lose thy love thereby.
But love me for love's sake, that evermore
Thou may'st love on through love's eternity.

XVII

My poet, thou canst touch on all the notes
God set between His After and Before,
And strike up and strike off the general roar
Of the rushing worlds a melody that floats
In a serene air purely. Antidotes
Of medicated music, answering for
Mankind's forlornest uses, thou canst pour
From thence into their ears. God's will devotes
Thine to such ends and mine to wait on thine!
How, Dearest, wilt thou have me for most use?
A hope, to sing by gladly? — or a fine
Sad memory, with thy songs to interfuse?
A shade, in which to sing — of palm or pine?
A grave on which to rest from singing? — Choose.

XX

Belovèd, my Belovèd, when I think
That thou wast in the world a year ago,
What time I sate alone here in the snow
And saw no footprint, heard the silence sink
No moment at thy voice, — but link by link
Went counting all my chains as if that so
They never could fall off at any blow
Struck by thy possible hand, — why, thus I drink
Of life's great cup of wonder. Wonderful,
Never to feel thee thrill the day or night
With personal act or speech, — nor ever cull
Some prescience of thee with the blossoms white
Thou sawest growing! Atheists are as dull,
Who cannot guess God's presence out of sight.

XXI

Say over again and yet once over again
That thou dost love me. Though the word repeated
Should seem "a cuckoo-song," as thou dost treat it,
Remember never to the hill or plain,
Valley and wood, without her cuckoo-strain,
Comes the fresh Spring in all her green completed!
Belovèd, I, amid the darkness greeted
By a doubtful spirit-voice, in that doubt's pain
Cry, "Speak once more, thou lovest!" Who can fear
Too many stars, though each in heaven shall roll —
Too many flowers, though each shall crown the year?
Say thou dost love me, love me, love me — toll
The silver iterance! — only minding, Dear,
To love me also in silence, with thy soul.

XXII

When our two souls stand up erect and strong,
Face to face, silent, drawing nigh and nigher,
Until the lengthening wings break into fire
At either curvèd point, — What bitter wrong
Can the earth do to us, that we should not long
Be here contented? Think. In mounting higher,
The angels would press on us, and aspire
To drop some golden orb of perfect song
Into our deep, dear silence. Let us stay
Rather on earth, Belovèd, — where the unfit,
Contrarious moods of men recoil away
And isolate pure spirits, and permit
A place to stand and love in for a day,
With darkness and the death-hour rounding it.

XXVIII

My letters all dead paper, mute and white!
And yet they seem alive and quivering
Against my tremulous hands which loose the string
And let them drop down on my knee to-night.
This said, he wished to have me in his sight
Once, as a friend; this fixed a day in spring
To come and touch my hand — a simple thing,
Yet I wept for it! — this — the paper's light —
Said, "*Dear*, I love thee"; and I sank and quailed
As if God's future thundered on my past:
This said, "I am thine" — and so its ink has paled
With lying at my heart that beat too fast:
And this — O Love, thy words have ill availed,
If, what this said, I dared repeat at last!

XLIII

How do I love thee? Let me count the ways.
I love thee to the depth and breadth and height
My soul can reach, when feeling out of sight
For the ends of Being and Ideal Grace.
I love thee to the level of everyday's
Most quiet need, by sun and candlelight.
I love thee freely, as men strive for Right
I love thee purely, as they turn from Praise;

I love thee with the passion put to use
In my old griefs, and with my childhood's faith;
I love thee with a love I seemed to lose
With my lost saints, — I love thee with the breath,
Smiles, tears, of all my life! — and, if God choose,
I shall but love thee better after death.

THE CRY OF THE CHILDREN

Do ye hear the children weeping, O my brothers,
Ere the sorrow comes with years?
They are leaning their young heads against their mothers,
And *that* cannot stop their tears.
The young lambs are bleating in the meadows:
The young birds are chirping in the nest;
The young fawns are playing with the shadows;
The young flowers are blowing toward the west —
But the young, young children, O my brothers,
They are weeping bitterly!
They are weeping in the playtime of the others,
In the country of the free.

Do you question the young children in their sorrow,
Why their tears are falling so?
The old man may weep for his to-morrow
Which is lost in Long Ago;
The old tree is leafless in the forest,
The old year is ending in the frost,
The old wound, if stricken, is the sorest,
The old hope is hardest to be lost:
But the young, young children, O my brothers,
Do you ask them why they stand
Weeping sore before the bosoms of their mothers,
In our happy Fatherland?

They look up with their pale and sunken faces,
And their looks are sad to see,
For the man's hoary anguish draws and presses
Down the cheeks of infancy;
"Your old earth," they say, "is very dreary,
Our young feet," they say, "are very weak!
Few paces have we taken, yet are weary —
Our grave-rest is very far to seek:
Ask the agèd why they weep, and not the children,
For the outside earth is cold,
And we young ones stand without, in our bewildering,
And the graves are for the old:

"True," say the children, "it may happen
That we die before our time:
Little Alice died last year, her grave is shapen
Like a snowball, in the rime.
We looked into the pit prepared to take her:
Was no room for any work in the close clay!
From the sleep wherein she lieth none will wake her
Crying, 'Get up, little Alice! it is day.'
If you listen by that grave, in sun and shower,
With your ear down, little Alice never cries;
Could we see her face, be sure we should not know her,
For a smile has time for growing in her eyes:
And merry go her moments, lulled and stilled in
The shroud by the kirk-chime.
It is good when it happens," say the children,
"That we die before our time."

Alas, alas, the children! they are seeking
Death in life as best to have:
They are binding up their hearts away from breaking,
With a cerement from the grave.
Go out, children, from the mine and from the city,
Sing out, children, as the little thrushes do;
Pluck your handfuls of the meadow-cowslips pretty,
Laugh aloud, to feel your fingers let them through!
But they answer, "Are your cowslips of the meadows
Like our weeds anear the mine?
Leave us quiet in the dark of the coal-shadows,
From your pleasures fair and fine!

"For oh," say the children, "we are weary,
And we cannot run or leap;
If we cared for any meadows, it were merely
To drop down in them and sleep.
Our knees tremble sorely in the stooping,
We fall upon our faces, trying to go;
And, underneath our heavy eyelids drooping,
The reddest flower would look as pale as snow.
For, all day, we drag our burden tiring,
Through the coal-dark, underground;
Or, all day, we drive the wheels of iron
In the factories, round and round.

"For, all day, the wheels are droning, turning;
Their wind comes in our faces,
Till our hearts turn, our heads, with pulses burning,
And the walls turn in their places:
Turns the sky in the high window, blank and reeling,
Turns the long light that drops adown the wall,

Turn the black flies that crawl along the ceiling:
All are turning, all the day, and we with all.
And all day the iron wheels are droning:
And sometimes we could pray,
'O ye wheels,' (breaking out in a mad moaning),
'Stop! be silent for to-day!'"

Ay, be silent! Let them hear each other breathing
For a moment, mouth to mouth!
Let them touch each other's hands, in a fresh wreathing
Of their tender human youth!
Let them feel that this cold metallic motion
Is not all the life God fashions or reveals:
Let them prove their living souls against the notion
That they live in you, or under you, O wheels!
Still, all day, the iron wheels go onward,
Grinding life down from its mark;
And the children's souls, which God is calling sunward,
Spin on blindly in the dark.

Now tell the poor young children, O my brothers,
To look up to Him and pray;
So the blessed One who blesseth all the others,
Will bless them another day.
They answer, "Who is God that He should hear us,
While the rushing of the iron wheels is stirred?
When we sob aloud, the human creatures near us
Pass by, hearing not, or answer not a word.
And *we* hear not (for the wheels in their resounding)
Strangers speaking at the door:
Is it likely God, with angels singing round Him,
Hears our weeping any more?

"Two words, indeed, of praying we remember;
And at midnight's hour of harm,
'Our Father,' looking upward in the chamber,
We say softly for a charm.
We know no other words, except 'Our Father,'
And we think that, in some pause of angels' song,
God may pluck them with the silence sweet to gather,
And hold both within His right hand which is strong.
'Our Father!' If He heard us, He would surely
(For they call Him good and mild)
Answer, smiling down the steep world very purely,
'Come and rest with me, my child.'

"But no!" say the children, weeping faster,
"He is speechless as a stone:
And they tell us, of His image is the master
Who commands us to work on.
Go to!" say the children, — "Up in Heaven,
Dark, wheel-like, turning clouds are all we find:
Do not mock us; grief has made us unbelieving:
We look up for God, but tears have made us blind."
Do you hear the children weeping and disproving,
O my brothers, what ye preach?
For God's possible is taught by His world's loving,
And the children doubt of each.

And well may the children weep before you!
They are weary ere they run;
They have never seen the sunshine, nor the glory
Which is brighter than the sun:
They know the grief of man, without its wisdom;
They sink in man's despair, without its calm;
And slaves, without the liberty in Christdom,
Are martyrs, by the pang without the palm:
Are worn as if with age, yet unretrievingly
The harvest of its memories cannot reap, —
Are orphans of the earthly love and heavenly.
Let them weep! let them weep!

They look up with their pale and sunken faces,
And their look is dread to see,
For they mind you of their angels in high places,
With eyes turned on Deity.
"How long," they say, "how long, O cruel nation,
Will you stand, to move the world, on a child's heart, —
Stifle down with a mailed heel its palpitation,
And tread onward to your throne amid the mart?
Our blood splashes upward, O gold-heaper,
And your purple shows your path!
But the child's sob in the silence curses deeper
Than the strong man in his wrath."

A CURSE FOR A NATION

PROLOGUE

I heard an angel speak last night
And he said, "Write!
Write a nation's curse for me,
And send it over the Western Sea."

I faltered, taking up the word:
"Not so, my lord!
If curses must be, choose another
To send thy curse against my brother.

"For I am bound by gratitude,
By love and blood,
To brothers of mine across the sea,
Who stretch out kindly hands to me."

"Therefore," the voice said, "shalt thou write
My curse to-night.
From the summits of love a curse is driven,
As lightning is from the tops of heaven."

"Not so," I answered. "Evermore
My heart is sore
For my own land's sins: for little feet
Of children bleeding along the street:

"For parked-up honours that gainsay
The right of way:
For almsgiving through a door that is
Not open enough for two friends to kiss:

"For love of freedom which abates
Beyond the Straits:
For patriot virtue starved to vice on
Self-praise, self-interest, and suspicion:

"For an oligarchic parliament,
And bribes well-meant.
What curse to another land assign,
When heavy-souled for the sins of mine?"

"Therefore," the voice said, "shalt thou write
My curse to-night.
Because thou hast strength to see and hate
A foul thing done *within* thy gate."

"Not so," I answered once again.
"To curse, choose men,
For I, a woman, have only known
How the heart melts and the tears run down."

"Therefore," the voice said, "shalt thou write
My curse to-night.
Some women weep and curse, I say
(And no one marvels), night and day,

"And thou shalt take their part to-night,
Weep and write,
A curse from the depths of womanhood
Is very salt, and bitter, and good."

So thus I wrote, and mourned indeed,
What all may read.
And thus, as was enjoined on me,
I send it over the Western Sea.

THE CURSE

I

Because ye have broken your own chain
With the strain
Of brave men climbing a nation's height,
Yet thence bear down with brand and thong
On souls of others, — for this wrong
This is the curse. Write.

Because yourselves are standing straight
In the state
Of Freedom's foremost acolyte,
Yet keep calm footing all the time
On writhing bond-slaves, — for this crime
This is the curse. Write.

Because ye prosper in God's name,
With a claim
To honour in the old world's sight,
Yet do the fiend's work perfectly
In strangling martyrs, — for this lie
This is the curse. Write.

II

Ye shall watch while kings conspire
Round the people's smouldering fire,
And, warm for your part,
Shall never dare — O shame!
To utter the thought into flame
Which burns at your heart.
This is the curse. Write.

Ye shall watch while nations strive
With the bloodhounds, die or survive,
Drop faint from their jaws,
Or throttle them backward to death,
And only under your breath
Shall favour the cause.
This is the curse. Write.

Ye shall watch while strong men draw
The nets of feudal law
To strangle the weak,
And, counting the sin for a sin,
Your soul shall be sadder within
Than the word ye shall speak.
This is the curse. Write.

When good men are praying erect
That Christ may avenge his elect
And deliver the earth,
The prayer in your ears, said low,
Shall sound like the tramp of a foe
That's driving you forth.
This is the curse. Write.

When wise men give you their praise.
They shall pause in the heat of the phrase,
As if carried too far.
When ye boast your own charters kept true,
Ye shall blush; for the thing which ye do
Derides what ye are.
This is the curse. Write.

When fools cast taunts at your gate,
Your scorn ye shall somewhat abate
As ye look o'er the wall;
For your conscience, tradition, and name
Explode with a deadlier blame
Than the worst of them all.
This is the curse. Write.

Go, wherever ill deeds shall be done,
Go, plant your flag in the sun
Beside the ill-doers!
And recoil from clenching the curse
Of God's witnessing Universe
With a curse of yours.
This is the curse. Write.

A MUSICAL INSTRUMENT

What was he doing, the great god Pan,
Down in the reeds by the river?
Spreading ruin and scattering ban,
Splashing and paddling with hoofs of a goat,
And breaking the golden lilies afloat
With the dragon-fly on the river?

He tore out a reed, the great god Pan,
From the deep cool bed of the river,
The limpid water turbidly ran,
And the broken lilies a-dying lay,
And the dragon-fly had fled away,
Ere he brought it out of the river.

High on the shore sat the great god Pan,
While turbidly flowed the river,
And hacked and hewed as a great god can
With his hard bleak steel at the patient reed,
Till there was not a sign of the leaf indeed
To prove it fresh from the river.

He cut it short, did the great god Pan,
(How tall it stood in the river!),
Then drew the pith, like the heart of a man,
Steadily from the outside ring,
And notched the poor dry empty thing
In holes as he sat by the river.

"This is the way," laughed the great god Pan,
(Laughed while he sat by the river).
"The only way since gods began
To make sweet music, they could succeed."
Then dropping his mouth to a hole in the reed,
He blew in power by the river.

Sweet, sweet, sweet, O Pan!
Piercing sweet by the river!
Blinding sweet, O great god Pan!
The sun on the hill forgot to die,
And the lilies revived, and the dragon-fly
Came back to dream on the river.

Yet half a beast is the great god Pan
To laugh, as he sits by the river,
Making a poet out of a man:
The true gods sigh for the cost and pain —
For the reed which grows never more again
As a reed with the reeds of the river.

A CHILD'S THOUGHT OF GOD

They say that God lives very high!
But if you look above the pines
You cannot see our God. And why?
And if you dig down in the mines
You never see Him in the gold,
Though from Him all that's glory shines.
God is so good, He wears a fold
Of heaven and earth across His face —
Like secrets kept, for love, untold.
But still I feel that His embrace
Slides down by thrills, through all things made,
Through sight and sound of every place:
As if my tender mother laid
On my shut lids, her kisses' pressure,
Half-waking me at night; and said,
"Who kissed you through the dark, dear guesser?"

EDWARD FITZGERALD (1809–1883)

From THE RUBAIYAT OF OMAR KHAYYAM

VII

Come, fill the Cup, and in the fire of Spring
Your Winter-garment of Repentance fling:
The Bird of Time has but a little way
To flutter — and the Bird is on the Wing.

VIII

Whether at Naishapur or Babylon,
Whether the Cup with sweet or bitter run,
The Wine of Life keeps oozing drop by drop,
The Leaves of Life keep falling one by one.

IX

Each Morn a thousand Roses brings, you say;
Yes, but where leaves the Rose of Yesterday?
And this first Summer month that brings the Rose
Shall take Jamshyd and Kaikobad away.

* * * * * * *

XII

A Book of Verses underneath the Bough,
A Jug of Wine, a Loaf of Bread — and Thou
Beside me singing in the Wilderness —
Oh, Wilderness were Paradise enow!

XIII

Some for the Glories of this World; and some
Sigh for the Prophet's Paradise to come;
Ah, take the Cash, and let the Credit go,
Nor heed the rumble of a distant Drum!

XIV

Look to the blowing Rose about us — "Lo,
Laughing," she says, "into the world I blow,
At once the silken tassel of my Purse
Tear, and its Treasure on the Garden throw."

XV

And those who husbanded the Golden grain,
And those who flung it to the winds like Rain,
Alike to no such aureate Earth are turn'd
As, buried once, Men want dug up again.

XVI

The Worldly Hope men set their Hearts upon
Turns Ashes — or it prospers; and anon,
Like Snow upon the Desert's dusty Face,
Lighting a little hour or two — was gone.

XVII

Think, in this batter'd Caravanserai
Whose Portals are alternate Night and Day,
How Sultan after Sultan with his Pomp
Abode his destin'd Hour, and went his way.

XVIII

They say the Lion and the Lizard keep
The Courts where Jamshyd gloried and drank deep:
And Bahram, that great Hunter — the Wild Ass
Stamps o'er his Head, but cannot break his Sleep.

XIX

I sometimes think that never blows so red
The Rose as where some buried Cæsar bled;
That every Hyacinth the Garden wears
Dropt in her Lap from some once lovely Head.

XX

And this reviving Herb whose tender Green
Fledges the River-Lip on which we lean —
Ah, lean upon it lightly! for who knows
From what once lovely Lip it springs unseen!

XXI

Oh, my Belovèd, fill the Cup that clears
To-day of past Regret and future Fears:
To-morrow! — Why, To-morrow I may be
Myself with Yesterday's Sev'n thousand Years.

XXII

For some we loved, the loveliest and the best
That from his Vintage rolling Time hath prest,
Have drunk their Cup a Round or two before
And one by one crept silently to rest.

XXIII

And we that now make merry in the Room
They left, and Summer dresses in new bloom,
Ourselves must we beneath the Couch of Earth
Descend — ourselves to make a Couch — for whom?

XXIV

Ah, make the most of what we yet may spend,
Before we too into the Dust descend;
Dust into Dust, and under Dust, to lie,
Sans Wine, sans Song, sans Singer, and — sans End!

* * * * * * *

XXVII

Myself when young did eagerly frequent
Doctor and Saint, and heard great argument
About it and about: but evermore
Came out by the same door where in I went.

XXVIII

With them the seed of Wisdom did I sow,
And with mine own hand wrought to make it grow;
And this was all the Harvest that I reap'd —
"I came like Water, and like Wind I go."

XXIX

Into this Universe, and WHY not knowing
Nor WHENCE, like Water willy-nilly flowing,
And out of it, as Wind along the Waste,
I know not WHITHER, willy-nilly blowing.

XXX

What, without asking, hither hurried WHENCE?
And, without asking, WHITHER hurried hence!
Oh, many a Cup of this forbidden Wine
Must drown the memory of that insolence!

XXXI

Up from Earth's Centre through the Seventh Gate
I rose, and on the Throne of Saturn sate,
And many a Knot unravel'd by the Road;
But not the Master-knot of Human Fate.

XXXII

There was the Door to which I found no Key;
There was the Veil through which I might not see:
Some little talk awhile of ME and THEE
There was — and then no more of THEE and ME.

* * * * * * *

XLIX

Would you that spangle of Existence spend
About THE SECRET — quick about it, Friend!
A Hair perhaps divides the False and True —
And upon what, prithee, does life depend?

L

A Hair perhaps divides the False and True;
Yes; and a single Alif were the clue —
Could you but find it — to the Treasure-house,
And peradventure to THE MASTER too;

LI

Whose secret Presence, through Creation's veins
Running Quicksilver-like eludes your pains;
Taking all shapes from Mah to Mahi; and
They change and perish all — but He remains;

LII

A moment guess'd — then back behind the Fold
Immerst of Darkness round the Drama roll'd
Which, for the Pastime of Eternity,
He doth Himself contrive, enact, behold.

* * * * * * *

LXVI

I sent my Soul through the Invisible
Some letter of that After-life to spell:
And by and by my Soul return'd to me,
And answer'd, "I Myself am Heav'n and Hell:"

LXVII

Heav'n but the Vision of fulfill'd Desire,
And Hell the Shadow from a Soul on fire
Cast on the Darkness into which Ourselves
So late emerg'd from, shall so soon expire.

LXVIII

We are no other than a moving row
Of Magic Shadow-shapes that come and go
Round with the Sun-illumin'd Lantern held
In Midnight by the Master of the Show;

LXIX

But helpless Pieces of the Game He plays
Upon this Chequer-board of Nights and Days;
Hither and thither moves, and checks, and slays,
And one by one back in the Closet lays.

LXX

The Ball no question makes of Ayes and Noes,
But here or there as strikes the Player goes;
And He that toss'd you down into the Field,
He knows about it all — HE knows — HE knows!

LXXI

The Moving Finger writes; and, having writ,
Moves on: nor all your Piety nor Wit
Shall lure it back to cancel half a Line
Nor all your Tears wash out a Word of it.

* * * * * * *

LXXVIII

What! out of senseless Nothing to provoke
A conscious Something to resent the yoke
Of unpermitted Pleasure, under pain
Of Everlasting Penalties, if broke!

* * * * * * *

LXXX

Oh Thou, who didst with pitfall and with gin
Beset the Road I was to wander in,
Thou wilt not with Predestin'd Evil round
Enmesh, and then impute my Fall to Sin!

LXXXI

Oh Thou, who Man of baser Earth didst make,
And ev'n with Paradise devise the Snake:
For all the sin wherewith the Face of Man
Is blackened — Man's forgiveness give — and take.

* * * * * * *

XCVI

Yet Ah, that Spring should vanish with the Rose
That Youth's sweet-scented manuscript should close!
The Nightingale that in the branches sang,
Oh whence, and whither flown again, who knows!

XCVII

Would but the Desert of the Fountain yield
One glimpse — if dimly, yet indeed, reveal'd,
To which the fainting Traveller might spring,
As springs the trampled herbage of the field!

XCVIII

Would but some wingèd Angel ere too late
Arrest the yet unfolded Roll of Fate,
And make the stern Recorder otherwise
Enregister, or quite obliterate!

XCIX

Ah Love! could you and I with Him conspire
To grasp this sorry Scheme of Things entire,
Would not we shatter it to bits — and then
Re-mould it nearer to the Heart's desire.

C

Yon rising Moon that looks for us again —
How oft hereafter will she wax and wane;
How oft hereafter rising look for us
Through this same Garden — and for one in vain!

CI

And when like her, oh Saki, you shall pass
Among the Guests Star-scatter'd on the Grass,
And in your joyous errand reach the spot
Where I made One — turn down an empty Glass!

ALFRED, LORD TENNYSON (1809–1892)

LILIAN

Airy, fairy Lilian,
Flitting, fairy Lilian,
When I ask her if she love me,
Clasps her tiny hands above me,
Laughing all she can;
She'll not tell me if she love me,
Cruel little Lilian.

When my passion seeks
Pleasance in love-sighs,
She, looking thro' and thro' me
Thoroughly to undo me,
Smiling, never speaks:
So innocent-arch, so cunning-simple,
From beneath her gathered wimple
Glancing with black-beaded eyes,
Till the lightning laughters dimple
The baby-roses in her cheeks;
Then away she flies.

Prithee weep, May Lilian!
Gaiety without eclipse
Wearieth me, May Lilian:
Thro' my very heart it thrilleth
When from crimson-threaded lips
Silver-treble laughter trilleth:
Prithee weep, May Lilian.
Praying all I can,
If prayers will not hush thee,
Airy Lilian,
Like a rose-leaf I will crush thee,
Fairy Lilian.

MARIANA

With blackest moss the flower-plots
Were thickly crusted, one and all:
The rusted nails fell from the knots
That held the pear to the gable-wall.
The broken sheds look'd sad and strange:
Unlifted was the clinking latch;
Weeded and worn the ancient thatch
Upon the lonely moated grange.
She only said, "My life is dreary,
He cometh not," she said;
She said, "I am aweary, aweary,
I would that I were dead!"

Her tears fell with the dews at even;
Her tears fell ere the dews were dried;
She could not look on the sweet heaven,
Either at morn or eventide.
After the flitting of the bats,
When thickest dark did trance the sky,
She drew her casement-curtain by,
And glanced athwart the glooming flats.
She only said, "The night is dreary,
He cometh not," she said;
She said, "I am aweary, aweary,
I would that I were dead!"

Upon the middle of the night,
  Waking she heard the night-fowl crow:
The cock sung out an hour ere light:
  From the dark fen the oxen's low
Came to her: without hope of change,
  In sleep she seem'd to walk forlorn,
  Till cold winds woke the grey-eyed morn
About the lonely moated grange.
    She only said, "The day is dreary,
      He cometh not," she said;
    She said, "I am aweary, aweary,
      I would that I were dead!"

About a stone-cast from the wall
  A sluice with blacken'd waters slept
And o'er it many, round and small,
  The cluster'd marish-mosses crept.
Hard by a poplar shook alway,
  All silver-green with gnarlèd bark:
  For leagues no other tree did mark
The level waste, the rounding grey.
    She only said, "My life is dreary,
      He cometh not," she said;
    She said, "I am aweary, aweary,
      I would that I were dead!"

And ever when the moon was low,
  And the shrill winds were up and away,
In the white curtain, to and fro,
  She saw the gusty shadow sway.
But when the moon was very low,
  And wild winds bound within their cell,
  The shadow of the poplar fell
Upon her bed, across her brow.
    She only said, "The night is dreary,
      He cometh not," she said;
    She said, "I am aweary, aweary,
      I would that I were dead!"

All day within the dreamy house,
  The doors upon their hinges creak'd;
The blue fly sung in the pane; the mouse
  Behind the mouldering wainscot shriek'd,
Or from the crevice peer'd about.
  Old faces glimmer'd thro' the doors,
  Old footsteps trod the upper floors,
Old voices called her from without.
    She only said, "My life is dreary,
      He cometh not," she said;
    She said, "I am aweary, aweary,
      I would that I were dead!"

The sparrows' chirrup on the roof,
  The slow clock ticking, and the sound
Which to the wooing wind aloof
  The poplar made, did all confound
Her sense; but most she loathed the hour
  When the thick-moated sunbeam lay
  Athwart the chambers, and the day
Was sloping toward his western bower.
    Then, said she, "I am very dreary,
      He will not come," she said;
    She wept, "I am aweary, aweary,
      Oh, God, that I were dead!"

THE LADY OF SHALOTT

PART I

On either side of the river lie
Long fields of barley and of rye,
That clothe the wold and meet the sky;
And thro' the field the road runs by
    To many-tower'd Camelot;
And up and down the people go,
Gazing where the lilies blow
Round an island there below,
    The island of Shalott.

Willows whiten, aspens quiver,
Little breezes dusk and shiver
Thro' the wave that runs forever
By the island in the river
    Flowing down to Camelot.
Four grey walls, and four grey towers,
Overlook a space of flowers,
And the silent isle imbowers
    The Lady of Shalott.

By the margin, willow-veil'd,
Slide the heavy barges trail'd
By slow horses; and unhail'd
The shallop flitteth silken-sail'd
    Skimming down to Camelot:
But who hath seen her wave her hand?
Or at the casement seen her stand?
Or is she known in all the land,
    The Lady of Shalott?

Only reapers, reaping early
In among the bearded barley,
Hear a song that echoes cheerly
From the river winding clearly,
    Down to tower'd Camelot:
And by the moon the reaper weary,
Piling sheaves in uplands airy,
Listening, whispers, "'Tis the fairy
    Lady of Shalott."

PART II

There she weaves by night and day
A magic web with colours gay.

She has heard a whisper say,
A curse is on her if she stay
To look down to Camelot.
She knows not what the curse may be,
And so she weaveth steadily,
And little other care hath she,
The Lady of Shalott.

And moving thro' a mirror clear
That hangs before her all the year,
Shadows of the world appear.
There she sees the highway near
Winding down to Camelot:
There the river eddy whirls,
And there the surly village-churls,
And the red cloaks of market girls,
Pass onward from Shalott.

Sometimes a troop of damsels glad,
An abbot on an ambling pad,
Sometimes a curly shepherd-lad,
Or long-hair'd page in crimson clad,
Goes by to tower'd Camelot;
And sometimes thro' the mirror blue
The knights come riding two and two;
She hath no loyal knight and true,
The Lady of Shalott.

But in her web she still delights
To weave the mirror's magic sights,
For often thro' the silent nights
A funeral, with plumes and lights
And music, went to Camelot:
Or when the moon was overhead,
Came two young lovers lately wed;
"I am half sick of shadows," said
The Lady of Shalott.

PART III

A bow-shot from her bower-eaves,
He rode between the barley-sheaves,
The sun came dazzling thro' the leaves,
And flamed upon the brazen greaves
Of bold Sir Lancelot.
A red-cross knight forever kneel'd
To a lady in his shield,
That sparkled on the yellow field,
Beside remote Shalott.

The gemmy bridle glitter'd free,
Like to some branch of stars we see
Hung in the golden Galaxy.
The bridle bells rang merrily
As he rode down to Camelot:
And from his blazon'd baldric slung
A mighty silver bugle hung,
And as he rode his armour rung,
Beside remote Shalott.

All in the blue unclouded weather
Thick-jewell'd shone the saddle-leather,
The helmet and the helmet-feather
Burn'd like one burning flame together,
As he rode down to Camelot.
As often thro' the purple night,
Below the starry clusters bright,
Some bearded meteor trailing light,
Moves over still Shalott.

His broad clear brow in sunlight glow'd;
On burnish'd hooves his war-horse strode;
From underneath his helmet flow'd
His coal-black curls as on he rode,
As he rode down to Camelot.
From the bank and from the river
He flash'd into the crystal mirror,
"Tirra lirra," by the river
Sang Sir Lancelot.

She left the web, she left the loom,
She made three paces thro' the room,
She saw the water-lily bloom,
She saw the helmet and the plume,
She look'd down to Camelot.
Out flew the web and floated wide;
The mirror crack'd from side to side;
"The curse is come upon me," cried
The Lady of Shalott.

PART IV

In the stormy east-wind straining,
The pale yellow woods were waning,
The broad stream in his banks complaining,
Heavily the low sky raining,
Over tower'd Camelot;
Down she came and found a boat
Beneath a willow left afloat,
And round about the prow she wrote
The Lady of Shalott.

And down the river's dim expanse
Like some bold seer in a trance,
Seeing all his own mischance —
With a glassy countenance
Did she look to Camelot.
And at the closing of the day
She loosed the chain, and down she lay;
The broad stream bore her far away,
The Lady of Shalott.

Lying, robed in snowy white,
That loosely flew to left and right —

The leaves upon her falling light —
Thro' the noises of the night
She floated down to Camelot:
And as the boat-head wound along
The willowy hills and fields among,
They heard her singing her last song,
The Lady of Shalott.

Heard a carol, mournful, holy,
Chanted loudly, chanted lowly,
Till her blood was frozen slowly,
And her eyes were darken'd wholly,
Turn'd to tower'd Camelot.
For ere she reach'd upon the tide
The first house by the water-side,
Singing in her song she died,
The Lady of Shalott.

Under tower and balcony,
By garden-wall and gallery,
A gleaming shape she floated by,
Dead-pale between the houses high,
Silent into Camelot.
Out upon the wharfs they came,
Knight and burgher, lord and dame,
And round the prow they read her name,
The Lady of Shalott.

Who is this? and what is here?
And in the lighted palace near
Died the sound of royal cheer;
And they cross'd themselves for fear,
All the knights at Camelot:
But Lancelot mused a little space;
He said, "She has a lovely face;
God in his mercy lend her grace,
The Lady of Shalott."

THE TWO VOICES

A still small voice spake unto me,
"Thou art so full of misery,
Were it not better not to be?"

Then to the still small voice I said;
"Let me not cast in endless shade
What is so wonderfully made."

To which the voice did urge reply;
"To-day I saw the dragon-fly
Come from the wells where he did lie.

"An inner impulse rent the veil
Of his old husk: from head to tail
Came out clear plates of sapphire mail.

"He dried his wings: like gauze they grew;
Thro' crofts and pastures wet with dew
A living flash of light he flew."

I said, "When first the world began,
Young Nature thro' five cycles ran,
And in the sixth she moulded man.

"She gave him mind, the lordliest
Proportion, and, above the rest,
Dominion in the head and breast."

Thereto the silent voice replied;
"Self-blinded are you by your pride;
Look up thro' night: the world is wide.

"This truth within thy mind rehearse,
That in a boundless universe
Is boundless better, boundless worse.

"Think you this mould of hopes and fears
Could find no statelier than his peers
In yonder hundred million spheres?"

It spake, moreover, in my mind.
"Tho' thou wert scatter'd to the wind,
Yet is there plenty of the kind."

Then did my response clearer fall:
"No compound of this earthly ball
Is like another, all in all."

To which he answer'd scoffingly:
"Good soul! suppose I grant it thee,
Who'll weep for thy deficiency?

"Or will one beam be less intense,
When thy peculiar difference
Is cancell'd in the world of sense?"

I would have said, "Thou canst not know,"
But my full heart, that work'd below,
Rain'd thro' my sight its overflow.

Again the voice spake unto me:
"Thou art so steep'd in misery,
Surely 'twere better not to be.

"Thine anguish will not let thee sleep,
Nor any train of reason keep:
Thou canst not think, but thou wilt weep."

I said, "The years with change advance:
If I make dark my countenance,
I shut my life from happier chance.

"Some turn this sickness yet might take,
Ev'n yet." But he: "What drug can make
A wither'd palsy cease to shake?"

I wept, "Tho' I should die, I know
That all about the thorn will blow
In tufts of rosy-tinted snow;

"And men, thro' novel spheres of thought
Still moving after truth long sought,
Will learn new things when I am not."

"Yet," said the secret voice, "some time,
Sooner or later, will gray prime
Make thy grass hoar with early rime.

"Not less swift souls that yearn for light,
Rapt after heaven's starry flight,
Would sweep the tracts of day and night.

"Not less the bee would range her cells,
The furzy prickle fire the dells,
The foxglove cluster dappled bells."

I said that "all the years invent;
Each month is various to present
The world with some development.

"Were this not well, to bide mine hour,
Tho' watching from a ruin'd tower
How grows the day of human power?"

"The highest-mounted mind," he said,
"Still sees the sacred morning spread
The silent summit overhead.

"Will thirty seasons render plain
Those lonely lights that still remain,
Just breaking over land and main?

"Or make that morn, from his cold crown
And crystal silence creeping down,
Flood with full daylight glebe and town?

"Forerun thy peers, thy time, and let
Thy feet, millenniums hence, be set
In midst of knowledge, dream'd not yet.

"Thou hast not gain'd a real height,
Nor art thou nearer to the light,
Because the scale is infinite.

"'Twere better not to breathe or speak,
Than cry for strength, remaining weak,
And seem to find, but still to seek.

"Moreover, but to seem to find
Asks what thou lackest, thought resign'd,
A healthy frame, a quiet mind."

I said, "When I am gone away,
'He dared not tarry,' men will say,
Doing dishonour to my clay."

"This is more vile," he made reply,
"To breathe and loathe, to live and sigh,
Than once from dread of pain to die.

"Sick art thou — a divided will
Still heaping on the fear of ill
The fear of men, a coward still.

"Do men love thee? Art thou so bound
To men, that how thy name may sound
Will vex thee lying underground?

"The memory of the wither'd leaf
In endless time is scarce more brief
Than of the garner'd Autumn-sheaf.

"Go, vexèd Spirit, sleep in trust;
The right ear, that is fill'd with dust,
Hears little of the false or just."

"Hard task, to pluck resolve," I cried,
"From emptiness and the waste wide
Of that abyss, or scornful pride!

"Nay — rather yet that I could raise
One hope that warm'd me in the days
While still I yearn'd for human praise.

"When, wide in soul and bold of tongue,
Among the tents I paused and sung,
The distant battle flash'd and rung.

"I sung the joyful Pæan clear,
And, sitting, burnish'd without fear
The brand, the buckler, and the spear —

"Waiting to strive a happy strife,
To war with falsehood to the knife,
And not to lose the good of life —

"Some hidden principle to move,
To put together, part and prove,
And mete the bounds of hate and love —

"As far as might be, to carve out
Free space for every human doubt,
That the whole mind might orb about —

"To search through all I felt or saw,
The springs of life, the depths of awe,
And reach the law within the law:

"At least, not rotting like a weed,
But, having sown some generous seed,
Fruitful of further thought and deed,

"To pass, when Life her light withdraws,
Not void of righteous self-applause,
Nor in a merely selfish cause —

"In some good cause, not in mine own,
To perish, wept for, honour'd, known,
And like a warrior overthrown;

"Whose eyes are dim with glorious tears,
When soil'd with noble dust, he hears
His country's war-song thrill his ears:

"Then dying of a mortal stroke,
What time the fóeman's line is broke,
And all the war is rolled in smoke."

"Yea!" said the voice, "thy dream was good,
While thou abodest in the bud.
It was the stirring of the blood.

"If Nature put not forth her power
About the opening of the flower,
Who is it that could live an hour?

"Then comes the check, the change, the fall,
Pain rises up, old pleasures pall.
There is one remedy for all.

"Yet hadst thou, thro' enduring pain,
Link'd month to month with such a chain
Of knitted purport, all were vain.

"Thou hadst not between death and birth
Dissolved the riddle of the earth.
So were thy labor little-worth.

"That men with knowledge merely play'd,
I told thee — hardly nigher made,
Tho' scaling slow from grade to grade;

"Much less this dreamer, deaf and blind,
Named man, may hope some truth to find,
That bears relation to the mind.

"For every worm beneath the moon
Draws different threads, and late and soon
Spins, toiling out his own cocoon.

"Cry, faint not: either Truth is born
Beyond the polar gleam forlorn,
Or in the gateways of the morn.

"Cry, faint not, climb: the summits slope
Beyond the furthest flights of hope,
Wrapt in dense cloud from base to cope.

"Sometimes a little corner shines,
As over rainy mist inclines
A gleaming crag with belts of pines.

"I will go forward, sayest thou,
I shall not fail to find her now.
Look up, the fold is on her brow.

"If straight thy track, or if oblique,
Thou know'st not. Shadows thou dost strike,
Embracing cloud, Ixion-like;

"And owning but a little more
Than beasts, abidest lame and poor,
Calling thyself a little lower

"Than angels. Cease to wail and brawl!
Why inch by inch to darkness crawl?
There is one remedy for all."

"O dull, one-sided voice," said I,
"Wilt thou make every thing a lie,
To flatter me that I may die?

"I know that age to age succeeds,
Blowing a noise of tongues and deeds,
A dust of systems and of creeds.

"I cannot hide that some have striven,
Achieving calm, to whom was given
The joy that mixes man with Heaven:

"Who, rowing hard against the stream,
Saw distant gates of Eden gleam,
And did not dream it was a dream;

"But heard, by secret transport led,
Ev'n in the charnels of the dead,
The murmur of the fountain-head —

"Which did accomplish their desire,
Bore and forbore, and did not tire,
Like Stephen, an unquenchèd fire.

"He heeded not reviling tones,
Nor sold his heart to idle moans,
Tho' cursed and scorn'd, and bruised with stones:

"But looking upward, full of grace,
He pray'd, and from a happy place
God's glory smote him on the face."

The sullen answer slid betwixt:
"Not that the grounds of hope were fix'd,
The elements were kindlier mix'd."

I said, "I toil beneath the curse,
But, knowing not the universe,
I fear to slide from bad to worse.

"And that, in seeking to undo
One riddle, and to find the true,
I knit a hundred others new:

"Or that this anguish fleeting hence,
Unmanacled from bonds of sense,
Be fix'd and froz'n to permanence:

"For I go, weak from suffering here:
Naked I go, and void of cheer:
What is it that I may not fear?"

"Consider well," the voice replied,
"His face, that two hours since hath died;
Wilt thou find passion, pain or pride?

"Will he obey when one commands?
Or answer should one press his hands?
He answers not, nor understands.

"His palms are folded on his breast:
There is no other thing express'd
But long disquiet merged in rest.

"His lips are very mild and meek:
Tho' one should smite him on the cheek,
And on the mouth, he will not speak.

"His little daughter, whose sweet face
He kiss'd, taking his last embrace,
Becomes dishonour to her race —

"His sons grow up that bear his name,
Some grow to honour, some to shame, —
But he is chill to praise or blame.

"He will not hear the north-wind rave,
Nor, moaning, household shelter crave
From winter rains that beat his grave.

"High up the vapours fold and swim:
About him broods the twilight dim:
The place he knew forgetteth him."

"If all be dark, vague voice," I said,
"These things are wrapt in doubt and dread,
Nor canst thou show the dead are dead.

"The sap dries up: the plant declines.
A deeper tale my heart divines.
Know I not Death? the outward signs?

"I found him when my years were few;
A shadow on the graves I knew,
And darkness in the village yew.

"From grave to grave the shadow crept:
In her still place the morning wept:
Touch'd by his feet the daisy slept.

"The simple senses crown'd his head.
'Omega! thou art Lord,' they said,
'We find no motion in the dead.'

"Why, if man rot in dreamless ease,
Should that plain fact, as taught by these,
Not make him sure that he shall cease?

"Who forged that other influence,
That heat of inward evidence,
By which he doubts against the sense?

"He owns the fatal gift of eyes,
That read his spirit blindly wise,
Not simple as a thing that dies.

"Here sits he shaping wings to fly:
His heart forebodes a mystery:
He names the name Eternity.

"That type of Perfect in his mind
In Nature can he nowhere find.
He sows himself on every wind.

"He seems to hear a Heavenly Friend,
And thro' thick veils to apprehend
A labour working to an end.

"The end and the beginning vex
His reason: many things perplex,
With motions, checks, and counter-checks.

"He knows a baseness in his blood
At such strange war with something good,
He may not do the thing he would.

"Heaven opens inward, chasms yawn,
Vast images in glimmering dawn,
Half shown, are broken and withdrawn.

"Ah! sure within him and without,
Could his dark wisdom find it out,
There must be answer to his doubt.

"But thou canst answer not again.
With thine own weapon art thou slain,
Or thou wilt answer but in vain.

"The doubt would rest, I dare not solve.
In the same circle we revolve.
Assurance only breeds resolve."

As when a billow, blown against,
Falls back, the voice with which I fenced
A little ceased, but recommenced.

"Where wert thou when thy father play'd
In his free field, and pastime made,
A merry boy in sun and shade?

"A merry boy they call'd him then,
He sat upon the knees of men
In days that never come again.

"Before the little ducts began
To feed thy bones with lime, and ran
Their course, till thou wert also man:

"Who took a wife, who rear'd his race,
Whose wrinkles gather'd on his face,
Whose troubles number with his days:

"A life of nothings, nothing-worth,
From that first nothing ere his birth
To that last nothing under earth!"

"These words," I said, "are like the rest·
No certain clearness, but at best
A vague suspicion of the breast:

"But if I grant, thou mightst defend
The thesis which thy words intend —
That to begin implies to end;

"Yet how should I for certain hold
Because my memory is so cold,
That I first was in human mould?

"I cannot make this matter plain,
But I would shoot, howe'er in vain
A random arrow from the brain.

"It may be that no life is found,
Which only to one engine bound
Falls off, but cycles always round.

"As old mythologies relate,
Some draught of Lethe might await
The slipping thro' from state to state.

"As here we find in trances, men
Forget the dream that happens then,
Until they fall in trance again.

"So might we, if our state were such
As one before, remember much,
For those two likes might meet and touch.

"But if I lapsed from nobler place,
Some legend of a fallen race
Alone might hint of my disgrace;

"Some vague emotion of delight
In gazing up an Alpine height,
Some yearning toward the lamps of night;

"Or if thro' lower lives I came —
Tho' all experience past became
Consolidate in mind and frame —

"I might forget my weaker lot;
For is not our first year forgot?
The haunts of memory echo not.

"And men, whose reason long was blind,
From cells of madness unconfined,
Oft lose whole years of darker mind.

"Much more, if first I floated free,
As naked essence, must I be
Incompetent of memory:

"For memory dealing but with time,
And he with matter, could she climb
Beyond her own material prime?

"Moreover, something is or seems,
That touches me with mystic gleams,
Like glimpses of forgotten dreams —

"Of something felt, like something here;
Of something done, I know not where;
Such as no language may declare."

The still voice laugh'd. "I talk," said he,
"Not with thy dreams. Suffice it thee
Thy pain is a reality."

"But thou," said I, "hast missed thy mark,
Who sought'st to wreck my mortal ark,
By making all the horizon dark.

"Why not set forth, if I should do
This rashness, that which might ensue
With this old soul in organs new?

"Whatever crazy sorrow saith,
No life that breathes with human breath
Has ever truly long'd for death.

"'Tis life, whereof our nerves are scant,
Oh life, not death, for which we pant;
More life, and fuller, that I want."

I ceased, and sat as one forlorn.
Then said the voice, in quiet scorn,
"Behold, it is the Sabbath morn."

And I arose, and I released
The casement, and the light increased
With freshness in the dawning east.

Like soften'd airs that blowing steal,
When meres begin to uncongeal,
The sweet church-bells began to peal.

On to God's house the people prest:
Passing the place where each must rest,
Each enter'd like a welcome guest.

One walk'd between his wife and child,
With measured footfall firm and mild,
And now and then he gravely smiled.

The prudent partner of his blood
Lean'd on him, faithful, gentle, good,
Wearing the rose of womanhood.

And in their double love secure,
The little maiden walk'd demure,
Pacing with downward eyelids pure.

These three made unity so sweet,
My frozen heart began to beat,
Remembering its ancient heat.

I blest them, and they wander'd on:
I spoke, but answer came there none:
The dull and bitter voice was gone.

A second voice was at mine ear,
A little whisper silver-clear,
A murmur, "Be of better cheer."

As from some blissful neighbourhood,
A notice faintly understood,
"I see the end, and know the good."

A little hint to solace woe,
A hint, a whisper breathing low,
"I may not speak of what I know."

Like an Æolian harp that wakes
No certain air, but overtakes
Far thought with music that it makes:

Such seem'd the whisper at my side:
"What is it thou knowest, sweet voice?" I cried.
"A hidden hope," the voice replied:

So heavenly-toned, that in that hour
From out my sullen heart a power
Broke, like the rainbow from the shower,

To feel, altho' no tongue can prove,
That every cloud, that spreads above
And veileth love, itself is love.

And forth into the fields I went,
And Nature's living motion lent
The pulse of hope to discontent.

I wonder'd at the bounteous hours,
The slow result of winter showers:
You scarce could see the grass for flowers.

I wonder'd while I paced along:
The woods were fill'd so full with song,
There seem'd no room for sense of wrong;

And all so variously wrought,
I marvell'd how the mind was brought
To anchor by one gloomy thought;

And wherefore rather I made choice
To commune with that barren voice,
Than him that said, "Rejoice! Rejoice!"

THE PALACE OF ART

I built my soul a lordly pleasure-house,
Wherein at ease for aye to dwell.
I said, "O Soul, make merry and carouse,
Dear soul, for all is well."

A huge crag-platform, smooth as burnish'd brass
I chose. The rangèd ramparts bright
From level meadow-bases of deep grass
Suddenly scaled the light.

Thereon I built it firm. Of ledge or shelf
The rock rose clear, or winding stair.
My soul would live alone unto herself
In her high palace there.

And "while the world runs round and round," I said,
"Reign thou apart, a quiet king,
Still as, while Saturn whirls, his steadfast shade
Sleeps on his luminous ring."

To which my soul made answer readily:
"Trust me, in bliss I shall abide
In this great mansion that is built for me,
So royal-rich and wide."

Four courts I made, East, West, and South and North,
In each a squarèd lawn, wherefrom
The golden gorge of dragons spouted forth
A flood of fountain-foam.

And round the cool green courts there ran a row
Of cloisters, branch'd like mighty woods,
Echoing all night to that sonorous flow
Of spouted fountain-floods.

And round the roofs a gilded gallery
That lent broad verge to distant lands,
Far as the wild swan wings, to where the sky
Dipt down to sea and sands.

From those four jets four currents in one swell
Across the mountain stream'd below
In misty folds, that floating as they fell
Lit up a torrent-bow.

And high on every peak a statue seem'd
To hang on tiptoe, tossing up
A cloud of incense of all odour steam'd
From out a golden cup.

So that she thought, "And who shall gaze upon
My palace with unblinded eyes,
While this great bow will waver in the sun,
And that sweet incense rise?"

For that sweet incense rose and never fail'd,
And, while day sank or mounted higher,
The light aërial gallery, golden-rail'd,
Burnt like a fringe of fire.

Likewise the deep-set windows, stain'd and traced,
Would seem slow-flaming crimson fires
From shadow'd grots of arches interlaced,
And tipt with frost-like spires.

Full of long-sounding corridors it was,
That over-vaulted grateful gloom,
Thro' which the livelong day my soul did pass,
Well-pleased, from room to room.

Full of great rooms and small the palace stood,
All various, each a perfect whole
From living Nature, fit for every mood
And change of my still soul.

For some were hung with arras green and blue,
Showing a gaudy summer-morn,
Where with puff'd cheek the belted hunter blew
His wreathèd bugle-horn.

One seem'd all dark and red — a tract of sand,
And some one pacing there alone,
Who paced forever in a glimmering land,
Lit with a low large moon.

One show'd an iron coast and angry waves,
You seem'd to hear them climb and fall
And roar rock-thwarted under bellowing caves,
Beneath the windy wall.

And one, a full-fed river winding slow
By herds upon an endless plain,
The ragged rims of thunder brooding low,
With shadow-streaks of rain.

And one, the reapers at their sultry toil.
In front they bound the sheaves. Behind
Were realms of upland, prodigal in oil,
And hoary to the wind.

And one, a foreground black with stones and slags,
Beyond, a line of heights, and higher,
All barr'd with long white cloud, the scornful crags,
And highest, snow and fire.

And one, an English home — grey twilight pour'd
On dewy pastures, dewy trees,
Softer than sleep — all things in order stored,
A haunt of ancient Peace.

Nor these alone, but every landscape fair,
As fit for every mood of mind,
Or gay, or grave, or sweet, or stern, was there
Not less than truth design'd.

Or the maid-mother by a crucifix,
In tracts of pasture sunny-warm,
Beneath branch-work of costly sardonyx
Sat smiling, babe in arm.

Or in a clear-wall'd city on the sea,
Near gilded organ-pipes, her hair
Wound with white roses, slept St. Cicily;
An angel look'd at her.

Or thronging all one porch of Paradise
A group of Houris bow'd to see
The dying Islamite, with hands and eyes
That said, We wait for thee.

Or mythic Uther's deeply-wounded son
In some fair space of sloping greens
Lay, dozing in the vale of Avalon,
And watch'd by weeping queens.

Or hollowing one hand against his ear,
To list a foot-fall, ere he saw
The wood-nymph, stay'd the Ausonian king to hear
Of wisdom and of law.

Or over hills with peaky tops engrail'd,
And many a tract of palm and rice,
The throne of Indian Cama slowly sail'd,
A summer fann'd with spice.

Or sweet Europa's mantle blew unclasp'd,
From off her shoulder backward borne:
From one hand dropp'd a crocus: one hand grasp'd
The mild bull's golden horn.

Or else flush'd Ganymede, his rosy thigh
Half-buried in the Eagle's down,
Sole as a flying star, shot thro' the sky
Above the pillar'd town.

Nor these alone: but every legend fair
Which the supreme Caucasian mind
Carved out of Nature for itself, was there,
Not less than life, design'd.

Then in the towers I placed great bells that swung,
Moved of themselves, with silver sound;
And with choice paintings of wise men I hung
The royal dais round.

For there was Milton like a seraph strong,
Beside him Shakespeare bland and mild;
And there the world-worn Dante grasp'd his song,
And somewhat grimly smiled.

And there the Ionian father of the rest;
A million wrinkles carv'd his skin;
A hundred winters snow'd upon his breast,
From cheek and throat and chin.

Above, the fair hall-ceiling stately-set
Many an arch high up did lift,
And angels rising and descending met
With interchange of gift.

Below was all mosaic choicely plann'd
With cycles of the human tale
Of this wide world, the times of every land
So wrought, they will not fail.

The people here, a beast of burden slow,
Toil'd onward, prick'd with goads and stings;
Here play'd, a tiger, rolling to and fro
The heads and crowns of kings;

Here rose, an athlete, strong to break or bind
All force in bonds that might endure,
And here once more like some sick man declined,
And trusted any cure.

But over these she trod: and those great bells
Began to chime. She took her throne:
She sat betwixt the shining Oriels,
To sing her songs alone.

And thro' the topmost Oriels' coloured flame
Two godlike faces gazed below;
Plato the wise, and large-brow'd Verulam,
The first of those who know.

And all those names, that in their motion were
Full-welling fountain-heads of change,
Betwixt the slender shafts were blazon'd fair
In diverse raiment strange:

Thro' which the lights, rose, amber, emerald, blue,
Flush'd in her temples, and her eyes.
And from her lips, as morn from Memnon, drew
Rivers of melodies.

No nightingale delighteth to prolong
Her low preamble all alone,
More than my soul to hear her echo'd song
Throb thro' the ribbèd stone;

Singing and murmuring in her feastful mirth,
Joying to feel herself alive,
Lord over Nature, Lord of the visible earth,
Lord of the senses five;

Communing with herself: "All these are mine,
And let the world have peace or wars,
'Tis one to me." She — when young night divine
Crown'd dying day with stars,

Making sweet close of his delicious toils —
Lit light in wreaths and anadems,
And pure quintessences of precious oils
In hollow'd moons of gems,

To mimic heaven; and clapt her hands and cried,
"I marvel if my still delight
In this great house so royal-rich, and wide,
Be flatter'd to the height.

"O all things fair to sate my various eyes!
O shapes and hues that please me well!
O silent faces of the Great and Wise,
My Gods, with whom I dwell!

"O God-like isolation which art mine,
I can but count thee perfect gain,
What time I watch the darkening droves of swine
That range on yonder plain.

"In filthy sloughs they roll a prurient skin,
They graze and wallow, breed and sleep;
And oft some brainless devil enters in,
And drives them to the deep."

Then of the moral instinct would she prate
And of the rising from the dead,
As hers by right of full-accomplish'd Fate;
And at the last she said:

"I take possession of man's mind and deed.
I care not what the sects may brawl.
I sit as God, holding no form of creed,
But contemplating all."

Full oft the riddle of the painful earth
Flash'd thro' her as she sat alone,
Yet not the less held she her solemn mirth,
And intellectual throne.

* * * * * * *
* * * * * * *

And so she throve and prosper'd: so three years
She prosper'd: on the fourth she fell,
Like Herod, when the shout was in his ears,
Struck thro' with pangs of hell.

Lest she should fail and perish utterly,
God, before whom ever lie bare
The abysmal deeps of Personality,
Plagued her with sore despair.

When she would think, where'er she turn'd her sight,
The airy hand confusion wrought,
Wrote, "Mene, mene," and divided quite
The kingdom of her thought.

Deep dread and loathing of her solitude
Fell on her, from which mood was born
Scorn of herself; again, from out that mood
Laughter at her self-scorn.

"What! is not this my place of strength," she said,
"My spacious mansion built for me,
Whereof the strong foundation-stones were laid
Since my first memory?"

But in dark corners of her palace stood
Uncertain shapes; and unawares
On white-eyed phantasms weeping tears of blood,
And horrible nightmares,

And hollow shades enclosing hearts of flame,
And, with dim fretted foreheads all,
On corpses three-months-old at noon she came,
That stood against the wall.

A spot of dull stagnation, without light
Or power of movement, seem'd my soul,
'Mid onward-sloping motions infinite
Making for one sure goal.

A still salt pool, lock'd in with bars of sand,
Left on the shore; that hears all night
The plunging seas draw backward from the land
Their moon-led waters white.

A star that with the choral starry dance
Join'd not, but stood, and standing saw
The hollow orb of moving Circumstance
Roll'd round by one fix'd law.

Back on herself her serpent pride had curl'd.
"No voice," she shriek'd in that lone hall,
"No voice breaks thro' the stillness of this world:
One deep, deep silence all!"

She, mouldering with the dull earth's mouldering sod,
Inwrapt tenfold in slothful shame,
Lay there exilèd from eternal God,
Lost to her place and name;

And death and life she hated equally,
And nothing saw, for her despair,
But dreadful time, dreadful eternity,
No comfort anywhere;

Remaining utterly confused with fears,
And ever worse with growing time,
And ever unrelieved by dismal tears,
And all alone in crime:

Shut up as in a crumbling tomb, girt round
With blackness as a solid wall,
Far off she seem'd to hear the dully sound
Of human footsteps fall.

As in strange lands a traveller walking slow,
In doubt and great perplexity,
A little before moon-rise hears the low
Moan of an unknown sea;

And knows not if it be thunder, or a sound
Of rocks thrown down, or one deep cry
Of great wild beasts; then thinketh, "I have found
A new land, but I die."

She howl'd aloud, "I am on fire within.
There comes no murmur of reply.
What is it that will take away my sin,
And save me, lest I die?"

So when four years were wholly finishèd,
She threw her royal robes away.
"Make me a cottage in the vale," she said,
"Where I may mourn and pray.

"Yet pull not down my palace towers, that are
So lightly, beautifully built:
Perchance I may return with others there,
When I have purged my guilt."

A DREAM OF FAIR WOMEN

I read, before my eyelids dropt their shade,
"The Legend of Good Women," long ago
Sung by the morning-star of song, who made
His music heard below;

Dan Chaucer, the first warbler, whose sweet breath
Preluded those melodious bursts that fill
The spacious times of great Elizabeth
With sounds that echo still.

And, for a while, the knowledge of his art
Held me above the subject, as strong gales
Hold swollen clouds from raining, tho' my heart,
Brimful of those wild tales,

Charged both mine eyes with tears. In every land
I saw, wherever light illumineth,
Beauty and anguish walking hand in hand
The downward slope to death.

Those far-renownèd brides of ancient song
Peopled the hollow dark, like burning stars,
And I heard sounds of insult, shame, and wrong,
And trumpets blown for wars;

And clattering flints batter'd with clanging hoofs;
And I saw crowds in column'd sanctuaries;
And forms that pass'd at windows and on roofs
Of marble palaces;

Corpses across the threshold; heroes tall
Dislodging pinnacle and parapet
Upon the tortoise creeping to the wall;
Lances in ambush set;

And high shrine-doors burst thro' with heated blasts
That run before the fluttering tongues of fire;
White surf wind-scatter'd over sails and masts,
And ever climbing higher;

Squadrons and squares of men in brazen plates,
Scaffolds, still sheets of water, divers woes,
Ranges of glimmering vaults with iron grates,
And hush'd seraglios.

So shape chased shape as swift as, when to land
Bluster the winds and tides the self-same way,
Crisp foam-flakes scud along the level sand,
Torn from the fringe of spray.

I started once, or seem'd to start in pain,
Resolved on noble things, and strove to speak,
As when a great thought strikes along the brain,
And flushes all the cheek.

And once my arm was lifted to hew down
A cavalier from off his saddle-bow,
That bore a lady from a leaguer'd town;
And then, I know not how,

All those sharp fancies, by down-lapsing thought
Stream'd onward, lost their edges, and did creep
Roll'd on each other, rounded, smooth'd, and brought
Into the gulfs of sleep.

At last methought that I had wander'd far
In an old wood: fresh-wash'd in coolest dew
The maiden splendours of the morning star
Shook in the steadfast blue.

Enormous elm-tree-boles did stoop and lean
Upon the dusky brushwood underneath
Their broad curved branches, fledged with clearest green,
New from its silken sheath.

The dim red morn had died, her journey done,
And with dead lips smiled at the twilight plain,
Half-fall'n across the threshold of the sun,
Never to rise again.

There was no motion in the dumb dead air,
Not any song of bird or sound of rill;
Gross darkness of the inner sepulchre
Is not so deadly still

As that wide forest. Growths of jasmine turn'd
Their humid arms festooning tree to tree,
And at the root thro' lush green grasses burn'd
The red anemone.

I knew the flowers, I knew the leaves, I knew
The tearful glimmer of the languid dawn
On those long, rank, dark wood-walks drench'd in dew,
Leading from lawn to lawn.

The smell of violets, hidden in the green,
Pour'd back into my empty soul and frame
The times when I remember to have been
Joyful and free from blame.

And from within me a clear undertone
Thrill'd thro' mine ears in that unblissful clime,
"Pass freely thro': the wood is all thine own,
Until the end of time."

At length I saw a lady within call,
Stiller than chisell'd marble, standing there;
A daughter of the gods, divinely tall,
And most divinely fair.

Her loveliness with shame and with surprise
Froze my swift speech: she turning on my face
The star-like sorrows of immortal eyes,
Spoke slowly in her place.

"I had great beauty: ask thou not my name:
No one can be more wise than destiny.
Many drew swords and died. Where'er I came
I brought calamity."

"No marvel, sovereign lady: in fair field
Myself for such a face had boldly died,"
I answer'd free; and turning I appeal'd
To one that stood beside.

But she, with sick and scornful looks averse,
To her full height her stately stature draws;
"My youth," she said, "was blasted with a curse:
This woman was the cause.

"I was cut off from hope in that sad place,
Which men call'd Aulis in those iron years:
My father held his hand upon his face;
I, blinded with my tears,

"Still strove to speak: my voice was thick with sighs
As in a dream. Dimly I could descry
The stern black-bearded kings with wolfish eyes,
Waiting to see me die.

"The high masts flicker'd as they lay afloat;
The crowds, the temples, waver'd, and the shore;
The bright death quiver'd at the victim's throat;
Touch'd; and I knew no more."

Whereto the other with a downward brow:
"I would the white cold heavy-plunging foam
Whirl'd by the wind, had roll'd me deep below
Then when I left my home."

Her slow full words sank thro' the silence drear,
As thunder-drops fall on a sleeping sea:
Sudden I heard a voice that cried "Come here,
That I may look on thee."

I turning saw, throned on a flowery rise,
One sitting on a crimson scarf unroll'd;
A queen, with swarthy cheeks and bold black eyes,
Brow-bound with burning gold.

She, flashing forth a haughty smile, began:
"I govern'd men by change, and so I sway'd
All moods. 'Tis long since I have seen a man.
Once, like the moon, I made

"The ever-shifting currents of the blood
According to my humour ebb and flow.
I have no men to govern in this wood:
That makes my only woe.

"Nay — yet it chafes me that I could not bend
One will; nor tame and tutor with mine eye
That dull cold-blooded Cæsar. Prythee, friend,
Where is Mark Antony?

"The man, my lover, with whom I rode sublime
On Fortune's neck: we sat as God by God:
The Nilus would have risen before his time
And flooded at our nod.

"We drank the Libyan Sun to sleep, and lit
Lamps which out-burn'd Canopus. O my life
In Egypt! O the dalliance and the wit,
The flattery and the strife,

"And the wild kiss, when fresh from war's alarms,
My Hercules, my Roman Antony,
My mailèd Bacchus leapt into my arms,
Contented there to die!

"And there he died: and when I heard my name
Sigh'd forth with life, I would not brook my fear
Of the other: with a worm I balk'd his fame.
What else was left? look here!"

(With that she tore her robe apart, and half
The polish'd argent of her breast to sight
Laid bare. Thereto she pointed with a laugh,
Showing the aspick's bite.)

"I died a Queen. The Roman soldier found
Me lying dead, my crown about my brows,
A name forever! — lying robed and crown'd,
Worthy a Roman spouse."

Her warbling voice, a lyre of widest range
Struck by all passion, did fall down and glance
From tone to tone, and glided thro' all change
Of liveliest utterance.

When she made pause I knew not for delight:
Because with sudden motion from the ground
She rais'd her piercing orbs, and fill'd with light
The interval of sound.

Still with their fires Love tipt his keenest darts;
As once they drew into two burning rings
All beams of Love, melting the mighty hearts
Of captains and of kings.

Slowly my sense undazzled. Then I heard
A noise of some one coming thro' the lawn,
And singing clearer than the crested bird
That claps his wings at dawn.

"The torrent brooks of hallow'd Israel
From craggy hollows pouring, late and soon,
Sound all night long, in falling thro' the dell,
Far-heard beneath the moon.

"The balmy moon of blessèd Israel
Floods all the deep-blue gloom with beams divine:
All night the splinter'd crags that wall the dell
With spires of silver shine."

As one that museth where broad sunshine laves
The lawn by some cathedral, thro' the door
Hearing the holy organ rolling waves
Of sound on roof and floor

Within, and anthem sung, is charm'd and tied
To where he stands, — so stood I, when that flow
Of music left the lips of her that died
To save her father's vow;

The daughter of the warrior Gileadite;
A maiden pure; as when she went along
From Mizpeh's tower'd gate with welcome light,
With timbrel and with song.

My words leapt forth: "Heaven heads the count of crimes
With that wild oath." She render'd answer high:
"Not so, nor once alone; a thousand times
I would be born and die.

"Single I grew, like some green plant, whose root
Creeps to the garden water-pipes beneath
Feeding the flower; but ere my flower to fruit
Changed, I was ripe for death.

"My God, my land, my father — these did move
Me from my bliss of life, that Nature gave,
Lower'd softly with a threefold cord of love
Down to a silent grave.

"And I went mourning, 'No fair Hebrew boy
Shall smile away my maiden blame among
The Hebrew mothers' — emptied of all joy,
Leaving the dance and song,

"Leaving the olive-gardens far below,
Leaving the promise of my bridal bower,
The valleys of grape-loaded vines that glow
Beneath the battled tower.

"The light white cloud swam over us. Anon
We heard the lion roaring from his den;
We saw the large white stars rise one by one,
Or, from the darken'd glen,

"Saw God divide the night with flying flame,
And thunder on the everlasting hills.
I heard Him, for He spake, and grief became
A solemn scorn of ills.

"When the next moon was roll'd into the sky,
Strength came to me that equall'd my desire.
How beautiful a thing it was to die
For God and for my sire!

"It comforts me in this one thought to dwell,
That I subdued me to my father's will;
Because the kiss he gave me, ere I fell,
Sweetens the spirit still.

"Moreover it is written that my race
Hew'd Ammon, hip and thigh, from Aroer
On Arnon unto Minneth," here her face
Glow'd as I look'd at her.

She lock'd her lips: she left me where I stood:
"Glory to God," she sang, and passed afar,
Thridding the sombre boskage of the wood,
Toward the morning-star.

Losing her carol I stood pensively,
As one that from a casement leans his head,
When midnight bells cease ringing suddenly,
And the old year is dead.

"Alas! alas!" a low voice, full of care,
Murmur'd beside me. "Turn and look on me:
I am that Rosamond, whom men call fair,
If what I was I be.

"Would I had been some maiden coarse and poor!
O me, that I should ever see the light!
Those dragon eyes of anger'd Eleanor
Do hunt me, day and night."

She ceased in tears, fallen from hope and trust:
To whom the Egyptian: "O, you tamely died!
You should have clung to Fulvia's waist, and thrust
The dagger thro' her side."

With that sharp sound the white dawn's creeping beams,
Stol'n to my brain, dissolved the mystery
Of folded sleep. The captain of my dreams
Ruled in the eastern sky.

Morn broaden'd on the borders of the dark,
Ere I saw her, who clasp'd in her last trance
Her murder'd father's head, or Joan of Arc,
A light of ancient France;

Or her who knew that Love can vanquish Death,
Who kneeling with one arm about her king,
Drew forth the poison with her balmy breath,
Sweet as new buds in Spring.

No memory labours longer from the deep
Gold-mines of thought to lift the hidden ore
That glimpses, moving up, than I from sleep
To gather and tell o'er

Each little sound and sight. With what dull pain
Compass'd, how eagerly I sought to strike
Into that wondrous track of dreams again!
But no two dreams are like.

As when a soul laments, which hath been blest,
Desiring what is mingled with past years,
In yearnings that can never be exprest
By sighs or groans or tears;

Because all words, tho' cull'd with choicest art,
Failing to give the bitter of the sweet,
Wither beneath the palate, and the heart
Faints, faded by its heat.

YOU ASK ME WHY

You ask me, why, tho' ill at ease,
Within this region I subsist,
Whose spirits falter in the mist,
And languish for the purple seas.

It is the land that freemen till,
That sober-suited Freedom chose,
The land, where girt with friends or foes
A man may speak the thing he will;

A land of settled government,
A land of just and old renown,
Where Freedom slowly broadens down
From precedent to precedent:

Where faction seldom gathers head,
But by degrees to fullness wrought,
The strength of some diffusive thought
Hath time and space to work and spread.

Should banded unions persecute
Opinion, and induce a time
When single thought is civil crime,
And individual freedom mute;

Tho' Power should make from land to land
The name of Britain trebly great —
Tho' every channel of the State
Should fill and choke with golden sand —

Yet waft me from the harbour-mouth,
Wild wind! I seek a warmer sky,
And I will see before I die
The palms and temples of the South.

MORTE D'ARTHUR

So all day long the noise of battle roll'd
Among the mountains by the winter sea;
Until King Arthur's table, man by man,
Had fallen in Lyonness about their Lord,
King Arthur: then, because his wound was deep,
The bold Sir Bedivere uplifted him,
Sir Bedivere, the last of all his knights,
And bore him to a chapel nigh the field,
A broken chancel with a broken cross,
That stood on a dark strait of barren land.
On one side lay the Ocean, and on one
Lay a great water, and the moon was full.
Then spake King Arthur to Sir Bedivere:
"The sequel of to-day unsolders all
The goodliest fellowship of famous knights
Whereof this world holds record. Such a sleep
They sleep — the men I loved. I think that we
Shall nevermore, at any future time,
Delight our souls with talk of knightly deeds,
Walking about the gardens and the halls
Of Camelot, as in the days that were.
I perish by this people which I made, —
Tho' Merlin sware that I should come again
To rule once more — but let what will be, be,
I am so deeply smitten thro' the helm
That without help I cannot last till morn.
Thou therefore take my brand Excalibur,
Which was my pride: for thou rememberest how
In those old days, one summer noon, an arm
Rose up from out the bosom of the lake,
Clothed in white samite, mystic, wonderful,
Holding the sword — and how I row'd across
And took it, and have worn it like a king:
And, wheresoever I am sung or told
In aftertime, this also shall be known:
But now delay not: take Excalibur,
And fling him far into the middle mere:
Watch what thou seest, and lightly bring me word."
To him replied the bold Sir Bedivere:
"It is not meet, Sir King, to leave thee thus,
Aidless, alone, and smitten thro' the helm.
A little thing may harm a wounded man.
Yet I thy hest will all perform at full,
Watch what I see, and lightly bring thee word."
So saying, from the ruin'd shrine he stept
And in the moon athwart the place of tombs,
Where lay the mighty bones of ancient men,
Old knights, and over them the sea-wind sang
Shrill, chill, with flakes of foam. He, stepping down
By zig-zag paths, and juts of pointed rock,
Came on the shining levels of the lake.
There drew he forth the brand Excalibur,

And o'er him, drawing it, the winter moon,
Brightening the skirts of a long cloud, ran forth
And sparkled keen with frost against the hilt:
For all the haft twinkled with diamond sparks,
Myriads of topaz-lights, and jacinth-work
Of subtlest jewellery. He gazed so long
That both his eyes were dazzled, as he stood,
This way and that dividing the swift mind,
In act to throw: but at the last it seem'd
Better to leave Excalibur conceal'd
There in the many-knotted water-flags,
That whistled stiff and dry about the marge.
So strode he back slow to the wounded King.
Then spake King Arthur to Sir Bedivere:
"Hast thou perform'd my mission which I gave?
What is it thou hast seen? or what hast heard?"
And answer made the bold Sir Bedivere:
"I heard the ripple washing in the reeds,
And the wild water lapping on the crag."
To whom replied King Arthur, faint and pale:
"Thou hast betray'd thy nature and thy name,
Not rendering true answer, as beseem'd
Thy fealty, nor like a noble knight:
For surer sign had follow'd, either hand,
Or voice, or else a motion of the mere.
This is a shameful thing for men to lie.
Yet now, I charge thee, quickly go again
As thou art lief and dear, and do the thing
I bade thee, watch, and lightly bring me word."
Then went Sir Bedivere the second time
Across the ridge, and paced beside the mere,
Counting the dewy pebbles, fix'd in thought;
But when he saw the wonder of the hilt,
How curiously and strangely chased, he smote
His palms together, and he cried aloud,
"And if indeed I cast the brand away,
Surely a precious thing, one worthy note,
Should thus be lost forever from the earth,
Which might have pleased the eyes of many men.
What good should follow this, if this were done?
What harm, undone? deep harm to disobey,
Seeing obedience is the bond of rule.
Were it well to obey then, if a king demand
An act unprofitable, against himself?
The King is sick, and knows not what he does.
What record, or what relic of my lord
Should be to aftertime, but empty breath
And rumours of a doubt? but were this kept,
Stored in some treasure-house of mighty kings,
Some one might show it at a joust of arms,
Saying, 'King Arthur's sword, Excalibur,
Wrought by the lonely maiden of the Lake.
Nine years she wrought it, sitting in the deeps
Upon the hidden bases of the hills.'
So might some old man speak in the aftertime
To all the people, winning reverence.
But now much honour and much fame were lost."
So spake he, clouded with his own conceit,
And hid Excalibur the second time,
And so strode back slow to the wounded King.
Then spoke King Arthur, breathing heavily:
"What is it thou hast seen? or what hast heard?"
And answer made the bold Sir Bedivere:
"I heard the water lapping on the crag,
And the long ripple washing in the reeds."
To whom replied King Arthur, much in wrath:
"Ah, miserable and unkind, untrue,
Unknightly, traitor-hearted! Woe is me!
Authority forgets a dying king,
Laid widow'd of the power in his eye
That bow'd the will. I see thee what thou art,
For thou, the latest-left of all my knights,
In whom should meet the offices of all,
Thou wouldst betray me for the precious hilt;
Either from lust of gold, or like a girl
Valuing the giddy pleasure of the eyes.
Yet, for a man may fail in duty twice,
And the third time may prosper, get thee hence:
But, if thou spare to fling Excalibur,
I will arise and slay thee with my hands."
Then quickly rose Sir Bedivere, and ran,
And, leaping down the ridges lightly, plunged
Among the bulrush-beds, and clutch'd the sword,
And strongly wheel'd and threw it. The great brand
Made lightnings in the splendour of the moon,
And flashing round and round, and whirl'd in an arch,
Shot like a streamer of the northern morn,
Seen where the moving isles of winter shock
By night, with noises of the northern sea.
So flash'd and fell the brand Excalibur:
But ere he dipt the surface, rose an arm
Clothed in white samite, mystic, wonderful,
And caught him by the hilt, and brandish'd him
Three times, and drew him under in the mere.
And lightly went the other to the King.
Then spoke King Arthur, drawing thicker breath:
"Now see I by thine eyes that this is done.
Speak out: what is it thou hast heard, or seen?"
And answer made the bold Sir Bedivere:
"Sir King, I closed mine eyelids, lest the gems
Should blind my purpose, for I never saw,
Nor shall see, here or elsewhere, till I die,
Not tho' I live three lives of mortal men,
So great a miracle as yonder hilt.
Then with both hands I flung him, wheeling him;
But when I look'd again, behold an arm,
Clothed in white samite, mystic, wonderful,
That caught him by the hilt, and brandish'd him
Three times, and drew him under in the mere."

And answer made King Arthur, breathing hard:
"My end draws nigh; 'tis time that I were gone.
Make broad thy shoulders to receive my weight,
And bear me to the margin; yet I fear
My wound hath taken cold, and I shall die."
So saying, from the pavement he half rose,
Slowly, with pain, reclining on his arm,
And looking wistfully with wide blue eyes
As in a picture. Him Sir Bedivere
Remorsefully regarded thro' his tears,
And would have spoken, but he found not words,
Then took with care, and kneeling on one knee,
O'er both his shoulders drew the languid hands,
And rising bore him thro' the place of tombs.
But, as he walk'd, King Arthur panted hard,
Like one that feels a nightmare on his bed
When all the house is mute. So sigh'd the King,
Muttering and murmuring at his ear, "Quick, quick!
I fear it is too late, and I shall die."
But the other swiftly strode from ridge to ridge,
Clothed with his breath, and looking, as he walk'd,
Larger than human on the frozen hills.
He heard the deep behind him, and a cry
Before. His own thought drove him, like a goad.
Dry clash'd his harness in the icy caves
And barren chasms, and all to left and right
The bare black cliff clang'd round him, as he based
His feet on juts of slippery crag that rang
Sharp-smitten with the dint of armèd heels —
And on a sudden, lo! the level lake,
And the long glories of the winter moon.
Then saw they how there hove a dusky barge,
Dark as a funeral scarf from stem to stern,
Beneath them; and descending they were ware
That all the decks were dense with stately forms
Black-stoled, black-hooded, like a dream — by these
Three Queens with crowns of gold — and from them rose
A cry that shiver'd to the tingling stars,
And, as it were one voice, an agony
Of lamentation, like a wind, that shrills
All night in a waste land, where no one comes,
Or hath come, since the making of the world.
Then murmur'd Arthur, "Place me in the barge,"
And to the barge they came. There those three Queens
Put forth their hands, and took the King, and wept.
But she, that rose the tallest of them all
And fairest, laid his head upon her lap,
And loosed the shatter'd casque, and chafed his hands,
And call'd him by his name, complaining loud,
And dropping bitter tears against his brow
Striped with dark blood: for all his face was white
And colourless, and like the wither'd moon
Smote by the fresh beam of the springing east;
And all his greaves and cuisses dash'd with drops
Of onset; and the light and lustrous curls —
That made his forehead like a rising sun
High from the dais-throne — were parch'd with dust;
Or, clotted into points and hanging loose,
Mix'd with the knightly growth that fringed his lips.
So like a shatter'd column lay the King;
Not like that Arthur who, with lance in rest,
From spur to plume a star of tournament,
Shot thro' the lists at Camelot, and charged
Before the eyes of ladies and of kings.
Then loudly cried the bold Sir Bedivere,
"Ah! my Lord Arthur, whither shall I go?
Where shall I hide my forehead and my eyes?
For now I see the true old times are dead,
When every morning brought a noble chance,
And every chance brought out a noble knight.
Such times have been not since the light that led
The holy Elders with the gift of myrrh.
But now the whole Round Table is dissolved
Which was an image of the mighty world;
And I, the last, go forth companionless,
And the days darken round me, and the years,
Among new men, strange faces, other minds."
And slowly answered Arthur from the barge:
"The old order changeth, yielding place to new,
And God fulfils Himself in many ways,
Lest one good custom should corrupt the world.
Comfort thyself: what comfort is in me?
I have lived my life, and that which I have done
May He within Himself make pure! but thou,
If thou shouldst never see my face again,
Pray for my soul. More things are wrought by prayer
Than this world dreams of. Wherefore, let thy voice
Rise like a fountain for me night and day.
For what are men better than sheep or goats
That nourish a blind life within the brain,
If, knowing God, they lift not hands of prayer
Both for themselves and those who call them friend?
For so the whole round earth is every way
Bound by gold chains about the feet of God.
But now farewell. I am going a long way
With these thou seest — if indeed I go —

(For all my mind is clouded with a doubt)
To the island-valley of Avilion;
Where falls not hail, or rain, or any snow,
Nor ever wind blows loudly; but it lies
Deep-meadow'd, happy, fair with orchard-lawns
And bowery hollows crown'd with summer sea,
Where I will heal me of my grievous wound."
So said he, and the barge with oar and sail
Moved from the brink, like some full-breasted swan
That, fluting a wild carol ere her death,
Ruffles her pure cold plume, and takes the flood
With swarthy webs. Long stood Sir Bedivere
Revolving many memories, till the hull
Look'd one black dot against the verge of dawn,
And on the mere the wailing died away.

ULYSSES

It little profits that an idle king,
By this still hearth, among these barren crags,
Match'd with an agèd wife, I mete and dole
Unequal laws unto a savage race,
That hoard, and sleep, and feed, and know not me.
I cannot rest from travel: I will drink
Life to the lees: all times I have enjoy'd
Greatly, have suffer'd greatly, both with those
That loved me, and alone; on shore, and when
Thro' scudding drifts the rainy Hyades
Vext the dim sea; I am become a name;
For always roaming with a hungry heart
Much have I seen and known; cities of men,
And manners, climates, councils, governments,
Myself not least, but honour'd of them all;
And drunk delight of battle with my peers,
Far on the ringing plains of windy Troy.
I am a part of all that I have met.
Yet all experience is an arch where-thro'
Gleams that untravell'd world, whose margin fades
Forever and forever when I move.
How dull it is to pause, to make an end,
To rust unburnish'd, not to shine in use!
As tho' to breathe were life. Life piled on life
Were all too little, and of one to me
Little remains: but every hour is saved
From that eternal silence, something more,
A bringer of new things; and vile it were
For some three suns to store and hoard myself,
And this grey spirit yearning in desire
To follow knowledge like a sinking star,
Beyond the utmost bound of human thought.
This is my son, mine own Telemachus,
To whom I leave the sceptre and the isle —
Well-loved of me, discerning to fulfil
This labour, by slow prudence to make mild
A rugged people, and thro' soft degrees
Subdue them to the useful and the good.
Most blameless is he, centred in the sphere
Of common duties, decent not to fail
In offices of tenderness, and pay
Meet adoration to my household gods,
When I am gone. He works his work, I mine.
There lies the port; the vessel puffs her sail:
There gloom the dark broad seas. My mariners,
Souls that have toil'd, and wrought, and thought with me —
That ever with a frolic welcome took
The thunder and the sunshine, and opposed
Free hearts, free foreheads — you and I are old;
Old age hath yet his honour and his toil;
Death closes all: but something ere the end,
Some work of noble note, may yet be done,
Not unbecoming men that strove with Gods.
The lights begin to twinkle from the rocks:
The long day wanes: the slow moon climbs: the deep
Moans round with many voices. Come, my friends,
'Tis not too late to seek a newer world.
Push off, and sitting well in order smite
The sounding furrows; for my purpose holds
To sail beyond the sunset, and the baths
Of all the western stars, until I die.
It may be that the gulfs will wash us down:
It may be we shall touch the Happy Isles,
And see the great Achilles, whom we knew.
Tho' much is taken, much abides; and tho'
We are not now that strength which in old days
Moved earth and heaven; that which we are, we are;
One equal temper of heroic hearts,
Made weak by time and fate, but strong in will
To strive, to seek, to find, and not to yield.

LOCKSLEY HALL

Comrades, leave me here a little, while as yet 'tis early morn:
Leave me here, and when you want me, sound upon the bugle-horn.

'Tis the place, and all around it, as of old, the curlews call,
Dreary gleams about the moorland flying over Locksley Hall;

Locksley Hall, that in the distance overlooks the sandy tracts,
And the hollow ocean-ridges roaring into cataracts.

Many a night from yonder ivied casement, ere I went to rest,
Did I look on great Orion sloping slowly to the West.

Many a night I saw the Pleiads, rising thro' the mellow shade,
Glitter like a swarm of fire-flies tangled in a silver braid.

Here about the beach I wander'd, nourishing a youth sublime
With the fairy tales of science, and the long result of Time;

When the centuries behind me like a fruitful land reposed;
When I clung to all the present for the promise that it closed:

When I dipt into the future far as human eye could see;
Saw the Vision of the world, and all the wonder that would be. —

In the Spring a fuller crimson comes upon the robin's breast;
In the Spring the wanton lapwing gets himself another crest;

In the Spring a livelier iris changes on the burnish'd dove;
In the Spring a young man's fancy lightly turns to thoughts of love.

Then her cheek was pale and thinner than should be for one so young,
And her eyes on all my motions with a mute observance hung.

And I said, "My cousin Amy, speak, and speak the truth to me,
Trust me, cousin, all the current of my being sets to thee."

On her pallid cheek and forehead came a colour and a light,
As I have seen the rosy red flushing in the northern night.

And she turn'd — her bosom shaken with a sudden storm of sighs —
All the spirit deeply dawning in the dark of hazel eyes —

Saying, "I have hid my feelings, fearing they should do me wrong";
Saying, "Dost thou love me, cousin?" weeping, "I have loved thee long."

Love took up the glass of Time, and turn'd it in his glowing hands;
Every moment, lightly shaken, ran itself in golden sands.

Love took up the harp of Life, and smote on all the chords with might;
Smote the chord of Self, that, trembling, pass'd in music out of sight.

Many a morning on the moorland did we hear the copses ring,
And her whisper throng'd my pulses with the fullness of the Spring.

Many an evening by the waters did we watch the stately ships,
And our spirits rush'd together at the touching of the lips.

O my cousin, shallow-hearted! O my Amy, mine no more!
O the dreary, dreary moorland! O the barren, barren shore!

Falser than all fancy fathoms, falser than all songs have sung,
Puppet to a father's threat, and servile to a shrewish tongue!

Is it well to wish thee happy? — having known me — to decline
On a range of lower feelings and a narrower heart than mine!

Yet it shall be: thou shalt lower to his level day by day,
What is fine within thee growing coarse to sympathise with clay.

As the husband is, the wife is: thou art mated with a clown,
And the grossness of his nature will have weight to drag thee down.

He will hold thee, when his passion shall have spent its novel force,
Something better than his dog, a little dearer than his horse.

What is this? his eyes are heavy; think not they are glazed with wine.
Go to him: it is thy duty: kiss him: take his hand in thine.

It may be my lord is weary, that his brain is overwrought;
Soothe him with thy finer fancies, touch him with thy lighter thought.

He will answer to the purpose, easy things to understand —
Better thou wert dead before me, tho' I slew thee with my hand!

Better thou and I were lying, hidden from the heart's disgrace,
Roll'd in one another's arms, and silent in a last embrace.

Cursed be the social wants that sin against the strength of youth!
Cursed be the social lies that warp us from the living truth!

Cursed be the sickly forms that err from honest Nature's rule!
Cursed be the gold that gilds the straiten'd forehead of the fool!

Well — 'tis well that I should bluster! — Hadst thou less unworthy proved —
Would to God — for I had loved thee more than ever wife was loved.

Am I mad, that I should cherish that which bears but bitter fruit?
I will pluck it from my bosom, tho' my heart be at the root.

Never, tho' my mortal summers to such length of years should come
As the many-winter'd crow that leads the clanging rookery home.

Where is comfort? in division of the records of the mind?
Can I part her from herself, and love her, as I knew her, kind?

I remember one that perish'd: sweetly did she speak and move:
Such a one do I remember, whom to look at was to love.

Can I think of her as dead, and love her for the love she bore?
No — she never loved me truly: love is love for evermore.

Comfort? comfort scorn'd of devils! this is truth the poet sings,
That a sorrow's crown of sorrow is remembering happier things.

Drug thy memories, lest thou learn it, lest thy heart be put to proof,
In the dead unhappy night, and when the rain is on the roof.

Like a dog, he hunts in dreams, and thou art staring at the wall,
Where the dying night-lamp flickers, and the shadows rise and fall.

Then a hand shall pass before thee, pointing to his drunken sleep,
To thy widow'd marriage-pillows, to the tears that thou wilt weep.

Thou shalt hear the "Never, never," whisper'd by the phantom years,
And a song from out the distance in the ringing of thine ears;

And an eye shall vex thee, looking ancient kindness on thy pain.
Turn thee, turn thee on thy pillow: get thee to thy rest again.

Nay, but Nature brings thee solace; for a tender voice will cry.
'Tis a purer life than thine; a lip to drain thy trouble dry.

Baby lips will laugh me down: my latest rival brings thee rest.
Baby fingers, waxen touches, press me from the mother's breast.

O, the child too clothes the father with a dearness not his due.
Half is thine and half is his: it will be worthy of the two.

O, I see thee old and formal, fitted to thy petty part,
With a little hoard of maxims preaching down a daughter's heart.

"They were dangerous guides the feelings — she herself was not exempt —
Truly, she herself had suffer'd" — Perish in thy self-contempt!

Overlive it — lower yet — be happy! wherefore should I care?
I myself must mix with action, lest I wither by despair.

What is that which I should turn to, lighting upon days like these?
Every door is barr'd with gold, and opens but to golden keys.

Every gate is throng'd with suitors, all the markets overflow.
I have but an angry fancy: what is that which I should do?

I had been content to perish, falling on the foeman's ground,
When the ranks are roll'd in vapour, and the winds are laid with sound.

But the jingling of the guinea helps the hurt that Honour feels,
And the nations do but murmur, snarling at each other's heels.

Can I but relive in sadness? I will turn that earlier page.
Hide me from thy deep emotion, O thou wondrous Mother-Age!

Make me feel the wild pulsation that I felt before the strife,
When I heard my days before me, and the tumult of my life;

Yearning for the large excitement that the coming years would yield,
Eager-hearted as a boy when first he leaves his father's field,

And at night along the dusky highway near and nearer drawn,
Sees in heaven the light of London flaring like a dreary dawn;

And his spirit leaps within him to be gone before him then,
Underneath the light he looks at, in among the throngs of men:

Men, my brothers, men the workers, ever reaping something new:
That which they have done but earnest of the things that they shall do:

For I dipt into the future, far as human eye could see,
Saw the Vision of the world, and all the wonder that would be;

Saw the heavens fill with commerce, argosies of magic sails,
Pilots of the purple twilight, dropping down with costly bales;

Heard the heavens fill with shouting, and there rain'd a ghastly dew
From the nations' airy navies grappling in the central blue;

Far along the world-wide whisper of the south-wind rushing warm,
With the standards of the peoples plunging thro' the thunder-storm;

Till the war-drum throbb'd no longer, and the battle-flags were furl'd
In the Parliament of man, the Federation of the world.

There the common sense of most shall hold a fretful realm in awe,
And the kindly earth shall slumber, lapt in universal law.

So I triumph'd ere my passion sweeping thro' me left me dry,
Left me with the palsied heart, and left me with the jaundiced eye;

Eye, to which all order festers, all things here are out of joint:
Science moves, but slowly slowly, creeping on from point to point:

Slowly comes a hungry people, as a lion creeping nigher,
Glares at one that nods and winks behind a slowly-dying fire.

Yet I doubt not thro' the ages one increasing purpose runs,
And the thoughts of men are widen'd with the process of the suns.

What is that to him that reaps not harvest of his youthful joys,
Tho' the deep heart of existence beat forever like a boy's?

Knowledge comes, but wisdom lingers, and I linger on the shore,
And the individual withers, and the world is more and more.

Knowledge comes, but wisdom lingers, and he bears a laden breast,
Full of sad experience, moving toward the stillness of his rest.

Hark, my merry comrades call me, sounding on the bugle-horn,
They to whom my foolish passion were a target for their scorn:

Shall it not be scorn to me to harp on such a moulder'd string?
I am shamed thro' all my nature to have loved so slight a thing.

Weakness to be wroth with weakness! woman's pleasure, woman's pain —
Nature made them blinder motions bounded in a shallower brain:

Woman is the lesser man, and all thy passions, match'd with mine,
Are as moonlight unto sunlight, and as water unto wine —

Here at least, where nature sickens, nothing. Ah, for some retreat
Deep in yonder shining Orient, where my life began to beat;

Where in wild Mahratta-battle fell my father evil-starr'd; —
I was left a trampled orphan, and a selfish uncle's ward.

Or to burst all links of habit — there to wander far away,
On from island unto island at the gateways of the day.

Larger constellations burning, mellow moons and happy skies,
Breadths of tropic shade and palms in cluster, knots of Paradise.

Never comes the trader, never floats an European flag,
Slides the bird o'er lustrous woodland, swings the trailer from the crag;

Droops the heavy-blossom'd bower, hangs the heavy-fruited tree —
Summer isles of Eden lying in dark-purple spheres of sea.

There methinks would be enjoyment more than in this march of mind,
In the steamship, in the railway, in the thoughts that shake mankind.

There the passions cramp'd no longer shall have scope and breathing space;
I will take some savage woman, she shall rear my dusky race.

Iron jointed, supple-sinew'd, they shall dive, and they shall run,
Catch the wild goat by the hair, and hurl their lances in the sun;

Whistle back the parrot's call, and leap the rainbows of the brooks,
Not with blinded eyesight poring over miserable books —

Fool, again the dream, the fancy! but I know my words are wild,
But I count the grey barbarian lower than the Christian child.

I, to herd with narrow foreheads, vacant of our glorious gains,
Like a beast with lower pleasures, like a beast with lower pains!

Mated with a squalid savage — what to me were sun or clime?
I the heir of all the ages, in the foremost files of time —

I that rather held it better men should perish one by one,
Than that earth should stand at gaze like Joshua's moon in Ajalon!

Not in vain the distance beacons. Forward, forward let us range,
Let the great world spin forever down the ringing grooves of change.

Thro' the shadow of the globe we sweep into the younger day:
Better fifty years of Europe than a cycle of Cathay.

Mother-Age (for mine I knew not), help me as when life begun:
Rift the hills, and roll the waters, flash the lightnings, weigh the Sun.

O, I see the crescent promise of my spirit hath not set.
Ancient founts of inspiration well thro' all my fancy yet.

Howsoever these things be, a long farewell to Locksley Hall!
Now for me the woods may wither, now for me the roof-tree fall.

Comes a vapour from the margin, blackening over heath and holt,
Cramming all the blast before it, in its breast a thunderbolt.

Let it fall on Locksley Hall, with rain or hail, or fire or snow;
For the mighty wind arises, roaring seaward, and I go.

ST. AGNES' EVE

Deep on the convent-roof the snows
  Are sparkling to the moon:
My breath to heaven like vapour goes:
  May my soul follow soon!
The shadows of the convent-towers
  Slant down the snowy sward,

Still creeping with the creeping hours
That lead me to my Lord:
Make Thou my spirit pure and clear
As are the frosty skies,
Or this first snowdrop of the year
That in my bosom lies.

As these white robes are soil'd and dark,
To yonder shining ground;
As this pale taper's earthly spark,
To yonder argent round;
So shows my soul before the Lamb,
My spirit before Thee;
So in mine earthly house I am,
To that I hope to be.
Break up the heavens, O Lord! and far,
Thro' all yon starlight keen,
Draw me, Thy bride, a glittering star,
In raiment white and clean.

He lifts me to the golden doors;
The flashes come and go;
All heaven bursts her starry floors,
And strows her lights below,
And deepens on and up! the gates
Roll back, and far within
For me the Heavenly Bridegroom waits,
To make me pure of sin.
The sabbaths of Eternity,
One sabbath deep and wide —
A light upon the shining sea —
The Bridegroom with His bride!

SIR GALAHAD

My good blade carves the casques of men,
My tough lance thrusteth sure,
My strength is as the strength of ten,
Because my heart is pure.
The shattering trumpet shrilleth high,
The hard brands shiver on the steel,
The splinter'd spear-shafts crack and fly,
The horse and rider reel:
They reel, they roll in clanging lists,
And when the tide of combat stands,
Perfume and flowers fall in showers,
That lightly rain from ladies' hands.

How sweet are looks that ladies bend
On whom their favours fall!
For them I battle till the end,
To save from shame and thrall:
But all my heart is drawn above,
My knees are bow'd in crypt and shrine:
I never felt the kiss of love,
Nor maiden's hand in mine.
More bounteous aspects on me beam,
Me mightier transports move and thrill;
So keep I fair thro' faith and prayer
A virgin heart in work and will.

When down the stormy crescent goes,
A light before me swims,
Between dark stems the forest glows,
I hear a noise of hymns:
Then by some secret shrine I ride;
I hear a voice but none are there;
The stalls are void, the doors are wide,
The tapers burning fair.
Fair gleams the snowy altar-cloth,
The silver vessels sparkle clean,
The shrill bell rings, the censer swings,
And solemn chants resound between.

Sometimes on lonely mountain-meres
I find a magic bark;
I leap on board: no helmsman steers:
I float till all is dark.
A gentle sound, an awful light!
Three angels bear the holy Grail:
With folded feet, in stoles of white,
On sleeping wings they sail.
Ah, blessed vision! blood of God!
My spirit beats her mortal bars,
As down dark tides the glory slides,
And star-like mingles with the stars.

When on my goodly charger borne
Thro' dreaming towns I go,
The cock crows ere the Christmas morn,
The streets are dumb with snow.
The tempest crackles on the leads,
And, ringing, springs from brand and mail;
But o'er the dark a glory spreads,
And gilds the driving hail.
I leave the plain, I climb the height;
No branchy thicket shelter yields;
But blessed forms in whistling storms
Fly o'er waste fens and windy fields.

A maiden knight — to me is given
Such hope, I know not fear;
I yearn to breathe the airs of heaven
That often meet me here.
I muse on joy that will not cease,
Pure spaces clothed in living beams,
Pure lilies of eternal peace,
Whose odours haunt my dreams;
And, stricken by an angel's hand,
This mortal armour that I wear,
This weight and size, this heart and eyes,
Are touch'd, are turn'd to finest air.

The clouds are broken in the sky,
  And thro' the mountain-walls
A rolling organ-harmony
  Swells up, and shakes and falls.
Then move the trees, the copses nod,
  Wings flutter, voices hover clear:
"O just and faithful knight of God!
  Ride on! the prize is near."
So pass I hostel, hall, and grange;
  By bridge and ford, by park and pale,
All-arm'd I ride, whate'er betide,
  Until I find the holy Grail.

BREAK, BREAK

Break, break, break,
  On thy cold grey stones, O Sea!
And I would that my tongue could utter
  The thoughts that arise in me.

O well for the fisherman's boy,
  That he shouts with his sister at play!
O well for the sailor lad,
  That he sings in his boat on the bay!

And the stately ships go on
  To their haven under the hill;
But O for the touch of a vanish'd hand,
  And the sound of a voice that is still!

Break, break, break,
  At the foot of thy crags, O Sea!
But the tender grace of a day that is dead
  Will never come back to me.

NORTHERN FARMER

NEW STYLE

Dosn't thou 'ear my 'erse's legs, as they canters awaäy?
Proputty, proputty, proputty — that's what I 'ears 'em saäy.
Proputty, proputty, proputty — Sam, thou's an ass for thy paaïns:
Theer's moor sense i' one o' 'is legs nor in all thy braaïns.

Woä — theer's a craw to pluck wi' tha, Sam: yon's parson's 'ouse —
Dosn't thou knaw that a man mun be eäther a man or a mouse?
Time to think on it then; for thou'll be twenty to weeäk.
Proputty, proputty — woä then, woä — let ma 'ear mysén speäk.

Me an' thy muther, Sammy, 'as beän a-talkin' o' thee;
Thou's beän talkin' to muther, an' she beän a tellin' it to me.
Thou'll not marry for munny — thou's sweet upo' parson's lass —
Noä — thou'll marry for luvv — an' we boäth on us thinks tha an ass.

Seeä'd her todaäy goä by — Saäint's daäy — they was ringing the bells.
She's a beauty thou thinks — an' soä is scoors o' gells,
Them as 'as munny an' all — wot's a beauty? — the flower as blaws.
But proputty, proputty sticks, an' proputty, proputty graws.

Do'ant be stunt: taäke time: I knaws what maäkes tha sa mad.
Warn't I craäzed fur the lasses mysén when I wur a lad?
But I knaw'd a Quaäker feller as often 'as towd ma this:
"Doänt thou marry for munny, but goä wheer munny is!"

An' I went wheer munny war: an' thy muther coom to 'and,
Wi' lots o' munny laaïd by, an' a nicetish bit o' land.
Maäybe she warn't a beauty — I niver giv it a thowt —
But warn't she as good to cuddle an' kiss as a lass as 'ant nowt?

Parson's lass 'ant nowt, an' she weänt 'a nowt when 'e's deäd,
Mun be a guvness, lad, or summut, and addle her breäd:
Why? fur 'e's nobbut a curate, an' weänt niver git naw 'igher;
An' 'e maäde the bed as 'e ligs on afoor e' coom'd to the shire.

An thin 'e coom'd to the parish wi' lots o' Varsity debt,
Stook to his taaïl they did, an' 'e 'ant got shut on 'em yet.
An' 'e ligs on 'is back i' the grip, wi' noän to lend 'im a shove,
Woorse nor a far-welter'd yowe: fur, Sammy, 'e married fur luvv.

Luvv? what's luvv? thou can luvv thy lass an' 'er munny too,
Maäkin' 'em goä togither as they've good right to do.

Could'n I luvv thy muther by cause o' 'er munny laaïd by?
Naäy — fur I luvv'd 'er a vast sight moor fur it: reäson why.

Ay an' thy muther says thou wants to marry the lass,
Cooms of a gentleman burn: an' we boäth on us thinks tha an ass.
Woä then, proputty, wiltha? — an ass as near as mays nowt —
Woä then, wiltha? dangtha! — the bees is as fell as owt.

Breäk me a bit o' the esh for his 'eäd, lad, out o' the fence!
Gentleman burn! what's gentleman burn? is it shillins an' pence?
Proputty, proputty's ivrything 'ere, an', Sammy, I'm blest
If it isn't the saäme oop yonder, for them as 'as it's the best.

Tis'n them as 'as munny as breäks into 'ouses an' steäls,
Them as 'as coäts to their backs an' taäkes their regular meäls.
Noä, but it's them as niver knaws wheer a meäl's to be 'ad.
Taäke my word for it, Sammy, the poor in a loomp is bad.

Them or thir feythers, tha sees, mun 'a beän a laäzy lot,
Fur work mun 'a gone to the gittin' whiniver munny was got.
Feyther 'ad ammost nowt; leastways 'is munny was 'id.
But 'e tued an' moil'd 'issén deäd, an 'e died a good un, 'e did.

Looök thou theer wheer Wrigglesby beck cooms out by the 'ill!
Feyther run oop to the farm, an' I runs oop to the mill;
An' I'll run oop to the brig, an' that thou'll live to see;
And if thou marries a good un I'll leäve the land to thee.

Thim's my noätions, Sammy, wheerby I means to stick;
But if thou marries a bad un, I'll leave the land to Dick. —
Coom oop, proputty, proputty — that's what I 'ears 'im saäy —
Proputty, proputty, proputty — canter an' canter awaäy.

WAGES

Glory of warrior, glory of orator, glory of song,
Paid with a voice flying by to be lost on an endless sea —
Glory of Virtue, to fight, to struggle, to right the wrong —
Nay, but she aim'd not at glory, no lover of glory she:
Give her the glory of going on, and still to be.

The wages of sin is death: if the wages of Virtue be dust,
Would she have heart to endure for the life of the worm and the fly?
She desires no isles of the blest, no quiet seats of the just,
To rest in a golden grove, or to bask in a summer sky:
Give her the wages of going on, and not to die.

THE HIGHER PANTHEISM

The sun, the moon, the stars, the seas, the hills and the plains —
Are not these, O Soul, the Vision of Him who reigns?

Is not the Vision He? tho' He be not that which He seems?
Dreams are true while they last, and do we not live in dreams?

Earth, these solid stars, this weight of body and limb,
Are they not sign and symbol of thy division from Him?

Dark is the world to thee: thyself art the reason why;
For is He not all but thou, that hast power to feel "I am I"?

Glory about thee, without thee; and thou fulfillest thy doom
Making Him broken gleams, and a stifled splendour and gloom.

Speak to Him thou for He hears, and Spirit with Spirit can meet —
Closer is He than breathing, and nearer than hands and feet.

God is law, say the wise; O Soul, and let us rejoice,
For if He thunder by law the thunder is yet His voice.

Law is God, say some: no God at all, says the fool;
For all we have power to see is a straight staff bent in a pool;

And the ear of man cannot hear, and the eye of man cannot see;
But if we could see and hear, this Vision — were it not He?

From Maud

XVIII

I have led her home, my love, my only friend,
There is none like her, none.
And never yet so warmly ran my blood
And sweetly, on and on
Calming itself to the long-wish'd-for end,
Full to the banks, close on the promised good.

None like her, none.
Just now the dry-tongued laurels' pattering talk
Seem'd her light foot along the garden walk,
And shook my heart to think she comes once more;
But even then I heard her close the door,
The gates of Heaven are closed, and she is gone.

There is none like her, none.
Nor will be when our summers have deceased.
O, art thou sighing for Lebanon
In the long breeze that streams to thy delicious East,
Sighing for Lebanon,
Dark cedar, tho' thy limbs have here increased,
Upon a pastoral slope as fair,
And looking to the South, and fed
With honey'd rain and delicate air,
And haunted by the starry head
Of her whose gentle will has changed my fate,
And made my life a perfumed altar-flame;
And over whom thy darkness must have spread
With such delight as theirs of old, thy great
Forefathers of the thornless garden, there
Shadowing the snow-limb'd Eve from whom she came.

Here will I lie, while these long branches sway,
And you fair stars that crown a happy day,
Go in and out as if at merry play,
Who am no more so all forlorn,
As when it seem'd far better to be born
To labour and the mattock-harden'd hand,
Than nursed at ease and brought to understand
A sad astrology, the boundless plan
That makes you tyrants in your iron skies,
Innumerable, pitiless, passionless eyes,
Cold fires, yet with power to burn and brand
His nothingness into man.

But now shine on, and what care I,
Who in this stormy gulf have found a pearl
The countercharm of space and hollow sky,
And do accept my madness, and would die
To save from some slight shame one simple girl.

Would die; for sullen-seeming Death may give
More life to Love than is or ever was
In our low world, where yet 'tis sweet to live.
Let no one ask me how it came to pass;
It seems that I am happy, that to me
A livelier emerald twinkles in the grass,
A purer sapphire melts into the sea.

Not die; but live a life of truest breath,
And teach true life to fight with mortal wrongs.
O, why should Love, like men in drinking-songs,
Spice his fair banquet with the dust of death?
Make answer, Maud my bliss,
Maud made my Maud by that long loving kiss,
Life of my life, wilt thou not answer this?
"The dusky strand of Death inwoven here
With dear Love's tie, makes Love himself more dear."

Is that enchanted moan only the swell
Of the long waves that roll in yonder bay?
And hark the clock within, the silver knell
Of twelve sweet hours that past in bridal white,
And died to live, long as my pulses play;
But now by this my love has closed her sight
And given false death her hand, and stol'n away
To dreamful wastes where footless fancies dwell
Among the fragments of the golden day.

May nothing there her maiden grace affright!
Dear heart, I feel with thee the drowsy spell.
My bride to be, my evermore delight,
My own heart's heart, my ownest own, farewell;
It is but for a little space I go:
And ye meanwhile far over moor and fell
Beat to the noiseless music of the night!
Has our whole earth gone nearer to the glow
Of your soft splendours that you look so bright?
I have climb'd nearer out of lonely Hell.
Beat, happy stars, timing with things below,
Beat with my heart more blest than heart can tell,
Blest, but for some dark undercurrent woe
That seems to draw — but it shall not be so:
Let all be well, be well.

XXII

Come into the garden, Maud,
  For the black bat, night, has flown,
Come into the garden, Maud,
  I am here at the gate alone;
And the woodbine spices are wafted abroad,
  And the musk of the rose is blown.

For a breeze of morning moves,
  And the planet of Love is on high,
Beginning to faint in the light that she loves
  On a bed of daffodil sky,
To faint in the light of the sun she loves,
  To faint in his light, and to die.

All night have the roses heard
  The flute, violin, bassoon;
All night has the casement jessamine stirr'd
  To the dancers dancing in tune;
Till a silence fell with the waking bird,
  And a hush with the setting moon.

I said to the lily, "There is but one
  With whom she has heart to be gay.
When will the dancers leave her alone?
  She is weary of dance and play."
Now half to the setting moon are gone,
  And half to the rising day;
Low on the sand and loud on the stone
  The last wheel echoes away.

I said to the rose, "The brief night goes
  In babble and revel and wine.
O young lord-lover, what sighs are those,
  For one that will never be thine?
But mine, but mine," so I sware to the rose,
  "For ever and ever, mine."

And the soul of the rose went into my blood,
  As the music clash'd in the hall;
And long by the garden lake I stood,
  For I heard your rivulet fall
From the lake to the meadow and on to the wood,
  Our wood, that is dearer than all;

From the meadow your walks have left so sweet
  That whenever a March-wind sighs
He sets the jewel-print of your feet
  In violets blue as your eyes,
To the woody hollows in which we meet
  And the valleys of Paradise.

The slender acacia would not shake
  One long milk-bloom on the tree;
The white lake-blossom fell into the lak
  As the pimpernel dozed on the lea;
But the rose was awake all night for your sake,
  Knowing your promise to me;
The lilies and roses were all awake,
  They sigh'd for the dawn and thee.

Queen rose of the rosebud garden of girls,
  Come hither, the dances are done,
In gloss of satin and glimmer of pearls,
  Queen lily and rose in one;
Shine out, little head, sunning over with curls,
  To the flowers, and be their sun.

There has fallen a splendid tear
  From the passion-flower at the gate.
She is coming, my dove, my dear;
  She is coming, my life, my fate;
The red rose cries, "She is near, she is near;"
  And the white rose weeps, "She is late;"
The larkspur listens, "I hear, I hear;"
  And the lily whispers, "I wait."

She is coming, my own, my sweet;
  Were it ever so airy a tread,
My heart would hear her and beat,
  Were it earth in an earthy bed;
My dust would hear her and beat,
  Had I lain for a century dead;
Would start and tremble under her feet,
  And blossom in purple and red.

FROM IN MEMORIAM

PROEM

Strong Son of God, immortal Love,
  Whom we, that have not seen thy face,
  By faith, and faith alone, embrace,
Believing where we cannot prove;

Thine are these orbs of light and shade;
  Thou madest Life in man and brute;
  Thou madest Death; and lo, thy foot
Is on the skull which thou hast made.

Thou wilt not leave us in the dust:
  Thou madest man, he knows not why,
  He thinks he was not made to die;
And thou hast made him: thou art just.

Thou seemest human and divine,
  The highest, holiest manhood, thou:
  Our wills are ours, we know not how;
Our wills are ours, to make them thine.

Our little systems have their day;
  They have their day and cease to be:
  They are but broken lights of thee,
And thou, O Lord, art more than they.

We have but faith: we cannot know;
For knowledge is of things we see;
And yet we trust it comes from thee,
A beam in darkness: let it grow.

Let knowledge grow from more to more,
But more of reverence in us dwell;
That mind and soul, according well,
May make one music as before,

But vaster. We are fools and slight;
We mock thee when we do not fear:
But help thy foolish ones to bear;
Help thy vain worlds to bear thy light.

Forgive what seem'd my sin in me;
What seem'd my worth since I began;
For merit lives from man to man,
And not from man, O Lord, to thee.

Forgive my grief for one removed,
Thy creature, whom I found so fair.
I trust he lives in thee, and there
I find him worthier to be loved.

Forgive these wild and wandering cries,
Confusions of a wasted youth;
Forgive them where they fail in truth,
And in thy wisdom make me wise.

I

I held it truth, with him who sings
To one clear harp in divers tones,
That men may rise on stepping-stones
Of their dead selves to higher things.

But who shall so forecast the years
And find in loss a gain to match?
Or reach a hand thro' time to catch
The far-off interest of tears?

Let Love clasp Grief lest both be drown'd,
Let darkness keep her raven gloss:
Ah, sweeter to be drunk with loss,
To dance with death, to beat the ground,

Than that the victor Hours should scorn
The long result of love, and boast,
"Behold the man that loved and lost,
But all he was is overworn.'

XXVII

I envy not in any moods
The captive void of noble rage,
The linnet born within the cage,
That never knew the summer woods:

I envy not the beast that takes
His license in the field of time,
Unfetter'd by the sense of crime,
To whom a conscience never wakes;

Nor, what may count itself as blest,
The heart that never plighted troth
But stagnates in the weeds of sloth;
Nor any want-begotten rest.

I hold it true, whate'er befall;
I feel it, when I sorrow most;
'Tis better to have loved and lost
Than never to have loved at all.

XXXI

When Lazarus left his charnel-cave,
And home to Mary's house return'd,
Was this demanded — if he yearn'd
To hear her weeping by his grave?

"Where wert thou, brother, those four days?"
There lives no record of reply,
Which telling what it is to die
Had surely added praise to praise.

From every house the neighbours met,
The streets were fill'd with joyful sound,
A solemn gladness even crown'd
The purple brows of Olivet.

Behold a man raised up by Christ!
The rest remaineth unreveal'd;
He told it not; or something seal'd
The lips of that Evangelist.

XXXII

Her eyes are homes of silent prayer,
Nor other thought her mind admits
But, he was dead, and there he sits,
And He that brought him back is there

Then one deep love doth supersede
All other, when her ardent gaze
Roves from the living brother's face,
And rests upon the Life indeed.

All subtle thought, all curious fears,
Borne down by gladness so complete,
She bows, she bathes the Saviour's feet
With costly spikenard and with tears.

Thrice blest whose lives are faithful prayers,
Whose loves in higher love endure;
What souls possess themselves so pure,
Or is there blessedness like theirs?

LIV

Oh yet we trust that somehow good
Will be the final goal of ill,
To pangs of nature, sins of will,
Defects of doubt, and taints of blood;

That nothing walks with aimless feet;
That not one life shall be destroy'd,
Or cast as rubbish to the void,
When God hath made the pile complete;

That not a worm is cloven in vain;
That not a moth with vain desire
Is shrivell'd in a fruitless fire,
Or but subserves another's gain.

Behold, we know not anything;
I can but trust that good shall fall
At last — far off — at last, to all,
And every winter change to spring.

So runs my dream; but what am I?
An infant crying in the night:
An infant crying for the light:
And with no language but a cry.

LVII

Peace; come away: the song of woe
Is after all an earthly song:
Peace; come away: we do him wrong
To sing so wildly: let us go.

Come; let us go: your cheeks are pale;
But half my life I leave behind:
Methinks my friend is richly shrined;
But I shall pass; my work will fail.

Yet in these ears, till hearing dies,
One set slow bell will seem to toll
The passing of the sweetest soul
That ever look'd with human eyes.

I hear it now, and o'er and o'er,
Eternal greetings to the dead;
And "Ave, Ave, Ave," said,
"Adieu, adieu" for evermore.

LXXVII

What hope is here for modern rhyme
To him, who turns a musing eye
On songs, and deeds, and lives, that lie
Foreshorten'd in the tract of time?

These mortal lullabies of pain
May bind a book, may line a box,
May serve to curl a maiden's locks;
Or when a thousand moons shall wane,

A man upon a stall may find,
And, passing, turn the page that tells
A grief, then changed to something else,
Sung by a long-forgotten mind.

But what of that? My darken'd ways
Shall ring with music all the same;
To breathe my loss is more than fame,
To utter love more sweet than praise.

XCVI

You say, but with no touch of scorn,
Sweet-hearted, you, whose light-blue eyes
Are tender over drowning flies,
You tell me, doubt is Devil-born.

I know not: one indeed I knew
In many a subtle question versed,
Who touch'd a jarring lyre at first,
But ever strove to make it true:

Perplext in faith, but pure in deeds,
At last he beat his music out.
There lives more faith in honest doubt,
Believe me, than in half the creeds.

He fought his doubts and gather'd strength,
He would not make his judgment blind,
He faced the spectres of the mind
And laid them: thus he came at length

To find a stronger faith his own;
And Power was with him in the night,
Which makes the darkness and the light,
And dwells not in the light alone,

But in the darkness and the cloud,
As over Sinai's peaks of old,
While Israel made their gods of gold,
Altho' the trumpet blew so loud.

CVI

Ring out, wild bells, to the wild sky,
The flying cloud, the frosty light:
The year is dying in the night;
Ring out, wild bells, and let him die.

Ring out the old, ring in the new,
Ring, happy bells, across the snow:
The year is going, let him go;
Ring out the false, ring in the true.

Ring out the grief that saps the mind,
For those that here we see no more;
Ring out the feud of rich and poor,
Ring in redress to all mankind.

Ring out a slowly dying cause,
  And ancient forms of party strife;
  Ring in the nobler modes of life,
With sweeter manners, purer laws.

Ring out the want, the care, the sin,
  The faithless coldness of the times;
  Ring out, ring out my mournful rhymes,
But ring the fuller minstrel in.

Ring out false pride in place and blood,
  The civic slander and the spite;
  Ring in the love of truth and right,
Ring in the common love of good.

Ring out old shapes of foul disease;
  Ring out the narrowing lust of gold;
  Ring out the thousand wars of old,
Ring in the thousand years of peace.

Ring in the valiant man and free,
  The larger heart, the kindlier hand;
  Ring out the darkness of the land,
Ring in the Christ that is to be.

CXXX

Thy voice is on the rolling air;
  I hear thee where the waters run;
  Thou standest in the rising sun,
And in the setting thou art fair.

What art thou then? I cannot guess;
  But tho' I seem in star and flower
  To feel thee some diffusive power,
I do not therefore love thee less:

My love involves the love before;
  My love is vaster passion now;
  Tho' mix'd with God and Nature thou,
I seem to love thee more and more.

Far off thou art, but ever nigh;
  I have thee still, and I rejoice;
  I prosper, circled with thy voice;
I shall not lose thee tho' I die.

From THE EPILOGUE

And rise, O moon, from yonder down,
  Till over down and over dale
  All night the shining vapour sail
And pass the silent-lighted town,

The white-faced halls, the glancing rills,
  And catch at every mountain head,
  And o'er the friths that branch and spread
Their sleeping silver thro' the hills;

And touch with shade the bridal doors,
  With tender gloom the roof, the wall;
  And breaking let the splendour fall
To spangle all the happy shores

By which they rest, and ocean sounds,
  And, star and system rolling past,
  A soul shall draw from out the vast
And strike his being into bounds,

And, moved thro' life of lower phase,
  Result in man, be born and think,
  And act and love, a closer link
Betwixt us and the crowning race

Of those that, eye to eye, shall look
  On knowledge; under whose command
  Is Earth and Earth's, and in their hand
Is Nature like an open book;

No longer half-akin to brute,
  For all we thought and loved and did,
  And hoped, and suffer'd, is but seed
Of what in them is flower and fruit;

Whereof the man, that with me trod
  This planet, was a noble type
  Appearing ere the times were ripe,
That friend of mine who lives in God,

That God, which ever lives and loves,
  One God, one law, one element,
  And one far-off divine event,
To which the whole creation moves.

SIR JOHN FRANKLIN

On the Cenotaph in Westminster Abbey

Not here! the white North has thy bones; and thou,
  Heroic sailor-soul,
Art passing on thine happier voyage now
  Toward no earthly pole.

TO DANTE

Written at Request of the Florentines

King, that hast reign'd six hundred years, and grown
In power, and ever growest! since thine own
Fair Florence honouring thy nativity,
Thy Florence now the crown of Italy,
Hath sought the tribute of a verse from me,
I, wearing but the garland of a day,
Cast at thy feet one flower that fades away.

THE SILENT VOICES

When the dumb Hour, clothed in black,
Brings the Dreams about my bed,
Call me not so often back,
Silent Voices of the dead,
Toward the lowland ways behind me,
And the sunlight that is gone!
Call me rather, silent voices,
Forward to the starry track
Glimmering up the heights beyond me
On, and always on!

MERLIN AND THE GLEAM

I

O young Mariner,
You from the haven
Under the sea-cliff,
You that are watching
The gray Magician
With eyes of wonder
I am Merlin,
And *I* am dying,
I am Merlin
Who follow The Gleam.

II

Mighty the Wizard
Who found me at sunrise
Sleeping, and woke me
And learn'd me Magic!
Great the Master,
And sweet the Magic,
When over the valley,
In early summers,
Over the mountain,
On human faces,
And all around me,
Moving to melody,
Floated The Gleam.

III

Once at the croak of a Raven who crost it,
A barbarous people,
Blind to the magic,
And deaf to the melody,
Snarl'd at and cursed me.
A demon vext me,
The light retreated,
The landskip darken'd,
The melody deaden'd,
The Master whisper'd
"Follow The Gleam."

IV

Then to the melody,
Over a wilderness
Gliding, and glancing at
Elf of the woodland,
Gnome of the cavern,
Griffin and Giant,
And dancing of Fairies
In desolate hollows,
And wraiths of the mountain,
And rolling of dragons
By warble of water,
Or cataract music
Of falling torrents,
Flitted The Gleam.

V

Down from the mountain
And over the level,
And streaming and shining on
Silent river,
Silvery willow,
Pasture and plowland,
Horses and oxen,
Innocent maidens,
Garrulous children,
Homestead and harvest,
Reaper and gleaner,
And rough-ruddy faces
Of lowly labour,
Slided The Gleam.—

VI

Then, with a melody
Stronger and statelier,
Led me at length
To the city and palace
Of Arthur the king;
Touch'd at the golden
Cross of the churches,
Flash'd on the Tournament,
Flicker'd and bicker'd
From helmet to helmet,
And last on the forehead
Of Arthur the blameless
Rested The Gleam.

VII

Clouds and darkness
Closed upon Camelot;
Arthur had vanish'd
I knew not whither,
The king who loved me,

And cannot die;
For out of the darkness
Silent and slowly
The Gleam, that had waned to a wintry glimmer
On icy fallow
And faded forest,
Drew to the valley
Named of the shadow,
And slowly brightening
Out of the glimmer,
And slowly moving again to a melody
Yearningly tender,
Fell on the shadow,
No longer a shadow,
But clothed with The Gleam.

VIII

And broader and brighter
The Gleam flying onward,
Wed to the melody,
Sang thro' the world;
And slower and fainter,
Old and weary,
But eager to follow,
I saw, whenever
In passing it glanced upon
Hamlet or city,
That under the Crosses
The dead man's garden,
The mortal hillock,
Would break into blossom;
And to the land's
Last limit I came —
And can no longer,
But die rejoicing,
For thro' the Magic
Of Him the Mighty,
Who taught me in childhood,
There on the border
Of boundless Ocean,
And all but in Heaven
Hovers The Gleam.

IX

Not of the sunlight,
Not of the moonlight,
Not of the starlight!
O young Mariner,
Down to the haven,
Call your companions,
Launch your vessel,
And crowd your canvas,
And, ere it vanishes
Over the margin,
After it, follow it,
Follow The Gleam.

BY AN EVOLUTIONIST

The Lord let the house of a brute to the soul of a man,
And the man said "Am I your debtor?"
And the Lord — "Not yet: but make it as clean as you can,
And then I will let you a better."

If my body come from brutes, my soul uncertain, or a fable,
Why not bask amid the senses while the sun of morning shines,
I, the finer brute rejoicing in my hounds, and in my stable,
Youth and health, and birth and wealth, and choice of women and of wines?

What hast thou done for me, grim Old Age, save breaking my bones on the rack?
Would I had past in the morning that looks so bright from afar!

Old Age

Done for thee? starved the wild beast that was linkt with thee eighty years back.
Less weight now for the ladder-of-heaven that hangs on a star.

If my body come from brutes, tho' somewhat finer than their own,
I am heir, and this my kingdom. Shall the royal voice be mute?
No, but if the rebel subject seek to drag me from the throne,
Hold the sceptre, Human Soul, and rule thy Province of the brute.

I have climb'd to the snows of Age, and I gaze at a field in the Past,
Where I sank with the body at times in the sloughs of a low desire,
But I hear no yelp of the beast, and the Man is quiet at last
As he stands on the heights of his life with a glimpse of a height that is higher.

CROSSING THE BAR

Sunset and evening star,
And one clear call for me!
And may there be no moaning of the bar,
When I put out to sea,

But such a tide as moving seems asleep,
  Too full for sound and foam,
When that which drew from out the boundless deep
  Turns again home.

Twilight and evening bell,
  And after that the dark!
And may there be no sadness of farewell,
  When I embark;

For tho' from out our bourne of Time and Place
  The flood may bear me far,
I hope to see my Pilot face to face
  When I have crost the bar.

ROBERT BROWNING (1812–1889)

CAVALIER TUNES

I. MARCHING ALONG

Kentish Sir Byng stood for his King,
Bidding the crop-headed Parliament swing:
And, pressing a troop unable to stoop
And see the rogues flourish and honest folk droop,
Marched them along, fifty-score strong,
Great-hearted gentlemen, singing this song.

God for King Charles! Pym and such carles
To the Devil that prompts 'em their treasonous parles!
Cavaliers, up! Lips from the cup,
Hands from the pasty, nor bite take nor sup
Till you're —
  CHORUS. — Marching along, fifty-score strong,
    Great-hearted gentlemen, singing this song.

Hampden to hell, and his obsequies' knell.
Serve Hazelrig, Fiennes, and young Harry as well!
England, good cheer! Rupert is near!
Kentish and loyalists, keep we not here,
  CHO. — Marching along, fifty-score strong,
    Great-hearted gentlemen, singing this song?

Then, God for King Charles! Pym and his snarls
To the Devil that pricks on such pestilent carles!
Hold by the right, you double your might;
So, onward to Nottingham, fresh for the fight,
  CHO. — March we along, fifty-score strong,
    Great-hearted gentlemen, singing this song!

II. GIVE A ROUSE

King Charles, and who'll do him right now?
King Charles, and who's ripe for fight now?
Give a rouse: here's, in hell's despite now,
King Charles!

Who gave me the goods that went since?
Who raised me the house that sank once?
Who helped me to gold I spent since?
Who found me in wine you drank once?
  CHO. — King Charles, and who'll do him right now?
    King Charles, and who's ripe for fight now?
    Give a rouse: here's, in hell's despite now,
    King Charles!

To whom used my boy George quaff else,
By the old fool's side that begot him?
For whom did he cheer and laugh else,
While Noll's damned troopers shot him?
  CHO. — King Charles, and who'll do him right now?
    King Charles, and who's ripe for fight now?
    Give a rouse: here's, in hell's despite now,
    King Charles!

III. BOOT AND SADDLE

Boot, saddle, to horse, and away!
Rescue my castle before the hot day
Brightens to blue from its silvery grey.
  CHO. — Boot, saddle, to horse, and away!

Ride past the suburbs, asleep as you'd say;
Many's the friend there, will listen and pray
"God's luck to gallants that strike up the lay —
  CHO. — Boot, saddle, to horse, and away!"

Forty miles off, like a roebuck at bay,
Flouts Castle Brancepeth the Roundheads' array:
Who laughs, "Good fellows ere this, by my fay,
  CHO. — Boot, saddle, to horse, and away!"

Who? My wife Gertrude; that, honest and gay,
Laughs when you talk of surrendering, "Nay!
I've better counsellors; what counsel they?
  CHO. — Boot, saddle, to horse, and away!"

THE LOST LEADER

Just for a handful of silver he left us,
Just for a riband to stick in his coat —
Found the one gift of which fortune bereft us,
Lost all the others she lets us devote;
They, with the gold to give, doled him out silver,
So much was theirs who so little allowed:
How all our copper had gone for his service!
Rags — were they purple, his heart had been proud!
We that had loved him so, followed him, honored him,
Lived in his mild and magnificent eye,
Learned his great language, caught his clear accents,
Made him our pattern to live and to die!
Shakespeare was of us, Milton was for us,
Burns, Shelley, were with us, — they watch from their graves!
He alone breaks from the van and the freemen,
— He alone sinks to the rear and the slaves!
We shall march prospering, — not through his presence;
Songs may inspirit us, — not from his lyre;
Deeds will be done, — while he boasts his quiescence,
Still bidding crouch whom the rest bade aspire:
Blot out his name, then, record one lost soul more,
One task more declined, one more footpath untrod,
One more devils'-triumph and sorrow for angels,
One wrong more to man, one more insult to God!
Life's night begins: let him never come back to us!
There would be doubt, hesitation and pain,
Forced praise on our part — the glimmer of twilight,
Never glad confident morning again!
Best fight on well, for we taught him — strike gallantly,
Menace our heart ere we master his own;
Then let him receive the new knowledge and wait us,
Pardoned in heaven, the first by the throne!

"HOW THEY BROUGHT THE GOOD NEWS FROM GHENT TO AIX"

(16—)

I sprang to the stirrup, and Joris, and he;
I galloped, Dirck galloped, we galloped all three;
"Good speed!" cried the watch, as the gate-bolts undrew;
"Speed!" echoed the wall to us galloping through;
Behind shut the postern, the lights sank to rest,
And into the midnight we galloped abreast.

Not a word to each other; we kept the great pace
Neck by neck, stride by stride, never changing our place;
I turned in my saddle and made its girths tight,
Then shortened each stirrup, and set the pique right,
Rebuckled the check-strap, chained slacker the bit,
Nor galloped less steadily Roland a whit.

'Twas moonset at starting; but while we drew near
Lokeren, the cocks crew and twilight dawned clear;
At Boom, a great yellow star came out to see;
At Düffeld, 'twas morning as plain as could be;
And from Mecheln church-steeple we heard the half-chime,
So Joris broke silence with, "Yet there is time!"

At Aershot, up leaped of a sudden the sun,
And against him the cattle stood black every one,
To stare through the mist at us galloping past,
And I saw my stout galloper Roland at last,
With resolute shoulders, each butting away
The haze, as some bluff river headland its spray:

And his low head and crest, just one sharp ear bent back
For my voice, and the other pricked out on his track;
And one eye's black intelligence, — ever that glance
O'er its white edge at me, his own master, askance!
And the thick heavy spume-flakes which aye and anon
His fierce lips shook upwards in galloping on.

By Hasselt, Dirck groaned; and cried Joris, "Stay spur!
Your Roos galloped bravely, the fault's not in her,
We'll remember at Aix" — for one heard the quick wheeze
Of her chest, saw the stretched neck and staggering knees,
And sunk tail, and horrible heave of the flank,
As down on her haunches she shuddered and sank.

So, we were left galloping, Joris and I,
Past Looz and past Tongres, no cloud in the sky;
The broad sun above laughed a pitiless laugh,
'Neath our feet broke the brittle bright stubble like chaff;

Till over by Dalhem a dome-spire sprang white,
And "Gallop," gasped Joris, "for Aix is in sight!" 42

"How they'll greet us!" — and all in a moment his roan
Rolled neck and croup over, lay dead as a stone;
And there was my Roland to bear the whole weight
Of the news which alone could save Aix from her fate,
With his nostrils like pits full of blood to the brim, 47
And with circles of red for his eye-sockets' rim.

Then I cast loose my buffcoat, each holster let fall,
Shook off both my jack-boots, let go belt and all,
Stood up in the stirrup, leaned, patted his ear,
Called my Roland his pet-name, my horse without peer;
Clapped my hands, laughed and sang, any noise, bad or good, 53
Till at length into Aix Roland galloped and stood.

And all I remember is — friends flocking round
As I sat with his head 'twixt my knees on the ground;
And no voice but was praising this Roland of mine,
As I poured down his throat our last measure of wine,
Which (the burgesses voted by common consent)
Was no more than his due who brought good news from Ghent. 60

MEETING AT NIGHT

The grey sea and the long black land;
And the yellow half-moon large and low;
And the startled little waves that leap
In fiery ringlets from their sleep,
As I gain the cove with pushing prow,
And quench its speed i' the slushy sand. 6

Then a mile of warm sea-scented beach;
Three fields to cross till a farm appears;
A tap at the pane, the quick sharp scratch
And blue spurt of a lighted match,
And a voice less loud, through its joys and fears,
Than the two hearts beating each to each! 12

PARTING AT MORNING

Round the cape of a sudden came the sea,
And the sun looked over the mountain's rim:
And straight was a path of gold for him,
And the need of a world of men for me. 4

SONG

Nay but you, who do not love her,
  Is she not pure gold, my mistress?
Holds earth aught — speak truth — above her?
  Aught like this tress, see, and this tress,
And this last fairest tress of all,
So fair, see, ere I let it fall? 6

Because you spend your lives in praising;
  To praise, you search the wide world over:
Then why not witness, calmly gazing,
  If earth holds aught — speak truth — above her?
Above this tress, and this, I touch
But cannot praise, I love so much! 12

EVELYN HOPE

Beautiful Evelyn Hope is dead!
  Sit and watch by her side an hour.
That is her book-shelf, this her bed;
  She plucked that piece of geranium-flower,
Beginning to die too, in the glass;
  Little has yet been changed, I think:
The shutters are shut, no light may pass
  Save two long rays through the hinge's chink. 8

Sixteen years old when she died!
  Perhaps she had scarcely heard my name;
It was not her time to love; beside,
  Her life had many a hope and aim,
Duties enough and little cares,
  And now was quiet, now astir,
Till God's hand beckoned unawares, —
  And the sweet white brow is all of her. 16

Is it too late then, Evelyn Hope?
  What, your soul was pure and true,
The good stars met in your horoscope,
  Made you of spirit, fire and dew —
And, just because I was thrice as old
  And our paths in the world diverged so wide,
Each was naught to each, must I be told?
  We were fellow mortals, naught beside? 24

No, indeed! for God above
  Is great to grant, as mighty to make,
And creates the love to reward the love:
  I claim you still, for my own love's sake!
Delayed it may be for more lives yet,
  Through worlds I shall traverse, not a few:
Much is to learn, much to forget
  Ere the time be come for taking you. 32

But the time will come, — at last it will,
When, Evelyn Hope, what meant (I shall say)
In the lower earth, in the years long still,
That body and soul so pure and gay?
Why your hair was amber, I shall divine,
And your mouth of your own geranium's red —
And what you would do with me, in fine,
In the new life come in the old one's stead.

I have lived (I shall say) so much since then,
Given up myself so many times,
Gained me the gains of various men,
Ransacked the ages, spoiled the climes;
Yet one thing, one, in my soul's full scope,
Either I missed or itself missed me:
And I want and find you, Evelyn Hope!
What is the issue? let us see!

I loved you, Evelyn, all the while!
My heart seemed full as it could hold;
There was place and to spare for the frank young smile,
And the red young mouth, and the hair's young gold.
So, hush, — I will give you this leaf to keep:
See, I shut it inside the sweet cold hand!
There, that is our secret: go to sleep!
You will wake, and remember, and understand.

HOME-THOUGHTS, FROM ABROAD

Oh, to be in England
Now that April's there,
And whoever wakes in England
Sees, some morning, unaware,
That the lowest boughs and the brush-wood sheaf
Round the elm-tree bole are in tiny leaf,
While the chaffinch sings on the orchard bough
In England — now!
And after April, when May follows,
And the whitethroat builds, and all the swallows!
Hark, where my blossomed pear-tree in the hedge
Leans to the field and scatters on the clover
Blossoms and dewdrops — at the bent spray's edge —
That's the wise thrush; he sings each song twice over,
Lest you should think he never could recapture
The first fine careless rapture!
And though the fields look rough with hoary dew,
All will be gay when noontide wakes anew
The buttercups, the little children's dower
— Far brighter than this gaudy melon-flower!

HOME-THOUGHTS, FROM THE SEA

Nobly, nobly Cape Saint Vincent to the North-west died away;
Sunset ran, one glorious blood-red, reeking into Cadiz Bay;
Bluish 'mid the burning water, full in face Trafalgar lay;
In the dimmest Northeast distance dawned Gibraltar grand and grey;
"Here and here did England help me: how can I help England?" — say,
Whoso turns as I, this evening, turn to God to praise and pray,
While Jove's planet rises yonder, silent over Africa.

FROM SAUL

XVII

"I have gone the whole round of creation: I saw and I spoke;
I, a work of God's hand for that purpose, received in my brain
And pronounced on the rest of his handwork — returned him again
His creation's approval or censure: I spoke as I saw:
I report, as a man may of God's work — all's love, yet all's law.
Now I lay down the judgeship he lent me. Each faculty tasked
To perceive him, has gained an abyss, where a dewdrop was asked.
Have I knowledge? confounded it shrivels at Wisdom laid bare.
Have I forethought? how purblind, how blank, to the Infinite Care!
Do I task any faculty highest, to image success?
I but open my eyes, — and perfection, no more and no less,
In the kind I imagined, full-fronts me, and God is seen God
In the star, in the stone, in the flesh, in the soul and the clod.
And thus looking within and around me, I ever renew
(With that stoop of the soul which in bending upraises it too)
The submission of man's nothing-perfect to God's all-complete,
As by each new obeisance in spirit, I climb to his feet.
Yet with all this abounding experience, this deity known,

I shall dare to discover some province, some gift of my own.
There's a faculty pleasant to exercise, hard to hoodwink,
I am faint to keep still in abeyance, (I laugh as I think)
Lest, insisting to claim and parade in it, wot ye, I worst
E'en the Giver in one gift. — Behold, I could love if I durst!
But I sink the pretension as fearing a man may o'ertake
God's own speed in the one way of love: I abstain for love's sake.
— What, my soul? see thus far and no farther? when doors great and small,
Nine-and-ninety flew ope at our touch, should the hundredth appall?
In the least things have faith, yet distrust in the greatest of all?
Do I find love so full in my nature, God's ultimate gift,
That I doubt his own love can compete with it? Here, the parts shift?
Here, the creature surpass the Creator, — the end, what Began?
Would I fain in my impotent yearning do all for this man,
And dare doubt he alone shall not help him, who yet alone can?
Would it ever have entered my mind, the bare will, much less power,
To bestow on this Saul what I sang of, the marvellous dower
Of the life he was gifted and filled with? to make such a soul,
Such a body, and then such an earth for insphering the whole?
And doth it not enter my mind (as my warm tears attest)
These good things being given, to go on, and give one more, the best?
Ay, to save and redeem and restore him, maintain at the height
This perfection, — succeed with life's day-spring, death's minute of night?
Interpose at the difficult minute, snatch Saul the mistake,
Saul the failure, the ruin he seems now, — and bid him awake
From the dream, the probation, the prelude, to find himself set
Clear and safe in new light and new life, — a new harmony yet
To be run, and continued, and ended — who knows? — or endure!
The man taught enough by life's dream, of the rest to make sure;
By the pain-throb, triumphantly winning intensified bliss,
And the next world's reward and repose, by the struggles in this.

XVIII

"I believe it! 'Tis thou, God, that givest, 'tis I who receive:
In the first is the last, in thy will is my power to believe.
All's one gift: thou canst grant it moreover, as prompt to my prayer
As I breathe out this breath, as I open these arms to the air.
From thy will stream the worlds, life and nature, thy dread Sabaoth:
I will? — the mere atoms despise me! Why am I not loth
To look that, even that in the face too? Why is it I dare
Think but lightly of such impuissance? What stops my despair?
This; — 'tis not what man Does which exalts him, but what man Would do!
See the King — I would help him but cannot, the wishes fall through.
Could I wrestle to raise him from sorrow, grow poor to enrich,
To fill up his life, starve my own out, I would — knowing which,
I know that my service is perfect. Oh, speak through me now!
Would I suffer for him that I love? So wouldst thou — so wilt thou!
So shall crown thee the topmost, ineffablest, uttermost crown —
And thy love fill infinitude wholly, nor leave up nor down
One spot for the creature to stand in! It is by no breath,
Turn of eye, wave of hand, that salvation joins issue with death!
As thy Love is discovered almighty, almighty be proved
Thy power, that exists with and for it, of being Beloved!
He who did most, shall bear most; the strongest shall stand the most weak.
'Tis the weakness in strength, that I cry for! my flesh, that I seek
In the Godhead! I seek and I find it. O Saul, it shall be

A Face like my face that receives thee; a Man like to me,
Thou shalt love and be loved by, forever: a Hand like this hand
Shall throw open the gates of new life to thee!
See the Christ stand!"

SONG

MY STAR

All that I know
Of a certain star
Is, it can throw
(Like the angled spar)
Now a dart of red,
Now a dart of blue;
Till my friends have said
They would fain see, too,
My star that dartles the red and the blue!
Then it stops like a bird: like a flower, hangs furled:
They must solace themselves with the Saturn above it.
What matter to me if their star is a world?
Mine has opened its soul to me; therefore I love it.

INCIDENT OF THE FRENCH CAMP

You know, we French stormed Ratisbon:
A mile or so away,
On a little mound, Napoleon
Stood on our storming-day;
With neck out-thrust, you fancy how,
Legs wide, arms locked behind,
As if to balance the prone brow
Oppressive with its mind.

Just as perhaps he mused "My plans
That soar, to earth may fall,
Let once my army-leader Lannes
Waver at yonder wall," —
Out 'twixt the battery-smokes there flew
A rider, bound on bound
Full-galloping; nor bridle drew
Until he reached the mound.

Then off there flung in smiling joy
And held himself erect
By just his horse's mane, a boy:
You hardly could suspect —
(So tight he kept his lips compressed
Scarce any blood came through)
You looked twice ere you saw his breast
Was all but shot in two.

"Well," cried he, "Emperor, by God's grace
We've got you Ratisbon!
The Marshal's in the market-place,
And you'll be there anon
To see your flag-bird flap his vans
Where I, to heart's desire,
Perched him!" The chief's eye flashed; his plans
Soared up again like fire.

The chief's eye flashed; but presently
Softened itself, as sheathes
A film the mother-eagle's eye
When her bruised eaglet breathes;
"You're wounded!" "Nay," the soldier's pride
Touched to the quick, he said:
"I'm killed, Sire!" And his chief beside,
Smiling the boy fell dead.

MY LAST DUCHESS

FERRARA

That's my last Duchess painted on the wall,
Looking as if she were alive. I call
That piece a wonder, now: Fra Pandolf's hands
Worked busily a day, and there she stands.
Will't please you sit and look at her? I said
"Fra Pandolf" by design, for never read
Strangers like you that pictured countenance,
The depth and passion of its earnest glance,
But to myself they turned (since none puts by
The curtain I have drawn for you, but I)
And seemed as they would ask me, if they durst,
How such a glance came there; so, not the first
Are you to turn and ask thus. Sir, 'twas not
Her husband's presence only, called that spot
Of joy into the Duchess' cheek: perhaps
Fra Pandolf chanced to say, "Her mantle laps
Over my lady's wrist too much," or "Paint
Must never hope to reproduce the faint
Half-flush that dies along her throat:" such stuff
Was courtesy, she thought, and cause enough
For calling up that spot of joy. She had
A heart — how shall I say? — too soon made glad,
Too easily impressed: she liked whate'er
She looked on, and her looks went everywhere.
Sir, 'twas all one! My favour at her breast,
The dropping of the daylight in the West,
The bough of cherries some officious fool
Broke in the orchard for her, the white mule
She rode with round the terrace — all and each
Would draw from her alike the approving speech,
Or blush, at least. She thanked men, — good! but thanked
Somehow — I know not how — as if she ranked

My gift of a nine-hundred-years-old name
With anybody's gift. Who'd stoop to blame
This sort of trifling? Even had you skill
In speech — (which I have not) — to make your will
Quite clear to such an one, and say, "Just this
Or that in you disgusts me; here you miss,
Or there exceed the mark" — and if she let
Herself be lessoned so, nor plainly set
Her wits to yours, forsooth, and made excuse,
— E'en then would be some stooping; and I choose
Never to stoop. Oh sir, she smiled, no doubt,
Whene'er I passed her; but who passed without
Much the same smile? This grew; I gave commands;
Then all smiles stopped together. There she stands
As if alive. Will't please you rise? We'll meet
The company below, then. I repeat,
The Count your master's known munificence
Is ample warrant that no just pretence
Of mine for dowry will be disallowed;
Though his fair daughter's self, as I avowed
At starting, is my object. Nay, we'll go
Together down, sir. Notice Neptune, though,
Taming a sea-horse, thought a rarity,
Which Claus of Innsbruck cast in bronze for me!

THE BOY AND THE ANGEL

Morning, evening, noon and night,
"Praise God!" sang Theocrite.

Then to his poor trade he turned,
Whereby the daily meal was earned.

Hard he laboured, long and well;
O'er his work the boy's curls fell.

But ever, at each period,
He stopped and sang, "Praise God!"

Then back again his curls he threw,
And cheerful turned to work anew.

Said Blaise, the listening monk, "Well done;
I doubt not thou art heard, my son:

"As well as if thy voice to-day
Were praising God, the Pope's great way.

"This Easter Day, the Pope at Rome
Praises God from Peter's dome."

Said Theocrite, "Would God that I
Might praise him that great way, and die!"

Night passed, day shone,
And Theocrite was gone,

With God a day endures alway,
A thousand years are but a day.

God said in heaven, "Nor day nor night
Now brings the voice of my delight."

Then Gabriel, like a rainbow's birth,
Spread his wings and sank to earth;

Entered, in flesh, the empty cell,
Lived there, and played the craftsman well;

And morning, evening, noon and night,
Praised God in place of Theocrite.

And from a boy, to youth he grew:
The man put off the stripling's hue:

The man matured and fell away
Into the season of decay:

And ever o'er the trade he bent,
And ever lived on earth content.

(He did God's will; to him, all one
If on the earth or in the sun.)

God said, "A praise is in mine ear;
There is no doubt in it, no fear:

"So sing old worlds, and so
New worlds that from my footstool go.

"Clearer loves sound other ways:
I miss my little human praise."

Then forth sprang Gabriel's wings, off fell
The flesh disguise, remained the cell.

'Twas Easter Day: he flew to Rome,
And paused above Saint Peter's dome.

In the tiring-room close by
The great outer gallery,

With his holy vestments dight,
Stood the new Pope, Theocrite:

And all his past career
Came back upon him clear,

Since when, a boy, he plied his trade,
Till on his life the sickness weighed;

And in his cell, when death drew near,
An angel in a dream brought cheer:

And rising from his sickness drear,
He grew a priest, and now stood here.

To the East with praise he turned,
And on his sight the angel burned.

"I bore thee from thy craftsman's cell,
And set thee here; I did not well.

"Vainly I left my angel-sphere,
Vain was thy dream of many a year.

"Thy voice's praise seemed weak; dropped —
Creation's chorus stopped!

"Go back and praise again
The early way, while I remain.

"With that weak voice of our disdain,
Take up creation's pausing strain.

"Back to the cell and poor employ:
Resume the craftsman and the boy!"

Theocrite grew old at home;
A new Pope dwelt in Peter's dome.

One vanished as the other died:
They sought God side by side.

THE LAST RIDE TOGETHER

I said — Then, dearest, since 'tis so,
Since now at length my fate I know,
Since nothing all my love avails,
Since all, my life seemed meant for, fails,
  Since this was written and needs must be —
My whole heart rises up to bless
Your name in pride and thankfulness!
Take back the hope you gave, — I claim
Only a memory of the same,
— And this beside, if you will not blame,
  Your leave for one more last ride with me.

My mistress bent that brow of hers;
Those deep dark eyes where pride demurs
When pity would be softening through,
Fixed me a breathing-while or two
  With life or death in the balance: right!
The blood replenished me again;
My last thought was at least not vain:
I and my mistress, side by side
Shall be together, breathe and ride,
So, one day more am I deified.
  Who knows but the world may end to-night?

Hush! if you saw some western cloud
All billowy-bosomed, over-bowed
By many benedictions — sun's
And moon's and evening-star's at once —
  And so, you, looking and loving best,
Conscious grew, your passion drew
Cloud, sunset, moonrise, star-shine too,
Down on you, near and yet more near,
Till flesh must fade for heaven was here! —
Thus leant she and lingered — joy and fear!
  Thus lay she a moment on my breast.

Then we began to ride. My soul
Smoothed itself out, a long-cramped scroll
Freshening and fluttering in the wind.
Past hopes already lay behind.
  What need to strive with a life awry?
Had I said that, had I done this,
So might I gain, so might I miss.
Might she have loved me? just as well
She might have hated, who can tell!
Where had I been now if the worst befell?
  And here we are riding, she and I.

Fail I alone, in words and deeds?
Why, all men strive, and who succeeds?
We rode; it seemed my spirit flew,
Saw other regions, cities new,
  As the world rushed by on either side.
I thought, — All labour, yet no less
Bear up beneath their unsuccess.
Look at the end of work, contrast
The petty done, the undone vast,
This present of theirs with the hopeful past!
  I hoped she would love me; here we ride.

What hand and brain went ever paired?
What heart alike conceived and dared?
What act proved all its thought had been?
What will but felt the fleshly screen?
  We ride and I see her bosom heave.
There's many a crown for who can reach.
Ten lines, a statesman's life in each!
The flag stuck on a heap of bones,
A soldier's doing! what atones?
They scratch his name on the Abbey-stones.
  My riding is better, by their leave.

What does it all mean, poet? Well,
Your brains beat into rhythm, you tell
What we felt only; you expressed
You hold things beautiful the best,
  And place them in rhyme so, side by side.
'Tis something, nay 'tis much: but then,
Have you yourself what's best for men?
Are you — poor, sick, old ere your time —
Nearer one whit your own sublime
Than we who never have turned a rhyme?
  Sing, riding's a joy! For me, I ride.

And you, great sculptor — so, you gave
A score of years to Art, her slave,
And that's your Venus, whence we turn
To yonder girl that fords the burn!

You acquiesce, and shall I repine?
What, man of music, you grown grey
With notes and nothing else to say,
Is this your sole praise from a friend,
"Greatly his opera's strains intend,
But in music we know how fashions end!"
I gave my youth; but we ride, in fine.

Who knows what's fit for us? Had fate
Proposed bliss here should sublimate
My being — had I signed the bond —
Still one must lead some life beyond,
Have a bliss to die with, dim-descried.
This foot once planted on the goal,
This glory-garland round my soul,
Could I descry such? Try and test!
I sink back shuddering from the quest.
Earth being so good, would heaven seem best?
Now, heaven and she are beyond this ride.

And yet — she has not spoke so long!
What if heaven be that, fair and strong
At life's best, with our eyes upturned
Whither life's flower is first discerned,
We, fixed so, ever should so abide?
What if we still ride on, we two,
With life forever old yet new,
Changed not in kind but in degree,
The instant made eternity, —
And heaven just prove that I and she
Ride, ride together, forever ride?

A GRAMMARIAN'S FUNERAL

SHORTLY AFTER THE REVIVAL OF LEARNING IN EUROPE

Let us begin and carry up this corpse,
Singing together.
Leave we the common crofts, the vulgar thorpes
Each in its tether
Sleeping safe on the bosom of the plain,
Cared-for till cock-crow:
Look out if yonder be not day again
Rimming the rock-row!
That's the appropriate country; there, man's thought,
Rarer, intenser,
Self-gathered for an outbreak, as it ought,
Chafes in the censer.
Leave we the unlettered plain its herd and crop;
Seek we sepulture
On a tall mountain, citied to the top,
Crowded with culture!
All the peaks soar, but one the rest excels;
Clouds overcome it;
No! yonder sparkle is the citadel's
Circling its summit.
Thither our path lies; wind we up the heights;
Wait ye the warning?
Our low life was the level's and the night's;
He's for the morning.
Step to a tune, square chests, erect each head,
'Ware the beholders!
This is our master, famous, calm and dead,
Borne on our shoulders.

Sleep, crop and herd! sleep, darkling thorpe and croft,
Safe from the weather!
He, whom we convoy to his grave aloft,
Singing together,
He was a man born with thy face and throat,
Lyric Apollo!
Long he lived nameless: how should Spring take note
Winter would follow?
Till lo, the little touch, and youth was gone!
Cramped and diminished,
Moaned he, "New measures, other feet anon!
My dance is finished"?
No, that's the world's way: (keep the mountain-side,
Make for the city!)
He knew the signal, and stepped on with pride
Over men's pity;
Left play for work, and grappled with the world
Bent on escaping:
"What's in the scroll," quoth he, "thou keepest furled?
Show me their shaping,
Theirs who most studied man, the bard and sage, —
Give!" — So, he gowned him,
Straight got by heart that book to its last page:
Learned, we found him.
Yea, but we found him bald too, eyes like lead,
Accents uncertain:
"Time to taste life," another would have said,
"Up with the curtain!"
This man said rather, "Actual life comes next?
Patience a moment!
Grant I have mastered learning's crabbed text,
Still there's the comment.
Let me know all! Prate not of most or least,
Painful or easy!
Even to the crumbs I'd fain eat up the feast,
Ay, nor feel queasy."
Oh, such a life as he resolved to live,
When he had learned it,
When he had gathered all books had to give!
Sooner, he spurned it.

Image the whole, then execute the parts —
Fancy the fabric
Quite, ere you build, ere steel strike fire from quartz,
Ere mortar dab brick!

(Here's the town-gate reached: there's the market-place
Gaping before us.)
Yea, this in him was the peculiar grace
(Hearten our chorus!)
That before living he'd learn how to live —
No end to learning:
Earn the means first — God surely will contrive
Use for our earning.
Others mistrust and say, "But time escapes:
Live now or never!"
He said, "What's time? Leave Now for dogs and apes!
Man has Forever."
Back to his book then: deeper drooped his head:
Calculus racked him:
Leaden before, his eyes grew dross of lead:
Tussis attacked him.
"Now, master, take a little rest!" — not he!
(Caution redoubled,
Step two abreast, the way winds narrowly!)
Not a whit troubled,
Back to his studies, fresher than at first,
Fierce as a dragon
He (soul-hydroptic with a sacred thirst)
Sucked at the flagon.
Oh, if we draw a circle premature,
Heedless of far gain,
Greedy for quick returns of profit, sure
Bad is our bargain!
Was it not great? did not he throw on God,
(He loves the burthen) —
God's task to make the heavenly period
Perfect the earthen?
Did not he magnify the mind, show clear
Just what it all meant?
He would not discount life, as fools do here,
Paid by instalment.
He ventured neck or nothing — heaven's success
Found, or earth's failure:
"Wilt thou trust death or not?" He answered "Yes!
Hence with life's pale lure!"
That low man seeks a little thing to do,
Sees it and does it:
This high man, with a great thing to pursue,
Dies ere he knows it.
That low man goes on adding one to one,
His hundred's soon hit:
This high man, aiming at a million,
Misses an unit.
That, has the world here — should he need the next,
Let the world mind him!
This, throws himself on God, and unperplexed
Seeking shall find him.
So, with the throttling hands of death at strife,
Ground he at grammar;
Still, through the rattle, parts of speech were rife:
While he could stammer
He settled *Hoti's* business — let it be! —
Properly based *Oun* —
Gave us the doctrine of the enclitic *De*,
Dead from the waist down.
Well, here's the platform, here's the proper place:
Hail to your purlieus,
All ye highfliers of the feathered race,
Swallows and curlews!
Here's the top-peak; the multitude below
Live, for they can, there:
This man decided not to Live but Know —
Bury this man there?
Here — here's his place, where meteors shoot, clouds form,
Lightnings are loosened,
Stars come and go! Let joy break with the storm,
Peace let the dew send!
Lofty designs must close in like effects:
Loftily lying,
Leave him — still loftier than the world suspects,
Living and dying.

"CHILDE ROLAND TO THE DARK TOWER CAME"

(See Edgar's song in *Lear*)

My first thought was, he lied in every word,
That hoary cripple, with malicious eye
Askance to watch the working of his lie
On mine, and mouth scarce able to afford
Suppression of the glee, that pursed and scored
Its edge, at one more victim gained thereby.

What else should he be set for with his staff?
What, save to waylay with his lies, ensnare
All travellers who might find him posted there,
And ask the road? I guessed what skull-like laugh
Would break, what crutch 'gin write my epitaph
For pastime in the dusty thoroughfare,

If at his counsel I should turn aside
Into that ominous tract which, all agree,
Hides the Dark Tower. Yet acquiescingly
I did turn as he pointed: neither pride
Nor hope rekindling at the end descried, 17
So much as gladness that some end might be.

For, what with my whole world-wide wandering,
What with my search drawn out through years, my hope
Dwindled into a ghost not fit to cope
With that obstreperous joy success would bring, —
I hardly tried now to rebuke the spring
My heart made, finding failure in its scope. 24

As when a sick man very near to death
Seems dead indeed, and feels begin and end
The tears, and takes the farewell of each friend,
And hears one bid the other go, draw breath
Freelier outside, ("since all is o'er," he saith, 29
"And the blow fallen no grieving can amend;")

While some discuss if near the other graves
Be room enough for this, and when a day
Suits best for carrying the corpse away,
With care about the banners, scarves and staves:
And still the man hears all, and only craves 35
He may not shame such tender love and stay.

Thus, I had so long suffered in this quest,
Heard failure prophesied so oft, been writ
So many times among "The Band" — to wit,
The knights who to the Dark Tower's search addressed
Their steps — that just to fail as they, seemed best,
And all the doubt was now — should I be fit?

So, quiet as despair, I turned from him, 43
That hateful cripple, out of his highway
Into the path he pointed. All the day
Had been a dreary one at best, and dim
Was settling to its close, yet shot one grim
Red leer to see the plain catch its estray. 48

For mark! no sooner was I fairly found
Pledged to the plain, after a pace or two,
Than, pausing to throw backward a last view
O'er the safe road, 'twas gone; grey plain all round:
Nothing but plain to the horizon's bound.
I might go on; naught else remained to do. 54

So, on I went. I think I never saw
Such starved ignoble nature; nothing throve:
For flowers — as well expect a cedar grove!
But cockle, spurge, according to their law
Might propagate their kind, with none to awe, 59
You'd think: a burr had been a treasure trove.

No! penury, inertness and grimace,
In some strange sort, were the land's portion. "See
Or shut your eyes," said Nature peevishly,
"It nothing skills: I cannot help my case:
'Tis the Last Judgment's fire must cure this place,
Calcine its clods and set my prisoners free." 66

If there pushed any ragged thistle-stalk
Above its mates, the head was chopped; the bents
Were jealous else. What made those holes and rents
In the dock's harsh swarth leaves, bruised as to balk
All hope of greenness? 'tis a brute must walk
Pashing their life out, with a brute's intents. 72

As for the grass, it grew as scant as hair
In leprosy; thin dry blades pricked the mud
Which underneath looked kneaded up with blood.
One stiff blind horse, his every bone a-stare,
Stood stupefied, however he came there: 77
Thrust out past service from the devil's stud!

Alive? he might be dead for aught I know,
With that red gaunt and colloped neck a-strain,
And shut eyes underneath the rusty mane;
Seldom went such grotesqueness with such woe;
I never saw a brute I hated so;
He must be wicked to deserve such pain. 84

I shut my eyes and turned them on my heart.
As a man calls for wine before he fights,
I asked one draught of earlier, happier sights,
Ere fitly I could hope to play my part.
Think first, fight afterwards — the soldier's art:
One taste of the old time sets all to rights. 90

Not it! I fancied Cuthbert's reddening face
Beneath its garniture of curly gold,
Dear fellow, till I almost felt him fold
An arm in mine to fix me to the place,
That way he used. Alas, one night's disgrace!
Out went my heart's new fire and left it cold. 96

Giles then, the soul of honour — there he stands
Frank as ten years ago when knighted first.
What honest man should dare (he said) he durst.
Good — but the scene shifts — faugh! what hangman hands
Pin to his breast a parchment? His own bands
Read it. Poor traitor, spit upon and curst!

Better this present than a past like that; 103
Back therefore to my darkening path again!

No sound, no sight as far as eye could strain.
Will the night send a howlet or a bat?
I asked: when something on the dismal flat
Came to arrest my thoughts and change their train. 108

A sudden little river crossed my path
As unexpected as a serpent comes.
No sluggish tide congenial to the glooms;
This, as it frothed by, might have been a bath
For the fiend's glowing hoof — to see the wrath
Of its black eddy bespate with flakes and spumes.

So petty yet so spiteful! All along, 115
Low scrubby alders kneeled down over it;
Drenched willows flung them headlong in a fit
Of mute despair, a suicidal throng:
The river which had done them all the wrong,
Whate'er that was, rolled by, deterred no whit.

Which, while I forded, — good saints, how I feared 121
To set my foot upon a dead man's cheek,
Each step, or feel the spear I thrust to seek
For hollows, tangled in his hair or beard!
— It may have been a water-rat I speared,
But, ugh! it sounded like a baby's shriek. 126

Glad was I when I reached the other bank.
Now for a better country. Vain presage!
Who were the strugglers, what war did they wage,
Whose savage trample thus could pad the dank
Soil to a plash? Toads in a poisoned tank,
Or wild cats in a red-hot iron cage — 132

The fight must so have seemed in that fell cirque.
What penned them there, with all the plain to choose?
No footprint leading to that horrid mews,
None out of it. Mad brewage set to work
Their brains, no doubt, like galley-slaves the Turk
Pits for his pastime, Christians against Jews.

And more than that — a furlong on — why, there! 139
What bad use was that engine for, that wheel,
Or brake, not wheel — that harrow fit to reel
Men's bodies out like silk? with all the air
Of Tophet's tool, on earth left unaware, 143
Or brought to sharpen its rusty teeth of steel.

Then came a bit of stubbed ground, once a wood,
Next a marsh, it would seem, and now mere earth
Desperate and done with: (so a fool finds mirth,
Makes a thing and then mars it, till his mood
Changes and off he goes!) within a rood —
Bog, clay and rubble, sand and stark black dearth. 150

Now blotches rankling, coloured gay and grim,
Now patches where some leanness of the soil's
Broke into moss or substances like boils;
Then came some palsied oak, a cleft in him
Like a distorted mouth that splits its rim
Gaping at death, and dies while it recoils. 156

And just as far as ever from the end!
Naught in the distance but the evening, naught
To point my footstep further! At the thought,
A great black bird, Apollyon's bosom-friend,
Sailed past, nor beat his wide wing dragon-penned
That brushed my cap — perchance the guide I sought. 162

For, looking up, aware I somehow grew,
'Spite of the dusk, the plain had given place
All round to mountains — with such name to grace
Mere ugly heights and heaps now stolen in view.
How thus they had surprised me, — solve it, you!
How to get from them was no clearer case. 168

Yet half I seemed to recognise some trick
Of mischief happened to me, God knows when —
In a bad dream perhaps. Here ended, then,
Progress this way. When, in the very nick
Of giving up, one time more, came a click 173
As when a trap shuts — you're inside the den!

Burningly it came on me all at once,
This was the place! those two hills on the right,
Crouched like two bulls locked horn in horn in fight;
While to the left, a tall scalped mountain . . . Dunce,
Dotard, a-dozing at the very nonce,
After a life spent training for the sight! 180

What in the midst lay but the Tower itself?
The round squat turret, blind as the fool's heart,
Built of brown stone, without a counterpart
In the whole world. The tempest's mocking elf
Points to the shipman thus the unseen shelf
He strikes on, only when the timbers start. 186

Not see? because of night perhaps? — why, day
Came back again for that! before it left,
The dying sunset kindled through a cleft:

The hills, like giants at a hunting, lay,
Chin upon hand, to see the game at bay, —
"Now stab and end the creature — to the heft!"

Not hear? when noise was everywhere! it tolled
Increasing like a bell. Names in my ears,
Of all the lost adventurers my peers, —
How such a one was strong, and such was bold,
And such was fortunate, yet each of old
Lost, lost! one moment knelled the woe of years.

There they stood, ranged along the hillsides, met
To view the last of me, a living frame
For one more picture! in a sheet of flame
I saw them and I knew them all. And yet
Dauntless the slug-horn to my lips I set,
And blew. "*Childe Roland to the Dark Tower came.*"

FRA LIPPO LIPPI

I am poor brother Lippo, by your leave!
You need not clap your torches to my face.
Zooks, what's to blame? you think you see a monk!
What, 'tis past midnight, and you go the rounds,
And here you catch me at an alley's end
Where sportive ladies leave their doors ajar?
The Carmine's my cloister: hunt it up,
Do, — harry out, if you must show your zeal,
Whatever rat, there, haps on his wrong hole,
And nip each softling of a wee white mouse,
Weke, weke, that's crept to keep him company!
Aha, you know your betters! Then, you'll take
Your hand away that's fiddling on my throat,
And please to know me likewise. Who am I?
Why, one, sir, who is lodging with a friend
Three streets off — he's a certain . . . how d'ye call?
Master — a . . . Cosimo of the Medici,
I' the house that caps the corner. Boh! you were best!
Remember and tell me, the day you're hanged,
How you affected such a gullet's-gripe!
But you, sir, it concerns you that your knaves
Pick up a manner nor discredit you:
Zooks, are we pilchards, that they sweep the streets
And count fair prize what comes into their net?
He's Judas to a tittle, that man is!
Just such a face! Why, sir, you make amends.
Lord, I'm not angry! Bid your hangdogs go
Drink out this quarter-florin to the health
Of the munificent House that harbours me
(And many more beside, lads! more beside!)
And all's come square again. I'd like his face —
His, elbowing on his comrade in the door
With the pike and lantern, — for the slave that holds
John Baptist's head a-dangle by the hair
With one hand ("Look you, now," as who should say)
And his weapon in the other, yet unwiped!
It's not your chance to have a bit of chalk,
A wood-coal or the like? or you should see!
Yes, I'm the painter, since you style me so.
What, brother Lippo's doings, up and down,
You know them and they take you? like enough!
I saw the proper twinkle in your eye —
'Tell you, I liked your looks at very first.
Let's sit and set things straight now, hip to haunch.
Here's spring come, and the nights one makes up bands
To roam the town and sing out carnival,
And I've been three weeks shut within my mew,
A-painting for the great man, saints and saints
And saints again. I could not paint all night —
Ouf! I leaned out of window for fresh air.
There came a hurry of feet and little feet,
A sweep of lute-strings, laughs, and whifts of song, —
Flower o' the broom,
Take away love, and our earth is a tomb!
Flower o' the quince,
I let Lisa go, and what good in life since?
Flower o' the thyme — and so on. Round they went.
Scarce had they turned the corner when a titter
Like the skipping of rabbits by moonlight, — three slim shapes,
And a face that looked up . . . zooks, sir, flesh and blood,
That's all I'm made of! Into shreds it went,
Curtain and counterpane and coverlet,
All the bed-furniture — a dozen knots,
There was a ladder! Down I let myself,
Hands and feet, scrambling somehow, and so dropped,
And after them. I came up with the fun
Hard by Saint Laurence, hail fellow, well met, —
Flower o' the rose,
If I've been merry, what matter who knows?
And so as I was stealing back again
To get to bed and have a bit of sleep
Ere I rise up to-morrow and go work
On Jerome knocking at his poor old breast
With his great round stone to subdue the flesh,
You snap me of the sudden. Ah, I see!

Though your eye twinkles still, you shake your head —
Mine's shaved — a monk, you say — the sting's in that!
If Master Cosimo announced himself,
Mum's the word naturally; but a monk!
Come, what am I a beast for? tell us, now!
I was a baby when my mother died
And father died and left me in the street.
I starved there, God knows how, a year or two
On fig-skins, melon-parings, rinds and shucks,
Refuse and rubbish. One fine frosty day,
My stomach being empty as your hat,
The wind doubled me up and down I went.
Old Aunt Lapaccia trussed me with one hand,
(Its fellow was a stinger as I knew)
And so along the wall, over the bridge,
By the straight cut to the convent. Six words there,
While I stood munching my first bread that month:
"So, boy, you're minded," quoth the good fat father,
Wiping his own mouth, 'twas refection-time, —
"To quit this very miserable world?
Will you renounce" . . . "the mouthful of bread?" thought I;
"By no means!" Brief, they made a monk of me;
I did renounce the world, its pride and greed,
Palace, farm, villa, shop, and banking-house,
Trash, such as these poor devils of Medici
Have given their hearts to — all at eight years old.
Well, sir, I found in time, you may be sure,
'Twas not for nothing — the good bellyful,
The warm serge and the rope that goes all round,
And day-long blessed idleness beside!
"Let's see what the urchin's fit for" — that came next.
Not overmuch their way, I must confess.
Such a to-do! They tried me with their books;
Lord, they'd have taught me Latin in pure waste!
Flower o' the clove,
All the Latin I construe is "amo," I love!
But, mind you, when a boy starves in the streets
Eight years together, as my fortune was,
Watching folk's faces to know who will fling
The bit of half-stripped grape-bunch he desires,
And who will curse or kick him for his pains, —
Which gentleman processional and fine,
Holding a candle to the Sacrament,
Will wink and let him lift a plate and catch
The droppings of the wax to sell again,
Or holla for the Eight and have him whipped, —
How say I? — nay, which dog bites, which lets drop
His bone from the heap of offal in the street, —
Why, soul and sense of him grow sharp alike,
He learns the look of things, and none the less
For admonition from the hunger-pinch.
I had a store of such remarks, be sure,
Which, after I found leisure, turned to use.
I drew men's faces on my copy-books,
Scrawled them within the antiphonary's marge,
Joined legs and arms to the long music-notes,
Found eyes and nose and chin for A's and B's,
And made a string of pictures of the world
Betwixt the ins and outs of verb and noun,
On the wall, the bench, the door. The monks looked black.
"Nay," quoth the Prior, "turn him out, d'ye say?
In no wise. Lose a crow and catch a lark.
What if at last we get our man of parts,
We Carmelites, like those Camaldolese
And Preaching Friars, to do our church up fine
And put the front on it that ought to be!"
And hereupon he bade me daub away.
Thank you! my head being crammed, the walls a blank,
Never was such prompt disemburdening.
First, every sort of monk, the black and white,
I drew them, fat and lean: then, folk at church,
From good old gossips waiting to confess
Their cribs of barrel-droppings, candle-ends, —
To the breathless fellow at the altar-foot,
Fresh from his murder, safe and sitting there
With the little children round him in a row
Of admiration, half for his beard and half
For that white anger of his victim's son
Shaking a fist at him with one fierce arm,
Signing himself with the other because of Christ
(Whose sad face on the cross sees only this
After the passion of a thousand years)
Till some poor girl, her apron o'er her head,
(Which the intense eyes looked through) came at eve
On tiptoe, said a word, dropped in a loaf,
Her pair of earrings and a bunch of flowers
(The brute took growling), prayed, and so was gone.
I painted all, then cried "'Tis ask and have;
Choose, for more's ready!" — laid the ladder flat,
And showed my covered bit of cloister-wall.
The monks closed in a circle and praised loud
Till checked, taught what to see and not to see,
Being simple bodies, — "That's the very man!
Look at the boy who stoops to pat the dog!
That woman's like the Prior's niece who comes
To care about his asthma: it's the life!"
But there my triumph's straw-fire flared and funked;
Their betters took their turn to see and say:

The Prior and the learned pulled a face
And stopped all that in no time. "How? what's here?
Quite from the mark of painting, bless us all!
Faces, arms, legs, and bodies like the true
As much as pea and pea! it's devil's-game!
Your business is not to catch men with show,
With homage to the perishable clay,
But lift them over it, ignore it all,
Make them forget there's such a thing as flesh.
Your business is to paint the souls of men —
Man's soul, and it's a fire, smoke . . . no, it's not . . .
It's vapour done up like a new-born babe —
(In that shape when you die it leaves your mouth)
It's . . . well, what matters talking, it's the soul!
Give us no more of body than shows soul!
Here's Giotto, with his Saint a-praising God,
That sets us praising, — why not stop with him?
Why put all thoughts of praise out of our head
With wonder at lines, colours, and what not?
Paint the soul, never mind the legs and arms!
Rub all out, try at it a second time.
Oh, that white smallish female with the breasts,
She's just my niece . . . Herodias, I would say, —
Who went and danced and got men's heads cut off!
Have it all out!" Now, is this sense, I ask?
A fine way to paint soul, by painting body
So ill, the eye can't stop there, must go further
And can't fare worse! Thus, yellow does for white
When what you put for yellow's simply black,
And any sort of meaning looks intense
When all beside itself means and looks naught.
Why can't a painter lift each foot in turn,
Left foot and right foot, go a double step,
Make his flesh liker and his soul more like,
Both in their order? Take the prettiest face,
The Prior's niece . . . patron-saint — is it so pretty
You can't discover if it means hope, fear,
Sorrow or joy? won't beauty go with these?
Suppose I've made her eyes all right and blue,
Can't I take breath and try to add life's flash,
And then add soul and heighten them three-fold?
Or say there's beauty with no soul at all —
(I never saw it — put the case the same —)
If you get simple beauty and naught else,
You get about the best thing God invents:
That's somewhat: and you'll find the soul you have missed,
Within yourself, when you return him thanks.
"Rub all out!" Well, well, there's my life, in short,
And so the thing has gone on ever since.
I'm grown a man no doubt, I've broken bounds:
You should not take a fellow eight years old
And make him swear to never kiss the girls.
I'm my own master, paint now as I please —
Having a friend, you see, in the Corner-house!
Lord, it's fast holding by the rings in front —
Those great rings serve more purposes than just
To plant a flag in, or tie up a horse!
And yet the old schooling sticks, the old grave eyes
Are peeping o'er my shoulder as I work,
The heads shake still — "It's art's decline, my son!
You're not of the true painters, great and old;
Brother Angelico's the man, you'll find;
Brother Lorenzo stands his single peer:
Fag on at flesh, you'll never make the third!"
Flower o' the pine,
You keep your mistr . . . manners, and I'll stick to mine!
I'm not the third, then: bless us, they must know!
Don't you think they're the likeliest to know,
They with their Latin? So, I swallow my rage,
Clench my teeth, suck my lips in tight, and paint
To please them — sometimes do and sometimes don't;
For, doing most, there's pretty sure to come
A turn, some warm eve finds me at my saints —
A laugh, a cry, the business of the world —
(*Flower o' the peach,*
Death for us all, and his own life for each!)
And my whole soul revolves, the cup runs over,
The world and life's too big to pass for a dream,
And I do these wild things in sheer despite,
And play the fooleries you catch me at,
In pure rage! The old mill-horse, out at grass
After hard years, throws up his stiff heels so,
Although the miller does not preach to him
The only good of grass is to make chaff.
What would men have? Do they like grass or no —
May they or mayn't they? all I want's the thing
Settled forever one way. As it is,
You tell too many lies and hurt yourself:
You don't like what you only like too much.
You do like what, if given you at your word,
You find abundantly detestable.
For me, I think I speak as I was taught;
I always see the garden and God there
A-making man's wife: and, my lesson learned,
The value and significance of flesh,
I can't unlearn ten minutes afterwards.

You understand me: I'm a beast, I know.
But see, now — why, I see as certainly

As that the morning-star's about to shine,
What will hap some day. We've a youngster here
Comes to our convent, studies what I do,
Slouches and stares and lets no atom drop:
His name is Guidi — he'll not mind the monks —
They call him Hulking Tom, he lets them talk —
He picks my practice up — he'll paint apace,
I hope so — though I never live so long,
I know what's sure to follow. You be judge!
You speak no Latin more than I, belike;
However, you're my man, you've seen the world
— The beauty and the wonder and the power,
The shapes of things, their colours, lights and shades,
Changes, surprises, — and God made it all!
— For what? Do you feel thankful, ay or no,
For this fair town's face, yonder river's line,
The mountain round it and the sky above,
Much more the figures of man, woman, child,
These are the frame to? What's it all about?
To be passed over, despised? or dwelt upon,
Wondered at? oh, this last of course! — you say.
But why not do as well as say, — paint these
Just as they are, careless what comes of it?
God's works — paint any one, and count it crime
To let a truth slip. Don't object, "His works
Are here already; nature is complete:
Suppose you reproduce her — (which you can't)
There's no advantage! you must beat her, then."
For, don't you mark? we're made so that we love
First when we see them painted, things we have passed
Perhaps a hundred times nor cared to see;
And so they are better, painted — better to us,
Which is the same thing. Art was given for that;
God uses us to help each other so,
Lending our minds out. Have you noticed, now,
Your cullion's hanging face? A bit of chalk,
And trust me but you should, though! How much more,
If I drew higher things with the same truth!
That were to take the Prior's pulpit-place,
Interpret God to all of you! Oh, oh,
It makes me mad to see what men shall do
And we in our graves! This world's no blot for us,
Nor blank; it means intensely, and means good:
To find its meaning is my meat and drink.
"Ay, but you don't so instigate to prayer!"
Strikes in the Prior: "when your meaning's plain
It does not say to folk — remember matins,
Or, mind you fast next Friday!" Why, for this
What need of art at all? A skull and bones,
Two bits of stick nailed crosswise, or, what's best,
A bell to chime the hour with, does as well.
I painted a Saint Laurence six months since
At Prato, splashed the fresco in fine style:
"How looks my painting, now the scaffold's down?"
I ask a brother: "Hugely," he returns —
"Already not one phiz of your three slaves
Who turn the Deacon off his toasted side,
But's scratched and prodded to our heart's content,
The pious people have so eased their own
With coming to say prayers there in a rage:
We get on fast to see the bricks beneath.
Expect another job this time next year,
For pity and religion grow i' the crowd —
Your painting serves its purpose!" Hang the fools!

— That is — you'll not mistake an idle word
Spoke in a huff by a poor monk, God wot,
Tasting the air this spicy night which turns
The unaccustomed head like Chianti wine!
Oh, the church knows! don't misreport me, now!
It's natural a poor monk out of bounds
Should have his apt word to excuse himself:
And hearken how I plot to make amends.
I have bethought me: I shall paint a piece
. . . There's for you! Give me six months, then go, see
Something in Sant' Ambrogio's! Bless the nuns!
They want a cast o' my office. I shall paint
God in the midst, Madonna and her babe,
Ringed by a bowery, flowery angel-brood,
Lilies and vestments and white faces, sweet
As puff on puff of grated orris-root
When ladies crowd to Church at midsummer.
And then i' the front, of course a saint or two —
Saint John, because he saves the Florentines,
Saint Ambrose, who puts down in black and white
The convent's friends and gives them a long day,
And Job, I must have him there past mistake,
The man of Uz (and Us without the z,
Painters who need his patience). Well, all these
Secured at their devotion, up shall come
Out of a corner when you least expect,
As one by a dark stair into a great light,
Music and talking, who but Lippo! I! —
Mazed, motionless, and moonstruck — I'm the man!
Back I shrink — what is this I see and hear?
I, caught up with my monk's-things by mistake,
My old serge gown and rope that goes all round,

I, in this presence, this pure company!
Where's a hole, where's a corner for escape?
Then steps a sweet, angelic slip of a thing
Forward, puts out a soft palm — "Not so fast!"
— Addresses the celestial presence, "nay —
He made you and devised you, after all,
Though he's none of you! Could Saint John there draw —
His camel-hair make up a painting-brush?
We come to brother Lippo for all that,
Iste perfecit opus!" So, all smile —
I shuffle sideways with my blushing face
Under the cover of a hundred wings
Thrown like a spread of kirtles when you're gay
And play hot cockles, all the doors being shut,
Till, wholly unexpected, in there pops
The hothead husband! Thus I scuttle off
To some safe bench behind, not letting go
The palm of her, the little lily thing
That spoke the good word for me in the nick,
Like the Prior's niece . . . Saint Lucy, I would say.
And so all's saved for me, and for the church
A pretty picture gained. Go, six months hence!
Your hand, sir, and good-by: no lights, no lights!
The street's hushed, and I know my own way back,
Don't fear me! There's the grey beginning. Zooks!

THE BISHOP ORDERS HIS TOMB AT SAINT PRAXED'S CHURCH

Rome, 15—

Vanity, saith the preacher, vanity!
Draw round my bed: is Anselm keeping back?
Nephews — sons mine . . . ah God, I know not! Well —
She, men would have to be your mother once,
Old Gandolf envied me, so fair she was!
What's done is done, and she is dead beside,
Dead long ago, and I am Bishop since,
And as she died so must we die ourselves,
And thence ye may perceive the world's a dream.
Life, how and what is it? As here I lie
In this state-chamber, dying by degrees,
Hours and long hours in the dead night, I ask
"Do I live, am I dead?" Peace, peace seems all.
Saint Praxed's ever was the church for peace;
And so, about this tomb of mine. I fought
With tooth and nail to save my niche, ye know:
— Old Gandolf cozened me, despite my care;
Shrewd was that snatch from out the corner South
He graced his carrion with, God curse the same!
Yet still my niche is not so cramped but thence
One sees the pulpit o' the epistle-side,
And somewhat of the choir, those silent seats,
And up into the aëry dome where live
The angels, and a sunbeam's sure to lurk:
And I shall fill my slab of basalt there,
And 'neath my tabernacle take my rest,
With those nine columns round me, two and two,
The odd one at my feet where Anselm stands:
Peach-blossom marble all, the rare, the ripe
As fresh-poured red wine of a mighty pulse.
— Old Gandolf with his paltry onion-stone,
Put me where I may look at him! True peach,
Rosy and flawless: how I earned the prize!
Draw close: that conflagration of my church
— What then? So much was saved if aught were missed!
My sons, ye would not be my death? Go dig
The white-grape vineyard where the oil-press stood,
Drop water gently till the surface sink,
And if ye find . . . Ah God, I know not, I! . . .
Bedded in store of rotten fig-leaves soft,
And corded up in a tight olive-frail,
Some lump, ah God, of *lapis lazuli*,
Big as a Jew's head cut off at the nape,
Blue as a vein o'er the Madonna's breast . . .
Sons, all have I bequeathed you, villas, all,
That brave Frascati villa with its bath,
So, let the blue lump poise between my knees,
Like God the Father's globe on both his hands
Ye worship in the Jesu Church so gay,
For Gandolf shall not choose but see and burst!
Swift as a weaver's shuttle fleet our years:
Man goeth to the grave, and where is he?
Did I say basalt for my slab, sons? Black —
'Twas ever antique-black I meant! How else
Shall ye contrast my frieze to come beneath?
The bas-relief in bronze ye promised me,
Those Pans and Nymphs ye wot of, and perchance
Some tripod, thyrsus, with a vase or so,
The Saviour at his sermon on the mount,
Saint Praxed in a glory, and one Pan
Ready to twitch the Nymph's last garment off,
And Moses with the tables . . . but I know
Ye mark me not! What do they whisper thee,
Child of my bowels, Anselm? Ah, ye hope
To revel down my villas while I gasp
Bricked o'er with beggar's mouldy travertine
Which Gandolf from his tomb-top chuckles at!
Nay, boys, ye love me — all of jasper, then!
'Tis jasper ye stand pledged to, lest I grieve
My bath must needs be left behind, alas!

One block, pure green as a pistachio-nut,
There's plenty jasper somewhere in the world —
And have I not Saint Praxed's ear to pray
Horses for ye, and brown Greek manuscripts,
And mistresses with great smooth marbly limbs?
— That's if ye carve my epitaph aright,
Choice Latin, picked phrase, Tully's every word,
No gaudy ware like Gandolf's second line —
Tully, my masters? Ulpian serves his need!
And then how I shall lie through centuries,
And hear the blessed mutter of the mass,
And see God made and eaten all day long,
And feel the steady candle-flame, and taste
Good strong, thick, stupefying incense-smoke!
For as I lie here, hours of the dead night,
Dying in state and by such slow degrees,
I fold my arms as if they clasped a crook,
And stretch my feet forth straight as stone can point,
And let the bedclothes, for a mortcloth, drop
Into great laps and folds of sculptor's-work:
And as yon tapers dwindle, and strange thoughts
Grow, with a certain humming in my ears,
About the life before I lived this life,
And this life too, popes, cardinals and priests,
Saint Praxed at his sermon on the mount,
Your tall pale mother with her talking eyes,
And new-found agate urns as fresh as day,
And marble's language, Latin pure, discreet,
— Aha, ELUCESCEBAT quoth our friend?
No Tully, said I, Ulpian at the best!
Evil and brief hath been my pilgrimage.
All *lapis*, all, sons! Else I give the Pope
My villas! Will ye ever eat my heart?
Ever your eyes were as a lizard's quick,
They glitter like your mother's for my soul,
Or ye would heighten my impoverished frieze,
Piece out its starved design, and fill my vase
With grapes, and add a visor and a Term,
And to the tripod ye would tie a lynx
That in his struggle throws the thyrsus down,
To comfort me on my entablature
Whereon I am to lie till I must ask
"Do I live, am I dead?" There, leave me, there!
For ye have stabbed me with ingratitude
To death — ye wish it — God, ye wish it! Stone —
Gritstone, a-crumble! Clammy squares which sweat
As if the corpse they keep were oozing through —
And no more *lapis* to delight the world!
Well, go! I bless ye. Fewer tapers there,
But in a row: and, going, turn your backs
— Ay, like departing altar-ministrants,
And leave me in my church, the church for peace,
That I may watch at leisure if he leers —
Old Gandolf — at me, from his onion-stone,
As still he envied me, so fair she was!

ONE WORD MORE

TO E. B. B.

London, September, 1855

I

There they are, my fifty men and women
Naming me the fifty poems finished!
Take them, Love, the book and me together;
Where the heart lies, let the brain lie also.

II

Rafael made a century of sonnets,
Made and wrote them in a certain volume
Dinted with the silver-pointed pencil
Else he only used to draw Madonnas:
These, the world might view — but one, the volume.
Who that one, you ask? Your heart instructs you.
Did she live and love it all her lifetime?
Did she drop, his lady of the sonnets,
Die, and let it drop beside her pillow
Where it lay in place of Rafael's glory,
Rafael's cheek so duteous and so loving —
Cheek, the world was wont to hail a painter's,
Rafael's cheek, her love had turned a poet's?

III

You and I would rather read that volume,
(Taken to his beating bosom by it)
Lean and list the bosom-beats of Rafael,
Would we not? than wonder at Madonnas —
Her, San Sisto names, and Her, Foligno,
Her, that visits Florence in a vision,
Her, that's left with lilies in the Louvre —
Seen by us and all the world in circle.

IV

You and I will never read that volume.
Guido Reni, like his own eye's apple
Guarded long the treasure-book and loved it.
Guido Reni dying, all Bologna
Cried, and the world cried too, "Ours, the treasure!"
Suddenly, as rare things will, it vanished.

V

Dante once prepared to paint an angel:
Whom to please? You whisper "Beatrice."
While he mused and traced it and retraced it,
(Peradventure with a pen corroded
Still by drops of that hot ink he dipped for,

When, his left-hand i' the hair o' the wicked,
Back he held the brow and pricked its stigma,
Bit into the live man's flesh for parchment,
Loosed him, laughed to see the writing rankle,
Let the wretch go festering through Florence) —
Dante, who loved well because he hated,
Hated wickedness that hinders loving,
Dante standing, studying his angel, —
In there broke the folk of his Inferno.
Says he — "Certain people of importance"
(Such he gave his daily dreadful line to)
"Entered and would seize, forsooth, the poet."
Says the poet — "Then I stopped my painting."

VI

You and I would rather see that angel,
Painted by the tenderness of Dante,
Would we not? — than read a fresh Inferno.

VII

You and I will never see that picture.
While he mused on love and Beatrice,
While he softened o'er his outlined angel,
In they broke, those "people of importance:"
We and Bice bear the loss forever.

VIII

What of Rafael's sonnets, Dante's picture?
This: no artist lives and loves, that longs not
Once, and only once, and for one only,
(Ah, the prize!) to find his love a language
Fit and fair and simple and sufficient —
Using nature that's an art to others,
Not, this one time, art that's turned his nature.
Ay, of all the artists living, loving,
None but would forego his proper dowry, —
Does he paint? he fain would write a poem, —
Does he write? he fain would paint a picture,
Put to proof art alien to the artist's,
Once, and only once, and for one only,
So to be the man and leave the artist,
Gain the man's joy, miss the artist's sorrow.

IX

Wherefore? Heaven's gift takes earth's abatement!
He who smites the rock and spreads the water,
Bidding drink and live a crowd beneath him,
Even he, the minute makes immortal,
Proves, perchance, but mortal in the minute,
Desecrates, belike, the deed in doing.
While he smites, how can he but remember,
So he smote before, in such a peril,
When they stood and mocked — "Shall smiting help us?"
When they drank and sneered — "A stroke is easy!"
When they wiped their mouths and went their journey,
Throwing him for thanks — "But drought was pleasant."
Thus old memories mar the actual triumph;
Thus the doing savours of disrelish;
Thus achievement lacks a gracious somewhat;
O'er-importuned brows becloud the mandate,
Carelessness or consciousness — the gesture.
For he bears an ancient wrong about him,
Sees and knows again those phalanxed faces,
Hears, yet one time more, the 'customed prelude —
"How shouldst thou of all men, smite, and save us?"
Guesses what is like to prove the sequel —
"Egypt's flesh-pots — nay, the drought was better."

X

Oh, the crowd must have emphatic warrant!
Theirs, the Sinai-forehead's cloven brilliance,
Right-arm's rod-sweep, tongue's imperial fiat.
Never dares the man put off the prophet.

XI

Did he love one face from out the thousands,
(Were she Jethro's daughter, white and wifely,
Were she but the Æthiopian bondslave,)
He would envy yon dumb patient camel,
Keeping a reserve of scanty water
Meant to save his own life in the desert;
Ready in the desert to deliver
(Kneeling down to let his breast be opened)
Hoard and life together for his mistress.

XII

I shall never, in the years remaining,
Paint you pictures, no, nor carve you statues,
Make you music that should all-express me;
So it seems: I stand on my attainment.
This of verse alone, one life allows me;
Verse and nothing else have I to give you.
Other heights in other lives, God willing:
All the gifts from all the heights, your own, Love!

XIII

Yet a semblance of resource avails us —
Shade so finely touched, love's sense must seize it.
Take these lines, look lovingly and nearly,
Lines I write the first time and the last time.
He who works in fresco, steals a hair-brush,
Curbs the liberal hand, subservient proudly,
Cramps his spirit, crowds its all in little,
Makes a strange art of an art familiar,
Fills his lady's missal-marge with flowerets.
He who blows through bronze, may breathe through silver,
Fitly serenade a slumbrous princess.
He who writes, may write for once as I do.

XIV

Love, you saw me gather men and women,
Live or dead or fashioned by my fancy,
Enter each and all, and use their service,
Speak from every mouth, — the speech, a poem.
Hardly shall I tell my joys and sorrows,
Hopes and fears, belief and disbelieving:
I am mine and yours — the rest be all men's,
Karshish, Cleon, Norbert, and the fifty.
Let me speak this once in my true person,
Not as Lippo, Roland, or Andrea,
Though the fruit of speech be just this sentence:
Pray you, look on these my men and women,
Take and keep my fifty poems finished;
Where my heart lies, let my brain lie also!
Poor the speech; be how I speak, for all things.

XV

Not but that you know me! Lo, the moon's self!
Here in London, yonder late in Florence,
Still we find her face, the thrice-transfigured.
Curving on a sky imbrued with colour,
Drifted over Fiesole by twilight,
Came she, our new crescent of a hair's-breadth.
Full she flared it, lamping Samminiato,
Rounder 'twixt the cypresses and rounder,
Perfect till the nightingales applauded.
Now, a piece of her old self, impoverished,
Hard to greet, she traverses the house-roofs,
Hurries with unhandsome thrift of silver,
Goes dispiritedly, glad to finish.

XVI

What, there's nothing in the moon noteworthy?
Nay: for if that moon could love a mortal,
Use, to charm him (so to fit a fancy),
All her magic ('tis the old sweet mythos),
She would turn a new side to her mortal,
Side unseen of herdsman, huntsman, steersman —
Blank to Zoroaster on his terrace,
Blind to Galileo on his turret,
Dumb to Homer, dumb to Keats — him, even!
Think, the wonder of the moonstruck mortal —
When she turns round, comes again in heaven,
Opens out anew for worse or better!
Proves she like some portent of an iceberg
Swimming full upon the ship it founders,
Hungry with huge teeth of splintered crystals?
Proves she as the paved work of a sapphire
Seen by Moses when he climbed the mountain?
Moses, Aaron, Nadab and Abihu
Climbed and saw the very God, the Highest,
Stand upon the paved work of a sapphire.
Like the bodied heaven in his clearness
Shone the stone, the sapphire of that paved work,
When they ate and drank and saw God also!

XVII

What were seen? None knows, none ever shall know.
Only this is sure — the sight were other,
Not the moon's same side, born late in Florence,
Dying now impoverished here in London.
God be thanked, the meanest of his creatures
Boasts two soul-sides, one to face the world with,
One to show a woman when he loves her!

XVIII

This I say of me, but think of you, Love!
This to you — yourself my moon of poets!
Ah, but that's the world's side, there's the wonder,
Thus they see you, praise you, think they know you!
There, in turn I stand with them and praise you —
Out of my own self, I dare to phrase it.
But the best is when I glide from out them,
Cross a step or two of dubious twilight,
Come out on the other side, the novel
Silent silver lights and darks undreamed of,
Where I hush and bless myself with silence.

XIX

Oh, their Rafael of the dear Madonnas,
Oh, their Dante of the dread Inferno,
Wrote one song — and in my brain I sing it,
Drew one angel — borne, see, on my bosom!
— R. B.

ABT VOGLER

AFTER HE HAS BEEN EXTEMPORISING UPON THE MUSICAL INSTRUMENT OF HIS INVENTION

Would that the structure brave, the manifold music I build,
  Bidding my organ obey, calling its keys to their work,
Claiming each slave of the sound, at a touch, as when Solomon willed
  Armies of angels that soar, legions of demons that lurk,
Man, brute, reptile, fly, — alien of end and of aim,
  Adverse, each from the other heaven-high, hell-deep removed, —
Should rush into sight at once as he named the ineffable Name,
  And pile him a palace straight, to pleasure the princess he loved!

Would it might tarry like his, the beautiful building of mine,
  This which my keys in a crowd pressed and importuned to raise!
Ah, one and all, how they helped, would dispart now and now combine,
  Zealous to hasten the work, heighten their master his praise!
And one would bury his brow with a blind plunge down to hell,
  Burrow awhile and build, broad on the roots of things,
Then up again swim into sight, having based me my palace well,
  Founded it, fearless of flame, flat on the nether springs.

And another would mount and march, like the excellent minion he was,
  Ay, another and yet another, one crowd but with many a crest,
Raising my rampired walls of gold as transparent as glass,
  Eager to do and die, yield each his place to the rest:
For higher still and higher (as a runner tips with fire,
  When a great illumination surprises a festal night —
Outlined round and round Rome's dome from space to spire)
  Up, the pinnacled glory reached, and the pride of my soul was in sight.

In sight? Not half! for it seemed, it was certain, to match man's birth,
  Nature in turn conceived, obeying an impulse as I;
And the emulous heaven yearned down, made effort to reach the earth,
  As the earth had done her best, in my passion, to scale the sky:
Novel splendours burst forth, grew familiar and dwelt with mine,
  Not a point nor peak but found and fixed its wandering star;
Meteor-moons, balls of blaze: and they did not pale nor pine,
  For earth had attained to heaven, there was no more near nor far.

Nay more; for there wanted not who walked in the glare and glow,
  Presences plain in the place; or, fresh from the Protoplast,
Furnished for ages to come, when a kindlier wind should blow,
  Lured now to begin and live, in a house to their liking at last;
Or else the wonderful Dead who have passed through the body and gone,
  But were back once more to breathe in an old world worth their new:
What never had been, was now; what was, as it shall be anon;
  And what is, — shall I say, matched both? for I was made perfect too.

All through my keys that gave their sounds to a wish of my soul,
  All through my soul that praised as its wish flowed visibly forth,
All through music and me! For think, had I painted the whole,
  Why, there it had stood, to see, nor the process so wonder-worth:
Had I written the same, made verse — still, effect proceeds from cause,
  Ye know why the forms are fair, ye hear how the tale is told;
It is all triumphant art, but art in obedience to laws,
  Painter and poet are proud in the artist-list enrolled: —

But here is the finger of God, a flash of the will that can,
  Existent behind all laws, that made them and, lo, they are!
And I know not if, save in this, such gift be allowed to man,

That out of three sounds he frame, not a fourth sound, but a star.
Consider it well: each tone of our scale in itself is naught:
It is everywhere in the world — loud, soft, and all is said:
Give it to me to use! I mix it with two in my thought:
And there! Ye have heard and seen: consider and bow the head!

Well, it is gone at last, the palace of music I reared;
Gone! and the good tears start, the praises that come too slow;
For one is assured at first, one scarce can say that he feared,
That he even gave it a thought, the gone thing was to go.
Never to be again! But many more of the kind
As good, nay, better perchance: is this your comfort to me?
To me, who must be saved because I cling with my mind
To the same, same self, same love, same God: ay, what was, shall be.

Therefore to whom turn I but to thee, the ineffable Name?
Builder and maker, thou, of houses not made with hands!
What, have fear of change from thee who art ever the same?
Doubt that thy power can fill the heart that thy power expands?
There shall never be one lost good! What was, shall live as before;
The evil is null, is naught, is silence implying sound;
What was good shall be good, with, for evil, so much good more;
On the earth the broken arcs; in the heaven a perfect round.

All we have willed or hoped or dreamed of good shall exist;
Not its semblance, but itself; no beauty, nor good, nor power
Whose voice has gone forth, but each survives for the melodist
When eternity affirms the conception of an hour.
The high that proved too high, the heroic for earth too hard,
The passion that left the ground to lose itself in the sky,
Are music sent up to God by the lover and the bard;
Enough that he heard it once: we shall hear it by and by.

And what is our failure here but a triumph's evidence
For the fullness of the days? Have we withered or agonized?
Why else was the pause prolonged but that singing might issue thence?
Why rushed the discords in, but that harmony should be prized?
Sorrow is hard to bear, and doubt is slow to clear,
Each sufferer says his say, his scheme of the weal and woe:
But God has a few of us whom he whispers in the ear;
The rest may reason and welcome: 'tis we musicians know.

Well, it is earth with me; silence resumes her reign:
I will be patient and proud, and soberly acquiesce.
Give me the keys. I feel for the common chord again,
Sliding by semitones till I sink to the minor, — yes,
And I blunt it into a ninth, and I stand on alien ground,
Surveying awhile the heights I rolled from into the deep;
Which, hark, I have dared and done, for my resting-place is found,
The C Major of this life: so, now I will try to sleep.

RABBI BEN EZRA

Grow old along with me!
The best is yet to be,
The last of life, for which the first was made:
Our times are in his hand
Who saith, "A whole I planned,
Youth shows but half; trust God: see all, nor be afraid!"

Not that, amassing flowers,
Youth sighed, "Which rose make ours,
Which lily leave and then as best recall?"
Not that, admiring stars,
It yearned, "Nor Jove, nor Mars;
Mine be some figured flame which blends, transcends them all!"

Not for such hopes and fears
Annulling youth's brief years,
Do I remonstrate: folly wide the mark!
Rather I prize the doubt
Low kinds exist without, 17
Finished and finite clods, untroubled by a spark.

Poor vaunt of life indeed,
Were man but formed to feed
On joy, to solely seek and find and feast:
Such feasting ended, then
As sure an end to men;
Irks care the crop-full bird? Frets doubt the maw-crammed beast? 24

Rejoice we are allied
To that which doth provide
And not partake, effect and not receive!
A spark disturbs our clod;
Nearer we hold of God
Who gives, than of his tribes that take, I must believe. 30

Then, welcome each rebuff
That turns earth's smoothness rough,
Each sting that bids nor sit nor stand but go!
Be our joys three-parts pain!
Strive, and hold cheap the strain;
Learn, nor account the pang; dare, never grudge the throe! 36

For thence, — a paradox
Which comforts while it mocks, —
Shall life succeed in that it seems to fail:
What I aspired to be,
And was not, comforts me:
A brute I might have been, but would not sink i' the scale. 42

What is he but a brute
Whose flesh has soul to suit,
Whose spirit works lest arms and legs want play?
To man, propose this test —
Thy body at its best,
How far can that project thy soul on its lone way? 48

Yet gifts should prove their use:
I own the Past profuse
Of power each side, perfection every turn:
Eyes, ears took in their dole,
Brain treasured up the whole;
Should not the heart beat once "How good to live and learn"? 54

Not once beat "Praise be thine!
I see the whole design,
I, who saw power, see now love perfect too:
Perfect I call thy plan:
Thanks that I was a man!
Maker, remake, complete, — I trust what thou shalt do"? 60

For pleasant is this flesh;
Our soul, in its rose-mesh
Pulled ever to the earth, still yearns for rest:
Would we some prize might hold
To match those manifold
Possessions of the brute, — gain most, as we did best! 66

Let us not always say,
"Spite of this flesh to-day
I strove, made head, gained ground upon the whole!"
As the bird wings and sings,
Let us cry, "All good things
Are ours, nor soul helps flesh more, now, than flesh helps soul!" 72

Therefore I summon age
To grant youth's heritage,
Life's struggle having so far reached its term:
Thence shall I pass, approved
A man, for aye removed
From the developed brute; a god, though in the germ. 78

And I shall thereupon
Take rest, ere I be gone
Once more on my adventure brave and new:
Fearless and unperplexed,
When I wage battle next,
What weapons to select, what armour to indue. 84

Youth ended, I shall try
My gain or loss thereby;
Leave the fire ashes, what survives is gold:
And I shall weigh the same,
Give life its praise or blame:
Young, all lay in dispute; I shall know, being old. 90

For note, when evening shuts,
A certain moment cuts
The deed off, calls the glory from the grey:
A whisper from the west
Shoots — "Add this to the rest,
Take it and try its worth: here dies another day." 96

So, still within this life,
Though lifted o'er its strife,
Let me discern, compare, pronounce at last,

"This rage was right i' the main,
That acquiescence vain:
The Future I may face now I have proved the Past." 102

For more is not reserved
To man, with soul just nerved
To act to-morrow what he learns to-day:
Here, work enough to watch
The Master work, and catch
Hints of the proper craft, tricks of the tool's true play. 108

As it was better, youth
Should strive, through acts uncouth,
Toward making, than repose on aught found made:
So, better, age, exempt
From strife, should know, than tempt
Further. Thou waitedst age: wait death nor be afraid! 114

Enough now, if the Right
And Good and Infinite
Be named here, as thou callest thy hand thine own,
With knowledge absolute,
Subject to no dispute
From fools that crowded youth, nor let thee feel alone. 120

Be there, for once and all,
Severed great minds from small,
Announced to each his station in the Past!
Was I, the world arraigned,
Were they, my soul disdained,
Right? Let age speak the truth and give us peace at last! 126

Now, who shall arbitrate?
Ten men love what I hate,
Shun what I follow, slight what I receive;
Ten, who in ears and eyes
Match me: we all surmise,
They this thing, and I that: whom shall my soul believe? 132

Not on the vulgar mass
Called "work," must sentence pass,
Things done, that took the eye and had the price;
O'er which, from level stand,
The low world laid its hand,
Found straightway to its mind, could value in a trice: 138

But all, the world's coarse thumb
And finger failed to plumb,
So passed in making up the main account;
All instincts immature,
All purposes unsure,
That weighed not as his work, yet swelled the man's amount: 144

Thoughts hardly to be packed
Into a narrow act,
Fancies that broke through language and escaped;
All I could never be,
All, men ignored in me,
This, I was worth to God, whose wheel the pitcher shaped. 150

Ay, note that Potter's wheel,
That metaphor! and feel
Why time spins fast, why passive lies our clay, —
Thou, to whom fools propound,
When the wine makes its round,
"Since life fleets, all is change; the Past gone, seize to-day!" 156

Fool! All that is, at all,
Lasts ever, past recall;
Earth changes, but thy soul and God stand sure:
What entered into thee,
That was, is, and shall be:
Time's wheel runs back or stops: Potter and clay endure. 162

He fixed thee 'mid this dance
Of plastic circumstance,
This Present, thou, forsooth, wouldst fain arrest:
Machinery just meant
To give thy soul its bent, 167
Try thee and turn thee forth, sufficiently impressed.

What though the earlier grooves,
Which ran the laughing loves
Around thy base, no longer pause and press?
What though, about thy rim,
Skull-things in order grim 173
Grow out, in graver mood, obey the sterner stress?

Look not thou down but up!
To uses of a cup,
The festal board, lamp's flash and trumpet's peal,
The new wine's foaming flow,
The Master's lips aglow!
Thou, heaven's consummate cup, what needst thou with earth's wheel? 180

But I need, now as then,
Thee, God, who mouldest men;
And since, not even while the whirl was worst,
Did I — to the wheel of life
With shapes and colours rife,
Bound dizzily — mistake my end, to slake thy thirst: 186

So, take and use thy work:
Amend what flaws may lurk,
What strain o' the stuff, what warpings past the aim!
My times be in thy hand!
Perfect the cup as planned!
Let age approve of youth, and death complete the same! 192

APPARITIONS

Such a starved bank of moss
Till, that May-morn,
Blue ran the flash across:
Violets were born!

Sky — what a scowl of cloud
Till, near and far,
Ray on ray split the shroud:
Splendid, a star!

World — how it walled about
Life with disgrace
Till God's own smile came out:
That was thy face!

WANTING IS — WHAT?

Wanting is — what?
Summer redundant,
Blueness abundant,
— Where is the blot?
Beamy the world, yet a blank all the same,
— Framework which waits for a picture to frame:
What of the leafage, what of the flower?
Roses embowering with naught they embower!
Come then, complete incompletion, O comer,
Pant through the blueness, perfect the summer!
Breathe but one breath 11
Rose-beauty above,
And all that was death
Grows life, grows love,
Grows love!

NEVER THE TIME AND THE PLACE

Never the time and the place
And the loved one all together!
This path — how soft to pace!
This May — what magic weather!
Where is the loved one's face?
In a dream that loved one's face meets mine,
But the house is narrow, the place is bleak
Where, outside, rain and wind combine
With a furtive ear, if I strive to speak,
With a hostile eye at my flushing cheek,
With a malice that marks each word, each sign!
O enemy sly and serpentine,
Uncoil thee from the waking man!
Do I hold the Past
Thus firm and fast,
Yet doubt if the Future hold I can?
This path so soft to pace shall lead
Through the magic of May to herself indeed!
Or narrow if needs the house must be,
Outside are the storms and strangers: we —
Oh, close, safe, warm sleep I and she, 21
— I and she!

THE EPILOGUE TO ASOLANDO

At the midnight in the silence of the sleep-time,
When you set your fancies free,
Will they pass to where — by death, fools think, imprisoned —
Low he lies who once so loved you, whom you loved so,
— Pity me?

Oh to love so, be so loved, yet so mistaken!
What had I on earth to do
With the slothful, with the mawkish, the unmanly?
Like the aimless, helpless, hopeless, did I drivel
—Being — who?

One who never turned his back but marched breast forward,
Never doubted clouds would break,
Never dreamed, though right were worsted, wrong would triumph,
Held we fall to rise, are baffled to fight better,
Sleep to wake.

No, at noonday in the bustle of man's work-time
Greet the unseen with a cheer!
Bid him forward, breast and back as either should be,
"Strive and thrive!" cry "Speed, — fight on, fare ever
There as here!"

PHILIP JAMES BAILEY (1816–1902)

FESTUS

From BOOK XV

Poets are all who love, who feel, great truths,
And tell them: and the truth of truths is love.
There was a time — oh, I remember well!
When, like a sea-shell with its sea-born strain,
My soul aye rang with the music of the lyre;
And my heart shed its lore as leaves their dew —

A honey dew, and throve on what it shed.
All things I loved; but song I loved in chief.
Imagination is the air of mind;
Judgment its earth and memory its main;
Passion its fire. I was at home in heaven.
Swift-like, I lived above; once touching earth,
The meanest thing might master me: long wings
But baffled. Still and still I harped on song.
Oh! to create within the mind is bliss;
And, shaping forth the lofty thought, or lovely,
We seek not, need not heaven: and when the thought,
Cloudy and shapeless, first forms on the mind,
Slow darkening into some gigantic make,
How the heart shakes with pride and fear, as heaven
Quakes under its own thunder; or as might,
Of old, the mortal mother of a god,
When first she saw him lessening up the skies.
And I began the toil divine of verse,
Which, like a burning bush, doth guest a god.
But this was only wing-flapping — not flight;
The pawing of a courser ere he win;
Till by degrees, from wrestling with my soul,
I gathered strength to keep the fleet thoughts fast,
And made them bless me. Yes, there was a time
When tones of ancient song held eye and heart;
Were the sole lore I recked of: the great bards
Of Greece, of Rome, and mine own master land,
And they who in the holy book are deathless;
Men who have vulgarised sublimity,
And bought up truth for the nations; held it whole;
Men who have forged gods — uttered — made them pass;
Sons of the sons of God, who, in olden days,
Did leave their passionless heaven for earth and woman,
Brought an immortal to a mortal breast,
And, rainbow-like the sweet earth clasping, left
A bright precipitate of soul, which lives
Ever; and through the lines of sullen men,
The dumb array of ages, speaks for all;
Flashing by fits, like fire from an enemy's front;
Whose thoughts, like bars of sunshine in shut rooms,
'Mid gloom, all glory, win the world to light;
Who make their very follies like their souls;
And like the young moon with a ragged edge,
Still, in their imperfection, beautiful;
Whose weaknesses are lovely as their strengths,
Like the white nebulous matter between stars,
Which, if not light, at least is likest light;
Men whom we build our love round like an arch
Of triumph, as they pass us on their way
To glory and to immortality;
Men whose great thoughts possess us like a passion
Through every limb and the whole heart; whose words
Haunt us, as eagles haunt the mountain air;
Whose thoughts command all coming times and minds,
As from a tower, a warden; fix themselves
Deep in the heart as meteor stones in earth,
Dropped from some higher sphere; the words of gods,
And fragments of the undeemed tongues of heaven;
Men who walk up to fame as to a friend,
Or their own house, which from the wrongful heir
They have wrested, from the world's hard hand and gripe;
Men who, like death, all bone but all unarmed,
Have ta'en the giant world by the throat, and thrown him;
And made him swear to maintain their name and fame
At peril of his life; who shed great thoughts
As easily as an oak looseneth its golden leaves
In a kindly largesse to the soil it grew on;
Whose names are ever on the world's broad tongue
Like sound upon the falling of a force;
Whose words, if wingèd are with angels' wings;
Who play upon the heart as on a harp,
And make our eyes bright as we speak of them;
Whose hearts have a look southward, and are open
To the whole noon of nature; these I have waked,
And wept o'er night by night; oft pondering thus:
Homer is gone; and where is Jove? and where
The rival cities seven? His song outlives
Time, tower, and god — all that then was, save heaven.

ARTHUR HUGH CLOUGH (1819–1861)

QUA CURSUM VENTUS

As ships, becalmed at eve, that lay
  With canvas drooping, side by side,
Two towers of sail at dawn of day
  Are scarce long leagues apart descried;

When fell the night, upsprung the breeze,
  And all the darkling hours they plied,
Nor dreamt but each the self-same seas
  By each was cleaving, side by side:

E'en so — but why the tale reveal
  Of those, whom year by year unchanged,
Brief absence joined anew to feel,
  Astounded, soul from soul estranged?

At dead of night their sails were filled,
And onward each rejoicing steered —
Ah, neither blame, for neither willed,
Or wist, what first with dawn appeared!

To veer, how vain! On, onward strain,
Brave barks! In light, in darkness too,
Through winds and tides one compass guides —
To that, and your own selves, be true.

But O blithe breeze; and O great seas,
Though ne'er, that earliest parting past,
On your wide plain they join again,
Together lead them home at last.

One port, methought, alike they sought,
One purpose hold where'er they fare, —
O bounding breeze, O rushing seas!
At last, at last, unite them there!

WITH WHOM IS NO VARIABLENESS, NEITHER SHADOW OF TURNING

It fortifies my soul to know
That, though I perish, Truth is so:
That, howsoe'er I stray and range,
Whate'er I do, Thou dost not change.
I steadier step when I recall
That, if I slip, Thou dost not fall.

EASTER DAY

I

Naples, 1849

Through the great sinful streets of Naples as I past,
With fiercer heat than flamed above my head
My heart was hot within me; till at last
My brain was lightened when my tongue had said —
Christ is not risen!

Christ is not risen, no —
He lies and moulders low;
Christ is not risen!

What though the stone were rolled away, and though
The grave found empty there? —
If not there, then elsewhere;
If not where Joseph laid Him first, why then
Where other men
Translaid Him after, in some humbler clay.
Long ere to-day
Corruption that sad perfect work hath done,
Which here she scarcely, lightly had begun:
The foul engendered worm
Feeds on the flesh of the life-giving form
Of our most Holy and Anointed One.
He is not risen, no —
He lies and moulders low;
Christ is not risen.

What if the women, ere the dawn was grey,
Saw one or more great angels, as they say
(Angels, or Him himself)? Yet neither there, nor then,
Nor afterwards, nor elsewhere, nor at all,
Hath He appeared to Peter or the Ten;
Nor, save in thunderous terror, to blind Saul;
Save in an after Gospel and late Creed,
He is not risen, indeed, —
Christ is not risen!

Or, what if e'en, as runs a tale, the Ten
Saw, heard, and touched, again and yet again?
What if at Emmaüs' inn, and by Capernaüm's Lake,
Came One, the bread that brake —
Came One that spake as never mortal spake,
And with them ate, and drank, and stood, and walked about?
Ah, "some" did well to "doubt"!
Ah! the true Christ, while these things came to pass,
Nor heard, nor spake, nor walked, nor lived, alas!
He was not risen, no —
He lay and mouldered low,
Christ was not risen!

. . . .

As circulates in some great city crowd
A rumour changeful, vague, importunate, and loud,
From no determined centre, or of fact
Or authorship exact,
Which no man can deny
Nor verify;
So spread the wondrous fame;
He all the same
Lay senseless, mouldering, low:
He was not risen, no —
Christ was not risen.

Ashes to ashes, dust to dust;
As of the unjust, also of the just —
Yea, of that Just One, too!
This is the one sad Gospel that is true —
Christ is not risen!

Is He not risen, and shall we not rise?
Oh, we unwise!
What did we dream, what wake we to discover?
Ye hills, fall on us, and ye mountains, cover!
In darkness and great gloom

Come ere we thought it is *our* day of doom;
From the cursed world, which is one tomb,
Christ is not risen!

Eat, drink, and play, and think that this is bliss:
There is no heaven but this;
There is no hell,
Save earth, which serves the purpose doubly well,
Seeing it visits still
With equalest apportionment of ill
Both good and bad alike, and brings to one same dust
The unjust and the just
With Christ, who is not risen.

Eat, drink, and die, for we are souls bereaved:
Of all the creatures under heaven's wide cope
We are most hopeless, who had once most hope,
And most beliefless, that had most believed.
Ashes to ashes, dust to dust;
As of the unjust, also of the just —
Yea, of that Just One too!
It is the one sad Gospel that is true —
Christ is not risen!

Weep not beside the tomb,
Ye women, unto whom
He was great solace while ye tended Him;
Ye who with napkin o'er the head
And folds of linen round each wounded limb
Laid out the Sacred Dead;
And thou that bar'st Him in thy wondering womb;
Yea, Daughters of Jerusalem, depart,
Bind up as best ye may your own sad bleeding heart:
Go to your homes, your living children tend,
Your earthly spouses love;
Set your affections *not* on things above,
Which moth and rust corrupt, which quickliest come to end:
Or pray, if pray ye must, and pray, if pray ye can,
For death; since dead is He whom ye deemed more than man,
Who is not risen: no —
But lies and moulders low —
Who is not risen.

Ye men of Galilee!
Why stand ye looking up to heaven, where Him ye ne'er may see,
Neither ascending hence, nor returning hither again?
Ye ignorant and idle fishermen!
Hence to your huts, and boats, and inland native shore,
And catch not men, but fish;
Whate'er things ye might wish,
Him neither here nor there ye e'er shall meet with more.
Ye poor deluded youths, go home,
Mend the old nets ye left to roam,
Tie the split oar, patch the torn sail:
It was indeed an "idle tale" —
He was not risen!

And, oh, good men of ages yet to be,
Who shall believe *because* ye did not see —
Oh, be ye warned, be wise!
No more with pleading eyes,
And sobs of strong desire,
Unto the empty vacant void aspire,
Seeking another and impossible birth
That is not of your own, and only mother earth.
But if there is no other life for you,
Sit down and be content, since this must even do:
He is not risen!

One look, and then depart,
Ye humble and ye holy men of heart;
And ye! ye ministers and stewards of a Word
Which ye would preach, because another heard —
Ye worshippers of that ye do not know,
Take these things hence and go: —
He is not risen!

Here, on our Easter Day
We rise, we come, and lo! we find Him not,
Gardener nor other, on the sacred spot:
Where they have laid Him there is none to say;
No sound, nor in, nor out — no word
Of where to seek the dead or meet the living Lord.
There is no glistering of an angel's wings,
There is no voice of heavenly clear behest:
Let us go hence, and think upon these things
In silence, which is best.
Is He not risen? No —
But lies and moulders low?
Christ is not risen?

EASTER DAY

II

So in the sinful streets, abstracted and alone,
I with my secret self held communing of mine own.
So in the southern city spake the tongue
Of one that somewhat overwildly sung,
But in a later hour I sat and heard
Another voice that spake — another graver word.
Weep not, it bade, whatever hath been said,

Though He be dead, He is not dead.
In the true creed
He is yet risen indeed;
Christ is yet risen.

Weep not beside His tomb,
Ye women unto whom
He was great comfort and yet greater grief;
Nor ye, ye faithful few that wont with Him to roam,
Seek sadly what for Him ye left, go hopeless to your home;
Nor ye despair, ye sharers yet to be of their belief;
Though He be dead, He is not dead,
Nor gone, though fled,
Not lost, though vanishèd;
Though He return not, though
He lies and moulders low;
In the true creed
He is yet risen indeed;
Christ is yet risen.

Sit if ye will, sit down upon the ground,
Yet not to weep and wail, but calmly look around.
Whate'er befell,
Earth is not hell;
Now, too, as when it first began,
Life is yet life, and man is man.
For all that breathe beneath the heaven's high cope,
Joy with grief mixes, with despondence hope.
Hope conquers cowardice, joy grief:
Or at least, faith unbelief.
Though dead, not dead;
Not gone, though fled;
Not lost, though vanishèd.
In the great gospel and true creed,
He is yet risen indeed;
Christ is yet risen.

"PERCHÈ PENSA? PENSANDO S'INVECCHIA"

To spend uncounted years of pain,
Again, again, and yet again,
In working out in heart and brain
The problem of our being here;
To gather facts from far and near,
Upon the mind to hold them clear,
And, knowing more may yet appear,
Unto one's latest breath to fear,
The premature result to draw —
Is this the object, end, and law,
And purpose of our being here?

THE QUESTIONING SPIRIT

The human spirits saw I on a day,
Sitting and looking each a different way;
And hardly tasking, subtly questioning,
Another spirit went around the ring
To each and each: and as he ceased his say,
Each after each, I heard them singly sing,
Some querulously high, some softly, sadly low,
We know not — what avails to know?
We know not — wherefore need we know?
This answer gave they still unto his suing,
We know not, let us do as we are doing.
Dost thou not know that these things only seem? —
I know not, let me dream my dream.
Are dust and ashes fit to make a treasure? —
I know not, let me take my pleasure.
What shall avail the knowledge thou hast sought? —
I know not, let me think my thought.
What is the end of strife? —
I know not, let me live my life.
How many days or e'er thou mean'st to move? —
I know not, let me love my love.
Were not things old once new? —
I know not, let me do as others do.
And when the rest were over-past,
I know not, I will do my duty, said the last.
Thy duty do? rejoined the voice,
Ah, do it, do it, and rejoice;
But shalt thou then, when all is done,
Enjoy a love, embrace a beauty
Like these, that may be seen and won
In life, whose course will then be run;
Or wilt thou be where there is none?
I know not, I will do my duty.

And taking up the word around, above, below,
Some querulously high, some softly, sadly low,
We know not, sang they all, nor ever need we know;
We know not, sang they, what avails to know?
Whereat the questioning spirit, some short space,
Though unabashed, stood quiet in his place.
But as the echoing chorus died away
And to their dreams the rest returned apace,
By the one spirit I saw him kneeling low,
And in a silvery whisper heard him say:
Truly, thou know'st not, and thou need'st not know;
Hope only, hope thou, and believe alway;
I also know not, and I need not know,
Only with questionings pass I to and fro,
Perplexing these that sleep, and in their folly
Imbreeding doubt and sceptic melancholy;
Till that, their dreams deserting, they with me
Come all to this true ignorance and thee.

BETHESDA

A SEQUEL

I saw again the spirits on a day,
Where on the earth in mournful case they lay;
Five porches were there, and a pool, and round,
Huddling in blankets, strewn upon the ground,
Tied-up and bandaged, weary, sore and spent,
The maimed and halt, diseased and impotent.
For a great angel came, 'twas said, and stirred
The pool at certain seasons, and the word
Was, with this people of the sick, that they
Who in the waters here their limbs should lay
Before the motion on the surface ceased
Should of their torment straightway be released.
So with shrunk bodies and with heads down-dropt,
Stretched on the steps, and at the pillars propt,
Watching by day and listening through the night,
They filled the place, a miserable sight.

And I beheld that on the stony floor
He too, that spoke of duty once before,
No otherwise than others here to-day,
Foredone and sick and sadly muttering lay.
"I know not, I will do — what is it I would say?
What was that word which once sufficed for all,
Which now I seek in vain, and never can recall?"
And then, as weary of in vain renewing
His question, thus his mournful thought pursuing,
"I know not, I must do as other men are doing."

But what the waters of that pool might be,
Of Lethe were they, or Philosophy;
And whether he, long waiting, did attain
Deliverance from the burden of his pain
There with the rest; or whether, yet before,
Some more diviner stranger passed the door
With his small company into that sad place,
And breathing hope into the sick man's face,
Bade him take up his bed, and rise and go,
What the end were, and whether it were so,
Further than this I saw not, neither know.

HOPE EVERMORE AND BELIEVE

Hope evermore and believe, O man, for e'en as thy thought
  So are the things that thou see'st; e'en as thy hope and belief.
Cowardly art thou and timid? they rise to provoke thee against them;
  Hast thou courage? enough, see them exulting to yield.
Yea, the rough rock, the dull earth, the wild sea's furying waters
  (Violent say'st thou and hard, mighty thou think'st to destroy),
All with ineffable longing are waiting their Invader,
  All, with one varying voice, call to him, Come and subdue;
Still for their Conqueror call, and but for the joy of being conquered
  (Rapture they will not forego), dare to resist and rebel;
Still, when resisting and raging, in soft under-voice say unto him,
  Fear not, retire not, O man; hope evermore and believe.

Go from the east to the west, as the sun and the stars direct thee.
  Go with the girdle of man, go and encompass the earth.
Not for the gain of the gold; for the getting, the hoarding, the having,
  But for the joy of the deed; but for the Duty to do.
Go with the spiritual life, the higher volition and action,
  With the great girdle of God, go and encompass the earth.
Go; say not in thy heart, And what then were it accomplished,
  Were the wild impulse allayed, what were the use or the good!
Go, when the instinct is stilled, and when the deed is accomplished,
  What thou hast done and shalt do, shall be declared to thee then.
Go with the sun and the stars, and yet evermore in thy spirit
  Say to thyself: It is good: yet is there better than it.
This that I see is not all, and this that I do is but little;
  Nevertheless it is good, though there is better than it.

SAY NOT THE STRUGGLE NOUGHT AVAILETH

Say not the struggle nought availeth,
  The labour and the wounds are vain,
The enemy faints not, nor faileth,
  And as things have been they remain.

If hopes were dupes, fears may be liars;
  It may be, in yon smoke concealed,
Your comrades chase e'en now the fliers,
  And, but for you, possess the field.

For while the tired waves, vainly breaking,
  Seem here no painful inch to gain,
Far back, through creeks and inlets making,
  Comes silent, flooding in, the main.

And not by eastern windows only,
  When daylight comes, comes in the light,
In front, the sun climbs slow, how slowly,
  But westward, look, the land is bright.

FREDERICK LOCKER-LAMPSON
(1821–1895)

TO MY GRANDMOTHER

Suggested by a picture by Mr. Romney

This Relative of mine,
Was she seventy-and-nine
    When she died?
By the canvas may be seen
How she look'd at seventeen,
    As a bride.

Beneath a summer tree
Her maiden reverie
    Has a charm;
Her ringlets are in taste;
What an arm! and what a waist
    For an arm!

With her bridal-wreath, bouquet,
Lace farthingale, and gay
    Falbala, —
If Romney's touch be true,
What a lucky dog were you,
    Grandpapa!

Her lips are sweet as love;
They are parting! Do they move?
    Are they dumb?
Her eyes are blue, and beam
Beseechingly, and seem
    To say, "Come!"

What funny fancy slips
From atween these cherry lips?
    Whisper me,
Fair Sorceress in paint,
What canon says I mayn't
    Marry thee?

That good-for-nothing Time
Has a confidence sublime!
    When I first
Saw this Lady, in my youth,
Her winters had, forsooth,
    Done their worst.

Her locks, as white as snow,
Once shamed the swarthy crow;
    By-and-by
That fowl's avenging sprite
Set his cruel foot for spite
    Near her eye.

Her rounded form was lean,
And her silk was bombazine;
    Well I wot
With her needles would she sit,
And for hours would she knit, —
    Would she not?

Ah perishable clay!
Her charms had dropt away
    One by one;
But if she heaved a sigh
With a burthen, it was, "Thy
    Will be done."

In travail, as in tears,
With the fardel of her years
    Overprest,
In mercy she was borne
Where the weary and the worn
    Are at rest.

Oh, if you now are there,
And sweet as once you were,
    Grandmamma,
This nether world agrees
You'll all the better please
    Grandpapa.

THE UNREALISED IDEAL

My only Love is always near, —
  In country or in town
I see her twinkling feet, I hear
  The whisper of her gown.

She foots it ever fair and young,
  Her locks are tied in haste,
And one is o'er her shoulder flung,
  And hangs below her waist.

She ran before me in the meads;
  And down this world-worn track
She leads me on; but while she leads
  She never gazes back.

And yet her voice is in my dreams,
  To witch me more and more;
That wooing voice! Ah me, it seems
  Less near me than of yore.

Lightly I sped when hope was high,
  And youth beguiled the chase;
I follow — follow still; but I
  Shall never see her Face.

MATTHEW ARNOLD (1822–1888)

TO A FRIEND

Who prop, thou ask'st, in these bad days, my mind?
He much, the old man, who, clearest-soul'd of men,
Saw The Wide Prospect, and the Asian Fen,
And Tmolus' hill, and Smyrna's bay, though blind.
Much he, whose friendship I not long since won,
That halting slave, who in Nicopolis
Taught Arrian, when Vespasian's brutal son
Clear'd Rome of what most sham'd him. But be his
My special thanks, whose even-balanc'd soul,
From first youth tested up to extreme old age,
Business could not make dull, nor Passion wild:
Who saw life steadily, and saw it whole:
The mellow glory of the Attic stage;
Singer of sweet Colonus, and its child.

SHAKESPEARE

Others abide our question. Thou art free.
We ask and ask: Thou smilest and art still,
Out-topping knowledge. For the loftiest hill
That to the stars uncrowns his majesty,
Planting his steadfast footsteps in the sea,
Making the Heaven of Heavens his dwelling-place,
Spares but the cloudy border of his base
To the foil'd searching of mortality:
And thou, who didst the stars and sunbeams know,
Self-school'd, self-scann'd, self-honour'd, self-secure,
Didst walk on Earth unguess'd at. Better so!
All pains the immortal spirit must endure,
All weakness that impairs, all griefs that bow,
Find their sole voice in that victorious brow.

STAGYRUS

Thou, who dost dwell alone —
Thou, who dost know thine own —
Thou to whom all are known
From the cradle to the grave —
    Save, oh save.
From the world's temptations,
From tribulations;
From that fierce anguish
Wherein we languish;
From that torpor deep
Wherein we lie asleep,
Heavy as death, cold as the grave;
    Save, oh save.

When the Soul, growing clearer,
  Sees God no nearer:
When the Soul, mounting higher,
  To God comes no nigher:
But the arch-fiend Pride
Mounts at her side,
Foiling her high emprize,
Sealing her eagle eyes,
And, when she fain would soar,
Makes idols to adore;
Changing the pure emotion
Of her high devotion,
To a skin-deep sense
Of her own eloquence:
Strong to deceive, strong to enslave —
    Save, oh save.

From the ingrain'd fashion
Of this earthly nature
That mars thy creature;
From grief, that is but passion;
From mirth, that is but feigning;
From tears, that bring no healing;
From wild and weak complaining;
Thine old strength revealing,
    Save, oh save.

From doubt, where all is double:
Where wise men are not strong:
Where comfort turns to trouble:
Where just men suffer wrong:
Where sorrow treads on joy:
Where sweet things soonest cloy:
Where faiths are built on dust:
Where Love is half mistrust,
Hungry, and barren, and sharp as the sea;
    Oh, set us free.
O let the false dream fly
Where our sick souls do lie
    Tossing continually.

O where thy voice doth come
  Let all doubts be dumb:
  Let all words be mild:
  All strifes be reconcil'd;
  All pains beguil'd.
Light bring no blindness;
Love no unkindness;

Knowledge no ruin;
Fear no undoing.
From the cradle to the grave,
Save, oh save.

THE FORSAKEN MERMAN

Come, dear children, let us away;
Down and away below.
Now my brothers call from the bay;
Now the great winds shorewards blow;
Now the salt tides seawards flow;
Now the wild white horses play,
Champ and chafe and toss in the spray.
Children dear, let us away.
This way, this way.

Call her once before you go.
Call once yet.
In a voice that she will know:
"Margaret! Margaret!"
Children's voices should be dear
(Call once more) to a mother's ear:
Children's voices, wild with pain.
Surely she will come again.
Call her once and come away.
This way, this way.
"Mother dear, we cannot stay."
The wild white horses foam and fret.
Margaret! Margaret!

Come, dear children, come away down.
Call no more.
One last look at the white-wall'd town,
And the little grey church on the windy shore.
Then come down.
She will not come though you call all day
Come away, come away.

Children dear, was it yesterday
We heard the sweet bells over the bay?
In the caverns where we lay,
Through the surf and through the swell
The far-off sound of a silver bell?
Sand-strewn caverns, cool and deep,
Where the winds are all asleep;
Where the spent lights quiver and gleam;
Where the salt weed sways in the stream;
Where the sea-beasts rang'd all round,
Feed in the ooze of their pasture-ground;
Where the sea-snakes coil and twine,
Dry their mail and bask in the brine;
Where great whales come sailing by,
Sail and sail, with unshut eye,
Round the world forever and aye?
When did music come this way?
Children dear, was it yesterday?

Children dear, was it yesterday
(Call yet once) that she went away?
Once she sate with you and me,
On a red gold throne in the heart of the sea,
And the youngest sate on her knee,
She comb'd its bright hair, and she tended it well,
When down swung the sound of the far-off bell.
She sigh'd, she look'd up through the clear green sea.
She said: "I must go, for my kinsfolk pray
In the little grey church on the shore to-day.
'Twill be Easter-time in the world — ah me!
And I lose my poor soul, Merman, here with thee."
I said: "Go up, dear heart, through the waves.
Say thy prayer, and come back to the kind sea-caves."
She smil'd, she went up through the surf in the bay.
Children dear, was it yesterday?

Children dear, were we long alone?
"The sea grows stormy, the little ones moan.
Long prayers," I said, "in the world they say.
Come," I said, and we rose through the surf in the bay.
We went up the beach, by the sandy down
Where the sea-stocks bloom, to the white-wall'd town.
Through the narrow pav'd streets, where all was still,
To the little grey church on the windy hill.
From the church came a murmur of folk at their prayers,
But we stood without in the cold blowing airs.
We climb'd on the graves, on the stones, worn with rains,
And we gaz'd up the aisle through the small leaded panes.
She sat by the pillar; we saw her clear:
"Margaret, hist! come quick, we are here.
Dear heart," I said, "we are long alone.
The sea grows stormy, the little ones moan."
But, ah, she gave me never a look,
For her eyes were seal'd to the holy book.
Loud prays the priest; shut stands the door.
Come away, children, call no more.
Come away, come down, call no more.

Down, down, down.
Down to the depths of the sea.
She sits at her wheel in the humming town,
Singing most joyfully.
Hark, what she sings; "O joy, O joy,
For the humming street, and the child with its toy.

For the priest, and the bell, and the holy well.
For the wheel where I spun,
And the blessed light of the sun."
And so she sings her fill,
Singing most joyfully,
Till the shuttle falls from her hand,
And the whizzing wheel stands still.
She steals to the window, and looks at the sand;
And over the sand at the sea;
And her eyes are set in a stare;
And anon there breaks a sigh,
And anon there drops a tear,
From a sorrow-clouded eye,
And a heart sorrow-laden,
A long, long sigh.
For the cold strange eyes of a little Mermaiden
And the gleam of her golden hair.

Come away, away, children.
Come, children, come down.
The salt tide rolls seaward.
Lights shine in the town.
She will start from her slumber
When gusts shake the door;
She will hear the winds howling
Will hear the waves roar.
We shall see, while above us
The waves roar and whirl,
A ceiling of amber,
A pavement of pearl.
Singing, "Here came a mortal,
But faithless was she.
And alone dwell forever
The kings of the sea."

But, children, at midnight,
When soft the winds blow;
When clear falls the moonlight;
When spring-tides are low;
When sweet airs come seaward
From heaths starr'd with broom;
And high rocks throw mildly
On the blanch'd sands a gloom:
Up the still, glistening beaches,
Up the creeks we will hie;
Over banks of bright seaweed
The ebb-tide leaves dry.
We will gaze, from the sand-hills,
At the white, sleeping town;
At the church on the hill-side —
And then come back down.
Singing, "There dwells a lov'd one,
But cruel is she.
She left lonely forever
The kings of the sea."

TO MARGUERITE

IN RETURNING A VOLUME OF THE LETTERS OF ORTIS

Yes: in the sea of life enisl'd,
With echoing straits between us thrown,
Dotting the shoreless watery wild,
We mortal millions live *alone*.
The islands feel the enclasping flow,
And then their endless bounds they know.

But when the moon their hollows lights
And they are swept by balms of spring,
And in their glens, on starry nights
The nightingales divinely sing,
And lovely notes, from shore to shore,
Across the sounds and channels pour;

Oh then a longing like despair
Is to their farthest caverns sent;
— For surely once, they feel, we were
Parts of a single continent.
Now round us spreads the watery plain —
Oh might our marges meet again!

Who order'd, that their longing's fire
Should be, as soon as kindled, cool'd?
Who renders vain their deep desire?
A God, a God their severance rul'd;
And bade betwixt their shores to be
The unplumb'd, salt, estranging sea.

MORALITY

We cannot kindle when we will
The fire that in the heart resides,
The spirit bloweth and is still,
In mystery our soul abides:
But tasks in hours of insight will'd
Can be through hours of gloom fulfill'd

With aching hands and bleeding feet
We dig and heap, lay stone on stone;
We bear the burden and the heat
Of the long day, and wish 'twere done.
Not till the hours of light return,
All we have built do we discern.

Then, when the clouds are off the soul,
When thou dost bask in Nature's eye,
Ask, how *she* view'd thy self-control,
Thy struggling task'd morality.
Nature, whose free, light, cheerful air,
Oft made thee, in thy gloom, despair.

And she, whose censure thou dost dread,
Whose eye thou wert afraid to seek,
See, on her face a glow is spread,
A strong emotion on her cheek.
"Ah child," she cries, "that strife divine —
Whence was it, for it is not mine?

"There is no effort on *my* brow —
I do not strive, I do not weep.
I rush with the swift spheres, and glow
In joy, and, when I will, I sleep. —
Yet that severe, that earnest air,
I saw, I felt it once — but where?"

"I knew not yet the gauge of Time,
Nor wore the manacles of Space.
I felt it in some other clime —
I saw it in some other place.
— 'Twas when the heavenly house I trod,
And lay upon the breast of God."

THE FUTURE

A wanderer is man from his birth.
He was born in a ship
On the breast of the River of Time.
Brimming with wonder and joy
He spreads out his arms to the light,
Rivets his gaze on the banks of the stream.

As what he sees is, so have his thoughts been.
Whether he wakes
Where the snowy mountainous pass
Echoing the screams of the eagles
Hems in its gorges the bed
Of the new-born clear-flowing stream:

Whether he first sees light
Where the river in gleaming rings
Sluggishly winds through the plain:
Whether in sound of the swallowing sea: —
As is the world on the banks
So is the mind of the man.

Vainly does each as he glides
Fable and dream
Of the lands which the River of Time
Had left ere he woke on its breast,
Or shall reach when his eyes have been clos'd
Only the tract where he sails
He wots of: only the thoughts,
Rais'd by the objects he passes, are his.

Who can see the green Earth any more
As she was by the sources of Time?
Who imagines her fields as they lay
In the sunshine, unworn by the plough?
Who thinks as they thought,
The tribes who then liv'd on her breast,
Her vigorous primitive sons?

What girl
Now reads in her bosom as clear
As Rebekah read, when she sate
At eve by the palm-shaded well?
Who guards in her breast
As deep, as pellucid a spring
Of feeling, as tranquil, as sure?

What Bard,
At the height of his vision, can deem
Of God, of the world, of the soul,
With a plainness as near,
As flashing as Moses felt,
When he lay in the night by his flock
On the starlit Arabian waste?
Can rise and obey
The beck of the Spirit like him?

This tract which the River of Time
Now flows through with us, is the Plain.
Gone is the calm of its earlier shore.
Border'd by cities and hoarse
With a thousand cries is its stream.
And we on its breast, our minds
Are confused as the cries which we hear,
Changing and shot as the sights which we see.

And we say that repose has fled
Forever the course of the River of Time.
That cities will crowd to its edge
In a blacker incessanter line;
That the din will be more on its banks,
Denser the trade on its stream,
Flatter the plain where it flows,
Fiercer the sun overhead;
That never will those on its breast
See an ennobling sight,
Drink of the feeling of quiet again.

But what was before us we know not,
And we know not what shall succeed.

Haply, the River of Time,
As it grows, as the towns on its marge
Fling their wavering lights
On a wider, statelier stream —
May acquire, if not the calm
Of its early mountainous shore,
Yet a solemn peace of its own.

And the width of the waters, the hush
Of the grey expanse where he floats,
Freshening its current and spotted with foam
As it draws to the Ocean, may strike
Peace to the soul of the man on its breast:
As the pale waste widens around him —
As the banks fade dimmer away —
As the stars come out, and the night-wind
Brings up the stream
Murmurs and scents of the infinite Sea.

SOHRAB AND RUSTUM

AN EPISODE

And the first grey of morning fill'd the east,
And the fog rose out of the Oxus stream.
But all the Tartar camp along the stream
Was hush'd, and still the men were plunged in sleep:
Sohrab alone, he slept not: all night long
He had lain wakeful, tossing on his bed;
But when the grey dawn stole into his tent,
He rose, and clad himself, and girt his sword,
And took his horseman's cloak, and left his tent,
And went abroad into the cold wet fog,
Through the dim camp to Peran-Wisa's tent.
Through the black Tartar tents he pass'd, which stood
Clustering like bee-hives on the low flat strand
Of Oxus, where the summer floods o'erflow
When the sun melts the snows in high Pamere:
Through the black tents he pass'd, o'er that low strand,
And to a hillock came, a little back
From the stream's brink, the spot where first a boat,
Crossing the stream in summer, scrapes the land.
The men of former times had crown'd the top
With a clay fort: but that was fall'n; and now
The Tartars built there Peran-Wisa's tent,
A dome of laths, and o'er it felts were spread.
And Sohrab came there, and went in, and stood
Upon the thick-pil'd carpets in the tent,
And found the old man sleeping on his bed
Of rugs and felts, and near him lay his arms.
And Peran-Wisa heard him, though the step
Was dull'd; for he slept light, an old man's sleep;
And he rose quickly on one arm, and said: —
"Who art thou? for it is not yet clear dawn.
Speak! is there news, or any night alarm?"
But Sohrab came to the bedside, and said: —
"Thou knowest me, Peran-Wisa: it is I.
The sun is not yet risen, and the foe
Sleep; but I sleep not; all night long I lie
Tossing and wakeful, and I come to thee.
For so did King Afrasiab bid me seek
Thy counsel, and to heed thee as thy son,
In Samarcand, before the army march'd;
And I will tell thee what my heart desires.
Thou know'st if, since from Ader-baijan first
I came among the Tartars, and bore arms,
I have still serv'd Afrasiab well, and shown,
At my boy's years, the courage of a man.
This too thou know'st, that, while I still bear on
The conquering Tartar ensigns through the world,
And beat the Persians back on every field,
I seek one man, one man, and one alone.
Rustum, my father; who, I hop'd, should greet,
Should one day greet, upon some well-fought field
His not unworthy, not inglorious son.
So I long hop'd, but him I never find.
Come then, hear now, and grant me what I ask.
Let the two armies rest to-day: but I
Will challenge forth the bravest Persian lords
To meet me, man to man: if I prevail,
Rustum will surely hear it; if I fall —
Old man, the dead need no one, claim no kin.
Dim is the rumour of a common fight,
Where host meets host, and many names are sunk:
But of a single combat Fame speaks clear."
He spoke: and Peran-Wisa took the hand
Of the young man in his, and sigh'd, and said: —
"O Sohrab, an unquiet heart is thine!
Canst thou not rest among the Tartar chiefs,
And share the battle's common chance with us.
Who love thee, but must press forever first,
In single fight incurring single risk,
To find a father thou hast never seen?
Or, if indeed this one desire rules all,
To seek out Rustum — seek him not through fight:
Seek him in peace, and carry to his arms,
O Sohrab, carry an unwounded son!
But far hence seek him, for he is not here.
For now it is not as when I was young,
When Rustum was in front of every fray:
But now he keeps apart, and sits at home,
In Seïstan, with Zal, his father old.
Whether that his own mighty strength at last
Feels the abhorr'd approaches of old age;
Or in some quarrel with the Persian King.
There go: — Thou wilt not? Yet my heart forebodes
Danger or death awaits thee on this field.
Fain would I know thee safe and well, though lost
To us: fain therefore send thee hence, in peace
To seek thy father, not seek single fights
In vain: — but who can keep the lion's cub
From ravening? and who govern Rustum's son?
Go: I will grant thee what thy heart desires."
So said he, and dropp'd Sohrab's hand, and left

His bed, and the warm rugs whereon he lay,
And o'er his chilly limbs his woollen coat
He pass'd, and tied his sandals on his feet,
And threw a white cloak round him, and he took
In his right hand a ruler's staff, no sword;
And on his head he placed his sheep-skin cap,
Black, glossy, curl'd, the fleece of Kara-Kul;
And rais'd the curtain of his tent, and call'd
His herald to his side, and went abroad.

The sun, by this, had risen, and clear'd the fog
From the broad Oxus and the glittering sands:
And from their tents the Tartar horsemen fil'd
Into the open plain; so Haman bade;
Haman, who next to Peran-Wisa rul'd
The host, and still was in his lusty prime.
From their black tents, long files of horse, they stream'd:
As when, some grey November morn, the files,
In marching order spread, of long-neck'd cranes,
Stream over Casbin, and the southern slopes
Of Elburz, from the Aralian estuaries,
Or some frore Caspian reed-bed, southward bound
For the warm Persian sea-board: so they stream'd.
The Tartars of the Oxus, the King's guard,
First, with black sheep-skin caps and with long spears;
Large men, large steeds; who from Bokhara come
And Khiva, and ferment the milk of mares.
Next the more temperate Toorkmuns of the south,
The Tukas, and the lances of Salore,
And those from Attruck and the Caspian sands;
Light men, and on light steeds, who only drink
The acrid milk of camels, and their wells.
And then a swarm of wandering horse, who came
From far, and a more doubtful service own'd;
The Tartars of Ferghana, from the banks
Of the Jaxartes, men with scanty beards
And close-set skull-caps; and those wilder hordes
Who roam o'er Kipchak and the northern waste,
Kalmuks and unkemp'd Kuzzaks, tribes who stray
Nearest the Pole, and wandering Kirghizzes,
Who come on shaggy ponies from Pamere.
These all fil'd out from camp into the plain.

And on the other side the Persians form'd:
First a light cloud of horse, Tartars they seem'd,
The Ilyats of Khorassan: and behind,
The royal troops of Persia, horse and foot,
Marshall'd battalions bright in burnished steel.

But Peran-Wisa with his herald came
Threading the Tartar squadrons to the front,
And with his staff kept back the foremost ranks.
And when Ferood, who led the Persians, saw
That Peran-Wisa kept the Tartars back,
He took his spear, and to the front he came,
And check'd his ranks, and fix'd them where they stood.
And the old Tartar came upon the sand
Betwixt the silent hosts, and spake, and said:—
"Ferood, and ye, Persians and Tartars, hear!
Let there be truce between the hosts to-day.
But choose a champion from the Persian lords
To fight our champion Sohrab, man to man."

As, in the country, on a morn in June,
When the dew glistens on the pearlèd ears,
A shiver runs through the deep corn for joy—
So, when they heard what Peran-Wisa said,
A thrill through all the Tartar squadrons ran
Of pride and hope for Sohrab, whom they lov'd.

But as a troop of peddlers, from Cabool,
Cross underneath the Indian Caucasus,
That vast sky-neighbouring mountain of milk snow;
Winding so high, that, as they mount, they pass
Long flocks of travelling birds dead on the snow,
Chok'd by the air, and scarce can they themselves
Slake their parch'd throats with sugar'd mulberries—
In single file they move, and stop their breath,
For fear they should dislodge the o'erhanging snows—
So the pale Persians held their breath with fear.

And to Ferood his brother Chiefs came up
To counsel: Gudurz and Zoarrah came,
And Feraburz, who rul'd the Persian host
Second, and was the uncle of the King:
These came and counsell'd; and then Gudurz said:—
"Ferood, shame bids us take their challenge up,
Yet champion have we none to match this youth.
He has the wild stag's foot, the lion's heart.
But Rustum came last night; aloof he sits
And sullen, and has pitched his tents apart:
Him will I seek, and carry to his ear
The Tartar challenge, and this young man's name.
Haply he will forget his wrath, and fight,
Stand forth the while, and take their challenge up."

So spake he; and Ferood stood forth and said:
"Old man, be it agreed as thou hast said.
Let Sohrab arm, and we will find a man."

He spoke; and Peran-Wisa turn'd, and strode
Back through the opening squadrons to his tent.
But through the anxious Persians Gudurz ran,
And cross'd the camp which lay behind, and reach'd,
Out on the sands beyond it, Rustum's tents.
Of scarlet cloth they were, and glittering gay,
Just pitch'd: the high pavilion in the midst
Was Rustum's, and his men lay camp'd around.
And Gudurz enter'd Rustum's tent, and found
Rustum: his morning meal was done, but still
The table stood beside him, charg'd with food;
A side of roasted sheep, and cakes of bread,

And dark green melons; and there Rustum sate
Listless, and held a falcon on his wrist,
And play'd with it; but Gudurz came and stood
Before him; and he look'd, and saw him stand;
And with a cry sprang up, and dropp'd the bird,
And greeted Gudurz with both hands, and said: —
"Welcome! these eyes could see no better sight.
What news? but sit down first, and eat and drink."
But Gudurz stood in the tent door, and said: —
"Not now: a time will come to eat and drink,
But not to-day: to-day has other needs.
The armies are drawn out, and stand at gaze:
For from the Tartars is a challenge brought
To pick a champion from the Persian lords
To fight their champion — and thou know'st his name —
Sohrab men call him, but his birth is hid.
O Rustum, like thy might is this young man's!
He has the wild stag's foot, the lion's heart.
And he is young, and Iran's Chiefs are old,
Or else too weak; and all eyes turn to thee.
Come down and help us, Rustum, or we lose."
He spoke: but Rustum answer'd with a smile: —
"Go to! if Iran's Chiefs are old, then I
Am older: if the young are weak, the King
Errs strangely: for the King, for Kai-Khosroo,
Himself is young, and honours younger men,
And lets the agèd moulder to their graves.
Rustum he loves no more, but loves the young —
The young may rise at Sohrab's vaunts, not I.
For what care I, though all speak Sohrab's fame?
For would that I myself had such a son,
And not that one slight helpless girl I have,
A son so fam'd, so brave, to send to war,
And I to tarry with the snow-hair'd Zal,
My father, whom the robber Afghans vex,
And clip his borders short, and drive his herds,
And he has none to guard his weak old age.
There would I go, and hang my armour up,
And with my great name fence that weak old man,
And spend the goodly treasures I have got,
And rest my age, and hear of Sohrab's fame,
And leave to death the hosts of thankless kings,
And with these slaughterous hands draw sword no more."
He spoke, and smiled; and Gudurz made reply:
"What then, O Rustum, will men say to this,
When Sohrab dares our bravest forth, and seeks
Thee most of all, and thou, whom most he seeks,
Hidest thy face? Take heed, lest men should say,
'Like some old miser, Rustum hoards his fame,
And shuns to peril it with younger men.'"
And, greatly mov'd, then Rustum made reply: —
"O Gudurz, wherefore dost thou say such words?
Thou knowest better words than this to say.
What is one more, one less, obscure or fam'd,
Valiant or craven, young or old, to me?
Are not they mortal, am not I myself?
But who for men of nought would do great deeds?
Come, thou shall see how Rustum hoards his fame.
But I will fight unknown, and in plain arms;
Let not men say of Rustum, he was match'd
In single fight with any mortal man."
He spoke, and frown'd; and Gudurz turn'd, and ran
Back quickly through the camp in fear and joy,
Fear at his wrath, but joy that Rustum came.
But Rustum strode to his tent door, and call'd
His followers in, and bade them bring his arms,
And clad himself in steel: the arms he chose
Were plain, and on his shield was no device,
Only his helm was rich, inlaid with gold,
And from the fluted spine atop, a plume
Of horsehair wav'd, a scarlet horsehair plume.
So arm'd, he issued forth; and Ruksh, his horse,
Follow'd him, like a faithful hound, at heel,
Ruksh, whose renown was nois'd through all the earth,
The horse, whom Rustum on a foray once
Did in Bokhara by the river find
A colt beneath its dam, and drove him home,
And rear'd him; a bright bay, with lofty crest;
Dight with a saddle-cloth of broider'd green
Crusted with gold, and on the ground were work'd
All beasts of chase, all beasts which hunters know:
So follow'd, Rustum left his tents, and cross'd
The camp, and to the Persian host appear'd.
And all the Persians knew him, and with shouts
Hail'd; but the Tartars knew not who he was.
And dear as the wet diver to the eyes
Of his pale wife who waits and weeps on shore,
By sandy Bahrein, in the Persian Gulf,
Plunging all day into the blue waves, at night,
Having made up his tale of precious pearls,
Rejoins her in their hut upon the sands —
So dear to the pale Persians Rustum came.
And Rustum to the Persian front advanc'd,
And Sohrab arm'd in Haman's tent, and came.
And as afield the reapers cut a swathe
Down through the middle of a rich man's corn,
And on each side are squares of standing corn,
And in the midst a stubble, short and bare;
So on each side were squares of men, with spears
Bristling, and in the midst, the open sand.
And Rustum came upon the sand, and cast
His eyes towards the Tartar tents, and saw
Sohrab come forth, and ey'd him as he came.
As some rich woman, on a winter's morn,
Eyes through her silken curtains the poor drudge
Who with numb blacken'd fingers makes her fire —
At cock-crow on a starlit winter's morn,

When the frost flowers the whiten'd window-panes —
And wonders how she lives, and what the thoughts
Of that poor drudge may be; so Rustum ey'd
The unknown adventurous Youth, who from afar
Came seeking Rustum, and defying forth
All the most valiant chiefs: long he perus'd
His spirited air, and wonder'd who he was.
For very young he seem'd, tenderly rear'd;
Like some young cypress, tall, and dark, and straight,
Which in a queen's secluded garden throws
Its slight dark shadow on the moonlit turf,
By midnight, to a bubbling fountain's sound —
So slender Sohrab seem'd, so softly rear'd.
And a deep pity enter'd Rustum's soul
As he beheld him coming; and he stood,
And beckon'd to him with his hand, and said: —
"O thou young man, the air of Heaven is soft,
And warm, and pleasant; but the grave is cold.
Heaven's air is better than the cold dead grave.
Behold me: I am vast, and clad in iron,
And tried; and I have stood on many a field
Of blood, and I have fought with many a foe:
Never was that field lost, or that foe sav'd.
O Sohrab, wherefore wilt thou rush on death?
Be govern'd: quit the Tartar host, and come
To Iran, and be as my son to me,
And fight beneath my banner till I die.
There are no youths in Iran brave as thou."
So he spake, mildly: Sohrab heard his voice,
The mighty voice of Rustum; and he saw
His giant figure planted on the sand,
Sole, like some single tower, which a chief
Has builded on the waste in former years
Against the robbers; and he saw that head,
Streak'd with its first grey hairs: hope fill'd his soul;
And he ran forwards and embrac'd his knees,
And clasp'd his hand within his own and said: —
"Oh, by thy father's head! by thine own soul!
Art thou not Rustum? Speak! art thou not he?"
But Rustum ey'd askance the kneeling youth,
And turn'd away, and spoke to his own soul: —
"Ah me, I muse what this young fox may mean.
False, wily, boastful, are these Tartar boys.
For if I now confess this thing he asks,
And hide it not, but say, 'Rustum is here,'
He will not yield indeed, nor quit our foes,
But he will find some pretext not to fight,
And praise my fame, and proffer courteous gifts,
A belt or sword perhaps, and go his way.
And on a feast day, in Afrasiab's hall,
In Samarcand, he will arise and cry —
'I challeng'd once, when the two armies camp'd
Beside the Oxus, all the Persian lords
To cope with me in single fight; but they
Shrank; only Rustum dar'd: then he and I
Chang'd gifts, and went on equal terms away.'
So will he speak, perhaps, while men applaud.
Then were the chiefs of Iran sham'd through me."
And then he turn'd, and sternly spake aloud: —
"Rise! wherefore dost thou vainly question thus
Of Rustum? I am here, whom thou hast call'd
By challenge forth: make good thy vaunt, or yield.
Is it with Rustum only thou wouldst fight?
Rash boy, men look on Rustum's face and flee.
For well I know, that did great Rustum stand
Before thy face this day, and were reveal'd,
There would be then no talk of fighting more.
But being what I am, I tell thee this;
Do thou record it in thine inmost soul:
Either thou shalt renounce thy vaunt, and yield;
Or else thy bones shall strew this sand, till winds
Bleach them, or Oxus with his summer floods,
Oxus in summer wash them all away."
He spoke: and Sohrab answer'd, on his feet: —
"Art thou so fierce? Thou wilt not fright me so.
I am no girl, to be made pale by words.
Yet this thou hast said well, did Rustum stand
Here on this field, there were no fighting then.
But Rustum is far hence, and we stand here.
Begin: thou art more vast, more dread than I,
And thou art prov'd, I know, and I am young —
But yet Success sways with the breath of Heaven.
And though thou thinkest that thou knowest sure
Thy victory, yet thou canst not surely know.
For we are all, like swimmers in the sea,
Pois'd on the top of a huge wave of Fate,
Which hangs uncertain to which side to fall.
And whether it will heave us up to land,
Or whether it will roll us out to sea,
Back out to sea, to the deep waves of death,
We know not, and no search will make us know:
Only the event will teach us in its hour."
He spoke; and Rustum answer'd not, but hurl'd
His spear: down from the shoulder, down it came
As on some partridge in the corn a hawk
That long has tower'd in the airy clouds
Drops like a plummet: Sohrab saw it come,
And sprang aside, quick as a flash: the spear
Hiss'd, and went quivering down into the sand,
Which it sent flying wide: — then Sohrab threw
In turn, and full struck Rustum's shield: sharp rang,
The iron plates rang sharp, but turn'd the spear.
And Rustum seiz'd his club, which none but he
Could wield: an unlopp'd trunk it was, and huge,
Still rough; like those which men in treeless plains
To build them boats fish from the flooded rivers,
Hyphasis or Hydaspes, when, high up

By their dark springs, the wind in winter-time
Has made in Himalayan forests wrack,
And strewn the channels with torn boughs; so huge
The club which Rustum lifted now, and struck
One stroke; but again Sohrab sprang aside
Lithe as the glancing snake, and the club came
Thundering to earth, and leapt from Rustum's hand.
And Rustum follow'd his own blow, and fell
To his knees, and with his fingers clutch'd the sand:
And now might Sohrab have unsheath'd his sword,
And pierc'd the mighty Rustum while he lay
Dizzy, and on his knees, and chok'd with sand:
But he look'd on, and smil'd, nor bar'd his sword,
But courteously drew back, and spoke, and said:—
"Thou strik'st too hard: that club of thine will float
Upon the summer-floods, and not my bones.
But rise, and be not wroth; not wroth am I:
No, when I see thee, wrath forsakes my soul.
Thou say'st thou art not Rustum: be it so.
Who art thou then, that canst so touch my soul?
Boy as I am, I have seen battles too;
Have waded foremost in their bloody waves,
And heard their hollow roar of dying men;
But never was my heart thus touch'd before.
Are they from Heaven, these softenings of the heart?
O thou old warrior, let us yield to Heaven!
Come, plant we here in earth our angry spears,
And make a truce, and sit upon this sand,
And pledge each other in red wine, like friends,
And thou shalt talk to me of Rustum's deeds.
There are enough foes in the Persian host
Whom I may meet, and strike, and feel no pang;
Champions enough Afrasiab has, whom thou
Mayst fight; fight them, when they confront thy spear.
But oh, let there be peace 'twixt thee and me!"
He ceas'd: but while he spake, Rustum had risen,
And stood erect, trembling with rage: his club
He left to lie, but had regain'd his spear,
Whose fiery point now in his mail'd right-hand
Blaz'd bright and baleful, like that autumn Star,
The baleful sign of fevers: dust had soil'd
His stately crest, and dimm'd his glittering arms.
His breast heav'd; his lips foam'd; and twice his voice
Was chok'd with rage: at last these words broke way:—
"Girl! Nimble with thy feet, not with thy hands!
Curl'd minion, dancer, coiner of sweet words!
Fight; let me hear thy hateful voice no more!
Thou art not in Afrasiab's gardens now
With Tartar girls, with whom thou art wont to dance;
But on the Oxus sands, and in the dance
Of battle, and with me, who make no play
Of war: I fight it out, and hand to hand.
Speak not to me of truce, and pledge, and wine!
Remember all thy valour: try thy feints
And cunning: all the pity I had is gone:
Because thou hast sham'd me before both the hosts
With thy light skipping tricks, and thy girl's wiles."
He spoke: and Sohrab kindled at his taunts,
And he too drew his sword: at once they rush'd
Together, as two eagles on one prey
Come rushing down together from the clouds,
One from the east, one from the west: their shields
Dash'd with a clang together, and a din
Rose, such as that the sinewy woodcutters
Make often in the forest's heart at morn,
Of hewing axes, crashing trees: such blows
Rustum and Sohrab on each other hail'd.
And you would say that sun and stars took part
In that unnatural conflict; for a cloud
Grew suddenly in Heaven, and dark'd the sun
Over the fighters' heads; and a wind rose
Under their feet, and moaning swept the plain,
And in a sandy whirlwind wrapp'd the pair.
In gloom they twain were wrapp'd, and they alone;
For both the on-looking hosts on either hand
Stood in broad daylight, and the sky was pure,
And the sun sparkled on the Oxus stream.
But in the gloom they fought, with bloodshot eyes
And labouring breath; first Rustum struck the shield
Which Sohrab held stiff out: the steel-spik'd spear
Rent the tough plates, but fail'd to reach the skin,
And Rustum pluck'd it back with angry groan.
Then Sohrab with his sword smote Rustum's helm,
Nor clove its steel quite through; but all the crest
He shore away, and that proud horsehair plume,
Never till now defil'd, sank to the dust;
And Rustum bow'd his head; but then the gloom
Grew blacker: thunder rumbled in the air,
And lightnings rent the cloud; and Ruksh, the horse,
Who stood at hand, utter'd a dreadful cry:
No horse's cry was that, most like the roar
Of some pain'd desert lion, who all day
Has trail'd the hunter's javelin in his side,
And comes at night to die upon the sand:—
The two hosts heard that cry, and quak'd for fear,
And Oxus curdled as it cross'd his stream.
But Sohrab heard, and quail'd not, but rush'd on,

And struck again; and again Rustum bow'd
His head; but this time all the blade, like glass,
Sprang in a thousand shivers on the helm,
And in his hand the hilt remain'd alone.
Then Rustum rais'd his head; his dreadful eyes
Glar'd, and he shook on high his menacing spear,
And shouted, "Rustum!" Sohrab heard that shout,
And shrank amaz'd: back he recoil'd one step,
And scann'd with blinking eyes the advancing Form:
And then he stood bewilder'd; and he dropp'd
His covering shield, and the spear pierc'd his side.
He reel'd, and staggering back, sunk to the ground.
And then the gloom dispers'd, and the wind fell,
And the bright sun broke forth, and melted all
The cloud; and the two armies saw the pair;
Saw Rustum standing, safe upon his feet,
And Sohrab, wounded, on the bloody sand.
  Then with a bitter smile, Rustum began: —
"Sohrab, thou thoughtest in thy mind to kill
A Persian lord this day, and strip his corpse,
And bear thy trophies to Afrasiab's tent.
Or else that the great Rustum would come down
Himself to fight, and that thy wiles would move
His heart to take a gift, and let thee go.
And then that all the Tartar host would praise
Thy courage or thy crafts, and spread thy fame,
To glad thy father in his weak old age.
Fool! thou art slain, and by an unknown man!
Dearer to the red jackals shalt thou be,
Than to thy friends, and to thy father old."
  And, with a fearless mien, Sohrab replied: —
"Unknown thou art; yet thy fierce vaunt is vain.
Thou dost not slay me, proud and boastful man!
No! Rustum slays me, and this filial heart.
For were I match'd with ten such men as thou,
And I were he who till to-day I was,
They should be lying here, I standing there.
But that belovèd name unnerv'd my arm —
That name, and something, I confess, in thee,
Which troubles all my heart, and made my shield
Fall; and thy spear transfix'd an unarm'd foe.
And now thou boastest, and insult'st my fate.
But hear thou this, fierce Man, tremble to hear!
The mighty Rustum shall avenge my death!
My father, whom I seek through all the world,
He shall avenge my death, and punish thee!"
  As when some hunter in the spring hath found
A breeding eagle sitting on her nest,
Upon the craggy isle of a hill-lake,
And pierc'd her with an arrow as she rose,
And follow'd her to find her where she fell
Far off; — anon her mate comes winging back
From hunting, and a great way off descries
His huddling young left sole; at that, he checks
His pinion, and with short uneasy sweeps
Circles above his eyry, with loud screams
Chiding his mate back to her nest; but she
Lies dying, with the arrow in her side,
In some far stony gorge out of his ken,
A heap of fluttering feathers: never more
Shall the lake glass her, flying over it;
Never the black and dripping precipices
Echo her stormy scream as she sails by: —
As that poor bird flies home, nor knows his loss —
So Rustum knew not his own loss, but stood
Over his dying son, and knew him not.
  But, with a cold, incredulous voice, he said: —
"What prate is this of fathers and revenge?
The mighty Rustum never had a son."
  And, with a failing voice, Sohrab replied: —
"Ah yes, he had! and that lost son am I.
Surely the news will one day reach his ear,
Reach Rustum, where he sits, and tarries long,
Somewhere, I know not where, but far from here;
And pierce him like a stab, and make him leap
To arms, and cry for vengeance upon thee.
Fierce Man, bethink thee, for an only son!
What will that grief, what will that vengeance be!
Oh, could I live, till I that grief had seen!
Yet him I pity not so much, but her,
My mother, who in Ader-baijan dwells
With that old King, her father, who grows grey
With age, and rules over the valiant Koords.
Her most I pity, who no more will see
Sohrab returning from the Tartar camp,
With spoils and honour, when the war is done.
But a dark rumour will be bruited up,
From tribe to tribe, until it reach her ear;
And then will that defenceless woman learn
That Sohrab will rejoice her sight no more;
But that in battle with a nameless foe,
By the far distant Oxus, he is slain."
  He spoke; and as he ceas'd he wept aloud,
Thinking of her he left, and his own death.
He spoke; but Rustum listen'd, plung'd in thought.
Nor did he yet believe it was his son
Who spoke, although he call'd back names he knew;
For he had had sure tidings that the babe,
Which was in Ader-baijan born to him,
Had been a puny girl, no boy at all:
So that sad mother sent him word, for fear
Rustum should take the boy, to train in arms;
And so he deem'd that either Sohrab took,
By a false boast, the style of Rustum's son;
Or that men gave it him, to swell his fame.
So deem'd he; yet he listen'd, plung'd in thought;
And his soul set to grief, as the vast tide
Of the bright rocking Ocean sets to shore
At the full moon: tears gathered in his eyes;

For he remember'd his own early youth,
And all its bounding rapture; as, at dawn,
The Shepherd from his mountain-lodge descries
A far bright City, smitten by the sun,
Through many rolling clouds; — so Rustum saw
His youth; saw Sohrab's mother, in her bloom;
And that old King, her father, who lov'd well
His wandering guest, and gave him his fair child
With joy; and all the pleasant life they led,
They three, in that long-distant summer-time —
The castle, and the dewy woods, and hunt
And hound, and morn on those delightful hills
In Ader-baijan. And he saw that Youth,
Of age and looks to be his own dear son,
Piteous and lovely, lying on the sand,
Like some rich hyacinth, which by the scythe
Of an unskilful gardener has been cut,
Mowing the garden grass-plots near its bed,
And lies, a fragrant tower of purple bloom,
On the mown, dying grass; — so Sohrab lay,
Lovely in death, upon the common sand.
And Rustum gaz'd on him with grief, and said: —
"O Sohrab, thou indeed art such a son
Whom Rustum, wert thou his, might well have lov'd!
Yet here thou errest, Sohrab, or else men
Have told thee false; — thou art not Rustum's son.
For Rustum had no son: one child he had —
But one — a girl: who with her mother now
Plies some light female task, nor dreams of us —
Of us she dreams not, nor of wounds, nor war."
But Sohrab answer'd him in wrath; for now
The anguish of the deep-fix'd spear grew fierce,
And he desired to draw forth the steel,
And let the blood flow free, and so to die;
But first he would convince his stubborn foe —
And, rising sternly on one arm, he said: —
"Man, who art thou who dost deny my words?
Truth sits upon the lips of dying men,
And Falsehood, while I liv'd, was far from mine.
I tell thee, prick'd upon this arm I bear
That seal which Rustum to my mother gave,
That she might prick it on the babe she bore."
He spoke: and all the blood left Rustum's cheeks;
And his knees totter'd, and he smote his hand,
Against his breast, his heavy mailèd hand,
That the hard iron corslet clank'd aloud:
And to his heart he press'd the other hand,
And in a hollow voice he spake, and said: —
"Sohrab, that were a proof which could not lie.
If thou shew this, then art thou Rustum's son."
Then, with weak hasty fingers, Sohrab loos'd
His belt, and near the shoulder bar'd his arm,
And shew'd a sign in faint vermilion points
Prick'd: as a cunning workman, in Pekin,
Pricks with vermilion some clear porcelain vase,
An emperor's gift — at early morn he paints,
And all day long, and, when night comes, the lamp
Lights up his studious forehead and thin hands: —
So delicately prick'd the sign appear'd
On Sohrab's arm, the sign of Rustum's seal.
It was that Griffin, which of old rear'd Zal,
Rustum's great father, whom they left to die,
A helpless babe, among the mountain rocks.
Him that kind Creature found, and rear'd, and lov'd —
Then Rustum took it for his glorious sign.
And Sohrab bar'd that figure on his arm,
And himself scann'd it long with mournful eyes,
And then he touch'd it with his hand and said: —
"How say'st thou? Is that sign the proper sign
Of Rustum's son, or of some other man's?"
He spoke: but Rustum gaz'd, and gaz'd, and stood
Speechless; and then he utter'd one sharp cry —
"O Boy — thy Father!" — and his voice chok'd there.
And then a dark cloud pass'd before his eyes,
And his head swam, and he sank down to earth.
But Sohrab crawl'd to where he lay, and cast
His arms about his neck, and kiss'd his lips,
And with fond faltering fingers strok'd his cheeks,
Trying to call him back to life: and life
Came back to Rustum, and he op'd his eyes,
And they stood wide with horror; and he seiz'd
In both his hands the dust which lay around,
And threw it on his head, and smirch'd his hair,
His hair, and face, and beard, and glittering arms:
And strong convulsive groanings shook his breast,
And his sobs chok'd him; and he clutch'd his sword,
To draw it, and forever let life out.
But Sohrab saw his thought, and held his hands,
And with a soothing voice he spoke, and said: —
"Father, forbear: for I but meet to-day
The doom that at my birth was written down
In Heaven, and thou art Heaven's unconscious hand.
Surely my heart cried out that it was thou,
When first I saw thee; and thy heart spoke too,
I know it: but Fate trod those promptings down
Under its iron heel; Fate, Fate engag'd
The strife, and hurl'd me on my father's spear.
But let us speak no more of this: I find
My father; let me feel that I have found.
Come, sit beside me on this sand, and take
My head betwixt thy hands, and kiss my cheeks,
And wash them with thy tears, and say: 'My son!'

Quick! quick! for number'd are my sands of life,
And swift; for like the lightning to this field
I came, and like the wind I go away —
Sudden, and swift, and like a passing wind.
But it was writ in Heaven that this should be."
So said he: and his voice releas'd the heart
Of Rustum, and his tears broke forth; he cast
His arms round his son's neck, and wept aloud,
And kiss'd him. And awe fell on both the hosts
When they saw Rustum's grief: and Ruksh, the horse,
With his head bowing to the ground, and mane
Sweeping the dust, came near, and in mute woe
First to the one, then to the other mov'd
His head, as if inquiring what their grief
Might mean; and from his dark, compassionate eyes,
The big warm tears roll'd down, and cak'd the sand.
But Rustum chid him with stern voice, and said: —
"Ruksh, now thou grievest; but, O Ruksh, thy feet
Should then have rotted on their nimble joints,
When first they bore thy Master to this field."
But Sohrab look'd upon the horse and said: —
"Is this then Ruksh? How often, in past days,
My mother told me of thee, thou brave Steed!
My terrible father's terrible horse; and said,
That I should one day find thy lord and thee.
Come, let me lay my hand upon thy mane.
O Ruksh, thou art more fortunate than I;
For thou hast gone where I shall never go,
And snuff'd the breezes of my father's home.
And thou hast trod the sands of Seïstan,
And seen the river of Helmund, and the Lake
Of Zirrah; and the aged Zal himself
Has often strok'd thy neck, and given thee food,
Corn in a golden platter soak'd with wine,
And said — 'O Ruksh! bear Rustum well!' — but I
Have never known my grandsire's furrow'd face,
Nor seen his lofty house in Seïstan,
Nor slak'd my thirst at the clear Helmund stream:
But lodg'd among my father's foes, and seen
Afrasiab's cities only, Samarcand,
Bokhara, and lone Khiva in the waste,
And the black Toorkmun tents; and only drunk
The desert rivers, Moorghab and Tejend,
Kohik, and where the Kalmuks feed their sheep,
The northern Sir; and this great Oxus stream —
The yellow Oxus, by whose brink I die."
And, with a heavy groan, Rustum replied: —
"Oh that its waves were flowing over me!
Oh that I saw its grains of yellow silt
Roll tumbling in the current o'er my head!"
And, with a grave mild voice, Sohrab replied: —
"Desire not that, my father: thou must live.
For some are born to do great deeds, and live,
As some are born to be obscur'd, and die.
Do thou the deeds I die too young to do,
And reap a second glory in thine age.
Thou art my father, and thy gain is mine.
But come: thou seest this great host of men
Which follow me; I pray thee, slay not these:
Let me entreat for them: what have they done?
They follow'd me, my hope, my fame, my star.
Let them all cross the Oxus back in peace.
But me thou must bear hence, not send with them,
But carry me with thee to Seïstan,
And place me on a bed, and mourn for me,
Thou, and the snow-hair'd Zal, and all thy friends.
And thou must lay me in that lovely earth,
And heap a stately mound above my bones,
And plant a far-seen pillar over all:
That so the passing horseman on the waste
May see my tomb a great way off, and say —
'Sohrab, the mighty Rustum's son, lies there,
Whom his great father did in ignorance kill' —
And I be not forgotten in my grave."
And, with a mournful voice, Rustum replied: —
"Fear not; as thou hast said, Sohrab, my son,
So shall it be; for I will burn my tents,
And quit the host, and bear thee hence with me,
And carry thee away to Seïstan,
And place thee on a bed, and mourn for thee,
With the snow-headed Zal, and all my friends.
And I will lay thee in that lovely earth,
And heap a stately mound above thy bones,
And plant a far-seen pillar over all:
And men shall not forget thee in thy grave.
And I will spare thy host: yea, let them go:
Let them all cross the Oxus back in peace.
What should I do with slaying any more?
For would that all whom I have ever slain
Might be once more alive; my bitterest foes,
And they who were call'd champions in their time,
And through whose death I won that fame I have;
And I were nothing but a common man,
A poor, mean soldier, and without renown;
So thou mightest live too, my Son, my Son!
Or rather would that I, even I myself,
Might now be lying on this bloody sand,
Near death, and by an ignorant stroke of thine,
Not thou of mine; and I might die, not thou;
And I, not thou, be borne to Seïstan;
And Zal might weep above my grave, not thine;
And say — 'O son, I weep thee not too sore,
For willingly, I know, thou met'st thine end.'
But now in blood and battles was my youth,
And full of blood and battles is my age;

And I shall never end this life of blood."
Then, at the point of death, Sohrab replied: —
"A life of blood indeed, thou dreadful Man!
But thou shalt yet have peace; only not now;
Not yet: but thou shalt have it on that day,
When thou shalt sail in a high-masted Ship,
Thou and the other peers of Kai-Khosroo,
Returning home over the salt blue sea,
From laying thy dear Master in his grave."
And Rustum gazed on Sohrab's face, and said: —
"Soon be that day, my Son, and deep that sea!
Till then, if Fate so wills, let me endure."
He spoke; and Sohrab smil'd on him, and took
The spear, and drew it from his side, and eased
His wound's imperious anguish: but the blood
Came welling from the open gash, and life
Flow'd with the stream; all down his cold white side
The crimson torrent pour'd, dim now and soil'd
Like the soil'd tissue of white violets
Left, freshly gather'd, on their native bank,
By romping children, whom their nurses call
From the hot fields at noon: his head droop'd low,
His limbs grew slack; motionless, white, he lay —
White, with eyes clos'd; only when heavy gasps,
Deep, heavy gasps, quivering through all his frame,
Convuls'd him back to life, he open'd them,
And fix'd them feebly on his father's face:
Till now all strength was ebb'd, and from his limbs
Unwillingly the spirit fled away,
Regretting the warm mansion which it left,
And youth and bloom, and this delightful world.
So, on the bloody sand, Sohrab lay dead.
And the great Rustum drew his horseman's cloak
Down o'er his face, and sate by his dead son.
As those black granite pillars, once high-rear'd
By Jemshid in Persepolis, to bear
His house, now, 'mid their broken flights of steps,
Lie prone, enormous, down the mountain side —
So in the sand lay Rustum by his son.
And night came down over the solemn waste,
And the two gazing hosts, and that sole pair,
And darken'd all; and a cold fog, with night,
Crept from the Oxus. Soon a hum arose,
As of a great assembly loosed, and fires
Began to twinkle through the fog: for now
Both armies moved to camp, and took their meal:
The Persians took it on the open sands
Southward; the Tartars by the river marge:
And Rustum and his son were left alone.
But the majestic River floated on,
Out of the mist and hum of that low land,
Into the frosty starlight, and there mov'd,
Rejoicing, through the hush'd Chorasmian waste,
Under the solitary moon: he flow'd
Right for the Polar Star, past Orgunjè,
Brimming, and bright, and large: then sands begin
To hem his watery march, and dam his streams,
And split his currents; that for many a league
The shorn and parcell'd Oxus strains along
Through beds of sand and matted rushy isles —
Oxus, forgetting the bright speed he had
In his high mountain cradle in Pamere,
A foil'd circuitous wanderer: — till at last
The long'd-for dash of waves is heard, and wide
His luminous home of waters opens, bright
And tranquil, from whose floor the new-bath'd stars
Emerge, and shine upon the Aral Sea.

PHILOMELA

Hark! ah, the Nightingale!
The tawny-throated!
Hark! from that moonlit cedar what a burst!
What triumph! hark — what pain!
O Wanderer from a Grecian shore,
Still, after many years, in distant lands,
Still nourishing in thy bewilder'd brain
That wild, unquench'd, deep-sunken, old-world pain —

Say, will it never heal?
And can this fragrant lawn
With its cool trees, and night,
And the sweet, tranquil Thames,
And moonshine, and the dew,
To thy rack'd heart and brain
Afford no balm?

Dost thou to-night behold
Here, through the moonlight on this English grass,
The unfriendly palace in the Thracian wild?
Dost thou again peruse
With hot cheeks and sear'd eyes
The too clear web, and thy dumb Sister's shame?
Dost thou once more assay
Thy flight, and feel come over thee,
Poor Fugitive, the feathery change
Once more, and once more seem to make resound
With love and hate, triumph and agony,
Lone Daulis, and the high Cephissian vale?
Listen, Eugenia —
How thick the bursts come crowding through the leaves!
Again — thou hearest!
Eternal Passion!
Eternal Pain!

THE SCHOLAR GIPSY

Go, for they call you, Shepherd, from the hill;
Go, Shepherd, and untie the wattled cotes:
No longer leave thy wistful flock unfed,
Nor let thy bawling fellows rack their throats,
Nor the cropp'd grasses shoot another head.
But when the fields are still,
And the tired men and dogs all gone to rest,
And only the white sheep are sometimes seen
Cross and recross the strips of moon-blanch'd green;
Come, Shepherd, and again renew the quest.

Here, where the reaper was at work of late,
In this high field's dark corner, where he leaves
His coat, his basket, and his earthen cruise,
And in the sun all morning binds the sheaves,
Then here, at noon, comes back his stores to use;
Here will I sit and wait,
While to my ear from uplands far away
The bleating of the folded flocks is borne;
With distant cries of reapers in the corn —
All the live murmur of a summer's day.

Screen'd is this nook o'er the high, half-reap'd field,
And here till sun-down, Shepherd, will I be.
Through the thick corn the scarlet poppies peep
And round green roots and yellowing stalks I see
Pale blue convolvulus in tendrils creep:
And air-swept lindens yield
Their scent, and rustle down their perfum'd showers
Of bloom on the bent grass where I am laid,
And bower me from the August sun with shade;
And the eye travels down to Oxford's towers.

And near me on the grass lies Glanvil's book —
Come, let me read the oft-read tale again,
The story of that Oxford scholar poor
Of pregnant parts and quick inventive brain,
Who, tired of knocking at Preferment's door,
One summer morn forsook
His friends, and went to learn the Gipsy lore,
And roam'd the world with that wild brotherhood,
And came, as most men deem'd, to little good,
But came to Oxford and his friends no more.

But once, years after, in the country lanes,
Two scholars whom at college erst he knew
Met him, and of his way of life enquir'd.
Whereat he answer'd, that the Gipsy crew,
His mates, had arts to rule as they desir'd
The workings of men's brains;
And they can bind them to what thoughts they will:
"And I," he said, "the secret of their art,
When fully learn'd, will to the world impart:
But it needs happy moments for this skill."

This said, he left them, and return'd no more,
But rumours hung about the country side
That the lost Scholar long was seen to stray,
Seen by rare glimpses pensive and tongue-tied,
In hat of antique shape, and cloak of grey,
The same the Gipsies wore.
Shepherds had met him on the Hurst in spring:
At some lone alehouse in the Berkshire moors,
On the warm ingle bench, the smock-frock'd boors
Had found him seated at their entering.

But, 'mid their drink and clatter, he would fly:
And I myself seem half to know thy looks,
And put the shepherds, Wanderer, on thy trace;
And boys who in lone wheatfields scare the rooks
I ask if thou hast pass'd their quiet place;
Or in my boat I lie
Moor'd to the cool bank in the summer heats,
'Mid wide grass meadows which the sunshine fills,
And watch the warm green-muffled Cumner hills,
And wonder if thou haunt'st their shy retreats.

For most, I know, thou lov'st retired ground.
Thee, at the ferry, Oxford riders blithe,
Returning home on summer nights, have met
Crossing the stripling Thames at Bab-lock-hithe,
Trailing in the cool stream thy fingers wet,
As the slow punt swings round:
And leaning backwards in a pensive dream,
And fostering in thy lap a heap of flowers
Pluck'd in shy fields and distant woodland bowers,
And thine eyes resting on the moonlit stream.

And then they land, and thou art seen no more.
Maidens who from the distant hamlets come
To dance around the Fyfield elm in May,

Oft through the darkening fields have seen thee roam,
Or cross a stile into the public way.
Oft thou hast given them store
Of flowers — the frail-leaf'd, white anemone —
Dark bluebells drench'd with dews of summer eves —
And purple orchises with spotted leaves —
But none has words she can report of thee.

And, above Godstow Bridge, when hay-time's here
In June, and many a scythe in sunshine flames,
Men who through those wide fields of breezy grass
Where black-wing'd swallows haunt the glittering Thames,
To bathe in the abandon'd lasher pass,
Have often pass'd thee near
Sitting upon the river bank o'ergrown:
Mark'd thine outlandish garb, thy figure spare,
Thy dark vague eyes, and soft abstracted air;
But, when they came from bathing, thou wert gone.

At some lone homestead in the Cumner hills,
Where at her open door the housewife darns,
Thou hast been seen, or hanging on a gate
To watch the threshers in the mossy barns.
Children, who early range these slopes and late
For cresses from the rills,
Have known thee watching, all an April day,
The springing pastures and the feeding kine;
And mark'd thee, when the stars come out and shine,
Through the long dewy grass move slow away.

In Autumn, on the skirts of Bagley Wood —
Where most the gipsies by the turf-edg'd way
Pitch their smok'd tents, and every bush you see
With scarlet patches tagg'd and shreds of grey,
Above the forest-ground called Thessaly —
The blackbird picking food
Sees thee, nor stops his meal, nor fears at all;
So often has he known thee past him stray,
Rapt, twirling in thy hand a wither'd spray,
And waiting for the spark from Heaven to fall.

And once, in winter, on the causeway chill
Where home through flooded fields foot-travellers go,
Have I not pass'd thee on the wooden bridge
Wrapt in thy cloak and battling with the snow,
Thy face towards Hinksey and its wintry ridge?
And thou hast climbed the hill,
And gain'd the white brow of the Cumner range,
Turn'd once to watch, while thick the snow-flakes fall,
The line of festal light in Christ-Church hall —
Then sought thy straw in some sequester'd grange.

But what — I dream! Two hundred years are flown
Since first thy story ran through Oxford halls,
And the grave Glanvil did the tale inscribe
That thou wert wander'd from the studious walls
To learn strange arts, and join a Gipsy tribe:
And thou from earth art gone
Long since, and in some quiet churchyard laid;
Some country nook, where o'er thy unknown grave
Tall grasses and white flowering nettles wave —
Under a dark red-fruited yew-tree's shade.

— No, no, thou hast not felt the lapse of hours.
For what wears out the life of mortal men?
'Tis that from change to change their being rolls:
'Tis that repeated shocks, again, again,
Exhaust the energy of strongest souls,
And numb the elastic powers.
Till having us'd our nerves with bliss and teen,
And tir'd upon a thousand schemes our wit,
To the just-pausing genius we remit
Our worn-out life, and are — what we have been.

Thou hast not liv'd, why should'st thou perish, so?
Thou hadst *one* aim, *one* business, *one* desire:
Else wert thou long since number'd with the dead —
Else hadst thou spent, like other men, thy fire.
The generations of thy peers are fled,
And we ourselves shall go;
But thou possessest an immortal lot,
And we imagine thee exempt from age
And living as thou liv'st on Glanvil's page,
Because thou hadst — what we, alas, have not!

For early didst thou leave the world, with powers
Fresh, undiverted to the world without,
Firm to their mark, not spent on other things;
Free from the sick fatigue, the languid doubt,
Which much to have tried, in much been baffled, brings.
O Life unlike to ours!
Who fluctuate idly without term or scope,
Of whom each strives, nor knows for what he strives,
And each half lives a hundred different lives;
Who wait like thee, but not, like thee, in hope.

Thou waitest for the spark from Heaven: and we,
Light half-believers of our casual creeds,
Who never deeply felt, nor clearly will'd,
Whose insight never has borne fruit in deeds,
Whose vague resolves never have been fulfill'd;
For whom each year we see
Breeds new beginnings, disappointments new;
Who hesitate and falter life away,
And lose to-morrow the ground won to-day —
Ah, do not we, Wanderer, await it too?

Yes, we await it, but it still delays,
And then we suffer; and amongst us One,
Who most has suffer'd, takes dejectedly
His seat upon the intellectual throne;
And all his store of sad experience he
Lays bare of wretched days;
Tells us his misery's birth and growth and signs,
And how the dying spark of hope was fed,
And how the breast was sooth'd, and how the head,
And all his hourly varied anodynes.

This for our wisest: and we others pine,
And wish the long unhappy dream would end,
And waive all claim to bliss, and try to bear
With close-lipp'd Patience for our only friend,
Sad Patience, too near neighbour to Despair:
But none has hope like thine.
Thou through the fields and through the woods dost stray,
Roaming the country side, a truant boy,
Nursing thy project in unclouded joy,
And every doubt long blown by time away.

O born in days when wits were fresh and clear,
And life ran gaily as the sparkling Thames;
Before this strange disease of modern life,
With its sick hurry, its divided aims,
Its heads o'ertax'd, its palsied hearts, was rife —
Fly hence, our contact fear!
Still fly, plunge deeper in the bowering wood!
Averse, as Dido did with gesture stern
From her false friend's approach in Hades turn,
Wave us away, and keep thy solitude.

Still nursing the unconquerable hope,
Still clutching the inviolable shade,
With a free outward impulse brushing through,
By night, the silver'd branches of the glade —
Far on the forest skirts, where none pursue,
On some mild pastoral slope
Emerge, and resting on the moonlit pales,
Freshen thy flowers, as in former years,
With dew, or listen with enchanted ears,
From the dark dingles, to the nightingales.

But fly our paths, our feverish contact fly!
For strong the infection of our mental strife,
Which, though it gives no bliss, yet spoils for rest;
And we should win thee from thy own fair life,
Like us distracted, and like us unblest.
Soon, soon thy cheer would die,
Thy hopes grow timorous, and unfix'd thy powers,
And thy clear aims be cross and shifting made:
And then thy glad perennial youth would fade,
Fade, and grow old at last and die like ours.

Then fly our greetings, fly our speech and smiles!
— As some grave Tyrian trader, from the sea,
Descried at sunrise an emerging prow
Lifting the cool-hair'd creepers stealthily,
The fringes of a southward-facing brow
Among the Ægean isles;
And saw the merry Grecian coaster come,
Freighted with amber grapes, and Chian wine,
Green bursting figs, and tunnies steep'd in brine;
And knew the intruders on his ancient home,

The young light-hearted Masters of the waves;
And snatch'd his rudder, and shook out more sail,
And day and night held on indignantly
O'er the blue Midland waters with the gale,

Betwixt the Syrtes and soft Sicily,
To where the Atlantic raves
Outside the Western Straits; and unbent sails
There, where down cloudy cliffs, through sheets of foam,
Shy traffickers, the dark Iberians come;
And on the beach undid his corded bales.

THE LAST WORD

Creep into thy narrow bed,
Creep, and let no more be said!
Vain thy onset! all stands fast.
Thou thyself must break at last.

Let the long contention cease!
Geese are swans, and swans are geese.
Let them have it how they will!
Thou art tired; best be still.

They out-talk'd thee, hiss'd thee, tore thee!
Better men fared thus before thee;
Fired their ringing shot and pass'd,
Hotly charged — and sank at last.

Charge once more, then, and be dumb!
Let the victors, when they come,
When the forts of folly fall,
Find thy body by the wall.

COVENTRY PATMORE (1823–1896)

FROM THE ANGEL IN THE HOUSE

BOOK I, CANTO III. PRELUDES

I. THE LOVER

He meets, by heavenly chance express,
The destined maid; some hidden hand
Unveils to him that loveliness
Which others cannot understand.
His merits in her presence grow,
To match the promise in her eyes,
And round her happy footsteps blow
The authentic airs of Paradise.
For joy of her he cannot sleep,
Her beauty haunts him all the night;
It melts his heart, it makes him weep
For wonder, worship, and delight.
O, paradox of love, he longs,
Most humble when he most aspires,
To suffer scorn and cruel wrongs
From her he honours and desires.
Her graces make him rich, and ask
No guerdon; this imperial style
Affronts him; he disdains to bask,
The pensioner of her priceless smile.
He prays for some hard thing to do,
Some work of fame and labour immense,
To stretch the languid bulk and thew
Of love's fresh-born magnipotence.
No smallest boon were bought too dear,
Though bartered for his love-sick life;
Yet trusts he, with undaunted cheer,
To vanquish heaven, and call her Wife.
He notes how queens of sweetness still
Neglect their crowns, and stoop to mate;
How, self-consign'd with lavish will,
They ask but love proportionate;
How swift pursuit by small degrees,
Love's tactic, works like miracle;
How valour, clothed in courtesies,
Brings down the loftiest citadel;
And therefore, though he merits not
To kiss the braid upon her skirt,
His hope discouraged ne'er a jot,
Out-soars all possible desert.

BOOK I, CANTO VIII. PRELUDES

I. LIFE OF LIFE

What's that, which, ere I spake, was gone:
So joyful and intense a spark
That, whilst o'erhead the wonder shone,
The day, before but dull, grew dark?
I do not know; but this I know,
That, had the splendour lived a year,
The truth that I some heavenly show
Did see, could not be now more clear.
This know I too: might mortal breath
Express the passion then inspired,
Evil would die a natural death,
And nothing transient be desired;
And error from the soul would pass,
And leave the senses pure and strong
As sunbeams. But the best, alas,
Has neither memory nor tongue!

II. THE REVELATION

An idle poet, here and there,
Looks round him; but, for all the rest,
The world, unfathomably fair,
Is duller than a witling's jest.
Love wakes men, once a life-time each;
They lift their heavy lids and look;
And, lo, what one sweet page can teach,
They read with joy, then shut the book.

And some give thanks, and some blaspheme,
And most forget; but, either way,
That and the Child's unheeded dream
Is all the light of all their day.

III. The Spirit's Epochs

Not in the crises of events,
Of compass'd hopes, or fears fulfill'd,
Or acts of gravest consequence,
Are life's delight and depth reveal'd.
The day of days was not the day;
That went before, or was postponed;
The night Death took our lamp away
Was not the night on which we groaned.
I drew my bride, beneath the moon,
Across my threshold; happy hour!
But, ah, the walk that afternoon
We saw the water-flags in flower!

BOOK I, CANTO X

Going to Church

Her soft voice, singularly heard
Beside me, in her chant, withstood
The roar of voices, like a bird
Sole warbling in a windy wood;
And, when we knelt, she seem'd to be
An angel teaching me to pray;
And all through the high Liturgy
My spirit rejoiced without allay,
Being, for once, borne clearly above
All banks and bars of ignorance
By this bright spring-tide of pure love,
And floated in a free expanse,
Whence it could see from side to side,
The obscurity from every part
Winnow'd away and purified
By the vibrations of my heart.

BOOK II, CANTO XII. PRELUDES

I. The Married Lover

Why, having won her, do I woo?
Because her spirit's vestal grace
Provokes me always to pursue,
But, spirit-like, eludes embrace;
Because her womanhood is such
That, as on court-days subjects kiss
The Queen's hand, yet so near a touch
Affirms no mean familiarness;
Nay, rather marks more fair the height
Which can with safety so neglect
To dread, as lower ladies might,
That grace could meet with disrespect;
Thus she with happy favour feeds
Allegiance from a love so high
That thence no false conceit proceeds
Of difference bridged, or state put by;
Because although in act and word
As lowly as a wife can be,
Her manners, when they call me lord,
Remind me 'tis by courtesy;
Not with her least consent of will,
Which would my proud affection hurt,
But by the noble style that still
Imputes an unattained desert;
Because her gay and lofty brows,
When all is won which hope can ask,
Reflect a light of hopeless snows
That bright in virgin ether bask;
Because, though free of the outer court
I am, this Temple keeps its shrine
Sacred to Heaven; because in short,
She's not and never can be mine.

From THE UNKNOWN EROS

THE TOYS

My little Son, who look'd from thoughtful eyes
And moved and spoke in quiet grown-up wise,
Having my law the seventh time disobey'd,
I struck him, and dismiss'd
With hard words and unkiss'd, —
His Mother, who was patient, being dead.
Then, fearing lest his grief should hinder sleep,
I visited his bed,
But found him slumbering deep,
With darken'd eyelids, and their lashes yet
From his late sobbing wet.
And I, with moan,
Kissing away his tears, left others of my own;
For, on a table drawn beside his head,
He had put, within his reach,
A box of counters and a red-vein'd stone,
A piece of glass abraded by the beach,
And six or seven shells,
A bottle with bluebells,
And two French copper coins, ranged there with careful art,
To comfort his sad heart.
So when that night I pray'd
To God, I wept, and said:
Ah, when at last we lie with trancèd breath,
Not vexing Thee in death,
And Thou rememberest of what toys
We made our joys,
How weakly understood
Thy great commanded good,

Then, fatherly not less
Than I whom Thou hast moulded from the clay,
Thou'lt leave Thy wrath, and say,
"I will be sorry for their childishness."

IF I WERE DEAD

"If I were dead, you'd sometimes say, Poor Child!"
The dear lips quiver'd as they spake,
And the tears brake
From eyes which, not to grieve me, brightly smiled.
Poor Child, poor Child!
I seem to hear your laugh, your talk, your song.
It is not true that Love will do no wrong.
Poor Child!
And did you think, when you so cried and smiled,
How I, in lonely nights, should lie awake,
And of those words your full avengers make?
Poor Child, poor Child!
And now unless it be
That sweet amends thrice told are come to thee,
O God, have Thou *no* mercy upon me!
Poor Child!

SIDNEY DOBELL (1824–1874)

IN WARTIME

A PRAYER OF THE UNDERSTANDING

Lo, this is night. Hast thou, O sun, refused
Thy countenance, or is thy golden arm
Shortened, or from thy shining place in heaven
Art thou put down and lost? Neither hast thou
Refused thy constant face, nor is thine arm
Shortened, nor from thy principality
Art thou deposed, O sun. Ours, ours, the sin,
The sorrow. From thy steadfast noon we turned
Into the eastern shade — and this is night.

Yet so revolves the axle of the world,
And by that brief aversion wheels us round
To morn, and rolls us on the larger paths
Of annual duty. Thou observant moon,
That dancest round the seasonable earth
As David round the ark, but half thy ring
In process, yet, complete, the circular whole
Promotes thee, and expedes thy right advance,
And all thy great desire of summer signs.
And thou, O sun, our centre, who thyself
Art satellite, and, conscious of the far
Archelion, in obedience of free will
And native duty, as the good man walks
Among the children's faces, with thine house
About thee, least and greatest, first and last,
Makest of the blue eternal holiday
Thy glad perambulation; and thou, far
Archelion, feudatory still, of one
Not sovran nor in fee of paramount power;
Moons round your worlds, worlds round your suns, suns round
Such satraps as in orderly degree
Confess a lordlier regent and pervade
A vaster cycle — ye, so moved, commoved,
Revolving and convolving, turn the heavens
Upon the pivot of that summery star,
Centre of all we know: and thou, O star,
Centre of all we know, chief crown of crowns,
Who art the one in all, the all in one,
And seest the ordered whole — nought uninvolved
But all involved to one direct result
Of multiform volition — in one pomp,
One power, one tune, one time, upon one path
Move with thee moving, thou, amid thy host
Marchest — ah whither?
O God, before Whom
We marshal thus Thy legioned works to take
The secret of Thy counsel, and array
Congress and progress, and, with multitude
As conquerors and to conquer, in consent
Of universal law, approach Thy bound,
Thine immemorial bound, and at Thy face
Heaven and earth flee away; O Thou Lord God,
Whether, O absolute existence, Thou,
The Maker, makest, and this fair we see
Be but the mote and dust of that unseen
Unsought unsearchable; or whether Thou
Whose goings forth are from of old, around
Thy going, in mere effluence, without care,
Breathest creation out into the cold
Beyond Thee, and, within Thine ambient breath,
So walkest everlasting as we walk
The unportioned snows; or whether, meditating
Eternity, self-centred, self-fulfilled,
Self-continent, Thou thinkest and we live,
A little while forgettest and we fade,
Rememberest and we are, and this bright vision
Wherein we move, nay all our total sum
And story, be to Thee as to a man
When in the drop and rising of a lid
Lo, the swift rack and fashion of a dream,
No more; O Thou inscrutable, whose ways
Are not as ours, whose form we know not, voice
Hear not, true work behold not, mystery
Conceive not, who — as thunder shakes the world
And rings a silver bell — hast sometime moved

The tongue of man, but in Thy proper speech
Wearest a human language on a word
As limpets on a rock, who, as Eternal,
Omnipotential, Infinite, Allwise,
In measure of Thine operation hast
No prime or term, in subject as in scheme
No final end, in eidol as in act
Nought but the perfect God; O Thou Supreme,
Inaudible, Invisible, Unknown,
Thy will be done.

AMERICA

Men say, Columbia, we shall hear thy guns.
But in what tongue shall be thy battle-cry?
Not that our sires did love in years gone by,
When all the Pilgrim Fathers were little sons
In merrie homes of Englaunde? Back, and see
Thy satchel'd ancestor! Behold, he runs
To mine, and, clasp'd, they tread the equal lea
To the same village-school, where side by side
They spell "our Father." Hard by, the twin-pride
Of that grey hall whose ancient oriel gleams
Thro' yon baronial pines, with looks of light
Our sister-mothers sit beneath one tree.
Meanwhile our Shakespeare wanders past and dreams
His Helena and Hermia. Shall we fight?

Nor force nor fraud shall sunder us! O ye
Who north or south, on east or western land,
Native to noble sounds, say truth for truth,
Freedom for freedom, love for love, and God
For God; O ye who in eternal youth
Speak with a living and creative flood
This universal English, and do stand
Its breathing book; live worthy of that grand
Heroic utterance — parted, yet a whole,
Far, yet unsevered, — children brave and free
Of the great Mother-tongue, and ye shall be
Lords of an Empire wide as Shakespeare's soul,
Sublime as Milton's immemorial theme,
And rich as Chaucer's speech, and fair as Spenser's dream.

DANTE GABRIEL ROSSETTI
(1828–1882)

THE BLESSED DAMOZEL

The blessed damozel leaned out
From the golden bar of Heaven;
Her eyes were deeper than the depth
Of waters stilled at even;
She had three lilies in her hand,
And the stars in her hair were seven.

Her robe, ungirt from clasp to hem,
No wrought flowers did adorn,
But a white rose of Mary's gift,
For service meetly worn;
Her hair that lay along her back
Was yellow like ripe corn.

Her seemed she scarce had been a day
One of God's choristers;
The wonder was not yet quite gone
From that still look of hers;
Albeit, to them she left, her day
Had counted as ten years.

(To one, it is ten years of years.
. . . Yet now, and in this place,
Surely she leaned o'er me — her hair
Fell all about my face. . . .
Nothing: the autumn fall of leaves.
The whole year sets apace.)

It was the rampart of God's house
That she was standing on;
By God built over the sheer depth
The which is Space begun;
So high, that looking downward thence
She scarce could see the sun.

It lies in Heaven, across the flood
Of ether, as a bridge.
Beneath, the tides of day and night
With flame and darkness ridge
The void, as low as where this earth
Spins like a fretful midge.

Around her, lovers, newly met
'Mid deathless love's acclaims,
Spoke evermore among themselves
Their heart-remembered names;
And the souls mounting up to God
Went by her like thin flames.

And still she bowed herself and stooped
Out of the circling charm;
Until her bosom must have made
The bar she leaned on warm,
And the lilies lay as if asleep
Along her bended arm.

From the fixed place of Heaven she saw
Time like a pulse shake fierce
Through all the world. Her gaze still strove
Within the gulf to pierce
Its path; and now she spoke as when
The stars sang in their spheres.

The sun was gone now; the curled moon
Was like a little feather

Fluttering far down the gulf; and now
She spoke through the still weather.
Her voice was like the voice the stars
Had when they sang together.

(Ah sweet! Even now, in that bird's song,
Strove not her accents there,
Fain to be hearkened? When those bells
Possessed the mid-day air,
Strove not her steps to reach my side
Down all the echoing stair?)

"I wish that he were come to me,
For he will come," she said.
"Have I not prayed in Heaven? — on earth,
Lord, Lord, has he not pray'd?
Are not two prayers a perfect strength?
And shall I feel afraid?

"When round his head the aureole clings,
And he is clothed in white,
I'll take his hand and go with him
To the deep wells of light;
As unto a stream we will step down,
And bathe there in God's sight.

"We two will stand beside that shrine,
Occult, withheld, untrod,
Whose lamps are stirred continually
With prayer sent up to God;
And see our old prayers, granted, melt
Each like a little cloud.

"We two will lie i' the shadow of
That living mystic tree
Within whose secret growth the Dove
Is sometimes felt to be,
While every leaf that His plumes touch
Saith His Name audibly.

"And I myself will teach to him,
I myself, lying so,
The songs I sing here; which his voice
Shall pause in, hushed and slow,
And find some knowledge at each pause,
Or some new thing to know."

(Alas! We two, we two, thou say'st!
Yea, one wast thou with me
That once of old. But shall God lift
To endless unity
The soul whose likeness with thy soul
Was but its love for thee?)

"We two," she said, "will seek the groves
Where the lady Mary is,
With her five handmaidens, whose names
Are five sweet symphonies,
Cecily, Gertrude, Magdalen,
Margaret and Rosalys.

"Circlewise sit they, with bound locks
And foreheads garlanded;
Into the fine cloth white like flame
Weaving the golden thread,
To fashion the birth-robes for them
Who are just born, being dead.

"He shall fear, haply, and be dumb:
Then will I lay my cheek
To his, and tell about our love,
Not once abashed or weak:
And the dear Mother will approve
My pride, and let me speak.

"Herself shall bring us, hand in hand,
To Him round whom all souls
Kneel, the clear-ranged unnumbered heads
Bowed with their aureoles:
And angels meeting us shall sing
To their citherns and citoles.

"There will I ask of Christ the Lord
Thus much for him and me: —
Only to live as once on earth
With Love, only to be,
As then awhile, forever now
Together, I and he."

She gazed and listened and then said,
Less sad of speech than mild, —
"All this is when he comes." She ceased.
The light thrilled towards her, fill'd
With angels in strong level flight.
Her eyes prayed, and she smil'd.

(I saw her smile.) But soon their path
Was vague in distant spheres:
And then she cast her arms along
The golden barriers,
And laid her face between her hands,
And wept. (I heard her tears.)

JENNY

"Vengeance of Jenny's case! Fie on her! Never name her, child!" — (*Mrs. Quickly.*)

Lazy laughing languid Jenny,
Fond of a kiss and fond of a guinea,
Whose head upon my knee to-night
Rests for a while, as if grown light
With all our dances and the sound
To which the wild tunes spun you round:
Fair Jenny mine, the thoughtless queen
Of kisses which the blush between

Could hardly make much daintier;
Whose eyes are as blue skies, whose hair
Is countless gold incomparable:
Fresh flower, scarce touched with signs that tell
Of Love's exuberant hotbed: — Nay,
Poor flower left torn since yesterday
Until to-morrow leave you bare;
Poor handful of bright spring-water
Flung in the whirlpool's shrieking face;
Poor shameful Jenny, full of grace
Thus with your head upon my knee; —
Whose person or whose purse may be
The lodestar of your reverie?

This room of yours, my Jenny, looks
A change from mine so full of books,
Whose serried ranks hold fast, forsooth,
So many captive hours of youth, —
The hours they thieve from day and night
To make one's cherished work come right,
And leave it wrong for all their theft,
Even as to-night my work was left:
Until I vowed that since my brain
And eyes of dancing seemed so fain,
My feet should have some dancing too: —
And thus it was I met with you.
Well, I suppose 'twas hard to part,
For here I am. And now, sweetheart
You seem too tired to get to bed.

It was a careless life I led
When rooms like this were scarce so strange
Not long ago. What breeds the change, —
The many aims or the few years?
Because to-night it all appears
Something I do not know again.

The cloud's not danced out of my brain, —
The cloud that made it turn and swim
While hour by hour the books grew dim.
Why, Jenny, as I watch you there, —
For all your wealth of loosened hair,
Your silk ungirdled and unlac'd,
And warm sweets open to the waist,
All golden in the lamplight's gleam, —
You know not what a book you seem,
Half-read by lightning in a dream!
How should you know, my Jenny? Nay,
And I should be ashamed to say:
Poor beauty, so well worth a kiss!
But while my thought runs on like this
With wasteful whims more than enough,
I wonder what you're thinking of.

If of myself you think at all,
What is the thought? — conjectural
On sorry matters best unsolved? —
Or inly is each grace revolved
To fit me with a lure? — or (sad
To think!) perhaps you're merely glad
That I'm not drunk or ruffianly,
And let you rest upon my knee.

For sometimes, were the truth confess'd,
You're thankful for a little rest, —
Glad from the crush to rest within,
From the heart-sickness and the din
Where envy's voice at virtue's pitch
Mocks you because your gown is rich;
And from the pale girl's dumb rebuke,
Whose ill-clad grace and toil-worn look
Proclaim the strength that keeps her weak,
And other nights than yours bespeak;
And from the wise unchildish elf,
To schoolmate lesser than himself,
Pointing you out, what thing you are: —
Yes, from the daily jeer and jar,
From shame and shame's outbraving too,
Is rest not sometimes sweet to you? —
But most from the hatefulness of man
Who spares not to end what he began,
Whose acts are ill and his speech ill,
Who, having used you at his will,
Thrusts you aside, as when I dine
I serve the dishes and the wine.

Well, handsome Jenny mine, sit up,
I've filled our glasses, let us sup,
And do not let me think of you,
Lest shame of yours suffice for two.
What, still so tired? Well, well then, keep
Your head there, so you do not sleep;
But that the weariness may pass
And leave you merry, take this glass.
Ah! lazy lily hand, more bless'd
If ne'er in rings it had been dress'd
Nor ever by a glove conceal'd!

Behold the lilies of the field,
They toil not neither do they spin;
(So doth the ancient text begin, —
Not of such rest as one of these
Can share.) Another rest and ease
Along each summer-sated path
From its new lord the garden hath,
Than that whose spring in blessings ran
Which praised the bounteous husbandman,
Ere yet, in days of hankering breath,
The lilies sickened unto death.

What, Jenny, are your lilies dead?
Aye, and the snow-white leaves are spread

Like winter on the garden-bed.
But you had roses left in May, —
They were not gone too. Jenny, nay,
But must your roses die, and those
Their purfled buds that should unclose?
Even so; the leaves are curled apart,
Still red as from the broken heart,
And here's the naked stem of thorns.

Nay, nay, mere words. Here nothing warns
As yet of winter. Sickness here
Or want alone could waken fear, —
Nothing but passion wrings a tear.
Except when there may rise unsought
Haply at times a passing thought
Of the old days which seem to be
Much older than any history
That is written in any book;
When she would lie in fields and look
Along the ground through the blown grass,
And wonder where the city was.
Far out of sight, whose broil and bale
They told her then for a child's tale.

Jenny, you know the city now.
A child can tell the tale there, how
Some things which are not yet enroll'd
In market-lists are bought and sold
Even till the early Sunday light,
When Saturday night is market-night
Everywhere, be it dry or wet,
And market-night in the Haymarket.
Our learned London children know,
Poor Jenny, all your pride and woe;
Have seen your lifted silken skirt
Advertise dainties through the dirt;
Have seen your coach-wheels splash rebuke
On virtue; and have learned your look
When, wealth and health slipped past, you stare
Along the streets alone, and there,
Round the long park, across the bridge,
The cold lamps at the pavement's edge
Wind on together and apart,
A fiery serpent for your heart.

Let the thoughts pass, an empty cloud!
Suppose I were to think aloud, —
What if to her all this were said?
Why, as a volume seldom read
Being opened half-way shuts again,
So might the pages of her brain
Be parted at such words, and thence
Close back upon the dusty sense.
For is there hue or shape defin'd
In Jenny's desecrated mind,
Where all contagious currents meet,
A Lethe of the middle street?
Nay, it reflects not any face,
Nor sound is in its sluggish pace,
But as they coil those eddies clot,
And night and day remember not.

Why, Jenny, you're asleep at last! —
Asleep, poor Jenny, hard and fast, —
So young and soft and tired; so fair,
With chin thus nestled in your hair,
Mouth quiet, eyelids almost blue
As if some sky of dreams shone through!

Just as another woman sleeps!
Enough to throw one's thoughts in heaps
Of doubt and horror, — what to say
Or think, — this awful secret sway,
The potter's power over the clay!
Of the same lump (it has been said)
For honour and dishonour made,
Two sister vessels. Here is one.

My cousin Nell is fond of fun,
And fond of dress, and change, and praise,
So mere a woman in her ways:
And if her sweet eyes rich in youth
Are like her lips that tell the truth,
My cousin Nell is fond of love.
And she's the girl I'm proudest of.
Who does not prize her, guard her well?
The love of change, in cousin Nell,
Shall find the best and hold it dear:
The unconquered mirth turn quieter
Not through her own, through others' woe:
The conscious pride of beauty glow
Beside another's pride in her,
One little part of all they share.
For Love himself shall ripen these
In a kind soil to just increase
Through years of fertilizing peace.

Of the same lump (as it is said)
For honour and dishonour made,
Two sister vessels. Here is one.

It makes a goblin of the sun.

So pure, — so fall'n! How dare to think
Of the first common kindred link?
Yet, Jenny, till the world shall burn
It seems that all things take their turn;
And who shall say but this fair tree
May need, in changes that may be,
Your children's children's charity?
Scorned then, no doubt, as you are scorn'd!
Shall no man hold his pride forewarn'd

Till in the end, the Day of Days,
At judgment, one of his own race,
As frail and lost as you, shall rise, —
His daughter, with his mother's eyes?

How Jenny's clock ticks on the shelf,
Might not the dial scorn itself
That has such hours to register?
Yet as to me, even so to her
Are golden sun and silver moon,
In daily largesse of earth's boon,
Counted for life-coins to one tune.
And if, as blindfold fates are toss'd,
Through some one man this life be lost,
Shall soul not somehow pay for soul?

Fair shines the gilded aureole
In which our highest painters place
Some living woman's simple face.
And the stilled features thus descried
As Jenny's long throat droops aside, —
The shadows where the cheeks are thin,
And pure wide curve from ear to chin, —
With Raffael's, Leonardo's hand
To show them to men's souls, might stand,
Whole ages long, the whole world through,
For preachings of what God can do.
What has man done here? How atone,
Great God, for this which man has done?
And for the body and soul which by
Man's pitiless doom must now comply
With lifelong hell, what lullaby
Of sweet forgetful second birth
Remains? All dark. No sign on earth
What measure of God's rest endows
The many mansions of his house.

If but a woman's heart might see
Such erring heart unerringly
For once! But that can never be.

Like a rose shut in a book
In which pure women may not look,
For its base pages claim control
To crush the flower within the soul;
Where through each dead rose-leaf that clings,
Pale as transparent psyche-wings,
To the vile text, are traced such things
As might make lady's cheek indeed
More than a living rose to read;
So nought save foolish foulness may
Watch with hard eyes the sure decay;
And so the life-blood of this rose,
Puddled with shameful knowledge, flows
Through leaves no chaste hand may unclose;
Yet still it keeps such faded show
Of when 'twas gathered long ago,
That the crushed petals' lovely grain,
The sweetness of the sanguine stain,
Seen of a woman's eyes, must make
Her pitiful heart, so prone to ache,
Love roses better for its sake: —
Only that this can never be: —
Even so unto her sex is she.

Yet, Jenny, looking long at you,
The woman almost fades from view.
A cipher of man's changeless sum
Of lust, past, present, and to come
Is left. A riddle that one shrinks
To challenge from the scornful sphinx.

Like a toad within a stone
Seated while Time crumbles on;
Which sits there since the earth was curs'd
For Man's transgression at the first;
Which, living through all centuries,
Not once has seen the sun arise;
Whose life, to its cold circle charmed,
The earth's whole summers have not warmed;
Which always — whitherso the stone
Be flung — sits there, deaf, blind, alone; —
Aye, and shall not be driven out
Till that which shuts him round about
Break at the very Master's stroke,
And the dust thereof vanish as smoke,
And the seed of Man vanish as dust: —
Even so within this world is Lust.

Come, come, what use in thoughts like this?
Poor little Jenny, good to kiss, —
You'd not believe by what strange roads
Thought travels, when your beauty goads
A man to-night to think of toads!
Jenny, wake up. . . . Why, there's the dawn!

And there's an early wagon drawn
To market, and some sheep that jog
Bleating before a barking dog;
And the old streets come peering through
Another night that London knew;
And all as ghostlike as the lamps.

So on the wings of day decamps
My last night's frolic. Glooms begin
To shiver off as lights creep in
Past the gauze curtains half drawn-to,
And the lamp's doubled shade grows blue, —
Your lamp, my Jenny, kept alight,
Like a wise virgin's, all one night!
And in the alcove coolly spread
Glimmers with dawn your empty bed;

And yonder your fair face I see
Reflected lying on my knee,
Where teems with first foreshadowings
Your pier-glass scrawled with diamond rings:
And on your bosom all night worn
Yesterday's rose now droops forlorn
But dies not yet this summer morn.

And now without, as if some word
Had called upon them that they heard,
The London sparrows far and nigh
Clamour together suddenly;
And Jenny's cage-bird grown awake
Here in their song his part must take,
Because here too the day doth break.

And somehow in myself the dawn
Among stirred clouds and veils withdrawn
Strikes greyly on her. Let her sleep.
But will it wake her if I heap
These cushions thus beneath her head
Where my knee was? No, — there's your bed,
My Jenny, while you dream. And there
I lay among your golden hair
Perhaps the subject of your dreams,
These golden coins.

For still one deems
That Jenny's flattering sleep confers
New magic on the magic purse, —
Grim web, how clogged with shrivelled flies!
Between the threads fine fumes arise
And shape their pictures in the brain.
There roll no streets in glare and rain,
Nor flagrant man-swine whets his tusk,
But delicately sighs in musk
The homage of the dim boudoir;
Or like a palpitating star
Thrilled into song, the opera-night
Breathes faint in the quick pulse of light;
Or at the carriage-window shine
Rich wares for choice; or, free to dine,
Whirls through its hour of health (divine
For her) the concourse of the Park.
And though in the discounted dark
Her functions there and here are one,
Beneath the lamps and in the sun
There reigns at least the acknowledged belle
Apparelled beyond parallel.
Ah, Jenny, yes, we know your dreams.

For even the Paphian Venus seems
A goddess o'er the realms of love,
When silver-shrined in shadowy grove:
Aye, or let offerings nicely placed
But hide Priapus to the waist,
And whoso look on him shall see
An eligible deity.

Why, Jenny, waking here alone
May help you to remember one,
Though all the memory's long outworn
Of many a double-pillowed morn.
I think I see you when you wake,
And rub your eyes for me, and shake
My gold, in rising, from your hair,
A Danaë for a moment there.

Jenny, my love rang true! for still
Love at first sight is vague, until
That tinkling makes him audible.

And must I mock you to the last,
Ashamed of my own shame, — aghast
Because some thoughts not born amiss
Rose at a poor fair face like this?
Well, of such thoughts so much I know:
In my life, as in hers, they show,
By a far gleam which I may near,
A dark path I can strive to clear.

Only one kiss. Good-bye, my dear.

SISTER HELEN

"Why did you melt your waxen man,
Sister Helen?
To-day is the third since you began."
"The time was long, yet the time ran,
Little brother."
(O Mother, Mary Mother,
Three days to-day, between Hell and Heaven!)

"But if you have done your work aright,
Sister Helen,
You'll let me play, for you said I might."
"Be very still in your play to-night,
Little brother."
(O Mother, Mary Mother,
Third night, to-night, between Hell and Heaven!)

"You said it must melt ere vesper-bell,
Sister Helen;
If now it be molten, all is well."
"Even so, — nay, peace! you cannot tell,
Little brother."
(O Mother, Mary Mother,
What is this, between Hell and Heaven?)

"Oh the waxen knave was plump to-day,
Sister Helen;

How like dead folk he has dropped away!"
"Nay now, of the dead what can you say,
Little brother?" 26
(*O Mother, Mary Mother,*
What of the dead, between Hell and Heaven?)

"See, see, the sunken pile of wood,
Sister Helen,
Shines through the thinned wax red as blood!"
"Nay now, when looked you yet on blood,
Little brother?" 33
(*O Mother, Mary Mother,*
How pale she is, between Hell and Heaven!)

"Now close your eyes, for they're sick and sore,
Sister Helen,
And I'll play without the gallery door."
"Aye, let me rest, — I'll lie on the floor,
Little brother." 40
(*O Mother, Mary Mother,*
What rest to-night between Hell and Heaven?)

"Here high up in the balcony,
Sister Helen,
The moon flies face to face with me,"
"Aye, look and say whatever you see,
Little brother." 47
(*O Mother, Mary Mother,*
What sight to-night, between Hell and Heaven?)

"Outside it's merry in the wind's wake,
Sister Helen;
In the shaken trees the chill stars shake."
"Hush, heard you a horse-tread as you spake,
Little brother?"
(*O Mother, Mary Mother,* 55
What sound to-night, between Hell and Heaven?)

"I hear a horse-tread, and I see,
Sister Helen,
Three horsemen that ride terribly."
"Little brother, whence come the three,
Little brother?"
(*O Mother, Mary Mother,*
Whence should they come, between Hell and Heaven?) 63

"They come by the hill-verge from Boyne Bar,
Sister Helen,
And one draws nigh, but two are afar."
"Look, look, do you know them who they are,
Little brother?" 68
(*O Mother, Mary Mother,*
Who should they be, between Hell and Heaven?)

"Oh, it's Keith of Eastholm rides so fast,
Sister Helen,
For I know the white mane on the blast."
"The hour has come, has come at last,
Little brother!"
(*O Mother, Mary Mother,*
Her hour at last, between Hell and Heaven!) 77

"He has made a sign and called Halloo!
Sister Helen,
And he says that he would speak with you."
"Oh tell him I fear the frozen dew,
Little brother." 82
(*O Mother, Mary Mother,*
Why laughs she thus, between Hell and Heaven?)

"The wind is loud, but I hear him cry,
Sister Helen,
That Keith of Ewern's like to die."
"And he and thou, and thou and I,
Little brother." 89
(*O Mother, Mary Mother,*
And they and we, between Hell and Heaven!)

"Three days ago, on his marriage-morn,
Sister Helen,
He sickened, and lies since then forlorn."
"For bridegroom's side is the bride a thorn,
Little brother?"
(*O Mother, Mary Mother,*
Cold bridal cheer, between Hell and Heaven!) 98

"Three days and nights he has lain abed,
Sister Helen,
And he prays in torment to be dead."
"The thing may chance, if he have prayed,
Little brother!" 103
(*O Mother, Mary Mother,*
If he have prayed, between Hell and Heaven!)

"But he has not ceased to cry to-day,
Sister Helen,
That you should take your curse away."
"*My* prayer was heard, — he need but pray,
Little brother!" 110
(*O Mother, Mary Mother,*
Shall God not hear, between Hell and Heaven?)

"But he says, till you take back your ban,
Sister Helen,
His soul would pass, yet never can."
"Nay then, shall I slay a living man,
Little brother?"
(*O Mother, Mary Mother,*
A living soul, between Hell and Heaven!) 119

"But he calls forever on your name,
Sister Helen,
And says that he melts before a flame."

"My heart for his pleasure fared the same,
Little brother."
(*O Mother, Mary Mother,*
Fire at the heart, between Hell and Heaven!) 126

"Here's Keith of Westholm riding fast,
Sister Helen,
For I know the white plume on the blast."
"The hour, the sweet hour I forecast,
Little brother!" 131
(*O Mother, Mary Mother,*
Is the hour sweet, between Hell and Heaven?)

"He stops to speak, and he stills his horse,
Sister Helen;
But his words are drowned in the wind's course."
"Nay hear, nay hear, you must hear perforce,
Little brother!" 138
(*O Mother, Mary Mother,*
What word now heard, between Hell and Heaven?)

"Oh, he says that Keith of Ewern's cry,
Sister Helen,
Is ever to see you ere he die."
"In all that his soul sees, there am I,
Little brother!"
(*O Mother, Mary Mother,* 146
The soul's one sight, between Hell and Heaven!)

"He sends a ring and a broken coin,
Sister Helen,
And bids you mind the banks of Boyne."
"What else he broke will he ever join,
Little brother?"
(*O Mother, Mary Mother,* 153
No, never joined, between Hell and Heaven!)

"He yields you these and craves full fain,
Sister Helen,
You pardon him in his mortal pain."
"What else he took will he give again,
Little brother?"
(*O Mother, Mary Mother,*
Not twice to give, between Hell and Heaven!) 161

"He calls your name in an agony,
Sister Helen,
That even dead Love must weep to see."
"Hate, born of Love, is blind as he,
Little brother!" 166
(*O Mother, Mary Mother,*
Love turned to hate, between Hell and Heaven!)

"Oh it's Keith of Keith now that rides fast,
Sister Helen,
For I know the white hair on the blast."
"The short, short hour will soon be past,
Little brother!" 173
(*O Mother, Mary Mother,*
Will soon be past, between Hell and Heaven!)

"He looks at me and he tries to speak,
Sister Helen,
But oh! his voice is sad and weak!"
"What here should the mighty Baron seek,
Little brother?"
(*O Mother, Mary Mother,*
Is this the end, between Hell and Heaven?) 182

"Oh his son still cries, if you forgive,
Sister Helen,
The body dies, but the soul shall live."
"Fire shall forgive me as I forgive,
Little brother!"
(*O Mother, Mary Mother,*
As she forgives, between Hell and Heaven!) 189

"Oh he prays you, as his heart would rive,
Sister Helen,
To save his dear son's soul alive."
"Fire cannot slay it, it shall thrive,
Little brother!"
(*O Mother, Mary Mother,*
Alas, alas, between Hell and Heaven!) 196

"He cries to you, kneeling in the road,
Sister Helen,
To go with him for the love of God!"
"The way is long to his son's abode,
Little brother." 201
(*O Mother, Mary Mother,*
The way is long, between Hell and Heaven!)

"A lady's here, by a dark steed brought,
Sister Helen,
So darkly clad, I saw her not."
"See her now or never see aught,
Little brother!" 208
(*O Mother, Mary Mother,*
What more to see, between Hell and Heaven!)

"Her hood falls back, and the moon shines fair,
Sister Helen,
On the Lady of Ewern's golden hair."
"Blest hour of my power and her despair,
Little brother!" 215
(*O Mother, Mary Mother,*
Hour blest and bann'd, between Hell and Heaven!)

"Pale, pale her cheeks, that in pride did glow,
Sister Helen,
'Neath the bridal-wreath three days ago."

"One morn for pride and three days for woe,
Little brother!" 222
(*O Mother, Mary Mother,*
Three days, three nights, between Hell and Heaven!

"Her clasped hands stretch from her bending head,
Sister Helen;
With the loud wind's wail her sobs are wed."
"What wedding-strains hath her bridal-bed,
Little brother?" 229
(*O Mother, Mary Mother,*
What strain but death's between Hell and Heaven?)

"She may not speak, she sinks in a swoon,
Sister Helen, —
She lifts her lips and gasps on the moon."
"Oh! might I but hear her soul's blithe tune,
Little brother!" 236
(*O Mother, Mary Mother,*
Her woe's dumb cry, between Hell and Heaven!)

"They've caught her to Westholm's saddle-bow,
Sister Helen,
And her moonlit hair gleams white in its flow."
"Let it turn whiter than winter snow,
Little brother!" 243
(*O Mother, Mary Mother,*
Woe-withered gold, between Hell and Heaven!)

"O Sister Helen, you heard the bell,
Sister Helen!
More loud than the vesper-chime it fell."
"No vesper-chime, but a dying knell,
Little brother!"
(*O Mother, Mary Mother,*
His dying knell, between Hell and Heaven!) 252

"Alas! but I fear the heavy sound,
Sister Helen;
Is it in the sky or in the ground?"
"Say, have they turned their horses round,
Little brother?" 257
(*O Mother, Mary Mother,*
What would she more, between Hell and Heaven?)

"They have raised the old man from his knee,
Sister Helen,
And they ride in silence hastily."
"More fast the naked soul doth flee,
Little brother!" 264
(*O Mother, Mary Mother,*
The naked soul, between Hell and Heaven!)

"Flank to flank are the three steeds gone,
Sister Helen,
But the lady's dark steed goes alone."
"And lonely her bridegroom's soul hath flown,
Little brother."
(*O Mother, Mary Mother,*
The lonely ghost, between Hell and Heaven!) 273

"Oh the wind is sad in the iron chill,
Sister Helen,
And weary sad they look by the hill."
"But he and I are sadder still,
Little brother!"
(*O Mother, Mary Mother,*
Most sad of all, between Hell and Heaven!) 280

"See, see, the wax has dropped from its place,
Sister Helen,
And the flames are winning up apace!"
"Yet here they burn but for a space,
Little brother!"
(*O Mother, Mary Mother,*
Here for a space, between Hell and Heaven!) 287

"Ah! what white thing at the door has cross'd,
Sister Helen,
Ah! what is this that sighs in the frost?"
"A soul that's lost as mine is lost,
Little brother!" 292
(*O Mother, Mary Mother,*
Lost, lost, all lost, between Hell and Heaven!)

THE BALLAD OF DEAD LADIES

(From FRANÇOIS VILLON)

Tell me now in what hidden way is
Lady Flora the lovely Roman?
Where's Hipparchia, and where is Thaïs,
Neither of them the fairer woman?
Where is Echo, beheld of no man,
Only heard on river and mere, —
She whose beauty was more than human? . . .
But where are the snows of yester-year? 8

Where's Héloise, the learned nun,
For whose sake Abeillard, I ween,
Lost manhood and put priesthood on?
(From Love he won such dule and teen!)
And where, I pray you, is the Queen
Who willed that Buridan should steer
Sewed in a sack's mouth down the Seine? . . .
But where are the snows of yester-year? 16

White Queen Blanche, like a queen of lilies,
With a voice like any mermaiden, —
Bertha Broadfoot, Beatrice, Alice,
And Ermengarde the lady of Maine, —
And that good Joan whom Englishmen
At Rouen doomed and burned her there, —

Mother of God, where are they then? . . .
But where are the snows of yester-year?

Nay, never ask this week, fair lord,
Where they are gone, nor yet this year,
Except with this for an overword, —
"But where are the snows of yester-year?"

FRANCESCA DA RIMINI

(From DANTE)

* * * * * * *

When I made answer, I began: "Alas!
How many sweet thoughts and how much desire
Led these two onward to the dolorous pass!"
Then turned to them, as who would fain inquire,
And said: "Francesca, these thine agonies
Wring tears for pity and grief that they inspire: —
But tell me, — in the season of sweet sighs,
When and what way did Love instruct you so
That he in your vague longings made you wise?"
Then she to me: "There is no greater woe
Than the remembrance brings of happy days
In Misery; and this thy guide doth know.
But if the first beginnings to retrace
Of our sad love can yield thee solace here,
So will I be as one that weeps and says.
One day we read, for pastime and sweet cheer,
Of Lancelot, how he found Love tyrannous:
We were alone and without any fear.
Our eyes were drawn together, reading thus,
Full oft, and still our cheeks would pale and glow;
But one sole point it was that conquered us.
For when we read of that great lover, how
He kissed the smile which he had longed to win, —
Then he whom nought can sever from me now
Forever, kissed my mouth, all quivering.
A Galahalt was the book, and he that writ:
Upon that day we read no more therein."
At the tale told, while one soul uttered it,
The other wept: a pang so pitiable
That I was seized, like death, in swooning-fit,
And even as a dead body falls, I fell.

ON REFUSAL OF AID BETWEEN NATIONS

Not that the earth is changing, O my God!
Nor that the seasons totter in their walk, —
Not that the virulent ill of act and talk
Seethes ever as a winepress ever trod, —
Not therefore are we certain that the rod
Weighs in thine hand to smite thy world; though now
Beneath thine hand so many nations bow,
So many kings: — not therefore, O my God! —
But because Man is parcelled out in men
To-day; because, for any wrongful blow,
No man not stricken asks, "I would be told
Why thou dost thus:" but his heart whispers then,
"He is he, I am I." By this we know
That the earth falls asunder, being old.

THE SONNET

A Sonnet is a moment's monument, —
Memorial from the Soul's eternity
To one dead deathless hour. Look that it be,
Whether for lustral rite or dire portent,
Of its own arduous fulness reverent:
Carve it in ivory or in ebony,
As Day or Night may rule; and let Time see
Its flowering crest impearled and orient.
A Sonnet is a coin: its face reveals
The soul, — its converse, to what Power 'tis due: —
Whether for tribute to the august appeals
Of Life, or dower in Love's high retinue,
It serve; or, 'mid the dark wharf's cavernous breath,
In Charon's palm it pay the toll to Death.

LOVE-SIGHT

When do I see thee most, belovèd one?
When in the light the spirits of mine eyes
Before thy face, their altar, solemnize
The worship of that Love through thee made known?
Or when in the dusk hours, (we two alone,)
Close-kissed and eloquent of still replies
Thy twilight-hidden glimmering visage lies,
And my soul only sees thy soul its own?
O love, my love! if I no more should see
Thyself, nor on the earth the shadow of thee,
Nor image of thine eyes in any spring, —
How then should sound upon Life's darkening slope
The ground-whirl of the perished leaves of Hope,
The wind of Death's imperishable wing?

LOVE-SWEETNESS

Sweet dimness of her loosened hair's downfall
About thy face; her sweet hands round thy head

In gracious fostering union garlanded;
Her tremulous smiles; her glances' sweet recall
Of love; her murmuring sighs memorial;
Her mouth's culled sweetness by thy kisses shed
On cheeks and neck and eyelids, and so led
Back to her mouth which answers there for all: —
What sweeter than these things, except the thing
In lacking which all these would lose their sweet: —
The confident heart's still fervour: the swift beat
And soft subsidence of the spirit's wing,
Then when it feels, in cloud-girt wayfaring,
The breath of kindred plumes against its feet?

MID-RAPTURE

Thou lovely and belovèd, thou my love;
Whose kiss seems still the first; whose summoning eyes,
Even now, as for our love-world's new sunrise,
Shed very dawn; whose voice, attuned above
All modulation of the deep-bowered dove,
Is like a hand laid softly on the soul;
Whose hand is like a sweet voice to control
Those worn tired brows it hath the keeping of: —
What word can answer to thy word, — what gaze
To thine, which now absorbs within its sphere
My worshipping face, till I am mirrored there
Light-circled in a heaven of deep-drawn rays?
What clasp, what kiss mine inmost heart can prove,
O lovely and belovèd, O my love?

SOUL-LIGHT

What other woman could be loved like you,
Or how of you should love possess his fill?
After the fullness of all rapture, still, —
As at the end of some deep avenue
A tender glamour of day, — there comes to view
Far in your eyes a yet more hungering thrill, —
Such fire as Love's soul-winnowing hands distil
Even from his inmost ark of light and dew.
And as the traveller triumphs with the sun,
Glorying in heat's mid-height, yet startide brings
Wonder new-born, and still fresh transport springs
From limpid lambent hours of day begun; —
Even so, through eyes and voice, your soul doth move
My soul with changeful light of infinite love.

STILLBORN LOVE

The hour which might have been yet might not be,
Which man's and woman's heart conceived and bore
Yet whereof life was barren, — on what shore
Bides it the breaking of Time's weary sea?
Bondchild of all consummate joys set free,
It somewhere sighs and serves, and mute before
The house of Love, hears through the echoing door
His hours elect in choral consonancy.
But lo! what wedded souls now hand in hand
Together tread at last the immortal strand
With eyes where burning memory lights love home?
Lo! how the little outcast hour has turned
And leaped to them and in their faces yearned: —
"I am your child: O parents, ye have come!"

INCLUSIVENESS

The changing guests, each in a different mood,
Sit at the roadside table and arise:
And every life among them in likewise
Is a soul's board set daily with new food.
What man has bent o'er his son's sleep, to brood
How that face shall watch his when cold it lies? —
Or thought, as his own mother kissed his eyes,
Of what her kiss was when his father wooed?
May not this ancient room thou sit'st in dwell
In separate living souls for joy or pain?
Nay, all its corners may be painted plain
Where Heaven shows pictures of some life spent well;
And may be stamped, a memory all in vain,
Upon the sight of lidless eyes in Hell.

KNOWN IN VAIN

As two whose love, first foolish, widening scope,
Knows suddenly, to music high and soft,
The Holy of holies; who because they scoff'd
Are now amazed with shame, nor dare to cope
With the whole truth aloud, lest heaven should ope;
Yet, at their meetings, laugh not as they laugh'd
In speech; nor speak, at length; but sitting oft
Together, within hopeless sight of hope
For hours are silent: — So it happeneth
When Work and Will awake too late, to gaze
After their life sailed by, and hold their breath.
Ah! who shall dare to search through what sad maze
Thenceforth their incommunicable ways
Follow the desultory feet of Death?

THE LANDMARK

Was *that* the landmark? What, — the foolish well
Whose wave, low down, I did not stoop to drink,
But sat and flung the pebbles from its brink
In sport to send its imaged skies pell-mell,
(And mine own image, had I noted well!) —
Was that my point of turning? — I had thought
The stations of my course should rise unsought,
As altar-stone or ensigned citadel.
But lo! the path is missed, I must go back,
And thirst to drink when next I reach the spring
Which once I stained, which since may have grown black.
Yet though no light be left nor bird now sing
As here I turn, I'll thank God, hastening,
That the same goal is still on the same track.

THE CHOICE

I

Eat thou and drink; to-morrow thou shalt die.
Surely the earth, that's wise being very old,
Needs not our help. Then loose me, love, and hold
Thy sultry hair up from my face; that I
May pour for thee this golden wine, brim-high,
Till round the glass thy fingers glow like gold.
We'll drown all hours: thy song, while hours are toll'd,
Shall leap, as fountains veil the changing sky.
Now kiss, and think that there are really those,
My own high-bosomed beauty, who increase
Vain gold, vain lore, and yet might choose our way!
Through many years they toil; then on a day
They die not, — for their life was death, — but cease;
And round their narrow lips the mould falls close.

II

Watch thou and fear; to-morrow thou shalt die.
Or art thou sure thou shalt have time for death?
Is not the day which God's word promiseth
To come man knows not when? In yonder sky,
Now while we speak, the sun speeds forth: can I
Or thou assure him of his goal? God's breath
Even at this moment haply quickeneth
The air to a flame; till spirits, always nigh
Though screened and hid, shall walk the daylight here.
And dost thou prate of all that man shall do?
Canst thou, who hast but plagues, presume to be
Glad in his gladness that comes after thee?
Will *his* strength slay *thy* worm in Hell? Go to:
Cover thy countenance, and watch, and fear.

III

Think thou and act; to-morrow thou shalt die.
Outstretch'd in the sun's warmth upon the shore,
Thou say'st: "Man's measured path is all gone o'er;
Up all his years, steeply, with strain and sigh,
Man clomb until he touched the truth; and I,
Even I, am he whom it was destined for."
How should this be? Art thou then so much more
Than they who sowed, that thou shouldst reap thereby?
Nay, come up hither. From this wave-washed mound
Unto the furthest flood-brim look with me;
Then reach on with thy thought till it be drown'd.
Miles and miles distant though the last line be,
And though thy soul sail leagues and leagues beyond, —
Still, leagues beyond those leagues, there is more sea.

VAIN VIRTUES

What is the sorriest thing that enters Hell?
None of the sins, — but this and that fair deed
Which a soul's sin at length could supersede.
These yet are virgins, whom death's timely knell
Might once have sainted; whom the fiends compel
Together now, in snake-bound shuddering sheaves
Of anguish, while the pit's pollution leaves
Their refuse maidenhood abominable.
Night sucks them down, the tribute of the pit,
Whose names, half entered in the book of Life,
Were God's desire at noon. And as their hair
And eyes sink last, the Torturer designs no whit
To gaze, but, yearning, waits his destined wife,
The Sin still blithe on earth that sent them there.

LOST DAYS

The lost days of my life until to-day,
What were they, could I see them on the street
Lie as they fell? Would they be ears of wheat

Sown once for food but trodden into clay?
Or golden coins squandered and still to-pay?
Or drops of blood dabbling the guilty feet?
Or such spilt water as in dreams must cheat
The undying throats of Hell, athirst alway?
I do not see them here; but after death
God knows I know the faces I shall see,
Each one a murdered self, with low last breath.
"I am thyself, — what hast thou done to me?"
"And I — and I — thyself," (lo! each one saith,)
"And thou thyself to all eternity!"

A SUPERSCRIPTION

Look in my face; my name is Might-have-been;
I am also called No-more, Too-late, Farewell;
Unto thine ear I hold the dead-sea shell
Cast up thy Life's foam-fretted feet between;
Unto thine eyes the glass where that is seen
Which had Life's form and Love's, but by my spell
Is now a shaken shadow intolerable,
Of ultimate things unuttered the frail screen.
Mark me, how still I am! But should there dart
One moment through thy soul the soft surprise
Of that winged Peace which lulls the breath of sighs, —
Then shalt thou see me smile, and turn apart
Thy visage to mine ambush at thy heart,
Sleepless with cold commemorative eyes.

THE ONE HOPE

When vain desire at last and vain regret
Go hand in hand to death, and all is vain,
What shall assuage the unforgotten pain
And teach the unforgetful to forget?
Shall Peace be still a sunk stream long unmet, —
Or may the soul at once in a green plain
Stoop through the spray of some sweet life-fountain
And cull the dew-drenched flowering amulet?
Ah! when the wan soul in that golden air
Between the scriptured petals softly blown
Peers breathless for the gift of grace unknown, —
Ah! let none other alien spell soe'er
But only the one Hope's one name be there, —
Not less nor more, but even that word alone.

CHIMES

I

Honey-flowers to the honey-comb
And the honey-bees from home.

A honey-comb and a honey-flower,
And the bee shall have his hour.

A honeyed heart for the honey-comb,
And the humming bee flies home.

A heavy heart in the honey-flower,
And the bee has had his hour.

VI

Buried bars in the breakwater
And bubble of the brimming weir.

Body's blood in the breakwater
And a buried body's bier.

Buried bones in the breakwater
And bubble of the brawling weir.

Bitter tears in the breakwater
And a breaking heart to bear.

THREE SHADOWS

I looked and saw your eyes
In the shadow of your hair,
As a traveller sees the stream
In the shadow of the wood;
And I said, "My faint heart sighs,
Ah me! to linger there,
To drink deep and to dream
In that sweet solitude."

I looked and saw your heart
In the shadow of your eyes,
As a seeker sees the gold
In the shadow of the stream;
And I said, "Ah me! what art
Should win the immortal prize,
Whose want must make life cold
And Heaven a hollow dream?"

I looked and saw your love
In the shadow of your heart,
As a diver sees the pearl
In the shadow of the sea;
And I murmured, not above
My breath, but all apart, —
"Ah! you can love, true girl,
And is your love for me?"

THE CLOUD CONFINES

The day is dark and the night
To him that would search their heart;
No lips of cloud that will part
Nor morning song in the light:
Only, gazing alone,
To him wild shadows are shown,
Deep under deep unknown
And height above unknown height.
Still we say as we go, —
"Strange to think by the way,
Whatever there is to know,
That shall we know one day."

The Past is over and fled;
Named new, we name it the old;
Thereof some tale hath been told,
But no word comes from the dead;
Whether at all they be,
Or whether as bond or free,
Or whether they too were we,
Or by what spell they have sped.
Still we say as we go, —
"Strange to think by the way,
Whatever there is to know,
That shall we know one day."

What of the heart of hate
That beats in thy breast, O Time? —
Red strife from the furthest prime,
And anguish of fierce debate;
War that shatters her slain,
And peace that grinds them as grain,
And eyes fixed ever in vain
On the pitiless eyes of Fate.
Still we say as we go, —
"Strange to think by the way,
Whatever there is to know,
That shall we know one day."

What of the heart of love
That bleeds in thy breast, O Man? —
Thy kisses snatched 'neath the ban
Of fangs that mock them above;
Thy bells prolonged unto knells,
Thy hope that a breath dispels,
Thy bitter forlorn farewells
And the empty echoes thereof?
Still we say as we go, —
"Strange to think by the way,
Whatever there is to know,
That shall we know one day."

The sky leans dumb on the sea,
Aweary with all its wings;
And oh! the song the sea sings
Is dark everlastingly.
Our past is clean forgot,
Our present is and is not,
Our future's a sealed seedplot,
And what betwixt them are we? —
We who say as we go, —
"Strange to think by the way,
Whatever there is to know,
That shall we know one day."

GEORGE MEREDITH (b. 1828)

LOVE IN THE VALLEY

Under yonder beech-tree single on the green-sward,
Couch'd with her arms behind her golden head,
Knees and tresses folded to slip and ripple idly,
Lies my young love sleeping in the shade.
Had I the heart to slide an arm beneath her,
Press her parting lips as her waist I gather slow,
Waking in amazement she could not but embrace me:
Then would she hold me and never let me go?

Shy as the squirrel and wayward as the swallow,
Swift as the swallow along the river's light
Circleting the surface to meet his mirror'd winglets,
Fleeter she seems in her stay than in her flight.
Shy as the squirrel that leaps among the pine-tops,
Wayward as the swallow overhead at set of sun,
She whom I love is hard to catch and conquer,
Hard, but oh the glory of the winning were she won!

When her mother tends her before the laughing mirror,
Tying up her laces, looping up her hair,
Often she thinks, were this wild thing wedded,
More love should I have, and much less care.
When her mother tends her before the lighted mirror,
Loosening her laces, combing down her curls,
Often she thinks, were this wild thing wedded,
I should miss but one for many boys and girls.

Heartless she is as the shadow in the meadows
Flying to the hills on a blue and breezy noon.
No, she is athirst and drinking up her wonder:
Earth to her is young as the slip of the new moon.
Deals she an unkindness, 'tis but her rapid measure,
Even as in a dance; and her smile can heal no less:

Like the swinging May-cloud that pelts the flowers with hailstones
Off a sunny border, she was made to bruise and bless.

Lovely are the curves of the white owl sweeping
Wavy in the dusk lit by one large star.
Lone on the fir-branch, his rattle-note unvaried,
Brooding o'er the gloom, spins the brown evejar.
Darker grows the valley, more and more forgetting:
So were it with me if forgetting could be will'd.
Tell the grassy hollow that holds the bubbling well-spring,
Tell it to forget the source that keeps it fill'd.

Stepping down the hill with her fair companions,
Arm in arm, all against the raying West,
Boldly she sings, to the merry tune she marches,
Brave is her shape, and sweeter unpossess'd.
Sweeter, for she is what my heart first awaking
Whisper'd the world was; morning light is she.
Love that so desires would fain keep her changeless;
Fain would fling the net, and fain have her free.

Happy happy time, when the white star hovers
Low over dim fields fresh with bloomy dew,
Near the face of dawn, that draws athwart the darkness,
Threading it with colour, like yewberries the yew.
Thicker crowd the shades as the grave East deepens
Glowing, and with crimson a long cloud swells.
Maiden still the morn is; and strange she is, and secret;
Strange her eyes; her cheeks are cold as cold sea-shells.

Sunrays, leaning on our southern hills and lighting
Wild cloud-mountains that drag the hills along,
Oft ends the day of your shifting brilliant laughter
Chill as a dull face frowning on a song.
Ay, but shows the South-West a ripple-feather'd bosom
Blown to silver while the clouds are shaken and ascend
Scaling the mid-heavens as they stream, there comes a sunset
Rich, deep like love in beauty without end.

When at dawn she sighs, and like an infant to the window
Turns grave eyes craving light, released from dreams,
Beautiful she looks, like a white water-lily
Bursting out of bud in havens of the streams.
When from bed she rises clothed from neck to ankle
In her long nightgown sweet as boughs of May,
Beautiful she looks, like a tall garden-lily
Pure from the night, and splendid for the day.

Mother of the dews, dark eye-lash'd twilight,
Low-lidded twilight, o'er the valley's brim,
Rounding on thy breast sings the dew-delighted skylark,
Clear as though the dew-drops had their voice in him,
Hidden where the rose-flush drinks the rayless planet,
Fountain-full he pours the spraying fountain-showers.
Let me hear her laughter, I would have her ever
Cool as dew in twilight, the lark above the flowers.

All the girls are out with their baskets for the primrose;
Up lanes, woods through, they troop in joyful bands.
My sweet leads: she knows not why, but now she loiters,
Eyes the bent anemones, and hangs her hands.
Such a look will tell that the violets are peeping,
Coming the rose: and unaware a cry
Springs in her bosom for odours and for colour,
Covert and the nightingale; she knows not why.

Kerchief'd head and chin she darts between her tulips,
Streaming like a willow grey in arrowy rain:
Some bend beaten cheek to gravel, and their angel
She will be; she lifts them, and on she speeds again.
Black the driving raincloud breasts the iron gateway:
She is forth to cheer a neighbour lacking mirth.
So when sky and grass met rolling dumb for thunder
Saw I once a white dove, sole light of earth.

Prim little scholars are the flowers of her garden,
Train'd to stand in rows, and asking if they please.
I might love them well but for loving more the wild ones:
O my wild ones! they tell me more than these.
You, my wild one, you tell of honied field-rose,
Violet, blushing eglantine in life; and even as they,
They by the wayside are earnest of your goodness,
You are of life's, on the banks that line the way.

Peering at her chamber the white crowns the red rose,
Jasmine winds the porch with stars two and three.
Parted is the window; she sleeps; the starry jasmine
Breathes a falling breath that carries thoughts of me.
Sweeter unpossess'd, have I said of her my sweetest?
Not while she sleeps: while she sleeps the jasmine breathes,
Luring her to love; she sleeps; the starry jasmine
Bears me to her pillow under white rose-wreaths.

Yellow with birdfoot-trefoil are the grass-glades;
Yellow with cinquefoil of the dew-grey leaf;
Yellow with stonecrop; the moss-mounds are yellow;
Blue-neck'd the wheat sways, yellowing to the sheaf.
Green-yellow, bursts from the copse the laughing yaffle;
Sharp as a sickle is the edge of shade and shine:
Earth in her heart laughs looking at the heavens,
Thinking of the harvest: I look and think of mine.

This I may know: her dressing and undressing
Such a change of light shows as when the skies in sport
Shift from cloud to moonlight; or edging over thunder
Slips a ray of sun; or sweeping into port
White sails furl; or on the ocean borders
White sails lean along the waves leaping green.
Visions of her shower before me, but from eyesight
Guarded she would be like the sun were she seen.

Front door and back of the moss'd old farmhouse
Open with the morn, and in a breezy link
Freshly sparkles garden to stripe-shadow'd orchard,
Green across a rill where on sand the minnows wink.
Busy in the grass the early sun of summer
Swarms, and the blackbird's mellow fluting notes
Call my darling up with round and roguish challenge:
Quaintest, richest carol of all the singing throats!

Cool was the woodside; cool as her white dairy
Keeping sweet the cream-pan; and there the boys from school,
Cricketing below, rush'd brown and red with sunshine;
O the dark translucence of the deep-eyed cool!
Spying from the farm, herself she fetch'd a pitcher
Full of milk, and tilted for each in turn the beak.
Then a little fellow, mouth up and on tiptoe,
Said, "I will kiss you": she laugh'd and lean'd her cheek.

Doves of the fir-wood walling high our red roof
Through the long noon coo, crooning through the coo.
Loose droop the leaves, and down the sleepy roadway
Sometimes pipes a chaffinch; loose droops the blue.
Cows flap a slow tail knee-deep in the river,
Breathless, given up to sun and gnat and fly.
Nowhere is she seen; and if I see her nowhere,
Lightning may come, straight rains and tiger sky.

O the golden sheaf, the rustling treasure-armful!
O the nutbrown tresses nodding interlaced!
O the treasure-tresses one another over
Nodding! O the girdle slack about the waist!
Slain are the poppies that shot their random scarlet
Quick amid the wheat-ears: wound about the waist,
Gather'd, see these brides of Earth one blush of ripeness!
O the nutbrown tresses nodding interlaced!

Large and smoky red the sun's cold disk drops,
Clipp'd by naked hills, on violet shaded snow:
Eastward large and still lights up a bower of moonrise,
Whence at her leisure steps the moon aglow.
Nightlong on black print-branches our beech-tree
Gazes in this whiteness: nightlong could I.
Here may life on death or death on life be painted.
Let me clasp her soul to know she cannot die!

Gossips count her faults; they scour a narrow chamber
Where there is no window, read not heaven or her.
"When she was a tiny," one agèd woman quavers,
Plucks at my heart and leads me by the ear.
Faults she had once as she learn'd to run and tumbled:
Faults of feature some see, beauty not complete.
Yet, good gossips, beauty that makes holy
Earth and air, may have faults from head to feet.

Hither she comes; she comes to me; she lingers,
Deepens her brown eyebrows, while in new surprise

High rise the lashes in wonder of a stranger;
  Yet am I the light and living of her eyes.
Something friends have told her fills her heart to brimming,
  Nets her in her blushes, and wounds her, and tames. —
Sure of her haven, O like a dove alighting,
  Arms up, she dropp'd: our souls were in our names.

Soon will she lie like a white frost sunrise.
  Yellow oats and brown wheat, barley pale as rye,
Long since your sheaves have yielded to the thresher,
  Felt the girdle loosen'd, seen the tresses fly.
Soon will she lie like a blood-red sunset.
  Swift with the to-morrow, green-wing'd Spring!
Sing from the South-west, bring her back the truants,
  Nightingale and swallow, song and dipping wing.

Soft new beech-leaves, up to beamy April
  Spreading bough on bough a primrose mountain, you
Lucid in the moon, raise lilies to the skyfields,
  Youngest green transfused in silver shining through:
Fairer than the lily, than the wild white cherry:
  Fair as in image my seraph love appears
Borne to me by dreams when dawn is at my eyelids:
  Fair as in the flesh she swims to me on tears.

Could I find a place to be alone with heaven,
  I would speak my heart out: heaven is my need.
Every woodland tree is flushing like the dogwood,
  Flashing like the whitebeam, swaying like the reed.
Flushing like the dogwood crimson in October;
  Streaming like the flag-reed South-west blown;
Flashing as in gusts the sudden-lighted whitebeam:
  All seem to know what is for heaven alone.

JUGGLING JERRY

Pitch here the tent, while the old horse grazes:
  By the old hedge-side we'll halt a stage.
It's nigh my last above the daisies:
  My next leaf'll be man's blank page.
Yes, my old girl! and it's no use crying:
  Juggler, constable, king, must bow.
One that outjuggles all's been spying
  Long to have me, and he has me now.

We've travelled times to this old common:
  Often we've hung our pots in the gorse.
We've had a stirring life, old woman!
  You, and I, and the old grey horse.
Races, and fairs, and royal occasions,
  Found us coming to their call:
Now they'll miss us at our stations:
  There's a Juggler outjuggles all!

Up goes the lark, as if all were jolly!
  Over the duck-pond the willow shakes.
Easy to think that grieving's folly,
  When the hand's firm as driven stakes!
Ay, when we're strong, and braced, and manful,
  Life's a sweet fiddle: but we're a batch
Born to become the Great Juggler's han'ful:
  Balls he shies up, and is safe to catch.

Here's where the lads of the village cricket:
  I was a lad not wide from here:
Couldn't I whip off the bale from the wicket?
  Like an old world those days appear!
Donkey, sheep, geese and thatched ale-house — I know them!
  They are old friends of my halts, and seem,
Somehow, as if kind thanks I owe them:
  Juggling don't hinder the heart's esteem.

Juggling's no sin, for we must have victual:
  Nature allows us to bait for the fool.
Holding one's own makes us juggle no little;
  But, to increase it, hard juggling's the rule.
You that are sneering at my profession,
  Haven't you juggled a vast amount?
There's the Prime Minister, in one Session,
  Juggles more games than my sins'll count.

I've murdered insects with mock thunder:
  Conscience, for that, in men don't quail.
I've made bread from the bump of wonder:
  That's my business, and there's my tale.
Fashion and rank all praised the professor:
  Ay! and I've had my smile from the Queen:
Bravo, Jerry! she meant: God bless her!
  Ain't this a sermon on that scene?

I've studied men from my topsy-turvy
  Close, and, I reckon, rather true.
Some are fine fellows: some, right scurvy:
  Most, a dash between the two.
But it's a woman, old girl, that makes me
  Think more kindly of the race:
And it's a woman, old girl, that shakes me
  When the Great Juggler I must face.

We two were married, due and legal:
  Honest we've lived since we've been one.
Lord! I could then jump like an eagle:

You danced bright as a bit o' the sun.
Birds in a May-bush we were! right merry!
All night we kiss'd, we juggled all day.
Joy was the heart of Juggling Jerry!
Now from his old girl he's juggled away.

It's past parsons to console us:
No, nor no doctor fetch for me:
I can die without my bolus;
Two of a trade, lass, never agree!
Parson and Doctor! — don't they love rarely,
Fighting the devil in other men's fields!
Stand up yourself and match him fairly:
Then see how the rascal yields!

I, lass, have lived no gipsy, flaunting
Finery while his poor helpmate grubs:
Coin I've stored, and you won't be wanting:
You sha'n't beg from the troughs and tubs.
Nobly you've stuck to me, though in his kitchen
Many a Marquis would hail you Cook!
Palaces you could have ruled and grown rich in,
But your old Jerry you never forsook.

Hand up the chirper! ripe ale winks in it;
Let's have comfort and be at peace.
Once a stout draught made me light as a linnet.
Cheer up! the Lord must have his lease.
May be — for none see in that black hollow —
It's just a place where we're held in pawn,
And, when the Great Juggler makes as to swallow,
It's just the sword-trick — I ain't quite gone.

Yonder came smells of the gorse, so nutty,
Gold-like and warm: it's the prime of May.
Better than mortar, brick, and putty,
Is God's house on a blowing day.
Lean me more up the mound; now I feel it:
All the old heath-smells! Ain't it strange?
There's the world laughing, as if to conceal it!
But He's by us, juggling the change.

I mind it well, by the sea-beach lying,
Once — it's long gone — when two gulls we beheld,
Which, as the moon got up, were flying
Down a big wave that sparked and swelled.
Crack went a gun: one fell: the second
Wheeled round him twice, and was off for new luck:
There in the dark her white wing beckon'd: —
Drop me a kiss — I'm the bird dead-struck!

BELLEROPHON

Maimed, beggared, grey; seeking an alms; with nod
Of palsy doing task of thanks for bread;
Upon the stature of a god,
He whom the Gods have struck bends low his head.

Weak words he has, that slip the nerveless tongue
Deformed, like his great frame: a broken arc:
Once radiant as the javelin flung
Right at the centre breastplate of his mark.

Oft pausing on his white-eyed inward look,
Some undermountain narrative he tells,
As gapped by Lykian heat the brook
Cut from the source that in the upland swells.

The cottagers who dole him fruit and crust,
With patient inattention hear him prate:
And comes the snow, and comes the dust,
Comes the old wanderer, more bent of late.

A crazy beggar grateful for a meal
Has ever of himself a world to say.
For them he is an ancient wheel
Spinning a knotted thread the livelong day.

He cannot, nor do they, the tale connect;
For never singer in the land has been
Who him for theme did not reject:
Spurned of the hoof that sprang the Hippocrene.

Albeit a theme of flame to bring them straight
The snorting white-winged brother of the wave,
They hear him as a thing by fate
Cursed in unholy babble to his grave.

As men that spied the wings, that heard the snort,
Their sires have told; and of a martial prince
Bestriding him; and old report
Speaks of a monster slain by one long since.

There is that story of the golden bit
By Goddess given to tame the lightning steed:
A mortal who could mount, and sit
Flying, and up Olympus midway speed.

He rose like the loosed fountain's utmost leap;
He played the star at span of heaven right o'er
Men's heads; they saw the snowy steep,
Saw the winged shoulders: him they saw not more.

He fell: and says the shattered man, "I fell":
And sweeps an arm the height an eagle wins;
And in his breast a mouthless well
Heaves the worn patches of his coat of skins.

Lo, this is he in whom the surgent springs
Of recollections richer than our skies
To feed the flow of tuneful strings,
Show but a pool of scum for shooting flies.

LUCIFER IN STARLIGHT

On a starred night Prince Lucifer uprose.
Tired of his dark dominion, swung the fiend
Above the rolling ball in cloud part screened,
Where sinners hugged their spectre of repose.
Poor prey to his hot fit of pride were those.
And now upon his western wing he leaned,
Now his huge bulk o'er Afric's sands careened,
Now the black planet shadowed Arctic snows.
Soaring through wider zones that pricked his scars
With memory of the old revolt from Awe,
He reached a middle height, and at the stars,
Which are the brain of heaven, he looked, and sank.
Around the ancient track marched, rank on rank,
The army of unalterable law.

From MODERN LOVE

XVI

In our old shipwrecked days there was an hour
When, in the firelight steadily aglow,
Joined slackly, we beheld the red chasm grow
Among the clicking coals. Our library-bower
That eve was left to us: and hushed we sat
As lovers to whom Time is whispering.
From sudden-opened doors we heard them sing:
The nodding elders mixed good wine with chat.
Well knew we that Life's greatest treasure lay
With us, and of it was our talk. "Ah, yes!
Love dies!" I said: I never thought it less.
She yearned to me that sentence to unsay.
Then when the fire domed blackening, I found
Her cheek was salt against my kiss, and swift
Up the sharp scale of sobs her breast did lift:—
Now am I haunted by that taste! that sound.

L

Thus piteously Love closed what he begat:
The union of this ever-diverse pair!
These two were rapid falcons in a snare,
Condemned to do the flitting of the bat.
Lovers beneath the singing sky of May,
They wandered once; clear as the dew on flowers.
But they fed not on the advancing hours:
Their hearts held cravings for the buried day.
Then each applied to each that fatal knife,
Deep questioning, which probes to endless dole.
Ah! what a dusty answer gets the soul
When hot for certainties in this our life!—
In tragic hints here see what evermore
Moves dark as yonder midnight ocean's force,
Thundering like ramping hosts of warrior horse,
To throw that faint thin line upon the shore.

ASK, IS LOVE DIVINE

Ask, is Love divine,
Voices all are, Ay.
Question for the sign,
There's a common sigh.

Would we through our years
Love forego,
Quit of scars and tears?
Ah, but no, no, no!

SONG OF THE SONGLESS

They have no song, the sedges dry,
And still they sing.
It is within my breast they sing,
As I pass by.
Within my breast they touch a spring,
They wake a sigh.
There is but sound of sedges dry;
In me they sing.

DIRGE IN WOODS

A wind sways the pines,
And below
Not a breath of wild air;
Still as the mosses that glow
On the flooring and over the lines
Of the roots here and there.
The pine-tree drops its dead;
They are quiet as under the sea.

Overhead, overhead
Rushes life in a race,
As the clouds the clouds chase:
And we go,
And we drop like the fruits of the tree,
Even we,
Even so.

CHRISTINA ROSSETTI (1830–1894)

THE BRIDE-SONG

From THE PRINCE'S PROGRESS

Too late for love, too late for joy!
Too late! too late!
You loitered on the road too long,
You trifled at the gate:
The enchanted dove upon her branch
Died without a mate;
The enchanted princess in her tower
Slept, died, behind the grate;
Her heart was starving all this while
You made it wait.

Ten years ago, five years ago,
One year ago, —
Even then you had arrived in time,
Though somewhat slow;
Then you had known her living face,
Which now you cannot know:
The frozen fountain would have leaped,
The buds gone on to blow,
The warm south wind would have awaked
To melt the snow.

Is she fair now as she lies?
Once she was fair;
Meet queen for any kingly king,
With gold-dust on her hair.
Now these are poppies in her locks,
White poppies she must wear;
Must wear a veil to shroud her face
And the want graven there:
Or is the hunger fed at length,
Cast off the care?

We never saw her with a smile
Or with a frown;
Her bed seemed never soft to her,
Though tossed of down;
She little heeded what she wore,
Kirtle, or wreath, or gown;
We think her white brows often ached
Beneath her crown,
Till silvery hairs showed in her locks
That used to be so brown.

We never heard her speak in haste:
Her tones were sweet,
And modulated just so much
As it was meet:
Her heart sat silent through the noise
And concourse of the street.
There was no hurry in her hands,
No hurry in her feet;
There was no bliss drew nigh to her,
That she might run to greet.

You should have wept her yesterday,
Wasting upon her bed:
But wherefore should you weep to-day
That she is dead?
Lo, we who love weep not to-day,
But crown her royal head.
Let be these poppies that we strew,
Your roses are too red:
Let be these poppies, not for you
Cut down and spread.

A BIRTHDAY

My heart is like a singing bird
Whose nest is in a watered shoot;
My heart is like an apple-tree
Whose boughs are bent with thick-set fruit;
My heart is like a rainbow shell
That paddles in a halcyon sea;
My heart is gladder than all these
Because my love is come to me.

Raise me a dais of silk and down;
Hang it with vair and purple dyes;
Carve it in doves and pomegranates,
And peacocks with a hundred eyes;
Work it in gold and silver grapes,
In leaves and silver fleur-de-lys;
Because the birthday of my life
Is come, my love is come to me.

SONG

When I am dead, my dearest,
Sing no sad songs for me;
Plant thou no roses at my head,
Nor shady cypress-tree:
Be the green grass above me
With showers and dewdrops wet;
And if thou wilt, remember,
And if thou wilt, forget.

I shall not see the shadows,
I shall not feel the rain;
I shall not hear the nightingale
Sing on, as if in pain:
And dreaming through the twilight
That doth not rise nor set,
Haply I may remember,
And haply may forget.

THE FIRST DAY

I wish I could remember that first day,
First hour, first moment of your meeting me,
If bright or dim the season, it might be
Summer or Winter for aught I can say;
So unrecorded did it slip away,
So blind was I to see and to foresee,
So dull to mark the budding of my tree
That would not blossom yet for many a May.
If only I could recollect it, such
A day of days! I let it come and go
As traceless as a thaw of bygone snow;
It seemed to mean so little, meant so much;
If only now I could recall that touch,
First touch of hand in hand — Did one but know?

REMEMBER

Remember me when I am gone away,
Gone far away into the silent land;
When you can no more hold me by the hand,
Nor I half turn to go, yet turning stay.
Remember me when no more, day by day,
You tell me of our future that you planned:
Only remember me; you understand
It will be late to counsel then or pray.
Yet if you should forget me for a while
And afterwards remember, do not grieve:
For if the darkness and corruption leave
A vestige of the thoughts that once I had,
Better by far you should forget and smile
Than that you should remember and be sad.

REST

O Earth, lie heavily upon her eyes;
Seal her sweet eyes weary of watching, Earth;
Lie close around her; leave no room for mirth
With its harsh laughter, nor for sound of sighs.
She hath no questions, she hath no replies,
Hushed in and curtained with a blessèd dearth
Of all that irked her from the hour of birth;
With stillness that is almost Paradise.
Darkness more clear than noonday holdeth her,
Silence more musical than any song;
Even her very heart has ceased to stir:
Until the morning of Eternity
Her rest shall not begin nor end, but be;
And when she wakes she will not think it long.

THE LOWEST PLACE

Give me the lowest place: not that I dare
Ask for that lowest place, but Thou hast died
That I might live and share
Thy glory by Thy side.

Give me the lowest place: or if for me
That lowest place too high, make one more low
Where I may sit and see
My God and love Thee so.

ROBERT, LORD LYTTON ["OWEN MEREDITH"] (1831–1892)

LUCILE

From CANTO III

II

Lucile de Nevers (if her riddle I read)
Was a woman of genius: whose genius, indeed,
With her life was at war. Once, but once, in that life
The chance had been hers to escape from this strife
In herself; finding peace in the life of another
From the passionate wants she, in hers, failed to smother.
But the chance fell too soon, when the crude restless power
Which had been to her nature so fatal a dower,
Only wearied the man it yet haunted and thrall'd;
And that moment, once lost, had been never recall'd.
Yet it left her heart sore: and, to shelter her heart
From approach, she then sought, in that delicate art
Of concealment, those thousand adroit strategies
Of feminine wit, which repel while they please,
A weapon, at once, and a shield, to conceal
And defend all that women can earnestly feel.
Thus, striving her instincts to hide and repress,
She felt frighten'd at times by her very success:
She pined for the hill-tops, the clouds, and the stars:
Golden wires may annoy us as much as steel bars,
If they keep us behind prison-windows: impassion'd
Her heart rose and burst the light cage she had fashion'd
Out of glittering trifles around it.
Unknown
To herself, all her instincts, without hesitation,
Embraced the idea of self-immolation.

The strong spirit in her, had her life but been blended
With some man's whose heart had her own comprehended,
All its wealth at his feet would have lavishly thrown.
For him she had struggled and striven alone;
For him had aspired; in him had transfused
All the gladness and grace of her nature; and used
For him only the spells of its delicate power:
Like the ministering fairy that brings from her bower
To some maze all the treasures, whose use the fond elf,
More enrich'd by her love, disregards for herself.
But standing apart, as she ever had done,
And her genius, which needed a vent, finding none
In the broad fields of action thrown wide to man's power,
She unconsciously made it her bulwark and tower,
And built in it her refuge, whence lightly she hurl'd
Her contempt at the fashions and forms of the world.

And the permanent cause why she now miss'd and fail'd
That firm hold upon life she so keenly assail'd,
Was, in all those diurnal occasions that place —
Say — the world and the woman opposed face to face,
Where the woman must yield, she, refusing to stir,
Offended the world, which in turn wounded her.

As before, in the old-fashion'd manner, I fit
To this character, also, its moral: to wit,
Say — the world is a nettle; disturb it, it stings:
Grasp it firmly, it stings not. On one of two things,
If you would not be stung, it behoves you to settle:
Avoid it, or crush it. She crush'd not the nettle;
For she could not; nor would she avoid it; she tried
With the weak hand of woman to thrust it aside,
And it stung her. A woman is too slight a thing
To trample the world without feeling its sting.

THE PORTRAIT

Midnight past! Not a sound of aught
 Thro' the silent house, but the wind at his prayers.
I sat by the dying fire, and thought
 Of the dear dead woman upstairs.

A night of tears! for the gusty rain
 Had ceased, but the eaves were dripping yet;
And the moon looked forth, as tho' in pain,
 With her face all white and wet:

Nobody with me, my watch to keep,
 But the friend of my bosom, the man I love:
And grief had sent him fast to sleep
 In the chamber up above.

Nobody else in the country place
 All round, that knew of my loss beside,
But the good young Priest with the Raphael-face
 Who confessed her when she died.

That good young Priest is of gentle nerve,
 And my grief had moved him beyond control;
For his lip grew white, as I could observe,
 When he speeded her parting soul.

I sat by the dreary hearth alone:
 I thought of the pleasant days of yore:
I said, "The staff of my life is gone:
 The woman I loved is no more.

"On her cold, dead bosom my portrait lies,
 Which next to her heart she used to wear —
Haunting it o'er with her tender eyes
 When my own face was not there.

"It is set all round with rubies red,
 And pearls which a Peri might have kept;
For each ruby there my heart hath bled:
 For each pearl my eyes have wept."

And I said — "The thing is precious to me:
 They will bury her soon in the churchyard clay;
It lies on her heart, and lost must be,
 If I do not take it away."

I lighted my lamp at the dying flame,
 And crept up the stairs that creak'd for fright,
Till into the chamber of death I came,
 Where she lay all in white.

The moon shone over her winding sheet.
 There, stark she lay on her carven bed;
Seven burning tapers about her feet,
 And seven about her head.

As I stretch'd my hand, I held my breath;
 I turn'd as I drew the curtains apart:
I dared not look on the face of death:
 I knew where to find her heart.

I thought, at first, as my touch fell there,
  It had warmed that heart to life, with love;
For the thing I touch'd was warm, I swear,
  And I could feel it move.

'Twas the hand of a man, that was moving slow
  O'er the heart of the dead, — from the other side:
And at once the sweat broke over my brow,
  "Who is robbing the corpse?" I cried.

Opposite me, by the tapers' light,
  The friend of my bosom, the man I loved,
Stood over the corpse, and all as white,
  And neither of us moved.

"What do you here, my friend?" . . . The man
  Look'd first at me, and then at the dead.
"There is a portrait here," he began;
  "There is. It is mine," I said.

Said the friend of my bosom, "Yours, no doubt,
  The portrait was, till a month ago,
When this suffering angel took that out,
  And placed mine there, I know."

"This woman she loved me well," said I.
  "A month ago," said my friend to me:
"And in your throat," I groaned, "you lie!"
  He answer'd . . . "Let us see."

"Enough!" I return'd, "let the dead decide:
  And whose soever the portrait prove,
His shall it be, when the cause is tried,
  Where Death is arraign'd by Love."

We found the portrait there, in its place:
  We open'd it by the tapers' shine:
The gems were all unchanged: the face
  Was — neither his nor mine.

"One nail drives out another, at least!
  The face of the portrait there," I cried,
"Is our friend's, the Raphael-faced young Priest,
  Who confess'd her when she died."

The setting is all of rubies red,
  And pearls which a Peri might have kept.
For each ruby there my heart hath bled:
  For each pearl my eyes have wept.

SIR EDWIN ARNOLD (1832–1904)

THE LIGHT OF ASIA

From BOOK I

The Mystery of Evil

But on another day the King said, "Come,
Sweet son! and see the pleasaunce of the spring,
And how the fruitful earth is wooed to yield
Its riches to the reaper; how my realm —
Which shall be thine when the pile flames for me —
Feeds all its mouths and keeps the King's chest filled.
Fair is the season with new leaves, bright blooms,
Green grass, and cries of plough-time." So they rode
Into a land of wells and gardens, where,
All up and down the rich red loam, the steers
Strained their strong shoulders in the creaking yoke
Dragging the ploughs; the fat soil rose and rolled
In smooth long waves back from the plough; who drove
Planted both feet upon the leaping share
To make the furrow deep; among the palms
The tinkle of the rippling water rang,
And where it ran the glad earth 'broidered it
With balsams and the spears of lemon-grass.
Elsewhere were sowers who went forth to sow;
And all the jungle laughed with nesting songs,
And all the thickets rustled with small life
Of lizard, bee, beetle, and creeping things
Pleased at the spring-time. In the mango-sprays
The sun-birds flashed; alone at his green forge
Toiled the loud copper-smith; bee-eaters hawked,
Chasing the purple butterflies; beneath,
Striped squirrels raced, the mynas perked and picked,
The seven brown sisters chattered in the thorn,
The pied fish-tiger hung above the pool,
The egrets stalked among the buffaloes,
The kites sailed circles in the golden air;
About the painted temple peacocks flew,
The blue doves cooed from every well, far off
The village drums beat for some marriage-feast;
All things spoke peace and plenty, and the Prince
Saw and rejoiced. But, looking deep, he saw
The thorns which grow upon this rose of life:
How the swart peasant sweated for his wage,
Toiling for leave to live; and how he urged
The great-eyed oxen through the flaming hours,
Goading their velvet flanks: then marked he, too,
How lizard fed on ant, and snake on him,
And kite on both; and how the fish-hawk robbed
The fish-tiger of that which it had seized;
The shrike chasing the bulbul, which did hunt
The jewelled butterflies; till everywhere

Each slew a slayer and in turn was slain,
Life living upon death. So the fair show
Veiled one vast, savage, grim conspiracy
Of mutual murder, from the worm to man,
Who himself kills his fellow; seeing which —
The hungry ploughman and his labouring kine,
Their dewlaps blistered with the bitter yoke,
The rage to live which makes all living strife —
The Prince Siddartha sighed. "Is this," he said,
"That happy earth they brought me forth to see?
How salt with sweat the peasant's bread! how hard
The oxen's service! in the brake how fierce
The war of weak and strong! i' th' air with plots!
No refuge e'en in water. Go aside
A space, and let me muse on what ye show."
So saying the good Lord Buddha seated him
Under a jambu-tree, with ankles crossed —
As holy statues sit — and first began
To meditate this deep disease of life,
What its far source and whence its remedy.
So vast a pity filled him, such wide love
For living things, such passion to heal pain,
That by their stress his princely spirit passed
To ecstasy, and, purged from mortal taint
Of sense and self, the boy attained thereat
Dhyâna, first step of "the path."

SIR LEWIS MORRIS (b. 1833)

AN ODE ON A FAIR SPRING MORNING

Come, friend, let us forget
The turmoil of the world a little while,
For now the soft skies smile,
The fields with flowers are set.
Let us away awhile
With fierce unrest and carking thoughts of care,
And breathe a little while the jocund air,
And sing the joyous measures sung
By those free singers, when the world was young.

For still the world is young; for still the spring
Renews itself, and still the lengthening hours
Bring back the month of flowers.
The leaves are green to-day as those of old
For Chaucer and for Shakespeare; still the gold
Of August gilds the rippling breadths of wheat;
Young maids are fair and sweet
As when they frolicked gay, with flashing feet,
Round the old May-pole. All young things rejoice.
No sorrow dulls the blackbird's mellow voice,
Thro' the clear summer dawns or twilights long.
With aspect not more dim
Thro' space the planets swim
Than of old time o'er the Chaldean plain.
We only, we alone,
Let jarring discords mar our song,
And find our music take a lower tone.
We only with dim eyes
And laboured vision feebly strain,
And flout the undying splendours of the skies.
Oh, see how glorious show,
On this fair morn in May, the clear-cut hills,
The dewy lawns, the hawthorns white,
Argent on plains of gold the growing light,
Pure as when first on the young earth
The faint warm sunlight came to birth.
There is a nameless air
Of sweet renewal over all, which fills
The earth and sky with life, and everywhere,
Before the scarce seen sun begins to glow,
The birds awake which slumbered all night long,
And with a gush of song,
First doubting of their strain, then full and wide
Raise their fresh hymns thro' all the country side;
Already, above the dewy clover,
The soaring lark begins to hover
Over his mate's low nest;
And soon, from childhood's early rest
In hall and cottage, to the casement rise
The little ones with their fresh morning eyes,
And gaze on the old Earth, which still grows new,
And see the tranquil heaven's unclouded blue,
And, since as yet no sight nor sound of toil
The fair-spread, peaceful picture comes to soil,
Look from their young and steadfast eyes
With such an artless sweet surprise
As Adam knew, when first on either hand
He saw the virgin landscapes of the morning land.

* * * * * * *

But grows the world then old?
Nay, all things that are born of time
Spring upwards, and expand from youth to prime,
Spring up from flower to fruit,
From song-tide till the days are mute,
Green blade to ear of gold.
But not the less through the eternal round
The sleep of winter wakes in days of spring,
And not the less the bare and frozen ground
Grows blithe with blooms that burst and birds that sing.
Nature is deathless; herb and tree,
Through time that has been and shall be,
Change not, although the outward form
Seem now the columned palm
Nourished in zones of calm,
And now the gnarled oak that defies the storm.
The cedar's thousand summers are no more
To her than are the fleeting petals gay
Which the young spring, ere March is o'er,
Scarce offered, takes away.
Eternal are her works. Unchanging she,
Alike in short-lived flower and ever-changing sea.

We too are deathless; we,
Eternal as the Earth,
We cannot cease to be,
While springtide comes or birth.
If our being cease to hold
Reflected lights divine
On budding lives, they day by day do shine
With unabated gold.
Though lost it may be to our mortal sight,
It cannot be that any perish quite —
Only the baser part forgets to be.
And if within the hidden Treasury
Of the great Ruler we awhile should rest,
Or issue with a higher stamp imprest,
With all our baser alloy purged and spent,
Were we not thus content?
Our thoughts too mighty are
To be within our span of years confined;
Too deep and wide and far,
The hopes, the fears, that crowd the labouring
mind;
The sorrows that oppress,
The sanctities that bless,
Are vaster than this petty stage of things.
The soaring fancy mounts on easy wings
Beyond the glimmer of the furthest star.
The watcher who with patient eye
Scans the illumined sky,
Knows when the outward rushing fire shall turn,
And in far ages hence shall brightly burn
For eyes to-day undreamt of. The clear voice
From Greece or Israel thro' the centuries heard
Still bids us tremble or rejoice,
Stronger than living look or word;
The love of home or race,
Which doth transfigure us, and seems to bring
On every heaven-lit face
Some shadow of the glory of our King,
Fades not on earth, nor with our years doth end;
Nay, even earth's poor physical powers transcend
The narrow bounds of space and time, —
The swift thought by some mystic sympathy
Speeding through desert sand, and storm-tost sea.
And shall we hold the range of mind
Is to our little lives confined;
That the pure heart in some blest sphere above,
Loves not which here was set on fire of love;
The clear eye scans not still, which here could scan
The confines of the Universal plan;
The seer nor speaks nor thinks his thoughts sublime,
And all of Homer is a speck of lime?
Nay, friend, let us forget
The conflicts of our doubt a little while,
Again our springs shall smile;
We shall not perish yet.
If God so guide our fate,
The nobler portions of ourselves shall last
Till all the lower rounds of life be past,
And we, regenerate.
We too again shall rise,
The same and not the same,
As daily rise upon the orient skies
New dawns with wheels of flame.
So, if it worthy prove,
Our being, self-perfected, shall upward move
To higher essence, and still higher grown;
Not sweeping idle harps before a throne,
Nor spending praise where is no need of praise;
But through unnumbered lives and ages come,
Of pure laborious days,
To an eternal home,
Where spring is not, nor birth, nor any dawn,
But life's full noontide never is withdrawn.

JAMES THOMSON (1834–1882)

From THE CITY OF DREADFUL NIGHT

As I came through the desert thus it was,
As I came through the desert: All was black,
In heaven no single star, on earth no track;
A brooding hush without a stir or note,
The air so thick it clotted in my throat;
And thus for hours; then some enormous things
Swooped past with savage cries and clanking wings:
But I strode on austere;
No hope could have no fear.

As I came through the desert thus it was,
As I came through the desert: Eyes of fire
Glared at me throbbing with a starved desire;
The hoarse and heavy and carnivorous breath
Was hot upon me from deep jaws of death;
Sharp claws, swift talons, fleshless fingers cold
Plucked at me from the bushes, tried to hold:
But I strode on austere;
No hope could have no fear.

As I came through the desert thus it was,
As I came through the desert: Lo you, there,
That hillock burning with a brazen glare;
Those myriad dusky flames with points a-glow
Which writhed and hissed and darted to and fro;
A Sabbath of the Serpents, heaped pell-mell
For Devil's roll-call and some fête of Hell:
Yet I strode on austere;
No hope could have no fear.

As I came through the desert thus it was,
As I came through the desert: Meteors ran
And crossed their javelins on the black sky-span;
The zenith opened to a gulf of flame,
The dreadful thunderbolts jarred earth's fixed
frame;

The ground all heaved in waves of fire that surged
And weltered round me sole there unsubmerged:
Yet I strode on austere;
No hope could have no fear.

As I came through the desert thus it was,
As I came through the desert: Air once more,
And I was close upon a wild sea-shore;
Enormous cliffs arose on either hand,
The deep tide thundered up a league-broad strand;
White foambelts seethed there, wan spray swept and flew;
The sky broke, moon and stars and clouds and blue:
And I strode on austere;
No hope could have no fear.

As I came through the desert thus it was,
As I came through the desert: On the left
The sun arose and crowned a broad crag-cleft;
There stopped and burned out black, except a rim,
A bleeding eyeless socket, red and dim;
Whereon the moon fell suddenly south-west,
And stood above the right-hand cliffs at rest:
Still I strode on austere;
No hope could have no fear.

As I came through the desert thus it was,
As I came through the desert: From the right
A shape came slowly with a ruddy light;
A woman with a red lamp in her hand,
Bareheaded and barefooted on that strand;
O desolation moving with such grace!
O anguish with such beauty in thy face!
I fell as on my bier,
Hope travailed with such fear.

As I came through the desert thus it was,
As I came through the desert: I was twain,
Two selves distinct that cannot join again;
One stood apart and knew but could not stir,
And watched the other stark in swoon and her;
And she came on, and never turned aside,
Between such sun and moon and roaring tide:
And as she came more near
My soul grew mad with fear.

As I came through the desert thus it was,
As I came through the desert: Hell is mild
And piteous matched with that accursèd wild;
A large black sign was on her breast that bowed,
A broad black band ran down her snow-white shroud;
That lamp she held was her own burning heart,
Whose blood-drops trickled step by step apart:
The mystery was clear;
Mad rage had swallowed fear.

As I came through the desert thus it was,
As I came through the desert: By the sea
She knelt and bent above that senseless me;
Those lamp-drops fell upon my white brow there,
She tried to cleanse them with her tears and hair;
She murmured words of pity, love, and woe,
She heeded not the level rushing flow:
And mad with rage and fear,
I stood stonebound so near.

As I came through the desert thus it was,
As I came through the desert: When the tide
Swept up to her there kneeling by my side,
She clasped that corpse-like me, and they were borne
Away, and this vile me was left forlorn;
I know the whole sea cannot quench that heart,
Or cleanse that brow, or wash those two apart:
They love; their doom is drear,
Yet they nor hope nor fear;
But I, what do I here?

From SUNDAY UP THE RIVER

XV

Give a man a horse he can ride,
Give a man a boat he can sail;
And his rank and wealth, his strength and health,
On sea nor shore shall fail.

Give a man a pipe he can smoke,
Give a man a book he can read;
And his home is bright with a calm delight,
Though the room be poor indeed.

Give a man a girl he can love,
As I, O my Love, love thee;
And his heart is great with the pulse of Fate,
At home, on land, on sea.

XVIII

The wine of Love is music,
And the feast of Love is song:
And when Love sits down to the banquet,
Love sits long:

Sits long and ariseth drunken,
But not with the feast and the wine;
He reeleth with his own heart,
That great rich Vine.

ART

I

What precious thing are you making fast
  In all these silken lines?
And where and to whom will it go at last?
  Such subtle knots and twines!

I am tying up all my love in this,
  With all its hopes and fears,
With all its anguish and all its bliss,
  And its hours as heavy as years.

I am going to send it afar, afar,
  To I know not where above;
To that sphere beyond the highest star
  Where dwells the soul of my Love.

But in vain, in vain, would I make it fast
  With countless subtle twines;
For ever its fire breaks out at last,
  And shrivels all the lines.

II

If you have a carrier-dove
  That can fly over land and sea;
And a message for your Love,
  "Lady, I love but thee!"

And this dove will never stir
  But straight from her to you,
And straight from you to her;
  As you know and she knows too.

Will you first ensure, O sage,
  Your dove that never tires
With your message in a cage,
  Though a cage of golden wires?

Or will you fling your dove:
  "Fly, darling, without rest,
Over land and sea to my Love,
  And fold your wings in her breast?"

III

Singing is sweet; but be sure of this,
Lips only sing when they cannot kiss.

Did he ever suspire a tender lay
While her presence took his breath away?

Had his fingers been able to toy with her hair
Would they then have written the verses fair?

Had she let his arm steal round her waist
Would the lovely portrait yet be traced?

Since he could not embrace it flushed and warm
He has carved in stone the perfect form.

Who gives the fine report of the feast?
He who got none and enjoyed it least.

Were the wine really slipping down his throat
Would his song of the wine advance a note?

Will you puff out the music that sways the whirl,
Or dance and make love with a pretty girl?

Who shall the great battle-story write?
Not the hero down in the thick of the fight.

Statues and pictures and verse may be grand,
But they are not the Life for which they stand.

WILLIAM MORRIS (1834–1896)

THE EARTHLY PARADISE

  Of Heaven or Hell I have no power to sing,
I cannot ease the burden of your fears,
Or make quick-coming death a little thing,
Or bring again the pleasure of past years,
Nor for my words shall ye forget your tears,
Or hope again for aught that I can say,
The idle singer of an empty day.

  But rather, when aweary of your mirth,
From full hearts still unsatisfied ye sigh,
And, feeling kindly unto all the earth,
Grudge every minute as it passes by,
Made the more mindful that the sweet days die —
— Remember me a little then, I pray,
The idle singer of an empty day.

  The heavy trouble, the bewildering care
That weighs us down who live and earn our bread,
These idle verses have no power to bear;
So let me sing of names rememberèd,
Because they, living not, can ne'er be dead,
Or long time take their memory quite away
From us poor singers of an empty day.

  Dreamer of dreams, born out of my due time,
Why should I strive to set the crooked straight?
Let it suffice me that my murmuring rhyme
Beats with light wing against the ivory gate,
Telling a tale not too importunate
To those who in the sleepy region stay,
Lulled by the singer of an empty day.

  Folk say, a wizard to a northern king
At Christmas-tide such wondrous things did show,
That through one window men beheld the spring,
And through another saw the summer glow,

And through a third the fruited vines a-row,
While still, unheard, but in its wonted way,
Piped the drear wind of that December day.

So with this Earthly Paradise it is,
If ye will read aright, and pardon me,
Who strive to build a shadowy isle of bliss
Midmost the beating of the steely sea,
Where tossed about all hearts of men must be;
Whose ravening monsters mighty men shall slay,
Not the poor singer of an empty day.

PROLOGUE

Forget six counties overhung with smoke,
Forget the snorting steam and piston stroke,
Forget the spreading of the hideous town;
Think rather of the pack-horse on the down,
And dream of London, small, and white, and clean,
The clear Thames bordered by its gardens green;
Think, that below bridge the green lapping waves
Smite some few keels that bear Levantine staves,
Cut from the yew wood on the burnt-up hill,
And pointed jars that Greek hands toiled to fill,
And treasured scanty spice from some far sea,
Florence gold cloth, and Ypres napery,
And cloth of Bruges, and hogsheads of Guienne;
While nigh the thronged wharf Geoffrey Chaucer's pen
Moves over bills of lading — mid such times
Shall dwell the hollow puppets of my rhymes.

A nameless city in a distant sea,
White as the changing walls of faerie,
Thronged with much people clad in ancient guise
I now am fain to set before your eyes;
There, leave the clear green water and the quays,
And pass betwixt its marble palaces,
Until ye come unto the chiefest square;
A bubbling conduit is set midmost there,
And round about it now the maidens throng,
With jest and laughter, and sweet broken song,
Making but light of labour new begun
While in their vessels gleams the morning sun.
On one side of the square a temple stands,
Wherein the gods worshipped in ancient lands
Still have their altars; a great market-place
Upon two other sides fills all the space,
And thence the busy hum of men comes forth;
But on the cold side looking toward the north
A pillared council-house may you behold,
Within whose porch are images of gold,
Gods of the nations who dwelt anciently
About the borders of the Grecian sea.
Pass now between them, push the brazen door,
And standing on the polished marble floor
Leave all the noises of the square behind;
Most calm that reverent chamber shall ye find,
Silent at first, but for the noise you made
When on the brazen door your hand you laid
To shut it after you — but now behold
The city rulers on their thrones of gold,
Clad in most fair attire, and in their hands
Long carven silver-banded ebony wands;
Then from the dais drop your eyes and see
Soldiers and peasants standing reverently
Before those elders, round a little band
Who bear such arms as guard the English land,
But battered, rent, and rusted sore and they,
The men themselves, are shrivelled, bent, and grey;
And as they lean with pain upon their spears
Their brows seem furrowed deep with more than years;
For sorrow dulls their heavy sunken eyes;
Bent are they less with time than miseries.

THE LADY OF THE LAND

It happened once, some men of Italy
Midst the Greek Islands went a sea-roving,
And much good fortune had they on the sea:
Of many a man they had the ransoming,
And many a chain they gat, and goodly thing;
And midst their voyage to an isle they came,
Whereof my story keepeth not the name.

Now though but little was there left to gain,
Because the richer folk had gone away,
Yet since by this of water they were fain
They came to anchor in a land-locked bay,
Whence in a while some went ashore to play,
Going but lightly armed in twos or threes,
For midst that folk they feared no enemies.

And of these fellows that thus went ashore,
One was there who left all his friends behind;
Who going inland ever more and more,
And being left quite alone, at last did find
A lonely valley sheltered from the wind,
Wherein, amidst an ancient cypress wood,
A long-deserted ruined castle stood.

The wood, once ordered in fair grove and glade,
With gardens overlooked by terraces,
And marble-pavèd pools for pleasure made,
Was tangled now, and choked with fallen trees;
And he who went there, with but little ease
Must stumble by the stream's side, once made meet
For tender women's dainty wandering feet.

The raven's croak, the low wind choked and drear,
The baffled stream, the grey wolf's doleful cry,
Were all the sounds that mariner could hear,
As through the wood he wandered painfully;
But as unto the house he drew anigh,
The pillars of a ruined shrine he saw,
The once fair temple of a fallen law.

No image was there left behind to tell
Before whose face the knees of men had bowed;
An altar of black stone, of old wrought well,
Alone beneath a ruined roof now showed
The goal whereto the folk were wont to crowd,
Seeking for things forgotten long ago,
Praying for heads long ages laid a-low.

Close to the temple was the castle-gate,
Doorless and crumbling; there our fellow turned,
Trembling indeed at what might chance to wait
The prey entrapped, yet with a heart that burned
To know the most of what might there be learned,
And hoping somewhat too, amid his fear,
To light on such things as all men hold dear.

Noble the house was, nor seemed built for war,
But rather like the work of other days,
When men, in better peace than now they are,
Had leisure on the world around to gaze,
And noted well the past times' changing ways;
And fair with sculptured stories it was wrought,
By lapse of time unto dim ruin brought.

Now as he looked about on all these things,
And strove to read the mouldering histories,
Above the door an image with wide wings,
Whose unclad limbs a serpent seemed to seize,
He dimly saw, although the western breeze,
And years of biting frost and washing rain,
Had made the carver's labour well-nigh vain.

But this, though perished sore, and worn away,
He noted well, because it seemed to be,
After the fashion of another day,
Some great man's badge of war, or armoury;
And round it a carved wreath he seemed to see:
But taking note of these things, at the last
The mariner beneath the gateway passed.

And there a lovely cloistered court he found,
A fountain in the midst o'erthrown and dry,
And in the cloister briers twining round
The slender shafts; the wondrous imagery
Outworn by more than many years gone by;
Because the country people, in their fear
Of wizardry, had wrought destruction here;

And piteously these fair things had been maimed;
There stood great Jove, lacking his head of might,
Here was the archer, swift Apollo, lamed;
The shapely limbs of Venus hid from sight
By weeds and shards; Diana's ankles light
Bound with the cable of some coasting ship;
And rusty nails through Helen's maddening lip.

Therefrom unto the chambers did he pass,
And found them fair still, midst of their decay,
Though in them now no sign of man there was,
And everything but stone had passed away
That made them lovely in that vanished day;
Nay, the mere walls themselves would soon be gone
And nought be left but heaps of mouldering stone.

But he, when all the place he had gone o'er,
And with much trouble clomb the broken stair,
And from the topmost turret seen the shore
And his good ship drawn up at anchor there,
Came down again, and found a crypt most fair
Built wonderfully beneath the greatest hall,
And there he saw a door within the wall,

Well-hinged, close shut; nor was there in that place
Another on its hinges, therefore he
Stood there and pondered for a little space,
And thought, "Perchance some marvel I shall see,
For surely here some dweller there must be,
Because this door seems whole, and new, and sound,
While nought but ruin I can see around."

So with that word, moved by a strong desire,
He tried the hasp, that yielded to his hand,
And in a strange place, lit as by a fire
Unseen but near, he presently did stand;
And by an odorous breeze his face was fanned,
As though in some Arabian plain he stood,
Anigh the border of a spice-tree wood.

He moved not for awhile, but looking round,
He wondered much to see the place so fair,
Because, unlike the castle above ground,
No pillager or wrecker had been there;
It seemed that time had passed on otherwhere,
Nor laid a finger on this hidden place,
Rich with the wealth of some forgotten race.

With hangings, fresh as when they left the loom,
The walls were hung a space above the head,
Slim ivory chairs were set about the room,
And in one corner was a dainty bed,

That seemed for some fair queen apparellèd;
And marble was the worst stone of the floor,
That with rich Indian webs was covered o'er.

The wanderer trembled when he saw all this,
Because he deemed by magic it was wrought;
Yet in his heart a longing for some bliss,
Whereof the hard and changing world knows nought,
Arose and urged him on, and dimmed the thought
That there perchance some devil lurked to slay
The heedless wanderer from the light of day.

Over against him was another door
Set in the wall; so, casting fear aside,
With hurried steps he crossed the varied floor,
And there again the silver latch he tried
And with no pain the door he opened wide,
And entering the new chamber cautiously
The glory of great heaps of gold could see.

Upon the floor uncounted medals lay,
Like things of little value; here and there
Stood golden caldrons, that might well outweigh
The biggest midst an emperor's copper-ware,
And golden cups were set on tables fair,
Themselves of gold; and in all hollow things
Were stored great gems, worthy the crowns of kings.

The walls and roof with gold were overlaid,
And precious raiment from the wall hung down;
The fall of kings that treasure might have stayed,
Or gained some longing conqueror great renown,
Or built again some god-destroyed old town;
What wonder, if this plunderer of the sea
Stood gazing at it long and dizzily?

But at the last his troubled eyes and dazed
He lifted from the glory of that gold,
And then the image, that well-nigh erased
Over the castle-gate he did behold,
Above a door well wrought in coloured gold
Again he saw; a naked girl with wings
Enfolded in a serpent's scaly rings.

And even as his eyes were fixed on it
A woman's voice came from the other side,
And through his heart strange hopes began to flit
That in some wondrous land he might abide
Not dying, master of a deathless bride,
So o'er the gold which now he scarce could see
He went, and passed this last door eagerly.

Then in a room he stood wherein there was
A marble bath, whose brimming water yet
Was scarcely still; a vessel of green glass
Half full of odorous ointment was there set
Upon the topmost step that still was wet,
And jewelled shoes and women's dainty gear,
Lay cast upon the varied pavement near.

In one quick glance these things his eyes did see,
But speedily they turned round to behold
Another sight, for throned on ivory
There sat a woman, whose wet tresses rolled
On to the floor in waves of gleaming gold,
Cast back from such a form as, erewhile shown
To one poor shepherd, lighted up Troy town.

Naked she was, the kisses of her feet
Upon the floor a dying path had made
From the full bath unto her ivory seat;
In her right hand, upon her bosom laid,
She held a golden comb, a mirror weighed
Her left hand down, aback her fair head lay
Dreaming awake of some long vanished day.

Her eyes were shut, but she seemed not to sleep,
Her lips were murmuring things unheard and low,
Or sometimes twitched as though she needs must weep
Though from her eyes the tears refused to flow,
And oft with heavenly red her cheek did glow,
As if remembrance of some half-sweet shame
Across the web of many memories came.

There stood the man, scarce daring to draw breath
For fear the lovely sight should fade away;
Forgetting heaven, forgetting life and death,
Trembling for fear lest something he should say
Unwitting, lest some sob should yet betray
His presence there, for to his eager eyes
Already did the tears begin to rise.

But as he gazed, she moved, and with a sigh
Bent forward, dropping down her golden head;
"Alas, alas! another day gone by,
Another day and no soul come," she said;
"Another year, and still I am not dead!"
And with that word once more her head she raised,
And on the trembling man with great eyes gazed.

Then he imploring hands to her did reach,
And toward her very slowly 'gan to move
And with wet eyes her pity did beseech,
And seeing her about to speak, he strove

From trembling lips to utter words of love;
But with a look she stayed his doubtful feet, 216
And made sweet music as their eyes did meet.

For now she spoke in gentle voice and clear,
Using the Greek tongue that he knew full well;
"What man art thou, that thus hast wandered here,
And found this lonely chamber where I dwell?
Beware, beware! for I have many a spell;
If greed of power and gold have led thee on,
Not lightly shall this untold wealth be won. 224

"But if thou com'st here, knowing of my tale,
In hope to bear away my body fair,
Stout must thine heart be, nor shall that avail
If thou a wicked soul in thee dost bear;
So once again I bid thee to beware,
Because no base man things like this may see,
And live thereafter long and happily." 231

"Lady," he said, "in Florence is my home,
And in my city noble is my name;
Neither on peddling voyage am I come,
But, like my fathers, bent to gather fame;
And though thy face has set my heart a-flame
Yet of thy story nothing do I know,
But here have wandered heedlessly enow. 238

"But since the sight of thee mine eyes did bless,
What can I be but thine? what wouldst thou have?
From those thy words, I deem from some distress
By deeds of mine thy dear life I might save;
O then, delay not! if one ever gave
His life to any, mine I give to thee;
Come, tell me what the price of love must be? 245

"Swift death, to be with thee a day and night
And with the earliest dawning to be slain?
Or better, a long year of great delight,
And many years of misery and pain?
Or worse, and this poor hour for all my gain?
A sorry merchant am I on this day,
E'en as thou willest so must I obey." 252

She said, "What brave words! nought divine am I,
But an unhappy and unheard-of maid
Compelled by evil fate and destiny
To live, who long ago should have been laid
Under the earth within the cypress shade.
Hearken awhile, and quickly shalt thou know
What deed I pray thee to accomplish now. 259

"God grant indeed thy words are not for nought!
Then shalt thou save me, since for many a day
To such a dreadful life I have been brought:
Nor will I spare with all my heart to pay
What man soever takes my grief away;
Ah! I will love thee, if thou lovest me
But well enough my saviour now to be. 266

"My father lived a many years agone
Lord of this land, master of all cunning,
Who ruddy gold could draw from out grey stone,
And gather wealth from many an uncouth thing;
He made the wilderness rejoice and sing,
And such a leech he was that none could say
Without his word what soul should pass away. 273

"Unto Diana such a gift he gave,
Goddess above, below, and on the earth,
That I should be her virgin and her slave
From the first hour of my most wretched birth;
Therefore my life had known but little mirth
When I had come unto my twentieth year
And the last time of hallowing drew anear. 280

"So in her temple had I lived and died
And all would long ago have passed away,
But ere that time came, did strange things betide,
Whereby I am alive unto this day;
Alas, the bitter words that I must say!
Ah! can I bring my wretched tongue to tell
How I was brought unto this fearful hell? 287

"A queen I was, what gods I knew I loved,
And nothing evil was there in my thought,
And yet by love my wretched heart was moved
Until to utter ruin I was brought!
Alas! thou sayest our gods were vain and nought;
Wait, wait, till thou hast heard this tale of mine,
Then shalt thou think them devilish or divine. 294

"Hearken! in spite of father and of vow
I loved a man; but for that sin I think
Men had forgiven me — yea, yea, even thou;
But from the gods the full cup must I drink,
And into misery unheard of sink, 299
Tormented, when their own names are forgot,
And men must doubt e'er if they lived or not.

"Glorious my lover was unto my sight,
Most beautiful, — of love we grew so fain
That we at last agreed, that on a night
We should be happy, but that he were slain
Or shut in hold; and neither joy nor pain
Should else forbid that hoped-for time to be; 307
So came the night that made a wretch of me.

"Ah! well do I remember all that night,
When through the window shone the orb of June,
And by the bed flickered the taper's light,
Whereby I trembled, gazing at the moon:
Ah me! the meeting that we had, when soon
Into his strong, well-trusted arms I fell,
And many a sorrow we began to tell.

"Ah me! what parting on that night we had!
I think the story of my great despair
A little while might merry folk make sad;
For, as he swept away my yellow hair
To make my shoulder and my bosom bare,
I raised mine eyes, and shuddering could behold
A shadow cast upon the bed of gold:

"Then suddenly was quenched my hot desire
And he untwined his arms; the moon so pale
A while ago, seemed changed to blood and fire,
And yet my limbs beneath me did not fail,
And neither had I strength to cry or wail,
But stood there helpless, bare, and shivering,
With staring eyes still fixed upon the thing.

"Because the shade that on the bed of gold
The changed and dreadful moon was throwing down
Was of Diana, whom I did behold,
With knotted hair, and shining girt-up gown,
And on the high white brow, a deadly frown
Bent upon us, who stood scarce drawing breath,
Striving to meet the horrible sure death.

"No word at all the dreadful goddess said,
But soon across my feet my lover lay,
And well indeed I knew that he was dead;
And would that I had died on that same day!
For in a while the image turned away,
And without words my doom I understood,
And felt a horror change my human blood.

"And there I fell, and on the floor I lay
By the dead man, till daylight came on me,
And not a word thenceforward could I say
For three years; till of grief and misery,
The lingering pest, the cruel enemy,
My father and his folk were dead and gone,
And in this castle I was left alone:

"And then the doom foreseen upon me fell,
For Queen Diana did my body change
Into a fork-tongued dragon, flesh and fell,
And through the island nightly do I range,
Or in the green sea mate with monsters strange,
When in the middle of the moonlit night
The sleepy mariner I do affright.

"But all day long upon this gold I lie
Within this place, where never mason's hand
Smote trowel on the marble noisily;
Drowsy I lie, no folk at my command,
Who once was called the Lady of the Land;
Who might have bought a kingdom with a kiss,
Yea, half the world with such a sight as this."

And therewithal, with rosy fingers light,
Backward her heavy-hanging hair she threw,
To give her naked beauty more to sight;
But when, forgetting all the things he knew,
Maddened with love unto the prize he drew,
She cried, "Nay, wait! for wherefore wilt thou die,
Why should we not be happy, thou and I?

"Wilt thou not save me? once in every year
This rightful form of mine that thou dost see
By favour of the goddess have I here
From sunrise unto sunset given me,
That some brave man may end my misery.
And thou — art thou not brave? can thy heart fail,
Whose eyes e'en now are weeping at my tale?

"Then listen! when this day is overpast,
A fearful monster shall I be again,
And thou mayst be my saviour at the last;
Unless, once more, thy words are nought and vain.
If thou of love and sovereignty art fain,
Come thou next morn, and when thou seest here
A hideous dragon, have thereof no fear,

"But take the loathsome head up in thine hands,
And kiss it, and be master presently
Of twice the wealth that is in all the lands
From Cathay to the head of Italy;
And master also, if it pleaseth thee,
Of all thou praisest as so fresh and bright,
Of what thou callest crown of all delight.

"Ah! with what joy then shall I see again
The sunlight on the green grass and the trees,
And hear the clatter of the summer rain,
And see the joyous folk beyond the seas.
Ah, me! to hold my child upon my knees,
After the weeping of unkindly tears,
And all the wrongs of these four hundred years.

"Go now, go quick! leave this grey heap of stone;
And from thy glad heart think upon thy way,
How I shall love thee — yea, love thee alone,
That bringest me from dark death unto day;
For this shall be thy wages and thy pay;
Unheard-of wealth, unheard-of love is near,
If thou hast heart a little dread to bear."

Therewith she turned to go; but he cried out,
"Ah! wilt thou leave me then without one kiss,
To slay the very seeds of fear and doubt,
That glad to-morrow may bring certain bliss?
Hast thou forgotten how love lives by this,
The memory of some hopeful close embrace, 412
Low whispered words within some lonely place?"

But she, when his bright glittering eyes she saw,
And burning cheeks, cried out, "Alas, alas!
Must I be quite undone, and wilt thou draw
A worse fate on me than the first one was?
O haste thee from this fatal place to pass!
Yet, ere thou goest, take this, lest thou shouldst deem
Thou hast been fooled by some strange midday dream." 420

So saying, blushing like a new-kissed maid,
From off her neck a little gem she drew,
That, 'twixt those snowy rose-tinged hillocks laid,
The secrets of her glorious beauty knew;
And ere he well perceived what she would do,
She touched his hand, the gem within it lay,
And, turning, from his sight she fled away. 427

Then at the doorway where her rosy heel
Had glanced and vanished, he awhile did stare,
And still upon his hand he seemed to feel
The varying kisses of her fingers fair;
Then turned he toward the dreary crypt and bare,
And dizzily throughout the castle passed,
Till by the ruined fane he stood at last. 434

Then weighing still the gem within his hand,
He stumbled backward through the cypress wood,
Thinking the while of some strange lovely land,
Where all his life should be most fair and good
Till on the valley's wall of hills he stood,
And slowly thence passed down unto the bay
Red with the death of that bewildering day. 441

The next day came, and he, who all the night
Had ceaselessly been turning in his bed,
Arose and clad himself in armour bright,
And many a danger he rememberèd;
Storming of towns, lone sieges full of dread,
That with renown his heart had borne him through
And this thing seemed a little thing to do. 448

So on he went, and on the way he thought
Of all the glorious things of yesterday,
Nought of the price whereat they must be bought,
But ever to himself did softly say,
"No roaming now, my wars are passed away;
No long dull days devoid of happiness, 454
When such a love my yearning heart shall bless."

Thus to the castle did he come at last,
But when unto the gateway he drew near,
And underneath its ruined archway passed
Into a court, a strange noise did he hear,
And through his heart there shot a pang of fear;
Trembling, he gat his sword into his hand,
And midmost of the cloisters took his stand. 462

But for a while that unknown noise increased,
A rattling, that with strident roars did blend,
And whining moans; but suddenly it ceased,
A fearful thing stood at the cloister's end,
And eyed him for a while, then 'gan to wend
Adown the cloisters, and began again 468
That rattling, and the moan like fiends in pain.

And as it came on towards him, with its teeth
The body of a slain goat did it tear,
The blood whereof in its hot jaws did seethe,
And on its tongue he saw the smoking hair;
Then his heart sank, and standing trembling there,
Throughout his mind wild thoughts and fearful ran,
"Some fiend she was," he said, "the bane of man." 476

Yet he abode her still, although his blood
Curdled within him: the thing dropped the goat,
And creeping on, came close to where he stood,
And raised its head to him, and wrinkled throat,
Then he cried out and wildly at her smote,
Shutting his eyes, and turned and from the place
Ran swiftly, with a white and ghastly face. 483

But little things rough stones and tree-trunks seemed,
And if he fell, he rose and ran on still;
No more he felt his hurts than if he dreamed,
He made no stay for valley or steep hill,
Heedless he dashed through many a foaming rill,
Until he came unto the ship at last
And with no word into the deep hold passed. 490

Meanwhile the dragon, seeing him clean gone,
Followed him not, but crying horribly,
Caught up within her jaws a block of stone
And ground it into powder, then turned she,
With cries that folk could hear far out at sea,
And reached the treasure set apart of old,
To brood above the hidden heaps of gold.

Yet was she seen again on many a day
By some half-waking mariner, or herd,
Playing amid the ripples of the bay,
Or on the hills making all things afeard,
Or in the wood, that did that castle gird,
But never any man again durst go
To seek her woman's form, and end her woe.

As for the man, who knows what things he bore?
What mournful faces peopled the sad night,
What wailings vexed him with reproaches sore,
What images of that nigh-gained delight!
What dreamed caresses from soft hands and white,
Turning to horrors ere they reached the best:
What struggles vain, what shame, what huge unrest?

No man he knew, three days he lay and raved,
And cried for death, until a lethargy
Fell on him, and his fellows thought him saved;
But on the third night he awoke to die;
And at Byzantium doth his body lie
Between two blossoming pomegranate trees,
Within the churchyard of the Genoese.

ALFRED AUSTIN (b. 1835)

PRIMROSES

I

Latest, earliest, of the year,
Primroses that still were here,
Snugly nestling round the boles
Of the cut-down chestnut poles,
When December's tottering tread
Rustled 'mong the deep leaves dead,
And with confident young faces
Peeped from out the sheltered places
When pale January lay
In its cradle day by day,
Dead or living, hard to say;
Now that mid-March blows and blusters,
Out you steal in tufts and clusters,
Making leafless lane and wood
Vernal with your hardihood.
Other lovely things are rare,
You are prodigal as fair.
First you come by ones, and ones,
Lastly in battalions;
Skirmish along hedge and bank,
Turn old Winter's wavering flank;
Round his flying footsteps hover,
Seize on hollow, ridge, and cover,
Leave nor slope nor hill unharried,
Till, his snowy trenches carried,
O'er his sepulchre you laugh,
Winter's joyous epitaph.

II

This, too, be your glory great,
Primroses, you do not wait,
As the other flowers do,
For the Spring to smile on you,
But with coming are content,
Asking no encouragement.
Ere the hardy crocus cleaves
Sunny borders 'neath the eaves;
Ere the thrush his song rehearse,
Sweeter than all poets' verse;
Ere the early bleating lambs
Cling like shadows to their dams;
Ere the blackthorn breaks to white,
Snowy-hooded anchorite;
Out from every hedge you look,
You are bright by every brook,
Wearing for your sole defence
Fearlessness of innocence.
While the daffodils still waver,
Ere the jonquil gets its savour;
While the linnets yet but pair,
You are fledged, and everywhere.
Nought can daunt you, nought distress,
Neither cold nor sunlessness.
You, when Lent sleet flies apace,
Look the tempest in the face
As descend the flakes more slow,
From your eyelids shake the snow,
And, when all the clouds have flown,
Meet the sun's smile with your own.
Nothing ever makes you less
Gracious to ungraciousness.
March may bluster up and down,
Pettish April sulk and frown;
Closer to their skirts you cling,
Coaxing Winter to be Spring.

III

Then, when your sweet task is done,
And the wild-flowers, one by one,
Here, there, everywhere do blow,
Primroses, you haste to go,

Satisfied with what you bring,
Fading morning-stars of Spring.
You have brightened doubtful days,
You have sweetened long delays,
Fooling our enchanted reason
To miscalculate the season.
But when doubt and fear are fled,
When the kine leave wintry shed,
And 'mong grasses green and tall
Find their fodder, make their stall;
When the wintering swallow flies
Homeward back from southern skies,
To the dear old cottage thatch
Where it loves to build and hatch,
That its young may understand,
Nor forget, this English land;
When the cuckoo, mocking rover,
Laughs that April loves are over;
When the hawthorn, all ablow,
Mimics the defeated snow;
Then you give one last look round,
Stir the sleepers underground,
Call the campion to awake,
Tell the speedwell courage take,
Bid the eyebright have no fear,
Whisper in the bluebell's ear
Time has come for it to flood
With its blue waves all the wood,
Mind the stitchwort of its pledge
To replace you in the hedge,
Bid the ladysmocks good-bye,
Close your bonnie lids and die;
And, without one look of blame,
Go as gently as you came.

ALGERNON CHARLES SWINBURNE
(b. 1837)

CHORUS FROM ATALANTA IN CALYDON

When the hounds of spring are on winter's traces,
  The mother of months in meadow or plain
Fills the shadows and windy places
  With lisp of leaves and ripple of rain;
And the brown bright nightingale amorous
Is half assuaged for Itylus,
For the Thracian ships and the foreign faces,
  The tongueless vigil, and all the pain.

Come with bows bent and with emptying of quivers,
  Maiden most perfect, lady of light,
With a noise of winds and many rivers,
  With a clamour of waters, and with might;
Bind on thy sandals, O thou most fleet,
Over the splendour and speed of thy feet;
For the faint east quickens, the wan west shivers,
  Round the feet of the day and the feet of the night.

Where shall we find her, how shall we sing to her,
  Fold our hands round her knees, and cling?
O that man's heart were as fire and could spring to her,
  Fire, or the strength of the streams that spring!
For the stars and the winds are unto her
As raiment, as songs of the harp-player;
For the risen stars and the fallen cling to her,
  And the southwest-wind and the west-wind sing.

For winter's rains and ruins are over,
  And all the season of snows and sins;
The days dividing lover and lover,
  The light that loses, the night that wins;
And time remember'd is grief forgotten,
And frosts are slain and flowers begotten,
And in green underwood and cover
  Blossom by blossom the spring begins.

The full streams feed on flower of rushes,
  Ripe grasses trammel a travelling foot,
The faint fresh flame of the young year flushes
  From leaf to flower and flower to fruit;
And fruit and leaf are as gold and fire,
And the oat is heard above the lyre,
And the hoofèd heel of a satyr crushes
  The chestnut-husk at the chestnut-root.

And Pan by noon and Bacchus by night,
  Fleeter of foot than the fleet-foot kid,
Follows with dancing and fills with delight
  The Mænad and the Bassarid;
And soft as lips that laugh and hide
The laughing leaves of the trees divide,
And screen from seeing and leave in sight
  The god pursuing, the maiden hid.

The ivy falls with the Bacchanal's hair
  Over her eyebrows hiding her eyes;
The wild vine slipping down leaves bare
  Her bright breast shortening into sighs;
The wild vine slips with the weight of its leaves,
But the berried ivy catches and cleaves
To the limbs that glitter, the feet that scare
  The wolf that follows, the fawn that flies.

THE GARDEN OF PROSERPINE

Here, where the world is quiet;
  Here, where all trouble seems
Dead winds' and spent waves' riot
  In doubtful dreams of dreams;

I watch the green field growing
For reaping folk and sowing,
For harvest-time and mowing,
  A sleepy world of streams.

I am tired of tears and laughter,
  And men that laugh and weep;
Of what may come hereafter
  For men that sow to reap:
I am weary of days and hours,
Blown buds of barren flowers,
Desires and dreams and powers
  And everything but sleep.

Here life has death for neighbour,
  And far from eye or ear
Wan waves and wet winds labour,
  Weak ships and spirits steer;
They drive adrift, and whither
They wot not who make thither;
But no such winds blow hither,
  And no such things grow here.

No growth of moor or coppice,
  No heather-flower or vine,
But bloomless buds of poppies,
  Green grapes of Proserpine,
Pale beds of blowing rushes,
Where no leaf blooms or blushes
Save this whereout she crushes
  For dead men deadly wine.

Pale, without name or number,
  In fruitless fields of corn,
They bow themselves and slumber
  All night till light is born;
And like a soul belated,
In hell and heaven unmated,
By cloud and mist abated
  Comes out of darkness morn.

Though one were strong as seven,
  He too with death shall dwell,
Nor wake with wings in heaven,
  Nor weep for pains in hell;
Though one were fair as roses,
His beauty clouds and closes;
And well though love reposes,
  In the end it is not well.

Pale, beyond porch and portal,
  Crowned with calm leaves, she stands
Who gathers all things mortal
  With cold immortal hands;
Her languid lips are sweeter
Than love's who fears to greet her
To men that mix and meet her
  From many times and lands.

She waits for each and other,
  She waits for all men born;
Forgets the earth her mother,
  The life of fruits and corn;
And spring and seed and swallow
Take wing for her and follow
Where summer song rings hollow
  And flowers are put to scorn.

There go the loves that wither,
  The old loves with wearier wings;
And all dead years draw thither,
  And all disastrous things;
Dead dreams of days forsaken,
Blind buds that snows have shaken,
Wild leaves that winds have taken,
  Red strays of ruined springs.

We are not sure of sorrow,
  And joy was never sure;
To-day will die to-morrow;
  Time stoops to no man's lure;
And love, grown faint and fretful,
With lips but half regretful
Sighs, and with eyes forgetful
  Weeps that no loves endure.

From too much love of living,
  From hope and fear set free,
We thank with brief thanksgiving
  Whatever gods may be
That no life lives forever;
That dead men rise up never;
That even the weariest river
  Winds somewhere safe to sea.

Then star nor sun shall waken,
  Nor any change of light:
Nor sound of waters shaken,
  Nor any sound or sight:
Nor wintry leaves nor vernal,
Nor days nor things diurnal;
Only the sleep eternal
  In an eternal night.

ITYLUS

Swallow, my sister, O sister swallow,
  How can thine heart be full of the spring?
    A thousand summers are over and dead.
What hast thou found in the spring to follow?
  What hast thou found in thy heart to sing?
    What wilt thou do when the summer is shed?

O swallow, sister, O fair swift swallow,
Why wilt thou fly after spring to the south,
The soft south whither thine heart is set?
Shall not the grief of the old time follow?
Shall not the song thereof cleave to thy mouth?
Hast thou forgotten ere I forget?

Sister, my sister, O fleet sweet swallow,
Thy way is long to the sun and the south;
But I, fulfill'd of my heart's desire,
Shedding my song upon height, upon hollow,
From tawny body and sweet small mouth
Feed the heart of the night with fire.

I the nightingale all spring through,
O swallow, sister, O changing swallow,
All spring through till the spring be done,
Clothed with the light of the night on the dew,
Sing, while the hours and the wild birds follow,
Take flight and follow and find the sun.

Sister, my sister, O soft light swallow,
Though all things feast in the spring's guest-chamber,
How hast thou heart to be glad thereof yet?
For where thou fliest I shall not follow,
Till life forget and death remember,
Till thou remember and I forget.

Swallow, my sister, O singing swallow,
I know not how thou hast heart to sing.
Hast thou the heart? is it all past over?
Thy lord the summer is good to follow,
And fair the feet of thy lover the spring:
But what wilt thou say to the spring thy lover?

O swallow, sister, O fleeting swallow,
My heart in me is a molten ember
And over my head the waves have met.
But thou wouldst tarry or I would follow
Could I forget or thou remember,
Couldst thou remember and I forget.

O sweet stray sister, O shifting swallow,
The heart's division divideth us.
Thy heart is light as a leaf of a tree;
But mine goes forth among sea-gulfs hollow
To the place of the slaying of Itylus,
The feast of Daulis, the Thracian sea.

O swallow, sister, O rapid swallow,
I pray thee sing not a little space.
Are not the roofs and the lintels wet?
The woven web that was plain to follow,
The small slain body, the flower-like face,
Can I remember if thou forget?

O sister, sister, thy first-begotten:
The hands that cling and the feet that follow,
The voice of the child's blood crying yet,
Who hath remember'd me? who hath forgotten?
Thou hast forgotten, O summer swallow,
But the world shall end when I forget.

From HERTHA

I am that which began;
Out of me the years roll;
Out of me God and man;
I am equal and whole;
God changes, and man, and the form of them bodily; I am the soul.

Before ever land was,
Before ever the sea,
Or soft hair of the grass,
Or fair limbs of the tree,
Or the flesh-coloured fruit of my branches, I was, and thy soul was in me.

* * * * * * *

Beside or above me
Naught is there to go;
Love or unlove me,
Unknow me or know;
I am that which unloves me and loves; I am stricken, and I am the blow.

* * * * * * *

I am that thing which blesses
My spirit elate;
That which caresses
With hands uncreate
My limbs unbegotten that measure the length of the measure of fate.

But what thing dost thou now,
Looking Godward, to cry,
"I am I, thou art thou;
I am low, thou art high"?
I am thou, whom thou seekest to find him: find thou but thyself, thou art I.

I the grain and the furrow,
The plough-cloven clod
And the plough-share drawn thorough,
The germ and the sod,
The deed and the doer, the seed and the sower, the dust which is God.

Hast thou known how I fashioned thee
Child, underground?
Fire that impassioned thee,
Iron that bound,

Dim changes of water, what thing of all these hast
thou known of or found?

Canst thou say in thine heart
Thou hast seen with thine eyes
With what cunning of art
Thou wast wrought in what wise,
By what force of what stuff thou wast shapen, and
shown on my breast to the skies?

Who hath given, who hath sold it thee,
Knowledge of me?
Has the wilderness told it thee?
Hast thou learnt of the sea?
Hast thou communed in spirit with night? have
the winds taken counsel with thee?

* * * * * * *

What is here, dost thou know it?
What was, hast thou known?
Prophet nor poet
Nor tripod nor throne
Nor spirit nor flesh can make answer, but only thy
mother alone.

Mother, not maker,
Born, and not made,
Though her children forsake her,
Allured or afraid,
Praying prayers to the God of their fashion, she
stirs not for all that have prayed.

A creed is a rod,
And a crown is of night;
But this thing is God,
To be man with thy might,
To grow straight in the strength of thy spirit, and
live out thy life as the light.

I am in thee to save thee,
As my soul in thee saith;
Give thou as I gave thee,
Thy life-blood and breath,
Green leaves of thy labour, white flowers of thy
thought, and red fruit of thy death.

Be the ways of thy giving
As mine were to thee;
The free life of thy living,
Be the gift of it free;
Not as servant to lord, nor as master to slave,
shalt thou give thee to me.

* * * * * * *

For Truth only is living,
Truth only is whole,
And the love of his giving
Man's pole-star and pole;
Man, pulse of my centre, and fruit of my body, and
seed of my soul.

One birth of my bosom;
One beam of mine eye;
One topmost blossom
That scales the sky;
Man, equal and one with me, man that is made of
me, man that is I.

THE ROUNDEL

A roundel is wrought as a ring or a starbright
sphere,
With craft of delight and with cunning of sound
unsought,
That the heart of the hearer may smile if to pleasure his ear
A roundel is wrought.

Its jewel of music is carven of all or of aught —
Love, laughter, or mourning — remembrance of
rapture or fear —
That fancy may fashion to hang in the ear of
thought.

As a bird's quick song runs round, and the hearts
in us hear
Pause answer to pause, and again the same strain
caught,
So moves the device whence, round as a pearl or
tear,
A roundel is wrought.

ÉTUDE RÉALISTE

I

A baby's feet, like sea-shells pink,
Might tempt, should heaven see meet,
An angel's lips to kiss, we think,
A baby's feet.

Like rose-hued sea-flowers toward the heat
They stretch and spread and wink
Their ten soft buds that part and meet.

No flower-bells that expand and shrink
Gleam half so heavenly sweet
As shine on life's untrodden brink
A baby's feet.

II

A baby's hands, like rosebuds furled
Whence yet no leaf expands.

Ope if you touch, though close upcurled,
A baby's hands.

Then, fast as warriors grip their brands
When battle's bolt is hurled,
They close, clenched hard like tightening bands.

No rosebuds yet by dawn impearled
Match, even in loveliest lands,
The sweetest flowers in all the world —
A baby's hands.

III

A baby's eyes, ere speech begin,
Ere lips learn words or sighs,
Bless all things bright enough to win
A baby's eyes.

Love, while the sweet thing laughs and lies,
And sleep flows out and in,
Sees perfect in them Paradise.

Their glance might cast out pain and sin,
Their speech make dumb the wise,
By mute glad godhead felt within
A baby's eyes.

THE SALT OF THE EARTH

If childhood were not in the world,
But only men and women grown;
No baby-locks in tendrils curled,
No baby-blossoms blown;

Though men were stronger, women fairer,
And nearer all delights in reach,
And verse and music uttered rarer
Tones of more godlike speech;

Though the utmost life of life's best hours
Found, as it cannot now find, words;
Though desert sands were sweet as flowers,
And flowers could sing like birds,

But children never heard them, never
They felt a child's foot leap and run;
This were a drearier star than ever
Yet looked upon the sun.

WHAT IS DEATH?

Looking on a page where stood
Graven of old on old-world wood
Death, and by the grave's edge grim,
Pale, the young man facing him,
Asked my well-beloved of me
Once what strange thing this might be,
Gaunt and great of limb.

Death, I told him: and, surprise
Deepening more his wildwood eyes
(Like some sweet fleet thing's whose breath
Speaks all spring though nought it saith),
Up he turned his rosebright face
Glorious with its seven years' grace,
Asking — What is death?

SONNETS

ON LAMB'S SPECIMENS OF DRAMATIC POETS

If all the flowers of all the fields on earth
By wonder-working summer were made one,
Its fragrance were not sweeter in the sun,
Its treasure-house of leaves were not more worth
Than those wherefrom thy light of musing mirth
Shone, till each leaf whereon thy pen would run
Breathed life, and all its breath was benison.
Beloved beyond all names of English birth,
More dear than mightier memories; gentlest name
That ever clothed itself with flower-sweet fame,
Or linked itself with loftiest names of old
By right and might of loving; I, that am
Less than the least of those within thy fold,
Give only thanks for them to thee, Charles Lamb.

BEN JONSON

Broad-based, broad-fronted, bounteous, multiform,
With many a valley impleached with ivy and vine,
Wherein the springs of all the streams run wine,
And many a crag full-faced against the storm,
The mountain where thy Muse's feet made warm
Those lawns that revelled with her dance divine
Shines yet with fire as it was wont to shine
From tossing torches round the dance a-swarm.
Nor less, high-stationed on the grey grave heights,
High-thoughted seers with heaven's heart-kindling lights
Hold converse: and the herd of meaner things
Knows or by fiery scourge or fiery shaft
When wrath on thy broad brows has risen, and laughed
Darkening thy soul with shadow of thunderous wings.

HOPE AND FEAR

Beneath the shadow of dawn's aërial cope,
With eyes enkindled as the sun's own sphere,
Hope from the front of youth in godlike cheer

Looks Godward, past the shades where blind men grope
Round the dark door that prayers nor dreams can ope,
And makes for joy the very darkness dear
That gives her wide wings play; nor dreams that fear
At noon may rise and pierce the heart of hope.
Then, when the soul leaves off to dream and yearn,
May truth first purge her eyesight to discern
What once being known leaves time no power to appal;
Till youth at last, ere yet youth be not, learn
The kind wise word that falls from years that fall —
"Hope thou not much, and fear thou not at all."

AFTER SUNSET

If light of life outlive the set of sun
That men call death and end of all things, then
How should not that which life held best for men
And proved most precious, though it seem undone
By force of death and woful victory won,
Be first and surest of revival, when
Death shall bow down to life arisen again?
So shall the soul seen be the self-same one
That looked and spake with even such lips and eyes
As love shall doubt not then to recognise,
And all bright thoughts and smiles of all time past
Revive, transfigured, but in spirit and sense
None other than we knew, for evidence
That love's last mortal word was not his last.

, 88, 129
211
7
Hampole, 14
of, 209
543
abriel, 524
Earl of Dor-
s, Lord Buck
57
346
s, 210
iam, 132
sshe, 394
m, 264

Shepherd Tony, 127
Sidney, Sir Philip, 104
Skelton, John, 61
Skinner, John, 304
Skirving, Adam, 307
Southey, Robert, 364
Southwell, Robert, 117
Spenser, Edmund, 90
Suckling, Sir John, 192
Surrey, Earl of, 82
Swift, Jonathan, 216
Swinburne, Algernon Charles, 558
Sylvester, Joshua, 120

Tennyson, Alfred, Lord, 441
Thomson, James, 255
Thomson, James, 548
Tickell, Thomas, 227

Vaughan, Henry, 200

Waller, Edmund, 174
Walsh, William, 215
Warner, William, 108
Warton, Thomas, 283
Watson, Thomas, 132
Watts, Isaac, 220
Wesley, Charles, 261
Wilmot, John, Earl of Rochester, 211
Winchilsea, Lady, 213
Wither, George, 165
Wolfe, Charles, 393
Wordsworth, William, 329
Wotton, Sir Henry, 146
Wyatt, Sir Thomas, 80

Young, Edward, 224

INDEX OF

Addison, Joseph, 218
Akenside, Mark, 277
Arnold, Sir Edwin, 546
Arnold, Matthew, 505
Austin, Alfred, 557

Bailey, Philip James, 498
Baillie, Joanna, 326
Barbauld, Anna Lætitia, 295
Barnfield, Richard, 127
Beattie, James, 294
Beaumont, Francis, 160
Beddoes, Thomas Lovell, 430
Blair, Robert, 254
Blake, William, 301
Breton, Nicholas, 127
Browne, William, 167
Browning, Elizabeth Barrett, 431
Browning, Robert, 474
Buckhurst, Lord, 85
Burns, Robert, 309
Butler, Samuel, 193
Byron, Lord, 378

Campbell, Thomas, 370
Campion, Thomas, 146
Carew, Thomas, 172
Chapman, George, 111
Chatterton, Thomas, 295
Chaucer, Geoffrey, 28
Churchill, Charles, 285
Clough, Arthur Hugh, 499
Coleridge, Samuel Taylor, 353
Collins, William, 272
Constable, Henry, 130
Cowley, Abraham, 197
Cowper, William, 285
Crabbe, George, 299
Crashaw, Richard, 194

Daniel, Samuel, 117
Davenant, Sir William, 174
Davies, Sir John, 147
Dekker, Thomas, 147
Denham, Sir John, 196
Dobell, Sidney, 523
Donne, John, 153

Dorset, Earl of, 209
Drayton, Michael, 1
Drummond, William
Dryden, John, 202
Dunbar, William, 58
Dyer, Sir Edward, 8
Dyer, John, 259

Elliot, Jane, 306

Fergusson, Robert, 30
Fitzgerald, Edward, 4
Fletcher, Giles, the el
Fletcher, John, 158
Ford, John, 163

Garth, Sir Samuel, 213
Gascoigne, George, 84
Gay, John, 225
Goldsmith, Oliver, 278
Gower, John, 22
Gray, Thomas, 265
Greene, Robert, 115
Guildford, Nicholas de,

Habington, William, 173
Hales, Thomas de, 10
Hall, Joseph, 156
Hamilton, William, of 260
Hawes, Stephen, 59
Hemans, Felicia Dorothe
Henryson, Robert, 52
Herbert, Edward, Lord, of bury, 161
Herbert, George, 171
Herrick, Robert, 168
Heywood, Thomas, 166
Hoccleve, Thomas, 47
Hood, Thomas, 425
Howard, Henry, Earl of S 82
Hunnis, William, 128
Hunt, Leigh, 376

James I of Scotland, 50
Johnson, Samuel, 262
Jonson, Ben, 149

Raleigh, Sir Walter
Ramsay, Allan, 228
Rochester, Earl of,
Rogers, Samuel, 32
Rolle, Richard, de
Roscommon, Earl
Rossetti, Christina
Rossetti, Dante G

Sackville, Charles, set, 209
Sackville, Thoma hurst, 85
Sandys, George,
Scott, Sir Walter,
Sedley, Sir Charl
Shakespeare, Wil
Shelley, Percy By
Shenstone, Willia

INDEX OF TITLES AND FIRST LINES

A baby's feet, like sea-shells pink.......... 561
A Bard's Epitaph........................ 319
A Birthday.............................. 543
A book was writ of late called Tetrachordon 183
Abou Ben Adhem (may his tribe increase!).. 377
Absalom and Achitophel............... 203
Abt Vogler.............................. 494
A Child's Thought of God.............. 438
Acon and Rhodope...................... 368
A Cradle Hymn........................ 220
A Curse for a Nation................... 436
Address to the Deil.................... 311
Address to the Unco Guid............... 318
A Description of One he would Love... 81
Adieu, farewell, earth's bliss............... 145
A Dirge................................ 412
A Dirge for Phyllip Sparowe........... 61
Admonition............................ 344
Adonais................................ 404
A Doubt of Martyrdom.................. 192
A Dream of Fair Women................. 452
Ae fond kiss, and then we sever............ 324
A face that should content me wondrous well.................................. 81
A Farewell to Tobacco.................. 367
A Fiesolan Idyl......................... 369
A flock of sheep that leisurely pass by...... 345
After Sunset............................ 563
A Garden............................... 376
A gentle knight was pricking on the plaine.. 99
A Grammarian's Funeral................ 482
Ah! County Guy, the hour is nigh......... 352
Ah for pittie, will rancke Winters rage...... 96
Ah, gentle shepherd, thine the lot to tend... 259
Ah me! full sorely is my heart forlorn...... 264
Ah, what avails the sceptred race.......... 369
Ah! what a weary race my feet have run..... 285
Ah, what is love? It is a pretty thing...... 116
A Hymn of Contentment................ 223
A Hymn to God the Father.............. 155
Airy, fairy Lilian........................ 441
Alas!—how light a cause may move........ 373
Alas, my lord, my haste was all too hot..... 84
Alas, 'tis true I have gone here and there... 142
Alastor................................. 394
Albion's England........................ 108
A Letter to Charles Lord Halifax..... 219
Alexander's Feast...................... 207
Alfred, A Masque...................... 258
Alle beon he blithe....................... 4
All in the Downs the fleet was moored..... 226
All my past life is mine no more........... 211
All that I know.......................... 479
All ye that lovely lovers be................ 108
A Lover's Complaint.................... 137
A Luve Ron............................. 10
Alysoun................................ 12
A Man's a Man for a' That............. 326
A Man's Requirements.................. 432
A mayde Cristes me bit yorne............. 10
Amazed he stands, nor voice nor body stirs.. 118
America................................ 524
Am I in Italy? Is this the Mincius........ 327
A milk-white Hind, immortal and unchanged 205
Amoretti................................ 90
A Musical Instrument.................. 438
An Account of the Greatest English Poets.............................. 218
An angel thus til him can sai.............. 9
A Naval Ode........................... 370
And are ye sure the news is true........... 305
And as the seed waits eagerly.............. 304
And now 'tis time; for their officious haste.. 202
And rise, O moon, from yonder down...... 471
And so bifel, whan comen was the tyme.... 28
And the first grey of morning fill'd the east. 509
And welcome now, great Monarch, to your own................................ 202
And when his bones are dust, his grave a blank.............................. 391
And [when man] was born til this werldys light 14
An Elegy of a Woman's Heart.......... 146
An Epitaph............................. 173
An Epitaph on Salathiel Pavy.......... 152
An Epithalamion........................ 92
An Essay on Criticism.................. 228
An Essay on Man....................... 240
An Essay on Translated Verse......... 209
An evil Spirit (your Beauty) haunts me still. 121
An Hymn in Honour of Beauty.......... 95
An Hymn of Heavenly Beauty.......... 96
An idle poet here and there................ 521
A Night-Piece on Death................ 222
Annus Mirabilis........................ 202
A noble range it was, of many a rood......... 376
A Nocturnal Reverie................... 215
An Ode for Music...................... 273
An Ode from the Norse Tongue........ 271
An Ode on a Fair Spring Morning...... 547
An Ode on the Superstitions of the Highlands.............................. 274
An Ode . . . whether Love should Continue Forever...................... 161
A Nymph's Disdain of Love............ 130

A Paraphrase upon the Psalms of David 157
A Paraphrase upon the Song of Solomon 158
A passing glance, a lightning 'long the skies 161
Apelles' Song 107
A Pindaric Ode 150
A Pindaric Ode 268
A Pindaric Ode 270
A Poet! — He hath put his heart to school 346
A Poison Tree 302
Apollo great, whose beams the greater world do light 106
Apparitions 498
A Renouncing of Love 80
A Robin Redbreast in a cage 302
A Roundel 45
A roundel is wrought as a ring or a starbright sphere 561
Art 550
Arthur for to Cornwale 2
Art thou poor, yet hast thou golden slumbers 148
A Satire Dissuading from Poetry 212
A Sea Dirge 145
As I came through the desert thus it was 548
As I in hoary winter's night stood shivering in the snow 117
A Simile 216
A simple child 329
As it fell upon a day 127
Ask, is Love divine 542
Ask me no more where Jove bestows 172
A slumber did my spirit seal 332
As Mailie an' her lambs thegither 309
A Snow Scene 255
A Soliloquy 260
A Song for St. Cecilia's Day 206
A Song from Shakespear's Cymbelyne 272
A sonnet is a moment's monument 533
As ships, becalmed at eve, that lay 499
A still small voice spake unto me 444
Astræa Redux 202
Astrophel and Stella 104
As two, whose love, first foolish, widening scope 534
A Superscription 536
At a dinner so various, at such a repast 282
At a posterne forth they gan to ryde 49
A Tear 328
At first a dusky wreath they seem to rise 256
A Thanksgiving to God for his House 170
A thing of beauty is a joy forever 417
At the Grave of Burns 335
At the midnight in the silence of the sleep-time 498
Auguries of Innocence 302
Auld Lang Syne 320
Auld Robin Gray 309
Autumn 256
Avenge, O Lord, thy slaughtered saints, whose bones 184
A Vision in a Dream 354
Awake, Æolian lyre, awake 268
Awake, my St. John! leave all meaner things 240
A wanderer is man from his birth 508
A well there is in the West country 366
A wind sways the pines 542
A Woman's Shortcomings 433

Balade de Bon Conseyl 45
Bards of passion and of mirth 415
Battle of the Baltic 371
Beautiful Evelyn Hope is dead 476
Beauty clear and fair 159
Beauty sat bathing in a spring 127
Before Sunrise in the Vale of Chamouni 353
Behind the Veil 200
Behind yon hills where Lugar flows 310
Behold her single in the field 336
Be it right or wrong, these men among 54
Bellerophon 541
Belovèd, my Belovèd, when I think 434
Beneath the shadow of dawn's aërial cope 562
Ben Jonson 562
Bethesda 503
Black-Eyed Susan 226
Blow, blow, thou winter wind 144
Bonie Doon 324
Bonie Lesley 324
Boot and Saddle 474
Boot, saddle, to horse, and away 474
Bound for holy Palestine 283
Branksome Hall 346
Brave infant of Saguntum, clear 150
Break, break, break 465
Bright Star of Beauty! on whose eyelids sit 120
Bright Star! would I were steadfast as thou art 417
Bristowe Tragedie 295
Britannia's Pastorals 167
Broad-based, broad-fronted, bounteous, multiform 562
Buried bars in the breakwater 536
But adoration! give me something more 224
But now the mindful messenger, come back 136
But, O my muse, what numbers wilt thou find 219
But on another day the King said, "Come 546
But who comes 327
By an Evolutionist 473
By Logan's streams that rin sae deep 307
By nature's law, what may be, may be now 224
By numbers here from shame or censure free 262
By the blue taper's trembling light 222
Bytuene Mersh and Averil 12

Caller Water 308
Calm on the bosom of thy God 412
Calm was the day, and through the trembling air 90
Can I forget the dismal night that gave 227
Can I see another's woe 301
Can you paint a thought? or number 164
Captain Car 76
Captain, or Colonel, or Knight in arms 183
Care-charmer Sleep, son of the sable Night 118
Care-charming Sleep, thou easer of all woes 159
Ca' the yowes to the knowes 306
Cavalier Tunes 474

How vainly men themselves amaze......... 199
H——, thou return'st from Thames, whose naiads long........................ 274
HUDIBRAS........................... 193
Hush! my dear, lie still and slumber........ 220
HYMN.............................. 220
HYMN BEFORE SUNRISE IN THE VALE OF CHAMOUNI........................ 353
HYMN TO APOLLO...................... 106
HYMN TO APOLLO...................... 107
HYMN TO INTELLECTUAL BEAUTY........... 396
HYPERION........................... 418

I am nae poet, in a sense................. 312
I am not one who much or oft delight...... 338
I am poor brother Lippo, by your leave.... 486
I am that which began.................... 560
I arise from dreams of thee............... 400
I bring fresh showers for the thirsting flowers 400
I built my soul a lordly pleasure house..... 449
I can love both fair and brown............ 153
Ich æm elder then ich wes a wintre and a lore 1
Ich was in one sumere dale............... 7
IDEA............................... 120
IDEAS OF GOOD AND EVIL............... 302
I did but look and love awhile............. 212
I did but prompt the age to quit their clogs. 183
I envy not in any moods.................. 469
If all the flowers of all the fields on earth.... 562
If all the world and love were young....... 131
If childhood were not in the world......... 562
"If I were dead, you'd sometimes say, Poor Child!"......................... 523
If Jove himself be subject unto Love....... 132
If light of life outlive the set of sun........ 563
If ought of oaten stop, or pastoral song..... 273
If poisonous minerals, and if that tree...... 155
If the quick spirits in your eye............ 173
If there were dreams to sell............... 430
If thou must love me, let it be for nought... 433
If thou survive my well-contented day...... 140
If you have a carrier-dove................ 550
I have gone the whole round of creation.... 477
I have had playmates, I have had companions 367
I have led her home, my love, my only friend 467
I have lost, and lately, these.............. 168
I heard an angel singing.................. 304
I heard an angel speak last night.......... 436
I hear some say, "This man is not in love!" 121
I held it truth, with him who sings........ 469
I long to talk with some old lover's ghost... 154
I looked and saw your eyes................ 536
IL PENSEROSO....................... 179
I met a traveller from an antique land...... 397
I'm wearin' awa', John.................. 328
In a somer sesun whon softe was the sonne.. 24
INCIDENT OF THE FRENCH CAMP.......... 479
INCLUSIVENESS...................... 534
INCONSTANCY....................... 368
INGRATEFUL BEAUTY THREATENED........ 173
IN IMITATION OF HAMLET.............. 260
IN IMITATION OF SPENSER.............. 264
Inland, within a hollow vale, I stood....... 343
In lowly dale, fast by a river's side......... 256
IN MEMORIAM....................... 468
In my poor mind it is most sweet to muse. 367
In my prosperity I said.................. 157
In our old shipwrecked days there was an hour.......................... 542
In Scotland there was a babie born......... 77
In such a night, when every louder wind.... 215
IN THE HOLY NATIVITY OF OUR LORD GOD 194
In the merry month of May.............. 127
In these deep solitudes and awful cells...... 239
INTIMATIONS OF IMMORTALITY........... 339
Into these Loves, who but for Passion looks 120
In vain you tell your parting lover.......... 215
INVITING A FRIEND TO SUPPER........... 152
INVOCATION TO SLEEP.................. 159
IN WARTIME......................... 523
In Xanadu did Kubla Khan.............. 354
I read before my eyelids dropt their shade.. 452
I said — Then, dearest, since 'tis so........ 481
I saw again the spirits on a day........... 503
I saw Eternity the other night............ 200
I sent for Ratcliffe; was so ill............ 216
I shiver, Spirit fierce and bold............ 335
I sprang to the saddle, and Joris and he.... 475
Is there a whim-inspirèd fool............. 319
Is there for honest poverty............... 326
Is this a fast, to keep................... 171
I strove with none, for none was worth my strife.......................... 370
I struck the board and cried, "No more; I will abroad......................... 172
ITALY.............................. 327
ITALY AND BERGAMO.................. 327
It befell at Martynmas.................. 76
It fortifies my soul to know............... 500
It happened once some men of Italy........ 551
I thought of thee, my partner and my guide........................... 345
I thought once how Theocritus had sung...... 433
It is a beauteous evening, calm and free.... 344
It is an ancient Mariner.................. 355
It is a place where poets crowned may feel the heart's decaying.................. 431
It keeps eternal whisperings around......... 417
It little profits that an idle king........... 459
It was a dismal and a fearful night..........197
It was a summer evening................. 365
It was the winter wild................... 175
ITYLUS............................. 559
I've heard them lilting, at our ewe-milking.. 306
I wandered lonely as a cloud............. 337
I was angry with my friend............... 302
I weep for Adonais — he is dead........... 404
I wish I could remember that first day...... 544

Jason, which sih his fader old............. 22
JENNY............................. 525
Jenny kissed me when we met............ 377
John Anderson my jo, John............... 320
JOHNNIE COPE....................... 307
JUGGLING JERRY..................... 540
Just for a handful of silver he left us...... 475

Kentish Sir Byng stood for his king....... 474
King Charles, and who'll do him right now.. 474
King Francis was a hearty king, and loved a royal sport.......................... 377
King Horn.......... 4
King, that hast reign'd six hundred years, and grown............................ 471
Know, Celia, since thou art so proud........ 173
KNOWN IN VAIN......................... 534
Know ye the land where the cypress and myrtle............................ 392
KUBLA KHAN............................ 354

LA BELLE DAME SANS MERCI.............. 416
LALLA ROOKH........................... 373
L'ALLEGRO............................. 178
LAMIA................................. 420
LAODAMIA.............................. 341
Latest, earliest, of the year............... 557
Lay a garland on my hearse............... 160
LAY OF ROSABELLE...................... 347
Lazy laughing languid Jenny............... 525
Lenten ys come with love to toune.......... 13
Lete holy chirche medle of the doctryne..... 47
Let me not to the marriage of true minds... 142
Let observation, with extensive view........ 262
Let others sing of Knights and Paladins.... 118
Let those who are in favour with their stars. 139
Let us begin and carry up this corpse....... 482
LICIA................................. 87
Life! I know not what thou art........... 295
LIFE OF LIFE.......................... 521
Life with yon lambs, like day, is just begun 346
Like as a ship, that through the ocean wide. 90
Like as the waves make towards the pebbled shore.............................. 140
Like Memnon's rock, touched with the rising sun............................... 87
Like to the falling of a star............... 160
LILIAN................................ 441
LINES COMPOSED NEAR TINTERN ABBEY.... 330
LINES ON THE MERMAID TAVERN.......... 415
LINES ON THE TOMBS IN WESTMINSTER..... 160
LINES PRINTED UNDER THE PORTRAIT OF MILTON.......................... 209
LINES TO JOHN LAPRAIK................. 312
LINES WRITTEN AMONG THE EUGANEAN HILLS............................. 397
LOCHINVAR............................. 347
LOCKSLEY HALL......................... 459
LOGAN BRAES........................... 307
LONDON................................ 262
LONDON, 1802........................... 344
LONDON LYCKPENNY...................... 48
Long had our dull forefathers slept supine.. 218
Look, Delia, how we esteem the half-blown rose.............................. 117
Looking on a page where stood........... 562
Look in my face; my name is Might-have-been........................... 536
LORD RANDAL.......................... 77
Lords, knights, and 'squires, the numerous band............................. 216
Lord, Thou hast given me a cell........... 170
LOSS FROM THE LEAST.................... 170
LOST DAYS............................. 535
Lo, this is night. Hast thou, O sun, refused 523
LOVE.................................. 172
LOVE AND LIFE......................... 211
Love bade me welcome; yet my soul drew back.............................. 172
Love in my bosom like a bee.............. 130
LOVE IN THE VALLEY.................... 537
LOVE IS DEAD.......................... 106
Lovely, lasting peace of mind................223
Love me, sweet, with all thou art.......... 432
LOVE'S DEITY.......................... 154
Love seeketh not itself to please........... 301
LOVE'S EMBLEMS........................ 159
LOVE-SIGHT............................ 533
LOVE'S SECRET......................... 304
Love still has something of the sea......... 210
LOVE-SWEETNESS........................ 533
LOVE'S YOUNG DREAM.................... 375
Love, that liveth and reigneth in my thought. 83
Loving in truth, and fain in verse my love to show............................ 104
Lo! where the rosy-bosom'd Hours......... 265
LUCIFER IN STARLIGHT.................. 542
Lucile de Nevers (if her riddle I read)....... 544
LUCY.................................. 332
LUCY GRAY............................. 333
Lully, lulley, lulley, lulley................ 65
LYCIDAS............................... 181

MADRIGAL I............................ 163
Maimed, beggared, grey; seeking an alms.. 541
Make rome, syrs, and let us be mery....... 65
Make we mery, bothe more and lasse....... 64
MAN................................... 225
Many a green isle needs must be.......... 397
MARCHING ALONG....................... 474
MARIANA............................... 441
MARMION............................... 347
MARMION AND DOUGLAS.................. 349
MARRIAGE HYMN........................ 160
Martial, the things that do attain.......... 83
MARY MORISON......................... 309
MASTER FRANCIS BEAUMONT'S LETTER TO BEN JONSON.......................... 161
MAUD.................................. 467
May! Be thou never graced with birds that sing............................ 168
May the Babylonish curse................ 367
MEDEA AND ESON....................... 22
MEETING AT NIGHT...................... 476
MENAPHON'S SONG...................... 116
Men call you fair, and you do credit it...... 90
Men say, Columbia, we shall hear thy guns. 524
MERLIN AND THE GLEAM................. 472
Midnight past! Not a sound of aught...... 545
MID-RAPTURE........................... 534
Milton! thou should'st be living at this hour 344
MODERN LOVE.......................... 542
Mon in the mone stond and strit........... 13
MORAL BALADE OF CHAUCER............. 46

MORAL ESSAYS........................... 247
MORALITY............................. 507
MORAL ODE............................ 1
More than most fair, full of the living fire.. 90
Morning, evening, noon and night.......... 480
Morpheus, the lively son of deadly Sleep.... 105
Mortality, behold and fear................ 160
MORTE D'ARTHUR...................... 456
Most sweet it is with unuplifted eyes....... 346
Much have I travell'd in the realms of gold 416
Music, when soft voices die................ 404
MUSOPHILUS........................... 119
My anxious soul is tore with doubtful strife. 260
My days among the Dead are past......... 366
My eye, descending from the hill, surveys... 196
My first thought was, he lied in every word 483
My good blade carves the casques of men... 464
My hair is gray, but not from years........ 386
My heart aches, and a drowsy numbness pains................................ 413
My heart is a-breaking, dear tittie........... 321
My heart is like a singing bird............. 543
My heart leaps up when I behold.......... 335
MY LAST DUCHESS.................... 479
My letters all dead paper, mute and white.. 434
My little Son, who look'd from thoughtful eyes.................................. 522
My lov'd, my honour'd, much respected friend............................... 316
My lute, awake, perform the last......... 80
My mind to me a kingdom is............. 88
My mother's maids, when they did sew and spin................................ 81
My name is Colyn Cloute................ 62
MY NANIE, O.......................... 310
My only Love is always near.............. 504
My Peggy is a young thing............... 228
My poet, thou canst touch on all the notes.. 434
MY STAR.............................. 479

Nay but you, who do not love her......... 476
Never seek to tell thy love................ 304
Never the time and the place.............. 498
NIGHT THOUGHTS...................... 224
No bliss can so contenting prove........... 166
Nobly, nobly Cape St. Vincent to the North-west died away...................... 477
No longer mourn for me when I am dead... 141
Nor can I not believe but that hereby....... 338
NORTHERN FARMER (NEW STYLE).......... 465
NOSCE TEIPSUM....................... 147
Not a drum was heard, not a funeral note..... 393
Not, Celia, that I juster am............... 210
Not far advanced was morning day......... 349
Not here! the white North has thy bones..... 471
Nothing so true as what you once let fall... 247
Not in the crises of events............... 522
Not marble, nor the gilded monuments..... 140
Not mine own fears, nor the prophetic soul.... 142
Not that the earth is changing, O my God.. 533
Now mirk December's dowie face.......... 307
Now riden this folk and walken on fote..... 27
Now the lusty spring is seen.............. 159
Now the storm begins to lower............. 271
Now, upon Syria's land of roses............ 373
Now Venus mounts her car, she shakes the reins................................ 226
Now was the Lord and Lady of the May... 167
Now welcom, somer, with thy sonne softe.. 45
NOX NOCTI INDICAT SCIENTIAM............ 173
Nu, broþerr Wallterr, broþerr min......... 2
Nuns fret not at their convent's narrow room.............................. 344
NYMPHIDIA........................... 124

O blithe New-comer! I have heard.......... 334
O, breathe not his name! let it sleep in the shade............................... 376
Obscurest night involved the sky........... 293
ODE ON A DISTANT PROSPECT OF ETON COLLEGE........................... 266
ODE ON A GRECIAN URN................. 414
ODE ON THE SPRING.................... 265
ODE TO A NIGHTINGALE................. 413
ODE TO DUTY......................... 337
ODE TO EVENING...................... 273
ODE TO THE WEST WIND................. 399
ODE UPON THE CENSURE OF HIS "NEW INN" 152
ODE WRITTEN IN THE BEGINNING OF THE YEAR 1746.......................... 272
O Earth, lie heavily upon her eyes......... 544
O erth! on erth it is a wonders case........ 59
O, fair sweet face! O, eyes celestial bright. 160
O, faithless World! and thy more faithless part............................... 146
Of all the thoughts of God that are........ 431
Of a' the airts the wind can blaw.......... 320
Of Heaven or Hell I have no power to sing.. 550
Of Man's first disobedience and the fruit... 184
Of Nelson and the North................. 371
O force of faith! O strength of virtuous will 364
O, for my sake do you with Fortune chide.. 142
O for some honest lover's ghost............ 192
OF THE DEATH OF SIR T. W............. 83
OF THE MEAN AND SURE ESTATE.......... 81
Of these the false Achitophel was first....... 203
OF THE SOUL OF MAN AND THE IMMORTALITY THEREOF............................ 147
Oft I had heard of Lucy Gray............. 333
Oft in the stilly night.................... 374
Oh, but, says one, Tradition set aside...... 205
Oh for a lodge in some vast wilderness..... 286
Oh that those lips had language!.......... 290
Oh! the days are gone when beauty bright.. 375
Oh, thou! in Hellas deem'd of heavenly birth 380
Oh, to be in England..................... 477
Oh, to what height will love of greatness drive. 156
Oh Venice! Venice! when thy marble walls 389
Oh yet we trust that somehow good........ 470
Old Adam, the carrion crow.............. 430
Old Chaucer doth of Topas tell............ 124
Old Chaucer, like the morning star......... 196
O Liberty, thou goddess heavenly bright.... 219
O Light! (which mak'st the light, which mak'st the day.......................... 147
O listen, listen, ladies gay................ 347

O maister deere and fadir reverent.......... 47
O Mary, at thy window be................ 309
O Mistress mine, where are you roaming... 144
On a Girdle.......................... 175
On Another's Sorrow.................. 301
On a starred night Prince Lucifer uprose... 542
Once did She hold the gorgeous east in fee.. 343
On Chaucer........................... 47
On Death............................. 370
On either side........................ 300
On either side of the river lie.............. 442
One more Unfortunate.................... 425
Ones yet agayne........................ 62
O, never say that I was false of heart...... 142
One word is too often profaned............ 410
One Word More........................ 491
On First Looking into Chapman's Homer. 416
On Hellespont, guilty of true love's blood..... 125
On his Blindness...................... 184
On his having Arrived at the Age of Twenty-three..................... 183
On his Seventy-fifth Birthday.......... 370
O Nightingale, that on yon bloomy spray... 183
On Lamb's Specimens of Dramatic Poets 562
On Linden, when the sun was low......... 370
On Man, on Nature, and on Human Life... 333
On Mr. Abraham Cowley's Death and Burial........................... 196
On my First Son....................... 152
O, no, Belov'd, I am most sure............ 161
On Refusal of Aid between Nations.... 533
On the Countess Dowager of Pembroke 168
On the Death of Mr. William Hervey.. 197
On the Detraction which followed . . . Certain Treatises............ 183
On the Extinction of the Venetian Republic............................. 343
On the Late Massacre in Piedmont..... 184
On the Life of Man.................. 160
On the Loss of the Royal George...... 289
On the Morning of Christ's Nativity... 175
On the Receipt of My Mother's Picture 290
On the Sea........................... 417
On the Sea-Shore Near Calais......... 344
On the Sonnet........................ 344
On the Sudden Restraint of . . . Earl of Somerset...................... 147
O Rose, thou art sick.................... 302
Or rushing thence, in one diffusive band.... 255
O saw ye bonie Lesley.................... 324
O! snatch'd away in beauty's bloom....... 393
O soft embalmer of the still midnight....... 416
O that the chemist's magic art............ 328
Others abide our question. Thou art free.. 505
O Thou that swing'st upon the waving hair. 197
O thou! whatever title suit thee........... 311
Out upon it, I have loved................ 192
Over hill, over dale..................... 143
Over the solitary hills he fared............ 420
O what can ail thee, knight-at-arms........ 416
O where hae ye been, Lord Randal, my son 77
O, wild West Wind, thou breath of Autumn's being............................ 399
O ye wha are sae guid yoursel............ 318
O, young Lochinvar is come out of the west. 347
O young Mariner........................ 472
Ozymandias............................ 397

Paradise and the Peri.................. 373
Paradise Lost......................... 184
Parting at Morning..................... 476
Passing from Italy to Greece, the tales...... 163
Passions are liken'd best to floods and streams 88
Pastyme with good companye.............. 65
Peace; come away: the song of woe........ 470
Pearl................................. 15
Peggy................................ 228
"Perché Pensa"....................... 502
Perle, plesaunte to prynces paye............ 15
Perplexed Music....................... 432
Personal Talk......................... 338
Persuasions to Joy: A Song............ 173
Phillis is my only joy..................... 211
Philomela............................ 517
Philomela's Ode...................... 115
Phœbus, arise.......................... 162
Phyllida and Corydon.................. 127
Phyllida's Love-Call to her Corydon.. 128
Phyllis! why should we delay............. 174
Piers the Plowman..................... 24
Pinch him, pinch him black and blue....... 107
Piping down the valleys wild.............. 301
Pitch here the tent, while the old horse grazes 540
Poets are all who love, who feel, great truths 498
Poor little, pretty, fluttering thing.......... 216
Poor soul, the centre of my sinful earth..... 143
Praise and Prayer..................... 174
Praise is devotion fit for mighty minds...... 174
Primroses............................ 557
Procrastination....................... 224
Prologue for an Amateur Performance of "The Honeymoon"............... 429
Prophetic Books....................... 304
Prothalamion......................... 90
Proverbs............................. 302
Psalm XXX, Part II.................... 157
Psalm XLVI........................... 158

Qua Cursum Ventus.................... 499
Quhare-as in ward full oft I wold bewaille... 50
Quhen Merch wes with variand windis past.. 58
Quho is at my windo? Quho? Quho.... 63
Quid petis, O fily........................ 64

Rabbi Ben Ezra........................ 495
Religio Laici.......................... 205
Remember me when I am gone away....... 544
Rest................................. 544
Resteth here, that quick could never rest..... 83
Restore thy tresses to the golden ore........ 117
Return, Content! for fondly I pursued....... 345
Ring out, wild bells, to the wild sky........ 470
Ring out your bells, let mourning shows be spread............................. 106
Robin Hood and Guy of Gisborne....... 66
Rondeau............................. 377

Rosalind's Madrigal.................... 130
Rose Aylmer.......................... 369
Roses at first were white.................. 169
Roses, their sharp spines being gone........ 160
Round the cape of a sudden came the sea... 476
Ruin seize thee, ruthless King............. 270
Rule Britannia........................ 258
Ruth.................................. 427

Sacred Religion! Mother of Form and Fear 119
Saul................................. 477
Say not the struggle nought availeth........ 503
Say over again and yet once over again..... 434
Scorn not the Sonnet; Critic, you have frowned......................... 346
Scots, wha hae wi' Wallace bled........... 325
Season of mists and mellow fruitfulness..... 414
See the chariot at hand here of Love....... 149
Sephestia's Song to her Child.......... 116
September, 1802, Near Dover........... 343
Seynt Stevene was a clerk in Kyng Herowdes halle.............................. 79
Shakespeare.......................... 505
Shall I compare thee to a summer's day.... 139
Shall I, wasting in despair................ 165
She dwelt among the untrodden ways....... 332
She has laughed as softly as if she sighed... 433
Shepherd, what's love, I pray thee tell...... 129
She stood breast-high amid the corn........ 427
She walks in beauty, like the night......... 393
She was a phantom of delight.............. 337
Should auld acquaintance be forgot......... 320
Shut, shut the door, good John! fatigued, I said.............................. 243
Sigh no more, ladies, sigh no more......... 144
Silent Nymph, with curious eye............ 259
Since all the riches of all this world........ 303
Since brass, nor stone, nor earth, nor boundless sea............................ 140
Since there's no help, come, let us kiss and part 121
Singing is sweet, but be sure of this........ 550
Sing to Apollo, god of day................ 107
Sir Galahad.......................... 464
Sir John Franklin..................... 471
Sir Patrick Spens...................... 75
Sister Helen......................... 529
Sitting by a river's side.................. 115
So all day long the noise of battle roll'd.... 456
Sohrab and Rustum.................... 509
So, in the sinful streets, abstracted and alone 501
Soldier, rest! thy warfare o'er............ 350
Sole listener, Duddon! to the breeze that played........................... 345
Solitude............................. 333
Some say Love........................ 116
Song from Old Fortunatus............. 148
Song from The Broken Heart.......... 164
Song from The Shoemaker's Holiday.... 147
Song of Paris and Œnone............. 107
Song of Solomon (Paraphrase)........... 158
Song of the Songless................. 542
Songs from Shakespeare's Plays......... 143
Songs of Experience.................. 301
Songs of Innocence.................. 301
Song. The Nightingale.............. 106
Song to Bacchus..................... 159
Song to Celia....................... 149
Sonnets from the Portuguese.......... 433
Sonnets to Delia..................... 117
Soul-Light........................... 534
Souls of Poets dead and gone............. 415
So, we'll go no more a-roving............. 393
Speak, goddess! since 'tis thou that best canst tell............................. 213
Sponsa.............................. 158
Spring.............................. 256
Spring's Welcome.................... 107
Springtime........................... 13
Squyer, com neer, if it your wille be........ 38
St. Agnes' Eve........................ 463
St. Agnes' Eve — Ah, bitter chill it was..... 421
Stagyrus............................ 505
Stanzas for Music.................... 393
Stanzas on Oliver Cromwell............ 202
Stanzas Written in his Library.......... 366
Stella's Birthday, March 13, 1726....... 218
Stern Daughter of the Voice of God........ 337
Stillborn Love....................... 534
Still must I hear? — shall hoarse Fitzgerald bawl.......................... 378
Storm in Harvest..................... 256
Stretched on my restless bed all night....... 158
Strong Son of God, immortal Love.......... 468
St. Stephen and Herod................. 79
St. Thomas the Apostle................ 411
Such a starved bank of moss.............. 498
Summer.............................. 255
Sunday Up the River.................. 549
Sunset and evening star.................. 473
Sure thou didst flourish once; and many springs........................... 201
Surrey to Geraldine.................. 123
Survivor sole, and hardly such, of all....... 291
Swallow, my sister, O sister swallow........ 559
Sweet are the thoughts that savour of content 115
Sweet Auburn! loveliest village of the plain 278
Sweet day, so cool, so calm, so bright....... 171
Sweet dimness of her loosened hair's downfall 533
Sweetest Melancholy.................. 158
Sweet Phosphor, Bring the Day........ 171
Swiftly walk o'er the western wave.......... 410
Syr Gawayn and the Grene Knyght.... 18
Syria................................ 373

Take, O, take those lips away............. 144
Tales............................... 300
Tam Glen............................ 321
Tam O' Shanter...................... 321
Tell me not, Sweet, I am unkind........... 196
Tell me now in what hidden way is........ 532
Tell me where is fancy bred............... 143
That's my last Duchess painted on the wall. 479
That time of year thou mayst in me behold.. 141
That which her slender waist confined...... 175
The Accounte of W. Canynges Feast... 299
The Angel in the House............... 521

The Apology........ 285
The awful shadow of some unseen Power... 396
The Ballad of Dead Ladies........ 532
The Bard........ 270
The Battle of Blenheim........ 365
The Battle of Otterburn........ 69
The Belle of the Ball-Room........ 428
The bell strikes one: we take no note of time 224
The Bishop Orders his Tomb........ 490
The blessed damozel leaned out........ 524
The Boy and the Angel........ 480
The breaking waves dashed high........ 413
The bride she is winsome and bonny........ 326
The Bride Song........ 543
The Bridge of Sighs........ 425
The Brut........ 2
The Brutons thus departed hence........ 108
The Burial of Sir John Moore at Corunna........ 393
The Burning Babe........ 117
The Campaign........ 219
The Canonization........ 153
The Canterbury Tales........ 32
The Castaway........ 293
The Castle of Indolence........ 256
The changing guests, each in a different mood 534
The Character of a Happy Life........ 146
The Charm........ 159
The Choice........ 535
The City of Dreadful Night........ 548
The Clod and the Pebble........ 301
The Cloud........ 400
The Cloud Confines........ 537
The Collar........ 172
The Coming of the Rain........ 256
The Complaint........ 224
The Complaint of Rosamond........ 118
The Compleint of Chaucer to his Empty Purse........ 46
The Computation........ 155
The Conclusion........ 89
The Constant Lover........ 192
The Cotter's Saturday Night........ 316
The Court of Fairy........ 124
The Crusade........ 283
The Cry of the Children........ 435
The Curfew tolls the knell of parting day... 267
The Curse of Kehama........ 364
The Daft Days........ 307
The day is dark and the night........ 537
The Day of Judgment........ 220
The Death and Dying Words of Poor Mailie........ 309
The Death-Bed........ 428
The Deserted Lover Consoleth Himself 80
The Deserted Village........ 278
The Dethe of Syr Charles Bawdin........ 295
The Dispensary........ 213
The Dream........ 154
The Dunciad........ 250
The Earthly Paradise........ 550
The Elegy on Addison........ 227
The Enchantment........ 212
The Epilogue to Asolando........ 498
The Epitaph of Graunde Amour........ 59
The Eve of St. Agnes........ 421
The Excusation of the Aucthoure........ 60
The Fable of Belling the Cat........ 26
The face of all the world is changed, I think 433
The Faerie Queene........ 99
The Fan........ 226
The feast was over in Branksome tower........ 346
The feathered songster chaunticleer........ 295
The Fire-Worshippers........ 373
The First Day........ 544
The firste stok, fader of gentilesse........ 46
The Fleece........ 259
The Flight into Egypt........ 9
The Flowers of the Forest........ 306
The Forsaken Merman........ 506
The forward violet thus did I chide........ 141
The Fruits of a Clear Conscience........ 120
The Funeral........ 155
The Future........ 508
The Garden........ 199
The Garden of Proserpine........ 558
The Glory that was Greece........ 392
The Glove and the Lions........ 377
The Grasshopper........ 197
The Grasshopper and the Cricket........ 416
The Grave........ 254
The gray sea and the long black land........ 476
The Hare with Many Friends........ 225
The harp that once through Tara's halls.... 375
The heaven doth not contain so many stars.. 162
The Herdman's Happy Life........ 131
The Higher Pantheism........ 466
The Hind and the Panther........ 205
The Holy Fair........ 313
The Homes of England........ 412
The hour which might have been yet might not be........ 534
The human spirits saw I on a day........ 502
The Hunting of the Cheviot........ 72
The Idle Singer of an Empty Day........ 550
The Iliad........ 252
The Indian Serenade........ 400
The Indifferent........ 153
The keener tempests come: and fuming dun 255
The Kingis Quair........ 50
The king sits in Dumferling toune........ 75
The Lady of Shalott........ 442
The Lady of the Lake........ 350
The Lady of the Land........ 551
The Landing of the Pilgrim Fathers... 413
The Landmark........ 535
The Land o' the Leal........ 328
The lark now leaves his wat'ry nest........ 174
The Last Ride Together........ 481
The Last Word........ 521
The Lay of Rosabelle........ 347
The Lay of the Last Minstrel........ 346
The Light of Asia........ 546
The Light of the Harem........ 373
The Lord let the house of a brute to the soul of a man........ 473

The lost days of my life until to-day........ 535
THE LOST LEADER........................ 475
THE LOVER.............................. 521
THE LOVER COMPLAINETH THAT HIS DREAM IS NOT LONGER.................... 80
THE LOVER COMPLAINETH THE UNKINDNESS OF HIS LOVE....................... 80
THE LOVER'S JOURNEY.................... 300
THE LOVER'S MELANCHOLY................. 163
THE LOWEST PLACE....................... 544
The lytyll, prety nyghtyngale.............. 66
THE MAN IN THE MOON.................... 13
THE MARIAGE BETWENE GRAUNDE AMOUR AND LABELL PUCELL................ 59
THE MARRIED LOVER...................... 522
The means, therefore, which unto us is lent.. 96
THE MEANS TO ATTAIN HAPPY LIFE....... 83
THE MINSTREL........................... 294
THE MIRROR FOR MAGISTRATES........... 85
The morn they look on with unwilling eyes.... 202
THE MOUSE AND THE PADDOCK............ 52
THE MYSTERY OF EVIL.................... 546
THE NIGHTINGALE........................ 277
The nightingale, as soon as April bringeth... 106
Then Perceveraunce in all goodly haste..... 59
Then thus. "Since man from beast by words is known............................ 250
THE NUTBROWNE MAIDE................... 54
THE NYMPH'S REPLY TO THE SHEPHERD... 131
THE OLD COQUETTE...................... 224
THE OLD FAMILIAR FACES................ 367
The old inventive Poets, had they seen..... 345
THE ONE HOPE........................... 536
THE ORMULUM........................... 2
THE OWL AND THE NIGHTINGALE.......... 7
THE PALACE OF ART...................... 449
THE PASSIONATE SHEPHERD TO HIS LOVE.. 131
THE PASSIONS........................... 273
THE PASTIME OF PLEASURE............... 59
The Persë owt off Northombarlonde........ 72
THE PETITION FOR AN ABSOLUTE RETREAT. 213
THE PLEASURES OF HOPE................ 372
THE POEMA MORALE...................... 1
The poetry of earth is never dead.......... 416
THE PORTRAIT........................... 545
THE POWER OF MUSIC.................... 207
THE PRICKE OF CONSCIENCE............. 14
THE PRINCE'S PROGRESS................. 543
THE PRISONER OF CHILLON.............. 385
THE PROGRESS OF POESY................. 268
THE QUESTIONING SPIRIT................ 502
THE RAPE OF LUCRECE................... 136
THE RAPE OF THE LOCK.................. 231
There be none of Beauty's daughters....... 393
There came to the beach a poor exile of Erin 371
THE RECLUSE........................... 333
There is a garden in her face.............. 146
There is delight in singing, though none hear 370
There lived in Gothic days, as legends tell.. 294
THE REMEDY WORSE THAN THE DISEASE.. 216
There often wanders one whom better days. 286
THERE'S NAE LUCK ABOUT THE HOUSE.... 305
THE RETALIATION....................... 282
There they are, my fifty men and women... 491
THE RETREAT........................... 200
THE RETREAT........................... 364
THE REVELATION........................ 521
There was a time when meadow, grove, and stream.............................. 339
THE RIME OF THE ANCIENT MARINER...... 355
THE RIVER DUDDON..................... 345
The rose had been washed, just washed in a shower............................ 290
THE ROUNDEL.......................... 561
The Rout is Folly's circle, which she draws.. 288
THE RUBAIYAT OF OMAR KHAYYAM........ 438
Ther wacz lokyng on lenthe, the lude to beholde.............................. 18
THE SALT OF THE EARTH................. 562
THE SCHOLAR GIPSY.................... 518
THE SCHOOL-MISTRESS.................. 264
THE SCOURGE OF VILLAINY.............. 157
THE SECOND THREE MEN'S SONG.......... 147
THE SHEEP-WASHING.................... 255
THE SHEPHEARDES CALENDER............ 96
THE SHEPHERD'S COMMENDATION OF HIS NYMPH............................... 129
THE SHEPHERD'S DESCRIPTION OF LOVE.... 129
THE SHEPHERD'S RESOLUTION IN LOVE.... 132
THE SHEPHERD'S WIFE'S SONG........... 116
THE SICK ROSE......................... 302
THE SILENT LOVER...................... 88
THE SILENT VOICES..................... 472
THE SIXTH BOOK OF HOMER'S ILIADS..... 111
THE SLEEP............................. 431
THE SLEEPING MISTRESS................. 160
THE SOLITARY REAPER................... 336
THE SONG OF THE SHIRT................. 426
THE SONNET............................ 533
The soote season that bud and bloom forth brings.............................. 82
THE SOUL'S EXPRESSION................ 432
The spacious firmament on high............ 220
THE SPIRIT OF SOLITUDE................ 394
THE SPIRIT'S EPOCHS................... 522
THE SPLENDID SHILLING................. 221
THE SQUIERES TALE..................... 38
The stage I choose — a subject fair and free 285
The stately homes of England............. 412
THE STEEL GLASS....................... 84
THE STORY OF PHŒBUS AND DAPHNE, APPLIED.............................. 174
THE STORY OF RIMINI.................. 376
THE STORY OF THEBES.................. 49
The sun hath twice brought forth his tender green................................ 82
The sun, the moon, the stars, the seas, the hills, and the plains................ 466
The sun (which doth the greatest comfort bring............................. 161
THE SWALLOW........................... 197
THE TABLES TURNED..................... 330
THE TASK.............................. 286
THE THRISSILL AND THE ROIS........... 58
THE TIGER............................. 302
THE TIMBER............................ 201

The time I've lost in wooing........... 374
THE TOYS........................... 522
THE TRIUMPH OF CHARIS................. 149
THE TWELFTH BOOK OF HOMER'S ODYSSEYS........................... 113
The twentieth year is well-nigh past........ 293
THE TWO SONGS......................... 304
THE TWO VOICES........................ 444
THE UNIVERSAL PRAYER.................. 249
THE UNKNOWN EROS...................... 522
THE UNREALIZED IDEAL.................. 504
THE VANITY OF HUMAN WISHES........... 262
THE VILLAGE........................... 299
THE WATERFALL......................... 412
THE WELL OF ST. KEYNE................. 366
The wine of Love is music.................. 549
THE WISH.............................. 198
THE WORLD............................. 200
The world is too much with us: late and soon 344
The world's great age begins anew......... 410
They are all gone into the world of light.... 200
The Year's twelve daughters had in turn gone by........................... 368
They have no song, the sedges dry.......... 542
They say that God lives very high.......... 438
They whisted all, with fixèd face attent.... 84
Think not, though, my Muse now sings.... 165
Think thou and act; to-morrow thou shalt die 535
This day, whate'er the Fates decree......... 218
This is the month, and this the happy morn 175
This life, which seems so fair.............. 163
This little vault, this narrow room.......... 173
This Relative of mine...................... 504
This said, he went to see.................. 111
This said, she hasteth to a myrtle grove.... 132
This way, this way come, and hear......... 159
THOMAS RYMER.......................... 78
Thorowe the halle the belle han sounde..... 299
THOUGHT OF A BRITON ON THE SUBJUGATION OF SWITZERLAND.................... 343
Thou ling'ring star, with less'ning ray...... 321
Thou lovely and belovèd, thou my love..... 534
Thou noblest monument of Albion's isle.... 284
Thou still unravish'd bride of quietness..... 414
Thou, who dost dwell alone............... 505
Three poets, in three distant ages born..... 209
THREE SHADOWS........................ 536
Three years she grew in sun and shower.... 332
Thrice happy he, who by some shady grove. 163
Through the great sinful streets of Naples as I past........................... 500
Thus piteously Love closed what he begat.. 542
Thyrsis, a youth of the inspired train....... 174
Thys ender night........................ 63
Thy voice is on the rolling air............. 471
Tiger, tiger, burning bright................ 302
TIME.................................. 224
Timely blossom, infant fair................ 221
Time the supreme! — Time is eternity..... 224
TINTERN ABBEY, LINES COMPOSED ABOVE.. 330
Tired with all these, for restful death I cry.. 141
'Tis hard to say, if greater want of skill..... 228
'Tis morning; and the sun with ruddy orb.. 288
'Tis so, 'twas ever so, since heretofore...... 212
'Tis the last rose of summer............... 375
'Tis the middle of the night by the castle clock 361
TO A CHILD OF QUALITY FIVE YEARS OLD.. 216
TO A FRIEND........................... 505
To all you ladies now at land............. 209
TO ALTHEA, FROM PRISON................ 197
TO A MOUNTAIN DAISY.................. 319
TO A MOUSE............................ 315
TO A SKY-LARK......................... 343
TO A SKYLARK.......................... 401
TO AUTUMN............................. 414
TO B. R. HAYDON....................... 345
TO CELIA.............................. 210
TO COLIN CLOUT........................ 127
TO CYRIACK SKINNER.................... 184
TO DAFFODILS.......................... 170
TO DANTE.............................. 471
To draw no envy, Shakespeare, on thy name 149
To fair Fidele's grassy tomb.............. 272
TO GEORGE SAND (A RECOGNITION)........ 432
TO HIS COY MISTRESS................... 199
TO HIS MISTRESS....................... 211
TO HIS SOUL........................... 216
TO KEEP A TRUE LENT................... 171
Toll for the brave....................... 289
To London once my steppes I bent......... 48
TO LUCASTA, GOING TO THE WARS......... 196
TO MARGUERITE......................... 507
TO MARY............................... 293
TO MARY IN HEAVEN..................... 321
TO MISS CHARLOTTE PULTENEY IN HER MOTHER'S ARMS.................... 221
TO MR. H. LAWES ON HIS AIRS........... 183
TO MY GRANDMOTHER.................... 504
TO NIGHT.............................. 410
To-night, grave sir, both my poor house and I 152
To-night retired, the queen of heaven....... 277
Too late for love, too late for joy........... 543
TO PHYLLIS............................ 174
TO ROBERT BROWNING................... 370
To see the world in a grain of sand.......... 302
To shine in silk, and glister all in gold...... 120
TO SIR JOHN OLDCASTLE................. 47
TO SLEEP.............................. 345
TO SLEEP.............................. 416
To spend uncounted years of pain.......... 502
TO THE CAMBRO-BRITANS: AGINCOURT..... 122
TO THE CUCKOO......................... 334
To thee, fair freedom! I retire............. 264
TO THE LORD GENERAL CROMWELL........ 184
TO THE MEMORY OF MY BELOVED MASTER, WILLIAM SHAKESPEARE.............. 149
TO THE NIGHTINGALE.................... 183
TO THE NIGHTINGALE.................... 214
TO THE VIRGINIAN VOYAGE............... 121
TO THE VIRGINS, TO MAKE MUCH OF TIME 169
TO TOUSSAINT L'OUVERTURE............. 343
Toussaint, the most unhappy man of men.. 343
To you, my purse, and to non other wight.. 46
TROILUS AND CRISEYDE................. 28
True genius, but true woman! dost deny.... 432
True Love in this differs from gold and clay 402

True Thomas lay oer yond grassy bank.... 78
TULLOCHGORUM.... 304
'Twas at the royal feast for Persia won..... 207
'Twas at the silent solemn hour.... 260
TWO KINDS OF RICHES.... 303
Two voices are there; one is of the sea..... 343

UBI SUNT QUI ANTE NOS FUERUNT.... 14
ULYSSES.... 459
Underneath this sable hearse.... 168
Under the greenwood tree.... 143
Under yonder beech-tree single on the greensward.... 537
UNIVERSAL HUMANITY.... 304
Unstable dream, according to the place..... 80
Unto all poetes I do me excuse.... 60
Upon a simmer Sunday morn.... 313
Upone a tyme as Ysop can report.... 52
UPON JULIA'S CLOTHES.... 170
UPON THE LOSS OF HIS MISTRESSES.... 168
Up! up! my friend, and quit your books.... 330
URANIA.... 163

Vain human kind! fantastic race.... 216
VAIN VIRTUES.... 535
Vanity, saith the preacher, vanity.... 490
VENUS AND ADONIS.... 132
VERSES ON THE DEATH OF DR. SWIFT.... 216
VIRGIL'S ÆNEID.... 84
VIRTUE.... 171
Virtue smiles: cry holiday.... 148

WAGES.... 466
Wanting is — what.... 498
Was that the landmark? What, — the foolish well.... 535
Watch thou and fear; to-morrow thou shalt die.... 535
WE ARE SEVEN.... 329
We cannot kindle when we will.... 507
Wee, modest, crimson-tippèd flow'r.... 319
Weep no more, nor sigh, nor groan.... 160
Weep not, my wanton, smile upon my knee. 116
Weep with me, all you that read.... 152
Wee, sleekit, cowrin, tim'rous beastie.... 315
We grant, altho' he had much wit.... 193
Well may'st thou halt — and gaze with brightening eye.... 344
Well then! I now do plainly see.... 198
Were beth they that biforen us weren.... 14
Were I as base as is the lowly plain.... 120
We the fairies blithe and antic.... 377
"We want" — the Duchess said to me to-day 429
We watched her breathing through the night 428
We were not by when Jesus came.... 411
Whan father Adie first pat spade in.... 308
Whan that Aprille with hise shoures soote... 32
What are we set on earth for? Say, to toil.... 432
What bird so sings, yet so does wail.... 107
What cher? Gud cher! gud cher, gud cher 65
What dire offence from amorous causes springs.... 231
What has this bugbear Death that's worth our care.... 215
What hope is here for modern rhyme.... 470
What if a day, or a month, or a year.... 146
What I have instanced only in the best..... 209
WHAT IS DEATH.... 562
What is the sorriest thing that enters Hell... 535
What other woman could be loved like you. 534
What pleasure have great princes.... 131
What precious thing are you making fast..... 550
What shepherd can express.... 129
What's that, which, ere I spake, was gone.. 521
What time this world's great Workmaster did cast.... 95
What was he doing, the great god Pan...... 438
Whenas in silks my Julia goes.... 170
When Britain first, at Heaven's command... 258
When chapman billies leave the street...... 321
When do I see thee most, belovèd one...... 533
When France in wrath her giant-limbs uprear'd.... 353
When I am dead, my dearest.... 543
When icicles hang by the wall.... 143
When I consider every thing that grows..... 139
When I consider how my light is spent..... 184
When I do count the clock that tells the time.... 138
When I have fears that I may cease to be.. 417
When I have seen by Time's fell hand defaced.... 140
When I made answer I began: "Alas...... 533
When, in disgrace with fortune and men's eyes.... 139
When in the chronicle of wasted time....... 141
When I survey the bright.... 173
When Lazarus left his charnel-cave.... 469
When lovely woman stoops to folly.... 282
When Love with unconfinèd wings.... 197
When Music, heav'nly maid, was young.... 273
When Nature made her chief work, Stella's eyes.... 104
When our two souls stand up erect and strong 434
When shawes beene sheene, and shradds full fayre.... 66
WHEN THE ASSAULT WAS INTENDED TO THE CITY.... 183
When the dumb Hour, clothed in black..... 472
When the fierce North-wind with his airy forces.... 220
When the hounds of spring are on winter's traces.... 558
When the lamp is shattered.... 411
When the sheep are in the fauld, and the kye at hame.... 309
When thy beauty appears.... 223
When to the sessions of sweet silent thought.. 139
When vain desire at last and vain regret.... 536
Where Barbarous hordes on Scythian mountains roam.... 372
Whereby I knew that she a goddess was.... 85
Where the bee sucks, there suck I.... 145
While some affect the sun, and some the shade.... 254

While summer suns o'er the gay prospect play'd ... 284
Whilst thus my pen strives to eternize thee .. 121
Whoever comes to shroud me, do not harm 155
Who is it that this dark night ... 105
Who is Silvia? what is she ... 143
Who prop, thou ask'st, in these bad days, my mind ... 505
Who shall have my fayr lady ... 63
Who will believe my verse in time to come .. 139
WHY ... 370
WHY COME YE NOT TO COURT ... 62
Why did you melt your waxen man ... 529
Why do our joys depart ... 370
Why dost thou shade thy lovely face? O why 211
Why, having won her, do I woo ... 522
Why so pale and wan, fond lover ... 193
Why, William, on that old grey stone ... 329
WILLIAM AND MARGARET ... 260
Will't ne'er be morning? Will that promised light ... 171
Wilt Thou forgive that sin where I begun .. 155
Wings have we, and as far as we can go ... 338
WINTER ... 255
With blackest moss the flower-plots ... 441
With fingers weary and worn ... 426
With how sad steps, O Moon, thou climb'st the skies ... 104
With sacrifice before the rising morn ... 341
With some pot-fury, ravish'd from their wit. 156
With stammering lips and insufficient sound 432
With that ran there a route of ratones at ones 26
WITH WHOM IS NO VARIABLENESS ... 500
WOO'D AND MARRIED AND A' ... 326
WOOING STUFF ... 106
WORK ... 432
Would I describe a preacher, such as Paul .. 287
Would'st thou hear what man can say ... 152
Would that the structure brave, the manifold music I build ... 494
Would you know what's soft? I dare ... 173
WRITTEN AT AN INN AT HENLEY ... 264
Wrong not, sweet empress of my heart ... 88

YARDLEY OAK ... 291
YARROW UNVISITED ... 336
Years — years ago, — ere yet my dreams ... 428
Ye banks, and braes, and streams around ... 325
Ye distant spires, ye antique towers ... 266
Ye flowery banks o' bonie Doon ... 324
Ye learned sisters, which have oftentimes ... 92
Ye little birds, that sit and sing ... 166
Ye mariners of England ... 370
Ye powers who rule the tongue, if such there are ... 285
Yes: in the sea of life enisl'd ... 507
Yet as when I with other swains have been. 167
Yet did I not, as some my equals did ... 137
"Yet life," you say, "is life" ... 338
Yet once more, O ye laurels, and once more 181
You ask me, why, tho' ill at ease ... 456
You brave heroic minds ... 121
You know, we French stormed Ratisbon ... 479
Your words, my friend, right healthful caustics, blame ... 104
You say, but with no touch of scorn ... 470
You that do search for every purling spring ... 104
Yt felle abowght the Lamasse tyde ... 69